ENVIRONMENTAL
ISSUES
for Architecture

ENVIRONMENTAL ISSUES
for Architecture

David Lee Smith

WILEY

John Wiley & Sons, Inc.

Library of Congress Cataloging-in-Publication Data:

Smith, David Lee, 1940–
    Environmental issues for architecture / David Lee Smith.
        p.   cm.
    Includes bibliographical references and index.
    ISBN 978-0-470-49709-8 (cloth : alk. paper); 978-0-470-64433-1 (ebk); 978-0-470-64434-8 (ebk); 978-0-470-64435-5 (ebk); 978-0-470-95106-4 (ebk); 978-0-470-95123-1 (ebk)
    1. Architecture–Human factors.   2. Buildings–Environmental engineering.   I. Title
NA2542.4.S535 2010
720′.47–dc22
                                                                                2010007962

Printed in the United States of America

10 9 8 7 6 5 4 3 2 1

CONTENTS

PREFACE

Since the beginning of time, living species have had to find ways to adapt to the natural environment. While some adaptation can be achieved physiologically or the need for it can be reduced through migration, many species, particularly humans, have also developed physical structures to help adjust the natural conditions to form an environment that can not only support life but also provide comfort. These constructions are the beginning of architecture, but for building to achieve this status, it must also embrace an emotional expression of intention or, as some would say, a sense of poetry.

Over time, designs intended merely as a way of providing functional adaptation to the natural environment often acquired an aesthetic quality that transcended their initial purpose. At times, perhaps when the intentions of these designs were no longer understood, the designs were applied to conditions for which they were not applicable or no longer relevant. As such, these designs acquired an intrinsic value in terms of their compositional or artistic expression rather than their functional potential.

With the development of modern technology, reliance on direct architectural intervention became less critical. The developing architectural form often was possible only because technology could not only adjust the natural environmental conditions but could also correct for the additional imposition of the architecture. The assumption was that technology made anything possible, and the intention of architectural design was no longer focused on environmental adaptation. For this reason, many designers felt that they were free to pursue poetic expression while relying on others to develop technological methods that could support this freedom. Unfortunately, this practice has given rise to a serious disconnect from the basic intentions of design.

The unfortunate result is that today architecture often seems to be part of our environmental problems rather than part of the necessary solution. Architectural design should be able to contribute to the solution of our environmental problems in a manner that is both effective and poetic. But for this to happen, architectural designers must be aware of the basic concepts and principles of the various environmental issues that are critical to sustaining life on this planet. While we as designers can embrace technology and utilize it to enhance our efforts, we must begin by understanding what is intended rather than focus on what is possible, particularly in terms of utilizing technology. Based on this belief, the title selected for this textbook was *Environmental Issues for Architecture*, for we must understand these issues if we are to realize the environmental contributions that can be achieved through effective architectural design. At the same time, we need to be knowledgeable about technology so that we can successfully integrate its potential into design. Architecture can then achieve its purpose and enhance the physical design.

As an architectural educator, it is important that I avoid the temptation of prescribing specific solutions to complex problems. Instead, my challenge in lectures and in the studio is to attempt to instill in my students an awareness of the critical issues that must be addressed, an understanding of the concepts and principles that underlie these issues, and a commitment to work to resolve them through responsible design. In this vein, I have written this book with the hope that it might inspire future designers to appreciate the potential that environmental issues have for architecture and to support that inspiration with the understanding and skill that can help them achieve this potential.

This intention was the basis for a conference held many years ago in Boston for architecture faculty teaching technology. The gathering started with a keynote address by Jerrold Zacharias, a professor of physics at MIT. He began his presentation by swinging one of two disks that hung behind a projection screen located above a huge chalkboard. As this disk swung back and forth, the second disk began moving in what appeared to be a somewhat erratic manner. Professor Zacharias began to compare the two motions and then suggested that we could analyze them mathematically in order to figure out what was causing the erratic movement. He then proceeded to fill the chalkboard with mathematical equations and finally exclaimed, "Now we know what's happening!"

As a nonengineer with a somewhat lazy mathematical mind, I had pretty much ignored his presentation, thinking instead about the wonderful things that I could do in Boston, but I continued to pay enough attention to be amazed that Professor Zacharias could fill the chalkboard and solve the problematic equation just before running out of space. I was also astonished that so many in the audience, who like me were teachers in architectural schools, seemed not only to be able to follow the presentation but apparently even relished the mathematical experience.

After Professor Zacharias's announcement that we now understood the conditions of the swinging disks, much of the audience, whom I assumed had an engineering background, initially seemed to agree. But then after a few moments of silence, it became apparent that while the equation had been solved, what was causing the two disks to move was still not clear. And then, at the right moment of bewilderment, Professor Zacharias raised the screen; there, to the amazement of the audience, was the explanation—a simple double pendulum with a stick connecting the two.

Professor Zacharias then talked about pendulums and vibrating strings, explaining that a guitar string is plucked and, depending on the type and length of the string, different pitches of sound can be produced. He then explained that with a violin, the desire is to sustain numerous repeated plucks of the strings; this is why a bow is used. Rosin is put on the bow, and as the bow is pulled across the strings, the rosin grabs a string and pulls it. Since the rosin cannot "hold on," as the bow is pulled across the string, a series of repeated plucks is established.

Once again, the audience seemed to understand. But again, Professor Zacharias would not let it rest. He said, "That's not the issue. The problem is that most of us didn't understand that there was a problem!"

While not necessarily problems, the various issues addressed in this book need to be understood in context with architectural design. In an attempt to help you grasp the connections between environmental issues and architecture, the discussion of each issue includes a short historic review to help you make connections with the general development of architecture that have occurred over time, especially since the Industrial Revolution. In addition, the order in which the various issues are organized is somewhat different from the traditional way in which environmental concerns are presented in most textbooks on environmental technology. While it is true that thermal issues are very important and have a major impact on design, this book begins with discussions of lighting and acoustics. This tends to parallel somewhat the way we actually experience space—through seeing and hearing. The expectation is that this order of presentation will further help you realize that *Environmental Issues for Architecture* can contribute to the foundations for architectural design. But since there is more than one way to approach design and since each issue is presented somewhat independently, you may consider each environmental issue in any order that makes sense to you.

ACKNOWLEDGMENTS

While the preparation of this book was essentially an individual effort, it was achieved with the help of many people to whom I am deeply indebted. Without their support, which has been provided in various ways, this publication would not have been possible.

Since this book covers material that I have taught for more than 40 years, I am most indebted to the many students who have taken my courses covering the various environmental technology topics. Not only did they provide the initial motivation to organize my lecture presentations of the different topics, but their requests to review my personal notes encouraged me to clarify and expand them as handouts that could help make connections between the assigned readings and class presentations. These handouts of my notes provided the initial draft of this book, although they have been expanded and, I trust, refined. So again, thanks to all of my students.

My knowledge of the various environmental issues is based in part on the work of many different authors who have effectively presented this material in their own books. While I have attempted to take a slightly different approach in this textbook, trying to emphasize the material from an architectural design point of view, my grasp of the material would not have been possible without my exposure to their publications, most of which are listed at the end of the chapters. I also want to acknowledge my association with the many members of the Society of Building Science Educators (SBSE). Through various gatherings and sharing of teaching materials, but especially through the ongoing dialogue on a broad range of important issues related to teaching on environmental controls and architectural design, the SBSE has been a great support and has encouraged me to pursue this effort.

I must also give thanks to my teaching colleagues. While my interaction with all of them has supported me over the years, I must give special recognition to my teaching buddy, my longtime officemate, and one of my dearest and closest friends, Richard Stevens. Dick is a mathematician and engineer who taught structures at the University of Cincinnati for many years, but his personal design sensitivity and aesthetic appreciation always emphasized the connection between technical considerations and architectural design.

I am also especially grateful to my colleagues Patrick Snadon and Jim Postell, both of whom strongly encouraged me to pursue the effort necessary to prepare this book.

Patrick, who is an accomplished historian of architecture and interior design and author of *The Domestic Architecture of Benjamin Henry Latrobe*, agreed to read an early draft of Chapter 8, which covers the history of thermal control. While he made many helpful critical comments, most importantly Patrick suggested that I take it further, although rather than focus on history, I decided to incorporate historical discussions related to each of the issues addressed in this comprehensive book on the full range of environmental concerns.

Jim persuaded me to follow up on Patrick's suggestion. Jim and I have taught together for many years in our foundation design studio in the School of Architecture and Interior Design, and building upon this association, we have also partnered on several actual design projects. Having recently completed an interesting and informative textbook, *Furniture Design*, Jim gave me the confidence to write this book, and he made it possible by connecting me with Paul Drougas at John Wiley & Sons. I also want to thank Paul and his colleagues at Wiley, especially Donna Conte, for their help and guidance in this effort.

I must also thank Donald Mouch, who was my graduate assistant as I began rewriting my notes. Not only did he relieve me of some of the work associated with my teaching, Donald also reviewed the early drafts of several chapters, providing helpful input that ultimately encouraged my rewriting; I trust it has helped clarify my presentation.

I must also give credit to my former teacher, mentor, and employer—Sidney J. Greenleaf. Sid introduced me to the environmental technologies as my professor when I was in graduate school. His classes instilled in me an understanding of the basic principles underlying the performance of these technologies and an appreciation of how this can inform architectural design. But more importantly, as my employer for a few years, he trusted in my understanding and ability, which provided me with an extraordinary opportunity to be involved in a critical way in a number of very interesting projects. This work forced me to expand my own explorations and gave me a wealth of experience in a relatively short time. Sid was also instrumental in making it possible for me to teach a course on climatological design at the Harvard Graduate School of Design (GSD) shortly after my graduation and then made contacts for me at the University of Cincinnati, where I have spent most of my teaching career.

I am also extremely indebted to my family, especially my dear wife, Susan, who not only encouraged me to complete this book, but supported me with love and understanding as I struggled with the difficult task of rewriting during the past year. I could not have succeeded without her understanding and compassion, not only in preparing this book and teaching and practicing architecture for many years but, more importantly, in achieving a life of happiness and fulfillment.

1 INTRODUCTION

INTRODUCTION

ENVIRONMENTAL AESTHETICS

THE INTENTIONS FOR ENVIRONMENTAL DESIGN

CONCLUSION

INTRODUCTION

This book presents basic information about the major environmental issues that impact on architectural design and attempts to do so in a manner that can guide and support the design process. These presentations are not intended merely to cover "required" information before they must be addressed, which for too many design projects done in school is during preparation of the presentation drawings. Unfortunately, the inclusion of environmental considerations often tends to be merely applied "window dressing" intended to make a project appear more "architectural." While there are legitimate reasons why an expansion of items addressed occurs at presentation time, an understanding of environmental issues, particularly in terms of concepts and principles, must be present at the beginning of the design process so that it can inform the initial schematic explorations. A response to the critical environmental issues must be at the core of any effective design, not merely an applied accommodation added later.

With an increased understanding of the basic concepts and principles of the different environmental topics, we should be better able to grasp the connection between these critical issues and effective architectural design. Although the presentation of these issues might at times be mathematical, these issues are definitely not external to effective design, nor should they be considered only as corrective measures that allow one to do something illogical in terms of design. In fact, an understanding of these principles is fundamental to design.

Unfortunately, the obvious significance to design of some of the material covered in this book might not become fully apparent until later in your studies or perhaps not until later in your design careers. But as with most of what we study, if we understand the underlying principles, these explorations of environmental issues will continue to be of value as we progress in our studies and throughout our professional careers.

ENVIRONMENTAL AESTHETICS

Nature can only be mastered by obeying its laws.

Roger Bacon (Thirteenth-century English philosopher and scientist)

Esthetic judgment constitutes the quintessential level of human consciousness.

James M. Fitch (Architectural historian and theorist)

The commitment of environmental designers (interior designers, architects, landscape architects, and urban designers) to the enhancement of the human experience can best be realized through designs that are both aesthetically pleasing and socially meaningful. In this effort, perhaps the most confusing task is to assign the proper significance to each concern so that the resulting design responds appropriately to the imposed conditions. To accomplish this effectively, designers must have an understanding of science and technology in addition to sensitivity for composition and form.

Science is much more than a body of knowledge. It is a way of thinking. This is central to its success. Science invites us to let the facts in, even when they don't conform to our preconceptions. It counsels us to carry alternative hypotheses in our heads and see which best match the facts. It urges on us a fine balance between no-holds-barred openness to new ideas, however heretical, and the most rigorous skeptical scrutiny of everything—new ideas and established wisdom.[1]

Carl Sagan (Renowned American scientist)

Many erroneously believe that science is based primarily on complex mathematical computations, and because of this, there is often a tendency to assume that science is imbued with a notion of certainty. On the other hand, art is generally considered to be nonspecific and nonscientific. As a result, designers often tend to avoid specific limitations, especially if they are expressed through the use of numbers, as if the acceptance of specificity might imply that they are not really concerned with the poetry of design or, even worse, that they are not really creative.

Calculations, the use of mathematical formulas, are merely a way to model certain aspects of the physical world. Math is a language that provides a simple way of expressing ideas, but many designers are uncomfortable with the mathematical language and cannot appropriately appreciate or effectively use a mathematical model. While rejection of mathematics is unfortunate, since it deprives designers of an effective means of modeling certain conditions, it is untenable if it encourages designers to concomitantly reject science or to go as far, as some do, as to exclaim, "Don't confuse me with the facts!"

Science is the ever-unfinished task of searching for facts, establishing relationships between things, and deciphering laws according to which things appear to occur. The main intention of science is to extract from the chaos and flux of phenomena a consistent, regular structure—that is, to find order. Similarly, effective environmental design should be committed to the discovery of pattern, structure, and order and to giving them viable expression in physical form.

Today there is some confusion over what is or should be the basic intentions of environmental design. This confusion is probably the result of various changes that began developing as long as 150 years ago with the general industrialization of the construction field. This industrialization has tended to separate the design process from what James Marston Fitch called "the healthy democratic base of popular participation."[2] As a result, the designer is now typically isolated from the consumer, increasing the "prevalence of the abstract, the formal, and the platitudinous in architectural design."[3] It is becoming increasingly clear that an attitude within many segments of the various design professions is "one of complacent laissez faire whose esthetic expression is a genial eclecticism. The result is a body of work as antipopular and aristocratic in its general impact as anything ordered by Frederick the Great or Louis XV."[4]

While many of the prominent voices in the design field seem to be consumed by a theoretical dialogue on stylistic intentions and priorities, the traditional leadership role that environmental designers have traditionally contributed has been significantly reduced. In fact, in many situations, oblivious to their fundamental responsibility to ensure that environmental development is nurturing and sustainable, the work of many designers continues to degrade rather than enhance the natural environment. At a time when the design professions should be actively involved in supporting rational, sustainable development, continued infatuation with a narrow set of design parameters might reasonably be interpreted as equivalent to rearranging the deck chairs on the *Titanic*.

Rather than narrowing our options, design professionals should be pursuing ways both to maintain traditional involvement in environmental design and to increase the level of participation through an expansion of professional services. We should take the opportunity to build upon the problem-solving methodology of the design field and substantially extend its realm of engagement. We should reinterpret the basic notion of what constitutes environmental design practice, and sustainable development provides a means to accomplish this.

The ultimate and quintessential role of environmental design is the interpretation of ideas through physical form for human habitation, and designing is the actual act of interpretation. The idea of the designer as a creative individual operating intuitively and independently in this effort of interpretation, although romantic, is unsubstantiated by fact and is a notion that inhibits realization of the architectural potential. While designing is obviously a critical responsibility of professional practice, there are numerous activities with which designers have regularly been involved and upon which designing relies. Just in

---

[1] Carl Sagan, *The Demon-Haunted World: Science as a Candle in the Dark* (Ballantine Books, New York, 1966), p. 27.

[2] James Marston Fitch, *American Building: The Environmental Forces That Shape It* (Houghton Mifflin Company, Boston, 1972), p. 316.
[3] Ibid., p. 317.
[4] Ibid., p. 318.

terms of traditional architectural practice, these usually include promoting and selling architectural services; educating the public, clients, and future professionals; preparing a project brief; developing contract documents; selecting contractors and determining costs; and inspecting construction progress. In addition to these activities, there are a number of allied services that are frequently associated with architectural practice.

Although these various activities collectively constitute the overwhelming portion of architectural practice, a presumption remains, even among many practicing architects, that designing is the most dominant aspect of professional architectural services. In reality, designing accounts for only around 10% of the actual effort expended in fulfilling the demands of most architectural practices! While the actual act of interpretation is critical, all efforts necessary to accomplish this interpretation are essential and crucial to the architectural endeavor, not merely the interpretation itself.

Regrettably, a distinction is sometimes made between the value and importance of "designing" and the "nondesign" efforts of contemporary environmental practice. This establishes an unfortunate hierarchy within the design professions that is extremely divisive and can undermine collaboration, which is essential for effective design that is responsive to the multiplicity of concerns in our complex world. While distinctions in the areas of involvement will remain, any assumed hierarchy will continue to be extremely disruptive to the environmental design professions. To remain effective, we can no longer indulge ourselves with a biased, myopic view of what is actually an extremely diverse responsibility that demands multiple skills and abilities.

Too many recent "prestigious" buildings have been designed in response to a rather narrow value system. While some of these buildings are clearly attractive, too often they are void of functional meaning or any significant social connotation. Only with an understanding of the technological propriety, tempered by a process of socialization, can the environmental design professions move from their recent role of "agent and spokesman for the elite"[5] to achieve more meaningful contact with and support for the popular community.

An understanding of technological propriety can only come from a sound theoretical scientific foundation. As Gary Stevens stated in *The Reasoning Architect*:

. . . although architecture is usually thought to be the product of acts of inspired creation, it is also the product of acts of inspired reason; to demonstrate that science

and mathematics are portions of our intellectual culture that cannot be set apart from architecture and left to the engineers to worry about, but are the concern of all of us.[6]

A distinction is often made also between art and craft. These dichotomies are in fact quite recent, about 200 years old, but as long as we do not take the boundary as hard-and-fast, and admit into each parts of the other, they are useful distinctions if only because scientists and artists do see themselves as carrying out quite different sorts of activities.

Though they may be different, it does not necessarily lead to the conclusion that they are opposed. The two can be unified in the one individual or pursuit.[7]

It is unfortunate, and perhaps even harmful, that in our society, art and science have come to be seen as opposites and antagonistic to one another. Perhaps this tension between the two cultures of art and science is most evident in the environmental design disciplines—that is, in architecture, broadly defined to include physical design extending from consideration of interior space to the urban environment. This confrontation between art and science is especially disturbing since effective environmental design depends on a collaboration of the two.

The wide-ranging criticism of science in architecture is based on the notion that science demands that design be predicated on the application of a set of operational rules that are devoid of any concern for humanistic values. But this criticism is founded on a fundamental confusion about the meaning of humanism and the nature of science. As expressed by Jacob Bronowski:

The scholar who dismisses science may speak in fun, but his fun is not quite a laughing matter. To think of science as a set of special tricks, to see the scientist as the manipulator of outlandish skills— this is the root of the poison that flourishes in the comic strip. There is no more threatening and no more degrading doctrine than the fancy that somehow we may shelve the responsibility for making the decisions of our society by passing it to a few scientists armoured with a special magic. [This is a] picture of a slave society, and should make us shiver whenever we hear a [person] of

[5]Ibid., p. 319.

[6]Gary Stevens, *The Reasoning Architect: Mathematics and Science in Design* (McGraw-Hill Companies, New York, 1990), p. 3.
[7]Ibid., p. 11.

sensibility dismiss science as someone else's concern. The world today is made, it is powered by science; and for any [individual] to abdicate an interest in science is to walk with open eyes towards slavery.[8]

Gary Stevens said:

[T]he fundamental fallacy . . . is in regarding creativity and reasoning as two watertight compartments of the human intellectual makeup. Since architecture is clearly a creative activity, it [is assumed to follow] that architecture cannot be about reasoning, and from this it is a straightforward step to conclude that it must not be about reasoning. The critique perpetuates the wholly wrong idea that creativity in architecture is the domain of design and design alone and that all the other components of architectural knowledge are just so many dry facts that are sometimes handy to the architect but preferably left to the consultant. The result of such attitudes, among other consequences, is that architects are doing less and less in the construction process, as the masters of all these dry facts chip away slowly but steadily at the architect's role.[9]

Only with an appreciation for human values and a committed sensitivity for nature, including both an understanding of its technological potential and an awareness of its ecological fragility, can we hope to achieve environmental design of significance and quality. But confusing any attempt of designers to address environmental concerns appropriately is their apparent failure to grasp the proper meaning of certain common terms: *visual, aesthetic,* and *taste.*

To address environmental concerns appropriately as we fulfill our commitment to design, we must grasp the proper meaning of *aesthetics* and *taste,* recognizing that they are based on more than personal choice and opinion.

Aesthetic Judgment

Aesthetic judgment deals with the issue of "beauty" as distinct from "moral" or "useful" issues, but "beauty" is not limited merely to visual concerns. Unfortunately, James Fitch's claim that "esthetic judgment constitutes the quintessential level of human consciousness"[10] is confus-

ing since it seems to be directly opposed to his stand against the obsession that many in the environmental design professions had, and still have, with visual aesthetics. However, any confusion that comes from this pithy comment derives from a narrow interpretation of aesthetic judgment and beauty. Since beauty entails a combination of qualities that pleases the aesthetic senses, "esthetic" judgment, as expressed by Fitch, is based on an interrelationship between all the physical senses, not just the visual. Aesthetic judgment also depends on personal interpretation of these sensations.

Assuming that aesthetic judgment is based only on visual phenomena leads to a serious misconception of the multidimensional aspect of aesthetic theory. "Far from being narrowly based upon any single sense of perception like vision, our response to a building derives from our body's total response to and perception of the environmental conditions which that building affords."[11] There are many examples of building types where the aesthetic judgment is clearly based on nonvisual concerns as well, and sometime perhaps instead of visual concerns. Even in the most beautiful symphonic hall, a building type that is primarily intended for the appreciation of auditory sensations, one cannot be truly aesthetically pleased if the acoustics are inadequate. In a ballet theater, one cannot be satisfied if one is unable to see the performance properly. There are also situations in which external issues impose on aesthetic judgment. For example, while an owner might recognize that a building incorporates certain positive physical qualities, if the costs far exceed expectations and/or the capacity to pay, it is questionable if there would be substantial appreciation, aesthetic or otherwise, of the structure.

It is inappropriate to attempt to qualify environmental design merely from visual phenomena. While we can, of course, analyze a building in terms of its compositional aspects, we should not confuse this with a comprehensive investigation of its overall aesthetic quality. Although we can derive information on certain nonvisual aspects of a structure from visual observation, we should not confuse issues.

An exploration of the broad issue of aesthetic judgment begins to clarify that there is an important distinction between architecture as object and architecture as experience. As object, architecture tends to exist external to us, and can be observed and interpreted dispassionately and objectively. It is beyond us. It exists for itself. However, as experience, the architectural object has significance only in that it provides the basis for a perceptual experience. It becomes part of us, and the actual physical substance of the object is not of paramount importance. Rather, it is only the effects of the object that are truly significant.

[8]Jacob Bronowski, *Science and Human Values* (Harper & Row, New York, 1965), p. 16.

[9]Stevens, *The Reasoning Architect*, p. 17.

[10]Fitch, *American Building*, p. 309.

[11]Stevens, *The Reasoning Architect*, p. 5.

Of course, the physical reality is important, but this importance is derived primarily from what it implies rather than what it might be physically. Its value and strength exist in its expressed ideas and in its meaning.

The distinction between architecture as object and architecture as experience is similar to the distinction between what can be referred to as "design from outside" and "design from within." While it would be desirable to further explore and clarify these differences, this is beyond the scope of this book; however, hopefully we can agree that the human-caused modification of the physical environment that we call architecture must be considered in terms of a complex composite structure formed of numerous distinct, yet interacting, elements including, but not limited to, its visual characteristics.

Aesthetic Taste

Taste deals with the value system on which we establish our aesthetic judgments. These judgments are based on established values that are developed by and representative of a culture. Since they are statements of cultural consciousness, aesthetic criteria are relative and are dependent on a particular culture. So, while there are specific individual responses that must be considered, aesthetic judgment is greatly affected by its particular social and cultural background. "Esthetic standards are expressions of social agreement, of a common outlook or attitude towards [a] particular aspect of human experience."[12] These standards may, and probably will, vary not only according to the society, but even within a society, according to the particular group or class, establishing a differentiation between what is called *popular taste* and *high style*.

While there is a sharp distinction between popular taste and high style, there is also an extremely important relationship between the two and a joint subordination of them to the exigencies of society as a whole. In certain situations, the connection between the two is complete. As Fitch mentioned, with handicraft methods of production, the aesthetic standards were constantly disciplined by the production method itself. Initially, the designer, producer, and consumer were one and the same, and there was no such thing as bad taste. With early societies basically isolated from other communities, there were no comparative values applied externally to an object, and it was on this basis that the unique aspects of primitive art evolved.

As society progressed from the primitive stage, a distinction between popular taste and high style started to emerge. It became more apparent and ultimately, following the Industrial Revolution, with an increase in automa-

tion, popular taste and high style tended to become totally separated and, at times, even in direct opposition to one another. Today, such opposition is often a conscious positioning by those choosing to suggest that their value set, which is obviously assumed to be high style, is different from and superior to that which is generally accepted.

Perception of the Physical Environment

In his book *American Building: The Environmental Forces That Shape It*, James Marston Fitch wrote about our perceptual experience. He suggested that while there might be a dominance of visual sensations or significance for our thermal experiences, our spatial perceptions are strongly influenced by all of our senses. Fitch listed six senses upon which our environmental perceptions are based: visual, auditory, olfactory, tactile, gustatory (taste), and proprioceptive (interactive). While the first five are reasonably understood, the proprioceptive or interactive sense is not commonly recognized. According to Fitch, this sense is activated by stimuli produced within the organism by movement of its own tissues. As intriguing and provocative as this sixth sense might be, another interpretation of the phenomena of perception was provided by Pierre von Meiss:

Be warned: for a person who has the use of all his senses, the experience of architecture is primarily visual and kinaesthetic [using the sense of movement of the parts of the body]. . . .That does not mean that you are allowed to be deaf and insensitive to smell and touch. That would be to deny oneself the fullness of sensations. Isn't it sometimes a failure on a single one of these points which are deemed to be of secondary importance which destroys all visual qualities? Aesthetic experiencing of the environment is a matter of all our senses and there are even some situations where hearing, smell, and tactility are more important than vision; they are experienced with extraordinary intensity. As designers we must never forget that! Let us try to imagine the echo in the spaces that we are designing, the smells that will be given off by the materials or the activities that will take place there, the tactile experience that they will arouse.[13]

While Fitch considered perception to be based on the five senses augmented by the proprioceptive or interactive sense, von Meiss reduced the number of basic senses by dropping the sense of taste and added the kinaesthetic

---

[12]Fitch, *American Building*, p. 31.

[13]Pierre von Meiss, *Elements of Architecture* [Van Nostrand Reinhold (International), London, 1990], p. 15.

sense as his special augmentation. More likely, our perceptions of the physical world are the result of the five physical senses of sight, sound, touch, smell, and taste, modified by our prior experiences, our expectations, and our intellectual capacity. Further, in agreement with both Fitch and von Meiss, our perceptions of the physical environment are established by the interaction of *all* of our senses. As Fitch said: "Far from being narrowly based upon any single sense of perception such as vision, our response to a building derives from our body's *total* response to and perception of the environmental conditions the building affords."[14]

As an extension of his classification of the senses, Fitch distinguished seven factors or areas upon which our environmental perceptions of the physical environment are based. He identified these as the thermal, atmospheric, aqueous, luminous, sonic, world of objects, and spatiogravitational. (For a further explanation of this, refer to the first chapter in Fitch's book.) While Fitch's division is helpful, especially since he used these to organize his book, assigning a chapter to each, in the discussion of environmental issues, the presentation is not generally organized on the basis of our perceptual experience. Rather, we usually organize the issues by the standard engineering subdivisions. These include HVAC (heating, ventilating, and air conditioning) or ECS (environmental control systems), lighting, and acoustics, plus the additional areas of plumbing, fire safety, electrical service, communications, movement systems, and others. This book uses these classifications, although the order in which they are arranged is somewhat different. Rather than begin with thermal issues and ECS, the discussion starts with lighting and then acoustics, and then addresses thermal issues, although there is no need to read the chapters in this order. The other issues are addressed afterward.

This arrangement aligns more closely with how we utilize our various sensations in developing spatial perception and, because of this, how we generally begin to develop an architectural design. In our discussion of the various environmental issues, we will explore basic physical phenomena and address how architectural design can be a means of addressing these, and since early design explorations tend to be more spatial than fully experiential, it makes sense to begin with lighting and acoustics since these issues most closely relate to how we predominantly develop our sense of space.

However the discussions of the various environmental issues are arranged, we should realize that our perceptual experiences are the result of all of our senses, although we tend to rely on each in different ways. Obviously, spatial perception is highly dependent on vision, followed perhaps by hearing, but it is also affected by thermal and atmospheric conditions. Olfactory senses also can have an effect that can be quite powerful, but generally this is because odors tend to trigger recollection of previous experiences, and often these do have spatial connotations. The tangible experience of touch can also influence how we experience space since it provides information on both the texture and substance of the materials, and these attributes are connected with issues of quality. However, it is usually sufficient to observe a texture or surface that we have touched previously to reconstruct the experience and then incorporate this in forming our perception. As for taste, although it is involved in assessing atmospheric conditions, we usually do not lick the space. However, as with touch, we might have actually had a taste. As infants, we probably did rely on taste as we initially explored our world, and these memories still have an impact on our interpretations.

THE INTENTIONS FOR ENVIRONMENTAL DESIGN

[The] ultimate task of architecture is to act in favor of human beings—to interpose itself between people and the natural environment in which they find themselves. . . . The successful interposition between people and their natural environment furnishes the material basis of all great architecture. To wrest the objective conditions for our optimal development and well-being from a Nature that only seldom provides them, to satisfy our physiological and psychological requirements at optimal levels— this, beyond question is the objective basis of any architecture that is both beautiful and good.[15]

James Marston Fitch

The main intention of environmental design, which includes urban design, architecture, interior design, and those other fields that deal with design of the physical environment, is the ordering of the physical environment to serve humankind. In order to serve humankind effectively, environmental design must be fundamentally scientific. Going beyond a dictionary definition,[16] science can

---

[14]Fitch, *American Building: The Environmental Forces That Shape It* (Oxford University Press, 1999), p. 4.

[15]Ibid., p. 3.

[16]*Webster* defines "science" as "1.) a branch of knowledge or study dealing with a body of facts or truths systematically arranged and showing the operation of general laws, 2.) systematic knowledge of the physical or

be explained as the ever-unfinished task of searching to discover facts, establishing relationships between things, and deciphering the laws according to which things occur.

The ultimate intention of environmental design is to achieve an environment that can support the fullest measure of human endeavor without the imposition of excessive external stress or, at the other extreme, the deprivation of necessary minimal sensory stimuli. To achieve this goal, designers must rely on science, although unfortunately, some design professions are unprepared to do this. Many designers do not adequately understand certain critical factors that significantly impact on the environment and, therefore, are unable to respond to them properly.

According to Fitch, this isolation from critical information is partially the consequence of the spread of industrialization and the resulting isolation of "design from the healthy democratic base of popular participation."[17] With increasing industrialization, the traditional connection between users and designers was set aside. The result of this division was the "increasing prevalence of the abstract, the formal, and the platitudinous in architectural and urban design."[18] It is probably fair to say that the aesthetic concern that has been the motivating force in the design of most of the recent prestigious buildings is an aesthetic void of any significant "functional-democratic connotations."[19] This has resulted in "a body of work as antipopular and aristocratic in its general impact as anything ordered by Frederick the Great or Louis XIV."[20] The environmental design professions must go beyond their current role as agents for the elite to provide meaningful professional service to the popular community. This demands that designers go through a process of socialization evolved from a broad theoretical foundation gained from a scientific education.

Some time ago, Dr. Jacob Bronowski presented an address to the Royal Institute of British Architects entitled "Architecture as a Science and Architecture as an Art." In this talk, Bronowski stated that "the architect bears the same responsibility for making science as well as art visible and familiar, and for having each influence and enter into the other. Architecture remains the cross-roads of new science and new art. If the architect is willing to make them one, by learning to live naturally in both, there will at last be fine modern buildings, and citizens wise enough to see

that they survive."[21] Or as Fitch stated: "Modern architectural problems can no more be solved by carpentry than can spacecraft be built by village blacksmiths."[22]

To be effective, environmental design must maintain or establish a symbiotic relationship between the physical structure and its occupancy. In this sense, occupancy includes both a human component and an operational component. As environmental designers, we can expect to achieve an appropriate and effective design expression only if we have a proper understanding of the technical issues that relate to environmental issues.

In *An Outline of Philosophy*, while commenting on mathematical modeling of the physical world, Bertrand Russell wrote, "Physics is mathematical not because we know so much about the physical world, but because we know so little; it is only its mathematical properties that we can discover."[23] Paraphrasing this comment to address the problems that face architecture today, we might suggest that architecture is evaluated on the basis of visual aesthetics, not because we know so much about design, but because we know so little. It is only the composition of form that we can readily observe and, therefore, attempt to control.

Another interpretation derived from Bertrand Russell's quotation is that, in general, we tend to be more attentive to those issues that are initially most apparent to us, not necessarily those issues that are most significant. Since we tend to deal first with obvious issues, we frequently avoid or miss those that are more difficult and may be more significant. As designers, we should recognize this and attempt to avoid the trap. We must be able to consider objectively all issues that impact on our task, not just the ones that we think of first or those in which we are interested. If we are to establish our design standards on a relatively firm factual base, we need to develop a more systematic and detailed investigation of the actual relationship between humankind and the physical environment.[24]

We should also recognize that we bring to the design task a great deal of valid understanding based on our prior experience. We should use this understanding or preconditioning, which some might choose to refer to as *common sense*, and build upon it. While our prior conceptions can guide us when we undertake the study of a new issue, they should not interfere with our expanding into new areas of understanding. We must be careful to keep our preconditioning from limiting our willingness to acquire new,

material world gained through observation and experimentation, . . . 4.) systematic knowledge in general, 5.) knowledge, as of facts or principles; knowledge gained by systematic study, ... 7.) skill, esp. reflecting a precise application of facts or principles; proficiency" (*Webster's Encyclopedic Unabridged Dictionary*, Gramercy Books, New York, 1996).

[17]Fitch, *American Building*, p. 354.

[18]Ibid., p. 355.

[19]Ibid., p. 356.

[20]Ibid., p. 356.

[21]Jacob Bronowski, "Architecture as a Science and Architecture as an Art," *R.I.B.A. Journal* (March 1955), pp. 183–189.

[22]Fitch, *American Building*, p. 357.

[23]Bertrand Russell, *An Outline of Philosophy* (Blackwell, Oxford, 1993), p. 125.

[24]Ibid., p. 24.

sometimes conflicting, information and formulating new concepts and ideas. In fact, they might give some relevance to these new concepts and ideas.

As designers, our ultimate concern should be the experiential reality of the physical environment that results from all of our senses.

Other Thoughts

The term *primitive* refers to being at the beginning, being original. According to Amos Rapoport, "Primitive building . . . refers to that produced by societies [which are] defined as primitive by anthropologists."[25] While these buildings might appear to us as rather elementary, "they are, in fact, built by people using their intelligence, ability . . . and resources to their fullest extent. The term primitive, therefore, does not refer to the builders' intentions or abilities, but rather to the society in which they build."[26] That is, a primitive building can be very sophisticated, especially from the vantage point of the builder!

According to the anthropologist Robert Redfield, *primitive* refers to a culture that is isolated and self-contained, if not in terms of other primitive cultures, then in terms of some higher culture. Primitive cultures have no knowledge of an outside higher culture. They are limited to their own devices. In the primitive society, there is a diffused knowledge of everything by everybody. In a primitive culture, there are prescribed ways of doing or not doing everything.

The term *vernacular* is distinct from primitive. Vernacular refers to a culture that coexists in association with a higher culture. Therefore, vernacular is related to *folk* and *peasant*, terms that clearly imply a distinction of cultural levels. In a sense, vernacular carries the connotation of *popular taste*.

In vernacular design, models are used as the basis of design, but these models are individually modified. They are not copied directly, as is done in primitive design. As mentioned before, in primitive design, individual adjustments of the prototype are not available. But while there is an important distinction between primitive design and vernacular design, this distinction is not as significant as that between vernacular design and high-style design. In vernacular design there is a "lack of theoretical or aesthetic pretensions; [and] working with the site and micro-climate; respect for other people and . . . the total environment, [human] made as well as natural; and working within an idiom and allowing variations only within a given order"[27] is the

acceptable standard. In high-style design, aesthetic pretensions tend to dominate, and concern for the environment is subjugated to the more ethereal concerns of the designer. Another distinction between vernacular and high-style design is that vernacular design has an additive and open-ended nature, whereas high-style design is basically closed and complete. Vernacular buildings can readily accept change and adapt to variations. This tends to contribute to the particular charm of such buildings. High-style buildings, on the other hand, cannot change or adapt without being conceptually modified.

With vernacular design, tradition is a regulator that helps establish the aesthetic norm. But today, the regulatory nature of tradition has basically disappeared, especially in the United States. It has been supplanted by stylistic pretensions that are not, unfortunately, generally concerned with adaptation to the natural environment. Even with all of the rhetoric concerning the need to change our ways and become better stewards of the environment, our actions tend to continue to impose on nature rather than work with it. While there are obviously many who are dedicated and committed, the majority seem unwilling to take even modest steps that could help in the near term, so it is our responsibility to lead as best we can.

Needs and Means

In vernacular design, the major intention is to achieve an honest solution to the fundamental requirements expected of the building. The designer, who is also usually the builder and the user, does not impose contradictory and extraneous considerations on the design. Rather, the designer attempts to accomplish a natural symbiosis with nature. In simpler times this natural symbiosis of vernacular design was easily achieved, generally through an intuitive process that resulted in a positive response to imposed requirements. This process should not be thought of in terms of blind trial and error. It was a logical process that depended on an understanding of the demands expected of the proposed building and the means available to meet these demands, as well as on a wealth of prior experience.

With the unbelievable expansion of knowledge that has occurred since the beginning of the twentieth century, an expansion considered to double every 15 years,[28] and with the increase in expectations and demands of our contemporary society, the intuitive design process cannot sustain effective architectural development. Today the architectural design process must be consciously rational

---

[25]Amos Rapoport, *House Form and Culture* (Prentice-Hall, Englewood Cliffs, NJ, 1969), p. 3.
[26]Ibid., p. 3.
[27]Ibid., p. 5.

---

[28]This would mean a more than 60-fold increase in knowledge since 1900.

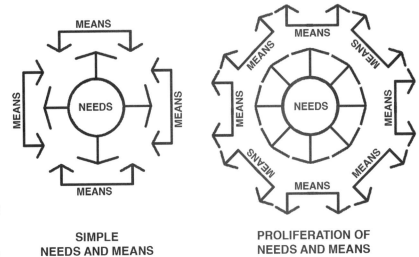

Figure 1.1 DIAGRAM OF NEEDS AND MEANS
James Marston Fitch stated that design should be the process of balancing the outward-pressing needs with the inward-pressing means that are available. While this balance was readily achieved in simpler times with limited needs and means, the increased complexity of needs and the expansion of the various means that are now possible have led to an explosion of possibilities and design chaos.

and scientific. In *American Building*, Fitch presented this thesis—the requirement for a rational and scientific design method. He suggested that prior to the general proliferation of design requirements and potentials that resulted from the industrial/technological revolution of the last 150-plus years, the building profession was disciplined and ordered by what Fitch called a "clear and comprehensible reference frame of needs and means."

As shown in the left-hand diagram in Figure 1.1, the needs that a building was to address, which were outward-pressing requirements, were relatively simple and basic, and they were readily defined. Also the means by which it was possible to respond to these needs, which were inward-pressing limitations, were easily identified and offered minimal opportunities for choice. Today, however, as indicated in the right-hand diagram, the balanced interface of needs and means has been exploded with the increase in both technological capability and programmatic demands. Without a balanced interface, chaos reigns supreme and the adaptation of the physical environment in humankind's favor, the primary objective of environmental design, cannot be achieved effectively.

Things have become more complex, and the challenge for environmental design is to embrace this complexity. We must develop a clear understanding of both sides of the needs–means interface and use this to reestablish a sustainable future where needs and means are again brought into balance, as indicated in Figure 1.2.

CONCLUSION

The aim of environmental design is to achieve a nurturing environment that can support the fullest measure

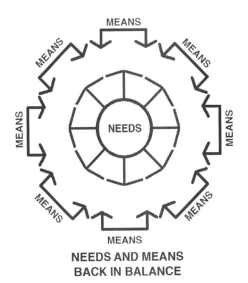

Figure 1.2 DIAGRAM OF NEEDS AND MEANS BACK IN BALANCE
With a clear understanding of the needs that environmental design must address and a solid grasp of not just what is possible but, more importantly, what is appropriate to address these complex needs, a balance between the two can be reestablished.

of human endeavor without imposing excessive external stress. The aim is to establish what Fitch called the *third environment*, in which there is a symbiotic relationship between the physical environment and the occupancy. If a designer's standards for judgment are to be firmly based, with more substantiation than is currently provided, the designer needs to understand the fields of physiology, psychology, anthropology, history, economics, and others. Architecture needs to have a broad knowledge base and a well-developed understanding of humankind's actual physical and emotional relationship with the environment.

Let us begin by learning more about the environmental issues that impact on architecture.

BIBLIOGRAPHY

Bronowski, J. " Architecture as a Science and Architecture as an Art." *R.I.B.A. Journal* (March 1955), 183–189.

Fitch, J.M. *American Building: The Environmental Forces That Shape It*. Houghton Mifflin Company, Boston, 1972.

Fitch, J.M. and W. Bobenhausen. *American Building: The Environmental Forces That Shape It* Oxford University Press, Boston, 1999.

Rapoport, A. *House Form and Culture*. Prentice-Hall, Englewood Cliffs, NJ, 1969.

Stevens, G. *The Reasoning Architect: Mathematics and Science in Design*. McGraw-Hill Companies, New York, 1990.

von Meiss, P. *Elements of Architecture*. Van Nostrand Reinhold (International), London, 1990.

2 LIGHTING PRINCIPLES

VISUAL PHENOMENA

Visual phenomena obviously deal with what is sensed by the eye; however, even in the area of design, they are not limited to issues of composition. Rather, visual experience relates to the broader issue of visual communication that extends well beyond mere visual sensation and enters into the realms of perception and conception that depend on interpretation of information gained through the visual senses. Visual communication is probably the major means by which information is transferred, although as we mature, verbal communication tends to supplant the dominance of visual data. However, even then, much of the verbal information is acquired through the visual senses—that is, through reading.

While we understand that our visual sensations allow us to discern the physical composition of the environment, we should recognize that these sensations also provide us with considerable data that convey important additional information about the environment. For example, we can often identify the function or purpose of a space from what we see, even when the space is devoid of people and furniture, or we can recognize the appropriate paths by which one may easily move through a space. We can even perceive the acoustical qualities and perhaps the thermal qualities of a space, and we can determine certain characteristics of the enclosing materials, such as whether they are soft or hard or whether they are smooth or rough. For instance, irregular light and dark areas on a surface are indicative of a rough surface texture, with the amount of irregularity of the light related to the relative degree of surface roughness.

Such interpretations of visual data are based on an understanding acquired from prior experience. Since individuals are unlikely to share similar previous experiences, common visual experiences do not typically result in identical interpretations. Each individual's interpretation of a particular visual condition is the result of the actual visual sensations of that condition combined with his/her own preconditioning. While we should be aware of the lack of uniformity in individual past histories and how these differences might affect spatial interpretations, we should also recognize that people often share many common experiences, especially with those within their own culture.

Understanding that people rely extensively on their previous experiences, we should realize that it is possible to establish visual statements that might suggest conditions that do not physically exist. For example, in this age of synthetic materials, the visual message of a rough-textured surface may be derived from a surface that is actually smooth, such as contact paper or plastic laminate (i.e., Formica), or an actual rough or irregular surface, such as one that might result from a poor finishing job of a gypsum board ceiling, can be rendered as a smooth, flat surface if the lighting is bilateral and eliminates all shadows. This is an important factor: as designers, we can manipulate the visual message to make it either consistent with or somewhat independent of the actual physical reality.

The complex processes used in visual communication are obviously very significant in establishing appreciation or lack of it for the physical environment. However, while not intending to diminish the significance that visual sensations have in formulating our spatial experiences, we might question the appropriateness of overemphasizing the importance of the visual qualities of design to the almost total exclusion of all other environmental qualities. We might also wonder about the current proclivity that certain design professionals seem to have for supplanting direct spatial experience with abstract, conjectural verbal commentary, sometimes referred to as *talkitecture*, which often seems to have very little connection with the actual physical realities.

As designers, it is important to understand visual perception and use this in the design process. The visual experience is a significant part of spatial perception, and understanding how this experience is formed should inform how a design intention might develop in terms of the placement, configuration, texture, and color of those objects that define the physical environment, not just in connection with the design of the lighting system. While the principles of composition are critical to this task, unless the visualization process is also considered in the development of a physical design, it is unlikely that the intended spatial perceptions will be achieved.

Reality or Illusion

When we "see" an object, unless it is actually emitting enough electromagnetic radiation that lies within the visible spectrum, what we actually sense is light that is reflected off the object, not light that actually comes from the object. That is, contrary to our normal way of thinking, we really do not see the object since we cannot sense any visible radiant energy that it emits. What we sense is actually the "negative" or the electromagnetic radiation that the object rejects, and we use this sensation to achieve our perception of the object. The image of the object received on the retina is also inverted since it is turned upside down in passing through the lens of the eye.

In terms of color perception, the visual process is similarly convoluted. When we see an object and assign a color

to it, we are really identifying the object by the color that it does not possess. Since the object absorbs certain colors and rejects others, the color of the object that we sense is actually the color that it rejects or reflects. That is, the color we call an object is that which it is not. As if this were not confusing enough, let us consider what happens when we observe something through glass.

Looking through glass is also not what it at first appears to be. The general theory suggests that when we look through glass, we really see only a reproduction of the original visual image that impinges on the glass since the specific light rays that are reflected off the object that we "see" do not actually pass through the glass. Rather, these rays are absorbed by the glass, which, in turn, emits new light rays. This sets up a chain reaction, somewhat like the movement of billiard balls. So again, we actually see a reproduction and not the real thing, but for all practical purposes, there really is no difference in terms of our experience. Of course, if the visual sensation is a construct that is not based on a physical reality, perhaps this also does not make much difference in our experience. Interestingly, in addition to establishing this magical experience of sight, the absorption and reemission of radiation in glass, or in any transparent medium, is what also causes the light to bend as it moves from one density to another (see Figure 2.1).

We are told that the cause for this bending of light is that the speed of light is reduced as light enters glass; but the speed of light is supposedly one of the fundamental constants of the universe, so how can it change? The more complete explanation is that the actual speed of light remains constant, but the absorption and reemission of the radiation in a transparent medium requires time, and this adjusts the apparent or effective speed of light. This delay in

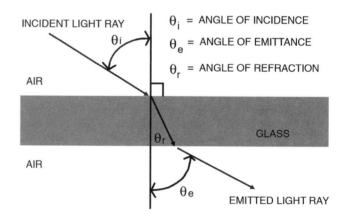

Figure 2.1 REFRACTION OF LIGHT

Light bends as it passes obliquely between the interface of two media of different densities. The light rays bend toward normal when the density increases and away from normal as it decreases, with the amount of the angular change related to the coefficient of refraction of the medium through which it passes.

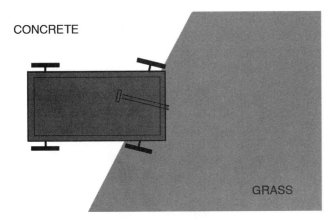

CONCRETE

GRASS

Figure 2.2 ANALOGY OF BENDING BY REFRACTION
Refraction of light is similar to what happens with a wagon moving across a paved surface onto grass. Assuming it comes at an angle, when one front wheel runs onto the grass, its speed is reduced while the other front wheel continues at a higher speed, which forces the wagon to turn.

passing through the transparent medium causes the light to bend, assuming that it enters at an oblique angle. The light bends when it enters and again when it leaves the glass because of the difference in the effective speed that occurs between the light rays at the interfacing planes of the denser glass and the air.

This bending is analogous to what occurs when a wagon rolls obliquely across a smooth concrete area onto grass. As diagrammed in Figure 2.2, as the first front wheel of the wagon leaves the smooth paved area, it slows down and the wagon turns slightly. The amount of turning is dependent on the difference between the speed of the wheel on the paved surface and on the grass and on the length of time that the first wheel is on the grass while the second wheel is still on the pavement, which is related to the angle of approach.

Even when not looking through glass, vision still relies on a similar reproductive process. The eye has an exterior covering called the *cornea*, a lens that focuses the entering light upon the retina and is itself filled with a transparent fluid called *vitreous humor*. As a result, the light rays that the eye initially receives do not actually strike the retina, so all visual perceptions are based on reproduced electromagnetic radiation. Since we do not see objects directly but rather experience energy fields that are merely influenced by the objects, it seems reasonable that, as designers, our major concern should be focused on the energy fields as the source of visual stimuli rather than on the physical objects themselves. We should be predominantly concerned about how the physical elements of a design affect the energy fields that are experienced instead of being obsessed with the tangible reality of the design. That is, if our primary concern is for a perceptual experience, our regard for the physical reality should be in terms of how it determines the

Figure 2.3 PERPENDICULAR LINES
Which of the images includes two lines of equal length? Interestingly, by comparing the two images with a square that has side dimensions equal to that of the vertical line, which is obviously equal in both images, we not only get verification of which image has lines of the same length, we also perceive the results in a way that mere measurement of the line length does not provide.

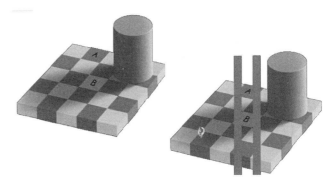

Figure 2.4 CHANGING SHADOWS
Are all of the light gray squares the same shade? While there might be some variation among the shades of the light or dark squares, clearly the light and dark squares are different from each other—or are they?

energy fields, especially in terms of lighting, upon which perceptual experience is established rather than on the physical reality itself. Or to say it otherwise, it is important to understand that the way an object is illuminated has a critical impact on how it is visually perceived. Recognizing this, perhaps rather than continue to assume that the purpose of lighting is merely to render the environment in a way that supports the perception of its actual reality, our intention might be to use lighting as a way to modify the appearance of physical reality and thereby create an illusion.

Perception also depends on interpretation, and there are a number of intriguing examples of how what we think we see is not substantiated by actual conditions. Figures 2.3 to 2.5 show several classic optical illusions.

Which of the perpendicular lines in Figure 2.3 are the same length—those in the left image or in the right image? Since the vertical line in the left image is clearly longer than the horizontal line, the equal lines must be in the right image, and these lines do appear to be the same length. However, since the vertical lines in both images are of the same length, by placing a square with sides of this length around each image, we can clearly show that the left image includes equal-length lines.

In Figure 2.4, the image on the left shows a checkerboard on which a shadow is cast by a cylinder. As we

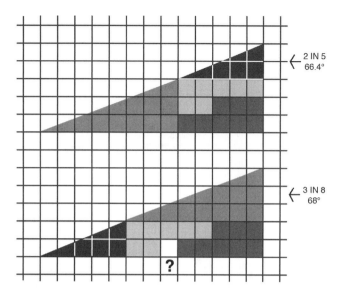

Figure 2.5　THE 7% RULE
Things are not always as they appear. While both of the larger triangles are comprised of two different-sized smaller triangles and two L-shaped blocks, when they are arranged differently, there is an extra grid square in the bottom 13 × 5 triangle. How is this possible?

Figure 2.6　LA GIOCONDA
The Mona Lisa presents an image that is quite familiar, although sometimes what we assume we see is not actually what we do see.

observe the various squares in the shadow of the cylinder, the A and B squares are clearly different colors, with the A square darker gray and the B square lighter gray. We perceive this, in part, since we know that the squares alternate on a checkerboard, but also because we accept that the lighter gray should be darker in the shadow of the cylinder. However, as we can readily observe in the image on the right, which has added dark gray bands to link the A and B squares, these two squares are the same gray.

Figure 2.5 contains two triangles on a grid. Each of these triangles contains the same four subcomponents, but these components are arranged differently in the two triangles. Interestingly, in the lower triangle, even though the same four components are used, there seems to be an extra square in the grid that is not covered by the rearranged components. How could this be possible, especially since these two triangles were actually developed by physically rearranging the different components?

The clue to solving the puzzle is provided at the right of the image. The top component of the upper triangle is itself a triangle. This smaller triangle has a base that extends for five grids and a height that is two grids, which, based on trigonometry, means that the slope of the hypotenuse of this smaller triangle is 66.4°. The upper triangle also includes another subtriangle, with a base of eight grids and a height of three grids, which relates to a slope of 68°.

The nontriangular subcomponents together include a total of 15 units of the grid. In the top composite triangle, they overlap and fill three five-unit rows, which is a total of 15 squares in the grid. In the bottom composite triangle

they are allocated to two rows or 8 units, which means that the 15 units cannot cover all 16 grid units. The "extra" square in the grid is not the result of changing the way the L-shaped blocks are arranged but of the different slopes of the subtriangles.

What we do not observe is that, since the hypotenuses of the two subtriangles in each figure are not at the same slope, the hypotenuse of each of the two larger triangles is not a straight line. This is not apparent to the eye, partly because of what is sometimes referred to as the *7% rule*, which states that when similar dimensions or angles have less than a 7% divergence, the difference is generally not perceived since our desire for order attempts to equalize conditions.

Another example of our tendency to perceive what we believe is there is provided by Figure 2.6. This image appears to be an inverted copy of the Mona Lisa by Leonardo da Vinci. While most people easily recognize this famous painting, few realize that the image has a serious flaw, but it is not because it is upside down. In fact, being inverted tends to conceal the flaw, which is that the eyes and the mouth in the image are inverted with respect to the overall orientation of the image.

Whether reality or illusion, environmental design is concerned with establishing a physical environment that is perceived primarily through the visual sensations derived from the impact of the various spatial definers (e.g., walls, floors, and ceilings) on the visual field. The way these spatial definers are illuminated clearly influences the way they are seen, and this, in turn, impacts on the spatial perception. While this is a cue that the design of the electric lighting system is important, we should understand that it actually has perhaps more to do with spatial design and how the physical components should be arranged so that they are seen in a way that will produce the intended spatial experience. Unfortunately, many designers do not adequately understand the processes by which we see, even though the visual experience is clearly the dominant force of architectural design.

As James Marston Fitch said:

The paradox is that, despite contemporary architects' obsession with the visible aspects of their work, they often have little knowledge or understanding of the visual performance field. This is expressed in many ways. For all the new means at their disposal, their use of color—either as pigment or as light—is both more timid and less expert than in many previous periods. For all their extravagant use of glass, they seldom recognize the basic optical fact that glass is only transparent under certain objective conditions. For all their wide use of [electric], non-daylit illumination, all too many buildings are poorly lit with improper fixtures for the task.

The field of lighting design has changed tremendously since the first energy crisis of 1973. All facets of technology have improved, including more efficient lamps, improved fixtures, and various controls to reduce waste. Laws, codes, standards, and basic operational economics have reduced the luminous power density of most buildings substantially. However, notwithstanding these changes and increased knowledge of insolation and orientation, many new buildings still display serious malfunction, expressed in glare, overheating, and faulty integration of natural and [electric] light sources. In short, the architect pays at once too much and too little attention to the visual world— too much to its formal superstructures, far too little to its experiential foundations.[1]

Too often it seems that designers, having only a limited understanding of visual perception, are incapable of realizing the potential of light and using it as an important part of the design palette. Instead, they increasingly turn to excessive spatial contortions as the way to develop spatial interest and excitement or, unwilling to take this tack, merely accept that spaces will be rather mundane and dull. If some designers do not seem to understand the basic principles of visual perception, then perhaps failure to recognize the tremendous significance that nonvisual stimuli

can have on our perception of the physical environment is to be expected, but hopefully not accepted.

BASIC PRINCIPLES OF LIGHTING

Over the last 40 years, considerable effort has been expended on determining the appropriate criteria for effective interior lighting. Prior to the Arab oil embargo in the early 1970s, the general tendency of the lighting profession was to continually increase levels of illumination. While several voices were questioning the logic of this approach to lighting design, the overwhelming momentum in the lighting industry was for higher and higher lighting levels to support greater and greater levels of visual performance. The Illuminating Engineering Society of North America (IESNA), which is the main professional organization in the lighting field, was calling for performance efficiencies[2] of 99%. According to the IESNA, this necessitated illumination levels of more than 100 foot-candles for general office work and more than twice that, 250 to 500 foot-candles, for detailed tasks such as drafting. Fortunately, in response to the general awareness of our energy limitations, the IESNA considerably reduced the recommended levels of illumination.

Four Factors That Affect Vision

While lighting levels have been reduced from those promoted by the IES prior to the 1970s, there is currently no clear agreement as to the amount of lighting that might be appropriate for various tasks. However, there is a general consensus that vision is improved when there is an increase in various factors:

1. Level of illumination
2. Contrast between a visual object and its background
3. Size of a visual object
4. Time of exposure

Level of Illumination: Up to certain levels of illumination, providing more light for a visual task generally improves vision. With an increase of illumination there is an increase in visual stimulation, which usually supports improved vision. However, with excessive levels of illumination, adaptation might actually result in a reduction

[1]James Marston Fitch with William Bobenhausen, *American Building: The Environmental Forces That Shape It* (Oxford University Press, New York, 1999), pp. 103–104.

[2]Performance efficiencies are based on the percentage of correct responses given by subjects as to the orientation of a specified form. Often the subjects are asked to identify the location (i.e., top, right, bottom, etc.) of an opening in what is referred to as a Landolt Ring, a small C-shaped figure that has a line thickness equal to one-fifth of the diameter of the circular shape. The width of the opening in the ring is also equal to one-fifth of the diameter.

of actual stimulation of the retina, resulting in decreased vision. For most visual tasks that are not highly demanding, 10–20 foot-candles of illumination, which correlates with 100–200 lux, is all that is actually required for adequate vision. While vision does tend to improve with higher illumination levels, there are data that suggest that above 30 foot-candles there is a diminishing benefit provided by increased levels of illumination and that above 120 foot-candles visual effectiveness might actually decline, especially if the illumination is not appropriately controlled.

Contrast Between a Visual Object and Its Background: Contrast is perhaps the single most important factor in visual acuity, especially when the outline or silhouette of the object provides the primary source of information. While providing an appropriate contrast is important, for ease of vision the average level of brightness within the visual field should be relatively in balance. Average brightness is what is provided within a particular portion of the field of vision to which our eyes adapt. For example, rather than the contrast between the letters in this book and the paper on which they are printed, which is critical to being able to distinguish the letters, the average brightness of this page of print is based on the combined effect of the black letters and the exposed white paper.

Any major difference in average brightness between adjacent surfaces should be avoided. This has often been stated in terms of ratios between the visual task and the surround, with recommendations that the ratio between brightness levels should not exceed 3:1 within the near surround, which is within the area of visual attention. It is also suggested that the task brightness be at a higher level than the background brightness, although this is not as critical as maintaining the 3:1 ratio. Within the total field of vision, the recommended maximum ratio should be 10:1, again with the task preferably at the higher level.

While contrast is effective in defining an object, contrast in brightness can also establish emphasis since the eye is naturally attracted to a level of luminance (brightness) that is significantly higher than the average brightness within the field of vision. A 10:1 ratio of brightness between two different surfaces will be clearly noticeable, with the brighter surface usually interpreted as being about twice as bright. A brightness ratio of 100:1 will produce a perceived emphasis on the brighter surface.

Size of a Visual Object: As the size of the visual image increases, the visual task becomes easier. With a reduction in the size of the task, the illumination level, the contrast, and/or the exposure time would have to increase in order to maintain comparable vision.

Time of Exposure: As the time available for a visual task increases, it generally becomes easier to discern things. With a reduction in the available time, the illumination level, the contrast, or the size would have to increase in order to maintain comparable vision, but additional time cannot always resolve inadequate illumination, contrast, and/or object size.

While we need to be aware of the interaction among these four factors, perhaps the most important thing to realize is that once minimal levels of illumination have been provided, improved visibility and visual comfort can often be more readily achieved by adjusting the contrast, increasing the size of the visual image, or expanding the time available for the task rather than by increasing the illumination level. For example, an original intention in suggesting increased illumination levels for the work environment was to enable effective reading of a fifth carbon copy generated by a manual typewriter. Today typewriters are hardly ever used, but if they are, they are probably electric rather than manual, and if we were intent on producing carbon copies, an electric typewriter will produce a stronger imprint and better copies. But rather than carbon paper, reproductions are now generated by photocopiers, and if the copy is not clear, it makes more sense to fix the copy machine than increase the level of illumination.

Although not one of the four basic factors of lighting control, another important aspect of visual perception is that in normal conditions the major plane of sight is horizontal. That is, we tend to look straight ahead, not up or down, and because of this, vertical surfaces comprise the most significant portion of the visual field. In most spaces, the walls are generally the dominant surfaces and, as a result, are the primary surfaces upon which spatial perceptions are based. This is especially true in normal-sized spaces. In large spaces, the ceiling and floor tend to become more visually dominant.

Sometimes lighting is identified as being either *natural* or *artificial*. Although there are differences between light emitted from the sun and light electrically generated, particularly in terms of wavelength composition, the significant distinction is the source of the light rather than the light itself. That is, light is a form of energy, particularly electromagnetic radiation with a wavelength between 380 and 760 nanometers. As a form of energy, it exists, and since it does, regardless of the manner in which it is generated, there is no such thing as artificial light. There is daylight and electric light, and sometimes even gas light, but whatever its source, light is light.

It is dubious whether the notion of artificial light is ever appropriate, but perhaps it is legitimate for light that is represented in a graphic manner or maybe when a sensation of light is experienced mentally independent of physical sensation. When light exists, it is real even though the characteristics of the light might differ.

PURPOSE OF ARCHITECTURAL LIGHTING

In addition to understanding these basic principles of lighting, it is also important to recognize that architectural lighting has a twofold purpose: spatial and task. Spatial lighting generally deals with visual ambiance, while task lighting deals with visual performance, and although at times these two roles of lighting continue to be handled together, they are distinct.

The role of spatial lighting is to define and enhance the spatial qualities of the physical environment. These qualities might be derived from the actual physical characteristics of the space, or they might not; in the latter case, the lighting system would attempt to modify the real physical configuration in order to achieve an intended effect. While spatial lighting basically involves illumination of the spatial definers, task lighting generally deals with lighting an implied surface on which a visual task is to be performed. This implied surface is assumed to be a horizontal illumination plane, often referred to as a *work plane*. This plane is usually set at 30 inches above the floor, which is the typical height of a desktop. The role of task lighting is to make a visual activity possible without imposing unnecessary effort. Of course, if the visual activity is to experience an aspect of the space, such as might occur in a building lobby or along a stair, then task lighting might be spatial lighting; however, normally the task is assumed to be something like reading or drafting, which requires illumination on the horizontal work plane.

As shown in Figure 2.7, in the early days of electric lighting, the electric lamps were often left exposed. While these exposed lamps could produce an interesting delineation of a space, the brightness of the lights could be a problem, especially when the lighting level was increased to provide better task lighting. In order to avoid this, indirect lighting was frequently used. The bright light sources were concealed from view, with the emitted light intentionally bounced off a room surface, usually the ceiling, to be reflected down to the illumination plane. As a result, with both of these early lighting methods, exposed lamps that outlined a space and indirect lighting, spatial lighting was often the means of providing task light. As the design of lighting fixtures improved, emphasis was placed on developing adequate light on the illumination plane, with spatial lighting often provided merely from the reflected task lighting, somewhat the reverse of indirect lighting. Unfortunately, the distinction between the two roles of lighting was not generally considered in the lighting design, and the approach was to light all areas to achieve the lighting level for the intended visual task level, letting the resulting reflected light serve as the source for spatial

Figure 2.7 PLUM STREET TEMPLE
This image of Plum Street Temple, located in Cincinnati, Ohio, and designed in 1866 by James Keyes Wilson, shows exposed incandescent lights that tend to outline the physical structure. This space, which is the home of American Reform Judaism, was originally illuminated by gas but was electrified around 1900.

lighting. With expanding awareness of the fragility of our natural environment and the negative effects of excessive energy consumption, the approach to lighting design is changing. Lighting all areas to task levels is being supplanted with a more focused approach to task lighting. These higher levels of illumination are now more typically provided only for those areas where the tasks are actually performed, with reasonable general levels of illumination now often achieved through intentional spatial lighting.

Whatever the motivation is, task lighting and spatial lighting should be approached distinctly in order to achieve the desired results. The lighting of a lecture hall in which digital presentations are shown is an example of a condition where the two should be handled separately. For example, taking notes demands an adjustable lighting system that can illuminate the tablet-arm surfaces so that students can see their notes during a presentation. In order not to affect the slides, this task lighting on the table arms should not spill off and illuminate the enclosing surfaces of the room, especially the screen. The spatial lighting system would be the system used to illuminate these surfaces. If there is a chalkboard on the front wall, the system for task lighting might also be part of the spatial lighting system.

If the enclosing surfaces of a space, such as the lecture hall, are illuminated, the space will appear to be brightly lit, even though there might not be adequate light for a particular task on the implied illumination plane. On the other hand, if there is proper illumination on the horizontal work plane that does not spill over onto the walls, the space might be perceived as not being adequately lit, although for the particular task, it is. But while these two purposes of lighting are different, spatial lighting can affect our expectations, which, in turn, can affect our visual performance.

Nela Park in Cleveland, Ohio, is the home of General Electric's Lighting and Electrical Institute. It began with the formation of the National Electric Lamp Association, primarily due to the efforts of Franklin S. Terry, from the Sunbeam Incandescent Lamp Company of Chicago, and Burton Gad Tremaine, who had business connections with the Fostoria Incandescent Lamp Company in Ohio. In the early days of electric lighting, without standardization, it was difficult for the various competing companies to gain a share of the lighting market, especially when contending with the major player in the lighting industry, the General Electric Company.

While we all know that Thomas Alva Edison was instrumental in the development of electric lighting, we might not realize that another sign of his innovative genius was his ability to form various companies to produce and support his invention. In 1889, Edison consolidated all of his companies under the Edison General Electric Company. Then in 1892, through a merger with the Thomson Houston Company, the General Electric Company was formed. Charles A. Coffin became the president of this new company, continuing in this position until 1913.

Coffin believed in competition, supposedly having different parts of GE compete against each other to improve the company's overall performance. His penchant for competition was well known, so the leaders of the smaller lighting companies came up with the audacious idea of approaching Coffin with a proposal that he endorse the formation of an association to standardize lighting components that would provide a more level field for broader competition. Coffin agreed, and the National Electric Lamp Association (NELA) was formed in 1901, with GE providing 75% of the financial backing although remaining a silent partner. While NELA essentially operated as an independent agency of the lighting industry, standardizing things and engaging in research, as a result of a U.S. government antitrust investigation, the major position of GE and the nonindependence of NELA were exposed. As a result, GE acquired the remaining 25% of NELA and converted it into its own research arm.

General Electric's Lighting and Electrical Institute at Nela Park provides resources and education support. This facility includes several demonstration lighting installations that dynamically adjust to show different lighting applications. While these demonstrations are quite effective in showing the different results that can be achieved, they also clearly show that work plane illumination and effective spatial lighting are best accomplished by different but coordinated lighting designs for each purpose.

Intentions of Lighting Design

William M. C. Lam, architect and lighting consultant, has been concerned with the architectural intentions of lighting design. He has presented his ideas in numerous publications, specifically in a series of articles entitled "Lighting for Architecture," originally published in *Architectural Record* and then reissued in *Environmental Control*, an Architectural Record Book edited by Robert E. Fischer. In a more recent publication, *Perception and Lighting as Formgivers for Architecture*, Lam again presented his ideas along with a number of well-documented case studies. Lam classified lighting according to six different objectives, one of them dealing with task lighting and five, with spatial lighting.

1. Light to see by: enough light for the purpose
2. The light you see: lighting for mood or atmosphere
3. The light you see: lighting for emphasis or to direct movement
4. The light you see: lighting to express intended use
5. The light you see: lighting to complement structure
6. The light you see: lighting to modify the appearance of space

Lam categorized lighting systems by the character of the lighting or the objective that the lighting achieves. While each of his six lighting categories has a particular emphasis, there is often an overlap among them. For example, the lighting design for a church that creates a mood conducive for a religious space might also establish a sense of movement toward the altar (see Figure 2.8). While *Perception and Lighting as Formgivers for Architecture* concentrates on electrical illumination, the lighting categories apply equally to day lighting.

In a slightly reordered manner, Figures 2.9 to 2.15 and associated commentary expand on the effects that Lam's various categories of lighting might have on one another.

Enough Light for the Purpose

While increasing lighting levels can improve vision, rather than merely increase light levels, it is usually more appropriate to provide a suitable level of illumination, in an appropriate manner, and to adjust other factors to enhance visual perception. Rather than rely on changes in lighting, the more practical approach to improve visual performance often involves altering the task. The return on increased lighting levels continually declines, and if excessive, it is also probable that higher lighting levels might actually reduce visibility (see Figure 2.9).

Figure 2.8 FIRST BAPTIST CHURCH, COLUMBUS, INDIANA
This church, designed by Harry Weese in 1965, is a simple space with a dramatic use of light. The intense daylight grazing down along the brick wall draws the eye forward and upward, while the deep, dark recesses in the wall impart a sense of wonder. The spiritual quality of the space comes from the manipulation of the light and would exist even without the prominent crucifix. There is natural up-light along both sides of the nave, further enhancing the special character of the chapel.

Lighting to Express Intended Use

The lighting system can suggest the desired use of a given space or even an area within a space. For example, the lighting system can define the circulation areas as distinct from the places of gathering. It is also possible to vary the lighting within the same room to denote a different intended type or level of activity. For instance, a restaurant for a fast-turnover lunch crowd can be converted into an intimate dining room by adjusting the level and type of illumination. During the day, a high level of cool light that illuminates the occupants will produce spatial vitality, whereas during the evening, low-level, warm light that illuminates the space rather than the occupants will suggest a relaxed, intimate environment (see Figure 2.10).

Lighting for Emphasis or to Direct Movement

Our attention is naturally drawn to higher levels of illumination. When a surface is brighter than other objects in the visual field, our attention is drawn to it. This difference in brightness levels offers the designer a means of establishing desired responses. However, it is important to recognize that it is the comparative brightness rather than the specific brightness that is operative. The control of lighting levels to establish emphasis can also result from induced movement, either implied or actual. For example, the spotlight during a theatrical performance draws our attention. Comparably, the bright lights over an information desk might actually stimulate us to move through a lobby. In addition to providing increased levels of illumination, lighting can direct movement by the use of repetitive light sources, such as a series of boulevard lights, or by the use of a moving light source, as is used on a theater marquee (see Figures 2.11 and 2.12).

Lighting for Mood or Atmosphere

The character of a space is predicated in large part on the lighting. While the physical objects that define the space are, of course, critical, the lighting has a significant impact on its perceived character. For example, within a given

Refrigerator Light

Cincinnati Union Terminal
Fellheimer & Wagner, Architects - 1933

Figure 2.9 LIGHT FOR THE PURPOSE
These two images are examples of light for a purpose. The image on the left is of a refrigerator with the light set forward near the line of the door. This is actually an improvement over more traditional lights that were set back in the box, leaving most of the items in silhouette. While the forward location does illuminate the items, it is obvious that the light is not very effective on the lower shelves. The image on the right is of an illuminated sign, which is clearly an example of light for a purpose.

Engineering Building Lobby   Executive Office Building Lobby
GM Tech Center, Eero Saarinen, Architect - 1949

Figure 2.10 LIGHT TO EXPRESS INTENDED USE
These two office building lobbies were designed by the same architect, Eero Saarinen, at the same time. The distinct character of these spaces, each of which relates to the type of activity that occurs in the building, is developed in large part by the lighting.

St. Charles Cathedral (Karlskirche), Vienna   Notre Dame du Haut, Ronchamp
Johann B. F. von Erlach, Architect - 1737   Le Corbusier, Architect - 1954

Figure 2.11 LIGHT FOR EMPHASIS
Generally, attention is automatically drawn to brighter objects or surfaces within the visual field. For the distinction to be effective, there should be at least a 10:1 ratio between the point of emphasis and the general visual field.

space, low levels of candlelight will produce an atmosphere quite different from that experienced under high levels of fluorescent lighting. And if the lighting is inverted and directed upward, such as is frequently done with landscape lighting, a very special ambiance is established. Although mood or atmospheric lighting might be considered in connection with spatial character, it also has a relationship with perceived physical factors, such as the size or even

the noise level of the space, both of which can have an effect on the ambiance of a space (see Figure 2.13).

Lighting to Complement Structure

While a designer often expends considerable effort establishing the intended physical juxtaposition of spatial defining elements, without appropriate illumination the results

Throne Room, Versailles   Hall of Mirrors
The Palace of Versailles, Louis Le Vau, Architect - 1669

Figure 2.12 LIGHT TO DIRECT MOVEMENT
Although both the Throne Room and the Hall of Mirrors at Versailles are very similar spaces in terms of form—a long linear space with a barrel-vaulted ceiling and comparable proportions—the different approach to lighting in each establishes a distinct spatial character that was appropriate for the particular purpose of the space.

Luxor Hotel Lobby, Las Vegas   Caesar's Palace Casino, Las Vegas
Veldon Simpson-Architect, Inc. - 1993   Melvin Grossman, Architect & Jo Harris, Designer
                                          1966

Figure 2.13 LIGHT FOR MOOD OR ATMOSPHERE
Las Vegas is a place of fantasy where electric lighting is clearly a major part of the design palette.

might not be visually appreciated. For example, if all surfaces are the same color and illuminated to the same level, it would be difficult to identify the spatial limits of a room, let alone the configuration of the space. All surfaces would tend to blend together, and surface articulation would not be accentuated. Clarity of spatial proportions and dimensions would be lost. On the other hand, by effectively delineating the physical qualities of a space and accentuating the compositional elements, a well-designed lighting system can dramatically enhance the design intentions.

Although this category of lighting is identified in terms of *structure*, we should not assume that this is limited to

the physical components of a structural system. While the dramatic example of "light to complement structure" from the Milwaukee Art Museum (Figure 2.14) clearly does entail supporting structural elements, this category relates to any physical element that articulates spatial enclosure.

Lighting to Modify the Appearance of Space

Lighting that can be effective in expressing structure can also be used to alter the appearance of a space. For example, with an increase in the level of illumination, the apparent physical dimensions of a space also tend to increase. The

Quadracci Pavilion, Milwaukee Art Museum, Santiago Calatrava, Architect - 2001

Figure 2.14 LIGHT TO COMPLEMENT STRUCTURE
When considerable effort is expended to develop interesting structural components to define architectural space, it makes sense to enhance the articulation of these components through effective lighting. (Images courtesy of Claire Shafer)

Daytime View   Nighttime View
Mercantile Center (Formica Building) Arcade, Cincinnati, OH
Harry Weese and Associates, Architect – 1970

Figure 2.15 LIGHT TO MODIFY THE APPEARANCE OF SPACE
As is apparent from these two images, changes in lighting can dramatically alter the appearance of a space. While this change clearly occurs each day when daylight is supplanted with electric light, various manipulations of light at any time can produce a significant change in spatial character.

brighter a space, the larger it generally appears. In addition, by accentuating a wall by lighting it intensely, the apparent physical configuration of a space can be modified such that a square room may be perceived as rectangular, or vice versa. Another interesting way of adjusting the appearance of space through lighting involves changing the way glazing is seen. When the view is the side with higher lighting levels, glass becomes black; when the view is from the other side, the glass is transparent (see Figure 2.15).

Light as Space and Light as Object

While not included as one of Lam's categories, light can also provide the primary means of defining space,

Bus Stop Shelter, Cincinnati, OH

Irwin Union Bank & Trust, Co., Columbus, IN
Eero Saarinen, Architect - 1954

Figure 2.16 LIGHT AS SPACE
While illuminating a space, which essentially means illuminating the physical elements that define that space, is often assumed to be the main objective of architectural lighting, in fact light itself can actually define space. Perhaps the most familiar example of this is the space that is created by a spotlight during a theatrical performance.

Figure 2.17 EMMETT KELLY, SR.
In his circus act, the great clown used light in a way that made it essentially a physical object. (Photo by H. W. Hannau)

independent of any physical delineators (see Figure 2.16). As a powerful energy field, light can not only define space, it can also project a sense of physical substance. Seeing light reflect off dust particles or smoke suggests that it has a physical substance, but perhaps the most dramatic expression of this characteristic of light was incorporated in the circus performance by the great clown Emmett Kelly, Sr., in his tramp-clown character Weary Willie (see Figure 2.17).

Between acts of the wonderful three-ring Ringling Brothers Barnum and Bailey Circus, Kelley would entertain the audience while the remnants from the previous acts were cleaned up and things were prepared for the next performances. Cleaning up often meant removing animal droppings, and Kelly made this part of his act, although rather than sweep up droppings, he would sweep the light from the spotlight into a waste pan. At the end of his per-

formance, he would start sweeping his spotlight inward. The light would get smaller and smaller, and then, when it was time for the beginning of the next acts, he would sweep the light away and the next performances would start. In Kelly's act, light essentially became a physical object.

PHYSICAL NATURE OF LIGHT

The intention of any effective lighting design is to help establish the desired visual ambiance while also providing the appropriate illumination levels required for the various tasks that are to be performed. To develop such a design, we must be knowledgeable about the various means of generating light. But since there are continual changes and additions to available light sources, we should understand the basic physical principles upon which all light sources are based rather than merely attempt to learn what light sources are now used.

While life experience and general science courses provide a reasonable grasp of the basics, a review of the physical principles of light can help establish a more solid base upon which we can utilize light as part of our design palette as we attempt to create architecture as experience rather than merely architecture as object.

As shown in Figure 2.18, light is electromagnetic radiation, a form of energy that extends from long-length radio waves to extremely short, high-intensity cosmic rays. While cosmic rays have wavelengths of only approximately 10×10^{-14} meters, radio waves are around 100 meters in length. Within this immensely wide range of wavelengths (a ratio of 10 trillion to 1), there is an extremely narrow range of electromagnetic radiation to which the human eye is sensitive. The portion of radiation that we call light has wavelengths between 3.8×10^{-7}

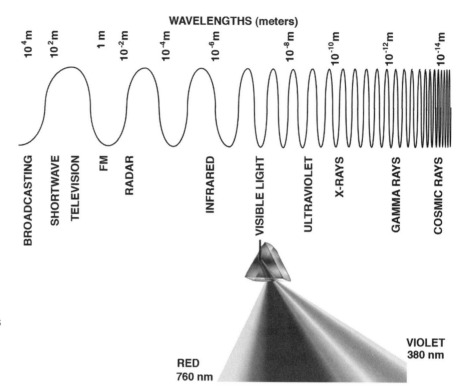

WAVELENGTHS (meters)

10^4 m 10^2 m 1 m 10^{-2} m 10^{-4} m 10^{-6} m 10^{-8} m 10^{-10} m 10^{-12} m 10^{-14} m

BROADCASTING SHORTWAVE TELEVISION FM RADAR INFRARED VISIBLE LIGHT ULTRAVIOLET X-RAYS GAMMA RAYS COSMIC RAYS

RED
760 nm

VIOLET
380 nm

Figure 2.18 WAVELENGTHS OF ELECTROMAGNETIC RADIATION
The range of electromagnetic radiation extends from the long wavelengths used for radio broadcasts to the minute wavelengths of cosmic rays. A narrow range within this extreme spread is associated with visible light, and within this limited range, the distinct colors of the spectrum are defined by the specific wavelengths of radiation.

and 7.6×10^{-7} meters. Vision relies on radiation within this narrow band of electromagnetic radiation entering the eye and stimulating the light-sensitive rods and cones on the retina.

Since the visible portion of electromagnetic radiation has extremely short wavelengths, they are usually measured in units called *nanometers* (380–760 nanometers) or angstroms (3800–7600 angstroms). There are 10 million nanometers or 100 million angstroms per meter. The shorter wavelength of light is at the violet end of the spectrum and the longer wavelength is at the red end of the spectrum.

While the human eye is sensitive to electromagnetic radiation within this limited range of wavelengths, unless there is an adequate amount of stimulation, the eye will not be able to sense it. The minimum level of stimulation to which the eye is sensitive occurs at an intensity of 1.5×10^{-11} watts per square foot, which can also be indicated as 1.0×10^{-8} foot-candles or 1.0×10^{-7} lux. Above this minimal intensity of energy, which is called the *threshold level*, the normal human eye will be sensitive to electromagnetic radiation between 380 and 760 nanometers, although sensitivity is greatest at the mid-range, at around 550 nanometers.

Foot-candles and *lux*, which are units of lighting intensity used, respectively, in the imperial and SI measurement systems, are adjusted to the sensitivity of the human eye. As a result, the conversion from watts per unit area to foot-candles or lux entails color correction that modifies the energy intensity to a perceived intensity.

If the amount of radiation increases excessively, it can damage the eye. The level of radiation considered excessive is generally accepted as the level of illumination that the direct sun provides, which is 10,000 foot-candles or 100,000 lux. This upper limit is 1 trillion or 1.0×10^{12} times the threshold level and is equal to approximately 15 watts per square foot.

Whatever the actual numbers may be (it is not important to memorize these interesting numerical figures), the human eye has an extraordinarily wide range of sensitivity. Within this range, which varies according to the wavelengths of light, our visual sensitivity is not based on arithmetic but rather logarithmic progression. As a result, approximately a 10-fold increase in intensity is required for the eye to perceive a doubling of the lighting level. This follows what is referred to as the Weber-Fechner Law, which suggests that human sensory response is based on changes in the ratio of the stimulus, not on the actual quantity of the stimulus. This is a very important fact that should have a major impact on our approach to design. As will be discussed later, doubling the actual energy level of lighting or sound will produce a change that is barely noticeable.

The speed of light is accepted as one of the basic constants of nature. This constant is the product of the wavelength times the number of waves, or cycles, that pass a

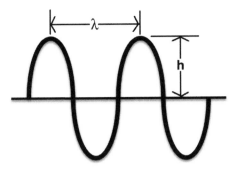

Where: λ = wavelength

h = amplitude

Figure 2.19 ELECTROMAGNETIC RADIATION WAVELENGTH AND AMPLITUDE
Electromagnetic radiation can be represented by means of a sinusoidal wave that represents the length and amplitude of the wave as indicated.

given point in a unit of time. This can be expressed by the formula

$$c = f \times \lambda$$

where:

c is the constant or speed of light

f is the frequency in cycles per second

λ is the wavelength

The speed of light is 186,000 miles per second or 300,000 kilometers per second. Since the various wavelengths of light all travel at this constant speed, a set number of waves, based on the length of the wave, must pass a point within a specific time period. That is, each wavelength of light has a specific frequency, which is usually referred to as *cycles per second*, noted as Hertz (Hz).[3] Since the speed of light must equal the wavelength times the cycles per second, light has frequencies between approximately 4.0×10^{14} Hz for the red end of the spectrum and 8.0×10^{14} Hz for the violet end of the spectrum. The actual wavelengths and frequencies must, of course, be correlated.

3800 ang $\times$ (7.9×10^{14} Hz) = 7600 ang
$\times$ (3.95×10^{14} Hz) = 300,000 km/sec

Figure 2.19 is the typical way to show the wavelength and amplitude of electromagnetic radiation.

As can be seen in Figure 2.18, electromagnetic radiation exists well beyond the frequencies and wavelengths

---

[3]Cycles per second are noted by the term Hertz (Hz), named after Heindrich Rudolph Hertz. Hertz was a German physicist who opened the way for the development of radio, television, and radar by his discovery of electromagnetic waves between 1886 and 1888. His work was based on the predictions of James Clerk Maxwell.

of light, although this radiation is not visible. At the lower frequencies, which correspond to wavelengths of around 1000 feet, the waves are radio waves on the AM band. At 10 feet, the waves are radio waves on the FM band. At higher frequencies, but still below the visible range, the radiation is infrared radiation, which we tend to sense as heat. While we cannot see it, we can feel it. The frequencies of ultraviolet radiation are immediately above the visible spectrum. At even higher frequencies, the radiation is what we know as x-rays, gamma rays, and cosmic rays. From our own intuitive understanding of the difference between these extremes, we should recognize that energy varies according to the frequency of the electromagnetic radiation, with higher energy levels provided by the higher frequencies.

Radio waves can be emitted and received by crystals, and some of the earliest radios were crystal receivers. These radios worked because a crystal vibrates at a frequency that is dependent on its size. This is somewhat similar to a bell or tuning fork. The smaller the crystal, the higher the frequency to which it is responsive. With a crystal, however, even at the higher frequencies, we are dealing with long-wave electromagnetic radiation that is well below the visible spectrum. If the size of the crystal were reduced to around the size of an atom or a molecule, the radiation produced would have a wavelength in the infrared range of the electromagnetic spectrum, although this radiation still would not be visible.

To be visible—that is, to have a frequency between around 4.0×10^{14} and 7.9×10^{14} Hz—the vibrating particle would have to be smaller than an atom. It would have to be an electron. Based on this, we understand that visible light is electromagnetic radiation that is emitted by the vibration of electrons. We should also realize that this vibration is the result of molecular activity that exists in all substances above thermodynamic zero. (Thermodynamic or absolute zero is $-273°$ C.)

When molecular activity exists, electrons vibrate and radiation is emitted. The temperature of the substance determines the rate of vibration, which, in turn, sets the radiation frequency. As the temperature rises, the rate of molecular activity and the radiation emitted increase commensurably, and this increase occurs in terms of both amount and energy level. With a higher temperature, both the energy intensity and the frequency of the radiation emitted are greater. When this radiation is within the visible range, it is referred to as *incandescent radiation*; therefore, an incandescent solid is an object that emits electromagnetic radiation within the visible range.

Incandescent radiation is actually emitted in a band of various frequencies. As indicated in Figure 2.20, this band peaks at a particular frequency that is temperature based. The distribution of radiation is in the form of what is

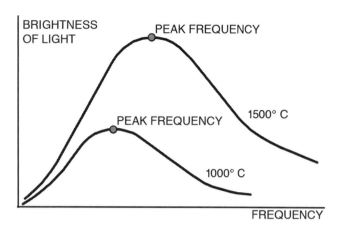

Figure 2.20 INCANDESCENT RADIATION CURVES
An incandescent solid emits radiation in a continuous spectrum. As the temperature of the solid increases, both the intensity and frequency of the emitted radiation increase.

Table 2.1: LIGHT TEMPERATURES

Degrees Kelvin	Light
1750 K	Candle Light
2000 K	Sunrise
2500 K	Incandescent Lamp
3500 K	Warm White Fluorescent
4000 K	White
4500 K	Cool White Fluorescent
5000 K	Noon Sunlight
7000 K	Overcast Sky
10000 K	Clear Blue Sky

generally referred to as a *bell curve*, with the majority of the distribution occurring at the center frequencies and dropping off at both sides. Since the emitted frequency increases with increased temperatures, if the temperature rises enough, some of the radiation emitted becomes visible. When just barely visible, a portion of the radiation is at the low end of the visible spectrum, resulting in emission of red light. If the temperature increases further, the shift results in a fuller spectrum of light, which we perceive as white; this is a balanced mixture of the various colors of light. Theoretically, if the temperature continued to increase, only the "tail end" of the spectrum would remain in the visible range, with the emitting light becoming blue. However, this is not generally possible since the incandescing solid will likely vaporize before such temperatures are attained.

A question often raised is why the emitted radiation follows a bell curve distribution of frequencies rather than one specific frequency based on the temperature of the solid. The classic explanation is that the radiation follows Planck's Law, although a possible answer is that we can assume that the temperature of a material is not an absolute for all elements within that material but is basically an average for these elements. While not accurate, this does relate to the actual reason, which is a little more complex and can be clarified after a further explanation of how light is generated is presented.

The emission of light from an incandescent solid is independent of the substance. As a result, all materials, except those with a shiny finish, are considered black body objects, and emit the same radiation and do so in a continuous spectrum; the color of light emitted is dependent on the object's temperature. In fact, as shown in Table 2.1, the color of light can be designated by the temperature of a solid object from which that color would be emitted.

Gases, unlike heated incandescent solids, emit electromagnetic radiation at specific frequencies. If an electron charge is passed through a gas, the charge will energize the gas, causing an emission of radiation. This radiation will occur at the specific wavelengths particular to that gas, and for wavelengths in the visible spectrum, particular colors will be emitted. This phenomenon has been used in spectroanalysis of distant gases in which the reduction of a particular part of a full-band spectrum of light is used to indicate the specific gas through which the light passes. If a full-band spectrum of light (i.e., white light) passes through a gas, the portions of the spectrum to which the gas is responsive are absorbed. This absorbed light is then reemitted, but in all directions, resulting in an apparent reduction in the intensity of radiation at those particular frequencies for the radiation that continues in the direction of radiation from the original light source. Therefore, passing a light through a gas produces dark bands within the color spectrum, whereas "charging" the gas produces light coincident with the frequency bands to which the gas is responsive.

Historic Review of Physical Principles

We lived in a world of light and shadow, ... but the shadow was almost as luminous as the light.[4]

Tennessee Williams, in Suddenly Last Summer

Although people have wondered about the nature of light since ancient times, scientific investigations of light began only some 350 years ago, and it was not until the early twentieth century that our current understanding

---

[4]Tennessee Williams, "Suddenly Last Summer," *Four Plays* (Signet Classics, Penguin Group [USA] Inc., New York, 2003), p. 21.

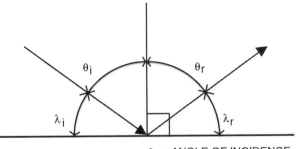

θ_i = ANGLE OF INCIDENCE

θ_r = ANGLE OF REFLECTANCE

Figure 2.21 ANGLE OF INCIDENCE EQUALS ANGLE OF REFLECTION
The angle of incidence of a ray of light is the angle drawn between that ray and a line normal to the surface. This angle is drawn on the plane that is defined by these intersecting lines. Similarly, the angle of reflectance, which from a specular surface equals the angle of incidence, is the angle defined by the reflected ray and the normal to the surface.

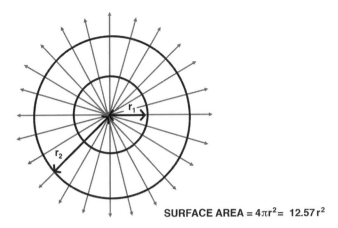

SURFACE AREA = $4\pi r^2$ = $12.57 r^2$

Figure 2.22 INVERSE SQUARE LAW
As light spreads out from a point source, it travels outward in straight lines, distributed over a spherical area that keeps increasing in proportion to the square of the radius of the sphere.

of the nature of light was firmly established. The ancient concern with the nature of light did not lead to any general conclusion. Rather, considerable disagreement arose and continued, on and off, until around 1900. The basic issue of contention was whether light is a waveform or a physical substance. The Aristotelians tended to support the waveform theory, while the Pythagoreans considered light as a series of particles, which is the basis of the corpuscular theory. Added to this polarization were other theories that only complicated the dialogue. For example, Plato believed that vision was dependent on a form of energy that was emitted by the eye itself. The apparent basis for his reasoning was that, unlike hearing, which is independent of orientation, vision relies on the viewer's eyes being directed toward the object seen.

Angle of Incidence Equals Angle of Reflection

While there might not have been agreement on or understanding of the basic nature of light, there was general consensus about certain aspects of light. For example, based on the studies of Hero of Alexandria, the ancient Greeks assumed that light travels in a straight line and that the angle of incidence is equal to the angle of reflection (see Figure 2.21). We should recognize that the angle of incidence, as well as the angle of reflection, is the angle between the ray of light and a line normal or perpendicular to the surface, and not the angle between the ray of light and the surface.[5]

---

[5] A ray of light and a line normal to a surface at the point where the light hits the surface form two intersecting lines, and two intersecting lines establish a plane. The angle between these two lines is then drawn on that plane. Since a line intersecting a flat plane (surface) does not define another plane, it is not clear how to determine the angle between a ray of light and a flat surface.

The observation that light travels in straight lines tended to support the corpuscular theory. While we intuitively understand that we cannot see around a corner and that sight lines can be used to determine straightness, we know and can readily observe that waveforms do bend. For example, a disturbance on a pond generates a wave that can readily go around an obstruction. From a simple experiment in which a water wave is interrupted by a perforated obstruction, we can see that any point on the wave is potentially a point of origin for a new wave, which is Huygens' Principle. Also, if we consider the behavior of sound, which can easily be shown to be a waveform, we realize that waves do travel around corners. So, if light travels in straight lines and does not seem to bend, which as we know a wave does, then light must not be a wave.

Inverse Square Law

The ancient Greeks also observed that the distribution of light follows the inverse square law. This law states that the intensity of illumination will vary inversely as the square of the distance between the source and the illuminated surface. This is based on the divergence of the light traveling in straight lines from a point source. As light from a point source, such as a candle, is emitted, it extends out from a point in a spherical shape. With the source at the center of an implied sphere, the light is assumed to spread out evenly across the sphere. The radius represents the distance that light travels from a point source, and the surface area of a sphere is equal to $4\pi r^2$.

As can be seen in Figures 2.22 and 2.23, as light spreads out from a point source, it is distributed over an implied spherical surface area that increases proportionally with the square of the distance. This means that the intensity of illumination from a point source of light varies inversely

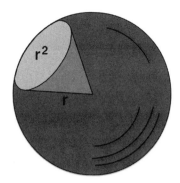

Figure 2.23 STERADIAN
A steradian is a solid angle. Specifically, it is a portion of a sphere that extends from the center and subtends a surface area equal to the square of the radius. A regular steradian takes the form of a cone, which means that the area subtended by the sides of the steradian is in the form of a circle, although a solid angle can subtend any surface shape that has an area equal to the distance from the apex of the angle. Since the surface area of a sphere equals $4\pi r^2$, there are 12.57 steradians in a sphere.

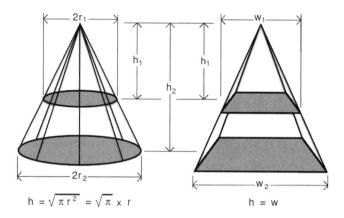

$$h = \sqrt{\pi r^2} = \sqrt{\pi} \times r \qquad h = w$$

Figure 2.24 STERADIAN DIMENSIONS
While it is easiest to visualize a regular solid angle, such as a cone or a pyramid, a solid angle need not be regular. Its base can take any form, and if its base has an area that equals the square of its height, then that solid angle is basically steradian. For practical purposes, we can assume that a steradian that has a regular pyramidal shape will have a height equal to the width of its base. A steradian that has a regular conical shape will have a height equal to the square root of π times the radius of the base.

as the square of the distance between the source and the illuminated surface. Furthermore, since 4π equals 12.57, a sphere with a 1-foot radius has a surface area of 12.57 square feet, which indicates that the illumination at a 1-foot distance from a point source of light will be equal to 1/12.57th of the total amount of light that is emitted by the source.

A pointed tapering shape, such as a cone or a pyramid, is a three-dimensional or solid angle. If a solid angle has a base area equal to the square of the distance from the apex to the base, it is called a *steradian*. While it is easiest to visualize a steradian by assuming a regular solid angle, such as a cone or a pyramid, as shown in Figure 2.24, any solid angle with a base area equal to the square of the apex-to-base dimension is a steradian. However, if the base of the solid angle is flat, the distance from the apex to the base will vary according to where on the base it is measured. Therefore, to maintain a constant dimension, a steradian legitimately has a curved base and is a segment or portion of a sphere, and since the surface area of a sphere equals $4\pi r^2$, there are 12.57 steradians in a sphere.

A steradian is used to determine the intensity of radiation from a light source, particularly a point source. Knowing the total amount of light that is emitted from a point source, since it will theoretically spread out evenly in all directions, the intensity of radiation will equal the total radiation divided by 12.57 times the square of the distance from the source. When determining illumination levels in this manner, it is unlikely that the illuminated surface will be curved, at least in terms of developing the calculation, so the "height" of the steradian is typically taken merely as the distance from the surface to the apex[6] of the solid angle.

<hr>

[6]The tip or point of a solid angle is referred to as either the *apex* or the *vertex*.

While a steradian is a particular-sized solid angle, generally the size of a solid angle is expressed in terms of a solid-angle fraction. In some ways this is similar to using degrees to indicate the spread of a planar angle, since a circle, which can be considered a complete planar angle, is set at a 360° degree. With a three-dimensional angle, however, there is a question as to what constitutes the "whole" on which the solid-angle fraction is based. Some choose to parallel the approach of planar angles and use the sphere as one solid angle, but generally the hemisphere is considered one solid angle.

The luminous intensity (I) on a surface is determined by the total luminous flux received divided by the area. The luminous flux is generally expressed in terms of lumens (L), so in the imperial system of measurement:

$$I = \frac{L}{sq\ ft},$$ which is expressed as lumens per square foot of illumination or as foot-candles

Since the base area of a steradian equals the square of the distance from the vertex to the base, h^2, luminous flux within a steradian produces a luminous intensity (I) equal to the total lumens in the steradian divided by the square of the distance (h^2).

$$I = \frac{L}{h^2},$$ so the intensity is inversely proportional to the square of the distance

The luminous flux in a steradian is called *candela*.

Figure 2.25 shows the distribution of light from various light sources: a point source, a linear source, and an area source. While the distribution of light from a point source of light is assumed to flow outward from the source equally

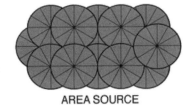

POINT
SOURCE   LINEAR SOURCE   AREA SOURCE

Figure 2.25 COMPARISON OF POINT, LINEAR, AND AREA LIGHT SOURCES
The intensity of illumination from a point source of light varies inversely as the square of the distance, which is the inverse square law. With a linear light source, which is essentially a series of point sources in a row, the intensity of illumination varies inversely as the distance. With an area light source, which is essentially a spread of point sources of light, the intensity of illumination does not vary with a change in distance. Similarly, if a source emits light in parallel rays in a particular direction, the intensity of illumination in that direction will not vary with a change in distance.

in all directions, following the inverse square law, the distribution, and therefore the intensity of illumination from a linear light source, such as a fluorescent tube or even more so a row of fluorescent lights, will vary according to the distance from the light source. In a sense, a linear light source is a row of point sources of light. As the light distributed from each point along this line diminishes according to the inverse square law, light from adjacent point sources is added to make up the loss on the line parallel to the line of assumed point sources of light. When the light is from an area light source, such as a balanced luminous ceiling, there is no reduction in intensity as the distance from the source increases. With an area source, as the incident illumination directly below an assumed point source of light is reduced, the loss is made up for by adjacent light sources, similar to the linear light source but now in all directions. If, rather than spreading the light out equally in all directions, as is assumed with a point source, a light fixture redirects the radiation into essentially parallel rays, the intensity of illumination will also not be reduced as the distance from the source increases.

While sunlight comes from a point source of light, after traveling the 93 million miles from the sun, the rays that reach the earth comprise an extremely small portion of the total emitted solar radiation; as a result, these rays are parallel to each other. Based on this, the intensity of sunlight does not vary with changes in distance, although, as with all radiation, the intensity of radiation received on a surface will depend on the angle of incidence on that surface. The intensity will vary as the cosine of the angle of incidence.

Speed of Light

While the confrontation between the wave and corpuscular theories of light began in ancient times, serious investigations of the nature of light did not began until early in the seventeenth century. The first explorations tried to answer a question that had fascinated humankind throughout the ages: "At what speed does light travel?"

Obviously, light travels at a very rapid rate, which is readily recognized by comparing its speed to that of sound. Anyone who has experienced a thunder and lightning storm realizes that there is a time delay between seeing the flash of light and hearing the clap of sound, but this delay only indicates that light travels more rapidly than sound. It does not provide any indication of its actual speed. (Of course, this assumes that a connection between the two has been made.) In ancient times, perhaps in comparison to what speeds could be conceived, it was generally thought that light traveled instantaneously. That is, the speed of light was assumed to be infinite—that no time was required for light to travel, even over great distances.

Supposedly, Galileo was the first person to seriously attempt to measure the speed of light. In the early 1600s, he set up an experiment to measure the time it took for light to travel to a mirror and back to the point of origin. Without the ability to develop a high-intensity light source or a mirror with nearly perfect reflection, the distance over which this experiment could be tried was limited. When Galileo's early attempts did not produce measurable results, with the help of members of the Florentine Academy he extended the experiment. Two lanterns were set up on two distant hilltops. Both lanterns were lit but were hidden from one another. One lantern was then uncovered, and when it was seen at the second location, the second lantern was uncovered. Measurements were taken of the time that had elapsed between uncovering the first lantern and then observing light from the second lantern, assuming that this was the time required for the light to travel between the two locations. While the basic idea was sound, obviously it was human reaction time that was actually being measured.

In the latter part of the century, relying on the conditions diagrammed in Figure 2.26, the Danish astronomer Olaus Roemer made the first effective estimation of the speed of light. Roemer observed that one of the moons of Jupiter appeared to emerge from behind the planet at successively later times when the Earth was receding from Jupiter and at correspondingly earlier times when the Earth

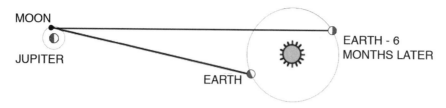

Figure 2.26 ROEMER'S DIAGRAM
Olaus Roemer used the phases of the moons of Jupiter to estimate the speed of light. He realized that while the period of the moon circling Jupiter was consistent, the time that it would take light to travel from Jupiter to Earth would vary according to the relative position between Jupiter and Earth. Using the estimated difference in travel distance, Roemer achieved the first effective estimation of the speed of light.

was approaching Jupiter. Accepting that the actual period of rotation of the moon was constant, Roemer assumed that the observed difference was due to the relative motion between the source and the observer, similar to the Doppler effect, which causes the pitch of a siren to change as an emergency vehicle approaches or leaves the observation point. Based on his understanding of this difference in the time when the moon of Jupiter would appear, Roemer determined that there would be nearly a 22-minute delay for the emergence of the moon from a position closest to the planet Jupiter to one farthest apart. He attributed this delay to the time that was required for the light to travel across the Earth's orbit.

In September 1676, prior to offering the above explanation, Roemer announced to the Academy of Science in Paris that the eclipse of one of the moons of Jupiter, which was expected to occur 45 seconds after 5:25 A.M. on November 9, would be exactly 10 minutes late. Needless to say, the Academy was skeptical of Roemer's prediction, but through careful measurements of the eclipse, it was indeed recorded as occurring exactly as Roemer had predicted.

Even with the demonstrated proof, Roemer's conclusions about the speed of light were not generally accepted. Shortly afterward, using Roemer's data, Huygens made the first calculation of the speed of light. Combining Roemer's 22-minute figure for the time of travel across the Earth's orbit with his own estimate of the diameter of the Earth's orbit, he obtained a value of 200,000,000 meters per second. Although this is only about two-thirds of the speed of light currently accepted, it was a considerable achievement for that time. While Galileo had been the first to suggest strongly that the speed of light is not instantaneous, Roemer's and Huygens' work firmly established that the propagation of light does require a finite time. This was the significance of their work, not the particular values they proposed for the speed of light.

In the eighteenth century, the English astronomer James Bradley attempted to measure the speed of light by applying the *aberration phenomenon*. This phenomenon is the apparent shift in the position of distant stars over the course of the year that causes the path of the stars to appear as small ellipses. The phenomenon is related to a common experience. When it is raining and we are standing still, we can usually protect ourselves by holding an umbrella overhead. However, if we walk forward while the rain continues to fall vertically, the combination of the vertical movement of the rain and our horizontal movement results in an apparent slantwise movement of the rain. As a result, in order to keep dry, we must tilt the umbrella forward. Similarly, in observing a distant star, the astronomer is forced to tilt the telescope to account for the movement of the Earth in its orbit. Over the course of a year, the tilt of the telescope would have to arc through an ellipse. This required tilt is the phenomenon of aberration and would have a specific angle that, although small, can be accurately measured. By relating the angle of aberration to the speed of the Earth in its orbit, Bradley expected to determine the speed of light.

In the mid-nineteenth century, the French experimenter Armand Fizeau was the first to succeed in measuring the speed of light. He adopted the method initially suggested by Galileo, but he replaced the second lantern with a polished mirror and used a pulsating light source. He established the light pulsations by passing the light through a rotating toothed wheel. With precise detail both in construction of the apparatus and in its even or regular operation, the toothed wheel released light at consistently controlled intervals. The pulsating light was directed toward a mirror located 5 miles away. The light reflected off the mirror then had to pass again through the revolving toothed wheel in order to be observed. Since the light had to pass through the toothed wheel twice, it could be observed only when the time required to travel the 10 miles to and from the distant mirror equaled the time required to move the toothed wheel to a position that would allow the returning light to pass unimpeded. Knowing the speed of rotation that allowed for this double pass through the toothed wheel, Fizeau was able to determine the speed of light.

Shortly after Fizeau's experiment, another French scientist, Foucault, refined the method by replacing the toothed wheel with a rotating "cylinder" regularly faceted

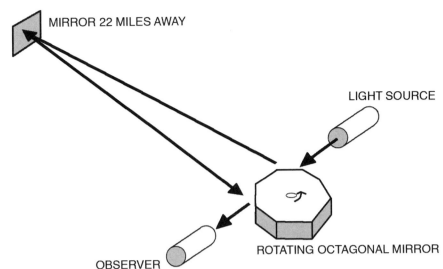

Figure 2.27 MICHELSON'S APPARATUS
Albert Michelson refined the pulsing-light approach to measuring the speed of light that was initially proposed by Galileo. While Galileo relied on people to manage the appearance of light and Fizeau used a spinning toothed wheel, Michelson used a spinning, highly refined octagonal mirror. Since light from the source would be visible at the observation point only at a specific RPM of the mirror, Michelson was able to achieve the first reasonably accurate measurement of the speed of light.

with mirrors. This apparatus, in the hands of the American physicist Albert Michelson, ultimately attained the highest level of precision.

Michelson's apparatus, which is diagrammed in Figure 2.27, included an extremely accurate octagonal mirrored cylindrical surface and a reflecting mirror located 22 miles away. When an intense light was directed onto one face of the octagon, it would be reflected off the octagon toward the distant mirror, from which it would then be reflected back to another face of the octagon and then to an observation post. As the octagonal cylinder was rotated, the reflected light could be observed only when the speed of rotation was such that the movement of the mirrored faces permitted the light to be reflected toward the distant mirror and then, upon return to the moving cylinder, be reflected to the observation post. This would occur only if the speed of rotation positioned a reflecting surface on the octagonal cylinder to both send and receive the light. By recording the particular rotational speed that would accomplish the correct triple reflection, Michelson was able to determine the speed of light. He achieved a precision level of better than 10,000 to 1. This precision was possible because of the extreme accuracy with which the various factors were determined. The distance of about 22 miles to the fixed reflecting mirror was measured by direct surveying techniques to within 4 inches, and the angles of the faces of the octagonal cylinder were within 1 part in a million.

In 1926, in recognition of his significant achievements in measuring the speed of light, Albert A. Michelson became the first American to receive a Nobel Prize. Michelson had determined the speed of light to be 299,776 kilometers per second. Today, we accept the speed as 299,792 kilometers per second, which is different from Michelson's figure by only 1/20,000. Generally, the speed is rounded

to 300,000 kilometers per second. In the imperial system, the speed of light is 186,282 miles per second, although this is usually rounded to 186,000 miles per second.

The major concern for an accurate measurement of the speed of light was based, in part, on the fact that modern physics ascribes to the velocity of light a fundamental significance that extends far beyond the field of optics. For one thing, the speed of light in a vacuum, which is noted as c, is considered to be a universal constant. As mentioned, it is the velocity of all electromagnetic radiation. It is also the theoretical maximum velocity at which any material object can move. But for our purposes, the ability to measure the speed of light provided the basis upon which it was possible to prove that light is a waveform.

Refraction

In 1621, shortly after Galileo's attempts to measure the speed of light, the Dutch mathematician Willdhehord Snell proposed that light would bend as it went from one medium to another. However, he was unable to explain why this occurred.

If light strikes the plane boundary of a transparent material at an oblique angle, part of the incident light will be reflected off the surface. That which is not reflected will enter the transparent material, changing its direction on passing through the boundary. This sudden change of direction is called *refraction*. In the case where the light passes into a denser medium, such as from air to water or glass, the light rays will be refracted, or bent, toward the normal. If light passes into a less dense medium, such as back into air, it is bent away from the normal. Actually, when this phenomenon is observed, the interpretation of what happens might be reversed. As diagrammed in Figure 2.28, if a straight stick is inserted into water, the stick will

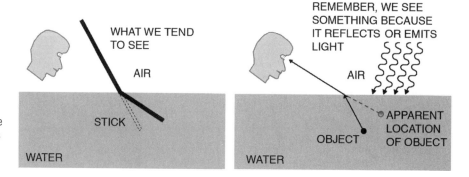

Figure 2.28 APPARENT BENDING IN WATER
The apparent position of an object in water can be confusing, not only in terms of where the object is actually located but also in demonstrating how refraction of light operates.

appear to bend upward below the surface of the water. Since we know that the stick does not actually bend, it could be assumed that the light rays bend upward on entering the water. However, on further analysis, it becomes clear that the reverse must be true. Although we look straight at an object, if the light rays bend downward on entering into the water, objects that are below a true straight line of vision will be seen and will appear to be above their actual location.

Since the angle of refraction is the same upon entering and leaving a material of different density, the rays that leave a flat plate of glass will be parallel to those entering the glass, although the leaving rays are shifted off the line of the entering rays.

The explanation of the phenomenon of refraction of light is directly tied to the determination of the nature of light. In 1637, the French philosopher, mathematician, and scientist René Descartes developed an analogy between the refraction of light passing into a denser material and the change of direction that occurs with a tennis ball passing through a net. When a tennis ball goes through a net, it slows down and is deflected toward the line of the net, whereas when light passes into a denser medium, it bends downward. Supposedly, Descartes reasoned from this analogy that because light rays bend downward, contrary to the tennis ball, the velocity of light in a denser material is increased. Interestingly, while this notion of increased velocity correlates with measurements obtained with sound waves passing through denser mediums, it actually became part of the justification of the corpuscular theory of light.

It must also have produced some confusion for Descartes himself, since he had previously asserted that light is always propagated instantaneously. Descartes, who is responsible for the existential comment "I think, therefore I am," had written in 1634 that light traveled instantaneously. Of this he was so "certain that if it could be proved false, [he would] be ready to confess that [he knew] absolutely nothing in philosophy." He also seems to have supported the Platonic notion that sight was dependent on

some energy that was emitted by the eye itself, all of which indicates that having one good idea is not a guarantee that all your ideas will be correct.

Isaac Newton believed that Descartes' notions of the nature of light supported the corpuscular theory. Newton reasoned that if light were comprised of particles, there would be a gravitational attraction between the particles and a denser transparent substance such as glass. This attraction would remain minimal until the light particles were close to the surface of the glass, at which time the gravitational pull would engage, increasing the velocity of the light particles and causing them to bend downward as they entered the glass. According to Newton, other properties of light also favored the corpuscular theory. For example, as will be discussed shortly, Newton used the refraction of light to experiment with color. When light was passed through a prism, the light refracted, bending and separating into its component colors. The fact that light could be separated into different colors tended to support the notion of light as particles. With Descartes' and Newton's strong support, reinforced by the common assumption that light travels in straight lines, there was a general popular acceptance of the corpuscular theory of light over the wave theory. However, in the scientific community, the debate continued.

In 1644, Thomas Hobbes proposed a pulse theory of light. This was not quite the wave theory as we understand it today since the periodic nature of the pulses had not been identified. Hobbes found that the pulse theory accounted for refraction in a more plausible way than the corpuscular theory if one assumed that, contrary to Descartes' assumption, the velocity of light was slower in a denser medium.

In 1690, the Dutch physicist Christian Huygens presented the idea in a more specific manner by considering light as impulses that travel as a wave front. He said that every point on a wave front may be regarded as a new source of waves, and by simple graphics he demonstrated the phenomenon of refraction. Simply stated, as the light enters the denser substance, the velocity decreases.

Assuming the notion of constant frequency, the wavelength must also decrease, resulting in the light bending downward. Huygens' belief that light is an impulse in a medium was in direct opposition to Newton's interpretations, but ironically, Newton had correctly suggested that light might have to be assigned periodic properties in order to account for the phenomena of color.

So, the question as to the relative speed of light as it enters a denser medium was significant. Today we accept that the apparent speed of light is reduced, not increased, upon entering a denser medium and that this reduction is the cause for the bending of the light rays. However, the rays of light also bend on leaving the denser medium, but in the reverse direction. If the light rays bend on entering due to slowing down, then the bending back to their original angle upon leaving the denser medium must be due to an increase in speed. The question, then, is not only what causes the decrease in velocity, but what induces the increase in velocity. If a fast-traveling particle, such as a bullet, flies through the air and penetrates a denser medium, it will slow down. However, if it emerges on the other side, it does not speed up but continues at its reduced velocity. In order for there to be an increase in speed, there would have to be an input of additional energy. So, how can light regain its initial velocity after slowing down by passing through a denser medium?

Combine this dilemma with the notion that the speed of light is a universal constant in nature. Of course, our acceptance of this "fact" might be analogous to Descartes' acceptance of light traveling instantaneously, but if we do accept that the speed of light is a constant, how can we assume that the velocity of light changes? Rather than a change in velocity, perhaps something interrupts or delays the transmission of light.[7]

As light strikes a surface, it can be reflected or absorbed. If it is reflected, it "bounces off" the surface. If it is not reflected, then the energy of the light is absorbed. If it is absorbed, it is either transformed into molecular activity (heat) or it is reemitted as electromagnetic radiation. When it is reemitted as electromagnetic radiation, it travels at the speed of light until it is again absorbed and perhaps reemitted. While the speed of light remains constant, the process of absorbing and then reemitting light is not instantaneous. The time required to absorb and reemit the light results in the apparent reduction in the velocity. Since on emerging from the denser material the absorption–reemission sequence no longer occurs, the light again travels at its initial velocity.

---

[7] Actually, when light passes through air, some absorption and reemission does occur, resulting in a reduction of the speed of light by 0.03% from the speed of light in a vacuum.

Light and Color

There is great fascination with the sparkling light and brilliant colors that are produced when sunlight strikes certain transparent gems and crystals. The sparkling effects and brilliant colors are the result of reflection and refraction, as well as the critical angle of the gem or crystal. If a narrow beam of light is obliquely incident onto a transparent material, the light rays will refract, or bend, upon entering the glass. The amount of refraction will depend on the material and will differ for each of the component colors of the light. Higher-frequency colors, ultraviolet and blue, will bend more than lower-frequency colors. The difference in refraction results in dispersing or spreading the light into a band of various colors. This band of colors is called a *spectrum*.

In 1666, shortly after Isaac Newton received his degree from Trinity College, Cambridge, there was a major outbreak of plague. The university was forced to close, and Newton retired for some 18 months to his home. During this enforced vacation, he pursued three major activities: the development of calculus, the formation of the theory of gravitation, and experiments in optics, particularly with the color of light.

At 24 years of age, Newton developed several experiments with prisms in order to investigate the color composition of light. He found that the angular configuration of the prism could increase the angular spread of the incident light and avoid reconversion. In addition to selecting a proper prism, by tilting the screen on which the emerging light was cast, Newton was able to achieve a further dispersion of the various wavelengths of light.

Having produced a major spread of the light into its component colors, Newton then placed another prism behind the first, but with an opaque screen between the two. The obstructing screen had a narrow slit so that only one segment of the spectrum produced by the light passing through the first prism could pass to the second prism. Using this arrangement, Newton attempted to divide a single color into the components that he observed comprised white light. He could not. Although the second prism refracted the light that passed through it, the light was not divided further but maintained the same color.

Having divided light into its component colors, Newton then experimented with the effects of combining single or monochromatic colors. Having separated white light into its component colors, he then selectively combined colors by reflecting them off a mirror onto a white screen. He found that combining different colors from the spectrum of sunlight produced new colors, but not white unless the full spectrum of light was recombined or the three primary colors of light came together. By passing the mixed light through another prism, he also found that the new apparent color produced by combining monochromatic colors could again be divided into its component colors. In this way, he demonstrated that the intermingled light was not itself monochromatic, although it might appear similar to a component of white light. For example, by combining red and green, Newton was able to produce a yellow light that was equal in appearance to the yellow light produced by the refraction of white light. From this Newton deduced the fundamental principle that our perception of color is not directly connected to the physical stimulus. While the physical stimulus obviously affects our perceptions, it does not determine them.

Newton also demonstrated that the various colors that comprise the full spectrum that produce white light do not react with each other but simply contribute to the resulting mixture. He did this by dispersing light through a prism and then inserting a narrow obstacle into the spectrum of light formed so that a single color was obstructed. The remaining light, which was deficient in that one color, was then recombined by passing it through a second prism. The intercepted color was found to be totally absent in the recombined light. This was observed by a change in color of the recombined light and was verified experimentally by again dispersing the recombined light by passing it through another prism. The obstructed color was not included in the dispersed light.

From these experiments, Newton concluded that white light consists of a mixture of colors that refract differently when they enter or leave a denser medium. This means that the index of refraction for a given material is slightly different for each color, being the lowest for red and the highest for violet.[8] In a dense transparent material the apparent speed of red light is therefore greater than that of violet, although the difference is not considerable.

The rainbow is probably the most familiar example of the refraction of light that occurs in nature. If, after a rain, the sun's rays fall upon slowly settling droplets of water, a colored arc is produced. This rainbow is the result of refraction of light as it enters the water droplets. The light is refracted on entering the water droplet, internally reflected, and then refracted again on leaving. As a result, the colored rays of the rainbow are seen coming in a direction opposite the sun.

While it is hard to imagine that Newton's fascination with optics and color was not based, at least in part, on being enamored of the beauty of a rainbow, there is no verification of this. Rather, his interest in these experiments supposedly began with his concern over the objectionable fringes of color that are sometimes apparent when using a refracting telescope. As will be discussed later, these disturbing color aberrations are a result of light waves, although Newton's experiments with colors were initially used to support the corpuscular theory of light. The assumption was that the dispersion of light into various colors showed that light is comprised of particulate matter, with each color of light related to a specific particle size. However, with further clarification that refraction of light is actually a result of the various wavelengths of light and the apparently different speed that each wavelength has in a transparent medium, it became apparent that Newton's experiments more properly indicated that light is a waveform.

If light enters or leaves a denser medium and its direction of travel is not perpendicular to the surface, the light rays will bend. The amount of bending is shown, by Snell's Law, to be determined by the index of refraction of the different media through which the light passes and the angle of incidence at which the light strikes the surface that divides the media. As mentioned, this is supposedly the result of the difference in the apparent speed of the various wavelengths of light. However, if the angle of incidence is zero, the light does not bend when it passes into a medium of different density. Does this mean that when there is no refraction the velocity of the different wavelengths of light is the same?

Although we might not have a complete grasp of all of the physical principles applicable to light, hopefully we now understand that what the eye perceives as the color of light is related to the wavelength of radiation. The wavelength of red light, which is the longest in the visible spectrum, is around 7600 angstroms. Violet has the shortest wavelength in the visible spectrum, at around 3800 angstroms.

There is no dispersion[9] of light in a vacuum, and the speed of light is a constant for all wavelengths. This can be observed whenever the moon passes in front of a distant star. As the moon obscures the star, the light is blocked suddenly, but without any apparent variation of color. If the speed of the different wavelengths of light were not constant, this condition could not occur.

As light passes through the atmosphere, dispersion does occur, which helps explain why the sky is blue and why the rising and setting sun casts a red veil over the

---

[8] Another important contribution by Newton to color theory was his arrangement of the various colors into the now familiar color wheel that connects the low end of the visible spectrum, red, to the high end, violet. In this, his critical contribution was the insertion of the color purple, which is not actually found in the dispersion of white light. By adding this new color, which he could produce by combining different monochromatic colors, Newton established an apparent continuum that allowed him to effectively connect the two ends of the visible spectrum to form a circle or wheel. Newton's color wheel is still accepted as a basis for color analysis.

[9] Dispersion of light, and in fact of all radiation, refers to the separation into the different wavelengths.

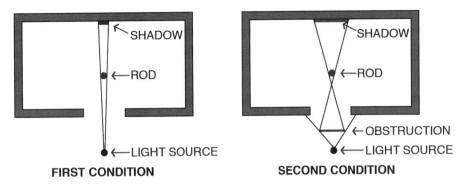

Figure 2.29 GRIMALDI'S DEMONSTRATION
Grimaldi developed a simple demonstration of diffraction. He set up two comparable conditions with one exception: in one condition, an obstruction panel was placed between the light source and the rod. Although direct light was obstructed, diffracted light that bent around the edge of the obstruction still managed to develop a shadow, although less intense and of wider configuration.

horizon. Dispersion also helps explain why the color blue tends to recede, while red tends to advance. While there is dispersion with light, sound waves do not show any clear indication of this phenomenon. Differently pitched sounds, which are indicative of different wavelengths, travel at the same speed even when they enter a denser medium at an angle. However, since the dispersion of light is understood to be proportional to the wavelength, becoming less with an increase in the wavelength, perhaps our failure to observe dispersion of sound is a factor of the relatively large size of sound waves.

Diffraction

The belief that light travels in straight lines tended to inhibit the acceptance of light as a waveform since waveforms are known to bend around corners or barriers. However, if light passes through a narrow slot, such as the space between two fingers, the light will be visible where the straight-line travel projections would not suggest. This simple observation suggests that light perhaps does bend, and in the mid-seventeenth century, the Italian scientist Francesco Grimaldi undertook what is recognized as the first attempt to prove that bending also occurs with light.

Grimaldi examined the shadow cast by an object that was illuminated by a narrow beam of sunlight that had passed through a small pinhole. He found, as with the double-finger slit, that the width of the shadow was wider than the theory of straight-line travel would indicate. He also found that the edges of the shadow were not as sharp as one would assume and were marked by alternating light and dark bands.

Grimaldi pursued his experiments, demonstrating that even if a light source is obscured, it can still produce a shadow of an object that is located beyond the obstruction. As shown in the left diagram in Figure 2.29, if a vertical rod is placed in front of the rear wall of a darkened room and a light source is placed outside the doorway, a shadow of the rod will be cast against the rear wall. When an obstruction is placed between the light source and the opening into the darkened room, as shown in the image on the right

of Figure 2.29, the shadow of the obstruction is cast over the shadow of the rod, but the shadow of the rod is still visible, although somewhat less clear. Obviously, the only way that the light can generate a shadow of the rod is if the light bends around the obstruction.

Grimaldi called the bending of light *diffraction*. The demonstration that the diffraction of light exists provided a clear indication that light is actually a wave phenomenon. Diffraction is the spreading of waves after they pass the edge of an obstacle or pass through a narrow opening, which means passing by two edges. In order to observe diffraction, the opening must not be much wider than the length of the wave. With sound, which has a relatively long wavelength, diffraction can be readily observed; however, with light, which has extremely short wavelengths, diffraction is difficult to discern. In order to demonstrate that a band of light has actually spread, the increase in the width of the light band would not only have to be measurable, it would also have to be a significant proportional increase. To achieve this, the aperture would have to be extremely narrow.

Newton, who was born when Grimaldi was 22, supposedly repeated Grimaldi's demonstration, but the true understanding of the observed effect was not achieved for almost 250 years.

While the bending of light rays around the edges of obstructions can be seen with special techniques and equipment,[10] it is also possible to observe this phenomenon in our everyday experiences. For example, when we look through a screened window, while the screen will affect the view, the screen is really only visible when focused on. This can be easily documented with a camera. To photograph through a screen or a fence, under the proper conditions,

---

[10] As discussed, a simple glass prism can be used to divide the light into its component wavelengths, but detailed analysis of a light source would be hindered by the tendency of the dispersed bands of light to merge together. Since a prism does not produce a very clear image, spectroscopes used for critical analysis generally rely on a diffraction screen rather than a prism. The diffraction screen includes a series of very narrow slits, each with a width of only about one-thousandth of an inch. As the light passes through these precise, narrow slits, it is dispersed into its component colors but without the problem of overlap. In this case, the dispersion of light is a result of diffraction rather than refraction.

we can obtain a reasonable clear shot by merely focusing beyond the obstruction, assuming that the open area of the obstructing screen or fence constitutes the major portion of the screen. If the screening material is relatively thin, the camera sees around the obstructions. Another relatively common opportunity to observe the phenomenon of light bending around obstructions occurs with the shadow produced by a deciduous tree in winter. Looking at the shadow and comparing it to the actual tree, we notice that the smaller branches of the tree do not produce shadows. Since the smaller branches do not seem to obstruct the light, the light apparently must bend around these small obstructions. Upon further consideration, we should realize that this is a significant factor that impacts on the collection of solar energy.

Since solar collection is often desired during the winter and not during the summer, the use of deciduous vegetation is frequently encouraged since the leaves will provide shade during the summer; then, during the winter, when insolation gain is desirable, the trees will have lost their leaves and the sun will not be blocked. The concept is that, as is indicated by its shadow, the leafless trees allow the sunlight to pass through, but the shadow is not an accurate illustration of the amount of light that can actually pass through the bare tree. While the shadow from a leafless tree might suggest that 85–90% of the sunlight is available, in actuality up to 50% of the insolation is actually blocked by the tree's branches, limbs, and twigs.

Diffraction is based on the principle that every point on a wave front may be considered the point of origin of a new wave. Huygens first proposed this principle in the second half of the seventeenth century, and at the beginning of the nineteenth century, the English scientist Thomas Young used this principle to demonstrate definitively that light is indeed a waveform. During the intervening 100 years between Huygens' and Young's work, the scientific community continued to argue back and forth between the corpuscular theory of light, which Descartes and Newton had endorsed, and the wave theory, which Huygens supported.

In order to understand better how Huygens' Principle can be used to explain the diffraction phenomenon, we might consider what would happen if a wave front were intercepted by an obstruction in which there was a narrow slit. If any point on the wave front is potentially the origin of a new wave, then a new wave should emerge through the slit and spread out from this point on the back side of the obstruction. However, if a new wave is not generated, the incident wave should merely pass through the opening and continue on in a narrow stream.

Huygens' Principle is easily demonstrated by a water wave. If the surface of a water body is disturbed, a wave will be formed, but if an obstruction is inserted into the water, the wave front will be blocked. However, if there is a narrow opening in the obstruction, a new wave will emerge through the opening. A similar experiment is possible with light. Although it is not possible to actually observe the waves, it should be possible to see that the light does spread as it passes through the narrow opening. This essentially is the experiment that Thomas Young performed in 1801. As Newton combined prisms, Young combined several obstructing panels in which there were narrow slits. His experiment is known as the *double-slit experiment*. In order to understand what Young observed, we should first introduce the notion of *interference*.

Without becoming too specific, a waveform deals with alternations of positive and negative energy. When a disturbance creates a wave in water, the water rises above and drops below the initial elevation of the water surface. Similarly, when the strings on a guitar are plucked, they vibrate up and down off the static position, generating waves in the strings that can create sound by causing the air to compress and expand.

Waves have both a positive and a negative aspect. If two identical waves that are in phase are joined together, they will interfere constructively or reinforce each other. The power of both waves will be added together. With water waves, this would result in increasing the height and depth of the peaks and troughs. However, if identical waves are combined out of phase, they will interfere destructively with each other. When the positive and negative aspects of the two waves overlap, they tend to cancel each other out. If the waves are identical and out of phase by one-half of a wavelength, then the positive waves will be opposed by equal negative waves. Theoretically, then, if two violins were played identically and simultaneously, but out of phase by half a wavelength, they would produce interfering waves of sound energy that would result in silence.

Figure 2.30 diagrammatically shows how similar waveforms can be combined in either a constructive or destructive manner. The double-slit experiment was based on this. Young understood that if light was a waveform, he should be able to use Huygens' Principle to divide the same light wave into two waves and then develop a series of light and dark bands as these two similar waves interfere constructively and destructively as they overlap.

Young set up three panels to demonstrate that light was a waveform (see Figure 2.31). The first panel had one small vertical slit, while the second had two, one on either side of the location of the opening in the first panel. The third panel was the screen on which the results were observed.

By placing a light source in front of the first panel, a point source of light emerged through the opening in that panel. If this light then passed through both openings in the middle panel, it could be due merely to the continuation of light rays that had passed through the first opening,

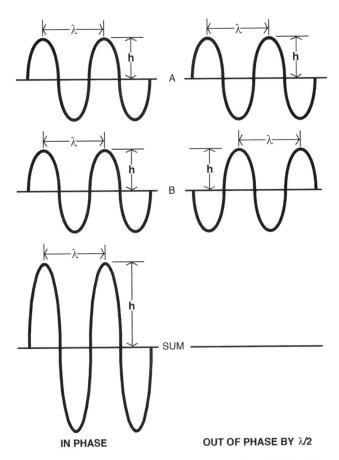

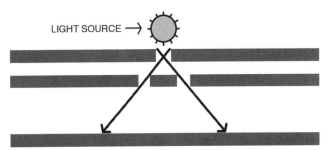

Figure 2.32 YOUNG'S DOUBLE-SLIT EXPERIMENT: DIRECT LIGHT RAYS
Assuming that light can only travel in a straight line, a single light source located beyond the outer panel should be able to project light onto the screen at only two points, each determined by a straight line drawn from the light source through the vertical slit in the outer panel and through one of the slits in the intermediate panel.

IN PHASE   OUT OF PHASE BY λ/2

Figure 2.30 WAVE INTERFERENCE: CONSTRUCTIVE AND DESTRUCTIVE
Combining waves can result in either constructive reinforcement or destructive cancellation. Since the sinusoidal waves extend both above and below the neutral line, the addition of two similar waves can result in anything from a full doubling of the intensity, both positive and negative, to a complete cancellation, with the positive negated by the negative. These extremes occur when the waves are in sync or when they are half a wavelength out of sync.

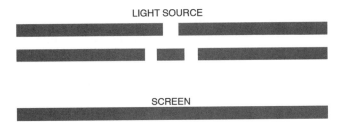

Figure 2.31 YOUNG'S DOUBLE-SLIT EXPERIMENT SETUP
The basic setup for Young's double-slit experiment involved two parallel panels placed in front of a screen that was also parallel to these panels. The outer panel had one vertical slit and the intermediate panel had two slits, each at the same distance from the opening in the outer panel.

to light that was somehow reflected within the interstitial space between the first and second panels, or to diffraction of light through the opening in the first panel and then through the two openings in the second. If the light that passed through both slits was a result of direct light rays, as diagrammed in Figure 2.32, then the light that ultimately reached the third panel would do so only at those points determined by drawing a straight line from the opening in the first panel through each opening in the second panel. However, this was not what was observed.

If light was being reflected within the interstitial space, then the light passing through the double slits would be diffused and spread out from each of the openings. However, this also did not happen, in part because reflection was intentionally reduced within this space. While light did get through, it was not as a result of either direct rays or reflected light, leaving the waveform characteristic of diffraction as the only remaining possibility. In addition, not only did the light get through, it did so in a way that could only be explained by the principle of interference (see Figure 2.33).

Young observed that while the light on the third panel was most intense directly opposite each of the openings in the middle panel, the light on the third panel actually consisted of many alternate bright and dark bands. Since only one light source was provided, all the light that ultimately passed through the middle panel would be in phase but would have to travel a different distance to the various points on the back panel. When the distance from the openings in the middle panel to a point on the back panel differed by half a wavelength, the overlapping, incident illumination would be out of phase, resulting in interference between the waves of light, each canceling the other. When the overlapping light arrived at the rear panel in phase, the light from each opening would reinforce the other, producing bright bands on the rear panel. In other words, as Huygens predicted, each opening in the middle panel acted as a source for a new wave based on the original wave. The constructive and destructive interference of the two coincident waves produced a pattern of light and dark bands, and by covering one of the openings in the middle panel, it was possible to verify the basis of the observed conditions.

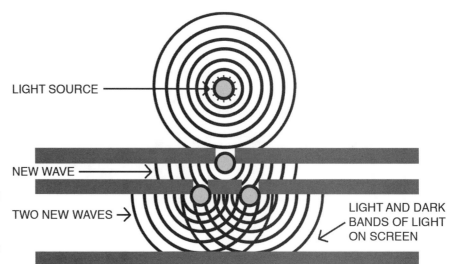

Figure 2.33 YOUNG'S DOUBLE-SLIT EXPERIMENT: WAVE PROPAGATION

In the actual experiment, a series of light and dark bands appeared across the center of the screen, clearly indicating that the light from the source was not traveling in straight lines but as a wave, establishing points of constructive and destructive interference.

LIGHT SOURCE

NEW WAVE

TWO NEW WAVES

LIGHT AND DARK BANDS OF LIGHT ON SCREEN

Although he apparently did not understand the basis for light interference, this phenomenon was actually critical to Newton's explorations into optics. As mentioned, his original investigations of optics and color began as a result of his concern over chromatic aberrations, a series of light and dark circular rings that were often visible when looking through the convex glass lenses of a telescope. While we understand that this is the result of interference between the light reflected off the top and bottom surfaces of a lens, Newton apparently failed to comprehend the significance of his observations, although today we call these aberrations *Newton's Rings*. Perhaps his acceptance of the corpuscular theory prevented him from drawing the proper conclusions.

A familiar example of the color rings produced by interference is the rich coloration of soap bubbles or films of oil. The color at any point is a composite of all the colors in the incident light that are not destroyed by interference. While these examples of light interference might be intriguing, observance of light interference can also be very annoying. Large windows are usually glazed with plate glass rather than sheet glass since in large areas sheet glass will tend to distort the view. The surfaces of sheet glass are somewhat irregular, but the opposing surfaces of plate glass are precise, parallel flat planes. However, if there are slight variations in the thickness of plate glass, or if the individual panels of insulating glass are slightly out of parallel, light interference can occur between the light that is reflected off the different near-parallel surfaces. If this happens, Newton's Rings will appear in the center of the view. Newton's Rings can also occur in photographic lenses; to avoid this problem, photographic lenses are usually coated with a thin layer of material specifically intended to reduce reflections.

Young's clear demonstration of the effects of light interference encouraged additional acceptance of the wave theory of light. Further support for the theory came, unwittingly, from the French mathematical physicist Simon Poisson. Poisson was one of the judges appointed by the French Academy of Science to examine a paper submitted by Augustin Fresnel in 1818. Fresnel, a young colleague of Thomas Young, had presented a paper that included mathematical equations explaining the diffraction of light waves around an obstacle. From his review of the paper, Poisson realized that if Fresnel's equations correctly described the behavior of light, then a small, opaque, round disk placed in a beam of light ought to produce a very peculiar thing. Based on the diffraction or bending theory of light, a bright spot should be produced in the center of the shadow as the diffracted light from the circular edges of the disk converged. This seemed illogical, and such a condition had never been reported. Poisson, who supported the corpuscular theory, felt that this prediction was totally absurd and believed that any attempted demonstration would lead to the clear refutation of the wave theory. He challenged Fresnel to do the experiment. Fresnel accepted the challenge, and the proof was provided. As indicated in Figure 2.34, a bright spot was indeed shown to exist in the center of the shadow!

With this demonstration and with the improved techniques for measuring the speed of light, which determined that it was apparently reduced when passing through a denser medium, support for the corpuscular theory crumbled. However, with the acceptance of the wave theory, there was still a question as to the nature of these waves. One of the difficulties with the wave theory of light was explaining what the waves were and in what they traveled. Generally, waves occur in a substance, and in fact, the wave is a disturbance of that substance such as water going up and down or, with sound, air being compressed and then expanded. Since it was assumed that if light were a wave, the wave had to exist "in" something, in response

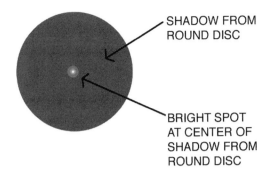

Figure 2.34 FRESNEL'S BRIGHT SPOT
Because of diffraction, light that passes by the edge of a circular disc will bend into the area assumed to be in shadow. If the disc is properly sized for the distance between the disc and a screen, the bending light will converge on the screen at the center of the projected circular area of the disc, producing a bright spot.

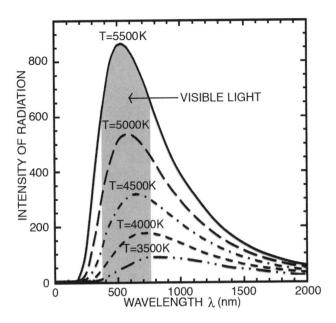

Figure 2.35 BLACKBODY RADIATION
As the temperature of a blackbody solid increases, both the intensity and frequency of the emitted radiation increase.

to this requirement, *ether* was proposed as the medium through which light traveled.

In 1864, James Clerk Maxwell, an English physicist, proposed the mathematical theory of electromagnetism. Maxwell, who used the notion of ether to help develop his theory of electromagnetic fields and waves, suggested that light travels as a vibrating electric charge through ether. This ultimately led to our understanding that light propagation occurs independent of any physical substance. In 1880, Heindrick Rudolph Hertz, a German physicist, confirmed Maxwell's predictions of electromagnetism. Hertz, whose name is used for the scientific notation of cycles per second (Hz), experimented with oscillating electric charges to produce ultra-high-frequency waves that could be transmitted across a distance from one wire to another. His work established the foundation for radio transmission. In 1887, Albert A. Michelson, the American physicist, began his attempts to measure the speed of light. His original intention was to investigate the effects of ether wind on the speed of light. But since his experiments indicated that there were no observable effects, they actually provided further proof that ether does not exist.

With the beginning of the twentieth century, the scientific investigations into the nature of light became more sophisticated and complex. The German physicist Max Planck realized that the radiation produced by an incandescent solid is emitted in a broadband, continuous spectrum and that there is a shift to higher frequencies with an increase in the temperature of the incandescent solid (see Figure 2.35). In 1900, Planck developed a formula that mathematically described this reaction. The formula, which he developed by trial and error, explained the shift to higher frequencies and demonstrated that the energy of light is proportional to its wavelength. Apparently, this contradicted the classical laws of physics. Planck was challenged to substantiate his formula. After further consid-

eration, he concluded that the formula, which he knew produced accurate results, could only be justified if one assumed that the energies of the vibrating electrons were restricted to distinct values. This meant that light energy had to occur in discrete bundles. Planck called these bundles *quanta*. This notion of quanta pointed again to the corpuscular theory of light, and it seemed that the old controversy was about to reemerge.

In 1905, Albert Einstein applied Planck's quantum theory to the wave theory. He explained, using the quantum theory, why light impinging on certain metals would cause the release of electrons, resulting in an electric current. He was dealing with what is referred to as the *photoelectric effect*, which allows us to measure light intensity by a meter and, with adjustments, to convert sunlight by photovoltaic cells into electric energy. Einstein helped explain that radiation is not emitted continuously but in units of energy that are equal to Planck's constant times the frequency of radiation. Brightness is not a result of the energy level of the light but of the number of quanta light units, which today we call *photons*. The energy of a photon is proportional to its frequency.

In 1913, building upon the work of others, the Danish physicist Neils Bohr helped provide what is still accepted as the basic explanation of how light is generated. He explained that light is emitted when electrons make a transition from a higher to a lower orbit around the nucleus of an atom (see Figure 2.36). His thesis was that electrons can travel only in certain successively larger orbits. As an electron drops from a higher to a lower orbit, it releases energy

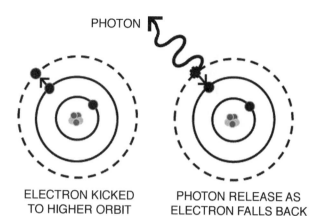

Figure 2.36 RELEASE OF ENERGY AS A PHOTON
This diagram shows the process by which a photon is released. If an electron is excited, which can result from an increase in temperature or by being hit by another electron, an electron in the outer valence is kicked into a higher orbit. Since the electron is not stable at this orbit, it drops back, releasing a photon of energy.

STABLE CONDITION

ELECTRON KICKED TO HIGHER ORBIT

PHOTON RELEASE AS ELECTRON FALLS BACK

in the form of electromagnetic radiation. The frequency of this radiation is determined by the energy released by the electron when it shifts orbits. The number of electrons dropping into a lower orbit determines the brightness or intensity of the radiation.

Lighting Terminology

The rate of flow of radiant energy is referred to as *radiant flux*, and the unit of measurement is the *watt*. Since the watt indicates a rate of flow, the unity of energy measurement is *kilowatt-hour* or *joule*.

While light is radiant energy with a frequency between 380 and 760 nanometers or 3800 and 7600 angstroms, it is also defined as radiant energy that is capable of exciting the retina and producing a visual sensation. In illuminating engineering, light is radiant energy weighted by the luminous efficiency of the human sensory system. While radiant energy between 380 and 760 nanometers is visible, human spectral sensitivity varies for the different wavelengths, being most sensitive at around 550 nanometers. In measuring the flow of radiant energy adjusted to human spectral sensitivity, the *lumen* is used instead of the watt and *luminous flux* is used rather than radiant flux. The major units and definitions used in illuminating engineering are listed in Table 2.2.

Light Meters

A light meter is a device that converts radiant energy into an electrical current and then, based on the current, indicates the intensity of the illumination. This conversion is accomplished by a photovoltaic cell, often made of selenium or silicone, that is able to develop direct current electricity from incident radiation. The typical light meter used to determine the level of illumination is both color corrected and cosine corrected. The color correction adjusts the radiant flux to the sensitivity of the human optical system. Since the human eye senses radiation only within a limited band and is less sensitive to the radiation at the extremes of this narrow band than it is to the radiation in the midrange, a filtering device is used to match this reduction in sensitivity. This device is usually a colored gel that is placed in front of the photovoltaic cell.

Cosine correction is accomplished by means of a diffusing plate through which the incident light must past before it can reach the cell. Since a perfectly diffusing material, either in reflection or transmission, follows the cosine law, a diffusing plate provides the necessary correction.

While General Electric continues to make a small analog handheld, triple-range light meter that measures approximate levels of illumination (Model 216 for lux measurements and Model 217 for foot-candles[11]), digital meters are more commonly used today. These digital meters, which usually can be adjusted for various intensity levels, often can read in either foot-candles or lux. In addition, the light sensors on these digital meters are often connected by a wire to the meter, allowing placement of the sensor at a remote point, reducing the chance that reading the meter will contaminate the reading of the level of illumination. Since without a remote sensor it is necessary to get close to the meter in order to get a reading, there is a chance that this will alter the actual lighting conditions.

---

[11]Model 217 has three scales. The lowest scale, which is activated when the switch on the side of the meter is in the bottom position, reads illumination levels from 10 to 50 foot-candles (fc). In this position, from 10 to 20 fc, the unit has an accuracy of ±15% and from 20 to 50 fc it has an accuracy of ±10%. The middle position of the switch provides midlevel readings, from 50 to 250 fc, with the accuracy basically similar to that of the lower level. When the switch is in the upper position, the meter reads from 200 to 1000 fc. In those instances when a higher illumination is to be measured or when the measurements are to be in lux rather than foot-candles, a metal perforated filter is installed over the diffusing plate. This filter allows 10% of the incident light to pass through so that the foot-candle readings are converted to lux values (e.g., 1:10) so that intense illumination, such as from the sun, can be read at one-tenth of its actual value (i.e., reading 200 fc for an actual 2000-fc illumination).

Table 2.2: DEFINITIONS OF TECHNICAL TERMS

Technical Term	Unit	Definition
Radiant Energy	Kilowatt-Hour (kWh) Joule (J)	Quantity of energy
Radiant Flux	Watt (W) Erg per Second	Time rate of energy flow
Luminous Flux	Lumen (lm)	Time rate of light energy flow adjusted to human visual sensitivity.
Luminous Efficacy	Lumens per Watt	The number of visible lumens per watt. At 550 nm, direct conversion between lumens and watts is 683 lm/watt. On the average across the visible spectrum, the conversion is 220 lm/watt.
Lumen (lm)		Unit of luminous flux.
Foot-candle (fc)	lm per sq. ft.	Unit of illumination equal to the luminous flux incident on each square foot of surface area of a 1 ft. radius sphere surrounding a light source of 1 candle power. Since the sphere has a surface area of $4\pi\ r^2$, there are 12.57 sq. ft. of surface area on a sphere with a 1 ft. radius. Therefore, a 1 candlepower light source emits a total of 12.57 lumens that are equally distributed in all directions.
Foot-lambert (fl)	lm per sq. ft.	Unit of luminous exitance equal to the uniform emittance from a perfectly diffusing surface that emits (or reflects) light at the rate of 1 lumen per square foot.
Lux (lx)	lm per m2	Unit of illumination that is equal to the luminous flux incident on each incident on each square meter of surface area of a 1 meter radius sphere. Since a 1 candle power source will equally distribute its lumens over a larger surface area if the radius of a sphere is one meter verses one foot, 1 fc is equal to 10.76 lux.
Illumination (E)	Foot-candle (fc)	Luminous flux density incident on a surface as lumens per unit area.
	Lux (lx)	In the imperial system, it is lumens per square foot or foot-candles. In the SI system, it is lumens per square meter or lux.
Luminance (L)	Candela per Unit Area	Luminous flux emitted or reflected from a point on a surface in a particular direction and within a solid angle of 1. $$M = \pi L = \text{Incident fl} \times \rho, \text{ while}$$ $$L = \frac{\text{Incident flux} \times r}{p}$$ In common usage, luminance is called "brightness."
Luminous Exitance (M), or Luminous Emittance	foot-lambert (fL) Apostillo (asb) [ρ = rho] [τ = tau]	Luminous flux density passing through or reflected by a surface. It was previously referred to as Luminance or Luminous Emittance. It is equal to Illumination times reflectance or transmission ($E\rho$ or $E\tau$). It is expressed as lumens per square foot or foot-lamberts in the imperial system and lumens per square meter in the SI system.
Luminous Intensity (I)	Lumens per Steradian	Luminous flux per steradian in a specific direction. A steradian is the unit.
	Candela (cd)	A of solid angle, and there are 12.57 steradians in a sphere.
Candela (cd)		The unit of luminous intensity. One candela is equal to one lumen per steradian and was formerly called "candle."
Candlepower (cp)		Luminous intensity of a light source expressed in candelas. A candle-power of 1 relates to equally distributed light of 1 candle emitted by a 12.57 lumen light source.
Glare		The sensation produced by luminance within the visual field that is sufficiently greater than the luminance to which the eyes are adapted and causes annoyance, discomfort, and/or loss in visual performance and visibility.
Luminance Contrast (C)		Relationship between the luminance of an object and its background. $$C = \frac{L_o - L_b}{L_b} \quad \text{or} \quad \frac{L_b - L_o}{L_b}$$
Steradian		A three-dimensional or solid angle that subtends an area that is equal to the square of the distance from the vertex of the angle to the surface.

A light meter typically is used to measure the level of illumination incident on a surface. The meter or the remote light sensor is place on the surface, with the diffusing plate parallel to the surface. When the meter is initially turned on, it might be necessary to wait a short time to allow the meter to "settle down" in order to obtain a reasonable measurement. When not in use, if the meter has an on-off switch, the meter should be turned off. If there is no switch, such as with the small General Electric meters, the meter should be set at the highest reading level so that any incident light will likely not exceed the meter setting and the sensor should be covered by its case, which is provided with most meters.

The typical light meter can also be used to determine the luminous exitance or brightness level of a diffuse surface. To obtain a reading of luminous exitance, hold the meter with its sensor close to and facing the surface. With a transmitting surface, the meter reading is the brightness in foot-lamberts. With a reflecting surface, slowly move the meter away from the surface and note if the reading remains constant. If it does, this is the luminous exitance in foot-lamberts. (Again, avoid interfering with the incident light on the surface.) Based on the cosine law, the level of luminous exitance should not change if the reflecting surface is reasonably large relative to the meter's sensor, so when the reading remains constant with adjustments in distance from the surface, the meter reading should be the foot-lamberts of luminous exitance from the surface.

To get a reading of luminous exitance off a surface with a typical light meter, it is necessary to get to the surface, which is not always feasible. Fortunately, there are also luminance meters that can directly record the luminous exitance off a surface and do so at a distance. These meters have a viewfinder similar to a camera's. The viewfinder includes a small dot, which represents a $2°$ view-angle that is to be set on the point being evaluated. For accurate measurements, the area of the surface defined by the $2°$ view-angle should fall within the overall area being measured.

To determine the transmittance (τ) or reflectance (ρ) of a surface, you can take readings of both the incident light (E) and the emitted light (L). The L/E ratio is the transmittance (τ) or the reflectance (ρ). An alternative is to refer to a table, such as a color or paint chart, that lists reflectance values.

LIGHT SOURCES

There are basically three methods of generating light. Incandescent and luminescent lighting, which rely, respectively, on incandescence and luminescence, are the two classic means of producing light. Solid-state lighting, which is a type of lighting that is developed from a solid object, is a relatively new means of generating light and is used in light-emitting diodes.

Incandescence

Incandescence results from the temperature-related molecular activity of a solid substance. This molecular activity includes the irregular excitation of free electrons that emit broadband radiation. As the temperature of the solid increases, the molecular activity also increases, resulting in a shift of the frequencies of radiation emitted. While incandescence involves radiation from a solid, sometimes the solid is relatively small. For example, the light emitted from a gas flame is actually a form of incandescence, referred to as *pyroluminescence.* The heat of the flame increases the temperature of the particulate matter within the gas stream, and this matter releases the visible incandescent radiation. As the cleanliness of the gas source and the efficiency of combustion are improved, there is less particulate matter and the amount of visible light produced is reduced. With improved efficiency, the temperature increases, and this shifts the color of the flame from red to white to blue. With a white flame, more radiation is emitted in the visible range, but the brightness of the light is generally less than with a red flame, for which only a small amount of the total radiation emitted is within the visible range.

In 1855, Robert Wilhelm Bunsen, a German chemist and professor, and his laboratory assistant, Peter Desaga, modified a laboratory gas burner to induce air into the gas supply in order to produce higher temperatures. While Michael Faraday had previously suggested a similar approach, there is a story that Bunsen came upon this idea by observing that a gas lighting fixture was not producing as much light as it should. On investigating the cause, Bunsen supposedly found that there was a small puncture in the gas line, and rather than gas leaking out of this opening, air was induced into the gas line, causing the flame to burn hotter but with less light. A gas flame produces light by heating particulate matter to the point where it emits radiation due to incandescence. With a relatively clean gas source, the particulate matter that emits the light is actually a portion of the fuel that is not fully consumed in the combustion process, but with an addition of air to the gas supply, the combustion process is improved. This leaves less unconsumed fuel, resulting in the production of more heat but less light.

There are four types of incandescence used for lighting—pyroluminescence (flame), candoluminescence (gas mantle), carbon arc, and incandescent filament—with the latter two developed through an electric current.

Today, the incandescent filament continues to be a major source of interior lighting, especially in residential applications. It is a familiar lamp that is a simple-to-operate, easy-to-control point source of light. Its emission of light results from passing an electric current through a highly resistant filament, generally made of tungsten. The electric current causes the temperature of the tungsten filament to increase to the point where visible radiation is emitted. Most of the radiation, however, is not in the visible range. Only about 10% of the energy consumed is emitted as visible light, with the major portion of energy converted into heat.[12] The light produced is rather red since the visible radiation is just entering the visible spectrum. Shifting the light into the higher end of the spectrum would require higher temperatures that, unfortunately, are generally beyond the capability of the normal incandescent lamp. At higher temperatures, the filament would not survive and glass would not be adequate for the bulb. In response to this latter limitation, in incandescent lamps that operate at higher temperatures, such as halogen lamps, quartz is usually used rather than glass for the bulb.

A traditional electric cooktop provides a classic demonstration of how incandescent light is generated. If an electric burner is turned on and set at a low or medium level, heat is produced. If nothing is on the burner, the emission of infrared, nonvisible radiant heat is quite noticeable. The burner remains its normal color. If the setting is raised to high, the emission of radiant heat continues but there is also visible radiation. The rings of the burner begin to glow red. The increased temperature of the burner raises the frequency of the emitted radiation, and some of it is at the low end of the visible spectrum.

An incandescent lamp, which is often erroneously called a *light bulb,* operates similarly to the electric burner but intentionally at a higher temperature. Since the incandescent filament is a wire much thinner than the metal rings used in an electric cooktop, the higher temperatures of the filament will quickly cause it to burn up if it is exposed to air, hence the need for the bulb. More on this later.

The sun may be considered to be an incandescent light source, although the radiation it generates comes from a superheated, high-density gas rather than from a solid (see Figure 2.37). The sun is a gaseous body with extremely high pressures and temperatures and is different from the

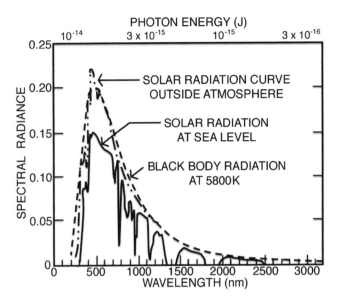

Figure 2.37 SOLAR RADIATION CURVES

vaporous form that gases usually take. The solar gases are actually in a plasma state, which is considered a fourth state of matter that has unique properties.

Solids, liquids, and gases, which are the ordinary forms of matter, have electrons that orbit an atomic nucleus and to which they are bound. If the temperature increases high enough, the outer electrons acquire enough kinetic energy to escape the bond. In this condition, the electrons are no longer trapped in orbits circling the atomic nucleus. But when a plasma is at an extremely high density, at least in terms of electromagnetic radiation, it behaves in a manner similar to that of a solid body and emits radiation in a broadband spectrum. That is, the high-density, ionized gases of the sun are in a plasma state and emit electromagnetic radiation in a *blackbody spectrum* similar to that of a solid. Although the sun is a body of gases, it emits radiation with a wavelength distribution that is similar to that from a blackbody solid at a temperature of 5800 K, the temperature of the sun.

Luminescence

Luminescence involves the release of a particular frequency of radiant energy resulting from the excitation of single-valence electrons of an atom in a gaseous or crystalline state or from an organic molecule. Instead of a continuous spectrum, luminescence produces particular wavelengths of radiation. There are two types of luminescence: photoluminescence and electroluminescence. Photoluminescence includes gaseous discharge, fluorescence, and phosphorescence. Electroluminescence is directly emitted radiation achieved by the passage of an

---

[12]Actually, except for the minute amount of light that might be used for vision, and therefore converted into visual energy, all of the consumed energy, including that which is released as visible light, is ultimately converted into heat. For this reason, incandescent lighting is a major source of heat gain in interior spaces. Similarly, essentially all of the consumed energy with other lighting systems (e.g., fluorescent or HID lighting) is also converted heat, but these other systems convert a larger percentage of the energy consumed into light, and as a result, they tend to cause less of a heat gain problem.

electric current through certain phosphors. Electroluminescence was thought to be the light source of the future, but it has not proved to be either efficient or aesthetically desirable.

In gaseous discharge, a flow of electrons is sent through a gas. These electrons hit outer-valence electrons of the gas and kick them into a higher orbit. As these excited electrons fall back to their previous orbits, they emit radiation. The energy involved in the shift in orbit is particular both to the gas and to its pressure, and the wavelength of radiation emitted as the electrons drop back is determined by these particulars. If the emitted radiation has a wavelength that is within the visible spectrum, it can be directly released from the lamp as light. However, if the radiation is not visible—for example if it is in the ultraviolet range of the spectrum—there would be no advantage to emit it from the lamp. Also, it could be harmful. Enclosing the lamp in glass, which is not effectively transparent to ultraviolet radiation, reduces the problem of harmful radiation. By coating the glass with fluorescent chemicals that can transpose radiation from a higher, nonvisible frequency to a lower, visible frequency, the energy of the radiation that is above the visible spectrum is transformed into visible light. The selection of the fluorescent chemicals determines the particular wavelengths of light that are produced.

A fluorescent material absorbs light and reradiates it at a frequency equal to or less than that of the original incident light. The incident photon of energy raises an electron to a higher energy level, where it remains only briefly. As it returns to its original level, it reradiates the energy, which it can do in more than one stage. If the reradiation occurs in one stage, it will be resonant with the incident radiation. If it takes more than one stage, it will be at a lower frequency.

Phosphorescence is similar to fluorescence, but it does not occur immediately. Normally, it entails a time delay between receiving the incident radiation and emitting the transposed radiation. While this phenomenon is very important, especially today in our various visual communication systems, it has not had a dominant impact on environmental design.

Light-Emitting Diodes

Light-emitting diodes (LEDs) provide what is called *solid-state lighting*. In a way, this means of generating light might be understood as falling between incandescence and photoluminescence. Incandescent light is produced by heating a solid element to increase molecular activity, which, when the temperature is high enough, causes emission of radiation in the visible spectrum. Photoluminescence, which is used by gaseous-discharge lamps, entails passing

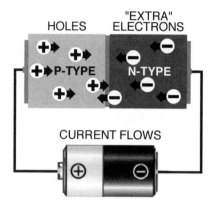

Figure 2.38 LED
This diagram shows the basics of an LED. As a direct current is applied across the diode, which is a doped semiconductor that has extra electrons on one side and missing electrons on the other, the flow of electricity results in the release of photons, or visible light. (Adapted from material from various sources, including howstuffworks.com.)

an electric current, which is a flow of electrons, through a nonsolid element, an ionized gas. This flow of electrons bombards the outer electrons of the ionized gas, causing emission of radiation that is visible or can be shifted into a frequency of visible light by fluorescence. Other than to pressurize the gas, photoluminescence does not require an increased temperature.

As with an incandescent lamp, generating light by an LED involves passing an electric current through a solid, but this solid is a semiconductor and particularly one that has been altered by doping. The semiconductor, typically aluminum-gallium-arsenide, has four electrons in its outer valence. It is coated on one side with a P-type material, which has only three electrons in its outer valence, and on the other side with an N-type material, which has five electrons in its outer electron shell. Based on this arrangement and relative to the four-electron semiconductor, it can be assumed that there are extra electrons on one side of the semiconductor and missing electrons, or holes, on the other. This forms a diode, which is basically the same arrangement used in a photovoltaic cell.

When a diode is connected to a positive charge on the side doped with a P-type material and a negative charge on the side doped with an N-type material, an electric current will flow (see Figure 2.38).[13] Rather than use this flow of current to increase temperature, as with an incandescent filament lamp, the current through the diode causes electrons to fall into the "holes," and as they fall, they release a photon of energy. Based on the material, this radiation can be visible light. While somewhat similar to photoluminescence, with an LED, the release of energy is caused by the movement of the electrons in the electric current

---

[13]If the connection to the diode is reversed, no current flows.

rather than another electron that is energized by an electric current.[14]

An electric current is a flow of electrons, and when these electrons flow across the diode, they "fall" into the holes that exist on the side of the diode doped with the P-type material. As each electron falls, it releases a photon of energy, and based on the physical composition of the diode, particular wavelengths or radiation are emitted. That is, the flow of current entails the direct release of radiation, which means that LEDs are a very efficient way of producing light and do so without generating significant heat. They also have an extended life, suggested to be up to 100,000 hours of operation. While this equates to more than 10 years of continuous output, the LEDs presently in use are usually rated for around 50,000 to 60,000 hours. With normal daily operation, these lamps can easily last for over 12 years.

BASIC SOURCES OF INTERIOR LIGHTING

The assumption for some time has been that there are three primary sources of interior illumination: the incandescent-filament lamp, the fluorescent lamp, and the various high-intensity discharge (HID) gas lamps. Unfortunately, one of the best and most energy-efficient light sources is not included in this group: daylight. In addition, this list does not include the LED, a source of electric light that promises high efficiency and long life. Each of these potential sources of interior illumination has particular characteristics, which for electric light sources involves color composition, the physical size of the generating device, electrical demands, operational efficiency, and length of life. As environmental designers, it is our responsibility to understand these sources so that they can be used effectively.

Lamps

While the term *lamp* is generally used to denote a non-fixed light fixture, technically this term refers to the actual source of light that is inserted into a light fixture, the *luminaire*. A lamp is commonly called a *bulb*; this is actu-

---

[14]With alternating current, the electrons keep moving back and forth, but with direct current, they continue to flow in the same direction. Generally, the flow of current for both alternating current and direct current relies on the billiard-ball effect of energy flow rather than physical movement of the electrons, and there is little difference in the effects produced by the two forms of electricity. However, LEDs work only with direct current, and the light that they produce is dependent on the physical flow of the electrons since it is that flow that directly generates the light.

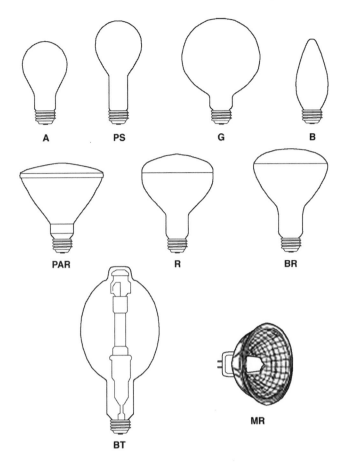

Figure 2.39 LAMP SHAPES
This figure includes some of the more commonly used lamp shapes, each of which has a particular notation. In addition to their shape, lamps are denoted in terms of their size, based on the number of $1/8$th-inch units.

ally merely the enclosing envelope of the lamp. The bulb is usually glass, but when the light generates very high temperatures, glass is usually replaced with quartz. This is typical with HID lamps, such as mercury, metal halide, and sodium vapor lamps, and with halogen incandescent lamps. It is important not to handle a quartz bulb without protection, since if any body oils are deposited on the bulb, which is somewhat porous, any absorbed oil will likely burn and damage the bulb.

Each lamp has both a particular shape and a particular size. The shape is indicated by a letter and the size by a number that is based on a $1/8$-inch unit (see Figure 2.39). The letters used to denote the shape of the bulb sometimes have a connection with the shape, whereas others do not seem to have any particular connection. PS is used for pear shape, G for globe, T for tube, and MR for mini-reflector. The regular-size reflector lamps are indicated by PAR for parabolic reflectors that have a heavy glass bulb and can be used outside and inside and by R for reflectors that have a thin glass bulb. BR refers to bulged reflectors, which are replacing the older R lamps since they have higher

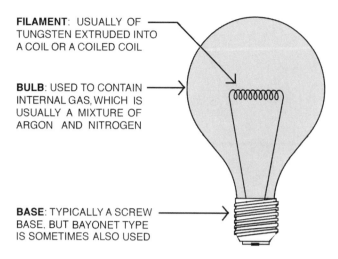

FILAMENT: USUALLY OF TUNGSTEN EXTRUDED INTO A COIL OR A COILED COIL

BULB: USED TO CONTAIN INTERNAL GAS, WHICH IS USUALLY A MIXTURE OF ARGON AND NITROGEN

BASE: TYPICALLY A SCREW BASE, BUT BAYONET TYPE IS SOMETIMES ALSO USED

Figure 2.40 INCANDESCENT LAMP
Since the early days of electric lighting, the incandescent lamp has been the mainstay of illumination, especially in residential applications.

efficiency. BR, MR, PAR, and R lamps come as floods or spots, depending on the spread of the output. While these reflector lamps tend to have a lower lumen output than comparable wattage lamps of other shapes, since the lumens are directed toward the surface being illuminated, the actual effective light output is often higher with these lamps. When the lamps do not direct the light output, the fixtures must do so to increase the efficiency of the lighting and to reduce the possibility of excessive brightness and visual glare.

The size of a lamp is indicated by its diameter in terms of the number of $1/8$-inch units. For example, fluorescent lamps are indicated as T12, T8, and T5, which means that the diameter of the tubes is, respectively, $1^1/_2$ inches, 1 inch, and $5/_8$ inch. The narrower fluorescents provide a more efficient light source.

Incandescent Lamp

Since the early days of electric lighting, the incandescent lamp has been the mainstay of illumination, especially in residential applications (see Figure 2.40). However, because of its low efficiency, various phaseout regulations have been adopted by a number of governments. As a result, the incandescent lamp is gradually being replaced with other lamps, particularly the compact fluorescent lamp (CFL). Still, the incandescent lamp continues to be used widely, in part because it is easily and effectively dimmed, which is not yet true of the CFL, and because it is rather inexpensive, at least on a first-cost basis. In addition to its low efficiency, it has one of the shortest life spans of any light source. There are two basic ways in which an incandescent lamp fails: failure of the seal of the bulb and deterioration of the tungsten filament.

U.S. legislation dealing with energy is complex and confusing, with a number of different acts and various moving targets. In general, the implication is that incandescent lamps will be banned in the near future. According to the Energy Independence and Security Act of 2007, incandescent lamps that produce 310 to 2600 lumens are to be phased out by 2014, with lamps that fall outside of this range being exempt. Supposedly, the intention is to initially phase out lamps that operate at less than 30% efficiency and then, by 2020, all lamps that are less than 70% efficient.

While Thomas Edison is often given credit for inventing the first practical incandescent lamp, for which he received a U.S. patent in 1880, a number of others were involved in the development of incandescent lighting. Sir Humphry Davy, perhaps the most celebrated British scientist of the early nineteenth century, was probably the first person to develop an incandescent electric light. He did this by connecting the poles of a large battery array, which forced an electric current through a thin metal strip, causing it to glow and emit light. The problem with this approach, which was supposedly demonstrated at the Royal Institution of Great Britain in 1802, was that the filament lasted for only a short time since the high temperatures in the presence of air consumed the glowing metal strip. To deal with this problem, Davy adjusted his approach, producing what is called an *arc light*. Rather than pass the electric current through a resistive conductor or filament, he allowed the current to arc between two electrodes. These electrodes were charcoal rods that were intended to be consumed. As long as there was an electric current and the distance between the rods was maintained, which meant advancing the rods as they were consumed, the arc light was sustained. Davy noticed that when the charcoal rods were horizontal, the actual light source tended to take the form of an arch. Based on this finding, he coined the term *arch lamp*, which over time was contracted to *arc lamp* and hence *arc light*.

While Davy accepted that the electrodes for the arc lamp would be consumed, others explored ways to sustain the filament of an incandescent light source. Joseph Swan, an English physicist and chemist, was the first to accomplish this, developing an effective incandescent lamp, for which he received a British patent for his lamp two years before Edison obtained his U.S. patent for essentially the same design. What both men did was to make an effective light bulb, literally. Both of them understood that the problem with the incandescent lamp was that the filament would burn up in the presence of air, but if it was heated in the absence of air, or specifically in the absence of oxygen, it should last a reasonable length of time. To accomplish this, the filament had to be contained within a volume that was void of oxygen. While today's incandescent lamps typically have bulbs that contain an inert gas, for Swan and Edison the bulb had to preserve a vacuum, and to do so while permitting electrical wires to penetrate into the bulb enclosure.

Both men initially used a carbonized thread for the incandescent filament, although Edison's was thinner and imposed a higher resistance than Swan's. This meant that Edison's lamp did not have to draw as much electric current to produce a comparable amount of light. While the carbonized thread worked as a filament, it was fragile, so the search for a better material was on. While a thin platinum wire had been used even before Swan and Edison's work, this proved to be too expensive. Other high-resistive metals were considered, and in the late 1890s, Carl Auer von Welsbach, an Austrian scientist and inventor, developed an effective metal filament incandescent lamp.

Welsbach is remembered today primarily for his work with rare earth elements, and more specifically for the incandescent gas mantle that bears his name, the Welsbach mantle. This mantle is essentially a gauze bag comprised of oxides that, when heated by a gas or kerosene flame, emit bright white light. When heated, the rare earth oxides of the mantle adjust the radiation of the flame, emitting bright visible light with little infrared radiation. When gas is used today as an intentional source of illumination rather than merely as nostalgic remembrance, it probably relies on a Welsbach mantle. Perhaps the Coleman lantern is the best-known continuous use of this remarkable device, although there are many communities that still retain gas street lamps that probably rely on the Welsbach mantle.

A Welsbach mantle starts as a flexible gauze bag comprised of silky threads that are impregnated with a mixture of thorium, cerium, and magnesium oxides. After it is attached to a gas fixture, the bag is ignited, burning away the silky threads to leave an extremely brittle ceramic shell of the oxides. In his attempt to develop a more durable mantle, Welsbach experimented with osmium, an exceptionally dense, hard, silvery metal, finding a way to convert pulverized osmium into a wire. He combined osmium oxide with rubber and sugar, forming a paste that could then be extruded into a linear form. He then burned away the paste, which formed the osmium into a fine wire.

While Welsbach's intention was to use this wire to weave a more durable gas mantle, he realized that if osmium wire could produce a more durable mantle, it could also be used as the filament in an electric incandescent lamp that would be more robust and last longer than other available filaments. Welsbach then redirected his efforts to electric light, and by the early twentieth century, he was commercially producing a metal filament incandescent lamp.

Osmium is rather rare and expensive, and producing osmium wire was complicated. Also, its maximum opera-

tional temperature was not very high, which limited the range of emitted visible light. The search for an effective metal filament continued. Ultimately, tungsten emerged as the material of choice, in part because it had a melting temperature that was higher than that of other materials, which meant that it could produce a whiter light. Although initial attempts to extrude this rather brittle material into wire were fraught with difficulties, improved methods were found. Today tungsten is extruded into a thin wire that can be coiled, and these coils can then be coiled again, producing a rather tight package of an extended wire filament. In addition, while tungsten conducts electricity, it does so at a high resistance, which means that an electric current produces a high temperature that emits visible light. Unfortunately, only about 10% of the consumed energy actually produces visible light, and much of this radiation is at the low or red end of the spectrum.

Even when surrounded by a vacuum or a volume of inert gas, as the tungsten is heated, some of the metal vaporizes. After a period of time, which for most standard incandescent lamps is after around 750 to 1000 hours of operation, the lost tungsten is sufficient to cause a break in the filament. Typically, when this happens in a based-down installation, the lost tungsten deposits on the top of the bulb and is clearly noticeable as a black spot on the interior of the bulb. Of course, if the lamp is used in a base-up position, the tungsten deposits are not apparent.

Table 2.3 includes data on a limited number of incandescent lamps. While this table can provide the initial lumen output of a particular lamp to use in calculating lighting levels, a review of these outputs indicates an interesting fact: as the wattage of an incandescent lamp increases, the luminous efficacy also increases.

Halogen gases, which include five nonmetallic gases (fluorine, chlorine, bromine, iodine, and astatine), react chemically with tungsten. Because of this, adding a small amount of halogen gas, usually bromine and/or iodine, to an incandescent lamp, will reduce the loss of tungsten from the filament. As a halogen lamp is energized, it operates generally the same way as a standard incandescent lamp. The temperature rises and some tungsten evaporates off of the filament, but with the added halogen gas, elevated to a high enough temperature, the vaporized tungsten combines chemically with halogen gas, producing tungsten halides. As the gases circulate within the bulb and the tungsten halides come in contact with the hot filament, the tungsten halides break down, releasing the halogen gas and depositing the tungsten back on the filament. As a result, the filament lasts longer; less tungsten is deposited on the wall of the bulb, so the light reduction from this film is less; and the lamp can be operated at a higher temperature, producing a more intense and whiter light.

Table 2.3: TYPICAL INCANDESCENT LAMP DATA

Standard Incandescent				
Watts	**Average Life (hrs)**	**Initial Lumens**	**Lumens[a] per Watt**	**Shape[b]**
6	1500	44	7.3	S-6
10	1500	80	8.0	S-14
15	2500	126	8.4	A-15
25	2500	235	9.4	A-19
25	1000	340	13.6	A-19
40	1500	455	11.4	A-19
50	1000	540	10.8	A-19
60	2500	750	12.5	A-19
60	1000	870	14.5	A-19
75	750	1190	15.9	A-19
100	1000	1280	12.8	A-21
100	750	1750	17.5	A-19
150	750	2880	19.2	A-21
200	750	4000	20.0	A-23
200	750	3710	18.6	PS-30
300	750	6110	20.4	PS-30
500	1000	10,850	21.7	PS-35
75	2000	800	10.7	BR-40
100	2000	935	9.4	BR-40
150	2000	1500	10.0	BR-40
Halogen Incandescent				
Watts	**Average Life (hrs)**	**Initial Lumens**	**Lumens[a] per Watt**	**Shape[b]**
50	2500	860	17.2	A-19
60	3000	965	16.1	A-19
75	3000	1330	17.7	A-19
100	3000	1800	18.0	A-19
150	3000	2850	19.0	A-19
60	2500	750	12.5	BR-30
75	2500	1020	13.6	BR-30
75	2500	1050	14.0	BR-40
100	2500	1500	15.0	BR-40
75	2500	1040	13.9	PAR-38
100	2500	1500	15.0	PAR-38

[a]Efficacy, in lumens per watt, increases with wattage.
[b]Bulb designations in which the letters refer to the shape of the bulb and numbers refer to the size in $1/8$th inch units. An A-19 bulb has a diameter of $2^3/_8$ inches.

With the higher operating temperature of a halogen lamp, the bulb that encloses the filament and the standard inert gases plus the halogen gas has to be quartz or a heat-resistant glass rather than the typical glass. This bulb also has to be smaller to ensure that the temperatures are high enough to allow for the chemical interactions. With the reduced bulb size, the gases can be at a higher pressure, which can reduce the rate of tungsten vaporization and extend the life of the lamp. Additionally, with the smaller bulb size, it becomes reasonable to replace argon, the standard inert gas used in incandescent lamps, with krypton or xenon, either of which can further slow the rate of tungsten vaporization. This can extend the life of the lamp even more and allow for a higher operating temperature, which will produce a more brilliant, whiter light.

With all of these advantages, halogen lamps cost more than standard incandescent lamps, but for the increased cost, they provide considerable benefits. They can last almost four times as long while producing whiter and brighter light for less energy. Since the bulb enclosing the filament is smaller than the bulb for standard lamps, halogen lamps are often enclosed within a second bulb comparable in size to standard lamps of the same wattage.

Fluorescent Lamp

While the incandescent lamp has been the main lighting source for residential occupancies, the workhorse in commercial applications has been the fluorescent lamp (see Figure 2.41). Early experiments with gaseous discharge lamps that utilized fluorescence and phosphorescence took place even before an effective incandescent light was developed by Edison and Swan, but a reasonably effective low-pressure mercury lamp, which is the basis of the fluorescent lamp, was not available until the early 1930s. It was not until 1938 that the first operational fluorescent lamp was introduced by General Electric under the leadership of George Inman.

While the fluorescent lamp was initially commercially available at the end of the Depression and at the build-up for World War II, this was not an auspicious time for building construction. However, after the war there was a construction boom, and with the higher efficiency of the fluorescent lamp, combined with the potential applications of air conditioning, which had also evolved during the Depression and the war, a major change in architectural design occurred. With a source of relatively low-heat lighting and a means of providing temperature control (cooling), it was possible to design buildings with extended interior space with no direct access to the exterior. With fluorescent lighting and air conditioning, occupiable space no longer had to be within around 20 feet from a window that could provide both daylight and ventilation.

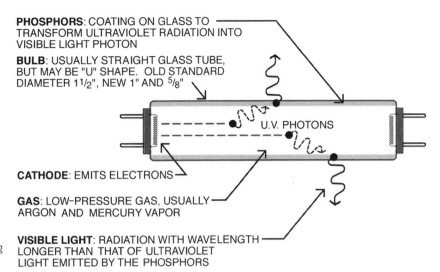

PHOSPHORS: COATING ON GLASS TO TRANSFORM ULTRAVIOLET RADIATION INTO VISIBLE LIGHT PHOTON

BULB: USUALLY STRAIGHT GLASS TUBE, BUT MAY BE "U" SHAPE. OLD STANDARD DIAMETER 1½", NEW 1" AND ⅝"

U.V. PHOTONS

CATHODE: EMITS ELECTRONS

GAS: LOW-PRESSURE GAS, USUALLY ARGON AND MERCURY VAPOR

VISIBLE LIGHT: RADIATION WITH WAVELENGTH LONGER THAN THAT OF ULTRAVIOLET LIGHT EMITTED BY THE PHOSPHORS

Figure 2.41 FLUORESCENT LAMP
The fluorescent lamp is the major light source used in nonresidential applications. While it first became commercially available in the late 1930s, major applications of fluorescent lighting did not begin until after World War II. Since then, it has become the lighting workhorse.

While the fluorescent lamp has been classified as a distinct light source separate from HID lamps, in actuality they are both gaseous discharge lamps, although with two main distinctions. One is that fluorescent lamps contain gas at low pressure (below atmospheric pressure), whereas HID lamps rely on high-pressure gases, although pressure variations are also significant in many HID lamps. The second distinction is that the electromagnetic radiation developed in a fluorescent lamp is above the visible range, so the lamp relies on fluorescence to convert this radiation into visible light. Fluorescence relates to the potential ability of a material to convert an absorbed photon of radiation into the emission of a longer-wavelength radiation. The difference between fluorescence and phosphorescence is the time it takes between the absorption of the incident radiation and the emission of the new radiation. The delay between absorption and emission for fluorescence is on the order of milliseconds,[15] whereas with phosphorescence the delay can be on the order of seconds, minutes, or even hours. But this distinction can be confusing since a fluorescent lamp relies on phosphors to emit visible light. The clarification is that fluorescence is a particular type of phosphorescence, so both are the result of the luminescence phenomenon that involves the excitation and deexcitation of electrons. See Table 2.4 for data on fluorescent lamps.

Some HID lamps also use fluorescence, although with higher internal pressures, HID lamps generally produce visible light directly. For example, both fluorescent lamps and mercury vapor HID lamps generate electromagnetic radiation by exciting the electrons of mercury vapor, but while at the low pressures of a fluorescent lamp this radiation is above the visible spectrum, with the higher pressure of the HID lamp a portion of the generated radiation

is within the visible spectrum. Some nonvisible radiation is also produced, and mercury vapor HID lamps often include a phosphorus coating to expand the range of light produced. Adding other gases to the lamp, as is done with metal halide lamps, is another way to expand the range of light waves produced, which, of course, will improve color rendition.

Fluorescent lamps are low-pressure, mercury-vapor, gaseous discharge lamps. These lamps are filled with argon gas and a small amount of mercury, although at lower temperatures, which generally means that before ignition, some of the mercury might be in a liquid form. On startup, all the mercury is vaporized and then ionized, after which a flow of electrons is released across the tube. As the electrons pass through the tube, they collide with ionized mercury vapor, exciting valence electrons that then drop back to their stable orbits as they release photons of ultraviolet radiation. This ultraviolet radiation, which is not visible light, then activates the phosphorus coating on the interior of the glass tube. The phosphors, in turn, convert the nonvisible ultraviolet radiation into visible light. The wavelengths of light that are produced depend on the particular composition of the phosphorus coating. Fortunately, the enclosing glass tube is not transparent to ultraviolet radiation, which can be harmful. When emission of ultraviolet radiation is desired—for example, with a germicidal light or a "black" light[16]—the glass tube is replaced with a material, such as quartz, that is transparent to ultraviolet radiation.

Older types of fluorescent fixtures use preheat lamps that rely on a starting sequence to initially activate the mercury vapor before a flow of electrons can be released through the lamp. This involves including a starter switch

---

[15]The time delay is believed to be 10^{-5} milliseconds or less for fluorescence.

[16]A black light is essentially a fluorescent lamp with a quartz rather than a glass tube and without the phosphorus coating.

Table 2.4: TYPICAL DATA FOR FLUORESCENT LAMP — 48″ NOMINAL LENGTH

Lamp	Nom. Watts	Average Life (Hrs)	Initial Lumens	Mean Lumens	Color Notation	General Color Temp.
F28T5	28	20,000	2900	2750	WW	3000 K
F28T5	28	20,000	2900	2750	WW	3500 K
F28T5	28	20,000	2900	2750	CW	4100 K
F54T5	49	25,000	5000	4750	WW	3000 K
F54T5	49	25,000	5000	4750	CW	4100 K
F54T5	49	25,000	4850	4625	D	5000 K
F32T8	32	30,000	2950	2800	WW	3000 K
F32T8	32	30,000	2950	2800	CW	4100 K
F32T8	32	30,000	2850	2700	D	5000 K
F32T8	32	30,000	2800	2660	WW	3000 K
F32T8	32	30,000	2800	2660	CW	4100 K
F32T8	32	30,000	2800	2660	CW	4100 K
F32T8	32	30,000	2700	2565	D	5000 K
F34T12	34	24,000	2650	2300	CW	4100 K
F34T12	34	24,000	2700	2350	WW	3000 K
F34T12	34	24,000	3100	2945	WW	3000 K
F34T12	34	24,000	3100	2945	CW	4100 K
F34T12	34	24,000	2950	2800	D	5000 K
F40T12	40	24,000	3600	3420	WW	3000 K
F40T12	40	24,000	3600	3420	CW	4100 K
F40T12	40	24,000	3450	3280	D	5000 K
F34T12	34	20,000	2800	2660	WW	3000 K
F34T12	34	20,000	2800	2660	CW	4100 K
F34T12	34	20,000	2650	2520	D	5000 K
F40T12	40	20,000	3200	3040	WW	3000 K
F40T12	40	20,000	3200	3040	CW	4100 K
F40T12	40	20,000	3050	2900	D	5000 K

CW Cool White with higher content of blue, used with higher levels of illumination.
WW Warm White with more red. Tends to "match" incandescent.
D Daylight
Source: Adapted from data from various manufacturers of fluorescent lamps.

in the fixture circuit that connects the two cathodes in series when the fixture is initially energized. This explains why there are two pins at either end of a typical fluorescent lamp; the current initially flows into and out of each cathode, heating up the gases in the fluorescent tube. After a short delay and a temperature increase, the starter switch opens, eliminating the connection between the cathodes. With each cathode still connected to the main electric circuit and the gases in the tube ionized, the current arcs from cathode to cathode.

The starting sequence and the continued operation of a fluorescent tube depend on the inclusion of a ballast within the fixture circuit. A ballast, which is essentially an electrical transformer, usually includes coiled wires that adjust the voltage and limit the current. These are magnetic ballasts, and the current they produce remains at the frequency of the electric service, which in the United States is 60 Hz. Newer ballast can be electronic, using solid-state components rather than coils to transform the voltage. Electronic ballasts can also change the frequency of the power to the lamp, thereby reducing any flicker that might occur.

During startup, the voltage through the cathodes is generally at low voltage, but when the electric current arcs between the cathodes, higher voltages are required, often above 200 volts. In addition, the ballast limits the amount of current that flows through the fixture. An interesting characteristic of any gaseous discharge lamp is that as it operates, its temperature and pressure increase, which in turn reduces the electrical resistance. This is the reverse of what happens with an incandescent lamp, which tends to be self-limiting in terms of current drawn. Without a current-limiting device, gaseous discharge lamps would continue to draw more and more current until they exceeded the capacity of the electrical service circuit and opened the protective circuit breaker.

Today, with more advanced ballasts, whether magnetic or electronic, rather than preheat lamps, fluorescents tend to be either rapid-start or instant-start lamps. Rapid-start lamps use special ballasts that can rapidly prepare the lamp gases. These generally require grounded fixtures, so when they are used in an older structure without grounded electric circuits, rapid-start lamps may not operate properly. Instant-start lamps use ballasts that can initially deliver a high voltage that can directly arc across the fluorescent tube. Generally, these lamps have only one pin on either end of the tube. An aspect of these lamps is that they generally operate a short time before they produce their rated lumen output.

When fluorescent lamps are use in locations where the temperatures can drop below 50° or 60° F, special provisions are required both to start and to operate the lights. In addition to special cold weather ballasts, fluorescent lamps are generally enclosed to allow the heat discharged from the lamps to maintain the tubes at appropriate operational temperatures. Optimal operation of fluorescent lamps occurs with internal temperatures of around 140° F, which relates to a temperature of around 110° to 110° F along the interior of the glass tube or 105° F on the outside of the lamp. As the internal temperature varies from these temperatures, either up or down, there is a considerable reduction in light output.

The standard or traditional fluorescent lamp is a tube with a $1^1/_2$-inch diameter and an overall nominal length of 48 inches. Other tube diameters, particularly 1 inch and $^5/_8$ inch, are now regularly used since they tend to have better luminous efficacy, which means that they produce more lumens per watt of electricity consumed. Fluorescent lamps also are available in a number of different lengths, including 15 inches, 18 inches, and 1-foot increments from 2 feet to 8 feet, plus several other special lengths. Some of the linear tubes are grooved in order to increase the output by causing the electric arc to travel a slightly longer distance. There are also U-shaped and circular tubes, which tend to reduce the overall size of the lamp, and there are small fluorescent lamps that are very compact—the CFLs.

CFLs are more than their name implies. Intended to be used in an incandescent luminaire, CFLs are small devices that include a fluorescent lamp and a ballast. With the

Table 2.5: COMPARISON OF OUTPUT FROM CFL AND INCANDESCENT LAMPS

CFL (watts)	Incandescent (watts)	Lumen Output
10	40	450
15	60	800
20	75	1100
29	100	1600
38	150	2600

Source: Adapted from information from Natural Resources Canada

typical fluorescent linear glass tube spiraled into a tight package, CFLs provide a compressed source of light with a lumen output that requires only around 25% of the energy of a comparable incandescent lamp, although there are some limitations with these light sources. As fluorescents, the emitted light does not parallel the incandescent spectrum, although a reasonable parity of color is possible if the CFL is properly selected. CFLs also do not turn on immediately, and even after they emit light, there is a further delay until full output is achieved (see Table 2.5). The intended color rendition is also not achieved until operational temperatures are attained, and while there are dimmable CFL lamps, the range of reduction is not comparable to that of an incandescent lamp; and as they dim, the color of the light does not adjust toward red.

CFLs are intended to be used as a way of converting an incandescent luminaire into a more efficient light fixture. With new construction, rather than take this approach, we should consider using a fluorescent fixture that can provide the light distribution and output that are desired. And since a "native" fluorescent fixture can include a ballast that is designed to dim the light output, using a fluorescent fixture will allow more effective control of lighting intensity than is available with a CFL, although the color adjustment is still not as we generally prefer.

HID Lamp

The principles of operation for high intensity discharge (HID) lamps are similar to those for fluorescent lamps, although HID lamps use high-pressure gases that can produce visible light directly and allow for a considerable reduction in lamp size. As such, HID lamps are essentially point sources of light that emit a large amount of lumens, hence the name *high intensity* (see Figure 2.42).

The high pressure is developed in part by the elevated temperatures at which HID lamps operate. It takes some time to reach these temperatures, so there is a delay between activating an HID lamp and delivery of the full lumen output at the intended wavelengths of radiation.

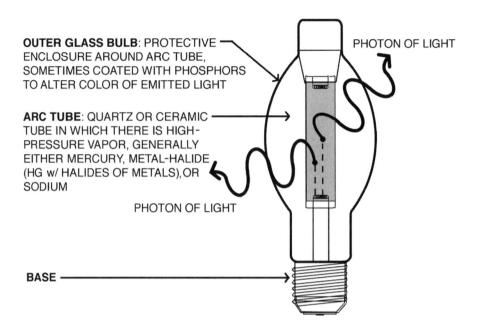

OUTER GLASS BULB: PROTECTIVE ENCLOSURE AROUND ARC TUBE, SOMETIMES COATED WITH PHOSPHORS TO ALTER COLOR OF EMITTED LIGHT

PHOTON OF LIGHT

ARC TUBE: QUARTZ OR CERAMIC TUBE IN WHICH THERE IS HIGH-PRESSURE VAPOR, GENERALLY EITHER MERCURY, METAL-HALIDE (HG w/ HALIDES OF METALS), OR SODIUM

PHOTON OF LIGHT

BASE

Figure 2.42 HID LAMP

Generally, it can take 5 to 8 minutes before the lamp is operating at design levels. Also, once extinguished, an HID lamp must cool down to allow the pressure to reduce before it can be turned on again. Otherwise, the startup cycle would draw excessive current, which could cause problems. Cooling down also takes several minutes, so if an HID lamp is extinguished, it may take up to 10 minutes, or perhaps even longer, until it is again operating at full lumen output. While there are some specially designed HID lamps and fixtures that will produce around 80% of their full output within 1 or 2 minutes after activation (referred to as *instant* restrike lamps, which do not require a cooldown period), most standard HID lamps are not appropriate for installations where the lights are regularly turned on and off (see Tables 2.6 to 2.9 for data on various types of HID lamps.)

LED Lamp

LEDs are often touted as the light source of the future. Clearly, they promise a great deal, particularly in terms of luminous efficacy, long life, color rendition, and effective control of light distribution. However, LEDs are expensive, particularly in terms of the initial costs. In terms of life-cycle costs, the overall expense becomes more reasonable, and in time, as the initial costs are reduced and there is a wider selection of lamps and luminaires, it is probable that LEDs will comprise a major portion of the lighting field (see Figure 2.43).

It is difficult to compare the output of LEDs with that of other light sources. Unlike the other sources, LED lamps are typically an assembly of a number of individual LEDs, each of which is rather small, with a low-lumen output. As

Table 2.6: TYPICAL HID. LAMP DATA

Lamp Type	Watts	Average Life (Hrs.)	Initial Lumens	Lumens[a] per Watt
Mercury Vapor				
H43AV-R75/DX	75	16,000	2800	32
H38JA-R100/WDX	100	24,000	3400	30
H39KC-R175/DX	175	24,000	8600	44
H33GL-R400/DX	400	24,000	22,500	51
H36GW-R1000/DX	1000	24,000	63,000	57
Metal Halide				
Metalarc	175	7,500	14,000	69
Super-Metalarc	175	10,000	15,000	77
Metalarc	400	15,000	34,000	77
Super-Metalarc	400	20,000	40,000	91
Metalarc	1000	12,000	110,000	100
High-Pressure Sodium				
Lumalux	150	24,000	16,000	79
Lumalux	400	24,000	50,000	104
Lumalux	1000	24,000	140,000	124

[a] Includes wattage for both lamp and ballast.

an assembly of smaller individual LEDs, the LED lamps can take a linear form or can be a tight-packed point source of light. Table 2.10 provides a comparison between LEDs, CFLs, and incandescent-filament lamps, although the basis of such assessments can be somewhat elusive.

The initial lumen output shown in the various lamp data tables usually indicates all of the lumens emitted from a lamp, whether or not these will be effective in providing illumination. Since a point-source lamp emits light in all

Table 2.7: TYPICAL MERCURY VAPOR LAMP DATA

Nom. Watts	ANSI Code	Bulb	Max. Length (inches)	Average Life (hr)	Approx. Initial	Lumens Mean	Efficacy[a]
Clear Lamps							
100	H38HT-100	E-23$\frac{1}{2}$	7$\frac{1}{2}$	24000	3850	3120	34
100	H38LL-100	A-23	5$\frac{7}{16}$	18000	3700	3000	32
175	H39KB-175	E-28	8$\frac{1}{4}$	24000	7950	7470	41
250	H37KB-250	E-28	8$\frac{1}{4}$	24000	11200	10300	38
400	H33CD-400	E-37	11$\frac{5}{16}$	24000	21000	19100	48
1000	H36GV-1000	BT-56	15$\frac{1}{16}$	24000	57000	48400	52
Deluxe White Lamps—Phosphor Coated							
40	H45AY-40/DX	E-17	5$\frac{7}{16}$	16000	1140	910	23
50	H45AY-50/DX	E-17	5$\frac{7}{16}$	16000	1575	1260	26
75	H43AV-75/DX	E-17	5$\frac{7}{16}$	16000	2800	2250	32
100	H38JA-100/DX	E-23$\frac{1}{2}$	7$\frac{1}{2}$	24000	4200	3530	35
100	H38MP-100/DX	A-23	5$\frac{7}{16}$	18000	4000	3040	37
175	H39KC-175/DX	E-28	8$\frac{1}{4}$	24000	8600	7650	44
250	H37KC-250/DX	E-28	8$\frac{1}{4}$	24000	12100	10400	42
400	H33GL-400/DX	E-37	11$\frac{5}{16}$	24000	22500	19100	51
1000	H36GW-1000/DX	BT-56	15$\frac{1}{16}$	24000	63000	47500	57
Warm Deluxe White Lamps—Phosphor Coated							
175	H39KC-175/WDX	E-28	8$\frac{1}{4}$	24000	6500	5760	34
250	H37KC-250/WDX	E-28	8$\frac{1}{4}$	24000	9500	7600	33
400	H33GL-400/WDX	E-37	11$\frac{5}{16}$	24000	20000	16400	46
1000	H36GW-1000/WDX	BT-56	15$\frac{1}{16}$	24000	58000	39440	52

[a]Efficacy or lumens per watt (LPW) includes the wattage of the ballast.

directions, some, if not most, of that luminous flux is not directed toward the surfaces that we intend to illuminate. However, when the lamp is a reflector, which includes the PAR, R, and BR lamps, the luminous flux is directed rather than spread out evenly, as from a point source, and the total lumens emitted from the lamp tend to be only around 70% of the lumens produced from a point source of equal wattage. While the output is less, the illumination from reflector lamps is often higher than that from same-wattage point-source lamps, such as a G, A, or PS lamp. Whether or not the lamp directs the light output, the light fixture in which it is placed generally also helps to redirect the luminous flux, except perhaps when a general diffusing distribution is desired.

LED lamps are often reflectors, so while they tend to have low wattage and low lumen output in comparison to other lamps, especially incandescent-filament lamps, the illumination they provide can be comparable—a lot of light from a small package. In addition, since LED lamps are typically small, a LED light fixture is generally more effective in controlling the light distribution, increasing the percentage of luminous flux emitted that is directed toward the surface being illuminated.

Luminaires

While the concept of a point source of light helps explain some basic lighting principles, a point source of light is not usually an effective way to provide illumination, whether for task lighting or spatial lighting. In practically all lighting design, the objective is to light surfaces that, by reflecting incident light, can be seen; this can be achieved best by controlling the distribution of the luminous flux from the light source. Merely increasing the lumen output and scattering it throughout a space, which is a shotgun method, will obviously allow us to see things, but without the refinement appropriate to the architectural design and/or the visual task.

In the early days of electric lighting, lighting fixtures were merely a means of providing an electrical connection. Light distribution was what the lamp provided, and

Table 2.8: TYPICAL METAL-HALIDE LAMP DATA

Nominal Watts	Description	Bulb	Average Life (hr)	Approx. Lumens		
				Initial	Mean	Efficacy[a]
Standard Design Lamps						
175	Clear	BT-28	7500	14500	10800	71
175	Phosphor Coated	BT-28	7500	14500	10200	71
250	Clear	BT-28	10000	20000	17000	73
250	Phosphor Coated	BT-28	10000	20000	17000	73
400	Clear	BT-37	15000	35000	27600	79
400	Phosphor Coated	BT-37	15000	35000	28600	79
1000	Clear	BT-56	18000	110000	88000	100
1000	Phosphor Coated	BT-56	18000	110000	85000	100
High-Output Lamps						
175	Clear	BT-28	10000	15500	12000	80
175	Phosphor Coated	BT-28	10000	15500	11000	80
175	Phosphor Coated	BT-28	10000	14000	10000	69
250	Phosphor Coated	BT-28	10000	21000	16000	75
400	Clear	BT-37	20000	39000	31000	89
400	Phosphor Coated	BT-37	20000	39000	30000	89
400	Phosphor Coated	BT-37	15000	37000	28000	84

[a]Efficacy or lumens per watt (LPW) includes the wattage of the ballast.

Table 2.9: TYPICAL HIGH-PRESSURE SODIUM (HPS) VAPOR LAMP DATA

Nominal Watts[a]		ANSI Code	Bulb	Max. Length (inches)	Average Life (hr)[b]	Approx. Lumens		
						Initial	Mean	Efficacy[c]
Clear Lamps								
50	CL	S68MS-50	E-23^1/$_2$	7^3/$_4$	24000	3300	2970	
50	CO	S68MY-50	E-23^1/$_2$	7^3/$_4$	24000	3150	2835	
70	CL	S62ME-70	E-23^1/$_2$	7^3/$_4$	24000	5800	5220	58
70	CO	S62MF-70	E-23^1/$_2$	7^3/$_4$	24000	5400	4860	54
100	CL	S54SB-100	E-23^1/$_2$	7^3/$_4$	24000	9500	8550	66
100	CO	S54MC-100	E-23^1/$_2$	7^3/$_4$	24000	8800	7920	61
150	CL	S55SC-150	E-23^1/$_2$	7^3/$_4$	24000	16000	14400	79
150	CO	S55MD-150	E-23^1/$_2$	7^3/$_4$	24000	15000	13500	74
250	CL	S50VA-250	E-18	9^3/$_4$	24000	27500	24750	90
250	CO	S50VC-250	E-28	9	24000	26000	23400	85
400	CL	S51WA-400	E-18	9^3/$_4$	24000	50000	45000	104
400	CO	S51WB-400	E-37	11^5/$_{16}$	24000	47500	42750	99
1000		S52XB-1000	E-25	15^1/$_{16}$	24000	140000	126000	124

[a]CL refers to clear, while CO refers to coated.
[b]Based on 10 hours minimum per start.
[c]Initial efficacy or lumens per watt (LPW) includes the wattage of the ballast.

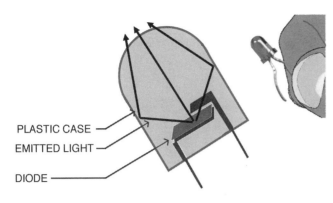

PLASTIC CASE
EMITTED LIGHT
DIODE

Figure 2.43 LED LAMP

Table 2.10: COMPARISON OF WATTS FOR LED, CFL AND INCANDESCENT LAMPS

Lumens	LED	CFL	Incandescent
50 lm	1 w	4 w	20 w
100 lm		5 w	25 w
200 lm		6–7 w	30–35 w
300 lm	4 w	8–9 w	40 w
400 lm		10 w	50 w
500 lm		11 w	60 w
600 lm	8 w	14 w	65 w

generally this was a shotgun distribution from what was essentially a point source of light. In terms of visual aesthetics, the bright lamps themselves often became visually prominent, as is demonstrated by the table lamps shown

in Figure 2.44. In time, various fixtures were designed for the electric lamp that provided a way of shielding the view of the bright lamp. These were often extraordinary works of art, but typically they were not effective in controlling light distribution.

Although there are still numerous light fixtures that are selected for their decorative qualities to enhance the design of a space, in general luminaires are selected to provide illumination and to do so without creating too much awareness of their presence. In this situation the luminaire has two purposes: to shield the view of the actual light source (which is typically rather bright) and to direct the luminous flux from that source to illuminate the task or room surfaces. For the latter purpose, particularly given our commitment to act responsibly in terms of the natural environment, the objective is often to maximize the efficiency of the lighting design. This should not only reduce energy consumption, it should also reduce heat gain, which can be a critical and difficult side effect of electric light. Unfortunately, these two purposes, shielding the source of light and providing efficacious illumination, are sometimes in conflict, but by understanding the basic principles of light distribution, we should be able to maximize both in the lighting design.

The recessed can fixture is a popular luminaire that provides a way to shield a point source of light. Figure 2.45 shows two different ways in which a can fixture controls the spread of light. Early can lights, as shown in the left diagram, used black baffles to shield the view of the lamp and control the spread of the light output. Unfortunately, while these fixtures were effective in obscuring the bright

Figure 2.44 EARLY TABLE LAMPS
These images represent two examples of table-lamp lighting fixtures that are wonderful works of art. In addition to their own beauty, both of these fixtures obscured a direct view of the electric lamp but they did little to control the light distribution. The fixture on the left is by Tiffany. The designer of the fixture shown on the right is unknown, but the table lamp was used in the Director's Office in the Cincinnati Union Terminal, designed by Alfred T. Fellheimer and Steward Wagner.

Tiffany Lamp

Director's Desk Lamp - Cincinnati Union Terminal

 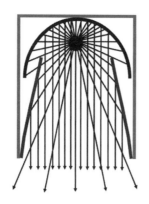 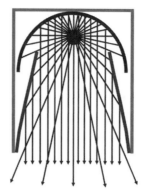 

Figure 2.45 SCHEMATIC CAN LUMINAIRES
The recessed can fixture provides an effective way to shield a point source of light. Early cans controlled the light spread by using black baffles. While effective, this method was very inefficient. A parabolic reflector controls the spread of light by redirecting it off of a parabolic reflector.

Figure 2.46 PLACEMENT OF A LAMP IN A LUMINAIRE
Controlled reflections are based on properly locating the light source with respect to the focus of the reflector's geometric form. When the lamp is the wrong physical size for the luminaire, less light may be emitted. This is true even if the replacement lamp has a higher wattage.

lamp and limiting the spread, they did so by absorbing much of the light, which meant operating less efficiently. By replacing the black baffles with a parabolic reflector, as shown in the right-hand diagram of Figure 2.45, the fixture can still shield the bright lamp and, rather than absorb the potentially problematic rays of light, the reflector can redirect these light rays so that they remain within the desired output spread, increasing the illumination level. This assumes that the optics of the luminaire are reasonably refined and that the appropriate lamp is used. When a recessed can light appears as a bright spot on the ceiling, one or both of these requirements have not been met.

The optics of most complex reflectors require placement of a point source of light at the focus of the geometric form. If the size, shape, and/or location of the lamp are not as prescribed for the fixture, the light distribution will not be as intended and the light output may be significantly reduced (see Figure 2.46). In fact, sometimes increasing the wattage of the lamp can actually result in reducing the light output. If the lamp with the higher wattage is larger than the proper lamp, the location of the light source will probably not be consistent with the optics of the luminaire. The more refined the luminaire optics, the more critical it is to use the lamp specified for the fixture.

Many luminaires stipulate a maximum wattage for the lamps used. While this can relate, in part, to selecting the appropriate lamp size for the optics of the fixture, the more significant issue is the temperature that the lamp will generate. All electric lamps generate heat, and in fact, except for the infinitesimal amount of radiant energy that might be converted into a visual sensation, the light that is produced ultimately is converted into heat. With incandescent lighting, only about 10% of the energy consumed is converted into luminous flux. A large portion of the energy also produces radiant flux outside the visible spectrum, which

we appreciate with heat lamps. While a major portion of the heat related to both visible and nonvisible radiation tends to leave the lighting fixture, a major portion of the energy consumed is involved in heating the filament, which is how the light is generated. With excessive wattage, more heat is generated, and if the heat becomes excessive, the insulation on the electric wiring supplying the fixture can be damaged.

Most fluorescent fixtures use lamps that are large. Rather than rely on reflectors to control the light distribution, fluorescent fixtures usually use a lens, although bare lamp fluorescent fixtures are often used (see Figure 2.47 for several diagrams showing various methods of controlling the light distribution from fluorescent fixtures). When the lamps are left exposed, the bright fluorescent tubes are visible, which some find objectionable. The simplest lens is a diffusing material that encloses the fluorescent lamps. This will reduce the brightness of the fixture and protect against dirt accumulation, but it does little to control the light distribution. In general, a diffusing lens should have at least 80% transmission, although to reduce the chance of seeing the image of the lamp, a lower transmission is sometimes used. Since this reduces the luminous efficacy of the lighting system and is actually prohibited by various jurisdictions, we can avoid the ghosting image of the lamps by either improving the reflection within the fixture or increasing the spacing between the lamp and the lens. With a luminous ceiling, a 6- to 8-inch spacing is recommended.

Using a prismatic lens can reduce the brightness of the fixture and control the light distribution. Depending on the coefficient of refraction of the lens material and the configuration of the lens, the light can be directed in various ways, although the performance of the lens cannot be determined by simple visual inspection. Different plastics might look similar, but their optical characteristics may

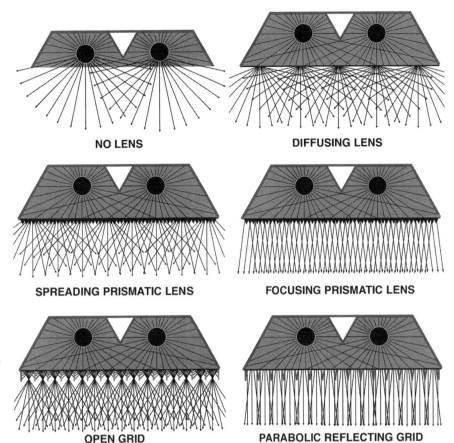

NO LENS   DIFFUSING LENS

SPREADING PRISMATIC LENS   FOCUSING PRISMATIC LENS

OPEN GRID   PARABOLIC REFLECTING GRID

Figure 2.47 SCHEMATICS OF DISTRIBUTION CONTROL FOR FLUORESCENT FIXTURES
While fluorescent lamps might be exposed, generally some device is used to shield the lamps from view and perhaps to control the way the light is distributed. These devices typically are either a lens or a grid. A lens might be a simple diffuser, which tends to be primarily a way to conceal the bright tubes, or it can be a prismatic refractor that provides some control over the distribution pattern, although the performance of a prismatic lens cannot be discerned by merely looking at it. Grids also might simply shield the lamps or, particularly if they are comprised of parabolic reflecting cells, they might also provide a reasonably controlled down light.

be quite distinct. For example, while not apparent in their appearance when new, there is a critical difference between styrene and acrylic plastics. Styrene will deteriorate and turn yellow when exposed to ultraviolet radiation. Although the glass bulbs used in fluorescent lamps tend to limit ultraviolet transmission, fluorescent lighting relies on ultraviolet radiation and some ultraviolet emission does occur; over time, this radiation will cause significant changes to styrene plastic.

Instead of a lens, many fixtures rely on an open grid to shield the view of the lamps. These grids can range from fins that are somewhat deep, around 4 inches, spread out across the face of the fixture, perhaps at a 6-inch spacing, to a tight grid, often referred to as an *egg-crate louver*, with a spacing as small as $1/2$ inch. Either way, the grid is an assemblage of vertical fins that allow light to pass through in a somewhat vertical direction but cut off both the light and the view at around a 45° angle (see Figure 2.48).

Although egg-crate louvers can effectively cut off the view of bright lamps, the grid itself can become rather bright, especially when it is white. The standard white egg-crate grid is also not very effective in controlling the light distribution. While the grid does not interrupt light that is emitted essentially downward, the light that it does interrupt is mostly reflected off of the grid, scattering in

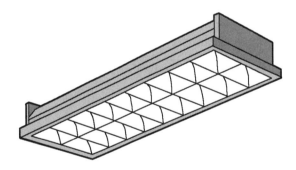

Figure 2.48 SCHEMATIC OF A FLUORESENT FIXTURE WITH A GRID

various directions, including horizontally. Instead of being formed from a series of regular rectangular cells, egg-crate louvers can consist of a series of parabolic cells. With the grid covered with a highly reflective coating, in addition to shielding the view of the lamps, a parabolic grid can effectively control the emission of light in a downward direction with very little horizontal spread. In fact, some find this ability to be a problem since, when viewed on the ceiling, parabolic egg-crate grids appear black.

Whatever luminaires we choose to use, it is important to explore their characteristic light distribution patterns. Every reputable manufacturer of lighting fixtures can

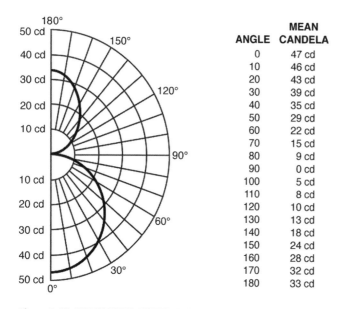

ANGLE	MEAN CANDELA
0	47 cd
10	46 cd
20	43 cd
30	39 cd
40	35 cd
50	29 cd
60	22 cd
70	15 cd
80	9 cd
90	0 cd
100	5 cd
110	8 cd
120	10 cd
130	13 cd
140	18 cd
150	24 cd
160	28 cd
170	32 cd
180	33 cd

Figure 2.49 PHOTOMETRIC DISTRIBUTION DATA
Each lighting manufacturer provides data on the photometric distribution for its luminaires. While a plot of lumen distribution provides a simple visual graphic that effectively indicates the basic distribution, not all manufacturers present the data in this format; many rely only on listed values.

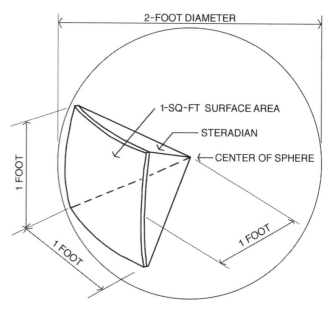

Figure 2.50 THE STERADIAN AND THE FOOT-CANDLE
The steradian, which is a solid angle that subtends an area equal to the square of the distance from the tip or apex of the solid angle to the surface subtended, is the basis of the foot-candle.

provide photometric data on its luminaires. It is also important to verify the specifications since, as with prismatic lenses, it is not feasible to grasp the difference in quality between different luminaires simply by looking at them. For example, a white finish on metal might be baked-on enamel or a simple coating of spray paint, and of course, once painted, it is no longer possible to determine the nature of the substrate. This can be a critical issue when the luminaire is to be installed in an area of high humidity.

Luminous Flux Distribution Curves

Each luminaire is tested in a laboratory to determine its output and photometric distribution. The apparatus basically includes a luminance meter that can record the luminous flux intensity at various points surrounding the fixture. Figure 2.49 shows a schematic of a typical distribution curve. When the luminaire is symmetrical, only one plot is typically provided, but with nonsymmetrical luminaires, which include most fluorescent fixtures, data are presented for both the width and length of the unit.[17]

ILLUMINATION

As has been discussed, and as shown in Figure 2.50, light from a point source spreads out equally in all direction, with 1/12.57th of the total lumens emitted traveling outward in each steradian. Since a steradian is actually a portion of a sphere, the surface it subtends, which is the "bottom" of the solid angle, is curved. Although this surface continues to be curved even as the distance between the vertex of the solid angle and the illuminated surface increases, in terms of illumination on a unit area of that surface the surface tends to flatten, and for practical purposes no correction is necessary. When determining the intensity of illumination on a surface, in addition to accepting that no correction is necessary for being flat, it is also assumed that the surface lies at the center of the steradian, which adjusts for conditions in which the light does not follow a pure point-source distribution. Based on this, the intensity of illumination on a surface from a point source of light is equal to the total luminous flux, in lumens, within a given steradian divided by the square of the distance. Since the lumens per steradian are indicated in *candela* units,[18]

---

[17]While there are fluorescent fixtures that intentionally control light distribution from the end of the fixture, most do not. As a general rule, it should be assumed that illumination from the end of a fluorescent fixture effectively extends only for about 2 feet. Based on this, fluorescent fixtures should not be spread more than 4 feet apart if they are installed in a row. Of course, when there is no separation between fixtures in a row, the wiring can run from fixture to fixture, eliminating the need to provide an electrical box for each fixture and the cost of this arrangement.

[18]The classic definition of candela is the luminous intensity in a given direction emitted by a monochromatic source of a frequency of 540×10^{12} Hz that has a radiant intensity in that direction of 1/683 watt per steradian. While the candela is the basic unit of luminous intensity adopted under the SI system of measurement, it is typically understood as lumens per steradian, and since a steradian is a form and not a measurement, candelas or lumens per steradian are equal for both the imperial and SI measurement systems.

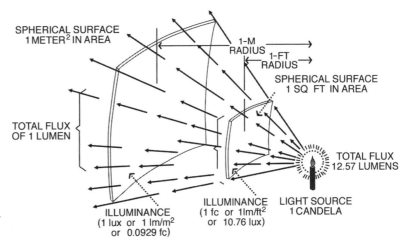

Figure 2.51 FOOT-CANDLE AND LUX DIAGRAM
If a candle, which is a point source of light, forms the apex of a steradian, the distribution of light within that steradian forms the basis of the unit of illumination: the foot-candle in the imperial measurement system and the lux in the SI system. (Adapted from a drawing in Stein, B., Reynolds, J. S., Grondzik, W. T., and Kwok, A. G.: *Mechanical and Electrical Equipment for Buildings*, John Wiley & Sons, Inc., Hoboken, NJ, 2006)

the illumination from a point source of light can be expressed by

$$\text{Point Source of Illumination} = \text{Candela}/\text{Distance}^2$$

The lumen is the basic unit in both the imperial and SI measurement systems to indicate the light distribution, the illumination (which is the light incident on a surface), and the brightness of a surface (which is the light emitted by or reflected off a surface). However, in the two systems, lumens per unit area are indicated by different terms. When illumination is in lumens per square foot, which indicates the imperial system, the term used is *foot-candle*. As shown in Figure 2.51, 1 foot-candle of illumination is the amount of light from a standard candle on a surface that is 1 foot away. When the distance is increased to 1 meter, the illumination intensity from a standard candle is 1 lumen per square meter, which is indicated as 1 *lux*.

Illuminance Levels

Illuminance levels are noted in terms of lumens per unit area. The foot-candle is the unit of illuminance intensity used in the imperial system, and the lux is the unit used in the SI system. Since 1 square meter equals essentially 10 square feet, 10 lux is equivalent to 1 foot-candle. The illumination levels that are appropriate are now usually presented in terms of the type of task for which lighting is to be provided, such as circulation areas, general areas, and tasks. While Table 2.11 presents recommended illuminance task levels, a more extensive exploration of the appropriate illumination levels can be found in various texts, including Lechner's *Heating, Cooling, Lighting: Design Methods for Architects* and the "MEEB" text, *Mechanical and Electrical Equipment for Buildings*. Unfortunately, these more extensive presentations often do not include any clear, definitive recommendations. Table 2.12 lists task luminance or brightness levels in foot-lamberts and the

Table 2.11: RECOMMENDED TASK ILLUMINANCE LEVELS

Task	Foot-Candles
Casual	10–20 fc
Ordinary	20–50 fc
Oderate	50–75 fc
Difficult	75–200 fc
Severe	200+ fc

Table 2.12: RECOMMENDED TASK ILLUMINANCE LEVELS

Task	Foot-Lamberts	$\rho - 0.50$	$\rho - 0.10$
Casual	5 fL	c. 10 fc	c. 50 fc
Ordinary	20 fL	c. 40 fc	c. 200 fc
Moderate	45 fL	c. 90 fc	c. 450 fc
Difficult	90 fL	c. 160 fc	c. 900 fc
Severe	120+ fL	c. 240 fc	c. 1200 fc

necessary foot-candles of illuminance, established by the illumination need to produce these luminance levels with the indicated reflectance of the surface or task. This list, which is a reasonable guide for establishing appropriate lighting levels, is based on the type of task to be performed.

Visual performance actually depends on the luminance or brightness of the task, and this is based on the reflectance of the task as well as on the illumination levels. So, while recommended illumination levels are important, they are not always appropriate since they are not usually connected to the reflectance of the task. For this reason, the recommended illumination levels are frequently higher than what might be reasonable in order to accommodate a range of probable values for task reflectance. This confusion is apparent if we compare the foot-candle recommendations listed in Table 2.11 with the suggested illumination indicated in Table 2.12.

Determining the illumination levels for a critical task can also help establish the illumination levels for general lighting and noncritical areas. The IESNA recommends that general lighting be set at one-third the task-lighting levels, although usually not below 20 foot-candles, and that the illumination in noncritical areas, such as circulation areas, should be set at one-third of the general lighting level, but not less than 10 foot-candles. While these recommendations seem reasonable as a way to balance lighting conditions, if the illumination in noncritical areas is at the minimum of 10 foot-candles, the general lighting levels should be at 30 foot-candles and the task lighting levels at 90 foot-candles, which is rather high for most tasks.

Today, with increased use of computers, which are themselves a source of task lighting, the issue of task lighting should be open to new interpretations. The traditional approach to lighting a space to a level that will permit a visual task no longer seems logical. Instead, it seems more appropriate to provide task lighting in connection with the task rather than with the space, and to do so in a way that allows the user to control the placement, operation, and intensity of the task lighting so that it is responsive to the task and the preference of the individual. Rather than base the overall lighting design on the level stipulated for task lighting, we should design the lighting system so that it can provide the illumination appropriate for the desired spatial ambiance and also include the means to accommodate reasonable task lighting.

Building codes generally establish minimum levels of illumination. In some jurisdictions, the lighting in all habitable and occupiable spaces is to be at least 6 foot-candles on average at 30 inches above floor level. This is to be provided by either natural or electrical sources. The average illumination in toilet rooms is to be at least 3 foot-candles, provided by electric lighting. And the emergency lighting should be at least 1 foot-candle, which is considered minimally adequate illumination for emergency egress, although the aisle illumination in movie theaters needs to be only 0.2 foot-candle. While this difference at first might seem inappropriate, perhaps when the factor of adaptation is considered, the lower theater illumination might be reasonable.

Determining whether lighting levels for a particular purpose are adequate is based in part on comparisons between lighting levels in adjacent areas and on expectations. For example, it is quite possible that the lighting levels in an interior space that has a strong visual connection to the outside might seem to be rather low, leading one to turn on the electric lights. While the electric lights might help, the feeling that the light is not adequate might continue. But then, at night, when outside conditions are rather dark, the electric lighting alone can seem rather bright. Obviously, the lighting level based only on the electric lights is

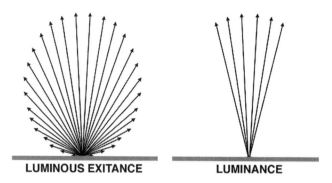

Figure 2.52 REFLECTED OR EMITTED LUMINOUS FLUX OFF A DIFFUSE SURFACE

less than what these lights plus daylight provide, but the experience can suggest a different interpretation.

Luminance and Luminous Exitance

As indicated in Figure 2.52, there are various ways to consider how light comes off of a surface. This light is also measured in lumens, but this can be the total diffused reflection or emission per unit area of the surface or the luminous flux in a particular direction, which is typically defined as candela for the steradian normal to the surface. When the light coming off of a surface is not directional, which is basically surface brightness, it is called *luminous exitance* or *luminous emittance*. Even though the term *exitance* is preferred, it is denoted by M, which seems to be a consideration for those who favored the use of *emittance*. In the SI system, luminous exitance is usually indicated simply in terms of lumens per square meter, although sometimes lux is used; this means that the same term is used for the intensity of luminous flux for both incident and leaving light. In the imperial system, the intensity of light leaving a surface is indicated by lumens per square foot, which is called *foot-lamberts*. In either case, the brightness is the incident light times the coefficient of reflection (ρ) or the coefficient of transmission (τ).

The reflected or emitted luminous flux from a surface in the steradian normal to the surface is *luminance*. While luminous exitance relates to brightness that we experience when viewing a surface, luminance is more of an engineering term in that it can be used to determine the luminous flux off of the surface as a secondary light source. Luminance equals the incident light times ρ or τ divided by π.

FOR REFLECTED LIGHT:

$$\text{Luminous Exitance } (M) = \text{Foot-Lamberts} = \text{Foot-Candles} \times \rho$$

$$\text{Luminance } (L) = \frac{\text{Foot-Candles} \times \rho}{\pi}$$

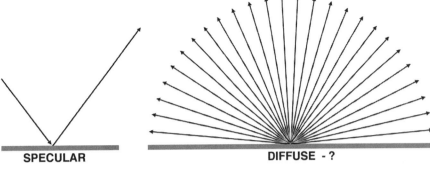

Figure 2.53 SPECULAR AND ASSUMED DIFFUSE REFLECTION

SPECULAR

DIFFUSE - ?

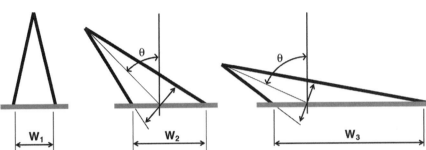

Figure 2.54 AREA SUBTENDED BY DIFFERENT ANGLES OF VIEW
As should be apparent from this series of diagrams, which shows a two-dimensional representation of a three-dimensional experience, as the view of a surface becomes increasingly oblique, the surface area that falls within the cone of vision keeps increasing.

W_1

θ

W_2

θ

W_3

FOR TRANSMITTED LIGHT:

$$\text{Luminous Exitance } (M) = \text{Foot-Lamberts} = \text{Foot-Candles} \times \rho$$

$$\text{Luminance } (L) = \frac{\text{Foot-Candles} \times \tau}{\pi}$$

The reflection off of a surface is usually thought to be either specular, which we assume when we consider that the angle of incidence equals the angle of reflection, or diffuse, which we believe is how light scatters off of a flat or matte-finish surface. While this difference is schematically shown in Figure 2.53, unfortunately the interpretation of diffuse reflection is not accurate, although it is representative of what we might actually experience. That is, while the light that we see coming off of a diffuse surface seems to be equal regardless of the angle of view, which is what is implied in the diagram, in actuality the reflection of light off of a matte finish follows a cosine distribution pattern, as shown schematically in the left image in Figure 2.52.

When we look at a diffuse surface, the light that we see reflected off of the surface and the brightness that we experience are determined in part by our cone of vision and by the angle at which we look at the surface. Since our cone of vision remains constant, as our view of a surface becomes more and more oblique, our eyes actually see an increasing amount of surface area, although the brightness of the diffuse surface remains consistent. This can only happen if the actual light emitted from the diffuse surface is reduced as the angle of emission becomes more oblique. This can be readily explained by a series of simple diagrams.

The three diagrams in Figure 2.54 all have the same cone shape. As the angle θ increases, the length of the line W also increases. Based on this, we can assume that the amount of light must continue to decrease as the angle between the emitted light ray and a line normal to the surface increases. By simple trigonometry, we should see that this reduction follows the cosine[19] of the angle at which the light is reflected or emitted. However, each point along the surface actually spreads light out in a diffuse pattern, so the brightness of the surface is based on the sum total of all of the light that actually enters the eye.

Figure 2.55 shows an implied cone of vision overlaid at three different angles on a single cosine distribution pattern. As we can surmise from these diagrams, in order to enter the eye, which is at the vertex of the cone of vision, the reflected or emitted rays of light must arrive at the vertex. The diagrams show neither the infinite number of rays coming off of each point on the surface nor the infinite number of points on the surface that send light to the eye.

While the diagram on the right in Figure 2.53 represents how we tend to think of diffuse reflection, in actuality Figure 2.56 is a more accurate representation. With diffuse reflection, each point emits light that follows the lambertian cosine law, named for the Swiss mathematician, Johann Heinrich Lambert (1728–1777), who developed the law. This law states that the radiant intensity observed from a diffuse surface is directly proportional to the cosine

---

[19]The cosine of an angle is the adjacent divided by the hypotenuse of a right triangle defined by that angle.

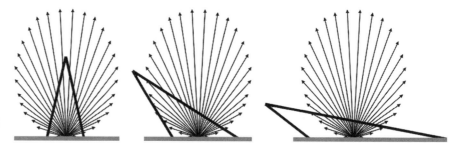

Figure 2.55 VIEWED DIFFUSE REFLECTION OR EMISSION OF LIGHT

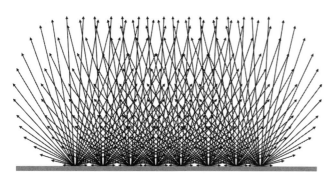

Figure 2.56 LAMBERTIAN DIFFUSION ROSETTES
Diffuse reflection follows the lambertian cosine law. This law states that the intensity of radiation from a diffuse surface is proportional to the cosine of the angle between an observer's line of sight of that surface and the normal to that surface at the point of sight. This law is named after the Swiss mathematician Johann Heinrich Lambert.

of the angle between an observer's line of sight and the surface normal.

Figure 2.57 diagrammatically shows the different light rays that the eye sees from each portion of the surface based on the angle of view. By combining the various light rays within each cone of vision, we can get an indication of the total amount of luminous flux that should enter the eye. As can be seen, the total luminous flux for each of the three scenarios is equal.

Whether light is reflected or emitted, as with a diffusing lens of a fluorescent luminaire, the luminous exitance from

a diffusing surface follows Lambert's cosine law. While the total amount light coming from the surface is equal to the lumens of incident illumination times the coefficient of reflection (ρ) or the coefficient of transmission (τ), the distribution of this total luminous flux is based on the cosine of the angle defined by the direction of the light ray and the line normal to the surface. The intensity of the luminous flux in a direction is determined by the light in the steradian normal to the surface times the cosine of the angle between the direction of radiation and the normal to the surface. See Table 2.13 for a list of cosine values

The luminance off of a surface, which is equal to the luminous exitance divided by π, can be used to determine the contribution of the reflected light to the illumination on another surface. Multiplying the luminance by the cosine of the angle between the normal to the surface and the line to the surface being illuminated determines the luminous flux in that direction (see Figure 2.58). This luminous flux can then be used to establish the foot-candles or lux of illumination, depending on the measuring system being used.

Table 2.13: COSINE VALUES

$\cos 90° = 0.00$	$\cos 80° = 0.17$	$\cos 70° = 0.34$
$\cos 60° = 0.50$	$\cos 50° = 0.64$	$\cos 40° = 0.77$
$\cos 30° = 0.87$	$\cos 20° = 0.94$	$\cos 10° = 0.99$

Figure 2.57 LUMINOUS FLUX IN EACH CONE OF VISION

Each of the three images schematically shows lines of luminous flux that reach the vertex of the cone and therefore are seen. As the angle of view becomes more oblique, more lines of radiation reach the vertex, but these lines, following lambertian distribution, are reduced by the cosine of the angle defined by the light ray and the line normal to the surface. When these lines in each cone are combined into a straight line, the overall lengths of these three lines are then compared, showing that the total flux within each cone is equal. This shows graphically that the brightness of a surface with diffuse reflection or emission does not vary with a change in the angle of view.

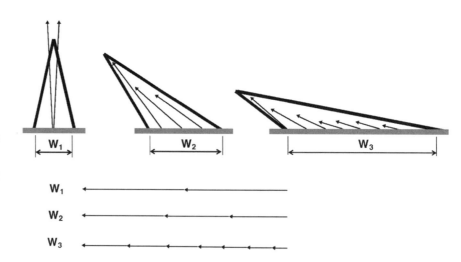

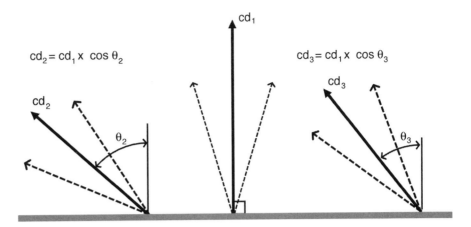

Figure 2.58 LUMINANCE AND ADJUSTED LUMINOUS FLUX

Point-to-Point Illumination

The amount of area seen when viewing a surface is based in part on the angle of view. This suggests that if the luminous flux incident on a surface is not normal to that surface, the intensity of illumination will be proportional to the cosine of the angle of incidence (see Figure 2.59). The greater the angle of incidence, the less the intensity will be in terms of lumens per unit area.

The luminous flux or candela in the steradian directed from a light source toward a surface determines the intensity of illumination. Since candela indicates the lumens per steradian, the intensity at the illuminated surface is equal to the candela in the steradian divided by the square of the distance from the point source to the point or surface being illuminated. When the distance is in feet, the intensity is in lumens per square foot or foot-candles. When the distance is in meters, the intensity is in lumens per square meter or lux. This, however, assumes that the surface is the "bottom" of the steradian. If the surface is at an angle with respect to the direction of the steradian, the intensity must be further reduced by the cosine of the angle of incidence.

$$\text{Point Source Illumination} = \text{Lumens per Unit Area}$$
$$= \frac{\text{Candela} \times \text{Cosine } \theta}{\text{Distance}^2}$$

With distance in feet, illumination is in lumens per square foot or foot-candles.

With distance in meters, illumination is in lumens per square meter or lux.

Lighting Systems

There are several ways to categorize lighting systems. One is by the way the light is generated, which typically means distinguishing between daylight and electrical light. Daylight can be provided by an overcast sky, a clear sky, or the

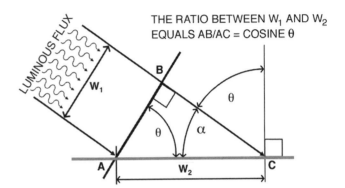

Figure 2.59 INTENSITY OF ILLUMINATION IS PROPORTIONAL TO COSINE
θ The intensity of illumination is proportional to the cosine of the angle of incidence. As shown in the diagram, the ratio of AB to AC is the cosine of angle θ in the triangle ABC. Since this is a right triangle and the two nonright angles must equal 90°, θ is clearly both the angle of incidence and the angle in the triangle that is adjacent to the hypotenuse.

direct rays of the sun, while electric light can be from an incandescent, fluorescent, HID, or LED source. Candles and gas lights are two other light sources still used occasionally. Unfortunately, light that does not rely on the sun is frequently called *artificial* light, but as has been discussed, light is a form of energy, and it either exists or it does not. It can vary in intensity and in wavelength composition, but if it exists, it is not artificial.

Another way to categorize lighting systems is by the way the generated light is distributed into the space. Since the typical situation involves electric lighting for the illumination of a horizontal work plane located below the lighting fixtures (luminaires), this categorization organizes lighting systems according to whether the light is emitted directly or indirectly toward the work plane. Actually, when the light distribution is called *direct* or *indirect*, the expectation is that 90% to 100% of the light is directed either down or up, respectively. In addition to these two clearly diverse systems, various intermediate lighting systems are recognized. Semidirect lighting has 60% to 90% of the light directed downward, with the balance directed

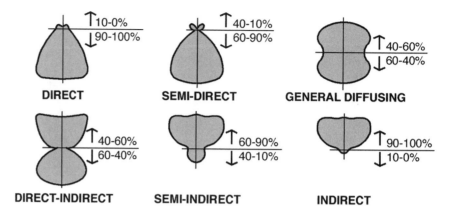

Figure 2.60 **LIGHT DISTRIBUTION**

upward. Direct-indirect lighting, which is sometimes referred to as *general diffused lighting*, has 40% to 60% of the light directed upward, with the balance directed downward. And, as you can guess, semi-indirect lighting has 60% to 90% of the light directed upward and the balance directed downward. Of course, in any classification, the total combined light is a maximum of 100% (see Figure 2.60).

When using a fixture with a major portion of its output distributed upward, the recommendation is to suspend the luminaire at least 18 inches below the ceiling in order to avoid developing hot spots on the ceiling. Of course, if the intention is to develop a highlighted area on the ceiling, it might be appropriate to reduce the distance between the ceiling and the fixture. If the up light is the primary source of illumination on the work plane, the surface off of which the light is reflected should have a fairly high reflectance (ρ). This surfaces acts as a secondary light source, and if it does not have a high reflectance, only a small portion of the incident light will be reflected, reducing the efficiency of the lighting system. Even with a high reflectance, indirect lighting should only be used to provide up to about 25 foot-candles of illumination on the horizontal work plane, which is adequate for most noncritical visual tasks. If this is not sufficient, a direct lighting system and/or localized task lighting should be provided. In fact, regardless of the general lighting design, it is often recommended that localized task lighting be provided for any visual task that requires an illumination level above 25 foot-candles.

Sometimes the selection of the lighting system is based, at least in part, on nonvisual factors. For example, in an open-office arrangement where numerous workstations are located in the same room, even when partial-height partitions are provided, there can be acoustical problems that can be affected by the lighting design. If direct lighting is provided by way of recessed fluorescent fixtures located in the ceiling, the fixtures will replace sound-absorbing acoustical tiles with what amounts to sound-reflecting surfaces. However, if indirect lighting is used, the acoustical absorption of the ceiling can be maximized and problematic reflecting panels avoided.

Maintenance is another factor that should influence the selection of the lighting system. One critical concern is how lamps within the fixtures can be replaced, which deals with whether there will be convenient access to the fixture after construction is complete and how the lamp is connected to the fixture. During construction, the contractors obviously need access to their work, and this might involve scaffolding, big ladders, or even cherry pickers, but after construction and occupancy, such access is typically no longer feasible. If the lamps are installed base up, it might be possible to use a lamp replacement tool that has an extended handle. While these devices are typically designed to work with lamps that have a screw base, there are tools that are designed to work with other types of connection. In some structures, access to the luminaires is provided by means of catwalks installed above the fixtures, but of course, this requires increased ceiling depth and adds considerable expense.

In the 1950s, Philip Johnson designed the Kneses Tifereth Israel Synagogue in Port Chester, New York (see Figure 2.61). By various accounts, Johnson was involved in pro-fascist activities in the 1930s, and he contributed his design services as a way of atoning for his previous indiscretion.[20] The synagogue design included one large volume of space that was 50 feet wide by 140 feet long and 40 feet high, with the ceiling providing a "floating" canopy that was reminiscent of a tent relating to wandering in the desert for 40 years. About half of the space had fixed seating, and this was the source of a problem.

The interior of the space was illuminated by numerous slit windows and HID lights. Sometime after the synagogue was finished, the HID lamps started to burn out, and the congregation had to decide how to replace them. While the ceiling floated below the structure, there was no catwalk to provide access to the lights, which was necessary

[20]Roger Kimball, "Philip Johnson: The Architect as Aesthete," *The New Criterion*, November 1994; David Samson, "Philip Johnson, Architecture and the Rebellion of the Text: 1930–1934," *Interfaces*, Holy Cross College, 2004; "New Acquisition to Go On View on September 2, 2007," The Jewish Museum Press release, August 29, 2007.

Figure 2.61 KNESES TIFERETH ISRAEL SYNAGOGUE
The lighting in the sanctuary of this temple, which is located in Port Chester, New York, and was designed by Philip Johnson, consisted of recessed ceiling lights that unfortunately could not be easily relamped. As a result, in a subsequent renovation, most of the original fixtures were replaced.

since the lamps apparently were installed in the luminaires horizontally. With fixed seating, it was not feasible to use ladders, so lamp replacement became a major undertaking, depending on an installation of scaffolding. In time, the congregation acquired a small cherry picker that provided access to each fixture by extending over the fixed seating, but unfortunately, this became part of the permanent furnishings of this elegant space.

Regular replacement of burned-out lamps is important to maintain the lighting system. Rather than merely considering the initial lighting levels when everything is new, clean, and operational, the general intention of a lighting design is to maintain average illumination levels for an extended period of time; however, over time, lamps burn out. If a number of lights are not operational, the average lighting level will be reduced proportionally. If an installation includes 15 fixtures of which 3 are burned out, the average lighting level will be lowered by 20%. While such a reduction is not usually acceptable, the illumination level below a burned-out fixture will likely be cut by significantly more than the 20% average reduction. When the lighting is provided by a number of smaller distributed light sources, the loss of a few might not be a problem, but when the system includes only a few high-intensity sources, the loss of one could be catastrophic.

Actually, some reduction in average illumination levels resulting from lamp burnout is accommodated by *engineering design*. When determining the amount of lumen output required for a particular level of illumination, the calculation procedures typically include correction factors for various ways in which available light will be reduced over time. One of these factors is lamp burnout, which is often addressed by including a 10% reduction factor. This, of course, means that the design is actually for a higher

level of illumination, 10% for potential burnouts. When all of the various factors are included—and there are eight factors to be considered—the initial illumination level will exceed what is considered will be maintained level. If each factor is assumed to provide only a 10% reduction, eight such minimal adjustments would account for an overall reduction of almost 60%.

$$0.90 \times 0.90 \times 0.90 \times 0.90 \times 0.90 \times 0.90$$
$$\times 0.90 \times 0.90 = 0.43$$

One way to address lamp burnout, especially in large lighting installations, is to establish a lamp replacement program. Each lamp has a projected operational life. While not every lamp will last as long as projected, most will, and many will actually continue to operate beyond this time limit, although likely at a reduced light output. The recommendation is to replace half of all of the lamps after they have operated for about one-half of their projected life and then to continue to replace one-half of the lamps prior to the end of their projected life. This will not only reduce the chance that a number of burnouts will occur in one portion of the lighting installation, it also tends to maintain lamp output. Following this replacement procedure, the lighting installation will be comprised of lamps that never exceed, on average, 75% of their projected operational life, when the lighting output of many lamps starts to decline significantly.

In addition to replacement, there is also the need to clean the lamps and luminaires, especially in environments that produce a lot of dust and dirt. While dust and dirt can accumulate on all surfaces regardless of orientation, the greatest accumulation typically occurs on upward-facing surfaces, which is often the lens of a fixture. As this accumulation increases, light output is reduced, but by enclosing the luminaire, the buildup of dirt can be reduced.

BIBLIOGRAPHY

Aronin, J.E. *Climate and Architecture*. Reinhold Publishing Corporation, New York, 1953.

Bennett, R. *Sun Angles for Design*. Robert Bennett, Bala Cynwyd, PA, 1978.

Brown, G.Z. *Sun, Wind, and Light: Architectural Design Strategies*. John Wiley & Sons, Inc, Hoboken, NJ, 1985.

Egan, M.D. *Concepts in Architectural Lighting*. McGraw-Hill Publishing Company, New York, 1983.

Egan, M.D., and V. Olgyay. *Architectural Lighting*. McGraw-Hill Companies, New York, 2002.

Evans, B.H. *Daylight in Architecture*. McGraw-Hill Publishing Company, New York, 1981.

Gordon, G., and K.L. Nuckolls. *Interior Lighting for Designers*. John Wiley & Sons, Inc., Hoboken, NJ, 1995.

Grondzik, W. T., Kwok, A. G., Stein, B., and Reynolds, J. S.: *Mechanical and Electrical Equipment for Buildings*. John Wiley & Sons, Inc., Hoboken, NJ, 2010.

Lam, W.M.C. *Perception and Lighting as Formgivers for Architecture*. McGraw-Hill Book Company, New York, 1977.

Lam, W.M.C. *Sunlighting as Formgiver for Architecture*. Van Nostrand Reinhold Company, Inc., New York, 1986.

Lechner, N., *Heating, Cooling, Lighting: Design Methods for Architects*, John Wiley & Sons, Hoboken, NJ, 2001.

Moore, F. *Concepts and Practice of Architectural Daylighting*. Van Nostrand Reinhold Company, Inc., New York, 1985.

Moore, F. *Environmental Control Systems: Heating, Cooling, Lighting*. McGraw-Hill, Inc., New York, 1993.

Steffy, G. *Architectural Lighting Design*. John Wiley & Sons, Inc, Hoboken, NJ, 2002.

3 LIGHTING CALCULATIONS

LIGHTING CALCULATION PROCEDURES

POINT-TO-POINT CALCULATIONS

ZONAL CAVITY CALCULATIONS

LIGHTING CALCULATIONS EXAMPLES

LIGHTING CALCULATION PROCEDURES

There are basically two approaches to determining illumination levels. One is the point-to-point method, which has already been discussed as part of our exploration of basic principles. This method indicates the illumination in lumens per unit area at a particular location. While we often assume that there is only one source of light, we can calculate the illumination levels from several light sources and add the results together to get the overall illumination level. While our perception of light might not follow an arithmetic ratio, light is additive.

The fact that light is additive allows us to determine, during the day, what the nighttime illumination levels will be for a space that is illuminated with daylight. If we take two measurements during a time when there is daylight, one with the electric lights on and the other with them off, the difference between the two should be the level of illumination at night with only the electric lights. Of course, the additivity of light also means that if there is more than one point-to-point source lighting an object or a surface, we need to determine the contribution from each and add the results together to obtain the overall illumination level.

POINT-TO-POINT CALCULATIONS

To calculate the illumination from a point source of light, we need to determine the candela emitted in the direction of the surface, the distance to the surface, and the angle of incidence on the surface.

$$\text{Lumens per Unit Area} = E = \frac{\text{Candela} \times \cos\theta}{\text{Distance}^2}$$

Assuming that the fixture is directed toward the surface, as shown in Figure 3.1, the candela will be the output of the fixture at the 0° direction. Using the generic can-light photometric distribution shown in Figure 3.2, the candela would be 2000 lumens. If the distance is 10 feet and the angle of incidence is 30°, the illumination on the surface would be 17.3 foot-candles.

$$E = \frac{\text{cd} \times \cos\theta}{D^2} = \frac{2000\ \text{cd} \times \cos 30°}{10\ \text{ft}^2}$$
$$= \frac{2000\ \text{lm} \times 0.866}{100\ \text{sq ft}} = 17.3\ \text{fc}$$

The photometric distribution from the generic luminaire in this example concentrates the light output within a relatively narrow beam. As a result, the candela in a direction falling between −30° and +30° will be relatively

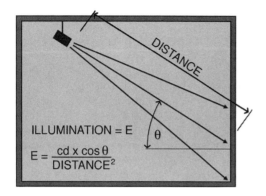

Figure 3.1 POINT-TO-POINT CALCULATION DIAGRAM
As indicated, the illumination from a spotlight or floodlight is typically based on the candela that is central to the fixture emission, but it is possible to determine the illumination for other portions of the emitted light. This requires adjustment of the lumens in that direction, the distance between the source and the illuminated plane, and the angle of incidence.

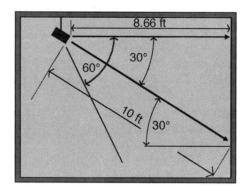

Figure 3.3 ALTERNATE ANGLES AND DIMENSIONS
While it is generally assumed that directed lighting is primarily concerned with the illumination provided by the central beam of light, the spread of light is also to be considered. When the point-to-point calculation method is used to determine the illumination levels established by the luminous flux from the various spread angles, the candela for those angles, the distance to the surface, and the angle of incidence all have to be adjusted from the values used in the central beam calculations.

consistent, from 1780 to 2000 candela, but even with this limited variation, the illumination on the surface provided by this light source will vary. At the effective edge of the beam of light, which we can assume has a spread of 60°, the luminous flux will be reduced to 1780 candela. In addition, both the distance to the surface and the angle of incidence will be different.

Figure 3.3 shows a possible lighting condition that we might wish to analyze. Since the angle of incidence on a vertical wall at the center of the light beam is 30°, we can surmise that the luminaire is angled downward at 30°. This means that the top edge of the 60° cone of light would be horizontal, and since this is the center of the beam of light, the angle of incidence on the surface

would be 0°. By simple trigonometry, as shown in Figure 3.3, the horizontal distance between the light and the surface can be found to be 8.66 feet,[1] and the candela to be 1780 candela. Based on this, the illumination at the top of the 60° cone of light would be 23.7 foot-candles. While the intensity of the luminous flux directed toward the spot on the wall is less, the light is incident at the normal to the surface and the distance is less, both of which increase the effective illumination from the light compared to the illumination at the 10-foot distance from the center of the beam.

$$E = \frac{cd \times \cos\theta}{D^2} = \frac{1780\ cd \times 1}{8.66\ ft^2}$$
$$= \frac{1780\ lm}{75\ sq\ ft} = 23.75\ fc$$

When the intention is to calculate the illumination level on the work plane, which is assumed to be at 30 inches above the floor (table height), and there are several lighting fixtures in the space, we can divide the space into a grid and then calculate the illumination levels at the center of each cell of the grid. This would require calculating the contribution from each of the fixtures, following the point-to-point method (see Figure 3.4). Assuming that the light is spread from each fixture, which would be reasonable if it is to contribute to the illumination of portions of the work plane that are not directly below the fixture, then we should also consider light that will be reflected off of the walls. This means that we would also have to divide the

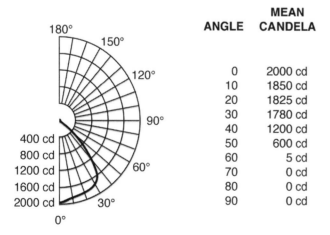

	ANGLE	MEAN CANDELA
	0	2000 cd
	10	1850 cd
	20	1825 cd
	30	1780 cd
	40	1200 cd
	50	600 cd
	60	5 cd
	70	0 cd
	80	0 cd
	90	0 cd

Figure 3.2 PHOTOMETRIC DISTRIBUTION—CAN LIGHT
This is a typical photometric distribution plot and listing for a can light fixture. As indicated, most of the light is downward within a 60° angle. Since there is only one plot, the fixture emits light in a symmetrical pattern.

---

[1] The distance from the fixture to the wall is the adjacent to the 30° angle in a right triangle with a 10-foot hypotenuse. Since the cosine of 30° is 0.866, the length of the line is 8.66 feet.

Figure 3.4 MULTIPLE POINT-TO-POINT CALCULATIONS FROM PRIMARY AND SECONDARY SOURCES
General space lighting usually involves several luminaires to disperse the light across the general area of a room. While this is quite different from the point-to-point approach used to illuminate a particular "spot," often on a wall, point-by-point calculations could be used to determine the general illumination levels. However, this would entail numerous calculations, not only for light that comes directly from a fixture but also for light reflected off of the various room surfaces.

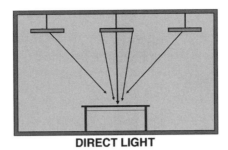

DIRECT LIGHT

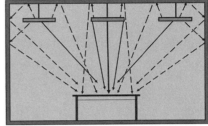

DIRECT AND REFLECTED LIGHT

walls into a grid, calculate the illumination on each wall cell, convert this to the luminance for that cell, and then use these values as secondary light sources directed toward each of the cells on the illumination plane. If the fixtures have a significant up-light component, then reflected light will also come from the ceiling.

This approach, as implied in Figure 3.4, would obviously be extremely tedious since it entails an excessive number of ray tracings. While using ray tracings is essentially how computer calculations are performed, it is not a reasonable method of gaining a general understanding of the critical issues on which to base a lighting proposal. In addition, attempting a computer calculation requires considerable input of information, much of which the preliminary lighting design proposal is trying to determine. We also need to gain an understanding of how various architectural design issues affect the lighting. Although the computer can give a reasonable indication of lighting levels or the number of fixtures required, it is difficult to understand how various design decisions impact on these factors. Most computer calculations require considerable front-end input and then, based on the conglomerate data, provide a response, so it is difficult to understand the effects of each design decision.

ZONAL CAVITY CALCULATIONS

The zonal cavity calculation method, also known as the *lumen method*, is a simple hands-on procedure that can help us determine the average lighting levels that will result from a particular design or guide us in developing a design to provide a prescribed level of illumination in foot-candles or lux. The process involves looking up information on several tables based on different conditions. In this process, we can readily grasp the impact of a variety of design choices, such as the type of lighting, the luminaire to be used, the number and spacing of the luminaires, the coefficient of reflection (colors) of the various room surfaces, and the proportions of the space itself.

Each of these is an architectural decision that affects the calculations.

Assuming that the intention is to determine the level of illumination that a lighting design will provide, we should begin by selecting a luminaire that seems appropriate for the design and then make an assumption about the number of fixtures and the lumens that each fixture should generate. Obviously, this requires some experience, but as with many design decisions, we should begin by making some assumptions and then explore various options that evolved from these assumptions, not committing to a design until we have completed several preliminary calculations.

When we have selected a luminaire, we can determine the coefficient of utilization (CU), which is the decimal portion of the generated lumens that will be available on the illumination plane. The CU is based on the photometric performance for the particular fixture and the characteristics of the space. Since over time there is a reduction in the lumens that the lighting system will provide, we should further reduce the expected lumens by applying a light loss factor (LLF). The lumens that are available to illuminate the work plane will be the total initial lumens produced by the lighting system adjusted by the CU and the LLF. Dividing these available lumens by the room area results in the lumens per square foot or foot-candles of illumination.

$$\text{Foot-Candles} = \frac{\text{Total Lumens Generated} \times \text{CU} \times \text{LLF}}{\text{Room Area in Square Feet}^2}$$

$$\text{Lux} = \frac{\text{Total Lumens Generated} \times \text{CU} \times \text{LLF}}{\text{Room Area in Square Meters}^2}$$

where:

Foot-candles = lumens per square foot

Lux = lumens per square meter

CU = coefficient of utilization

LLF = light loss factor

While this is what is entailed in the zonal cavity method, further clarification of the procedure is obviously appropriate. Before we delve into a further explanation, we

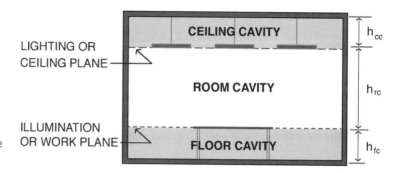

Figure 3.5 THREE ZONAL CAVITIES
The basic assumption of the zonal cavity method is that there are three possible zones in a space, with each zone comprising a volume of space, referred to as a *cavity*.

should realize that while the zonal cavity method provides reasonable results, like many design tools it is merely a design aid. It does not impose definitive or specific requirements. For example, the procedure often indicates that a number other than a whole number of fixtures are required to provide the desired foot-candles of illumination, but partial fixtures are not usually available.[2] Also, while adjusting the lamp wattage can alter the lumens per fixture, the wattages are limited to prescribed sizes, so it is probable that the specific lumens that each luminaire can provide will not match the calculation results. In addition, although the zonal cavity method entails a recommendation for the spacing of fixtures based on their mounting height above the implied work plane, the designer must decide how to arrange the fixtures. If the calculations suggest 20 fixtures, it might be appropriate to have four rows of 5 fixtures or two rows of 10 fixtures; perhaps it might be more logical to add a fixture and have three rows of 7 fixtures. Once we understand the implications of a calculation, not just the average foot-candles provided or the number of fixtures and the lumen output required, we can revise the design and test how these revisions might affect the lighting performance. It is just another part of the design process.

Zonal Cavity Procedures

To simplify the calculations, the zonal cavity method assumes that the space is divided into three zones, as shown in Figure 3.5, hence the name of this approach to calculating the illumination levels. The assumption is that the illumination on the implied work plane is from light that is emitted from an implied plane, sometimes called the *ceiling plane* although it is a lighting plane, and that both the emitted and received light are evenly distributed across these implied planes. These planes are essentially projections of the ceiling and the floor, so the area of each

is equal to the area of the space unless the walls are not vertical.

The space between these lighting planes is considered the room cavity, although the height of this cavity is not based on the floor-to-ceiling dimension but rather on the spacing between the two implied planes, the lighting plane and the illumination plane. If the illumination plane is at +30 inches, then the bottom of the room cavity is at this plane, and the volume between it and the floor constitutes a floor cavity. If the intention is to light the floor, as perhaps in a lobby, then the implied illumination plane is the floor, there is no floor cavity, and the height of the room cavity is from the floor to the implied lighting plane. If the lights are suspended, the lighting plane is at the level of the suspended lights, and the volume of space above this implied plane constitutes the ceiling cavity. Of course, if the lights are mounted on the ceiling or are recessed into it, the lighting plane is the actual ceiling of the space, and there is no ceiling cavity.

Based on the various possible arrangements, spaces with the same overall dimensions might have different cavity conditions (see Figure 3.6). Even if they all have three cavities (ceiling cavity, room cavity, and floor cavity), the heights of the comparable cavities in each space might vary. For example, the distance from the ceiling to the suspended fixtures in each room might be different for some reason.[3] The height of the work plane might also vary. If one space is used for drafting, the work plane might be at +36 inches rather than at the desk-height norm of +30 inches.

As suggested in Figure 3.7, the zonal cavity method assumes that the light or luminous flux coming from the lighting plane is evenly distributed across that plane. Since this is comparable to a luminous ceiling, theoretically the intensity of illumination should not change with an adjustment in distance between the lighting plane and the illumination plane. However, if the distance between the two planes increases, the proportions of the room cavity

---

[2]The standard fluorescent fixture is 48 inches long, but fixtures are available in 12-inch increments. When selecting a smaller or larger fixture, do not assume that things will remain proportional. Check the CU for that fixture and the lumen output for the lamp.

[3]A suspended fixture that has a significant upward component should be installed at least 12 inches below the ceiling, with 18 inches recommended in order to avoid ceiling hot spots.

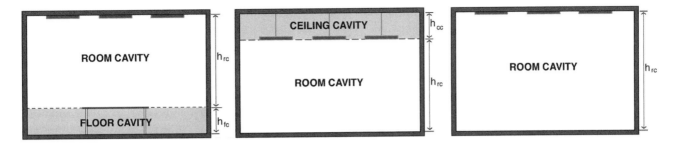

Figure 3.6 THREE VARIATIONS OF ZONAL CAVITIES
While a space might have three cavities, this assumes that the luminaires are suspended below the ceiling, which is often not the condition. When the lights are surface mounted or recessed, there is no ceiling cavity. It is also possible that rather than an elevated work plane, the intended illumination is on the floor—for example, in a lobby or circulation space. In this condition there is no floor cavity.

would change. This would result in more reflection of light off of the walls, reducing the amount of light that actually reaches the illumination plane. In addition to the proportions of the cavity, the amount of light reflecting off the walls of the room cavity will depend on the average coefficient of reflection of those walls. Similarly, the proportions of the floor and ceiling cavities and the coefficients of reflection in those cavities will affect how these components of the equivalent space contribute to the available light (see Figure 3.7).

Cavity Ratios

The cavity ratio of a zone compares the floor area to the wall area in that cavity (see Figure 3.8). In order to increase the range of values, the quotient achieved by dividing the wall area by the floor area is multiplied by 2.5 to derive the cavity ratio. The general formula is:

$$\text{Cavity Ratio} = 2.5 \times \frac{\text{Wall Area}}{\text{"Floor" Area}}$$

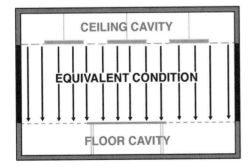

Figure 3.7 ZONAL CAVITY EQUIVALENT CONDITIONS
The zonal cavity method converts actual conditions into the equivalent condition of a lighting plane that evenly emits light essentially directed toward the illumination plane. The actual amount of generated lumens of light that reaches the illumination plane is determined by the CU and the LLF, and dividing this number by the square-foot area provides the foot-candles of illumination.

For a rectangular space, the cavity ratio of each zone can be found by the following formula:

$$\text{Cavity Ratio} = 2.5 \times \frac{2(\text{Length} + \text{Width})(\text{Cavity Height})}{\text{Length} \times \text{Width}}$$

$$= 5 \times \frac{(\text{Cavity Height})(\text{Length} + \text{Width})}{\text{Length} \times \text{Width}}$$

For a circular space, the cavity ratio of each zone can be found by the following formula:

$$\text{Cavity Ratio} = 2.5 \times \frac{(\text{Cavity Height})(2\pi r)}{\pi^2}$$

$$= 5 \times \frac{\text{Cavity Height}}{r}$$

Although rather obvious, it is important to recognize that more internal reflections occur within a zone that has a high cavity ratio. With more reflections, less light reaches the illumination plane. Also, the proportion of light that is reflected off the walls is based on the average coefficient of reflection for the walls (ρ_w). As a result, the CU for a luminaire will depend on the room cavity ratio (RCR) and the average coefficient of reflection for the walls in the room cavity. The CU tables include adjustments for RCR and the average coefficient of reflectance of the walls. And since light is reflected off of the floor and perhaps off of the

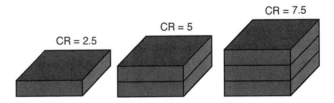

Figure 3.8 COMPARISON OF VARIOUS CAVITY RATIOS
The cavity ratio compares the wall area to the floor area of a zonal cavity, which is used in the zonal cavity method of calculating the average illumination levels for a space. The actual ratio of wall area to floor area is multiplied by 2.5. Higher cavity ratios indicate that there will be more light reflection off of the walls within a zone.

ceiling, the coefficients of reflectance for these surfaces also have an impact on the effective CU for each luminaire.

In reality, rather than the reflectance off of the actual ceiling or floor, the CU tables use reflectance values for the ceiling cavity and the floor cavity since these represent the implied planes that form the equivalent condition on which the zonal cavity method is based (see Figure 3.7). If the lighting fixtures are not suspended, there is no ceiling cavity, so the coefficient of reflectance for the ceiling cavity (ρ_{cc}) is merely the coefficient of reflectance of the ceiling. If there is no floor cavity, then the coefficient of reflectance for the floor cavity (ρ_{fc}) is the reflectance of the actual floor.

The zonal cavity method deals with average conditions, and the CU tables use average reflectance for the walls. As a result, the actual illumination varies for different locations within a space. In large spaces, assuming an equal distribution of the luminaires, the illumination levels near the walls will be less than those available in the center of the room. The difference will be based on the average wall coefficient of reflectance (ρ_w). With low ρ_w, less light is reflected, so there will be a greater difference in the illumination levels along the edges of a space compared to the room center. Of course, while ρ_w is an average, there would be more foot-candles of illumination at a location next to a wall with a higher coefficient of reflectance than at a location next to a wall with a lower coefficient of reflection.

Glass has a low coefficient of reflection, generally around 0.10. As a result, a location near a window will benefit from a high level of daylight during the day, but then at night, when electric light is the only light source, the lighting levels will be lower than those in the major portion of the space unless the lighting design is adjusted to address this issue. Rather than increase the output of electric lighting along the windows, which would be inefficient since around 90% of the light striking the glazing would be lost from the space, we should address the design of the overall lighting system, which includes daylight and electric light. One simple solution is to install light-colored venetian blinds. During the day, the blinds can help control the distribution of daylight within the space.[4] Then at night, the blinds can be adjusted so that they provide a reflective surface that can redirect the electric light to the illumination plane.

While it is not effective in determining specific levels of illumination within a space, the zonal cavity method is a very useful design tool, especially if we avoid excessive detail or minutia. Form 3.1 provides guidance for the zonal cavity calculation procedure.

Form 3.1 Lighting Design Information Form

Space and Activity:_____

Proposed Illumination Level:_____

Type of Lighting:_____

Fixture Number:_____ Spacing/Mounting Height:_____

Lamps per Fixture:_____ Lumens per Lamp:_____

Lumens per Fixture:_____

Maintenance Issues:_____

_____

Table 3.3, "Coefficients of Utilization for Several Generic Luminaires," includes a great deal of information. While the basic purpose of referring to this table is assumed to be to find the CU value for a particular application, in actuality what we can gain by reading the table may be more important than the particular CU needed to complete a calculation. For example, as shown in Figure 3.9 for Luminaire 1, the CU table includes a diagram for each luminaire as well as a simple photometric graph of the lumen distribution. It also indicates the maintenance category[5] for the fixture, which is used to determine the LLF, and a recommendation for the maximum spacing to mounting height (S/MH) ratio.

The zonal cavity method assumes that the light is evenly distributed across the illumination plane. The distribution pattern and the spacing of fixtures are critical to this assumption. If the fixture placement exceeds the S/MH ratio, there will be areas that are not adequately illuminated, which also means that other areas will be at an illumination level that exceeds the foot-candle target. In terms of the S/MH ratio, the mounting height is not the actual height above the floor at which the fixtures are installed but rather the height between the assumed illumination plane and the lighting plane, which is also the height of the room cavity. For luminaires that do not have a symmetrical distribution pattern, two S/MH ratios are indicated.

While our intention is to calculate the lighting level by merely selecting a fixture and determining its maximum S/MH ratio, we have most of the information necessary for a preliminary lighting design. As indicated in Figure 3.9, which relates to Luminaire 1 from Table 3.3, the maximum S/MH is shown, along with a diagram of the basic form of the fixture and its maintenance category. Unfortunately, when lighting calculations are developed, since the focus is on determining the total lumens required and the potential lumens per fixture, the critical S/MH ratio might

---

[4]The suggestion that the blinds can help control daylight is based on the notion that exterior shading is preferred, particularly in terms of thermal issues.

[5]The maintenance category is related to the LLF and is addressed in Table 3.12.

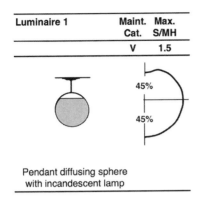

Luminaire 1	Maint. Cat.	Max. S/MH
	V	1.5

45%

45%

Pendant diffusing sphere
with incandescent lamp

Figure 3.9 CU TABLE DETAIL

be overlooked. This can result in a very uneven lighting design.

When we have selected a luminaire and have confirmed that the spacing to mounting height and the number and distribution of lighting fixtures suggested are compatible for our general design intentions, we can proceed to select the CU. As we explore Table 3.3, we can see that the CUs for each luminaire are based on the RCR and the coefficients of reflection for the ceiling cavity (ρ_{cc}), the walls (ρ_{w}), and the floor cavity (ρ_{fc}). As shown in Figure 3.10, RCR is listed in the left-hand column of numbers, the ρ_{cc} is located along the top of each section, and various ρ_{w} values are included below each ρ_{c}. As noted below the ρ_{w} values, ρ_{fc} is assumed to be 20%.

While there are several options for both ρ_{cc} and ρ_{w}, the CU values for each luminaire are based on an effective floor cavity reflectance of 20%. If the ρ_{fc} is not 20%, then the selected CU must be adjusted by the appropriate factor from Table 3.1. To adjust for 30% effective floor cavity reflectance, we must multiply the selected CU by the appropriate factor. To adjust for 10% effective floor cavity reflectance, we must divide the CU by the appropriate factor. For intermediate floor cavities, we can interpolate, but we need not become excessively detailed since this is an approximation at best.

A review of Table 3.1 suggests that if a space is rather large, which relates to a low RCR, and the effective reflectance of the ceiling cavity is high, a luminaire with its major component of light distributed downward would have a higher effective CU if the floor cavity reflectance is significantly higher than 20%. Assuming an off-white floor with an effective reflectance of 70%, the CU listed in Table 3.3 could be increased by almost 50%. However, if the actual floor cavity reflectance is between 10% and 30%, it is doubtful that a correction from the assumed 20% reflectance would be justified since the actual number of luminaires and lumens per fixture cannot be selected to specifically match the calculation results, especially when

these are intended as a way to test the appropriateness of a design proposal rather than actually engineer the system.

As suggested by Figures 3.5 and 3.7, to obtain a CU, we must first determine the cavity ratio for the room and the cavity ratios and effective reflectance for the ceiling and floor cavities. The ceiling cavity is the spatial volume defined by the plane of the luminaires, the actual ceiling plane, and the intervening enclosing walls. If the lights are installed at the ceiling, there is no ceiling cavity and the actual average ceiling reflectance is used. The floor cavity is the spatial volume defined by the illumination or work plane, the actual floor plane, and the intervening enclosing walls. Again, if the plane on which illumination is being calculated is the actual floor, there is no floor cavity, and the actual average floor reflectance is used.

The wall reflectance (ρ_{w}) used by the CU table is the average reflectance of all vertical surfaces of the room cavity. If half of the wall area is at $\rho_{w} = 0.50$ and the other half is at $\rho_{w} = 0.70$, the effective average coefficient of reflectance for the walls, ρ_{w}, would be 0.60. If a quarter of the wall surface is at $\rho_{w} = 0.50$ and the remaining three-quarters is at $\rho_{w} = 0.70$, the effective ρ_{w} is 0.65.

To determine the effective reflectance for the ceiling cavity or floor cavity, we need to consider the reflectance values of the actual ceiling or floor and the walls that line the cavity (see Table 3.2). The effective coefficient of reflectance of the cavity is based on multiple reflections of light off of the walls and the horizontal surface. Because of the interaction of these surfaces, the ρ_{cc} and ρ_{fc} are generally somewhat less than what might be assumed.

If there is a ceiling or floor cavity, there will be multiple reflections within the cavity. Along the perimeter of the cavity, the light would reflect off the ceiling or floor plane and then onto the walls. If the horizontal dimensions of the cavity are large compared to the cavity height, then the wall reflectance in the cavity has little impact on the effective cavity reflectance, and the effective reflectance of the cavity would be close to the reflectance of the actual ceiling plane or floor plane. However, if the height of the cavity is large in comparison to its horizontal dimensions, then there is ample wall area within the cavity, and this will have a considerable impact on the effective cavity reflectance. Because of the internal cavity reflections, the amount of reflected light would be diminished, resulting in an effective cavity reflectance that is less than that of the flat ceiling plane or floor plane.

To determine the effective cavity reflectance for a ceiling cavity or a floor cavity, we must first determine the cavity ratio, the reflectance of the ceiling or floor plane, and, depending on the nature of the cavity, the average reflectance of all the vertical surfaces within the cavity. With these data, we can then use Table 3.2 to select the

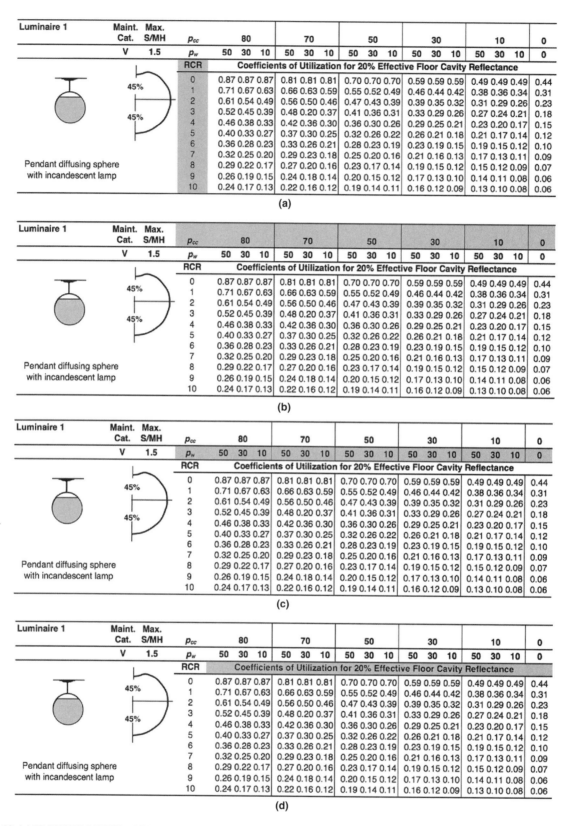

Figure 3.10 (a) CU TABLE 3.3 DETAIL – RCR. (b) CU TABLE 3.3 DETAIL – CEILING CAVITY REFLECTANCE (ρ_{cc}). (c) CU TABLE 3.3 DETAIL – AVEARAGE WALL REFLECTANCE (ρ_w). (d) CU TABLE 3.3 DETAIL – FLOOR CAVITY REFLECTANCE (ρ_{fc})

Table 3.1: FACTORS FOR FLOOR CAVITY REFLECTANCE OTHER THAN 20%

Room Cavity Ratio (RCR)	Percent Effective Ceiling Cavity Reflectance, ρ_{cc}			
	80	70	50	10
1	1.08	1.06	1.04	1.01
2	1.06	1.05	1.03	1.01
3	1.04	1.04	1.03	1.01
4	1.03	1.03	1.02	1.01
5	1.03	1.02	1.02	1.01
6	1.02	1.02	1.02	1.01
7	1.02	1.02	1.01	1.01
8	1.02	1.02	1.01	1.01
9	1.01	1.01	1.01	1.01
10	1.01	1.01	1.01	1.01

Note: When ρ_{fc}, is other than 20% the CU must be corrected. The adjustment factors listed in this table are for each 10% change in ρ_{fc}. If ρ_{fc}, is higher than 20%, multiply the CU found in the CU table by the factor from this table for each 10% of increase. If less than 20%, divide the CU by the factor from this table for each 10% of decrease.

appropriate cavity reflectance, ρ_{cc} or ρfc, to use in the CU tables.

The CU indicates the operational efficiency of a luminaire. As is obvious from a review of Table 3.3, the CU values vary for different luminaires and a particular fixture will have different CU values. CU values tend to vary inversely both with the reflectance of the room surfaces (ρ) and with the RCR. The latter inverse ratio occurs since as the RCR increases, a larger percentage of the light will be reflected off of the room surfaces before reaching the horizontal illumination plane.

In general, we can see the range of efficiencies that a particular fixture has by comparing the values at the top left and the bottom right. These CU variations, which essentially are the result of architectural decisions, can be quite significant. As shown in the example in Figure 3.11, the same fixture can deliver 87% of the generated lumens or only 8%, depending on the architectural conditions of the space in which the fixture is used!

A review of the various luminaires included in Table 3.3 indicates that the range of CUs for a fixture based on architectural conditions varies according to how the light from the fixture is distributed. As might be expected, the range of possible CUs for a particular luminaire is smallest for those fixtures that direct the light downward toward the illumination plane and greatest for those that spread the light outward, relying on indirect lighting. The low range is about 2:1 (Luminaire 5), while the high range is 28:1 (Luminaire 2).

Table 3.3 includes information for various generic luminaires that can help us select an actual fixture to use in a design. However, this choice is usually based on a number of additional factors, including the intentions of the architectural design, the nature of the activity that will occur in the space, personal aesthetic preference and previous experience, as well as the lighting performance. This should include a review of the manufacturer's literature, including the fixture specifications, as well as a visual inspection of sample luminaires and, hopefully, comparable installations. While a visual inspection of the fixtures can provide obvious important information about their appearance, it is often unreliable for determining their actual performance, especially over an extended time period. As mentioned before, although the lenses from two different fixtures might appear to be similar, the actual distribution patterns of each lens might be considerably different, to say nothing of the deterioration that might occur through use. Also, the finished surfaces of different fixtures might appear to be similar, but over a period of exposure to various elements, the performance of a fixture with painted steel will probably not match that of a fixture with enameled galvanized steel or made from stainless steel.

The CU indicates the decimal portion of the total lumens generated that are available on the work plane. The CU, which is specific for each luminaire, is also based on the particular room, including its size, its proportions, and the reflectivity of the various surfaces. While each lighting fixture manufacturer produces CU data for its luminaires, Table 3.3 provides data for selected generic fixtures. Specific CU data are usually extended to three-number accuracy (0.###), while the generic data are listed with only two-number accuracy (0.##).

In either approach to lighting calculations, to determine the foot-candles of illumination that a lighting system should provide the number of fixtures necessary to produce a desired lighting level, we should be accurate while avoiding excessive detail or minutia.

Light Loss Factor

The LLF is used to adjust the initial lumens to the average lumens maintained. LLF is the product of various depreciation factors, such as lamp lumen depreciation (LLD), luminaire dirt depreciation (LDD), luminaire ambient temperature (LAT), voltage (V), luminaire surface depreciation (LSD), nonstandard components, room surface dirt (RSD), and burnouts. The individual depreciation factors are multiplied together to derive the total LLF. While the actual LLF should be determined, for estimating purposes an average LLF of 0.65 is frequently used.

The illumination levels provided by any lighting system depend on the number of lumens that each lamp

Table 3.2: EFFECTIVE COEFFICIENTS OF REFLECTANCE FOR CEILING AND FLOOR CAVITIES

Percent Ceiling or Floor Reflectance:	90				80				70			50			30				10		
Percent Wall Reflectance:	90	70	50	30	80	70	50	30	70	50	30	70	50	30	65	50	30	10	50	30	10
0.0	0.90	0.90	0.90	0.90	0.80	0.80	0.80	0.80	0.70	0.70	0.70	0.50	0.50	0.50	0.30	0.30	0.30	0.30	0.10	0.1	0.1
0.2	0.89	0.88	0.86	0.85	0.79	0.78	0.77	0.76	0.68	0.67	0.66	0.49	0.48	0.47	0.30	0.29	0.29	0.28	0.10	0.1	0.9
0.4	0.88	0.86	0.83	0.81	0.78	0.76	0.74	0.72	0.67	0.65	0.63	0.48	0.46	0.45	0.30	0.29	0.27	0.26	0.11	0.1	0.9
0.6	0.88	0.84	0.80	0.76	0.77	0.75	0.71	0.68	0.65	0.62	0.59	0.47	0.45	0.43	0.29	0.28	0.26	0.25	0.11	0.1	0.9
0.8	0.87	0.82	0.77	0.73	0.75	0.73	0.69	0.65	0.64	0.60	0.56	0.47	0.43	0.41	0.29	0.27	0.25	0.23	0.11	0.1	0.8
1.0	0.86	0.80	0.74	0.69	0.74	0.71	0.66	0.61	0.63	0.58	0.53	0.46	0.42	0.39	0.29	0.27	0.24	0.22	0.11	0.9	0.8
1.2	0.86	0.78	0.72	0.65	0.73	0.70	0.64	0.58	0.61	0.56	0.50	0.45	0.41	0.37	0.29	0.26	0.23	0.20	0.12	0.9	0.7
1.4	0.85	0.77	0.69	0.62	0.72	0.68	0.62	0.55	0.60	0.54	0.48	0.45	0.40	0.35	0.28	0.26	0.22	0.19	0.12	0.9	0.7
1.6	0.85	0.75	0.66	0.59	0.71	0.67	0.60	0.53	0.59	0.52	0.45	0.44	0.39	0.33	0.28	0.25	0.21	0.18	0.12	0.9	0.7
1.8	0.84	0.73	0.64	0.56	0.70	0.65	0.58	0.50	0.57	0.50	0.43	0.43	0.37	0.32	0.28	0.25	0.21	0.17	0.12	0.9	0.6
2.0	0.83	0.72	0.62	0.53	0.68	0.64	0.56	0.48	0.56	0.48	0.41	0.43	0.37	0.30	0.28	0.24	0.20	0.16	0.12	0.9	0.6
2.2	0.83	0.70	0.60	0.51	0.67	0.63	0.54	0.45	0.55	0.46	0.39	0.42	0.36	0.29	0.28	0.24	0.19	0.15	0.13	0.9	0.6
2.4	0.82	0.68	0.58	0.48	0.65	0.61	0.52	0.43	0.54	0.45	0.37	0.42	0.35	0.27	0.28	0.24	0.19	0.14	0.13	0.9	0.6
2.6	0.82	0.67	0.56	0.46	0.66	0.60	0.50	0.41	0.53	0.43	0.35	0.41	0.34	0.26	0.27	0.23	0.18	0.13	0.13	0.9	0.5
2.8	0.81	0.66	0.54	0.44	0.66	0.59	0.48	0.39	0.52	0.42	0.33	0.41	0.33	0.25	0.27	0.23	0.18	0.13	0.13	0.9	0.5
3.0	0.81	0.64	0.52	0.42	0.65	0.58	0.47	0.38	0.51	0.40	0.32	0.40	0.32	0.24	0.27	0.22	0.17	0.12	0.13	0.8	0.5
3.5	0.79	0.61	0.48	0.37	0.63	0.55	0.43	0.33	0.48	0.38	0.29	0.39	0.30	0.22	0.26	0.22	0.16	0.11	0.13	0.8	0.5
4.0	0.78	0.58	0.44	0.33	0.61	0.52	0.40	0.30	0.46	0.35	0.26	0.38	0.29	0.20	0.26	0.21	0.15	0.9	0.13	0.8	0.4
4.5	0.77	0.55	0.41	0.30	0.59	0.50	0.37	0.27	0.45	0.33	0.24	0.37	0.27	0.19	0.25	0.20	0.14	0.8	0.14	0.8	0.4
5.0	0.76	0.53	0.38	0.27	0.57	0.48	0.35	0.25	0.43	0.32	0.22	0.36	0.26	0.17	0.25	0.19	0.13	0.7	0.14	0.8	0.4

(Rows 1.2 through 2.0 fall under the category **Ceiling or Floor Cavity Ratios**.)

Source: The data in this table are based on information available from various sources including the IESNA *Lighting Handbook*. The effective coefficient of reflectance of a cavity is based on the cavity ratio and the average reflectance coefficients for the major horizontal surface and the walls within the cavity. The major horizontal surface reflectance values, which are indicated in the top row of the table, relate to the ceiling or floor depending on which cavity is involved.

produces, but this varies over time. While the output of an incandescent lamp tends to remain relatively consistent throughout its life, the output from fluorescent lamps and HID lamps varies considerably over their life. Fluorescents deliver a high initial lumen output that declines somewhat rapidly over the first 100 hours of operation and continues to decline over its remaining life, which is generally around 20,000 hours. To adjust the calculations to identify the maintained levels of illumination, either the mean lumens of output should be used or a correction factor should be included. This factor is generally called the LLD.

Another factor to consider is the LDD, which is based on the maintenance category noted in the CU table for each luminaire. These are shown in Table 3.4. The maintenance categories relate to the type of luminaire and its tendency to collect dirt. An enclosed fixture with a downward-facing lens will obviously collect less dirt than an open upward-facing fixture. The LDD tends to reduce the percentage

of the generated lumens that are actually available in an installation due to the accumulation of dirt on and in the fixtures.

As noted in Table 3.4, there is a range of LDD adjustments for each category. Since the basic assumption is a normal condition in terms of cleanliness of the space and a 12-month cycle of cleaning, if the lighting is located in a space that is rather dirty and/or the cleaning is not scheduled on even a yearly basis, the LDD factor would be lowered. If the conditions are better than assumed, then the LDD factor would be increased.

The LAT becomes a factor in cold temperatures or when return air is drawn through the fixture. The output of a standard fluorescent lamp peaks at an ambient air temperature of 77° F, and any change of temperature results in a drop in light output. While the impact of cold temperatures is considerable, resulting not only in a significant lowering of lumen output (to slightly less than 20% at 0° F, 40% at 20° F, and 80% at 40° F) but also in starting difficulty, a

Table 3.3: COEFFICIENTS OF UTILIZATION FOR SEVERAL GENERIC LUMINAIRES

Luminaire 1	Maint. Cat.	Max. S/MH	ρ_{cc}	80			70			50			30			10			0
	V	1.5	ρ_w	50	30	10	50	30	10	50	30	10	50	30	10	50	30	10	0
			RCR	Coefficients of Utilization for 20% Effective Floor Cavity Reflectance															
			0	0.87	0.87	0.87	0.81	0.81	0.81	0.70	0.70	0.70	0.59	0.59	0.59	0.49	0.49	0.49	0.44
			1	0.71	0.67	0.63	0.66	0.63	0.59	0.55	0.52	0.49	0.46	0.44	0.42	0.38	0.36	0.34	0.31
			2	0.61	0.54	0.49	0.56	0.50	0.46	0.47	0.43	0.39	0.39	0.35	0.32	0.31	0.29	0.26	0.23
			3	0.52	0.45	0.39	0.48	0.20	0.37	0.41	0.36	0.31	0.33	0.29	0.26	0.27	0.24	0.21	0.18
			4	0.46	0.38	0.33	0.42	0.36	0.30	0.36	0.30	0.26	0.29	0.25	0.21	0.23	0.20	0.17	0.15
			5	0.40	0.33	0.27	0.37	0.30	0.25	0.32	0.26	0.22	0.26	0.21	0.18	0.21	0.17	0.14	0.12
			6	0.36	0.28	0.23	0.33	0.26	0.21	0.28	0.23	0.19	0.23	0.19	0.15	0.19	0.15	0.12	0.10
			7	0.32	0.25	0.20	0.29	0.23	0.18	0.25	0.20	0.16	0.21	0.16	0.13	0.17	0.13	0.11	0.09
			8	0.29	0.22	0.17	0.27	0.20	0.16	0.23	0.17	0.14	0.19	0.15	0.12	0.15	0.12	0.09	0.07
			9	0.26	0.19	0.15	0.24	0.18	0.14	0.20	0.15	0.12	0.17	0.13	0.10	0.14	0.11	0.08	0.06
			10	0.24	0.17	0.13	0.22	0.16	0.12	0.19	0.14	0.11	0.16	0.12	0.09	0.13	0.10	0.08	0.06

Pendant diffusing sphere with incandescent lamp (45%, 45%)

Luminaire 2	Maint. Cat.	Max. S/MH	ρ_{cc}	80			70			50			30			10			0
	IV	1.5	ρ_w	50	30	10	50	30	10	50	30	10	50	30	10	50	30	10	0
			RCR	Coefficients of Utilization for 20% Effective Floor Cavity Reflectance															
			0	0.83	0.83	0.83	0.72	0.72	0.72	0.50	0.50	0.50	0.30	0.30	0.30	0.12	0.12	0.12	0.03
			1	0.72	0.69	0.66	0.62	0.60	0.57	0.43	0.42	0.40	0.26	0.25	0.25	0.10	0.10	0.10	0.03
			2	0.63	0.58	0.54	0.54	0.50	0.47	0.38	0.35	0.33	0.23	0.22	0.20	0.09	0.09	0.08	0.02
			3	0.55	0.49	0.45	0.47	0.43	0.39	0.33	0.30	0.28	0.20	0.19	0.17	0.08	0.07	0.07	0.02
			4	0.46	0.42	0.37	0.42	0.37	0.33	0.29	0.26	0.23	0.18	0.16	0.15	0.07	0.06	0.06	0.02
			5	0.43	0.36	0.32	0.37	0.32	0.28	0.26	0.23	0.20	0.16	0.14	0.12	0.06	0.06	0.05	0.01
			6	0.38	0.32	0.27	0.33	0.26	0.24	0.23	0.20	0.17	0.14	0.12	0.11	0.06	0.05	0.04	0.01
			7	0.34	0.28	0.23	0.30	0.24	0.21	0.21	0.17	0.15	0.13	0.11	0.09	0.05	0.04	0.04	0.01
			8	0.31	0.25	0.20	0.27	0.21	0.18	0.19	0.15	0.13	0.12	0.10	0.08	0.05	0.04	0.03	0.01
			9	0.28	0.22	0.18	0.24	0.19	0.16	0.17	0.14	0.11	0.10	0.09	0.07	0.04	0.03	0.03	0.01
			10	0.25	0.20	0.16	0.22	0.17	0.14	0.16	0.12	0.10	0.10	0.06	0.06	0.04	0.03	0.03	0.01

Concentric ring unit incandescent silver-bowl lamp (83%, 3½%)

Luminaire 3	Maint. Cat.	Max. S/MH	ρ_{cc}	80			70			50			30			10			0
	IV	1.5	ρ_w	50	30	10	50	30	10	50	30	10	50	30	10	50	30	10	0
			RCR	Coefficients of Utilization for 20% Effective Floor Cavity Reflectance															
			0	0.99	0.99	0.99	0.97	0.97	0.97	0.92	0.92	0.92	0.89	0.89	0.89	0.85	0.85	0.85	0.83
			1	0.88	0.85	0.82	0.86	0.83	0.81	0.83	0.80	0.78	0.79	0.76	0.74	0.76	0.74	0.72	0.72
			2	0.78	0.73	0.68	0.76	0.72	0.67	0.73	0.69	0.66	0.69	0.65	0.62	0.66	0.63	0.60	0.61
			3	0.69	0.62	0.57	0.67	0.61	0.57	0.65	0.60	0.56	0.60	0.56	0.52	0.58	0.54	0.51	0.52
			4	0.61	0.54	0.49	0.60	0.53	0.48	0.58	0.52	0.48	0.53	0.48	0.44	0.51	0.47	0.43	0.45
			5	0.54	0.47	0.41	0.53	0.46	0.41	0.51	0.45	0.41	0.47	0.42	0.37	0.46	0.41	0.37	0.38
			6	0.48	0.41	0.35	0.47	0.40	0.35	0.46	0.39	0.35	0.43	0.37	0.33	0.41	0.36	0.32	0.32
			7	0.43	0.35	0.30	0.42	0.35	0.30	0.41	0.34	0.30	0.39	0.33	0.29	0.38	0.32	0.28	0.25
			8	0.38	0.31	0.26	0.38	0.31	0.26	0.37	0.30	0.26	0.35	0.30	0.25	0.34	0.29	0.25	0.24
			9	0.35	0.28	0.23	0.34	0.27	0.23	0.33	0.27	0.23	0.32	0.27	0.23	0.32	0.26	0.23	0.21
			10	0.32	0.25	0.21	0.32	0.25	0.21	0.31	0.25	0.21	0.30	0.24	0.21	0.29	0.24	0.20	0.19

Porcelain-enameled ventilated standard dome with incandescent lamp (10%, 85%)

Luminaire 4	Maint. Cat.	Max. S/MH	ρ_{cc}	80			70			50			30			10			0
	IV	1.5	ρ_w	50	30	10	50	30	10	50	30	10	50	30	10	50	30	10	0
			RCR	Coefficients of Utilization for 20% Effective Floor Cavity Reflectance															
			0	1.01	1.01	1.01	0.99	0.99	0.99	0.94	0.94	0.94	0.90	0.90	0.90	0.87	0.87	0.87	0.82
			1	0.95	0.93	0.91	0.93	0.91	0.89	0.89	0.88	0.87	0.86	0.85	0.84	0.83	0.82	0.82	0.80
			2	0.89	0.86	0.83	0.87	0.84	0.82	0.85	0.82	0.80	0.82	0.80	0.79	0.80	0.78	0.77	0.76
			3	0.83	0.80	0.77	0.82	0.79	0.76	0.80	0.77	0.75	0.78	0.76	0.74	0.76	0.74	0.72	0.71
			4	0.79	0.74	0.71	0.78	0.74	0.71	0.76	0.73	0.70	0.74	0.71	0.69	0.73	0.70	0.68	0.67
			5	0.74	0.70	0.67	0.74	0.69	0.66	0.72	0.68	0.66	0.71	0.68	0.65	0.69	0.67	0.65	0.63
			6	0.70	0.66	0.62	0.70	0.65	0.92	0.68	0.65	0.62	0.67	0.64	0.61	0.66	0.63	0.61	0.60
			7	0.67	0.62	0.59	0.66	0.62	0.59	0.65	0.61	0.58	0.64	0.61	0.58	0.63	0.60	0.58	0.57
			8	0.63	0.59	0.56	0.63	0.58	0.55	0.62	0.58	0.55	0.61	0.58	0.55	0.60	0.57	0.55	0.54
			9	0.60	0.56	0.53	0.60	0.56	0.53	0.59	0.55	0.52	0.58	0.55	0.52	0.58	0.54	0.52	0.51
			10	0.57	0.53	0.50	0.57	0.53	0.50	0.56	0.52	0.50	0.56	0.52	0.50	0.55	0.52	0.49	0.48

R-40 flood with specular anodized reflector 45° cutoff (0%, 85%)

(Continued)

Table 3.3 (*Continued*)

Luminaire 5

Maint. Cat.	Max. S/MH																
		ρ_{cc}	80			70			50			30			10			0
IV	1.5	ρ_w	50	30	10	50	30	10	50	30	10	50	30	10	50	30	10	0
		RCR	Coefficients of Utilization for 20% Effective Floor Cavity Reflectance															
0% / 43½%		0	0.52	0.52	0.52	0.51	0.51	0.51	0.48	0.48	0.48	0.48	0.46	0.46	0.45	0.45	0.44	0.44
		1	0.49	0.48	0.48	0.48	0.47	0.46	0.46	0.45	0.45	0.44	0.44	0.43	0.43	0.43	0.41	0.41
		2	0.47	0.46	0.45	0.45	0.44	0.43	0.45	0.43	0.42	0.43	0.42	0.41	0.41	0.41	0.40	0.39
		3	0.45	0.44	0.43	0.43	0.41	0.40	0.42	0.42	0.42	0.41	0.39	0.38	0.40	0.39	0.38	0.37
		4	0.43	0.42	0.41	0.41	0.39	0.37	0.42	0.40	0.39	0.39	0.37	0.36	0.38	0.37	0.36	0.35
		5	0.42	0.40	0.39	0.93	0.37	0.35	0.40	0.38	0.37	0.37	0.36	0.34	0.36	0.35	0.34	0.34
		6	0.40	0.39	0.37	0.37	0.35	0.33	0.38	0.36	0.35	0.35	0.34	0.33	0.35	0.34	0.32	0.32
		7	0.39	0.37	0.36	0.35	0.33	0.31	0.34	0.33	0.31	0.34	0.32	0.31	0.33	0.32	0.31	0.30
		8	0.37	0.36	0.34	0.33	0.31	0.30	0.33	0.31	0.30	0.32	0.31	0.29	0.32	0.31	0.29	0.29
		9	0.36	0.34	0.33	0.32	0.30	0.28	0.31	0.30	0.28	0.31	0.29	0.28	0.31	0.29	0.28	0.28
		10	0.31	0.28	0.27	0.31	0.28	0.27	0.30	0.28	0.27	0.30	0.28	0.27	0.30	0.28	0.27	0.26

EAR-38 lamp above 2 in. diam. aperture

Luminaire 6

Maint. Cat.	Max. S/MH																
		ρ_{cc}	80			70			50			30			10			0
III	1.5	ρ_w	50	30	10	50	30	10	50	30	10	50	30	10	50	30	10	0
		RCR	Coefficients of Utilization for 20% Effective Floor Cavity Reflectance															
½% / 77½%		0	0.93	0.93	0.93	0.91	0.91	0.91	0.87	0.87	0.87	0.83	0.83	0.83	0.79	0.79	0.79	0.78
		1	0.85	0.82	0.80	0.83	0.81	0.79	0.79	0.78	0.76	0.76	0.74	0.73	0.73	0.72	0.70	0.70
		2	0.77	0.73	0.70	0.76	0.72	0.69	0.73	0.70	0.67	0.68	0.66	0.63	0.66	0.64	0.62	0.63
		3	0.70	0.65	0.61	0.68	0.64	0.60	0.66	0.62	0.59	0.61	0.58	0.55	0.59	0.56	0.54	0.56
		4	0.63	0.58	0.53	0.62	0.57	0.53	0.60	0.56	0.52	0.55	0.51	0.48	0.54	0.50	0.47	0.49
		5	0.57	0.51	0.47	0.56	0.51	0.47	0.55	0.50	0.46	0.50	0.45	0.42	0.49	0.45	0.41	0.44
		6	0.51	0.45	0.41	0.51	0.45	0.41	0.49	0.44	0.40	0.45	0.41	0.37	0.44	0.40	0.37	0.38
		7	0.46	0.40	0.35	0.45	0.39	0.35	0.44	0.39	0.35	0.41	0.36	0.33	0.40	0.36	0.33	0.33
		8	0.41	0.35	0.31	0.41	0.35	0.31	0.40	0.34	0.31	0.38	0.33	0.29	0.37	0.32	0.29	0.29
		9	0.37	0.31	0.27	0.37	0.31	0.27	0.36	0.30	0.27	0.35	0.30	0.26	0.34	0.29	0.26	0.25
		10	0.34	0.28	0.24	0.34	0.28	0.24	0.33	0.28	0.24	0.32	0.27	0.24	0.31	0.27	0.24	0.22

High-bay wide-distribution, ventilated reflector with clear HID lamp

Luminaire 7

Maint. Cat.	Max. S/MH																
		ρ_{cc}	80			70			50			30			10			0
II	1.5/1.3	ρ_w	50	30	10	50	30	10	50	30	10	50	30	10	50	30	10	0
		RCR	Coefficients of Utilization for 20% Effective Floor Cavity Reflectance															
17% / 66%		0	0.95	0.95	0.95	0.91	0.91	0.91	0.83	0.83	0.83	0.76	0.76	0.76	0.69	0.69	0.69	0.66
		1	0.85	0.82	0.80	0.82	0.79	0.77	0.75	0.73	0.72	0.69	0.67	0.66	0.63	0.62	0.61	0.59
		2	0.76	0.72	0.68	0.74	0.70	0.66	0.68	0.65	0.62	0.62	0.59	0.57	0.57	0.55	0.53	0.52
		3	0.69	0.63	0.59	0.66	0.61	0.57	0.62	0.58	0.54	0.55	0.52	0.49	0.51	0.49	0.46	0.46
		4	0.62	0.56	0.51	0.60	0.54	0.50	0.56	0.51	0.47	0.50	0.46	0.43	0.46	0.43	0.41	0.41
		5	0.55	0.49	0.44	0.53	0.48	0.43	0.50	0.45	0.41	0.45	0.41	0.38	0.42	0.39	0.36	0.36
		6	0.50	0.43	0.39	0.48	0.42	0.38	0.45	0.40	0.36	0.41	0.37	0.33	0.38	0.35	0.32	0.31
		7	0.45	0.38	0.34	0.43	0.37	0.33	0.41	0.36	0.32	0.38	0.33	0.30	0.35	0.31	0.28	0.27
		8	0.40	0.34	0.29	0.39	0.33	0.29	0.37	0.31	0.28	34.0	0.30	0.27	0.32	0.28	0.26	0.24
		9	0.37	0.31	0.26	0.36	0.30	0.26	0.34	0.29	0.25	0.32	0.27	0.24	0.30	0.26	0.23	0.21
		10	0.34	0.28	0.24	0.33	0.27	0.23	0.31	0.26	0.23	0.29	0.25	0.22	0.28	0.24	0.21	0.19

Diffuse aluminum reflector with 35° crosswise shielding

Luminaire 8

Maint. Cat.	Max. S/MH																
		ρ_{cc}	80			70			50			30			10			0
II	1.5/1.1	ρ_w	50	30	10	50	30	10	50	30	10	50	30	10	50	30	10	0
		RCR	Coefficients of Utilization for 20% Effective Floor Cavity Reflectance															
17% / 56½%		0	0.83	0.83	0.83	0.79	0.79	0.79	0.72	0.72	0.72	0.65	0.65	0.65	0.59	0.59	0.59	0.56
		1	0.75	0.72	0.70	0.72	0.69	0.67	0.65	0.64	0.62	0.59	0.58	0.57	0.54	0.53	0.52	0.50
		2	0.67	0.63	0.60	0.65	0.61	0.58	0.59	0.57	0.54	0.54	0.51	0.49	0.49	0.47	0.46	0.45
		3	0.61	0.56	0.52	0.58	0.54	0.51	0.54	0.50	0.48	0.48	0.46	0.43	0.45	0.42	0.40	0.40
		4	0.55	0.49	0.45	0.53	0.48	0.44	0.49	0.45	0.42	0.44	0.41	0.38	0.40	0.38	0.36	0.36
		5	0.49	0.44	0.40	0.47	0.42	0.39	0.44	0.40	0.37	0.40	0.36	0.33	0.37	0.34	0.32	0.31
		6	0.45	0.39	0.35	0.43	0.38	0.34	0.40	0.36	0.33	0.36	0.33	0.30	0.34	0.31	0.28	0.28
		7	0.40	0.35	0.31	0.39	0.34	0.30	0.36	0.32	0.29	0.33	0.30	0.27	0.31	0.28	0.25	0.25
		8	0.36	0.31	0.27	0.35	0.30	0.26	0.33	0.28	0.25	0.31	0.27	0.24	0.29	0.25	0.23	0.21
		9	0.33	0.27	0.23	0.32	0.26	0.23	0.29	0.25	0.22	0.28	0.24	0.22	0.26	0.23	0.21	0.19
		10	0.31	0.25	0.22	0.30	0.25	0.22	0.28	0.24	0.21	0.26	0.22	0.20	0.25	0.21	0.19	0.18

Diffuse aluminum reflector with 35° crosswise and 35° lengthwise shielding

Table 3.3 (*Continued*)

Luminaire 9	Maint. Cat.	Max. S/MH	ρ_{cc}	80			70			50			30			10			0
	VI	N.A.	ρ_w	50	30	10	50	30	10	50	30	10	50	30	10	50	30	10	0
			RCR	Coefficients of Utilization for 20% Effective Floor Cavity Reflectance															
			0	0.77	0.77	0.77	0.68	0.68	0.68	0.50	0.50	0.50	0.34	0.34	0.34	0.19	0.19	0.19	0.12
			1	0.67	0.64	0.62	0.59	0.57	0.54	0.44	0.42	0.41	0.29	0.29	0.28	0.17	0.16	0.16	0.10
			2	0.59	0.54	0.50	0.52	0.48	0.45	0.38	0.36	0.34	0.26	0.24	0.23	0.14	0.14	0.13	0.09
			3	0.51	0.46	0.42	0.45	0.41	0.37	0.34	0.31	0.28	0.23	0.21	0.19	0.13	0.12	0.11	0.07
			4	0.45	0.40	0.35	0.40	0.35	0.31	0.30	0.27	0.24	0.20	0.18	0.17	0.11	0.10	0.10	0.06
			5	0.40	0.34	0.30	0.35	0.30	0.27	0.26	0.23	0.20	0.18	0.16	0.14	0.10	0.09	0.08	0.05
			6	0.36	0.30	0.26	0.32	0.27	0.23	0.24	0.20	0.18	0.16	0.14	0.12	0.09	0.08	0.07	0.05
			7	0.32	0.26	0.22	0.28	0.23	0.20	0.21	0.18	0.15	0.15	0.12	0.11	0.08	0.07	0.01	0.04
			8	0.29	0.23	0.19	0.25	0.21	0.17	0.19	0.16	0.13	0.13	0.11	0.09	0.08	0.06	0.06	0.03
			9	0.26	0.20	0.17	0.23	0.18	0.15	0.17	0.14	0.12	0.12	0.10	0.08	0.07	0.06	0.05	0.03
			10	0.24	0.19	0.15	0.21	0.17	0.13	0.16	0.13	0.10	0.11	0.01	0.07	0.06	0.05	0.04	0.03

Luminous-bottom suspended unit with very-high-output lamp (66% / 12%)

Luminaire 10	Maint. Cat.	Max. S/MH	ρ_{cc}	80			70			50			30			10			0
	V	1.5/1.2	ρ_w	50	30	10	50	30	10	50	30	10	50	30	10	50	30	10	0
			RCR	Coefficients of Utilization for 20% Effective Floor Cavity Reflectance															
			0	0.81	0.81	0.81	0.78	0.78	0.78	0.72	0.72	0.72	0.66	0.66	0.66	0.61	0.61	0.61	0.59
			1	0.71	0.69	0.66	0.69	0.66	0.64	0.64	0.62	0.60	0.58	0.57	0.56	0.54	0.53	0.52	0.50
			2	0.64	0.59	0.56	0.61	0.58	0.54	0.57	0.54	0.51	0.52	0.50	0.47	0.48	0.46	0.45	0.44
			3	0.57	0.52	0.48	0.55	0.50	0.47	0.51	0.48	0.45	0.47	0.43	0.41	0.43	0.41	0.39	0.38
			4	0.51	0.46	0.41	0.49	0.44	0.41	0.46	0.42	0.39	0.42	0.38	0.35	0.39	0.36	0.34	0.34
			5	0.46	0.40	0.36	0.44	0.39	0.35	0.41	0.37	0.34	0.38	0.34	0.31	0.35	0.32	0.30	0.29
			6	0.41	0.35	0.31	0.40	0.35	0.31	0.38	0.33	0.30	0.34	0.30	0.27	0.32	0.29	0.26	0.26
			7	0.37	0.31	0.27	0.36	0.31	0.27	0.34	0.29	0.26	0.31	0.27	0.24	0.30	0.26	0.23	0.23
			8	0.33	0.28	0.24	0.32	0.27	0.23	0.30	0.26	0.22	0.29	0.25	0.22	0.27	0.24	0.21	0.19
			9	0.20	0.24	0.20	0.29	0.24	0.20	0.27	0.23	0.19	0.26	0.23	0.20	0.25	0.22	0.19	0.17
			10	0.28	0.23	0.12	0.27	0.22	0.19	0.26	0.21	0.18	0.24	0.21	0.18	0.23	0.20	0.17	0.16

Two-lamp prismatic wraparound; multiply by 0.95 for four lamps (11½% / 58½%)

Luminaire 11	Maint. Cat.	Max. S/MH	ρ_{cc}	80			70			50			30			10			0
	V	1.4/1.2	ρ_w	50	30	10	50	30	10	50	30	10	50	30	10	50	30	10	0
			RCR	Coefficients of Utilization for 20% Effective Floor Cavity Reflectance															
			0	0.75	0.75	0.75	0.73	0.73	0.73	0.70	0.70	0.70	0.67	0.67	0.67	0.64	0.64	0.64	0.63
			1	0.67	0.65	0.63	0.66	0.64	0.62	0.63	0.62	0.60	0.60	0.59	0.58	0.58	0.57	0.56	0.55
			2	0.60	0.57	0.54	0.59	0.56	0.53	0.57	0.54	0.52	0.54	0.52	0.49	0.52	0.50	0.48	0.49
			3	0.54	0.50	0.47	0.53	0.49	0.46	0.52	0.48	0.45	0.48	0.45	0.43	0.47	0.44	0.42	0.43
			4	0.49	0.44	0.40	0.48	0.44	0.40	0.47	0.43	0.40	0.44	0.40	0.37	0.42	0.39	0.37	0.37
			5	0.44	0.39	0.35	0.43	0.38	0.35	0.42	0.38	0.34	0.39	0.36	0.33	0.38	0.35	0.32	0.33
			6	0.40	0.34	0.31	0.39	0.34	0.31	0.38	0.34	0.30	0.36	0.32	0.29	0.35	0.31	0.29	0.29
			7	0.35	0.30	0.26	0.35	0.30	0.26	0.34	0.29	0.26	0.33	0.29	0.26	0.32	0.38	0.26	0.25
			8	0.32	0.27	0.24	0.32	0.27	0.23	0.30	0.26	0.23	0.30	0.26	0.23	0.29	0.36	0.23	0.22
			9	0.30	0.25	0.21	0.29	0.24	0.21	0.28	0.24	0.21	0.28	0.24	0.21	0.27	0.34	0.21	0.20
			10	0.27	0.22	0.19	0.27	0.22	0.19	0.26	0.22	0.19	0.26	0.22	0.19	0.25	0.22	0.19	0.18

Fluorescent unit with flat prismatic lens, four-lamp 2 ft. wide (0% / 60% / 63%)

Luminaire 12	Maint. Cat.	Max. S/MH	ρ_{cc}	80			70			50			30			10			0
	IV	N.A.	ρ_w	50	30	10	50	30	10	50	30	10	50	30	10	50	30	10	0
			RCR	Coefficients of Utilization for 20% Effective Floor Cavity Reflectance															
			0	0.71	0.71	0.71	0.70	0.70	0.70	0.66	0.66	0.66	0.64	0.64	0.64	0.61	0.61	0.61	0.60
			1	0.64	0.62	0.60	0.63	0.61	0.60	0.60	0.59	0.58	0.58	0.57	0.56	0.56	0.55	0.54	0.53
			2	0.57	0.54	0.51	0.56	0.53	0.51	0.54	0.52	0.50	0.52	0.50	0.48	0.51	0.49	0.47	0.46
			3	0.51	0.47	0.44	0.50	0.46	0.43	0.49	0.45	0.43	0.47	0.44	0.42	0.46	0.43	0.41	0.40
			4	0.46	0.41	0.38	0.45	0.41	0.37	0.44	0.40	0.37	0.42	0.39	0.36	0.41	0.38	0.36	0.35
			5	0.41	0.38	0.33	0.40	0.36	0.32	0.39	0.35	0.32	0.38	0.35	0.32	0.37	0.34	0.31	0.30
			6	0.37	0.32	0.28	0.36	0.32	0.28	0.35	0.31	0.28	0.34	0.31	0.28	0.34	0.30	0.28	0.27
			7	0.33	0.29	0.25	0.33	0.28	0.25	0.33	0.28	0.25	0.31	0.27	0.25	0.30	0.27	0.24	0.23
			8	0.30	0.26	0.22	0.30	0.25	0.22	0.29	0.25	0.22	0.28	0.25	0.22	0.28	0.24	0.22	0.21
			9	0.28	0.23	0.20	0.27	0.23	0.20	0.27	0.23	0.20	0.26	0.22	0.20	0.25	0.22	0.19	0.18
			10	0.25	0.21	0.18	0.25	0.21	0.18	0.24	0.20	0.18	0.24	0.20	0.18	0.23	0.20	0.18	0.17

Bilateral batwing distribution (0% / 60% / 45%)

(Continued)

Table 3.3 (*Continued*)

Luminaire 13 Maint. Cat.	Max. S/MH		80			70			50			30			10			0
V	N.A.	ρ_w	50	30	10	50	30	10	50	30	10	50	30	10	50	30	10	0
		RCR	\multicolumn{16}{Coefficients of Utilization for 20% Effective Floor Cavity Reflectance}														
Radial batwing four-lamp 2 ft. wide fluorescent w/ flat prismatic lens (48%, 45%)		0	0.57	0.57	0.57	0.56	0.56	0.56	0.53	0.53	0.53	0.51	0.51	0.50	0.49	0.49	0.49	0.48
		1	0.50	0.48	0.46	0.49	0.47	0.46	0.47	0.45	0.44	0.45	0.43	0.42	0.43	0.42	0.41	0.40
		2	0.43	0.40	0.37	0.42	0.39	0.28	0.40	0.38	0.37	0.39	0.37	0.35	0.37	0.36	0.34	0.33
		3	0.37	0.33	0.30	0.37	0.33	0.31	0.35	0.32	0.31	0.34	0.31	0.29	0.33	0.30	0.28	0.27
		4	0.33	0.28	0.25	0.32	0.28	0.26	0.31	0.27	0.26	0.30	0.27	0.24	0.29	0.26	0.24	0.23
		5	0.29	0.24	0.21	0.28	0.24	0.22	0.27	0.24	0.22	0.26	0.23	0.20	0.25	0.23	0.20	0.19
		6	0.26	0.21	0.18	0.25	0.21	0.18	0.24	0.21	0.18	0.24	0.20	0.18	0.23	0.20	0.17	0.16
		7	0.23	0.19	0.16	0.23	0.18	0.16	0.22	0.18	0.16	0.21	0.18	0.15	0.21	0.17	0.15	0.14
		8	0.21	0.17	0.14	0.21	0.16	0.13	0.20	0.16	0.15	0.19	0.16	0.13	0.19	0.16	0.13	0.12
		9	0.19	0.15	0.12	0.19	0.15	0.12	0.18	0.14	0.12	0.18	0.14	0.12	0.17	0.14	0.12	0.11
		10	0.17	0.13	0.11	0.17	0.13	0.11	0.17	0.13	0.11	0.16	0.13	0.11	0.16	0.13	0.10	0.10

Luminaire 14 Maint. Cat.	Max. S/MH	ρ_{cc}	80			70			50			30			10			0
I	1.6/1.2	ρ_w	50	30	10	50	30	10	50	30	10	50	30	10	50	30	10	0
		RCR	\multicolumn{16}{Coefficients of Utilization for 20% Effective Floor Cavity Reflectance}														
Two-lamp fluorescent strip unit (20½%, 68%)		0	1.01	1.01	1.01	0.96	0.96	0.96	0.87	0.87	0.87	0.79	0.79	0.79	0.72	0.72	0.72	0.68
		1	0.85	0.81	0.77	0.81	0.77	0.73	0.73	0.70	0.67	0.65	0.63	0.60	0.59	0.57	0.55	0.53
		2	0.73	0.66	0.61	0.69	0.63	0.58	0.63	0.58	0.54	0.56	0.52	0.48	0.50	0.47	0.44	0.42
		3	0.63	0.56	0.50	0.60	0.53	0.48	0.55	0.49	0.44	0.48	0.43	0.39	0.43	0.39	0.36	0.35
		4	0.56	0.47	0.41	0.53	0.46	0.40	0.48	0.42	0.37	0.42	0.37	0.33	0.38	0.34	0.30	0.29
		5	0.49	0.40	0.34	0.46	0.39	0.33	0.42	0.36	0.31	0.38	0.32	0.28	0.34	0.29	0.26	0.24
		6	0.43	0.35	0.29	0.41	0.34	0.28	0.38	0.31	0.26	0.34	0.28	0.24	0.30	0.26	0.22	0.20
		7	0.39	0.31	0.25	0.37	0.29	0.24	0.34	0.27	0.23	0.31	0.25	0.21	0.28	0.23	0.19	0.17
		8	0.34	0.27	0.21	0.33	0.26	0.21	0.30	0.24	0.19	0.28	0.22	0.18	0.25	0.21	0.17	0.15
		9	0.31	0.23	0.18	0.30	0.23	0.18	0.27	0.21	0.17	0.26	0.20	0.16	0.23	0.19	0.15	0.12
		10	0.29	0.22	0.17	0.28	0.21	0.17	0.26	0.20	0.16	0.24	0.18	0.15	0.22	0.17	0.14	0.11

Source: The data in this generic table of CU values are adapted from information available from various sources including the *IESNA Lighting Handbook*.

problem with high temperatures also exists. Since the light fixture generates heat, the temperature surrounding the fluorescent tubes is usually considerably higher than the room air temperature, and this higher temperature also reduces lumen output. At 100° F to 120° F the lumen output is only around 75–80% of that at an ambient air temperature of 77° F. But if the room air, which is cooler, is drawn through the light fixture as it is being returned to the air handling unit or being exhausted, this cooler air will cool the fluorescent tubes and produce increased light output.

Although each factor might not represent a significant reduction in maintained lighting levels, since the LLF is the product of all of the individual factors, the result of the various adjustments can be a major reduction in lighting levels. If each of the eight factors were 0.95, then the LLF would be 0.95^8 or 0.66.

Number of Luminaires

Although the total lumens required is important, a more critical design issue is often the number of lighting fixtures

Luminaire 1	Maint. Cat.	Max. S/MH	ρ_{cc}	80			70			50			30			10			0
	V	1.5	ρ_w	50	30	10	50	30	10	50	30	10	50	30	10	50	30	10	0
			RCR	\multicolumn{16}{Coefficients of Utilization for 20% Effective Floor Cavity Reflectance}														
Pendant diffusing sphere with incandescent lamp (45%, 45%)			0	0.87	0.87	0.87	0.81	0.81	0.81	0.70	0.70	0.70	0.59	0.59	0.59	0.49	0.49	0.49	0.44
			1	0.71	0.67	0.63	0.66	0.63	0.59	0.55	0.52	0.49	0.46	0.44	0.42	0.38	0.36	0.34	0.31
			2	0.61	0.54	0.49	0.56	0.50	0.46	0.47	0.43	0.39	0.39	0.35	0.32	0.31	0.29	0.26	0.23
			3	0.52	0.45	0.39	0.48	0.42	0.37	0.41	0.36	0.31	0.33	0.29	0.26	0.27	0.24	0.21	0.18
			4	0.46	0.38	0.33	0.42	0.36	0.31	0.36	0.30	0.26	0.29	0.25	0.21	0.23	0.20	0.17	0.15
			5	0.40	0.33	0.27	0.37	0.30	0.25	0.32	0.26	0.22	0.26	0.21	0.18	0.21	0.17	0.14	0.12
			6	0.36	0.28	0.23	0.33	0.26	0.21	0.28	0.23	0.19	0.23	0.19	0.15	0.19	0.15	0.12	0.10
			7	0.32	0.25	0.20	0.29	0.23	0.18	0.25	0.20	0.16	0.21	0.16	0.13	0.17	0.13	0.11	0.09
			8	0.29	0.22	0.17	0.27	0.20	0.16	0.23	0.17	0.14	0.19	0.14	0.11	0.15	0.12	0.09	0.07
			9	0.26	0.19	0.15	0.24	0.18	0.14	0.20	0.15	0.12	0.17	0.13	0.10	0.14	0.11	0.08	0.06
			10	0.24	0.17	0.13	0.22	0.16	0.12	0.19	0.14	0.11	0.16	0.12	0.09	0.13	0.10	0.08	0.06

Figure 3.11 CU TABLE VARIATIONS—MAXIMUM TO MINIMUM

Table 3.4: LUMINAIRE DIRT DEPRECIATION

Maintenance Category	LDD
I	0.88 ± 0.10
II	0.90 ± 0.08
III	0.85 ± 0.07
IV	0.80 ± 0.15
V	0.83 ± 0.10
VI	0.78 ± 0.12

Source: Based on information from Stein, B., J.S. Reynolds, W.T. Grondzik, and A.G. Kwok. 2006, *Mechanical and Electrical Equipment for Buildings.* John Wiley & Sons, Inc., Hoboken, NJ.

that must be provided in order to develop the appropriate level of illumination. To determine the number of fixtures, or *luminaires*, to use the more proper term, the following formula can be used:

$$\text{No. of Luminaires} = \frac{\text{fc} \times \text{Area}}{\text{Lumens per Fixture} \times \text{CU} \times \text{LLF}}$$

Obviously, in selecting the actual number of luminaires, we will select a whole number and might adjust the calculated figure up or down to achieve a distribution design appropriate for the space. Since the calculation procedure assumes a number of generalizations, a slight increase or decrease in the calculated lumens required and/or the number of luminaires will usually not result in significant adjustments in the lighting levels, especially when the notion of maintained versus initial illumination is considered.

The lumens per luminaire are based on the number of lamps included in the fixture and the lumens per lamp. Lamp lumens are available from various manufacturers. They are also listed in the simplified tables included under Light Sources (Tables 2.3 to 2.9).

Wall and Ceiling Brightness

The zonal cavity method can also provide an indication of the average wall or ceiling brightness based on the design of the electric lighting system. The procedure is very similar to the illumination calculations except that the CU is replaced with an exitance coefficient (EC). Table 3.5 includes EC values for the same generic fixtures included in Table 3.3. There are two sections of this table. One lists the EC for ceilings and the other the EC for walls.

Like the calculation of illumination levels, the calculations using EC rather than CU also provide only the average brightness of the wall surfaces or the ceiling cavity. Since

the calculations use an average coefficient of reflectance, the brightness values will be for those averages. To find the brightness of a particular wall surface, we need to adjust the calculated value based on the average coefficient of reflection to the actual coefficient of reflection for the particular wall surface.

For example, if a space has four equal-sized walls, each with a different coefficient of reflectance (ρ_w), the average ρ_w would be equal to the sum of the four values divided by 4.

Assume:

$$\rho_{w_1} = 0.30$$
$$\rho_{w_2} = 0.40$$
$$\rho_{w_3} = 0.50$$
$$\rho_{w_4} = 0.60$$
$$\rho_{w\text{-average}} = 0.45$$

If the calculated brightness of the walls in this space was 120 foot-lamberts, the adjusted brightness for each of the walls would be based on $\rho_w/0.45$:

WALL 1:

$$\text{fl}_1 = 0.30/0.45 \times 120\,\text{fl} = 80\,\text{fl}$$

WALL 2:

$$\text{fl}_2 = 0.40/0.45 \times 120\,\text{fl} = 106\,\text{fl}$$

WALL 3:

$$\text{fl}_3 = 0.50/0.45 \times 120\,\text{fl} = 133\,\text{fl}$$

WALL 4:

$$\text{fl}_4 = 0.60/0.45 \times 120\,\text{fl} = 160\,\text{fl}$$

The calculation procedure for wall and ceiling brightness uses EC values from Table 3.5 rather than CU values from Table 3.3 to determine foot-lamberts of surface brightness, but, otherwise, the process is the same as that used to determine average foot-candles of illumination.

$$\text{Average Maintained Ceiling Luminous Exitance} = \frac{\text{Total Bare Lamp Lumens} \times \text{Ceilling Cavity EC} \times \text{LLF}}{\text{Floor Area}}$$

$$\text{Average Maintained Wall Luminous Exitance} = \frac{\text{Total Bare Lamp Lumens} \times \text{Wall EC} \times \text{LLF}}{\text{Floor Area}}$$

$$\text{Exitance for a Specific Wall Surface Reflectance} = \frac{\text{Average Wall Exitance} \times \text{Reflectance of Surface}}{\text{Average Wall Reflectance}}$$

Table 3.5: EXITANCE COEFFICIENTS FOR SEVERAL GENERIC LUMINAIRES

Luminaire 1	Maint. Cat.	Max. S/MH	ρ_{cc}	80			50			30			10		
	V	1.5	ρ_w	50	30	10	50	30	10	50	30	10	50	30	10
			RCR	Ceiling Exitance Coefficient for 20% Effective Floor Cavity Reflectance											
			0	0.42	0.42	0.42	0.25	0.25	0.25	0.14	0.14	0.14	0.05	0.05	0.05
			1	0.42	0.40	0.37	0.25	0.23	0.22	0.14	0.14	0.13	0.05	0.04	0.04
			2	0.42	0.38	0.35	0.25	0.23	0.21	0.14	0.13	0.12	0.05	0.04	0.04
			3	0.41	0.37	0.33	0.24	0.22	0.20	0.14	0.13	0.12	0.05	0.04	0.04
			4	0.41	0.36	0.32	0.24	0.22	0.20	0.14	0.13	0.12	0.05	0.04	0.04
			5	0.40	0.35	0.31	0.24	0.21	0.19	0.14	0.12	0.11	0.04	0.04	0.04
			6	0.39	0.34	0.31	0.23	0.21	0.19	0.14	0.12	0.11	0.04	0.04	0.04
			7	0.39	0.34	0.31	0.23	0.21	0.17	0.13	0.12	0.11	0.04	0.04	0.04
			8	0.38	0.34	0.30	0.23	0.20	0.17	0.13	0.12	0.11	0.04	0.04	0.04
			9	0.32	0.33	0.30	0.23	0.20	0.19	0.13	0.12	0.11	0.04	0.04	0.04
			10	0.37	0.33	0.30	0.22	0.20	0.17	0.13	0.12	0.11	0.04	0.04	0.04

45%
45%

Luminaire 2	Maint. Cat.	Max. S/MH	ρ_{cc}	80			50			30			10		
	IV	1.3	ρ_w	50	30	10	50	30	10	50	30	10	50	30	10
			RCR	Ceiling Exitance Coefficient for 20% Effective Floor Cavity Reflectance											
			0	0.80	0.80	0.80	0.46	0.46	0.46	0.27	0.27	0.27	0.09	0.07	0.09
			1	0.79	0.77	0.76	0.46	0.46	0.45	0.27	0.26	0.25	0.09	0.09	0.09
			2	0.78	0.76	0.73	0.46	0.45	0.44	0.27	0.26	0.26	0.09	0.09	0.08
			3	0.78	0.74	0.72	0.46	0.45	0.44	0.27	0.26	0.26	0.09	0.08	0.08
			4	0.77	0.73	0.70	0.46	0.44	0.43	0.26	0.26	0.26	0.09	0.08	0.08
			5	0.77	0.73	0.70	0.46	0.44	0.43	0.28	0.26	0.25	0.09	0.08	0.08
			6	0.76	0.72	0.69	0.45	0.44	0.43	0.25	0.26	0.25	0.09	0.08	0.08
			7	0.76	0.72	0.69	0.45	0.44	0.42	0.25	0.26	0.25	0.09	0.08	0.08
			8	0.76	0.71	0.68	0.45	0.43	0.42	0.25	0.26	0.25	0.09	0.08	0.08
			9	0.75	0.71	0.68	0.45	0.43	0.42	0.26	0.26	0.25	0.09	0.08	0.08
			10	0.75	0.71	0.68	0.45	0.43	0.42	0.26	0.26	0.25	0.08	0.08	0.08

83%
3½%

Luminaire 3	Maint. Cat.	Max. S/MH	ρ_{cc}	80			50			30			10		
	IV	1.3	ρ_w	50	30	10	50	30	10	50	30	10	50	30	10
			RCR	Ceiling Exitance Coefficient for 20% Effective Floor Cavity Reflectance											
			0	0.16	0.16	0.16	0.09	0.09	0.09	0.05	0.05	0.05	0.02	0.02	0.02
			1	0.15	0.13	0.11	0.09	0.08	0.07	0.05	0.05	0.04	0.02	0.01	0.01
			2	0.14	0.11	0.08	0.08	0.07	0.05	0.05	0.04	0.03	0.02	0.01	0.01
			3	0.14	0.10	0.06	0.08	0.06	0.04	0.05	0.03	0.02	0.02	0.01	0.01
			4	0.13	0.08	0.05	0.08	0.05	0.03	0.05	0.03	0.02	0.01	0.01	0.01
			5	0.13	0.08	0.04	0.07	0.05	0.02	0.04	0.03	0.01	0.01	0.01	0.01
			6	0.12	0.09	0.03	0.07	0.04	0.02	0.04	0.03	0.01	0.01	0.01	0.01
			7	0.11	0.06	0.03	0.07	0.04	0.02	0.04	0.02	0.01	0.01	0.01	0.01
			8	0.11	0.06	0.02	0.09	0.04	0.02	0.04	0.02	0.01	0.01	0.01	0.01
			9	0.10	0.05	0.02	0.06	0.03	0.01	0.04	0.02	0.01	0.01	0.01	0.01
			10	0.10	0.05	0.02	0.06	0.03	0.01	0.03	0.02	0.01	0.01	0.01	0.01

10%
85%

Luminaire 4	Maint. Cat.	Max. S/MH	ρ_{cc}	80			50			30			10		
	IV	0.7	ρ_w	50	30	10	50	30	10	50	30	10	50	30	10
			RCR	Ceiling Exitance Coefficient for 20% Effective Floor Cavity Reflectance											
			0	0.16	0.16	0.16	0.09	0.09	0.09	0.05	0.05	0.05	0.02	0.02	0.02
			1	0.14	0.13	0.12	0.08	0.08	0.07	0.05	0.05	0.04	0.02	0.02	0.01
			2	0.13	0.11	0.10	0.08	0.07	0.06	0.04	0.04	0.03	0.01	0.01	0.01
			3	0.12	0.10	0.08	0.07	0.06	0.05	0.04	0.03	0.03	0.01	0.01	0.01
			4	0.11	0.08	0.05	0.09	0.05	0.04	0.04	0.03	0.02	0.01	0.01	0.01
			5	0.10	0.07	0.05	0.06	0.04	0.03	0.04	0.03	0.02	0.01	0.01	0.01
			6	0.10	0.07	0.04	0.06	0.04	0.03	0.03	0.02	0.02	0.01	0.01	0.01
			7	0.09	0.06	0.04	0.05	0.04	0.02	0.03	0.02	0.01	0.01	0.01	0.01
			8	0.07	0.05	0.03	0.05	0.03	0.02	0.03	0.02	0.01	0.01	0.01	0.01
			9	0.08	0.05	0.03	0.05	0.03	0.02	0.03	0.02	0.01	0.01	0.01	0.01
			10	0.08	0.05	0.02	0.05	0.03	0.02	0.03	0.02	0.01	0.01	0.01	0.01

0%
85%

Table 3.5 (*Continued*)

Luminaire 1

ρ_{cc}	80			70			50			30			10		
ρ_w	50	30	10	50	30	10	50	30	10	50	30	10	50	30	10
RCR	Wall Exitance Coefficient for 20% Effective Floor Cavity Reflectance														
0															
1	0.33	0.19	0.06	0.31	0.18	0.06	0.28	0.16	0.05	0.25	0.15	0.05	0.23	0.13	0.04
2	0.28	0.15	0.05	0.26	0.14	0.04	0.23	0.13	0.04	0.21	0.12	0.04	0.18	0.10	0.03
3	0.24	0.13	0.04	0.23	0.12	0.04	0.20	0.11	0.03	0.18	0.10	0.03	0.15	0.09	0.03
4	0.21	0.11	0.03	0.20	0.11	0.03	0.18	0.09	0.03	0.16	0.08	0.03	0.14	0.07	0.02
5	0.19	0.10	0.03	0.18	0.09	0.03	0.18	0.08	0.02	0.14	0.07	0.02	0.12	0.08	0.02
6	0.18	0.09	0.03	0.19	0.08	0.02	0.15	0.07	0.02	0.13	0.07	0.02	0.11	0.06	0.02
7	0.15	0.08	0.02	0.15	0.08	0.02	0.13	0.07	0.02	0.12	0.06	0.02	0.10	0.05	0.02
8	0.15	0.07	0.02	0.14	0.09	0.02	0.12	0.06	0.02	0.11	0.05	0.02	0.09	0.05	0.01
9	0.14	0.07	0.02	0.13	0.06	0.02	0.12	0.06	0.02	0.10	0.05	0.01	0.09	0.04	0.01
10	0.13	0.06	0.02	0.12	0.06	0.02	0.11	0.05	0.02	0.09	0.05	0.01	0.08	0.04	0.01

Luminaire 2

ρ_{cc}	80			70			50			30			10		
ρ_w	50	30	10	50	30	10	50	30	10	50	30	10	50	30	10
RCR	Wall Exitance Coefficient for 20% Effective Floor Cavity Reflectance														
0															
1	0.23	0.13	0.04	0.20	0.11	0.04	0.14	0.08	0.03	0.08	0.05	0.02	0.03	0.02	0.01
2	0.21	0.11	0.04	0.18	0.10	0.03	0.13	0.07	0.02	0.08	0.04	0.01	0.03	0.02	0.01
3	0.19	0.10	0.03	0.19	0.09	0.03	0.12	0.06	0.02	0.07	0.04	0.01	0.03	0.02	0.01
4	0.18	0.09	0.03	0.15	0.08	0.02	0.11	0.06	0.02	0.07	0.04	0.01	0.03	0.01	0.01
5	0.16	0.08	0.02	0.14	0.07	0.02	0.10	0.05	0.02	0.06	0.03	0.01	0.03	0.01	0.01
6	0.15	0.08	0.02	0.13	0.07	0.02	0.09	0.05	0.01	0.06	0.03	0.01	0.02	0.01	0.01
7	0.14	0.07	0.02	0.12	0.06	0.02	0.09	0.04	0.01	0.05	0.03	0.01	0.02	0.01	0.01
8	0.13	0.07	0.02	0.12	0.06	0.02	0.08	0.04	0.01	0.05	0.03	0.01	0.02	0.01	0.01
9	0.13	0.06	0.02	0.11	0.05	0.02	0.08	0.04	0.01	0.05	0.02	0.01	0.02	0.01	0.01
10	0.12	0.06	0.02	0.10	0.05	0.01	0.07	0.04	0.01	0.05	0.02	0.01	0.02	0.01	0.01

Luminaire 3

ρ_{cc}	80			70			50			30			10		
ρ_w	50	30	10	50	30	10	50	30	10	50	30	10	50	30	10
RCR	Wall Exitance Coefficient for 20% Effective Floor Cavity Reflectance														
0															
1	0.25	0.14	0.05	0.24	0.14	0.04	0.23	0.13	0.04	0.22	0.13	0.04	0.21	0.12	0.04
2	0.24	0.13	0.04	0.24	0.13	0.04	0.21	0.12	0.04	0.20	0.11	0.04	0.20	0.11	0.04
3	0.23	0.12	0.04	0.22	0.12	0.04	0.21	0.12	0.04	0.20	0.11	0.03	0.20	0.11	0.03
4	0.21	0.11	0.03	0.21	0.11	0.03	0.20	0.11	0.03	0.19	0.10	0.03	0.18	0.10	0.03
5	0.19	0.10	0.03	0.19	0.10	0.03	0.18	0.10	0.03	0.18	0.09	0.03	0.17	0.09	0.03
6	0.18	0.09	0.03	0.18	0.09	0.03	0.17	0.09	0.03	0.17	0.09	0.03	0.16	0.08	0.03
7	0.17	0.08	0.02	0.19	0.08	0.02	0.16	0.08	0.02	0.16	0.08	0.02	0.15	0.08	0.02
8	0.16	0.08	0.02	0.16	0.08	0.02	0.16	0.08	0.02	0.15	0.07	0.02	0.14	0.07	0.02
9	0.15	0.07	0.02	0.15	0.07	0.02	0.14	0.07	0.02	0.14	0.07	0.02	0.13	0.07	0.02
10	0.14	0.07	0.02	0.14	0.07	0.02	0.13	0.09	0.02	0.13	0.06	0.02	0.13	0.06	0.02

Luminaire 4

ρ_{cc}	80			70			50			30			10		
ρ_w	50	30	10	50	30	10	50	30	10	50	30	10	50	30	10
RCR	Wall Exitance Coefficient for 20% Effective Floor Cavity Reflectance														
0															
1	0.14	0.08	0.03	0.13	0.08	0.02	0.12	0.07	0.02	0.11	0.09	0.02	0.10	0.06	0.02
2	0.13	0.07	0.02	0.13	0.07	0.02	0.12	0.07	0.02	0.11	0.06	0.02	0.10	0.06	0.02
3	0.13	0.09	0.02	0.12	0.09	0.02	0.11	0.06	0.02	0.11	0.06	0.02	0.10	0.06	0.02
4	0.12	0.06	0.02	0.12	0.06	0.02	0.11	0.06	0.02	0.10	0.06	0.02	0.10	0.05	0.02
5	0.11	0.06	0.02	0.11	0.06	0.02	0.11	0.06	0.02	0.10	0.05	0.02	0.10	0.05	0.02
6	0.11	0.06	0.02	0.11	0.05	0.02	0.10	0.05	0.02	0.10	0.05	0.02	0.09	0.01	0.01
7	0.10	0.05	0.02	0.10	0.05	0.01	0.10	0.05	0.01	0.09	0.05	0.01	0.09	0.05	0.01
8	0.10	0.05	0.01	0.10	0.05	0.01	0.09	0.05	0.01	0.09	0.05	0.01	0.09	0.05	0.01
9	0.10	0.05	0.01	0.09	0.05	0.01	0.09	0.05	0.01	0.09	0.04	0.01	0.08	0.04	0.01
10	0.092	0.044	0.012	0.091	0.044	0.012	0.088	0.043	0.012	0.085	0.042	0.012	0.082	0.041	0.012

(*Continued*)

Table 3.5 (*Continued*)

Luminaire 5

Maint. Cat.	Max. S/MH												
IV	0.7	ρ_{cc}		80			50			30			10	
		ρ_w	50	30	10	50	30	10	50	30	10	50	30	10

0% up, 43½% down

RCR	Ceiling Exitance Coefficient for 20% Effective Floor Cavity Reflectance											
0	0.08	0.08	0.08	0.05	0.05	0.05	0.03	0.03	0.03	0.01	0.01	0.01
1	0.07	0.07	0.06	0.04	0.04	0.01	0.03	0.02	0.02	0.01	0.01	0.01
2	0.07	0.06	.0SO	0.04	0.03	0.03	0.02	0.02	0.02	0.01	0.01	0.01
3	0.06	0.05	0.04	0.04	0.03	0.03	0.02	0.02	0.01	0.01	0.01	0.01
4	0.06	0.04	0.03	0.03	0.03	0.02	0.02	0.02	0.01	0.01	0.01	0.01
5	0.05	0.04	0.03	0.03	0.02	0.02	0.02	0.01	0.01	0.01	0.01	0.01
6	0.05	0.03	0.02	0.03	0.02	0.01	0.02	0.01	0.01	0.01	0.01	0.01
7	0.05	0.03	0.02	0.03	0.02	0.01	0.02	0.01	0.01	0.01	0.01	0.01
8	0.04	0.03	0.02	0.03	0.02	0.01	0.02	0.01	0.01	0.01	0.01	0.01
9	0.04	0.03	0.01	0.02	0.02	0.01	0.01	0.01	0.01	0.01	0.01	0.01
10	0.04	0.02	0.01	0.02	0.01	0.01	0.01	0.01	0.01	0.01	0.01	0.01

Luminaire 6

Maint. Cat.	Max. S/MH												
III	1.5	ρ_{cc}		80			50			30			10	
		ρ_w	50	30	10	50	30	10	50	30	10	50	30	10

½% up, 77½% down

RCR	Ceiling Exitance Coefficient for 20% Effective Floor Cavity Reflectance											
0	0.15	0.15	0.15	0.09	0.09	0.09	0.05	0.05	0.05	0.02	0.02	0.02
1	0.14	0.01	0.12	0.06	0.08	0.07	0.05	0.04	0.04	0.02	0.01	0.01
2	0.14	0.11	0.07	0.08	0.09	0.05	0.05	0.04	0.03	0.02	0.01	0.01
3	0.13	0.10	0.07	0.08	0.06	0.04	0.04	0.03	0.02	0.01	0.01	0.01
4	0.12	0.08	0.06	0.07	0.05	0.03	0.04	0.03	0.02	0.01	0.01	0.01
5	0.12	0.08	0.05	0.07	0.05	0.03	0.04	0.03	0.02	0.01	0.01	0.01
6	0.11	0.07	0.04	0.07	0.04	0.02	0.04	0.03	0.01	0.01	0.01	0.01
7	0.11	0.06	0.03	0.08	0.04	0.02	0.04	0.02	0.01	0.01	0.01	0.01
8	0.10	0.06	0.03	0.06	0.04	0.02	0.04	0.02	0.01	0.01	0.01	0.01
9	0.10	0.06	0.03	0.06	0.03	0.01	0.03	0.02	0.01	0.01	0.01	0.01
10	0.09	0.05	0.02	0.06	0.03	0.02	0.03	0.02	0.01	0.01	0.01	0.01

Luminaire 7

Maint. Cat.	Max. S/MH												
II	1.5/1.3	ρ_{cc}		80			50			30			10	
		ρ_w	50	30	10	50	30	10	50	30	10	50	30	10

17% up, 66% down

RCR	Ceiling Exitance Coefficient for 20% Effective Floor Cavity Reflectance											
0	0.29	0.29	0.29	0.17	0.17	0.17	0.10	0.10	0.10	0.03	0.03	0.03
1	0.28	0.26	0.24	0.16	0.15	0.15	0.09	0.09	0.06	0.03	0.03	0.03
2	0.27	0.24	0.22	0.16	0.14	0.13	0.09	0.08	0.08	0.03	0.03	0.03
3	0.26	0.23	0.20	0.15	0.14	0.12	0.09	0.08	0.07	0.03	0.03	0.02
4	0.25	0.21	0.18	0.15	0.13	0.11	0.09	0.08	0.07	0.03	0.03	0.02
5	0.25	0.21	0.17	0.15	0.12	0.11	0.09	0.07	0.08	0.03	0.02	0.02
6	0.24	0.20	0.17	0.14	0.12	0.10	0.08	0.07	0.06	0.03	0.02	0.02
7	0.24	0.19	0.16	0.14	0.12	0.10	0.08	0.07	0.06	0.03	0.02	0.02
8	0.23	0.19	0.16	0.14	0.12	0.10	0.08	0.09	0.06	0.03	0.02	0.02
9	0.23	0.19	0.16	0.14	0.11	0.10	0.08	0.07	0.06	0.03	0.02	0.02
10	0.23	0.18	0.15	0.14	0.11	0.10	0.08	0.07	0.06	0.03	0.02	0.02

Luminaire 8

Maint. Cat.	Max. S/MH												
II	1.5/1.1	ρ_{cc}		80			50			30			10	
		ρ_w	50	30	10	50	30	10	50	30	10	50	30	10

17% up, 56½% down

RCR	Ceiling Exitance Coefficient for 20% Effective Floor Cavity Reflectance											
0	0.27	0.27	0.27	0.16	0.16	0.16	0.09	0.09	0.09	0.03	0.03	0.03
1	0.26	0.25	0.23	0.15	0.14	0.14	0.09	0.08	0.08	0.03	0.03	0.03
2	0.25	0.23	0.21	0.15	0.14	0.13	0.09	0.08	0.07	0.03	0.03	0.02
3	0.25	0.22	0.19	0.14	0.13	0.12	0.08	0.08	0.09	0.03	0.02	0.02
4	0.24	0.21	0.18	0.14	0.12	0.11	0.08	0.07	0.07	0.03	0.02	0.02
5	0.24	0.20	0.17	0.14	0.12	0.11	0.08	0.07	0.06	0.03	0.02	0.02
6	0.23	0.19	0.17	0.14	0.12	0.10	0.08	0.07	0.06	0.03	0.02	0.02
7	0.23	0.19	0.16	0.13	0.11	0.10	0.08	0.07	0.06	0.03	0.02	0.02
8	0.22	0.18	0.16	0.13	0.11	0.10	0.08	0.07	0.07	0.03	0.02	0.02
9	0.22	0.18	0.15	0.13	0.11	0.10	0.08	0.07	0.06	0.03	0.02	0.02
10	0.21	0.18	0.15	0.13	0.11	0.09	0.08	0.06	0.06	0.02	0.02	0.02

Table 3.5 (*Continued*)

Luminaire 5 ρ_{cc}	80			70			50			30			10		
ρ_w	50	30	10	50	30	10	50	30	10	50	30	10	50	30	10
RCR	Wall Exitance Coefficient for 20% Effective Floor Cavity Reflectance														
0															
1	0.07	0.04	0.01	0.07	0.04	0.01	0.06	0.04	0.01	0.06	0.03	0.01	0.05	0.03	0.01
2	0.07	0.04	0.01	0.06	0.04	0.01	0.06	0.03	0.01	0.05	0.03	0.01	0.05	0.03	0.01
3	0.06	0.03	0.01	0.06	0.03	0.01	0.06	0.03	0.01	0.05	0.03	0.01	0.05	0.03	0.01
4	0.06	0.03	0.01	0.06	0.03	0.01	0.05	0.03	0.01	0.05	0.03	0.01	0.05	0.03	0.01
5	0.06	0.03	0.01	0.05	0.03	0.01	0.05	0.03	0.01	0.05	0.03	0.01	0.05	0.05	0.01
6	0.05	0.03	0.01	0.05	0.03	0.01	0.05	0.03	0.01	0.05	0.03	0.01	0.05	0.02	0.01
7	0.05	0.03	0.01	0.05	0.03	0.01	0.05	0.02	0.01	0.05	0.02	0.01	0.04	0.02	0.01
8	0.05	0.02	0.01	0.05	0.02	0.01	0.05	0.02	0.01	0.04	0.02	0.01	0.04	0.02	0.01
9	0.05	0.02	0.01	0.05	0.02	0.01	0.04	0.02	0.01	0.04	0.02	0.01	0.04	0.02	0.01
10	0.05	0.02	0.01	0.05	0.02	0.01	0.04	0.02	0.01	0.04	0.02	0.01	0.04	0.02	0.01

Luminaire 6 ρ_{cc}	80			70			50			30			10		
ρ_w	50	30	10	50	30	10	50	30	10	50	30	10	50	30	10
RCR	Wall Exitance Coefficient for 20% Effective Floor Cavity Reflectance														
0															
1	0.19	0.11	0.03	0.18	0.10	0.03	0.17	0.10	0.03	0.16	0.09	0.03	0.15	0.07	0.03
2	0.19	0.10	0.03	0.18	0.10	0.03	0.17	0.10	0.03	0.16	0.09	0.03	0.16	0.09	0.03
3	0.18	0.10	0.03	0.17	0.09	0.03	0.17	0.09	0.03	0.16	0.09	0.03	0.15	0.08	0.03
4	0.17	0.09	0.03	0.17	0.09	0.03	0.16	0.08	0.03	0.15	0.08	0.03	0.15	0.08	0.02
5	0.16	0.08	0.02	0.16	0.08	0.02	0.15	0.08	0.02	0.15	0.08	0.02	0.14	0.07	0.02
6	0.15	0.08	0.02	0.15	0.08	0.02	0.14	0.07	0.02	0.14	0.07	0.02	0.13	0.07	0.02
7	0.14	0.07	0.02	0.14	0.07	0.02	0.14	0.09	0.02	0.13	0.07	0.02	0.13	0.07	0.02
8	0.14	0.07	0.02	0.13	0.07	0.02	0.13	0.08	0.02	0.12	0.06	0.02	0.12	0.05	0.02
9	0.13	0.06	0.02	0.13	0.06	0.02	0.12	0.05	0.02	0.12	0.06	0.02	0.14	0.06	0.02
10	0.12	0.06	0.02	0.12	0.06	0.02	0.12	0.06	0.02	0.11	0.06	0.02	0.11	0.06	0.02

Luminaire 7 ρ_{cc}	80			70			50			30			10		
ρ_w	50	30	10	50	30	10	50	30	10	50	30	10	50	30	10
RCR	Wall Exitance Coefficient for 20% Effective Floor Cavity Reflectance														
0															
1	0.21	0.12	0.04	0.20	0.11	0.04	0.18	0.10	0.03	0.16	0.09	0.03	0.14	0.08	0.03
2	0.20	0.11	0.03	0.19	0.11	0.03	0.17	0.10	0.03	0.16	0.09	0.03	0.14	0.08	0.03
3	0.19	0.10	0.03	0.18	0.10	0.03	0.16	0.09	0.03	0.15	0.08	0.03	0.14	0.08	0.02
4	0.18	0.09	0.03	0.17	0.09	0.03	0.16	0.08	0.03	0.14	0.08	0.02	0.13	0.07	0.02
5	0.17	0.09	0.03	0.16	0.08	0.02	0.15	0.08	0.02	0.13	0.07	0.02	0.12	0.07	0.02
6	0.16	0.08	0.02	0.15	0.08	0.02	0.14	0.07	0.02	0.13	0.07	0.02	0.12	0.06	0.02
7	0.15	0.07	0.02	0.14	0.07	0.02	0.13	0.07	0.02	0.12	0.08	0.02	0.11	0.06	0.02
8	0.14	0.09	0.02	0.14	0.09	0.02	0.12	0.06	0.02	0.11	0.06	0.02	0.11	0.05	0.02
9	0.13	0.06	0.02	0.13	0.06	0.02	0.12	0.06	0.02	0.11	0.05	0.02	0.10	0.05	0.02
10	0.13	0.06	0.02	0.12	0.09	0.02	0.11	0.06	0.02	0.10	0.05	0.02	0.10	0.05	0.01

Luminaire 8 ρ_{cc}	80			70			50			30			10		
ρ_w	50	30	10	50	30	10	50	30	10	50	30	10	50	30	10
RCR	Wall Exitance Coefficient for 20% Effective Floor Cavity Reflectance														
0															
1	0.18	0.10	0.03	0.17	0.10	0.03	0.15	0.09	0.03	0.13	0.08	0.03	0.12	0.07	0.02
2	0.17	0.10	0.03	0.16	0.09	0.03	0.15	0.08	0.03	0.13	0.07	0.02	0.12	0.07	0.02
3	0.16	0.09	0.03	0.16	0.08	0.03	0.14	0.08	0.02	0.13	.08'	0.02	0.11	0.06	0.02
4	0.15	0.08	0.02	0.15	0.08	0.02	0.13	0.07	0.02	0.12	0.06	0.02	0.11	0.06	0.02
5	0.14	0.07	0.02	0.14	0.07	0.02	0.13	0.07	0.02	0.11	0.06	0.02	0.10	0.05	0.02
6	0.14	0.07	0.02	0.13	0.07	0.02	0.12	0.06	0.02	0.11	0.06	0.02	0.10	0.05	0.02
7	0.13	0.06	0.02	0.12	0.06	0.02	0.11	0.06	0.02	0.10	0.05	0.02	0.09	0.05	0.01
8	0.12	0.06	0.02	0.12	0.06	0.02	0.11	0.05	0.02	0.10	0.05	0.01	0.09	0.05	0.01
9	0.11	0.06	0.02	0.11	0.05	0.02	0.10	0.05	0.01	0.09	0.05	0.01	0.08	0.04	0.01
10	0.11	0.05	0.01	0.10	0.05	0.01	0.10	0.05	0.01	0.09	0.04	0.01	0.08	0.04	0.01

(*Continued*)

Table 3.5 (*Continued*)

Luminaire 9

Maint. Cat.	Max. S/MH	ρ_{cc}	80			50			30			10		
VI	N.A.	ρ_w	50	30	10	50	30	10	50	30	10	50	30	10
		RCR	Ceiling Exitance Coefficient for 20% Effective Floor Cavity Reflectance											
		0	0.65	0.65	0.65	0.38	0.38	0.38	0.22	0.22	0.22	0.07	0.07	0.07
		1	0.65	0.63	0.62	0.38	0.37	0.37	0.22	0.22	0.21	0.07	0.07	0.07
		2	0.64	0.62	0.59	0.38	0.39	0.36	0.22	0.21	0.21	0.07	0.07	0.07
		3	0.64	0.60	0.58	0.37	0.36	0.35	0.22	0.21	0.21	0.07	0.07	0.07
		4	0.63	0.60	0.57	0.37	0.36	0.35	0.22	0.21	0.21	0.07	0.07	0.07
		5	0.63	0.59	0.56	0.37	0.36	0.34	0.22	0.21	0.20	0.07	0.07	0.07
		6	0.62	0.58	0.55	0.39	0.35	0.34	0.21	0.21	0.20	0.07	0.07	0.07
		7	0.62	0.58	0.55	0.37	0.35	0.34	0.21	0.21	0.20	0.07	0.07	0.07
		8	0.61	0.58	0.55	0.37	0.35	0.34	0.21	0.21	0.20	0.07	0.07	0.07
		9	0.61	0.57	0.55	0.36	0.35	0.34	0.21	0.21	0.20	0.07	0.07	0.07
		10	0.61	0.57	0.54	0.36	0.35	0.34	0.21	0.21	0.20	0.07	0.07	0.07

66%
12%

Luminaire 10

Maint. Cat.	Max. S/MH	ρ_{cc}	80			50			30			10		
V	1.5/1.2	ρ_w	50	30	10	50	30	10	50	30	10	50	30	10
		RCR	Ceiling Exitance Coefficient for 20% Effective Floor Cavity Reflectance											
		0	0.22	0.22	0.22	0.13	0.13	0.13	0.07	0.07	0.07	0.02	0.02	0.02
		1	0.21	0.20	0.18	0.13	0.12	0.11	0.07	0.07	0.06	0.02	0.02	0.02
		2	0.21	0.18	0.16	0.12	0.11	0.10	0.07	0.06	0.06	0.02	0.02	0.02
		3	0.20	0.17	0.14	0.12	0.10	0.09	0.07	0.06	0.05	0.02	0.02	0.02
		4	0.20	0.16	0.13	0.12	0.10	0.08	0.07	0.06	0.05	0.02	0.02	0.02
		5	0.19	0.15	0.13	0.11	0.09	0.08	0.07	0.05	0.02	0.02	0.02	0.02
		6	0.19	0.15	0.12	0.11	0.09	0.07	0.06	0.05	0.04	0.02	0.02	0.01
		7	0.18	0.14	0.12	0.11	0.09	0.07	0.06	0.05	0.04	0.02	0.02	0.01
		8	0.18	0.14	0.11	0.11	0.08	0.07	0.06	0.05	0.04	0.02	0.02	0.01
		9	0.17	0.14	0.11	0.10	0.08	0.07	0.06	0.05	0.04	0.02	0.02	0.01
		10	0.17	0.13	0.11	0.10	0.08	0.07	0.06	0.05	0.04	0.02	0.02	0.01

11½%
58½%

Luminaire 11

Maint. Cat.	Max. S/MH	ρ_{cc}	80			50			30			10		
V	1.4/1.2	ρ_w	50	30	10	50	30	10	50	30	10	50	30	10
		RCR	Ceiling Exitance Coefficient for 20% Effective Floor Cavity Reflectance											
		0	0.12	0.12	0.12	0.07	0.07	0.07	0.04	0.04	0.04	0.01	0.01	0.01
		1	0.11	0.10	0.09	0.17	0.06	0.05	0.04	0.03	0.03	0.01	0.01	0.01
		2	0.11	0.08	0.06	0.06	0.05	0.04	0.04	0.03	0.02	0.01	0.01	0.01
		3	0.10	0.07	0.05	0.06	0.04	0.03	0.03	0.03	0.02	0.01	0.01	0.01
		4	0.10	0.06	0.04	0.06	0.04	0.02	0.03	0.02	0.01	0.01	0.01	0.01
		5	0.09	0.06	0.03	0.05	0.03	0.02	0.03	0.02	0.01	0.01	0.01	0.01
		6	0.09	0.05	0.03	0.05	0.03	0.02	0.03	0.02	0.01	0.01	0.01	0.01
		7	0.08	0.05	0.02	0.05	0.03	0.01	0.03	0.02	0.01	0.01	0.01	0.01
		8	0.08	0.04	0.02	0.05	0.03	0.01	0.03	0.02	0.01	0.01	0.01	0.01
		9	0.08	0.04	0.02	0.05	0.02	0.01	0.03	0.01	0.01	0.01	0.01	0.01
		10	0.07	0.04	0.02	0.04	0.02	0.01	0.03	0.01	0.01	0.01	0.01	0.01

0%
63%
60%

Luminaire 12

Maint. Cat.	Max. S/MH	ρ_{cc}	80			50			30			10		
IV	N.A.	ρ_w	50	30	10	50	30	10	50	30	10	50	30	10
		RCR	Ceiling Exitance Coefficient for 20% Effective Floor Cavity Reflectance											
		0	0.11	0.11	0.11	0.07	0.07	0.07	0.04	0.04	0.04	0.01	0.01	0.01
		1	0.11	0.09	0.08	0.06	0.06	0.05	0.04	0.03	0.03	0.01	0.01	0.01
		2	0.10	0.08	0.06	0.06	0.05	0.04	0.03	0.03	0.02	0.01	0.01	0.01
		3	0.09	0.07	0.05	0.06	0.04	0.03	0.03	0.02	0.02	0.01	0.01	0.01
		4	0.09	0.06	0.04	0.05	0.04	0.02	0.03	0.02	0.01	0.01	0.01	0.01
		5	0.09	0.05	0.03	0.05	0.03	0.02	0.03	0.02	0.01	0.01	0.01	0.01
		6	0.08	0.05	0.03	0.05	0.03	0.02	0.03	0.02	0.01	0.01	0.01	0.01
		7	0.08	0.04	0.02	0.05	0.03	0.01	0.03	0.02	0.01	0.01	0.01	0.01
		8	0.08	0.04	0.02	0.04	0.03	0.01	0.03	0.02	0.01	0.01	0.01	0.01
		9	0.07	0.04	0.02	0.04	0.02	0.01	0.03	0.01	0.01	0.01	0.01	0.01
		10	0.07	0.04	0.01	0.04	0.02	0.01	0.02	0.01	0.01	0.01	0.01	0.01

0%
60%
45%

Table 3.5 (*Continued*)

Luminaire 9 ρ_{cc}	80			70			50			30			10		
ρ_w	50	30	10	50	30	10	50	30	10	50	30	10	50	30	10
RCR	Wall Exitance Coefficient for 20% Effective Floor Cavity Reflectance														
0															
1	0.21	0.12	0.04	0.18	0.10	0.03	0.13	0.08	0.02	0.09	0.05	0.02	0.05	0.03	0.01
2	0.19	0.10	0.03	0.17	0.09	0.03	0.12	0.07	0.02	0.08	0.05	0.02	0.05	0.03	0.01
3	0.18	0.09	0.03	0.16	0.08	0.03	0.12	0.06	0.02	0.08	0.04	0.01	0.04	0.02	0.01
4	0.16	0.09	0.03	0.14	0.08	0.02	0.11	0.06	0.02	0.07	0.04	0.01	0.04	0.02	0.01
5	0.15	0.01	0.02	0.13	0.07	0.02	0.10	0.05	0.02	0.07	0.04	0.01	0.04	0.02	0.01
6	0.14	0.07	0.02	0.12	0.06	0.02	0.09	0.05	0.01	0.06	0.03	0.01	0.04	0.02	0.01
7	0.13	0.09	0.02	0.12	0.06	0.02	0.09	0.04	0.01	0.06	0.03	0.01	0.03	0.02	0.01
8	0.12	0.06	0.02	0.11	0.05	0.02	0.08	0.04	0.01	0.06	0.03	0.01	0.03	0.02	0.01
9	0.12	0.06	0.02	0.10	0.05	0.01	0.08	0.04	0.01	0.05	0.03	0.01	0.03	0.02	0.01
10	0.11	0.05	0.02	0.10	0.05	0.01	0.07	0.04	0.01	0.05	0.03	0.01	0.03	0.01	0.01

Luminaire 10 ρ_{cc}	80			70			50			30			10		
ρ_w	50	30	10	50	30	10	50	30	10	50	30	10	50	30	10
RCR	Wall Exitance Coefficient for 20% Effective Floor Cavity Reflectance														
0															
1	0.20	0.12	0.04	0.19	0.11	0.04	0.18	0.10	0.03	0.16	0.09	0.03	0.16	0.09	0.03
2	0.19	0.10	0.03	0.18	0.10	0.03	0.16	0.09	0.03	0.15	0.09	0.03	0.14	0.08	0.03
3	0.17	0.09	0.03	0.17	0.09	0.03	0.15	0.08	0.03	0.14	0.08	0.02	0.13	0.07	0.02
4	0.16	0.08	0.02	0.15	0.08	0.02	0.14	0.08	0.02	0.13	0.07	0.02	0.12	0.07	0.02
5	0.15	0.08	0.02	0.14	0.07	0.02	0.13	0.07	0.20	0.12	0.07	0.02	0.11	0.06	0.02
6	0.14	0.07	0.02	0.13	0.07	0.02	0.12	0.06	0.02	0.12	0.06	0.02	0.11	0.06	0.02
7	0.13	0.06	0.02	0.13	0.06	0.02	0.12	0.06	0.02	0.11	0.06	0.02	0.10	0.05	0.02
8	0.12	0.06	0.02	0.12	0.06	0.02	0.11	0.06	0.02	0.10	0.05	0.02	0.10	0.05	0.01
9	0.12	0.06	0.02	0.11	0.05	0.02	0.10	0.05	0.02	0.10	0.05	0.01	0.09	0.05	0.01
10	0.11	0.05	0.01	0.11	0.05	0.01	0.10	0.05	0.01	0.09	0.05	0.01	0.09	0.04	0.01

Luminaire 11 ρ_{cc}	80			70			50			30			10		
ρ_w	50	30	10	50	30	10	50	30	10	50	30	10	50	30	10
RCR	Wall Exitance Coefficient for 20% Effective Floor Cavity Reflectance														
0															
1	0.17	0.10	0.03	0.16	0.09	0.03	0.17	0.09	0.03	0.15	0.09	0.03	0.14	0.08	0.03
2	0.16	0.09	0.03	0.16	0.09	0.03	0.15	0.08	0.03	0.14	0.08	0.03	0.14	0.08	0.02
3	0.15	0.08	0.02	0.15	0.08	0.02	0.14	0.08	0.02	0.14	0.08	0.02	0.13	0.07	0.02
4	0.14	0.07	0.02	0.14	0.07	0.02	0.13	0.07	0.02	0.13	0.07	0.02	0.12	0.07	0.02
5	0.13	0.07	0.02	0.13	0.07	0.02	0.13	0.07	0.02	0.12	0.06	0.02	0.12	0.06	0.02
6	0.13	0.06	0.02	0.12	0.06	0.02	0.12	0.06	0.02	0.11	0.06	0.17	0.11	0.06	0.02
7	0.12	0.06	0.02	0.12	0.06	0.02	0.11	0.06	0.02	0.11	0.06	0.02	0.10	0.05	0.02
8	0.11	0.05	0.02	0.11	0.05	0.02	0.11	0.05	0.02	0.10	0.05	0.02	0.10	0.05	0.02
9	0.10	0.05	0.01	0.10	0.05	0.01	0.10	0.05	0.01	0.10	0.05	0.01	0.09	0.05	0.01
10	0.10	0.05	0.01	0.10	0.05	0.01	0.09	0.05	0.01	0.09	0.05	0.01	0.09	0.05	0.01

Luminaire 12 ρ_{cc}	80			70			50			30			10		
ρ_w	50	30	10	50	30	10	50	30	10	50	30	10	50	30	10
RCR	Wall Exitance Coefficient for 20% Effective Floor Cavity Reflectance														
0															
1	0.14	0.08	0.03	0.14	0.08	0.03	0.13	0.08	0.02	0.13	0.07	0.02	0.12	0.07	0.02
2	0.14	0.08	0.02	0.14	0.08	0.02	0.13	0.07	0.02	0.13	0.07	0.02	0.12	0.07	0.02
3	0.14	0.07	0.02	0.13	0.07	0.02	0.13	0.07	0.02	0.12	0.07	0.02	0.12	0.06	0.02
4	0.13	0.07	0.02	0.13	0.07	0.02	0.12	0.07	0.02	0.12	0.06	0.02	0.11	0.06	0.02
5	0.12	0.06	0.02	0.12	0.06	0.02	0.12	0.06	0.02	0.11	0.06	0.02	0.11	0.06	0.02
6	0.12	0.06	0.02	0.12	0.06	0.02	0.11	0.06	0.02	0.11	0.06	0.02	0.10	0.06	0.02
7	0.11	0.06	0.02	0.11	0.05	0.02	0.11	0.05	0.02	0.10	0.05	0.02	0.10	0.05	0.02
8	0.11	0.05	0.01	0.10	0.05	0.01	0.10	0.05	0.01	0.10	0.05	0.01	0.09	0.05	0.01
9	0.10	0.05	0.01	0.10	0.05	0.01	0.10	0.05	0.01	0.09	0.05	0.01	0.09	0.05	0.01
10	0.09	0.05	0.01	0.09	0.05	0.01	0.09	0.04	0.01	0.09	0.04	0.01	0.09	0.04	0.01

(*Continued*)

Table 3.5 (*Continued*)

Luminaire 13	Maint. Cat.	Max. S/MH	ρcc	80			50			30			10		
	V	N.A.	ρw	50	30	10	50	30	10	50	30	10	50	30	10
			RCR	Ceiling Exitance Coefficient for 20% Effective Floor Cavity Reflectance											
			0	0.09	0.09	0.09	0.06	0.05	0.05	0.03	0.03	0.03	0.01	0.01	0.01
			1	0.09	0.08	0.06	0.05	0.04	0.04	0.03	0.03	0.02	0.01	0.01	0.01
			2	0.08	0.06	0.05	0.05	0.04	0.03	0.03	0.02	0.02	0.01	0.01	0.01
			3	0.08	0.06	0.04	0.05	0.03	0.02	0.03	0.02	0.01	0.01	0.01	0.01
			4	0.08	0.05	0.03	0.05	0.03	0.02	0.03	0.02	0.01	0.01	0.01	0.01
			5	0.07	0.04	0.02	0.04	0.03	0.01	0.03	0.02	0.01	0.01	0.01	0.01
			6	0.07	0.04	0.02	0.04	0.02	0.01	0.02	0.01	0.01	0.01	0.01	0.01
			7	0.07	0.04	0.02	0.04	0.02	0.01	0.02	0.01	0.01	0.01	0.01	0.01
			8	0.06	0.03	0.01	0.04	0.02	0.01	0.02	0.01	0.01	0.01	0.01	0.01
			9	0.06	0.03	0.01	0.04	0.02	0.01	0.02	0.01	0.01	0.01	0.01	
			10	0.06	0.03	0.01	0.04	0.02	0.01	0.02	0.01	0.01	0.01	0.01	

Luminaire 14	Maint. Cat.	Max. S/MH	ρcc	80			50			30			10		
	I	1.6/1.2	ρw	50	30	10	50	30	10	50	30	10	50	30	10
			RCR	Ceiling Exitance Coefficient for 20% Effective Floor Cavity Reflectance											
			0	0.33	0.33	0.33	0.17	0.17	0.17	0.11	0.11	0.11	0.04	0.04	0.04
			1	0.32	0.30	0.27	0.19	0.17	0.16	0.11	0.10	0.09	0.04	0.03	0.03
			2	0.32	0.28	0.24	0.17	0.16	0.15	0.11	0.10	0.09	0.03	0.03	0.03
			3	0.31	0.28	0.22	0.18	0.16	0.14	0.11	0.09	0.08	0.03	0.03	0.03
			4	0.30	0.25	0.21	0.18	0.15	0.13	0.10	0.09	0.08	0.03	0.03	0.03
			5	0.30	0.24	0.20	0.18	0.15	0.12	0.10	0.09	0.07	0.03	0.03	0.02
			6	0.29	0.23	0.20	0.17	0.14	0.12	0.10	0.08	0.07	0.03	0.03	0.02
			7	0.28	0.23	0.19	0.17	0.14	0.12	0.10	0.08	0.07	0.03	0.03	0.02
			8	0.28	0.22	0.19	0.17	0.14	0.12	0.10	0.08	0.07	0.03	0.03	0.02
			9	0.27	0.22	0.18	0.16	0.13	0.11	0.10	0.08	0.07	0.03	0.03	0.02
			10	0.27	0.22	0.18	0.16	0.13	0.11	0.09	0.08	0.07	0.03	0.03	0.02

Table 3.5: WALL EXITANCE COEFFICIENTS FOR SEVERAL GENERIC LUMINAIRES (*Continued*)

Luminaire 13 ρcc	80			70			50			30			10		
ρw	50	30	10	50	30	10	50	30	10	50	30	10	50	30	10
RCR	Wall Exitance Coefficient for 20% Effective Floor Cavity Reflectance														
0															
1	0.15	0.09	0.03	0.15	0.09	0.03	0.14	0.08	0.03	0.14	0.08	0.03	0.13	0.08	0.03
2	0.15	0.08	0.02	0.14	0.08	0.02	0.14	0.08	0.02	0.13	0.07	0.02	0.13	0.07	0.02
3	0.14	0.07	0.02	0.13	0.07	0.02	0.13	0.07	0.02	0.12	0.07	0.02	0.12	0.06	0.02
4	0.13	0.06	0.02	0.12	0.06	0.02	0.12	0.06	0.02	0.11	0.06	0.02	0.11	0.06	0.02
5	0.12	0.06	0.02	0.11	0.06	0.02	0.11	0.06	0.02	0.11	0.06	0.02	0.10	0.06	0.02
6	0.11	0.05	0.02	0.11	0.05	0.02	0.10	0.05	0.02	0.10	0.05	0.02	0.10	0.05	0.02
7	0.10	0.05	0.01	0.10	0.05	0.01	0.10	0.05	0.01	0.09	0.05	0.01	0.09	0.05	0.01
8	0.09	0.05	0.01	0.09	0.05	0.01	0.09	0.04	0.01	0.09	0.04	0.01	0.08	0.04	0.01
9	0.09	0.04	0.01	0.09	0.04	0.01	0.08	0.04	0.01	0.08	0.04	0.01	0.08	0.04	0.01
10	0.08	0.04	0.01	0.08	0.04	0.01	0.08	0.04	0.01	0.08	0.04	0.01	0.07	0.04	0.01

Luminaire 14 ρcc	80			70			50			30			10		
ρw	50	30	10	50	30	10	50	30	10	50	30	10	50	30	10
RCR	Coefficient for 20% Effective Floor Cavity Reflectance														
0															
1	0.34	0.19	0.06	0.32	0.18	0.06	0.30	0.17	0.06	0.28	0.16	0.05	0.26	0.15	0.05
2	0.29	0.16	0.05	0.28	0.16	0.05	0.26	0.05	0.05	0.24	0.14	0.04	0.22	0.13	0.04
3	0.26	0.14	0.04	0.25	0.14	0.04	0.23	0.13	0.04	0.21	0.12	0.04	0.20	0.11	0.03
4	0.24	0.12	0.04	0.23	0.12	0.04	0.21	0.11	0.03	0.19	0.10	0.03	0.18	0.10	0.03
5	0.22	0.11	0.03	0.21	0.11	0.03	0.19	0.10	0.03	0.18	0.09	0.03	0.16	0.09	0.03
6	0.20	0.10	0.03	0.19	0.10	0.03	0.17	0.09	0.03	0.16	0.06	0.02	0.15	0.08	0.02
7	0.18	0.09	0.03	0.17	0.09	0.03	0.16	0.08	0.02	0.15	0.08	0.02	0.14	0.07	0.02
8	0.17	0.08	0.02	0.16	0.08	0.02	0.15	0.08	0.02	0.14	0.07	0.02	0.13	0.07	0.02
9	0.16	0.08	0.02	0.15	0.07	0.02	0.14	0.07	0.02	0.13	0.06	0.02	0.12	0.06	0.02
10	0.15	0.07	0.02	0.14	0.07	0.02	0.13	0.06	0.02	0.12	0.06	0.02	0.11	0.06	0.02

Source: The data in this generic table of EC values are based on information available from various sources including the *IESNA Lighting Handbook*

Luminaire 9

ρ_{cc}	80			70			50			30			10			0
ρ_w	50	30	10	50	30	10	50	30	10	50	30	10	50	30	10	0
RCR	Coefficients of Utilization for 20% Effective Floor Cavity Reflectance															
0	0.77	0.77	0.77	0.68	0.68	0.68	0.50	0.50	0.50	0.34	0.34	0.34	0.19	0.19	0.19	0.12
1	0.67	0.64	0.62	0.59	0.57	0.54	0.44	0.42	0.41	0.29	0.29	0.28	0.17	0.16	0.16	0.10
2	0.59	0.54	0.50	0.52	0.48	0.45	0.38	0.36	0.34	0.26	0.24	0.23	0.14	0.14	0.13	0.09
3	0.51	0.46	0.42	0.45	0.41	0.37	0.34	0.31	0.28	0.23	0.21	0.19	0.13	0.12	0.11	0.07
4	0.45	0.40	0.35	0.40	0.35	0.31	0.30	0.27	0.24	0.20	0.18	0.17	0.11	0.10	0.10	0.06
5	0.40	0.34	0.30	0.35	0.30	0.27	0.26	0.23	0.20	0.18	0.16	0.14	0.10	0.09	0.08	0.05
6	0.36	0.30	0.26	0.32	0.27	0.23	0.24	0.20	0.18	0.16	0.14	0.12	0.09	0.08	0.07	0.05
7	0.32	0.26	0.22	0.28	0.23	0.20	0.21	0.18	0.15	0.15	0.12	0.11	0.08	0.07	0.01	0.04
8	0.29	0.23	0.19	0.25	0.21	0.17	0.19	0.16	0.13	0.13	0.11	0.09	0.08	0.06	0.06	0.03
9	0.26	0.20	0.17	0.23	0.18	0.15	0.17	0.14	0.12	0.12	0.10	0.08	0.07	0.06	0.05	0.03
10	0.24	0.19	0.15	0.21	0.17	0.13	0.16	0.13	0.10	0.11	0.01	0.07	0.06	0.05	0.04	0.03

Figure 3.12 RANGE OF VALUES FOR THE CU

Interpolation

When there is a ceiling cavity, the average maintained luminous exitance is for the ceiling cavity. Unfortunately, because of the complicated internal reflections that occur within the cavity, we cannot readily determine the brightness of a particular surface within the cavity. However, if there is no cavity, then we can determine the brightness for a particular portion of the ceiling, assuming that there is variation in the finish of the ceiling. Of course, if the ceiling finish is consistent, then the calculated foot-lamberts value indicates the average ceiling luminous exitance of the ceiling.

Interpolation

Often the reflectance of the ceiling cavity, the reflectance of the walls, or the cavity ratio for a particular design is not exactly equal to the values listed in the CU tables. When this occurs, we have to interpolate between the CUs indicated for the listed values to obtain the proper value for the actual conditions. Assume that we plan to use Luminaire No. 9 and that the reflectance of the ceiling cavity (ρ_{cc}) is 60%, the average reflectance of the walls (ρ_w) is 40%, and the RCR is 4.5; what would be the adjusted CU? In order to determine this, we must first select the proper sections of the CU tables and determine the range within which the actual conditions should fall (see Figure 3.12).

Having identified the range of CUs, as shown in Figure 3.12, we must then establish the sequence by which to interpolate between the listed CU values to obtain the CU for the actual conditions. While one approach is indicated in Figure 3.13, there are often several different methods that can be used to provide the desired interpolation.

When a sequence has been chosen, we interpolate by finding the difference between the CU values listed for the two conditions between which the actual condition exists, properly proportioning this difference, and adding this proportion to the lower value. This is done in a step-by-step manner until the CU for the actual condition is ultimately determined (Figure 3.14).

While, as shown in Figure 3.14, the interpolation between two values can be done by merely proportioning the difference between the values, it is also possible to interpolate by using a simple formula.

$$IV = V_1 + [(V_2 - V_1) \times (\text{Ratio})]$$

Luminaire 9

ρ_{cc}	80			70			50			30			10			0
ρ_w	50	30	10	50	30	10	50	30	10	50	30	10	50	30	10	0
RCR	Coefficients of Utilization for 20% Effective Floor Cavity Reflectance															
0	0.77	0.77	0.77	0.68	0.68	0.68	0.50	0.50	0.50	0.34	0.34	0.34	0.19	0.19	0.19	0.12
1	0.67	0.64	0.62	0.59	0.57	0.54	0.44	0.42	0.41	0.29	0.29	0.28	0.17	0.16	0.16	0.10
2	0.59	0.54	0.50	0.52	0.48	0.45	0.38	0.36	0.34	0.26	0.24	0.23	0.14	0.14	0.13	0.09
3	0.51	0.46	0.42	0.45	0.41	0.37	0.34	0.31	0.28	0.23	0.21	0.19	0.13	0.12	0.11	0.07
4	0.45	0.40	0.35	0.40	0.35	0.31	0.30	0.27	0.24	0.20	0.18	0.17	0.11	0.10	0.10	0.06
5	0.40	0.34	0.30	0.35	0.30	0.27	0.26	0.23	0.20	0.18	0.16	0.14	0.10	0.09	0.08	0.05
6	0.36	0.30	0.26	0.32	0.27	0.23	0.24	0.20	0.18	0.16	0.14	0.12	0.09	0.08	0.07	0.05
7	0.32	0.26	0.22	0.28	0.23	0.20	0.21	0.18	0.15	0.15	0.12	0.11	0.08	0.07	0.01	0.04
8	0.29	0.23	0.19	0.25	0.21	0.17	0.19	0.16	0.13	0.13	0.11	0.09	0.08	0.06	0.06	0.03
9	0.26	0.20	0.17	0.23	0.18	0.15	0.17	0.14	0.12	0.12	0.10	0.08	0.07	0.06	0.05	0.03
10	0.24	0.19	0.15	0.21	0.17	0.13	0.16	0.13	0.10	0.11	0.01	0.07	0.06	0.05	0.04	0.03

Figure 3.13 RANGE OF VALUES FOR THE CU

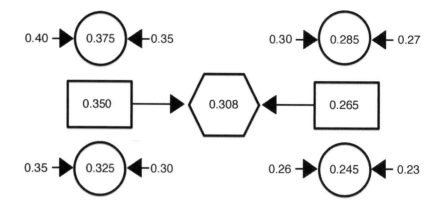

Figure 3.14 INTERPOLATION SEQUENCE

where:

> IV is the interpolated value to be used (e.g., CU)
> V_1 is the listed value for the lower condition (C_1)
> V_2 is the listed value for the higher condition (C_2)

$$\text{Ratio} = \frac{C_{act} - C_1}{C_2 - C_1}$$

with:

> C_{act} as the actual condition (e.g., $\rho = 40$)
> C_1 as the lower condition (e.g., $\rho = 30$)
> C_2 as the higher condition (e.g., $\rho = 50$)

We should note that if the value for the higher condition is less than that for the lower condition, this would result in a negative number that would be added to V_1. That is, this formula gives correct answers regardless of the values. However, it still tends to be easier to simply proportion the difference between two values and sequence through the necessary number of steps needed to derive the proper interpolated value.

For example, as shown in the upper right interpolation above, if the actual wall reflectance (C_{act}) is $\rho_{act} = 40\%$, but the tables values are for $\rho_1 = 30\%$ with a CU_1 of 0.27 and $\rho_2 = 50\%$ with a CU_2 of 0.30, then the calculated

interpolated CU value would be:

$$CU = CU_1 + \left[(CU_2 - CU_1) \times \left(\frac{\rho_{act} - \rho_1}{\rho_2 - \rho_1} \right) \right]$$
$$= 0.27 + \left[(0.30 - 0.27) \times \left(\frac{40 - 30}{50 - 30} \right) \right] = 0.285$$

If, as for the conditions listed above, the actual condition falls midway between the listed CU values, then the interpolated CU can be found by adding the individual CUs and dividing by the number of CUs added. That is, by adding the eight CU values within which the actual CU would fall and dividing by 8, the actual CU, rounded to three significant figures, can be found. But note that this only works when each step of interpolation is to find the value midway between two values.

$$\begin{aligned} CU & \\ &= \frac{0.40 + 0.35 + 0.30 + 0.27 + 0.35 + 0.30 + 0.26 + 0.23}{8} \\ &= 0.308 \end{aligned}$$

Sometimes the conditions fall beyond the values provided in the tables. When this occurs, it is necessary to extrapolate or to project from the known changes that are documented a probable change that will occur (see Figure 3.15). For example, if the average wall reflectance (ρ_w)

Luminaire 9

ρ_{cc}	80			70			50			30			10			0
ρ_w	50	30	10	50	30	10	50	30	10	50	30	10	50	30	10	0
RCR	Coefficients of Utilization for 20% Effective Floor Cavity Reflectance															
0	0.77	0.77	0.77	0.68	0.68	0.68	0.50	0.50	0.50	0.34	0.34	0.34	0.19	0.19	0.19	0.12
1	0.67	0.64	0.62	0.59	0.57	0.54	0.44	0.42	0.41	0.29	0.29	0.28	0.17	0.16	0.16	0.10
2	0.59	0.54	0.50	0.52	0.48	0.45	0.38	0.36	0.34	0.26	0.24	0.23	0.14	0.14	0.13	0.09
3	0.51	0.46	0.42	0.45	0.41	0.37	0.34	0.31	0.28	0.23	0.21	0.19	0.13	0.12	0.11	0.07
4	0.45	0.40	0.35	0.40	0.35	0.31	0.30	0.27	0.24	0.20	0.18	0.17	0.11	0.10	0.10	0.06
5	0.40	0.34	0.30	0.35	0.30	0.27	0.26	0.23	0.20	0.18	0.16	0.14	0.10	0.09	0.08	0.05
6	0.36	0.30	0.26	0.32	0.27	0.23	0.24	0.20	0.18	0.16	0.14	0.12	0.09	0.08	0.07	0.05
7	0.32	0.26	0.22	0.28	0.23	0.20	0.21	0.18	0.15	0.15	0.12	0.11	0.08	0.07	0.01	0.04
8	0.29	0.23	0.19	0.25	0.21	0.17	0.19	0.16	0.13	0.13	0.11	0.09	0.08	0.06	0.06	0.03
9	0.26	0.20	0.17	0.23	0.18	0.15	0.17	0.14	0.12	0.12	0.10	0.08	0.07	0.06	0.05	0.03
10	0.24	0.19	0.15	0.21	0.17	0.13	0.16	0.13	0.10	0.11	0.01	0.07	0.06	0.05	0.04	0.03

Figure 3.15 EXTRAPOLATION OF THE CU

is 60%, it would be reasonable to find out what the conditions for a wall reflectance of 40% would be and then add the difference between a ρ_w of 50% and a ρ_w of 40% to the CU found for a ρ_w of 50%.

Again assuming Luminaire 9, if the RCR is 3 and the ρ_{cc} is 80%, ρ_w is 60%, and ρ_{fc} is 20%, what would be the appropriate CU?

The difference between the CU for a ρ_w of 50% and a ρ_w of 30% is 0.05.

$$0.51 - 0.46 = 0.05 \text{ and } \frac{0.05}{2} = 0.025$$

If we assume that the rate of change is essentially consistent both above and below a ρ_w of 50%, at a ρ_w of 60% the CU should be higher than 0.51 by 0.025. Based on this, the CU for a ρ_{cc} of 80%, a ρ_w of 60%, and a ρ_{fc} of 20% is 0.0535, which, rounded to three significant figures, is 0.054.

LIGHTING CALCULATIONS EXAMPLES

As previously discussed, the intensity of illumination changes with a change in the angle of incidence. This change of illumination is proportional to the cosine of the angle of incidence, the angle drawn between the ray of incident light and the normal to the surface at the point of incidence. In addition, if the illumination comes from a point source of light, the intensity follows the inverse square law. As a result, the basic formula to determine the illumination from a point source on a surface is:

$$\text{Foot-candles or Lux} = \text{Lumens per Unit Area} = E$$
$$E = \frac{1 \times \cos\theta}{\text{Distance}^2}$$

When the light is from a linear source, the inverse square law no longer applies and the formula is changed to respond to reduction according to the change in distance:

$$\text{Foot-candles or Lux} = \text{Lumens per Unit Area} = E$$
$$E = \frac{1 \times \cos\theta}{\text{Distance}}$$

When the light is from an area source, the formula is changed:

$$\text{Foot-candles or Lux} = \text{Lumens per Unit Area} = E$$
$$E = 1 \times \cos q$$

POINT-TO-POINT METHOD—CALCULATION EXAMPLES

1. If the luminous flux from a point source of light is 10,000 candela (lumens per steradian), what would be the illumination on a surface located 15 feet from the source if the angle of incidence (θ) is 20°?

2. If the luminous flux from a point source of light is 12,566 candela, what would be the illumination on a surface located 8 feet from the source if the angle of incidence (θ) is 15°?

3. If the luminous flux from a point source of light is 75,000 candela, what would be the illumination on a surface located 25 feet from the source if the angle of incidence (θ) is 33°?

4. If the conditions of Example 3 are the same except that the angle of incidence is 67° rather than 33°, what would be the illumination?

5. If the luminous flux from a point source of light is 15,000 candela, what would be the illumination on a surface located 20 feet from the source if the angle of incidence (θ) is 30°?

6. If the luminous flux from a point source of light is 25,132 candela, what would be the illumination on a surface located 10 feet from the source if the angle of incidence (θ) is 10°?

7. If the luminous flux from a point source of light is 120,000 candela, what would be the illumination on a surface located 15 feet from the source if the angle of incidence (θ) is 45°?

8. If the conditions of Example 7 were the same except that the angle of incidence is 67° rather than 45°, what would be the illumination?

9. If a linear light source emits a luminous flux of 8500 candela, what would be the illumination on a surface located 6 feet from the source if the angle of incidence (θ) is 65°?

10. If a linear light source emits a luminous flux of 4500 candela, what would be the illumination on a surface located 8 feet from the source if the angle of incidence (θ) is 25°?

11. If the luminous flux directed downward from an area light source is 300 candela, what would be the illumination on a horizontal surface located 15 feet below the area source?

12. If the luminous flux directed downward from an area light source is 750 candela, what would be the illumination on a horizontal surface located 7 feet below the area source?

Answers

1. $E = \dfrac{1000 \times \cos 20°}{15^2} = \dfrac{1000 \times 0.9397}{225} = 41.76 \text{ fc}$

2. $E = \dfrac{1000 \times \cos 15°}{8^2} = \dfrac{1000 \times 0.9659}{64} = 189.7 \text{ fc}$

3. $E = \dfrac{7500 \times \cos 33°}{25^2} = \dfrac{7500 \times 0.8387}{625} = 100.6 \text{ fc}$

4. $E = \dfrac{75,000 \times \cos 67°}{25^2} = \dfrac{75,000 \times 0.3907}{625} = 46.9 \text{ fc}$

5. $E = \dfrac{15,000 \times \cos 30°}{20^2} = \dfrac{15,000 \times 866}{400} = 32.48 \text{ fc}$

6. $E = \dfrac{25,132 \times \cos 10°}{10^2} = \dfrac{25,032 \times 0.9848}{100} = 247.5 \text{ fc}$

7. $E = \dfrac{120,000 \times \cos 45°}{15^2} = \dfrac{120,000 \times 0.7071}{225} = 377.1 \text{ fc}$

8. $E = \dfrac{120,000 \times \cos 67°}{15^2} = \dfrac{120,000 \times 0.3907}{225} = 208.4 \text{ fc}$

9. $E = \dfrac{8500 \times \cos 65°}{6} = \dfrac{8500 \times 0.4226}{6} = 599 \text{ fc}$

10. $E = \dfrac{4500 \times \cos 25°}{8} = \dfrac{4500 \times 0.9063}{8} = 510 \text{ fc}$

11. $E = 300 \times \cos 0° = 300 \text{ fc}$

12. $E = 750 \times \cos 0° = 750 \text{ fc}$

ZONAL CAVITY METHOD—CALCULATION EXAMPLES

1. For a room with a floor area of 500 square feet, how many lumens of generated light are required to develop a general illumination level of 100 foot-candles if the light fixture used is Luminaire No. 1 in Table 3.3 and the LLF is 0.80, the RCR is 4.0, the average ρ_w is 50, the ρ_{cc} is 70, and the ρ_{fc} is 20?

2. If the lamp used in the above example is a 150-watt lamp with an A-21 bulb, how many luminaires would be required to achieve 148,810 lumens?

3. What would be the average luminous exitance from the walls and the ceiling?

4. What would be the adjusted CU for Luminaire No. 11 if the reflectance of the ceiling cavity (ρ_{cc}) is 65%, the average reflectance of the walls (ρ_w) is 35%, and the RCR is 6.5?
5–7. (See Figure 3.16.)

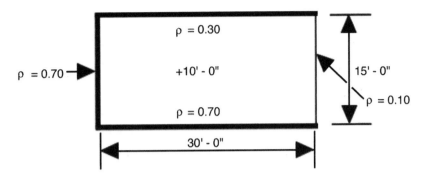

Figure 3.16 ROOM CONDITIONS FOR QUESTIONS 5–7

5. How many light fixtures (luminaires) would be required to develop 50 foot-candles of illumination at the standard work plane elevation in a room that has overall dimensions of 15 feet by 30 feet and a height of 10 feet? Assume that the fixture to be used is Luminaire No. 4 from Table 3.3 and that a 150-watt, A-21 incandescent lamp will be used. Also assume that the coefficient of reflection (ρ) of the ceiling is 0.70 and that of the floor is 0.15, and that the walls consist of one 30-foot wall with $\rho = 0.70$, the other 30-foot wall with $\rho = 0.30$, one of the 15-foot walls with $\rho = 0.10$ (window wall) and the other with $\rho = 0.70$, and that the LLF is 0.60.

6. How many luminaires would be required if Luminaire No. 6 with a 175-watt BT-28 metal halide lamp were used?

7. Based on the answers to the above questions, what would be the average luminous exitance of the walls and the ceiling for each lighting system?

Answers

1. CU = 0.42

$$\text{Req. Lm} = \frac{\text{fc} \times \text{area}}{\text{CU} \times \text{LLF}} = \frac{100 \text{ fc} \times 500}{0.42 \times 0.80}$$

$$= 148{,}810 \text{ lm}$$

2. No. of Luminaires $= \dfrac{148{,}810 \text{ lm}}{2880 \text{ lm/lamp}} = 52 \text{ Luminaires}$

3. EC for Wall = 0.201

$$\text{Wall Luminous Exitance} = \frac{52 \times 2880 \text{ lm/lamp} \times 0.201}{500 \text{ sq ft}}$$

$$= 60.2 \text{ fl}$$

EC for ceiling = 0.348

$$\text{Ceiling Luminous Exitance} = \frac{52 \times 2880 \text{ lm/lamp} \times 0.348}{500 \text{ sq ft}}$$

$$= 104.2 \text{ fl}$$

4. (See Figures 3.17 and 3.18.)

Luminaire 11

ρ_{cc}	80			70 (65 ↓)			50			30			10			0
ρ_w	50	30	10	50	30	10	50	30	10	50	30	10	50	30	10	0
RCR	Coefficients of Utilization for 20% Effective Floor Cavity Reflectance															
0	0.75	0.75	0.75	0.73	0.73	0.73	0.70	0.70	0.70	0.67	0.67	0.67	0.64	0.64	0.64	0.63
1	0.67	0.65	0.63	0.66	0.64	0.62	0.63	0.62	0.60	0.60	0.59	0.58	0.58	0.57	0.56	0.55
2	0.60	0.57	0.54	0.59	0.56	0.53	0.57	0.54	0.52	0.54	0.52	0.49	0.52	0.50	0.48	0.49
3	0.54	0.50	0.47	0.53	0.49	0.46	0.52	0.48	0.45	0.48	0.45	0.43	0.47	0.44	0.42	0.43
4	0.49	0.44	0.40	0.48	0.44	0.40	0.47	0.43	0.40	0.44	0.40	0.37	0.42	0.39	0.37	0.37
5	0.44	0.39	0.35	0.43	0.38	0.35	0.42	0.38	0.34	0.39	0.36	0.33	0.38	0.35	0.32	0.33
6.5 → 6	0.40	0.34	0.31	**0.39**	**0.34**	0.31	**0.38**	**0.34**	0.30	0.36	0.32	0.29	0.35	0.31	0.29	0.29
7	0.35	0.30	0.26	**0.35**	**0.30**	0.26	**0.34**	**0.29**	0.26	0.33	0.29	0.26	0.32	0.38	0.26	0.25
8	0.32	0.27	0.24	0.32	0.27	0.23	0.30	0.26	0.23	0.30	0.26	0.23	0.29	0.36	0.23	0.22
9	0.30	0.25	0.21	0.29	0.24	0.21	0.28	0.24	0.21	0.28	0.24	0.21	0.27	0.34	0.21	0.20
10	0.27	0.22	0.19	0.27	0.22	0.19	0.26	0.22	0.19	0.26	0.22	0.19	0.25	0.22	0.19	0.18
				↑ 35			↑ 35									

Figure 3.17 INTERPOLATION FOR QUESTION 4

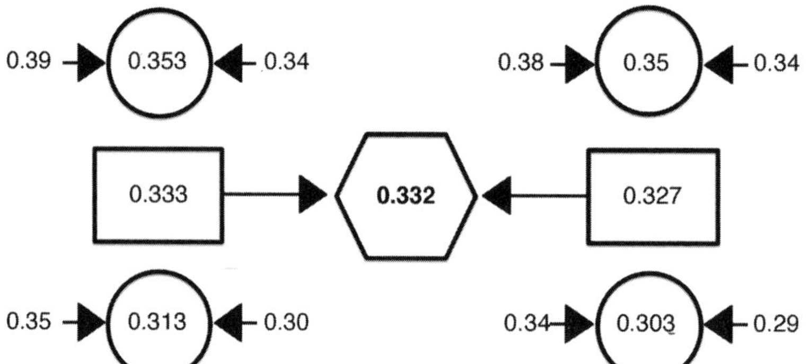

Figure 3.18 INTERPOLATION STEPS FOR QUESTION 4

In this example, the interpolation for the RCR is between 6 and 7, but with ρ_w at 35%, the interpolation is one-quarter of the difference between 30% and 50% from the 30% values. And with ρ_{cc} at 65%, the interpolation is one-quarter of the difference between 50% and 70%, but this time it is from the 70% or higher value.

We should note that while this step-by-step method of interpolation provides proper results, when the actual conditions fall midway between listed values, we can add the listed values and divide by the number of values. For example, if the conditions for this problem were for an RCR of 6.5, ρ_{cc} of 60%, ρ_w of 40%, and ρ_{fc} of 20%, the CU would be the sum of the eight CUs divided by 8.

$$\text{CU} = \frac{0.39 + 0.34 + 0.38 + 0.34 + 0.35 + 0.30 + 0.34 + 0.29}{8} = 0.3413$$

5. Average Wall Reflectance:

$$\rho_W = \frac{(15 \times 0.10) + (15 \times 0.70) + (30 \times 0.70) + (30 \times 0.30)}{90}$$

$$= 0.47$$

$$\text{Cavity Ratios: FCR} = 5\,\frac{(30 + 15) \times 2.5}{30 \times 15} = 1.25$$

$$\text{RCR} = 5\,\frac{(30 + 15) \times 7.5}{30 \times 15} = 3.75$$

Effective Floor Cavity Reflectance: Refer to Table 3.2: Effective Coefficients of Reflectance for Ceiling and Floor Cavities.

Partial Table of Percent Effective Floor Cavity Reflectance for Various Reflactance Combinations

Percent Ceiling or Floor Reflectance		30			10		
Percent Wall Reflectance		50	30	10	50	30	10
	1.2	26	23	20	12	9	7
FCR	1.4	26	22	19	12	9	7
	1.6	25	21	18	12	9	7

Since $\rho fl = 0.15$, we must interpolate between 0.30 and 0.10. Since $\rho_w = 0.47$, we must interpolate between 0.50 and 0.30. And since FCR = 1.25, we must interpolate between 1.2 and 1.4.

> $\rho fl = 0.15$, so we must interpolate between 0.30 and 0.10
> $\rho_w = 0.47$, so we must interpolate between 0.50 and 0.30
> FCR = 1.25, so we must interpolate between 1.2 and 1.4

As suggested above, the interpolation can be accomplished by a simple formula:

$$IV = V_1 + [(V_2 - V_1) \times (\text{Ratio})]$$

where:

> IV is the interpolated value to be used
> V_1 is the listed value for the lower condition)
> V_2 is the listed value for the higher condition

$$\text{Ratio} = \frac{C_{act} - C_1}{C_2 - C_1}$$

with:

> C_{act} as the actual condition
> C_1 as the lower condition
> C_2 as the upper condition

For $\rho fl = 0.30$, $\rho_w = 0.47$, and FCR = 1.2
$$\text{Ratio} = \frac{C_{act} - C_1}{C_2 - C_1} = \frac{0.47 - 0.30}{0.50 - 0.30} = 0.85$$
$$23 + [(26 - 23) \times (0.85)] = 25.55$$
For $\rho fl = 0.30$, $\rho_w = 0.47$, and FCR = 1.4
$$\text{Ratio} = \frac{C_{act} - C_1}{C_2 - C_1} = \frac{0.47 - 0.30}{0.50 - 0.30} = 0.85$$
$$22 + [(26 - 22) \times (0.85)] = 25.4$$
For $\rho fl = 0.30$, $\rho_w = 0.47$, and FCR = 1.25
$$\text{Ratio} = \frac{C_{act} - C_1}{C_2 - C_1} = \frac{1.25 - 1.2}{1.4 - 1.2} = 0.25$$
$$25.55 + [(25.4 - 25.55) \times (0.25)] = 25.51$$
For $\rho fl = 0.10$, $\rho_w = 0.47$, and FCR = 1.2
$$\text{Ratio} = \frac{C_{act} - C_1}{C_2 - C_1} = \frac{0.47 - 0.30}{0.50 - 0.30} = 0.85$$
$$9 + [(12 - 9) \times (0.85)] = 11.55$$
For $\rho fl = 0.10$, $\rho_w = 0.47$, and FCR = 1.4
$$\text{Ratio} = \frac{C_{act} - C_1}{C_2 - C_1} = \frac{0.47 - 0.30}{0.50 - 0.30} = 0.85$$
$$9 + [(12 - 9) \times (0.85)] = 11.55$$

For $\rho\,fl = 0.10$, $\rho_w = 0.47$, and FCR $= 1.25$

$$\text{Ratio} = \frac{C_{act} - C_1}{C_2 - C_1} = \frac{1.25 - 1.2}{1.4 - 1.2} = 0.25$$

$$11.55 + [(11.55 - 11.55) \times (0.25)] = 11.55$$

For $\rho\,fl = 0.15$, $\rho_w = 0.47$, and FCR $= 1.25$

$$\text{Ratio} = \frac{C_{act} - C_1}{C_2 - C_1} = \frac{0.15 - 0.10}{0.30 - 0.10} = 0.25$$

$$11.55 + [(25.51 - 11.55) \times (0.25)] = 15.04$$

Effective Floor Cavity Reflectance $= 15.04$

This is a lot of effort for a refinement that accounts for only a minor adjustment in the CU. But note that if the effective reflectance were for the ceiling, the interpolation would be more significant than for the floor cavity. We will use the adjusted reflectance for the floor cavity by applying the correction factor found in Table 3.1 to the CU value selected.

A simple graphic technique, shown in Figure 3.19, provides an alternative to the formal interpolation calculation.

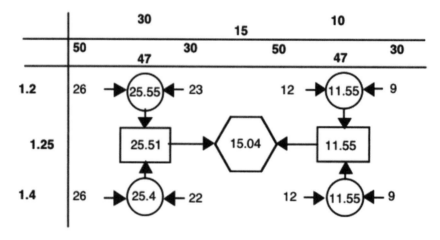

Figure 3.19 INTERPORATION FOR QUESTION 5

Correction Factor for Effective FCR of 15.04:
For RCR $= 3$ and $\rho_{cc} = 0.70$, Factor $= 1.04$
For RCR $= 4$ and $\rho_{cc} = 0.70$, Factor $= 1.03$
For RCR $= 3.75$ and $\rho_{cc} = 0.70$, Factor $= 1.0325$ for a 10% variation
For a 50% variation (*rflc* difference of approximately 5 versus 10 off the standard of 20% ρflc)

Correction Factor $= 1 + [(0.5)(1.0325 - 1.0)] = 1.0163$, the value by which the CU is to be *divided*. Again, this is a lot of work to identify a relatively small adjustment.

Now for the CUs for the two different luminaires.

Luminaire No. 4:

$r_w = 0.47$, $\rho_{cc} = 0.70$, RCR $= 3.75$
For RCR 3 and $\rho_w = 0.50$: CU $= 0.45$

For RCR 3 and $\rho_w = 0.30$: CU = 0.43

For RCR 3, $\rho_w = 0.47$, and

$$\text{Ratio} = \frac{0.47 - 0.30}{0.50 - 0.30} = 0.85 : \text{CU} = 0.43 + (0.85 \times 0.02) = 0.447,$$

$\text{orCU} = 0.45(3/20 \times 0.02) = 0.447$

For RCR 4 and $\rho_w = 0.50$: CU = 0.43

For RCR 4 and $\rho_w = 0.30$: CU = 0.41

For RCR 4, $\rho_w = 0.47$, and

$$\text{Ratio} = \frac{0.47 - 0.30}{0.50 - 0.30} = 0.85 : \text{CU} = 0.41 + (0.85 \times 0.02) = 0.427$$

For RCR 3.75, $\rho_w = 0.47$, and

$$\text{Ratio} = \frac{3.75 - 3.0}{4.0 - 3.0} = 0.75 : \text{CU} = 0.447 + [(0.427 - 0.447) \times 0.75] = 0.432$$

Corrected CU:

$$\frac{0.432}{1.0163} = 0.425$$

Luminaire No. 6:

$r_w = 0.47$, $\rho_{cc} = 0.70$, RCR = 3.75

For RCR 3 and $\rho_w = 0.50$: CU = 0.68

For RCR 3 and $\rho_w = 0.30$: CU = 0.64

For RCR 3, $\rho_w = 0.47$, and Ratio = 0.85 : CU = $0.68 - (3/20 \times 0.04) = 0.674$

For RCR 4 and $\rho_w = 0.50$: CU = 0.62

For RCR 4 and $\rho_w = 0.30$: CU = 0.57

For RCR 4, $\rho_w = 0.47$, and Ratio = 0.85 : CU = $0.62 - (3/20 \times 0.05) = 0.613$

For RCR 3.75, $\rho_w = 0.47$, and Ratio = 0.75 : CU = $0.674 + [(0.613 - 0.674) \times 0.75] = 0.628$

Corrected CU:

$$\frac{0.628}{1.0163} = 0.618$$

Next, determine the number of fixtures required for the two luminaires.

5. **Luminaire No. 4:**

$$\text{Correct CU} = 0.425$$

1 – 150-watt, A-21 incandescent lamp – 2880 lumens per lamp

$$\text{No. of Luminaires} = \frac{50 \text{ fc} \times (15' - 0'' \times 30' - 0'')}{0.425 \times 2880 \text{ lm} \times 0.60 \text{ LLF}} = 30.64$$

This is a lot of fixtures for the space and would require them to be placed on $4'-0''$ centers (actually, at $3'-10\frac{1}{2}''$). With a maximum spacing to mounting height (S/MH) of 0.7 and a mounting height of $7'-6''$ above the work plane, the spacing of Luminaire No. 7 should be $5'-3''$, so perhaps we should increase the lumens per luminaire by changing from the 150-watt lamp to a lamp with 3809 lumens, based on comparing the ratio of $3'-10\frac{1}{2}'' : 5'-3''$. The closest choice provided by the text would be a 200-watt, A-23 lamp with 4000 lumens.

$$\text{No. of Luminaires} = \frac{50 \text{ fc} \times (15' - 0'' \times 30' - 0'')}{0.425 \times 4000 \text{ lm} \times 0.60 \text{ LLF}} = 22.06$$

So, in order to achieve the desired spacing and lighting level, perhaps we should assume 24 luminaires placed in three rows of 8 fixtures each. This should result in about a 10% increase in lighting since light is additive.

6. Luminaire No. 6:

$$\text{Correct CU} = 0.618$$

1 – 175-watt BT-28 Phosphor-Coated Metal Halide Lamp – 14,500 Lumens per Lamp

$$\text{No. of Luminaires} = \frac{50 \text{ fc} \times (15' - 0'' \times 30' - 0'')}{0.618 \times 14{,}500 \text{ lm} \times 0.60 \text{ LLF}} = 4.19$$

The maximum S/MH is indicated as 1.5 for Luminaire No. 18. This suggests that a fixture must be provided for each 11'–3" × 11'–3" area or each 126.6 square feet. Since the room is 15'–0" × 30'–0" and has an area of 450 square feet, this spacing indicates the need for 3.6 or, more properly, 4 fixtures; that essentially is the number calculated. The placement, however, will be a little off since the space is not square. For best placement within the space, perhaps six or eight fixtures might be used, located in relation to the geometry of the space, but this would require reduced lumens per fixture.

The 175-watt BT-28 is the smallest metal halide lamp for which we have data. If we use six fixtures, each fixture would need to generate 10,125 lumens.

$$\frac{4.19 \times 14.500 \text{ lm}}{6 \text{ flxtures}} = 10{,}125 \text{ lm}$$

Based on 10,125 lumens per lamp, we might choose to use a mercury vapor lamp, but it would require a 250-watt lamp to generate the required lumens. As a result, we would need 1500 watts of mercury vapor lighting in comparison with only 700 watts of metal halide lighting. So, let's assume that we can manage with four fixtures, each with a 175-watt metal halide lamp.

7.   Based on the above answers, we can calculate the average luminous exitance for the walls and ceiling for each condition. Since this procedure indicates only approximate brightness, the calculations need not be too specific. Therefore, we will not attempt to interpolate for the reflectance values and will assume that $\rho_w = 0.50$, $\rho_{cc} = 0.70$, and $\rho_{fc} = 0.20$. We will, however, use an RCR of 3.75 and interpolate between the RCR values of 3.0 and 4.0.

Luminaire No. 4:

$$\text{EC for Wall} = 0.058$$

$$\text{Wall Luminous Exitance} = \frac{24 \times 4000 \text{ lm/lamp} \times 0.058}{450 \text{ sq ft}} = 12.4 \text{ fl}$$

$$\text{EC for Ceiling} = 0.049$$

$$\text{Ceiling Luminous Exitance} = \frac{24 \times 4000 \text{ lm/lamp} \times 0.049}{450 \text{ sq ft}} = 10.5 \text{ fl}$$

Luminaire No. 6:

$$\text{EC for Wall} = 0.168$$

$$\text{Wall Luminous Exitance} = \frac{4 \times 14{,}500 \text{ lm/lamp} \times 0.168}{450 \text{ sq ft}} = 21.7 \text{ fl}$$

$$\text{EC for Ceiling} = 0.106$$

$$\text{Ceiling Luminous Exitance} = \frac{4 \times 14{,}500 \text{ lm/lamp} \times 0.106}{450 \text{ sq ft}} = 13.7 \text{ fl}$$

BIBLIOGRAPHY

Aronin, J.E. *Climate and Architecture*. Reinhold Publishing Corporation, New York, 1953.

Bennett, R. *Sun Angles for Design*. Robert Bennett, Bala Cynwyd, PA, 1978.

Brown, G.Z. *Sun, Wind, and Light: Architectural Design Strategies*. John Wiley & Sons, Hoboken, New Jersey, 1985.

Egan, M.D. *Concepts in Architectural Lighting*. McGraw-Hill Publishing Company, New York, 1983.

Egan, M.D., and V. Olgyay. *Architectural Lighting*. McGraw-Hill Companies, New York, 2002.

Evans, B.H. *Daylight in Architecture*. McGraw-Hill Publishing Company, New York, 1981.

Gordon, G., and K.L. Nuckolls. *Interior Lighting for Designers*. John Wiley & Sons, Hoboken, New Jersey, 1995.

Grondzik, W. T., Kwok, A. G., Stein, B., and Reynolds, J. S. *Mechanical and Electrical Equipment for Buildings*. John Wiley & Sons, Hoboken, New Jersey, 2010.

Lam, W.M.C. *Perception and Lighting as Formgivers for Architecture*. McGraw-Hill Book Company, New York, 1977.

Lam, W.M.C. *Sunlighting as Formgiver for Architecture*. Van Nostrand Reinhold Company, Inc., New York, 1986.

Lechner, N., *Heating, Cooling, Lighting: Design Methods for Architects*, John Wiley & Sons, Hoboken, New Jersey, 2001.

Moore, F. *Concepts and Practice of Architectural Daylighting*. Van Nostrand Reinhold Company, Inc., New York, 1985.

Moore, F. *Environmental Control Systems: Heating Cooling Lighting*. McGraw-Hill, Inc., New York, 1993.

Steffy, G. *Architectural Lighting Design*. John Wiley & Sons, Hoboken, New Jersey, 2002.

4 DAYLIGHTING

INTRODUCTION

DESIGN INTENTIONS FOR DAYLIGHTING

DAYLIGHT CALCULATIONS

DAYLIGHTING DIAGRAMS

INTRODUCTION

When all buildings were designed around a single, fixed light source— the sun— the difference between great architecture and mere building could be measured to a large degree by the skill with which that source was used. The shapes and sizes of rooms, and the materials and details in them, were determined largely by the appearance the room would take on when rendered by daylight. Light was not always simply applied to structural innovations; more often, the structures themselves were developed to make possible desired lighting and spatial effects.[1]

Even with its extraordinary size, the sun is essentially a point source of light, especially in term of the solar system. Even though solar radiation continually spreads outward, from our perspective 93 million miles away, the radiation the Earth receives from the sun is comprised of essentially parallel rays. Of course, at this tremendous distance, these solar rays constitute an extremely small portion of the total energy that the sun emits. Spreading out from the sun, the intensity of the solar radiation reaching the Earth

is reduced by a factor of about 10^{16}, but this is still great enough so that the Earth receives each hour more solar energy than the whole world consumes every year!

While solar radiation is reasonably constant, as a result of the continual movement of the Earth and its particular tilt with respect to the sun, the incident solar radiation striking the Earth's surface is not constant. For one thing, due to our daily rotation, the sun continually comes and goes. Since there are 360° in a circle and 24 hours in a day, the Earth rotates at a rate of 15° every hour. For another, since the Earth is tilted with respect to the sun, as the Earth follows its yearly path around the sun, it tilts toward and then away from the sun. Actually, in terms of the Earth as a spherical body, the total solar radiation does not change significantly, except that the adjustment from the Earth's path around the sun is not symmetrical. The Earth is actually about 7% closer to the sun during the month of January than during the month of July. But while the Earth as a total body tends to be exposed to comparable radiation throughout the year, the tilt of the Earth means that the incident solar radiation in the Northern Hemisphere is different from that in the Southern Hemisphere, except at the solar *equinox*. Regardless of the hemisphere, we refer to the time when the tilt results in more intense solar radiation as *summer* and when the tilt results in less intense radiation as *winter*.

The tilt of the Earth, which is referred to as its *angle of declination*, extends from minus 23.5° to plus 23.5° (see Table 4.1). At the time of the equinox, around the 20th

---

[1]William M.C. Lam, *Perception and Lighting as Formgivers for Architecture* (McGraw-Hill Book Company, New York, 1977), p. 10.

Table 4.1: ANGLES OF DECLINATION

Season	Angle
Fall Equinox	0°
Winter Solstice	−23.5°
Spring Equinox	0°
Summer Solstice	+23.5°

of March and the 20th of September, the beginning of spring and fall, respectively, there is essentially no tilt, and the plane of the equator is parallel to the incident solar radiation. At the winter solstice, around the 20th of December, the tilt is 23.5° away from the sun, and at the summer solstice, around the 20th of June, the tilt is 23.5° toward the sun. Of course, this is related to location, and while the Northern Hemisphere is in winter, the Southern Hemisphere is in summer.

Incident solar radiation is frequently referred to as *insolation* (i.e., in-sol-ation). The intensity of the insolation is usually determined by the latitude of the site, the season of the year (angle of declination), the depth of atmosphere through which the radiation must travel, the orientation and slope of the ground surface, and the weather conditions (e.g., cloud cover). The various solar angles include the angle of declination, the angle of incidence, the azimuth angle, the altitude, and the profile angle.

Solar Angles

The position of the sun is defined by various angles (see Figure 4.1). These angles typically establish the position of a solar ray relative to a particular point on Earth. The *angle of incidence* is the angle that the solar ray makes with a line normal to the surface under consideration. The *azimuth angle* is the angle used to indicate the bearing of the sun

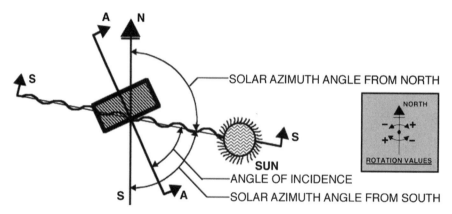

PLAN DRAWING WITH SUN PROJECTED ON HORIZONTAL PLANE

ANGLE OF INCIDENCE: THE ANGLE BETWEEN A SOLAR RAY AND THE NORMAL TO THE ARCHITECTURAL SURFACE MEASURED ON THE PLANE DEFINED BY THE NORMAL AND THAT INTERSECTING SOLAR RAY

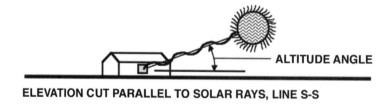

ELEVATION CUT PARALLEL TO SOLAR RAYS, LINE S-S

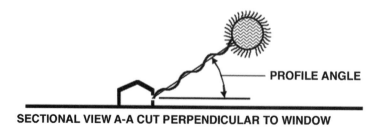

Figure 4.1 SOLAR ANGLES   **SECTIONAL VIEW A-A CUT PERPENDICULAR TO WINDOW**

relative to the north-south axis. Sometimes the bearing is taken from the north, but for our purposes it is usually taken from the south. The *altitude angle* indicates the elevation of the solar ray above the horizontal Earth plane. Again, this angle can be taken in various ways. If the viewing section is cut on the solar ray, it is the true altitude. If it is taken from a section cut on the north-south axis, it is the altitude with respect to that axis. And if it is taken from another section—for example, from a section cut through an architectural exposure—it is called the *profile angle*. The profile angle is an indication of the altitude, but as seen in terms of a sectional cut that is usually based on a building orientation rather than the sun or the north-south axis. As a result, the profile angle is higher than the altitude angle, which is taken on the vertical plane defined by the solar ray and a line normal to the surface of the Earth at the location being studied.

The *angle of declination* is the angle of the tilt of the Earth's axis with respect to an assumed horizontal plane, one within which the Earth tends to move as it circles around the sun. Based on this and the geometry of the Earth's spherical shape, the 12 noon altitude angle is equal to 90° minus the latitude angle of the location plus the angle of declination.

12 Noon Altitude Angle
= [(90° − Latitude Angle) + Angle of Declination]

The amount of radiation that is actually available at any location depends on a number of factors, the most important of which is the angle of incidence. The more normal the solar radiation is to a surface, the greater its intensity. This is true whether the surface is the ground or an exposure of a building.

Although the tilt of the Earth relative to the sun changes continually throughout the year as the Earth moves in its orbit around the sun, the 12 noon solar radiation at the solar equinox is normal to the Earth's surface at the equator.[2] As the earth circles around the sun, the relative tilt of the earth with respect to the sun changes, and the latitude at which the 12 noon radiation is normal also changes. Since the tilt of the earth, or angle of declination as it is formally referred to, changes by $23\frac{1}{2}°$ from the equinox to the solstice, the annual angular adjustment is 47°. On December 21, the winter solstice for the Northern Hemisphere, the solar radiation at 12 noon is normal to the Earth's surface at south latitude of $23\frac{1}{2}°$. On June 21, the summer solstice for the Northern Hemisphere, it is normal to the Earth's surface at north latitude of $23\frac{1}{2}°$. That is, the seasonal shift in the tilt of the Earth or change in the

angle of declination is $23\frac{1}{2}°$, so that at the *winter solstice*, regardless of the hemisphere, there is a $23\frac{1}{2}°$ shift *away* from the sun, and at the *summer solstice* there is a $23\frac{1}{2}°$ shift *toward* the sun. At the spring and fall equinox, the angle of declination is 0°.

As diagrammed in Figure 4.2, the solar angles for a particular location are also determined, in part, by the latitude of that location. At 40° north latitude, which is basically at the center of the continental United States, the 12 noon solar altitude on December 21 is $26\frac{1}{2}°$ above the horizon, and the 12 noon solar altitude on June 21 is $73\frac{1}{2}°$. On the solar equinox, the 12 noon altitude at 40° north latitude is 50°. The 12 noon altitude for any day and any latitude can be found by the following formula:

12 Noon Altitude Angle
= [90° − Latitude Angle] + Angle of Declination

where the angle of declination is positive (+) for the summer season and negative (−) for the winter season.

As can also be seen in Figure 4.2, the depth of atmosphere through which solar radiation must pass before hitting the Earth's surface depends on the latitude. At the equinox, the farther away you are from the equator, the longer the path through the atmosphere. As the axis of the Earth tilts with respect to the sun, the length of travel through the atmosphere at each latitude also changes such that, in addition to hitting the Earth at a more oblique angle during the winter, the sun must also pass through an increased depth of atmosphere before hitting the Earth's surface, further reducing the intensity of the received solar radiation.

In terms of solar gain on the ground, the latitude of the site is the primary controlling element, but the slope of the ground itself can also have a significant effect on solar intensity. As a result, in a valley running east-west, the microclimate on the north side of the valley will be quite different from that on the south. Since these distinctions in climate, like those at different latitudes, are based on the angle at which the solar radiation impinges on the ground, we should understand that when physical structures are added to the landscape, access to the sun is also altered considerably.

For one thing, structures establish shadows, and based on the orientation and configuration of the structure, some areas adjacent to a building might be in permanent shadow. As can be seen in Figure 4.3, the same form with different orientations can produce quite different results. While a cruciform structure implies four equal building wings, in terms of solar access there is a great deal of difference between each wing and each exposure of each wing. As indicated in the shadow diagram, there are areas on the ground adjacent to the "rotated" structure that will always

---

[2]The plane of the equator cutting through the Earth is parallel to the plane of the Earth's horizontal movement around the sun at the time of the solar equinox.

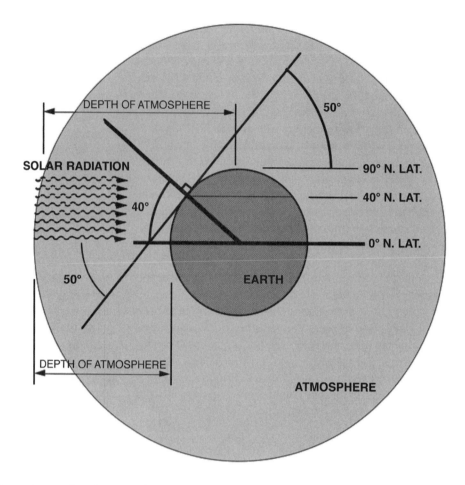

Figure 4.2 LATITUDE AND SOLAR ANGLES

be in shadow, even early in the morning or late in the afternoon in the summer, when the range of solar movement is greatest. There are also portions of the building's façade that will never receive any direct sun, which will obviously diminish the quality of the interior space and the potential for direct solar gain.

When solar radiation strikes a surface, its intensity is proportional to the cosine of the angle of incidence. Based on this, as shown in Table 4.2, the relative intensity of the available solar radiation is quite different on a south-facing vertical surface than on the ground, and this basically changes the seasonal conditions. That is, relative to a south-facing vertical surface in the Northern Hemisphere, the peak of "summer" occurs in December and January.

With 360° in a circle and 24 hours per day, the hourly rotational movement of the Earth on its axis is 15°, although the hourly movement of the sun across the sky is not 15°. With the complexity of geometry and the changing angle of declination, the apparent hourly angular movement of the sun varies. As shown in Figure 4.4, which is a sun chart from the original Libbey-Owens-Ford (LOF) Sun Angle Calculator, at 40° north latitude on the summer solstice, the range of the solar azimuth angle from sunrise to sunset is from around 120° east of south to 120° west of south, or a total movement of 240° over about 14.5 hours.

This correlates with an hourly angular movement of over 16.5°. On the winter solstice, the azimuth range is only 120°, which is basically half the range on the summer solstice, in just over 9 hours. This relates to an hourly angular movement of only 13.33°. On the equinox,[3] when the axis of the Earth is "vertical," the hourly angular movement of the sun is 15°.

There are several ways that we can determine the various solar angles. Some of them are based on horizontal projection of the sun's path, while others use a vertical projection. The Sun Angle Calculator, which uses a horizontal projection, was developed in 1951 by LOF. It is an effective hands-on tool that provides critical information about solar angles. It is still available through the Society of Building Science Educators (SBSE) under the authority of Pilkington North America, Inc., which acquired LOF in 1986. As a physical device, which in many ways is a positive attribute, the calculator is limited to particular locations: eight north latitudes including 24°, 28°, 32°, 36°, 40°, 44°, 48°, and 52°. Horizontal plots for other locations are available from the University of Oregon Solar Radiation

---

[3]The autumnal equinox generally occurs on September 23 and the vernal on March 20. On this day, which some erroneously claim is the only time of the year when an egg will stand upright, there are 12 hours of sunlight and 12 hours of night; night (*nox*) is equal to day.

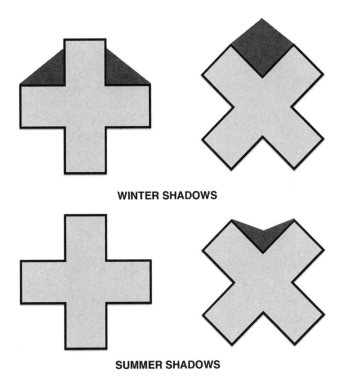

WINTER SHADOWS

SUMMER SHADOWS

Figure 4.3 PERMANENT SEASONAL SHADOWS
Based on its configuration and orientation, a structure can establish ground areas and portions of the building façade that will be in permanent shadow throughout a season, typically the winter or even always. Interestingly, permanent shadows often occur in buildings that are designed symmetrically, which, of course, raises a conundrum: symmetry of form can cause major imbalance in access to daylighting,

Monitoring Laboratory. These plots are for a particular location, based on latitude and longitude or zip code for U.S. locations. The Solar Radiation Monitoring Laboratory can also provide vertical plots on the same basis. There are also many publications, including *Architectural Graphic Standards,* that include solar data, and there are various spreadsheets that can determine the various solar angles based on input of location, surface orientation, and solar time. In addition, most CAD programs have the capacity to represent the solar angles for a particular location and time. So, in various ways, whether by means of a physical device, a graphical representation, numerical listings, and/or CAD, information on solar angles is readily available.

Table 4.2: RELATIVE INTENSITY OF AVAILABLE SOLAR RADIATION—40° N LAT.

Solar Altitude Surface		On Horizontal Surface		On South-Facing Vertical	
Summer	$73\frac{1}{2}°$	$\cos 16\frac{1}{2}°$	0.96	$\cos 73\frac{1}{2}°$	0.28
Equinox	50°	$\cos 40°$	0.77	$\cos 50°$	0.64
Winter	$26\frac{1}{2}°$	$\cos 63\frac{1}{2}°$	0.45	$\cos 26\frac{1}{2}°$	0.90

A further review of the LOF Sun Angle Calculator for 40° north latitude provides some other rather interesting and important information regarding the apparent movement of the sun (see Figure 4.5). The critical hours of solar access for a south-facing surface are the 4 hours between 10 A.M. and 2 P.M. solar time. Over these 4 hours, the movement of the sun on the summer solstice is from about 65° east of south at 10 A.M. to about 65° west of south at 2 P.M. So, the summer angular movement of the sun from 10 A.M. until 2 P.M. is 131°. On the winter solstice, the angular movement of the sun for the same 4-hour period is from about 29° east of south at 10 A.M. to about 29° west of south at 2 P.M., for an angle spread of only 58°. For the equinox, angular spread is approximately 80° for the same 4 hours.

Based on this difference in solar angular movement, we should realize that vertical shading on the south makes a great deal of sense if that shading obscures direct solar penetration from azimuth angles that are greater than 30° from north-south while not interrupting solar penetration within the 60° range centered on north-south. With this approach, all 4 hours of solar gain should be accessible during the colder period of the year when such gain is desirable, and only about 1 hour of solar gain between 10 A.M. and 2 P.M. will be unshaded during the same 4 hours in the overheated period of the year, which, of course, is when solar gain is not effective in terms of thermal comfort. In addition, with effectively designed horizontal shading, all direct solar gain on the south orientation should be eliminated during the overheated period of the year.

DESIGN INTENTIONS FOR DAYLIGHTING

Recognizing that the sun is continually moving with respect to any site on Earth, resulting in various qualities of available light, it seems logical that we should design for these changing conditions. As designers, we should consider the quality of light that might be appropriate for a particular activity and also when this light might be necessary. It is not uncommon for different spaces to be used for different activities and at different times of the day. Based on this fact, a simple analysis can produce an effective planning guide that would indicate the appropriate orientation for various spaces. This can be presented in a simple format, as shown in Table 4.3 and originally proposed by Jeffery Ellis Aronin in his book *Climate and Architecture* (1953).

While the orientations for the spaces presented in Table 4.3 might not be appropriate for all residences, the identification of preferred orientation is something that should

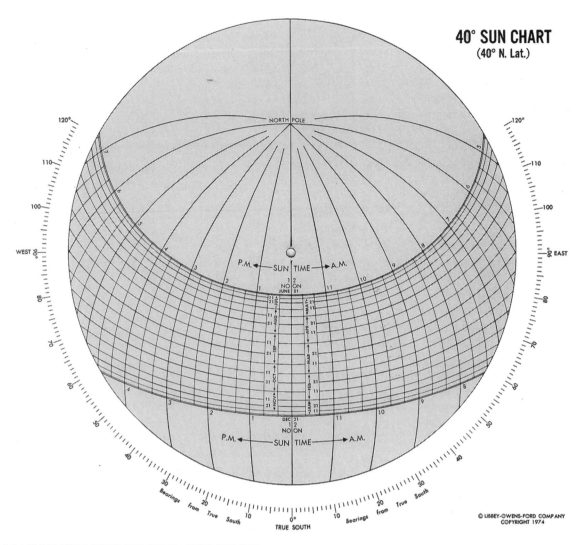

Figure 4.4 LOF SUN ANGLE CALCULATOR FOR 40° NORTH LATITIUDE
This is one of eight solar plots included in the LOF Sun Angle Calculator. The calculator includes sun charts for 24°, 28°, 32°, 36°, 40°, 44°, 48°, and 52° north latitude. Similar plots are available from the University of Oregon Solar Radiation Monitoring Laboratory. Used by permission from Pilkington North America, Inc.

be explored in the design process. The assumption is that daylighting is desired when a space is being used, and since there are times during the day when primary use of a space is likely to occur, the orientation of that space should be responsive to this condition. For example, even though a child's bedroom will be used at various hours throughout the day, exposure to the early morning sun, or perhaps sunrise, can be a helpful motivator in terms of waking up. The critical issue might not be which orientation is best, but the fact that this is considered in our designs.

Since daylighting clearly has an impact on the spatial qualities of any room, it is a wonder that in multifamily housing with repetitive unit designs, these units are often arranged without any consideration for solar orientation. The plan and window placement remain consistent regardless of exposure, although the daylighting and, therefore, the nature and quality of the space change significantly.

When the probable difference in the view is also considered, the consistency of design is even more confounding!

Clearly, we should design with consideration for daylighting, including a distinction between the diffuse light that comes from the sky, which we call *skylight*, and direct sunlight. Furthermore, we should recognize that skylight occurs during overcast days as well as clear days, although sunlight is limited to clear days and is dependent on orientation. With an overcast sky, exterior horizontal illumination can range from around 500 to 2000 foot-candles. With a clear sky, the illumination provided by the sky is often not this high, but with the additive element of the direct sun, exterior horizontal illumination can range from 6000 to 10,000 foot-candles in open, exposed locations.

On overcast days, daylighting tends to produce a more even level of interior lighting, whereas with the movement of the sun and the relatively dark portions of the sky dome,

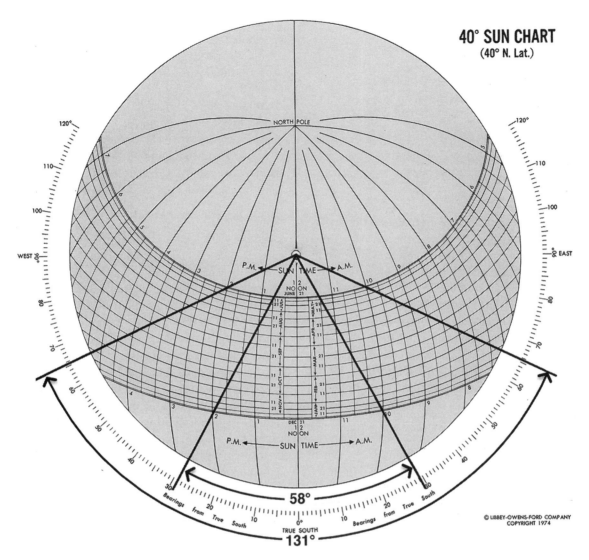

40° SUN CHART
(40° N. Lat.)

© LIBBEY-OWENS-FORD COMPANY
COPYRIGHT 1974

Figure 4.5 LOF SUN ANGLE CALCULATOR FOR 40° NORTH LATITUDE WITH OVERLAY
The sun chart includes the angular movement for the winter and summer solstices. Base chart used by permission from Pilkington North America, Inc.

Table 4.3: PREFERRED SPATIAL ORIENTATION BASED IN ACTIVITY

Space	N	NE	E	SE	S	SW	W	NW
Living Room					•			
Dining Room						•	•	•
Den			•	•	•			
Kitchen	•	•	•	•	•	•	•	•
Breakfast Room			•					
Child's Bedroom		•	•					
Master Bedroom		•	•	•	•	•	•	

This chart, which is based on a proposal by Jeffery Ellis Aronin, includes assumptions that might or might not be appropriate for a particular residential design. For example, the orientation for the dining room is shown as being toward the west, but if the major use of that space were for mid-day meals rather than evening meals, the preferred orientation might be the south.

clear days can result in changing interior lighting conditions, which can be quite dramatic, although for some activities rather problematic.

In dealing with interior illumination, especially that which is developed from daylight, it is generally appropriate to consider relative levels of illumination rather than absolute levels. Human visual perception is very adaptable, and when a visual task is performed, the context establishes a base from which expectations are derived. If one were aware that the exterior lighting was rather diminished, as might occur on an overcast day, then the expected interior lighting level would be diminished compared to what would be expected on a bright, clear day. Based on this fact and compounded by the variability of available daylight, in referring to daylight illumination it is preferable to use daylight factors rather than foot-candles

Table 4.4: RECOMMENDED MINIMUM DAYLIGHT FACTORS

Activity	DF
ART STUDIO, GALLERIES	4 – 6
FACTORIES, LABORATORIES	3 – 5
OFFICES, CLASSROOMS	2
LOBBIES, LOUNGES	1
CORRIDORS, BEDROOMS	0.5

of illumination. The daylight factor (DF) is a decimal proportion of the exterior horizontal illumination that will be available at an interior location. Sometimes the DF is noted as a decimal (0.02) and sometimes merely as a whole integer (2), but in either case, it refers to a particular ratio between interior and exterior illumination. While average illumination levels from overcast skies are available from various sources, recommended minimal daylight factors for various activities are listed in Table 4.4.

On first consideration, a DF of 2, which means only 2% of the exterior illumination, might seem rather low. But even on an extremely overcast day that would have an exterior illumination of only 500 foot-candles, this would result in an interior illumination level of 10 foot-candles, which is adequate for a number of noncritical visual tasks. Since the recommendations are for minimum DFs, which generally means at a location somewhat removed from the lighting source, the window, the average DF for a space will usually be quite a bit higher than the recommended minimum. Unlike the assumption with the design of elec-

tric lighting systems, which is that the lighting is evenly distributed across the space, daylighting is not generally evenly distributed, which is often considered one of the attributes of this means of illumination. When more balanced daylight distribution is desired, there are various techniques that can help achieve this result.

As suggested by Figure 4.6, a window will typically provide an adequate level of illumination for a room depth of up to two to two and one-half times the height of the window head above the floor. As indicated in Figure 4.7, it is the height of the head of the window rather than the height of the window that extablishes the depth of illumination. The assumption is also that the window is reasonably distributed across the width of the room, which can be accomplished by configuring the window in a strip extending across the room's width or by providing a series of separate window openings distributed across the room. Furthermore, the area of the window opening should be at least 8% to 10% of the floor area of the space. In fact, most building codes require all habitable spaces to have this amount of glazed opening. While a larger amount of open area may prove to be beneficial, the recommended maximum amount of glazed opening is around 20% to 25% of the floor area. Above this, the levels of lighting tend to be excessive, to say nothing of the potential for excessive heat gain and heat loss. Actually, the 25% of the floor area in glazed opening facing south is the ballpark recommendation for solar exposure in space that is to be heated by the sun.

As the distance from a side window increases, the illumination levels drop, as can be seen in Figure 4.8. When

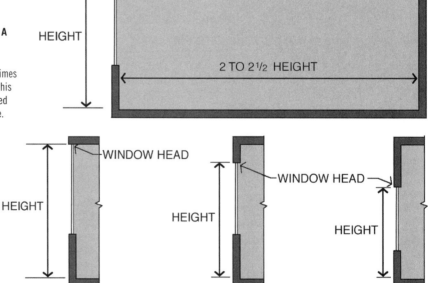

Figure 4.6 DEPTH OF DAYLIGHT AVAILABLE FROM A WINDOW
The illumination available from a window is generally sufficient for a depth of up to two to two and one-half times the height of the window head above the floor. Beyond this depth, the reduction in lighting levels and the associated variation in lighting intensity are typically not adequate.

Figure 4.7 HEIGHT OF THE WINDOW HEAD
In determining the depth to which daylight illumination will be effective, the height of the window head is based on the distance between the top of the window and the floor and is independent of the actual height of the window.

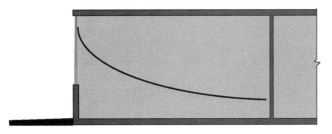

Figure 4.8 REDUCING LEVELS OF DAYLIGHT ILLUMINATION
The illumination levels from single-sided exposure to daylight continually drop as the distance from the window increases.

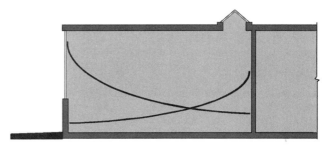

Figure 4.10 ALTERNATIVE ACCESS TO BILATERAL DAYLIGHT—SKYLIGHT
Bilateral lighting can be provided through skylights when the space is at the top level of a building.

bilateral lighting is possible, a more even distribution of light across the space is possible. While bilateral lighting is most easily provided with double exposure, which requires a rather narrow building configuration comprised of only one room, when the space is not below another level or when there is a possibility of including light wells, bilateral lighting might still be feasible.

The variations in illumination levels that daylighting typically provides, such as happen as the conditions of sunlight change and at different locations within a space with respect to the daylight opening that provides daylight access to the space, are often appreciated. Sometimes, however, particularly when task lighting is the objective, a more balanced distribution of light might be desired. There are several ways that this can be achieved. When a space has exposure on opposite sides, bilateral lighting will tend to balance the lighting levels (see Figure 4.9).

If a space does not have double exposure, it is still possible to gain bilateral access to daylight. If the space is at the top floor, then we can install skylights at the interior side. In this way, the illumination from the skylight would be located primarily at the portion of the space that has less illumination from the windows. Clerestory windows can also work if the adjacent portions of the building are lower than the height of the space. While this is relatively easy when the space is at the top floor, as shown in Figure 4.10, there are other options when this is not the case, such as suggested in Figure 4.11.

Unfortunately, sometimes designers include skylights along the perimeter of a building, even above windows, which makes no sense, at least in terms of enhancing the quality of lighting. Although light is additive, it is perceived in terms of logarithmic progression. If skylights are added above windows, while they might be objects of visual interest, they will not be an effective means of increasing lighting levels. However, as seen in Figure 4.12, if skylights are added to a space that has windows that provide daylight illumination, they should be located internal to the space. Not only will this tend to balance the overall distribution of the light, it will also make the light contributed by the skylights more significant. When it comes from a location where windows are not obvious, the light will draw attention to the source.

An important aspect of visual perception is that in normal conditions the major plane of sight is horizontal. While as designers we often see things because we are looking for them, and with our focus on the physical components of the design we might be enamored of their significance, laypersons typically are not as spatially inquisitive. Often they totally fail to observe particular components of a design composition. It is generally the spatial experience, rather than any specific compositional elements, that tends to move them. While designers might appreciate the compositional aspects of a row of skylights located over a line of

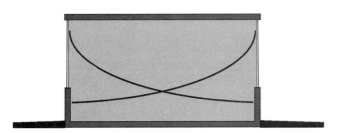

Figure 4.9 MORE EVEN LEVELS OF BILATERAL DAYLIGHT ILLUMINATION
With bilateral lighting, the overall lighting levels tend to be more balanced than lighting provided from a single exposure.

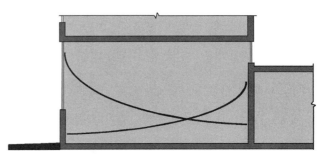

Figure 4.11 ALTERNATIVE ACCESS TO BILATERAL DAYLIGHT—CLERESTORY
Bilateral lighting can be provided through clerestory windows installed above adjacent lower-height extended portions of the same structure.

Figure 4.12 ALTERNATIVE SKYLIGHT PLACEMENTS

Placing skylights directly above windows does not make sense in terms of enhancing the quality or distribution of the daylighting. Skylights should be added to provide daylight at locations where windows are feasible, as a potential means to balance the light distribution within a space, and/or as a design element both in terms of the light they provide and as a component of the visual composition.

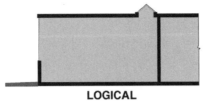

LOGICAL

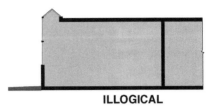

ILLOGICAL

windows, the skylights will not contribute significantly to the quality of lighting, will probably be a negative factor in terms of thermal performance, and might not even be seen by most people.

While skylights can provide access to light from above, the horizontal exposure receives maximum solar intensity during the summer and only limited solar intensity during the winter. However, if, rather than a skylight, overhead access to light is provided by a roof monitor, exposure can be to the south, which will have maximum solar intensity during the winter and reduced solar intensity during the summer, the reverse of the situation with the skylight. In addition to the benefits provided by southern exposure, a vertical clerestory window in the roof monitor allows for effective solar shading that can further maximize the solar potential (see Figures 4.13 to 4.15).

A roof monitor can provide greater benefits than a horizontal skylight since it can be oriented to maximize solar radiation, but that alone is not sufficient in terms of control. Although the solar radiation that is admitted is generally adjusted to somewhat match the seasonal demands, direct sun can still pass through a clerestory window and can cause problems. Often the intention is to raise the opening within the monitor so that direct solar radiation cannot

enter the occupied space until it has been reflected off of the monitor walls. The walls of the monitor can also be angled to increase the spread of the diffuse reflections.

Internal elements can also be added to the monitor to minimize the penetration of direct rays into the occupied space. Grids can be added at the bottom of the monitor, which essentially works as a number of reflective panels. However, it is also possible to create a grid of translucent material that can both reflect and transmit diffuse light.

Although internal devices can provide effective light control, in general external solar shading is preferable, particularly for minimizing solar heat gain. While the assumption is that external solar control will intercept the radiation, it can actually increase the amount of radiation that can enter a light opening and do so in a way that will be responsive to seasonal variations—increasing radiation during the underheated period of the year but decreasing it during the overheated period. As shown in Figure 4.16, a reflective surface sloping downward in front of a roof monitor can reflect the low-angle winter sun into the window opening while reflecting the high-angle summer sun away from the window while also reducing the solar heat gain on the roof.

Figure 4.13 SKYLIGHT AND ROOF MONITOR

In general, light from above can be provided through skylights, for which the glazing is basically horizontal, or through roof monitors, for which the glazing is essentially vertical with a particular orientation.

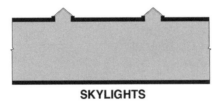

SKYLIGHTS

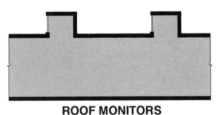

ROOF MONITORS

Figure 4.14 ROOF MONITOR INTERCEPTS DIRECT SOLAR RAYS

Through various arrangements, the solar rays can be controlled, both in terms of admission and distribution.

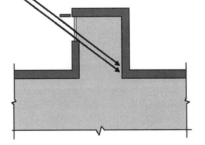

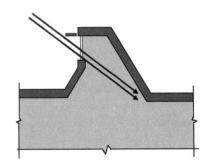

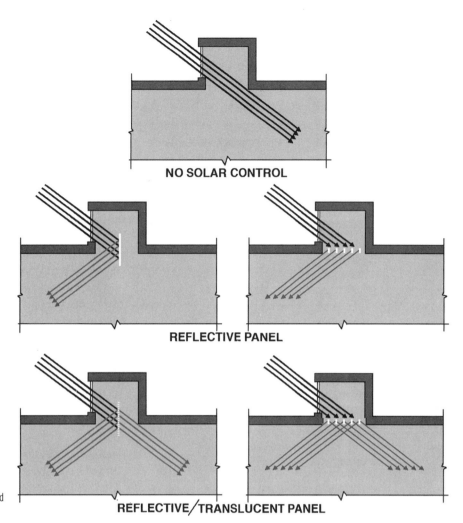

Figure 4.15 ALTERNATIVE METHODS OF CLERESTORY LIGHT CONTROL

As suggested in Fuller Moore, *Concepts and Practice of Architectural Daylighting,* Van Nostrand Reinhold Company, New York, 1985, p. 37.

NO SOLAR CONTROL

REFLECTIVE PANEL

REFLECTIVE/TRANSLUCENT PANEL

Similarly, placing a specially configured reflective shading device above a window can shade the opening when this is appropriate while also increasing the amount of sunlight that passes through the opening when this is needed. Since this shading device tends to be rather large, as shown in Figure 4.17, it can also house exterior rolling shutters.

Light shelves can also provide an effective way to shade sun at locations close to the window while projecting sunlight deeper into the space (see Figure 4.18). The direct sunlight and skylight that enter a window tend not to ex-

tend very far into the room before reflecting off of the floor, and with the low reflectance that floors generally have, this reflected light does not contribute much to the daylight illumination deep in the space. By adding a reflective surface close to the window, inside or outside of the glazing, and perhaps tilting it slightly, the sunlight can be reflected up to the ceiling and then downward deeper in the space.

While exterior ground reflection can also be effective, most ground surfaces are not very reflective, some considerably less than the 20% assumed for the floor. The major exception is, of course, after a fresh snow, when

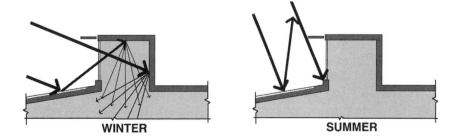

Figure 4.16 USING A REFLECTIVE SURFACE TO ENHANCE SOLAR CONTROL

WINTER

SUMMER

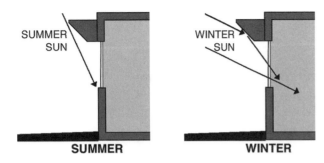

Figure 4.17 WINDOW SHADING AND ENHANCEMENT

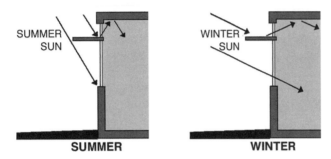

Figure 4.18 LIGHT SHELF SOLAR SHADING AND REFLECTION

the exterior reflected daylight establishes a rather unique quality of illumination within a space (see Table 4.5).

By placing shading devices outside of the space, not only can we minimize the solar gain, we can also achieve a functional yet aesthetically pleasing addition to our design palette. Effective shading devices should be responsive to the different orientations and perhaps also adjustable to seasonal variations. Rather than being fixed and unchangeable, a building can be dynamic and responsive to environmental conditions and, as a result, establish spaces that are truly enlivened and building façades that are clearly contextual.

Unfortunately, shading devices that are exposed to the elements generally require continual maintenance. The components of the shading system, especially those that might be movable and/or are lightweight, will deteriorate

over time as a result of environmental pollution and can be damaged if they are exposed to freezing temperatures. Pollution can also reduce the reflective qualities of elements such as light shelves. The accumulation of dirt, however, can be limited by effectively sloping the surfaces so that they are somewhat self-cleaning when exposed to precipitation or an intentional water spray.

Internal movable shading devices, such as venetian blinds, can also be quite effective. Typically, the blinds are made from a solid material that is opaque to light transmission, so blinds are an effective way to stop the sun. However, venetian blinds can also redirect the radiation, but to do this the blinds should be reflective. In a sense, the blinds are multiple light shelves that can be adjusted to meet various lighting demands. For example, at night, the tilt of the venetian blinds can be reversed so that they reflect the electric light back into the space.

Dark venetian blinds offer little benefit in terms of either light or thermal control. Standard glass is approximately 90% transparent, so interior blinds should not only stop unwanted solar radiation from continuing into the space, they should also reflect the shortwave radiation back through the glazing, thereby reducing the thermal gain. While there will be more gain than would occur with exterior shading, light-colored blinds will reflect a good portion of the radiation back through the glazing. However, if dark blinds are used, they will absorb the radiation, and this energy will be trapped within the enclosed space. They can also be a source of glare.

To avoid glare, or at least to minimize visual interference, the cross section of the window framing elements should be reduced, and these elements should be of light color. Before large sheets of glass were readily available, windows were often comprised of several lites separated by mullions and muntins, and even without power tools, these supporting elements were typically reduced in cross section. Unfortunately, today, windows are often set within dark frames with a 2-inch or greater width. Like dark blinds, these thick, dark elements tend to establish a visual grid that, as a result of the strong contrast with the bright images seen through them, tends to add visual noise.

Window openings that pierce an opaque wall are naturally a potential source of glare from the bright exterior view in contrast with the surrounding wall that does not receive any direct illumination. To minimize this contrast, not only should the wall be a light color, the opening might be splayed to spread the light (see Figure 4.19).

We can also reduce glare by placing windows close to the ceiling or a sidewall, surfaces that extend into the space. In this way, an adjacent surface is illuminated, reducing the contrast of the bright image seen through the opening against the surrounding surfaces.

Table 4.5: COEFFICIENTS OF REFLECTION FOR GROUND SURFACES

Surface	Coefficient of Reflectance
Water Body	0.07
Weathered Blacktop	0.10
Soil	0.15
Weathered Concrete	0.20
Grass	0.26
Fresh Snow	0.75

Figure 4.19 SPLAYED VERSUS SQUARE WINDOW OPENING

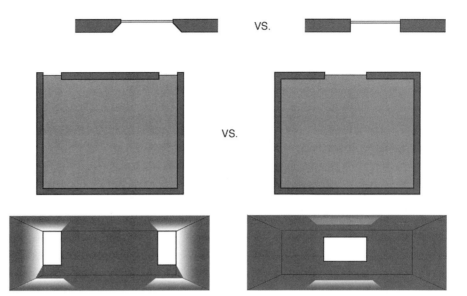

Figure 4.20 MINIMIZING GLARE BY WINDOW PLACEMENT
Locating a window opening adjacent to a reflecting surface can reduce the glare generally associated with a "puncture" window.

Interestingly, when we observe a wall that is clearly illuminated by a window, such as indicated in the lower left image in Figure 4.20, the change in sidewall brightness levels as the distance from the window increases is not really perceived. Because we recognize how the illumination is provided, the change in brightness levels is typically not perceived as unbalanced. However, when a wall is illuminated by electric lights that are concealed, perhaps located in a recess in the ceiling, comparable variations in brightness are quite obvious and generally considered problematic. That is, the way we react to a lighting condition is based in part on what we understand, which is often only at an unconscious level.

While there are various considerations of which we must be aware to develop appropriate daylighting, perhaps one of the most important is that the electric lighting should be developed as a supplement to daylighting. This can mean that the design of the electric lighting is consistent with the design intentions of the daylighting when necessary. That is, the electric light extends the design qualities of daylight when daylight is not adequate. It can also mean that when daylight is not adequate, electric lighting is used to provide illumination but in a manner that is clearly in contrast to daylighting.

Whatever the design intentions, electric lighting should be considered as a supplement to daylighting. This is at times referred to as *permanent supplementary artificial lighting of interiors* (PSALI). While the idea is correct, of course, it would be more appropriate and consistent with the intentions to revise this term to *permanent supplementary electric lighting of interiors* (PSELI).

As with most design intentions, as a project develops, we need to continually verify that the lighting intentions are being fulfilled and, if not, to adjust the design or confirm that the changes are appropriate. In terms of daylighting,

we can attempt to observe how a design will work by using hand sketches or computer modeling, but perhaps the best approach is physical modeling of the design. With a model at a scale of $1/_2'' = 1'-0''$ and using a sundial to orient the model for particular solar conditions, we can get a reasonable representation of the daylighting in conjunction with an effective way to study the overall qualities of a spatial design.

DAYLIGHT CALCULATIONS

There are a number of procedures by which we can obtain a reasonable indication of the illumination levels that will be produced by daylight, whether in terms of foot-candles or DF. However, with the dynamic changes in daylight that continually occur, it is questionable how much detail or specificity is necessary, particularly with respect to basic architectural design.

The original approach to hand calculations of daylight illumination suggested by the Illuminating Engineering Society of North America (IESNA) entailed three different lighting components: a sky component (SC), an exterior-reflected component (ERC), and an interior-reflected component (IRC). As suggested by Figure 4.21, the IRC was essentially a ground-reflected component that was reflected off of the ceiling and tended to make the smallest contribution to the lighting level on the work plane. This approach also did not include direct sunlight since it was assumed that if direct sun did penetrate into the space, it would do so only for a short time, and when it did, it would generally be a problem for task lighting and would need to be controlled.

In a sense, this approach is still used, but as the basic approach with most of the computer calculation programs that are actually ray-tracing efforts similar to the process

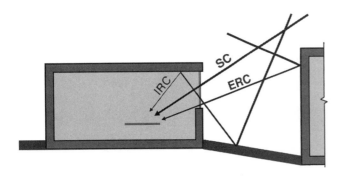

Figure 4.21 IESNA DAYLIGHT CALCULATION COMPONENTS
Interior illumination is assumed to be the result of three components: a sky component, an exterior-reflected component, and an interior-reflected component.

used for graphic rendering. Many computer programs are available to calculate daylight illumination, including Radiance, developed by Greg Ward Larson while he was at the Lawrence Berkeley National Laboratory; ECOTECT, available from Autodesk; Lumen Micro, by Lighting Technologies, Inc.; and AGi32, by Lighting Analysts, Inc.

In *Concepts and Practice of Architectural Daylighting* (1985), Fuller Moore included descriptions of a number of classic hands-on, graphical procedures to determine daylight illumination. One of the more intriguing of these procedures, which was developed by the British Research Station (BRS), is the Daylight Factor Protractor. Rather than merely determine the angular spread of a window opening based on a particular location, which is what a basic protractor would do, the BRS Daylight Factor Protractor determines the amount and angular location of skylight that will be seen. Using the BRS Protractor to determine the particular exposure angles for both the plan and sec-

tion for a location provides a reasonable indication of the DF for that location. Although not very refined and limited by the assumed exterior lighting conditions, the process is based on the critical factor that the greater the exposure to the sky, the greater will be the daylight illumination. Figure 4.22 provides a simplified diagram that suggests the procedure.

As William M.C. Lam suggested in the introduction to *Perception and Lighting as Formgivers for Architecture* (1986), the skill with which a designer uses daylight to define "the shapes and sizes of rooms, and the materials and details in them" (p. 10) is perhaps the basis of all great architecture. But even with this recognition, Lam embraced electric lighting as the preferred means of illuminating architectural space, at least until an emerging general concern for the environment increased support for reduced energy consumption.

In *Daylight in Architecture* (1981), published in the early days of energy consciousness following the 1973 OPEC oil embargo, Benjamin Evans presented some simple diagrams illustrating fundamental principles that should be followed in dealing with daylight. A number of the following diagrams (Figures 4.23 to 4.28) are derived from Evans. Some of Evans' diagrams suggested using daylight as an extension of electric lighting. While this might seem to be a peculiar reversal of the current emphasis, we should recognize that for a long time, daylighting was considered to be more of a problem than an advantage for good interior illumination. Daylight is always a variable, and the intensity of direct sunlight is often in conflict with visual performance. From our own experience, we should understand that while direct sunlight can be an object of interest within a space, it is rarely an effective means of providing task illumination.

Figure 4.22 BRS DAYLIGHT FACTOR PROTRACTOR DIAGRAM
This is a schematic of the BRS Daylight Factor Protractor approach to determining the DF. As the diagram indicates, the protractor can determine the angular exposures to the sky component (SC) for both the plan and section for a particular location. Since light is additive, if there is more than one opening, the DF would be determined for each opening and these values would then be added together to obtain the effective DF for a particular location.

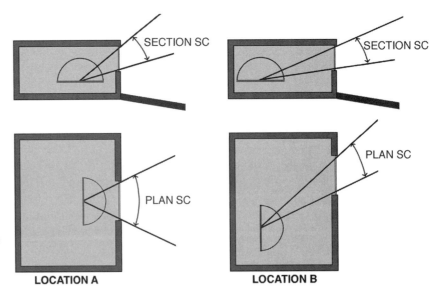

With a desire for constancy, which seems to be an attribute of high-style design, for many designers, encouraged by those who stood to benefit from increased energy consumption, electric lighting reigned supreme and daylight, although prevalent in the curtained wall towers that dominated much of the architectural landscape, was discounted. So, when Evans suggested that daylighting and electric lighting might be handled together, he tended to suggest that daylighting should supplement electric lighting. We should appreciate that Evans was endorsing the use of daylight at a time when this was not in vogue, although, of course, today we believe that electric lighting should supplement daylighting.

Daylight is a variable, but when effectively controlled through appropriate architectural design, it can provide effective illumination that can fulfill the dual purpose of architectural lighting—spatial ambiance and visual performance. While direct sunlight can enliven a space, if there are critical visual tasks to be performed, its intensity can be a problem. However, by intercepting the direct rays and bouncing them off of room surfaces and lighting control devices, the beam of light can be spread out and its intensity can be softened. Of course, a northern exposure will minimize the entry of direct sunlight and should provide balanced and consistent lighting throughout the hours of daylight. This might be appropriate for task lighting, but it is not the quality of light that is generally preferred for architectural purposes.

DAYLIGHTING DIAGRAMS

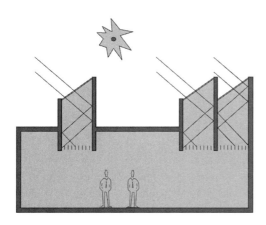

Figure 4.23 SKYLIGHT ORIENTATION AND LIGHT CONTROL
The orientation of a skylight can affect the amount of captured direct sunlight and solar thermal gain, but it has little impact on the amount of the diffuse skylight that is received. When the orientation indicates that direct sunlight will be captured, light control mechanisms must be included to minimize potential problems. This diagram is adapted, in part, from Evans, *Daylight in Architecture* (1981), Figure 4.61.

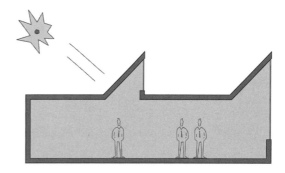

Figure 4.24 NORTHERN ORIENTATION FOR CONSISTENT LIGHTING
A northern orientation tends to provide relatively consistent daylight illumination throughout the day. Without exposure to direct sunlight, except in the early and late hours of the day during the summer months, the lighting is essentially only from the sky component and provides reasonable uniformity over the day for both illumination levels and lighting color. Based on this, a northern exposure might be preferred for artists' studios and factory environments, but it will minimize the dynamic aspects of daylight that can effectively energize a space.

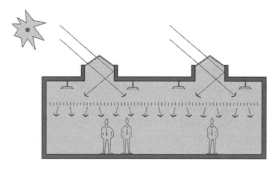

Figure 4.25 INTEGRATION OF DAYLIGHT AND ELECTRIC LIGHT
In designing electric lighting as a supplement to daylighting, it is possible to integrate the two systems such that the lighting within a space is essentially the same with either or both sources of light. This will establish relative consistency in the spatial character, which, of course, might be contrary to the intention of maximizing the dynamic potentials that daylight illumination provides. This diagram is adapted from Evans, *Daylight in Architecture* (1981), Figure 3.4.

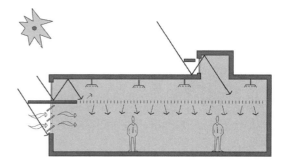

Figure 4.26 INTEGRATION OF DAYLIGHT WITH OTHER ENVIRONMENTAL ISSUES
Daylight illumination is naturally connected with other environmental issues. During the underheated period of the year, solar energy can be a beneficial direct source of heat as well as light, and during the overheated period, daylight provides the coolest source of illumination available. With daylight, almost all of the energy is connected with light, whereas with electric light sources, heat is a major by-product of the generation of light. Since daylight must come from outside, generally the opening that admits light can also be useful as a means of ventilation. This diagram is adapted from Evans, *Daylight in Architecture* (1981), Figures 3.5 and 4.6.

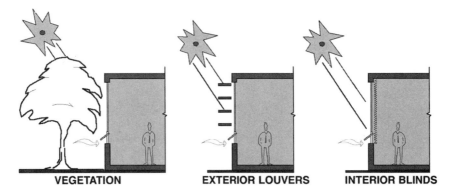

VEGETATION   **EXTERIOR LOUVERS**   **INTERIOR BLINDS**

Figure 4.27 SOLAR SHADING
While exterior shading methods tend to reduce the thermal impact of solar gain, interior shading devices are typically controlled more easily. This diagram is adapted from various diagrams in Evans, *Daylight in Architecture* (1981).

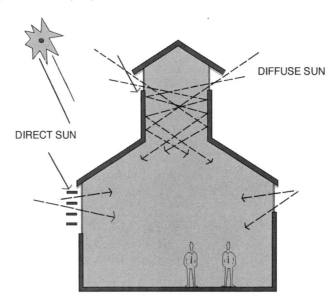

DIFFUSE SUN

DIRECT SUN

Figure 4.28 CONTROL OF DIRECT SUNLIGHT TO SOFTEN THE LIGHT
While there are situations in which the intensity of direct sunlight is desired to dynamically enliven a space, when daylight is used as the source of general illumination, it is better to diffuse it. As expressed by Benjamin Evans, we can choose to "bring daylight in high and let it down softly." This diagram is adapted from Evans, *Daylight in Architecture* (1981),

BIBLIOGRAPHY

Aronin, J.E. *Climate and Architecture*. Reinhold Publishing Corporation, New York, 1953.

Bennett, R. *Sun Angles for Design*. Robert Bennett, Bala Cynwyd, PA, 1978.

Brown, G.Z. *Sun, Wind, and Light: Architectural Design Strategies*. John Wiley & Sons, Hoboken, New Jersey, 1985.

Egan, M.D. *Concepts in Architectural Lighting*. McGraw-Hill Book Company, New York, 1983.

Egan, M.D., and V. Olgyay. *Architectural Lighting*. McGraw-Hill Co., New York, 2002.

Evans, B.H. *Daylight in Architecture*. McGraw-Hill Book Company, New York, 1981.

Gordon, G., and K.L. Nuckolls. *Interior Lighting for Designers*. John Wiley & Sons, Hoboken, New Jersey, 1995.

Lam, W.M.C. *Perception and Lighting as Formgivers for Architecture*. McGraw-Hill Book Company, New York, 1977.

Lam, W. M.C. *Sunlighting as Formgiver for Architecture*. Van Nostrand Reinhold Company, Inc., New York, 1986.

Moore, F. *Concepts and Practice of Architectural Daylighting*. Van Nostrand Reinhold Company, Inc., New York, 1985.

Moore, F. *Environmental Control Systems: Heating, Cooling, Lighting*. McGraw-Hill New York, 1993.

Steffy, G. *Architectural Lighting Design*. John Wiley & Sons, Hoboken, New Jersey, 2002.

5 ACOUSTICS

INTRODUCTION
PHYSICS OF SOUND
ARCHITECTURAL ACOUSTICS
SOUND DISTRIBUTION
SOUND ISOLATION

INTRODUCTION

Although the nature of sound and human sensitivity to it have remained constant, the field of architectural acoustics and its impact on building design have changed significantly in recent years. These changes are based on modifications of the type and level of sounds that exist in contemporary environments, alterations in methods of building construction, and variations in the intentions and techniques of architectural planning.

The population density in many urban locations has reached a new high, resulting in considerably higher sound levels. While this concentration of population is significant, it is not as critical in producing higher levels of environmental noise as the plethora of new sound sources that now exist. Automobiles, planes, and trains are modern transportation systems that add to the general sound level. While many support this notion of increased noise levels, an alternative view was presented in Jack Finney's intriguing novel about time travel, *Time and Again*:

We were at the intersection where Broadway crosses Fifth, and vehicles were pouring from Broadway to join our traffic stream, which was just possible, or to fight their way across it, which was almost impossible. Nearly every vehicle had four wheels and every wheel was wrapped in iron that smashed and rang against

---

the cobbles, every horse had four iron-shod hoofs that did the same, and there was no control whatsoever. Wheels clattered, wood groaned, chains rattled, leather creaked, whips cracked against horseflesh, men shouted and cursed, and no street I've ever seen of the twentieth century made even half that brain-numbing sound.[1]

Whether or not traffic noise is louder than in the past, today we increasingly utilize various noise-emitting machines to reduce our physical labor and depend on rather noisy mechanical systems to provide reasonable levels of interior thermal comfort. There are also numerous electronic sound sources that some people might think is "music to our ears" but that others might consider to be objectionable noise and an environmental nuisance. There is also the somewhat newer sound problem associated with the use of cell phones—people talking loudly on their phones in public spaces, often sharing personal information about themselves that we are forced to hear (perhaps a reason to appreciate text messaging?).

As if all of these increases in sound sources that seem to continually bombard us were not enough, our noise problems are compounded by modern construction techniques that generally employ lighter materials, often in

---

[1] Jack Finney, *Time and Again* (Simon & Schuster, New York, 1970), p. 126.

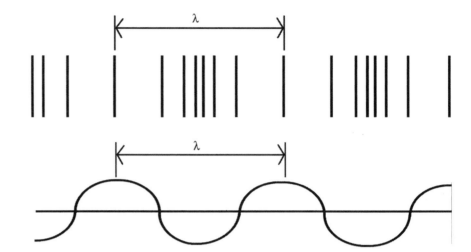

Figure 5.1 LONGITUDINAL WAVE

Figure 5.2 TRANSVERSE WAVE/SINE WAVE

prefabricated assemblies. Instead of enclosing our build-ings in heavy masonry walls that have a few window open-ings, today we are likely to use curtain walls comprised of large glass panels and lightweight wall assemblies. Instead of plaster ceilings within the walls of each space, we are apt to spread an acoustical tile ceiling across a large area and then subdivide the space with wall partitions that, even if they do extend up to the ceiling, generally allow sound to pass above. Compounding these problems, for conve-nience, we frequently place in close proximity activities that, in terms of acoustics, are often not very compatible. Combined with changes in our lifestyle, these various con-struction and design practices tend to reduce considerably our ability to provide effective sound isolation from noise, whether within the space we occupy, from another space within the building, or from the outside. However, while our acoustical problems are somewhat exacerbated today, the nature of sound remains the same.

PHYSICS OF SOUND

"If a tree falls in the forest and there is no one there to hear it, is there any sound?" So goes the old riddle, but what do we mean by the term *sound*? Does it refer to acoustical en-ergy, which is identified as objective sound, or to hearing, which is subjective sound? While as designers our ultimate concern is for the subjective nature of sound, unless we un-derstand the nature of sound in the objective sense, we will be unable to control the subjective experience effectively.

The normal human ear is sensitive to a wide range of frequencies or cycles per second that extends from around 20 to 20,000 Hertz (Hz), but even within this range, an audible sound must have an intensity that exceeds the threshold level of human perception, which is 10^{-16} watts per square centimeter (10^{-16} w cm^{-2}).

Sound energy occurs in the form of a longitudinal wave. The fluctuation of energy entails sequential compressions and rarefactions of an elastic medium, which occur in the direction of travel, as is diagrammed in Figure 5.1. A way to visualize a longitudinal wave is to think of a spring that has been compressed and then allowed to expand but with these oscillations continuing. Perhaps you might have even played with a "Slinky" toy in an accordion fash-ion. If you have, then you have experienced a longitudinal wave directly.

While the distortion of a longitudinal wave occurs in the direction of travel, it is often represented by a sine wave, such as shown in Figure 5.2. Although this is more repre-sentative of a transverse wave, which occurs perpendicular to the direction of travel, a sine wave provides a clear way of indicating the sequential change in energy level from positive to negative.

However it is represented, in the objective sense, sound is an audible signal that can be, but is not necessarily, heard. The audible signal is a form of energy that involves the vibration within an elastic medium, with a frequency and intensity that fall within the human auditory range. That is, sound is a range of vibrations to which the human auditory system is specifically sensitive.

The speed of sound in air, at standard atmospheric conditions and a temperature of around 68° F, is 1130 feet per second. If audible sound has a frequency of between 20 and 20,000 Hz, then the wavelengths of audible sound will be between 50 feet for low-frequency sounds and $^1/_2$ inch for high-frequency sounds.

The speed of sound is proportional to the elasticity and inversely proportional to the density of the medium in which it travels. Although the speed of sound traveling through various materials seems to indicate that the speed increases as the weight of the material increases, it is the effect of the increase in elasticity that usually overwhelms the "negative" effect of increased density. Note that while

Table 5.1: SPEED OF SOUND IN VARIOUS MEDIA

Medium	Speed (FPS)
Air	1130 fps
Water	4625 fps
Concrete	12,000 fps
Steel	16,000 fps
Aluminum	19,000 fps

the increase in the speed of sound for the materials listed in Table 5.1 seems to suggest that there is a proportional relationship between speed and density, the continued increase for aluminum over steel indicates that this presumption is not accurate.

Since sound travels through various media, we should recognize that it is the variation in pressure that travels through the media, not the media themselves. Although we have all probably seen waves moving through water

and perhaps have even experienced the physical force they can exert when swimming in the ocean or another large body of water, there is really no major horizontal movement or dislocation of the water. While the water moves up and down, causing floating objects to flow forward, the water itself actually remains pretty much in its initial location. As a result, while sound can travel through air, the actual movement of air is not critical to sound transmission.

Figure 5.3 shows common sounds in terms of loudness and frequency. Although the range of frequencies to which the human ear is sensitive extends from 20 to 20,000 Hz, the human ear tends to be more sensitive to the midrange frequencies. That is, the ear does not respond equally to changes in sound pressure at all frequencies. The optimum sensitivity occurs between 500 and 6000 Hz, with maximum sensitivity at 4000 Hz. The critical range of human speech is between 300 and 4000 Hz, but while the sensitivity of the human ear tends to be best at midrange frequencies, diminishing at the extremes, the decrease in

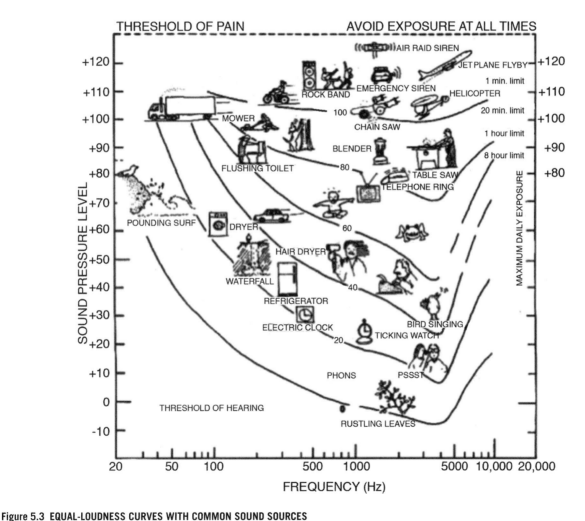

Figure 5.3 EQUAL-LOUDNESS CURVES WITH COMMON SOUND SOURCES

Adapted from B. Stein, J.S. Reynolds, W.T. Grondzik, and A.G. Kwok, *Mechanical and Electrical Equipment for Buildings* (John Wiley & Sons, Inc., Hoboken, New Jersey, 2006), Figure 17.8.

sensitivity is most pronounced at the lower frequencies. In addition, there is often a pronounced reduction in auditory sensitivity with increasing age, occurring mainly at the higher frequencies.

For convenience, the broad range of sound is divided into distinct frequency bands. Each band is noted by its geometric mean: 31.5 Hz, 63 Hz, 125 Hz, 250 Hz, 500 Hz, 1000 Hz, 2000 Hz, 4000 Hz, 8000 Hz, and 16,000 Hz. The division between two adjacent frequency or octave bands is defined as the geometric mean of the lower frequency multiplied by the square root of 2 or the geometric mean of the higher frequency divided by the square root of 2. For example, the division between the 500-Hz and 1000-Hz octave bands is 700.11 ($500 \times \sqrt{2} = 1000 \div \sqrt{2} = 700.11$). Similarly, the division between the 4000-Hz and 8000-Hz octave bands is 5656.85 ($4000 \times \sqrt{2} = 8000 \div \sqrt{2} = 5656.85$).

If a sound is heard twice, with the second hearing coming 0.07 second (70 milliseconds) or more after the first, although these sounds will likely be understood to be related, the second sound will be sensed as a separate, distinct sound that we call an *echo*. If the delay in hearing the second sound is within 0.035 second, the second sound will reinforce the first and will not be distinguished as a separate sound. However, even though a delayed sound that is heard within 0.035 second after the initial sound will reinforce the initial sound, the human ear can actually detect two distinct sounds, such as clicks, that occur as close as 0.001 second apart.

The basic unit of acoustical energy is the watt. Watts per unit area provides an indication of sound intensity, usually measured in watts cm^{-2} and generally noted by I. The minimum intensity of sound energy to which the human ear is sensitive, that is, the minimal energy intensity that will cause adequate movement in the auditory system to be perceived as sound, is 10^{-16} watts cm^{-2}. This minimal level of sound intensity is generally noted as I_o. The maximum intensity to which the human ear is exposed should not exceed 10^{-3} watts cm^{-2}. Even below this intensity, serious pain and actual physical damage can occur. In fact, sounds with an intensity above 10^{-7} watts cm^{-2} can cause problems.

Very high sound levels might not only be painful, they can cause temporary and even permanent hearing loss. When exposed to sound levels with an intensity of 10^{-7} watts cm^{-2} (90 dB) or higher over an extended period of time, special precautions must be taken. This is required by law. Fortunately, much of the hearing loss we experience as a result of a short exposure to excessive sound intensity levels is temporary, and we can regain most of the hearing loss over time. Frequently, some sensory loss is retained, especially if the exposure occurs over a sustained period of time, and with advancing age, our ability to regain a hearing loss diminishes rapidly; even limited exposure could have lasting repercussions.

Sound loudness or, more specifically, sound intensity level, is generally designated by decibels, which are based on the base 10 logarithmic scale. The decibel value of a particular sound intensity is actually 10 times the $\log_{10}$ of the ratio of that sound to the threshold sound intensity (10^{-16} watts cm^{-2}).

Decibels (dB) are used to indicate sound levels since human sensitivity to sound intensity, like other stimulation, is generally perceived in terms of a logarithmic rather than an arithmetic progression. We refer to this phenomenon of human sensory response as the Weber-Fechner Law.

While the actual ratio between the minimum and maximum sound intensity to which the human auditory system is responsive is 10,000,000,000,000 to 1 (10^{-16} to 10^{-3} watts cm^{-2}), the decibel range is merely from 1 to 130 dB. That is, although the ratio in basic energy units of the maximum to minimum sound to which we are responsive is 10 trillion to 1, the range of decibels is only 130 to 1.

Decibels are based on a ratio. If the ratio is between a sound intensity and the threshold intensity, the decibel notation is an indication of the loudness of that sound. If the ratio is between two conditions or changes in sound intensity, the decibels indicate the change in sound intensity level.

Based on general theory, the minimal sound source power that is audible is noted as W_o and equals 10^{-12} watts, but the minimal audible intensity, I_o, is 10^{-16} watts. What is the relationship between W_o at 10^{-12} watts and at 10^{-16} watts cm^{-2}? Recognizing that the dispersal of a sound wave is analogous to the dispersal of a light wave, we should realize that the intensity of sound at a particular location is developed from a sound source located at the center or origin of the sound waves, and that these waves spread out from the source in spherical form. Therefore, as the distance from the sound source increases, the spherical area across which the sound is spread increases and the intensity of a sound is reduced. Since the spherical area increases as the square of the distance, this intensity reduction follows the inverse square law.

The numerical connection between W_o at 10^{-12} watts and I_o at 10^{-16} watts cm^{-2} (e.g., watts/cm²) is based on the sound intensity located approximately 1 foot from the sound source. Since the surface area of a sphere is $4\pi r^2$, if the radius of the sphere is 1 foot, which in SI units would be 30.5 centimeters, the surface area would be 11,690 square centimeters. Rounding off, the surface area of a 1-foot sphere is approximately 10,000 square centimeters or 10^4 cm², which means that the intensity of

Table 5.2: ACOUSTIC TERMS

Term	Units	Description
Sound Power (W)	watts	total sound energy
Sound Power Level (PWL)	dB	$PWL = 10 \log (W/10^{-12})$
Sound Intensity (I)	watts cm^{-2}	sound energy in a given direction per unit area
Sound Intensity Level (SIL)	dB	$SIL = 10 \log(I/10^{-16})$ dB
Sound Pressure (P)	microns or newtons cm^{-2}	similar to sound intensity
Sound Pressure Level (SPL)	dB	$SPL = 10 \log^2 dB$ $= 20 \log dB$

a 10^{-12} watts sound would be 10^{-16} watts cm^{-2}.

$$\frac{10^{-12} \text{ watts}}{10^4 \text{ cm}^2} = 10^{-16} \text{ watts cm}^{-2}$$

If this mingling of the English and SI systems is not confusing enough, sound is really sensed as pressure and not intensity (power/unit area). Table 5.2 should help clarify terms.

Sound Levels

If 0 dB is the threshold level of sound and 130 dB is the maximum level to which the human ear may be exposed without causing serious damage, what is the response to the intermediate sound levels? Table 5.3 indicates the basic values of various decibel levels and the effects of change in sound levels. It also indicates the sound level of various types of speech.

While these various sound-level listings may help you understand how we tend to interpret different sound levels and changes within them (see Table 5.4), the actual energy levels involved are not easily grasped. How can we understand the amount of energy connected with the threshold power (P_o) of 10^{-12} watts or the threshold intensity (I_o) of 10^{-16} watts cm^{-2}? How much energy is involved? Perhaps if we consider a known condition, we can clarify this concept.

Let's consider 100,000 screaming fans at a football stadium. While normal speech averages between 40 and 60 dB at a $3'-0''$ distance, yelling typically measures around 90 dB. Since 90 dB represents a sound intensity of 10^{-7} watts cm^{-2}, the power that would produce such an intensity at a $3'-0''$ distance from the source would be approximately 10^{-2} watts. This is based on the fact that a sphere with a $3'-0''$ diameter would have a surface area

Table 5.3: RESPONSE TO CHANGES IN SOUND INTENSITY LEVELS

Sound Level		Response
10 dB	–	very faint
20 – 40 dB	–	faint
40 – 60 dB	–	moderate
60 – 80 dB	–	loud
80 – 100 dB	–	very loud
100 – 120 dB	–	deafening
Sound Levels of Speech		**SIL**
Soft Whisper	–	30 dB
Normal Speech	–	40 – 50 dB
Loud Speech	–	60 dB
Shouting	–	80 dB
Screaming	–	90 dB
Apparent Difference		**Change in Intensity**
Reasonable Perception	–	3 dB
Clearly Noticeable	–	5 dB
Twice as Loud/Half as Loud	–	10 dB
Much Louder	–	15 dB
Very Much Louder	–	20 dB

Table 5.4: TYPICAL AVERAGE SOUND LEVELS

Sound Source	Sound Level (dB)
Watch Ticking	20
Quiet Garden	30
Low Conversation @ 3 ft	40
Average Quiet Home	42
Quiet Residential Street	48
Private Business Office	50
Landscaped or Open Planned Office	53
Large Conventional Office	60
Normal Conversation @ 3 ft	60
Passenger Car in City Traffic @ 20 ft	70
Quiet Factory	70
Loud Conversation @ 3 ft	76
Noisy Factory	80
Business Machines @ 3 ft	80
10-hp Outboard Motor @ 50 ft	88
Rush-Hour City Traffic @ 10 ft	90
Large Jet Taking Off @ 3,000 ft	90
Diesel Bus or Truck @ 30 ft	94
Power Gas Mower @ 10 ft	105
Large Jet Taking Off @ 500 ft	115
50-hp Siren @ 100 ft	138

of 113.1 square feet or approximately 100,000 square centimeters. If one person yelling generates 10^{-2} watts of acoustical power, then 100,000 people yelling would generate only 10^3 watts of acoustical power, which is hardly enough energy to fry an egg!

We should not confuse the energy required to produce the 90-dB sound level with the energy of that sound. That is, much more effort is required to generate a 90-dB sound than is actually contained within it. Even though sound does not represent a high level of energy, it can produce a considerable effect, especially in terms of the human response, which can be positive or negative.

When a sound is an annoyance or is unwanted, it is often referred to as *noise*. Normally, sounds are more annoying when they are louder or intermittent (noncontinuous). Higher-frequency sounds tend to be more bothersome than lower-frequency sounds, as are pure tones compared to broadband sounds. Also, if the sound source is moving or unlocatable, it tends to be more annoying. In addition, intelligence-bearing sounds, such as the bark of a dog, the horn of a car, or an emergency siren, can be more irritating than general sounds, and speech can be quite bothersome when it is loud enough to be audible but not loud enough to be intelligible.

While the range of frequencies to which we are sensitive extends from 20 to 20,000 Hz, the human auditory system is not equally sensitive to all of these frequencies. In general, we are more sensitive to the middle range of frequencies, with a pronounced drop at the higher frequencies and a gradual reduction at the lower frequencies. This is similar to how we respond to light. Our sensitivity to light within the visible spectrum is greatest in the yellow-green range, so we use a color-corrected meter to measure light levels. In this way, the actual radiant flux, which is the energy flow, is adjusted to match the luminous flux that relates to human sensitivity. With acoustics, however, the distinction between the two—sound energy and sound perception—is not necessarily clear.

In addition, the difference in sensitivity to different frequencies tends to vary as the sound intensity changes. This complex changing sensitivity to sound is shown by the equal loudness curves, which provide a means of correlating actual sound levels with perceived loudness (see Figure 5.4). The measured sound levels are indicated in terms of decibels, whereas the perceived sound levels are indicated in terms of phons. As a result, these curves are sometimes referred to as *phons curves.*

To be accurate, sound pressure or sound intensity relates to the sound energy, and when compared to our threshold sensitivity, is described in terms of decibels dB, whereas the loudness of a sound—that is, how we perceive a sound—should be described in phons. This distinction has been expressed as the difference between a *physical* unit, the decibel, and a *psychophysical* unit, the phon.

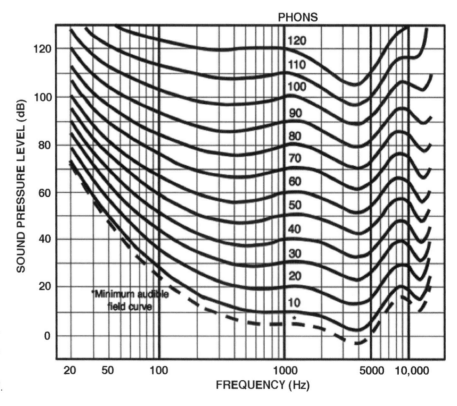

Figure 5.4 EQUAL LOUDNESS CURVES
These curves indicate the typical perceived sound loudness of various sound levels. The perceived loudness, which is denoted in terms of phons, varies according to the sound frequency with the variations between frequencies reducing at higher sound levels. Adapted from B. Stein, J.S. Reynolds, W.T. Grondzik, and A.G. Kwok, *Mechanical and Electrical Equipment for Buildings* (John Wiley & Sons, Inc., Hoboken, New Jersey, 2006), Figure 17.7.

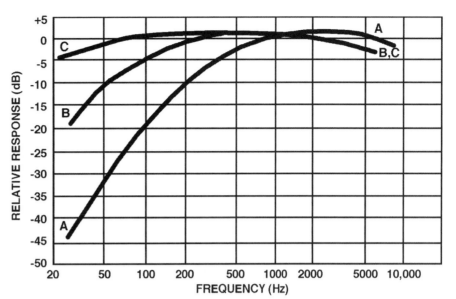

Figure 5.5 STANDARDIZED dBA, dBB, and dBC CURVES
There are three filters used to adjust the measured sound levels to indicate perceived loudness. Since phon curves tend to flatten at higher sound levels, the dBA filter should be applied at "normal" levels with the dBB and dBC filters applied at higher sound levels. Adapted from B. Stein, J.S. Reynolds, W.T. Grondzik, and A.G. Kwok, *Mechanical and Electrical Equipment for Buildings* (John Wiley & Sons, Inc., Hoboken, New Jersey, 2006), Figure 17.16.

However, since the curves relate measured decibels with perceived phons values that are slightly different from the measured decibels, phons are often referred to as *decibels*. This is further encouraged by the use of adjusted decibel scales that directly relate decibels of measured sound intensity with decibels, generally dBA, of perceived sound.

There are other quirks with the equal loudness or phons curves. One is that the curves tend to flatten out as the sound levels increase. Another is that the correlation between the sensitivity curves and the measured decibel levels is set at 1000 Hz, although human sensitivity to sound is maximized at 4000 Hz. That is, while the curves are intended to indicate our sensitivity to sound, the way in which they have been set is somewhat arbitrary.

Equal loudness curves, which are contours of relatively consistent interpreted loudness, indicate perceived sound levels at various frequencies. These curves are reasonably accurate for normal hearing, and the subjective loudness of each curve is indicated in terms of phons. The sound intensity level (SIL) at 1000 Hz determines the phons value. As a result of the curves, the same SIL will be perceived at quite different phons values. For example, an SIL of 60 dB corresponds to 30 phons at 50 Hz, 50 phons at 100 Hz, 63 phons at 500 Hz, 60 phons at 1000 Hz, 68 phons at 4000 Hz, and 60 phons at 6000 Hz.

While it is relatively easy to grasp what the equal loudness curves indicate, using them to adjust measured SILs to the loudness with which a sound will be perceived (phons) is somewhat complicated since most sounds involve various frequencies that collectively combine to establish the perceived loudness. To use equal loudness curves to determine the perceived loudness, we would need to measure the SIL for each of the octave bands, converting each of the measured decibel value to an appropriate phons value. We would then have to add these together to determine the overall perceived loudness.

Neither decibels nor phons, both of which are based on logarithmic ratios, should be added together. Since logarithms are the exponential values of the log base number, adding logarithms together is equivalent to multiplication. In order to combine the various loudness levels for the different octave bands, we need to determine the intensity level (watts cm^{-2}) related to each phon value, add these together, and then find the decibel equivalent of the ratio of this total to the threshold level (10^{-16} watts cm^{-2}).

Rather than use equal loudness or phons curves to adjust measured acoustical energy intensity levels to determine perceived sound loudness, we can measure SILs using a filter that adjusts the measurements to somewhat match human sensitivity at the various frequencies. The perceived SIL is measured in decibels denoted by one of the three filters generally used: dBA, dBB, and dBC. The dBA scale, which tends to be the inverse of the typical phons curve in the normal range of sound intensities, is used most often. At higher sound levels, it is appropriate to use the dBB or dBC scales, both of which flatten out, similar to the equal loudness curves, increasing response to lower frequencies (see Figure 5.5).

Logarithms

While the use of decibels provides a better indication of the human response to sound levels than direct energy measurements in watts cm^{-2}, the decibel is not a convenient unit for adding together different sounds. Since decibels are based on logarithms, adding decibel levels would actually be analogous to multiplying actual sound levels. So, in order to add sounds that are noted in decibel units, we must first convert the sounds into basic intensity units.

If two sounds of the same SIL are added together, the combined results should be equal to twice that SIL. In logarithms, since $\log_{10} 2 = 0.3$, when two equal sounds are combined, the resulting decibel level should be equal to 3 dB more than the base sound. Remember that the addition of logarithmic values is equivalent to arithmetic multiplication, so a doubling of a decibel value can be determined by adding 3 dB.

$$\text{if } 40\,\text{dB} = 10\,\log_{10}\left(\frac{10^{-12}\,\text{w cm}^{-2}}{10^{-16}\,\text{w cm}^{-2}}\right), \quad \text{then}$$

$$40\,\text{dB} + 40\,\text{dB} = 10\,\log_{10}\left(\frac{2 \times 10^{-12}\,\text{w cm}^{-2}}{10^{-16}\,\text{w cm}^{-2}}\right), \text{ or}$$

$$10\,\log_{10} 2 + 10\,\log_{10}\left(\frac{10^{-12}\,\text{w cm}^{-2}}{10^{-16}\,\text{w cm}^{-2}}\right)$$

Since $10\,\log_{10} 2 = 3$,

$$40\,\text{dB} + 40\,\text{dB} = 43 \text{ dB}.$$

The rule of thumb relating to the combination of sound levels in decibel units is as follows:

1. When the difference between the two sound levels is 1 dB or less, add 3 dB to the higher level to determine the combined sound level.
2. When the difference is 2 to 3 dB, add 2 dB to the higher level.
3. When the difference is 4 to 8 dB, add 1 dB to the higher level.
4. When the difference is 9 dB or more, since the combined sound level will not exceed the higher level, ignore the effect of the lower sound level.

Prior to the development of the convenient electronic calculator, mathematical calculations were often done by means of a slide rule, a graphic device that provides a means of manipulating logarithms. The logarithm of a number is the exponent of the base number that would provide the same numerical value as the number. For example, since we will be using logarithms to base 10 ($\log_{10}$), we could equate $5 = 10^{0.7}$ and $6 = 10^{0.78}$. Therefore, since multiplication of numbers with the same exponential base is accomplished by adding the exponents, if we wish to find the product of 5 times 6, we could merely add the exponents of the comparable base 10 values to determine

Table 5.5: SIMPLIFIED TABLE OF LOGARITHMS

Condensed Logarithm Chart	
$\log_{10} 1 = 0.0$	$\log_{10} 6 = 0.78$
$\log_{10} 2 = 0.3$	$\log_{10} 7 = 0.85$
$\log_{10} 3 = 0.48$	$\log_{10} 8 = 0.90$
$\log_{10} 4 = 0.60$	$\log_{10} 9 = 0.95$
$\log_{10} 5 = 0.70$	$\log_{10} 10 = 1.0$
Condensed 10 × Log Chart	
$10\,\log_{10} 1 = 0.0$	$10\,\log_{10} 6 = 7.8$
$10\,\log_{10} 2 = 3.0$	$10\,\log_{10} 7 = 8.5$
$10\,\log_{10} 3 = 4.8$	$10\,\log_{10} 8 = 9.0$
$10\,\log_{10} 4 = 6.0$	$10\,\log_{10} 9 = 9.5$
$10\,\log_{10} 5 = 7.0$	$10\,\log_{10} 10 = 10.0$

the answer.

Since $5 = 10^{0.7}$ and $6 = 10^{0.78}$,

$5 \times 6 = 10^{(0.7+0.78)} = 10^{1.48} = 30$.

Note also that $10^{1.48} = 10^{1.0} \times 10^{0.48} = 10 \times 3 = 30$.

Obviously, in this example it would be easier to merely multiply 5 and 6, but as numbers become larger or if we wish to determine the power or root values of a number, logarithms can make calculations easier.

Directly stated, a logarithm to base 10 is merely the exponent of 10 that gives the same numerical value. When a number is larger than 10, we can convert it into a number less than 10 multiplied by 10 taken to some whole number exponent. For example:

$$467{,}510 = 4.6751 \times 100{,}000 = 4.6751 \times 10^5$$
$$= 10^{0.6698} \times 10^5 = 10^{(0.6698+5)}$$
$$= 10^{5.6698}, \text{ so}$$
$$\log_{10} 467610 = 5.6698$$

While most calculators include a base 10 log function, most acoustic calculations can be accomplished by merely using basic logarithms. Table 5.5 includes some of the basic log values, which are generally adequate for simple acoustical calculations.

Since the decibel is a unit equal to 10 bels, its values are 10 times the log values. These values are also included in Table 5.5 for your convenience.

ARCHITECTURAL ACOUSTICS

The discussion of architectural acoustics can be reasonably subdivided into four areas of concern: room acoustics, sound systems, sound isolation, and mechanical equipment. Although this subdivision has proven to be a helpful way of organizing the subject of acoustics, a more effective way of ordering acoustics in terms of its architectural aspects is to divide the subject into two parts: the acoustical quality within a space and the isolation of sound within and between spaces.

Aspects of Architectural Acoustics

I. ROOM ACOUSTICS: SOUND DISTRIBUTION AND QUALITY
    A. Spatial quality: volume
        1. Shape
        2. Finishes
    B. Sound distribution: reflecting surfaces
        1. Electronic sound systems
II. SOUND ISOLATION
    A. Sound transmission: mass
        1. Resiliency
        2. Tightness
    B. Mechanical equipment: noise
        1. Vibration
        2. Connectivity

The acoustical quality of a space is a result of its shape, volume, and finishes. Once a sound is generated, it is distributed outward from the source until it impinges on the surrounding room surfaces. When the sound reaches an enclosing surface, it is either absorbed, transmitted, or reflected. The portion of the sound that is absorbed or transmitted is lost, but the reflected sound is sustained within the space and contributes to the perceived sound level. Therefore, the more sound that is reflected, the louder the space will tend to be.

In theory, each space has three acoustical fields: a near field, a free field, and a reverberant field (see Figure 5.6). In the near field, which extends from the source to a distance equal to the longest wavelength of that sound, things are rather complicated. In a sense, within this field, you are actually "within" the sound, and it is difficult to analyze the conditions. In the free field, the sound is essentially only what is coming from the sound source, without any sound reflected off of the surfaces enclosing the space. As a result, the intensity of the sound follows the inverse square law and diminishes as the distance from the source increases. As the distance doubles, the sound is only one-quarter the intensity, which means a 6-dB reduction for each doubling. The free field is largest in spaces that are highly absorptive, but in most spaces, the free field, if it even exists, is rather limited. As a result, most spaces consist mainly of a reverberant field in which the initial and reflective sounds commingle.

While absorption and transmission are different, in terms of their impact on a space they are related and tend to be considered comparably. In fact, the unit of sound absorption, the Sabin (A), is defined as being equal to 1 square foot of total absorption or 1 square foot of open window. That is, 1 Sabin, which represents no sound being reflected, is equivalent to 100% of total sound "lost" from 1 square foot. If the sound absorption of an enclosing surface were 50% or 33% per square foot, 2 or 3 square feet, respectively, of that surface would provide 1 Sabin. Although 1 square foot of total sound absorption is equal to 1 Sabin, the story is that the initial Sabin unit was actually set to be equal to the absorption provided by one seat cushion from Sanders Theater, a lecture hall with excellent acoustics located in Memorial Hall, built in 1878 for Harvard University.

Seventeen years later, in 1895, Harvard opened a new museum, the Fogg Museum, designed by the architect Richard Morris Hunt on a site across the street from Memorial Hall. By 1925 the Harvard collection had increased, and the Fogg Museum moved into a new building designed by the Boston firm Coolidge, Shepley, Bulfinch, and Abbot. Hunt's building, renamed for him, began its long service as one of the buildings used by the Harvard Graduate School of Design (GSD). Unfortunately, in 1970, following the construction of Gund Hall, the present home of the GSD that was designed by John Andrews, Hunt Hall was demolished to make way for a new student dormitory.

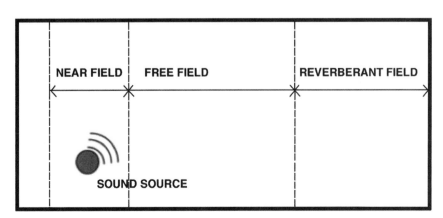

Figure 5.6 ACOUSTICAL FIELDS WITHIN A SPACE

The old Fogg Museum included a lecture hall of semi-circular design in which the speaker's platform was located along the flat edge of the space (see Figure 5.7). While this design was similar in many ways to that of a classical Roman theater, the lecture room was an interior, not an exterior space, with a relatively flat seating area as distinct from the steeply inclined seats traditionally provided in the historic exemplars. As a result, a major portion of the sound would travel unimpeded to the curved rear wall, be reflected off the semicircular, hard plaster surface back into the lecture space, focused back to the presentation area. This focused sound reflection and the associated extended reverberation time caused quite a problem, and members of the Harvard Physics Department were asked to help fix it.

Wallace Clement Sabine was a young member of the Physics Department, and after the more senior faculty chose not to respond, he accepted the task of trying to resolve the problem. Sabine apparently didn't limit his efforts to solving the acoustical problems in the Fogg Lecture Hall. As an academic, he attempted to determine the basis for the difference between the bad acoustics in the Fogg Lecture Hall and the acceptable acoustics in other lecture spaces, including Sander Theater, which was in a number of ways similar to the Fogg. In the process, he founded the field of architectural acoustics.

Sabine apparently took a number of acoustical measurements for different sound frequencies in the Fogg Lecture Hall. He also modified the conditions in the space by bringing horsehair seat cushions from Sander Theater into the hall. The story is that during the night, he and a number of students would carry the seat cushion across the street to the Fogg, Sabine would conduct his measurements, and then he and his students would return the cushions to Sander Theater so that they would be in place for lectures the next day. From these explorations, Sabine was able to clarify the relationship between acoustical quality, the size of a space, and the amount of sound absorption present. Based on his findings, he was able to prescribe the addition of sound absorption to the Fogg Lecture Hall that reduced the focused reflections of sound and lowered the reverberation time.

Sabine supposedly assigned one sound absorption unit to each of the horsehair seat cushions from Sander Theater. This unit, fortuitously, was basically equal to 1 square foot of total sound absorption. The cushions were around 1 foot wide and 6 feet long, indicating that the sound absorption coefficient for the cushions would have been around 0.17.

Sound Absorption

The basic unit of sound absorption is the Sabin, named in recognition of the contributions of Wallace Clement Sabine, who is called the father of architectural acoustics. One Sabin is equivalent to 1 square foot of total absorption. Therefore, if 1 square foot of a material has an absorptivity (α) of 0.20, 5 square feet of this material will provide 1 Sabin ($5 \times 0.20 = 1.0$). While the amount of absorption is noted in Sabin units (A), the decimal portion of the incident sound that will be absorbed notes the absorptivity of a surface. This can be found by comparing the absorbed to the incident sound intensity.

$$\alpha = \frac{I_a}{I_i} \qquad A = \sum S\alpha$$

To determine the total sound absorption of a space, we must identify the various surfaces, their coefficients of sound absorption (α), and their surface areas (S). By summing the product of each surface area times its coefficient of absorption, we can find the total Sabins of sound absorption.

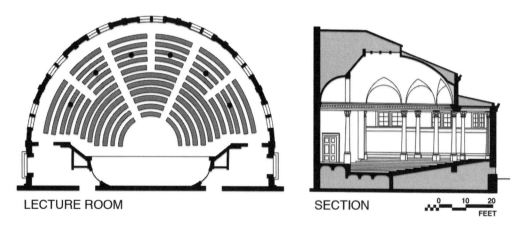

LECTURE ROOM   SECTION

Figure 5.7 LECTURE HALLL AT FOGG MUSEUM
The lecture room in the original Fogg Museum at Harvard University was designed by Richard Morris Hunt and opened in 1895. With the construction of a new building in 1926, the building, called Hunt Hall, was used as the home of the Graduate School of Design until 1969. The building was demolished in 1973.

The absorption of sound is frequency dependent. Materials that may absorb a large percentage of high-frequency sound may not absorb a significant portion of low-frequency sound. In fact, because of this, various techniques and devices are used to achieve sound absorption at particular frequencies. Fuzzy materials that readily absorb high- and medium-frequency sounds are not very effective in absorbing low-frequency sounds. For these sounds, panel resonators are usually required. For sounds of a particular frequency, cavity resonators that can be "tuned" to certain frequencies might be necessary.

A panel resonator is essentially a large, flat box, often with small openings distributed along its sides. As a sound approaches the exposed surface of the box, the impinging compression and rarefaction of the air moves the panel cover in and out, and if the box has openings, this movement forces air out of and then into the box. As a result, some of the acoustical energy is converted into the physical movement of the panel and the air and into heat.

Cavity resonators work by using the sound itself to reduce the intensity. The resonator has a small opening into a contained volume. Sounds entering the cavity are reflected off of the containing surfaces and must reemerge from the opening. If the distance between the entry and the reflecting surface is equal to one-quarter of the wavelength of the sound, the emerging sound and the entering sound are one-half wavelength out of sync, and as a result they cancel each other.

Table 5.6 lists sound absorption coefficients and noise reduction coefficients (NRC) for various building materials. How sound absorption materials are installed can affect their performance. This is particularly critical with acoustic ceiling tiles. Different methods of installation are shown in Figure 5.8, with the mounting type E denoting the installation assumed in Table 5.6. If there is a cavity behind the acoustic tile or if the tile is thick, the sound absorption tends to be higher as well as somewhat more uniform across the frequency spectrum of the sound. Perforated metal covers can affect high-frequency sound absorption but tend to have little impact on low-frequency sounds. Diffraction tends to allow low-frequency sounds to pass through the perforated panel with little reduction. With high-frequency sounds, the size and spacing of the openings influence the absorption, with larger holes at closer spacing having greater high-frequency absorption. Increasing the thickness and density of the absorptive blanket will also increase the sound absorption and reduce variation in response at different frequencies.

Since sound absorption is frequency dependent, we need to complete a number of calculations for any reasonably detailed analysis. However, for general purposes, we can use the NRC rather than the coefficients of sound absorption (α) for the different octave bands. The NRC is an average of α at 250, 500, 1000, and 2000 Hz. While the NRC can give reasonable results, we should realize that materials with the same NRC might absorb sounds quite differently. For example, one material might absorb more lower-frequency sounds, while another might do better with sounds at higher frequencies. So, while the NRC provides reasonable information on sound absorption in a space, it is not definitive. If we need a detailed analysis of sound absorption, we should undertake a series of calculations for each octave band, although perhaps it would be more appropriate to collaborate with an acoustical specialist.

The usual assumption is that sound absorption is provided merely by the characteristics of the various surfaces that define a particular space. However, it is also possible to "float" sound absorption material within a space. This can be quite effective since it can significantly increase the total number of Sabins of sound absorption, thereby reducing the sound level within the space. Of course, furniture and finishes, such as rugs and draperies, can also provide additional sound absorption.

Noise Reduction

If the absorption of sound in a space is increased, there is less reflected sound contributing to the sound level within the space. This results in noise reduction (NR), which can be determined by comparing the Sabins of sound absorption for the two different conditions.

$$NR = 10 \log_{10}(A_1/A_2)$$

where:

  NR is a decibel value

  A_1 is the total sound absorption for the initial conditions

  A_2 is the total sound absorption for the revised conditions

As noted, the calculation is based on the ratio of total Sabins of sound absorption in the revised and initial conditions. We can find the total sound absorption for each condition by multiplying the surface area by the NRC for each surface of the space. If there is furniture or other items within the space that can absorb sound, we should also include the Sabins of absorption that they provide for each condition. Again, if we need a more definitive understanding of the noise reduction that will result from a change in overall sound absorption, we could use the sound absorption coefficient (α) for each octave band for each surface material or consult with a specialist.

Table 5.6: SOUND ABSORPTION COEFFICIENTS (A) AND NRC FOR SELECTED INTERIOR SURFACE MATERIALS

Typical Wall Materials		125 Hz	250 Hz	500 Hz	1000 Hz	2000 Hz	4000 Hz	NRC[a]
High Reflectance								
Brick, unglazed and unpainted		0.03	0.03	0.03	0.04	0.05	0.07	0.04
Brick, unglazed and painted		0.01	0.01	0.02	0.02	0.02	0.03	0.02
Marble or glazed tile		0.01	0.01	0.01	0.01	0.02	0.02	0.01
Plaster, gypsum or lime, smooth finish on brick or tile		0.013	0.015	0.02	0.03	0.04	0.05	0.03
Smooth gypsum or lime plaster on lath		0.013	0.015	0.02	0.03	0.04	0.05	0.03
Rough gypsum or lime plaster on lath		0.14	0.10	0.06	0.05	0.04	0.03	0.06
$\frac{1}{2}$-in. gypsum board (GWB), nailed to 2 × 4 studs 16″ oc		0.29	0.10	0.05	0.04	0.07	0.09	0.07
$\frac{3}{8}$-in. plywood paneling on studs		0.28	0.22	0.17	0.09	0.10	0.11	0.15
Concrete block, painted		0.10	0.05	0.06	0.07	0.09	0.08	0.07
High Absorption								
Concrete block, unpainted		0.36	0.44	0.31	0.29	0.39	0.25	0.36
Tack-board		0.42	0.49	0.33	0.22	0.19	0.17	0.31
Rough wood as tongue and groove cedar		0.24	0.19	0.14	0.08	0.13	0.10	0.14
Light wt. drapery or tapestry, flat on wall		0.03	0.04	0.11	0.17	0.24	0.35	0.14
Medium wt. drapery, draped to half wall area		0.07	0.31	0.49	0.75	0.70	0.60	0.56
Heavy wt. drapery, draped to half wall area		0.14	0.35	0.55	0.72	0.70	0.65	0.58
Glass								
Ordinary window glass		0.35	0.25	0.18	0.12	0.07	0.04	0.16
Heavy plate glass		0.18	0.06	0.04	0.03	0.02	0.02	0.04
Typical Floor and Ground Materials		**125 Hz**	**250 Hz**	**500 Hz**	**1000 Hz**	**2000 Hz**	**4000 Hz**	**NRC[a]**
High Reflectance								
Marble or glazed tile		0.01	0.01	0.01	0.01	0.02	0.02	0.01
Concrete or terrazzo		0.01	0.01	0.02	0.02	0.02	0.02	0.02
Tile on concrete		0.02	0.03	0.03	0.03	0.03	0.02	0.03
Linoleum, asphalt, rubber, or cork tile on concrete		0.02	0.03	0.03	0.03	0.03	0.02	0.03
Wood		0.15	0.11	0.10	0.07	0.06	0.07	0.09
High Absorption								
Carpet, heavy, on concrete		0.02	0.06	0.14	0.37	0.60	0.65	0.29
Carpet, heavy, on foam padding		0.08	0.24	0.57	0.69	0.71	0.73	0.55
Indoor-outdoor carpet		0.01	0.05	0.10	0.20	0.45	0.65	0.20
Typical Ceiling Materials		**125 Hz**	**250 Hz**	**500 Hz**	**1000 Hz**	**2000 Hz**	**4000 Hz**	**NRC[a]**
High Reflectance								
Concrete		0.01	0.01	0.015	0.02	0.02	0.02	0.02
Smooth gypsum or lime plaster on lath		0.013	0.015	0.02	0.03	0.04	0.05	0.03
Rough gypsum or lime plaster on lath		0.14	0.10	0.06	0.05	0.04	0.03	0.06
$\frac{1}{2}$-in. gypsum board (GWB) on joists		0.29	0.10	0.05	0.04	0.07	0.09	0.07
$\frac{3}{8}$-in. plywood paneling on joists		0.28	0.22	0.17	0.09	0.10	0.11	0.15
Recessed 2′ × 4′ fluorescent w/ plastic lens		0.30	0.22	0.17	0.10	0.10	0.10	0.15
High Absorption								
$1\frac{1}{2}$-in. glass fiber tile		0.75	0.8	0.85	1	1	1	0.91
Vinyl-faced fiberglass ceiling panels								
1 in. thick	E405	0.73	0.88	0.71	0.98	0.96	0.77	0.88
$1\frac{1}{2}$-in. thick	E405	0.79	0.98	0.83	1.03	0.98	0.80	0.96
Painted nubby glass cloth panels								
$\frac{3}{4}$-in. thick	E405	0.81	0.94	0.65	0.87	1.00	0.96	0.87
1 in. thick	E405	0.78	0.92	0.79	1.00	1.03	1.10	0.94
Random fissured $\frac{3}{4}$-in. thick panels	E405	0.52	0.58	0.60	0.80	0.92	0.80	0.73
Perforated metal panel with infill 1 in. thick	E405	0.70	0.86	0.74	0.88	0.95	0.86	0.86
Typical averages, mineral fiber tiles and panels								
$\frac{3}{4}$-in. fissured tile	E405	0.47	0.50	0.52	0.76	0.86	0.81	0.66
$\frac{3}{4}$-in. fissured tile	E400	0.57	0.60	0.65	0.83	0.94	0.98	0.76
$\frac{3}{4}$-in. textured tile	E405	0.49	0.55	0.53	0.80	0.94	0.83	0.71
$\frac{5}{8}$-in. fissured tile	E405	0.28	0.33	0.66	0.73	0.74	0.75	0.62
$\frac{5}{8}$-in. fissured tile	E400	0.33	0.39	0.53	0.77	0.86	0.80	0.64
$\frac{5}{8}$-in. textured tile	E405	0.29	0.35	0.66	0.63	0.44	0.34	0.52
$\frac{5}{8}$-in. perforated tile	E405	0.27	0.29	0.55	0.78	0.69	0.53	0.58
3 in. thick × 16 in. square on 24-in. centers	A	0.40	0.61	1.92	2.54	2.62	2.60	

(Continued)

Table 5.6 *(Continued)*

Miscellaneous	125 Hz	250 Hz	500 Hz	1000 Hz	2000 Hz	4000 Hz	NRC[a]
Typical Absorption of Air	–	–	–	–	3.5	3.5	
Fabrics							
Light velour, 10 oz/yd, hung straight, in contact with wall	0.03	0.04	0.11	0.17	0.24	0.35	0.14
Medium velour, 14 oz/yd, draped to half area	0.07	0.31	0.49	0.75	0.70	0.60	0.56
Heavy velour, 18 oz/yd, draped to half area	0.14	0.35	0.55	0.72	0.70	0.65	0.58
Openings							
Stage, depending on furnishings				0.25–0.75			
Deep balcony, upholstered seats				0.50–1.00			
Grilles, ventilating				0.15–0.50			
Slightly vibrating surface (e.g., hollow core door)	0.02	0.02	0.03	0.03	0.04	0.05	0.03
Readily vibrating surface (e.g., thin wood paneling on studs)	0.10	0.07	0.05	0.04	0.04	0.05	0.05
Water surface (pool or pond)	0.008	0.008	0.013	0.015	0.02	0.025	0.01
Typical Seating Materials	**125 Hz**	**250 Hz**	**500 Hz**	**1000 Hz**	**2000 Hz**	**4000 Hz**	**NRC[a]**
Upholstered Seating, Occupied, per sq.ft. of floor area	0.60	0.74	0.88	0.96	0.93	0.85	0.88
Upholstered Seating, Unoccupied, per sq.ft. of floor area	0.49	0.66	0.80	0.88	0.82	0.70	0.79
Wooden Pews, Fully Occupied, per sq.ft. of floor area	0.57	0.61	0.75	0.86	0.91	0.86	0.78
Student Tablet-Armchairs, Occupied, per sq.ft. of floor area	0.30	0.42	0.50	0.85	0.85	0.84	0.66
Leather Seating, Unoccupied	0.44	0.54	0.60	0.62	0.58	0.50	0.59

[a]Noise Reduction Coefficient (NRC) is the arithmetic average of absorption coefficients (α) at 250, 500, 1000, & 2000. (Based on various sources including Cavanaugh, W. J. and Wilkes, J. A.: *Architectural Acoustics – Principles and Practice*, John Wiley & Sons, Inc., Hoboken, New Jersey, 1999.)

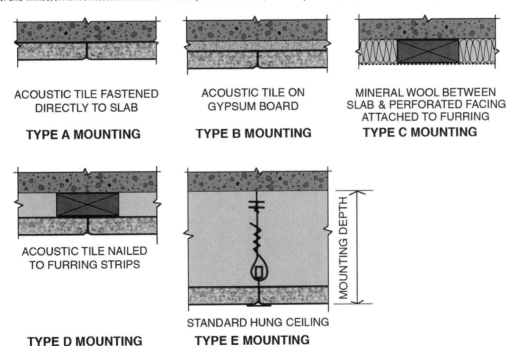

ACOUSTIC TILE FASTENED
DIRECTLY TO SLAB

TYPE A MOUNTING

ACOUSTIC TILE ON
GYPSUM BOARD

TYPE B MOUNTING

MINERAL WOOL BETWEEN
SLAB & PERFORATED FACING
ATTACHED TO FURRING

TYPE C MOUNTING

ACOUSTIC TILE NAILED
TO FURRING STRIPS

TYPE D MOUNTING

STANDARD HUNG CEILING

TYPE E MOUNTING

MOUNTING DEPTH

Figure 5.8 ACOUSTIC TILE MOUNTING

These are the standard methods of mounting sound-absorptive materials used to determine sound absorption. The number following the mounting type, usually E, indicates the mounting depth, which is the distance in millimeters from the slab surface to the face of the acoustical treatment. Table 5.6 indicates mounting methods for various acoustical ceiling tiles.

CALCULATION PROBLEMS—NOISE REDUCTION

1. A space is 20 feet by 20 feet by 20 feet. In the initial condition, all surfaces are concrete, with an NRC rating of 0.01. In the proposed revised condition, all surfaces will be treated with a magical sound absorption material that has an NRC rating of 0.99. What would be the NR developed as a result of the addition of this amazing material to all of the enclosing room surfaces?

2. What would be the NR if the revised condition in the previous problem were changed to a space with an acoustical tile ceiling, carpeted floor, and plaster walls? Assume that the NRC of the tile ceiling is 0.75, that of the floor is 0.29, and that of the walls is 0.05.

3. What would be the NR if the initial condition was the revised absorption of the previous problem (ceiling NRC of 0.75, floor NRC of 0.29, and wall NRC of 0.05), and it was changed to the revised conditions of the first problem (NRC of all surfaces of 0.99)?

4. A space is 30 feet by 30 feet by 10 feet. In the initial condition, all wall surfaces are concrete block, with an NRC of 0.35, the floor is vinyl tile with an NRC of 0.05, and the ceiling is plaster with an NRC of 0.05. In the proposed revised condition, the ceiling surface will be covered with acoustical tile with an NRC of 0.95. What would be the NR?

Answers

1. $NR = 10 \log_{10} \dfrac{A_{rev}}{A_{initial}}$

   Total surface area of space $= 6 \, (20'\text{-}0'' \times 20'\text{-}0'') = 6 \times 400$ sq ft $= 2400$ sq ft

   Total Sabins of sound absorption:

   Initial: $A_{initial} = 2400$ sq ft $\times 0.01 = 24$ Sabins

   Revised: $A_{rev} = 2400$ sq ft $\times 0.99 = 2376$ Sabins

   $$NR = 10 \log_{10} \frac{2376}{24} = 10 \log_{10} 99 = 19.956$$
   $$\approx 20 \, dB$$

2. $NR = 10 \log_{10} \dfrac{A_{rev}}{A_{initial}}$

   Total Sabins of sound absorption:

   Initial: $A_{initial} = 2400$ sq ft $\times 0.01 = 24$ Sabins

   Revised: $A_{rev} = 400$ sq ft $\times 0.75 = 300$ Sabins

   $\qquad\qquad + 400$ sq ft $\times 0.29 = 116$ Sabins

   $\qquad\qquad + 1600$ sq ft $\times 0.05 = 80$ Sabins

   $\qquad\qquad = 496$ Sabins

   $$NR = 10 \log_{10} \frac{496}{24} = 10 \log_{10} 20.67 = 13.15$$
   $$\approx 13 \, dB$$

3. $NR = 10 \log_{10} \dfrac{A_{rev}}{A_{initial}}$

   Total Sabins of sound absorption:

   Initial: $A_{initial} = 400$ sq ft $\times 0.75 = 300$ Sabins

   $\qquad\qquad + 400$ sq ft $\times 0.29 = 116$ Sabins

   $\qquad\qquad + 1600$ sq ft $\times 0.05 = 80$ Sabins

   $\qquad\qquad = 496$ Sabins

   Revised: $A_{rev} = 2400$ sq ft $\times 0.99 = 2376$ Sabins

   $$NR = 10 \log_{10} \frac{2376}{496} = 10 \log_{10} 4.79 = 6.8 \approx 7 \, dB$$

4. $NR = 10 \log_{10} \dfrac{A_{rev}}{A_{initial}}$

   Surface areas of space:

   Ceiling $= (30' - 0'' \times 30' - 0'') = 900$ sq ft

   Floor $= (30' - 0'' \times 30' - 0'') = 900$ sq ft

   Walls $= 4(30' - 0'' \times 10' - 0'') = 1200$ sq ft

   Total Sabins of sound absorption:

   Initial: $A_{initial} = (900$ sq ft $\times 0.05)$

   $\qquad\qquad + (900$ sq ft $\times 0.05)$

   $\qquad\qquad + (1200$ sq ft $\times 0.35)$

   $\qquad\qquad = 510$ Sabins

   Revised: $A_{rev} = (900$ sq ft $\times 0.95)$

   $\qquad\qquad + (900$ sq ft $\times 0.05)$

   $\qquad\qquad + (1200$ sq ft $\times 0.35)$

   $\qquad\qquad = 1320$ Sabins

   $$NR = 10 \log_{10} \frac{1320}{510} = 10 \log_{10} 2.59 = 4.13 \approx 4 \, dB$$

Note that the change in the second problem from the "concrete bunker" to a somewhat reasonable acoustical treatment entails a change in total sound absorption, from 24 to 496 Sabins. This change is based on an addition of 472 Sabins, which produces a ratio of 1:20 and relates to a 13-dB NR. The change in the third problem is from 496 to 2376 Sabins, which requires an addition of 1880 Sabins. This is four times as much additional

sound absorption as in the second problem, but it produces a ratio of only 1:4.8 that results in only a 7-dB NR. What these simple problems indicate, beyond the calculation procedures, is that it is comparatively easy to obtain a significant NR if we start with very little sound absorption but quite difficult if the existing conditions include even a reasonable amount of sound absorption.

Room Sound Quality

There are essentially two bases for the acoustical quality of a space: background noise level and reverberation time. The background noise level is the general noise level within a space excluding the contribution from any sound related to the intended use of the space, such as holding a discussion in a classroom or listening to music in a lounge area. The reverberation time is the amount of time a sound can be sustained within a space. The longer a sound is sustained, the "fuller" it tends to be, although with certain sounds, such as speech, if the sound continues too long, it can reduce intelligibility.

Background Noise Level

In order to be heard, a sound needs to be louder than the background noise level. For clear audibility, it is recommended that the difference in sound level be about 20 dB or more. Since our sensitivity to sound is not constant, acceptable background sound levels are adjusted for the different sound frequencies in a manner somewhat similar to that of the equal loudness curves.

In the 1950s, Leo Beranek, one of the founding partners of the acoustic consulting firm Bolt, Beranek, and Newman, developed a background noise rating system that accounted for our reduced sensitivity to noise at lower frequencies. This system included a series of curves, which Beranek called *noise criteria* (NC) curves. These curves, which are shown in Figure 5.9, are related to different background noise levels. Like equal loudness curves, NC curves are related to sound pressure levels (SPLs); however, NC curves represent the maximum sound level that can exist for each NC rating, whereas equal loudness or phons curves indicate a perceived loudness based on the actual energy level of a sound at the various frequencies. Another distinction is that the correlation between the NC curves and the actual SPL is not clear. It is generally at 1500 Hz, not 4000 Hz, at which we are most sensitive, or 1000 Hz, which is the correlation frequency for the actual SPL and the equal loudness curves.

While NC curves continue to be used, a number of similar curves are also used to determine allowable background noise levels. In 1971, preferred noise criteria (PNC) curves were developed. These curves, which are shown in Figure 5.10, were extended to include lower frequencies, somewhat reduced the allowable levels for low- and high-frequency sounds, and switched the "correlation" frequency to 1000 Hz. The room criteria (RC) curves, which were adopted by ASHRAE, also extend to lower frequencies. This system bases the rating of background noise on a set of straight lines that approximate variations in our hearing sensitivity rather than the curves and were proposed as a basis for determining the acceptable sound levels from mechanical equipment. The RC straight lines slope downward at −5 dB for each octave band as the frequency increases. Other means of rating background noise levels include the noise rating (NR) curves, which are mainly used outside of the United States, and the balanced noise criteria (NCB) curves.

While there are some differences among these systems for rating a background noise level, the NC and PNC curves are quite similar and are used the same way. The background sound level for each of the different octave bands is measured, and these values are plotted on the curves. Assuming use of the NC curves, the appropriate NC rating is the NC curve that defines the upper limit of the plotted spectrum—the lowest NC curve that is not exceeded by any point of the plotted spectrum. As indicated in Figure 5.11, a plot of the measured noise within a space, shown by the dashed line, has its highest point at the NC-40 curve, indicating that this condition has an NC rating of 40.

Of course, we select a rating system and then use it to find what the adjusted background noise rating will be in order to determine whether conditions will be acceptable for the intended use of a space. In general terms, NC curves 35 and below are indicative of very quiet to quiet conditions. Spaces that comply with NC curves between 35 and 55 are considered to be moderately noisy to noisy, and spaces that comply with NC curves between 55 and 65 are considered to be very noisy. Those that comply with NC curves above 65 are considered to be extremely

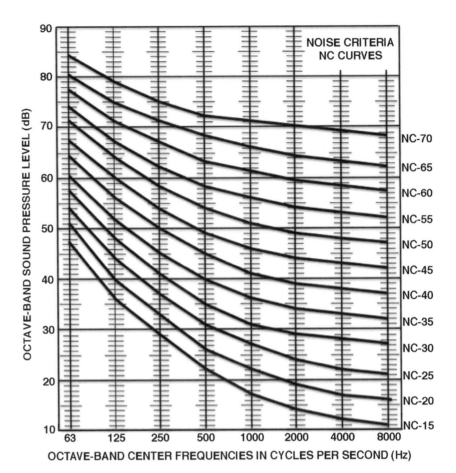

Figure 5.9 NC CURVES

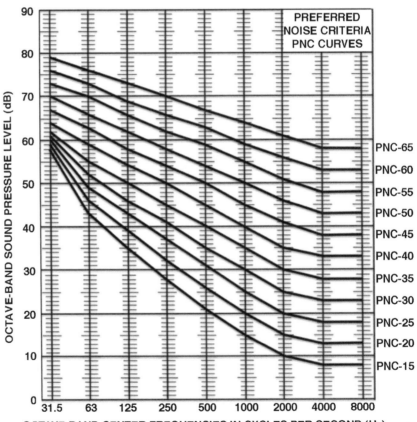

Figure 5.10 PREFERRED NOISE CRITERIA CURVES

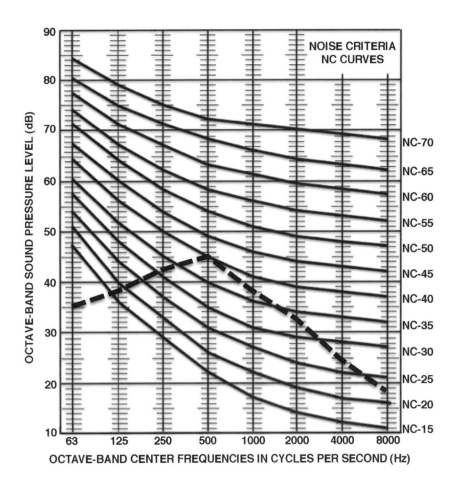

Figure 5.11 NC CURVES WITH PLOTTED SOUND

noisy. Of course, these are relative interpretations that are somewhat dependent on the nature of the activity.

The background noise level in a space is a result of the noise being generated within that space, such as from mechanical equipment, and of noises that are transmitted into that space from outside or adjacent spaces. This background noise level is also affected by the Sabins of sound absorption within the space. So, to meet the appropriate background NC, we should take several actions. First, we should attempt to eliminate or at least reduce the sources of noise within the space. While this deals directly with control of the sound sources, as we have seen above, increasing sound absorption within the space will also reduce the sound level. Another action is to provide good sound isolation for the space by reducing the transmission of these outside noises into the space. Of course, these outside noises, which could be from sources within the building or outside it, might also be reduced by lowering the power of the source, increasing the separation distance, and/or adding sound absorption in the source space to effectively reduce the sound level of that source.

Table 5.7 lists appropriate background-noise criteria or NC ratings that are recommended for various types of space or activity. These recommended NC levels are presented in a range of sound levels, most of which entail a 5-dB spread, although a few exceed this amount. Since a 5-dB change represents a clearly noticeable difference, it should be apparent that there is considerable latitude in defining background noise levels. Table 5.7 also includes the equivalent dBA sound level associated with each of the listed NC levels. The differences between the two levels indicate that the NC curves and the dBA or phons curves are uncorrelated, on average, by about 10 dB.

This difference between the recommended NC level and the equivalent dBA sound level is based primarily on the difference in the way NC levels and dBA sound levels are established. NC levels are determined by comparing curves of measured background sound energy levels for each octave band with the NC curves. As such, they are set essentially by only the measured sound level of one octave band. On the other hand, sound levels denoted by the dBA scale are based on the combined sound levels of all octave bands, although these octave levels are adjusted to respond to the sensitivity of the human auditory system. Since eight octave bands are used for the NC curve, only one of which sets the NC level, the equivalent sound level in dBA is established by essentially eight times the energy level used for the recommended NC level, hence the 10-dB difference.

Table 5.7: RECOMMENDED BACKGROUND-NOISE CRITERIA FOR SPACES

Type of Space or Activity	Recommended NC Level	Equivalent Sound Level dBA
Assembly Halls	25–30	35–40
Concert and Recital Halls	15–20	25–30
Legitimate Theaters	20–25	30–65
Motion Picture Theaters	30–35	40–45
Church, Synagogue, or Mosque	30–35	40–45
Court Rooms	30–40	40–50
Libraries	35–40	40–50
Restaurants	40–45	50–55
Offices		
Conference Rooms	25–30	35–40
Private	30–35	40–45
Open-plan Areas	35–40	45–50
Schools		
Lecture and Classrooms	25–30	35–40
Open-plan Classrooms	35–40	45–50
Housing		
Apartments	25–35	35–45
Private Residences	25–35	35–45
Hotels/Motels		
Individual Rooms or Suites	25–35	35–45
Meeting or Banquet Rooms	25–35	35–45
Service and Support Areas	40–45	45–50
Halls, Corridors, Lobbies	35–40	50–55
Computers/Business Machines	40–45	50–55
Hospitals and Clinics		
Private Rooms	25–30	35–40
Operating Rooms	25–30	35–40
Wards	30–35	40–45
Laboratories	35–40	45–50
Corridors	30–35	40–45
Public Areas	35–40	45–50
Factories	40–65	50–75
Sport Coliseums	45–55	55–65
Recording Studios	15–20	25–30
Sound Broadcasting	15–20	25–30
TV Broadcast Studios	15–25	25–35

Source: Adapted from various tables including one developed by The Engineering ToolBox and included in Egan M. D.; *Architectural Acoustics*, McGraw-Hill Inc., New York, 1988 and a table in Cavanaugh, W. J. and Wilkes, J. A.: *Architectural Acoustics – Principles and Practice*, John Wiley & Sons, Inc., Hoboken, NJ, 1999.

For convenience, let us assume that the measured sound levels for all eight octave bands, shown in Table 5.8, follow the 40-dB NC curve. If we determine the decibel value indicated by the NC curve for each octave band and apply the dBA adjustment to these values, we can find the sound intensity in watts per square centimeter of the perceived sound. This is the sum of the adjusted sound intensity for each of the octave bands. For this assumption,

Table 5.8: ADJUSTMENTS BETWEEN NC CURVES AND DBA LEVELS

40 NC Curve	dBA Adjustment	Octave Band dBA	dBA Sound Intensity
65 dB @ 63 Hz.	−27	38 dB	6.3×10^{-13} w cm^{-2}
56 dB @ 125 Hz.	−16	40 dB	10^{-12} w cm^{-2}
50 dB @ 250 Hz.	−8	42 dB	1.6×10^{-12} w cm^{-2}
45 dB @ 500 Hz.	−3	49 dB	7.9×10^{-12} w cm^{-2}
41 dB @ 1,000 Hz.	0	41 dB	1.3×10^{-12} w cm^{-2}
39 dB @ 2,000 Hz.	+2	41 dB	1.3×10^{-12} w cm^{-2}
38 dB @ 4,000 Hz.	+2	40 dB	10^{-12} w cm^{-2}
37 dB @ 8,000 Hz.	−2	35 dB	3.25×10^{-13} w cm^{-2}

This table lists the differentials between the NC curve and dBA ratings for 40 dB.

the total of the combined intensities is 1.5×10^{-11} w cm^{-2}. This correlates with 51 dB, which is about 10 dB higher than the 40-dB NC rating.

One of the concerns in terms of background noise level is how speech is heard. Unless we are dealing with performance spaces, the critical issue is whether or not the sound level of the speech will be adequate, which typically means louder than the background noise level by around 20 dB. Table 5.9, based on the work of William J. Cavanaugh, presents the nature of speech possible for various background noise levels.

There is also a question of the maximum allowable exposure to high sound levels. In the United States, these are set by the Occupational Safety and Health Administration (OSHA). The permitted hours of exposure each day to various sound levels are presented in Table 5.10. However, currently the intention is to reduce each level by 5 dB, thereby setting 85 dBA[2] as the loudest exposure without ear protection. Of course, if we wear ear protection that effectively reduces the sound level, we can be exposed to excessive sound levels for longer periods of time.

Exposure to loud sounds tends to cause hearing loss. The amount of hearing loss and the length of time that it might remain are based on the level of the sound to which one is exposed, the duration of exposure to the sound, and the age of the individual. Unfortunately, as we age, exposure to loud sounds tends, even for a limited time, to cause permanent hearing loss.

Reverberation Time

Travel time of an energy waveform is based on both its speed and the length of travel. With light, which travels extremely fast, there is no perceived difference in travel

---

[2] While dBA is generally used for OSHA limitations, the difference in our auditory sensibility for different frequencies tends to flatten out at higher sound levels. This suggests that it would be more appropriate to use the dBB and dBC scales for these OSHA regulations.

Table 5.9: NATURE OF SPEECH FOR VARIOUS BACKGROUND NOISE LEVELS

Background Sound Level dBA	Voice Effort Required and Distance	Nature of Communication Possible	Telephone Use
55	Normal Voice @ 10 ft	Relaxed Communication	Satisfactory
65	Normal Voice @ 3 ft	Continuous Communication	Satisfactory
	Raised Voice @ 6 ft		
	Very Loud Voice @ 12 ft		
75	Raised Voice @ 2 ft	Intermittent Communication	Marginal
	Very Loud Voice @ 12 ft		
	Shouting @ 8 ft		
85	Very Loud Voice @ 1 ft Shouting @ 2–3 ft	Minimal Communication (restricted prearranged vocabulary desirable)	Impossible

Source: Based on a table in Cavanaugh, W. J. and Wilkes, J. A.: *Architectural Acoustics – Principles and Practice*, John Wiley & Sons, Inc., Hoboken, NJ, 1999.

Table 5.10: OSHA ALLOWABLE SOUND EXPOSURE

Hours of Duration Per Day	Allowable Sound Level dBA
0.25 or less	115
0.5	110
1	105
1.5	102
2	100
3	97
4	95
6	92
8	90

Source: Based on a table in Cavanaugh, W. J. and Wilkes, J. A.: *Architectural Acoustics – Principles and Practice*, John Wiley & Sons, Inc., Hoboken, NJ, 1999.

time for the dimensions with which we are generally working in architectural design, but with sound, the difference can be pronounced for even relatively small dimensional variations.

Sound travels through air at a rate of 1130 feet per second, which is a relatively slow speed. As a result, there can be a noticeable difference in the time that it takes a sound to travel across spaces with different physical dimensions. The time that it takes for a sound to travel across a room and back, combined with the amount of sound that will be reflected off the surfaces that define the space, has a definite effect on the sound quality of that space. That is, both the physical size of the space and the amount of sound absorption in that space determine the length of time that a sound will be sustained, and the time delay between hearing the sound that comes directly from a sound source and hearing the sound reflected off the enclosing room surfaces will determine the acoustical ambiance of the space.

That is, the acoustical ambiance of a space is affected by the length of time that a sound is sustained and the time delay between hearing the sound that comes directly from a sound source and hearing the sound reflected off the

enclosing room surfaces. These are determined by several spatial factors: the dimensions of the space, its configuration, and the amount and placement of sound absorption.

Reverberation time (T_r), which indicates how long a sound will be sustained in a space, is defined as the time that it would take for a sound level to diminish by 60 dB. T_r can be calculated as follows:

$$T_r = 0.05 \frac{V}{A} \text{ sec,}$$

where:

V = room volume in cubic feet (for volume in cubic meters, replace 0.05 with 0.16)

A = total room absorption in Sabins

The longer sounds are sustained within a space by continued sound reflections, the "livelier" the space will be. Since large spaces and/or spaces with little sound absorption tend to sustain sound for a longer period of time, the reverberation time of a space strongly influences its perceived spatial character. Understanding this helps us recognize that acoustical design can either contribute to or fight against architectural intentions.

Appropriate reverberation times (T_r) are shown in Figure 5.12. As indicated, there is a considerable variation in the T_r that is deemed appropriate for different types of activity. Generally, the acceptable T_r for music is longer than the T_r for speech, since with extended reverberation the fullness of a sound is increased, while its intelligibility is reduced. Even with music there are preferred variations. Gregorian chant and organ music should be performed in space with rather long reverberation times, well over 2 seconds, while chamber music is more appropriate in spaces with reverberation times well below 2 seconds. If we consider the distinctions between these two forms of music, we realize that Gregorian chant music and much of the early organ music was performed in large stone cathedrals, whereas chamber music, as its name implies,

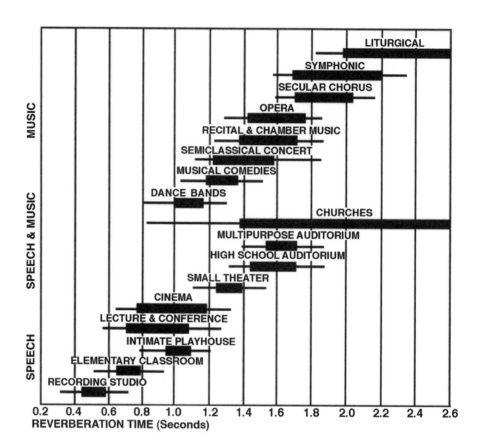

Figure 5.12 REVERBERATION TIMES
Based on a graph initially developed by Robert Newman and included in J.H. Callender (ed.), *Time-Saver Standards for Architectural Design Data* (McGraw-Hill, 1974), Figure 8.

was intended to be performed in much smaller and less acoustically hard rooms.

Spaces are often used for various activities for which distinct reverberation times might be appropriate. Fortunately, it is possible to adjust conditions to change the reverberation. One way is to augment conditions electronically. If a space that is relatively nonreverberant, or "dead," has an electronic sound reinforcement system, it is possible to add reverberation to the electronic signal. However, while this will work, it is not an architectural response. Rather than depend on a technological method, we can adjust the reverberation time architecturally. There are two basic approaches that we can follow: adjusting the acoustical volume of the space or altering the amount of sound absorption within the space.

Acoustical volume adjustment entails coupling spaces together when a greater reverberation time is desired and then separating them when the reverberation time should be less. A wonderful example of this approach was used at the Cincinnati Music Hall for many years until the original pipe organ was replaced with an electronic organ to make room for the opera company. While the electronic organ now provides its own reverberation, the pipe organ relied on coupling the auditorium with the attic. As shown in Figure 5.13, the ceiling of the auditorium has a slight central dome from which a grand chandelier hangs. The chandelier is suspended from the center of a grilled, open

escutcheon, above which there was a box that could be opened or closed, making it possible to connect the attic with the auditorium. Since the volume of the attic is about equal to the volume of the house, coupling the two spaces essentially doubled the reverberation time when the organ was played compared to the reverberation time for the symphony orchestra.

Reverberation time can also be changed by adjusting the amount of sound absorption within a space. As indicated in the basic formula, the change in reverberation time (*Tr*) is proportional to the change in Sabins of absorption. Figures 5.14 and 5.15 show a variety of ways for you to adjust sound absorption. While the methods shown in Figure 5.14 involve various ways of opening or closing off sound absorption materials by adjusting wall panels, some of which alter the visual appearance of the space, Figure 5.15 shows how it is possible to have moveable acoustic panels that can drop down into a space when lower reverberation times are deemed appropriate. While all of the methods can be quite effective in adjusting the reverberation time, the retracting sound-absorption panel can easily adjust the amount of sound absorption from none to all or any point in between.

The preferred reverberation time for speech is generally around 1 second; an extended time would mean that the sound is repeated in a way that would reduce intelligibility (delayed longer than 0.035 second). There is also a

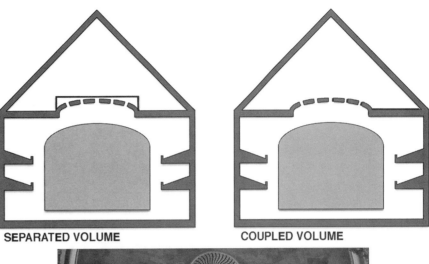

SEPARATED VOLUME   COUPLED VOLUME

Figure 5.13 ADJUSTABLE REVERBERATION VOLUME

The reverberation time of a space is proportional to the volume of the space, which means the effective contained volume rather than the visual spatial volume. Thus, it is possible to link two spaces together. When they are combined, the reverberation time within a space will increase compared to when it stands alone. The lower image shows this approach, which was used in the Cincinnati Music Hall before the pipe organ was replaced with an electronic organ during renovations to accommodate summer opera.

connection between the reverberation time we expect and the size of the space. In fact, we have a tendency to match spatial volume and reverberation time perceptually, so we expect and prefer longer reverberation times with larger spaces. That is, the preferred reverberation time for speech is not based merely on sound intelligibility. It is also based on the characteristics of the space.

The following empirical formula helps to determine the appropriate reverberation time (T_r) for a space to be used for speech presentation:

$$T_r = 0.3 \log_{10} \left(\frac{V}{350} \right) \text{ sec}$$

where:
$V =$ room volume, ft^3

$$T_r = 0.3 \log_{10} \left(\frac{V}{10} \right) \text{ sec}$$

where:
$V =$ room volume, m^3

Understanding all of this, we might still question how to determine what might be the appropriate amount of

sound absorption that should be provided for a space. Assuming that speech is probably the most critical sound for which we need to design in most nonperformance spaces, we can choose an appropriate T_r for a space, which would generally be around 1 second, and then use the basic reverberation time formula to establish a total sound absorption target. Accepting a T_r of 1 second, the proposed total room absorption in Sabins would be equal to 0.05 times the volume of the space.

$$T_r = 0.05 \left\{ \frac{\text{Volume in ft}^3}{\text{Total Sabins of Absorption}} \right\}$$

$$\text{Total Sabins of Absorption} = 0.05 \left\{ \frac{\text{Volume in ft}^3}{T_r} \right\}$$

$$= 0.06 \left\{ \frac{\text{Volume in ft}^3}{1.0} \right\} = 0.05 \times \text{Volume in ft}^3$$

If the desired reverberation time is not 1 second, then we can adjust the "constant" in the above formula, as indicated in Table 5.11.

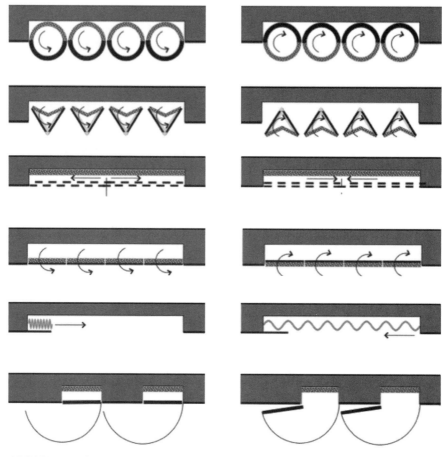

Figure 5.14 EXAMPLES OF ADJUSTABLE SOUND ABSORPTION

There are various ways to adjust the sound absorption of an exposure, many that can give a visual articulation of the changing conditions. Adapted from L.L. Doelle, *Environmental Acoustics* (McGraw-Hill Book Company, New York, 1972), Figure 5.24.

ABSORPTIVE SURFACE CONCEALED   **ABSORPTIVE SURFACE EXPOSED**

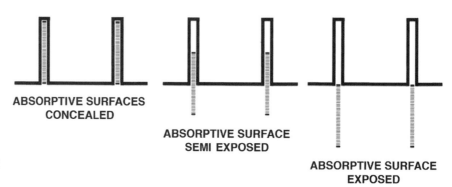

Figure 5.15 ADJUSTABLE CEILING SOUND ABSORPTION PANELS

With a lower ceiling, it is possible to adjust room sound absorption by moving sound absorption panels into and out of holding pockets since the surface area providing absorption is not limited to the exposed area of the conventional elements that define the space.

ABSORPTIVE SURFACES CONCEALED

ABSORPTIVE SURFACE SEMI EXPOSED

ABSORPTIVE SURFACE EXPOSED

Table 5.11: REVERBERATION-TIME CONSTANTS

T_r		Constant	T_r		Constant
0.5 sec	–	0.10	1.0 sec	–	0.05
1.5 sec	–	0.033	2.0 sec	–	0.025
2.5 sec	–	0.02	3.0 sec	–	0.017

CALCULATION PROBLEMS—REVERBERATION

1. If a space were 40 feet by 80 feet, with a ceiling height of 12 feet, what would be the appropriate reverberation time for speech?

2. Assume that there is a space that is 40 feet by 60 feet by 20 feet. If the ceiling in the space has an NRC of 0.80, the walls have an NRC average of 0.05, and the floor has an NRC of 0.10, what would be the reverberation time for the space?

3. What would be the preferred or optimum reverberation time for the above space for speech?

4. Since the calculated optimum reverberation time for speech is less than the reverberation time of the space, what could be done to achieve a reverberation time that is acceptable for speech? How might we actually achieve this improvement? What changes in the sound absorption of the floor might we expect if we used carpeting?

5. Assume that there is a space that is 10 feet by 15 feet by 8 feet high. If the ceiling in the space has an NRC of 0.95, the walls have an NRC average of 0.05, and the floor has an NRC of 0.05, what would be the reverberation time for the space?

6. What would be the preferred or optimum reverberation time for the above space for speech? What could be done with this space to achieve a reverberation time that is acceptable for speech?

Answers

1.
$$T_r = 0.3 \log_{10} \left(\frac{40' \times 80' \times 12'}{350} \right) = 0.6 \, \text{sec}$$

2. Surface area of space:

Ceiling = 40′ − 0″ × 60′ − 0″ = 2400 sq ft
Floor = 40′ − 0″ × 60′ − 0″ = 2400 sq ft
Walls = 20′ − 0″ × (40′ + 40′ + 60′ + 60′)
= 4000 sq ft

Volume of space:

2400 sq ft × 20′ − 0″ = 48,000 cu ft

Total Sabins of sound absorption:

Ceiling = 2400 sq ft × 0.80 = 1920 Sabins
Floor = 2400 sq ft × 0.10 = 240 Sabins
Wall = 4000 sq ft × 0.05 = 200 Sabins
= 2360 Sabins

$$\text{Reverberation Time } (T_r) = 0.05 \frac{V}{A}$$
$$= 0.05 \frac{48,000 \, \text{cu ft}}{2360 A} = 1.017 \, \text{sec}$$

3. Optimum reverberation time for speech, with volume in cubic feet:
$$0.3 \log \frac{V}{350} = 0.3 \log_{10} \frac{48,000 \, \text{cu ft}}{350} = 0.642 \, \text{sec}$$

4. While it might be possible to reduce the volume of the space, this would also reduce the calculated optimum reverberation time for speech. A more successful method of improving speech quality would be to increase the sound absorption within the space. Since the existing T_r of 1.017 seconds should be changed to a T_r of 0.642 seconds, we would have to increase the total number of Sabins from 2360A by a factor of 1.58 to a new total number of Sabins of 3740A.

$$\frac{1.017}{0.642} = 1.58$$

With this new amount of Sabins of sound absorption, the reverberation time would be:

$$\text{Reverberation Time } (T_r) = 0.05 \frac{48,000 \, \text{cu ft}}{3740 A}$$
$$= 0.642 \, \text{sec}$$

To achieve this improvement, we might consider adding carpeting. The existing floor has an NRC of 0.10 and a floor area of 2400 square feet. To obtain an increase in sound absorption of 1380A (i.e., 3740A − 2360A), we would have to obtain a new NRC for the floor of 0.675 (i.e., $\frac{1380A}{2400 \, \text{sq ft}} + 0.10$). By referring to Table 5.6, we see that heavy carpeting on a pad would have an NRC of 0.55. While this will help, it will not be sufficient. We still need to add 300 Sabins of sound absorption (i.e., 1380A − [2400 sq ft × (0.55 − 0.10)]). We should be able to accomplish this addition by selecting a slightly improved ceiling tile. Alternatively, we could just accept the reverberation time achieved with the addition of carpet on the pad since it will be close to the calculated optimum reverberation time for speech.

$$\text{Reverberation Time } (T_r) = 0.05 \frac{48,000 \text{ cu ft}}{3440\,A}$$
$$\approx 0.7 \text{ sec}$$

5. Reverberation Time $(T_r) = 0.05\dfrac{V}{A}$

Surface area of space:

$$\begin{aligned}
\text{Ceiling} &= 10' - 0'' \times 15' - 0'' = 150 \text{ sq ft} \\
\text{Floor} &= 10' - 0'' \times 15' - 0'' = 150 \text{ sq ft} \\
\text{Walls} &= 8' - 0'' \times (10' + 10' + 15' + 15') \\
&= 400 \text{ sq ft}
\end{aligned}$$

Volume of space:

$$150 \text{ sq ft} \times 8' - 0'' = 1200 \text{ cu ft}$$

Total Sabins of sound absorption:

$$\begin{aligned}
\text{Ceiling} &= 150 \text{ sq ft} \times 0.95 = 142.5 \text{ Sabins} \\
\text{Floor} &= 150 \text{ sq ft} \times 0.05 = 7.5 \text{ Sabins} \\
\text{Wall} &= 400 \text{ sq ft} \times 0.05 = 20.0 \text{ Sabins} \\
&= 170.0 \text{ Sabins}
\end{aligned}$$

$$\text{Reverberation Time } (T_r) = 0.05\,\frac{1200 \text{ cu ft}}{170}$$
$$= 0.35 \text{ sec}$$

6. Optimum reverberation time for speech, with volume in cubic feet: $0.3\log\frac{V}{350} = 0.3\log\frac{1200\text{ cu ft}}{350} = 0.16$ sec

While it might be possible to increase the sound absorption to come closer to the calculated optimum reverberation time for speech, since the reverberation time is already rather low and since the space is small, an adjustment does not seem appropriate. In fact, the use of the optimum reverberation time calculation is not for small spaces but rather for lecture halls and theaters. So, no adjustment is suggested.

SOUND DISTRIBUTION

The study of sound distribution within a space is often based on straight-line ray distribution diagrams. Since the angle of reflection generally equals the angle of incidence, a simple ray distribution diagram, as shown in Figure 5.16, can provide a reasonable representation of the probable sound distribution. Sometimes the study of sound distribution can reasonably be accomplished with scale models in which light rays are used to represent sound waves. While light and sound are not the same, effective results can be achieved with ray studies based on light. The reflectivity of the surfaces to light can be modeled to represent the acoustical reflectivity. The use of actual sound in model studies is also possible as long as the frequency is adjusted to compensate for the scale difference. Because the wavelengths of sound extend between about $1/2$ inch at high frequencies to around 50 feet at low frequencies, the frequency of the sound used in scale models must be adjusted proportionally with the change in scale, which is rather complicated since the adjusted higher frequencies are not audible. Another complication is that the sound absorption is also frequency dependent. With computer enhancements and electronic measurements, acoustical studies through scale model simulations have produced reasonable indications of acoustical performance in the actual spaces.

In studying sound distribution within a space, we must remain cognizant of the maximum 0.035 second that should exist between an initially heard sound and a delayed reflected sound that will reinforce the initial sound

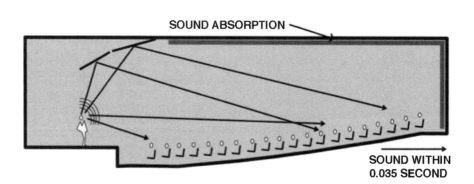

SOUND ABSORPTION

SOUND WITHIN 0.035 SECOND

Figure 5.16 RAY DIAGRAM

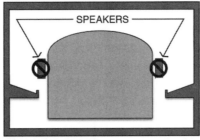 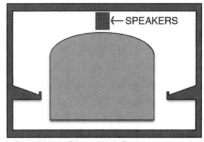

SPLIT SPEAKERS   **CENTRAL SPEAKERS**

Figure 5.17 ELECTRONIC SPEAKER LOCATIONS

rather than impair it. If a sound, which travels in air at 1130 feet per second (fps), takes a circuitous route between the source and the receiver, the difference in length of travel must be less than 40 feet in order to arrive no later than 0.035 second after the initial sound.

$$40 \text{ ft} = 1130 \text{ fps} \times 0.035 \text{ sec}$$

In addition to the time delay that might occur between the arrival of a direct sound and a reflected sound, we must consider the appropriate size of the reflecting surface. In order for a surface to reflect a sound, the surface must be larger than the sound wave. For example, a 300-Hz sound wave, which is at the bottom of the critical range for human speech, has a wavelength just under 4'-0" in length. Therefore, a panel that is intended to reflect speech should be at least around 4'-0" square. If the intention is to reinforce symphonic music, which includes critical lower-frequency sound, the reflecting panel should be larger, at least 8'-0" square, if not more.

Since surfaces can reflect sound and, based on the orientation of the surface, direct the reflected sound to an intended location, we should also be aware of the possible reflections of unwanted sounds, such as might occur from the audience. As a result, we should consider adding sound absorption to those surfaces that could cause a problem. That is, we need to reflect the sounds that are desired while absorbing those that are not.

As architectural designers, we can do a lot to provide effective sound reinforcement through appropriate design and the proper selection of surfaces and finishes. At times, however, we might have to incorporate electronic sound reinforcement. When we do, we should use it as a means of enhancing our design efforts rather than supplanting them. In taking this approach, we need to ensure that, whenever possible, the initial sound that one hears is a direct nonelectronic sound from the source and that any electronic reinforcement comes after the direct "real" sound. This is important since the initial sound that we hear determines how we locate the source of the sound. Properly designed, delayed sound reinforcement can increase the perceived sound level without supplanting the recognition of the initial real sound.

As a result, if we must incorporate electronic sound reinforcement, we should design the sound system so that the electronic sound arrives after the direct sound. In this way, the origin of the sound will be set by the actual sound source, and the electronic sound will reinforce it.

For effective sound reinforcement, we should locate the speakers centrally over the actual performance area rather than on either side (see Figure 5.17). On first thought, this might seem contrary to what we normally do when we are arranging speakers for a home sound system—place the speakers at either side of the room. With a home sound system, we should also position ourselves at a distance from the speakers so that we can hear a balanced sound from both speakers, but in a theater or auditorium, while it is likely that part of the audience will be far enough from the side speakers so that the electronic sound will be balanced and arrive after the direct sound, it is also probable that there will be others who are located near one of the side speakers. As a result, these individuals will perceive that the original sound emanates from the nearby speaker and, based on the way that the actual sound is distributed to the two side speakers, might not hear a balanced reproduction of the real sound.

If the electronic reinforcement comes from speakers located above the performance area, the electronic sound will appear to come from the original source and will likely arrive slightly after the direct sound. As a result, the real sound will be enhanced.

At times, we might have to rely on ceiling speakers to achieve acceptable sound distribution in a theater or auditorium. For example, if there is a balcony that is not configured in a way that redirects sound, the balcony will tend to prevent a major portion of the sound from reaching the audience sitting underneath the overhang. This can happen whether the sound comes directly from the source or from front electronic speakers.

This problem can be reduced by incorporating ceiling speakers under the balcony. If the ceiling speakers are delayed so that the sound they emit arrives after the direct sound, they will effectively reinforce that direct sound, but if the speakers are not electronically delayed, their sound will be interpreted as the sound source. Since the initially

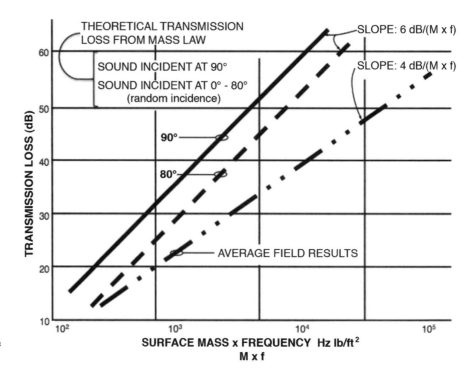

Figure 5.18 MASS LAW ATTENUATION
Adapted from B. Stein, J.S. Reynolds, W.T. Grondzik, and A.G. Kwok, *Mechanical and Electrical Equipment for Buildings* (John Wiley & Sons, Inc., New Jersey, 2006), Figure 19.12.

heard sound establishes the origin of the sound, the perception is that the source is above and perhaps even behind the listener—not a very effective hearing experience.

SOUND ISOLATION

The isolation of sound within an architectural environment is generally dependent on three factors: mass, resiliency, and tightness. The mass of an isolating architectural barrier is important since the construction assembly essentially acts as diaphragm that absorbs the source sound and then reemits it. For other than impact sounds, which is a special area of architectural acoustics, the sound incident on the isolating barrier usually entails the compression and rarefaction of air. As this variation in the air pressure impinges on the barrier, it sets the barrier in motion. The heavier the barrier, the less likely that the variation in air pressure will produce a significant vibration in the barrier, and with less barrier movement, less sound will be transmitted across the barrier.

The theoretical mass law suggests that with each doubling of the mass of an acoustical barrier, there is a 6-dB increase in the transmission loss. (Note that an increase in the transmission loss means a reduction in the amount of sound transmitted.) At times, this is shown by the following formula that has been found to work for 500 Hz:

$$TL_{500 \text{ Hz.}} = 20 + 20 \log_{10}(\text{wt of Barrier in lb/sq ft})$$

While we continue to refer to the theoretical mass law, the actual adjustment in transmission loss of a sound barrier is based on mass times frequency. Therefore, if the product of mass times frequency is doubled, there is a 6-dB increase. This is shown in Figure 5.18, which also indicates that the angle of incidence at which the sound enters a sound barrier is also a factor that affects the transmission. When this angle of incidence is close to 90°, the 6-dB slope holds true. With average conditions that include various angles of incidence, the change in transmission loss tends to be closer to 4 dB for each doubling of mass times frequency.

While the change in the product of mass times frequency does tend to correlate with a general change in sound transmission for much of a sound barrier, whether at a 6-dB or a 4-dB slope, other factors also have an impact on the way sound at different frequencies can be transmitted across a wall or through a ceiling/floor assembly. Based on the construction of the barrier, stiffness, resonance, and critical frequency can cause sudden adjustments in sound transmission. As shown in Figure 5.19, resonance and critical frequency tend to increase sound transfer, whereas stiffness tends to resist movement within the barrier, decreasing sound transfer.

As shown in Figure 5.20, the critical frequency of a barrier is a function of both its thickness and the materials from which it is constructed. Of course, most partitions do not consist of only one homogeneous material. For this reason, and because of the effects of stiffness, resonance, and coincidence, the actual expected attenuation for a

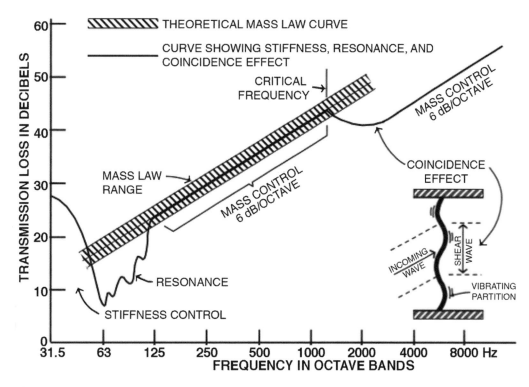

Figure 5.19 MASS LAW PARTITION ATTENUATION

While a partition generally adheres to the theoretical mass law, at low frequencies there is some resonance and at higher frequencies a coincidence effect, both of which tend to increase sound transmission. Adapted from B. Stein, J.S. Reynolds, W.T. Grondzik, and A.G. Kwok, *Mechanical and Electrical Equipment for Buildings* (John Wiley & Sons, Inc., Hoboken, New Jersey, 2006), Figure 19.13

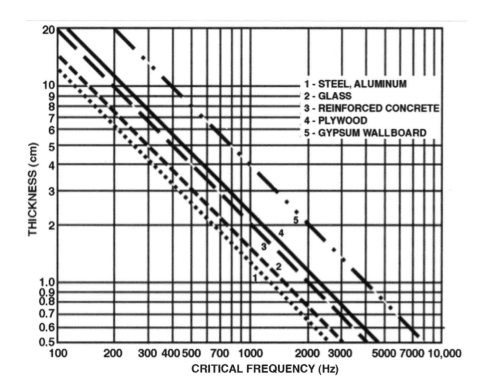

Figure 5.20 CRITICAL FREQUENCY AS A FUNCTION OF MATERIAL AND THICKNESS

Adapted from B. Stein, B., J.S. Reynolds, W.T. Grondzik, and A.G. Kwok, *Mechanical and Electrical Equipment for Buildings* (John Wiley & Sons, Inc., Hoboken, New Jersey, 2006), Figure 19.14 .

partition must be determined by testing in a laboratory rather than on theoretical projections, although these projections are helpful in proposing modifications to a standard design or perhaps even developing a rather unique new partition configuration.

While increasing mass can reduce sound transmission, each subsequent increase provides a diminishing return. For example, if the effective TL for a 3-inch concrete wall is 47 dB, based on the theoretical mass law the effective TL for a 6-inch concrete wall would be 6 dB higher, or 53 dB. If this wall is then doubled to 12 inches, the improvement is again only 6 dB for a total of 59 dB. While not quite legitimate, if we divide the *TL* improvement for each inch of added concrete thicknesses, we see that for the initial 3-inch wall, each inch of concrete appears to provide 16 dB of transmission loss. For the second condition, since 3 inches provide a 6-dB improvement, each additional inch accounts for only 2 dB. In the third condition, 6 inches provide a 6-dB improvement, or only 1dB per added inch of concrete.

Besides diminishing returns, another factor to consider about increasing mass as the way to reduce sound transmission is that added weight increases structural loads. Fortunately, there are ways in which we can improve sound isolation without adding mass. Another way of reducing sound transmission is through resiliency. In this method, rather than rely on the mass of the barrier to inhibit sound transmission, the construction assembly uses resilient connections so that impinging sounds do not establish direct movement through the barrier. If a resilient component is provided within the assembly, the movement of one side of the barrier is not directly transmitted to the opposing side. As a result, the sound is effectively dampened, and less sound is transmitted. Table 5.12 shows the increase in TL at various frequencies for several depths of air space.

Adding an air space is a simple way to gain resiliency in a sound barrier. For example, if we used a wall comprised of two 4-inch brick wythes separated by a $1^1/_2$-inch air space rather than a solid 8-inch brick wall, we would improve the transmission loss, on average, by more than 6 dB. That is, a $9^1/_2$-inch wall with 8 inches of masonry would provide sound isolation equivalent to that of a solid 16-inch brick wall. To be effective, the air space must allow for independent movement of the two wythes. If we used rigid metal ties to link the wythes, we would effectively lose the improvement in TL.

Staggered-stud and double-stud walls also separate the wall components and add resiliency. Staggered studs entail two rows of studs, each set at 16 inches o.c. or 24 inches o.c. With 2 × 4 top and sole plates, the studs are generally 2 × 3, and for 2 × 4 studs, we usually use 2 × 6 plates.

Table 5.12: IMPROVEMENT IN TL RESULTING FROM AIR SPACES

Frequency	Depth or Thickness of Air Space		
	1.5"	3"	6"
500 Hz.	2 dB	6 dB	11 dB
1000 Hz.	6 dB	10 dB	15 dB
2000 Hz.	9 dB	14 dB	19 dB
4000 Hz.	12 dB	17 dB	22 dB

While this reduces the movement of one side of the stud wall to cause movement on the other side, sharing the top and sole plates actually limits the reduction. With a double-stud wall, with different plates for each row of studs, the TL is higher.

Using mounting clips or metal channels, as shown in Figure 5.21, is a third way to add resiliency. In this approach, panelized materials, such as gypsum board or wood fiberboard, are attached to the structural support in a way that limits the direct transmission of movement between the panels and the structure, typically framing studs. Resilient channels are usually thin metal around $^1/_2$ inch high.

Adding sound-absorptive materials within a sound barrier can also increase the effective sound transmission loss by around 4 to 6 dB. This is usually accomplished by adding sound insulation to an air space that exists within the construction assembly. While there is special sound insulation, this is essentially standard fiberglass batt insulation and does not perform significantly better.

Actually, sound insulation is not effective in stopping sound transmission. Sound insulation is a sound absorber, and it works as such because it is porous and the sound can pass through it. As it does, some of the sound is converted

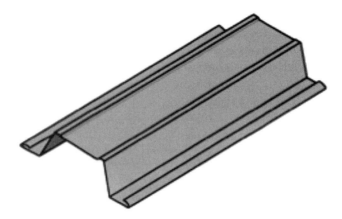

Figure 5.21 RESILIENT METAL CHANNEL
A light-gauge metal channel can provide a way to attach gypsum board with added resiliency.

into heat and the acoustical energy is reduced. So, rather than stopping sound transmission, the insulation absorbs sound within the air space, thereby lowering the sound level in the space and, as a result, reducing the amount of sound that is transmitted. While this process might seem convoluted, it is important to understand how sound insulation works, since if we attempted to use sound insulation by itself as a way to stop sound transmission, it would not be effective.

The following situation provides another example of how sound absorption can impact sound transmission, but in this case the absorption material is added to the surface of the sound barrier.

If sound coming from an adjacent space is a problem, adding sound absorption on the noise-source side of the common wall between the two spaces would effectively reduce the sound coming through the wall. We might assume that since the sound coming through the wall is reduced, the added sound absorption effectively increased the transmission loss of the common wall. This assumption would be wrong. Again, it is not that the sound transmission has been reduced, but rather that the added sound absorption in the source room has effectively reduced the sound level in that room, and as a result, the transmitted sound is also less. If the same amount of sound absorption had been added in the sound-source room but on a surface other than the common wall, the same reduction in sound would have occurred.

Transmission loss between spaces, like sound absorption within a space, is dependent on sound frequency. While separate calculations can be executed for each octave band, typically an average transmission loss is used. This average is provided by the sound transmission class (STC), which is adjusted for human sensitivity and is used for general sound transmission loss calculations. Unlike the NRC, which is merely an average of the absorption for different frequencies (between 250 and 2000 Hz), the STC is found by comparing the sound transmission at the various octave-band frequencies with a standardized curve, which are shown in Figure 5.22. This is somewhat similar to the way we use NC curves to determine the background noise level.

While the high point of the plotted measurements of noise level sets the NC curve for background noise levels, the procedure to determine the STC for a sound barrier is a little more involved (see Figure 5.23). We begin by finding the sound transmission for each octave band and plotting these values on the STC graph. However, rather than set the high point of the plot against an STC curve, we need to find an STC curve for which no point on the plotted measurements is more than 8 dB below the curve and the total area of the plotted measurements below the

curve does not exceed the area equal to an STC curve that is 1 dB below the selected STC curve.

For this reason, sound barriers with the same STC can perform quite differently. Figure 5.24 presents the sound transmission plots for two different sound barriers. While the sounds that can pass through these barriers appear to be quite different, both of the barriers have an STC of 45. Although the barrier with the higher plot transmits less sound, because the plot dips down at around 700 Hz, its STC is only 45. The lower plot, which will obviously transmit more sound, also ends up with an STC of 45 even though it seems to be considerably below that curve. As Figure 5.24 shows, the total area below the 45 STC curve only amounts to the area of a 1-dB difference, which is shown in the curve that is below the plot of the sound transmission.

Standardized STC curves extend from 125 to 4000 Hz, and the STC rating for each is set at 500 Hz.

While the transmission loss for each octave band should be analyzed for critical installations, architectural sound isolation calculations are typically executed merely on the basis of STC values. Rather than having to use the STC standardized curves, we can access listings of STC values for various interior wall construction assemblies. These are included in Tables 5.13 and Table 5.14. These tables list the sound transmission loss at the different frequencies for various construction assemblies and their appropriate STC values.

As we can see by reviewing these values, since the STC is not an average of the sound transmission losses at the different frequencies, it does not necessarily relate to these losses. In fact, because of the different requirements, the STC for a partition could be quite different from what the various octave-band losses might suggest.

By reviewing the STC tables, we can see a number of things. Increasing the mass, which is possible by increasing the thickness of gypsum boards or even doubling them, will improve the STC rating. Adding sound insulation is also effective, often by 6 dB or more. Resilient mounting, staggered studs, and especially double-stud walls are also effective, and metal stud walls perform better that wood stud walls.

While Table 5.14 includes STC ratings for a few exterior walls, there are some who believe that STC should only be used for interior partitions and floor/ceiling assemblies. The reasoning is that outside sounds are different from interior sounds, and since these sounds include noises from vehicular traffic and airplanes, the STC rating is not appropriate. Several alternative classifications have been proposed.

The outside-inside transmission class (OITC) rating has been proposed as the method to classify exterior-interior

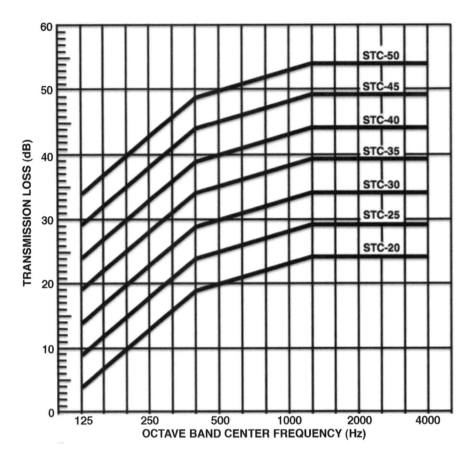

Figure 5.22 STANDARDIZED CURVES FOR SOUND TRANSMISSION CLASS (STC)

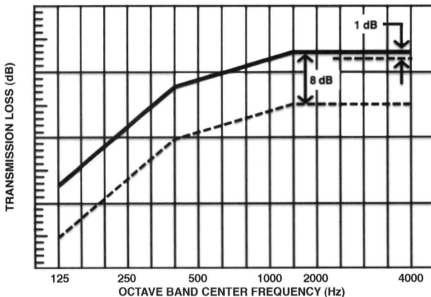

Figure 5.23 STC ADJUSTMENTS
The STC rating for a constructed assembly is ultimately determined by comparing measured sound transmission against a standardized curve. The STC rating is based on the STC curve that is no higher than 8 dB above any point on the line representing the measured transmission and for which the area between the STC curve and that line does not exceed the area representing an average of 1 dB.

sound transmission of glazing. The suggested difference between this and STC is in terms of the sound frequencies. Whereas STC ratings are based on "white" noise, which is a broadband spectrum of sound, OITC ratings utilize a sound source distribution that combines aircraft and truck traffic and is weighted more to the lower frequencies.

The exterior wall rating (EWR) has also been proposed for exterior-interior sound transmissions. While this system is similar to the STC system, it is distinct in terms of adjusting the spectrum of noise against which the ratings are based. There is also the exterior wall noise rating (EWNR), which is based on the A-weighted decibel response curve

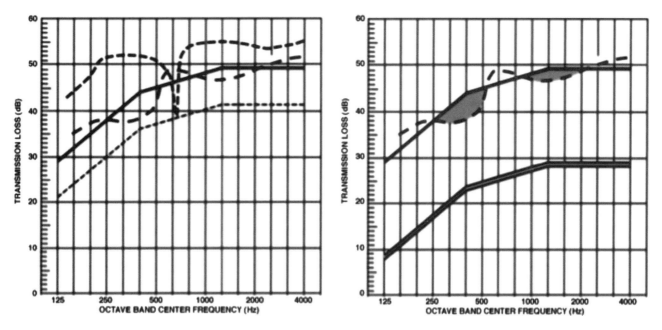

Figure 5.24 STC COMPARISONS
The same STC rating might be assigned to barriers that have considerably different transmissions. As shown, one STC is based on the 8 dB rule, while the other is based on an average of no more than 1dB area below the STC curve.

or, more specifically, the 40-dB or phons equal loudness contour. This curve correlates more closely with exterior traffic noises.

While sound transmission and STC ratings are appropriate for a particular construction assembly, actual conditions might be somewhat different. For example, sound transmission often occurs across a composite barrier, such as a wall in which there is a door or window.

Figure 5.25 includes a graph that we can use to determine the effective performance of a composite acoustical barrier. While the original of this graph was in terms of transmission loss (TL), since we usually use only STC ratings, Figure 5.25 has been converted into these units. The procedure for using this graph is relatively straightforward. First, we need to determine the percentage of the overall barrier comprised of each component. Usually the smaller unit has a lower STC rating, which makes sense. There are two critical factors that determine the combined performance: the lower STC rating and the larger area. If the larger area has the lower STC rating, then the smaller component with the higher STC rating will have only a negligible impact in terms of improving the combined STC rating.

Once we have determined the percentages of the two components, we must find the difference between the STC ratings. With this value, we can locate the point on the abscissa where we enter the graph, rise up to the proper percentage curve, and then find the amount by which the higher STC rating will lowered on the ordinate.

For example, if a 200-square-foot wall with a basic STC rating of 50 dB includes a 60-square-foot window with an STC rating of 26 dB, what is the effective STC rating of the overall partition? The window amounts to 30% of the wall, and the difference between the STC ratings of the two components of the barrier is 24 dB. As a result, as shown in Figure 5.26, the combined STC rating will be 19 dB less than that of the opaque wall, or 31 dB.

This example shows that it doesn't make sense to develop a composite sound barrier that includes a major component with an excellent STC rating if the second component has a significantly lower STC rating. The effective STC rating of a composite barrier with components that have quite different STC ratings tends to be determined increasingly by the lower STC component. With an increase in the percentage of the lower STC-rated component and/or the difference between the STC ratings, the weaker part of the sound barrier has a greater impact on the overall barrier performance. With sound barriers, it is better to keep things in balance rather than try to average an excellent sound barrier with a poor one.

Although Figure 5.25 is easy to use, we might attempt to approximate the STC rating for a composite barrier by simply proportioning the individual STC ratings. This will not work. Since STCs are presented as decibels, they are logarithms and cannot be manipulated mathematically in a conventional manner. For the above example, the combined STC is not equal to 70% at 50 dB (35 dB) plus 30% at 26 dB (7.8), or 42.8 dB.

Table 5.13: SOUND TRANSMISSION LOSS CHARACTERISTICS FOR SELECTED INTERIOR BARRIERS

	\multicolumn{7}{c}{Typical Transmission Loss (dB) @ Octave Band Center Frequencies (Hz)}						
	125	250	500	1000	2000	4000	STC
Representative Construction Assemblies							
$\frac{1}{8}$-in. single-pane float glass	18	21	26	31	33	22	26
$\frac{1}{4}$-in. single-pane float glass	25	28	31	34	30	37	31
$\frac{1}{2}$-in. insulated glass ($\frac{1}{8}$-in-$\frac{1}{4}$-in air space-$\frac{1}{8}$-in)	21	26	24	33	44	34	28
$\frac{3}{8}$-in. plywood	14	18	22	20	21	26	22
$\frac{1}{2}$-in. GWB	15	20	25	31	33	27	28
3-in. solid poured concrete wall	35	40	44	53	58	64	47
6-in. lt. wt. hollow concrete block wall, painted	30	33	36	41	46	51	41
6-in. hollow concrete block wall, unpainted	32	33	40	47	51	48	43
6-in. hollow concrete block wall, painted	37	36	42	49	55	58	45
6-in. solid concrete w/ $\frac{1}{2}$-in. plaster both sides	39	42	50	58	64	–	53
6-in. lt. wt. hollow concrete w/ $\frac{1}{2}$-in. plaster resilient mtd. one side	35	42	50	64	67	65	53
8-in. lt. wt. hollow concrete block wall, painted	34	40	44	49	59	64	49
12-in. solid brick wall	45	45	53	58	60	61	56
2 × 4 wood studs w/ $\frac{1}{2}$-in. GWB both sides	21	28	35	42	45	41	39*
2 × 4 wood studs w/ $\frac{1}{2}$-in. GWB both sides, insulated	39	40	42	47.5	55	51.5	46*
2 × 4 wood studs w/ dbl. $\frac{3}{8}$-in. GWB both sides	27	31	39	45	52.5	48	40
2 × 4 wd studs w/ $\frac{5}{8}$-in. GWB resilient mtd both sides	30	40	46	50	49	49	47
2 × 3 staggered wd studs w/ $\frac{1}{2}$-in. GWB both sides	36	36	40	47	52	45	44*
2 × 3 staggered wd studs w/ dbl. $\frac{5}{8}$-in. GWB both sides	41	41	46	49	41	54	44
2 × 4 mtl studs w/ $\frac{5}{8}$-in. GWB screwed both sides	29	36	40	46	40	46	41
Louvered door, 25 to 30% open	10	12	12	12	12	11	12
$1\frac{3}{4}$-in. hollow-core wood door, $\frac{1}{2}$-in undercut	7	9	13	14	13	12	15
$1\frac{3}{4}$-in. hollow -core wood door, no gaskets	14	19	23	18	17	21	19
$1\frac{3}{4}$-in. solid-core wood door, no gaskets	22	25	25	26	30	34	29
$1\frac{3}{4}$-in. solid core wood door, with gaskets & drop seal	29	31	31	31	39	43	35
$1\frac{3}{4}$-in. hollow-core 16 ga. steel door, with gaskets & drop seal	23	28	36	41	39	44	38
$1\frac{3}{4}$-in. special double panel acoustically rated door	31	33	37	40	44	44	40

Note: This table, which presents sound transmission data, is compiled from various sources. While the *TL* indicated are representative of actual performance and provide an indication of differences in sound transmission that occurs with different but similar construction, due to the variation in source, the listed data might not be totally accurate.

* These values vary from those for comparable partitions in the extended STC table, Table 5.14.

Converting back to basic w cm^{-2} values, while considerably more complicated, also will not work; 50 dB is equivalent to $(10^{-11}\,\text{watts cm}^{-2})/(10^{-16}\,\text{watts cm}^{-2})$, and 26 dB is equivalent to $(4 \times 10^{-14}\,\text{watts cm}^{-2})/(10^{-16}\,\text{watts cm}^{-2})$. Adjusting each of these basic values to the percentage that each comprises in the composite barrier would result in $(701.2 \times 10^{-14}\,\text{watts cm}^{-2})/(10^{-16}\,\text{watts cm}^{-2})$, which converts to 48.5 dB, quite different than the actual 31 dB.

We can reduce sound transmission by increasing mass and/or by adding resiliency to the sound partition. An-

other critical method to ensure effective sound isolation entails eliminating or at least minimizing any opening in the sound barrier.

The amount of sound that can pass through an opening, even a very small one, can be quite significant. In part because of Huygens' Principle, which indicates that any point on a wave front is the potential origin of a new wave, any sound that passes through an opening within an acoustical barrier will spread out from the point of entry and fill the space. An opening of merely one-tenth of 1% (0.1%) of the barrier area will permit enough sound

Table 5.14: STC VALUES FOR SELECTED ACOUSTICAL BARRIERS

Interior Partitions
Wood Stud Partition

Representative Construction Assemblies	Weight in lb./sq. ft.	STC
2 × 4 wood studs, 16-in. o.c., with 1/4-in. plywood both sides	1.5	24
2 × 4 wood studs, 16-in o.c., with 1/2-in. gypsum board both sides	4.2	33
2 × 4 wood studs, 16-in. o.c., with 2-in. cavity insulation and 1/2-in. gypsum board both sides	4.7	36
2 × 4 wood studs, 16-in. o.c., with 5/8-in. gypsum board both sides	5.4	34
2 × 4 wood studs, 16-in. o.c., with 2-in. cavity insulation and 5/8-in. gypsum board both sides	5.9	38
2 × 4 wood studs, 16-in. o.c., with 5/8-in. gypsum board, double on one sides and single on other	8.5	36
2 × 4 wood studs, 16-in. o.c., with 2-in. cavity insulation and 5/8-in. gypsum board, double on one sides and single on other	9.0	39
2 × 4 wood studs, 16-in. o.c., with 5/8-in. gypsum board both sides, one side mounted on resilient channel	5.6	38
2 × 4 wood studs, 16-in. o.c., with 2-in. cavity insulation and 5/8-in. gypsum board both sides, one side mounted on resilient channel	6.1	47
2 × 4 wood studs, 16-in. o.c., with 5/8-in. gypsum board mounted on resilient channel both sides	5.8	39
2 × 4 wood studs, 16-in. o.c., with 2-in. cavity insulation and 5/8-in. gypsum board mounted on resilient channel both sides	6.3	49
2 × 4 wood studs, 16-in. o.c., with 5/8-in. gypsum board mounted on resilient channel one side and double 5/8-in. gypsum board on other side	8.9	43
2 × 4 wood studs, 16-in. o.c., with 2-in. cavity insulation, 5/8-in. gypsum board mounted on resilient channel one sides and double 5/8-in. gypsum board on other side	9.2	50
2 × 4 wood studs, 16-in. o.c., with 1/2-in. gypsum board one side mounted on 1/2-in. wood fiberboard and other side on studs	5.8	36
2 × 4 wood studs, 16-in. o.c., with 1/2-in. gypsum board mounted on 1/2-in. wood fiberboard both sides	6.6	42
2 × 4 wood studs, 16-in. o.c., with 1/2-in. plaster on 3/8-in. gypsum lath both sides	13.1	50
2 × 4 wood studs, 16-in. o.c., with 1/2-in. plaster on resiliently mounted 3/8-in. gypsum lath both sides	14.0	50
2 × 4 wood studs, 24-in o.c., with 1/2-in. gypsum board both sides	4.2	35
2 × 4 wood studs, 24-in o.c., with 2-in. cavity insulation and 1/2-in. gypsum board both sides	4.7	40
2 × 4 wood studs, 24-in. o.c., with 5/8-in. gypsum board both sides	5.4	36
2 × 4 wood studs, 24-in. o.c., with 2-in. cavity insulation and 5/8-in. gypsum board both sides	5.9	39
2 × 4 wood studs, 24-in. o.c., with single 1/2-in. gypsum board on one side and double 1/2-in gypsum board on other side	6.7	39
2 × 4 wood studs, 24-in. o.c., with double 1/2-in. gypsum board both sides	9.2	41
2 × 4 wood staggered studs, 8-in o.c., with 5/8-in. gypsum board both sides	5.5	39
2 × 4 staggered wood studs, 8-in. o.c., with double 5/8-in. gypsum board both sides	11.7	44
2 × 4 wood staggered studs, 8-in o.c., with 1/2-in. plaster on 3/8-in. gypsum lath both sides	13.5	45
2 × 4 wood staggered studs, 8-in o.c., with 2-in. cavity insulation and 1/2-in. gypsum board both sides	4.7	46
2 × 4 wood staggered studs, 8-in o.c. with 2-in. cavity insulation and 1/2-in. gypsum board one side and 1/2-in. and 5/8-in. gypsum boards on other side	7.4	50
2 × 4 wood studs,16-in o.c., with 1/2-in. gypsum board laminated on 5/8-in. gypsum board on resilient channels both sides	9.8	48
2 × 4 wood studs, 16-in. o.c., with 3-in. cavity insulation, 5/8-in. gypsum board both sides, and one side screwed to resilient channels	6.5	52
Double 2 × 4 wood studs, 16-in. o.c., with 9-in. cavity insulation and 1/2-in. gypsum board both sides	6.2	54

(Continued)

Table 5.14 *(Continued)*

Metal Stud Partition		
Representative Construction Assemblies	**Weight in lb./sq. ft.**	**STC**
$2\frac{1}{2}$-in. metal channel studs, 24-in o.c., with $\frac{1}{2}$-in. gypsum board both sides	4.2	36
$2\frac{1}{2}$-in. metal channel studs, 24-in o.c., with 2-in. cavity insulation, and $\frac{1}{2}$-in. gypsum board both sides	4.7	44
$2\frac{1}{2}$-in. metal channel studs, 24-in o.c., with $\frac{5}{8}$-in. gypsum board both sides	5.4	40
$2\frac{1}{2}$-in. metal channel studs, 24-in o.c., with 2-in. cavity insulation and $\frac{5}{8}$-in. gypsum board both sides	5.9	46
$3\frac{5}{8}$-in. metal channel studs, 24-in o.c., with $\frac{1}{2}$-in. gypsum board both sides	4.2	37
$3\frac{5}{8}$-in. metal channel studs, 24-in o.c., with 2-in. cavity insulation and $\frac{1}{2}$-in. gypsum board both sides	4.7	46
$3\frac{5}{8}$-in. metal channel studs, 24-in o.c., with $\frac{1}{2}$-in. gypsum board both sides, one side with lead sheet @ 1 lb/ft^2	5.2	40
$3\frac{5}{8}$-in. metal channel studs, 24-in o.c., with 2-in. cavity insulationand $\frac{1}{2}$-in. gypsum board both sides, one side with lead sheet @ 1 lb/ft^2	5.7	48
$3\frac{5}{8}$-in. metal channel studs, 24-in o.c., with $\frac{5}{8}$-in. gypsum board both sides	5.4	39
$3\frac{5}{8}$-in. metal channel studs, 24-in o.c., with 2-in. cavity insulation and $\frac{5}{8}$-in. gypsum board both sides	5.9	47
$3\frac{5}{8}$-in. metal channel studs, 24-in o.c., with double $\frac{1}{2}$-in. gypsum board one side and single $\frac{1}{2}$-in. gypsum board other side	6.2	42
$3\frac{5}{8}$-in. metal channel studs, 24-in o.c., with 2-in. cavity insulation and double $\frac{1}{2}$-in. gypsum board one side and single $\frac{1}{2}$-in. gypsum board other side	6.7	48
$3\frac{5}{8}$-in. metal channel studs, 24-in o.c., with double $\frac{1}{2}$-in. gypsum board both sides	8.3	45
$3\frac{5}{8}$-in. metal channel studs, 24-in o.c., with 2-in. cavity insulation and double $\frac{1}{2}$-in. gypsum board both sides	8.8	51
$2\frac{1}{2}$-in. staggered metal studs, 8-in o.c., with double $\frac{5}{8}$-in. gypsum board both sides	10.9	36
$2\frac{1}{2}$-in. staggered metal studs, 8-in o.c., with 2-in. cavity insulation and double $\frac{5}{8}$-in. gypsum board both sides	11.4	41
Double $2\frac{1}{2}$-in. metal channel studs, 24-in o.c and $\frac{1}{2}$-in. gap. with 2-in. cavity insulation and $\frac{5}{8}$-in. gypsum board both sides	6.0	52
Double $2\frac{1}{2}$-in. metal channel studs, 24-in o.c and $\frac{1}{2}$-in. gap. with 2-in. cavity insulation and double $\frac{5}{8}$-in. gypsum board both sides	11.2	57
Masonry Partition		
Representative Construction Assemblies	**Weight in lb./sq. ft.**	**STC**
2-in. gypsum perlite plaster on metal mesh	16.0	31
2-in. sanded gypsum plaster on metal mesh	18.5	36
$2\frac{1}{4}$-in. laminated gypsum board comprised of $\frac{1}{2}$-in. gypsum board both sides of 1-in. core	9.5	34
$2\frac{1}{2}$-in. laminated gypsum board comprised of $\frac{5}{8}$-in. gypsum board both sides of 1-in. core	10.5	36
4-in. solid concrete	50.0	41
6-in. solid concrete	75.0	46
8-in. solid concrete	100.0	51
10-in. solid concrete	125.0	52
12-in. solid concrete	150.0	56
4-in. brick	40.0	41
6-in. brick	60.0	45
8-in. brick	80.0	49
12-in. brick	120.0	56
4-in. brick with $\frac{1}{2}$-in. plaster both sides	44.0	40

Table 5.14 *(Continued)*

Masonry Partition		
Representative Construction Assemblies	**Weight in lb./sq. ft.**	**STC**
Double 4-in. brick with 2-in. airspace	100.0	54
Double 4-in. brick with 2-in. airspace with wire ties and $1/2$-in. plaster both sides	104.0	49
Double 4-in. brick with 2-in. airspace without wire ties and $1/2$-in. plaster both sides	104.0	54
4-in. brick, 2-in. air space, and 4-in. lightweight 3-cell concrete block	60.0	54
4-in. brick, 2-in. air space, and 4-in. lightweight 3-cell concrete block with $1/2$-in. gypsum board on furring strips	62.0	56
4-in. lightweight 3-cell concrete block, unpainted	15-20	40
4-in. lightweight 3-cell concrete block, painted	15-20	43
4-in. 3-cell concrete block, unpainted	20-30	41
4-in. 3-cell concrete block, painted	20-30	44
6-in. lightweight 3-cell concrete block, unpainted	20-30	41
6-in. lightweight 3-cell concrete block, painted	20-30	44
6-in. 3-cell concrete block, unpainted	30-40	43
6-in. 3-cell concrete block, painted	30-40	46
8-in. lightweight 3-cell concrete block, unpainted	30-35	43
8-in. lightweight 3-cell concrete block, painted	30-35	46
8-in. 3-cell concrete block, unpainted	40-50	45
8-in. 3-cell concrete block, painted	40-50	48
8-in. 3-cell concrete block with $1/2$-in. gypsum board on furring strips both sides	45-55	50+
10-in. lightweight 3-cell concrete block, unpainted	35-40	44
10-in. lightweight 3-cell concrete block, painted	35-40	47
10-in. 3-cell concrete block, unpainted	50-60	45
10-in. 3-cell concrete block, painted	50-60	49
12-in. lightweight 3-cell concrete block, unpainted	40-50	47
12-in. lightweight 3-cell concrete block, painted	40-50	50
12-in. 3-cell concrete block, unpainted	60-70	48
12-in. 3-cell concrete block, painted	60-70	51
8-in. brick with $1/2$-in. plaster both sides	100.0	48
Double 4-in. brick wall with 2-in. wire-tied cavity and $1/2$-in. plaster both outsides	100.0	49
Double 4-in. brick wall with 2-in. cavity (no wire ties) and $1/2$-in. plaster both outsides	100.0	54
Double 4-in. face brick with insulated 2-in. air space and plaster on both sides	100.0	59
Double 4-in. brick wall with 6-in. cavity (no wire ties) and $1/2$-in. plaster on wood fiberboard both outsides	110.0	62

Exterior Walls		
Representative Construction Assemblies	**Weight in lb./sq. ft.**	**STC**
2 × 4 wood studs, 16-in. o.c. with 1-in. exterior stucco on metal lath and $1/2$-in. gypsum board on interior	6.0	42
2 × 4 wood studs, 16-in. o.c. with $3^1/2$-in. cavity insulation, 1-in. exterior stucco on metal lath, and $1/2$-in. gypsum board on interior	7.0	50

(Continued)

Table 5.14 *(Continued)*

Doors	
Representative Construction Assemblies	**STC**
$1\frac{1}{2}$-in. hollow core wood door	22
$1\frac{1}{2}$-in. hollow core wood door, gasketed	25
$1\frac{3}{4}$-in. filled metal door	32
$1\frac{3}{4}$-in. hollow core metal door	30
$1\frac{3}{4}$-in. solid core wood door	29
$1\frac{3}{4}$-in. solid core wood door, gasketed	35
4-in. rated acoustical metal door	53
Any door undercut by 2-in.	17
Louvered door with 25–30% opening	12
Two hollow core doors, gasketed all around, with sound lock	45
Two solid core doors, gasketed all around, with sound lock	55
Windows and Glass	
Representative Construction Assemblies	**STC**
$\frac{1}{8}$-in. single glass	21
$\frac{1}{4}$-in. single glass	26
$\frac{1}{4}$-in. single laminated glass	32
$\frac{3}{8}$-in. single laminated glass	34
$\frac{1}{2}$-in. insulating glass with $\frac{1}{8}$-in. glass and $\frac{1}{4}$-in. airspace	26
$\frac{1}{8}$-in. glass - $\frac{1}{4}$-in. airspace - $\frac{1}{8}$-in. glass	27
$\frac{1}{8}$-in. glass - $\frac{3}{8}$-in. airspace - $\frac{1}{8}$-in. glass	31
$\frac{1}{4}$-in. glass - $\frac{1}{2}$-in. airspace - $\frac{1}{4}$-in. glass	35
$\frac{1}{4}$-in. glass - 1-in. airspace - $\frac{1}{4}$-in. glass	37
$\frac{1}{4}$-in. glass - $\frac{1}{2}$-in. airspace - $\frac{1}{4}$-in. laminated glass	39
$\frac{1}{4}$-in. laminated glass - $\frac{1}{2}$-in. airspace - $\frac{1}{4}$-in. laminated glass	42
Operable wood sash, $\frac{1}{8}$-in. glass, unsealed	23
Operable wood sash, $\frac{1}{4}$-in. glass, unsealed	25
Operable wood sash, $\frac{1}{4}$-in. glass, gasketed	30
Operable wood sash, laminated glass, unsealed	28
Operable wood sash, laminated glass, gasketed	33
Operable wood sash with insulating glass ($\frac{1}{8}$-in. glass - $\frac{3}{8}$-in. airspace - $\frac{1}{8}$-in. glass),gasketed	29
Single-pane glass with storm window	35
Dual-pane glass with storm window	40
Double soundproof window over dual-pane	55
4-in. glass block	40
"Soundproof" window over dual-pane	46
"Soundproof" window over single-pane	42

Table 5.14 *(Continued)*

Floor/Ceiling Construction			
Representative Construction Assemblies	Weight in lb./sq. ft.	STC	IIC
Standard oak flooring with $\frac{1}{2}$-in. plywood subfloor on 2 × 10 wood joists, 16-in. o.c.	7.7	25	20
Standard oak flooring with $\frac{1}{2}$-in. plywood subfloor on 2 × 10 wood joists, 16-in. o.c., with $\frac{5}{8}$-in. gypsum board ceiling	9.7	37	32
Standard oak flooring with $\frac{1}{2}$-in. plywood subfloor on 2 × 10 wood joists, 16-in. o.c., with $\frac{5}{8}$-in. gypsum board ceiling attached to resilient channels crossing joists @ 24-in. o.c.	10.3	45	39
Standard oak flooring with $\frac{1}{2}$-in. plywood subfloor on 2 × 10 wood joists with 3-in. cavity insulation, 16-in. o.c., with $\frac{5}{8}$-in. gypsum board ceiling attached to resilient channels crossing joists @ 24-in. o.c.	11.0	49	46
Standard oak flooring on furring strips over $\frac{1}{2}$-in. fiberboard on $\frac{1}{2}$-in. plywood subfloor on 2 × 10 wood joists, 16-in. o.c. with 3-in. cavity insulation, with $\frac{5}{8}$-in. gypsum board ceiling suspended on resilient channels	13.0	53	51
Carpeting with padding on double $\frac{5}{8}$-in. plywood with felt between panels, on 2 × 10 wood joists, 16-in. o.c. with 3-in. cavity insulation, with $\frac{1}{2}$-in. gypsum plaster ceiling on $\frac{3}{8}$-in. gypsum lath suspended on resilient channels	12.0	50	68
2 to $2\frac{1}{2}$-in. concrete slab on cellular metal decking on steel joists with $\frac{1}{8}$-in. resilient floor tile and $\frac{1}{2}$-in. gypsum board ceiling	41.0	48	35
2 to $2\frac{1}{2}$-in. concrete slab on cellular metal decking on steel joists with carpeting on pad and $\frac{1}{2}$-in. gypsum board ceiling	41.0	49	64
4-in. reinforced concrete slab	53.0	44	25
4-in. reinforced concrete slab with $\frac{1}{8}$-in. resilient tile	54.0	44	28
4-in. reinforced concrete slab with $\frac{1}{2}$-in. oak flooring	55.0	44	45
4-in. reinforced concrete slab with $\frac{1}{2}$-in. oak flooring on $\frac{1}{2}$-in. fiberboard	56.0	44	45
4-in. reinforced concrete slab with carpeting on padding	54.0	44	80
4-in. reinforced concrete slab with carpeting on padding over $\frac{1}{2}$-in. oak flooring	56.0	44	84
6-in. reinforced concrete slab	75.0	55	34
6-in. reinforced concrete slab with $\frac{3}{4}$-in. T&G wood flooring on $1\frac{1}{2}$ × 2 wooden battens floated on 1-in. glass fiber	78.0	55	57
6-in. hollow-core concrete panel with $1\frac{1}{2}$-in. lightweight concrete	55.0	50	23
6-in. hollow-core concrete panel with $1\frac{1}{2}$-in. lightweight concrete and carpeting on pad	56.0	51	69
8-in. hollow-core concrete panel with $1\frac{1}{2}$-in. lightweight concrete	67.0	52	24
6-in. hollow-core concrete panel with $1\frac{1}{2}$-in. lightweight concrete and carpeting on padding	68.0	52	74
Heavy carpet laid on pad over $1\frac{5}{8}$-in. concrete slab on $\frac{5}{8}$-in. plywood on 18-in. steel joist, 16-in. o.c., with $\frac{5}{8}$-in. gypsum board ceiling attached to joists		47	62
2-in. concrete topping on 14-in. precast concrete tees with 2-in. thick slab	75.0	54	24
2-in. concrete topping on 14-in. precast concrete tees with 2-in. thick slab and carpeting on padding	75.0	54	72

Note: This table is compiled from various sources to provide an indication of differences in STC that occurs with different but similar construction. Due to the variation in source, the listed data might not be totally accurate.

to pass through a sound barrier so that the effective maximum transmission loss across the barrier, regardless of its STC rating, would be less than 30 dB. If the opening were 1% of the total area, the effective maximum transmission loss for the barrier would be only 20 dB. This clearly indicates that it makes no sense to choose a partition with a high STC rating unless we are also committed to ensuring that the partition is properly sealed along all edges, such as the ceiling, floor, and adjacent walls, and that there are no holes within the partition, such as back-to-back electric outlets.

While Figure 5.25 can also be used to indicate the transmission loss if there is an opening within the barrier, another graph, Figure 5.27, shows the performance for

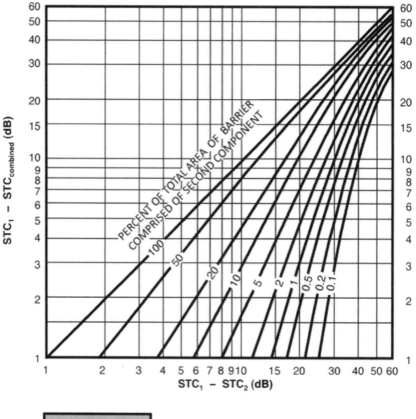

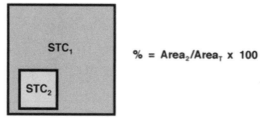

Figure 5.25 TRANSMISSION LOSS OF A TWO-ELEMENT COMPOSITE BARRIER

Adapted from a graph initially developed by Robert Newman and included in J.H. Callender (ed.), *Time-Saver Standards for Architectural Design Data* (McGraw-Hill Book Company, New York, 1974), Figure 21.

$$\% = Area_2/Area_T \times 100$$

various percentages of opening for barriers with different TL or STC ratings.

When any acoustical barrier is assembled, an opening within it or around it can undermine its effectiveness. All of the curves in Figure 5.27, each of which relates to a percentage of the opening within the partition, tend to flatten out as the STC rating of the partition increases. This indicates a greater reduction in the sound isolation and then, ultimately, the maximum effective STC for the partition. Once the flat section of the curve is reached, which is based on the percentage of opening, improvements in sound isolation are not possible unless the size of the opening is reduced. At a 35 STC rating for the partition, all of the curves in Figure 5.27 are flat. This suggests that unless we are able to eliminate all openings within a sound barrier, the maximum effective STC rating will be 35 dB. As the percentage of opening increases, the STC rating will be lower. With only a 1% opening the maximum STC rating is 20 dB, regardless of the nature of the barrier construction.

Once the transmission loss of the construction assembly is determined, the effective noise reduction (NR) can be calculated. *Noise reduction* refers to the difference in the sound level in the source space and the sound level in the receiving space. While this difference is largely dependent on the transmission loss as the sound passes through the sound isolation barrier that the two spaces share, it is also affected by the amount of sound absorption within the receiving space. Since sound absorption within a space lowers the sound level of that space, sound absorption within the receiving space will effectively reduce the level of any transmitted sound. In addition, the amount of transmitted sound will be adjusted by the size of the common barrier between the spaces. As this area increases, more sound is likely to be transmitted.

Therefore, to determine the noise reduction between two spaces, we must include the influence of both the size of the connecting barrier and the sound absorption in the receiving space in addition to the actual transmission loss.

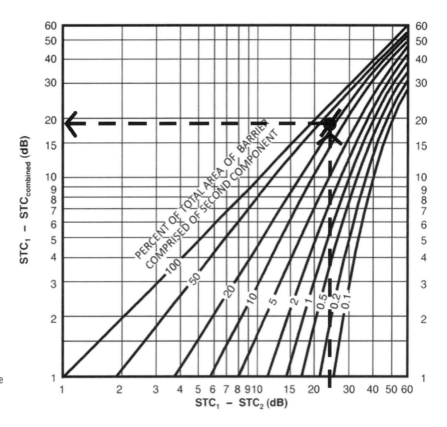

Figure 5.26 EXAMPLE USING THE TWO-ELEMENT COMPOSITE BARRIER

This plot is for the example with a composite barrier in which the difference in the STC ratings is 26 dB and the component with the lower rating comprises 30% of the overall barrier.

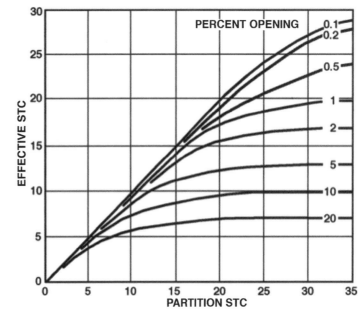

Figure 5.27 TRANSMISSION LOSS OF A BARRIER WITH AN OPENING

Adapted from E.B. Magrab, *Environmental Noise Control* (John Wiley & Sons, Inc., Hoboken, New Jersey, 1975, Figure 7-47.

The basic formula for noise reduction between two spaces is:

$$NR = TL + 10\log_{10}\frac{A_r}{S}$$

Since we are not likely to be undertaking a detailed acoustical analysis, we should use STC rather than TL and substitute the STC values for the TL values. Since we are

using logarithms, we could restate the formula as:

$$NR = STC + 10\log_{10}\frac{A_r}{S}$$

We should also note that since we are using logarithms, the formula could also be written a little differently:

$$NR = STC - 10\log_{10}\frac{S}{A_r}$$

CALCULATION EXAMPLES—SOUND ISOLATION

1. Assume that there are two spaces separated by a sound barrier that is 20'-0" by 10'-0" high and comprised of 160 square feet of wall (2 × 4 wood studs with $\frac{1}{2}$-inch gypsum board both sides) and a 40-square-foot, $\frac{1}{8}$-inch glazed, unsealed window. What would be the noise reduction (NR) between these two spaces if the receiving room were 20 feet by 20 feet by 10 feet high? Assume that the ceiling of the receiving room has an NRC of 0.80, the floor has an NRC of 0.20, and the walls have an average NRC of 0.10.

2. Assume that there are two spaces separated by a wall that is 30'-0" by 12'-0" high and comprised of 2 × 4 staggered wood with $\frac{1}{2}$-inch plaster on $\frac{3}{8}$-inch gypsum lath both sides in which there is a 3'-0" × 7'-0" $1\frac{3}{4}$-inch solid wood door that has a 2'-0" × 2'-0" louver. What would be the noise reduction (NR) between these two spaces if the receiving room were 30 feet by 15 feet by 12 feet high? Assume that the ceiling of the receiving room has an NRC of 0.80, the floor has an NRC of 0.10, and the walls have an average NRC of 0.05.

Answers

1. The basic formula to determine the NR between spaces is:

$$\text{NR} = \text{STC} + 10\log_{10}\frac{A_r}{S}$$

The STC rating of the barrier are:

$$\frac{1}{2} - \text{inch gypsum board each side on 2} \times \text{4 wood studs} \ -\text{STC} = 33$$
$$\frac{1}{8} - \text{inch glazed, unsealed window} \qquad\quad -\text{STC} = 23$$

The effective STC rating of the composite barrier is based on:
    80% with an STC$_{\text{wall}}$ of 33 and
    20% with an STC$_{\text{window}}$ of 23.
From Figure 5.25, we find that the composite STC would be $33 - 4.5 \approx 28$ dB.
The total sound absorption in the receiving room and the area of the partition:

$$A_r = (20' \times 20' \times 0.80) + (20' \times 20' \times 0.20) + (20' \times 10' \times 4 \times 0.10)$$
$$= 320 + 80 + 80 = 480 \text{ Sabins}$$
$$S = 20' \times 10' = 200 \text{ sq ft,}\quad \text{so}$$
$$\text{NR} = 28 + 10\log_{10}\frac{480 \text{ Sabins}}{200 \text{ sq feet}} = 28 + 3.8 \approx 32 \text{ dB}$$

2. The STC ratings of the barrier are:

$$2 \times \text{4 stag.wd studs w/} \frac{1}{2}\text{-inch plaster on } \frac{3}{8}\text{-inch gypsum lath both sides-STC} = 45$$
$$3'0'' \times 7'0'' 1\frac{3}{4}\text{-inch solid wood door with louver-STC} = 12$$

The effective STC rating of the composite barrier is based on:
94% with an STC$_{\text{wall}}$ of 45 and
6% with an STC$_{\text{door}}$ of 12.
From Figure 5.25, we find that the composite STC would be $45 - 18 \approx 27$ dB.
The total sound absorption in the receiving room and the area of the partition:

$$A_r = (30' \times 15' \times 0.80) + (30' \times 15' \times 0.10) + (30' \times 12' \times 4 \times 0.05)$$
$$= 360 + 45' + 72 = 477 \text{ Sabins}$$
$$S = 30', 12' = 360 \text{ sq ft,}\quad \text{so}$$
$$\text{NR} = 28 + 10\log_{10}\frac{477 \text{ Sabins}}{360 \text{ sq feet}} = 27 + 1.2 \approx 28 \text{ dB}$$

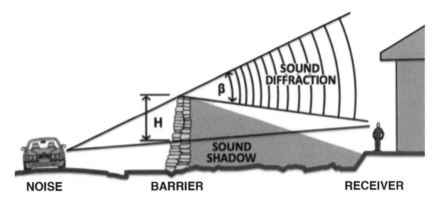

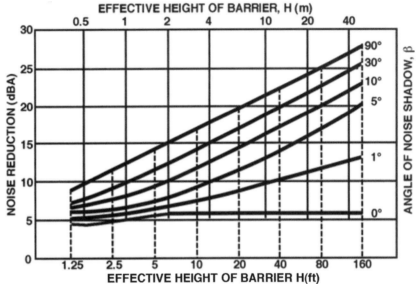

Figure 5.28 SOUND BARRIER DIFFRACTION
Adapted from L.L. Doelle, *Environmental Acoustics* (McGraw-Hill Book Company, New York, 1972), Figure 13.10.

Sound Barriers

A solid sound barrier will block some sound propagation. However, since sound is a waveform that follows Huygens' Principle, as the sound passes over the barrier it will diffract and bend downward. Since the direct sound will not readily pass through the barrier, there will be a sound shadow behind the barrier. However, since the sound will also diffract as it passes over the barrier, the sound will spread out on the leeward side. The behavior of this sound diffraction, which is shown in Figures 5.28 and 5.29, is described by an empirical formula that was developed by Zyun-iti Maekawa:

$$NR = 20 \log_{10} \left[\frac{2\pi N}{\tanh \sqrt{2\pi N}} \right] + 5 \text{ dB}$$

where:

NR = noise reduction in decibels

$N = (F/565)(A + B - d)$

F = frequency in Hertz

$A + B$ = shortest path around the barrier (see Figure 5.29)

d = straight-line path through the barrier

Rather than calculate the sound reduction with the Maekawa formula, we can use a nomograph based on that formula and graphically determine the expected sound reduction (see Figure 5.30).

The maximum sound attenuation by a barrier wall in an exterior situation is 24 dB, although 20 dB is the highest sound reduction generally achieved. In interior locations, since there tends to be more reflection of the sound, particularly from a ceiling even if it has high absorption, the maximum sound attenuation by a partial-height partition is 15 dB.

Anyone who has driven down an interstate highway that passes through a congested residential area has seen sound barriers that were installed to reduce the sound levels on the property adjacent to the highway. From an analysis using either the Maekawa formula or a

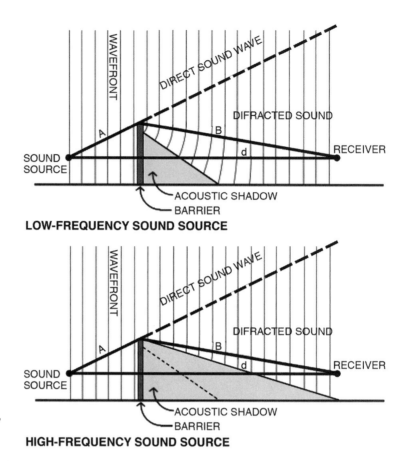

Figure 5.29 SOUND BARRIER DIFFRACTION
Adapted from B. Stein, J.S. Reynolds, W.T. Grondzik, and A.G. Kwok, *Mechanical and Electrical Equipment for Buildings* (John Wiley & Sons, Inc., Hoboken, New Jersey, 2006), Figure 19.32.

nomograph, we can see that the significant sound reduction from these walls actually occurs in the area immediately behind the barrier in the sound shadow. As the distance on the sound "backside" of the barrier increases, the actual effect of the barrier is reduced, particularly in comparison with the "standard" exterior sound reduction of around 6 dB that occurs with every doubling of the distance from a sound source. So, although significant efforts have been expended in constructing all of these sound barriers, the reduction in sound levels is generally not significant if the occupied residence is at a reasonable distance from the highway.

In open-plan offices, which are sometimes referred to as *landscaped* offices, partial-height partitions help limit spread of sound through the space. The partitions can reduce direct sound travel, particularly if they are at least 5'-6" to 6'-0" in height; higher units tend to increase sound attenuation by about 1 to 3 dB. However, the effectiveness of the partitions is less in terms of their STC ratings and more in terms of the sound absorption that they provide. General guidelines for open-plan office design are presented in Figure 5.31.

Open-plan offices should have a minimum 9'-0" clear ceiling height. It is also recommended that the ceiling be constructed with highly sound-absorptive materials and that any potential sound-reflecting surfaces be avoided. That is, we should avoid using typical 2' × 4' fluorescent lighting fixtures, which usually include a flat lens, since these would become sound-reflecting panels. In maximizing the ceiling sound absorption, we should provide above the ceiling a plenum that has a height of at least 3'-0" and a full layer of sound absorption blankets.

There should also be carpeting in the space to reduce footfall sound generation and to increase the overall sound absorption. The furniture should also be located and oriented so that it is less likely that the sounds generated in the space, mainly from conversation, will travel beyond the individual cubicles.

With this approach, sound will tend to be reduced by around 6 dB for each doubling of distance. Assuming somewhat loud normal speech at 60 dB at 3 feet, the sound level would be reduced to around 50 dB at a 9-foot distance within the same cubicle and to around 42 dB at a 15-foot distance in an adjacent cubicle. According to these reductions, and as is shown in Figure 5.31, the actual measured attenuation tends to be somewhat greater than the theoretical 6-dB reduction based on the inverse square law for each doubling of distance.

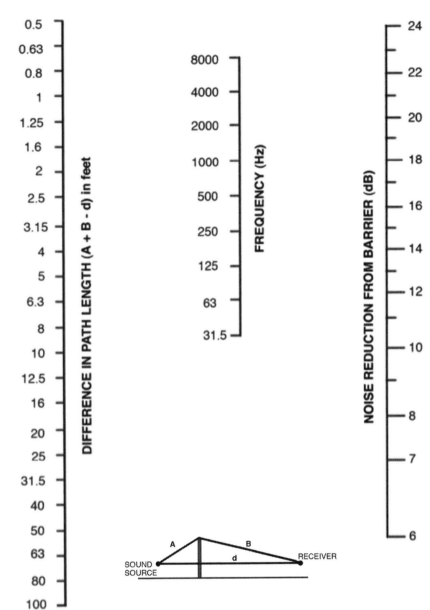

Figure 5.30 SOUND BARRIER NOMOGRAPH
This nomograph can be used to estimate the noise reduction from a freestanding barrier. A is the distance from the source to the top of the barrier, and B is the distance from the top of the barrier to the receiver location; d is the direct distance between the source and the receiver. Adapted from B. Stein, J.S. Reynolds, W.T. Grondzik, and A.G. Kwok, *Mechanical and Electrical Equipment for Buildings* (John Wiley & Sons, Inc., Hoboken, New Jersey, 2006), Figure 19.33.

Impact Noise

Impact noise is another source of sound within structures. In most occupancies, the source of impact noise is people walking across the floor above. This can be quite a problem with hard-surfaced floors, and as a result, the use of resilient flooring (e.g., resilient tiling) has been standard in most multistory commercial structures. However, where impact sound can be a serious problem, such as in residential occupancies, carpeting has become the flooring of choice, especially since it is now often one of the least expensive finished floorings.

Where a hard surface is required or where there is a potential problem of impact noise, it may be necessary to float a floor above the actual structural support. In this way, while the impact might establish sound generation within the floor, this sound will not travel directly through the structural system. However, this can become rather complicated and costly.

Criteria for Sound Isolation

The Federal Housing Administration (FHA) of the U.S. Department of Housing and Urban Development (HUD) has established extensive requirements for sound isolation. These are generally divided into requirements for walls and for floors and are arranged in terms of three different grades.

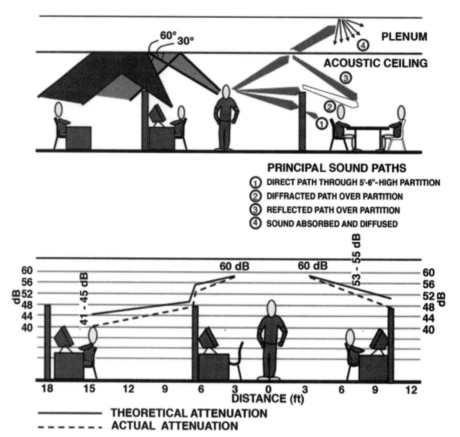

Figure 5.31 OPEN-PLAN OFFICE CONDITIONS
Adapted from B. Stein, J.S. Reynolds, W.T. Grondzik, and A.G. Kwok, *Mechanical and Electrical Equipment for Buildings*, Figure 19.40 (John Wiley & Sons, Inc., Hoboken, New Jersey, 2006).

Grade I is generally appropriate for suburban areas that are considered to be reasonably quiet—with a nighttime general exterior noise level of around 35 to 40 dBA or lower. Since street noise is a major sound source in urban locations, Grade I is also considered to be applicable for dwelling units on upper floors of high-rise structures, generally for the tenth floor and higher. For residential structures in locations with a higher outside noise level, Grades II and III are considered more appropriate. Grade II applies to the more typical condition in which the exterior nighttime noise level is between 40 and 45 dBA, whereas Grade III applies where there are higher exterior nighttime noise levels—55 dBA or more. Some sources denote the three grades I, II, and III as "Luxury," "Average," and "Minimum."

We might question why nighttime general noise levels are used rather than daytime levels. It would seem that since outside noise levels tend to be higher during the day, we should set our sound isolation targets for these higher values. As if this weren't confusing enough, we might also wonder why the "best" grade of sound isolation is actually used for the quietest location. These standards are intended to reduce the direct effect of noise that might be transmitted into a dwelling unit. When there is a high general background noise level, this noise tends to mask other noises. As a result, these other noises are usually less problematic.

When the general noise levels are lower, specific sounds are more audible. So, evening or nighttime outside noise levels are used since they occur during the period of the day when the general noise level tends to be much lower and therefore provide less sound masking than might exist during the more active part of the day.

Table 5.15 lists both STC and IIC ratings. Since STC ratings are for airborne sound transmission, these ratings apply to walls and floors, whereas the IIC ratings are applicable only to impact sound transmission from above through the floor to the unit below. As indicated, the recommended STC and IIC ratings are lowest when comparable room functions are paired together.

Mechanical Equipment Noise

Today most structures rely on various mechanical systems in order to maintain acceptable interior environmental conditions. Unfortunately, these systems are often a major source of significant noise in addition to providing various pathways that can transmit noise, both that generated by the systems and that which might come from other activities.

Air ducts, which are prevalent in most buildings, especially nonresidential structures, can readily transmit

Table 5.15: CRITERIA FOR AIRBORNE & IMPACT SOUND ISOLATION

Sound Isolation Between Dwellings			Luxury Grade I		Average Grade Ii		Minimum Grade Iii	
APT. A		APT. B	STC	IIC	STC	IIC	STC	IIC
Bedroom	to/above	Bedroom	55	55	52	52	48	48
Living Room	to/above	Bedroom	57	60	54	57	50	53
Kitchen	to/above	Bedroom	58	65	55	62	52	58
Family Room	to/above	Bedroom	60	65	56	62	52	58
Corridor	to/above	Bedroom	55	65	52	62	48	58
Bedroom	to/above	Living Room	57	55	54	52	50	48
Living Room	to/above	Living Room	55	55	52	52	48	48
Kitchen	to/above	Living Room	55	60	52	57	48	53
Family Room	to/above	Living Room	58	62	54	60	52	56
Corridor	to/above	Living Room	55	60	52	57	48	53
Bedroom	to/above	Kitchen	58	52	55	50	52	46
Living Room	to/above	Kitchen	55	55	52	52	48	48
Kitchen	to/above	Kitchen	52	55	50	52	46	48
Bath Room	to/above	Kitchen	55	55	52	52	48	48
Family Room	to/above	Kitchen	55	60	52	58	48	54
Corridor	to/above	Kitchen	50	55	48	52	46	48
Bedroom	to/above	Family Room	60	50	56	48	52	46
Living Room	to/above	Family Room	58	52	54	50	52	48
Kitchen	to/above	Family Room	55	55	52	52	48	50
Bath Room	to/above	Bath Room	52	52	50	50	48	48
Corridor	to/above	Corridor	50	50	48	48	46	46

sounds, if not directly through the ducts then through the openings through which the ducts pass. For example, if return air is pulled from two different spaces into a common duct, it is quite possible that this will establish a major connection between the two spaces. Therefore, it is recommended that when such a duct connection might occur, the connecting ducts between the two spaces should be lined with acoustical sound absorption and include at least three, if not four, elbows. Of course, the longer the duct is that separates the two spaces, the greater the sound attenuation.

When air ducts and other distribution elements, such as plumbing and heating pipes and electrical conduits, pass through walls and floors, we must take care to close off the openings surrounding these components. While we should close off the openings to stop sound transmission, we must still allow for possible thermal expansion and contraction and avoid establishing a physical connection that could transmit any vibrations in the mechanical components into the structure.

Robert Newman, one of the founding partners of the renowned acoustical consulting firm of Bolt, Beranek and Newman, who also taught acoustics at both Harvard and

MIT, used to tell a story about the Harvard Graduate Center, which is also known as Harkness Commons. This complex, which opened in 1950 and was one of the first major projects designed by The Architects Collaborative, the firm organized by Walter Gropius, was primarily a dormitory for students in Harvard Law School. Unfortunately, after it opened, there were numerous complaints about the noise transmitted between students' rooms. To address the problem, the university decided to improve the sound isolation of the walls separating the dorm rooms. Although the walls were 4-inch concrete block and should have had a rather good STC rating (about 40 STC), the decision was made to add a resiliently mounted layer of $5/8$-inch gypsum board to each wall separating dorm rooms.

The modifications were completed one summer, but when the dorm reopened in the fall, the noise problem supposedly remained. On further, or perhaps the initial, exploration to find out what might be causing the problem, someone decided to remove the continuous fin tube radiation enclosure that ran from wall to wall under the windows. Once the covers were removed, it was clear that the problem was the result of oversized wall sleeves through which the hot water heating line ran. Packing the sleeves

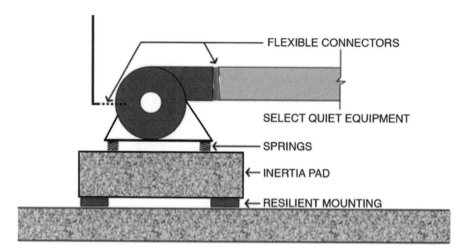

Figure 5.32 SCHEMATIC EQUIPMENT NOISE CONTROL

in a way that closed the opening yet allowed for thermal expansion and contraction of the water line solved the problem.

In addition to reducing sound transmission, we must also try to minimize the noise from the systems themselves and ensure that any noise they might generate is not exacerbated by being transmitted through the building structure. Therefore, it is necessary to select quiet equipment and reduce the potential of transmitting into the building structure any noise or vibrations produced.

Even if we select quiet equipment, it is probable that there will be some noise and vibration. For example, water draining through a copper pipe, which flows in a spiral pattern down the stacks, will likely produce some vibration in the pipe and, as a result, potential noise. Rather than a drainage pipe, perhaps there is a duct carrying air at high velocity. High-velocity air generally means air turbulence, duct vibrations, and noise. In either case, if such a pipe or duct were rigidly attached to the structure, even slight vibrations could be transmitted into the building structure. To avoid generating sound when vibrating equipment is present, we need to keep things "loose" and avoid connecting to the potential sounding board of the building structure.

Consider what happens if we hit a string. If it is loose, the string will merely move. However, it the string is stretched tightly, then our action would be like a pluck that would set up a series of vibrations. If this stretched string is on a guitar, a very clear sound will be established. While the string itself doesn't produce much sound, when connected to the neck that is attached to a sounding board, the vibrating string produces a very noticeable sound.

As indicated in Figure 5.32, the intention is to avoid rigid connections that might allow vibrations to be transmitted into the building structure. In addition, the figure shows the use of an inertia pad that, as a result of its mass, can reduce the motion of the equipment—in this example a centrifugal fan.

Possible Future Sound Cancellation

We began our discussion of acoustics by considering the physical theory of sound. We saw that a sound wave can theoretically cancel itself out. If a sound wave is reproduced and the two waves meet when they are out of sync by half a wavelength, the positive pressure of one sound wave will be matched by the negative pressure of the second wave. As they converge, the sound will be eliminated.

This is not only theoretical, it is actual. In fact, there are headphones that you can now purchase that reduce external sounds by recording sounds and reemitting them at a time delay so that they cancel each other. While this works most effectively when the sound source is a continuous "white" sound, such as what we experience in an airplane, it is also possible that an electronic approach to sound control will be developed. While this might be possible, as architects and designers, rather than hope for technological advances to solve the environmental problems that confront us, we should attempt to minimize environmental problems through our effective design efforts and explore the architectural potentials that might evolve.

Architecture as part of the solution—not a bad idea!

BIBLIOGRAPHY

Cavanaugh, W.J. and J.A. Wilkes. *Architectural Acoustics – Principles and Practice*. John Wiley & Sons, Inc., New Jersey, 1999.

Doelle, L.L. *Environmental Acoustics*. McGraw-Hill Book Company, New York, 1972.

Egan, M.D. *Architectural Acoustics*. McGraw-Hill Book Company, New York, 1988.

Magrab, E.B. *Environmental Noise Control*. John Wiley & Sons, Inc., Hoboken, New Jersey, 1975.

Newman, R.B. "Acoustics," in Callender, J.H., ed., *Time-Saver Standards for Architectural Design Data*. McGraw-Hill Book Company, New York, 1974.

Stein, B., J.S. Reynolds, W.T. Grondzik, and A.G. Kwok. *Mechanical and Electrical Equipment for Buildings*. John Wiley & Sons, Inc., Hoboken, New Jersey, 2006.

6 THE THERMAL ENVIRONMENT

THEORY OF HEAT: AN HISTORIC REVIEW

All nature then, as it exists by itself, is founded on two things: there are bodies and there is void in which these bodies are placed and through which they move.

Lucretius

The Nature of Heat

Ever since the discovery of fire in ancient times, the nature of heat has been a source of interest and wonder. Since fire possesses certain mystical qualities that extend beyond humankind's conception, many ancient societies considered fire to be the embodiment of a god. While they tended to ascribe spiritual qualities to those things that they could not understand, these people were inquisitive about the nature of things and frequently persisted in their intellectual inquiry. About 2500 years ago, this inquiry led the ancient Greeks, specifically Democritus and Leucippus, to propose

an atomistic theory of matter. And shortly thereafter, at least in terms of historic perspective, the ancient Roman poet Lucretius wrote the above statement. While this is essentially the fundamental concept behind the atomistic theory, which is currently generally accepted as the valid explanation of matter, it was not broadly accepted until around 170 years ago when, in 1840, Mayer and Joule proposed the Law of Conservation of Energy and provided a quantitative experiment demonstrating that there is a direct relationship between work and temperature. Mayer and Joule's experiment clearly indicated that heat is a form of energy. It provided the first concrete substantiation of the ancient theory that matter is comprised of atomic particles moving through space.

Temperature and work have a direct relationship. Today, as expressed by Lucretius, we readily accept that in nature "there are bodies and there is void . . . through which they move," and we have come to understand that the temperature of a substance is an indication of its level of molecular energy. Of course, this theory is supported by a more substantial explanation that involves atoms and molecules as well as electrons, protons, and neutrons.

The theory that solid matter is actually comprised of minuscule particles spinning through a void is probably understandable to you in almost an intuitive sense, whereas for me, introduced this concept in school, it is something that I had to learn and that remains a concept of wonder and amazement. And for my parents, the notion of molecular activity was perhaps an accepted fact, but I doubt that they ever really understood it. That is, you were raised on this theory, I was taught it, and my parents were told that it was so. But while you might intuitively accept the atomistic theory of matter, I am not certain that you necessarily grasp its implications.

Interestingly, some of our confusion regarding the nature of matter might be an inheritance from the ancient Greek philosopher Aristotle. He was one of the greatest thinkers of all ages and initially proposed many of the ideas that we accept today. One of his ideas was that there are four basic elements—water, earth, fire, and air—and all things are comprised of them. While on first consideration this notion seems to support the atomistic theory of matter, on further reflection certain problems emerge, at least in terms of how we understand this theory today. For one thing, air, one of Aristotle's basic elements, is analogous to void or space, especially in terms of understandings in ancient times. But if air is an element, how can it be the void in which the elements move? Fire, which is analogous to heat, is another of Aristotle's elements and, as a result, is a substance. But this substantiates the fluid theory of heat, which is in direct opposition to the atomic theory of matter. The fluid theory, which at times is referred to as the *caloric theory of heat*, is based on the concept of heat as a substance that occupies space and possesses weight. While this might seem implausible to us today, it was a pretty good theory as most theories go. For one thing, it clearly explained several things: why heat can only flow from a higher-temperature substance to a lower-temperature substance, why a material expands when it is heated, and why most operations that we observe demonstrate limited heat capacity.

That heat can only flow from a higher intensity level to a lower intensity level is known as the Second Law of Thermodynamics. The First Law of Thermodynamics states that heat can be neither created nor destroyed; this is the thermal statement of the Law of Conservation of Energy.

In the fluid theory, the element of heat was called *caloric*. Since a substance that got warmer would have to acquire more caloric, the theory clearly provided a reasonable explanation for thermal expansion. And since a warmer substance tends to have excess caloric that it will lose to a cooler substance, the theory also explained why heat can only flow from a higher intensity to a lower one.

Actually, the question of thermal expansion and thermal transfer led to a rather intriguing proposal: that of mutual repulsion and diverse attraction. The following question was raised: why do various substances, although they all tend to expand when heated, do so at different rates? While the absorption of caloric, the heat substance, explained expansion, it did not clarify the disparity in the amount of expansion that was observed in different materials. Obviously, some other factor must be operating, and this was the notion that caloric is mutually repulsive. Therefore, based on the cohesiveness of the material that absorbed the caloric, there would be a variation in the amount of observed expansion. The caloric was attracted to the other substance to which it would adhere, but since it would attempt to repel other caloric, the force of repulsion compared to the force of attraction of the other substance would determine the amount of expansion of the material.

While the supporters of the fluid theory of heat managed to present certain convincing arguments, some questions remained without adequate explanation. Perhaps the major question was why a substance that acquired additional heat did not increase in weight. If caloric was a substance, its weight should be measurable. But if you are a zealot supporting a concept that seems essentially correct, you do not let little contradictions destroy your beliefs. You either ignore the inconsistencies or you explain them away. Following this approach, supporters of the fluid theory hypothesized that the reason a substance did not get noticeably heavier when it got warmer was that caloric is extremely light. They proposed that the problem was the inaccuracy of available scales, not the concept.

Although some ancient philosophers rejected the caloric theory of heat and endorsed an atomistic theory of matter, this theory was not generally accepted, in part because it tended to undermine its own credibility. By assuming that heat is one of the basic elements, they had to accept that heat must also be a substance, which, of course, is fundamental to the fluid or caloric theory of heat; therefore, a basic understanding of the principle of the atomistic theory of matter was denied. Until they understood that heat is a form of energy rather than a substance, the philosophers and scientists could not develop a plausible atomistic theory.

Of course, the inherent contradiction of the atomistic theory encouraged the continued acceptance of the fluid theory of heat. In addition, the atomistic theory was generally regarded as contrary to the basic teachings of the Christian Church. The theory, which suggested a rational interplay and structure among material bodies, professed to explain the nature of existence in a manner not dependent on the notion of divine intervention. Even the attempts in the seventeenth century to suggest that atoms are not self-animated but rather are inert pieces of matter that require a divine agency to set them in motion did not modify the Church's negative view of the atomistic theory. And without Church acceptance, there was no possibility for general acceptance in the Western world.

While the fluid theory had its problems of explanation, so did the atomistic theory. If all matter was comprised of small particles moving through a void, why didn't the particles just fly apart? What kept them together? Today we believe that the answer to these questions derives from the principle of gravitation, which, when developed by Sir Isaac Newton, tended to offer increased support for the atomistic theory. But we should also note that Newton, who tended not to stray too far from accepted doctrines of the Church, did not himself endorse the atomistic theory of matter. Another obstacle to the acceptance of the atomistic theory came from the fact that radiant transfer is one of the three ways that heat can be transferred—the three ways being conduction, convection, and radiation. But radiation is comparable to light, which, as we recall, was thought to be a physical substance. If heat could be transferred in a manner similar to the way light was transferred, then it followed that heat must be similar to light and therefore must also be a substance.

All this confusion!

In the seventeenth century, although not generally accepted, increasing support for the atomistic theory started to develop in the scientific community. The work of Roger Bacon, Galileo Galilei, Robert Boyle, and even Isaac Newton added to this growing support. Then in 1738, the Swiss physicist Daniel Bernoulli published a paper in which he claimed, "It is admitted that heat may be considered as an increasing internal motion of particles." And 60 years later, in 1798, while touring a cannon factory in Munich, Count Rumford[1] observed that, in the process of boring out the barrel of the cannon, heat was continually released. Based on this observation, Rumford suggested that heat could be explained by "very old doctrines which rest on nothing but a vibratory motion taking place among the particles of the body." While Rumford was a leading and respected figure in the scientific community, he did not present any definitive quantitative support for his conclusions. Such confirmation did not occur for another 40 years when, in 1840, James Prescott Joule, using the apparatus diagrammed in Figure 6.1, clearly demonstrated a direct relationship between work and temperature—that heat is, in fact, a form of energy related to molecular activity.

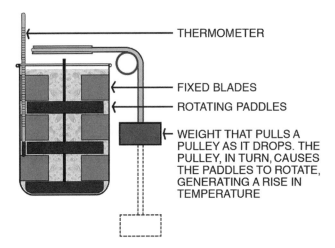

THERMOMETER

FIXED BLADES
ROTATING PADDLES

WEIGHT THAT PULLS A PULLEY AS IT DROPS. THE PULLEY, IN TURN, CAUSES THE PADDLES TO ROTATE, GENERATING A RISE IN TEMPERATURE

Figure 6.1 DIAGRAM OF JOULE'S EXPERIMENTAL APPARATUS
This simple apparatus was used to demonstrate the connection between work and heat, providing the foundation for the Law of Conservation of Energy.

Although Joule generally gets the credit for this concept, a few years earlier the German physicist Julius Robert von Mayer had independently made the same discovery. It was Mayer who stated that "energy can be neither created nor destroyed," and today we mainly remember him for his work in terms of the Law of Conservation of Energy, also known as the First Law of Thermodynamics.

Temperature Measurement

Even with the confusion concerning the nature of heat and long before the current atomistic or kinetic theory was accepted, it was possible to obtain an indication of the amount of heat in a substance by measuring its temperature. This measurement relied on the notion that materials do indeed expand when heated. In order to develop a reliable means for measuring temperature, it was necessary to find a material that would expand at a relatively constant rate and remain stable, not altering its state during the temperature change. It was also necessary to devise a scale against which to measure the change. Since the expanding material had to be measured against a scale, the notion of using a liquid held within a glass tube was very popular. While various liquids were tried, alcohol and mercury were most often used.

The astronomer Galileo supposedly produced the first temperature-recording device in 1593. While apparently it was not very reliable, 50 years later some reasonably acceptable thermometers were being made. Usually each person interested in pursuing temperature measurements was responsible for constructing his own device or thermometer and establishing the scale that would be used. In the early 1700s, the German scientist Gabriel Daniel

---

[1] Count Rumford (1753–1814) was an American expatriate. He was born Benjamin Thompson in Massachusetts but sided with the British during the Revolution. By 1798 a refugee from his native country, he was knighted by King George III and was employed by the Elector of Bavaria as Minister of War, Minister of Police, and Chamberlain. For more information on this fascinating individual, refer to Sanborn Brown, *Count Rumford: Physicist Extraordinary* (Greenwood Press Reprint, Westport, CT, 1975).

Fahrenheit (1686–1736) apparently developed a reliable and accurate mercury thermometer. Stories suggest that various members of the scientific community, having learned that Fahrenheit's thermometers were extremely reliable, desired to obtain one, and as their use increased, the Fahrenheit scale of temperature measurement became a standard. But why did Fahrenheit set 32° as the freezing temperature of water and 212° as the boiling temperature? These seem to be rather arbitrary points on a numerical scale for such significant temperatures.

It is suggested that Fahrenheit set up a scale based on 0° to 100°, with 0° established in one of the following ways. Living near the sea where temperatures never get very low due to the thermal mass of the water, Fahrenheit experienced a day that he felt was perhaps the coldest ever and chose to assign that temperature to the zero point on his scale. More likely, he realized that if you place ice into a saltwater solution and stir, the temperature of the water would drop, and he used this freezing temperature of saltwater as his 0°. This explanation makes sense since this was the method used to obtain the lowest temperature in the laboratory at that time—0°. As for his 100° mark, a reasonable explanation is that he chose to record his own temperature, and, because he was rather excited over the event, his temperature slightly exceeded the norm that we all know as 98.6° F. But for whatever reasons Fahrenheit established his temperature scale, it became the standard for most scientific work in the Western world until it was ultimately replaced with the more rational centigrade scale that established 0° as the freezing temperature and 100° as the boiling temperature of unsalted water. Today the centigrade scale is called the Celsius scale after Anders Celsius, the Swedish astronomer who originally developed it in 1742. How lucky we are that *centigrade* and *Celsius* both begin with a *c*!

While we are familiar with liquid thermometers, gas thermometers provide a more accurate means of recording temperature, at least within a range. This reliability is based on two fundamental laws of physics: Boyle's Law and Charles' Law.

Robert Boyle (1627–1691), an Irish scientist, was one of the leading figures involved in the study of the behavior of gases. In 1662, he published results of his innovative work in the study of vacuums that suggested that variations in the height of a closed column of mercury were the result of changes in atmospheric pressure rather than a mystical response to the basic distaste of nature for a vacuum. The Aristotelian philosophers had proposed that "Nature abhors a vacuum." They used this notion to explain why two containers, like rubber suction cups, which were placed together and from which the air had been exhausted, could not be readily separated. They also observed that if you fill a tube with water and then invert it into a dish of water, the water will remain in the tube. Again, this was explained by the natural abhorrence of a vacuum. Because the glass was sealed, if the water did not remain in the tube, a vacuum would result above the column of water if the water did not continue to fill the inverted container. Interestingly, this distaste for a vacuum was sustained only as long as the column of water did not exceed 30 feet.

Evangelista Torricelli, a pupil of Galileo, realized that the atmosphere exerts a pressure at the surface of the Earth and that this pressure, which results from the height of the atmosphere above the ground, accounts for the elevation of the water in the glass tube rather than an abhorrence of a vacuum (see Figure 6.2). He also realized that mercury, a liquid nearly 14 times as heavy as water, would provide a more convenient experimental vehicle. Not only did he demonstrate his theory concerning atmospheric pressure, he also showed that it was not a vacuum that caused the liquid to remain in the tube.

Torricelli made two barometers similar to those shown in Figure 6.3, one with a narrow top and one with a large, bulbous top. Although there was quite a difference in the sizes of the vacuums produced, the height of the mercury column was the same in both tubes. This, of course, would not be the case if an abhorrence of a vacuum was the operational force.

Boyle published his own observations, based on the earlier work of Torricelli, that the height of a column of mercury would change with changes in atmospheric pressure. On reviewing his paper, Franciscus Linus, a Jesuit scientist, challenged Boyle's thesis. Linus asserted that a column of mercury or water was actually pulled up the tube by the *finiculus*, or the pulling effect that the vacuum

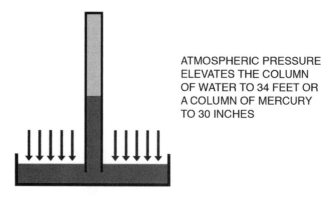

ATMOSPHERIC PRESSURE ELEVATES THE COLUMN OF WATER TO 34 FEET OR A COLUMN OF MERCURY TO 30 INCHES

Figure 6.2 DIAGRAM OF A BAROMETER
The weight of the atmosphere imposes downward pressure. If an inverted enclosed vessel is inserted into a liquid, this pressure on the liquid causes the liquid to rise into the inverted vessel. The height of the column of liquid is therefore an indication of the atmospheric pressure.

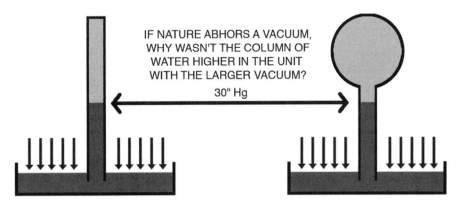

Figure 6.3 COMPARISON BETWEEN TWO BAROMETERS

Torricelli compared two barometers that differed in terms of the volume contained within the inverted vessel. Since the height of the liquid in each barometer was the same, it was apparent that the downward pressure of the atmosphere was the force that raised the liquid in the barometer, not that "nature abhors a vaccum."

exerted. In response to this challenge, Boyle continued with his experiments and developed the law that defines the quantitative relation between the pressure and the volume of a gas. Boyle found that when a gas is compressed at a constant temperature, its pressure rises in inverse proportion to the compression. This law, called Boyle's Law, states that the product of the pressure and volume of a gas is constant at a constant temperature.

$$PV = \text{Constant at a Constant Temperature, or}$$
$$P_1 V_1 = P_2 V_2$$

Around 100 years later, in 1787, the French chemist Jacques Alexandre Cesar Charles proposed that the expansion of a gas is proportional to a change in temperature. Charles did not publish this theory, but he explained it to Joseph Gay-Lussac, who then published it in 1802. It is known as Charles' Law or sometimes as Gay-Lussac's Law. It is expressed mathematically as:

$$V/T = \text{Constant, with } T \text{ in absolute temperature}$$

When a gas is heated at a constant pressure, its volume increases in proportion to its absolute temperature.

From these laws, we can develop a combined formula that explains the proportional relationship of gas pressure, volume, and temperature:

$$PV = \text{Constant} \times T, \text{ with } T \text{ in absolute temperature, or}$$
$$P_1 V_1 / T_1 = P_2 V_2 / T_2$$

We can readily develop a simple experiment to observe the physical phenomena represented by these formulas. If we take an easily stretched balloon and fill it with any gas, we will have a container with equal pressure inside and outside. If we then heat the balloon, it will expand, indicating an increase in the internal volume. Through careful measurements with various gases, a startling fact will be observed: the fractional increase of the total contained volume will be the same for all the gases for each degree of temperature change. More interestingly, the increase will be 1/273th of the gas volume that exists at 0° C for each 1° C increase in temperature.

An ideal gas obeys both Boyle's Law and Charles' Law with complete precision. If we assume that this ideal gas does not change state by becoming a liquid or a solid as it cools, then when we lower the temperature of the gas to −273° C, as shown in Figure 6.4, the gas should theoretically contract to a zero volume. Therefore, at −273° C we would have absolute zero, a theoretical minimum temperature that, according to certain theories, is impossible

Figure 6.4 TEMPERATURE GRAPH

For each degree Celsius change in the temperature of a gas, the volume of the gas will change by 1/273th of the volume at 0° C. Projecting this from 0° C suggests that at −273° C the volume of the gas should be zero, indicating that −273° C must be the limit of low temperature. Since this is the lowest temperature that is theoretically possible based on this change in volume, it was called *absolute zero*, although now it is referred to as *thermodynamic zero*.

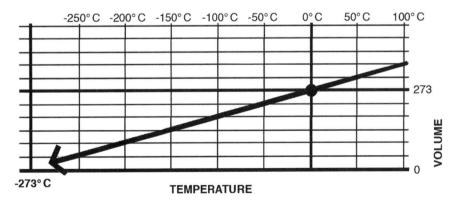

to achieve. Today we call this minimum temperature *thermodynamic zero* and assign it a value of −273.15° C.

The idea of zero volume may be difficult to understand, but by referring back to the mathematical formulas that explain the relationship between volume, pressure, and temperature, we can see that if any item becomes zero, it is probable that they all will. If the temperature is thermodynamic zero, then molecular activity must cease since temperature is an indication of molecular activity, and if there is no molecular movement, then there is no pressure since pressure is merely the cumulative effect of the forces produced by the molecular movement of the individual particles. If there is no pressure because there is no temperature, then the molecular particles will be drawn together by gravity. They will collapse, if not into nothing, into a minimal volume. This would be somewhat like a black hole in space. With a 1/273 reduction in the volume of a gas for each degree Celsius drop in temperature, −273° C is established as the lowest temperature that can theoretically exist in order for matter to remain as we know it.

All of this should make it easy for us to understand both Boyle's Law and Charles' Law. Temperature is an indication of molecular activity. Pressure is the result of molecules hitting the sides of a container. So, as the temperature increases as a result of increased molecular activity, either the molecules will spread out to occupy the expanded volume or, if expansion is not possible, the rate of impact or pressure on the enclosing container will increase. That is, there is a necessary relationship between temperature, pressure, and volume because they all relate to the level of molecular activity. By understanding this, we should realize that the vibratory motion of molecules is the energy that we refer to as *heat*. Temperature provides an indication of the intensity of this energy. It is noted by degrees, whether they are Fahrenheit, Celsius, Rankin, or Kelvin (the last two being based on thermodynamic zero in the Fahrenheit and Celsius scales, respectively).

Since theoretically a gas has a constant rate of expansion for each degree of temperature increase, a gas thermometer should provide a rather accurate way to measure temperature. Unfortunately, its size and the complexity of actually accommodating expansion and measuring the amount that has occurred preclude general use of gas thermometers. Liquid thermometers, while not as accurate, work quite well, especially if the variations in volumetric expansion at different temperature ranges are accounted for in the scale. We also need to limit the range of temperatures to those for which the material we use remains a liquid. But if temperature is an indication of thermal energy based on the rate of molecular activity, why do we rely on thermal expansion rather than devise a means of direct measurement?

A thermocouple can measure the flow of energy that occurs as a result of a temperature differential. It relies on the principle that an electric current is a flow of electrons, that molecular activity involves movement of electrons, and that there is a difference in electric conductivity in a conductor and a semiconductor. As shown in Figure 6.5, we can connect a semiconductor to a conductor in such a way that they form a continuous loop. If we then place the junctions between these two different types of conductors, which are called *thermocouples*, in water at two different temperatures, we will observe, as Johann Seebeck did in 1821, that an electric current is established. Of course, we would have to add some means to let us know that there is a current since we cannot see the flow of electricity.

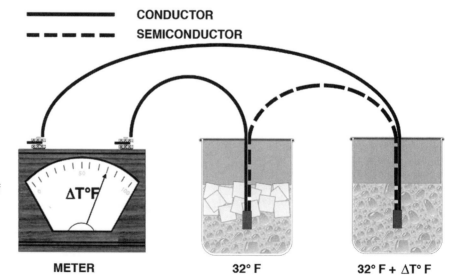

Figure 6.5 THERMOCOUPLE THERMOMETER
A thermocouple is a junction between a conductor and a semiconductor. If two such junctions are connected in a circuit and they are placed at two different temperatures, as shown, by immersing them in water at different temperatures, an electric current will be formed. Since the temperature difference establishes the pressure of the current, measuring the voltage provides a direct indication of the pressure differential, that is, of the temperature difference. If the temperature of one of the water samples is known (perhaps it is water with ice), the temperature of the other sample can be readily determined.

The principle should be relatively easy to grasp. With each of the junctions of a conductor and a semiconductor at a different temperature, there is also a difference in molecular activity. The more active electrons in the higher-temperature junction flow outward along the conductor to the lower-temperature junction and in this way establish an electric current. Since the voltage differential in the circuit is directly related to the temperature differential between the two thermocouple junctions, a voltage meter added to the circuit will provide an indication of the temperature differential. Based on this simple explanation, if one thermocouple junction is at a known temperature, the temperature of the second junction can be determined by the voltage of the developed current. This is known as the *Seebeck effect*, and when the electrical potential of the thermocouple system is known, a thermoelectric thermometer can provide a direct and accurate indication of the temperature of a thermocouple junction without the need to maintain the other junction at a known temperature.

Thermal Energy

A man once complained to the servant at his boarding house that his room was too cold. "The thermometer stands at only 50 degrees," he complained to her.

"Ah, but for this little room," the servant replied, "40 degrees would be quite enough!"

Whereas temperature indicates the relative *intensity* of thermal energy, as this conversation implies, it does not indicate the *quantity* of energy. For this we must establish a unit of energy that is based on a measurable change in the temperature of a specific quantity of a specific substance. The quantity of the substance and the energy change should both be measured in basic units. For example, the unit of the substance can be either 1 gram, if we are using the metric system or the International System of Units (SI), or 1 pound if we are operating in the U.S. customary units or the imperial system. The imperial system is also sometimes referred to as the *British system* or the *English system* since this system of measurement units was originally defined by the British Weights and Measures Act of 1824.

The unit of temperature can be either 1° F or 1° C. While these are obvious units of measurement, any agreed-upon units could be used. Similarly, any substance could be used as the base or reference material for thermal measurements, but since water is already used in establishing the standard temperature scale, readily changes from solid to liquid and from liquid to gas, and is generally available,

water is the accepted reference material used for thermal measurements. Water is also the logical choice since it has one of the highest thermal capacities of all materials.

The unit of thermal energy is set as the amount of energy required to cause a specific change in temperature of a specific quantity of a material. This unit is the amount of energy that will cause a unit change in temperature (i.e., 1° Fahrenheit or 1° C) of a unit amount of water (i.e., one unit of weight, pound or gram).

In the imperial system, this basic unit of thermal energy is the British Thermal Unit (BTU) and is defined as the amount of energy required to raise the temperature of 1 pound of water by 1° Fahrenheit, between 63° F and 64° F. In the International System, the basic unit of thermal energy is the calorie (c), which is defined as the amount of energy required to raise the temperature of 1 gram of water by 1° Celsius, between 14.5° C and 15.5° C. The kilocalorie, which is also used, is noted as the Calorie (C). A Calorie is the amount of energy required to raise the temperature of 1 kilogram of water by 1° Celsius.

There is a specific temperature range for which the definitions of BTU, c, and C apply (i.e., between 63° and 64° F or between 14.5° and 15.5° C), but since the variation that exists at other temperatures for liquid water (i.e., between freezing and boiling) is not significant, it is normally accepted that the thermal unit is the energy required to establish a 1° change in temperature of a unit of weight of liquid water. One BTU is equal to 252 calories or 0.252 kilocalories. One kilocalorie is approximately equal to 4 BTU (3.968 BTU).

Having established the basic unit of thermal energy that relates to thermal content or quantity, we can develop the following formulas.

$$\text{BTU} = \text{Weight in Pounds} \times \text{Specific Heat} \times \text{Temperature Differential in } °F$$

$$\text{Calorie} = \text{Weight in Kilograms} \times \text{Specific Heat} \times \text{Temperature Differential in } °C$$

In the International System, if the weight is in grams rather than kilograms, then the unit of thermal energy is the calorie (c).

$$\text{Calorie} = \text{Weight in Grams} \times \text{Specific Heat} \times \text{Temperature Differential in } °C$$

Reference to the British Thermal Unit (BTU), Calorie, or calorie indicates thermal quantity. Reference to temperature, whether in degrees Fahrenheit or degrees Celsius, indicates thermal intensity. There is a difference. For example, let us assume that we have two samples of water, both at 70° F. One sample is 1 pound and the other is 10 pounds. If we add an equal quantity of thermal energy to each, say 50 BTU, we will find that the 1-pound sample will reach a thermal intensity (i.e., temperature) of 120° F, while the 10-pound sample will reach a temperature of only 75° F. The same quantity of added thermal energy will result in a considerable difference in thermal intensity.

All substances do not have the same capacity for heat, weight for weight, that water has. If they did, the addition of 1 BTU of energy to 1 pound of any material would result in a 1° F temperature increase, but this is not the normal condition. The amount of thermal energy (i.e., heat) required to raise the temperature of 1 pound of any substance by 1° F (or 1 gram by 1° C) is called the *specific heat* of that substance. The specific heat provides a comparison of a substance's thermal capacity with that of water. The unit of specific heat in the imperial system is BTU per pound per °F. In the International System it is Calories per kilogram per °C or calories per gram per °C. We should note that the specific heat of a substance is the same quantitatively in both the imperial system and the International System since they are both comparisons of the substance to water and that comparison remains constant, independent of the measurement system. The specific heat of water is 1.

The specific heat of nearly all other substances is less than that of water. The one notable exception is hydrogen, which has a specific heat of 3.40. With gases, there are two specific heats, one for a constant volume and one for a constant pressure. This makes sense since with a constant pressure some of the added thermal energy is used to expand the gas, whereas with a constant volume, all of it essentially goes to a temperature increase.

If the BTU is constant, then the two gases, one with a constant volume and one with a constant pressure, can be compared.

$$BTU = Wt \times Spec\ Ht_1 \times Temp\ Dif_1$$
$$= Wt \times Spec\ Ht_2 \times Temp\ Dif_2$$

Since the first sample has a constant volume, all added thermal energy is used to increase the temperature, whereas in the second sample, which has constant pressure and an expanding volume, some energy is used for the expansion. So, the temperature differential of the first sample would be greater than that of the second for the same energy input.

If

$$Temp\ Dif_1 > Temp\ Dif_2$$

and

$$Wt \times Spec\ Ht_1 \times \Delta T_1 = Wt \times Spec\ Ht_2 \times \Delta T_2$$

then

$$Spec\ Ht_1 < Spec\ Ht_2,\ or$$
$$\frac{Spec\ Ht\ of\ Constant}{Volume} < \frac{Spec\ Ht\ of\ Constant}{Pressure}$$

The specific heat for some materials with which environmental designers should be concerned are as follows:

Water 1.0
Ice 0.50
Steam 0.47
Air 0.24
Concrete 0.20

By definition, the basic thermal unit is the amount of energy required to raise the temperature of one unit of weight of water one degree. In the imperial system, the unit of weight is a pound and the degrees are in Fahrenheit. In the International System (SI), the unit of weight is the kilogram and the degrees are in Celsius. Specific heat provides a comparison of the thermal capacity of a material with that of water. As such, the basic formula for thermal transfer can be restated as:

$$BTU = Wt\ in\ lb \times Spec\ Ht \times \Delta T\ in\ °F$$

Of course, this is based on the imperial system of measurement. If we use the SI measurements, the formula would be restated:

$$Calorie = Wt\ in\ Kg \times Spec\ Ht \times \Delta T\ in\ °C$$

Both of these formulas use a change in standard temperature. As a result, they indicate the amount of thermal energy required to develop that change in temperature or, if the formulas were reversed, the change in temperature that would result from a change in thermal energy. Understanding the basic premise expressed by these formulas, we might assume that it should be possible to determine the actual thermal content of a substance if we replace the temperature differential with the particular thermodynamic or absolute temperature of that substance. Since the thermodynamic temperature, whether in degrees Rankin or degrees Kelvin, represents a change in temperature from the base point of zero, this should give the total thermal content of the substance. While in theory this might make sense, there is a question as to whether the comparison of a substance to water that exists within a normal range of temperature remains consistent for all temperatures. There is also the issue that most materials actually go through a change of state in going from thermodynamic zero to the temperatures that we generally experience in the natural environment. As a result, the above formulas and thermodynamic temperatures cannot be used to determine the actual thermal content of a substance.

Change of State—Sensible and Latent Heat

There are two types of thermal energy: sensible and latent. *Sensible heat* is heat that we can sense and measure with a thermometer. *Latent heat*, which we cannot measure directly, is heat that is associated with a change in the state of a material. For example, when water transforms from the solid state we call ice to a liquid, it absorbs thermal energy with no temperature increase, which is why putting ice in a drink tends to keep it cold for a while. Similarly, when water goes from a liquid to a gas, energy is added to the water, but again without producing a temperature increase. This is why food does not burn when it is boiled, although it might still be overcooked.

What is the required input of energy to heat 1 pound of water from 0° to 300° F?

The specific heat of ice is 0.50. As a result, 16 BTU are required to heat 1 pound of ice from 0° F to 32° F. If we continue to add BTU, the ice will begin to melt but the temperature will not increase. In fact, until all of the ice has melted, there will be no increase in the temperature of either the ice or the liquid water. They will remain at 32° F. By measuring the BTU that we add, we find that we would have to add 144 BTU in order to melt the whole pound of ice. If we continue to add BTU after all the ice has melted, the temperature of the water will again rise, but now there will be a 1° increase for each added BTU since the specific heat of water as a liquid is 1.0. Since there are 180° between the freezing temperature and the boiling temperature of water, 180 BTU will be required to go from 32° F to 212° F. When the water reaches 212° F, it will begin to boil and the temperature will again stop increasing. It will take a total of 970 BTU for the total pound of water to boil. If we conduct our experiment in a closed system, the temperature of the water in its gaseous

form (i.e., the temperature of the steam) will remain at 212° F until all of the water boils. If we continue to add heat to the system, the temperature will again rise, with an increase of about 2° F for each BTU added since the specific heat of steam is 0.47 (see Figure 6.6).

The distinction between sensible heat and latent heat can be clarified by considering the change in the physical arrangement of water as it transforms from ice to fluid and then to steam, but first, we need to understand the physical arrangement in each of these three states: solid, liquid, and gaseous. In the solid state, the molecules of a substance are in a fixed position relative to each other in terms of both distance and position. In the liquid state, while the distance relationship between the molecules is set, there is no fixed position. The molecules are free to move as long as they remain at the same relative distance from each other. In the gaseous state, the molecules are not fixed in terms of distance or position, and they are independent and widely separated. This clarifies why a gas will expand to fill its container. It also explains why humidity, which is the water vapor in the mixture we call air, tends to distribute itself relatively evenly throughout a space or even a group of spaces that are connected.

While we can sense or measure the energy required in order to increase the vibratory motion of the molecules, we cannot do so directly for the energy required to break the linkage between the molecules. We know that this second type of heat energy, which is what we call latent heat, does exist, since we can measure the amount of energy that we put into a system—for example, when we heat water and boil it—and compare this with the amount of energy involved in the observed change in temperature. The comparison will show that more energy has been added to the system, and based on the Law of Conservation of Energy, we know that the "excess" energy that went into the system did not merely disappear. Although we cannot measure it directly, we can surmise that the energy that was not related to the temperature increase must be the

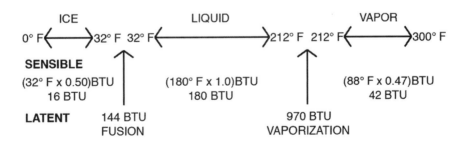

Figure 6.6 THE THERMAL JOURNEY OF WATER
Water can exist in three different forms or states. In order to change state, there must be an exchange of thermal energy, although without any apparent change in the temperature of the water. Since this energy does not relate to a change in temperature that can be measured, it is called *latent heat*. Latent heat of fusion is the energy required to change water from a solid, ice, to a liquid, and latent heat of vaporization is the energy required to change water from a liquid to a vapor or gas. As noted, in heating a sample of water from 0° F to 300° F, considerably more energy will be entailed in the latent heat exchange than in raising the temperature of the water in its three states.

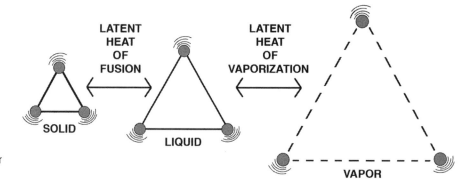

Figure 6.7 CHANGE OF STATE
There must be an exchange of latent heat as a material changes state from a solid to a liquid or from a liquid to a solid.

latent heat entailed in the change of state—the conversion from liquid water into water vapor.

When a material changes its state, its molecular structure is altered. In a sense, as shown in Figure 6.7, we can assume that the alteration involves moving the molecules apart from each other or at least releasing the bond between them. This would make sense, since in going from a solid to a liquid and then from a liquid to a gas, the relationship between molecules is "reduced." While sensible heat is related to the vibration of the molecules, which is indicated by temperature, latent heat is the energy required to reduce the bond that links the molecules. Since particles are physical entities that should abide by the laws of gravity and naturally collapse, an input of energy is required to increase their separation, such as when ice melts into a liquid or water boils into a vapor. When the change of state is reversed, that is, when water vapor condenses or water freezes, the molecules fall back or condense somewhat, releasing energy.

For crystalline solids such as ice, the change of state occurs at a definite temperature. For noncrystalline amorphous solids, such as waxes or fats, there is no specific melting point. When heated, these materials gradually soften throughout the whole mass, becoming first pasty and then less viscous as the temperature is raised. For this type of change of state, latent heat is still required but in a gradual manner as the molecular arrangement slowly adjusts. Therefore, when melting begins in an amorphous solid, some of the added energy is used for the change of state and some for a temperature increase. While the material is going through its change, the temperature rise for each added BTU will decrease. This could be interpreted as a change in the specific heat of the substance, although it is actually only an indication that some of the added thermal energy is transformed into a latent form and some is maintained in the kinetic form.

In the liquid state, with the rearrangement of the molecules, the forces between the molecules are no longer strong enough to hold them in a fixed position. They can only attain a fixed average distance. The molecules oscil-

late about this average distance with increased activity as the temperature increases. The molecules move farther and farther apart as the temperature increases until at last they reach the limit of their effective bond. Any further addition of thermal energy results in a separation or breaking apart of the molecules and the formation of a gas. If the internal pressure of the liquid equals the atmospheric pressure, the liquid boils as it becomes a gas.

All liquids are without specific form, have distinct boiling points, and require a large quantity of energy to change into a gas. It takes 970 BTU per pound at 212° F and standard atmospheric pressure to transform (boil) 1 pound of water into 1 pound of vapor, whereas only 180 BTU are required to heat 1 pound of water from the melting temperature to the boiling temperature, that is, from 32° F to 212° F.

Even if the internal pressure of a liquid does not reach the atmospheric pressure, a change of state can occur. Whenever the internal pressure of the liquid exceeds the vapor pressure of the air, as distinct from the atmospheric pressure, a portion of the liquid will change into a gas. This will continue until the internal pressure and the external vapor pressure are equal. In this case, rather than boil, the liquid evaporates. Whether it boils or only evaporates, it still requires the addition of latent heat.

In the gaseous state, the molecules are released from all effective restraint and move about independently. In 1738, Daniel Bernoulli suggested that a gas could expand indefinitely. It was this observation that began the development of the modern theory of heat and led to the acceptance of the atomistic theory of matter.

While Bernoulli's work was extremely instrumental in advancing our understanding of thermodynamics, he is primarily remembered for what we call Bernoulli's Principle. Kinetic energy plus potential energy is a constant. While this is very applicable in thermodynamics, with sensible heat being kinetic energy and latent heat potential energy, it also relates to the issue of airflow. According to Bernoulli's Principle, the total of static pressure plus the velocity pressure in an air stream remains a constant.

Therefore, when the wind is deflected over a building, since it cannot travel in its original configuration, its cross section is constricted and its velocity is increased. To allow for this increased velocity, the static pressure is reduced. This, in turn, results in the potential for the wind to actually suck off the roof. We now understand why, when we see roofs that have been damaged by high winds in a storm, the shingles or roofing seem to have been torn off the surface. Bernoulli's Principle also explains why planes can fly.

To reiterate, sensible heat is the energy related to the molecular activity of a material. It is the heat energy that we measure with a thermometer. Latent heat is the energy required to change the physical state of a material. Latent heat is a form of potential energy and cannot be directly recorded on a thermometer. However, if we surround the bulb of a thermometer with a wet wick, converting the standard thermometer, which we accurately call a *dry bulb thermometer*, we obtain a way of indirectly measuring the latent heat, at least the heat in an air sample. This second thermometer is called a *wet bulb thermometer.*

PSYCHROMETRIC CHART

An air sample normally contains some water in a gaseous state. The amount of water vapor that can be contained will depend, somewhat proportionally, on the temperature of the air sample. The psychrometric chart, which is presented schematically in Figure 6.8, is a graphic representation of the thermal characteristics of air. It is a plot of various combinations of sensible heat and latent heat and the characteristics of each combination.

Sensible thermal energy is plotted on the abscissa, or horizontal scale, of the chart. Since temperature is an in-

dication of sensible energy contained in an air sample, the abscissa scale typically represents the dry bulb temperature (DBT) in degrees F. We should note that movement from left to right indicates an increase in sensible energy, so the intersection of the sensible and latent energy lines does not represent the origin of the chart. The origin of the chart, if 0° F were the base, would occur somewhat to the left. If the intention were to plot the actual thermal energy contained in the air sample, the origin, which would occur at thermodynamic zero, would be considerably farther removed!

Latent thermal energy, which is generally referred to either as *specific humidity* or *vapor pressure*, is plotted on the ordinate, or vertical scale. Latent energy, limited to that contained in the water vapor, is measured either by weight of water vapor per weight of air (i.e., pounds of water vapor per pound of dry air) or by vapor pressure (i.e., inches of mercury). Upward movement denotes an increase in latent energy.

An air sample actually contains additional latent heat since all the gases that comprise the mixture of air also have had to go through a phase change to become a vapor. However, since water is the only component of the air mixture that can naturally exist in various physical states within the range of standard environmental temperatures and pressures (i.e., exist either as a solid, a liquid, or a vapor), the representation of latent heat in the psychrometric chart is limited to that energy contained in the water vapor. While the sensible heat represented in the psychrometric chart includes the sensible thermal energy of all the gases that comprise the air mixture, latent heat is limited to the energy contained in the water vapor.

As shown in Figure 6.8, a diagonal line is noted as the *adiabatic process line*. Since the term *adiabatic* means

Figure 6.8 SCHEMATIC PSYCHROMETRIC CHART

The psychrometric chart is a graphic representation of the thermal properties of an air sample. An air sample is a mixture of various gases, including water vapor. However, in terms of the psychrometric chart and general thermal considerations, water vapor is considered separately from the rest of the mixture. Water vapor is the only component of an air mixture that might normally exist other than as a gas at standard temperatures and atmospheric pressures; therefore, the amount of water vapor in an air sample varies according to temperature and pressure. The energy related to the presence of water vapor is the latent heat of vaporization for the weight of water vapor that exists per pound of dry air.

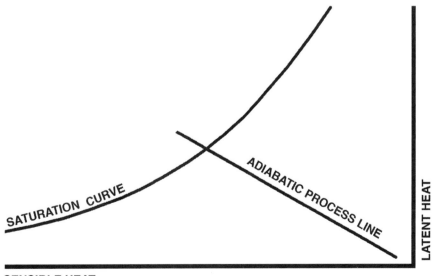

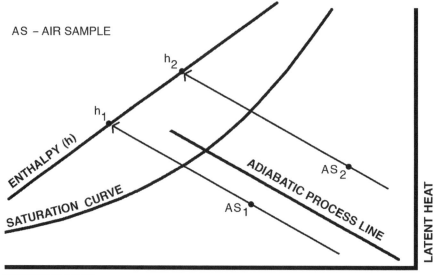

AS – AIR SAMPLE

Figure 6.9 ENTHALPY ON THE SCHEMATIC PSYCHROMETRIC CHART
Enthalpy is an indication of the relative thermal energy, both latent and sensible, contained within an air sample. It is denoted in terms of BTU per pound of air. Since *adiabatic* means no change in energy and since the psychrometric chart is a plot of sensible and latent energy, a particular slope of a line on the chart indicates a change in latent energy that is equal but opposite to a change in sensible energy. Each such line, called an *adiabatic process line*, therefore relates to constant total energy or a particular enthalpy value. Extending the adiabatic process line that passes through an air sample to the enthalpy scale provides an indication of the relative enthalpy for that air sample.[2]

no change in thermal energy content, this line, or more specifically the slope of the line in the psychrometric chart, represents movement for which there would be no change in the total amount of thermal energy contained in the air sample. Any change in the temperature of an air sample that follows the slope of the adiabatic line would have to entail an opposite change in the specific humidity of that air sample. That is, with movement along the adiabatic process line, a change in sensible energy is balanced by a comparable but opposite change in latent energy, so the thermal content of the air sample remains constant.

The slope of the adiabatic process line relates horizontal movement to vertical movement within the psychrometric chart. The psychrometric chart actually includes a number of parallel lines at the same slope of the adiabatic process, and when a change in temperature and humidity follows one of these lines, the change is adiabatic and the total energy in the air sample remains constant. Although the proportion that is sensible or latent heat would differ, they would all have the same total BTU per pound of air. Therefore, these process lines provide the means of denoting the total content of thermal energy in BTU for an air sample. As shown in Figure 6.9, if we plot a particular condition of air on the psychrometric chart, we can then move up the adiabatic process line that passes through the plotted point to another scale that represents the total thermal energy content. We call this total energy content *enthalpy* (*h*), which is BTUsensible and latent per pound of air.

Since both horizontal and vertical movement relate to a change in BTU per pound of air, we might question why the adiabatic lines are not drawn at a 45° angle. If the psychrometric chart were drawn so that equal movement on either the sensible or latent energy scales represented an equal change in energy, as shown on the left side of Figure 6.10, the adiabatic process lines would be drawn at a 45° angle. Because the psychrometric chart has been deformed, probably to fit on standard $8\frac{1}{2} \times 11$-inch paper, the adiabatic process lines are not drawn at 45°. As a result, a unit of horizontal movement represents a greater energy change than a unit of vertical movement, and the slopes of the adiabatic lines are at an angle that is less than 45°.

The psychrometric chart also includes a curved line called the *saturation curve*. This curve, which indicates that the amount of moisture that an air sample can contain increases with a rise in temperature, is defined by the air conditions that correlate with 100% relative humidity, which is the maximum water vapor that can be contained at each temperature. At any DBT, the height of the vertical line between the abscissa and the saturation curve represents 100% humidity for that temperature. Proportioning this vertical line provides an indication of the relative humidity[3] for that temperature. By doing this for all temperatures, a set of relative humidity curves is developed. While the schematic chart in Figure 6.11 only shows the curve for 50% relative humidity, standard psychrometric charts include additional curves, generally at 10% increments.

In order to determine where a particular air sample falls on the psychrometric chart, we need to know at least two

---

[2]While extending the adiabatic process lines to the enthalpy scale should indicate the total energy in an air sample, this is not quite accurate since there is a minor adjustment in the thermal content as the conditions of air change. This refinement is incorporated in the Trane psychrometric chart, although for most practical applications, particularly those with which we are likely to be involved, this level of specificity is not critical.

[3]Relative humidity is the percentage of maximum humidity that can be contained at a particular temperature. The "relative" reference connects the percentage of humidity to a particular temperature.

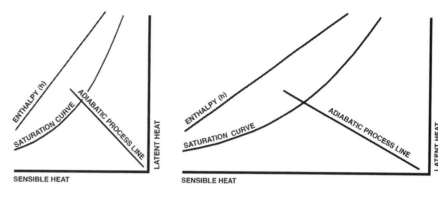

Figure 6.10 PROPORTIONAL RELATIONSHIPS OF THE PSYCHROMETRIC CHART

Horizontal and vertical movement on the psychrometric chart does not represent equal change in energy. As a result of the geometry of the chart, horizontal movement, which relates to a change in sensible energy, must be larger than vertical movement, which relates to a change in latent energy. This means that the slope of the adiabatic process lines is less than 45°, which is the slope that would be expected if horizontal and vertical movement were equal.

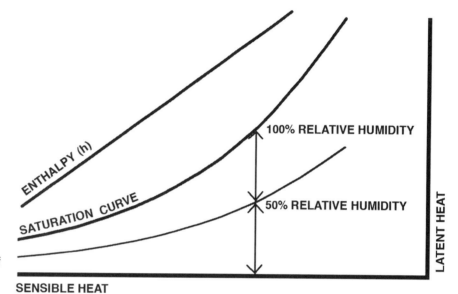

Figure 6.11 RELATIVE HUMIDTY ON THE PSYCHROMETRIC CHART

The maximum amount of water vapor that can be contained within an air sample is based on atmospheric pressure and air temperature. This maximum varies for different temperatures, increasing as the temperature increases. A plot of these maximum amounts of water vapor establishes a plot, which is a curve rather than a straight line. This curve is the saturation or 100% relative humidity curve. Proportioning the height of this saturation curve at each temperature establishes a series of relative humidity curves.

characteristics of that air sample. One that is easy to measure is the DBT. Measuring the DBT with a thermometer defines a vertical line along which a number of different air samples can lie. To know where on that line the particular air sample lies, we need to identify a second characteristic that defines another line. The wet bulb temperature (WBT) is a good choice. It defines a specific adiabatic process line, and the particular air sample will lie at the intersection of this line and the vertical line drawn at the point of the DBT.

If moisture is added to an air sample adiabatically, there is an exchange of sensible energy for latent energy and the air sample moves up the adiabatic process line. As the moisture evaporates into the air adiabatically, the temperature drops as the humidity increases. This adiabatic exchange will continue until saturation occurs and additional evaporation is no longer possible. At that point the maximum exchange of sensible for latent energy will have occurred, and the lowest temperature attainable through adiabatic evaporation will have been reached. This lowest attainable temperature is called the *wet bulb temperature* (WBT). The

classic definition of WBT is the temperature to which an air sample can be brought through the adiabatic evaporation of water.

If we put a wick on the end of a thermometer and wet it, the water will evaporate adiabatically, causing an exchange of sensible heat for latent heat. As a result, the temperature will drop until it reaches the temperature related to the point where the adiabatic line crosses the saturation curve. This is the WBT. We generally record both the WBT and the DBT by a *sling psychrometer*. As shown in Figure 6.12, this device includes two thermometers, one a dry bulb and the other a wet bulb, in such a way that they can be swung around. If the thermometers are moved, the wet bulb thermometer does not remain in the same location in which the water evaporates, thereby providing a slightly better measurement. A hygrometer is similar to a sling psychrometer in having two thermometers, one with a wet wick; however, the *hygrometer* does not move. Once we have determined both the WBT and the DBT of an air sample, we can readily plot the air sample on the psychrometric chart (see Figure 6.13).

Figure 6.12 SLING PSYCHROMETER
The sling psychrometer includes two thermometers, one of which has a wick attached to its end. If the wick is wet, some of the water will evaporate, and since latent heat of vaporization must be acquired, the temperature will go down. Spinning the psychrometer continually moves the wet wick away from the air sample that has acquired the increased moisture, producing a more accurate indication of the rate of evaporation and the associated drop in temperature. A hygrometer is similar to the sling psychrometer but is stationary. This image is of the 1330PJ psychrometer by Taylor Precision Products Inc. and is used with permission.

Figure 6.14 shows that once the air sample is located on the psychrometric chart, the other characteristics of that sample can be determined. Moving horizontally to the left indicates the temperature at which condensation will occur. This is noted as the *dew point temperature* (DPT). Moving horizontally to the right reveals the specific humidity and the vapor pressure. And as mentioned above, by moving along the adiabatic process line up to the enthalpy scale, it is also possible to establish the total thermal energy

contained in the air sample. The relative humidity is found by interpolating between the two relative humidity curves that pass on either side of the plotted air sample. Obviously, we do not have to interpolate between two curves if the air sample lies on one of the relative humidity lines. Of course, if the air sample is initially defined by two other characteristics, then the DBT and the WBT can also be determined from the psychrometric chart.

Given any two distinct thermal characteristics of an air sample, we can plot the air sample on the psychrometric chart and then determine the other thermal values for that sample. Various thermal characteristics of the air sample will lie on the same line and, therefore, cannot be used to specify a particular location on the psychrometric chart. For example, enthalpy and WBT would not suffice since they lie on the same sloping line. DPT, specific humidity, and vapor pressure also would not work because they also lie on the same line, although this line is horizontal.

We recognize Willis Carrier as the individual who initially developed the connections between temperature and humidity that are the bases of the psychrometric chart. Shortly after receiving his master's degree in mechanical engineering from Cornell University in 1901, he started working for the Buffalo Forge Company. One of his first assignments was to determine how to solve a problem that a Brooklyn printing company was having as a result of its inability to control humidity in its plant. Since, at that time, color printing required sequential printing of the various primary ink colors, variations in humidity altered the dimensions of the paper, which, in turn, made it difficult to achieve accurate results. Supposedly, while standing on a railroad platform one winter evening in 1902 in Pittsburgh, observing that steam was condensing on cold

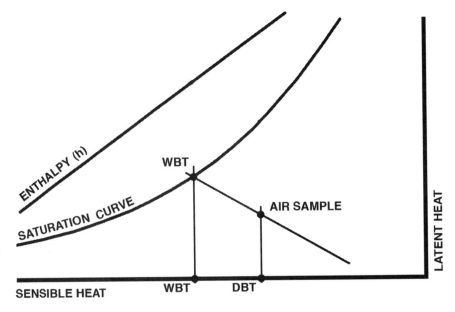

Figure 6.13 FINDING AN AIR SAMPLE ON THE PSYCHROMETRIC CHART
The DBT and WBT of an air sample define two lines on the psychrometric chart that intersect at a point. This point indicates the conditions of the air sample.

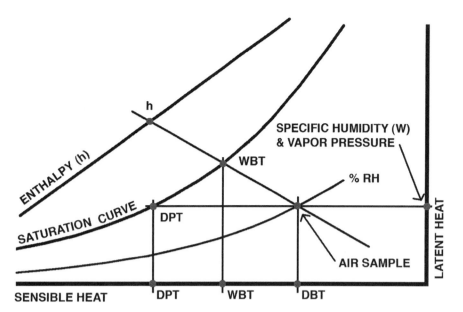

Figure 6.14 CHARACTERISTICS OF AN AIR SAMPLE ON THE PSYCHROMETRIC CHART
If two distinct characteristics of an air sample are plotted on the psychrometric chart, the other characteristics of that air sample can be identified.

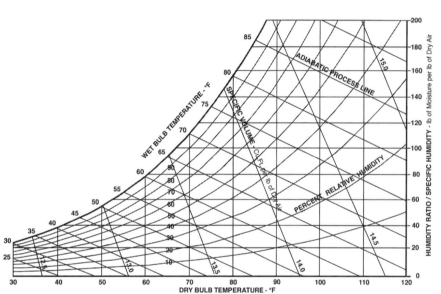

Figure 6.15 PSYCHROMETRIC CHART
This chart is based on the psychrometric chart by Carrier Corporation.

surfaces, Carrier grasped the link between temperature and humidity. He went on to describe mathematically the phenomena he had observed, thereby establishing the science of psychrometrics, which is graphically shown by the psychrometric chart (see Figure 6.15).

One aspect of the connection between temperature and humidity that Carrier discovered was that as air temperature drops, air can no longer contain the same amount of moisture. Ultimately, if the temperature of the air drops enough, conditions reach saturation or 100% relative humidity, and any further drop in temperature forces some moisture to condense out of the air. We call the water that condenses out of the air *dew*, so the temperature at which this occurs is referred to as the *dew point temperature* (DPT). While this principle is important and was used to lower the

humidity, merely lowering the temperature to reduce the amount of water vapor contained in the air does not allow close control of air temperature or relative humidity.

While he understood this, the critical realization that came to Carrier on that fateful evening in 1902 was that in addition to lowering the temperature, it is possible to attain saturation by adiabatic evaporation of water. Spraying water into the air, which is what Carrier essentially saw on the railroad platform, results in an exchange of sensible for latent heat; the air temperature drops, and saturation is achieved. This brings the air sample to a specific lower temperature, which is called the *wet bulb temperature* (WBT), and as a result, it is possible to control both temperature and humidity. Willis Carrier developed his "Apparatus for Treating Air," for which he obtained a patent in 1906, and

Figure 6.A CONDUCTION

Figure 6.B CONVECTION

Figure 6.C RADIATION

modern control of temperature and humidity, which we now call *air conditioning*, was possible.[4]

THERMAL TRANSFER

There are four ways in which thermal energy can be exchanged. These include the three classic methods of thermal transfer, conduction, convection, and radiation, plus evaporation.

Conduction (see Figure 6.A) is the method of thermal transfer whereby the molecular activity of a substance is transferred, particle by particle, through the substance. A molecule whose oscillation is increased above the mean for the substance, as a result of an addition of thermal energy, will collide with adjacent molecules, causing their oscillations to increase. Somewhat similar to the action of billiard balls, a chain reaction develops and energy in the form of increased molecular activity travels through the substance. With conductive transfer, the relative position of the particles of the substance is maintained while the energy moves by "jumping" from molecule to molecule. In general, materials that are good electrical conductors are also good thermal conductors. Glass is an obvious exception. Glass, which is a reasonably good thermal conductor, is often used as an electric isolator, as a glance at an electrical pole will probably confirm.

Convection (see Figure 6.B) is the transfer of thermal energy by fluid flow. Within a liquid or a gas, but not within a rigid solid, the addition of heat will cause an increase in molecular activity that normally results in some expansion of the substance. As the substance expands, its density is reduced. Since the molecules are not held in a rigid position in either a liquid or a gas, the less dense molecules will rise and be displaced by other, more dense molecules. These "new" molecules will then be heated, assuming that the addition of thermal energy continues, and they will similarly be displaced as they expand and become less dense. In convection the thermal energy is carried through the material by the movement of the molecules—hence the term *fluid flow.*

Radiation (see Figure 6.C) is the transfer of thermal energy by electromagnetic radiation. This is directly related to the transfer of light and entails the release or reception of energy in the form of a photon. The emission of radiation occurs when the molecular activity at the surface of a substance releases a photon. The radiation that is emitted from a substance is related to its absolute or thermodynamic temperature, as well as to its ability to emit radiation, which is called *emissivity* (E). While not specifically the same, the emissivity of a material is generally equal to its *absorptivity* (A). The absorption of radiation is, of course, dependent on the absorptivity of the receiving surface. Since the absorptivity is equal to 1 minus the reflectivity (R), we can write the following formula:

$$E = A = 1 - R$$

We should recognize that since thermal radiation is related to light, the emissivity and absorptivity of a substance will depend on the wavelength. While a surface might emit or absorb certain wavelengths of radiation, this does not mean that it will be equally responsive to all wavelengths. In fact, we can observe that there is usually a clear distinction of both the emissivity and the absorptivity to different wavelengths of radiation.

Interestingly enough, there is a significant variation in how some materials respond to radiation, depending on if the radiation is emitted from a surface above or below 450°F, which is about the temperature at which wood begins to emit volatiles and combustion can occur. Radiation emitted from a surface that is above 450° F is considered to be shortwave radiation and generally means solar radiation and visible light. Radiation emitted from a surface below 450° F, which includes almost all surface-emitting radiation in our physical environment, is longwave radiation.

The short wavelengths of solar radiation, which we sometimes refer to as *insolation*,[5] can readily pass through some substances that will not transmit the long

---

[4]Carrier's Apparatus for Treating Air relied on a wet spray to move the air up the adiabatic line to reach saturation while lowering the air temperature. Today, as a result of our developed understanding of psychrometrics and a better grasp of the actual cooling process that occurs as air passes over dry cooling coils, we rarely use spray cooling coils, relying primarily on dry cooling coils.

[5]Insolation, with an *o* and not a *u*, refers to solar radiation but is used predominantly in terms of thermal performance as distinct from illumination.

wavelengths of radiation emitted from the surfaces in our physical environment that are at less than 450° F. Glass is such a material. It allows insolation to pass through, but it does not allow the longwave radiation emitted from the surfaces that have been heated by the sun to pass. Therefore, glass operates essentially as a one-way filter and delivers what is often referred to as the *greenhouse effect*. High humidity in the atmosphere behaves somewhat similarly to glass, thereby creating a heat trap. The solar radiation that arrives during the day can pass through the high humidity, but the longwave radiation emitted by the Earth's surface during the day and night cannot pass through the humidity and, therefore, the solar gain is retained. This explains why temperatures do not vary significantly (day and night) in areas of high humidity, whereas they do vary greatly in dry areas, especially desert regions.

A glass cover on a solar collector generally serves as an effective one-way filter. It allows solar radiation to pass through to be absorbed on a black collecting surface, but it does not permit the longer-wavelength radiation emitted by the collecting surface to pass through. It also provides a means of isolating the warmer temperatures within the collector from the exterior, often cooler temperatures.

While not one of the classic methods of thermal transfer, *evaporation* does account for thermal exchange. This is especially significant when the evaporation occurs within a closed system of constant thermal energy content so that energy is neither gained nor lost. In such a condition, all thermal exchanges are essentially adiabatic, at least in terms of the closed system. While the total amount of energy in BTU remains constant, there can still be an exchange between sensible and latent energy. In an adiabatic system, evaporation, which always requires that the evaporating material gain latent heat, results in a reduction of the sensible heat within the closed system.

To fully appreciate the importance of the thermal exchange that occurs with evaporation, we must recognize that materials can change in state from a liquid to a gas without the input of additional heat. Our normal observation of vaporization occurs with the boiling of water at 212° F. At that temperature, which in our environment always relies on the input of additional heat, the internal pressure of the hot water equals that of the atmosphere.[6] When this occurs, bubbles appear as gas pockets because of vaporization within the actual liquid. That is, since the internal pressure exceeds the external atmospheric pressure, some of the liquid flashes into a gas before it escapes into the air above, and as it does, it creates a vapor bubble.[7]

If we take a bowl of water and place it in a room, we would find that in due time the bowl would be empty. The water would evaporate; however, the temperature of the room would never even approach 212° F. This simple experiment confirms that vaporization occurs at temperatures well below 212° F, even at standard atmospheric pressures. We generally call the vaporization that occurs below the normal boiling temperature of water *evaporation.*

If, rather than leaving the bowl of water in the room uncovered, we covered it with a bell jar, we would most likely observe that the water in the bowl would diminish, but it would not totally evaporate. In this closed system, the evaporation would occur adiabatically and would continue only as long as the internal vapor pressure of the water was greater than the vapor pressure of the air contained within the bell jar. When the two pressures are equal, effective evaporation ceases. Any additional evaporation of water would have to be matched by a comparable condensation of water vapor out of the air. At the condition of equal pressures, the air sample contained in the bell jar would be saturated. It would be at 100% humidity. The air would contain as much water vapor as can be contained at that particular temperature. However, if we increased the temperature of the bell jar system, additional water evaporation would occur.

Relative humidity is defined as the percentage of the maximum amount of water vapor that can exist at a particular temperature and pressure that does exist. It is essentially the ratio of the amount of water vapor in an air sample compared to the amount at saturation. The percentage is based on the mass of water or the vapor pressure at the relative and saturated conditions. In addition to relative humidity, which is temperature dependent, there is specific humidity and absolute humidity. *Specific humidity*, as previously stated, is the amount of water vapor in the air sample measured in weight of water per weight of air. In the International System, specific humidity is noted in terms of grams of water vapor per gram of air. In the imperial system, it is pounds of water vapor per pound of dry air.[8] Specific humidity is also at times referred to as *humidity ratio*. *Absolute humidity* is given in terms of weight of water vapor in a unit of volume of the air sample, such as pounds of water vapor per cubic foot of dry air. Since absolute

---

[6]With an increase or decrease in atmospheric pressure, there is a comparable adjustment in the boiling temperature of water.

[7]While we can tell that water has reached the boiling temperature by seeing these bubbles, we also sometimes determine that the water has boiled by seeing the discharge coming off the water, especially when we are using an opaque kettle that has a small spout and that damnable whistle no longer works. In this situation, we generally assume that we see the steam or water vapor, but of course we cannot. Gases are not visible, and we do not have any superhuman ability to see them. So, what do we see? We actually see suspended water droplets that have condensed out of the steam. As these droplets dissipate through the air, they generally revaporize and disappear.

[8]Since the weight of water vapor is minimal, sometimes instead of pounds, the weight of water vapor is listed in grains, with 7000 grains equal to 1 pound.

humidity entails mixed units, it does not really live up to its name and is not often, and should not be, used.

Basic Thermal Terminology

Various terms are used in discussing thermal issues. Following are short definitions for most of these terms. This inventory of terms is organized by relationships, although there are connections between terms that might be separated in the listing.

Sensible Heat: Heat energy measured on a dry bulb thermometer (kinetic).

Latent Heat: Heat energy required to change the physical state of a material (potential). Solid–liquid changes involve latent heat of fusion. Liquid–vapor changes entail latent heat of vaporization.

Temperature of Water	Latent Heat of Vaporization	Pressure (PSI)	ATM
32° F	1075.8 BTU	0.09	
40° F	1071.3 BTU	0.12	
60° F	1059.9 BTU	0.25	
70° F	1054.3 BTU	0.36	
80° F	1048.6 BTU	0.51	
100° F	1037.2 BTU	0.95	
200° F	977.9 BTU	11.5	
212° F	970.3 BTU	14.7	1+
250° F	945.5 BTU	29.8	2+
500° F	714.0 BTU	690.8	4+
705° F	0.0 BTU	3206.2	200+

Specific Heat: The quantity of heat energy necessary to produce a unit temperature change in a unit mass of a given material.

British Thermal Unit (BTU): The basic unit of heat energy. One BTU is the amount of heat energy required to raise the temperature of 1 pound of water 1° F, between 32° F and 212° F.

Calorie: The basic metric unit of heat energy. One calorie (1 c) is the amount of heat energy required to raise the temperature of 1 gram of water 1° C, between 0° C and 1° C. One kilocalorie (1 C) is the amount of heat energy required to raise the temperature of 1 kilogram of water 1° C, between 0° C and 1° C. (1 C is equivalent to 3.966 BTU.)

Enthalpy: The measurement, in BTU per pound, of total heat quantity, both sensible and latent.

Figure 6.D EVAPORATION

Figure 6.E CONDUCTION

Dry Bulb Temperature (DBT): The measurement of sensible heat intensity.

Dew Point Temperature (DPT): The temperature at which the condensation of water vapor would begin for a particular specific humidity.

Wet Bulb Temperature (WBT): The temperature to which an air sample can be brought by the adiabatic evaporation of water. WBT is an indication of temperature and humidity.

Specific Humidity (W): The amount of water vapor in the air measured in pounds of water per pound of dry air (or grains of water per pound of dry air). Specific humidity is also called the *humidity ratio*.

Relative Humidity: The amount of water vapor in an air sample, at a particular temperature and pressure, measured as a percentage of the maximum water vapor that the air sample at the same temperature and pressure could contain at saturation.

Absolute Humidity: The weight of water vapor in the air measured in pounds per unit volume.

Water Vapor: The gaseous form of water or "low-pressure" steam.

Condensation: The process of water changing from a gaseous state to a liquid state, requiring the release of latent heat of vaporization.

Evaporation: The process of water vaporizing into a gas at below the boiling temperature, requiring a change from sensible heat to latent heat (see Figure 6.D).

Conduction: The transmission of heat energy by the collision of active "heated" molecules with slower "unheated" neighboring molecules. Movement of heat through materials from particle to particle (see Figure 6.E).

Convection: The transmission of heat energy by fluid flow resulting from movement caused by density variation or forced motion (see Figure 6.F).

Radiation: The transmission of heat energy by electromagnetic waves. This method of transmission is

Figure 6.F CONVECTION

Figure 6.G RADIATION

in the form of radiant energy that becomes thermal energy upon absorption (see Figure 6.G).

Mean Radiant Temperature (MRT): The average temperature of all surfaces that define a given place. The MRT can be estimated by multiplying each surface area by the surface temperature and dividing the total by the total area of the enclosing surfaces. The actual MRT will vary from point to point within the space.

Adiabatic: Without a change in energy content.

Atmospheric Pressure: At sea level, 30 inches of mercury, 34 feet of water, 14.7 psia, 0 psig.

ENVIRONMENTAL CONTROL

A major intention of environmental design is to establish conditions that provide thermal comfort. Essentially, this means controlling the environmental factors that determine thermal conditions in a way that allows us to achieve a thermal balance and to do so without being conscious of the processes involved. Considering how design can establish conditions that will result in thermal comfort, it is helpful to recognize that there are four basic classifications of the various means of controlling the thermal conditions, all of which have definite architectural aspects:

- Physiology
- Climatology
- Construction
- Technology

While the construction category is traditionally considered the realm of architecture, to be effective, architecture must also be responsive to physiology and climate and must appropriately utilize technology.

Physiology

A heat engine is a device that transforms heat energy into energy of motion. Thermodynamics indicates that all heat engines require three components: a source of heat at a high temperature, an agency that can transform heat energy into motion, and a colder source or reservoir that can absorb the excess heat. In simple parlance, a heat engine is a device that can convert a portion of heat energy into motion as that heat energy flows through the engine as it drops from a higher intensity to a lower intensity. The process of transforming heat into motion is never 100% efficient. The Watt steam engine, which essentially enabled the Industrial Revolution, had an efficiency of around 5%, but this was a tremendous improvement over the Newcomen engine. The Newcomen engine, which essentially made coal mining possible by being the first safe steam engine that provided a way to continuously pump water out of the mines, had an efficiency rating of only around 1% to 2%.[9]

The efficiency of modern steam engines is much higher than anything Watt could achieve, with smaller engines operating at around 8% efficiency and larger units at around 17%. Modern steam turbines significantly improve even on these figures, achieving an efficiency of 28%. The gasoline internal combustion engine generally operates at an efficiency of around 22% to 24%, while a diesel engine runs at an efficiency of around 35%.

The human body is also basically a heat engine. As such, it has the same three requirements of all such devices. Our source of heat is the food we consume. Our metabolism combines sugars, fats, and protein supplied by the food with the oxygen that we breathe in to establish a source of energy. We essentially burn the food we eat to produce this energy, which our body then converts physiologically into action.

While the human body is remarkable in many ways, as a heat engine it is condemned to perform physiological functions, mental activities, and physical activities at less than 100% efficiency. In fact, the average efficiency of the human heat engine is considerably less than that of many modern engines. Its efficiency is only around 20%, which means that humans have to release to the environment in which they exist 80% of the heat they generate.

The recommended average daily food consumption for people who are moderately active is around 2200 Calories for women and 3000 Calories for men. Since 1 Calorie equals about 4 BTU, this average daily intake equals 8800 to 12,000 BTU. Based on a 20% efficiency, this means that each day we need to release to the environment

---

[9]James Watt actually developed his steam engine as a way to improve the efficiency of the Newcomen engine.

approximately 7000 to 9600 BTU, which on an hourly basis equals approximately 290 to 400 BTU per hour (BTUH). However, when we sleep, which is usually for around 8 hours each night or about one-third of the time, our activity is reduced to almost basal metabolism. As a result, we generally accept that the average heat loss to the environment during the day is around 400 to 500 BTUH, with about half as sensible heat and half as latent heat.

How much energy does 400 to 500 BTUH represent? Since 1 watt of energy is equivalent to 3.412 BTU, 400 to 500 BTUH is equal to around 115 to 145 watt-hours, or somewhat more than the heat given off by a 100-watt incandescent light bulb (lamp) every hour.[10] Perhaps this helps us understand the amount of heat that we continually release to the environment. It might also give us a new appreciation for the cartoon image of a light bulb drawn over a person. While this is meant to represent having an idea, if we have ever touched a hot light bulb, it should also remind us how much heat a bulb gives off. If this does not help, then knowing that 1 BTU equals 778 foot-pounds might provide a clearer sense of the energy entailed in our body heat loss. But perhaps the best way of impressing on us the significance of our hourly heat loss, on a per unit weight, is the knowledge that the human body supposedly gives off more heat than the sun.

Since all people must continually dissipate their excess body heat, control of a building's thermal environment entails establishing conditions that allow the occupants to lose their excess body heat at the rate at which they generate it, and to do so without imposing any stress or even awareness of the process involved in cooling their bodies. If the environment absorbs heat faster than it is generated, chilling of the body will be experienced. If the environment absorbs heat more slowly than it is generated, overheating of the body will be experienced. When the rate of thermal transfer from our bodies to the surrounding environment matches the rate at which we generate excess heat and the transfer does not impose any stress on us, we experience thermal comfort. That is, thermal balance is the basis of thermal comfort.

The physiological processes by which our bodies maintain a thermal balance are rather complex, but we tend to rely on them to succeed. In fact, if our internal body temperature varies from the standard 98.6° F by even a small amount, we generally interpret this as a sign of a physical problem. While our personal normal temperature might be slightly different from 98.6° F, when it rises to 100° F or higher, we accept that we have a fever, which means we are sick. If our body temperature rises to 104° F, the situation is serious, and at 106° F, which is only about a 10% variation from normal, we will probably die unless we get immediate medical attention. Lower than normal temperatures are also an indication of trouble. While abnormally low body temperatures can be life-threatening, alcohol or drug use, shock, certain metabolic disorders, and exposure to a cold environment can result in reduced body temperatures. Some infections, particularly in elderly persons and newborns, may also cause a reduction in body temperature, but generally infections result in an increase in body temperature.

When we are sick or have an infection, our bodies try to heal us and, as a result, there is less control of body temperature. Blood flow is the basic means by which we attain thermal balance. By vasomotor regulation, we are able to adjust the distribution of blood throughout the body. When excess heat is not being lost and we may possibly overheat, our blood vessels dilate and more blood is sent to the body's perimeter. With more blood there is more heat, which raises the temperature of the skin, and with higher skin temperatures, more heat should be lost to the surrounding environment. If we lose heat more rapidly than we generate it, vasomotor regulation again comes to our defense. The blood vessels constrict, less blood is sent to the body's perimeter, and the temperature of the extremities will drop. The reduced surface temperature results in a reduction of body heat loss.

Our blood flow does not exist merely to maintain our body temperature. It is the way that nutrients are supplied to all of our cells, and when there is an infection the cells need more blood, so less blood is available for temperature control and we are likely to have a fever, often determined by merely sensing that our skin is warmer. Under normal unstressed conditions, our body skin temperature is around 90° F. Our body surface temperature affects how much heat we can transfer to the surrounding environment by convection and radiation. The rate of thermal exchange by convection is determined by the temperature differential between our body surface temperature and the air temperature. The greater the differential, the higher the rate of heat transfer. Of course, if the air temperature is higher than 98.6° F, rather than lose heat by convection, we can actually gain additional heat. We can also lose or gain heat by radiation. The rate of radiant transfer is based on the difference in the mean radiant temperature (MRT) of the space we are in and our body surface temperature, although the actual computation of the amount of transfer is based on the thermodynamic temperature scale. As with convection, sometimes rather than remove excess body heat, radiation can add to our body heat.

---

[10]An incandescent lamp generally converts only around 10% of the consumed electricity into light. As a result, 90% is released merely as heat, which equals 0.90×100 watts $\times 3.412$ BTU/watt. However, except for the extremely small portion of the generated light that is actually converted into another form of energy, such as our vision, the light that is generated is also ultimately converted into heat. At 100% conversion between watts and BTU, the heat produced each hour by a 100-watt incandescent lamp is around 340 BTUH.

When convection and radiation are not adequate, fortunately evaporative heat transfer can maintain our necessary body heat loss. In fact, we always lose at least around 25% of our excess heat by evaporative transfer. When we breathe, we exhale air that includes water vapor; since water vapor contains heat of vaporization, this results in some heat loss. In addition, although we are not aware of it, we continually lose some moisture through our skin. This insensible perspiration, which is a cleansing as well as a cooling action, releases water through pores in our skin. This water carries away body impurities and quickly evaporates, cooling us as it acquires latent heat of vaporization. The minimal evaporative heat loss is basically split equally between the loss by respiration and the loss by unnoticeable perspiration.

To provide any thermal benefit, the water that we lose by perspiration has to evaporate. When we become wet with sweat, the process is not working effectively; this often happens when the humidity is high. In a dry environment, sweat evaporates rapidly and keeps us cool, and if we drink enough water, we can avoid the effects of dehydration. Unfortunately, there is no clear indication of when dehydration starts, so rather than wait until we are thirsty, whenever we are in a hot, dry environment, we should drink large quantities of water even if this does not seem necessary.

If we cannot lose our excess heat, our internal body temperature increases. When it rises above 104° F, we can suffer from heat stroke. As more blood is pumped to the extremities, less goes to the brain. If the brain does not get enough blood, the results can be fatal. While very serious and undesirable, heat stroke restores our basal metabolism, which means that we do the least possible amount of physical activity necessary for survival.

When conditions are such that body heat loss exceeds heat generation and vasomotor constriction of the blood vessels cannot regain thermal balance, we generally experience involuntary muscular tension. This is what we call *shivering*, which is a way to intensify physical activity in order to increase body heat production. Another adjustment comes from the development of goose bumps. While this is generally assumed to be a remaining vestige of our hairier form, in which the physiological action that causes goose bumps would have fluffed our surface hair to provide more insulation, there is some indication that this action also entails the secretion of a liquid that increases the thermal resistance of our subcutaneous layer of fat.

Although not physiological, clothing is obviously part of our thermal-balance arsenal. But when thermal balance cannot be maintained by physiological means and clothing, it is necessary to either move to a more favorable climate or develop architectural controls of the natural environment.

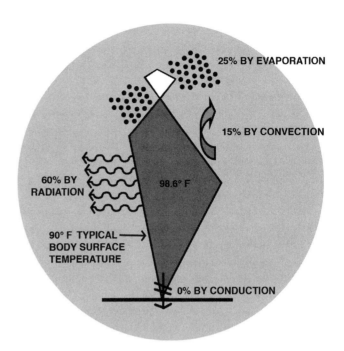

Figure 6.16 THERMAL ENVIRONMENTAL SPHERE AND HEAT TRANSFER
The human body is essentially a heat engine situated within an environmental sphere. As a heat engine, the body must be able to release to this environmental sphere around 80% of the heat it generates so that the internal body temperature remains at 98.6° F. To maintain this temperature, body heat can be transferred by conduction, convection, radiation, and evaporation. In unstressed comfort conditions, the rate of transfer is basically as indicated in the diagram.

Thermal comfort never requires us to heat the building's occupants, even on the coldest days. Rather, our challenge is to establish an environment that allows them to cool down, to dissipate their excess body heat, and to do so at the rate at which this heat is generated. While four means of thermal transfer are available, generally we cannot rely on conduction as a way to lose body heat since only a very small part of the body's surface is typically in direct contact with a surface to which heat can be conducted. Although when we sit down we might initially conduct heat to the surfaces we sit on, after a short period of time these surfaces essentially become extensions of our body. An exception in which conduction might be an effective way of losing body heat is lying down on a waterbed, which has a major thermal mass.

The means of establishing body heat loss are shown in Figure 6.16. As indicated in the diagram, which assumes no effective loss by conduction, we must depend on only convection, radiation, and evaporation to lose our excess body heat to the surrounding environment. Generally when not thermally stressed, we achieve thermal balance primarily through radiant transfer. Although we might assume that air temperature is the critical thermal characteristic of the environment and, as a result, that convection is the major way in which we lose body heat, in

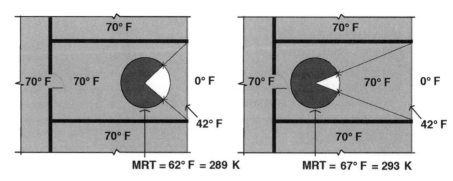

Figure 6.17 MRT BASED ON LOCATION WITHIN A SPACE
The MRT depends on the particular location within a space since the percentage of the environmental sphere comprised by the different physical elements is based on location. As indicated in the diagram, as one moves farther away from a cold window surface, this surface represents a smaller portion of the total environmental sphere, which changes the effective MRT.

reality convection accounts for only around 15% of our total heat loss. In an unstressed condition, in which the body surface temperature is 90° F, around 25% of our excess body heat is lost by evaporation, which includes perspiration and respiration, leaving about 60% to be handled by radiant transfer.

These percentages obviously are not rigid. As environmental conditions change, it is likely that the rate of loss by each method will also change, and it is possible that convection and/or radiation might actually account for an addition of heat to the body. This might require us evaporative transfer to handle 100% of body heat loss.

Considering how each of the methods of thermal transfer work, we can see that convective loss is primarily dependent on the difference between the temperature of the body surface and the ambient air, but we should realize that it is also affected by air velocity. While a temperature differential can set up a convective loss, which is loss by means of fluid flow, if there is forced airflow, by mechanical means or natural forces, the warmer surface will be continually bathed in cooler air and the convective loss will increase.

Radiant Transfer

Radiant transfer is set by the difference in surface temperatures, based on the thermodynamic temperature scale, usually in degrees Kelvin, and by the surface characteristics of absorptivity and emissivity. For body heat loss, the temperature differential is between the body surface temperature and the MRT of the space, which is based on the temperature of each surface adjusted by the percentage of total environmental exposure comprised by each. This makes MRT a variable based on the location within the space. Things are further complicated by the fact that the thermal resistance of any space-defining element that is an exterior wall or roof will affect the actual surface temperature. While we can assume that any interior space-defining element will basically be at the interior air temperature, elements located along the building's perimeter will have a surface temperature somewhere between the interior air temperature and the exterior air temperature. The higher

the overall thermal resistance across the enclosing element, the closer the interior surface temperature will be to the interior air temperature. With the standard resistances that are now prescribed for walls and roofs, the major impact on establishing a difference between the interior air temperature and the MRT comes from windows, and based on their location within a space, as shown in Figure 6.17, this is a variable. The greater the window's percentage of one's environmental sphere, the greater its impact on the MRT for that location. While the percentage of the total environmental sphere that each surface comprises is based on three-dimensional space, the two-dimensional diagrams in Figure 6.17 demonstrate the importance of location.

While the difference between 289 K and 293 K does not seem to be significant, we should remember that we are concerned with mean radiant loss, and this depends on the difference in thermodynamic temperature between the body's surface temperature and the MRT of the surrounding surfaces. When the body is not under thermal stress, the body surface temperature is basically held at 90° F, which is equal to 305 K. Therefore, the radiant transfer would be based on a temperature differential for the left-hand condition of 16 K and only 12 K for the right-hand condition, which indicates an approximate ratio of 4:3. Assuming a 60% body heat loss by radiant transfer, a person in the left-hand location would have around a 20% greater heat loss than a person in the right-hand location. As a result, two people in the same space with the same room-air temperature and humidity would experience quite different thermal conditions.

This example assumes insulated glazing. With single glazing, the difference in thermal conditions would be even greater. The interior temperature of the windows would be around 20° F rather than 42° F, so the MRT values for the two room locations would be 283 K and 290 K, which means that the difference in radiant temperature between the occupant's body surface temperature and the location's MRT would be 22 K and 15 K, respectively. As a result, the overall increased heat loss with single glazing would be almost 30% higher in the location closer to the window. This is another good reason for using insulated glazing—the thermal conditions within a space do not vary that much.

Realizing that there is a linkage between the various methods of thermal transfer and environmental conditions, we should understand that if body heat loss becomes a problem due to a low MRT, we can counter this by raising the air temperature, which should not only reduce the convective loss of body heat but also raise the MRT. A number of years ago, Dr. Clarence Mills, professor of experimental medicine at the University of Cincinnati, explored the effects of pollution and climate on health. His research helped established the above-mentioned percentage heat loss by the various thermal transfer methods and led to his development of a way to heat and cool space solely by radiant methods. Rather than control air temperature, which was and is the usual approach for thermal conditioning, Mills' system controlled the MRT and did so in a rather interesting way.[11]

Dr. Mills began by lining each space with materials that were highly reflective. He essentially used aluminum foil with a "selective coating," which was similar to some wrapping paper, often red or green, that we might use during Christmas. Mills' idea was that since the body loses so much heat by radiant transfer, the reflective surfaces would bounce the radiant energy added by the occupants around the space and then back to the occupants. Rather than heat the space to the normal thermal comfort range of around 70° F, the space could remain considerably cooler and yet the occupants would be comfortable. If not, Dr. Mills included a radiant system, but not as is typically done today. His radiant system involved a continuous pipe that ran around each room in a valance located high on the walls. In the colder seasons, warm water ran through the pipes, effectively raising the MRT. In the warmer seasons, chilled water ran through the pipes, effectively lowering the MRT.

Dr. Mills retrofitted several buildings with his system and actually built his own home using it. While he continued to believe in his approach, others did not. The main problem was that while his system might have been effective in establishing thermal balance in terms of body heat loss, it did not provide thermal comfort. With no air movement or humidity control, the spaces were not very pleasant. However, while Mills' assumption that thermal comfort could be achieved merely through the control of MRT was not justified, MRT control is critical to achieve thermal comfort, and this is primarily an architectural task. Although there are engineering techniques that affect MRT, such as radiant panel heating, the design of the building envelope and the selection of interior surfaces are the more critical means of MRT control.

While Dr. Mills emphasized MRT, others accepted his basic premise: thermal comfort is based on a combination of various environmental factors and if some of them are not in the comfort range, acceptable conditions can be achieved by adjusting others. Unfortunately, for many years, the assumption was that control of relative humidity could compensate for temperature, suggesting that raising humidity when the temperature was low or lowering it when the temperature was high could establish comfort. This was the basis of the initial Effective Temperature scale developed by the American Society of Heating, Refrigerating and Air-Conditioning Engineers (ASHRAE). Based on this initial Effective Temperature scale, it was assumed that adjustments in humidity were effective across the range of humidity.[12] Subsequent studies by the Olgyay brothers (1957, 1963) and P. Ole Fanger (1972) showed that the impact of humidity on what we call thermal comfort actually occurs only below 20% and above 60% to 75%. Under unstressed conditions—that is, within a temperature range between 70° F and 80° F, with an MRT of basically the same intensity and an airflow of 15 to 25 feet per minute—around 25% of body heat is lost through evaporation. As long as relative humidity is not excessively high, above 60% to 75%, we have no difficulty in releasing this amount of body heat, so variations in humidity have no thermal impact at less than these percentages. When the humidity becomes too low, while this does not affect us thermally, it does start to cause drying of nasal passages and skin. It can also cause problems with many materials, such as the changes that occur in wood if it loses too much moisture content. So, while not actually a thermal problem, very low humidity is to be avoided.

ENVIRONMENTAL COMFORT

While ASHRAE's focus was and continues to be on mechanical environmental control, Victor and Aladar Olgyay were interested in exploring how architectural design can

---

[11]Dr. Mills demonstrated that controlling MRT can establish comfort well beyond the normal range of temperatures considered comfortable. Realizing that radiant transfer across polyethylene is the same for longwave and shortwave radiation, he constructed several spaces enclosed by polyethylene. He controlled the air temperature and humidity inside the enclosures, and independently the effective MRT within the spaces, by controlling the surface temperatures outside the enclosures. This allowed him to adjust the temperatures inside the spaces well beyond the comfort range, sometimes above and sometimes below, while simultaneously adjusting the MRT in the opposite way. The polyethylene did not affect the radiant transfer but did separate the thermal air conditions inside and outside the enclosures.

[12]According to the ASHRAE comfort chart, which was developed in the 1950s and attempted to indicate graphically the conditions of temperature and humidity that would be comparably perceived, winter comfort would exist between 69° F and 80% relative humidity and 76° F and 20% relative humidity.

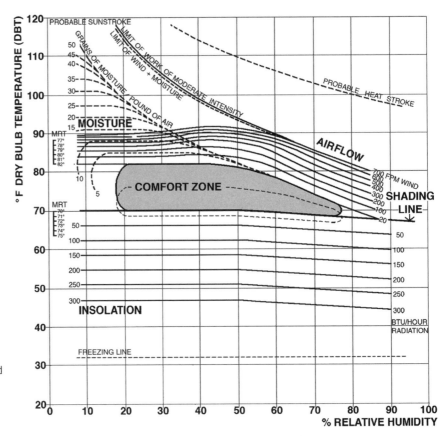

Figure 6.18 BIOCLIMATIC CHART
Adapted from the bioclimatic chart initially presented
Figure 47 in A. Olgyay and V. Olgyay, *Solar Control
and Shading Devices* (Princeton University Press,
Princeton, New Jersey, 1957),
p. 20

effectively moderate the natural environment in order to establish comfort conditions. In *Solar Control and Shading Devices* (1957), they presented a graphic method of determining ways to effectively adjust conditions that fall outside of the thermal comfort zone to regain comfort. They called this graph the *bioclimatic chart*, a representation of which is shown in Figure 6.18.

The bioclimatic chart, which is based on DBT and relative humidity, presents a wealth of important information. First, it defines the thermal comfort zone as conditions of temperature and humidity. The acceptable range of temperatures is between 70° F and 82° F, although with increased clothing during the cooler seasons, the suggestion is that the comfort zone is compressed somewhat and lowered a few degrees. The comfort range of relative humidity runs from around 20% to 75%, although the upper limit of acceptable humidity is reduced as the temperatures rise. While it is around 75% for the low 70s° F, it is reduced to 60% at the upper air temperatures of the comfort zone.

The bottom of the standard comfort zone is noted as the shading line, which implies that MRT equals DBT. This is significant. While it helps explain why temperatures in the low 80s° F can be considered comfortable, more importantly it should make it clear that it is critical to provide solar shading to achieve comfort during the warmer seasons. Furthermore, when the natural conditions of tem-

perature and humidity fall below the shading line, added insulation can adjust to conditions to regain thermal comfort. As indicated, if the air temperature was 50° F, we could reestablish thermal comfort by adding around 260 BTUH of solar radiation.

If conditions lie above the comfort zone, we could improve them by using two methods. By increasing airflow, which is often feasible by various architectural means,[13] we can counteract higher temperatures or higher humidity. By increasing the velocity of air passing over the

---

[13]We can increase airflow by raising a building up on stilts in order to get above the drag effect of the ground. This can also redirect the air, forcing it to constrict, thereby increasing its velocity. We can also deflect the air over and around the structure as a way to establish a draft by inducing airflow as a result of the venturi effect. Of course, thoughtful placement, sizing, and design of window openings can also improve airflow, potentially increasing the air velocity passing over the occupants. In addition to enhancing airflow when there is some wind, we can establish air movement by harnessing the stack effect that is formed by vertical displacement. However, when vertical airflow is based on increased temperatures, it is likely that any corrective value is gained because of a basic failure. That is, rather than improve the natural conditions during the overheated period of the year, the interior temperatures are higher than the exterior temperatures. While it might not make sense to rely on a temperature differential as the way to establish airflow to counteract high temperatures or humidity, it is appropriate to harness the temperature differential that occurs during the night, when the exterior temperatures have dropped, as a way to ventilate the interior and cool it down.

occupants, we can increase both convective and evaporative heat loss, but this improvement increases only up to 700 FPM, which is equivalent to almost 8 MPH. The bioclimatic chart indicates that evaporative cooling is another way of improving thermal conditions. If the humidity is low, which means that the temperature and humidity conditions lie on the left side of the chart, adding moisture adiabatically will lower the DBT. While this will also increase the humidity, as long as the resulting humidity does not exceed the acceptable limits of the comfort zone, the thermal exchange is beneficial.

The Olgyays suggested that by using the bioclimatic chart to plot the combinations of temperature and relative humidity that typically occur over the year for a particular location, it is possible to see the overall thermal conditions of that location, when comfort conditions should exist, and if and when they do not, what means of adjusting the natural conditions might exist to achieve thermal comfort. In this presentation, they suggested that there are essentially four different thermal regions—cool, temperate, hot arid, and hot humid—each having a particular appropriate architectural response that we can readily see from the plots of the yearly temperature and humidity conditions. Figure 6.19 presents an example of yearly plots of the monthly temperature and humidity for Minneapolis, New York, Phoenix, and Miami, with these cities

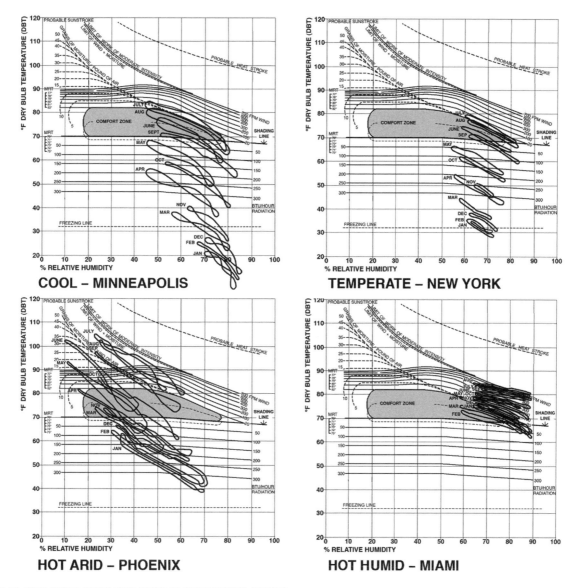

Figure 6.19 BIOCLIMATIC CHART WITH PLOTS OF FOUR THERMAL REGIONS
Plotting the climatic conditions for a particular location on the bioclimatic chart indicates possible adjustments in the natural environment that will reestablish comfort conditions. Comparing plots for different locations provides a clear indication of the different architectural approaches that might be appropriate. Adapted from the bioclimatic chart initially presented in A. Olgyay and V. Olgyay, *Solar Control and Shading Devices* (Princeton University Press, Princeton, New Jersey, 1957).

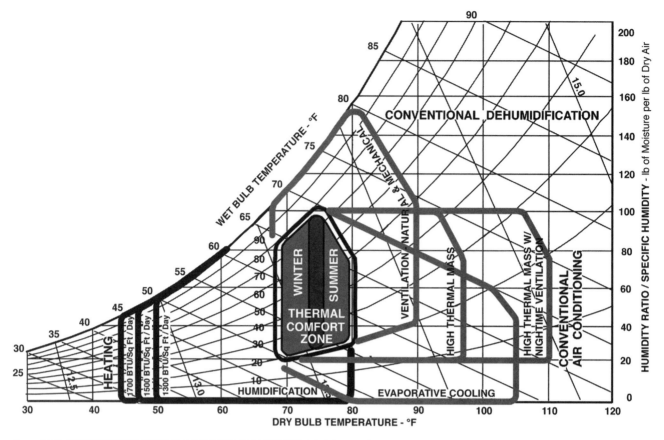

Figure 6.20 ENVIRONMENTAL CONTROL STRATEGIES AS A FUNCTION OF AMBIENT CONDITIONS
Adapted from Figures 5 and 6 in Milne and Givoni (1979), pp. 102 and 104.

representing, respectively, one of the climatic zones: cool, temperate, hot arid, and hot humid.

In "Architectural Design Based on Climate" (1979), Murray Milne and Baruch Givoni transcribed the basic information included in the bioclimatic chart from the temperature and relative humidity plot that the Olgyays used to the psychrometric chart. While quite similar, the Milne–Givoni responses to conditions that lie beyond the comfort zone have also been adjusted from basic thermal processes, such as the grains of moisture to be added, to more architectural means of environmental control, including conventional heating and cooling. Again, by plotting the natural conditions that are likely to occur for a particular location on this chart, which are shown in Figure 6.20, we can identify architectural responses that would help to achieve thermal comfort.

Beyond our limited ability to adapt physiologically to different environmental conditions, thermal comfort, whether achieved through beneficial natural conditions, passive architectural means, reliance on energy-consuming mechanical devices, or some combination of these methods, is based on controlling five environmental factors:

- Temperature of the ambient air (DBT)
- Humidity of the ambient air (WBT, specific humidity, vapor pressure, or relative humidity)
- MRT of the location
- Air velocity
- Air quality

While we can compensate for a deficiency in one factor by adjusting one or more of the others, generally there is a limited acceptable range for each of these factors. If this range is exceeded, real comfort probably cannot be achieved.

Air quality is not a true thermal factor, but our reaction to it is strongly related to our perception of thermal conditions. Interestingly, before science and physiological experiments provided a clear explanation of our thermal experience, it was thought that the discomfort that we now realize is due to air contamination was actually the result of high temperatures and humidity. It makes sense to include air quality among the factors that determine the thermal environment since the methods we use to control the four basic thermal factors are often connected with the management of air quality.

CLIMATE

Thoughts on Its Architectural Significance

[F]or architecture, the solution of experiential problems is the only source of valid form.[14]

[A]n esthetically rich and sensuously satisfying architecture can only be derived from the closest attention to and respect for its actual terrestrial environment, especially at the microclimatic scale.[15]

James Marston Fitch

Unfortunately, even with our current concern for environmental issues, architectural design still often demonstrates profound misunderstanding of the ecological realities of the environment. Today, as James Marston Fitch wrote a number of years ago in *American Building: The Environmental Forces That Shape It*, there are two sorts of errors that designers continue to make. "One is a lack of comprehension of the absolute inter-relatedness of all the component elements of the natural environment—an interdependence that makes it impossible to manipulate one factor without setting in motion a complex chain reaction that usually extends far beyond the individual designer's sphere of action.... The other professional error is the consistent tendency of [many] architects and engineers grossly to underestimate the magnitude of the natural forces of the environment— or, contrariwise, grossly to overestimate the magnitude of manmade capacities at their disposal."[16] While there has been increasing recognition in the design field of the benefits that can accrue from a positive interaction with the natural environment, many designers still erroneously believe that any set of interior conditions can be achieved by mechanical means regardless of the actual conditions imposed by the natural environment. Instead of approaching design with the expectation that we can depend on complex, energy-consuming mechanical systems to provide acceptable thermal conditions, regardless of how environmentally irresponsible we might choose to be in our design, we must begin with a commitment to maximize the architectural potential to establish comfortable conditions through passive means that do not rely on energy consumption. In this approach, the intention is to use mechanical systems to supplement architectural contributions rather than to correct architectural problems.

The design process should include early consideration of the site in terms of its thermal effects. First of all, the site itself should be selected for its microclimatic advantages. While at times this might include selecting the region where the project is to be located, normally our site location decisions are limited to the selection of a particular property in a given area and/or the identification of the specific location on which to build within that property.

Having selected the site, we should then consider ways in which we can modify the existing conditions in order to minimize the environmental problems and maximize the environmental potentials. While this should affect the actual design of the structure, it should also influence how we develop the site in terms of movement of earth, placement of roadways, and location and selection of vegetation. As for the actual building design, we should arrange the massing, configuration, and orientation to take full advantage of the natural conditions, which means capturing the positive aspects, enhancing the potentials, and avoiding the problems. With an understanding of the natural conditions of the site, and through considered placement of the various activities in response to orientation and the selection of appropriate enclosing membranes, we can establish a positive relationship between the interior space and the exterior environment. Only after we have exhausted these potentials should we consider incorporating mechanical systems to solve environmental problems.

In *Heating, Cooling, Lighting: Design Methods for Architects* (2001), Norbert Lechner includes a good presentation of this approach. While environmentally responsive design might be seen as something new, primitive buildings usually resulted from this type of design. Perhaps this was an imposed approach developed out of necessity due to the relatively unsophisticated mechanical devices available, but whatever the reason, we can readily see that primitive buildings typically reflect the designer's fairly detailed and precise understanding of the local conditions in terms of climate, performance of available building materials, and building traditions. Using their understanding of these three issues, primitive builders often built more wisely than we seem to be able to do today. They followed principles of design that we either ignore or of which we are unaware. Realizing that our failure to consider these issues has had a strongly negative effect on our designs, we still should not merely copy from these primitive examples of effective climatic adaptation. Rather, we should study these examples of effective climatic response with the intent of gaining an understanding of the principles involved so that we can apply them appropriately today. In this way, we will be able to improve our own design efforts in a manner that is responsive to our time.

[14]James Marston Fitch with William Bobenhausen, *American Building: The Environmental Forces That Shape It* (Oxford University Press, New York, 1999), p. 290.
[15]Ibid., p. 271.
[16]Ibid., p. 259.

In his book *Mainsprings of Civilization*, the scientist, historian, and philosopher Ellsworth Huntington presented an analysis of the influence that both biological inheritance and the physical environment have had on the course of history. He began with the claim that "the course of history may be summed up in two main statements. First, for thousands of years civilization has been persistently advancing along certain definite lines. Second, the rate of march varies incessantly, both from time to time and place to place."[17] As to what causes these incessant variations, Huntington claimed that there were three causal factors: "biological inheritance, physical environment, and cultural endowment."[18] By combining the factors of biological inheritance and cultural endowment together under the title of heredity and dividing the physical environment into geography and climate, we obtain another listing of the important factors that the text presents as having had a strong influence on the evolution of civilization: heredity, geography, and climate.

It is important to suggest that these factors are *influences* rather than *determinants* since they have not had a direct causal effect on the evolution of civilization. Amos Rapoport addressed the issue of determinants versus influences in *House Form and Culture*. Even though he was not dealing with the broader issue of civilization itself but rather with house forms that have been used by a civilization, Rapoport rejected the notion that there are finite determining forces. "We should speak of coincidences rather than causal 'relations,' since the complexity of forces precludes our being able to attribute (results directly) to given forces or variables."[19] In the section of his book entitled "General Criticism of the Physical Determinist View," he went on to state that "since possibilities have to be used, there can be no physical determinism. The physical setting only provides possibilities, not imperatives. It is man—not site or climate—that decides."[20]

This is an extremely important observation that has a great deal of relevance for the field of architecture. While as designers we should be concerned with the influence that various factors have on the development of architectural form, we must realize that their actual impact is the result of our intervention and not some direct, forced response. Some designers seem to exclude themselves from direct involvement in the design process by assuming that certain factors are *form determinants* rather than merely influences that can affect the development of the architectural form. In fact, sometimes designers use the expression "What does

the —— want to be?" as if the object being designed had a will of its own.

"What does the building want to be?" This is an expression that has been attributed to the architect Louis I. Kahn. But how can a building, an inanimate object, have consciousness? Obviously, it cannot, and to assume so is irrational. If a designer grants consciousness to an object, one might rightly question the designer's level of development or intellectual ability. Children of toddler age or individuals who are part of a society generally referred to as primitive often assume that objects that move possess life, and life is a precondition for consciousness. So, if a designer assumes that even a nonmoving object possesses consciousness in that it "wants" something, it might be appropriate to question the designer's position on the ladder of development.

Even if we agree that a designer is probably on difficult ground by assuming that a building "wants to be" something, there is a certain enticing aspect about this way of considering the influences that affect architectural design. There is a strong logic in considering design decisions not only in terms of how those decisions respond to existing factors but also how they might affect new ones. That is, it is important for us as designers to consider what new forces are generated by each design decision and then to respond to these new forces. When suggesting that an inanimate object might have an influence on its own intentions, we are not really considering the object itself; rather, we are dealing with the conceptual interpretation of the object by those individuals who will experience it. By considering the ways in which the object will be used and perceived and then allowing this to influence the development of the design, we can respond to conditions rather than imposing upon them. Understanding this approach can be helpful in terms of designing in response to climate, particularly at the micro-climatic scale, since any new building will alter the natural conditions and result in different conditions. This is an important issue that should guide us in our design efforts. It is closely related to an idea suggested a number of years ago by the Dutch architect Jacob Berend Bakema, although his concern was not specifically climate related.

Bakema talked about the need to consider how a building that we are designing might influence the environment after it is added to the existing ecological system and to modify our design so that the completed building would promote or lessen the projected effects. For example, as diagrammed in Figure 6.21, if we were designing a new hotel near an existing transportation terminal, the existing traffic patterns might change because of the new building. Although an existing major thoroughfare might suggest that we should locate the main entry to the new hotel off of this thoroughfare, if there was a secondary roadway,

---

[17] Ellsworth Huntington, *Mainsprings of Civilization* (John Wiley & Sons, Hoboken, New Jersey, 1945), p. 13.

[18] Ibid., p. 19.

[19] Amos Rapoport, *House Form and Culture* (University of Wisconsin Press, Milwaukee, 1969), p. 17.

[20] Ibid., p. 42.

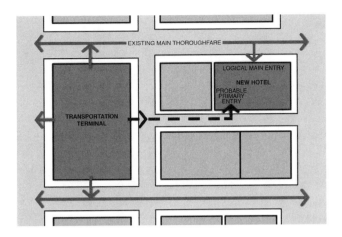

Figure 6.21 THE BAKEMA PRINCIPLE
The imposition of a new structure generally alters the preexisting conditions. As a result, while design of a structure should be responsive to existing conditions, it is also important for the design to be responsive to the conditions that are established by the structure once it is built. Since this consideration was often discussed by the Dutch architect Jacob Berend Bakema, it is referred to as the *Bakema Principle.*

this might provide a more direct connection between the hotel and the transportation center. This "alley" connection might become more significant upon the completion of the new hotel, so it would be proper for us to consider whether or not it would be reasonable to accept this entry and develop our design accordingly. If we include an entry at that location, it will likely become a major, if not primary, entrance, so we should develop our design to respond to this condition. If we do not think that this alley entry is appropriate, we should intentionally not locate an entrance at that point. This is based on the Bakema Principle, which basically says that we should not assume that the preexisting conditions will continue to dominate; instead, we should explore how our design will alter the existing conditions and design for these conditions.

Understanding this notion of design influence, we can recognize the significance of Huntington's thesis that civilizations have been strongly affected by the climates in which they exist. Huntington wrote that "1.) Aside from the distribution of land and sea, climate appears to be the most important physical factor in determining the habitability, occupation, and mode of life in different parts of the world; 2.) No other known physical factor, when considered directly and indirectly, has so great an influence upon health and vigor; 3.) No other feature of the physical environment is so variable from one period to another, as well as from place to place; 4.) We . . . found that both in the U.S. and the world at large, climate seems to set a basic pattern of civilization upon which other factors impose variations with all degrees of magnitude."[21] Later on, he added that

"among all factors which influence people's modes of life, the two that seem to be most dominant are climate and the stage of culture already attained."[22]

Huntington claimed that all progressive civilizations throughout the ages have been located in temperate climates where the temperature is on the cool side. He said that "most of the world's main civilizations have grown up where the majority of the months have average temperatures near or below the (63°–73° F) optimum."[23] The simple basis for this claim is that in environments where the temperature is too hot, lethargy pervades and there is no adequate incentive for a level of activity on which advancement of society can be developed. In places where the temperature is too cold, mere survival consumes the majority of effort. However, in places where it is slightly cool, such as exist with what Huntington called the "optimal conditions for societal advancement," the climate is invigorating and encourages maximum human effort.

While this theory seems fairly reasonable, we might question the connection between it and the developments that occurred in the ancient Babylonian and Egyptian civilizations or, perhaps, between it and the industrialized development in the southern United States. However, on reflection, we realize that the current climatic conditions of the Middle East are not those that were described for the land between the Tigris and Euphrates or for the fertile Nile Valley at the time these civilizations achieved their significance. Similarly, the conditions that have supported the industrialization of the American South are not those of excessive warmth but rather those that resulted from the use of human-made mechanical refrigeration. Interestingly, Huntington suggested that the issue of slavery was also strongly influenced by climatic conditions. Simply stated, in times when air conditioning was not available, the South was not a place conducive to physical labor, so a system was found to provide it—slavery. In the North, however, physical labor during the warmer seasons was less physiologically demanding, and the seasonal changes limited slave productivity in the predominantly agricultural economy to only a portion of the year. As a result, in the North, there was less incentive to support the system of slavery.

While Huntington discussed climate in terms of civilization, Rapoport introduced climate as one of the three major modifying factors of house form. The other two are sociocultural and technological. Rapoport wrote that "while climatic determinism fails to account for the range and diversity of house form, climate is nevertheless an important aspect of the form-generating forces, and has major effects

[21] Huntington, *Mainsprings of Civilization*, p. 272.

[22] Ibid., p. 290.
[23] Ibid., p. 278.

Figure 6.22 *DYCKIA BREVIFOLIA* AND *ALOE BREVIFOLIA*

Vegetation evolves in response to the natural environment. At times, different species from quite different geographic locations with similar climatic conditions display comparable form.

DYCKIA BREVIFOLIA
(PINEAPPLE FAMILY)
BRAZIL

ALOE BREVIFOLIA
(LILIACEAE FAMILY)
SOUTH AFRICA

on the forms man may wish to create for himself."[24] We should remember that Rapoport was writing about preindustrial societies with no advanced technology that could allow humankind's domination over nature, so adaptation was necessary, and the impact that climatic adaptation had on building form tended to increase proportionally with the severity of the environmental conditions.

While Rapoport identified considerable variations in the architectural forms developed by different societies for similar environmental conditions, we should not ignore the fact that these were primitive cultures that lived in isolation, with no outside influences. Therefore, while we should recognize the differences, we should also try to understand and appreciate the similarities that emerged individually and independently in response to similar environmental forces. While it is interesting to compare design similarities in structures that were built by remotely separated, independent primitive cultures that happened to

share equivalent climatic conditions, it is also intriguing to see that different plant species from remote locations with similar climates have evolved into comparable forms (see Figures 6.22 and 6.23).

Although his book was written long before our current interest in ecology and a rational use of natural resources began to reemerge early in the 1970s, Rapoport condemned the idea of using mechanical modifications of the environment in lieu of effective architectural adaptation. He said that "we cannot ignore the physical environment, and that we [should not] underestimate its continued effect on our cities and buildings."[25] These are words of advice that we should follow.

Solar Radiation

Solar angles were discussed in Chapter 4. While this presentation was related to daylighting, the basic information

---

[24]Rapoport, *House Form and Culture*, p. 83.

[25]Ibid., p. 84.

EUPHORBIA FEROX
(SURGE FAMILY)
AFRICA

ECHINOCEREUS MARITIMUS
(CACTUS FAMILY)
MEXICO

Figure 6.23 *EUPHORBIA FEROX* **AND** *ECHINOCEREUS MARITIMUS*

As seen at the Arizona-Senora Desert Museum outside of Tucson, distinct species of vegetation often display quite comparable forms as a way to adapt to similar environmental conditions.

obviously applies as well to thermal considerations. However, there are some considerations that are more specific to thermal conditions.

At the outer atmosphere, the solar constant is 2 calories cm^{-2} mm^{-1} or about 450 BTUH/SF. At the Earth's surface, this is reduced to about 1 calorie cm^{-2} mm^{-1} or about 225 BTUH/SF, which is referred to as *1 Langley*. The actual amount of solar energy that strikes the surface of the Earth varies based on the depth of the atmosphere through which the radiation must pass, the conditions of the atmosphere, and the angle at which the radiation strikes the Earth's surface.

In December, solar radiation must pass through an increased depth of atmosphere in order to reach the Earth's surface in the Northern Hemisphere. Also, at the higher latitudes, the depth of atmosphere through which the sun must pass before it strikes the ground is greater (see Figure 6.24). This increased depth of atmosphere reduces the intensity of radiation that is available. The distance that solar radiation must travel through the atmosphere is shortest when it is most normal to the Earth's surface. At the solar equinox, this occurs at the equator, whereas at the solstice in December, it occurs at the Tropic of Capricorn ($23^1/_2°$ south of the equator), and at the solstice in June, it occurs at the Tropic of Cancer ($23^1/_2°$ north of the equator).

The angle of the sun above the horizon is generally considered as the *altitude angle*. At 12 noon sun time,[26] the altitude is equal to 90° minus the latitude plus or minus the angle of declination. Based on this, at 40° north latitude the noon altitude angle is $73^1/_2°$ at the summer solstice, 50° at the equinox, and $26^1/_2°$ at the winter solstice.

The angle of incidence also impacts on the thermal conditions. Since the intensity of solar radiation is proportional to the cosine of the angle of incidence, the more normal the radiation is to a surface, the greater is the solar intensity on that surface.[27] As a result, once the angle of incidence

---

[26] Sun time is used rather than clock time. 12 noon sun time occurs when the sun is due south and casts the shortest shadow. Generally sun time equals clock time minus the proportion of an hour determined by proportional distance from the beginning of the time zone, adjusted for daylight savings time if appropriate.

[27] The intensity of solar radiation is proportional to the cosine of the angle of incidence.

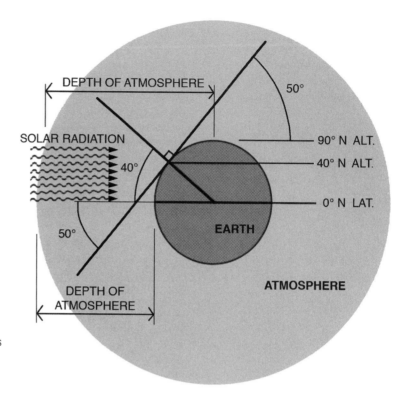

Figure 6.24 LATITUDE AND SOLAR ANGLES
The latitude of a site is based on the angle that the horizon plane of the site is above the plane of the equator, although the degrees of latitude are equal to 90° minus this angle between the planes. The 12 noon solar altitude is equal to 90° minus the degrees of latitude of the location.

is known, the relative intensity of the available solar radiation can be determined. Table 6.1 lists basic 12-noon solar intensities on the ground and on a vertical south-facing surface for each season at 30°, 40°, and 50° north latitude.

As shown in Table 6.1, at 40° north latitude, solar intensity on the ground during the winter is approximately half the summer intensity, and as a result, outside temperatures vary during the different seasons. But as we can also see, on a vertical south-facing wall or window, the solar intensity on a southern exposure in the winter is more than three times the intensity in the summer! The greatest amount of potential solar gain for a south-facing interior space occurs during the coldest season of the year, and due to the high angle of the sun during the summer, this same space would have the least solar heat gain during the

Table 6.1: 12 Noon Solar Intensity at 30°, 40°, and 50° North Latitude

	Altitude Angle	Angle of Incidence on Ground	Solar Intensity on	
			Horizontal Surface	South-Facing Vertical Surface
30° North Latitude				
Summer	$83^1/_2°$	$6^1/_2°$	0.99	0.28
Equinox	60°	30°	0.87	0.64
Winter	$36^1/_2°$	$53^1/_2°$	0.60	0.90
40° North Latitude				
Summer	$73^1/_2°$	$16^1/_2°$	0.96	0.28
Equinox	50°	40°	0.77	0.64
Winter	$26^1/_2°$	$63^1/_2°$	0.45	0.90
50° North Latitude				
Summer	$63^1/_2°$	$26^1/_2°$	0.90	0.28
Equinox	40°	50°	0.64	0.64
Winter	$16^1/_2°$	$73^1/_2°$	0.28	0.90

hottest season of the year. These data assume full sun, but overcast conditions do exist, and when they do, they can significantly reduce solar intensity.

Airflow

While it is possible to modify airflow by a thoughtful design, generally the natural conditions are a major determinant of whether there is adequate wind that can be harnessed as a means of cooling or, at the other end of the spectrum, too much airflow that could exacerbate heat loss during the underheated period of the year. Accepting that these parameters do exist, there are still ways in which we can maximize the potential contribution of airflow control to thermal comfort.

When air flows over and around a structure, pressure variations occur. As the wind approaches the structure on the windward side, positive pressures are formed. The air is deflected by the physical obstacle, which establishes higher velocities since the volume of air must not pass through a reduced area. As the higher-velocity air flows around the edges, the sides of the structure in plan or the roof in section (see Figure 6.25), it forms a negative pressure, which is consistent with Bernoulli's Principle, but then, as it continues, it can again establish a positive pressure. Then as the air passes by the structure, a negative pressure is formed on the leeward side of the structure, and based on the Venturi effect, reversing eddies of airflow are likely to occur.

Although we cannot specifically establish the direction or velocity of the natural wind currents, we can maximize the internal airflow by selecting the ventilation openings. The first principle is that for air to flow into a structure, it must also flow out, so it is always necessary to have both an inlet and an outlet. Generally, this is best achieved by at least two separate openings, with the inlet located at a point of positive exterior pressure and the outlet at a point of negative pressure. If we are ventilating a single space, this usually means that the room must have at least two exposures in which the openings are located. When a space has only one exposure, cross ventilation probably will depend on other spaces with which the ventilated space is connected. Transoms over doors were traditionally used to establish such connections while maintaining visual privacy. Of course, in an arrangement in which cross ventilation depends on combing spaces, one space probably serves as the inlet and the other as the outlet, so fresh air will actually enter only one space. If it is not possible to establish airflow by linking two separate ventilation openings located at different pressures, it is possible to use one window, but this relies on the window itself forming a pressure differential. Double-hung windows can do this, but both the upper and lower sashes must operate. When both are open, some air will flow as a result of the stack effect based on the change in elevation and temperature differential, although the limited difference in pressure that these will establish will not set up a significant airflow. As indicated in Figure 6.26, architectural projected casements can harness a natural airflow by establishing both an inlet and

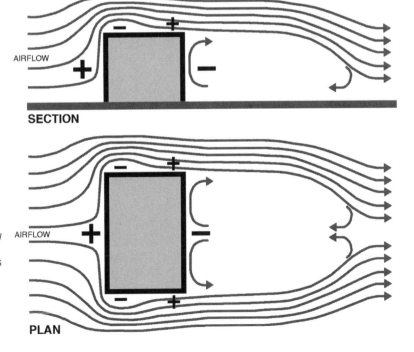

Figure 6.25 AIRFLOW PRESSURES
Air flowing around a structure establishes pressure variations, with positive pressures generally on the windward side and negative pressures on the leeward side. As the air flows along the sides or roof of a structure, a negative pressure is generally formed beyond the leading edge as the air is deflected away from the edge and then a positive pressure as the air converges toward the original airflow path. To maximize internal airflow, the inlet should be located at a point of positive pressure and the outlet at a point of negative pressure, although once the structure is penetrated, the basic locations of positive and negative pressure can be altered.

**Figure 6.26 WINDOW VENTILATION –
CAPTURED OR EXTRACTED**

A single window can provide both an inlet and an outlet. A double-hung window does so by providing both a low and a high opening that allow natural convective airflow. An architecturally projected window that moves the hinged side of a swing-opening sash into the opening provides two openings that respond to airflow, establishing a positive and negative pressure differential that will induce air circulation through the interior space.

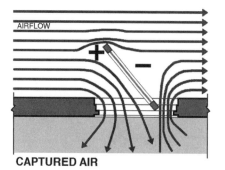
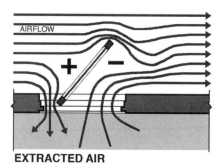

CAPTURED AIR   EXTRACTED AIR

**Figure 6.27 VENTILATION AIRFLOW RATES
BASED ON OPENINGS**

Airflow requires both an inlet at a point of positive pressure and an outlet at a point of negative pressure. With only one of the two, even if it is with positive pressure, airflow will be limited if it exists at all. For maximum airflow, both the inlet and outlet should be located at the appropriate pressures and be as large as possible. For maximum velocity, the inlet opening should be reduced in size, maintaining a large outlet. For large airflow at reduced velocity, the setup should be reversed, with a large inlet opening and a smaller outlet.

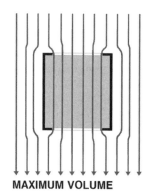
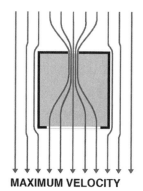
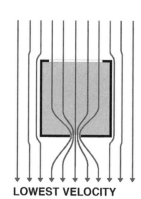

MAXIMUM VOLUME   MAXIMUM VELOCITY   LOWEST VELOCITY

an outlet. This type of window typically opens outward, and as the wind passes across the open sash, positive and negative pressure will be formed. Either way the window opens with respect to the direction of the natural breeze, as the air flows across the sash, a positive and negative pressure will be established. As a result, an architectural projected casement provides both an inlet and an outlet, although when the sash opens into the breeze, it does tend to provide increased ventilation. The projected sash of a standard casement, which is hinged along one side, even if it opens into the breeze, cannot supply effective ventilation by itself. Without an outlet provided by another opening, there will not be sufficient airflow regardless of which way the sash opens.

Since the airflow is based on the pressure differential between the inlet and the outlet, we can maximize the volume of ventilation air by placing the intended air inlet at a point of positive pressure and the outlet at a point of negative pressure. When located in this manner, the larger the openings, the greater the volume of air that will flow. With a smaller inlet and a larger outlet, not only will there be a good pressure differential, the constricted inlet means that the entering ventilation air will flow at high velocity. By reversing the opening sizes, with a large inlet and a smaller outlet, the overall volume of air will be essentially the same but the velocity within the space will be lower (see Figure 6.27). Increased air velocity can provide more cooling if it passes over the occupants, but it also can create problems, such as disrupting papers, so we should

select a ventilation arrangement to deliver the intended results.

This has been a rather cursory coverage of climatic concerns. There are a number of worthwhile publications that pursue this critical issue much further. In addition to the Olgyay and Lechner books, which have been mentioned, V. Bradshaw's *The Building Environment: Active and Passive Control Systems* (2006), G. Z. Brown and Mark DeKay's *Sun, Wind, and Light: Architectural Design Strategies* (2004), and W. T. Grondzik, A. G. Kwok, B. Stein, and J. S. Reynolds's *Mechanical and Electrical Equipment for Buildings* (2010) are recommended for expanded coverage of this important material.

BIBLIOGRAPHY

Bradshaw, V. *The Building Environment: Active and Passive Control Systems.* John Wiley & Sons, Inc., Hoboken, NJ, 2006.

Brown, G.Z., and M. DeKay. *Sun, Wind, and Light: Architectural Design Strategies.* John Wiley & Sons, Inc., Hoboken, NJ, 2004.

Fanger, P. O. *Thermal Comfort: Analysis and Applications in Environmental Engineering,* McGraw-Hill Book Company, New York, 1972.

Fitch, J.M., with W. Bobenhausen, *American Building: The Environmental Forces That Shape It.* Oxford University Press, New York, 1999.

Huntington, E. *Mainsprings of Civilization.* John Wiley & Sons, Inc., Hoboken, NJ, 1945.

Lechner, N. *Heating, Cooling, Lighting: Design Methods for Architects.* John Wiley & Sons, Inc., Hoboken, NJ, 2001.

Milne, M., and B. Givoni. "Architectural Design Based on Climate." In Donald Watson (ed.), *Energy Conservation through Building Design*. McGraw-Hill Book Company, New York, 1979.

Olgyay, V. *Design with Climate: Bioclimatic Approach to Architectural Regionalism*. Princeton University Press, Princeton, NJ, 1963.

Olgyay, A., and V. Olgyay. *Solar Control and Shading Devices*. Princeton University Press, Princeton, NJ, 1957.

Rapoport, A. *House Form and Culture*. University of Wisconsin Press, Milwaukee, WI, 1969.

Stein, B., J.S. Reynolds, W.T. Grondzik, and A.G. Kwok. *Mechanical and Electrical Equipment for Buildings*. John Wiley & Sons, Inc., Hoboken, NJ, 2006.

7 THERMAL CALCULATIONS

HEAT LOSS

CODE COMPLIANCE

ANNUAL HEATING DEMAND

HEAT GAIN

HEAT LOSS

Heat loss calculations provide an effective way to analyze the contributions made by various architectural components to the thermal performance of a structure. Without this understanding, effective architectural design is elusive. Generally, the calculations are used to determine the worst probable conditions that a building will experience. In terms of heat loss, this means that it is assumed that (1) there are no solar contributions or interior heat gain, (2) the exterior wind velocity is 15 mph, and (3) the exterior temperature is the lowest that legitimately can be expected for the area. According to the American Society of Heating, Refrigerating and Air-Conditioning Engineers (ASHRAE), this lowest temperature is the temperature above which actual winter temperature conditions should exist for either 99% or 97.5% of the time. That is, the lowest temperature is that temperature projected to occur only 1.0% or 2.5% of the time in a three-month winter season. From the ASHRAE tables, a reasonable winter exterior design temperature for basic calculation might be 0° F for the 99% base or 5° F for the 97.5% base. Also, assuming an interior temperature of around 68° F to 70° F, the maximum differential between the interior and exterior temperatures would be between 62° F and 69° F. Based on this and for convenience, we might assume a 70° F temperature differential (ΔT). Obviously, for a heat loss calculation for an actual project, we should use the appropriate exterior and interior temperatures rather than this generalized assumption.

Heat Transfer

Understanding the basic means by which thermal energy can be transferred is helpful in distinguishing the various components of the thermal barrier. While we have identified evaporation as an important means by which the human body transfers its excess body heat and as an effective means of adjusting for excessive heat in a dry environment (refer to the bioclimatic chart developed by the Olgyay brothers shown in Figure 6.18), the classic means of thermal transfer include only conduction, convection, and radiation. Remember the definitions of these terms and their standard graphic notations.

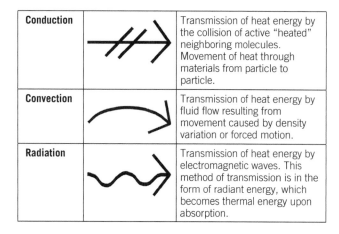

Conduction		Transmission of heat energy by the collision of active "heated" neighboring molecules. Movement of heat through materials from particle to particle.
Convection		Transmission of heat energy by fluid flow resulting from movement caused by density variation or forced motion.
Radiation		Transmission of heat energy by electromagnetic waves. This method of transmission is in the form of radiant energy, which becomes thermal energy upon absorption.

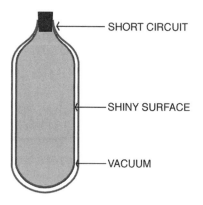

Figure 7.1 THERMOS BOTTLE
The thermos bottle relies on a sealed vacuum that is combined with a shiny surface. The vacuum minimizes the transfer by both conduction and convection, and the shiny surface reduces radiant transfer since a shiny surface neither absorbs nor emits thermal radiation. The interesting question is whether the thermos bottle will keep a cold liquid cold longer or a hot liquid hot longer.

Recognizing that there are three modes of thermal transfer, we should realize that the way to minimize the thermal transfer across a construction assembly is to reduce the ability of the assembly to conduct, convect, and radiate heat. To reduce thermal conduction, we should use materials that are not effective thermal conductors, and we should avoid creating thermal short circuits, which would have conductive materials passing completely through a construction assembly. That is, if conductive materials are used as part of a thermal barrier, thermal breaks should be used to avoid establishing a direct path across which thermal energy can readily conduct. The best way to reduce conduction, which would also reduce convection, would be to create a vacuum. If there were a vacuum, there would be no vapor or any other substance that could either conduct or convect thermal energy across the space. And if, in addition to a vacuum, the space were surrounded by highly reflective surfaces that would neither absorb nor emit radiation, then we would have the best condition. This tends to be the condition that exists in an original thermos bottle[1] (see Figure 7.1).

While a vacuum might be preferred, an air space that is not too wide can offer considerable resistance to thermal transfer. If the space is not wide, the natural friction of the physical surfaces that bound the air space tends to inhibit air movement within the space, limiting convective transfer across the air space. Since air is a gas and its "particles" are greatly spread out, thermal conduction across the air space will also be minimized. In addition, if the air space were provided with at least one surface that is highly reflective, then radiant transfer will be reduced because of either limited emission or limited absorption. The surface selected for the reflective coating does not really matter, although it is important that in a horizontal air space the reflective surface is not positioned so that dust and dirt might collect on it. If a reflective surface gets covered, then the reflective advantage is lost.

"U" Coefficients

The total heat loss is the combined thermal transmission that will occur across all of the environmental enclosures (e.g., walls, roofs, and floors) plus the amount of heat that will be lost as a result of outside air infiltrating into the interior. To determine the thermal transmission that will occur across each enclosing element, it is first necessary to determine the rate at which transmission will occur. This transmission is referred to as the *"U" coefficient*. When we multiply it by the actual area of the appropriate enclosing element and the maximum expected temperature differential between the interior and the exterior, we get the heat loss contribution from that element. This procedure is shown by the following formula:

$$\text{BTUH} = \text{Area} \times \text{"U" Coefficient} \times \Delta T$$

Procedures for Calculating "U" Coefficients

A thermal barrier's effectiveness, which is known as the *heat transfer coefficient* or *"U" coefficient*, is based on its particular components and how these are assembled. Specifically, a "U" coefficient indicates the hourly rate of thermal energy transfer, per degree temperature differential, per unit of surface area of the thermal barrier. In the imperial or British notational system, this is noted in terms of the number of BTUH that are transmitted across 1 square foot of the thermal barrier for each degree Fahrenheit of temperature differential that exists across the barrier.

---

[1] The thermos bottle was invented in 1892 by Sir James Dewar, a scientist at Oxford University, but it wasn't commercially available until 1904. Initially called *vacuum flask*, a contest was held to name it. The winning name, Thermos, was based on the Greek word *therme* meaning *heat*.

In the international measurement system (SI), the "U" coefficient is noted in watt-hours per square meter per degree Celsius.

Imperial Measurement System:

"U" Coefficient $= \dfrac{\text{BTUH}}{\text{sq ft} \times {}^\circ\text{F}}$

International Measurement System:

"U" Coefficient $= \dfrac{\text{watt-hours}}{\text{m}^2 \times {}^\circ\text{C}}$

Since no thermal barrier can eliminate all thermal flow, if no heating or cooling is provided, the interior temperature would eventually approximate the exterior temperature. That is, there would be no temperature differential between the inside and outside; however, in most situations, it is assumed that there is heating in the winter and cooling in the summer and that this maintains the interior temperature. As a result, even though there is thermal transfer, the calculations presume that the thermal barrier continues to separate the inside ambient conditions from the outside ambient conditions.

While there are numerous tables of "U" coefficients for various wall, roof, and floor assemblies, these tables do not generally provide a designer with clear information about the thermal performance that occurs within the assembly. They merely indicate overall results that can be used to size mechanical equipment. While we should be interested in these overall results, as architects and designers we should be more concerned with how this information can help us in designing an appropriate thermal barrier. Therefore, we need to know what determines a "U" coefficient so that we can understand the effects that various materials and construction assemblies have on thermal performance.

All exterior enclosing elements (i.e., walls, roofs, and floors), regardless of the particulars of their construction, separate the interior thermal conditions from the exterior thermal conditions. For example, any exterior wall, whether it is comprised of a piece of paper, a stud wall assembly, or 12 inches of solid concrete, will establish a physical separation between the inside ambient air conditions and the outside ambient air conditions. If the inside and the outside are at different temperatures, some thermal transfer will occur across the barrier; however, the rate at which this transfer occurs will vary according to the thermal resistance offered by the particular thermal barrier and the temperature differential between the inside and the outside. The amount of transfer, as distinct from the rate of transfer, will also depend on the size of the barrier.

The "U" coefficient of a thermal barrier indicates its overall *thermal transmittance*, or the rate of thermal flow that will occur in 1 hour across 1 square foot of area of the barrier for each degree Fahrenheit of temperature differential. When the area of the barrier is multiplied by its "U" coefficient and the expected temperature differential between the inside and the outside, the amount of thermal energy that will be transmitted or conducted across the thermal barrier can be determined.

BTUH $=$ Area $\times$ "U" $\times \Delta T\,{}^\circ\text{F}$

[Watts $=$ Area $\times$ "U" $\times \Delta T\,{}^\circ\text{C}$]

In attempting to determine the total thermal energy that will flow across a thermal barrier, we could test the actual construction assembly and measure the rate of transfer based on known conditions. While this would give us the necessary information, it would be rather difficult to physically model and test every construction assembly that we might wish to consider. Instead, we can measure the conductance that occurs across particular materials and then use these data to calculate the thermal transmittance that might be expected to occur in a particular construction assembly. That is, if we can determine the performance of the individual components of a construction assembly, we should be able to ascertain the combined effects of all the components through basic calculations.

To do this, we first need to understand that resistance is the reciprocal of conductance, and vice versa (i.e., $R = 1/C$ and $C = 1/R$). This relationship is important since, although we are interested in obtaining the overall conductance, we cannot add the conductance values of the various components together. Instead, we have to determine the conductance values of each component and then calculate the reciprocal of each, which is the resistance. We then add the resistance values together and find the reciprocal of this total. This reciprocal is the overall thermal transmittance or "U" coefficient, which, in the imperial measurement system, indicates the transmission of heat in BTU per hour per degree Fahrenheit per square foot of area.

We might question why, if we want to find total conductance, we do not just add the individual conductance values together, especially since, in testing the actual materials to determine their thermal performance, we measure conductance rather than resistance. Perhaps a little further reflection is appropriate.

Consider how a 1-foot-thick material would compare to a 2-foot-thick material. If we only tested a 1-foot thickness, what would we have to do to determine the conductance through 2 feet? If we tested the 1-foot-thick material and measured the conductance as half of the incident energy, say 10 units, it would be wrong to double this amount to determine the conductance across the 2-foot-thick material. If 10 units got through the first foot, it is illogical to

$$\frac{1}{R} = U$$

assume that 20 units would get through 2 feet. More properly, if half, or 10 units, got through 1 foot, 5 units, or only a quarter, would get through 2 feet. If initially only one-fifth of the incident units got through the first foot— say, 50 units were reduced to 10 units—then it is reasonable to assume that only 2 units, or one-fifth, would get through the second foot.

That is, in order to determine the overall transmittance of a thermal barrier, rather than add together the conductance values of all the various components that comprise the barrier, we must first determine the resistance of each of the components, add these resistance values together, and from the total resistance determine the overall transmittance. Actually, if we measure the conductance through a 1-inch thickness of a homogeneous material, we would refer to this as the conductivity of the material. Conductivity is the capacity of a material to conduct, as distinct from the specific quantity conducted. As the reciprocal of conductance is resistance, the reciprocal of conductivity is resistivity.

If we know the resistivity of a material, the resistance of a particular thickness of that material can be determined by multiplying the thickness in inches by the resistivity per inch.

Since the resistivity of poured-in-place concrete is 0.08 per inch, the resistance of 8 inches of poured-in-place concrete is 8 inches × 0.08, or 0.64. Although not usually indicated, the units of resistivity are the reciprocal of the units of conductivity, which are BTUH, per inch of thickness, per degree Fahrenheit, per square foot of area (BTUH/inch × °F × square foot of area).

$$\text{Resistivity} = \frac{1\text{in.} \times 1°F \times 1 \text{ sq ft of area}}{BTUH} = \frac{1}{C}$$

$$\text{Conductivity} = \frac{BTUH}{1\text{in.} \times 1°F \times 1 \text{ sq ft of area}} = \frac{1}{R}$$

Generally, in calculating the "U" coefficient of a thermal barrier, the resistivity of the various materials is used unless a material is nonhomogeneous or is of a specific dimension. For example, resistivity would be used for poured-in-place concrete, which is a homogeneous material, whereas resistance would be used for concrete block since it is nonhomogeneous and has a specific thickness. At certain points within a concrete block—that is, at the webs—the concrete extends across the full thickness of the block, but elsewhere, the center of the block is an air space. In addition, the concrete wythes, or the exterior walls of the block that bound this air space, tend to be of the same thickness regardless of the overall thickness of the block. That is, a 4-inch concrete block, which actually has a thickness of $3^5/_8$ inches, has surface wythes that are comparable to the surface wythes of an 8-inch block, which actually has a thickness of $7^5/_8$ inches.

To calculate the "U" coefficient of a thermal barrier, we must first distinguish all of the components of the barrier that offer some resistance to thermal transfer and identify the resistance of each. Then we must add these various resistances together to find the total resistance for the barrier and take the reciprocal of this total.

$$\text{"U" Coeffficient} = \frac{1}{\text{Total Resistance}}$$

Table 7.1 lists the basic resistance values for different air spaces that are either reflective or nonreflective. The assumption is that an air space is nonreflective unless it is noted otherwise since this is the normal condition. Also, as indicated in the table, the orientation of the air space and the direction of thermal flow affect the resistance. The least resistance occurs if the air space is in a horizontal position and the thermal transfer is upward. The highest resistance occurs again with a horizontal placement but with the thermal transfer downward, which is contrary to the natural convective flow based on thermal forces.

Air spaces are effective in reducing thermal transfer, and not only when they comprise a part of the interstices of a construction assembly. Most thermal insulations rely on the fact that they consist primarily of air. This reduces conductive transfer, and with the air often contained within small pockets or voids, convection is also limited.

Air films that cover the outside surfaces of a thermal barrier also tend to reduce thermal transfer. An air film is a thin layer of stagnant air that is attached on each exposed surface of a construction assembly. The relative thickness of air film depends on the air velocity to which the surface is exposed. With the exterior air velocity assumed to be 15 mph, which converts to 1320 feet per minute (fpm), and with the interior airflow being around 15 to 25 fpm, which converts to around 0.20 to 0.25 mph, a strong distinction might be expected between these two exposures. As with

Table 7.1: RESISTANCE OF AIR SPACES

Surface Orientation	Direction of Flow	Thickness	Nonreflective	Reflective
Horizontal	Upward	.75–4 in.	0.80	1.84
Sloping (45°)	Upward	.75–4 in.	0.85	2.08
Vertical	Horizontal	.75–4 in.	0.92	2.64
Sloping (45°)	Downward	.75–4 in.	1.00	3.36
Horizontal	Downward	.75 in.	1.02	3.57
		4 in.	1.23	8.94

Source: Adapted from a table in the ASHRAE Handbook—Fundamentals.

Table 7.2: RESISTANCE OF SURFACE AIR FILMS

Position of Surface	Direction of Heat Flow	Nonreflective $\varepsilon = 0.90$	Reflective	
			$\varepsilon = 0.20$	$\varepsilon = 0.05$
Still Air				
Horizontal	Upward	0.61	1.10	1.32
Sloping (45°)	Upward	0.62	1.14	1.37
Vertical	Horizontal	0.68	1.35	1.70
Sloping (45°)	Downward	0.76	1.67	2.22
Horizontal	Downward	0.92	2.70	4.55
Moving Air				
15 mph (for winter)	Any		0.17	
7.5 mph (for summer)	Any		0.25	

Source: Adapted from a table in the *ASHRAE Handbook—Fundamentals.*

an air space, in addition to the thickness of the air film, the position of the film and the direction of thermal flow both affect the rate of transfer. The resistance values for air films are listed in Table 7.2.

Since radiation provides a significant means of thermal transfer across an air space or an air film, surface reflectivity and/or emissivity, depending on the direction of flow, will affect the resistance of both air spaces and air films. When a shiny surface is provided, either the received radiation is reflected back or the emitted radiation is not released. In either case, there is greater resistance to the thermal transfer. While typical building materials are nonreflective, in certain circumstances reflective materials are used to achieve this improved resistance. But to be effective, the shiny surface must face an air space or be exposed. As mentioned above, the shiny surface should be located so that its reflectivity or emissivity is not reduced over time, such as would occur if it faced upward. Table 7.3 indicates the reflectivity of various materials.

To calculate the overall thermal transmittance ("U" coefficient) of a thermal barrier, it is generally best to begin by listing *all* of the components of the barrier. These include all physical components of the construction assembly, any possible air spaces, and the surface air films. Since the air spaces, and especially the air films, are not actual physical components, it is helpful to begin with them so that they are not overlooked. Once the list of all thermal components is complete, we can enter the appropriate resistance values for the surface air films and for any air spaces that might exist. We must consider carefully whether there are any reflective surfaces, although since these are not standard, if there are reflective surfaces, this should be clearly noted. If not, we should assume nonreflective conditions. After recording the resistances for the air films

Table 7.3: SURFACE REFLECTIVITY & EMISSIVITY AND EFFECTIVE AIR SPACE EMISSIVITY

Surface	Reflectivity (in %)	Average Emissivity	Effective Air Space Emissivity
Aluminum foil, bright	92 to 97	0.05	0.05
Aluminum sheet	80 to 95	0.12	0.01
Aluminum coated paper, polished	75 to 84	0.20	0.20
Steel, bright galvanized	70 to 80	0.25	0.24
Aluminum paint	30 to 70	0.50	0.47
Standard building materials: wood paper, glass, masonry, etc.	5 to 15	0.90	0.82

Source: Adapted from a table in the *ASHRAE Handbook—Fundamentals.*

and any air spaces, we need to enter the resistance values for the remaining components of the construction assembly. Extended listings of thermal resistances are included in various textbooks; a condensed listing is provided in Table 7.4.

For certain construction assemblies, rather than calculate the "U" coefficient by adding together the various component resistances, the appropriate values can be selected from available tables. Doors and windows especially fall into this category since their coefficients of thermal transmittance are more accurately determined by measuring their actual performance in a laboratory. In general, the winter "U" coefficient for single glazing is 1.10, while that for double glazing is between 0.49 and 0.62. Table 7.5 lists data for a number of different doors. Table 7.6 includes data for fenestration materials, and Table 7.7 includes data for windows and skylights.

U & R Values

Table 7.4: THERMAL PROPERTIES OF SELECTED BUILDING MATERIALS

Description		Density (lb/ft³)	Conductivity (per inch) (k)	Conductance (for listed thickness) (C)	Resistance (R) (1/k)	Resistance (R) (1/C)
Building Board						
Gypsum Wall Board	0.375 in.	50	–	3.10	–	0.32
	0.5 in.	50	–	2.22	–	0.45
	0.625 in.	50	–	1.78	–	0.56
Plywood (Douglas Fir)		34	0.80	–	1.25	–
	0.25 in.	34	–	3.20	–	0.31
	0.5 in.	34	–	1.60	–	0.62
	0.75 in.	34	–	1.07	–	0.93
Vegetable Fiber Board						
Sheathing, regular density	0.5 in.	18	–	0.76	–	1.32
Sheathing, regular density	0.75 in.	18	–	0.49	–	2.06
Sheathing, intermediate density	0.5 in.	22	–	0.82	–	1.22
Tile and lay-in panels, plain or acoustic		18	0.40	–	2.50	–
	0.5 in.	18	–	0.80	–	1.25
	0.75 in.	18	–	0.53	–	1.89
Hardboard						
Medium density		50	0.73	–	1.37	–
High density		55	0.82	–	1.22	–
Particle Board						
Low density		37	0.54	–	1.85	–
Medium density		50	0.94	–	1.06	–
High density		62.5	1.18	–	0.85	–
Underlayment	0.625 in.	40	–	1.22	–	0.82
Wood Subfloor	0.75 in.		–	1.06	–	0.94
Building Membrane						
Building Paper			–	–	–	0.05
Vapor Barrier						
Permeable felt			–	16.70	–	0.06
2 layers 15–lb felt			–	8.35	–	0.12
Plastic film			–	–	–	Negl.
Insulating Materials						
Blanket and Batt						
Mineral fiber	approx. 3 – 3.5	0.3 – 2.0	–	0.091	–	11.0
	approx. 5.5 – 6.5 in.	0.3 – 2.0	–	0.05	–	19.0
	approx. 8.5 in.	0.3 – 2.0	–	0.03	–	30.0
	approx. 11.5 in.	0.3 – 2.0	–	0.03	–	38.0
Board and Slabs						
Cellular glass		8.5	0.38	–	2.63	–
Expanded polystyrene extruded, cut cell surface		4.5	0.22	–	4.55	–
Expanded polystyrene extruded, smooth skin						
"Styrofoam"	1 in. or more	2.2	0.20	–	5.00	–
	less than 1 in.	2.22	0.25	–	4.00	–
Expanded polystyrene extruded, smooth skin						
High-density "Styrofoam"		3.5	0.19	–	5.26	–
Expanded polystyrene extruded, molded beads		1.0	0.28	–	3.57	–
Loose Fill						
Cellulose		2.3 – 3.2	0.27 – 0.32	–	3.13 – 3.70	–
Mineral fiber	approx. 3.75 – 5 in.	0.6 – 2.0	–	–	–	11.0
	approx. 6.5 – 8.75 in.	0.6 – 2.0	–	–	–	19.0
	approx. 7.5 – 10 in.	0.6 – 2.0	–	–	–	22.0
	approx. 10.25 – 13.75 in.	0.6 – 2.0	–	–	–	30.0
Roof Insulation						
Preformed, for use above deck				0.72 – 0.12		1.39 – 8.33
Masonry Materials						
Concrete						
Sand & gravel aggregate (not dried)		140	12.0	–	0.08	–
Sand & gravel aggregate (oven dried)		140	9.0	–	0.11	–
Lightweight aggregates		120	5.2	–	0.19	–
		100	3.6	–	0.28	–
		80	2.5	–	0.40	–
		60	1.7	–	0.59	–

Table 7.4 *(Continued)*

Description		Density (lb/ft³)	Conductivity (per inch) (k)	Conductance (for listed thickness) (C)	Resistance (R) (1/k)	Resistance (R) (1/C)
Masonry Units						
Brick						
Common		120	5.0	–	0.20	–
Face		130	9.0	–	0.11	–
Concrete Block						
Regular Density (sand & gravel agg.)	4-in.		–	1.40	–	0.71
	8-in.		–	0.90	–	1.11
	12-in.		–	0.78	–	1.28
Lightweight	4-in.		–	0.67	–	1.50
	8-in.		–	0.50	–	2.00
	12-in.		–	0.44	–	2.27
Stone			12.50	–	0.08	–
Plastering Materials						
Cement plaster, sand aggregate		116	5.0	–	0.20	–
	0.75-in.		–	13.30	–	0.08
Gypsum plaster, lightweight aggregate		45	1.56	–	0.64	–
	0.5-in.	45	–	3.12	–	0.32
	0.75-in.	45	–	2.13	–	0.47
Gypsum plaster, sand aggregate		105	5.60	–	0.18	–
	0.5-in.	105	–	11.10	–	0.09
	0.75-in.	105	–	7.70	–	0.13
Roofing						
Asphalt roll roofing		70	–	6.50	–	0.15
Asphalt shingles		70	–	2.27	–	0.44
Built-up roofing		70	–	3.00	–	0.33
Slate	0.375-in.		–	20.00	–	0.05
Wood shingles	0.5-in.		–	1.06	–	0.94
Siding Materials						
Shingles						
Wood,	16-in., 7.5-in. exposure		–	1.15	–	0.87
Wood, double	16-in., 12-in. exposure		–	0.84	–	1.19
Siding						
Hardboard siding		40	1.49	–	0.67	
Wood bevel	0.5 × 8-in., lapped		–	1.23	–	0.81
Wood bevel	0.75 × 10-in., lapped		–	0.95	–	1.05
Wood plywood,	0.375-in., lapped		–	1.59	–	0.59
Metal						
Over sheathing			–	1.61	–	0.61
With 0.375-in. insulating-board backing			–	0.55	–	1.82
With 0.375-in. insulating-board backing w/ foil			–	0.34	–	2.96
Architectural Glass			–	10.00	–	0.10
Woods						
Hardwoods (maple, oak, etc.)		45	1.10	–	0.91	–
Softwoods (fir, pine, etc.)		32	0.80	–	1.25	–
	0.75-in.		–	1.06	–	0.94
	1.5-in.		–	0.53	–	1.89
	2.5-in.		–	0.32	–	3.12
	3.5-in.		–	0.23	–	4.35
Flooring						
Carpet and fibrous pad			–	0.48	–	2.08
Carpet and rubber pad			–	0.81	–	1.23
Terrazzo	1-in.		–	12.50	–	0.08
Tile, asphalt, vinyl, etc.			–	20.00	–	0.05
Hardwood	0.75-in.		–	1.47	–	0.68
Acoustical Ceiling Tiles						
Mineral fiber tile			0.35	–	2.86	–
Wood fiber tile	0.5-in.		–	0.80	–	1.25
	0.75-in.		–	0.53	–	1.89

Source: Derived from a table in the *ASHRAE Handbook—Fundamentals.*

Table 7.5: OVERALL COEFFICIENTS OF TRANSMISSION OF DOORS (BTUH/SQ FT)

| Door Thickness | Description | No Storm Door | Winter | | Summer |
			Wood Storm Door	Metal Storm Door	No Storm Door
$1\frac{3}{8}$ in.	Hollow-core, flush wood door	0.47	0.30	0.32	0.45
$1\frac{3}{8}$ in.	Solid-core, flush wood door	0.39	0.26	0.28	0.38
$1\frac{3}{8}$ in.	Panel wood door w/ $7/16$ in. panels	0.57	0.33	0.37	0.54
$1\frac{3}{4}$ in.	Hollow-core, flush wood door with single glazing @ 17% op'g	0.46 0.58	0.29 0.33	0.32 0.36	0.44 0.54
$1\frac{3}{4}$ in.	Solid-core, flush wood door with single glazing @ 17% op'g with insulated glazing @ 17% op'g	0.33 0.46 0.37	0.28 0.29 0.25	0.25 0.32 0.27	0.32 0.44 0.36
$1\frac{3}{4}$ in.	Steel door with fiberglass core	0.60	–	–	–
$1\frac{3}{4}$ in.	Steel door with paper honeycomb core	0.56	–	–	–
$1\frac{3}{4}$ in.	Steel door with solid urethane foam core without thermal break with thermal break	 0.40 0.19	 – –	 – –	 – –

Source: Adapted from various sources including the *ASHRAE Handbook—Fundamentals* and *Mechanical and Electrical Equipment for Buildings* (2006).

Table 7.6: OVERALL COEFFICIENTS OF TRANSMISSION OF VARIOUS FENESTRATION MATERIALS

| Glazing Type | | | Glass Only | | Aluminum Frame No Thermal Break | | | Aluminum Frame Thermal Break | | | Wood or Vinyl Frame | |
					R	C		R	C		R	C
Vertical Installation												
Single glazing			1.10		1.31	1.23		1.09	1.10		0.90	0.98
Double glass												
$\frac{1}{4}$" air space			0.58		0.92	0.78		0.70	0.65		0.54	0.55
$\frac{1}{2}$" air space			0.49		0.87	0.72		0.64	0.59		0.49	0.49
Double glass, $\varepsilon = 0.40$												
$\frac{1}{4}$" air space			0.50		0.87	0.73		0.65	0.59		0.49	0.50
$\frac{1}{2}$" air space			0.38		0.81	0.65		0.58	0.52		0.43	0.42
Double glass, $\varepsilon = 0.15$												
$\frac{1}{4}$" air space			0.45		0.84	0.68		0.61	0.55		0.46	0.46
$\frac{1}{2}$" air space			0.32		0.76	0.60		0.54	0.46		0.39	0.37
Triple glass												
$\frac{1}{4}$" air space			0.39		0.79	0.64		0.57	0.50		0.42	0.41
$\frac{1}{2}$" air space			0.31		0.75	0.58		0.53	0.45		0.38	0.36
Triple glazing, with polyester film with $\varepsilon = 0.40$ suspended in middle												
$\frac{1}{4}$" air space			0.33		0.76	0.59		0.53	0.45		0.39	0.37
$\frac{1}{2}$" air space			0.24		0.70	0.52		0.48	0.39		0.34	0.30
Triple glazing, with polyester film with $\varepsilon = 0.15$ suspended in middle												
$\frac{1}{4}$" air space			0.28		0.73	0.55		0.53	0.42		0.36	0.33
$\frac{1}{2}$" air space			0.19		0.67	0.48		0.45	0.35		0.31	0.26
Conversions for Sloping Installation (Upward Heat Flow)												
90° (vertical)	0.10	0.20	0.30	0.40	0.50	0.60	0.70	0.80	0.90	1.00	1.10	1.20	1.30
45°	0.14	0.25	0.36	0.47	0.57	0.68	0.79	0.90	1.00	1.11	1.22	1.33	1.44
0° (horizontal)	0.19	0.29	0.40	0.51	0.61	0.72	0.82	0.93	1.04	1.14	1.25	1.35	1.46

R refers to residential style with smaller glazed area at around 65-70% or less of the opening area.
C refers to commercial style with larger glazed area at around 70% or more of the opening area

Source: Adapted from various sources including the *ASHRAE Handbook—Fundamentals* and *Mechanical and Electrical Equipment for Buildings*.

Table 7.7: COEFFICIENT OF TRANSMISSION: WINDOWS AND SKYLIGHTS

Vertical Panels	Exterior		
Description	**Winter**	**Summer**	**Interior**
Flat Glass			
Single Glass	1.10	1.04	0.73
Insulating Glass — Double			
0.1875-in. air space	0.62	0.65	0.51
0.25-in. air space	0.58	0.61	0.49
0.5-in. air space	0.49	0.56	0.46
0.5-in. air space, low emittance coating			
$\varepsilon = 0.20$	0.32	—	0.38
$\varepsilon = 0.40$	0.38	0.45	0.38
$\varepsilon = 0.60$	0.43	0.51	0.42
Insulating Glass — Triple			
0.25-in. air space	0.39	0.44	0.38
0.5-in. air space	0.31	0.39	0.30
Storm Windows — 1-in. to 4-in. air space	0.50	0.50	0.44
Plastic Sheet — Single			
0.125-in. thick	1.06	0.98	—
0.25-in. thick	0.96	0.89	—
0.5-in. thick	0.81	0.76	—
Plastic Sheet — Double			
0.25-in. thick	0.55	0.56	—
0.5-in. thick	0.43	0.45	—
Glass Block			
6 × 6 × 4-in. thick	0.60	0.57	0.46
8 × 8 × 4-in. thick	0.56	0.54	0.44
with cavity divider	0.48	0.46	0.38
12 × 12 × 4-in. thick	0.52	0.50	0.41
with cavity divider	0.44	0.42	0.36
12 × 12 × 12-in. thick	0.60	0.57	0.46

Horizontal Panels	Exterior		
Description	**Winter**	**Summer**	**Interior**
Flat Glass			
Single Glass	1.23	0.83	0.96
Insulating Glass — Double			
0.1875-in. air space	0.70	0.57	0.62
0.25-in. air space	0.65	0.54	0.59
0.5-in. air space	0.59	0.49	0.56
0.5-in. air space, low emittance coating			
$\varepsilon = 0.20$	0.48	0.36	0.39
$\varepsilon = 0.40$	0.52	0.42	0.45
$\varepsilon = 0.60$	0.56	0.46	0.50
Glass Block			
11 × 11 × 3-in. thick			
with cavity divider	0.53	0.35	0.04
12 × 12 × 4-in. thick			
with cavity divider	0.51	0.34	0.42
Plastic Domes			
Single—walled	1.15	0.80	—
Double-walled	0.70	0.46	—

Adjustment Factors to Multiply by Which to Above U Values			
Description	**Single Glass**	**Double or Triple Glass**	**Storm Windows**
Windows			
All Glass	1.00	1.00	1.00
Wood Sash — 80% Glass	0.90	0.95	0.90
Wood Sash — 60% Glass	0.80	0.85	0.80
Metal Sash — 80% Glass with thermal break	0.90	1.00	1.00
Metal Sash — 80% Glass w/o thermal break	1.00	1.20	1.20
Sliding Patio Doors			
Wood Frame	0.95	1.00	—
Metal Frame with thermal break	0.90	1.00	—
Metal Frame w/o thermal break	1.00	1.10	—

Source: Adapted from a table in the *ASHRAE Handbook—Fundamentals.*

"U" COEFFICIENT CALCULATION EXAMPLE

The "U" coefficient of the wall assembly shown in Figure 7.2 can be determined by finding the total resistance of all of the wall components and then finding the reciprocal of the total resistance.

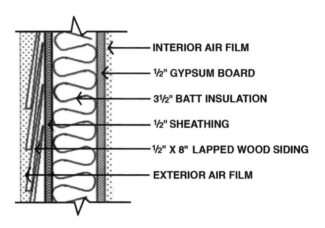

INTERIOR AIR FILM
½" GYPSUM BOARD
3½" BATT INSULATION
½" SHEATHING
½" X 8" LAPPED WOOD SIDING
EXTERIOR AIR FILM

Figure 7.2 WALL SECTION
A typical 2×4 stud wall used in residential construction. Note that there are air films on the exterior and interior surfaces.

Thermal Barrier Components Resistance	
Interior air film	0.68
$^1/_2$-in. gypsum wall board	0.48
$3^1/_2$-in. batt insulation	11.00
$^1/_2$-in. sheathing	1.32
$^1/_2$-in. × 8-in. lapped wood siding	0.81
Exterior air film	0.17
Total Resistance	**14.46**
"U" Coefficient	**0.069**

Surface Temperatures

Having calculated the "U" coefficient, we can then determine how the temperature will drop across the thermal barrier. The total temperature drop across the thermal barrier will be the difference between the interior ambient air temperature and the exterior ambient air temperature regardless of the effectiveness of the thermal barrier. While the "U" coefficient might indicate a large or small rate of thermal transmittance, the temperature drop within the thermal barrier will be proportional to the relative position within the barrier in relation to the overall resistance, as distinct from the physical location. As a result, a clear graphic representation of the temperature drop can be developed by drawing each of the various components of the thermal barrier in terms of its resistance rather than in terms of its physical dimensions.

In Figure 7.3, in the section with the actual dimensions (left image), the line that represents the temperature drop keeps changing slope as it is drawn across the construction assembly from inside to outside, while in the section drawn according to resistance values (on the right), the slope of the line representing the temperature drop remains constant.

While we can use a graphic representation, by recognizing how the temperature drops across a thermal barrier, we can readily calculate what the temperature will be at any point within the assembly by developing a simple proportioning ratio. Since the temperature drop is proportional to the resistance, we can express the temperature mathematically at any surface within the assembly.

$$\frac{T_i - T_o}{R_t} = \frac{T_i - T_p}{R_{i-p}} = \frac{T_p - T_o}{R_{p-o}}$$

where:

T_i = interior ambient air temperature

T_o = exterior ambient air temperature

T_p = temperature of a point within the assembly

R_t = total resistance of the thermal barrier from interior to exterior

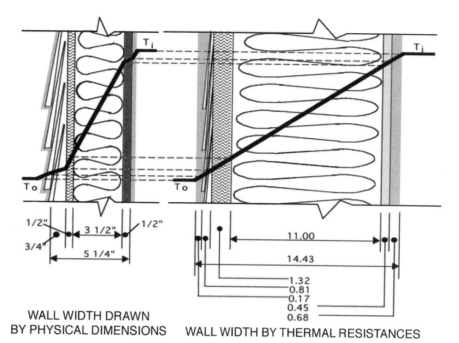

Figure 7.3 WALL SECTION DRAWN BY PHYSICAL DIMENSIONS AND BY THERMAL RESISTANCE VALUES

As shown in the left image above, the temperature drop across a thermal barrier can be plotted on a conventional wall section that is drawn according to the physical dimensions. If the wall section is drawn representing each component of the thermal barrier by its thermal resistance rather than its physical dimensions, the temperature drop will be a straight line, which will indicate the actual temperature at each point across the barrier.

WALL WIDTH DRAWN
BY PHYSICAL DIMENSIONS

WALL WIDTH BY THERMAL RESISTANCES

R_{i-p} = resistance from the interior ambient air to the point

R_{p-o} = resistance from the point to the exterior ambient air

Of course, rather than compare temperature drop to resistance, the above relationships could have been written in terms of ratios of resistances to ratios of temperature drops.

$$\frac{T_i - T_p}{T_i - T_o} = \frac{R_{i-p}}{R_t} \text{ or } \frac{T_i - T_p}{T_p - T_o} = \frac{R_{i-p}}{R_{p-o}}$$

For those who prefer a graphic representation, Figure 7.4, which provides a simpler diagram than Figure 7.3, might be a clearer way to represent the same relationships.

Whether graphically or by using a mathematical formula, the temperature drop across any portion of the thermal barrier can be determined by proportioning the partial temperature drop to the partial resistance as the total temperature drop relates to the total resistance. Alternatively, we could proportion the partial temperature drop to the partial resistance as the total temperature drop relates to the total resistance. Using this simple proportioning system, basing our measurements on the interior temperature, and recognizing that $U = 1/R_t$, we can mathematically express the temperature at a particular point within the assembly by the following formula:

$$\frac{T_i - T_o}{R_t} = \frac{T_i - T_p}{R_{i-p}}$$

But $\frac{1}{R_t}$ = "U" Coefficient, so

$$[(T_i - T_o)(R_{i-p})(U)] = (T_i - T_p)$$

$$T_p = T_i[(T_i - T_o) \times R_{i-p} \times U]$$

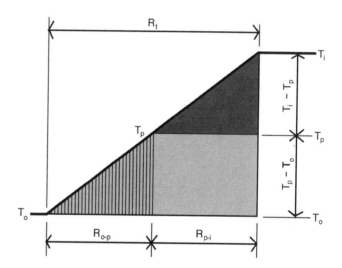

Figure 7.4 PROPORTIONAL RELATIONSHIP BETWEEN TEMPERATURE DROP AND THERMAL RESISTANCE

A triangle drawn with the vertical height representing the overall temperature differential across a thermal barrier, from inside to outside (ΔT_{i-o}), and the base width determined by the total resistance of the barrier (R_t), establishes a slope of line that represents a consistent ratio between the two. Any subtriangle will retain that slope of line, which relates to the ratio of ΔT to ΔR. As a result, each partial triangle indicates the change in temperature associated with a change in resistance.

where:

T_p = temperature of a particular point within the assembly

T_i = indoor temperature of the heated space.

T_o = outdoor temperature.

R_{i-p} = resistance from the interior to the particular point

U = "U" coefficient of the overall construction assembly

While the calculation will find the temperature of a particular point within the thermal barrier, often the intention is to find the temperature of the interior physical surface of a wall or ceiling, which will affect the mean radiant temperature of the space, or the temperature at the face of a component within a construction assembly. As a result, rather than use the more generic notion of the temperature at a particular point within a construction assembly, that is, T_p, surface temperature (T_s) is typically assumed and the formula is called the *surface temperature formula* and is restated as follows.

$$T_s = T_i - [(T_i - T_o) \times R_{i-s} \times U]$$

Example Problems—"U" Coefficients and Surface Temperatures

Calculate the overall thermal transmittance ("U" coefficient) and the interior surface temperature for the following thermal barriers. Remember that there are air films and air spaces that contribute to the total resistance. For the surface temperature calculations, assume an interior ambient air temperature of 70° F and an exterior ambient air temperature of 0° F.

1. 8 in. of poured-in-place concrete

2. 8 in. of lightweight concrete block

3. 8 in. of poured-in-place concrete
    $^{3}/_{4}$ in. of Styrofoam insulation
    $^{1}/_{2}$ in. of gypsum wall board (GWB)

4. 8 in. of lightweight concrete block
    $3^{1}/_{2}$ in. of batt insulation
    $^{1}/_{2}$ in. of GWB

5. 4 in. of face brick
    $^{3}/_{4}$-in. air space
    8 in. of concrete block

6. Lapped wood siding
    $^{1}/_{2}$-in. sheathing
    $3^{1}/_{2}$ in. of air space (wood studs)
    $^{1}/_{2}$ in. of GWB with foil-faced backing

7. Lapped wood siding
    $^{1}/_{2}$-in. sheathing
    5 in. of batt insulation with foil face
    $^{3}/_{4}$-in. air space

8. Lapped wood siding
    $^{1}/_{2}$-in. sheathing
    $5^{1}/_{2}$ in. of batt insulation
    $^{1}/_{2}$-in. GWB

9. Built-up roofing (flat)
    6 in. of concrete
    4-in. air space
    in. of batt insulation
    $^{3}/_{4}$-in. wood fiber acoustic tile

10. Asphalt shingles on a 3:1 slope
    $^{1}/_{2}$ in. of plywood
    2-in. air space
    9 in. of batt insulation
    $^{3}/_{8}$in. of GWB

Answers

Total Resistance	"U" Coefficient	Surface Temperature
1. $R_t = 1.49$	$U = 0.67$	$T_s = 38.1$
2. $R_t = 2.85$	$U = 0.352$	$T_s = 53.3$
3. $R_t = 4.94$	$U = 0.203$	$T_s = 60.3$
4. $R_t = 14.30$	$U = 0.07$	$T_s = 66.67$
5. $R_t = 3.28$	$U = 0.31$	$T_s = 55.2$
6. $R_t = 6.07$	$U = 0.165$	$T_s = 62.2$
7. $R_t = 25.07$	$U = 0.04$	$T_s = 68.1$
8. $R_t = 22.43$	$U = 0.045$	$T_s = 67.9$
9. $R_t = 34.28$	$U = 0.029$	$T_s = 68.8$
10. $R_t = 33.01$	$U = 0.03$	$T_s = 68.7$

Slab Edges Loss and Basement Heat Loss

A major loss of heat from a building can occur through its foundation, whether it is a slab on grade, a crawl space, or a full basement. The problem with the slab on grade is that the slab is usually poured concrete, which is a good thermal conductor, and it is not readily insulated to minimize thermal transfer. As indicated in Figure 7.5, although there might not be significant exposure in terms of surface

area, a slab on grade can be responsible for considerable heat loss and can cause condensation.

Figure 7.6 shows various ways of providing exterior insulation for slab-on-grade construction. Rigid-board insulation, such as expanded polystyrene (e.g., Styrofoam), can be installed on the exterior of the foundation, which is about the only way to effectively insulate if the slab and footing are poured integrally. The board should be at least 2 inches thick and 2 feet wide. Any exposed insulation should be covered since exposure to sunlight can cause deterioration. Usually a thin sheet of cementitious material is attached by mastic to the portion of the exposed portion of the insulation that is above grade, with some extension below grade. If there is an independent foundation, insulation can be installed between the floor slab and the exposed foundation wall (see Figure 7.7).

While the installation of edge insulation can be somewhat problematic, the calculation procedure is relatively simple. Rather than having to find the individual resistances, determine the "U" coefficient and then calculate the heat loss; the amount of slab edge heat loss is available in terms of BTUH per linear foot of slab edge. While various detailed tables are available, Table 7.8 gives some generalized heat loss figures in BTUH per linear foot of slab edge. These figures are actually based on heat loss measurements of a 25-foot by 25-foot structure. After accounting for the heat loss through the walls and the roof, both the edge loss and the slab loss to the ground, which is at a temperature of around 50° F to 55° F, were assigned to 100 linear feet of exposed edge. Therefore, the figures in the table tend to include some heat loss through the floor slab in addition to the edge loss. If there is a large interior area—for example, if the building's dimensions are greater than 40 feet by 40 feet, there is some heat loss through the slab, usually at around 2 BTUH per square foot based on a ground

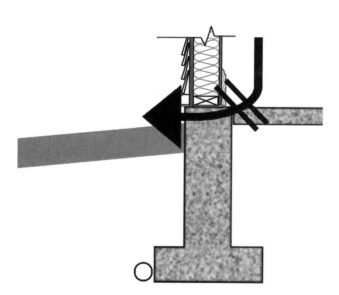

Figure 7.5 NO SLAB EDGE INSULATION
Without any edge insulation, the concrete slab and foundation establish a highly conductive short circuit for heat loss. Since the resistivity of concrete is 0.08 per inch, even 12 inches of concrete, including the surface air films, has a "U" coefficient of 0.67. As a result, the heat loss through each linear foot of slab exposure actually exceeds the loss through the full-height opaque wall above the edge since the standard "U" coefficient for a typical stud wall is 0.069.

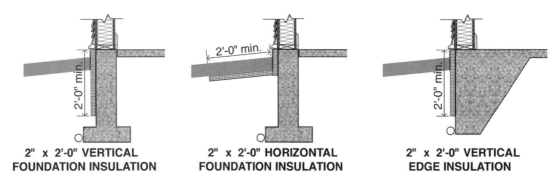

Figure 7.6 FOUNDATION AND EXPOSED EDGE INSULATION
Edge insulation of 2 × 2′ − 0″ is recommended. Care must be taken to ensure that no insulation is exposed to the elements, particularly if it is expanded polystyrene, since over time it will deteriorate if exposed to sunlight.

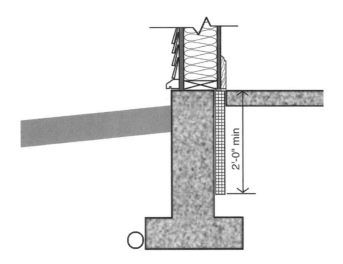

Figure 7.7 INTERIOR FOUNDATION INSULATION
Rigid insulation can be installed on the inside of the foundation, but to be effective, it should also insulate the concrete slab. With 2-inch insulation, this will leave a wide gap between the foundation and the slab that should be covered, which is feasible with 2 × 6 framing set on an 8-inch foundation wall.

suming that above each foot of slab exposure there is a wall, which has a "U" coefficient of 0.05 and extends upward 8′-0″, the overall heat loss through a linear foot of wall would be less than 30 BTUH, or only half of the edge loss. If the wall consisted of 25% window with a "U" coefficient of 0.50, then each linear foot of the wall would have a heat loss of basically 90 BTUH, or only about 50% more than the edge loss. Simply stated, a considerable amount of heat is lost through the slab edge, even with insulation.

SLAB EDGE LOSS PER LINEAR FOOT

$$1 \text{ linear ft} \times 60 \text{ BTUH/linear ft} = 60 \text{ BTUH}$$

OPAQUE WALL LOSS PER LINEAR FOOT

$$8 \text{ sq ft} \times 0.05 \times 70° \text{ F} \Delta T = 28 \text{ BTUH}$$

WALL AND WINDOW LOSS PER LINEAR FOOT

$$[(6 \text{ sq ft} \times 0.05) + (2 \text{ sq ft} \times 0.50)] \times 70° \text{ F} \Delta T$$
$$= 91 \text{ BTUH}$$

Since concrete is an effective thermal conductor, the surface temperature at the outside edge of a concrete slab, especially when the slab is poured integrally with the foundation footing, will be significantly lower than the interior ambient air temperature. Assuming that the slab is covered with carpet on a foam pad, the temperature can be considerably lower than the room DPT. This will result

temperature of 50° F to 55° F, that should be added to the slab edge loss.

Without insulation that is properly installed, slab edge loss can be a serious source of heat loss as well as the cause of other problems. As shown in Table 7.8, an uninsulated slab would have a 60-BTUH loss for every linear foot of exposure in an area with a 0° F outside temperature. As-

Table 7.8: HEAT LOSS PER FOOT OF EXPOSED EDGE, BTUH

Outdoor Design Temperature °F	2-in. × 2-ft Edge Insulation	1-in. × 2-ft Edge Insulation	1-in. × 1-ft Edge Insulation	No Edge Insulation
−20 to −30	50	55	60	75
−10 to −20	45	50	55	65
0 to −10	40	45	50	60

Source: Adapted from a table in the *ASHRAE Handbook – Fundamentals* (1977).

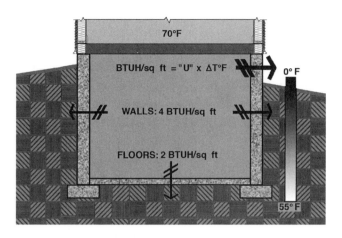

Figure 7.8 BASEMENT HEAT LOSS
The rule of thumb for heat loss through below-grade basement walls is 4 BTUH per square foot. For the slab, it is 2 BTUH per square foot. Above-grade walls are handled as standard walls, which means "U" coefficient times $\Delta T\,°F$.

in water condensation and associated moisture problems (e.g., mold and mildew) that might be assumed to be the result of foundation leaks rather than thermal transfer.

Basement heat loss, although also related to a structure's foundation, is handled differently than slab edge loss. As suggested by Figure 7.8, it involves the loss of heat from the basement through various enclosing elements: the floor slab, the foundation walls below grade, and the foundation walls above grade. Various tables present data that can be used to determine basement heat loss, but rather than go through extended calculations, it is reasonable to determine basement heat loss in terms of BTUH per square foot of the below-grade basement wall and the basement slab. With this approach, the portion of the basement wall that is above grade must be handled by using a "U" coefficient multiplied by the temperature differential between the inside and outside.

For below-grade basement walls, the heat loss is generally assumed to be 4 BTUH per square foot, and for the basement slab, 2 BTUH per square foot. Both of these values are based on no insulation and an assumed effective "U" coefficient of 0.10 for the construction and the earth. Since the ground temperature below the basement slab is normally between 50° F and 55° F, an interior temperature of 70° F to 75° F would mean a 20° F temperature differential, which, when multiplied by the 0.10 "U" coefficient value, results in 2 BTUH per square foot of slab heat loss. Through the walls, without insulation and with an average temperature somewhere between an exterior ambient air temperature of 0° F and a ground temperature of 50° F to 55° F, a heat loss of 4 BTUH per square foot is reasonable. Of course, if the basement wall below grade were insulated, this 4-BTUH value would have to be adjusted. If 1 inch of expanded polystyrene, such as Styrofoam, were

used, the effective heat loss per square foot would be about 3 BTUH per square foot, and with 2 inches of insulation, it would be about 2 BTUH per square foot.

Vapor Barriers

Calculating the overall thermal transmittance of a construction assembly, rather than merely using a "U" coefficient table, provides important information, specifically in terms of how the temperature will drop across the assembly. The temperature drops from higher to lower ambient air conditions. So, in the winter, this drop is from higher interior temperatures to lower exterior temperatures, but in the summer, with higher exterior temperatures, the direction of the temperature drop reverses. Regardless of the direction, if the temperature drop is sufficient and the humidity is high enough, chances are that the DPT will be reached at some point within the construction assembly. There is a strong probability that this will occur during the winter season with the large change in temperature, but it is also possible during the summer, particularly in areas of high exterior humidity when the interior is cooled significantly below the outdoor temperature. If the DPT does occur within the construction assembly that does not have an adequate vapor barrier, there is a potential for condensation and the associated problems that this can cause. Determining where the dew point might occur can be critical in protecting against these potential problems.

If water does condense, in addition to causing severe problems of material deterioration, it tends to fill any air pockets that exist, such as those on which most types of insulation rely to provide their added thermal resistance. As a result, the resistance of the insulation will decrease, thereby increasing thermal transmittance. In order to minimize this condensation problem, it is best to install a vapor barrier as close as possible to the warmer interior and to have the construction assembly beyond the vapor barrier reasonably permeable to vapor flow so that any moisture that might pass through the vapor barrier can continue to pass out of the construction assembly before it is trapped and condenses. This assumes that there will be less condensation if the flow of vapor beyond the vapor barrier is unimpeded, which is similar to running water that tends not to freeze except at temperatures considerably lower than 32° F.

The general recommendation is to install a vapor barrier immediately behind the interior finish material, which is often gypsum board. As indicated in Figure 7.9, this will place the barrier close to the warmer side of the construction assembly while protecting it. The barrier can be a vapor-impermeable material, such as aluminum foil,

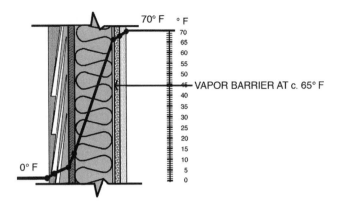

Figure 7.9 VAPOR BARRIER LOCATION
A vapor barrier should be placed as close as possible to the interior surface. This generally means just behind the gypsum board. The vapor barrier can be a sheet of polyethylene or foil backing on gypsum board. While the standard asphalt-impregnated facing of the batt insulation does resist moisture migration, it meets the expected performance level for a vapor barrier. Although double vapor barriers are to be avoided, with the two barriers (polyethylene and impregnated facing of the insulation) next to each other, they should not trap any moisture, especially with the less permeable polyethylene on the warmer side.

attached to the back side of the gypsum board or a plastic film, such as polyethylene, installed on the interior sides of the wall studs. Appropriately locating and installing a vapor barrier is relatively easy, but ensuring that the barrier is not breached is somewhat more complicated. Every opening within a barrier is a potential point where the barrier can be broken, as are electric outlet boxes.

Before the possibility of space cooling, condensation during the warmer periods of the year was not generally a problem except perhaps with ice storage houses. With their interior temperatures below 32° F, these structures often suffered from excessive condensation. Typically, they were insulated with cork, which is both organic and permeable to water vapor. As a result, condensation and interior deterioration occurred; the solution was simply to accept that this would occur and to replace the insulation every few years. With modern rigid-board insulations, which are usually impervious to the flow of water vapor, insulation is now available that can also effectively serve as a vapor barrier.

With the present use of mechanical refrigeration to lower the interior temperatures of most spaces during the summer, what used to be essentially only a winter problem, except for cold storage buildings, can now become a summer issue. Since winter conditions usually demand a warm-side vapor barrier with vapor-permeable materials on the exterior side of the barrier, when summer conditions might also result in condensation, it is difficult to control things without compromising the winter conditions. Fortunately, unless the interior summer temperatures are set unreasonably low, if the dew point is reached within a

construction assembly, it is often for only a short period of time. Any condensation that might occur will likely revaporize before any serious problems develop. However, when summer conditions are less benign, it is difficult to control things unless we again rely on rigid, non-vapor-permeable insulation that establishes a vapor barrier on the warm side, regardless of the direction of thermal flow.

If the desired interior thermal conditions call for 70° F and a relative humidity of 30%, the DPT will be 37° F. Based on this information, where would the vapor barrier have to be placed in a wall that has the currently expected "U" coefficient of 0.05 or less, assuming that the outside temperature is 0° F? Transposing the standard surface temperature formula, we can find the resistance limits to locate the vapor barrier.

Given:

$$Interior\ temperature = 70°\ F$$
$$Dew\ point\ temperature = 37°\ F$$
$$Outside\ temperature = 0°\ F$$
$$Relative\ humidity = 30\%$$

$$\text{"U" Coefficient} = 0.05$$
$$T_s = T_i - [(T_i - T_o) \times R_{i-s} \times U]$$

$$R_{i-s} = \frac{T_i - T_s}{(T_i - T_o) \times U}$$

$$= \frac{70°\ F - 37°\ F}{(70°\ F - 0°\ F) \times 0.05}$$

$$= \frac{33°\ F\Delta T}{70°\ F\Delta T \times 0.05}$$

$$R_{i-s} = 9.43$$

Since the overall "U" coefficient is 0.05, the total resistance of the thermal barrier in this example is 20 (i.e., 20 = 1/0.05), and the resistance from the interior ambient air to the point in the assembly where the dew point will occur is 9.43. Therefore, the vapor barrier must be located at a point where the resistance from that point to the interior ambient air is less than 9.43. Assuming that the thermal barrier is a wall with an interior surface comprised of $1/2$-inch gypsum board, the resistance from the interior ambient air to the back side of the gypsum board would be 1.13 (i.e., 0.68 for the interior air film and 0.45 for the gypsum board), well within the allowed 9.43 resistance. So, it makes sense to install the vapor barrier immediately behind the gypsum wallboard.

If, in attempting to achieve low overall thermal transmittance, the exterior sheathing used was expanded polystyrene insulation, then there might be a problem. As discussed, this type of insulation is an effective vapor barrier since it consists of foamed plastic, which, although it has numerous air pockets, creates a continuous vapor-resistant membrane. In fact, one of the early demonstrations used to show the benefits of this type of insulation was to weigh a sample of the material, immerse it in a container of water for a day, and then reweigh it, showing that no water was absorbed. While this characteristic of expanded polystyrene is, in certain ways, beneficial, if the material is installed toward the outside of a construction assembly, especially if it is beyond the DPT, it acts as a trap for any moisture that might have passed through the vapor barrier on the warm side of the construction. As a result, condensation could occur. Let us explore how this would happen.

Assuming that some sort of exterior siding is applied over the exterior insulated sheathing and the sheathing is 1-inch-thick expanded polystyrene, the total resistance from the exterior ambient air to the interior side of the sheathing would be as follows:

Resistance from Exterior to Interior Side of Insulated Sheathing

Exterior air film	0.17
Siding	0.81 ±
1-inch insulated sheathing	5.00
Resistance$_{o-s}$	5.98

With 5.98 as the resistance from the outside ambient air to the interior of the sheathing and 20.0 as the total resistance of the thermal barrier, the resistance from the interior ambient air to the interior side of the insulated sheathing (R_{i-p}) is 14.02, considerably more than what is allowed (e.g., 9.43, as calculated above). As a result, it is perhaps better to avoid using expanded polystyrene as sheathing. On the other hand, we could determine the exterior temperature at which the interior surface of the sheathing would drop to the DPT of 37° F.

Again, transposing the standard formula, we can determine the exterior temperature for which T_s will be 37° F.

$$T_s = T_i - [(T_i - T_o) \times R_{i-s} \times U]$$

$$T_o = T_i - \left[\frac{T_i - T_s}{R_{i-s} \times U} \right] = 70° \text{ F} - \left[\frac{70° \text{ F} - 37° \text{ F}}{14.02 \times 0.05} \right]$$
$$= 23° \text{ F}$$

While the "minimum" exterior temperature of 0° F occurs infrequently, 23° F is not uncommon. As a result, it is quite likely that there could be some condensation on the inside surface of the sheathing. However, if the interior humidity were lowered to 20% relative humidity, the DPT would be 27° F, adjusting the lowest allowable exterior temperature to avoid condensation on the inside surface of the sheathing to around 9° F.

$$T_o = 70° \text{ F} \left[\frac{70° \text{ F} - 27° \text{ F}}{14.02 \times 0.05} \right] = 8.66° \text{ F}$$

But outside temperatures of less than 9° F do occur. A mitigating factor that keeps expanded polystyrene sheathing from causing serious condensation problems is that the interior vapor barrier tends to reduce the amount of moisture that can enter the wall, effectively lowering the apparent interior relative humidity. That is, less moisture gets past the interior vapor barrier, so the critical DPT within the wall might be less than the above-assumed 27° F. However, if the interior vapor barrier is breached, which might and often does occur around window openings, there could be serious condensation problems.

This use of rigid polystyrene insulation as exterior sheathing is common with the Exterior Insulation Finishing System (EIFS), which is sometimes erroneously referred to as "synthetic stucco." Dryvit is a proprietary EIFS system named for Dryvit Systems, Inc., the original U.S. manufacturer to provide this approach to providing an exterior finish. Unfortunately, moisture problems with EIFS are rather prevalent. The problems generally occur around window openings, and it is assumed that they result from faulty flashing and exterior leaks. While some of the problems might result from such failures, they are often caused by interior moisture migrating into the walls, being trapped, and condensing, producing mold and mildew.

Exterior sheathing is not the only place where problems might occur due to double vapor barriers. Roofing requires that a waterproof membrane be installed on the exterior to protect against the entrance of water, and such membranes often also act as vapor barriers. The traditional roof design places the waterproof membrane on the exterior or cold side of the assembly, whereas with the *inverted roof membrane assembly* (IRMA), also known as the *protected membrane roof* (PMR), the waterproof membrane is located below an exterior layer of rigid expanded polystyrene that is covered with gravel or some sort of paving stone. With a conventional roof, the membrane is exposed to a wide range of temperatures, some well below the DPT. To protect the construction assembly from condensation, a vapor barrier should be installed on the warm side of the roof assembly, perhaps just above the ceiling material. This results in double vapor barriers, and in this instance, the outer vapor barrier is clearly beyond the DPT. To solve this problem, it is recommended that the roof assembly be vented above the insulation. While this is readily accomplished with the conventional truss construction used in residential construction, having the insulation installed immediately above the ceiling and venting the attic space, venting can also be provided if the ceiling is installed on the bottom of inclined rafters. Assuming wood rafters of adequate depth, a 2-inch air space can be provided above the insulation, and this space can be vented below the eaves and at the roof ridge. Unfortunately, to get an adequate joist depth, since at least 9 inches of batt insulation are recommended, the joists should be 2×12, considerably more than what is probably required for structural support.

While the surface temperature formula can help to determine at what point within the construction assembly the DPT might occur, it is also useful to identify the highest relative humidity that can exist in the interior space so that condensation does not occur on the interior of the windows. For example, if single glazing is used, with a "U" coefficient of 1.10 and an interior air film resistance of 0.68, the interior surface of the glass would be around $17.5°$ F when the exterior temperature is $0°$ F and the interior temperature is $70°$ F. And for a DPT of $17.5°$ F, the maximum relative humidity would only be around 12%. If double glazing were used, with a "U" coefficient of 0.62, the interior surface of the glass would be around $40.5°$ F and the maximum relative humidity would be around 35%.

GENERAL FORMULA

$$T_s = T_i - [(T_i - T_o) \times R_{i-s} \times U]$$

FOR SINGLE GLAZING

$$T_s = 70° F - [(70° F - 0° F) \times 0.68 \times 1.10] = 17.64° F$$

FOR DOUBLE GLAZING

$$T_s = 70° F - [(70° F - 0° F) \times 0.68 \times 0.62] = 40.49° F$$

Clearly, using the surface temperature calculations to determine when and where condensation might occur is an effective way to guide design development in order to reduce the probability that the serious problems it can cause will arise. These calculations can also give us a better sense of the thermal conditions within a space. As discussed previously, radiant heat loss is the major means by which we lose excess body heat, and the amount of heat lost through this means of thermal transfer is based on the surface temperatures of the spaces we occupy. When the walls and ceilings defining a space also separate the interior from the exterior, higher overall resistance values mean that the surface temperatures of these elements will be closer to the interior ambient air temperature.

Before the emergence of energy consciousness in the 1970s, appropriate "U" coefficients were often determined more for thermal comfort than for energy savings. At that time, the suggested maximum "U" coefficient for an opaque enclosing element was 0.30, with 0.20 set as a reasonable value and 0.10 as the preferred value. Based on these "U" values, the interior surface temperatures of a wall or ceiling with a $70°$ F to $0°$ F temperature differential

would be as follows.

$$T_{s-0.30} = 70° F - (70° F \times 0.68 \times 0.30) = 55.72° F$$
$$T_{s-0.20} = 70° F - (70° F \times 0.68 \times 0.20) = 60.48° F$$
$$T_{s-0.10} = 70° F - (70° F \times 0.68 \times 0.10) = 65.24° F$$

With the current recommended "U" coefficients for an opaque wall or ceiling of 0.05 and 0.03, respectively, the interior surface temperatures are higher and, as a result, so are the thermal comfort conditions.

$$T_{s-0.05} = 70° F - (70° F \times 0.68 \times 0.05) = 67.62° F$$
$$T_{s-0.03} = 70° F - (70° F \times 0.61 \times 0.03) = 68.72° F$$

Similarly, the "U" coefficient for insulated glazing, especially when combined with a low-emissivity coating, is considerably less than that for single glazing with commensurate higher interior surface temperatures.

SINGLE GLAZING

$$T_{s-1.10} = 70° F - (70° F \times 0.68 \times 1.10) = 17.64° F$$

INSULATED GLAZING

$$T_{s-0.49} = 70° F - (70° F \times 0.68 \times 0.49) = 46.68° F$$

LOW AND INSULATED GLAZING

$$T_{s-0.32} = 70° F - (70° F \times 0.68 \times 0.32) = 54.77° F$$

Improved interior thermal comfort conditions are provided with better "U" coefficients. As obvious as this might be, sometimes the implications are not adequately understood, particularly when mere numbers are the focal consideration rather than overall experience. For example, many years ago, a woman called the consulting engineer who had designed the heating system for her new house located outside of Boston. The house, which was expensive and elegant, was essentially a glass box with only single glazing, which was not unusual for the times. The woman's concern was that whenever the outside temperature dropped, she had to raise the setting on the thermostat in order to remain comfortable.

The engineer with whom she talked said that raising the thermostat was not necessary since once it was set, it would maintain that temperature. After their conversation, the engineer criticized her supposed foolishness. What he did not say was that the woman was correct and that he was wrong, at least in terms of addressing her complaint. While it is true that a thermostat should maintain the temperature once it is set, assuming that the heating system has adequate capacity, as the outside temperature drops, the interior mean radiant temperature (MRT) in a space with a significant amount of single glazing will also drop. Raising the thermostat setting can help to compensate for the lower MRT.

While increasing the total resistance of a thermal barrier is generally worthwhile, if it is not done appropriately, adding insulation can be the wrong solution. This is likely to be the result if the added insulation adjusts conditions so an existing vapor barrier is effectively re-located well beyond where the DPT will be reached. Even the placement of furniture can have a deleterious effect. For example, if a bookcase is placed against an exterior wall, it can add resistance to the effective overall thermal barrier. In this situation, a normally acceptable interior humidity could result in moisture collecting behind the bookcase.

Infiltration

In addition to transfer across thermal barriers, heat loss occurs as a result of infiltration. As the wind blows against a building, some unheated exterior air infiltrates into the interior by passing through cracks in windows, doors, and various construction joints. This unheated air adds to the overall heat loss.

To determine the amount of heat loss attributed to infiltration, it is first necessary to establish the amount of air that will infiltrate. This can be accomplished by using the generalized air change method or the more detailed crack method. In the air change method, the amount of infiltration is based on an assumed number of air changes that would occur, based on the exterior temperature, the number of exposures that the space has, and the general classification of construction. These are shown in Table 7.9 in terms of air changes per hour for tight, medium, and loose construction.

Alternatively, the air changes that will occur can be estimated from the more simplified Table 7.10, which bases the number of air changes merely on the number of exposures that exist in a space. And for an even simpler approach, we might assume that there will be one air change

Table 7.10: AIR CHANGES OCCURRING FOR CONDITIONS IN RESIDENCES

Kind of Room	Number of Air Changes per Hour
Rooms with no windows or exterior doors	0.5
Rooms with windows or exterior doors on one side	1
Rooms with windows or exterior doors on two sides	1.5
Rooms with windows or exterior doors on three sides	2
Entrance halls	2
For rooms with weather-stripped windows or storm windows, use $^2/_3$ of these values.	

Source: Adapted from a table in the *ASHRAE Handbook—Fundamentals.*

per hour for standard construction and one-half of an air change per hour for tight construction in the winter and in general for all construction in the summer.

Knowing the number of air changes per hour, the volume of infiltration is found by multiplying the number of air changes by the volume of the space for which the calculation is being done. Knowing the volume of infiltration, we can determine the BTUH heat loss from sensible infiltration using the following formula:

$$\text{BTUH}_{\text{sens. infil.}} = \text{CFH} \times 0.075 \times 0.24 \times \Delta T°\text{F}$$
$$= \text{CFH} \times 0.018 \times T°\text{F}$$

where:

$\quad$ CFH = volume of air in cubic feet per hour

$\quad$ 0.075 = density of standard air in pounds per cubic foot

$\quad$ 0.24 = specific heat of air

$\quad$ 0.018 = product of 0.075 × 0.24

$\quad$ $\Delta T°$F = temperature differential between the interior and exterior

Table 7.9: ESTIMATED INFILTRATION AIR CHANGE RATES FOR SMALL BUILDINGS

Construction Type	Winter Outdoor Design Temperature w/ 15 mph wind									
	50	40	30	20	10	0	−10	−20	−30	−40
Tight	0.4	0.5	0.6	0.6	0.7	0.8	0.8	0.9	0.9	1.0
Medium	0.6	0.7	0.8	0.9	1	1.1	1.2	1.2	1.3	1.4
Loose	0.8	0.9	1	1.2	1.3	1.4	1.5	1.6	1.8	1.9

Construction Type	Summer Outdoor Design Temperature w/ 7.5 mph wind					
	85	90	95	100	105	110
Tight	0.3	0.3	0.3	0.4	0.4	0.4
Medium	0.4	0.4	0.5	0.5	0.5	0.6
Loose	0.4	0.5	0.6	0.6	0.7	0.8

Source: Adapted from a table in *Mechanical and Electrical Equipment in Buildings.*

If the flow of air is in terms of minutes rather than hours, then 0.018 is multiplied by 60 minutes per hour and the constant is $1.08 (0.075 \times 0.24 \times 60 \text{ min/hr})$.

$$BTUH_{\text{sens. infil.}} = CFH \times 0.018 \times \Delta T° F$$
$$BTUH_{\text{sens. infil.}} = CFM \times 1.08 \times \Delta T° F$$

Although the air change method provides a reasonable estimation of infiltration, the crack method offers a more accurate indication of the amount of air that would infiltrate. In using this method, it is first necessary to determine the length of the crack that exists. This involves measuring the total length of the crack in the various penetrations of the façade. Sometimes this includes the crack between the window frame and the opening in which the frame is set, although this crack should be effectively sealed with caulking. More typically, crack measurements are limited to the perimeter of each operating sash or door. Once the length of the crack is known, the expected infiltration in cubic feet per hour per linear foot of crack can be determined based on wind velocity and the type of opening. These data are specific to the type of fenestration device (e.g., wood, vinyl, or metal window) and are supplied by the manufacturer.

When using the crack method for spaces with multiple exposures, it is important to use the worst exposure of that space rather than all of the exposures since it is unlikely that the wind will be coming from more than one direction at the same time. If the wind comes at a 45° angle and thereby strikes two adjacent exposures, based on the adjusted pressures that result, the actual infiltration will be less than that experienced with the wind striking only the one exposure that has the greatest length of crack. However, if three or more exposures exist, it is normal to compare the infiltration through the single exposure with the largest crack length with half of the total infiltration, assuming that the wind comes directly at all exposures, and to use the higher of these two volumes of infiltration. Of course, when using the data from Table 7.10 for the air change method, these adjustments are not necessary since they are already considered in selecting the proper infiltration rates.

While infiltration must be considered in calculating heat loss, if a mechanical ventilation system is to be used (which is true for most commercial structures), it is reasonable to pressurize the interior space by supplying more air than is returned or exhausted. This will pressurize the space, so rather than infiltration, some exfiltration will occur. Although this would essentially eliminate the infiltration load that needs to be added to the transmission heat loss, it does not eliminate the ventilation load. If outside air is used as the source of ventilation and it is at a colder temperature, then the heating system must be able

to condition this outside air before it is distributed into the building. So, with mechanical ventilation, we substitute the heat loss that results from infiltration with the energy required to heat the ventilation air. Knowing the amount of fresh air (i.e., outside air) required for ventilation, we use the same basic formula to determine the BTUH load.

If we were to consider latent load, we would then use the difference in specific humidity between the outside air and the desired interior conditions in one of the following formulas:

$$BTUH_{\text{latent infiltration}} = CFH \times 0.075 \times 1060 \times \Delta W$$

where:

CFH = volume of air in cubic feet per hour

0.075 = density of standard air in pounds per cubic feet

1060 = latent heat of vaporization per pound of air at c. 75° F

ΔW = difference in specific humidity between the interior and exterior

$$BTUH_{\text{latent infiltration}} = CFH \times 79.5 \times \Delta W$$
$$BTUH_{\text{latent infiltration}} = CFM \times 4840 \times \Delta W$$

Estimating Temperatures in Adjacent Unheated Spaces

The amount of transmission that occurs across a thermal barrier is dependent on the "U" coefficient of the barrier and the temperature difference between the ambient air on either side of the barrier. Generally, this temperature difference is taken between the interior and exterior ambient conditions, but in certain situations the thermal barrier separates the interior from an adjacent unheated space, such as an attic or a crawl space. In these situations, it is necessary to ascertain the temperature of the adjacent unheated space in order to determine the amount of transmission. The temperature of the adjacent unheated space, which is located somewhere between the interior and exterior, can be found the following formula:

$$T_u = \frac{T_i(A_1 U_1 + A_2 U_2 + A_3 U_3 + \text{etc.}) + T_o(A_a U_a + A_b U_b + A_c U_c + \text{etc.})}{(A_1 U_1 + A_2 U_2 + A_3 U_3 + \text{etc.}) + (A_a U_a + A_b U_b + A_c U_c + \text{etc.})}$$

where:

T_u = temperature of the unheated space

T_i = indoor temperature of the heated space

T_o = outdoor temperature

A_1, A_2, A_3 = surface areas of unheated space adjacent to heated space

A_a, A_b, A_c = surface areas of unheated space adjacent to outdoors

U_1, U_2, U_3 = heat transfer coefficients of $A_1, A_2, A_3,$ etc.

U_a, U_b, U_c = heat transfer coefficients of $A_a, A_b, A_c,$ etc.

When the unheated space is an attic above a flat ceiling, the formula is simplified somewhat:

$$T_a = \frac{T_i(A_cU_c) + T_o(A_rU_r + A_wU_w + A_gU_g)}{(A_cU_c + A_rU_r + A_wU_w + A_gU_g)}$$

where:

T_a = temperature of the unheated attic

T_i = indoor temperature of the heated space

T_o = outdoor temperature

A_r = surface areas of attic roof

A_w = surface areas of vertical walls in attic

A_g = surface areas of glass in attic

U_r = heat transfer coefficients of attic roof

U_w = heat transfer coefficients of vertical walls in attic

U_g = heat transfer coefficients of glass in attic

Sometimes there is an exchange of outside air in the unheated space. For example, an attic will have a ventilation rate of 0.1 to 0.5 cubic feet per minute per square foot of attic floor area, with the higher number typically occurring when the attic is intentionally ventilated in order to reduce potential moisture condensation. If outside air does infiltrate into the unheated space, the temperature difference between the heated interior and the unheated space is to be reduced by 10% for each 0.1 CFM per square foot of airflow that occurs.

Figure 7.10 shows various ways to provide reasonable attic ventilation that will minimize potential problems of winter moisture condensation as well as reduce summer heat gain.

Ventilation should also be provided for crawl spaces. Not only might some moisture migrate from the heated interior, especially when there is no effective vapor barrier, it is also likely that ground moisture will disperse into the crawl space. While any condensation will fall back onto the ground, the higher humidity in the crawl space can lead to mold and mildew. Even with a vapor barrier in the floor construction assembly above the crawl space and a continuous vapor-impermeable ground sheet, the crawl space should be ventilated.

Obviously, when an attic or crawl space is ventilated, the temperature in that unheated space will be closer to the outdoor air temperature, but with most of the insulation located between the controlled interior space and the unheated attic or crawl space, this does not pose a problem. With an overall thermal resistance of 20 or higher, which is readily achieved with at least 6 inches of batt insulation, and assuming minimal thermal resistance between the unheated space and the outside, the temperature in the attic or crawl space will naturally be fairly close to the exterior temperature even without ventilation.

Reasonable attic ventilation can be achieved by providing openings that have a free area equal to 1/150th of the attic floor area. While gable vents can provide the necessary opening area, placing half of the openings at a low point, such as with continuous eave vents, and the other half at a high point, with a continuous ridge vent, is preferred since this will take advantage of natural thermal convective flow.

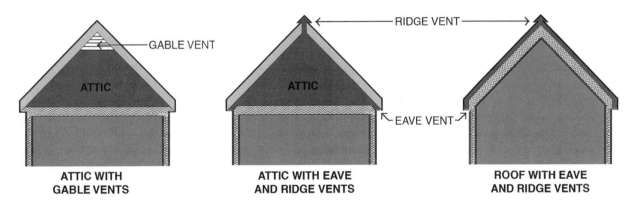

Figure 7.10 ATTIC VENTILATION
Attic ventilation is critical for avoiding moisture problems during the underheated period of the year and reducing excessive solar heat buildup that can impose a considerable load during any time of major insolation gain, particularly during the overheated period of the year.

CODE COMPLIANCE

To enhance the quality of the interior space, the building siting, configuration, fenestration, and construction details of any building should be responsive to the principles of sustainable development; at times, however, these responses are not provided. As a result, various requirements and standards have been established in order to ensure reasonable action. Most building codes now contain minimum requirements for energy conservation that apply to all new construction, including single-family residences.

Standards, which in many jurisdictions are the basis for the building code requirements, include those of ASHRAE, IESNA, and the U.S. Department of Energy (DOE), particularly the International Energy Conservation Code (IECC) and the International Residential Code (IRC). Perhaps the most broadly accepted requirements are presented in the ANSI/ASHRAE/IESNA Standards 90.1 and 90.2, which mandate resistance or "U" coefficients for construction assemblies and infiltration rates. For the latter, they stipulate minimum air leakage, which is usually not to exceed 0.30 cubic feet per minute (CFM) per linear foot of sash crack for operable windows, 0.15 CFM per square foot for nonoperable windows, 1.25 CFM per square foot for commercial entries, and 0.5 CFM per square foot for residential doors. In addition, the interior lighting power load should be 1 to 2.5 watts per square foot, depending on the building occupancy. (You might recall that in single-family residential occupancies, 3 watts per square foot is assumed when calculating the electrical demand.)

While the energy code has prescriptive requirements, it is possible to demonstrate code compliance by comparing the performance of the actual design to the performance that would result from the prescriptive requirements. That is, we can get around the prescriptive requirements if we can show that the calculated heat loss for the actual conditions is less than or equal to the heat loss that the code requirements would demand for the spatial composition.

The effective average "U" coefficient can be found from the following equation:

$$U_o = [U_w A_w + U_g A_g + U_d A_d + \cdots]/A_o$$

where:

U_o = effective average or combined thermal transmittance of the overall exterior wall area

A_o = gross area of the exterior wall

U_w = thermal transmittance of the opaque wall area

A_w = opaque wall area

U_g = thermal transmittance of the glazing area

A_g = glazing area

U_d = thermal transmittance of the door opening

A_d = door area

For example, let us assume that the code requires that "U" coefficients not exceed 0.05 for the roof or 0.228 for the overall walls. Accepting that a roof with excellent insulation will have, at best, a "U" coefficient of 0.03 and that an insulated skylight with a low-emittance coating will have a "U" coefficient of 0.48, this would only permit a skylight with an area less than 5% of the floor area. In order to have a skylight larger than 5% of the floor area, a trade-off would be required. If the effective average wall "U" coefficient is less than the required 0.228, the improvements in the wall could be applied against the increased skylight in the roof. What will the overall "U" coefficient have to be for the walls?

First of all, let us assume that the building is a two-story structure that is 40 feet square and that each floor has an overall height of 10 feet. Based on this configuration, the roof has a total area of 1600 square feet and the exterior wall area is 3200 square feet. According to code, the prescribed overall heat loss per degree Fahrenheit temperature differential should not exceed 809.6 BTUH.

$$\text{BTUH}/^\circ\text{F} = (1600 \text{ sq ft} \times 0.05) + (3200 \text{ sq ft} \times 0.228)$$
$$= 809.6 \text{ BTUH}/^\circ\text{F}$$

If the skylight comprises 10% of the roof, there will be 160 square feet of skylight and 1440 square feet of solid roof; the overall "U" coefficient of the roof will be 0.075, and the roof heat loss per degree Fahrenheit will be 120 BTUH. This means that the maximum heat loss through the walls must be no greater than 689.6 BTUH.

$$U_o = \frac{(160 \text{ sq ft} \times 0.48) + (1440 \text{ sq ft} \times 0.03)}{1600 \text{ sq ft}} = 0.075$$
$$\text{BTUH}/^\circ\text{F} = 1600 \text{ sq ft} \times 0.075 = 120 \text{ BTUH}/^\circ\text{F}$$

With a total area of 3200 square feet, a heat loss of 689.6 BTUH per degree Fahrenheit correlates with an overall "U" coefficient of 0.216.

$$\text{"U" Coefficient of Walls} = \frac{689.6 \text{ BTUH}/^\circ\text{F}}{3200 \text{ sq ft}} = 0.2155$$

Based on this and assuming that the "U" coefficients will not exceed 0.05 for the opaque walls or 0.50 for any windows, the walls could contain a window area of up to around 35%. With 35% of the gross wall area comprised of windows with a "U" coefficient of 0.50, the average "U" coefficient for the gross wall area would be 0.208, or

Table 7.11: CRITERIA FOR THERMAL ENVELOPE OF LOW-RISE RESIDENTIAL STRUCTURES

Low-Rise Residential																
Opaque Elements	**Maximum "U"**								**Minimum R-Value**							
Zone	1	2	3	4	5	6	7	8	1	2	3	4	5	6	7	8
Roof																
Attic																
Wood Framing	0.03	0.03	0.03	0.03	0.02	0.02	0.02	0.02	30	30	30	38	43	49	49	52
Metal Framing	0.03	0.03	0.03	0.03	0.02	0.02	0.02	0.02	30	30	30	38	43	49	49	52
No Attic																
Wood Framing	0.08	0.05	0.05	0.05	0.04	0.03	0.03	0.03	13	22	22	22	26	38	38	38
Metal Framing	0.05	0.05	0.05	0.05	0.04	0.03	0.03	0.03	19	19	22	22	26	38	38	38
Walls, Above-Grade																
Wood Framing - Cavity	0.08	0.07	0.07	0.05	0.05	0.04	0.03	0.03	13	15	15	15	21	15	21	21
Wood Framing - Continuous[b]	-	-	-	-	-	-	-	-	0	0	0	5	0	10	10	10
Steel Framing - Cavity	0.07	0.05	0.04	0.04	0.03	0.03	0.03	0.03	15	21	15	15	21	21	21	21
Steel Framing - Continuous[b]	-	-	-	-	-	-	-	-	0	0	7.5	7.5	10	10	10	10
Mass Exterior Insulation																
Walls, Below-Grade																
Continuous Exterior	*	-	-	-	-	-	-	-	NR	NR	NR	0	5.4	8.1	10.8	10.8
Interior	-	-	-	-	-	-	-	-	NR	NR	NR	0	11	11	11	11
Floors																
Wood Frame Over Exterior	0.07	0.05	0.05	0.05	0.04	0.04	0.03	0.03	15	19	19	21	25	25	38	38
Steel Frame Over Exterior	0.05	0.05	0.03	0.03	0.03	0.03	0.03	0.03	22	22	30	38	38	38	38	38
Wood Frame Over Unheated	0.08	0.08	0.05	0.05	0.04	0.04	0.03	0.03	13	13	19	19	25	25	30	30
Steel Frame Over Unheated	0.07	0.07	0.03	0.03	0.03	0.03	0.03	0.03	15	15	30	30	38	38	38	38
Slab-on-Grade Floors																
Perimeter Insulation									NR	NR	NR	NR	NR	NR	NR	NR
Opaque Doors																
Nonwood	0.39	0.39	0.39	0.39	0.39	0.39	0.39	0.39								
Fenestration	**Maximum "U"**								**Assembly Max. SHGC.**							
Zone	1	2	3	4	5	6	7	8	1	2	3	4	5	6	7	8
Vertical Glazing	0.67	0.67	0.47	0.35	0.35	0.35	0.35	0.35	0.37	0.37	0.4	NR	NR	NR	NR	NR
Skylight	1.60	1.05	0.90	0.60	0.60	0.60	0.60	0.60	0.4	0.4	0.4	NR	NR	NR	NR	NR

[a]"U" coefficients shown for cavity include continuous insulation when required.
[b]Continuos insulation is to be added in addition to the cavity insulation.
Source: This table is based on information from ANSI/ASHRAE/IESNA Standard 90.2-2007.

less than 0.216, which would allow 10% of the roof to be comprised of skylights.

$$0.2155 = \frac{(W \text{ sq ft} \times 0.50) + ((3200 - W) \text{ sq ft} \times 0.05)}{3200 \text{ sq ft}}$$

$$0.2155 \times 3200 = 689.66 = 0.50W - 0.50W + 160$$

$$0.45W = 529.6$$

Window Area with "U" of 0.50 = 1175 sq ft

Opaque Wall Area with "U" of 0.05 = 2025 sq ft

1175/3200 = 0.367

While there are various things that we can learn from this short exercise, the important message here is that we should attempt to ensure that the "U" coefficients for the various portions of the thermal envelope meet code requirements. However, since these are minimal requirements, perhaps we should attempt to go beyond what might be required. In general, for opaque thermal barriers, 0.05 for walls and 0.03 for roofs are reasonable targets for much of the U.S. regardless of the particular code stipulations.

Tables 7.11, 7.12, and 7.13 present the basic requirements stipulated by ANSI/ASHRAE/IESNA Standards 90.1 and 90.2. These are adjusted for various climatic conditions, which are presented in Figure 7.11 or Table 7.14.

ANNUAL HEATING DEMAND

Degree Days

Heat loss calculations are generally based on the lowest exterior temperatures that legitimately can be expected to occur about every 10 years, not the lowest recorded temperature. As a result, they do not result in the worst possible conditions that might actually be expected to occur, but since they are also not based on the mean or average

Table 7.12: CRITERIA FOR THERMAL ENVELOPE OF RESIDENTIAL STRUCTURES

Residential — Opaque Elements

Opaque Elements	Maximum "U"								Minimum R-Value							
Zone	1	2	3	4	5	6	7	8	1	2	3	4	5	6	7	8
Roof																
Metal Building	0.065	0.065	0.065	0.065	0.065	0.065	0.065	0.049	19	19	19	19	19	19	19	13+19 ci
Attic and Other	0.027	0.027	0.027	0.027	0.027	0.027	0.027	0.021	38	38	38	38	38	38	38	49
Walls, Above-Grade																
Mass	0.151	0.123	0.104	0.090	0.080	0.071	0.071	0.052	5.7 ci	7.6 ci	9.5 ci	11.4 ci	13.3 ci	15.2 ci	15.2 ci	25 ci
Metal Building	0.113	0.113	0.113	0.113	0.057	0.570	0.052	0.057	13	13	13	13	13+13 ci	13+13 ci	13+13 ci	13+13 ci
Steel-Framed	0.124	0.064	0.064	0.064	0.064	0.640	0.042	0.037	13	13	13	13+7.5 ci	13+7.5 ci	13+7.5 ci	13+15.6 ci	13+18.8 ci
Wood-Framed & Other	0.089	0.089	0.089	0.064	0.051	0.051	0.051	0.036	13	13	13	13+3.8 ci	13+7.5 ci	13+7.5 ci	13+7.5 ci	13+15.6 ci
Walls, Below-Grade																
Wall	0.322	0.087	0.089	0.074	0.064	0.057	0.051	0.051	NR	NR	NR	7.5 ci	7.5 ci	7.5 ci	10 ci	12.5 ci
Floors																
Mass	0.350	0.052	0.052	0.038	0.038	0.032	0.032	0.032	8.3 ci	8.3 ci	8.3 ci	10.4 ci	12.5 ci	14.6 ci	16.7 ci	16.7 ci
Steel-Framed	0.282	0.033	0.033	0.033	0.033	0.033	0.033	0.033	NR	19	19	30	30	38	38	38
Wood-Framed & Other	0.282	0.033	0.033	0.033	0.033	0.033	0.033	0.033	NR	30	30	30	30	30	30	30
Slab-on-Grade Floors																
Unheated									NR	NR	NR	10/24"	10/24"	15/24"	15/24"	20/24"
Heated									7.5/12"	7.5/12"	10/24"	15/24"	15/24"	20/48"	20/48"	20/48"
Opaque Doors																
Swinging	0.700	0.700	0.700	0.700	0.500	0.500	0.500	0.500								
Non-swinging	1.450	0.500	0.500	0.500	0.500	0.500	0.500	0.500								

Residential — Fenestration

Fenestration	Maximum "U"								Assembly Max. SHGC[c]							
Zone	1	2	3	4	5	6	7	8	1	2	3	4	5	6	7	8
Vertical Glazing[a]																
Nonmetal Framing	1.20	0.75	0.65	0.40	0.35	0.35	0.35	0.35	0.25	0.25	0.25	0.40	0.40	0.40	NR	NR
Metal Framed Store Front	1.20	0.70	0.60	0.50	0.45	0.45	0.40	0.40								
Metal Framed Entry Door	1.20	1.10	0.90	0.85	0.80	0.80	0.80	0.80								
Metal Framing	1.20	0.75	0.65	0.55	0.55	0.55	0.45	0.45								
Skylight[b]																
Glass w/ curb	1.98	1.98	1.17	1.17	0.98	0.98	0.98	0.98	0.19 - 0.16	0.19	0.36 - 0.19	0.36 - 0.19	0.49 - 0.39	0.46 - 0.36	0.64	NR
Plastic w/ curb	1.90	1.90	1.30	1.30	1.10	0.74	0.61	0.61	0.27	0.27	0.27	0.27	0.77 - 0.62	0.65 - 0.55	0.77	NR
Without curb	1.36	1.36	0.69	0.58	0.58	0.58	0.58	0.58	0.19	0.19	0.36 - 0.19	0.36 - 0.19	0.49 - 0.39	0.49 - 0.39	0.64	NR

(The Assembly Max. SHGC values listed for Vertical Glazing apply to all vertical glazing framing types.)

[a] Vertical fenestration should not exceed 40% of the gross wall area. The listed values are the equivalent "U" or SHGC for the roof opening and include the curbs, if they exist.

[b] Skylight area should not exceed 5% of the gross roof area.

[c] If SHGC is shown by two number separated by a dash, the first number refers to a skylight with 0% to 2% of gross roof area and the second number to a skylight with 2% to 5% of gross roof area.

ci — continuous insulation extending over framing.

Source: This table is based on information from ANSI/ASHRAE/IESNA Standard 90.1-2007.

Table 7.13: CRITERIA FOR THERMAL ENVELOPE OF NONRESIDENTIAL STRUCTURES

Nonresidential

Opaque Elements

Opaque Elements	Maximum "U"								Minimum R-Value							
Zone	1	2	3	4	5	6	7	8	1	2	3	4	5	6	7	8
Roof																
Metal Building	0.065	0.065	0.065	0.065	0.065	0.065	0.065	0.049	19	19	19	19	19	19	19	13 + 19 ci
Attic and Other	0.034	0.027	0.027	0.027	0.027	0.027	0.027	0.021	30	38	38	38	38	38	38	49
Walls, Above-Grade																
Mass	0.580	0.151	0.123	0.104	0.090	0.080	0.071	0.071	NR	5.7 ci	7.6 ci	9.5 ci	11.4 ci	13.3 ci	15.2 ci	15.2 ci
Metal Building	0.113	0.113	0.113	0.113	0.113	0.113	0.057	0.057	13	13	13	13	13	13	13 + 13 ci	13 + 13 ci
Steel-Framed	0.124	0.124	0.084	0.064	0.064	0.064	0.064	0.064	13	13	13 + 3.8 ci	13	13 + 7.5 ci	13 + 7.5 ci	13 + 7.5 ci	13 + 7.5 ci
Wood-Framed and Other	0.089	0.089	0.089	0.089	0.064	0.051	0.051	0.036	13	13	13	13	13 + 3.8 ci	13 + 7.5 ci	13 + 7.5 ci	13 + 15.6 ci
Walls, Below-Grade																
Wall									NR	NR	NR	NR	7.5 ci	7.5 ci	7.5 ci	7.5 ci
Floors																
Mass	0.322	0.107	0.107	0.087	0.074	0.064	0.064	0.057	NR	6.3 ci	6.3 ci	8.3 ci	10.4 ci	12.5 ci	12.5 ci	14.6 ci
Steel-Framed	0.350	0.052	0.052	0.038	0.038	0.038	0.038	0.032	NR	19	19	30	30	30	30	38
Wood-Framed and Other	0.282	0.051	0.051	0.033	0.033	0.033	0.033	0.033	NR	19	19	30	30	30	30	30
Slab-on-Grade Floors																
Unheated									NR	NR	NR	NR	NR	10/24"	15/24"	15/24"
Heated									7.5/12"	7.5/12"	10/24"	15/24"	15/24"	15/24"	20/24"	20/48"
Opaque Doors																
Swinging	0.700	0.700	0.700	0.700	0.700	0.700	0.500	0.500								
Nonswinging	1.450	1.450	1.450	1.500	0.500	0.500	0.500	0.500								

Fenestration

Fenestration	Maximum "U"								Assembly Max. SHGC[c]							
Zone	1	2	3	4	5	6	7	8	1	2	3	4	5	6	7	8
Vertical Glazing[a]																
Nonmetal Framing	1.20	0.75	0.65	0.40	0.35	0.35	0.35	0.35	0.25	0.25	0.25	0.40	0.40	0.40	0.45	0.45
Metal-Framed Store Front	1.20	0.70	0.60	0.50	0.45	0.45	0.40	0.40								
Metal-Framed Entry Door	1.20	1.10	0.90	0.85	0.80	0.80	0.80	0.80								
Metal Framing	1.20	0.75	0.65	0.55	0.55	0.55	0.45	0.45								
Skylight[b]																
Glass w/ curb	1.98	1.98	1.17	1.17	1.17	1.17	1.17	0.98	0.36 - 0.19	0.36 - 0.19	0.39 - 0.19	0.49 - 0.39	0.49 - 0.39	0.49	0.68 - 0.64	NR
Plastic w/ curb	1.90	1.90	1.30	1.30	1.10	0.87	0.87	0.61	0.34 - 0.27	0.39 - 0.34	0.65 - 0.34	0.65 - 0.34	0.77 - 0.62	0.71 - 0.58	0.77 - 0.71	NR
Without curb	1.36	1.36	0.69	0.69	0.69	0.69	0.69	0.58	0.36 - 0.19	0.36 - 0.19	0.39 - 0.19	0.49 - 0.39	0.49 - 0.39	0.49	0.68 - 0.64	NR

[a] Vertical fenestration should not exceed 40% of the gross wall area.

[b] Skylight area should not exceed 5% of the gross roof area. The listed values are the equivalent "U" or SHGC for the roof opening and include the curbs, if they exist.

[c] If SHGC is shown by two number separated by a dash, the first number refers to a skylight with 0% to 2% of gross roof area and the second number to a skylight with 2% to 5% of gross roof area.

ci — continuous insulation extending over framing.

Source: This table is based on information from ANSI/ASHRAE/IESNA Standard 90.1-2007.

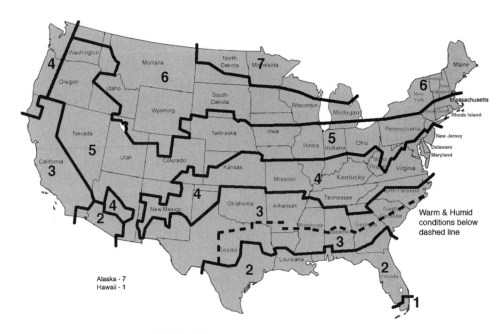

Figure 7.11 SCHEMATIC MAP OF U.S. THERMAL CLIMATE ZONES
The various climatic zones shown are used for Tables 7.11 to 7.13. The zones are also presented in Table 7.14, which lists selected U.S. cities by state. This map is based on information from ANSI/ASHRAE/IESNA Standard 90.1-2007.

exterior temperatures, they do not indicate the average conditions of heat loss that can be expected either. Rather, the heat loss calculations for a building are performed to determine the appropriate size for the heating system. The assumption is that this system, including both the central heating device and the distribution system, is large enough to perform adequately when normal seasonal low temperatures do occur.

If we wanted to determine the annual heating load in BTU required for the heating season as distinct from the BTUH heating load that might be required at the lowest exterior temperature, then we should calculate the heat loss for the average exterior winter temperature rather than for the expected worst condition. By identifying the average hourly heat loss, based on the winter's average exterior temperature, we could then theoretically calculate the annual heating load by multiplying the average hourly heat loss by the total number of hours that exist during the winter heating season.

An alternative method for determining the annual heating load is to identify the BTUH heat loss per degree Fahrenheit temperature differential between the interior and the exterior and then multiply this hourly rate by 24 hours per day and the location's seasonal degree days. The number of *degree days* (DD) is the sum of each day's average or mean temperature difference from the degree day base. The degree day base, which is traditionally set at 65° F, is the average daily temperature above which heating

would be not required. It is assumed that with the typical residential unit, if the average exterior temperature did not fall below the base, the building mass would essentially level the actual daily temperature variations and, combined with reasonable daily solar gain and the interior, heat-generating activities that normally exist, would preclude the need for any heating. Therefore, it is assumed that heating is necessary only when the average exterior temperature drops below the degree day base temperature. Since the temperature averaging is limited to one 24-hour period, no benefit is assumed for those days when the average exterior temperature exceeds the base. If the average exterior temperature for a day is higher than the base, that day's contribution to the total number of degree days is zero, not minus the difference. That is, when the daily average temperature is above the degree day base, we assume that no heating is required that day, and regardless of how warm the average temperature might be, we assume that there is no carryover of stored heat. Each 24-hour period is considered on its own, whether or not heating is required.

Since degree days are based on the daily average temperature, we must multiply the degree day value for each day by 24, the number of hours in a day, in order to use degree days in a formula based on BTUH. The appropriate formula to determine the heating demand for a building over a period of time is:

$$\text{Total BTU Load} = \frac{\text{BTUH}}{°\text{F}} \times 24 \text{ Hours/Day} \times \text{DD}$$

Table 7.14: THERMAL CLIMATE ZONES FOR SELECTED U.S. CITIES

Location	Zone	Location	Zone	Location	Zone
Alabama		**Iowa**		**North Carolina**	
Huntsville	3A	Des Moines	5A	Asheville	4A
Mobile	2A	Sioux City	6A	Cape Hatteras	4A
Montgomery	3A	Waterloo	5A	Charlotte	4A
Alaska		**Kansas**		Raleigh	4A
Anchorage	7	Dodge City	4A	**North Dakota**	
Fairbanks	8	Topeka	4A	Bismarck	7A
Arizona		Wichita	4A	Fargo	7A
Flagstaff	3B	**Kentucky**		Grand Forks	7A
Phoenix	3B	Jackson	4A	**Ohio**	
Tucson	3B	Lexington	4A	Cincinnati	5A
Arkansas		Louisville	4A	Cleveland	5A
Fort Smith	3A	**Louisiana**		Columbus	5a
Little Rock	3A	Baton Rouge	2A	Dayton	5A
California		New Orleans	2A	Toledo	5A
Bakersfield	3B	**Maine**		**Oklahoma**	
Bishop	3B	Portland	6A	Oklahoma City	3A
Fresno	3B	**Maryland**		Tulsa	3A
Long Beach	3B	Baltimore	4A	**Oregon**	
Los Angeles	3B	**Massachusetts**		Eugene	4C
Sacramento	3B	Boston	5A	Portland	4C
San Diego	3B	Worcester	5A	Salem	4C
San Francisco	3C	**Michigan**		**Pennsylvania**	
Santa Barbara	3B	Detroit	5A	Erie	5A
Colorado		Flint	5A	Harrisburg	5A
Colorado Springs	5B	Grand Rapids	5A	Philadelphia	4A
Denver	5B	Lansing	5A	Pittsburgh	5A
Grand Junction	5B	Marquette	6A	**Rhode Island**	
Connecticut		**Minnesota**		Providence	5A
Bridgeport	5A	Duluth	6A	**South Carolina**	
Hartford	5A	Minneapolis–St.Paul	6A	Charleston	3A
Delaware		Rochester	6A	Columbia	3A
Wilmington	4A	**Mississippi**		Greenville-Spartanburg	3A
District of Columbia		Jackson	2A	**South Dakota**	
Washington, D.C.	4A	Meridian	3A	Aberdeen	6A
Florida		Tupelo	3A	Rapid City	6A
Daytona Beach	2A	**Missouri**		Sioux Falls	6A
Fort Myers	2A	Columbia	4A	**Tennessee**	
Gainesville	2A	Kansas City	4A	Chattanooga	4A
Jacksonville	2A	St. Louis	4A	Knoxville	4A
Key West	1A	Springfield	4A	Memphis	4A
Miami	1A	**Montana**		Nashville	4A
Orlando	2A	Billings	6B	**Texas**	
Pensacola	2A	Helena	6B	Abilene	3A
Tallahassee	2A	Missoula	6B	Austin	2A
Tampa	2A	**Nebraska**		Dallas–Fort Worth	3A
Georgia		Lincoln	5A	Houston	2A
Atlanta	3A	North Platte	5A	San Antonio	3A
Augusta	3A	Omaha	5A	**Utah**	
Macon	3A	**Nevada**		Salt Lake City	5B
Savannah	3A	Elko	5B	**Vermont**	
Hawaii		Ely	5B	Burlington	6A
Honolulu	1A	Las Vegas	5B	**Virginia**	
Kahului	1A	Reno	5B	Norfolk	4A
Lihue	1A	Winnemucca	5B	Richmond	4A
Idaho		**New Hampshire**		Roanoke	4A
Boise	6B	Concord	6A	**Washington**	
Lewiston	6B	**New Jersey**		Seattle	5B
Illinois		Atlantic City	4A	Spokane	5B
Chicago	5A	Newark	4A	**West Virginia**	
Peoria	5A	**New Mexico**		Charleston	5A
Rockford	5A	Albuquerque	5B	Huntington	5A
Springfield	5A	Taos	5B	**Wisconsin**	
Indiana		**New York**		Madison	6A
Evansville	5A	Albany	5A	Milwaukee	6A
Fort Wayne	5A	Buffalo	5A	**Wyoming**	
Indianapolis	5A	New York	5A	Casper	5B
South Bend	5A	Syracuse	5A	Cheyenne	5B

The zones vary from 1 to 8 with lower temperatures generally associated with higher zone numbers. Also "A" indicates a moist zone, "B" a dry zone, and "C" a "maritime" zone, which essentially means the northwest coastal region. (Based on a listing of cities included in ANSI/ASHRAE/IESNA Standards 90.1.)

where:

BTUH/° F = building's hourly heat loss for each degree of temperature difference between the interior and the exterior

DD = total number of degree days for the period of time that usually is the total heating season, but could be any number of days or months

The term degree day is somewhat difficult to grasp. Essentially, it is the sum of the number of degrees below the base point that occur within each day over a period of time. For example, assuming a 65° F base, 150 DD would occur during a 1-month period during which the average temperature each day for the 30 days in the month was 60° F or during 1 day when the average temperature was −85° F.

$$30 \text{ days} \times (65° \text{ F} − 60° \text{ F}) = 30 \text{ days} \times 5° \text{ F} = 150 \text{ DD}$$
$$1 \text{ day} \times [65° \text{ F} − (−85° \text{ F})] = 1 \text{ day} \times 150° \text{ F} = 150 \text{ DD}$$

If we want to work directly from the calculated maximum heat loss for a building, we can slightly modify the above equation. By dividing the calculated maximum heat loss by the temperature differential used in the calculations, we can obtain the heat loss per degree Fahrenheit for all of the means of heat loss, including the transmission loss across thermal barriers, slab edge loss, and infiltration.

$$\text{Total BTU Load} = \frac{\text{BTUH}_{max}}{\Delta T_{i−o}} \times 24 \text{ Hours/Day} \times \text{DD}$$

where:

BTUH$_{max}$ = the building's hourly heat loss based on a maximum temperature difference between the interior and the exterior

$\Delta T_{i−o}$ = the maximum temperature differential used

Once the total BTU heating load is determined for a particular period of time, the heating costs for that time period can be calculated for different fuels. Typically, the period of time is the overall winter season, and in determining the cost to meet this demand, we must account for the effective efficiency of the heating system. Except for electric resistance heating within the occupied space, heating systems generally do not operate at 100% efficiency. While certain high-efficiency gas furnaces claim nearly 100% efficiency, most central heating systems operate at between 75% and 95% efficiency, and a heat pump system can achieve an overall winter season efficiency of around 200% since this device, as its name implies, pumps heat rather than generates it.

In determining heating costs, it is also important to recognize that fuel costs vary according to location and also fluctuate over time.

$$\text{Total Fuel Demand} = \frac{\text{Total BTU Heating Load}}{\text{BTU per Unit of Fuel}} \times \text{Efficiency}$$

$$\text{Seasonal Heating Costs} = \text{Total Fuel Demand} \times \text{Cost per Unit of Fuel}$$

These two formulas are often combined:

$$\text{Seasonal Heating Costs} = \frac{\text{BTU Heating Load} \times \text{Cost/Unit of Fuel}}{\text{BTU/Unit of Fuel} \times \text{Effficiency}}$$

In general, we might assume that a typical single-family residence of around 2000 to 2500 square feet will have a maximum heat loss of around 50,000 BTUH based on a 70° F temperature differential between inside and outside. If this residence is situated in a location with a 5000-DD winter season, we can readily calculate the total winter season BTU load, as well as the fuel demand and the cost. For these last calculations, we might assume a 90% efficiency of operation and natural gas as the fuel source, with 100,000 BTU produced from each 100 cubic feet of gas, referred to as a *therm*. While the cost of 1 therm of natural gas varies, let us assume that it is $1.25.[2]

$$\text{Seasonal Heating Demand} = \frac{50,000 \text{ BTUH}_{max} \times 24 \text{hr/day} \times 5000 \text{ DD}}{70° \text{ F} \Delta T_{i−o}}$$
$$= 85,714,285 \text{ BTU} \approx 86,000,000$$
$$\text{Seasonal Heating Costs} = \frac{86,000,000 \text{ BTU} \times \$1.25/\text{Therm}}{100,000 \text{ BTU/Therm} \times 90\%}$$
$$= \$1194.44 \approx \$1200.00$$

HEAT GAIN

A basic assumption for heat loss calculations is that the environmental conditions represent the worst probable situation for heat loss and that these conditions exist for an extended period of time. In doing heat gain calculations, there is again an assumption of the worst probable situation, but because this should involve solar gain, the notion that these worst conditions are stable must be set aside. If there is a solar factor, the environmental conditions cannot remain stable since the relative position of the sun is continually changing. Once consideration of the

---

[2]$1.25 is more than the cost at the time of writing but less than what it was a few years ago and maybe what it currently costs.

sun's relative movement enters into the calculations, the season and the time of the day, as well as the orientation and the relative absorptivity of the surfaces that might receive incident solar radiation, must all be factored in. In addition, since we are attempting to determine the maximum heat gain, we must also include any internal loads, such as people and lights, that will also contribute to the total heat gain. As a result, calculations for heat gain tend to be more complicated than those for heat loss. However, if we understand the basic calculation procedures, then the complication is related mainly to added factors that must be accounted for rather than increased mathematical complexity.

In doing heat loss calculations, some attention should be paid to possible humidity problems such as might occur if very dry air infiltrates directly into the controlled environment or is supplied by mechanical ventilation. But while we might consider humidity issues in heat loss calculations, in heat gain calculations humidity is often a major concern and must be included. Like sensible loads, humidity or latent loads are expressed in terms of BTU; however, the methods used to control latent loads are quite different from those used to control sensible loads. Sensible loads are controlled by either adding or removing heat, usually accomplished by increasing or decreasing the temperature of the air in the controlled environment, while latent loads are controlled by adding moisture to or removing it from the air. Since the proper mechanical responses to $BTU_{sensible}$ and BTU_{latent} loads are quite different, the calculation of these two loads should be done separately and combined only to find the ultimate, total load on a system.

Sensible Heat Gain Loads

As with heat loss, the sensible heat gain loads that result from natural environmental conditions can be divided into transmittance gains and infiltration (or ventilation) gains. In addition to the actual temperature difference between the exterior and interior ambient conditions, transmittance heat gains must include the effects of solar radiation. While transparent or translucent materials can transmit all or at least a major portion of the solar radiation directly, opaque materials tend to absorb incident solar radiation, which causes an increase in effective temperature. When an opaque thermal barrier is exposed to the sun, its exterior surface temperature tends to increase above the exterior ambient air temperature. Because of this, the effective heat flow across the thermal barrier is increased. The impact of this solar radiation and of the resulting temperature increase varies according to the color or absorptivity of the exposed surface and to the overall mass of the thermal barrier.

The absorptivity and reflectivity of an exposed surface determine the relative amount of incident solar radiation that will be absorbed and reflected. If the exposed surface is dark, it will absorb much of the solar radiation. When the radiation is absorbed by this surface, it is converted from radiant energy into sensible energy, increasing the temperature of the surface. With an increased temperature, the exterior surface will tend to radiate heat outward while also transferring heat by conduction and convection both out to the exterior ambient air, which is at a lower temperature since the air itself does not tend to absorb significant quantities of solar radiation, and into the thermal barrier. That is, some of the increased sensible energy gained from the solar radiation will start to flow into the thermal barrier, toward the interior space. While the rate at which this flow will occur is based on the "U" coefficient, the time that it will take to migrate across the thermal barrier will depend on the mass of the barrier since the thermal energy gained from the solar radiation will have to heat up the materials within the thermal barrier sequentially as the heat flows across the thermal barrier. If the materials are of considerable mass, they will tend to soak up much of the thermal energy, delaying the time it takes the temperature to migrate across the barrier. The explanation for this delay in thermal transfer is provided in the following basic formula:

$$BTU = Weight \times Specific\ Heat \times \Delta T$$

If the temperature flow across the barrier is delayed, it is probable that the sun will have moved, and without the added solar intensity, it is likely that the effective exterior surface temperature of the barrier will have dropped. When this happens, if all the thermal energy has not yet passed through the barrier, some of it might flow back toward the outside since the exterior temperature of the barrier will now be less than the temperature within the barrier. That is, the raised temperature inside the barrier will now flow in both directions, back to the outside and to the inside. Based on this, the amount of internal heat gained as a result of the incident solar radiation on the exterior of the thermal barrier will depend on various barrier factors: the "U" coefficient, the absorptivity of the exterior surface, its mass, and its time lag, which is a result of this mass.

The following must be considered in determining the amount of transmitted heat gain:

- The temperature difference between interior and exterior ambient air
- "U" coefficient of the barrier
- Mass of the barrier and the time lag factor
- Effects of insolation

  - Site location
  - Time of season

Table 7.15A: HOURLY OUTDOOR TEMPERATURE

Solar Time	1	2	3	4	5	6	7	8	9	10	11	12	13	14	15	16	17	18	19	20	21	22	23	24
°F	76	75	75	75	76	78	80	82	85	88	90	92	94	95	95	95	94	92	90	88	85	82	80	78
°C	25	24	24	24	25	26	27	28	29	31	32	33	34	35	35	35	34	33	32	31	29	28	27	26

Based on a 95° F or 35° C maximum exterior temperature and a 20° F. or 11° C diurnal range (DR). Celsius temperatures were calculated based on formula,[3] $T_o = T_{15} - \frac{DR}{2}\left[1 - \sin\frac{(\theta\pi - 9\pi)}{12}\right]$, with θ equal to solar time. Fahrenheit temperatures were converted from calculated Celsius temperatures.

Table 7.15B: HOURLY TEMPERATURE DIFFERENTIALS

Solar Time	1	2	3	4	5	6	7	8	9	10	11	12	13	14	15	16	17	18	19	20	21	22	23	24
°F	−2	−3	−3	−3	−2	0	2	4	7	10	12	14	16	17	17	17	16	14	12	10	7	4	2	0
°C	−1	−1	−2	−1	−1	0	1	2	4	5	7	8	9	9	9	9	8	7	5	4	2	1	0	

Based on the calculated hourly outdoor temperatures (95° F or 35° C maximum exterior temperature and 20° F. or 11° C diurnal range) and an interior design temperature of 78°F.or 28°C.

- Hour of day
- Surface orientation
- Surface absorptivity

Temperature Differential

The maximum temperature differential between the interior and exterior ambient air is usually used in heat loss calculations. By using this differential, it is possible to determine the size of heating equipment that is required to counteract the coldest conditions that are likely to exist. Although these conditions, in terms of temperature and airflow, might occur for only short periods of time during the heating season, the assumption is that these worst conditions do occur and that they continue to exist long enough to establish stable conditions of thermal transfer.[3]

Since we also assume the worst conditions with heat gain calculations, which means that we have to include the effects of direct solar radiation, the conditions are not stable. Not only does the sun continually move, continually changing the insolation that is gained on each exposure, but the outdoor temperature also fluctuates during the day. Each day as the sun rises, travels across the sky, and then sets in the evening, the ambient air temperature is affected, generally producing a 20° daily temperature change. Therefore, the actual temperature differential, which is used in a detailed heat gain calculation, must be based on the time of day and the expected daily range of temperatures. With the average 20° daily range, the temperature tends to peak at around 2 P.M. solar time and follows a standard bell curve from that point. Of course, in regions of low humidity, especially when there are clear

evening skies, this daily range tends to exceed 20° F. In regions of high humidity or if there is excessive cloud cover, the daily temperature range is usually considerably less, often only around 5° F.

Tables 7.15A and 7.15B list the standard temperature differences between an interior at 78° F and an exterior with a maximum daily temperature of 95° F and a daily range of 20° F. Note that the listed temperature differentials do not specifically equate to the expressed parameters. The maximum and minimum $\Delta T°$ F values are 14° and -2°, and based on an interior temperature of 78° F, this suggests that the maximum and minimum exterior temperatures are 92° F and 76° F, not the implied 95° F and 74° F. However, since we are trying to get a sense of thermal performance in order to help develop a design, we should not worry about the minor inconsistencies and use the values listed in these tables.

We should also note that the summer interior temperature is assumed to be 78° F, which is around 10° F higher than the interior temperature assumed for the winter. While 78° F − 80° F is suggested for the summer interior temperature and 68° F − 70° F for the winter interior temperature, unfortunately thermostats are often set lower in the summer and higher in the winter. When the summer interior temperatures are specified to be other than 78° F, we need to subtract the specified temperature from 78° F and add the difference to the hourly temperature differentials shown in Table 7.15A or calculate the hourly temperature differentials based on the values in Table 7.15B and the specified interior design temperature.

Summer "U" Coefficient

The calculation procedure used to determine the summer "U" coefficients is the same as that used for the winter "U" coefficient, but the exterior wind velocity is usually

[3] W.P. Jones, *Air Conditioning Application and Design* (Butterworth-Heinemann, Oxford, 1996), p. 8.

indicated as $7^1/_2$ mph rather than the winter velocity of 15 mph and the direction of heat flow is reversed. With horizontally positioned thermal barriers, this reversal results in a change in the resistance of the surface air films and air spaces. In winter, heat is usually flowing up through the roof, whereas in summer it is flowing down. The change in air velocity and direction will result in changes in "U" coefficients, although this change will not be substantial if the thermal barrier includes a significant amount of insulation.

Heat Gain Calculation Methods

There are several different hand calculation methods plus a number of effective computer programs available to calculate heat gain. As with heat loss, our major intention in exploring heat gain calculations is to develop a better understanding of the ways in which heat gain occurs to guide our architectural design efforts. With this purpose in mind, we will concentrate on the instantaneous heat gain method (IHGM), which deals with the various sources of gain, rather than on the space design cooling load method (SDCLM) currently endorsed by ASHRAE, which is oriented toward sizing the cooling system, or any of the effective computer programs, which provide excellent results but again are intended primarily to size equipment and to produce overall end results rather than identify the causes for heat gain. Since we will emphasize the IHGM, it is perhaps appropriate to first clarify how this approach differs from the SDCLM.

Unlike IHGM, SDCLM includes an adjustment of the actual thermal gain to account for the thermal mass of the construction. This method basically evolved from the realization that the heat gain suggested by IHGM, the traditional ASHRAE approach, seemed to exceed somewhat the heat gain indicated by other methods of calculation used outside of the United States and, more importantly, resulted in oversizing the equipment to some extent.

The assumption with IHGM is that the sensible heat gain results in an increase of the interior air temperature. While this is partially true, as the air temperature increases, the temperatures of the building materials and the building contents also increase. Based on their mass, the rate of increase in the air temperature is adjusted. With heavy mass, a considerable amount of thermal energy is admitted into the structure and building contents. As a result of this, which has been referred to as *admittance theory*, increases in air temperature are counteracted by minor increases in the temperature of the construction mass. By allowing a slight increase in the ambient air temperature, the size of the cooling system can be reduced considerably. That is, sizing the environmental control system to match the instantaneous heat gain tends to result in excessive cooling

capacity, although the IHGM provides a clear indication of how the heat gain occurs and is, therefore, a better initial design guide.

Let us explore the admittance theory further.

Admittance Theory

Admittance theory deals with the thermal transfer that occurs as the temperature varies. Basically, it is an expression of the Second Law of Thermodynamics, which states that heat can flow only from a higher intensity to a lower intensity. There is also the Zeroth Law of Thermodynamics, which follows from both the First and Second Laws and states that if two objects with different temperatures are brought into physical contact, the temperatures of these objects will move toward thermal equilibrium. Based on this, we can consider how temperatures will stabilize within a space that experiences heat gain.

If a room that is 20 foot square and 10 feet high has an hourly heat gain of 12,000 $BTUH_{sensible}$, the interior temperature would tend to increase by over 165° F if all the gain were added only to the air. However, if the space were surrounded with at least 1 inch of masonry on all six exposures, the theoretical temperature increase from the same heat gain would be less than 3° F. This is based on the assumption that the heat gain is distributed into both the ambient air and the surrounding masonry.

$$BTUH = Weight \times Specific\ Heat \times \Delta T$$
$$\Delta T = \frac{BTUH}{Weight \times Specific\ Heat}$$

The interior volume of the room is 4000 cubic feet. Since air has a specific heat of 0.24 and a density of 0.075 pound per cubic foot, the 12,000 $BTUH_{sensible}$ heat gain would result in a temperature increase of 166.67° F if the gain is absorbed solely by the room air.

$$\Delta T = \frac{12,000\ BTU}{4000\ cu\ ft \times 0.075\ lb/cu\ ft \times 0.24\ BTU/lb°\ F}$$
$$= \frac{12,000\ BTU}{4000\ cu\ ft \times 0.018\ BTU/cu\ ft°\ F} = \frac{12,000\ BTU}{72\ BTU/°\ F}$$
$$= 166.67°\ F$$

The interior surfaces of the room are all masonry with a total area of 1600 square feet. This is based on 80 linear feet of wall with a 10-foot height plus both the floor and ceiling, each at 20 feet by 20 feet. We will assume only 1 inch of masonry on the room surfaces since the time lag for the masonry to absorb increased thermal energy suggests that the thermal transfer with the masonry will not extend more than 1 inch in 1 hour. Based on this, the effective volume of masonry is 1600 square feet at a 1-inch depth, or 133.33 cubic feet. Since masonry, which has a specific heat of 0.20, typically weighs 150 pounds per cubic foot, there are 20,000 pounds of masonry lining the room. With the 12,000 BTUH$_{sensible}$ heat gain absorbed by the room air and the 1 inch of masonry on all six exposures, the temperature increase would be only 2.95° F.

$$\Delta T = \frac{12,000 \text{ BTU}}{72 \text{ BTU/}°F + [(1600 \text{ sq ft} \times 0.083 \text{ ft}) \times 150 \text{ lb/cu ft} \times 0.20 \text{ BTU/lb}°F]}$$

$$= \frac{12,000 \text{ BTU}}{72 \text{ BTU/}°F + 4000 \text{ BTU/}°F} = \frac{12,000 \text{ BTU}}{4072 \text{ BTU/}°F} = 2.95°F$$

Instantaneous Heat Gain Method

IHGM, which is the traditional way of calculating heat gain, does as its name suggests—it calculates the instantaneous heat gain that occurs during a particular hour. Since IHGM does not incorporate thermal mass as a means to adjust the size of the cooling load, it tends to somewhat overestimate the size of the mechanical system, but it does provide results that can be used for an initial estimate of equipment size. This is not a problem because the actual size of the equipment, for which we are not normally responsible, must also be established on the basis of operational factors as well as heat gain. More importantly, while it might tend to overestimate the cooling load, IHGM provides an excellent indication of the various sources of heat gain, and an understanding of this information is critical for an effective architectural design.

A basic premise of this method is that there are two sources of external heat gain—the temperature differential between inside and outside and the impact of insolation. With a transparent enclosure, these two sources operate differently. The flow of heat based on the temperature differential is calculated similarly to heat loss, whereas the solar contribution is handled as a direct entry of thermal energy through the glazing. Of course, this direct solar gain has to be adjusted for the transparency of the particular glazing and any shading that might exist. With opaque enclosing elements, the solar factor is assumed to establish an elevated surface temperature, so rather than use the actual temperature differential between the interior and exterior, an effective temperature difference is used. Although IHGM does not use thermal mass to adjust the size of the cooling load, some consideration is given to thermal mass in terms of this effective temperature differential. Since both transparent and opaque enclosing elements have a solar factor, the exposure orientation and the time are critical to the ultimate gain.

TRANSPARENT BARRIER GAIN

Transfer: BTUH = Area × "U" Coefficient × $\Delta T°F$
Direct: BTUH = Area × SHGF × SC

OPAQUE BARRIER GAIN

Transfer: BTUH = Area × "U" Coefficient × ETD

where:
SHGF = solar heat gain factor in BTUH per square feet
SC = shading coefficient
ETD = equivalent temperature differential

A more extensive outline of the IHGM is provided in the following table.

PROCEDURE FOR CALCULATING INSTANTANEOUS HEAT GAIN

How to calc. heat gain

Load Source	Equation	Reference, Table, Description	
External			
Glass Solar	BTUH = A(SC) SHGF	A:	Glass Area Calculated from Architectural Plans
		SC:	Shading Coefficient for Combination of Glass and Internal Shading **(Tables 7.18–7.20)**
		SHGF:	Solar Heat Gain Factor for the Particular Latitude, Time, and Orientation **(Table 7.16)**
			For Externally Shaded Glass, Compute the Shaded Area and Use SHGF for north Orientation
Glass Conduction	BTUH = UA (HTD)	U:	Based on the Type of Window, Glazing, and Interior Shading, if Used
		A:	Glass Area Calculated from Architectural Plans
		HTD:	Hourly Temperature Difference, Inside to Outside **(Table 7.15A)** Correct for Outside DBT and Daily Range Correct for Inside DBT
		U:	Designed Heat Transmission Coefficients
		A:	Areas Calculated from Architectural Plans
Walls	BTUH = UA (ETD)	ETD:	Equivalent Temperature Differential **(Table 7.22)** Correct for Outside DBT and Daily Range Correct for Inside DBT
		U:	Designed Heat Transmission Coefficients
		A:	Areas Calculated from Architectural Plans

PROCEDURE FOR CALCULATING INSTANTANEOUS HEAT GAIN (*Continued*)

Load Source	Equation	Reference, Table, Description		
Roofs	BTUH = UA (ETD)	ETD:	Equivalent Temperature Differential (**Table 7.23**) Correct for Outside DBT and Daily Range Correct for Inside DBT	
		U:	Designed Heat Transmission Coefficients	
Ceilings & Floors	BTUH = UA (ΔT)	A:	Areas Calculated from Architectural Plans	
		ΔT:	Design Temperature Difference	
Internal				
Lights	BTUH = Wattage (3.412 BTUH)	Wattage Input Rating Is Based on Electrical and Lighting from Plans at 3.412 BTUH per Watt-Hour		
People Sensible Latent	$BTUH_s$ = No. (Sens. H.G.) $BTUH_l$ = No. (Lat. H.G.)	No. Is the Number of People in the Space Based on Occupancy Standards Sensible Heat Gain from Occupants (**Tables 7.23 and 7.24**) Latent Heat Gain from Occupants (**Tables 7.23 and 7.24**)		
Appliances Sensible Latent	$BTUH_s$ = Heat Gain $BTUH_l$ = Heat Gain	Sensible Heat Gain from Appliances and Equipment Latent Heat Gain from Appliances and Equipment		
Infiltration or Ventilation				
Sensible	$BTUH_s$ = 1.08 CFM (ΔT) = 0.018 CFH ΔT	CFM and CFH:	Infiltration Air Circulation Change Method	
		ΔT:	Inside-Outside Air Temperature Difference, °F	
Latent	$BTUH_l$ = 4840 CFM (ΔW) = 79.5 CFH (ΔW)	ΔW:	Inside-Outside Air Humidity Ratio Difference, lb/lb, Determined from a Psychrometric Chart on Interior and Maximum Exterior Conditions	

Notes:

SC is the shading coefficient and is the same value used when the specific solar heat gain factor for a particular time is used.

SHGF is the solar heat gain factor for a particular orientation, latitude, month of the year, and time of day.

ETD is the equivalent temperature differential and establishes a temperature differential between the interior and the exterior that accommodates the actual temperature differential and the effects of insolation, modified by aspects of the construction assembly.

ΔW_{i-o} indicates the change in specific humidity, in pounds of water per pound of dry air, between the interior and exterior conditions. The assumption is that the outside specific humidity remains essentially constant throughout the day, so the daily maximum exterior DBT and WBT establish W_o.

Solar Heat Gain Factor

In general, in doing heat gain calculations, transparent materials are handled separately from opaque materials since the effects of solar radiation are quite different for these different types of material. Tables are used that list the amount of solar gain, in BTUH per square foot, that is expected to pass through single clear glazing into the interior space. The primary source for this information is the Solar Intensity and Solar Heat Gain Factor Tables, which are based on conditions for the 21st day of each month for different latitudes. These tables are derived from the *ASHRAE Fundamentals Handbook* and are found in various textbooks. Table 7.16 includes the annual solar gain for seven north latitudes, ranging from 16° N to 64° N in steps of 8°.

The following is a condensed representation of 1 month's values taken from this table for 40°N lattitude.

SHGF FOR 40° NORTH LATITUDE FOR DS SHEET GLASS

Date	Solar Time (a.m.)	Direct Normal (BUTH/ft^2)	N	E	S	W	HOR	Solar Time (p.m.)
21-Jan	8	142	5	111	75	5	14	4
	9	239	12	154	160	12	55	3
	10	274	16	124	213	16	96	2
	11	289	19	61	244	19	124	1
	12	294	20	21	254	21	133	12
Half-Day Totals			62	461	819	63	356	
	(a.m.)	(BUTH/ft^2)	N	E	S	W	HOR	(p.m.)

In this table, the times are listed at both the left and right sides. The left side lists morning times (a.m.) and is correlated with the exposures listed at the top. The right side lists the afternoon times (p.m.) and is correlated with the exposures listed at the bottom. Since the sun's path is symmetrical with respect to the north-south axis, the morning solar gains on the east are the same as the afternoon solar gains on the west.

MORNING ORIENTATIONS

Date	Solar Time (a.m.)	Direct Normal (BUTH/ft²)	N	E	S	W	HOR	Solar Time (p.m.)
21-Jan	8	142	5	111	75	5	14	4
	9	239	12	154	160	12	55	3
	10	274	16	124	213	16	96	2
	11	289	19	61	244	19	124	1
	12	294	20	21	254	21	133	12
Half-Day Totals			62	461	819	63	356	
	(a.m.)		N	W	S	E	HOR	(p.m.)

AFTERNOON ORIENTATIONS

Date	Solar Time (a.m.)	Direct Normal (BUTH/ft²)	N	E	S	W	HOR	Solar Time (p.m.)
21-Jan	8	142	5	111	75	5	14	4
	9	239	12	154	160	12	55	3
	10	274	16	124	213	16	96	2
	11	289	19	61	244	19	124	1
	12	294	20	21	254	21	133	12
Half-Day Totals			62	461	819	63	356	
	(a.m.)		N	W	S	E	HOR	(p.m.)

The chart could have been shown as below, although this would include considerable repetition of data.

ALL-DAY ORIENTATIONS

Date	Solar Time (a.m.)	Direct Normal (BUTH/ft²)	N	E	S	W	HOR	Solar Time (p.m.)
21-Jan	8	142	5	111	75	5	14	8
	9	239	12	154	160	12	55	9
	10	274	16	124	213	16	96	10
	11	289	19	61	244	19	124	11
	12	294	20	21	254	21	133	12
	1	142	19	19	244	61	124	1
	2	239	16	16	213	124	96	2
	3	274	12	12	160	154	55	3
	4	289	5	5	75	111	14	4
Full-Day Totals			124	524	1638	524	712	

Instead, the tables are usually condensed. In the condensed form, in addition to having the morning and afternoon exposures flip-flopped, the totals are only for half a day for each exposure. The half-day values are the sum of half of the 12 noon gain plus the gain for all the other listed hours. Only half of the 12 noon value is included since 12 noon is listed for both the morning and afternoon times. By combining the half-day totals for a morning exposure, as listed at the top of the table, with those for the same exposure in the afternoon, which are listed at the bottom of the table, the full-day solar radiation gain can be readily obtained. Interestingly, there might be a slight discrepancy in the full-day totals obtained by adding the gain for each hour, as shown above, or by combining the morning and afternoon half-day totals. If a discrepancy does exist, it should be merely the result of the way the 12 noon gains are rounded off when included in the half-day totals.

Table 7.16 lists the BTUH heat gain through a square foot of double-strength single glazing oriented as noted. If the glazing is not single and/or if it has some sort of shading, then a correction, known as the *shading coefficient* (SC), must be applied to the values found. Other tables indicate the various SCs that are to be used with the solar heat gain factor (SHGF) for unshaded glazing. Table 7.17 indicates the SCs for glass without shading, and Tables 7.18 and 7.19 are for glass with shading. Table 7.20 is for horizontal skylights. To determine the amount of sensible heat gain in BTUH per square foot of glazing, multiply the SHGF by the SC.

$$\text{BTUH per square foot of glazing} = (SC)\,SHGF$$

The SCs are intended for use with glazing that is exposed to solar radiation. When the glazing itself is shaded by an external shading device, whether this device is architectural or natural (e.g., a tree), then we should use the SHGF for the northern exposure for those portions of the glazing that are in the shadow of the exterior shading device. We should recognize that while the direct rays from the sun are blocked, diffuse radiation still exists, although the shaded solar gain should be less than the northern exposure since there is no direct exposure to the sky dome. However, the northern exposure provides a reasonable indication of the solar gain with exterior shading for latitudes of 24° north latitude or higher. At latitudes below 24° north, a northern exposure can have considerable direct solar gain in the early morning and late afternoon.

Conduction Across Glazing

While the majority of heat gain across any glazed opening occurs as a result of insolation, since the glazing is not normally an effective insulator, consideration must also be given to the thermal transfer that occurs due to the inside–outside temperature differential. This is accomplished as with heat loss calculations but with the

Table 7.16A: SOLAR HEAT GAIN FACTOR FOR 16° NORTH LATITUDE FOR DS SHEET GLASS

Date	Solar Time (am)	Direct Normal (BUTH/ft²)	N	NNE	NE	ENE	E	ESE	SE	SSE	S	SSW	SW	WSW	W	WNW	NW	NNW	HOR	Solar Time (pm)
21-Jan	7	141	5	6	44	92	124	134	126	96	49	6	5	5	5	5	5	5	14	5
	8	262	14	15	55	147	210	240	233	189	114	25	14	14	14	14	14	14	79	4
	9	300	21	21	32	122	200	244	251	219	152	58	22	21	21	21	21	21	150	3
	10	317	26	26	27	66	150	209	233	223	178	102	31	26	26	26	26	26	203	2
	11	325	29	29	29	31	77	148	195	210	194	146	75	31	29	29	29	29	36	1
	12	327	30	30	30	30	32	73	139	184	199	184	138	72	32	30	30	30	248	12
HALF-DAY TOTALS			**110**	**112**	**202**	**473**	**777**	**1012**	**1108**	**1029**	**787**	**429**	**216**	**133**	**111**	**110**	**110**	**110**	**606**	
21-Feb	7	182	8	17	84	138	169	172	150	103	36	8	8	8	8	8	8	8	25	65
	8	273	17	19	96	180	231	247	224	166	77	18	17	17	17	17	17	17	101	4
	9	305	23	24	64	153	214	242	233	188	110	30	23	23	23	23	23	23	174	3
	10	319	28	29	33	92	16	202	211	188	134	61	30	28	28	28	28	28	229	2
	11	326	32	32	32	37	83	136	167	172	149	102	49	33	32	32	32	32	263	1
	12	328	33	33	33	33	34	60	107	142	154	142	106	60	34	33	33	33	275	12
HALF-DAY TOTALS			**125**	**138**	**326**	**617**	**730**	**1029**	**1039**	**888**	**583**	**290**	**180**	**139**	**125**	**125**	**125**	**125**	**930**	
21-Mar	7	201	11	53	124	172	192	183	145	82	15	10	10	10	10	10	10	10	40	5
	8	272	20	50	140	205	239	235	195	123	35	19	19	19	19	19	19	19	120	4
	9	299	26	35	109	179	218	225	197	138	57	27	26	26	26	26	26	26	192	3
	10	312	31	33	61	120	165	182	172	134	76	34	32	31	31	31	31	31	247	2
	11	318	34	35	36	53	87	114	125	116	89	55	36	35	34	34	34	34	280	1
	12	320	35	35	36	36	37	47	69	87	93	86	68	47	37	38	36	36	291	12
HALF-DAY TOTALS			**140**	**224**	**488**	**747**	**920**	**963**	**869**	**637**	**319**	**188**	**157**	**145**	**139**	**139**	**138**	**138**	**1025**	
21-Apr	6	14	2	8	12	14	14	12	8	2	1	1	1	1	1	1	1	1	1	6
	7	197	24	94	153	187	191	167	117	45	14	13	13	13	13	13	13	13	53	5
	8	256	27	99	172	216	227	204	150	69	24	22	22	22	22	22	22	22	131	4
	9	280	31	79	149	193	208	193	147	77	31	29	29	29	29	29	29	29	197	3
	10	293	35	54	102	141	158	151	120	73	37	34	33	33	33	33	33	33	249	2
	11	299	38	40	54	72	86	88	78	60	43	38	38	36	36	36	36	37	279	1
	12	301	39	39	39	40	40	41	43	45	45	45	43	41	40	39	39	39	289	12
HALF-DAY TOTALS			**177**	**394**	**662**	**843**	**904**	**836**	**642**	**349**	**173**	**160**	**158**	**155**	**154**	**154**	**154**	**155**	**1055**	
21-May	6	44	14	30	41	45	43	34	19	4	3	3	3	3	3	3	3	3	5	6
	7	193	50	120	168	19	185	150	92	24	16	16	16	16	16	16	16	17	62	5
	8	244	52	132	189	218	215	179	115	38	25	24	24	24	24	24	24	25	135	4
	9	268	49	116	171	198	197	167	109	45	32	30	30	30	30	30	30	32	197	3
	10	280	47	89	130	151	150	126	84	44	37	35	35	35	35	35	35	37	245	2
	11	286	47	63	79	87	83	70	52	41	40	39	38	38	38	39	39	41	273	1
	12	288	46	46	44	43	42	41	41	41	41	41	41	41	42	43	44	46	282	12
HALF-DAY TOTALS			**282**	**573**	**800**	**740**	**894**	**747**	**492**	**217**	**174**	**168**	**167**	**167**	**167**	**169**	**169**	**178**	**1058**	
21-Jun	6	53	20	39	52	55	51	39	20	4	4	4	4	4	4	4	4	4	7	6
	7	188	62	128	172	190	179	141	80	20	16	16	16	16	16	16	16	18	64	5
	8	238	66	142	184	217	207	167	99	31	25	25	25	25	25	25	25	27	135	4
	9	261	63	130	178	198	190	154	93	37	31	31	31	31	31	31	31	33	194	3
	10	273	59	104	140	154	145	115	70	39	37	36	36	36	36	36	36	38	241	2
	11	279	57	76	90	92	82	63	46	41	40	39	39	39	39	40	41	43	268	1
	12	281	57	55	50	45	43	42	41	41	41	41	41	42	42	45	50	55	277	12
HALF-DAY TOTALS			**356**	**647**	**841**	**929**	**876**	**700**	**429**	**193**	**174**	**172**	**172**	**172**	**172**	**175**	**178**	**191**	**1048**	
	(am)		N	NNW	NW	WNW	W	WSW	SW	SSW	S	SSE	SE	ESE	E	ENE	NE	NNE	HOR	(pm)

Table 7.16A (*Continued*)

Date	Solar Time (am)	Direct Normal (BUTH/ft²)	N	NNE	NE	ENE	E	ESE	SE	SSE	S	SSW	SW	WSW	W	WNW	NW	NNW	HOR	Solar Time (pm)
21-Jul	6	41	14	29	39	42	40	31	18	4	3	3	3	3	3	3	3	3	6	6
	7	184	51	118	164	185	179	145	88	23	16	16	16	16	16	16	16	17	62	5
	8	236	55	132	187	214	210	174	111	37	25	25	25	25	25	25	25	26	133	4
	9	259	52	117	170	196	193	163	106	44	32	31	31	31	31	31	31	33	194	3
	10	272	50	92	131	151	148	123	81	44	38	36	36	36	36	36	36	38	241	2
	11	278	49	66	81	88	83	69	52	42	41	40	39	39	39	40	40	42	289	1
	12	279	49	48	46	44	43	42	42	42	42	42	42	42	43	44	46	48	277	12
HALF-DAY TOTALS			296	578	795	898	875	726	477	215	176	172	171	171	172	173	174	183	1064	
21-Aug	6	11	2	7	10	12	12	10	6	2	1	1	1	1	1	1	1	1	1	6
	7	180	26	92	145	176	180	156	109	42	15	14	14	14	14	14	14	14	53	5
	8	240	30	100	168	209	219	196	143	65	25	23	23	23	23	23	23	23	128	4
	9	266	33	82	148	190	203	187	142	74	33	30	30	30	30	30	30	30	193	3
	10	279	37	58	104	140	155	147	117	71	39	36	35	35	35	35	35	35	243	2
	11	285	40	43	57	75	86	87	76	59	44	40	39	38	38	38	38	39	273	1
	12	287	41	41	41	42	42	43	44	45	46	45	44	43	42	41	41	41	282	12
HALF-DAY TOTALS			189	403	653	823	876	805	615	336	180	167	164	163	162	162	162	163	1032	
21-Sep	7	179	12	50	114	158	176	168	133	76	15	11	11	11	11	11	11	11	39	5
	8	253	21	49	134	196	227	224	186	119	36	20	20	20	20	20	20	20	116	4
	9	281	28	36	106	173	211	217	191	134	57	28	27	27	27	27	27	27	185	3
	10	295	32	34	61	118	16	178	168	132	76	35	33	32	32	32	32	32	236	2
	11	302	35	36	37	54	86	113	123	114	88	56	38	36	35	35	35	35	271	1
	12	304	36	36	37	38	39	49	69	86	93	86	69	48	39	38	37	36	282	12
HALF-DAY TOTALS			146	223	471	718	736	925	836	618	319	193	164	150	145	144	144	143	988	
21-Oct	7	166	8	18	79	128	156	159	139	95	33	9	8	8	8	8	8	8	25	5
	8	259	17	20	95	174	223	237	215	159	74	19	17	17	17	17	17	17	99	4
	9	292	24	25	65	150	209	235	225	187	106	31	24	24	24	24	24	24	170	3
	10	307	29	30	34	92	158	197	205	183	130	60	31	29	29	29	29	29	224	2
	11	314	32	32	33	39	83	133	163	167	145	100	49	34	32	32	32	32	258	1
	12	316	33	33	33	34	35	60	105	139	150	138	104	60	35	34	33	33	270	12
HALF-DAY TOTALS			127	142	323	600	847	991	1000	861	563	288	181	142	128	127	127	127	911	
21-Nov	7	134	2	6	43	89	119	129	120	92	47	6	5	5	5	5	5	5	14	5
	8	255	115	15	55	145	206	235	228	185	111	25	15	15	15	15	15	15	78	4
	9	295	21	21	33	121	197	241	247	215	150	57	22	21	21	21	21	21	149	3
	10	312	26	26	28	67	147	206	230	220	176	100	31	26	26	26	26	26	201	2
	11	320	29	29	29	31	77	146	192	207	191	144	74	31	29	29	29	29	234	1
	12	322	30	30	30	30	32	72	137	181	196	181	137	72	32	30	30	30	246	12
HALF-DAY TOTALS			108	112	203	468	762	993	1086	1010	773	423	216	134	112	111	111	111	799	
21-Dec	7	118	4	5	30	72	101	112	107	85	48	7	4	4	4	4	4	4	10	5
	8	255	13	14	41	132	198	233	231	193	124	33	13	13	13	13	13	13	69	4
	9	297	20	20	25	108	191	241	254	227	165	72	21	20	20	20	20	20	138	3
	10	315	25	25	26	56	144	208	239	233	192	117	35	25	25	25	25	25	191	2
	11	323	28	28	28	29	73	150	202	221	207	161	86	30	28	28	28	28	223	1
	12	325	29	29	29	29	30	77	149	197	212	196	149	76	30	29	29	29	234	12
HALF-DAY TOTALS			105	107	165	412	722	983	1108	1058	842	488	234	130	105	105	105	105	748	
	(am)		N	NNW	NW	WNW	W	WSW	SW	SSW	S	SSE	SE	ESE	E	ENE	NE	NNE	HOR	(pm)

Table 7.16B: SOLAR HEAT GAIN FACTOR FOR 24° NORTH LATITUDE FOR DS SHEET GLASS

Date	Solar Time (am)	Direct Normal (BUTH/ft²)	N	NNE	NE	ENE	E	ESE	SE	SSE	S	SSW	SW	WSW	W	WNW	NW	NNW	HOR	Solar Time (pm)
21-Jan	7	71	2	3	21	45	62	67	63	49	25	3	2	2	2	2	2	2	5	5
	8	239	12	12	41	128	190	221	218	181	114	28	12	12	12	12	12	12	55	4
	9	288	18	18	23	106	190	240	253	227	166	73	19	18	18	18	18	18	121	3
	10	308	23	23	24	53	144	211	245	241	200	125	38	24	23	23	23	23	172	2
	11	317	26	26	26	27	73	156	211	234	220	173	95	29	26	26	26	26	204	1
	12	320	27	27	27	27	29	82	160	210	227	210	160	81	29	27	27	27	214	12
HALF-DAY TOTALS			**95**	**96**	**149**	**373**	**674**	**936**	**1070**	**1037**	**839**	**507**	**246**	**126**	**96**	**95**	**95**	**95**	**664**	
21-Feb	7	153	6	12	67	114	141	145	128	90	33	6	6	6	6	6	6	6	17	65
	8	262	15	16	80	165	220	240	224	172	89	17	15	15	15	15	15	15	83	4
	9	297	21	22	46	138	208	244	243	205	133	42	22	21	21	21	21	21	153	3
	10	314	26	26	28	76	157	209	228	213	165	87	28	26	26	26	26	26	205	2
	11	321	29	29	29	31	80	148	191	203	185	137	68	31	29	29	29	29	238	1
	12	323	30	30	30	30	32	70	134	177	192	177	133	70	32	30	30	30	249	12
HALF-DAY TOTALS			**112**	**120**	**265**	**539**	**822**	**1021**	**1081**	**972**	**701**	**378**	**206**	**134**	**113**	**112**	**112**	**112**	**821**	
21-Mar	7	194	11	45	115	164	186	180	145	86	17	10	10	10	10	10	10	10	36	5
	8	267	18	35	124	195	234	237	204	138	48	19	18	18	18	18	18	18	112	4
	9	295	25	27	85	165	215	232	214	163	82	27	25	25	25	25	25	25	180	3
	10	309	30	31	41	103	162	194	195	168	112	47	31	30	30	30	30	30	232	2
	11	315	33	33	34	42	85	129	154	155	139	86	43	34	33	33	33	33	264	1
	12	317	34	34	34	34	35	56	96	126	137	126	95	56	35	34	34	34	275	12
HALF-DAY TOTALS			**134**	**188**	**416**	**686**	**900**	**1000**	**960**	**773**	**467**	**252**	**175**	**145**	**134**	**133**	**133**	**133**	**962**	
21-Apr	6	40	6	21	33	39	39	33	22	7	2	2	2	2	2	2	2	2	4	6
	7	203	20	88	151	189	197	176	127	55	15	14	14	14	14	14	14	14	58	5
	8	256	24	80	159	209	228	212	164	88	24	22	22	22	22	22	22	22	132	4
	9	280	30	54	126	181	208	203	169	105	39	29	28	28	28	28	28	28	195	3
	10	292	34	37	75	125	157	165	148	107	56	35	33	33	33	33	33	33	244	2
	11	298	36	37	40	59	85	103	106	94	70	45	38	37	36	36	36	36	274	1
	12	299	37	37	38	38	39	46	59	70	75	70	58	45	39	38	38	37	283	12
HALF-DAY TOTALS			**169**	**336**	**603**	**821**	**934**	**915**	**766**	**491**	**244**	**182**	**166**	**159**	**155**	**154**	**154**	**154**	**1049**	
21-May	6	86	25	57	79	87	84	66	38	8	6	6	6	6	6	6	6	6	13	6
	7	203	43	117	171	199	196	163	105	32	17	17	17	17	17	17	17	18	73	5
	8	248	38/	114	178	214	218	190	132	54	26	25	25	25	25	25	25	26	142	4
	9	269	35	88	150	188	198	179	132	66	33	31	31	31	31	31	31	31	301	3
	10	280	38	59	103	137	150	141	111	67	39	36	35	35	35	35	35	36	247	2
	11	286	40	43	55	72	83	84	75	58	44	40	39	38	38	38	38	39	274	1
	12	288	41	41	41	41	42	43	44	46	46	46	44	43	42	42	42	42	282	12
HALF-DAY TOTALS			**202**	**499**	**757**	**918**	**950**	**845**	**615**	**308**	**188**	**178**	**175**	**174**	**173**	**173**	**173**	**177**	**1191**	
21-Jun	6	97	36	70	93	101	94	73	39	8	7	7	7	7	7	7	7	8	17	6
	7	201	55	127	177	199	192	155	94	26	18	18	18	18	18	18	18	20	77	5
	8	242	50	126	184	214	212	179	117	43	27	26	26	26	26	26	26	27	145	4
	9	263	43	102	158	189	192	168	116	53	34	32	32	32	32	32	32	33	201	3
	10	274	41	72	113	140	146	131	96	55	39	36	36	36	36	36	36	38	245	2
	11	279	42	50	65	77	82	77	64	49	42	41	40	39	39	39	40	41	271	1
	12	281	43	43	43	43	43	43	43	43	43	43	43	43	43	43	43	43	279	12
HALF-DAY TOTALS			**289**	**569**	**812**	**942**	**940**	**805**	**548**	**256**	**189**	**182**	**181**	**180**	**180**	**180**	**181**	**189**	**1096**	
	(am)		N	NNW	NW	WNW	W	WSW	SW	SSW	S	SSE	SE	ESE	E	ENE	NE	NNE	HOR	(pm)

Table 7.16B (*Continued*)

Date	Solar Time (am)	Direct Normal (BUTH/ft²)	N	NNE	NE	ENE	E	ESE	SE	SSE	S	SSW	SW	WSW	W	WNW	NW	NNW	HOR	Solar Time (pm)
21-Jul	6	81	26	56	76	84	80	63	36	8	6	6	6	6	6	6	6	6	12	6
	7	195	45	116	168	194	190	158	101	31	18	18	18	18	18	18	18	18	73	5
	8	239	41	115	176	210	213	185	128	52	27	26	26	26	26	26	26	26	141	4
	9	261	37	90	150	186	195	175	129	64	34	32	32	32	32	32	32	32	198	3
	10	272	39	62	104	137	149	139	108	65	39	37	36	36	36	36	36	37	243	2
	11	278	41	44	58	73	83	83	73	57	44	41	40	39	39	39	39	40	270	1
	12	280	42	42	42	43	43	44	45	46	46	46	45	43	43	42	42	42	278	12
HALF-DAY TOTALS			**250**	**504**	**753**	**906**	**932**	**825**	**598**	**300**	**191**	**183**	**181**	**179**	**179**	**178**	**178**	**180**	**1076**	
21-Aug	6	35	6	20	30	35	35	30	19	6	2	2	2	2	2	2	2	2	4	6
	7	186	22	87	144	179	186	165	119	51	16	15	15	15	15	15	15	15	58	5
	8	241	26	82	156	203	220	204	157	84	26	24	24	24	24	24	24	24	130	4
	9	265	32	57	126	178	202	197	162	101	39	31	30	30	30	30	30	30	191	3
	10	278	36	40	78	125	155	161	143	103	55	37	35	35	35	35	35	35	239	2
	11	284	38	39	42	61	85	101	104	91	68	46	40	38	37	37	37	37	268	1
	12	286	38	39	40	40	41	47	58	69	72	68	58	47	41	40	40	39	277	12
HALF-DAY TOTALS			**179**	**345**	**596**	**801**	**904**	**882**	**733**	**471**	**242**	**189**	**175**	**168**	**164**	**163**	**163**	**163**	**1029**	
21-Sep	8	248	19	36	119	185	222	225	194	132	48	20	19	19	19	19	19	19	108	4
	9	278	26	28	84	160	207	223	206	158	81	28	26	26	26	26	26	26	174	3
	10	292	31	32	42	101	158	188	190	163	110	48	32	31	31	31	31	31	224	2
	11	299	34	34	35	43	84	127	151	151	128	86	44	35	34	34	34	34	256	1
	12	301	35	35	35	36	37	57	95	124	134	124	94	57	37	36	36	36	266	12
HALF-DAY TOTALS			**128**	**148**	**298**	**507**	**690**	**792**	**789**	**666**	**434**	**244**	**168**	**140**	**129**	**128**	**128**	**128**	**895**	
21-Oct	7	138	6	12	62	104	129	133	117	82	31	7	6	6	6	6	6	6	17	5
	8	247	16	17	79	159	211	230	214	164	85	17	16	16	16	16	16	16	82	4
	9	284	22	23	47	135	202	237	235	198	128	41	23	22	22	22	22	22	150	3
	10	301	27	27	29	77	154	204	222	207	160	85	29	27	27	27	27	27	201	2
	11	309	30	30	30	33	80	145	186	198	180	133	67	32	30	30	30	30	233	1
	12	311	31	31	31	31	33	70	131	173	187	172	130	69	33	31	31	31	244	12
HALF-DAY TOTALS			**117**	**125**	**263**	**524**	**793**	**984**	**1040**	**936**	**678**	**369**	**206**	**138**	**118**	**117**	**117**	**117**	**805**	
21-Nov	7	67	2	3	20	43	59	64	60	46	24	3	2	2	2	2	2	2	5	5
	8	232	12	13	42	126	186	216	213	177	111	28	12	12	12	12	12	12	55	4
	9	282	19	19	23	106	187	236	249	223	163	71	20	19	19	19	19	19	120	3
	10	303	23	23	24	53	143	209	241	237	197	123	37	24	23	23	23	23	171	2
	11	312	26	26	26	28	73	154	209	230	217	171	93	29	26	26	26	26	202	1
	12	315	27	27	27	27	29	81	158	207	224	207	158	80	29	27	27	27	213	12
HALF-DAY TOTALS			**96**	**98**	**149**	**370**	**663**	**920**	**1051**	**1017**	**824**	**500**	**243**	**126**	**97**	**96**	**96**	**96**	**660**	
21-Dec	7	30	1	1	7	18	25	28	27	21	12	2	1	1	1	1	1	1	2	5
	8	225	10	10	29	112	174	208	209	178	118	35	11	10	10	10	10	10	44	4
	9	281	17	17	19	93	180	234	252	231	174	84	18	17	17	17	17	17	107	3
	10	304	22	22	22	44	137	209	247	247	209	137	44	22	22	22	22	22	157	2
	11	314	25	25	25	26	69	156	216	241	230	183	104	29	25	25	25	25	188	1
	12	317	26	26	26	26	27	85	167	219	237	219	167	84	27	26	26	26	199	12
HALF-DAY TOTALS			**88**	**88**	**115**	**306**	**599**	**878**	**1035**	**1028**	**862**	**551**	**262**	**121**	**89**	**88**	**88**	**88**	**598**	
	(am)		N	NNW	NW	WNW	W	WSW	SW	SSW	S	SSE	SE	ESE	E	ENE	NE	NNE	HOR	(pm)

Table 7.16C: SOLAR HEAT GAIN FACTOR FOR 32° NORTH LATITUDE FOR DS SHEET GLASS

Date	Solar Time (am)	Direct Normal (BUTH/ft²)	N	NNE	NE	ENE	E	ESE	SE	SSE	S	SSW	SW	WSW	W	WNW	NW	NNW	HOR	Solar Time (pm)
21-Jan	7	1	0	0	0	1	1	1	1	1	0	0	0	0	0	0	0	0	0	5
	8	203	9	9	29	105	160	189	189	159	103	28	9	9	9	9	9	9	32	4
	9	269	15	15	17	91	175	229	246	225	169	82	17	15	15	15	15	15	88	3
	10	295	20	20	20	41	135	209	249	250	212	141	46	20	20	20	20	20	136	2
	11	306	23	23	23	24	25	159	221	249	238	191	110	29	23	23	23	23	166	1
	12	310	24	24	24	24	25	88	174	228	246	228	174	88	25	24	24	24	176	12
HALF-DAY TOTALS			79	79	101	274	509	831	993	998	845	556	269	117	80	79	79	79	510	
21-Feb	7	112	4	7	47	82	102	106	95	67	26	4	4	4	4	4	4	4	9	5
	8	245	13	14	65	149	205	228	216	170	95	17	13	13	13	13	13	13	64	4
	9	287	19	19	32	122	199	242	248	216	149	55	20	19	19	19	19	19	127	3
	10	305	24	24	25	62	151	213	241	232	189	112	31	24	24	24	24	24	176	2
	11	314	26	26	26	28	76	156	208	227	212	165	87	28	26	26	26	26	207	1
	12	316	27	27	27	27	29	79	155	204	221	204	155	79	29	27	27	27	217	12
HALF-DAY TOTALS			100	104	209	457	748	985	1086	1014	782	455	233	128	101	100	100	100	692	
21-Mar	7	185	10	37	105	153	176	173	142	88	20	9	9	9	9	9	9	9	32	5
	8	260	17	25	107	183	227	237	209	150	62	18	17	17	17	17	17	17	100	4
	9	290	23	25	64	151	210	237	227	183	107	30	23	23	23	23	23	23	164	3
	10	304	28	28	30	87	158	202	215	195	144	70	29	28	28	28	28	28	211	2
	11	311	31	31	31	34	82	142	179	188	168	120	59	32	31	31	31	31	242	1
	12	313	32	32	32	32	33	66	122	162	176	162	122	66	33	32	32	32	252	12
HALF-DAY TOTALS			125	162	353	624	870	1024	1033	885	589	328	198	142	125	124	124	124	875	
21-Apr	6	66	9	35	54	65	66	56	38	12	4	3	3	3	3	3	3	3	7	6
	7	206	17	80	146	188	200	182	136	65	16	14	14	14	14	14	14	14	61	5
	8	255	23	61	144	200	227	219	177	107	30	22	22	22	22	22	22	22	129	4
	9	278	28	36	103	168	206	212	187	133	58	29	28	28	28	28	28	28	188	3
	10	290	32	34	52	108	155	177	172	141	87	39	33	32	32	32	32	32	233	2
	11	295	35	35	36	47	83	118	135	132	108	70	40	36	35	35	35	35	262	1
	12	297	36	36	36	37	38	53	82	106	115	106	82	53	38	37	36	36	271	12
HALF-DAY TOTALS			162	299	553	795	956	991	886	643	361	230	181	162	153	153	152	152	1016	
21-May	6	119	33	77	108	121	116	94	56	13	8	8	8	8	8	8	8	9	21	6
	7	211	36	111	170	202	204	174	118	42	19	18	18	18	18	18	18	19	81	5
	8	250	29	94	165	208	220	199	149	73	27	25	25	25	25	25	25	25	146	4
	9	269	33	61	128	177	198	190	155	93	37	32	31	31	31	31	31	31	201	3
	10	280	36	40	76	121	150	156	138	99	54	37	35	35	35	35	35	35	243	2
	11	285	38	39	42	59	83	99	102	90	68	47	40	39	37	37	37	37	269	1
	12	286	38	39	40	40	41	47	59	70	74	70	59	47	41	40	40	39	277	12
HALF-DAY TOTALS			224	442	709	908	992	936	748	445	250	202	187	180	175	174	174	176	1100	
21-Jun	6	1331	44	92	123	135	127	99	55	12	10	10	10	10	10	10	10	11	28	6
	7	210	47	122	176	204	201	168	108	35	20	20	20	20	20	20	20	21	88	5
	8	245	36	106	171	208	214	189	135	60	28	27	27	27	27	27	27	27	151	4
	9	264	35	74	137	178	193	180	139	77	35	32	32	32	32	32	32	32	204	3
	10	274	38	47	86	125	146	145	123	83	45	38	36	36	36	36	36	36	244	2
	11	279	40	41	47	64	82	91	89	75	56	43	41	40	39	39	39	39	269	1
	12	280	41	41	41	42	42	46	52	58	60	58	52	46	42	42	41	41	276	12
HALF-DAY TOTALS			261	503	761	935	984	895	675	371	224	199	192	188	185	185	185	187	1122	
	(am)		N	NNW	NW	WNW	W	WSW	SW	SSW	S	SSE	SE	ESE	E	ENE	NE	NNE	HOR	(pm)

Table 7.16C (*Continued*)

Date	Solar Time (am)	Direct Normal (BUTH/ft²)	N	NNE	NE	ENE	E	ESE	SE	SSE	S	SSW	SW	WSW	W	WNW	NW	NNW	HOR	Solar Time (pm)
21-Jul	6	113	34	76	105	117	113	90	53	12	9	9	9	9	9	9	9	9	22	6
	7	203	38	111	167	198	198	169	114	41	20	19	19	19	19	19	19	19	81	5
	8	241	31	95	163	204	215	194	145	70	28	26	26	26	26	26	26	26	145	4
	9	261	34	64	129	175	195	186	150	90	37	32	32	32	32	32	32	32	198	3
	10	271	37	42	78	121	148	153	134	96	53	38	36	36	36	36	36	36	240	2
	11	277	39	40	43	60	83	98	99	88	66	47	41	40	38	38	38	38	265	1
	12	279	40	40	41	41	42	48	58	68	72	68	58	48	42	41	41	40	273	12
HALF-DAY TOTALS			**233**	**448**	**706**	**896**	**973**	**914**	**724**	**431**	**249**	**205**	**192**	**186**	**181**	**181**	**181**	**180**	**1088**	
21-Aug	6	59	10	33	50	60	60	51	34	11	4	4	4	4	4	4	4	4	8	6
	7	190	19	79	141	179	190	172	128	61	17	15	15	15	15	15	18	15	61	5
	8	240	25	63	141	195	219	210	170	102	31	23	23	23	23	23	24	23	128	4
	9	263	30	39	104	166	200	206	181	127	57	31	29	29	29	29	29	29	185	3
	10	276	34	36	55	109	153	173	167	136	84	40	35	34	34	34	34	34	229	2
	11	282	36	37	39	50	84	116	131	127	104	69	41	38	36	36	36	36	256	1
	12	284	37	37	37	39	40	54	81	103	111	103	81	54	40	39	37	37	265	12
HALF-DAY TOTALS			**173**	**306**	**549**	**779**	**926**	**955**	**852**	**616**	**353**	**234**	**188**	**170**	**161**	**161**	**164**	**160**	**1000**	
21-Sep	7	163	10	35	96	139	159	156	128	80	20	10	10	10	10	10	10	10	31	5
	8	240	18	26	103	173	215	224	198	143	60	19	18	18	18	18	18	18	96	4
	9	272	24	26	64	146	202	227	218	177	105	31	24	24	24	24	24	24	158	3
	10	287	29	29	32	86	154	196	208	189	141	70	31	29	29	29	29	29	204	2
	11	294	23	32	32	36	81	139	174	182	163	118	59	34	32	32	32	32	234	1
	12	296	22	33	33	33	35	66	120	158	171	158	120	66	35	33	33	33	244	12
HALF-DAY TOTALS			**115**	**165**	**344**	**597**	**829**	**975**	**986**	**850**	**575**	**327**	**202**	**148**	**131**	**130**	**130**	**130**	**845**	
21-Oct	7	99	4	7	43	74	92	96	85	60	24	5	4	4	4	4	4	4	10	5
	8	229	13	15	63	143	195	217	206	162	90	17	13	13	13	13	13	13	63	4
	9	273	20	20	33	120	193	234	239	208	144	54	21	20	20	20	20	20	125	3
	10	293	24	24	26	62	147	207	234	225	183	109	32	24	24	24	24	24	173	2
	11	302	27	27	27	29	76	152	203	221	207	160	85	29	27	27	27	27	203	1
	12	304	28	28	28	28	30	78	151	199	215	199	151	78	30	28	28	28	213	12
HALF-DAY TOTALS			**102**	**107**	**206**	**442**	**718**	**945**	**1043**	**976**	**756**	**445**	**231**	**129**	**103**	**102**	**102**	**102**	**681**	
21-Nov	7	2	0	0	0	1	1	1	1	1	1	0	0	0	0	0	0	0	0	5
	8	196	9	9	29	103	156	184	184	155	100	27	9	9	9	9	9	9	32	4
	9	263	16	16	17	90	173	225	241	221	166	80	17	16	16	16	16	16	88	3
	10	289	20	20	21	41	134	206	245	246	209	138	45	21	20	20	20	20	136	2
	11	301	23	23	23	24	67	157	218	245	234	188	109	29	23	23	23	23	165	1
	12	304	24	24	24	24	25	87	171	224	243	224	171	87	25	24	24	24	175	12
HALF-DAY TOTALS			**80**	**80**	**102**	**271**	**544**	**817**	**975**	**980**	**832**	**545**	**266**	**119**	**81**	**80**	**80**	**80**	**509**	
21-Dec	8	176	7	7	19	84	135	163	166	143	97	31	7	7	7	7	7	7	22	4
	9	257	14	14	15	77	162	218	238	222	171	89	15	14	14	14	14	14	72	3
	10	288	18	18	18	34	127	204	246	251	216	148	52	19	18	18	18	18	119	2
	11	301	21	21	21	22	63	157	222	252	243	197	116	29	21	21	21	21	148	1
	12	304	22	22	22	22	23	89	177	232	252	232	177	89	23	22	22	22	158	12
HALF-DAY TOTALS			**71**	**71**	**84**	**228**	**499**	**787**	**961**	**984**	**853**	**581**	**279**	**114**	**72**	**71**	**71**	**71**	**440**	
	(am)		N	NNW	NW	WNW	W	WSW	SW	SSW	S	SSE	SE	ESE	E	ENE	NE	NNE	HOR	(pm)

Table 7.16D: SOLAR HEAT GAIN FACTOR FOR 40° NORTH LATITUDE FOR DS SHEET GLASS

Date	Solar Time (am)	Direct Normal (BUTH/ft²)	N	NNE	NE	ENE	E	ESE	SE	SSE	S	SSW	SW	WSW	W	WNW	NW	NNW	HOR	Solar Time (pm)
21-Jan	8	142	5	5	17	71	111	132	133	114	75	22	6	5	5	5	5	5	14	4
	9	239	12	12	13	74	154	205	224	209	160	82	13	12	12	12	12	12	55	3
	10	274	16	16	16	31	124	199	241	246	213	146	51	17	16	16	16	16	96	2
	11	289	19	19	19	20	61	156	222	252	244	198	118	28	19	19	19	19	124	1
	12	294	20	20	20	20	21	90	179	234	254	234	179	90	21	20	20	20	133	12
HALF-DAY TOTALS			**62**	**62**	**75**	**206**	**461**	**737**	**910**	**938**	**819**	**565**	**278**	**107**	**63**	**62**	**62**	**62**	**356**	
21-Feb	7	55	2	3	23	40	51	53	47	34	14	2	2	2	2	2	2	2	4	5
	8	219	10	11	50	129	183	206	199	160	94	18	10	10	10	10	10	10	43	4
	9	271	16	16	22	107	186	234	245	218	157	66	17	16	16	16	16	16	98	3
	10	294	21	21	21	49	143	211	246	243	203	129	38	21	21	21	21	21	143	2
	11	304	23	23	23	24	71	160	219	244	231	184	103	27	23	23	23	23	171	1
	12	307	24	24	24	24	25	86	170	222	241	222	170	86	25	24	24	24	180	12
HALF-DAY TOTALS			**84**	**86**	**151**	**361**	**647**	**907**	**1041**	**1010**	**820**	**510**	**255**	**119**	**85**	**84**	**84**	**84**	**549**	
21-Mar	7	171	9	29	93	140	163	161	135	86	22	8	8	8	8	8	8	8	22	5
	8	250	16	18	91	169	218	232	211	157	74	17	16	16	16	16	16	16	85	4
	9	282	21	22	47	136	203	238	236	198	128	40	22	21	21	21	21	21	143	3
	10	297	25	25	27	72	153	207	229	216	171	95	29	25	25	25	25	25	186	2
	11	305	28	28	28	30	78	195	198	213	197	150	77	30	28	28	28	28	213	1
	12	307	29	29	29	29	31	75	145	191	206	191	145	75	31	29	29	29	223	12
HALF-DAY TOTALS			**114**	**137**	**301**	**562**	**831**	**891**	**1082**	**880**	**695**	**506**	**225**	**138**	**114**	**113**	**113**	**113**	**761**	
21-Apr	6	89	11	46	72	87	88	76	52	18	5	5	5	5	5	5	5	5	11	6
	7	206	16	71	140	185	201	186	143	75	16	14	14	14	14	14	14	14	61	5
	8	252	22	44	128	190	224	223	188	124	41	22	21	21	21	21	21	21	123	4
	9	274	27	29	80	155	202	219	203	156	83	29	27	27	27	27	27	27	177	3
	10	286	31	31	37	92	152	187	193	170	121	56	32	31	31	31	31	41	217	2
	11	292	33	33	34	39	81	130	160	166	146	102	52	35	33	33	33	33	243	1
	12	293	34	34	34	34	36	62	108	142	154	142	108	62	36	34	34	34	252	12
HALF-DAY TOTALS			**157**	**271**	**508**	**765**	**966**	**1052**	**993**	**780**	**489**	**299**	**205**	**164**	**149**	**148**	**148**	**158**	**958**	
21-May	5	1	0	1	1	1	1	1	0	0	0	0	0	0	0	0	0	0	0	7
	6	144	36	90	128	145	141	115	71	18	10	10	10	10	10	10	10	11	31	6
	7	216	28	102	165	202	209	184	131	54	20	19	19	19	19	19	19	19	87	5
	8	250	27	73	149	199	220	208	164	93	29	25	25	25	25	25	25	25	146	4
	9	267	31	42	105	164	197	200	175	121	53	32	30	30	30	30	30	30	195	3
	10	277	34	36	54	105	148	168	163	133	83	40	35	34	34	34	34	34	234	2
	11	283	36	36	38	48	81	113	130	127	105	70	42	38	36	36	36	36	257	1
	12	284	37	37	37	38	40	54	82	104	113	104	82	54	40	38	37	37	265	12
HALF-DAY TOTALS			**211**	**399**	**659**	**1033**	**1017**	**1016**	**875**	**598**	**357**	**248**	**202**	**183**	**174**	**173**	**173**	**174**	**1083**	
21-Jun	5	22	10	17	21	22	20	14	6	2	1	1	1	1	1	1	1	2	3	7
	6	155	48	104	143	159	151	121	70	17	13	13	13	13	13	13	13	14	40	6
	7	216	28	102	165	202	209	184	131	54	20	19	19	19	19	19	19	19	87	5
	8	246	30	85	156	201	216	199	152	80	29	27	27	27	27	27	27	27	153	4
	9	263	33	51	114	166	192	190	161	105	45	33	32	32	32	32	32	32	201	3
	10	272	35	38	63	109	145	158	148	116	69	39	36	35	35	35	35	35	238	2
	11	277	38	39	40	52	81	105	115	110	88	60	41	39	38	38	38	38	260	1
	12	279	38	38	38	40	41	52	72	89	95	89	72	52	41	40	38	38	267	12
HALF-DAY TOTALS			**241**	**455**	**721**	**931**	**1035**	**997**	**819**	**529**	**313**	**237**	**205**	**192**	**186**	**185**	**184**	**186**	**1116**	
	(am)		N	NNW	NW	WNW	W	WSW	SW	SSW	S	SSE	SE	ESE	E	ENE	NE	NNE	HOR	(pm)

Table 7.16D (*Continued*)

Date	Solar Time (am)	Direct Normal (BUTH/ft²)	N	NNE	NE	ENE	E	ESE	SE	SSE	S	SSW	SW	WSW	W	WNW	NW	NNW	HOR	Solar Time (pm)
21-Jul	5	2	1	2	2	2	2	1	1	0	0	0	0	0	0	0	0	0	0	7
	6	138	37	89	125	142	137	112	68	18	11	11	11	11	11	11	11	12	32	6
	7	208	30	102	163	198	204	179	127	53	21	20	20	20	20	20	20	20	88	5
	8	241	28	75	148	196	216	203	160	90	30	26	26	26	26	26	26	26	145	4
	9	259	32	44	106	163	193	196	170	118	52	33	31	31	31	31	31	31	194	3
	10	269	35	37	56	106	146	165	159	129	81	41	36	35	35	35	35	35	231	2
	11	275	37	38	40	50	81	111	127	123	102	69	43	39	37	37	37	37	254	1
	12	276	38	38	338	40	41	55	80	101	109	101	80	55	41	40	38	38	262	12
HALF-DAY TOTALS			219	406	809	877	1000	995	852	582	352	251	207	190	181	180	179	180	1075	
21-Aug	6	81	12	44	68	81	82	71	48	17	6	5	5	5	5	5	5	5	12	6
	7	191	17	71	135	177	191	177	135	70	17	16	16	16	16	16	16	16	62	5
	8	237	24	47	126	185	216	214	180	118	41	23	23	23	23	23	23	23	122	4
	9	260	28	31	82	153	197	212	196	151	80	31	28	28	28	28	28	28	174	3
	10	272	32	33	40	93	150	182	187	165	116	56	64	62	62	62	62	62	214	2
	11	278	35	35	36	41	81	128	156	160	141	99	52	37	35	35	35	35	239	1
	12	280	35	35	35	36	38	63	106	138	149	138	106	63	38	36	35	35	247	12
HALF-DAY TOTALS			166	279	505	748	936	1016	955	750	476	299	241	203	188	187	187	187	947	
21-Sep	7	149	9	27	84	125	146	144	121	77	21	9	9	9	9	9	9	9	25	5
	8	230	17	19	87	160	205	218	199	148	71	18	17	17	17	17	17	17	82	4
	9	263	22	23	47	131	194	227	226	190	124	41	23	22	22	22	22	22	138	3
	10	280	27	27	28	71	148	200	221	209	165	93	30	27	27	27	27	27	180	2
	11	287	29	29	29	31	78	147	192	207	191	146	77	31	29	29	29	29	206	1
	12	290	30	30	30	30	32	75	142	185	200	185	142	75	32	30	30	30	215	12
HALF-DAY TOTALS			119	140	290	533	787	974	1030	924	672	400	227	144	120	119	119	119	739	
21-Oct	7	48	2	3	20	36	45	47	42	30	12	2	2	2	2	2	2	2	4	5
	8	204	11	12	49	123	173	195	188	151	89	18	11	11	11	11	11	11	43	4
	9	257	17	17	23	104	180	225	235	209	151	64	18	17	17	17'	17	17	97	3
	10	280	21	21	22	50	139	205	238	235	196	125	38	22	21'	21	21	21	140	2
	11	291	24	24	24	25	71	156	212	236	224	178	101	28	24	24	24	24	168	1
	12	294	25	25	25	25	27	85	165	216	234	216	165	85	27	25	25	25	177	12
HALF-DAY TOTALS			88	90	151	351	622	871	998	969	789	495	253	123	68	71	88	88	541	
21-Nov	8	136	5	5	18	69	108	128	129	110	72	21	6	5	5	5	5	5	14	4
	9	232	12	12	13	73	151	201	219	204	156	80	13	12	12	12	12	12	55	3
	10	268	16	16	16	31	122	196	237	242	209	143	50	17	16	16	16	16	96	2
	11	283	19	19	19	20	61	154	218	248	240	194	116	28	19	19	19	19	123	1
	12	288	20	20	20	20	21	89	176	231	250	231	176	89	21	20	20	20	132	12
HALF-DAY TOTALS			62	62	76	203	453	724	891	920	802	554	273	107	63	62	62	62	354	
21-Dec	8	89	3	3	8	41	67	82	84	73	50	17	3	3	3	3	3	3	6	4
	9	217	10	10	11	60	135	185	205	194	151	83	13	10	10	10	10	10	39	3
	10	261	14	14	14	25	113	188	232	239	210	146	55	15	14	14	14	14	77	2
	11	280	17	17	17	17	56	151	217	249	242	198	120	28	17	17	17	17	104	1
	12	285	18	18	18	18	19	89	178	233	253	233	178	89	19	18	18	18	113	12
HALF-DAY TOTALS			53	53	59	152	381	651	827	872	780	561	280	101	54	53	53	53	283	
	(am)		N	NNW	NW	WNW	W	WSW	SW	SSW	S	SSE	SE	ESE	E	ENE	NE	NNE	HOR	(pm)

Table 7.16E: SOLAR HEAT GAIN FACTOR FOR 48° NORTH LATITUDE FOR DS SHEET GLASS

Date	Solar Time (am)	Direct Normal (BUTH/ft²)	N	NNE	NE	ENE	E	ESE	SE	SSE	S	SSW	SW	WSW	W	WNW	NW	NNW	HOR	Solar Time (pm)
21-Jan	8	37	1	1	4	18	29	34	35	30	20	6	1	1	1	1	1	1	2	4
	9	185	8	8	8	53	118	160	176	166	129	69	10	8	8	8	8	8	25	3
	10	239	12	12	12	22	106	17	216	223	195	136	50	12	12	12	12	12	55	2
	11	261	14	14	14	15	53	144	208	239	233	190	116	26	14	14	14	14	77	1
	12	267	15	15	15	15	16	86	171	226	245	226	171	86	16	15	15	15	85	12
HALF-DAY TOTALS			43	43	46	116	314	398	721	771	700	514	263	90	43	43	43	43	202	
21-Feb	7	4	0	0	1	3	3	3	3	2	1	0	0	0	0	0	0	0	3	5
	8	180	8	8	36	103	149	170	166	136	82	17	8	8	8	8	8	8	25	4
	9	247	13	13	16	90	168	216	230	209	155	71	14	13	13	13	13	13	66	3
	10	275	17	17	17	38	131	203	242	244	207	138	44	18	17	17	17	17	105	2
	11	288	19	19	19	20	65	158	221	249	239	192	113	27	19	19	19	19	130	1
	12	292	20	20	20	20	22	89	176	231	250	231	176	89	22	20	20	20	138	12
HALF-DAY TOTALS			67	67	99	264	527	795	950	956	809	534	267	111	68	67	67	67	398	
21-Mar	7	153	7	22	80	123	145	145	123	80	23	7	7	7	7	7	7	7	20	5
	8	236	14	15	76	154	204	222	206	158	82	15	14	14	14	14	14	14	38	4
	9	270	19	19	3	121	193	134	239	207	142	52	20	19	19	19	19	19	118	3
	10	287	23	23	24	58	146	208	237	231	189	115	33	23	23	23	23	23	156	2
	11	295	25	25	25	26	74	156	210	232	218	172	94	28	25	25	25	25	180	1
	12	298	26	26	26	26	17	83	161	211	228	211	161	83	27	26	26	26	188	12
HALF-DAY TOTALS			101	117	221	495	771	907	1096	1014	768	467	249	133	102	101	101	101	606	
21-Apr	6	108	12	53	86	105	107	93	64	23	6	6	6	6	6	6	6	6	15	6
	7	205	15	61	132	180	199	189	148	84	18	14	14	14	14	14	14	14	60	5
	8	247	20	32	111	179	219	225	196	138	55	21	20	20	20	20	20	20	114	4
	9	268	25	26	60	141	197	223	215	176	106	33	25	25	25	25	25	25	161	3
	10	280	28	28	31	77	148	193	209	194	150	80	31	28	28	28	28	28	196	2
	11	286	31	31	31	33	78	140	181	193	177	133	69	33	31	31	31	31	218	1
	12	288	31	31	31	31	34	71	131	172	186	172	1321	71	34	31	31	31	226	12
HALF-DAY TOTALS			147	247	467	731	965	1099	1079	894	605	373	826	162	141	140	140	140	877	
21-May	5	41	17	31	40	42	39	29	14	3	3	3	3	3	3	3	3	3	5	7
	6	162	35	97	141	162	160	133	85	24	12	12	12	12	12	12	12	16	40	6
	7	219	23	90	158	200	212	191	142	68	21	19	19	19	19	19	19	19	91	5
	8	248	26	54	132	190	218	214	178	113	38	25	25	25	25	25	25	25	142	4
	9	264	29	32	82	151	194	208	192	147	77	32	29	29	29	29	29	29	185	3
	10	274	33	34	39	90	145	178	184	163	116	57	35	33	33	33	33	33	219	2
	11	279	35	35	36	40	79	126	155	160	142	101	54	37	35	35	35	35	240	1
	12	280	35	35	35	36	38	63	107	139	150	139	107	63	38	36	35	35	247	12
HALF-DAY TOTALS			216	391	646	893	1066	1111	1004	748	484	319	231	190	175	174	174	178	1046	
21-Jun	5	77	35	61	76	80	70	53	24	6	5	5	5	5	5	5	5	8	12	7
	6	172	46	110	155	175	169	138	84	22	14	14	14	14	14	14	14	16	51	6
	7	220	29	101	165	204	211	187	135	60	23	21	21	21	21	21	21	21	103	5
	8	246	29	64	139	191	215	206	168	101	34	27	27	27	27	27	27	27	152	4
	9	261	31	36	91	153	190	199	180	133	66	33	31	31	31	31	31	31	193	3
	10	269	34	36	45	94	143	169	171	148	101	50	36	34	34	34	34	34	225	2
	11	274	36	36	38	44	79	118	142	145	126	88	49	38	36	36	36	36	246	1
	12	275	37	37	37	38	40	60	96	124	134	124	96	60	40	38	37	37	252	12
HALF-DAY TOTALS			259	463	728	960	1097	1100	952	677	436	300	231	200	188	187	187	192	1108	
	(am)		N	NNW	NW	WNW	W	WSW	SW	SSW	S	SSE	SE	ESE	E	ENE	NE	NNE	HOR	(pm)

Table 7.16E (*Continued*)

Date	Solar Time (am)	Direct Normal (BUTH/ft²)	N	NNE	NE	ENE	E	ESE	SE	SSE	S	SSW	SW	WSW	W	WNW	NW	NNW	HOR	Solar Time (pm)
21-Jul	5	43	18	33	42	45	41	30	15	3	3	3	3	3	3	3	3	4	6	7
	6	156	37	96	138	159	156	129	82	24	13	13	13	13	13	13	13	14	41	6
	7	211	25	90	156	196	207	186	138	66	22	20	20	20	20	20	20	20	92	5
	8	240	27	56	132	187	214	209	174	110	38	26	26	26	26	26	26	26	142	4
	9	256	30	34	83	149	191	204	187	143	75	33	30	30	30	30	30	30	184	3
	10	266	34	35	41	90	143	174	180	158	113	56	36	34	34	34	34	34	417	2
	11	271	36	36	37	42	79	124	151	156	138	99	54	38	36	36	36	36	437	1
	12	272	36	36	36	37	39	63	104	136	146	136	104	63	39	37	36	36	244	12
HALF-DAY TOTALS			225	398	647	887	1051	1088	979	728	475	318	234	196	182	181	180	182	1441	
21-Aug	6	99	13	51	81	98	100	87	60	22	7	7	7	7	7	7	7	7	16	6
	7	190	17	61	128	172	190	179	141	79	19	15	15	15	15	15	15	15	61	5
	8	232	22	34	110	174	211	216	188	132	53	23	22	22	22	22	22	22	114	4
	9	154	27	28	63	139	192	216	108	169	102	34	27	27	27	27	27	27	159	3
	10	266	30	30	33	78	145	188	203	188	144	78	33	30	30	30	30	30	215	2
	11	272	32	32	32	36	78	137	175	187	171	129	68	35	32	32	32	32	223	1
	12	274	33	33	33	33	36	71	128	167	189	167	128	71	36	33	33	33	869	12
HALF-DAY TOTALS			158	253	464	714	934	1059	939	861	591	370	236	172	151	150	150	150	1223	
21-Sep	7	131	8	21	71	108	128	128	108	71	21	8	7	7	7	7	7	7	20	5
	8	215	15	16	72	144	191	207	193	148	77	16	15	15	15	15	15	15	65	4
	9	251	20	20	34	116	184	223	227	197	136	52	21	20	20	20	20	20	114	3
	10	269	24	24	25	58	141	200	228	221	182	112	34	24	24	24	24	24	151	2
	11	278	25	26	26	28	73	151	203	223	210	166	92	29	26	26	26	26	174	1
	12	280	27	27	27	27	29	82	156	204	220	204	156	82	29	27	27	27	182	12
HALF-DAY TOTALS			106	121	242	468	732	950	1037	962	736	456	247	136	107	106	106	106	615	
21-Oct	7	4	0	0	2	3	4	4	3	126	1	0	0	0	0	0	0	0	0	5
	8	165	8	9	35	96	139	159	155	199	77	16	8	8	8	8	8	8	25	4
	9	233	14	14	16	88	161	207	220	234	148	68	15	14	14	14	14	14	66	3
	10	262	18	18	18	39	128	196	233	241	199	133	43	18	18	18	18	18	104	2
	11	274	20	20	20	21	64	153	213	223	231	186	109	27	20	20	20	20	128	1
	12	278	21	21	21	21	23	87	171	925	242	223	171	87	23	21	21	21	136	12
HALF-DAY TOTALS			71	72	102	258	508	763	910	1486	777	515	261	111	72	71	71	71	391	
21-Nov	8	36	1	1	4	18	29	64	65	161	20	6	1	1	1	1	1	1	2	4
	9	179	8	8	9	52	115	156	171	218	125	67	10	8	8	8	8	8	26	3
	10	233	12	12	12	22	104	172	212	234	191	133	49	13	12	12	12	12	55	2
	11	255	15	15	15	15	52	142	204	222	228	186	114	26	15	15	15	15	77	1
	12	261	15	15	15	15	17	85	168	760	240	222	168	85	17	15	15	15	85	12
HALF-DAY TOTALS			44	44	48	115	309	577	736	1215	684	503	258	91	45	44	44	44	203	
21-Dec	9	140	5	5	6	36	86	120	133	127	100	56	8	5	5	5	5	5	13	3
	10	214	10	10	10	16	91	156	194	201	179	126	49	10	10	10	10	10	38	2
	11	242	12	12	12	13	46	134	195	225	220	180	111	25	12	12	12	12	57	1
	12	250	13	13	13	13	14	81	163	215	233	215	168	81	14	13	13	13	65	12
HALF-DAY TOTALS			34	34	35	72	230	451	604	661	616	470	252	81	34	34	34	34	141	
	(am)		N	NNW	NW	WNW	W	WSW	SW	SSW	S	SSE	SE	ESE	E	ENE	NE	NNE	HOR	(pm)

Table 7.16F: SOLAR HEAT GAIN FACTOR FOR 56° NORTH LATITUDE FOR DS SHEET GLASS

Date	Solar Time (am)	Direct Normal (BUTH/ft²)	N	NNE	NE	ENE	E	ESE	SE	SSE	S	SSW	SW	WSW	W	WNW	NW	NNW	HOR	Solar Time (pm)
21-Jan	9	78	3	3	3	21	49	67	74	70	55	30	4	3	3	3	3	3	5	3
	10	170	7	7	7	13	74	126	156	162	143	100	38	7	7	7	7	7	21	2
	11	207	9	9	9	10	40	116	169	194	190	156	96	21	9	9	9	9	34	1
	12	217	10	10	10	10	11	71	144	190	205	190	144	71	11	10	10	10	40	12
HALF-DAY TOTALS			24	24	24	49	169	345	471	521	491	381	210	67	25	24	24	24	80	
21-Feb	8	115	4	4	21	64	95	109	107	88	55	12	4	4	4	4	4	4	10	4
	9	203	10	10	11	71	139	183	197	182	136	66	10	10	10	10	10	10	36	3
	10	246	13	13	13	28	115	184	223	227	196	133	45	14	13	13	13	13	65	2
	11	262	15	15	15	16	57	148	210	239	232	188	112	25	15	15	15	15	84	1
	12	267	16	16	16	16	17	86	171	225	244	225	171	86	17	16	16	16	91	12
HALF-DAY TOTALS			50	50	68	187	415	667	823	849	741	512	257	96	51	50	50	50	241	
21-Mar	7	128	6	16	65	101	121	122	105	70	21	6	6	6	6	6	6	6	14	5
	8	215	12	13	61	136	185	205	194	152	84	15	12	12	12	12	12	12	49	4
	9	253	16	16	23	105	179	224	233	207	148	61	17	16	16	16	16	16	89	3
	10	272	19	19	20	46	136	203	238	236	198	128	39	20	19	19	19	19	122	2
	11	282	21	21	21	22	68	156	215	241	230	184	106	27	21	21	21	21	142	1
	12	284	22	22	22	22	24	86	170	222	241	222	170	86	24	22	22	22	149	12
HALF-DAY TOTALS			85	96	201	421	701	953	1070	1017	802	505	265	124	86	85	85	85	491	
21-Apr	6	122	13	58	95	118	121	107	75	29	7	7	7	7	7	7	7	7	18	6
	7	201	15	51	123	173	195	188	152	91	21	14	14	14	14	14	14	14	56	5
	8	239	19	23	95	167	211	223	201	148	68	20	19	19	19	19	19	19	101	4
	9	260	23	24	44	126	190	223	223	189	126	44	24	23	23	23	23	23	140	3
	10	272	26	26	27	63	142	196	220	212	171	102	33	26	26	26	26	26	170	2
	11	278	28	28	28	30	74	147	195	213	200	156	86	31	28	28	28	28	189	1
	12	280	28	28	28	28	31	79	149	194	210	194	149	79	31	28	28	28	195	12
HALF-DAY TOTALS			138	224	426	691	949	1124	1141	979	698	440	258	160	133	131	131	131	772	
21-May	5	93	36	68	89	95	88	66	33	7	6	6	6	6	6	6	6	7	14	7
	6	175	33	99	148	174	173	147	97	31	14	14	14	14	14	14	14	14	48	6
	7	219	21	77	149	195	212	197	152	81	22	19	19	19	19	19	19	19	92	5
	8	244	25	38	115	179	215	218	189	131	52	25	24	24	24	24	24	24	135	4
	9	259	28	30	62	136	189	213	206	168	102	36	28	28	28	28	28	28	171	3
	10	268	31	31	33	75	141	185	200	187	145	80	33	31	31	31	31	31	199	2
	11	273	32	32	32	35	76	135	174	187	172	131	71	35	32	32	32	32	216	1
	12	275	33	33	33	33	36	71	129	168	181	168	129	71	36	33	33	33	222	12
HALF-DAY TOTALS			223	392	645	906	1112	1197	1116	876	604	395	260	193	172	171	171	172	986	
21-Jun	4	21	13	19	12	21	18	11	3	1	1	1	1	1	1	1	2	5	3	8
	5	122	53	94	119	126	115	85	40	10	9	9	9	9	9	9	9	12	25	7
	6	285	42	111	160	185	182	152	97	30	16	16	16	16	16	16	16	17	62	6
	7	222	25	86	156	199	213	195	147	74	24	22	22	22	22	22	22	22	105	5
	8	243	27	46	122	181	219	213	181	122	46	27	26	26	26	26	26	26	146	4
	9	257	30	32	69	139	187	206	196	156	91	34	30	30	30	30	30	30	181	3
	10	265	33	33	36	79	139	178	190	174	132	71	35	33	33	33	33	33	208	2
	11	269	34	34	35	38	76	129	164	174	159	119	65	37	34	34	34	34	225	1
	12	271	35	35	35	35	38	68	119	155	168	155	119	68	38	35	35	35	231	12
HALF-DAY TOTALS			275	473	738	989	1162	1207	1082	822	562	376	160	103	190	189	189	196	1070	
	(am)		N	NNW	NW	WNW	W	WSW	SW	SSW	S	SSE	SE	ESE	E	ENE	NE	NNE	HOR	(pm)

Table 7.16F (*Continued*)

Date	Solar Time (am)	Direct Normal (BUTH/ft²)	N	NNE	NE	ENE	E	ESE	SE	SSE	S	SSW	SW	WSW	W	WNW	NW	NNW	HOR	Solar Time (pm)
21-Jul	5	91	37	69	89	95	88	66	33	8	7	7	7	7	7	7	7	8	16	7
	6	169	34	98	145	170	170	143	95	31	15	14	14	14	14	14	14	15	50	6
	7	212	23	77	147	192	208	193	148	79	23	20	20	20	20	20	20	20	93	5
	8	237	26	40	115	177	211	214	185	128	51	26	25	25	25	25	25	25	135	4
	9	252	29	31	63	135	186	209	201	164	99	36	29	29	29	29	29	29	171	3
	10	261	32	32	64	76	139	181	196	182	142	78	35	32	32	32	32	32	198	2
	11	265	33	33	66	37	76	133	171	183	168	128	70	36	33	33	33	33	215	1
	12	267	34	34	64	34	37	71	126	164	177	164	126	71	37	34	34	34	221	12
HALF-DAY TOTALS			**231**	**397**	**721**	**899**	**1097**	**1175**	**1092**	**857**	**594**	**391**	**263**	**199**	**179**	**177**	**177**	**179**	**989**	
21-Aug	5	1	0	1	1	1	1	1	0	0	0	0	0	0	0	0	0	0	0	7
	6	112	14	56	91	111	114	101	71	28	8	8	8	8	8	8	8	8	20	6
	7	187	16	51	119	165	186	179	144	86	22	15	15	15	15	15	15	15	58	5
	8	225	20	25	94	162	203	214	192	142	66	22	20	20	20	20	20	20	101	4
	9	246	25	26	46	124	184	216	215	182	121	44	26	25	25	25	25	25	140	3
	10	258	28	28	30	65	139	191	213	204	165	99	34	28	28	28	28	28	169	2
	11	264	30	30	30	32	74	143	189	206	193	152	84	33	30	30	30	30	187	1
	12	266	30	30	30	30	30	78	145	188	203	188	145	78	33	30	30	30	198	12
HALF-DAY TOTALS			**148**	**232**	**426**	**675**	**916**	**1084**	**1097**	**942**	**677**	**434**	**260**	**168**	**143**	**141**	**141**	**141**	**774**	
21-Sep	7	107	6	15	56	87	104	105	90	60	19	6	6	6	6	6	6	6	14	5
	8	194	12	14	58	126	171	189	179	140	78	16	12	12	12	12	12	12	48	4
	9	233	17	17	24	100	170	211	220	195	140	59	18	17	17	17	17	17	86	3
	10	253	20	20	21	46	131	194	227	225	189	123	39	21	20	20	20	20	118	2
	11	263	22	22	22	24	67	150	206	230	220	176	103	28	22	22	22	22	137	1
	12	266	23	23	23	23	25	85	163	213	231	213	163	85	25	23	23	23	144	12
HALF-DAY TOTALS			**89**	**100**	**193**	**395**	**656**	**892**	**1004**	**957**	**762**	**487**	**260**	**127**	**90**	**89**	**89**	**89**	**475**	
21-Oct	8	104	4	5	20	59	87	100	98	81	50	11	4	4	4	4	4	4	10	4
	9	193	10	10	11	68	132	173	186	171	129	63	11	10	10	10	10	10	37	3
	10	231	14	14	14	28	111	176	213	216	186	127	44	14	14	14	14	14	64	2
	11	248	16	16	16	17	56	142	202	229	222	180	108	25	16	16	16	16	84	1
	12	253	16	16	16	16	18	83	164	216	234	216	164	83	18	16	16	16	91	12
HALF-DAY TOTALS			**52**	**53**	**69**	**180**	**395**	**633**	**781**	**805**	**704**	**489**	**249**	**95**	**53**	**52**	**52**	**52**	**241**	
21-Nov	9	76	3	3	3	21	48	66	72	69	54	29	4	3	3	3	3	3	6	3
	10	165	7	7	7	13	72	122	152	157	139	98	37	7	7	7	7	7	21	2
	11	201	9	9	9	10	39	113	165	190	186	152	94	21	9	9	9	9	35	1
	12	211	10	10	10	10	11	70	140	186	200	186	140	70	11	10	10	10	40	12
HALF-DAY TOTALS			**24**	**24**	**24**	**49**	**165**	**336**	**459**	**509**	**479**	**372**	**205**	**66**	**25**	**24**	**24**	**24**	**82**	
21-Dec	9	5	0	0	0	1	3	4	5	5	4	2	0	0	0	0	0	0	0	3
	10	113	4	4	4	7	47	82	103	107	96	68	27	4	4	4	4	4	9	2
	11	166	6	6	6	7	30	92	135	156	154	127	78	17	6	6	6	6	19	1
	12	180	7	7	7	7	8	59	120	159	171	159	120	59	8	7	7	7	23	12
HALF-DAY TOTALS			**14**	**14**	**14**	**19**	**84**	**208**	**303**	**348**	**340**	**277**	**165**	**51**	**14**	**14**	**14**	**14**	**40**	
	(am)		N	NNW	NW	WNW	W	WSW	SW	SSW	S	SSE	SE	ESE	E	ENE	NE	NNE	HOR	(pm)

Table 7.16G: SOLAR HEAT GAIN FACTOR FOR 64° NORTH LATITUDE FOR DS SHEET GLASS

Date	Solar Time (am)	Direct Normal (BUTH/ft²)	N	NNE	NE	ENE	E	ESE	SE	SSE	S	SSW	SW	WSW	W	WNW	NW	NNW	HOR	Solar Time (pm)
21-Jan	10	22	1	1	1	1	9	16	20	21	19	13	5	1	1	1	1	1	1	2
	11	81	3	3	3	3	15	45	67	77	75	62	38	8	3	3	3	3	6	1
	12	100	3	3	3	3	4	33	67	89	96	89	67	33	4	3	3	3	8	12
HALF-DAY TOTALS			6	6	6	6	26	78	121	143	142	120	77	26	6	6	6	6	11	
21-Feb	8	18	1	1	3	10	15	17	17	14	9	2	1	1	1	1	1	1	1	4
	9	134	5	5	6	43	8	118	128	119	90	45	6	5	5	5	5	5	13	3
	10	190	8	8	8	18	87	144	176	180	157	108	38	9	8	8	8	8	28	2
	11	215	10	10	10	11	44	122	177	202	197	160	97	20	10	10	10	10	41	1
	12	222	11	11	11	11	12	73	147	194	210	194	147	73	12	11	11	11	45	12
HALF-DAY TOTALS			30	30	33	88	160	438	572	612	558	412	216	72	30	30	30	30	106	
21-Mar	7	95	4	11	47	74	90	91	79	53	17	4	4	4	4	4	4	4	9	5
	8	185	9	10	46	113	158	177	170	135	78	14	9	9	9	9	9	9	32	4
	9	277	13	13	16	88	159	203	215	194	143	64	14	13	13	13	13	13	59	3
	10	249	16	16	16	35	122	190	226	215	194	130	42	16	16	16	16	16	84	2
	11	260	17	17	17	18	60	148	209	236	228	184	109	25	17	17	17	17	99	1
	12	263	18	18	18	18	19	852	168	221	239	221	168	85	19	18	18	18	105	12
HALF-DAY TOTALS			68	76	151	337	599	1235	983	944	780	507	262	110	69	68	68	68	336	
21-Apr	5	27	8	18	24	27	26	20	12	2	1	1	1	1	1	1	1	1	2	7
	6	133	12	59	102	127	132	118	84	35	8	8	8	8	8	8	8	8	21	6
	7	194	14	41	113	163	189	185	153	96	25	13	13	13	13	13	13	13	51	5
	8	228	17	19	79	153	201	217	201	153	79	19	17	17	17	17	17	17	85	4
	9	248	21	21	32	111	180	219	225	197	138	55	22	21	21	21	21	21	116	3
	10	260	23	23	24	51	134	194	225	221	185	118	38	24	23	23	23	23	140	2
	11	266	24	24	24	26	68	148	202	225	214	171	99	29	24	24	24	24	155	1
	12	268	25	25	25	25	27	83	159	208	224	208	159	83	27	25	25	25	160	12
HALF-DAY TOTALS			132	218	411	671	944	1143	1182	1033	762	489	278	155	121	120	120	120	650	
21-May	4	51	30	44	51	51	43	28	8	3	3	3	3	3	3	3	3	10	6	8
	5	132	48	95	125	135	125	96	50	11	9	9	9	9	9	9	9	11	26	7
	6	185	28	97	150	181	183	158	109	40	15	15	15	15	15	15	15	15	55	6
	7	218	24	63	138	189	211	201	161	94	19	19	19	19	19	19	19	19	90	5
	8	239	23	28	97	167	209	220	198	146	68	25	23	23	23	23	23	23	124	4
	9	252	26	27	45	122	183	215	215	184	123	46	27	26	26	26	26	26	152	3
	10	261	28	28	30	61	135	188	212	205	167	102	36	28	28	28	28	28	174	2
	11	265	30	30	30	32	72	141	188	207	195	154	87	33	30	30	30	30	188	1
	12	267	30	30	30	30	33	78	146	189	204	189	146	78	33	30	30	30	192	12
HALF-DAY TOTALS			252	427	681	953	1178	1286	1214	985	706	468	292	195	170	168	168	177	911	
21-Jun	4	93	53	83	96	94	78	50	14	7	7	7	7	7	7	7	7	21	16	8
	5	154	62	114	148	158	158	145	55	14	12	12	12	12	12	12	14	14	39	7
	6	194	36	107	162	191	192	192	110	39	18	17	17	17	17	17	18	18	71	6
	7	221	24	71	145	193	213	213	158	89	25	22	22	22	22	22	22	22	105	5
	8	239	25	33	104	170	208	208	192	139	62	27	25	25	25	25	25	25	137	4
	9	251	28	29	51	124	181	181	208	175	115	43	29	28	28	28	28	28	165	3
	10	258	30	30	32	65	134	134	204	195	157	94	36	30	30	30	30	30	186	2
	11	262	32	32	32	34	72	72	180	196	184	144	92	35	32	32	32	32	199	1
	12	263	32	32	32	32	35	35	138	179	193	179	138	76	35	32	32	32	203	12
HALF-DAY TOTALS			306	515	786	1045	1254	1213	1190	944	677	456	309	214	191	189	189	206	1020	
	(am)		N	NNW	NW	WNW	W	WSW	SW	SSW	S	SSE	SE	ESE	E	ENE	NE	NNE	HOR	(pm)

Table 7.16G (*Continued*)

Date	Solar Time (am)	Direct Normal (BUTH/ft²)	N	NNE	NE	ENE	E	ESE	SE	SSE	S	SSW	SW	WSW	W	WNW	NW	NNW	HOR	Solar Time (pm)
21-Jul	4	53	32	47	55	54	46	29	9	4	4	4	4	4	4	4	4	11	8	8
	5	128	49	94	123	133	124	95	50	11	10	10	10	10	10	10	10	11	28	7
	6	179	30	96	148	177	180	155	106	39	16	15	15	15	15	15	15	15	57	6
	7	211	22	64	137	186	207	197	157	92	25	20	20	20	20	20	20	20	92	5
	8	231	24	30	97	165	205	215	193	142	67	26	24	24	24	24	24	24	124	4
	9	245	27	28	47	121	180	211	211	179	120	46	28	27	27	27	27	27	152	3
	10	253	29	29	31	62	134	185	208	200	164	100	37	29	29	29	29	29	174	2
	11	257	31	31	31	33	72	139	185	202	191	151	86	34	31	31	31	31	187	1
	12	259	31	31	31	31	34	78	143	185	200	185	143	78	34	31	31	31	192	12
HALF-DAY TOTALS			**260**	**435**	**685**	**947**	**1165**	**1265**	**1191**	**962**	**697**	**465**	**296**	**202**	**177**	**176**	**176**	**184**	**918**	
21-Aug	5	29	9	20	27	30	28	22	13	2	2	2	2	2	2	2	2	3		7
	6	123	13	58	97	121	125	111	80	34	9	9	9	9	9	9	9	23		6
	7	181	15	42	109	157	180	176	145	92	26	14	14	14	19	14	14	14	53	5
	8	214	19	21	78	148	193	208	192	147	76	21	19	19	19	19	19	19	87	4
	9	234	22	22	34	109	174	211	217	189	133	55	23	22	22	22	22	22	117	3
	10	246	25	25	26	52	131	188	217	214	178	114	39	25	25	25	25	25	140	2
	11	252	26	26	26	28	69	144	196	217	207	166	97	31	26	26	26	26	154	1
	12	254	27	27	27	27	29	82	155	201	217	201	155	82	29	27	27	27	159	12
HALF-DAY TOTALS			**143**	**228**	**411**	**659**	**915**	**1101**	**1138**	**996**	**740**	**482**	**281**	**163**	**137**	**131**	**131**	**131**	**657**	
21-Sep	7	77	4	10	39	62	74	75	65	44	15	4	4	4	4	4	4	4	8	5
	8	163	10	10	43	103	143	160	154	123	71	14	10	10	10	10	10	10	31	4
	9	206	14	14	17	83	148	189	200	181	133	61	15	14	14	14	14	14	57	3
	10	229	16	16	17	35	116	179	213	214	183	123	41	17	16	16	16	16	81	2
	11	240	18	18	18	19	59	141	198	224	216	174	104	26	18	18	18	18	96	1
	12	244	19	19	19	19	21	82	160	209	227	209	160	82	19	19	19	19	101	12
HALF-DAY TOTALS			**72**	**78**	**144**	**312**	**551**	**785**	**910**	**891**	**732**	**481**	**254**	**112**	**73**	**72**	**72**	**72**	**324**	
21-Oct	8	17	1	1	3	10	14	16	16	13	8	2	1	1	1	1	1	1	1	4
	9	122	5	5	6	40	82	109	118	110	83	42	3	5	5	5	5	5	13	3
	10	176	9	9	9	18	83	135	165	169	147	102	36	9	9	9	9	9	29	2
	11	201	11	11	11	11	43	116	167	191	186	152	92	20	11	11	11	11	41	1
	12	208	11	11	11	11	13	70	140	184	199	184	140	70	13	11	11	11	46	12
HALF-DAY TOTALS			**32**	**32**	**35**	**85**	**229**	**411**	**536**	**575**	**524**	**390**	**202**	**70**	**33**	**32**	**32**	**32**	**107**	
21-Nov	10	23	1	1	1	10	17	21	22	20	14	5	1	1	1	1	1	1	1	2
	11	79	3	3	3	15	44	65	75	74	61	37	8	2	3	3	3	3	6	1
	12	97	4	4	4	4	32	66	87	93	87	66	32	4	4	4	4	4	8	12
HALF-DAY TOTALS			**6**	**6**	**6**	**27**	**77**	**119**	**141**	**141**	**119**	**75**	**25**	**5**	**6**	**6**	**6**	**6**	**11**	
21-Dec	11	4	0	0	0	0	1	2	3	4	4	3	2	0	0	0	0	0	0	1
	12	16	0	0	0	0	1	5	11	14	15	14	11	5	1	0	0	0	1	12
HALF-DAY TOTALS			**0**	**0**	**0**	**0**	**2**	**5**	**9**	**11**	**12**	**10**	**8**	**3**	**1**	**0**	**0**	**0**	**1**	
	(am)		N	NNW	NW	WNW	W	WSW	SW	SSW	S	SSE	SE	ESE	E	ENE	NE	NNE	HOR	(pm)

temperature differential being adjusted for the varying time of day. The hourly temperature differentials (HTDs) listed in Table 7.15B indicate the temperature differentials to be used in the standard formula, where the HTD is substituted for the standard temperature differential. [Note that HTD is used with glazing and infiltration, whereas equivalent temperature differential (ETD) is used with walls and roofs and other opaque thermal barriers.]

$$BTUH_{sensible} = Area \times U \times HTD$$

While Table 7.15A lists the outdoor temperatures based on a 20° F diurnal temperature range and a high

Table 7.17: SHADING COEFFICIENTS FOR SINGLE AND INSULATING GLASS WITHOUT INTERIOR OR EXTERIOR SHADING TO BE APPLIED TO THE SOLAR HEAT GAIN FACTORS (SHGF)

Type of Glass	Nominal Thickness	Solar Trans.	Shading Coefficient
Single Glass			
Clear	$\frac{1}{8}$ in.	0.86	1.00
	$\frac{1}{4}$ in.	0.78	0.94
	$\frac{3}{8}$ in.	0.72	0.90
	$\frac{1}{2}$ in.	0.67	0.87
Heat Absorbing	$\frac{1}{8}$ in.	0.64	0.83
	$\frac{1}{4}$ in.	0.46	0.69
	$\frac{3}{8}$ in.	0.33	0.60
	$\frac{1}{2}$ in.	0.24	0.53
Insulating Glass			
Clear Out, Clear In	$\frac{1}{8}$ in.	0.71	0.83
Clear Out, Clear In	$\frac{1}{4}$ in.	0.61	0.81
Ht. Abs. Out, Clear In	$\frac{1}{4}$ in.	0.36	0.55

Source: Adapted from Table 5.37 in B. Stein, J.S. Reynolds, and W.J. McGuinness, *Mechanical and Electrical Equipment for Buildings* (John Wiley & Sons, Inc., New York, 1992).

temperature of 95° F, Table 7.15B indicates the temperature differential based on the same outdoor conditions and an assumed interior design temperature of 78° F. That is, Table 7.15A merely lists the outdoor temperatures, whereas Table 7.15B lists the temperature differentials for the assumed conditions. Unlike opaque barriers, solar radiation contributions to heat gain are handled by the SHGF, and because of the light weight of glass, there is no need to account for any significant thermal storage resulting from any absorbed solar radiation. That is, the transmission across the glass is based merely on the temperature differential.

Table 7.19: SHADING COEFFICIENTS FOR SINGLE & INSULATING GLASS WITH DRAPERIES TO BE USED WITH SOLAR HEAT GAIN FACTORS (SHGF)

Drapery Fabrics				
			Transmittance	
			High	Low
			Reflectance	
Type of Glass	Glass	SC	Low	High
Single Glass				
Clear	$\frac{1}{8}$ in.	1.00	0.87	0.37
Clear	$\frac{1}{4}$ in.	0.95	0.80	0.35
Heat Absorbing	$\frac{1}{4}$ in.	0.67	0.57	0.33
Reflective Coated		0.60	0.57	0.33
Reflective Coated		0.50	0.46	0.31
Reflective Coated		0.40	0.36	0.26
Reflective Coated		0.30	0.25	0.20
Insulating Glass				
Clear Out, Clear In		0.83	0.66	0.35
Heat Abs. Out, Clear In		0.55	0.49	0.32
Reflective Coated		0.40	0.38	0.28
Reflective Coated		0.30	0.29	0.24
Reflective Coated		0.20	0.19	0.16

Source: Adapted from Table 5.38 in B. Stein, J.S. Reynolds, and W.J. McGuinness, *Mechanical and Electrical Equipment for Buildings* (John Wiley & Sons, Inc., New York, 1992).

If we choose to use Table 7.15B and the daily mean temperature is different from 85° F, we should add half of the difference between the actual daily mean temperature and 85° F. Note that if the daily mean temperature is less than 85° F, this will result in a lower HTD. If the interior design temperature is not the assumed 78° F or if the outside maximum temperature is not 95° F, we have to adjust the HTD values. If the interior temperature is not 78° F,

Table 7.18: SHADING COEFFICIENTS FOR SINGLE GLASS WITH INTERIOR SHADING BY VENETIAN BLINDS OR ROLLER SHADES TO BE USED WITH SOLAR HEAT GAIN FACTORS (SHGF)

Type of Glass	Arrangement	Venetian Blinds		Roller Shades		
				Opaque		Translucent
		Medium	Light	Dark	White	Light
Single Glass						
Clear	open 45°	0.74	0.67			
Heat Absorbing	closed	0.63	0.58	0.59	0.25	0.39
Tinted	tightly closed	0.29	0.25			
Heat Absorbing		0.57	0.53	0.45	0.30	0.36
Insulating Glass						
Clear Out, Clear In	open 45°	0.62	0.58			
Clear Out, Clear In	closed	0.63	0.58	0.71	0.35	0.40
Heat Abs. Out, Clear In		0.39	0.36	0.40	0.22	0.30
Shading between Double Glazing						
Clear Out, Clear In		0.36	0.33			
Heat Abs. Out, Clear In		0.30	0.28			

Source: Adapted from Table 5.39 in B. Stein, J.S. Reynolds, and W.J. McGuinness, *Mechanical and Electrical Equipment for Buildings* (John Wiley & Sons, Inc., New York, 1992).

Table 7.20: SHADING COEFFICIENTS FOR DOMES SKYLIGHTS

Dome	U Coefficient at Center	Light Diffuser	Shading Coefficient
Clear ($\tau = 0.86$)	0.43	Yes	0.58
Clear ($\tau = 0.86$)	0.8	No	0.88
	0.7	No	0.80
Translucent ($\tau = 0.52$)	0.8	No	0.57
	0.7	No	0.46
Translucent ($\tau = 0.27$)	0.8	No	0.34
	0.7	No	0.28

Source: Adapted from Table 5.41 in B. Stein, J.S. Reynolds, and W.J. McGuinness, *Mechanical and Electrical Equipment for Buildings* (John Wiley & Sons, Inc., New York, 1992).

we should subtract the design temperature from $78°$ F and add the difference to the HTD. If the maximum exterior temperature is other than $95°$ F, we should subtract $95°$ F from the maximum temperature and add the difference to the HTD values. If the daily range of exterior temperatures is not $20°$ F, we also need to adjust the HTD values by subtracting half the difference from the temperature differentials listed in Table 7.15B. If we choose to use the values in Table 7.15A or calculate the outdoor temperatures using the formula presented in the note to this table, these corrections are not necessary. Of course, since the intention is to determine what is contributing to the heat gain rather than develop a detailed analysis of the heat gain to size the control system, it might not be necessary to do any correction.

Transmittance Across Opaque Construction Assemblies

Heat gain across opaque construction assemblies is determined in the same manner as heat loss except that the actual temperature differential is replaced with an equivalent temperature differential (ETD) that takes into consideration the effects of solar radiation. ETD, which is based on the particular type of construction in terms of mass, thermal storage, color, orientation of the exposure, and time of day, can be found in Tables 7.21 and 7.22.

Table 7.21 provides ETD values for sunlit walls. This table is divided into sections according to the relative weight of construction, with the lightest-weight walls at the top. In similar tables, the order in which the various types of construction are listed might be reversed, with the heaviest walls placed at the top.

Table 7.22 provides ETD values for roofs. This table is divided into six sections. The first three are for different roofs based on the relative weight of the construction, although within each section there is a further breakdown. The fourth and fifth sections are for roofs with a water pond or a water spray, respectively. The last section is for a roof

in shade, again with further distinctions based on weight of construction.

$$\text{BTUH}_{sens} = \text{Area} \times \text{"U" Coefficient} \times \text{ETD}$$

To find the heat gain across a square foot of an opaque barrier, we multiply the ETD by the appropriate "U" coefficient. However, since code requirements tend to limit the "U" coefficient for opaque construction to 0.05 or less, the resulting amount of heat transmitted is often not significant. So, even if the ETD is at the maximum, the heat gain per square foot is generally less than 2.5 BTUH per square foot.

For example, the maximum ETD listed for walls is $48°$. Since the sensible heat transmission per square foot equals the "U" coefficient times ETD, if the "U" coefficient equals 0.05, the heat transmission per square foot would be only 2.4 BTUH.

$$\text{BTUH}_{sens} = 0.05 \times 48 \text{ ETD} = 2.4 \text{ BTUH}$$

Generally, the ETD for a wall is considerably less than this maximum of $48°$. This is also true for most roofs. Although the maximum ETD for a roof can reach $62°$, the heat gain would only be 3.1 BTUH per square foot, based on a "U" coefficient of 0.05, and, of course, it would be less at the recommended "U" coefficient of 0.03. As a result, the heat gain through most opaque barriers is not the major factor in heat gain. Direct insolation is the major source of transmitted heat gain, although for interior spaces the internal heat gain from people, lights, and equipment might form the dominant load.

Edge Gains

In heat gain calculations, slab edge gains, the heat gain equivalent to slab edge loss incorporated in heat loss calculations, are not usually included. Although there might be some heat gain from the exposed slab edges that are above grade, since much of the slab is in contact with the ground, any gain will not be significant. In fact, with a ground temperature at $55°$ F, the slab might actually account for a minor heat loss.

Infiltration

In addition to the transmitted heat gains through glazed openings and opaque barrier, there is also heat gain as a result of direct infiltration or forced ventilation. Like heat loss, these gains will probably be both sensible and latent in nature, and therefore they need to be handled separately.

Sensible and latent heat gains from infiltration are based on the same formulas used in heat loss. For sensible infiltration, however, the temperature differential is based on the hourly temperature differentials listed in Table 7.15B. This is used in the standard formula. For

Table 7.21: EQUIVALENT TEMPERATURE DIFFERENTIALS FOR SUNLIT WALLS

N Latitude	Sun Time																	
	8		10		12		2		4		6		8		10		12	
	Exterior color of wall: D = dark, L = light																	
	D	L	D	L	D	L	D	L	D	L	D	L	D	L	D	L	D	L
Frame																		
NE	22	10	24	12	14	10	12	10	14	14	14	14	10	10	6	4	2	2
E	30	14	36	18	32	16	12	12	14	14	14	14	10	10	6	6	2	2
SE	13	6	26	16	28	18	24	16	16	14	14	14	10	10	6	4	2	2
S	−4	−4	4	0	22	12	30	20	26	30	16	14	10	10	6	6	2	2
SW	−4	−4	0	−2	6	4	26	22	40	28	42	28	24	20	6	4	2	2
W	−4	−4	0	0	6	6	20	12	40	28	48	34	22	22	8	8	2	2
NW	−4	−4	0	−2	6	4	12	10	24	20	40	26	34	24	6	4	2	2
N (Shade)	−4	−4	−2	−2	4	4	10	10	14	14	12	12	8	8	4	4	0	0
4" Masonry plus Frame																		
NE	−2	−4	24	12	20	10	10	6	12	10	14	14	21	12	10	10	6	4
E	2	0	30	14	31	17	14	14	12	12	14	14	12	12	10	8	6	6
SE	2	−2	20	10	28	16	26	16	17	14	14	14	12	12	10	8	6	6
S	−4	−4	−2	−2	12	6	24	16	26	18	20	16	12	12	8	8	4	4
SW	0	−2	0	−2	2	2	12	8	32	22	36	26	34	24	10	8	6	6
W	0	−2	0	0	4	2	10	8	26	18	40	28	42	28	16	14	6	6
NW	−4	−4	−2	−2	2	2	8	6	12	12	30	22	34	24	12	10	6	6
N (Shade)	−4	−4	−2	−2	0	0	6	6	10	10	12	12	12	12	8	8	4	4
8" Concrete or Stone or 6" to 8" Concrete Block																		
NE	4	2	4	0	16	8	14	8	10	6	12	8	12	10	10	8	8	6
E	6	4	14	8	24	12	24	12	18	10	14	10	14	10	12	10	10	8
SE	6	2	6	4	16	10	18	12	18	12	14	12	12	10	12	10	10	8
S	2	1	2	1	4	1	12	6	16	12	18	12	14	12	10	8	8	6
SW	6	2	4	2	6	2	8	4	14	10	22	16	24	16	22	16	10	8
W	6	4	6	4	6	4	8	6	12	8	20	14	28	18	26	18	14	10
NW	4	2	4	0	4	2	4	4	6	6	12	10	20	14	22	16	8	6
N (Shade)	0	0	0	0	0	0	2	2	4	4	6	6	8	8	6	6	4	4
8" Hollow Tile or 8" Cinder Block																		
NE	0	0	0	0	20	10	16	10	10	6	12	10	14	12	12	10	8	8
E	4	2	12	4	24	12	26	14	20	12	12	10	14	12	14	10	10	8
SE	2	0	2	0	16	8	20	12	20	14	14	12	14	12	12	10	8	8
S	0	0	0	0	2	0	12	6	24	14	26	16	20	14	12	10	8	6
SW	2	0	2	0	2	0	6	4	12	10	26	18	30	20	26	18	8	6
W	4	2	4	2	4	2	6	4	10	8	18	14	30	22	32	22	18	14
NW	0	0	0	0	2	0	4	2	8	6	12	10	22	18	30	22	10	8
N (Shade)	−2	−2	−2	−2	−2	−2	0	0	6	6	10	10	10	10	10	10	6	6
8" Brick or 12" Hollow Tile or 12" Cinder Block																		
NE	2	2	2	2	10	2	16	8	14	8	10	6	10	8	10	10	10	8
E	8	6	8	6	14	8	18	10	18	10	14	8	14	10	14	10	12	10
SE	8	4	6	4	6	4	14	10	18	12	16	12	12	10	12	10	12	10
S	4	2	4	2	4	2	4	2	10	6	16	10	16	12	12	10	10	8
SW	8	4	6	4	6	4	8	4	10	6	12	8	20	12	24	16	20	14
W	8	4	6	4	6	6	8	6	10	6	14	8	20	16	24	16	24	16
W	2	2	2	2	2	2	4	2	6	4	8	6	10	8	16	14	18	14
N (Shade)	0	0	0	0	0	0	0	0	2	2	6	6	8	8	8	8	6	6

[1]The table is based on a maximum daily exterior temperature of 95° F and an interior temperature of 80° F and a diurnal range of 20° F. Adjustment for a different temperature differential other than 95° and 80° — add difference to listed values. Adjustment for a different diurnal range — apply half of the difference to the listed values.

[2]Use values for light walls only where conditions indicate that the light color will be sustained. For medium colors, interpolate between listed values for L and D.

Source: Adapted from various sources including prior editions of the *Mechanical and Electrical Equipment for Buildings* and the *ASHRAE Handbook—Fundamentals.*

Table 7.22: EQUIVALENT TEMPERATURE DIFFERENTIALS FOR ROOFS

Description of Construction	AM			PM					
	8	10	12	2	4	6	8	10	12
Light Construction Roofs — Exposed to Sun									
1" Wood w/ or w/o 1" or 2" insulation	12	38	54	62	50	26	10	4	0
Medium Construction Roofs — Exposed to Sun									
2" Concrete w/ or w/o 1" or 2" insulation or 2" Wood or 2" Gypsum w/ or w/o + 1" insulation	6	30	48	58	50	32	14	6	2
1" Wood or 2" Wood + 4" batt insulation or 2" Concrete or 2" Gypsum	0	20	40	52	54	42	20	10	6
4" Concrete w/ or w/o 2" insulation	0	20	38	50	52	40	22	12	6
Heavy Construction Roofs — Exposed to Sun									
6" Concrete w/ or w/o 2" insulation	4	6	24	38	46	44	32	18	12
	6	6	20	34	42	44	34	20	14
Roofs Covered with Water — Exposed to Sun									
Light Roof w/ 1" Water	0	4	16	22	18	14	10	2	0
Heavy Roof w/ 1" Water	−2	−2	−4	10	14	16	14	10	6
Any Roof w/ 6" Water	−2	0	0	6	10	10	8	4	0
Roofs with Water Spray — Exposed to Sun									
Light Construction	0	4	12	18	16	14	10	2	0
Heavy Construction	−2	−2	2	8	12	14	12	10	6
Roofs in Shade									
Light Construction	−4	0	6	12	14	12	8	2	0
Medium Construction	−4	−2	2	8	12	12	10	6	2
Heavy Construction	−2	−2	0	4	8	10	10	8	4

[1]This table is based on a maximum daily exterior temperature of 95° F and an interior temperature of 80° F and a diurnal range of 20° F Adjustments for other temperature conditions should be made by adding the changed temperature differential to the listed values (e.g., if interior is at 70° F, add 10° F to ETD values in table). Adjustments for a diurnal range other than 20°F should be made by adding the difference between the actual daily exterior mean temperature and 85° F, the base for this chart (e.g., if daily range is 24° F and the maximum temperature remains at 95° F, subtract 2° F from ETD values in table).

[2]If an attic exists with an insulated ceiling and forced attic ventilation, reduce the values of this table by 25%.

Source: Adapted from various sources including prior editions of the *Mechanical and Electrical Equipment for Buildings* and the *ASHRAE Handbook – Fundamentals.*

latent infiltration, the change in specific humidity (W) is the difference between the desired interior humidity and the maximum daily exterior humidity, both as found in the psychrometric chart.

$$\text{BTUH}_{\text{sensible infiltration}} = \text{CFH} \times 0.018 \times \text{HTD}$$
$$\text{BTUH}_{\text{latent infiltration}} = \text{CFH} \times 79.5 \times \Delta W$$

The rate of airflow can be based on either the air change method or on the crack method. However, since heat gain calculations are often done with the intention of incorporating a mechanical cooling system, which in turn usually means that an air supply will be utilized, infiltration heat gain is frequently replaced by forced mechanical ventilation. If the amount of fresh air that is distributed mechanically into the occupied spaces exceeds the amount of air that is exhausted, internal pressurization basically eliminates infiltration. While there might be no direct infiltration into the occupied spaces, there still would be a load on the system as a result of the ventilation, and this ventilation load would include both a sensible and a latent component.

Internal Heat Gains

In addition to external heat loads, heat gains are produced by internal loads. People, lights, and equipment all contribute to the heat gain, with people and many types of equipment contributing latent as well as sensible gains. These internal loads must be accounted for when doing a heat gain calculation.

One kilowatt of electricity is equivalent to 3412 BTUH. So, if a lighting system's total wattage or the wattage of a piece of equipment is known, it is relatively easy to convert this into a $\text{BTUH}_{\text{sensible}}$ heat gain. If the equipment results in latent as well as sensible loads, however, it is usually necessary to refer to tables that list the heat gain from equipment.

Lights

The traditional method of dealing with heat gain from lighting is to find the total wattage used and multiply this by 3.412 BTUH per watt-hour. The heat gain from incandescent lighting is based merely on the lamp wattage. With fluorescent and HID lighting, heat gain results from the ballasts as well as the lamps. For ease of calculation, ballast wattage can be assumed to be around 20% of lamp wattage, so the wattage of fluorescent or HID fixtures is found by multiplying the lamp wattage by a factor of 1.2. This fixture wattage is then multiplied by 3.412 BTUH per watt-hour. But since $1.2 \times 3.214 = \approx 4$, we can multiply the lamp wattage of a fluorescent or HID fixture by 4 BTUH per watt-hour to determine the heat gain contribution.

Given a lighting wattage of 5000 watts, what would be the heat gain from these lights? If they were incandescent lamps, the heat gain would be:

$$5000 \text{ watts} \times 3.412 \text{ BTUH/watt-hour}$$
$$= 17{,}060 \text{ BTUH}$$

Table 7.23: RATES OF HEAT GAIN FROM OCCUPANTS OF CONDITIONED SPACES

Degree of Activity	Typical Application	Adj. Total Heat BTUH	Sensible BTUH$_{sens}$	Latent BTUH$_{lat}$
Seated at rest	Theater, movie	350	210	140
Very light work seated	Office, hotels, apartments	420	230	190
Seated, eating	Restaurant	580	255	325
Light work — seated, typing	Office, hotels, apartments	510	255	255
Light work — standing or walking slowly	Retail store bank	640	315	325
Walking, 3 mph or Light bench work	Factory	780	345	435
Moderate Dancing	Dance Hall	1280	405	875
Heavy work	Factory	1600	565	1035
Very Heavy work, athletics	Gymnasium	1800	635	1165

Source: Adapted from Table 26.30 in *ASHRAE Guide and Data Book—Fundamentals and Equipment* (1963).

Table 7.24: RATES OF HEAT GAIN FROM OCCUPANTS OF CONDITIONED SPACES

Level of Activity	Typical Application	Total	Heat gain, BTUH Sensible	Latent
Seated, at rest	Theater	350	245	105
Seated, light work	Office	400	245	155
Moderate office work	Office	450	250	200
Standing, walking	Sales clerk	500	250	250
Light bench work	Factory	750	275	475
Dancing	Nightclub	850	305	545
Heavy work	Factory	1450	580	870

Source: Adapted from Table 25.16 in the *ASHRAE Handbook—Fundamentals* (1977). There values are adjusted for a normal percentage of men, women, and children.

If they were fluorescent lamps, the load would be:

$$5000 \text{ watts} \times 1.2 \times 3.412 \text{ BTUH/watt-hour}$$
$$= 20{,}472 \text{ BTUH, or}$$
$$5000 \text{ watts} \times 4 \text{ BTUH/watt - hour} \approx 20{,}000 \text{ BTUH.}$$

Equipment

As mentioned, the heat contribution from equipment is generally found from appropriate tables. Various tables exist that list a variety of equipment and appliances. The heat gain may be both sensible and latent. With detailed calculations, it is appropriate to factor in the length of time that both equipment and lights might operate, but for our purposes, this refinement is not critical.

People

Each person is essentially a heat engine that must continually release generated excess heat to the surrounding environment. The rate of this release and its breakdown between sensible and latent energy will vary according to the type of activity in which an individual is engaged. The basic heat gains from occupants of conditioned spaces are listed in Tables 7.23 and 7.24. The listed gains in Table 7.24 are adjusted for a normal percentage of men, women, and children. Based on the differences between the listed heat gains in these two tables, it should be clear that these tables merely represent approximate gains from occupants.

Alternative Heat Gain Procedure— Space Design Cooling Load

Although IHGM produces a reasonable indication of the overall heat gain, particularly in terms of insolation, and does so in a way that can effectively inform the architectural design, it tends to overestimate the actual load for the environmental control system. Rather than maximize the heat gain and then size the equipment to match the instantaneous heat gain load, SDCLM accepts a slight increase in DBTs and a connected storage of heat gain in the construction thermal mass.

SDCLM, while somewhat more obscure in terms of the thermal processes, can effectively estimate the load on the environmental control system. The basic procedures for SDCLM are presented here merely for comparison and reference. If we wish to use SDCLM to calculate the cooling

PROCEDURES FOR CALCULATING THE SPACE DESIGN COOLING LOAD

Load Source	Equation	Description
External		
Glass Solar	BTUH = A (SC) SCL	A: Glass Area Calculated from Architectural Plans SC: Shading Coefficient SCL: Solar Cooling Load Factor – Table Data For Externally Shaded Glass, Use North Orientation for Shaded Area
Conduction	BTUH = UA (CLTD)	U: "U" Coefficient for Glazing A: Glass Area Calculated from Architectural Plans CLTD: Conduction Load through Glass – Table Data Correct for Outside DBT and Daily Range Correct for Inside DBT
Walls	BTUH = UA (CLTD)	U: Design Heat Transmission Coefficients A: Areas Calculated from Architectural Plans Wall: Type Classifications – Table Data CLTD: Cooling Load Temperature Difference for Walls – Table Data Correct for Outside DBT and Daily Range Correct for Inside DBT
Roof	BTUH = UA (CLTD)	U: Design Heat Transmission Coefficients A: Areas Calculated from Architectural Plans Roof: Type Classifications – Table Data CLTD: Cooling Load Temperature for Roof – Table Data Correct for Outside DBT and Daily Range Correct for Inside DBT
Ceilings & Floors	BTUH = UA (TD)	U: Design Heat Transmission Coefficients A: Areas Calculated from Architectural Plans TD: Design Temperature Difference
Internal		
Lights	BTUH = INPUT (CLF)	Input Rating from Electrical and Lighting Plans Zone Type – Table Data CLF: Cooling Load Factor Based on Total Hours of Operation and Time – Table Data
People Sensible	$BTUH_s$ = No. (Sens. H.G.) CLF	No.: Number of People in Space from Occupancy Standards Sensible Heat Gain from Occupants – Table Data Zone Type – Table Data CLF: Cooling Load Factor for People; Based on Duration of Occupancy and Time from Entry – Table Data Correct for Space Temperature and/or Density of Occupants CLF = 1.0 if There Is Variable Space Temperature and/or High Density
People Latent	$BTUH_l$ = No. (Lat. H.G.)	Latent Heat Gain from Occupants – Table Data
Appliances Sensible	$BTUH_s$ = (Heat Gain) CLF	Recommended Rate of Heat Gain - Sensible Heat CLF: Cooling Load Factor for Sensible Heat Gain – Table Data
Latent	$BTUH_l$ = Heat Gain	Recommended Rate of Heat Gain – Latent Heat
Infiltration		
Sensible	$BTUH_s$ = 1.08 CFM (ΔT) CLF = 0.018 CFH ΔT) CLF	CFM & CFH: Infiltration Air - Air Change Method ΔT: Inside-Outside Air Temperature Difference, °F – Table Data CLF: Cooling Load Factor for Sensible Infiltration
Latent	$BTUH_l$ = 4840 CFM (ΔW) =79.5 CFH (ΔW)	ΔW: Inside-Outside Air Humidity Ratio Difference, lb/lb, Determined from Psychrometric Chart on Interior and Max. Exterior Conditions

The data necessary for calculating SDCL are available in various references, including the *ASHRAE Handbook—Fundamentals* and Stein et al. (2006).

load, we will have to refer to tables available in other publications, such as the ASHRAE *Handbook—Fundamentals* or Grondzik et al. (2010).

SDCLM was developed to provide a more reasonable indication of the cooling load that the environmental control system must control. This method, which follows the same basic procedures used in instantaneous heat gain calculations, includes consideration of the potential of the physical mass of the structure to absorb some of the heat gains, particularly at the peaks, and thereby reduce the load on the equipment. The procedures and tables used in SDCLM are outlined below.

The cooling load temperature differential (CLTD) replaces the ETD used in IHGM for opaque barriers, and the solar cooling load (SCL) factor is used rather than the SHGF. While an initial cooling load calculation procedure used a maximum solar gain factor that then had to be adjusted for various conditions of time and orientation, the SCL is selected for a particular orientation, time of day, time of year, and latitude, similar to the SHGF used with IHGM, although SCL also is based on the relative mass of the construction. As with the IHGM, the SCL has to be adjusted by an appropriate SC. In fact, basically the same SCs are used for both IHGM and SDCLM.

Winter Solar Gain

Insolation is the most significant factor in terms of heat gain from external forces. Since this source of heat gain can be modified by a number of different architectural responses, control of the interior thermal conditions need not be totally, or even perhaps primarily, reliant on energy-consumptive environmental control systems. Proper building orientation and placement and sizing of openings are the first steps in developing a positive response to the potential advantages and problems posed by insolation. Other design responses that can contribute to the development of positive internal thermal conditions include effective shading, which can actually enhance the intentions for the opening while minimizing any associated complications, and the incorporation of thermal storage within the construction. Effectively incorporated into the architectural design, these can contribute to the overall visual qualities of a design while improving the thermal characteristics of the space.

A major benefit of using the IHGM and the SHGF tables is the exposure to information regarding incident solar radiation for all the months of the year. As designers, we can use these data to refine a design so that it can respond effectively to thermal exchange, particularly in terms of insolation. This generally means developing a design to capture solar radiation during the colder periods of the year while minimizing the solar gain during the warmer periods. In order to benefit from this approach, particularly in terms of capturing solar gain, we need to provide a way of storing the solar gain so that it does not overheat the space when the sun is shining and is available when there is no direct sun. This generally means adding thermal mass.

Although SDCLM incorporates consideration of thermal mass, the basic response to environmental forces is not as clearly addressed in this heat gain method as in IHGM, so appropriate design responses are not as clear. However, the basic principle of thermal storage used by SDCLM has important architectural design implications, particularly in connection with direct solar gain. With increased thermal mass, the impact of solar radiation on the internal thermal conditions can be modified. If solar gain is absorbed by the mass of the construction, there will be less of an increase in the interior ambient air temperature. As a result, the insolation will not create as much of a load on the mechanical system during the overheated period of the year, and it can provide an effective heat source for the underheated periods. Without thermal mass, any solar gain, even in the middle of the winter, can result in excessive heat gain.

A simple rule of thumb is that 1 cubic foot of exposed thermal mass should be provided for each square foot of south-facing glazing. Recognizing that there is a time lag associated with thermal absorption, the cubic foot of mass, which might be concrete or masonry, should be spread out. This is most easily accomplished by providing 3 square feet of at least 4-inch thickness of the mass material. Water or a phase-change material can also provide the necessary thermal mass. With a phase-change material, the distributed material should be equivalent to 4 inches of masonry, which usually can be provided with much less material since the phase-change process typically entails considerable exchange of thermal energy. With water, since thermal absorption involves convective transfer, the mass does not need to be distributed across a larger area, although it is better if the water is directly exposed to the sun. Location of the thermal mass generally requires merely that the exposed mass be positioned so there is a clear line of sight between the mass and the glazed opening, not that the direct sun must strike the mass. With water, however, since the mass is more concentrated, some closer connection between sun and storage mass is preferred.

Review of the SHGF information presented in Tables 7.16A–G can clarify some basic objectives of proper solar design. First of all, in terms of heat gain, we can see that the July 21st gain in the morning for an eastern exposure or in the afternoon for a western exposure is 1000 BTUH, and for the full day it is 1181 BTUH, although for a southern exposure the comparable values are 352 and 704 BTUH.

So, during the overheated period of the year, the gain in 1 day for the southern exposure is only about one-half as much as for the eastern or western exposure. Further exploration indicates that the maximum July 21st hourly gain, which is typically the basis for sizing the cooling system, is 216 BTUH per square foot for an eastern or western exposure but only 109 BTUH per square foot for

SHGF FOR 40° NORTH LATITUDE FOR DS SHEET GLASS

Date	Solar Time (a.m.)	Direct Normal (BUTH/ft²)	N	E	S	W	HOR	Solar Time (p.m.)
21 Jan	8	142	5	111	75	5	14	4
	9	239	12	154	160	12	55	3
	10	274	16	124	213	16	96	2
	11	289	19	61	244	19	124	1
	12	294	20	21	254	21	133	12
Half-Day Totals			**62**	**461**	**819**	**63**	**356**	
21 July	5	2	1	2	0	0	0	7
	6	138	37	137	11	11	32	6
	7	208	30	204	21	20	88	5
	8	241	28	216	30	26	145	4
	9	259	32	193	52	31	194	3
	10	269	35	146	81	35	231	2
	11	275	37	81	102	37	254	1
	12	276	38	41	109	41	262	12
Half-Day Totals			**219**	**1000**	**352**	**181**	**1075**	
	(a.m.)	(BUTH/ft²)	N	E	S	W	HOR	(p.m.)

a southern exposure, although the higher half-day totals compare on a 3-to-1 basis: 1000:352.

Another critical comparison is between the southern exposure for January 21, with a half-day total of 819, and July 21, with a half-day total of only 352. This indicates that during the colder period of the year, a southern exposure has a potential solar gain that is almost two and a half times the gain during the overheated period of the year. In fact, the full-day gain for a southern exposure is 1638 BTUH per square foot of single glazing, whereas the full-day gain on July 21 for an eastern or western exposure is only 1181 BTUH per square foot. That is, the most critical exposures in terms of heat gain during the summer receive less insolation than does a southern exposure in the middle of the winter! No wonder the maximum cooling for a south-facing space with considerable glazing might occur in the winter rather than the summer.

These comparisons are very informative, but they do not tell the full story. If the southern exposure is provided with exterior shading that essentially eliminates all direct solar access during the warmer periods while not diminishing the solar exposure during the colder periods, which is relatively easy to do if we understand the movement of the sun each day over the year (see the discussion on daylighting), the comparison between heat gain for a southern exposure in January versus July is even more dramatic. On January 21, the daily gain is still 1638 BTUH per square foot, but on July 21, with shading, we should use the northern exposure and the full-day gain is only 438 BTUH per square foot, a ratio of about 4 to 1!

EXAMPLE PROBLEMS

1. What are the appropriate terms/units associated with each of the following notations and standard numerical values used in heat loss and heat gain calculations?

   a. ΔT _____   b. ΔW _____
   c. Δh _____   d. 0.075 _____
   e. 0.24 _____   f. 60 _____
   f. 0.018 _____   g. 1.08 _____

2. Since BTU = Weight × Specific Heat × Temperature Differential is the basic formula for thermal exchange, which of the following is/are not appropriate expression(s) for the thermal energy exchange in calculating an air system? (Note that although not all units are indicated, you should still check that the adjustments for different time units are proper.)
   1. BTUH = CFH × 0.018 × ΔT
   2. BTUH = CFM × 1.08 × ΔT
   3. BTUH = CFM × 0.075 × 0.24 × 60 × ΔT
   4. BTUH = CFH × 0.075 × 0.24 × ΔT

3. Recognizing that 1 gallon of water weighs 8.33 pounds, what would be the proper formula to relate British Thermal Units per hour (BTUH), gallons per minute (GPM), and temperature differential (ΔT)?

4. If the total heat gain, both sensible and latent, for a space is 240,000 BTUH and the sensible heat ratio (SHR) is 0.67, how much air would you have to circulate to condition the space if ΔT is 24° F?

5. If the total heat gain, both sensible and latent, for a space is 240,000 BTUH and the SHR is 0.67, how much air would you have to circulate to condition the space if the difference in specific humidity (ΔW) between the room air and the supply air is 0.0025 pound of water per pound of dry air?

6. If the total heat gain, both sensible and latent, for a space is 240,000 BTUH, how much air would you have to circulate to condition the space if the enthalpy of the room air (RA) and the supply air (SA) are 31.5 BTU per pound and 24 BTU per pound, respectively, and the SA volume is 13.2 cubic feet per pound?

7. If the sensible heat gain for a space is 150,000 BTUH, how much air would you have to circulate to condition the space if the ΔT between the RA and the SA is 20° F?

8. A 2000-square-foot house, which has a maximum heat loss of 50,000 BTUH, is to be conditioned by warm air based on the standard ratio of CFM per square foot. What would have to be the maximum temperature differential between the SA and the RA?

9. What would be the annual heating demand for a structure, located in a region that has an annual total of 6400 degree days, if the maximum heat loss at 70° F is 120,000 BTUH?

10. If #2 oil, which has a 140,000 BTU-per-gallon heat value, is to be used as the fuel to heat a home that has an *annual* BTU heating load of 150,000,000 BTU, approximately how much will it cost to heat the home for a year? Assume that the overall efficiency of the heating system is 85% and that heating oil costs $2 per gallon.

Answers

1.
  a. ΔT – change in temperature, generally in degrees Fahrenheit (°F)
  b. ΔW – change in specific humidity (lb/lb)
  c. Δh – change in enthalpy (BTU/lb of air)
  d. 0.075 – lb/cu ft of air at standard atmospheric pressure
  e. 0.24 – specific heat of air
  f. 60 – minutes per hour
  g. 0.018 – 0.075 lb/cu ft × 0.24 specific heat of air
  h. 1.08 – 0.075 lb/cu ft × 0.24 specific heat of air × 60 min/hr

2. They are all proper expressions used to equate a change in temperature for a volume of air with the BTUH entailed in that change.
  a. $BTUH = CFH \times 0.018 \times \Delta T$
  b. $BTUH = CFM \times 1.08 \times \Delta T$
  c. $BTUH = CFM \times 0.075 \times 0.24 \times 60 \times \Delta T$
  d. $BTUH = CFH \times 0.075 \times 0.24 \times \Delta T$

3. $BTUH = \text{Weight of Water per Hour} \times \Delta T$

$$GPM \times 8.33 \text{ lb/gal} \times 60 \text{ min/hr} \times \Delta T = GPM \times 500 \text{ lb min/gal - hr} \times \Delta T$$

4.
$$CFM = \frac{BTUH_{sens}}{1.08 \times \Delta T} = \frac{2.4 \times 10^5 BTUH \times 0.67}{1.08 \times 24°F}$$
$$= \frac{1.6 \times 10^5 BTUH}{1.08 \times 24°F} = 6203.7 \text{ CFM} = 6200 \text{ CFM}$$

5.
$$CFM = \frac{BTUH_{latent}}{4840 \times \Delta W} = \frac{2.4 \times 10^5 BTUH \times (1 - 0.67)}{4840 \times 0.0025 \text{ lb/lb}}$$
$$= \frac{8 \times 10^4 BTUH}{4840 \times 0.0025 \text{ lb/lb}} = 6611.6 \text{ CFM} = c. \ 6600 \text{ CFM}$$

6.
$$CFM = \frac{BTUH \times CF/lb}{60 \text{ min/hr} \times \Delta h} = \frac{2.4 \times 10^5 BTUH \times 13.2 \text{ CF/lb}}{60 \text{ min/hr} \times (31.5 - 24) BTU/lb} = 7040 \text{CFM} = c.7050 \text{CFM}$$

7.
$$CFM = \frac{BTUH_{sensible}}{1.08 \times \Delta T} = \frac{1.5 \times 10^5 \text{ BTUH}}{1.08 \times 20°F} = 6,944 \text{CFM} = c.6950 \text{CFM}$$

8.
$$\Delta T = \frac{BTUH_{sensible}}{1.08 \times CFM} = \frac{5 \times 10^4 \text{ BTUH}}{1.08 \times 2000 \text{ CFM}} = 23.2°F$$

9.
$$BTUH \text{ Demand} = \frac{1.2 \times 10^5 \text{ BTUH}}{70° \text{ F}} \times 6400 \text{ DD} \times 24 \text{ hr/day} = 263,314,285 \text{ BTU}$$

10.
$$\text{Cost} = \frac{1.5 \times 10^8 BTU \times \$2 \text{ per gal.}}{85\% \times 1.4 \times 10^5 BTU/gal.} = \$2521 \approx \$2500$$

HEAT LOSS/HEAT GAIN CALCULATIONS

Example

Calculate the maximum hourly heat loss in BTUH that would occur for the small structure shown in Figures 7.12A and 7.12B if the interior ambient air temperature is to be maintained at 68° F and the exterior ambient air temperature is 0° F. Include the heat loss from the edge of the slab and from infiltration based on an exterior wind velocity of 15 mph. Use the air change method, assuming medium tightness. In addition to the maximum hourly heat loss, you should also determine the annual BTU heating demand if the structure were at a location with a 5000–degree day heating season. Since you will also be expected to determine the hourly heat gain in BTUH for this structure, you should organize your calculations according to the various exposures. Determine the area of exterior wall and window facing north, east, south, and west separately.

Calculate the maximum instantaneous hourly heat gain on July 21 for 40° north latitude. Assume that the interior ambient air temperature is to be maintained at 75° F and 40% relative humidity and that the maximum daily exterior ambient air temperature is 95° F, at which time the exterior WBT is 85° F. You should also recognize that for this calculation there are a total of eight people in the structure involved in work at a moderate level and that the electric lighting is based on 6 watts per square foot. Assume that the exterior wall are of an intermediate color.

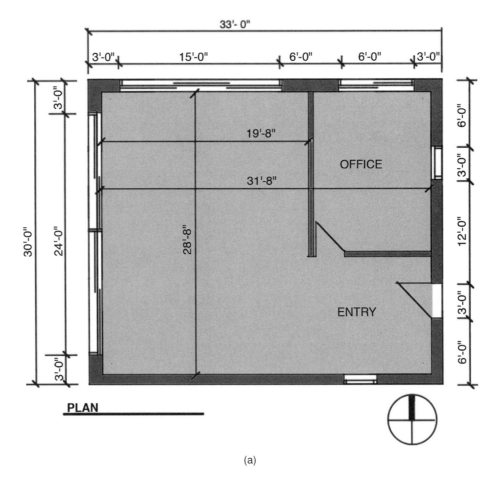

(a)

Figure 7.12A: EXAMPLE ONE FLOOR PLAN

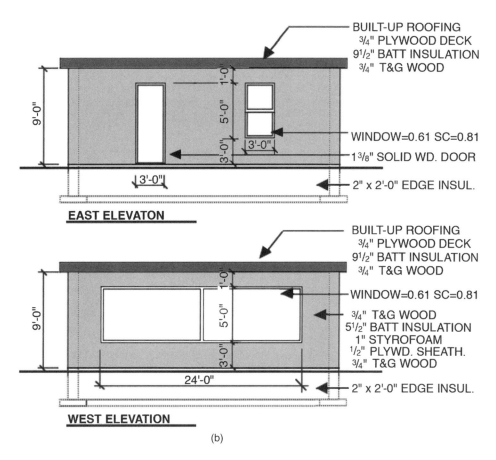

Figure 7.12B: **EXAMPLE ONE ELEVATIONS**

Heat Loss Calculations

Indoor Temp.: 68° F Outdoor Temp.: 0° F

Winter "U" Coefficients

Wall		Roof	
Inside Air Film	00.68	Inside Air Film	00.61
³/₄″ T&G Wd.	00.94	³/₄″ T&G Wd.	00.94
5¹/₂″ Insulation	19.00	9¹/₂″ Insulation	30.00
1″ Styrofoam	05.00	³/₄″ Plywood	00.93
¹/₂″ Plywood	00.62	B.U.R.	00.33
³/₄″ T&G Wd.	00.94	Outside Air Film	<u>00.17</u>
Outside Air Film	<u>00.17</u>	Total R	32.98
Total R	27.35		
$U = 1/R_t = 0.037$		$U = 1/R_t = 0.030$	
Window		**Door**	
$U = 0.61$		$U = 0.39$	

Maximum Btuh Heat Loss Calculations

North Wall		
	Length: 31.67 ft	Height: 9 ft
	Gross Area: 285 sq ft	
Window	Window Area: 105 sq ft	"U" Coef: 0.61
	BTUH = Area × U × ΔT	4355 BTUH
Wall	Net Area: 180 sq ft	"U" Coef: 0.037
	BTUH = Area × U × ΔT	448 BTUH

East Wall		
	Length: 28.67 ft	Height: 9 ft
	Gross Area: 258 sq ft	
Window	Window Area: 15 sq ft	"U" Coef: 0.61
	BTUH = Area × U × ΔT	622 BTUH
Wall	Net Area: 219 sq ft	"U" Coef: 0.037
	BTUH = Area × U × ΔT = 545 BTUH	
Door	Door Area: 24 sq ft	"U" Coef: 0.39
	BTUH = Area × U × ΔT = 636 BTUH	

South Wall		
	Length: 31.67 ft	Height: 9 ft
	Gross Area: 285 sq ft	
Window	Window Area: 15 sq ft	"U" Coef: 0.61
	BTUH = Area × U × ΔT = 622 BTUH	
Wall	Net Area: 270 sq ft	"U" Coef: 0.037
	BTUH = Area × U × ΔT = 671 BTUH	

West Wall		
	Length: 28.67 ft	Height: 9 ft
	Gross Area: 258 sq ft	
Window	Window Area: 120 sq ft	"U" Coef: 0.61
	BTUH = Area × U × ΔT = 4978 BTUH	
Wall	Net Area: 138 sq ft	"U" Coef: 0.037
	BTUH = Area × U × ΔT = 343 BTUH	

Ceiling		
	Length: 31.67 ft	Width: 28.67 ft
	Gross Area: 908 sq ft	"U" Coef: 0.030
	BTUH = Area × U × ΔT = 1872 BTUH	
Edge		
	Length: 31.67 ft	Width: 28.67 ft
	Linear Length: 120.68 ft	40 BTUH/L.F.
	BTUH = Linear Length × BTUH/lin. ft = 4827 BTUH	

Infiltration		
	Assume Medium Construction	
	Width: 28.67 ft	Length: 31.67 ft Height: 9 ft
	Volume: 8,170 cu ft	Air Change: 1.1 A.C./hr
		(Adjusted for °F)
	BTUH = Volume × A.C./hr × 0.018 × ΔT = 11,003 BTUH	

Maximum Hourly Heat Loss	**30,922 BTUH**

Annual Heating Demand

Degree Days: 5000

BTU = $BTUH_{max}$/°F × DD × 24 hr/day = 54,568,235 BTU

Heat Gain Calculations

4 p.m.	Indoor:	75° F	40% RH	$W = 0.0074$ lb/lb
Lights turned on at 8 a.m. and on for 8 hours per day				
	Outdoor$_{Max}$:	95° F	85° F WBT	$W = 0.0240$ lb/lb
People enter at 8 a.m. and remain for 8 hours per day				

Summer "U" Coefficients

Wall			Roof	
Inside Air Film	00.68		Inside Air Film	00.92
$3/4''$ T&G Wd.	00.94		$3/4''$ T&G Wd.	00.94
$5^1/2''$ Insulation	19.00		$9^1/2''$ Insulation	30.00
1″ Styrofoam	05.00		$3/4''$ Plywood	00.93
$1/2''$ Plywood	00.62		B.U.R.	00.33
$3/4''$ T&G Wd.	00.94		Outside Air Film	00.25
Outside Air Film	00.25		Total R	33.37
Total R	27.43			
$U = 1/R_t = 0.036$			$U = 1/R_t = 0.030$	
Window			**Door**	
$U = 0.58$			$U = 0.38$	

Maximum Instantaneous Heat Gain Calculations

North Wall

	Length: 31.67 ft Gross Area: 285 sq ft	Height: 9 ft	
Window	Area: 105 sq ft $BTUH_{trans} = Area \times U \times HTD = 1035$ $BTUH_{sensible}$ SC: 0.81 $BTUH_{solar} = Area \times SC \times SHGF = 2381$ $BTUH_{sensible}$	HTD: 17° F SHGF: 28 BTUH/sq ft	"U" Coef: 0.58
Wall	Net Area = 180 sq ft $BTUH_{trans} = Area \times U \times ETD = 125$ $BTUH_{sensible}$	ETD: 19° F	"U" Coef: 0.036

East Wall

	Length: 28.67 ft	Height: 9 ft	
	Gross Area: 258 sq ft		
Window	Area: 15 sq ft $BTUH_{trans} = Area \times U \times HTD = 148$ $BTUH_{sensible}$ SHGF: 26 BTUH/sq ft $BTUH_{solar} = Area \times SC \times SHGF = 316$ $BTUH_{sensible}$	HTD: 17° F	"U" Coef: 0.58 SC: 0.81
Door	Area: 24 sq ft $BTUH_{trans} = Area \times U \times ETD = 173$ $BTUH_{sensible}$	ETD: 19° F	"U" Coef: 0.38
Wall	Net Area: 192 sq ft $BTUH_{trans} = Area \times U \times ETD = 152$ $BTUH_{sensible}$	ETD: 19° F	"U" Coef: 0.036

South Wall

	Length: 31.67 ft	Height: 9 ft	
	Gross Area: 285 sq ft		
Window	Area: 15 sq ft	HTD: 17° F	"U" Coef: 0.58
	$BTUH_{trans} = Area \times U \times HTD = 148\ BTUH_{sensible}$		
	SC: 0.81		
	SHGF: 30 BTUH/sq ft		
	$BTUH_{solar} = Area \times SC \times SHGF = 365\ BTUH_{sensible}$		
Wall	Net Area: 270 sq ft	ETD: 28° F	"U" Coef: 0.036
	$BTUH_{trans} = Area \times U \times ETD = 276\ BTUH_{sensible}$		

West Wall

	Length: 28.67 ft	Height: 9 ft	
	Gross Area: 258 sq ft		
Window	Area: 120 sq ft	HTD: 17° F	"U" Coef: 0.58
	$BTUH_{trans} = Area \times U \times HTD = 1183\ BTUH_{sensible}$	SC: 0.81	
	SHGF: 216 BTUH/sq ft		
	$BTUH_{solar} = Area \times SC \times SHGF = 20{,}995$		
	$BTUH_{sensible}$		
Wall	Net Area: 138 sq ft	ETD: 39° F	"U" Coef: 0.036
	$BTUH_{trans} = Area \times$ "U" $\times ETD = 196\ BTUH_{sensible}$		

Ceiling

Length: 31.67 ft	Width: 28.67 ft
Gross Area: 908 sq ft	
"U" Coef: 0.030	ETD: 55° F
$BTUH_{trans} = Area \times U \times ETD = 1497\ BTUH_{sensible}$	

Infiltration

	Assume Medium Construction	
	Air Change: 0.5 (Adjusted for 95° F & 7.5 mph)	
	Width: 28.67 ft	Length: 31.67 ft Height: 9 ft
	HTD: 17° F	ΔW: 0.0166
		(Adjusted for 4 p.m.)
Sensible	$BTUH_{sensible} = Volume \times A.C./hr \times 0.018 \times HTD$	
	$= 8172\ CF \times 0.5\ A.C./hr \times 0.018 \times 17°\ F = 1250$	
	$BTUH_{sensible}$	
Latent	$BTUH_{latent} = Volume \times A.C./hr \times 79.5 \times \Delta W$	
	$= 8172\ CF \times 0.5\ A.C./hr \times 79.5 \times 0.0166 = 5392$	
	$BTUH_{latent}$	

Lights

Width: 28.67 ft	Length: 31.67 ft 6.00 watts/sq ft
$BTUH_{sensible} = Area \times watts/sq\ ft \times 3.412$	
$BTUH/watt$	
$= 18{,}588\ BTUH_{sensible}$	

People

Number of People: 8	
Sensible	$BTUH_{sensible}/person$: 255 $BTUH_{sensible}$
	$BTUH_{sensible} = 8 \times 255\ BTUH = 2040\ BTUH_{sensible}$
Latent	$BTUH_{latent}/person$: 255 $BTUH_{lat}$
	$BTUH_{latent} = 8 \times 255\ BTUH = 2040\ BTUH_{latent}$

Maximum Instantaneous Total Hourly Heat Gain @ 4 pm

Sensible	50,868 $BTUH_{sensible}$
Latent	7432 $BTUH_{latent}$
Total	**58,300 BTUH**

Instantaneous Heat Gain Calculations (other times)

While the significant amount of west-facing glass in the structure indicates that the maximum heat gain would probably occur at 4 p.m., you might attempt to determine the maximum heat gain at other times of the day as well. Below are the total values for different times.

8 a.m.	Sensible	30,136 BTUH$_{sensible}$
	Latent	7432 BTUH$_{latent}$
	Total	37,568 BTUH
10 a.m.	Sensible	33,146 BTUH$_{sensible}$
	Latent	7432 BTUH$_{latent}$
	Total	40,578 BTUH
12 p.m.	Sensible	34,758 BTUH$_{sensible}$
	Latent	7432 BTUH$_{latent}$
	Total	42,190 BTUH
2 p.m.	Sensible	44,923 BTUH$_{sensible}$
	Latent	7432 BTUH$_{latent}$
	Total	52,355 BTUH
6 p.m.	Sensible	42,389 BTUH$_{sensible}$
	Latent	7432 BTUH$_{latent}$
	Total	49,821 BTUH

BIBLIOGRAPHY

Publications of the American Society of Heating, Refrigeration and Air-Conditioning Engineers, Inc., Atlanta, GA: *ASHRAE Handbook — Fundamentals* (2005).

ASHRAE Standard 62.1 — 2004: *Ventilation for Acceptable Indoor Air Quality.*

ASHRAE Standard 62.2 — 2004: *Ventilation for Acceptable Indoor Air Quality in Low-Rise Residential Buildings.*

ANSI/ASHRAE/IESNA Standard 90.1 — 2004: *Energy Standard for Buildings Except Low-Rise Residential Buildings.*

ANSI/ASHRAE Standard 90.2 — 2004: *Efficient Design of Low-Rise Residential Buildings.*

Bradshaw, V. *The Building Environment: Active and Passive Control Systems.* John Wiley & Sons, Inc., New Jersey, 2006.

Heerwagen, D. *Passive and Active Environmental Controls,* McGraw-Hill Book Company, New York, 2004.

Jones, W.P. *Air Conditioning Applications and Design.* Butterworth-Heinemann, Oxford, 1996.

Shuttleworth, R. *Mechanical and Electrical Systems for Construction,* McGraw-Hill Book Company, New York, 1983.

Grondzik, W.T., A.G. Kwok., Stein, B., and J.S. Reynolds. *Mechanical and Electrical Equipment for Buildings.* John Wiley & Sons, Inc., New Jersey, 2010.

8 HISTORIC REVIEW

INTRODUCTION
HISTORY OF HEATING
CENTRAL HEATING
HISTORY OF COOLING

INTRODUCTION

This chapter reviews the historical development of the various methods of heating and cooling, and the effects these methods have had on the development of architecture. Perhaps the main reason we design and construct buildings has always been to control the natural environment, which is often not very conducive to human comfort. While a building structure can contribute to improving or enhancing the natural conditions that exist, control of the thermal environment in the colder climates has typically depended on some sort of heating system. And while our ability to effectively control conditions in the hotter climates is relatively recent, there have been various means, in addition to providing appropriate architectural designs and materials, to act in response to overheated conditions.

The different systems that have been used for this adjustment of the natural conditions have had an impact on the development of architectural form. This impact has occurred both in terms of the various architectural responses necessary to accommodate these systems and in terms of the design opportunities afforded by these systems, which allow for less dependency on strict environmental constraints.

To begin this historic exploration, it is appropriate to consider what Vitruvius wrote more than 2000 years ago.

Vitruvius, the Ten Books on Architecture

BOOK II, CHAPTER I: THE ORIGINS OF THE DWELLING HOUSE

1. *The men of old were born like the wild beasts, in woods, caves, and groves, and lived on savage fare. As time went on, the thickly crowded trees in a certain place, tossed by storms and winds, and rubbing their branches against one another, caught fire, and so the inhabitants of the place were put to flight, being terrified by the furious flame. After it subsided, they drew near, and observing that they were very comfortable standing before the warm fire, they put on logs and, while thus keeping it alive, brought up other people to it, showing them by signs how much comfort they got from it. In that gathering of men, at a time when utterance of sound was purely individual, from daily habits they fixed upon articulate words just as these had happened to come; then, from indicating by name things in common use, the result was that in this chance way they began to talk, and thus originated conversation with one another.*

2. *Therefore, it was the discovery of fire that originally gave rise to the coming together of men, to the deliberative assembly, and to social intercourse. And so, as they kept coming together in greater numbers into one place, finding themselves naturally gifted beyond other animals in not being obliged to walk with faces to the ground, but upright and gazing upon the splendour of the starry firmament, and also in being able to do with ease whatever they chose with their hands and fingers, they began in that first assembly to construct shelters. Some made them of green boughs, others dug caves on mountain sides, and some, in imitation of the nests of swallows and the way they built, made places of refuge out of mud and twigs. Next, by observing the shelters of others and adding new details to their own inceptions, they constructed better and better kinds of huts as time went on.*

3. *And since they were of imitative and teachable nature, they would daily point out to each other the results of their building, boasting of the novelties in it; and thus, with their natural gifts sharpened by emulation, their standards improved daily. At first they set up forked stakes connected by twigs and covered these walls with mud. Others made walls of lumps of dried mud, covering them with reeds and leaves to keep out the rain and the heat. Finding that such roofs could not stand the rain during the storms of winter, they built them with peaks daubed with mud, the roofs sloping and projecting so as to carry off the rain water*

4. *That houses originated as I have written above, we can see for ourselves from the buildings that are to this day constructed of like materials by foreign tribes: for instance, in Gaul, Spain, Portugal, and Aquitaine, roofed with oak shingles or thatched....*

6. *... Furthermore, as men made progress by becoming daily more expert in building, and as their ingenuity was increased by their dexterity so that from habit they attained to considerable skill, their intelligence was enlarged by their industry until the more proficient adopted the trade of carpenters. From these early beginnings, and from the fact that nature had not only endowed the human race with senses like the rest of the animals, but had also equipped their minds with the powers of thought and understanding, thus putting all other animals under their sway, they next gradually advanced from the construction of buildings to the other arts and sciences, and so*

passed from a rude and barbarous mode of life to civilization and refinement.
Vitruvius, *The Ten Books on Architecture*, pp. 38–40

It is ironic that architects often continue to utilize design elements that were initially developed in response to a particular purpose long after that purpose has ceased to exist or, perhaps, is even remembered. The fireplace, while not quite yet in this category, is an example of such confusion. The central hearth, which traditionally was the focus of environmentally controlled space during the cold season, was celebrated in the Prairie School houses of Frank Lloyd Wright. However, Wright's use of the fireplace as a significant spatial element in his open-planned designs was possible only because these houses had central heating. Without this modern means of providing thermal control, open planning is not feasible in colder climates, which, of course, is the appropriate location in which to use a fireplace as a spatial focus.

By investigating the evolution of the fireplace, which is the quintessential means of environmental control, and studying its effects on the development of central heating, we can better understand the connection between technological change and architectural design.

The intention of this chapter is to focus on thermal issues, avoiding direct discussion of the important social aspects of fire. The ephemeral and mysterious qualities of the fire's flame have always intrigued and fascinated humankind, imparting an important ceremonial significance to fire. While this significance has obvious architectural implications that should not be denied, our purpose here is to consider the important architectural design implications of effective and knowledgeable use of fire's thermal potential.

Background

Interior space is not heated to warm us, even on the coldest days. On the contrary, the environment is controlled to maintain thermal conditions that allow us to lose our excess body heat, and to do so at the rate at which we produce it. Rather than being heated by the surrounding space, we heat the space!

The human body is essentially a heat engine that must maintain an internal temperature of 98.6° F. The body, like all heat engines, is not 100% efficient. As a result, it can utilize only a portion of the energy that it generates and must dissipate the energy that it cannot use to the surrounding environment. The body transfers this

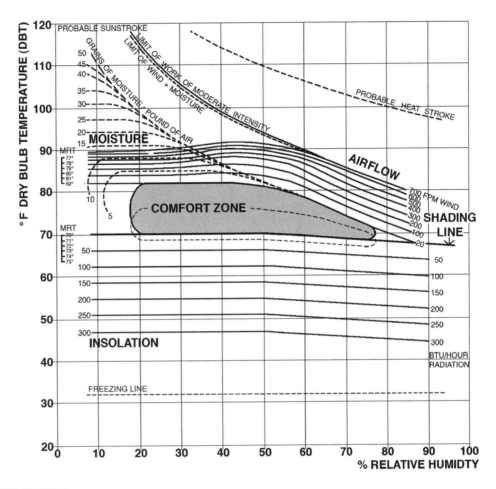

Figure 8.1 BIOCLIMATIC CHART
Adapted from the bioclimatic chart initially presented as Figure 47 in A. Olgyay and V. Olgyay, *Solar Control and Shading Devices* (Princeton University Press, Princeton, NJ, 1957), p. 20.

excess heat to its surrounding environment by the thermal processes of conduction, convection, radiation, and evaporation. When the body is able to dissipate its excess heat at the rate at which it is generated, and to do so without imposing any physiological stress or drawing conscious attention, thermal comfort is attained.

In order to maintain conditions that provide thermal comfort, we must control four factors of the interior environment: the dry bulb temperature (DBT), the humidity or the wet bulb temperature (WBT), the mean radiant temperature (MRT), and the air velocity. These four factors establish what is referred to as the *interior thermal environment*. They influence the processes of thermal transfer through which we interact with the spaces we occupy. In an ideal location, the natural thermal environment would match our body's need for thermal exchange. When the natural conditions do not meet these needs, effective architectural design can sometimes achieve environmental adjustments that are adequate for thermal comfort.

The bioclimatic chart, which was initially presented in Chapter 6 and is shown again in Figure 8.1, was developed by Aladar and Victor Olgyay and initially introduced in their publication *Solar Control and Shading Devices*;[1] it clearly presents the design responses that can effectively reestablish comfortable conditions. These responses were further developed in Victor Olgyay's book *Design with Climate*.[2] Murray Milne and Baruch Givoni, in their article "Architectural Design Based on Climate," presented in *Energy Conservation through Building Design*,[3] translated these responses into a set of appropriate climate-based architectural design approaches.

---

[1] A. Olgyay and V. Olgyay, *Solar Control and Shading Devices* (Princeton University Press, Princeton, NJ, 1957).

[2] V. Olgyay, *Design with Climate: Bioclimatic Approach to Architectural Regionalism* (Princeton University Press, Princeton, NJ, 1963).

[3] M. Milne and B. Givoni, "Architectural Design Based on Climate," in D. Watson, ed., *Energy Conservation through Building Design* (McGraw Hill Book Company, New York, 1979), pp. 96–113.

HISTORY OF HEATING

When environmentally responsive design efforts are not adequate, or when they are not properly developed, thermal comfort conditions are achieved only through the use of some form of energy-consumptive device, what we generally refer to as an *environmental control system* (ECS). Since ancient times, building designers have attempted to ameliorate the natural conditions through building design, but when this was not adequate, they have relied on various "mechanical" devices to achieve acceptable conditions for thermal comfort. The most fundamental of these is fire.[4]

The Fireplace

The open fire was the original means of providing thermal control. As such, it is the initial ECS. In ancient times, during cold weather, heating was achieved by simply placing a fire in the center of the space to be warmed. In fact, one theory suggests that the embryonic beginnings of architecture involved attempts to control the heating potential of such an open fire.[5] In order to enhance the warming potential of the fire, barriers or walls were placed around the fire to increase the thermal benefits it provided. The barriers deflected the draft of air pulled in by the flame, as well as absorbing and reemitting some of the radiant heat emitted by the fire.

Whether or not the earliest architecture was actually intended only as a means of capturing and enhancing the warmth of the fire, we do know that in ancient times fires were usually placed in the center of the spaces that were to be heated. Ruins from ancient Troy, dating from around 2000 B.C.E., show that a central, fixed place was provided

Figure 8.2 OPEN HEARTH AT PENSHURST CASTLE
Heating in the Great Hall at Penshurst Castle, Kent, was by an open hearth that was located in the center of the hall.

for the fire, although no special allowance for venting the smoke was included. The central open hearth, as shown in Figure 8.2, continued in use and was found in other locations. With this approach, if a means was provided to remove the smoke, it was merely an opening located either in the roof or high on an exterior wall. It was not until the Middle Ages that chimneys started to be used to control fires intended for space heating.[6]

The twelfth-century Fontevrault Abbey in Anjou, France, the burial site of Richard the Lion-Hearted and his parents, Henry II and Eleanor of Acquitaine, has perhaps the oldest chimneys still existing.[7] However, these chimneys, shown in Figure 8.3, were intended as vents for the kitchen, built in 1115, rather than as vents for space-heating devices. The Abbey of Senanque in St. Gilles, near Arles, France, built in 1150, did include a fireplace, which was intended as a means of space heating, that had a chimney.[8] In addition to these French examples, Sir Bannister Fletcher suggests that there were early English uses of the chimney at Little Wenham Hall, Suffolk, built in 1270–1280, and at Stokesay Castle, Shropshire, built in 1285–1305, although the plan of Stokesay Castle, shown in Figure 8.4, indicates that there was also a central hearth similar to the one at Penshurst Castle.

While the construction materials that were placed close to the fire had to be noncombustible, the roof, which was not directly in contact with temperatures that were above its combustion point, could be constructed of almost any material. Of course, when combustible materials were used, sparks released from the fire could potentially cause

---

[4]By reviewing the evolution of architectural responses to the use of fire for environmental conditioning, we can begin to address what are perhaps the truly significant questions regarding the relationship between architecture and mechanical systems. (a) When are mechanical systems that modify the physical environment (i.e., H.V.A.C.) integral architectural components and when are they independent devices that are imposed on the architecture? Is there a distinction and, if so, should there be one? (b) In what ways does the physical structure of a building fulfill the need to modify the physical environment thermally? Can the physical structure of a building be considered part of the mechanical system? (c) What are the architectural effects of employing nonarchitectural mechanical devices for the control of the environment? There are two aspects of this question: (i) How has the use of mechanical systems altered architectural form? That is, in what ways has the incorporation of mechanical systems necessitated change in architectural form? (ii) In what ways has architectural form been able to evolve because of the availability of mechanical systems? That is, what is the architectural potential of mechanical systems? Or, put another way, how has the development of advanced mechanical potential permitted greater freedom of architectural expression?

[5]L.A. Shuffrey, *The English Fireplace and Its Accessories* (E. T. Batsford, London, 1912), p. 1.

[6]Henry J. Cowan, *An Historical Outline of Architectural Science* (Elsevier Publishing Company, New York, 1966), p. 102.

[7]Robert Wernick, "Where There's Fire There Is Smoke—And Usually a 'Chimney,'" *Smithsonian* (Washington, DC), September 1987, 143.

[8]Sir Bannister Fletcher, *A History of Architecture on the Comparative Method* (Charles Scribner's Sons, New York, 1961), p. 347.

Figure 8.3 FONTEVRAULT ABBEY
Fontevrault Abbey in Anjou, France, has perhaps the oldest existing chimneys.
Photo by Maria Loranger and used with permission.

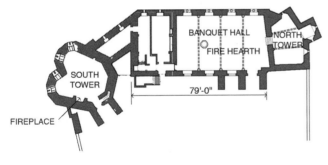

Figure 8.4 PLAN OF STOKESAY CASTLE, SHROPSHIRE
The main banquet hall was heated by a central fire hearth. The castle also
included one of the earliest examples of a fireplace. The fireplace, which included
a chimney, was located in the south tower.

problems and often did. Therefore, for significant buildings where destruction by fire was to be avoided, noncombustible masonry construction was preferred. This preference for greater permanence probably provided the major impetus for the development of early masonry structural design.

In ancient times, fire was more than just a source of environmental warmth. It was also the source of light at night and a means of protection against wild beasts and enemies. Due to its importance for continued survival, it usually was the focus of the family, if not of the whole community. Primitive societies respected the importance of fire, often in the form of religious veneration. Since they could not easily make fire, maintaining the flame was a sacred ritual. Even today, this reverence for fire can still be seen. The eternal lights that are found in all Jewish synagogues, the numerous votive candles that are lit in Christian churches, and the flame, the symbol of the Olympics that every four years is so dramatically carried from Mount Olympus in Greece to the site of athletic competition, are only a few of the more obvious examples of this reverence.

As societies developed, social structures tended to become more complex. Often this resulted in the provision of a communal fire that was used during the day and from which hot coals would be taken to provide warmth for individual sleeping areas during the night. In nomadic tribes, there would have been an outside central fire that was used to cook the meals and around which the community would gather. On retiring for the night, hot coals would be taken from this fire for continued warmth in the individual tents. In agrarian societies, where social structures were often more complex, there would have been a central fire for a building complex. Hot coals would be taken from this central fire to provide warmth in the individual spaces at night. The device used to hold these hot coals is called a *brazier*. It was usually a simple container in which the hot embers from the central fire could be placed and then carried into the individual spaces. Often the brazier included some form of cover, such as a perforated metal lid, which would maintain the heat source for several hours. When the fire was covered, the air required for combustion would be reduced, allowing the embers to continue to burn longer. Covering the fire in order to have it burn longer was a major advance. In the Middle Ages this became the general practice, especially in the cold northern European climate, where the cover was usually an earthen pot. The French word for this pot was *couvre feu* (literally, "fire cover"), and from this term comes the English term *curfew*. In 1068, William the Conqueror introduced a law in England requiring that a cover be put over the fire before retiring for the evening.

As mentioned before, the chimney was not developed until the Middle Ages, at first only as a means for releasing smoke and not as a device for controlling the draft. It has been suggested that the first chimneys might actually have been vents that were added to braziers. When covered, the braziers would produce considerable smoke, and the first chimneys might have been merely a way to vent smoke from the occupied room. If this were the case, then these vented braziers would have been the predecessor of the heating stove. While this is plausible, the more traditional theory suggests that the chimney was developed in response to the problem of using wooden floor construction in multistory residential structures.

In his heroic text *A History of Architecture on the Comparative Method*, Sir Bannister Fletcher wrote:

As in the Norman period, ground floor halls had a central hearth for an open fire . . . the smoke escaping by a louvre in the roof timbers above, or through small gablets at the two ends of the roof apex in the case of hipped roofs. In the case of the two-floored manor houses, wall fireplaces had been in use since late Norman times; when they are not present, braziers would have served.[9]

Earlier in the text, Fletcher wrote:

In the country, besides castles and manor houses of the nobility and gentry, there were the homesteads of small free-holders or yeomen of the Middle Ages, which were based on the manor-house model, having a centrally-placed hall or "house-part," usually combining the function of kitchen in later days, flanked at one end by service rooms and at the other by private rooms. . . . Wall fireplaces did not become usual in yeomen's houses until Tudor times, which then gave complete freedom to add an upper floor.[10]

Locating an open fire in the center of a space caused no serious problems as long as the floor was either dirt or masonry, even with a wooden roof structure. When the floor was wood, however, which was possible in multistory buildings, placing a fire in the middle of the floor obviously posed a serious problem. In order to avoid a potential disaster, something had to be done. At times, this merely entailed adding a masonry platform to the wood floor, but when the walls were masonry, which was likely for multistory structures, a more effective response was to form a recess in the exterior masonry wall and relocate the fire in it. Sometimes, rather than a recess, a masonry shelf was added to the exterior wall. Either way, in order to avoid direct contact with the wooden floor, the fire was relocated from the center of the room. This provided another advantage. With the fire at the exterior edge of the space, as shown in Figure 8.5, it was possible to add an opening through the exterior wall that could vent the smoke.

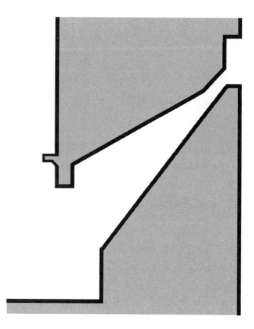

Figure 8.5 SECTION THROUGH A WALL FIREPLACE
The initial fireplace vents were merely openings in the exterior wall behind the fire. In time, these openings were extended vertically up to the roof in order to reduce the ability of wind to blow into the opening, which also established an updraft that increased airflow and enhanced the combustion process.

Initially, these opening might have sloped upward, but they were essentially only holes in the wall. It is assumed that through various attempts to improve the venting, the modern chimney developed. By increasing the height of the opening that was initially intended only to release the smoke, it was found that the draft would improve. Ultimately, the vent was extended up to the roof through a vertical shaft added to or in the exterior masonry wall. This effectively reduced the problem of backdrafts that often resulted from the wind blowing against the side-wall vents, and it also increased the flow of air due to the vertical extension of the stack. This draft, which is the result of the stack effect, improved the basic combustion of the large logs of wood that were the preferred fuel at this time.[11] Elevating the logs above the hearth by placing them on iron grates also increased the flow of air and improved combustion.

As a result of these various adjustments, we find that by the end of the Middle Ages, space heating in northern Europe was usually accomplished by log fires located on iron grates placed in special recesses in the exterior masonry walls. These recesses were vented upward, through the roof, to the outside. In other words, space heating was provided by burning wood in fireplaces that had chimneys.

---

[9]Ibid., p. 447.
[10]Ibid., p. 394.

[11]Large logs were preferred, since they not only burned for a long time but also did not require multiple cuts. Remember that, at this time, cutting wood was a manual effort.

Figure 8.6 WEST BANQUETING HOUSE, CHIPPING CAMPDEN, ENGLAND
This is the West Banqueting House that was part of the home and gardens built by Sir Baptist Hicks in the early 1600s. When it was built, it was in the latest style, although this was obviously influenced by the exuberant sugar twist chimneys that are shown here and were also on the East Banqueting House that still stands across from what were formal gardens.

Actually, rather than a *fireplace*, especially in accordance with the general contemporary meaning of this term, *chimneypiece* is probably a more appropriate term for denoting these early examples of recessed places where fires were burned since the depth of the recess in the masonry wall was nominal. A hood or projecting shelf extending from the wall above the fire collected the combustion products from the fire and directed them into the chimney opening.

Most of these developments in space heating occurred outside of what might be referred to as *high-style* design, an area of architecture that tends to rely on precedent for acceptable form. With few exceptions, the architecture of ancient times evolved in response to relatively mild climates, at least in terms of heating requirements. The Renaissance also began in Italy, a part of Europe where no major provisions for space heating are required. Since classical architectural precedents usually did not celebrate special accommodations for heating, it is questionable whether the advances in fireplace design would have occurred if stylistic considerations were predominant.[12] Of course, the same question might be raised concerning most of the major technological advances that have occurred in architecture.

With the interest in classical precedents that emerged in the seventeenth and eighteenth centuries in England, where heating is required, some interesting compromises between aesthetic preference and practical necessity often occurred. In the process of transposing architectural styles from one environment to another and from one technological age to another, designers frequently did not appreciate the intentions of the exemplar and, as a result, developed some rather confusing and/or contradictory architectural statements. The West Banqueting house at Chipping Campden, shown in Figure 8.6, shows such confusion. Even today, with our continuing interest in historic exemplars, similar confusion often seems to exist. For example, it is doubtful that there is much logic in current attempts to achieve an expression of heavy masonry construction by using lightweight frame construction enclosed in walls made of light plastic insulation covered with thin cementitious material.[13]

Refinements in Fireplace Design

When the fire was moved from the center of a room to a recess in a masonry wall at the edge of the space, fewer people could congregate around the hearth. Perhaps as a way to increase the number of people who could gather around the fire, or more likely as a way to continue using large logs, which, of course, required less effort to cut, early chimneypieces were usually rather large. In fact,

[12]During the Italian Renaissance, there was an apparent preference to emphasize the building facade. Roofs were usually kept flat or low so that they would not play a major part in the design and compete with the facade. "Even chimneys were masked, except at Venice" (Fletcher, *A History of Architecture*, p. 801). Carpaccio's "Miracle of the True Cross," a painting of that time, includes a dramatic view of Venice along the Grand Canal clearly showing "funnel shaped chimneys jutting sharply into the sky" (Wernick, "Where There's Fire," p. 144). In contrast, in the French Renaissance, "high roofs, [often] with lofty chimney stacks were usual, intending to provide a picturesque skyline" (Fletcher, ibid., p. 801). Chimneys were generally used and architecturally displayed. One of the most celebrated uses of the chimney at that time was at "the Chateau of Chambord which Francis I started in 1519, [and which had] 365 chimney [pieces], each different, each decked out with sculpted shields, wreaths, columns, animals, or nymphs" (Wernick, ibid., p. 144).

[13]For example, the Exterior Insulation Finishing System (EIFS). Perhaps a more important question that we should consider is whether it is acceptable to use architectural forms that were developed as an expression of a society whose basic social values we cannot accept.

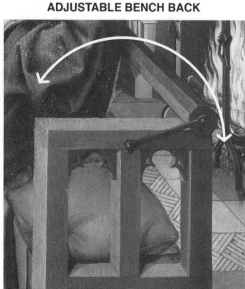

ADJUSTABLE BENCH BACK

Figure 8.7 SANTA BARBARA AND ADJUSTABLE BENCH

The reproduction of the painting by Robert Campin (1438) of Santa Barbara that hangs in the Museo del Prado in Madrid shows the saint sitting in front of a fire with her back to the flame. As shown in the right image, the bench on which she sits has an adjustable back rail that would allow for reorientation. Interestingly, while there is a fire, the window shutters and the windows themselves are apparently open, since the lower sash does not show the leaded glass of the transom.

SAINT BARBARA IN FRONT OF FIRE, FACING AWAY

early chimneypieces were often as much as 12 feet wide and frequently were high enough to stand under.

These huge chimneypieces and their equally large fires caused great differences in thermal conditions relative to one's location with respect to the fire. With the chimneys venting away the large volumes of hot combustion gases, essentially all of the heat that entered the occupied space did so by radiation. So, if one were not directly exposed to the fire, little radiant heat would be gained but there might be considerable draft. The larger the fire was, the larger the area that emitted the radiation and generally the more intense the emitting heat source.

The extremely large fire also demanded considerable combustion air. Since this air would be drawn from the exterior through the occupied space, it caused a large draft that, when not tempered by radiation emitted from the fire, produced a great deal of chilling. In order to deal with these difficulties, one had to adjust one's position in the space. When someone was close to the flames, the radiant heat could be extreme, but as one moved away from the fire or was shielded from it, the radiant heat would be reduced, although the draft would likely continue. Certain furniture designs were developed in response to the need to control the heat. One example was a bench with a back that could be reversed, like the backs of the seats in old trolley cars that switched orientation to allow for the change in direction of travel. Such a bench, an example of which is shown in Figure 8.7, allowed one to sit either facing the fire, during periods of chill, or turning away from the fire,

during periods of warmth. If the back of the bench was solid, it would also either trap or block the radiant heat.

There are other examples of furniture designed specifically to provide thermal comfort. At one extreme are the wing-backed chair and the butler's lobby chair, both of which tend to enclose the occupant; at the other extreme is the wicker rocking chair, which not only allows air to flow through the chair but also adds its own movement to increase airflow. There are also the fireplace screens, two of which are shown in Figure 8.8. While today we might assume that these were similar to the screens that are placed in front of an open fireplace to keep sparks from flying into the room, in earlier times these were movable panels that were intended to block radiant emissions, which are essentially the only way a conventional fireplace can provide heat for the space. With the hot combustion gases going up the chimney, carrying away all of the heat generated unless there is a convection insert, and with the flue gases inducing cold air to flow through the occupied space into the open face of the fireplace unless there is a direct supply of outside air, the only way that a fireplace provides heat for the room is by radiation.

Sometimes heavy curtains were used to divide a large space into areas of varying thermal conditions and privacy. In medieval times, it was not unusual for everyone to gather together to sleep in the large manor hall to avoid the cold of a winter night. Somewhat like gathering around the campfire, all the residents of the manor—the lord and lady as well as their servants and vassals—would often all

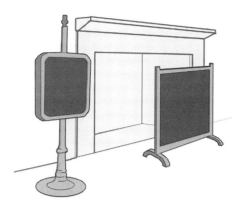

Figure 8.8 FIREPLACE SCREENS
This rough sketch shows two fireplace screens that were often used to block the radiation from a fire. Such screens were often needlepoint panels that could be arranged according to the needs of the occupants. The screen on the left was intended to prevent radiant heat from striking a woman's face, which was often enhanced with wax-based makeup that would melt if exposed to the heat.

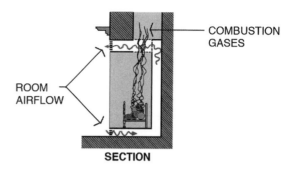

Figure 8.9 SAVOT'S CONVECTION FIREPLACE INSERT
Savot's fireplace insert reduced the size of the firebox and exchanged heat from the hot combustion gases with room air. The insert was iron and formed an air passage through which air from the room could circulate around the outside of the firebox to pick up heat from the hot metal and then return to the room.

sleep in the main hall to enjoy the warmth of the large central fire. Sometimes curtains would be hung to provide some privacy for the lord and lady; this approach apparently led to enclosing their bed, which was typically rather large, with curtains. While the privacy curtains were originally hung from the ceiling, the bed evolved, with the addition of a frame that could support the curtains and a canopy.[14] In time, others emulated the nobility, adopting the canopy bed as a sign of prosperity even when it was used in a private sleeping room.

While the location within the heated space allowed for adjustment of the thermal conditions, particularly in terms of balancing the cold draft with the radiant heat gain, in rooms adjacent to the main space the cooling from the draft existed but with no chance of modification by radiant energy. These peripheral spaces were only cooled by the infiltration of exterior air drawn by the fire's draft.

In order to avoid the problem of drafts caused by the combustion process, the German chemist Johanne Rudolph Glauber (1604–1670)[15] proposed supplying outside air directly to the fireplace. This suggestion, which dates from the early 1600s, was not generally incorporated in most fireplaces, although it is now required by

most codes. This simple adjustment considerably increases heating efficiency while basically eliminating the problem of drafts. While there is considerable variation among fireplaces, it is fair to say that the standard fireplace at best has an efficiency of only around 10%. With exterior air directly supplied to the combustion area, the efficiency might increase to around 20–30%. For comparison, one should note that today's high-tech airtight stoves operate at an efficiency of approximately 65%.[16]

In 1624, Louis Savot developed a device that could capture heat from the hot combustion gases that generally escaped up the chimney. The device was a box made from metal plates. As indicated in Figure 8.9, when it was inserted into a fireplace, it formed an air passage that surrounded the fire while still permitting the escape of combustion gases up the chimney. The fire heated the iron plates that formed the insert. The heated plates then warmed the air behind them, which set up a convective airflow that would draw in room air. This air was heated by the hot metal plates and then flowed into the occupied space. The design of the Savot fireplace insert, which established heat exchange between the hot combustion gases and room air, is very similar to the modern *heat-o-later* fireplace that captures heat contained in the combustion gases, significantly improving the efficiency of the fireplace.

The next major improvement to the wood-burning fireplace occurred some 200 years later when Count Rumford proposed what is still the basis of the design of most fireplaces today. He suggested that the firebox be reduced in size and provided with splayed sidewalls that would more effectively radiate heat out of the masonry recess into the room. His proposal for redesigning the fireplace, which is

---

[14]F. Gies and J. Gies, *Life in a Medieval Castle* (Harper and Row, Publishers, New York, 1974), pp. 67, 68.

[15]It is interesting to note that the idea of saving energy by directly supplying combustion air to the fireplace was initially proposed by Glauber. Today we are more likely to remember this scientist in connection with the compound of sodium sulfate and water that carries his name: *Glauber salt*. Interestingly, although this compound was originally proposed for use as a laxative, today it is recognized as an important material that, due to its tendency to change its state from a solid to a liquid at temperatures close to those in occupied spaces, can be effectively used for thermal storage in passive solar systems.

[16]Larry Gay, *The Complete Book of Heating with Wood* (Garden Way Publishing, Charlotte, VT, 1974), p. 89.

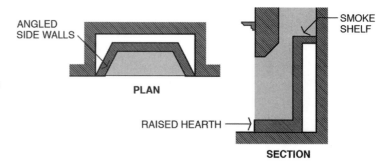

Figure 8.10 RUMFORD FIREPLACE CONVERSION
Rumford's conversion to the fireplace reduced the size of the firebox, established a smoke shelf that tended to counteract potential downdrafts, and angled the sides of the firebox in order to allow these heated surfaces to radiate heat out of the firebox into the room. While the design was initially a way of converting an existing fireplace, it soon became the method for new construction, including a back wall that was splayed forward in order to form the smoke shelf and reduce the flue opening.

diagrammed in Figure 8.10, also included a smoke shelf at the bottom of the chimney to reduce the problem of back-draft. This reduced the opening to the flue, which lowered the amount of draft.

Reducing the size of the firebox and the opening into the flue lowered the amount of air that had to be drawn up the chimney flue to keep the by-products of the combustion process from entering the occupied space. Typically, to maintain a proper draw, the cross-sectional area of a chimney flue should be about 10% of the front opening into the fireplace. In addition, with a smaller firebox, a greater percentage of the air is drawn through the fire, which enhances the combustion process.

Conversion to Coal

The 1973 oil crisis was not the first energy crisis that humankind has had to endure. Around 1600, the forests of England were beginning to be depleted, and alternative fuels had to be used. While peat was available, it was not a very desirable fuel. It had relatively low heat content, and it did not burn very well. Coal, which had been used in ancient times and had been reintroduced in England as early as 1200, was also available. While it was better than peat, it was not as convenient to use as wood.

Coal is difficult to ignite, requires a strong draft to support combustion, and provides an intense (compact) source of heat. Therefore, the conversion from wood to coal necessitated major revisions in the design of the fireplace. Although a raised grate was usually used with wood, with coal's need for increased airflow, it was a necessity. Also, due to the greater density of coal, the size of the firebox had to be reduced even more than for the Rumford fireplace.

The thermal value of coal is generally accepted as around 13,000 BTU per pound, although poor grades of coal might have considerably lower values. Wood, on the other hand, has a thermal value of approximately 7000 BTU per pound. Interestingly, different species of wood have basically the same thermal value per pound. A cord of hickory has a fuel value of 30.8 million BTU, while a cord of pine has a fuel value of only 15.8 million BTU, but a cord of hickory weighs twice as much as a cord of pine, 4400 pounds versus 2200 pounds. Also, a ton of coal has a volume of approximately 40 cubic feet, whereas, based on the dimensions of a cord of wood as 4 feet by 8 feet by 4 feet (128 cubic feet) and an average weight of 3300 pounds per cord, a ton of wood would comprise a volume of approximately 80 cubic feet. By simple mathematics, we see that as a fuel, coal is around four times as dense as wood.

As long as an adequate supply of wood was available, because of the ease with which it could be acquired and used, it remained the preferred fuel. (Our current continuing wasteful practice of depleting fossil fuel resources is not unique!) With the declining availability of wood, coal found ever-increasing use as a heating fuel, and this necessitated a change in the design of the fireplace.

In 1678, Prince Rupert, Count Palatine of the Rhine and Duke of Bavaria, developed a means of both adjusting the draft and improving the heat transfer of a coal-burning fireplace. Rupert was a "17th century Renaissance man, an incongruous pastiche of Sir Galahad and Cyrano de Bergerac."[17] In addition to being responsible for the formation of the Hudson's Bay Company, he was a successful inventor.[18] To improve the coal-burning fireplace, he suggested reducing the size of the firebox and installing movable metal panels at the front of the fireplace and at its connection to the flue (see Figure 8.11). A strong draft of air is required when igniting coal, and Rupert's design accomplished this by repositioning metal panels in order to constrict the room's opening to the fireplace and to provide a direct connection to the flue. After the coal was ignited, the front metal panel would then be swung back, which would both enlarge the fireplace opening, reducing

---

[17]Peter C. Newman, "Canada's Fur-Trading Empire," *National Geographic* (Washington, DC), August 1987, 205.

[18]Prince Rupert should also be remembered for his invention of glass globules that led to the development of tempered safety glass.

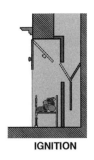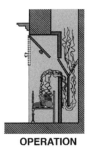

IGNITION   **OPERATION**

Figure 8.11 RUPERT FIREPLACE

Figure 8.12 COAL CONVERSION GRATE

This conversion grate is from Kelmscott Manor. The original farmhouse was built in the late 1500s, and an addition was added in 1665. Some 200 years later, it became the home of William Morris.

the velocity of the draft, and provide a tilted surface that would reflect radiant heat from the top of the fire into the room. The flue damper would also be adjusted so that the exhausting gases would have to circulate downward before rising up the chimney, thereby providing additional thermal transfer into the room.

When coal is heated, it releases volatile gases. Unfortunately, some of these gases are lost before they are burned. By forcing the combustion gases to travel downward before they are discharged up the chimney, more of the volatile gases will burn, thereby increasing the output of the fire.

By 1700, while coal had become the major fuel used in England, the fireplace, although modified for coal, essentially retained its design as a wood-burning device. The fireplace had apparently become an aesthetically desirable object for which a preference was retained even after conversion to coal as the fuel of choice. This conversion basically involved adding a cast iron insert that included a grate or "basket" to hold the coal and reduce the fireplace opening (see Figure 8.12).

In the late 1700s, there was also a shortage of wood in the American colonies, including the area around Philadelphia. This threat of a fuel shortage led Benjamin Franklin to propose modifications to the traditional wood-burning fireplace, which led to what is referred to as the *Pennsylvanian fireplace* (see Figure 8.13). Franklin hoped that with the use of his more efficient design, an adequate supply of firewood could be sustained.

Franklin recognized that most of the heat produced from a wood fire went up the chimney in the combustion gases. While burning an open fire in the middle of the room allowed for the capture of some of this heat, the problems of smoke and dirt did not justify the possible improvement in thermal efficiency. In a sense, the Pennsylvanian fireplace achieved some of the benefits of a centrally located open fire without its various problems. Similar to Louis Savot's convection fireplace, Franklin's design had the hot combustion

gases from the fire pass over and around a metal unit that contained a series of internal passageways through which air could flow. As the hot gases passed over the metal, the heat would be transferred to the metal and then to the air inside the air chambers. The air would be heated without any cross-contamination with the combustion gases and then flow into the occupied room. While this air could be supplied from the room, Franklin also proposed that it come from either the cellar or the outside. While this meant that cold air would have to be heated, it provided a means of controlled ventilation. In addition, the combustion air was to be drawn from outside the heated room and supplied directly to the fire, which meant that the combustion air was not drawn through the occupied spaces. As a result, the drafts caused by the draw of combustion air that usually occurs with an open fire were eliminated.

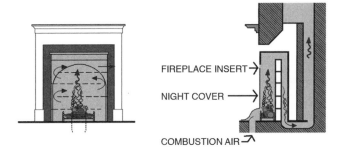

FIREPLACE INSERT

NIGHT COVER

COMBUSTION AIR

Figure 8.13 PENNSYLVANIAN FIREPLACE

Benjamin Franklin's Pennsylvanian fireplace, which was intended as a fireplace insert and was essentially the same as the Franklin stove, incorporated most of the fireplace improvements already discussed.

Figure 8.14 PENNSYLVANIAN FIREPLACE AND FRANKLIN STOVE
While the Pennsylvanian fireplace was intended as an insert to be placed in a conventional fireplace, the Franklin stove, although basically the same type of heating device, was a freestanding device. Also, while Franklin's designs included a means of supplying combustion air from the basement, neither of these examples includes this feature.

PENNSYLVANIAN FIREPLACE   **FRANKLIN STOVE**

The Pennsylvanian fireplace forced the combustion gases to pass downward before rising in the chimney, thereby capturing heat from any volatile gases that were released from the fuel before full combustion. Like coal, wood releases combustible gases when heated, although these gases tend to be consumed more readily with wood than with coal. Franklin's device also included a metal shield that was to be used at times when the fire was extinguished. By using the shield to close off the opening into the unit, the warm interior air would not be lost up the chimney. Of course, closing a chimney damper provides the same benefit.

The Pennsylvanian fireplace, shown in Figure 8.14, was actually an insert that was to be placed in a traditional wood-burning fireplace. With some minor adjustments, the design was the same as that of the Franklin stove, a freestanding unit that is still recognized as one of the more efficient devices used for burning wood. In fact, although, as a fireplace insert or a freestanding stove, it was part of the room to be heated, Franklin's design incorporated essentially all the attributes of a modern central heating system: a direct supply of outside combustion air, the addition of ventilation air, full burning of the fuel, and maximized exchange of heat from the hot combustion gases to the supply air. This last attribute was attained by passing the combustion gases over the heat exchanger twice and by including a series of air passes of the supply air.

Benjamin Franklin's inventiveness is legendary. Another of his innovations led to the improved combustion of coal. In 1757, he was sent to London as a delegate from the Pennsylvania legislature to speak for the colony on the matter of taxes. He remained in Britain until 1775, serving as an unofficial American ambassador. During those 18 years, he had to deal personally with the moist, cold English winters, using coal as the only available fuel source. He knew that, as with wood, much of the potential heat from a coal fire is lost in the hot exhaust gases, but he also recognized that with coal an additional problem often

occurs since, when it is heated, a lot of combustible gases are released before they attain the temperature of ignition. In order to benefit from the thermal values of these released gases, Franklin understood that these gases should be forced to pass through the fire, where they would be ignited and burned. As a result, rather than going up the chimney before they reached ignition, these combustible gases would pass through the fire and be ignited and consumed, providing additional heat output.

Franklin proposed using a downdraft stove to capture these gases. While the Pennsylvanian fireplace forced the combustion gases downward before they were released up the chimney, the actual combustion process occurred with the flames rising upward. With the downdraft stove, even the basic combustion process was inverted, so there was no chance that any combustible coal gases would be released upward in front of the flames. This invention, which is diagrammed in Figure 8.15, was known both as the *smoke-consuming stove* and as Franklin's *vase stove*. Unfortunately, it was difficult to operate, as indicated by Franklin's own suggestion "that 'ignorant servants' not be permitted to tend the stove."[19] Franklin prepared directions on how to light the stove, indicating that it was best to do so when there was a downdraft existing with warm room air passing up the flue, which he felt would be most pronounced without the stove ignited early in the morning.[20] While the downdraft stove had its problems, his simple rotating grate, which he subsequently developed as a simplified smoke-consuming device for the common people, permitted one to add coal "at the top of the grate and turning it one half of a revolution [so that] fresh fuel thus had to pass up through the layer of coals where

[19]Gay, *The Complete Book of Heating with Wood*, p. 71.

[20]B. Franklin, W.T. Franklin, and W. Duane, *Memoirs of Benjamin Franklin V2: With His Social Epistolary Correspondence, Philosophical, Political, and Moral Letters and Essays* (1859) (Kessinger Publishing, 2008), pp. 414–420.

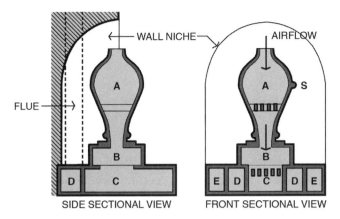

Figure 8.15 FRANKLIN'S DOWNDRAFT COAL STOVE

Although known for having been extremely difficult to ignite, Franklin's downdraft coal stove, also known as his *vase stove*, adopted some of the attributes of the Pennsylvanian fireplace. The combustion air would initially flow downward to pass across the burning coals, assuming they were ignited. This downdraft, which would be established by the draft up the flue, would pull the volatile gases released from the fresh coal as they were heated down through the flames, where they would burn. The hot combustion gases would then pass through various horizontal passages, where they would exchange heat to room air that was passing in adjacent passages, and then up the flue. Room air would also be heated as it passed over the hot vase section, A, in which the coal was burning.

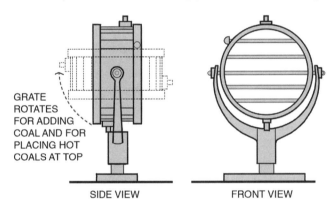

Figure 8.16 FRANKLIN'S REVOLVING COAL GRATE

Considerably simpler than his inverted coal-burning stove, Franklin's revolving coal grate would be tilted on its side for adding coal and then flipped so that the fresh coal would be at the bottom of the grate. As a result, the heat from the hot coals would drive out combustible gases from the freshly added coal, and since these gases would rise up through the burning coal, they would be ignited, thereby increasing the amount of heat generated.

they burned."[21] This revolving grate, which is shown in Figure 8.16, readily reduced the amount of volatile gases lost before they were consumed. It was an ingeniously simple response to the problem of burning coal effectively.

Design Preference

As mentioned above, the English developed a very strong aesthetic preference for the fireplace. Perhaps this was

[21] Gay, *The Complete Book of Heating with Wood*, p. 74.

a transference of the fascination people have with fire. But whatever the reason, when they had to convert from wood to coal, the English continued to use the fireplace even though the closed stove was fairly well developed and proved to be a more effective device for obtaining heat from a coal fire. The fireplace had become an important element in the architectural language. It was retained, and its design was even embellished long after it was understood to be ineffective for providing space heating.

The English preference for the fireplace was adopted in the New World. Even after the formation of the Republic, Americans tended to follow the British in their pursuit of high-style design. Interestingly, while there was a fairly abundant supply of wood in America, in certain high-style designs the fireplace was sometimes converted, in the English manner, for burning coal. This is an obvious example of the confusion of intention that often exists when one attempts to emulate a previous design without understanding the basis upon which the precedent was developed.

The modern metal fireplace can be seen as a similar example of confusion over design intention. Over many years, the central open fire was moved to the edge of the space, enclosed, and vented in order to improve its efficiency. Through a series of further transformations, the fireplace gradually evolved into the metal stove. In some instances, the stove currently seems to be reverting back to the fireplace, although now made out of metal. Perhaps this is merely a means to regain some of the fascination that an open flame provides, or maybe it is an attempt to establish a stronger connection with historic exemplars of high-style English design. Whatever the motivation was behind these efforts, there seems to be little technical benefit gained from attempting to make a stove appear to be a fireplace. If it is only the visual appearance of a fireplace that the designer wishes to achieve, it might be equally appropriate to merely place an electric light behind fluttering paper cutouts, which can sometimes be quite effective.

In terms of design intentions, it is also interesting to consider the assumption that *masonry* normally implies fireplace, while *metal* implies stove. While this assumption tends to be valid from an English or western European perspective, in terms of the colder regions of eastern Europe it is clearly not appropriate. A better perspective on this issue might be gained if we recognize that while the open fire or perhaps metal stoves were preferred in England and in those American regions colonized by the English, closed masonry stoves have long been the preferred means of providing space heating in the colder parts of Europe and America where the temperatures are less likely to fluctuate. In regions where it gets cold and stays cold, the masonry stove is a logical source of heat since, although it takes time after being ignited before it can provide much heat, once it does start releasing heat, it continues to emit an even warmth and to do so for some time without the need for continual refueling.

While a masonry stove might not be an appropriate heating device for locations where exterior temperatures tend to fluctuate, in areas where winter temperatures tend to be rather cold and remain stable at these low levels, the masonry stove is indeed effective. Russia is a country renowned for its cold winters and its extensive use of masonry stoves, often called *Russian stoves*. In other cold countries, masonry stoves are also call *Finnish stoves, Swedish stoves,* and *German stoves*. Whatever their name, they are all essentially the same type of heating device—a large assembly of heavy masonry that, although it takes time before it starts to release heat, provides a continuous, relatively low-level output of heat from only one or two firings per day. Also, since these stoves typically involve a series of passages through which the combustion gases flow, the heat in these gases is effectively captured. As a result, many Russian stoves operate at around 90% efficiency, whereas the typical fireplace has at best only around 10% efficiency and, in fact, is often a net loser of heat. However, fireplace efficiency can be increased to around 65% or even higher with combustion air supplied directly from the outside, an enclosed firebox usually accomplished by adding a glass door, and the addition of a heat-o-later type of double-jacket steel insert that exchanges heat from the hot combustion gases to air that is circulated to the room air. Of course, after all this, the resemblance to the conventional fireplace is decreased.

While they are often referred to by the country where they are used, since they are often finished in beautiful decorative ceramic tiles (see Figure 8.17), masonry stoves are also often called *ceramic stoves, tile stoves,* or *kachelofens,* which simply means "tile stoves" in German. These stoves were, and still are, designed as ornamental yet functional devices. Of course, there are also metal stoves that were obviously designed with consideration of their visual aesthetic potential, but generally these were not intended for use as decorative elements in high-style design. They were usually mere celebrations of themselves.

Fireplace Location

The placement of a fireplace within the occupied space is an important concern for the space designer. Today, while some designers might be concerned mainly with the thermal potential and operational efficiency of the fireplace, in general a fireplace is desired primarily to provide a social focus for a space. As such, its placement in the space is influenced by the intended use of the space. For example, the fireplace is normally located in a living room so that seating can be arranged around the hearth rather than in a location where it would not be possible to gather. While

Figure 8.17 CERAMIC STOVE AT CATHERINE'S PALACE
While there are many examples of wonderful ceramic stoves, perhaps none exceeds the elegance and beauty of those located at Catherine's Palace in Pushkin, about 17 miles outside of St. Petersburg, Russia.

it is important to recognize the significance of nonthermal concerns in locating a fireplace, this should not be considered a reason to avoid responding appropriately to the thermal factors as well.

In terms of thermal considerations, should the fireplace be located on an exterior or an interior wall? In England the fireplace was usually placed on an exterior wall, while in America, particularly in the northern colonial settlements where winters were rather severe, it was more likely to be located in a central position. When the fireplace was located in a central position, more heat was retained in the house. The back of the chimney tended to release whatever heat it did lose to the interior of the house rather than to the exterior. Also, and probably more significantly, when the fireplace was located in the center of the house, people tended to gather around it in the winter and, as a result, reduced their contact with the cold exterior walls. Being at a distance, the cold exterior walls comprised less of the "environmental sphere" and had less impact on the mean radiant temperature experienced, especially when walls were not usually insulated. This was not merely an American phenomenon. In eastern Europe, where cold

LINCOLN'S BOYHOOD HOME
KNOB CREEK, KY

Figure 8.18 LOG CHIMNEYS
Log chimneys were often used in the American frontier. Sometimes the log chimney sat above a stone base that served as the firebox, but in many cases the whole construction was made from logs. Typically, the interior of the logs was lined with clay that, through exposure to the heat of the fire, baked to a hard finish that protected the wood against probable ignition.

FORT HARROD, HARRODSBURG, KY

exterior temperatures prevail during the winter season, the ceramic stoves were also usually located toward the center of the structure, and often served not only as a focal point for social gatherings but also as a warm surface on which people might actually sit. Also, in the southern American colonies, where the winters were warmer, fireplaces were often located on the exterior walls.[22]

In pondering the appropriate location of the fireplace, we might also wish to consider whether it is appropriate to change the orientation of a space from winter to summer.[23] If so, even if the winter is not severe, the fireplace might be located on an interior wall, providing an increased sense of enclosure during the colder season of the year, when the occupants are oriented toward the fireplace, and allowing an easy connection with the outside during the warmer season of the year, when the tendency is to turn away from the fireplace. In addition, by moving away from the fireplace in the warmer season, there is a greater potential to benefit from the breezes coming through the opened windows.

Obviously, the placement of the fireplace is partially a response to climatic conditions. But it has also been suggested that whether a fireplace is located in the center of a house or along an exterior wall is also, in part, a response to the construction materials. In England, masonry was usually used to construct the exterior walls. Therefore, it was natural to locate the fireplace along the exterior wall. In America, on the other hand, wood frame construction was prevalent. Therefore, since commonality of materials was not an issue, it was often more logical to use a centrally

located masonry shaft that would permit collection of the flues from all the spaces in the house.

The notion that the location of the fireplace is somewhat based on the construction materials used can be supported by examples of log cabins that had wooden chimneys built as part of the exterior log walls. (That's right, wooden chimneys!—see Figure 8.18) Many such log cabins were built in the American wilderness. Abraham Lincoln's birthplace is an example of this dangerous design. But perhaps the location of the wooden chimney on the exterior wall was not really a response to combining common materials but rather the most astute way of using a wooden chimney—outside the structure! Actually, the interior of these log chimneys was usually coated with clay that, through exposure to the combustion gases, baked into a reasonably durable lining that protected the logs. Also, if the heat from the combustion process, which usually occurred in a stone firebox, was sufficiently transferred into the stone mass, the exhaust gases passing up the chimney would have cooled somewhat. As a result, if the log cabin survived, we might assume that the heating efficiency was reasonable, at least for a fireplace.

Central Heating

The major contribution to space heating since the Industrial Revolution has been the development of central heating. Although modern hot-air heating systems rely on separation of the combustion gases from the hot air that is circulated into the occupied space, this was not a new innovation. As we have seen, Benjamin Franklin proposed this in his design for the Pennsylvanian fireplace, as did Louis Savot with his fireplace insert. The primary difference between modern hot-air heating and previous means of providing thermal control is that with modern systems the combustion process is located outside of the occupied space, in a central location. This is usually in a service area

---

[22]Although still important, with the benefits of modern insulated glass and insulation, thermal comfort is not as dependent on room location as it used to be.

[23]Patrick Snadon, author of *The Domestic Architecture of Benjamin Henry Latrobe* (which Snadon coauthored with Michael Fazio), chooses to refer to the "inboard" versus the "outboard" orientation of a space, including the placement of a fireplace.

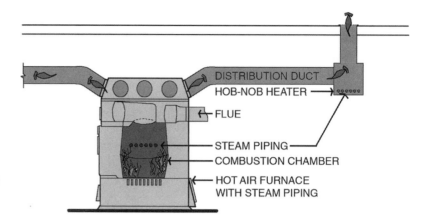

Figure 8.19 HOB-NOB HEATING SYSTEM
This warm-air heating system provided a way to enhance the air distribution in a system that relied on differences in air density to move the air.

of the building. The air is heated at this central location and is then distributed to the various spaces throughout the occupied structure in air ducts. In early central hot-air systems, distribution relied on convective currents produced by the warmer air temperatures. These systems are usually referred to as *gravity systems*, but with the pressure differentials that were available, the air runs were limited. This often meant that the warm-air outlets had to be located centrally rather than along the exterior walls.

The *hob-nob system*, diagrammed in Figure 8.19, provided a way to increase the air runs in a gravity warm-air system. While the heating was still provided by warm air, the movement of the air was enhanced by steam or hot water heating coils. These coils were installed in an enlarged air duct at the bottom of a vertical riser. With the added heat, the air would be drawn horizontally through the supply air duct and then forced upward to the supply air outlet in the floors above.

Since the beginning of the twentieth century, with the availability of electricity and small motors, fans have usually been added to control the airflow. These systems, which are sometimes called *fan-forced systems*, permit much longer duct runs. They also make it possible to move cold air, which is not feasible by gravity flow since, with the limited temperature differentials, the density differences are minimal and, if this were not a problem, these systems would be effective only in causing the air to drop rather than rise. This might work if the cooling unit were located on the roof or on an upper floor but not otherwise.

Alternative Fuels

A switch in fuels was another change that occurred with the development of modern heating systems. In addition to wood and coal, there are other fuels that can be used for space heating. As was mentioned before, peat is one such fuel. This is partly decayed plant matter found in swamp and marsh areas throughout the world. While it

is still used in certain areas, including Ireland and Russia, the more generally used alternative fuels are gas and oil. In the modern industrial areas of the world, these have now become the major fuels used for space heating in most buildings, particularly with central systems.

Gas

Today, gas as a heating fuel probably means natural gas, but this has been used since ancient times. The Chinese used natural gas. They captured the gas, which rose from the ground in certain areas, and moved it in bamboo pipes. They used it mainly to boil seawater to produce salt. When first used in Europe in the early seventeenth century, gas was a by-product of manufacturing coke from coal. It was not used in any significant amount until the nineteenth century, and then it was employed mainly for lighting applications rather than for space heating. The use of gas for lighting made sense since other fuels were available for space heating that did not need the high level of investment required by manufactured gas. Light, on the other hand, which could be effectively generated only from fuels that were also expensive, could benefit particularly from using gas, since it could be easily distributed through small pipes to points of use. Although it was used mainly for illumination, an early recorded use of gas for heating occurred around 1830, but this was for cooking rather than for space conditioning. Cooking is often intermittent and of short duration, while space heating entails a longer operation. Therefore, it was logical to use gas for cooking since, compared to wood and coal, it was simple to ignite, readily adjusted, and easily extinguished.

In 1855, Baron Bunsen proposed modifying the gaslight burner to make it into an improved heating divide by inducing air into the gas supply. The story is that he observed that the flame from a gas lighting jet was not producing as much light as usual. On investigating the problem, he found that there was a puncture in the gas line that was inducing air into the gas flow, resulting in less light from the flame. A gas flame produces light by heating particulate matter to the point where it emits radiation due to incandescence. With a relatively clean gas source, the particulate matter that emits the light is actually a portion of the fuel that is not consumed in the combustion process. With the addition of air to the gas supply, the combustion process is improved, which leaves less unconsumed fuel. As a result, more heat is produced but less light.

With the development of the Bunsen burner and the availability of manufactured gas, gas became a desirable heat source, but predominantly for cooking rather than for space heating. By the late nineteenth century, gas stoves had become fairly popular additions to the modern home. It was not until natural gas, which is a by-product of petroleum, became available that gas was widely used for space heating purposes. This had to wait until the introduction of the electrically welded, seamless steel pipe in the 1920s that allowed high-pressure gas distribution lines to run from the wellhead to the places of use. Even today, in those locations where it is available, natural gas is usually the preferred heating fuel.

Initially, gas was sold for its illuminating capacity. It was not until 1914 that the thermal values of gas were determined. These values are generally expressed in terms of a therm, which is basically equivalent to 100 cubic feet of natural gas and 100,000 BTU. In the 1920s, gas started to be sold by therms rather than on the basis of its illuminating value. Of course, both systems relied on the volume of gas consumed, but with therms this was measured in units of 100 cubic feet.

Oil

While oil has been used since ancient times, especially in the Middle East and in China, its use was limited and typically, as with gas, was primarily for lighting. With the discovery of oil in Titusville, Pennsylvania in 1859, petroleum became available as an alternative fuel source, particularly in the United States. However, in its natural form there are limits to how it can be used. But with the development of various means of refining this thick, gooey liquid into more usable forms, the diverse potentials that oil provided started to be realized.

Through refinement, the thick, viscous substance that emerges from the ground can be altered into various forms ranging from an even thicker molasses-like, tarry substance to a volatile liquid, kerosene. This more refined and volatile form of petroleum became the preferred form for this new fuel, although it was primarily used as a source of light. Kerosene could also be used for space heating, although usually in a freestanding stove. As a result, the major impact of kerosene has been through its application as a light source rather than a heating source.

In the early days of petroleum use, the products other than kerosene were often merely discarded. With the arrival of the automobile, gasoline became the major petroleum product, with the by-product oil a resultant that ultimately became an effective heating fuel. Various weights of oil can be produced through the refining process. Kerosene is the lightest, sometimes called #1, although #2 oil is often considered the lightest stage that is classified as oil. Number 2 oil is generally used for space heating, typically in central heating systems. Since it is somewhat viscous, #2 oil is not really combustible unless it is sprayed into small droplets that are then mixed with air. This combustible mixture of oil and air is generally accomplished by a gun-oil burner. The burner includes a pump, which forces the oil through a spray nozzle, and a fan, which develops an air stream that picks up the oil droplets and then delivers the combustible mixture into the combustion chamber where it is burned.

The heavier oils, typically #4, #5, and #6, are also used for heating. However, converting these heavier oils into a combustible form is somewhat more complicated. Generally, this is accomplished by a rotary-cup burner, but before this happens, the oil often needs to be heated to reduce its viscosity. Even when heated, the oil is too thick to be sprayed, so it is dropped onto a spinning truncated cone called a *rotary cup*. As the oil drops onto the spinning cup, it flies off in droplets. Again, there is an air stream that carries the droplets of oil into the combustion chamber. While this system works quite well, if it is not operated for a while the oil coagulates, requiring maintenance before it can be used again. As a result, these heavier oils are not appropriate unless full-time maintenance people are available. This is unfortunate since the heating value per gallon of these heavy oils is higher than for #2 and the cost is less.

While in the form of kerosene it has been used in individual space heaters, generally oil is burned within a central system and then heated steam, water, or air is distributed to the various spaces.

Electricity

Electricity became available as a feasible energy source in the late nineteenth century with the development of dependable electrical generation and distribution systems. Like gas and kerosene, electricity was first used primarily for lighting. It was not until the end of the nineteenth century that proposals for using electricity as a heat source started to emerge. Then, as with gas, it was for cooking rather than for space heating purposes. In 1887, an electric saucepan was produced in Canada, and in 1891 an electric fair was held at the Crystal Palace in London featuring, among other things, electric cooking. At the

1893 Columbian Exposition in Chicago, a model electric kitchen was displayed. It is interesting to note that while the Chicago Exposition, with its *mercantile classicism*, was strongly criticized for its lack of architectural innovation, the exposition actually provided one of the earliest major applications of electrical illumination. Not only did this new light source provide interior illumination, it was also used to turn night into day by floodlighting the exterior of most of the buildings. Contrary to most claims, the Columbian Exposition did provide a technological breakthrough that has had a tremendous impact on architecture, although this important breakthrough was concealed by an architectural design of historical regression.

Today electricity is often used for space heating in both electric resistance units and heat pumps. While resistance heating usually occurs within the occupied space with 100% efficiency, in terms of the fuel used to generate the electricity, the overall efficiency is only around 30%. Compared to the efficiency generally available from oil and gas heating, which is around 85% and 95%, respectively, it seems questionable to use our limited natural resources at such low efficiency. It also seems inappropriate to generate electricity, a very high-intensity form of energy, only to maintain temperatures of around 70° F. But there are some beneficial aspects of electric resistance heating. The distribution of electricity requires very little space or special accommodations. Also, each space can be readily controlled individually, which is not easily done with other systems. In addition to the personal choice that individual control can provide, there is also the potential for improved efficiency since the temperatures in unoccupied spaces can be reduced. Still, if electricity is to be used, it is usually more reasonable to do so in a heat pump. In a heat pump, rather than generating heat, electricity only moves heat from a lower intensity level to a higher, more useful level. In this process the performance of the heat pump is extremely efficient, releasing two to four times as much heat as could be generated by direct resistance.

From an open log flame, a gas-burning furnace, a central oil-fired boiler, or by the compression and condensation of a refrigerant, heat can be produced to thermally control the occupied environment. The methods of heat generation and the means of heat transfer are numerous. Their requirements and potentials offer many architectural design opportunities. Our task is to understand these opportunities and to respond appropriately.

CENTRAL HEATING

Modes of Environmental Management

In his book *Architecture of the Well-Tempered Environment*, Reyner Banham suggests that there are three modes of

environmental management: *conservative, selective,* and *regenerative.*

Banham named the conservative mode "in honour of the 'Conservative Wall' at Chatsworth, devised by that master-environmentalist Sir Joseph Paxton, in 1846."[24] This mode, which he says is the norm in European culture, entails the use of a heavy, massive structure, usually masonry, that can absorb and store the energy necessary to maintain comfort.

In contrast, "the 'Selective' mode . . . employs structure not just to retain desirable environmental conditions, but to admit desirable conditions from outside." That is, the selective mode attempts to modify the natural environment in order to establish comfort conditions.

The regenerative mode is distinct from the other modes in that it consumes power. According to Banham, the regenerative mode is predominantly an American development of the last 100 years; it was approximately 100 years ago that electric lighting and electric power first became available. This energy consumption expanded with the widespread adoption of fluorescent lighting and air conditioning, which are major components of the regenerative mode, although perhaps *generative* might have been more appropriate given the implications that Banham assigned to this mode of environmental management.

In general, if the conservative mode is indicative of massive structures and the selective mode of structures that interact and attempt to enhance the natural environmental forces, the regenerative mode is indicative of lightweight structures and climate extremes, matched by a pioneering, non-culture-bound society that is free to experiment with different ways of doing things. While these classifications of energy management provide a helpful way of identifying the architectural means of achieving thermal comfort, Banham's suggestion that the regenerative mode is essentially American does not properly reveal that the foundations are, in fact, of European origin.

The Hypocaust[25]

In ancient Rome, the public bath became the social focus of the community. These baths were called *thermae*, and according to Sir Bannister Fletcher, they were "evidences of the luxury which contributed to the decline and fall of the Empire."[26]

---

[24]Reyner Banham, *Architecture of the Well-Tempered Environment* (University of Chicago Press, Chicago, 1969), p. 23.

[25]The term *hypocaust* (Latin *hypocaustum*) literally means "heat from below." It derives from Greek, *hypokauston,* from *hypo,* which means "under," plus *kauston,* which means "to burn."

[26]Fletcher, *A History of Architecture on the Comparative Method,* 1961, p. 8.

Figure 8.20 ROMAN HYPOCAUST AT FIESOLE
The hypocaust system involved a raised floor and flues embedded in the walls. Hot combustion gases were produced in a furnace, and then these gases would pass under the floor and up through the wall flues, surrounding the space with high temperatures. Since these spaces were often not fully enclosed, the use of radiant heating could effectively compensate for temperatures that might not represent the desired warm conditions.

RAISED FLOOR

WALL FLUES

The thermae *or palatial public baths of Imperial Rome, which were probably derived from the Greek* gymnasia, *portray, even in their ruin, the manners and customs of the pleasure-loving populace, and are as characteristic of Roman civilization as are the amphitheatres. . . . The* thermae *were not only designed for luxurious bathing, but were resorted to for news and gossip, and served, like a modern club, as a rendezvous of social life besides being used for lectures and athletic sports, and indeed entered largely into the daily life.*[27]

The thermae *were generally raised on a high platform within an enclosing wall, and underneath were . . . the vaulted store-chambers, corridors, furnaces, hypocausts and hot-air ducts for heating the building.*[28]

As the Roman Empire grew, the symbols of Roman culture—the baths, the amphitheaters, the temples—were replicated across the conquered lands, but throughout the empire, except for the northern extremes, the climate was relatively mild. Therefore, heating was not a major requirement for comfortable conditions in most situations. While some heating was surely used, thermal adjustment was usually provided by clothing. However, the ritual of the public bath required not only removal of clothing but also the intentional experience of three large bath chambers, each with different temperature conditions: the hot *calidarium*, the warm *tepidarium*, and the cold *frigidarium*. That is, temperature control was an integral part of the ritual and necessitated an effective means of thermal control of the interior environment.

To achieve the proper interior thermal conditions, the regenerative mode of energy management was used, predominantly in the form of the hypocaust. This was an extremely sophisticated means of thermal control, and it was perhaps the first example of central heating. The hypocaust system was "originated in the 1st century B.C., and subsequently became standard equipment in Roman baths and in many villas."[29] The system entailed a central furnace that was connected to a series of air passages through which the hot combustion gases passed. These air passages were located under the floor and within the walls enclosing the spaces to be heated.

Aspects of the hypocaust system are shown in Figures 8.20 and 8.21. The air passages under the floor were formed by raising the floor up on short masonry piers that were about 2 feet high and placed about 2 feet on center. The floor was constructed of a series of 2-foot-square slabs, above which was usually a poured concrete floor that was then finished with tiles or mosaics. The flues in the wall were made of clay tiles, sometimes square and sometimes rectangular. These flues were located within the enclosing walls, usually just behind the interior finish wythe, which was often marble. The flues provided a vertical passage through which the hot combustion gases could rise and then be released at the top of the wall, sometimes merely to the interior of the conditioned space. Since there are no Roman baths that remain in their completed form, the conditions of the tops of the flues can only be surmised.

The hypocaust system was an extremely effective means of managing the interior conditions, achieved by control of the radiant temperatures. As has been previously discussed, radiation is the major means the body uses for thermal exchange with its surrounding environment under normal comfort conditions. Often, under normal environmental conditions, radiant transfer is responsible for 60% of overall body heat loss. And when the body is not fully clothed, as was the tradition in the Roman *thermae*, radiant temperature control becomes even more significant. Add to this the lack of an effective means of glazing the large openings to provide a physical separation between interior and exterior, and the dependence on radiant control become critical.

In addition to the regenerative mode, interior thermal comfort of the Roman baths was achieved by both the conservative and selective modes of environmental management. The orientation of the structures and the use of materials considerably enhanced the interior thermal conditions. While this was helpful in terms of capturing and

[27]Ibid., p. 202.
[28]Ibid., p. 205.
[29]Henry J. Cowan, *An Historical Outline of Architectural Science* (Elsevier Publishing Company, New York, 1966), pp. 103–104.

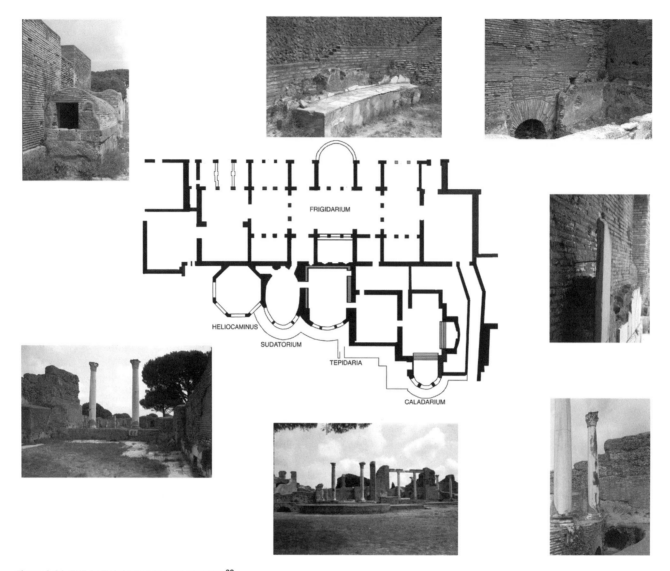

Figure 8.21 THE BATHS OF THE FORUM AT OSTIA[30]

There were a number of public baths at the Roman seaport town of Ostia, but none quite as extensive as the Baths of the Forum. This structure was altered several times, with much effort expended to maximize the solar gain for the various warm spaces. In addition to solar gain there was the hypocaust system, which was used not only to warm the spaces but also to heat the pools of water.

maintaining as much heat as possible from the sun, it was critical in terms of establishing the environmental conditions required for the *frigidarium*, the cold room. Generally, the *frigidarium* was located so that it had a northeastern exposure. In addition, it was designed to maximize the cooling potential of the ground and often included water sprays.

In other buildings, if heat was required, the ancient Romans usually located an open fire only in the center of the space. There are some ruins that indicate the use of a hearth along an exterior wall, but without a flue

to release the gases. And as indicated above, in a few more affluent houses, the hypocaust was used for space heating.

With the fall of the Roman Empire and the loss of Roman organization and administration, the level of building technology fell considerably and the notion of central heating was lost. Perhaps the loss of central heating was also an intentional rejection of the excesses of Rome. If the *thermae* were the epitome of these excesses, then the rejection of the hypocaust would have been a logical part of an overall redirection. It is also possible that the notion of central heating was lost merely because the need that it fulfilled no longer existed. Whatever the cause, following the fall of the Roman Empire, space heating, if provided at all, was generally limited to open fires for individual rooms.

[30]The baths at Ostia are an excellent example of this *passive* response and have been documented in several articles, including Edwin Daisley Thatcher, "Solar and Radiant Heating—Roman Style: The Open Rooms at the Terme del Foro at Ostia," *A.I.A. Journal* (1958), pp. 116–129.

While the hypocaust went out of use after the fall of the Roman Empire, a similar heating system existed in Korea and has continued to be used to this day. This system is *ondol* or *gudeul* and developed, quite independently of the hypocaust, more than 2000 years ago in the Goguryeo Kingdom, which lasted from 38 B.C.E to 668 C.E. and encompassed northern Korea and southern Manchuria. When Frank Lloyd Wright was in Japan while working on the Imperial Hotel in Tokyo, he became familiar with a modern *ondol* installation, and this apparently influenced him to employ radiant floor heating.[31]

Steam Heating

Central heating applications did not reemerge until the middle of the eighteenth century. However, much earlier, in 1594, Sir Hugh Platt suggested the idea of using steam for central heating of a structure. Platt was an observer of Elizabethan husbandry and gardening and published regularly on gardening. In support of the interest in propagating plant species that were not indigenous to the English climate, Platt proposed using steam as a way to force plants, but he also suggested it as a means to provide space heating. Many of his writings were compiled in his 1608 publication *Floraes Paradise*. While this did not sell well, a revised edition in 1655 was renamed *The Garden of Eden* and was successful, although there is no indication that his idea of steam heating for a structure was actually pursued, at least not for some time.

Steam is a logical medium for central heating since, as a gas, it will rise readily from a central source to a remote location. In addition, after it has released its heat, primarily by condensing into water, the water can easily flow back to the point of origin if the pipes have been properly sloped. Unlike water and air, steam can use the same pipe for both supply and return.

In 1745, 150 years after Platt's suggestion, Colonel William Cook installed a central steam heating system in his eight-room cottage.[32] The benefits of this installation are not known, but since we are not aware of other systems that were similar to his, we must assume that it was not an overwhelming success.

In 1784, James Watt followed up on Cook's experiment by installing a steam heating system in his office,[33] a room that was 20 feet square and apparently cold and damp. Apparently, the results of this installation were dis-

appointing.[34] From a drawing showing Watt in his office, we can surmise that he used a serpentine pipe mounted on the wall as the heat transfer device. If this is correct, then it is understandable why his steam heating system was not effective. By coiling the steam pipe, the bottom loops would fill with condensate, forming traps that would inhibit proper steam circulation. Since the drawing that shows the coiled pipe is from the Bundy Tubing Company collection, it might be that the source is biased. In *Changing Ideals in Modern Architecture*, Peter Collins suggests that, rather than using a coiled piped, Watt "heated his office by means of a hollow iron box fed with steam from a boiler in the basement."[35]

Another suggested possible problem with Watt's heating system for his office might have been the high temperatures that would have resulted if he had used high-pressure steam. While it is possible that Watt, whom we remember primarily as the person who developed the first effective steam engine, used high-pressure steam that could have resulted in intense temperatures that would have been problematic, especially in a relatively small space, it is unlikely. What made Watt's steam engine effective was that it did not require high-pressure steam, but relied on condensing low-pressure steam to establish a vacuum.

A more likely problem with Watt's initial experiments was controlling the release of steam and air from the system. When steam was used as a heat source for horticultural purposes, some of it was usually released into the greenhouse. This obviously increased the humidity in the house, which would be helpful for the plants but undesirable in a relatively small office, especially if it was already damp. On the other hand, if Watt had effectively sealed the system so that steam could not escape, then the steam would not have been able to circulate into the "hollow iron box" that Collins suggested was used or through the coiled piping that others have suggested. (Of course, Watt might have experimented with both.)

In order for steam to move through the system, the air must be evacuated. If the system is not sealed, the rising steam will force the air out of the system, but steam will also be dispersed into the occupied space, which is not acceptable. On the other hand, if the system is effectively sealed, the steam will not be released into the occupied space but neither will the air, which will keep the steam from circulating. To resolve this conundrum, an effective means of venting the air but not the steam was required. While this could be accomplished by manually opening the vent as a heating cycle began and then closing it as the

[31]S. Smith and J. Sweet, "Brief History of Radiant Heating," *Plumbing & Mechanical*, June, 2006.

[32]Robert Bruegmann, "Central Heating and Forced Ventilation: Origins and Effects on Architectural Design," *Journal of the Society of Architectural Historians*, October 1978, p. 146.

[33]Cowan, *An Historical Outline of Architectural Science*, p. 105.

[34]"How to Lock Out Air, the Heat Thief" (Hoffman Specialty Company, Inc., Waterbury, CT, 1927), p. 7.

[35]Peter Collins, *Changing Ideals in Modern Architecture, 1750–1950* (McGill-Queen's University Press, Montreal, 1965), p. 236.

system filled with steam, the automatic air-venting valve was a much better solution, although this was not developed until around 1890. This vent, which is typically located at about one-third the height of the radiator, will release any air that comes in contact with the valve but will close in the presence of steam or water. In addition, to be effective, the valve should keep the system purged of air. That is, it should be able to release any air within the system but not any steam, and it must not allow air to return. Otherwise, as the steam begins to rise, it must again purge the system of air, which requires enough steam pressure to overcome the 14.7 psig exerted by the air. Although this is not difficult to accomplish, it both extends the time before heat can be delivered into the space and consumes energy. In fact, the claim is that a properly vented steam system can save around one-third of the energy required.[36]

Some 20 years before his experiments with steam heating, Watt was working at the University of Glasgow as a maker of mathematical instruments. In 1763, he was asked to repair a model of the Newcomen steam engine, which, although developed 50 years previously, still represented the latest in steam engine development.

Thomas Savery had received the patent for the first practical steam engine in 1698. The primary use for this engine was in pumping water out of coal mines, but since it used high-pressure steam, there were frequent explosions. At the time, the engines relied on cast iron since steel was not yet available, and cast iron has low tensile strength, which is necessary to resist internal pressures. In response to this problem, Thomas Newcomen worked to develop a steam engine that operated at low pressure. Rather than rely on steam to develop a positive pressure to force a piston to move by pushing, Newcomen used the partial vacuum that resulted from steam condensing from a gas back into a liquid. In his engine, the cylinder was filled with steam and then cold water was sprayed into the cylinder, causing the steam to condense. As the steam condensed, a negative pressure was formed that pulled the piston down into the cylinder. The first recorded installation of the Newcomen engine was in 1712 near Dudley Castle, Staffordshire, and it was still the engine of choice some 50 years later when Watt was asked to repair the model.

While Watt was able to repair the model of the Newcomen steam engine, he realized that by cooling the cylinder itself, considerable additional heat was required by the engine. Watt was not satisfied with the engine, and he tried to find a way to improve its efficiency. His idea was to provide a separate condenser in which to establish the partial vacuum rather than in the actual piston cylinder, which was constructed from rather massive iron. This avoided having to cool down this mass, which increased the en-

gine's efficiency. As a result of these modifications, Watt was able to double the efficiency of the Newcomen steam engine. His innovations produced a steam engine that operated at around 5% efficiency, and at this efficiency, steam became an effective source of motive power. Watt received a patent on his revised engine in 1769, which gave him exclusive rights for 14 years, but Watt basically did nothing other than construct an experimental engine to exploit these rights in the first 6 years of the patent.[37]

Matthew Boulton was a successful manufacturer from Manchester who took an interest in Watt's work, particularly in the potential commercial opportunities connected with his patent on his steam engine. In 1774, Boulton entered into partnership with Watt.[38] Realizing that the patent provided a financial potential that had not been realized, Boulton and Watt somehow managed to convince Parliament to extend the patent so that they would have 24 years of exclusive development rights.[39] Together, Watt and Boulton both manufactured steam engines and leased the patent rights to other manufacturers. In addition, they became involved in manufacturing iron for structural purposes.

In *Space, Time, and Architecture*, Sigfried Giedion stated that "the cotton mill of Philip and Lee, built at Salford, Manchester, in 1801 … represents the first experiment in the use of iron pillars and beams for the whole interior framework of a building…. This truly extraordinary feat for builders of that date … was accomplished by Boulton and Watt's Soho foundry."[40] Giedion went on to mention that the drawings, which still exist, show "the construction of the hollow cast-iron pillars, each of which had an outside diameter of nine inches. This extremely careful treatment reflects the experience acquired by Boulton and Watt in the making of steam engines. The details of the assembly of pillar and socket show a precision that had been learned in machinery construction."[41]

[36]Hoffman Specialty, "How to Lock Out Air," pp. 17–19.

[37]Samuel Smiles, *Lives of Boulton and Watt. Principally from the Original Soho mss. Comprising Also a History of the Invention and Introduction of the Steam Engine* (John Murray, London, 1865; Scholarly Publishing Office, University of Michigan Library, 2005), Ann Arbor, p. 206.

[38]Watt realized that he did not have business acumen. He therefore initially entered into partnership with Dr. John Roebuck to develop the potentials of the patent for his steam engine, but this venture was not very successful. In addition, Roebuck got into personal financial difficulty. He owed money to Matthew Boulton and was able to get released from this debt by transferring his share in Watt's patent to Boulton. This was not merely an altruistic move by Bolton. He was part owner of the Soho Manufactory, and even before Watt received his patent, he had become interested in the advantages that were possible by adapting Watt's steam engine to power the machinery at this iron works.

[39]Smiles, *Lives of Boulton and Watt*, p. 217.

[40]Sigfried Giedion, *Space, Time, and Architecture* (Harvard University Press, Cambridge, MA, 1956), p. 189.

[41]Ibid., p. 190.

The Philip and Lee Mill in Salford was not built until just after Watt's patent expired, but Watt had been experimenting with steam heating, as had Boulton. In 1789, Boulton installed a steam system to heat a room in his house and, later, to heat his bath. In 1795, he apparently installed a central steam heating system in the house of one of his friends.

Following these personal experiments with steam heating, Watt and Boulton began installing steam heating in factory buildings.[42] While Giedion did not mention anything about it (his interest was in the structural impact on the development of architectural form, and he tended to discount almost all other factors), the Philip and Lee Mill was where Boulton and Watt achieved their first major steam heating installation. The columns, which Giedion mentioned were joined together with extraordinary precision, were not only used for structural support but were also the means of distributing the steam for heating. This is a unique example of true architectural integration!

The steam that was used for heating was not the discharge from the steam engines that were used to power the machinery in the mill. Remember, Watt's steam engine achieved its efficiency and advantage by condensing the steam into water, not by harnessing its pressure and then releasing it. It was the condensation of the vapor in the attached condenser that created a vacuum that pulled the piston rather than steam pressure that pushed the piston. However, it is probable that the boiler that provided the steam for the engines also provided the steam for heating. While Watt did not use by-product steam, it was used at other locations. In 1811 in Middletown, Connecticut, a factory was built using exhaust steam from a high-pressure steam engine, and a year later, another factory near Baltimore, Maryland, was similarly heated.

As the development of steam power led to improvements in space heating, the need to control the temperature in greenhouses also brought about considerable advancement in heating systems that were adapted for environmental control systems intended to provide comfort for humans. In the late eighteenth century in England, botanical interests became the rage of society, which led to major advances in environmental control.[43] Of course, since England has a climate that is anything but tropical, the major focus of this botanical interest was tropical plants. Since these plants would not survive outdoors, much of the horticultural activity occurred in the *greenhouse* or *conservatory.* Another term for this glass-enclosed structure is *hothouse*, a name that clearly indicates its purpose, although this is often expressed merely as *house*, which

causes some confusion since the usual understanding of this term is somewhat different. Whatever it was called, in addition to maximizing solar gain, generally some form of heat was required during the colder period of the year.

As a result, while Boulton and Watt were pursuing their interest in steam applications in mills, others were considering the use of steam for horticulture. A.M. Wakefield of Liverpool is "purported to be the first to use steam for forcing"[44] plant growth in 1788. And three years later, in 1791, a Mr. Hoyle of Halifax obtained a patent on a steam heating system, which he proposed for use in greenhouses and other buildings.

John Claudius Loudon was another individual who was instrumental in advancing steam heating. Loudon was one of the most important and influential persons in the horticultural field in the nineteenth century. He not only personally developed some of the important advances in conservatory construction, he also published widely and therefore had a great deal of influence. At first, Loudon rejected steam as a viable source of heat for conservatories. Apparently, he reacted against the opened steam systems that were sometimes used at this time. These systems merely discharged the vapor into the space to be heated. This resulted in extremely high humidity and produced serious problems of condensation. However, by 1817, having become aware of the more sophisticated uses of steam that limited the release of vapor, Loudon became a major support of steam heating.

Loudon's interest in steam heating was not limited to its application in horticulture. He believed that by using a central boiler, steam could be an "all-purpose power source for small country estates," providing heating for all of the spaces, not just the conservatories, and also supplying the power for the working machinery. He also developed a scheme for using steam from a central boiler to heat a housing complex containing 80 cottages. These ideas were presented in his 1833 publication, *An Encyclopedia of Cottage, Farm, and Villa.*[45]

In 1819, an engineer named Hague from Spital Field designed a system that generated steam in a pressurized boiler. The steam was distributed under pressure to terminal devices that used both radiation and convection for heat transfer. The condensate was then returned to the boiler. This system, for which Hague received a patent, was used to heat a factory run by a Joseph Hayward.

Another individual who pioneered the use of steam heating was Joseph Paxton. Architects generally know him from his contributions to the design and

---

[42]Bruegmann, "Central Heating and Forced Ventilation," p. 147.

[43]A rather detailed discussion of these developments in included in John Hix's *The Glass House* (MIT Press, Cambridge, MA, 1974).

[44]Ibid., p. 34.

[45]Loudon later supported the use of hot-water heat. In his publication *The Gardener's Magazine*, volume IV, 1828, he included a discussion of Marquis de Chabannes' *calorifère fumivore* fireplace and hot-water heater.

Figure 8.22 VICTORIA REGIA LILY AT CHATSWORTH

This drawing is from *The Illustrated London News* of November 17, 1849, showing the Victoria Regia lily that Joseph Paxton was able to propagate in the conservatory at Chatsworth.

construction of the 1851 Crystal Palace, the central structure of The Great London Exhibition in 1851.[46] This structure, which enclosed an area of almost 20 acres, was designed and built in the incredibly short time of only six months. It was the first example of large-scale prefabricated construction. It was built with a framework that was made of both cast iron and wrought iron and supported a "ridge and furrow" greenhouse enclosure, such as the one developed by Loudon. The whole design was based on a 4-foot-long sheet of glass that was the largest standard glass size available at that time. Interestingly, while the Crystal Palace is important in terms of architectural technology, it did not contribute to the advancement of central heating since it was not heated. The Great Exhibition was held during the summer, and the Crystal Palace was only intended to remain standing during the exhibition. However, the structure was so highly regarded that, after the exhibition, it was dismantled at its Hyde Park location and rebuilt at Sydenham. It remained in use until 1935, when it was tragically destroyed by fire. When it was rebuilt at Sydenham, the structure was expanded and a central heating system was added.

While Paxton is remembered for the Crystal Palace that did not have a central heating system, he achieved his original recognition because of his propagation of the highly prized Victoria Regia lily at Chatsworth, shown in Figure 8.22. He was able to accomplish this because of the steam system that he designed to control both the temperature and the humidity in the conservatory.

While we have been discussing the development of steam heating in England, there are clear indications that this method of environmental control was used elsewhere as well. For example, it is suggested that the first major use of steam heating in France was in 1828 at the Bourse in Paris, the French stock exchange.[47] Interestingly, while a considerable amount has been written about the Greek Revival design of the building, there is only a passing comment about the fact that the structure was provided with a central heating system.

By the second half of the nineteenth century, steam heating was a common means of providing thermal comfort in many major buildings. It even found use in what is sometimes referred to as *district heating*. In 1876, Mr. Birdsell Holly of Lockport, New York, installed a central steam distribution system at his farm. With the success of this installation, the next year he proposed a central steam distribution system for a residential and commercial complex in Lockport. The most notable installation of district heating was that of Thomas A. Edison in 1882 in New York City. While Edison is generally given credit for developing the first successful incandescent lamp, for which he received a U.S. patent, the English physicist Sir Joseph Wilson Swan had concurrently also developed a successful incandescent lamp. While his achievements in refining the incandescent lamp were important, perhaps Edison's significant contribution was his development of electric generation and distribution. He realized that without a source of electricity, the electric lamp would have limited application. Based on his understanding gained from his work with the telegraph, he organized the central generation and district distribution of electricity. His first

---

[46]Folke T. Kihlstedt, "The Crystal Palace," *Scientific American*, October 1984.

[47]Emmanuelle Gallo, "Lessons Drawn from the History of Heating: A French Perspective," Centre of Energy and Society Conference on Energy and Culture, 2007, Esbjerg, Denmark, p. 6.

installation was in New York City. Interestingly, perhaps because he was competing with gas as a source of illumination, Edison decided that the electrical distribution should be below grade. It is suggested that he had said that since gas piping was not installed on poles, electricity also should not be distributed in this manner. For whatever reason, he decided to distribute the electricity below grade. Along with the electricity, Edison also distributed the steam that was a by-product of the electrical generation. Since steam cannot return to the boiler, its vapor must condense into a liquid before it can be reheated to generate adequate steam pressure to turn the turbines, so steam discharged from the generators either had to be condensed by some means of cooling or used in a functional way that would result in condensation—for example, as the source of steam heating. As the steam condenses, it must release its latent heat of vaporization, which is equivalent to approximately 8000 BTU for each gallon of water, which is a considerable amount of energy. Obviously, it makes sense to use this energy effectively; today, however, this is not generally done. In most locations, the steam that exits the generating turbines is condensed back into liquid, either in large cooling towers or through heat exchange with a large body of water. As a result, most of the energy involved in generating the electricity is not actually used but is thrown away, producing considerable environmental thermal pollution. But as Edison demonstrated, it is possible to use the by-product steam effectively. When this is done, it is generally referred to as *cogeneration*, although the term *total energy* is also sometimes used to denote this procedure of effective utilization of the energy consumed by electrical generation.

Hot Water Heating

Today, when we refer to *hydronic* space heating rather than *steam*, we are probably considering hot water heating.[48] With the development of electric power and efficient circulation pumps, water has become a most effective heating source. Not only can the temperature of water be readily adjusted, the rate of flow can also be attuned to variations in heating demand.

The first recorded use of hot water for space heating in the Western world occurred more than 200 years ago

and relied on gravity flow. Interestingly, this application of hot water heating was for a chicken incubator built near Paris by the Frenchman Bonnemiam in 1770.[49] While this system apparently continued to work, generally hot water heating was not adopted in France, although in 1818 the Marquis de Chabannes did propose using a water-jacketed boiler for a hot water system to heat a hothouse. Across the Channel, Joseph Bramah installed a hot water heating system for Westminster Hospital in 1795. There are also some indications that Watt and Boulton might have experimented with hot water heat before 1800, and 10 years after Chabannes, Thomas Tredgold proposed a design for a hot water heating system.[50] By the 1830s, hot water was fairly well recognized as a heat source.[51]

Jacob Perkins is one of the more prominent names associated with the development of hot water heating. He was raised in Massachusetts but arrived in Philadelphia around 1815. There he joined some of the more inventive people who were following in the direction initiated by Benjamin Franklin. Perkins became interested in the potential of high-pressure steam and pursued it for several decades, but mainly in England, to which he emigrated in 1819.

Perkins became a successful plumber in his new home country. As his son, Angier Marsh Perkins, matured, he acquired Perkins' interest in scientific investigation and joined him in his professional endeavors. However, Angier March Perkins seems to have switched from high-pressure steam to high-pressure hot water, and in 1831 he obtained an English patent for a high-pressure hot water heating system.

This system was rather unconventional. For one thing, other hot water systems relied on variations of density developed by the temperature differential to establish convective flow in the water, which required rather large-diameter piping, around $3\frac{1}{2}$ inches or more. Perkins' system, on the other hand, used small-bore pipe of around $3/4$-inch interior diameter. Also, while other systems were usually open at the top to allow for the thermal expansion of the water (today we generally use a closed expansion tank in which air provides a cushion against which the water can expand), Perkins' system was hermetically sealed. As a result, when the temperature exceeded 212° F, the water could not flash into a gas. It remained as a liquid with increased pressure. As the temperature increased, so did the pressure. At 350° F the interior pressure would be around 125 pounds per square

[48]The preference for the type of heating system to use varies according to the region where one is located. In part, this is a response to environmental conditions, but it is also a reaction to tradition and/or individuals. Suppose that in a particular region there are two heating contractors. Further, assume that the better contractor tends to install steam systems, while the other contractor tends to install hot water systems. As a result of this difference of both talent and choice, it is probable that in that region a preference will develop for steam heating systems.

[49]Bruegmann, "Central Heating and Forced Ventilation," p. 148.
[50]Ibid.
[51]Since electric pumps were not yet available, these hot water systems relied on the variation in density resulting from a difference in temperature to establish natural convective flow to move the water through the supply and return pipes.

inch (psi) or 8.5 atmospheres (atm), at 500° F it would rise to around 700 psi, or almost 50 atm, and at 636° F it would reach 2000 psi, or 135 atms. And these high temperatures and pressures were, in fact, produced!

Such high pressures cause concern today. One hundred fifty years ago, with the then available materials and technology, it is inconceivable that Perkins' system was even a potential possibility, let alone actually achieved. However, the system was apparently very successful and was used in a number of installations both in England and in the United States. Supposedly, a Perkins small-bore, high-pressure hot water heating system was installed in John Soane's house and museum, although apparently it had no impact on the design of this intriguing building complex. Perkins' system was added to the house and museum after several other methods of heating had been tried and abandoned. It is suggested that Soane, like many designers today, had little awareness of what types of systems were available, particularly in what way they might influence the architectural form. Instead, he was fortunate to have available the engineering support to make his formal explorations feasible.[52]

The extension of Perkins' ideas to the United States was the result of Joseph Nason. In 1837, when he was 22 years old, Nason, a native of Boston, Massachusetts, went to London to work for Angier Marsh Perkins. Four years later, with the experience he had gained, he returned to America, where he became a recognized expert in the area of heating and ventilation, and was engaged as the consultant for the heating and ventilating of the expanded U.S. Capitol in the mid-1800s. While Nason initially proposed a Perkins small-bore system, he ultimately switched his design from high-pressure water to low-pressure steam.

Warm Air Heating and Ventilation

As mentioned before, the first central heating system that used warm air as the heating medium was the ancient Roman hypocaust system. This was a radiant heating system and does not fit into the normal category of warm air heating, even though John Loudon proposed using such a system in a cottage in the eighteenth century, a comparable system has been used consistently in Korea, and similar systems have been proposed more recently. Warm air heating, as used today, is considered to be a development of the notion of separating the hot combustion gases from the air in the occupied space that Louis Savot used for his fireplace insert and Benjamin Franklin used in his Pennsylvanian stove. Usually warm air heating entails re-

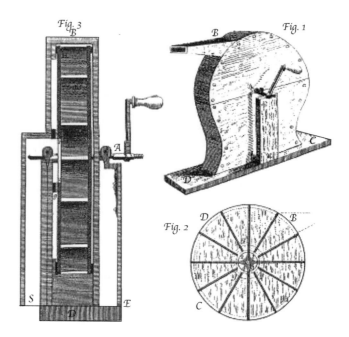

Figure 8.23 DESAGULIERS' VENTILATION FAN
Desaguliers' ventilation apparatus (1735) was installed in the House of Commons and gave rise to the term *ventilator*, although this was initially used to describe the person employed to turn the crank handle of the fan rather than the device.

placing the ambient air in the occupied space with air that has been conditioned. While we usually attempt to recirculate room air, sometimes this air is exhausted and is replaced with air drawn in from the outside, which is what Franklin recommended. When outside air, often referred to as *fresh air* (although this becomes more debatable with increased environmental pollution), is brought into the occupied space, the process is referred to as *ventilation.* This ability of an air system to replace contaminated interior air was a benefit that initially motivated the development of warm air heating.

Today, when we consider air systems, we are conscious of the importance of electric fans incirculating the air, although as we have seen, prior to the availability of a reliable source of electricity, air movement was achieved by employing thermal forces or even animal labor. In 1734, Dr. Joseph Theophilus Desaguliers designed a ventilation system for the House of Commons in London.[53] This system used a centrifugal fan that is shown in Figure 8.23. This fan, which had a diameter of 7 feet, was operated by a man turning a crank that rotated the fan's impeller. This man was called the *ventilator*, although this term now denotes the equipment used to circulate the air (see Figure 8.23). This system was intended to remove the vitiated air that contaminated the House of Commons without necessarily heating it. Therefore, the system, with its equipment on the

---

[52]It is suggested that for the Bank of England, Soane relied on steam pipes buried in the floor.

[53]Bruegmann, "Central Heating and Forced Ventilation," p. 149.

lower levels, could not rely on the principle of rising warm air. Unfortunately, this system was not properly operated because the janitor, an important individual who was truly the custodian of the House of Commons and responsible for the operation of the building, was angry that the ventilation apparatus was located in a room that he considered his domain. He claimed that the system would compound the problem of air quality in the House of Commons.

Some 100 years later, in 1840, Dr. David Boswell Reid,[54] again in response to the need to provide adequate ventilation for the House of Commons, proposed moving the air by harnessing the draft drawn by the combustion process. This type of ventilation system is referred to as *thermal siphon extract* in Banham's *Architecture of the Well-Tempered Environment* and as *thermo-ventilation* in Peter Collins' *Changing Ideals in Modern Architecture.* This system was used in a number of buildings, including the Pentoville Prison built in London in 1841. In this application, the fires were located in the attic, drawing combustion from the occupied spaces, which induced the flow of ventilation air (see Figure 8.24).

Interestingly, Desaguliers had initially proposed using this method to provide ventilation for the House of Commons. He apparently "installed ventilating fires in the already existing pyramidal air tubes in the roof,"[55] but this system was unsuccessful. This same approach was also attempted by Sir Humphrey Davy, but it was also a failure.

In the 1840s, when Sir Charles Barry was rebuilding the House of Commons in the Palace of Westminster, Dr. Reid again proposed providing ventilation by using thermal siphon extract. Unfortunately, this proposal, which entailed cleaning, heating, and even cooling the ventilation air by drawing it through a spray of water, was never fully installed.[56] Apparently, Barry objected to the amount of building volume required by Reid's system, which was one of the first recorded arguments between architect and mechanical engineer and resulted in the rejection of the environmental control potentials in favor of a visual aesthetic. Of course, Barry's objection might have been stimulated by the previous failures of Desaguliers and Davy.

Dr. Reid, who was a Scottish physician and lectured on chemistry at Edinburgh University, pursued his ideas for environmental control after his disagreement with Barry. In 1850 he designed the control system for St. George's Hall in Liverpool with the architect Harvey Lonsdale Elme.

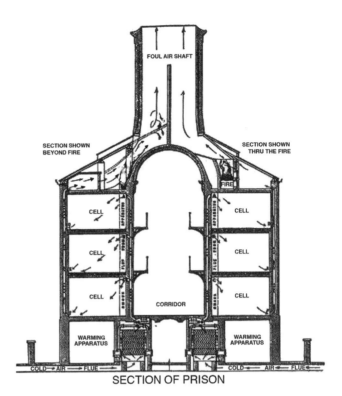

Figure 8.24 PENTOVILLE PRISON

This section shows how thermal siphon extraction provides ventilation. At the Pentoville Prison in London, a fire in the attic induced outside air through the prison cells. While this air provided year-round ventilation, in the colder seasons the air would be heated by passing over heating coils. While this induced air included the combustion air, it also included air induced by the rising draft from the fire. In smaller structures, sometimes the kitchen stove, located on the lower level rather than in the attic, was the means of inducing the flow of ventilation air.

However, in this installation, large fans run by steam engines circulated the air.

According to Peter Collins, Sir Charles Barry did not totally abandon Reid's ideas in rebuilding the House of Commons. In fact, Collins claims that the ventilation shafts that Reid initially proposed had considerable influence on the building form of the Palace of Westminster that Barry finally designed.

The Marquis de Chabannes emigrated to England in the late eighteenth century, and he continued to write and work on heating and ventilation. He worked on Covent Garden, ventilating it using thermal siphon extraction as well as heat from its four gas chandeliers.[57] His use of the heat from the chandeliers became common in subsequent theaters and meeting halls, providing a means of releasing the heat as well as inducing ventilation air.

Before these examples of induced ventilation, gravity warm air heating systems had been used for space heating.

---

[54]It is interesting to note that both Desaguliers and Reid were medical doctors attempting to improve air quality.

[55]Bruegmann, "Central Heating and Forced Ventilation," p. 149.

[56]While we recognize the spray cooling coil as the device that Willis Carrier initially used, this was the method of cleaning the air that Dr. Reid proposed. For cooling, he suggested using the cool water from the Thames or, when this was not adequate, passing air over bags of ice.

[57]Marquis de Chabannes, "On Air and Its Properties Relative to Respiration," *The Repertory of Arts, Manufactures, and Agriculture* (Reportory Office, Hatton Garden, London, 1818), pp. 225–227, 281–285.

William Strut, of Derbyshire, installed a warm air heating system in a mill in 1792 and in the Derbyshire Infirmary in 1806. In 1830, Charles Sylvester apparently modified Strut's system. According to Peter Collins, Sylvester developed a system that ventilated the infirmary by bringing in fresh air through a 200-yard-long underground tunnel, which provided some cooling of the ventilation air.

In 1820, John Vallance received a patent for a most peculiar warm air system. He proposed isolating the interior by using revolving doors at the entries and sealing all windows. In response to this idea, the editor of the *London Journal of Arts and Sciences* commented: "Among the many wild schemes and theories which are occasionally dignified with the title of patent, we have rarely met with any more impracticable and ridiculous."

A system similar to that proposed by John Vallance was installed in the 1850s renovation of the U.S. Capitol. While the design was the responsibility of Captain Montgomery C. Meigs, Joseph Nason was responsible for the system used to control the interior thermal environment. Since Meigs believed that the primary purpose of the Capitol was debate, he felt that the legislators should not be distracted in any way by extraneous events. As a result, he chose to isolate the legislative halls from the exterior, which required total reliance on mechanical means to provide for interior environmental control. While Nason's design included ventilation, the senators who had to occupy the space found the conditions intolerable. Lewis Leeds, a popular lecturer of the time, stated:

It appears to have been originally designed to exclude the main halls as much as possible from all external influences, and to have all the currents, the heating and the lighting, under perfect artificial control.

But if the whole nation could be taught the valuable lesson of the great folly of attempting to produce artificial light, artificial heat, and artificial mixed air that shall equal that which our Creator has provided for us, that knowledge would be cheaply bought at the great price paid for these buildings.[58]

The folly of the Capitol is discussed in an article by Eugene S. Ferguson, "An Historical Sketch of Central Heating: 1800–1860," which was published in *Building Early America*. In this article, Ferguson mentions what he sees as the tendency of technical virtuosity, over a period of time, to defeat itself and collapse.[59]

---

[58]Charles E. Peterson, ed., *Building Early America* (Chilton Book Company, Randor, PA, 1976), pp. 178–179.
[59]Ibid., p. 166.

Interestingly, such sealed systems are often installed in many of today's large buildings, probably with no more logic than was employed by Vallance and Nason. One justification for such a system today is that with an air distribution system in a high-rise structure, opening windows can cause major problems from the stack effect. A high-rise building with openings at the bottom and at the top of the structure acts as a vertical stack or chimney. Essentially this is what is achieved with the tall cooling towers frequently located at electric generating plants. In such cooling towers or in chimneys, the updraft is relied on to cause the desired air movement. In a building, however, especially one heated and cooled by a central air system, such an updraft can wreak havoc on the distribution system.

By 1860, the B. F. Sturtevant Company was manufacturing reliable engine-driven fans, and fan-forced heating systems became fairly standard in new construction for large buildings. These early fans relied on steam power, but with the proliferation of electric motors in the late nineteenth century, air systems became effective as a means of environmental control for all buildings. Today, with our attempts to cool as well as to heat the interiors of our buildings and with our need to control humidity, air systems are often the preferred means of environmental control.

HISTORY OF COOLING

Thermal control includes both heating and cooling. Both approaches basically involve controlling the environmental conditions when the natural surroundings are either cooler or warmer than desired for human comfort. When they are cooler, both heat and humidity are generally added to the interior space, along with various ways to improve the air quality; when the natural conditions are warmer than desired, in addition to continuing to improve air quality, today this usually means that the air is cooled and the humidity is adjusted to maintain interior conditions within a range of comfort, which usually means dehumidification.

Therefore, it should be clear that for both heating and cooling, the intention is to provide thermal comfort by adjusting the condition of the interior space, that is, to condition the interior air. This is *air conditioning*; however, beginning with the early applications of mechanical refrigeration to provide cooling, this term has been usurped to imply the cycle of control to counteract overheated conditions.

On January 2, 1906, Willis Haviland Carrier was issued a patent for what he called an "Apparatus for Treating Air." This system used a fine spray of cool water, an idea that was "so revolutionary that it was greeted with incredulity and, in some cases, with ridicule,"[60] especially since the primary reason for using the water spray was to dehumidify the air. While Carrier's system was not the first to provide interior space cooling (this had been accomplished in numerous ways since ancient times) or even the first to control interior humidity effectively, it was the first system to control both humidity and temperature in a prescribed manner. As a result of his innovations, Carrier is recognized as the father of air conditioning, although he himself did not like the term *air conditioning*, which was first coined by one of his early competitors, Stuart W. Cramer. It is suggested that Carrier preferred the term *man-made weather*, although in 1908 he helped form one of the first companies specifically established to address the control of the interior thermal environment, namely, the Carrier Air Conditioning Company of America, a subsidiary of the Buffalo Forge Company.

Long before the development of the earliest artificial refrigeration systems in the nineteenth century, various methods were used to cool space; however, prior to refrigeration, they all had to rely on natural forces to reduce the thermal intensity and/or its effects. Basically, nature provides four ways to improve an overheated environment—shade, increasing airflow, evaporative cooling, and storage of *coolth*. Since cold is the absence, or more properly a reduction, of heat, in terms of acquiring a lower temperature the term *coolth* is often used as an indication of what would be obtained if cold were a substance.

Shade

Perhaps the first way to improve overheated conditions is to provide shade. As discussed in connection with the bioclimatic chart, overheating often results from exposure to the sun rather than the actual air temperature. And if the air temperature is excessive, adding solar gain will exacerbate the already undesirable conditions.

Air Movement

During overheated periods, increased air movement can improve thermal comfort. While it is not easy to change the basic natural air patterns, it is possible to modify airflow through the selection and location of vegetation and the design of the structure in order to maximize the cooling effects from air movement. Of course, it is also possible to use a fan to increase air movement, but until modern

times this was usually accomplished by the exploitation of people. Figure 8.25 shows an example of a ceiling fan from the Mehrangarh Fort in Jodhpur, India, that was manipulated by a servant as a way to cool the Maharajah.

Harnessing the airflow has led to some rather interesting architectural responses, some of the most notable perhaps being the wind scoops of Hyderabad Sind in Pakistan (see Figure 8.26). There are similar uses of prevailing breezes from the Middle East to southern Asia. In Iran there are examples of structures that are comfortably maintained by the use of wind towers that capture the winds and then force the air down through below-grade spaces where the air is cooled by the lower temperatures of the ground, which are often further lowered by evaporative cooling of water from underground streams or on the surface of porous earthen jugs filled with water.

In a more direct manner, windows were, of course, also used to provide air movement during overheated times. To take advantage of an open window, there had to be a means for the air already in the space to escape before fresh air could enter. While this can be accomplished with only one exposure if special consideration is given to the window design, cross ventilation provides a much better means for ensuring airflow. As a result, when airflow was critical for establishing reasonable conditions, multiple exposures were provided for each space. When this was not feasible, cross ventilation was established by adding transoms (see Figure 8.27) or louvered doors so that airflow could be maintained through a sequence of spaces.

In the heat of the Thar Desert in Rajasthan, India, the need for shade, privacy, and airflow produced some extraordinary architectural details in the *haveli*, the private homes of the wealthy (see Figure 8.28). In addition to the architectural responses to enhance airflow, in many places slaves and servants were often required to manipulate various forms of fans to cool their masters (see Figure 8.25).

Extraordinary as the window treatment shown in Figure 8.28 is, the window shutter seems to have become merely a form of window decoration. Today, shutters usually are fixed to the sides of the window and often no longer have a clear proportional relationship to the opening, although window shutters actually derive from an effective way to help ameliorate environmental conditions. This potential is clearly shown in the shutters that have been used in southern Europe for many years and continue to be used there (see Figure 8.29).

Evaporative Cooling

Evaporative cooling, which is still often used in hot, arid regions, is another natural means of cooling. The thermal process is one that we have all personally experienced after

[60]Margaret Ingels, *The Father of Air Conditioning* (Country Life Press, Garden City, NY, 1952), p. 23.

Figure 8.25 CEILING FAN OVER A BED
This image of a sleeping porch in the Mehrangarh Fort in Jodhpur, India, shows a large fan over the bed. This fan was moved manually by servants as the maharaja slept. This is perhaps a forerunner of the ceiling fans that have become popular as a way to establish slight airflow through a bedroom.

a swim or a shower. Before we dry off, some of the water on our skin evaporates, cooling us. Of course, this is also the effective operation of perspiration or the use of traditional clay pottery before it was sanitized by being sealed so that liquid would not ooze through the porous material.[61]

Evaporative cooling was often accomplished by spraying water into the air in the place where the cooling was desired. When this spray was within a contained space, such as the Court of the Lions at the Alhambra, shown in Figure 8.30, the cooler air settled within the space and the conditions were improved. Since evaporation requires the transformation of sensible energy into latent energy, the temperature of the air is lowered as water evaporates. While a spray of water can provide effective cooling when the humidity is low, if the humidity is high, evaporative cooling can make the conditions worse even though the temperature is lowered, especially since high humidity is often more oppressive than a high tempera-

ture. However, evaporative cooling can also be beneficial even in areas of high humidity if the cooling is accomplished outside of the occupied space. By spraying water on the outside of the structure, as with a spray-pond roof, the increased humidity is not imposed on the occupants. This was a very popular method of environmental control in hot, humid Florida before the general availability of mechanical refrigeration.

While not as elegant or aesthetically pleasing, thatch shutters have also been used to provide evaporative cooling (see Figure 8.31). A mat of thatch is placed in front of a window, and water is poured over the thatch. As the air flows through the mat, it is cooled evaporatively. At Kibbutz Beit Hashita in the eastern Jezreel Valley in Israel, this traditional method of cooling was modernized by placing the thatch material in a metal frame covered with chicken wire, forming a shutter that could be readily opened and closed, although new interior shutters and air conditioning now have replaced this traditional means of cooling.

Thermal Storage

A fourth method of natural cooling relies on the fact that nature itself does not maintain constant thermal

---

[61] When I was a youngster, I use to go camping with the Boy Scouts. One of the pieces of equipment I always brought along was my father's old canvas water bag. The outside of the bag was always damp and somewhat dirty, and the water had a peculiar flavor, but when the weather was hot, the water stayed cool and was truly refreshing. Today, if I go camping, I bring along a large collapsible, plastic water jug. The jug stays dry and clean, and there is very little change in the taste of the water, but on hot days the water is also hot.

Figure 8.26 WIND SCOOPS AT HYDERABAD SIND, PAKISTAN
Where prevailing breezes come from a consistent direction, wind scoops can capture these streams of air and cause them to flow through a structure. In dry climates, this air is often passed over water from various sources to provide additional cooling. Photo by Dr. Martin Hürlimann and included in Martin Hürlimann, *India: The Landscpe, the Monuments and the People* (B. Westerman, NY, 1928) and in Bernard Rudofsky, *Architecture without Architects* (Museum of Modern Art, NY, 1964).

Figure 8.27 DOOR WITH TRANSOM
A transom over a door, which is now primarily considered a design detail, was originally intended to provide for air circulation without opening the door. As shown, this meant that the transom was operable and, therefore, could establish cross ventilation. While this figure shows a transom over an exterior door, transoms or louvered doors were also provided for interior doors serving rooms with only one exposure.

conditions. Temperatures change according to, among other things, the location of the sun, the season, and the topology. Comfort can be increased by capturing a condition that occurs in one situation and moving it to or saving it for another. One such basic method of thermal control entails the use of a thermal mass, sometimes referred to as a *thermal flywheel*. This has generally involved building with heavy masonry material, particularly in hot, arid locations where the daily fluctuations of temperature mean that the heavy thermal mass can reduce midday heat gain and allow for tempering of the colder temperatures at night. The use of adobe in the American Southwest is a good example of this approach (see Figure 8.32).

In addition to the use of a thermal mass, taking advantage of changes in environmental conditions has also meant collecting ice in its natural formation and storing it, or even transporting it, to be used when or where desired. Some 3000 years ago, the Chinese harvested ice in the win-

ter and stored it for use in the summer. The ancient Greeks and Romans also harvested snow and ice for use during the warmer seasons of the year. They transported snow and ice from the high mountains to their cities, where it was stored in insulated structures. Often these structures were dug out of the earth, surrounded with heavy logs or stone, and insulated with layers of straw. Since considerable effort and expense were involved in this endeavor, only the more affluent and socially prominent members of these ancient civilizations could benefit from this cooling source.

While this captured snow or ice was not generally used for environmental conditioning, sometimes it was. Al-Mahdi, Caliph of Baghdad, for example, was able to benefit from this approach in the late eighth century. He apparently "had a summer residence built with double walls between which imported snow was packed."[62] Use

---

[62]Ingels, op. cit., p. 14.

Figure 8.28 HAVELI IN JAISALMER, RAJASTHAN, INDIA
This is the Patwon-Ji-Ki Haveli in Jaisalmer, at the edge of the Thar Desert in Rajasthan, India. The *haveli* was the private residence of a wealthy merchant and typically, as shown here, was provided with highly embellished screens that could provide shade and privacy yet allow for airflow.

Figure 8.29 WINDOW SHUTTER
Adjustable window shutters have long been used in southern Europe. This shutter, which is from northern Italy, can provide various levels of shading and airflow. The shutter can be opened or closed, and when it is closed, the lower portions can be adjusted. In addition, the slats can be manually adjusted.

of stored coolth was also sometimes combined with manual airflow, as shown in Figure 8.33.

The desire for a source of cooling in the warmer climates created an American industry of harvesting winter ice, storing it, and then shipping it to warmer regions, although this ice was generally not used for space conditioning but rather for the preservation of food. The ice was cut into large blocks from the frozen northern lakes (see Figure 8.34), placed in the holds of ships that were insulated with sawdust or straw, and then sent by sea to markets in warmer locations. In 1799, ice was shipped from New York City to Charleston, South Carolina. Following the success of this venture, transporting ice from the cold northeastern part of the United States to the southern U.S. states, the West Indies, South America, and even India developed into a profitable industry. Frederic Tudor was a leader in this endeavor. Known as the "Ice King," he made a fortune harvesting ice in the area around Boston and then shipping it to various locations, near and far. One of the places where Tudor harvested was Walden Pond in Concord, Massachusetts (see Figure 8.34).

The practice of harvesting ice in the winter and storing it for later use, often at remote locations, continued to flourish until it was replaced by advancing technology. With the introduction of refrigeration ice plants in the 1870s, manufactured ice started to replace this historic industry, although ice harvesting was still done through the early twentieth century, often for personal use in colder climates, where this meant storing the ice in an insulated structure (see Figure 8.35).

Figure 8.30 COURT OF THE LIONS AT THE ALHAMBRA
The Court of the Lions at the Alhambra is cooled by evaporation of the water sprayed in the fountain. As the water evaporates and cools the air, the air settles within the close courtyard, providing improved thermal conditions. The spray of water also produces a wonderful soothing sound that embellishes the environmental effects.

Figure 8.31 THATCH SHUTTERS
When water is poured over the thatch shutters and air flows through, evaporative cooling occurs. This system has been used in various locations in the Middle East, as shown in these images. The previous application at Beit Hashita is shown on the right.

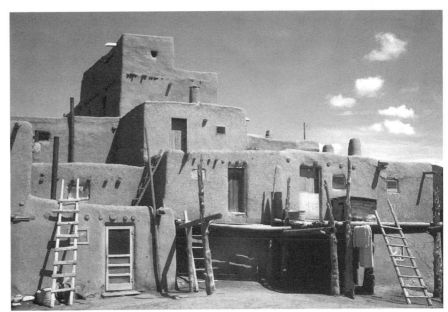

Figure 8.32 TAOS PUEBLO
The use of adobe construction, especially when massed tightly together, provides effective thermal storage that ameliorates the daily changes in temperature that are prevalent in hot, arid regions.

Figure 8.33 SLAVE-POWERED AIR COOLING USING CAKES OF SNOW
This cartoon shows an image from Bagdad from around 775 C.E. with slaves fanning air over blocks of snow that can drop down onto the sultan below. This combines the initial notion of increased air movement with the third means of natural cooling that entails storing coolth.
Used with permission.

Figure 8.35 ICEHOUSE AT GRACELAND
This icehouse, which was used until 1923, was built in 1890 for Senator Stephen Elkins of West Virginia. During the winter, ice was harvested from a pond on his summer estate, known as Graceland. The ice was stored in this structure to be used during the summer, when he and his family resided at Graceland.

Figure 8.34 ICE HARVESTING
This picture shows men harvesting ice in New England.

Figure 8.36 LARKIN BUILDING
This building was designed by Frank Lloyd Wright in 1904 for the Larkin Soap Company in Buffalo, New York. It was a sealed structure that relied on an environmental control system that, along with the fire stairs, gave rise to the architectural form. The structure was unfortunately demolished in 1950.

Photo © The Frank Lloyd Wright Foundation, AZ/Art Resource, NY, © 2010 Frank Lloyd Wright Foundation, Scottsdale, AZ, Artists Rights Society (ARS), NY and used with permission from Art Resources, NY and Artists Rights Society, NY.

Today, with the availability of effective refrigeration systems, most of us think of storing and using ice only in connection with a cold drink. However, there are situations in which using stored ice to cool a space might still be appropriate. A space such as a church is used intermittently. When it is used, it requires considerable cooling. Such a space might take advantage of a system that can produce ice for an extended period and then use this accumulated ice to cool the space during the short time when it is occupied. It is also possible for a building that uses a heat pump for winter space conditioning to be cooled during the summer by ice produced during the heating season. This means that during the winter, rather than extract heat from the outside air, the heat pump provides space heating by extracting heat from water. This way of providing heat will actually increase the efficiency of the heating operation, since the low temperature is set at 32° F while also producing a considerable amount of ice that can be used for summer cooling. This approach is basically the Annual Cycle Energy System (ACES) that was studied from 1977 to 1980 at the Oak Ridge National Laboratory in Tennessee.

Somewhat less exotic than storing and using ice but related to the notion of using natural forces is the use of groundwater for cooling purposes. While this is still used today, often in connection with a heat pump, before the development of reliable refrigeration equipment, environmental control systems often had to rely on cool water pumped from artesian wells to provide some interior space cooling. There are several classic examples of this approach. In 1848, Dr. David Boswell Reid had suggested circulating artesian well water through the steam heating pipes in the British House of Commons during the summer. In 1902, in his design for Sackett-Wilhelm's Lithographing

Figure 8.37 NATURAL AIR CONDITIONING
The canvas awnings on these balconies of an apartment building in northern Italy are an example of a natural air conditioning system. While both awnings are shown draped over the balcony railings, which maintain shading while allowing airflow, at times they are hung vertically in front of the opening, which limits airflow, and at other times they are pushed aside, leaving the opening free and clear. In addition to this ability to adjust both shading and airflow, the awnings serve as a source of evaporative cooling when water is poured over the canvas. As shown by the shadows, these balconies are facing basically south, which means that during the cooler periods the glass doors can be closed, reducing all airflow while capturing solar gain.

Figure 8.38 MILAM BUILDING
The Milam Building in San Antonio, Texas, was designed by George Willis and was completed in 1928. While its design is consistent with the need for all occupied space to have direct access to light and air, this is the first structure in the United States that included a central air conditioning system when it was constructed. Photo by Paul Heaton and used with permission.

and Publishing Company in Brooklyn, New York, considered to be "the world's initial scientific air conditioning installation,"[63] Willis Carrier called for the circulation of naturally cool artesian well water along with water chilled by the mechanical refrigeration unit. In Frank Lloyd Wright's 1904 Larkin Building in Buffalo, New York, which incorporated an advanced environmental control system, cooling was initially provided by groundwater. This building, shown in Figure 8.36, was a sealed environment, which seems appropriate considering that its site was adjacent to the Buffalo railroad yards. Being sealed, the building required a complex environmental control system, and the building's "final form was imposed by the method of environmental management employed . . . in a masterly manner [by] which Wright managed to turn those impositions to his architectural purposes."[64]

Since the building was sealed, cooling was critical, and groundwater apparently was not up to the task since

mechanical refrigeration was installed in 1909. Unfortunately, this important building was demolished in 1950.[65]

Even with the potentials of modern refrigeration and environmental control systems, the historic methods of improving thermal conditions by applying the natural means of shading, airflow, evaporative cooling, and thermal storage can still be effective (see Figure 8.37). The critical question is how this approach can inform the development of architectural form. Reflecting on how natural methods have been used is perhaps a good beginning, which is a reason for this historic review.

Generally, when natural adaptation is used to achieve thermal comfort, the occupants of the building must be involved, to some extent, in adjusting these methods to the varying environmental conditions, whereas most modern technical systems operate independent of such participation. While this automation might be convenient and capable of establishing rather consistent conditions, it reduces the appreciation that can be derived from a more direct interaction with environmental control.

Figure 8.39 PSFS BUILDING
The PSFS Building in Philadelphia was designed by George Howe and completed in 1932. While not the first structure to have been constructed with air conditioning, it is perhaps the first building whose design is responsive to being centrally air conditioned.

[63]Ibid., p. 19.
[64]Banham, *The Architecture of the Well-Tempered Environment*, p. 91.

[65]Ibid., pp. 90–91.

Air Conditioning

While there are numerous ways to improve the interior thermal environment, today we tend to rely predominantly on energy-consumptive methods. The first building built with a central mechanical system for both space heating and cooling was the Milam Building in San Antonio, Texas (see Figure 8.38). The architect was George Willis and the building was built in 1928. However, rather than responding to the potentials provided by the environmental control system, the design of the Milam Building was based on the traditional need to provide direct access to light and air in all occupied spaces, a requirement of non-air-conditioned structures. The first building with a design that was truly responsive to its central air conditioning system was the 1932 PSFS Building in Philadelphia, which was designed by George Howe (see Figure 8.39).

BIBLIOGRAPHY

Appendix to the Marquis de Chabannes' publication, on conducting air by forced ventilation, and equalizing the temperature of dwellings; published in 1818. [London] To be had at the Patent Calorifere Fumivore Manufactory and Foundry, [1820?]. The Making of the Modern World. Gale 2009. Gale, Cengage Learning. University of Cincinnati Libraries.

Baden-Powell, C. *Fireplace Design and Construction.* George Godwin, London, 1984.

Banham, R. *Architecture of the Well-Tempered Environment.* University of Chicago Press, Chicago, 1969.

Bruegmann, R. "Central Heating and Forced Ventilation: Origins and Effects on Architectural Design." *Journal of the Society of Architectural Historians,* October 1978.

Collins, P. *Changing Ideals in Modern Architecture 1750–1950.* McGill University Press, Montreal, 1965.

Cowan, H.J. *An Historical Outline of Architectural Science.* Elsevier Publishing Company, New York, 1966.

Ferguson, E.S. "An Historical Sketch of Central Heating: 1800–1860," in *Building Early America, Contributions Towards the History of a Great Industry.* Chilton Book Company, Radnor, PA, 1976.

Fletcher, Sir B. *A History of Architecture on the Comparative Method.* Charles Scribner's Sons, New York, 1963.

Gallo, E. "Lessons Drawn from the History of Heating: A French Perspective." Centre of Energy and Society Conference on Energy and Culture, Esbjerg, Denmark, 2007.

Giedion, S. *Mechanization Takes Command: A Contribution to Anonymous History.* Oxford University Press, New York, 1948.

Giedion, S. *Space, Time, and Architecture.* Harvard University Press, Cambridge, MA, 1956.

Hix, J. *The Glass House.* MIT Press, Cambridge, MA, 1974.

Ingels, M. *Willis Haviland Carrier, Father of Air Conditioning.* Country Life Press, Garden City, NY, 1952.

Marquis de Chabannes. "On Air and Its Properties Relative to Respiration," in *The Repertory of Arts, Manufactures, and Agriculture.* Repertory Office, Hatton Garden, London, 1818.

Marquis de Chabannes. "On the Advantage of Warming and Ventilating Houses, Mines, Ships, etc.," in *The Repertory of Arts, Manufactures, and Agriculture.* Repertory Office, Hatton Garden, London, 1818.

Mucciagrosso, R. "Technology and Modern Architecture," in *Technology in the Twentieth Century.* Kendall Hunt Publishing Company, Dubuque, IA, 1983.

Smiles, S. *Lives of Boulton and Watt. Principally from the Original Soho mss. Comprising Also a History of the Invention and Introduction of the Steam Engine.* John Murray, London, 1865 (Scholarly Publishing Office, University of Michigan Library, Ann Arbor, MI, 2005).

Vitruvius. *The Ten Books on Architecture,* trans. Morris Hicky Morgan. Dover Publications, New York, 1960.

Wernick, R. "Where There's Fire There Is Smoke—-and Usually a Chimney,'" *Smithsonian* (Washington, DC), September 1987, p.143.

Wright, L. *Home Fires Burning: The History of Domestic Heating and Cooking.* Routledge & Kegan Paul, London, 1964.

9 ECS DESIGN INTENTIONS

ARCHITECTURAL VERSUS MECHANICAL CONTROL
OF THE ENVIRONMENT

ECS ZONING

THE BEST ECS

We can't solve problems by using the same kind of thinking we used when we created them.

Albert Einstein, physicist, Nobel laureate

ARCHITECTURAL VERSUS MECHANICAL CONTROL OF THE ENVIRONMENT

In our discussions on heating and cooling calculations, the principal concern has not been sizing environmental control systems but what is generally referred to as *nonmechanical* or *passive* means of providing environmental control. Perhaps it is more appropriate to call these the *architectural* means of environmental control. These methods usually do not consume energy in their operation even though energy is probably consumed in their construction.

We should understand that we can gain important information from the analysis of potential heat loss and heat gain for a structure. This not only indicates the heating and cooling loads that will exist, it also provides information that is critical to effective architectural design. Understanding how a building will perform thermally should provide guidance in selecting an appropriate building site,

arranging proper massing and configuration, developing an environmentally responsive fenestration design, opting for sustainable materials, and supporting an efficient construction process. Although the intention should be to minimize the thermal loads through appropriate design, in most situations, even with effective architectural intervention, it is probable that some mechanical heating and cooling will be required to maintain reasonable thermal conditions.

As we explore the basic design of environmental control systems (ECS), we should keep in mind that the intention is not to learn enough to act as "little engineers" so that, sometime in our professional careers, we can avoid engaging an engineer and paying the associated consulting fees. Rather, the intention is to help us understand the design implications of ECS, both positive and negative. That is, our goal is to become mature designers.

Toward this end, we should address certain questions:

1. When are ECS used to modify the physical environment's integral architectural components and when are they independent devices imposed on the architecture? Is there a distinction and, if so, should there be one?

2. In what ways does the physical structure of a building fulfill the need to thermally modify the physical environment? Can the physical structure be considered part of the ECS?

3. What are the architectural effects of employing nonarchitectural, mechanical devices for the control of the environment? There are two parts to this question:

a. How has the use of ECS altered architectural form?

b. In what ways has architectural form been able to evolve because of the availability of ECS? That is, what is the architectural reaction to and potential of ECS? To put it another way, how has the contemporary potential for controlling the interior thermal environment through the use of energy-consumptive devices permitted greater freedom of architectural expression?

Hopefully, we will keep these overarching questions in mind as we explore the various systems that are used to control the interior thermal environment. In doing so, it is important to clarify the meaning of different terms.

The systems used to control the interior thermal environment are logically called *environmental control systems* (ECS). Although these systems are generally assumed to be the technical or mechanical systems that entail some form of energy consumption in order to provide heating, ventilating, and air conditioning (HVAC), since architecture is often referred to as *environmental design*, it should be clear that both architecture and ECS are connected and that they are jointly involved in the control of the environment. Any distinction between the two is not, or at least should not be, significant. The distinction is related to the means by which the same objectives are achieved, although even this might not be obvious.

Building on this understanding, we should be able to accept that environmental design is the overall umbrella that encompasses both architecture and mechanical systems. How might we define these ideas?

■ *Environmental design* is concerned with modification of the physical environment in order to support habitation. This modification, which should be done in a sustainable manner, should be both responsive to and expressive of the nature of the habitation to be accommodated.

■ A classic definition of *architecture* is "1: the act or science of building . . . 2: formation or construction resulting from or as if from a conscious act."[1]

■ A *mechanical system* is considered a "system of elements that interact on mechanical principles."[2]

Expanding on this, *Webster's OnLine Dictionary* defines *mechanical* as "1 a (1): of or relating to machinery or tools (2): produced or operated by a machine or tool b: of or relating to manual operations 2: of or relating to artisans or machinists 3 a: done as if by machine: seemingly uninfluenced by the mind or emotions: automatic b: of or relating to technicalities or petty matters."[3] While the reference here to *manual operations* is intriguing, the critical word in the definition is probably *machine*, which in turn can be defined as "a system used to alter, transmit, and direct applied forces in a predetermined manner to accomplish a specific objective."[4] *System*, which is not only a part of the term we are trying to define but is also included in the definition of *mechanical*, is defined as "an assemblage of objects (or elements) united by some form of regular interaction or interdependence."[5]

Based on these definitions, a *mechanical system* can be defined as an assemblage of objects used to alter, transmit, and direct applied forces in a predetermined manner to accomplish a specific objective. However, when we use the term *mechanical system* or refer to *mechanical means*, we are generally alluding to the use of machinery that is propelled by an applied external force. While this could be a human or an animal force, today we tend to assume that the source of this external force is probably some energy-consumptive device. So, while we would readily accept that a refrigeration unit, which consumes energy to pump heat out of a space, is a mechanical system, would we be willing to accept that a canvas awning, which is used to block out direct solar rays and thereby keep the interior space cool, is a mechanical system? Is it a mechanical means of providing environmental control?

Perhaps most people would accept that a canvas awning, which is usually raised and lowered according to the position of the sun and the interior environmental needs, is mechanical in that it moves. But movement is not a requirement for a mechanical system, at least by its basic definition. Movement is not incorporated in the definition, only the ability to transmit forces. If we think about a structural system, this becomes obvious, for if that system moved, it probably would mean failure.

So, even a fixed awning can be considered a mechanical device, as can, therefore, a thatched roof on a primitive hut in a hot, humid climate. Such a roof shields the interior from both the intense sun and the heavy tropical rains. The roof alters the applied forces of solar radiation and precipitation in a desired way, and since the roof is one of the primary architectural elements, it should be apparent that *architecture* and *mechanical systems* are integrally connected. If we are more descriptive and use the terms

---

[1] *Merriam-Webster's OnLine Dictionary*, http://www.merriam-webster.com/dictionary/architecture.

[2] *The Free Dictionary*, http://www.thefreedictionary.com/mechanical+system.

[3] *Merriam-Webster's OnLine Dictionary*, op. cit.

[4] Ibid.

[5] Ibid.

environmental design and *environmental control systems*, the basic connection between the two should be even clearer.

Since we are having so much fun with these definitions, what about the word *technology*? Technology refers to applied science, and since *science* is defined as "the state of knowing: knowledge as distinguished from ignorance or misunderstanding,"[6] technology merely means the application of knowledge. If we approached it from an analysis of the roots of the word (*techno* refers to art, skill, or craft and *logy* refers to a doctrine or theory), we see that technology is the theory of a skill or a craft.

From a liberal interpretation of the above, we can see that architecture is, and always has been, a form of technology that employs ECS or devices in order to achieve the appropriate objectives. So, the use of mechanical means to modify the physical environment is not antithetical to architecture. However, ECS are not necessarily architectonic.

Normally, regardless of formal definitions, technology is assumed to refer to the high-level, sophisticated science of recent times, although even this is relative. The control of fire by prehistoric societies was clearly a major technological achievement for that time, and the current reemerging interest in effective environmental adaptation (sometimes referred to as *passive solar design, green design, sustainable design*, etc.) is involved with new technological breakthroughs, although in an area where activity has existed for ages.

All of this suggests that one of the major concerns that should underpin an exploration of ECS is this question: when are ECS used to modify interior thermal conditions integral architectural components and when are they independent devices that are imposed on the architecture? Is there a distinction, and should there be one?

Even with the obvious connections, there often appears to be an assumption that architecture and ECS are distinctly different. There seems to be an unwritten professional preference for a separation between the two. This is probably the result of many environmental designers' failure to seriously pursue an understanding of the technology of the times and, based on their limited understanding, to incorporate the concerns of technology adequately into the design milieu. As a result of this narrow-minded approach, engineers have been encouraged to fill the void left by designer myopia.

Throughout history, a particular design responses to a pragmatic requirement often resulted in the development of an aesthetic preference that long outlived the viability of the design itself. Even worse than that, this preference actually came to counteract the initial pragmatic concern upon which it was based. Examples of such misplaced aesthetic preference are our continued affection for fireplaces, which are usually negative heaters (i.e., the heat they lose as a result of the need for combustion air exceeds the heat they emit to the occupied space, especially to rooms other than those in which they exist), our infatuation with fixed, nonoperable window shutters and with removable plastic window muttins intended to replicate small panes of glass, and our continuing utilization of *porte cocheres* at building entries where we are unable to disembark and are actually required to park our own vehicles and then approach on foot.

Conflicts between aesthetic preference and pragmatic necessity must be resolved if effective design is to be achieved. However, if the designer attempts to resolve such conflicts by neglecting pragmatic necessities, others will accept the responsibility and will then impose their values on the design. Since aesthetic preferences often have pragmatic origins, it seems reasonable and logical to try to initially develop an understanding of the fundamental requirements to which a design should respond and then, based on this understanding, attempt to establish an appropriate aesthetic response.

The Transition between the Interior and the Exterior

In the textbook *Mechanical and Electrical Equipment in Buildings*, the envelope of a building is presented as being more than merely a set of two-dimensional exterior surfaces.[7] It is suggested that the envelope of the building comprises a "transition space" that exists between the exterior, natural environmental conditions and the interior, controlled conditions. In recognition of what occurs within the environmental envelope, perhaps this should be called a *transition mechanism* or perhaps a *transition place* in deference to the architectural meaning of the term *space*. While *transition place* tends to focus on the location in which the transition occurs, *transition mechanism* tends to emphasize the operations that are involved.

Christian Norberg-Schulz talked about architecture in terms of controlling the environment in order to make interaction and collaboration possible. While he introduced several different aspects by which such control is achieved, he identified the thermal environment as the most elementary.

---

[6]Ibid.

[7]B. Stein, J.S. Reynolds, W.T. Grondzik, and A.G. Kwok, *Mechanical and Electrical Equipment for Buildings* (John Wiley & Sons, Inc., Hoboken, New Jersey, 2006), p. 171.

"In general we may say that architecture controls the environment in order to make interaction and collaboration possible. This control has several different aspects. The most elementary is the creation of an 'artificial climate,' protecting man against rain, wind, cold, heat, moisture, noise, insects, wild animals, enemies, and other evils in the surroundings. We will call this aspect 'physical control.' Another aspect of the *physical milieu* is the participation of buildings in human actions. This problem we will study under the heading 'functional frame.' The actions, however, are socially determined, and the physical objects participating (e.g. the buildings) therefore manifest social meanings. The buildings form a part of the 'social milieu.' Finally, architecture may represent cultural objects like religious, philosophical, or cosmological conceptions. Together with the social aspects, this 'cultural symbolization' makes up the *symbol-milieu*. The building task thus will be studied in further detail by means of four dimensions of comparison."

PHYSICAL CONTROL

The physical control is the better understood aspect of the building task. Acoustics, illumination, heating, and air conditioning have become highly developed specialties where the architect only in part is competent. In the following we will not enter upon particular problems of these fields, but limit ourselves to some general remarks on the role of the physical control within the building task. It is expedient to take the existing specialties as a point of departure, because the specialties are functions of the physiological constitution of man. We thus distinguish between the control of:

Climate (air, humidity, temperature, wind, rainfall, etc.)
Light
Sound
Smell
Things (dust, smoke, insects, animals, persons)
(Radio-activity)

Most of these factors are 'geographical,' and we understand that the physical control above all is concerned with the relations between the building and its surroundings. The environment affects the building with energies, which have to be controlled. . . . We may, however, also study the physical control as an 'exchange of energies.' To permit this, we will introduce the concepts 'filter,' 'connector,' 'barrier,' and 'switch.' "[8]

According to Norberg-Schulz, the nature of the transition that occurs between the conditions that exist on either side of a building's envelope can be classified in terms of the envelope being either a *connector*, a *filter*, a *switch*, or a *barrier*. The implications of a barrier are that the exterior and the interior are effectively separated into two totally distinct and different environments. At the other extreme, the implications of a connector are that it provides a direct link between both conditions so that the exterior and the interior are effectively unified. In contrast to the barrier and the connector, the filter selectively connects the conditions of both the exterior and the interior. This results in two distinct environments that share certain selected common elements. And the switch, which can be referred

to as a *regulating connector*, tends to share conditions that are modified as they are transmitted across the envelope.

If the aim is to make the interior appear as the exterior, we might wonder why we cannot merely utilize the existing natural conditions. However, even if we were somehow able to solve this problem, it should be clear that the interior and exterior can never be totally unified and over time must become increasingly distinct as the effects of the different environmental conditions take their toll. If a design were able to initially establish continuity between the exterior and the interior, separating the two conditions with minimal architectural expression, the separation would create variations in conditions. Weathering and pollution would occur, so any initial similarity between the interior and exterior would be diminished considerably over time. For example, if the same material were used to pave adjacent interior and exterior areas, the detailing required for water drainage and thermal adjustments on the exterior

[8]Christian Norberg-Shulz, *Intentions in Architecture* (MIT Press, Cambridge, MA, 1965), pp. 111–113.

Figure 9.1 KRESGE AUDITORIUM

Kresge Auditorium at the Massachusetts Institute of Technology, designed by Eero Saarinen in the early 1950s. The basic structure is thin-shell concrete equaling one-eighth of a sphere with three sides, each enclosed in glass. As shown in the right image, while brick paving tended to connect the interior and exterior, structural bracing of the shell, water drainage, and weathering over time, in addition to the window framing, established a significant separation between the two locations.

would be different from that required for interior maintenance. Even if these differences were somehow effectively concealed, the exterior conditions would ultimately make the different conditions increasingly apparent.

Of course, if the attempt to connect the interior and the exterior were successful and there was no obvious distinction between the two, occupants might be enticed to physically breach the connector, which could be extremely hazardous. For example, if wall-to-wall, floor-to-ceiling glass were used in such a way that the intended connection was effectively achieved, there would be a potential danger of people walking into the glass as they tried to move between the two zones. In order to avoid this, some means of denoting the presence of the glazed divider, such as a crash bar or a series of cute dots placed on the glass, would be necessary. If such demarcation were not required, while the glass might be transparent during the day when looking out toward the brighter exterior, there would not be a sense of connection from the exterior. During the day, glass fenestration tends to appear from the outside as a black solid, not a transparent opening. Again at night, if the interior and exterior were not illuminated to the same level, the presence of a glazed opening, while it might provide a visual connection between the interior and the exterior, would be quite apparent.

Eero Saarinen's design for MIT's Kresge Auditorium, shown in Figure 9.1, was an early attempt to connect the interior and the exterior. The major architectural component of the design was a long-span, thin-shell concrete dome, and the interior and exterior were to be separated merely by expansive glazing. Unfortunately, the potential movement of the shell as a result of temperature changes

required the addition of heavy vertical framing to stabilize the edges of the shell so that the window glazing would be retained in place. This framing created more of a visual separation than desired. Even with these heavy steel members forming an edge to the space, Saarinen minimized the sill so that the brick paving used both inside and outside would seem to flow together. While initially there was some sense that the paving did continue, after a few years the interior paving, which had grouted joints and was cleaned and polished, appeared quite different from the exterior paving, which had open joints for water control and acquired a weathered patina. The continuous trench drain that surrounded the shell also violated the sense of connection.

Total or absolute isolation of interior and exterior is also not achievable and generally not desirable. Generally, any space that is located along a building perimeter should take advantage of the daylighting potentials and views, but even when this is not desired and considerable thermal insulation is added to the exterior envelope, some heat exchange is likely. As in larger buildings with major segments of interior space that are architecturally isolated from the exterior, some connections must still be established with the outside in order to condition these spaces adequately. For example, fresh air must be provided from the outside in order to ventilate the interior space, and the internal heat gains, which are a necessary by-product of occupancy, must be dissipated to the exterior by means of some mechanical device.

While the design intentions for a building's envelope might be to achieve total connection or total isolation between the exterior and the interior, such intentions are

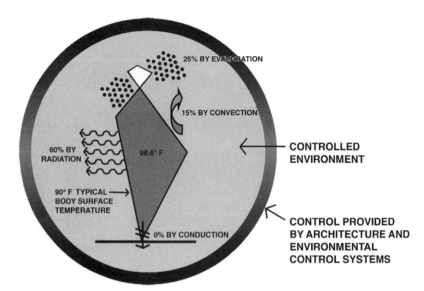

Figure 9.2 THERMAL BALANCE DIAGRAM
As shown in the diagram, the human body releases its excess heat by the classic thermal transfer means of conduction, convection, radiation, and evaporation, although, under most conditions, conduction does not contribute to the heat loss. To maintain the rate of transfer as shown, which relates to conditions of comfort, the environment needs to be controlled through architecture, in conjunction with and supplemented by ECS.

seldom fully attainable. In most contemporary structures, rather than acting as a connector or a barrier, the building envelope operates partially as a filter, providing certain connections between the interior and the exterior, and partially as a switch, ameliorating the flow of forces between the two environments. While the architecture tends to play both of these roles, the role of switch is also fulfilled largely by the building's mechanical ECS. The ECS are intended to counteract the natural flow of energy between the interior and the exterior, and to be effective, they should accomplish this at the point of this energy flow. Rather than merely achieve some sort of thermal balance, an ECS should control any thermal problems at their source. If the building envelope is allowing a flow of energy between the exterior and the interior, which conflicts with the desired interior conditions, then the ECS should counteract this flow. They do this by adding to or extracting from the interior environment the energy that is being lost or gained, and they should do this at the point where this "natural" exchange is occurring. This fundamental principle establishes what is perhaps the primary requirement of any effective, mechanical thermal control system: provide the environmental control at the point of heat gain or heat loss.

Basic Intentions of ECS

The basic requirement for thermal comfort is the loss of excess body heat at the rate at which it is produced and to do so without imposing any stress. This thermal exchange between the body and the environment, which is diagrammed in Figure 9.2, relies on the basic forms of thermal transfer: conduction, convection, radiation, and, for heat loss, evaporation. The effectiveness of each of these

methods in exchanging the excess heat to the surrounding environment is based on five environmental factors:

■ Dry bulb temperature (DBT)
■ Humidity or wet bulb temperature (WBT)
■ Mean radiant temperature (MRT)
■ Air velocity
■ Air quality

While not particularly a thermal factor, air quality is generally included in the group, partly because the response to air quality is somewhat related to thermal reactions but, more importantly, because the means of controlling the other four factors is often also the way air quality is controlled—through an air system.

The basic intention of effective environmental design is to maximize the architectural control of these five factors, relying on ECS as a way to extend these means. That is, the architectural response should be the initial means of providing thermal control. Architectural design should be part of the solution, not part of the problem!

Unfortunately, basic as this might seem, architectural design often tends to compound the negative aspects of the environment. While not specifically architectural, Figure 9.3 clearly presents an example of how misdirected we can be. As shown in the image, while the people are exposed to the intense sunlight, the dogs have found an appropriate use of the lounge chairs—shade. Interestingly, even though an umbrella is available to provide shade, the people lying under it are not in its shade but are still exposed to the direct sun.

Although there are preferred ranges for each of the five environmental factors in terms of thermal comfort (see Figure 9.4), when one or two of these factors exceed these limits, there is some latitude in compensating for these conditions by adjusting one or more of the other

Figure 9.3 THE BEACH ON THE ISLAND OF SANTORINI, GREECE
On the beach just north of Akrotiri on the island of Santorini, Greece, the dogs seem to have a better understanding of how to respond to the natural environment than the people, who are exposed to the intense Mediterranean sun.

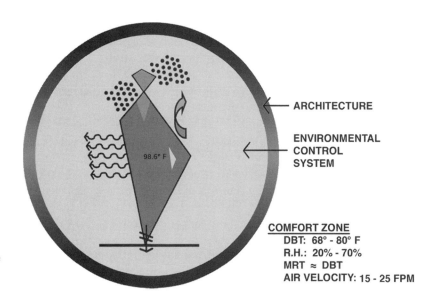

ARCHITECTURE

ENVIRONMENTAL CONTROL SYSTEM

COMFORT ZONE
DBT: 68° - 80° F
R.H.: 20% - 70%
MRT ≈ DBT
AIR VELOCITY: 15 - 25 FPM

Figure 9.4 THERMAL CONTROL DIAGRAM
The controlled environment is based on five factors, four of which have a direct connection with the establishment of thermal balance. Air quality, although related to the others and to our sensation of thermal conditions, is not specifically a factor in terms of thermal balance. The range of comfort as shown is based on the interaction of the four factors.

factors, which might mean that they should exceed the normal limits.

When architectural means are used to establish thermal comfort, the intention is essentially to harness the beneficial environmental conditions while minimizing the impact of the negative conditions. When we incorporate mechanical systems into our design to extend the means of environmental control, the intention should be the same—to enhance the positive conditions and to counteract the problems, and to be effective, this should be done at the source. Rather than merely provide thermal balance, ECS control should be responsive to the way any gain or loss occurs.

The Conundrum of Mechanical Expression

Another important issue for all environmental control systems is the level of awareness that the building occupants should have of the systems.

Successful as we might be in maximizing the natural environmental potential for thermal comfort through architectural design, it is probable that some energy-consumptive ECS will be required. ECS are a reality of most buildings today, so if we do not wish to have them impose on our designs, we must be able to incorporate them into our design. This raises an interesting conundrum: the more we dislike ECS, particularly their overt expression in our designs, the more we need to understand about ECS.

While not specifically included, the principle that thermal control should be provided at the point of gain or loss implies that the occupants of a building should not be aware of the operation of the ECS, especially in terms of experiencing thermal stress. While we might accept that ECS should accomplish their task without imposing negatively on building occupants, what is the basis for a negative interpretation? Are there ways in which an awareness of the ECS might be appropriate?

There is a range of possible responses to these questions. For some, any awareness of ECS is deemed inappropriate; for others, ECS might be embraced as a major positive design component that can impact effectively on the spatial experience. While the latter position generally merely encourages a positive and significant integration of mechanical devices with the design vocabulary, it might actually go as far as to accept a conscious awareness of the operation of the ECS. Being exposed to drafts or having to endure the noise and vibration that ECS can produce is not the usual intention of mechanical expression. However, rejecting all forms of overt mechanical expression in the architectural aesthetic does not eliminate the need to understand ECS. On the contrary, it probably increases it.

If we embrace the aesthetics that mechanical systems can contribute to environmental design, we will probably have no difficulty in accommodating the physical requirements of these systems in our designs. While hopefully we will understand what is necessary, our appreciation for the potential aesthetic contributions of the technical systems allows for a more open, interactive collaboration with our consulting engineers. On the other hand, if we find mechanical expression distasteful, then we need to know more about ECS, how they work and what they require, so that we can develop our designs to incorporate these systems as part of the architectural expression while ensuring that they will perform appropriately and not impose on the design aesthetic.

For example, to accommodate the size of an air duct necessary to supply enough air to control a space, we need to have a good idea of the appropriate duct size, the route that the air supply will likely take to do what is required, and the way the air can be supplied to heat and/or cool the space properly. Of course, there are also the issues of return air, air velocity, insulation, duct installation, and others. And if the ECS components are not to be expressed, they should be included within the building *poché*, which must be sized adequately and located appropriately for both the system's operation and the intent of the architectural design. Although the final design of the ECS will likely involve collaboration with a consulting engineer, the basic architectural design should be responsive to the demands of the ECS or the ultimate inclusion of the system will be difficult. We cannot wait until the contract document phase of a project to learn that a dropped soffit might be required to accommodate the air ducts or that a vertical chase must be added in the center of a major space.

Whether or not we appreciate a mechanical aesthetic, we need to understand ECS and use this understanding to inform our design efforts. However, if our appreciation does not tend to include mechanical expression, then we must be more knowledgeable so that we can accommodate the ECS as an integral part of the architecture rather than as an imposition.

ECS ZONING

While there is a range of reasonable options for the expression of ECS within architectural design, the premise of all these options rests on the notion that architectural design offers a medium through which articulation can be achieved. It is assumed that a major intention of architectural design is to provide a physical statement of the essential nature of the purposes for which the building exists. In developing such an expression, the designer is encouraged to identify these purposes and, in order to achieve a meaningful articulation, to organize them according to some level of commonality. While the "language" of any design is partially based on the standards that exist for a particular culture, location, and time, its particular statement is formed primarily from the relative comparisons established among its various components. That is, while there are some architectural forms or articulations for which there might be a limited agreed-upon meaning, generally any meaning that is conveyed through design is achieved by comparative relationships.

Since the potential for specific articulation in architectural form is extremely limited, the spatial divisions that are appropriate for environmental control can help establish a basis for comparative relationships. Alternatively, relationships among the various components of a design, which might be formulated in response to other intentions, can also provide an effective rationale for the design of the ECS. But whatever the basis of the intended design, there should be a reasonable consistency of expression.

An ECS should be designed so that it is responsive to the actual loads on the system, the operational demands for the system, and the different environmental conditions expected from the system. To accomplish this, it is generally necessary to identify areas of commonality and then to subdivide or zone the overall system so that there can be an effective response to the particular needs of each

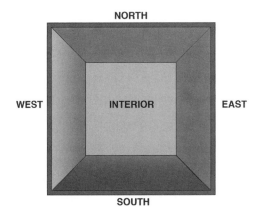

Figure 9.5 ENVIRONMENTAL FORCES
In general terms, there are basically five environmental zones, one for each of the four cardinal orientations plus the interior. However, if the building is oriented other than north-south or if the building configuration is not rectangular, the number of zones might need to be adjusted. Also, the building fenestration might influence the number of exterior zones.

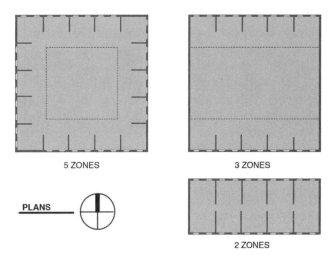

Figure 9.6 VARIABLE ENVIRONMENTAL ZONES
A major intention of environmental control is to respond to the natural forces that impose on a structure. Since at times each building exposure experiences different environmental forces, the control system must be able to adjust to these distinctions, and this establishes the need for different ECS zones.

common grouping or zone. Based on this arrangement, there are six bases of commonality used to establish appropriate environmental zones:

- Environmental forces
- Function
- Patterns of use
- Ownership
- Architectural design
- ECS potential

Environmental Forces

As diagrammed in Figure 9.5, the environmental forces typically result in five distinct zones: an interior zone, which is surrounded by conditioned spaces that are maintained at the desired interior thermal conditions, and four exterior or perimeter zones, one for each orientation (i.e., north, east, south, and west). The architectural design, of course, will impact on these zones. If the design does not include an interior habitable space that is isolated from the exterior, there will be only four orientation zones. Obviously the siting of the building could also switch the orientation of these zones off the cardinal points, or the basic design could suggest an adjustment in the actual number of zones.

For example, an octagonal form would imply eight distinct perimeter zones rather than the standard four, whereas a long, narrow rectangular building might have only two perimeter zones, one for each major exposure. Similarly, if the design included an area with considerable roof exposure, this too might indicate a separate zone.

In addition to these basic design influences, the construction details can affect the determination of environmental zones. While an elongated rectangular structure might suggest the presence of two zones, one for each major exposure, if windows were located on only one wall and the remaining exposures were heavily insulated, it might be appropriate to consider that there is only one exterior zone. In the same way, while a square structure would imply four equal exterior zones, if there are windows in only two of the exterior walls, the number of zones might also be reduced to two.

While the simple diagrams in Figure 9.6 do not stipulate orientation, different orientations would obviously experience quite different environmental conditions, particularly as a result of solar radiation. This is perhaps most obvious from the two-zone diagram. If oriented as shown, it is clear that the southern exposure will experience solar gain while the northern exposure does not. As a result, this might mean that at the same time that the southern-oriented spaces require cooling, the northern-oriented spaces need heating. As mentioned previously, this diverse situation might occur during the coldest period of the year. Although this is an extreme condition—heating and cooling at the same time—the variation in exposure can readily establish different intensities of solar gain that would convert into quite distinct demands on the ECS.

If the two-zone plan were oriented with major exposures to the east and west, a distinction in the demands on the ECS would exist on most days. When the eastern exposure is exposed to direct solar gain, which would produce a maximum heat gain, the western exposure would clearly not have the same forces imposed. As a result, it is quite probable that when the eastern spaces demand maximum cooling, the western spaces do not and, in fact, might actually require some heating if the exterior temperatures are low. On the same day, when the sun has moved to the western part of the sky, the western spaces would then require maximum cooling while the eastern spaces might now require some heating. Even if heating is not necessary, the cooling load would be significantly less than that for the western zone. Obviously, from such a simple consideration, we should clearly recognize that the ECS should be designed to respond to the various environmental forces.

In most large buildings, in addition to the zones for each exposure, there is an interior zone. Generally, this zone is delineated by surrounding walls, although this arrangement is not required. When a physical separation exists between the interior and exterior zones, it usually determines the depth of the exterior zone, which could be as little as about 10 feet or as large as 30 feet. When the distance from a building's exterior exceeds approximately 30 feet, an interior zone condition exists whether or not there is a physical separation. Since, as mentioned above, the primary intention of any ECS is to provide thermal control at the point of heat gain or heat loss, at 30 feet from the building's edge the demands on the system should no longer entail control of the exterior thermal loads. Generally, since an interior has no heat loss because it is surrounded by conditioned spaces, typically there is no access to daylight either. As a result, illumination depends on electric lights that add considerable heat. Any occupants or operating equipment will also add heat to the space, so cooling is required for an interior zone at all times of the year.

Sometimes, when renovating a building, it might make sense to subdivide a large space located along a building perimeter into a number of smaller spaces, as suggested in Figure 9.7. The design could either subdivide the larger space into several smaller spaces with exterior exposure (scheme A), create several interior spaces that no longer have any connection to the building perimeter (scheme B), or some combination of the two (scheme C). Since all of these schemes divide one space into five different spaces, some adjustment to the ECS will be required by each scheme; however, schemes B and C both pose a new environmental concern—interior thermal zones. Assuming that the previous open space was effectively heated and cooled as the yearly seasons changed, only minor adjustments to delivery of the supply air will probably be required by scheme A, but with the other approaches that create interior zones, cooling is probably necessary even during the winter period. Without any heat loss, the interior heat gains from lights and people constitute continuous heat

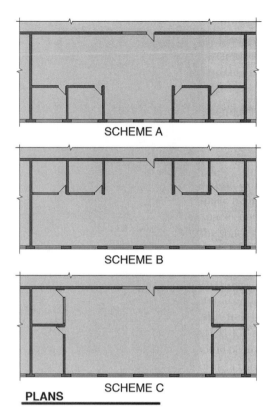

Figure 9.7 ALTERNATIVE RENOVATION PLANS
Three different schemes are presented showing how a large exterior space might be renovated to provide four private offices and a reception/general office area. Assuming that the current space is conditioned by linear-feed, perimeter baseboard radiation combined with a ceiling-supplied air system, which scheme would require the most adjustment to the ECS?

gains during occupancy, and what might have been a simple renovation now requires a major adjustment to the ECS.

Function

The building functions also suggest areas of commonality. Various activities often require different environmental conditions and, at the same time, impose unique loads on the systems. Therefore, in laying out an ECS it is appropriate to consider distinct system responses that might be necessary to respond to the intended or potential activities. One of the more dramatic examples of how different functions or activities can demand distinct thermal control is provided by a sports area, perhaps for basketball at a university that has a team that tries hard but does not do very well and yet maintains loyal support from the students and alumni. At most games, the stands are sparsely filled with hopeful but somewhat reserved spectators who watch a small group of extremely active players under bright lights, but at some games between major rivals, the stands are full with actively cheering fans. Between games, during practice, the same central court activity might continue while the stands are empty. Although there is only one large space, within that space are zones that have quite different thermal demands, and these vary according to the activity.

When considering how different functions might impose on the design of ECS, the notion of commonality is probably more specifically related to distinctions among functional demands. A good example of this, which has become less of a problem with changes in law and behavior, is how to separate smoking from nonsmoking areas. Merely locating the smokers away from the nonsmokers does not solve the problem, especially if thermal control is provided by a central air system, unless the system does not return any air from the smoking area.

Patterns of Use

Although similar to function, the pattern of use of a space offers a distinct basis of commonality. This might be a response to the different times that individual businesses might operate, some remaining open seven days a week, from early morning to late evening, while others close on the weekend and have limited hours each day. Specific patterns of use also frequently exist within a given organization; perhaps the most notable one is the computer center that might operate continuously, 24-7, while the remaining activities of the organization tend to operate only during normal business hours.

Large places of public assembly, such as restaurants and lecture halls, are other examples of spaces whose patterns of use often require a particular response by the ECS. These spaces could be fully occupied for a period of time and then totally empty. Since the use of the adjoining spaces probably would not follow the same pattern, there could be problems if they are served by the same ECS.

When an assembly space is fully occupied, the concentration of people often demands both maximum ventilation and maximum cooling, even during the winter season. As a result, while heating is required for adjacent spaces, there could be an alternating demand between maximum heating and maximum cooling in the assembly space, along with an associated adjustment required in rates of ventilation. In addition, since the assembly space might be used during hours when the remaining portions of the structure are unoccupied—for example, on evenings or weekends—it might be appropriate to be able to operate its ECS independently of the system(s) used for the rest of the structure.

Ownership

Ownership, which in terms of ECS refers specifically to the responsibility for payment rather than to holding title to the property, also influences how ECS should be divided into distinct zones. In many buildings, similar activities, which by themselves might not imply a need for separate zoning, are often associated with different businesses, each of which usually demands separate utility billing. To respond to this demand, separate zones, if not individual systems, should be provided. Of course, depending upon the business and/or the design of the space, each of these "ownership" zones or systems might require additional subzones that are capable of responding to the various conditions of that occupancy.

The basis of payment also has an influence on energy efficiency. When a tenant is responsible only for its own energy use, there is an incentive to be efficient, whereas when operational expenses are shared, individual efficiency might not be rewarded.

Architectural Design

The particular architectural *parti*, or design idea, provides another basis of commonality. While the design *parti* is hopefully a response to and reinforcement of the other three bases of commonality, it generally implies a distinctive approach. If architectural design were merely a result of a set of prescribed responses to various demands of environmental conditions and functionality needs, then design could be achieved by formula, but such is not the case. Each architectural design provides its own individualized statement and an expressed order to which the ECS should be sympathetic. That is, the intentions of the design of the ECS of any building should be consistent with its architectural intentions.

For example, a school could be designed as a single building or as a series of buildings in what is called a *campus plan*, as is shown in Figure 9.8. There are legitimate reasons for each approach, and these reasons should also inform the design of the ECS. While environmental control for the single-building design might be provided by a multizone air-handling unit, separate air-handling units would be logical for the campus plan since this would be more consistent with the intentions of the architectural design. While other arrangements of the ECS for the campus plan might also be reasonable, there are some approaches that might work technologically but would be inconsistent with the architectural intentions.

As suggested by Figure 9.8, with the common areas for the school located within a central structure, it might

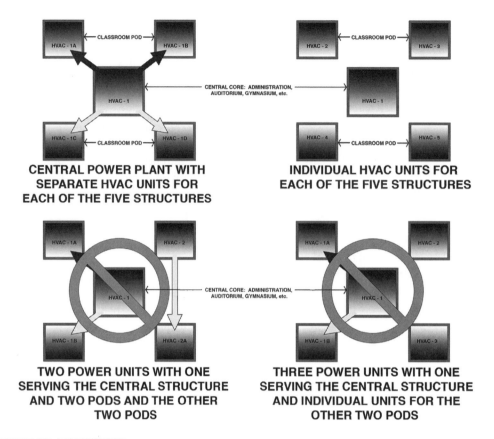

Figure 9.8 ALTERNATIVE ECS ARRANGEMENTS
Four different schemes are presented of possible layouts of the ECS for a campus plan school, two that are consistent with the architectural *parti* and two that are not.

make sense to include a central power plant and then control each building with independent air-handling units, which, based on the design, might be multizoned units or a series of individual units for each space. In this approach, the central power plant could supply hot and chilled water to each air-handling unit. An alternative approach would be to have each air-handling unit be an independent unit with its own heating and cooling capacity, perhaps by means of a heat pump, which would clearly make sense if electricity is the primary energy source. While these approaches or others that are responsive to the architectural arrangement are reasonable, dividing the ECS components purely on the basis of equipment capacity, such as having one unit for the central structure and two pods plus another unit for the other two pods, does not make sense. Although such an ECS approach might be more economical or energy efficient, it is questionable whether these same values are applicable to the architectural design. It does not make sense to impose different fundamental criteria on different aspects of the same design. If economy and energy are critical, which is likely, then they should also apply to the architectural *parti*.

ECS Potential

Finally, ECS provide another basis of commonality since there are limits beyond which systems cannot be expected to perform properly. For example, although the horizontal distribution for a water system can generally extend over a considerable distance,[9] the vertical displacement is often limited to around 15 to 16 stories. Since atmospheric pressure of 14.7 psi can raise a column of water to a height of approximately 30 feet, we should realize that a 15- to 16-story column of water would exert a pressure of approximately 100 psi, which is about the maximum internal pressure for most standard water valves. In order to operate the internal mechanisms of a valve, the valve

[9] Early plumbing systems often relied on hollowed-out wooden logs to convey water under pressure. Since these pipes were unable to resist much pressure, the length of distribution was rather limited unless they were merely conduits for water flowing downward. While cast iron and then wrought iron pipes could resist higher internal pressures than wood pipes, it was not until welded steel pipe and extruded copper pipe were developed that high pressures could be contained, allowing for a considerable increase in internal pressure and distribution distance.

stem must physically pass from the inside of the valve to an actuator, which might be a valve handle or an automatic controller. While the valve stem is surrounded by packing to prevent leakage of fluid, there is a limit to the internal pressures that the packing can resist. This establishes the 15- to 16-floor maximum rise, but this could also be a drop. With both a rise and a drop, typically a mechanical floor is needed every 30 to 32 floors. This also works with the limitations for air distribution.

Air systems have similar limitations, again based on the maximum allowable internal pressure. The maximum length of run for a low-pressure air system is normally around 150 linear feet. Since high-pressure systems use air ducts that are considerably stronger than those used in low-pressure systems, the maximum length for high-pressure systems is approximately 400 linear feet.

In addition to the length of run, an air system is limited to a maximum capacity set by the largest circulating fans. Air movement in a duct results from pressure produced by a fan, generally a centrifugal fan, which requires a level of precision that cannot generally be achieved in the field. As a result, fans are typically constructed in a factory and shipped completely assembled to the building site. Since there are limitations on the size of items that can be transported readily on the highways, there are limits on the maximum size of an air-handling unit. If the fan will be used in what is referred to as a *built-up* air-handling unit, one that is assembled at the building site, the largest fan that meets the transportation regulations will be able to circulate a maximum air volume of around 100,000 cubic feet per minute (CFM). Since we require approximately 1 CFM for each square foot of occupied space, this largest fan could condition up to 100,000 square feet of space. This then becomes the largest floor area that can be included within a single environmental zone within an air system.

If the fan is used in a packaged air-handling unit, one that is assembled at the factory and then shipped to the building site, the fan has to be smaller so that it can fit within the maximum allowable size of the unit that can be transported. This normally is a fan with up to a 25,000-CFM capacity, meaning that the largest environmental zone for such a packaged air-handling unit is around 25,000 square feet.

Obviously, the environmental system must be responsive to these system limitations, but so should the architectural design. Put another way, while the design of the ECS of any building should be responsive to its architectural design, in addition to the other factors of environmental forces, function, patterns of use, and ownership, the architectural design should be responsive to the requirements and potentials of the ECS. Truly effective, quality architectural design can be achieved only through a positive integration of architectural intentions and the potentials and limitations of the ECS.

THE BEST ECS

Often a basic question raised when considering environmental control systems for a building project is: what is the best system to use? The assumption seems to be that since ECS are technical systems, there is some predetermined "best" approach that needs to be identified. However, this assumption is no more valid for the ECS design than it is for the architectural design.

Accepting that the overall thermal conditions are based on the five basic environmental factors of DBT, WBT, MRT, air velocity, and air quality, we might assume that the preferred system would be determined by how many of these factors the system can control. Based on this assumption, the logical best system would be an air system, since this can readily control four of the five factors and, with special considerations, can even affect MRT.[10] However, if control of MRT is the critical issue, which is likely for a structure with a considerable amount of glazing that is located in a cool region where heat loss dominates, an air system would probably not be as effective as a hot water radiation system. Even if an air system might be reasonable for counteracting the loads on a structure, a water system might be more appropriate if the building design does not provide space to accommodate the air ducts.

Even with an air system, there are various possibilities. Thermal control might be provided by a central air system that requires distributing supply air from the central equipment and then returning the air to the same location. Alternatively, an air system might merely entail circulating the air within each space to be conditioned, but even with this approach, there are several possibilities. The heating and cooling can be provided by hot and chilled water supplied from a central source to each air-handling unit located in the conditioned spaces or by independent, self-contained units, such as heat pumps, that can both heat and cool.

In addition to the thermal issues and architectural design factors, the preferred ECS might be set by the custom, or *minhag,* of the area where a structure is located. A good example of this from early central heating days is whether a hydronic system meant steam or hot water. While there

---

[10]The hypocaust system that the Romans used in the baths was an air system that provided thermal control primarily by managing the MRT.

are definite advantages for each, the selection of one over the other was often based merely on the preference of the local contractors, particularly the better contractors, who basically set the standard. As a result, two comparable locations, at least in terms of thermal conditions, might differ, one of which might rely predominantly on steam as the source of heat and the other, on using hot water. This is similar to architectural preferences, such as for brick versus clapboard siding.

BIBLIOGRAPHY

Greenleaf, S.J. "Design Parameters," in *Progressive Architecture* (Reinhold Publishing Corporation, New York, October 1963), pp. 150–155.

Grondzik, W.T., A.G. Kwok, B. Stein, and J.S. Reynolds,. *Mechanical and Electrical Equipment for Buildings*. John Wiley & Sons, Inc., Hoboken, NJ, 2010.

Norberg-Shulz, C. *Intentions in Architecture*. MIT Press, Cambridge, MA, 1965.

CHAPTER

10 ENVIRONMENTAL CONTROL SYSTEMS

CATEGORIES OF ECS

ECS can be organized into various categories, although within each category there might be further subdivision. A major division of ECS is between *central systems* and *distributed systems*, yet we have to understand that these are relative terms. A series of buildings, such as might exist on a university campus, might be supplied with centrally generated hot and chilled water that is then utilized in each individual structure, which in turn might be conditioned by a central unit or by a series of individual units, perhaps for different major zones or for each individual space. While there are different aspects in terms of whether the ECS is central, distributed, or some sort of combination, the distinction, which can be related to similar distinctions pursued in architectural design, can be very helpful in developing an appropriate design for the ECS.

Another major division of ECS is between *hydronic systems* and *air systems*. While today *hydronic* tends to mean a water system, it actually includes both water and steam systems. Of course, as was discussed previously, while there is a distinction between air systems and hydronic systems, many large air systems employ steam, hot water, and/or chilled water as the source of energy transfer, although air systems might include a means of heat generation and cooling. A typical residential furnace or a heat pump is an example of such.

A third distinction of ECS is between *heating* and *cooling*. While many, if not most, systems today have both a heating and a cooling capacity, there are still ECS that can only heat or cool. Sometimes this is a factor of location, which might mean that the climatic conditions of the building site do not require one or the other, or perhaps both, thermal control needs. Of course, with effective architectural design, even

Figure 10.1 WATER-TUBE BOILER
This is a simple diagram of a two-pass water-tube boiler with the water flowing through pipes that are surrounded by the hot combustion gases. The piping is arranged so that the cool water is surrounded by the cooler combustion gases and the hot water by the hotter combustion gases. This establishes a temperature differential between the water and the combustion gases that will achieve the greatest thermal exchange. Since the heated water will deposit chemicals within the pipes, access must be provided for maintenance. This generally requires a free area equal to the size of the boiler so that the tubes can be serviced and/or removed.

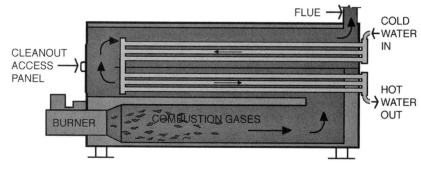

sites with marginal climatic conditions might avoid the need for conventional ECS.

HEAT GENERATION PROCESS

Heat input for an ECS is usually the result of the combustion process. When combustion occurs in a device that directly heats air, the device is called a *furnace*, and when it heats water, the device is called a *boiler*. While the term *boiler* implies steam, it is used for both steam and hot water generators, although some prefer to use the term *hot water heater* or sometimes *hot water boiler* to clarify that the device does not produce steam. Since the heater for domestic hot water is also called a *hot water heater*, there can be some confusion in the terms we use.

The control gauges for a steam boiler and a hot water boiler are different. While both should include pressure release valves, the operation of a hot water boiler is typically managed by temperature, whereas that of a steam boiler relies on pressure, although a steam boiler will also be maintained at near-boiling temperatures during the heating season so that there is no major delay before steam can be generated and heat can be delivered. Similarly, a hot water boiler is usually maintained at near-operational temperatures, relying on room thermostats to initiate the operation of the water pumps for space heating to occur.

Although typically steam is distributed by means of natural variations in density and water by pumps, pumps can be added to a steam system and differences in water density can establish what is referred to as a *gravity-flow water system*. Water boils at 212° F at standard atmospheric pressure, but by adjusting the pressures within a steam system, boiling can occur at a lower or higher temperature than 212° F. When such a system is employed, the system is a *variable vacuum steam system*, which provides for slightly improved temperature control. However, if pumps, which are pressure-producing devices, are to be included, it is generally more reasonable to use a water system since it can be controlled in terms of both temperature and flow, resulting in better operational control.

Early hot water systems often were gravity systems, relying on variations in water density established by temperature differences to set up the water flow. This required large-diameter piping through which the hot water would circulate, but this would occur based on water temperature rather than the space thermostat. As the water was heated, it would circulate even if space heating was not required. While this was not a problem at times or in areas that were consistently cold, it did cause some problems during more mild conditions. As a result, most gravity systems were converted to pumped distribution systems, adding a flow valve so that water would circulate only when heating was required and the pump was activated.

Whether the heating device heats air or water, the process entails heat exchange between the hot combustion gases and the medium being heated. The more interaction that is established between the hot gases and the heated medium, the higher the efficiency of operation. With boilers, this efficiency is expressed in terms of the number of passes between the combustion gases and the water, with three passes recommended. Also, as shown in Figures 10.1 and 10.2, the boiler can be either a fire-tube unit or a water-tube unit. In a fire-tube unit, the combustion gases travel through a flue that is surrounded by water. In a water-tube boiler, the water is in pipes that pass through the path of the combustion gases. Since the combustion gases are hotter than the water, a fire-tube boiler tends to be somewhat more efficient.

REFRIGERATION PROCESS

In the effort to control the interior environment, it is sometimes necessary to add and at other times to remove thermal energy from the space to be conditioned. Since the Second Law of Thermodynamics indicates that thermal energy can flow naturally only from a higher to a lower intensity level, the heating process is relatively easy but the

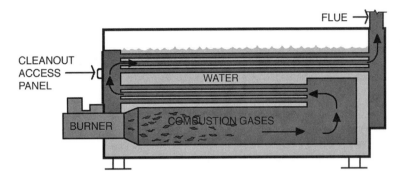

Figure 10.2 FIRE-TUBE BOILER
This is a simple diagram of a three-pass fire-tube boiler with the combustion gases flowing through passages that are surrounded by the water to be heated. Since combustion by-products can deposit within the fire tubes, access must be provided for maintenance. This generally requires a free area equal to the size of the boiler so that the tubes can be serviced and/or removed.

cooling process is another matter. In order to heat a space, we merely have to establish a source of thermal energy at an intensity level (i.e., temperature) higher than that of the space we wish to heat and then allow the energy to flow from this elevated level into the space. Since most combustion processes operate at above 450° F, we simply have to burn a fuel to establish this higher temperature source. To cool a space is not as simple since it is not possible to create cold. *Cold* is not a substance but the absence of heat. (Some people use the term *coolth* when referring to cold as a substance.) In addition, if a lower-temperature source were available, we could remove excessive heat in a space we wish to condition by merely allowing the heat to flow to this lower-temperature reservoir. If this were possible, there would be no need for refrigeration. In the winter, this is true. While an interior space that is surrounded by conditioned spaces will require cooling due to the internal heat gains from lights, equipment, and people, we can often cool the space by "dumping" the excess heat to the colder outside. Since in the warmer seasons, when we need to cool a space, there generally is no cooler reservoir to which the excess heat can flow naturally, we must develop a means to extract heat from the interior space by transferring it to a higher level of thermal intensity. That is, we must use refrigeration.

Refrigeration is a means by which it is possible to pump thermal energy from a lower to a higher intensity level (see Figure 10.3). All refrigeration systems entail a change in pressure to force a cooling effect, and there are essentially two ways that this change in pressure can be produced: one that entails a chemical reaction and the other a physical or mechanical action.

In the early 1820s, the British scientist Michael Faraday experimented with various gases, demonstrating how releasing the pressure on a liquefied gas would produce a cooling effect. While Faraday's work is often considered to have established the basis of practical refrigeration, an American inventor, Oliver Evans, proposed a design for a refrigeration device in the early 1800s. In 1834, apparently expanding on Evans' proposal, Jacob Perkins, who

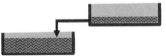

HEAT, LIKE WATER, CAN FLOW NATURALLY FROM A HIGHER LEVEL TO A LOWER LEVEL

BUT NEITHER WATER NOR HEAT CAN FLOW NATURALLY FROM A LOWER LEVEL TO A HIGHER LEVEL

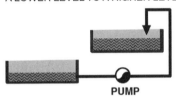

PUMP
BOTH WATER AND HEAT MUST BE "PUMPED" TO GET FROM A LOWER LEVEL TO A HIGHER LEVEL

Figure 10.3 REFRIGERATION ANALOGY WITH WATER FLOW
Thermal energy or heat can only flow naturally from a higher intensity level to a lower intensity level, which is analogous to the flow of water. As with water, in order to raise heat from a lower level to a higher level, some means of pumping the heat upward is required. Refrigeration provides the means to pump heat upward.

has been mentioned in connection with hot water heating, developed a closed system that used a hand-operated compressor to force a refrigerant, ether, to liquefy; then, by releasing the pressure, the ether would evaporate, producing a drop in temperature.[1] Several years later, John Gorrie, an American physician, developed a working mechanical refrigeration system. Gorrie lived in Florida, and through his efforts to treat subtropical diseases he became convinced that "bad air" (*mal-aria* in Italian) was the cause and that it could be corrected by creating cooler temperatures; Gorrie accomplished this by placing blocks of ice in a

[1] W.C. Whitman, W.M. Johnson, and J. Tomczyk, *Refrigeration and Air Conditioning Technology*, (Thomson Delmar Learning, Clifton Park, NY, 2004), p. xxvi.

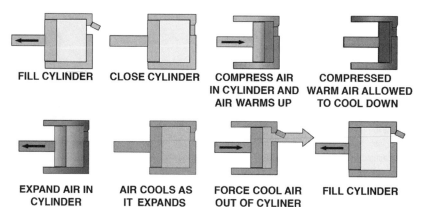

Figure 10.4 SCHEMATIC OF GORRIE'S COMPRESSION REFRIGERATION SYSTEM
This system relied on the thermal changes produced by compressing and expanding a gas. Initially, air was compressed within a closed cylinder. This increased the temperature of the air and the cylinder, which were allowed to remain for a short time in the compressed position, dissipating the increased temperature to the surrounding air. Once cooled, the piston was pulled back, expanding and cooling the air within the cylinder. The piston was then compressed again, but with the door open, thereby releasing the cool air.

FILL CYLINDER   CLOSE CYLINDER   COMPRESS AIR IN CYLINDER AND AIR WARMS UP   COMPRESSED WARM AIR ALLOWED TO COOL DOWN

EXPAND AIR IN CYLINDER   AIR COOLS AS IT EXPANDS   FORCE COOL AIR OUT OF CYLINER   FILL CYLINDER

room. This was in mid-1840s, and while ice was available, it was rather expensive since it was typically only winter-harvested ice that came from quite a distance.

Convinced that there was a better way of obtaining ice, Gorrie gave up his medical practice and concentrated on developing a refrigeration system that could generate ice locally. His system, which is diagrammed in Figure 10.4, worked, although at a relatively low efficiency. While he was granted a U.S. patent for his ice machine in 1851, there was not much of a demand for this device, and Gorrie never realized any financial return from his efforts.

While various individuals explored ways to pump heat from a lower to a higher intensity, Ferdinand Carré, a French engineer, is credited with developing the first effective refrigeration device in 1859. His unit, which built on the previous work of his brother, Edmond Carré, relied on ammonia as the cooling agent.

Carré's artificial ice machine, which is shown in Figure 10.5, boiled a solution of ammonia and water. Since ammonia boils at 92° F, heating the solution released the ammonia as a vapor. The vapor was allowed to condense and then reevaporated when it was combined again with water. As the ammonia vaporized, it absorbed latent heat of vaporization, producing the desired cooling. This is essentially the same cycle as the modern absorption refrigeration cycle, although in the modern absorption unit ammonia, which is quite toxic, has been replaced with lithium bromide, which is more benign. With this change from ammonia to lithium bromide, water is the material that is released from the solution, condensed, and then re-evaporated to produce the refrigeration effect. That is, while ammonia is the refrigerant in the ammonia-water unit, water is the refrigerant in the water–lithium bromide cycle. As a result, an ammonia-water system can achieve lower temperatures than a water–lithium bromide system. However, for ECS applications, the water–lithium bromide cycle is quite effective and somewhat simpler than the ammonia-water cycle, which continues to be used for industrial ap-

Figure 10.5 FERDINAND CARRÉ'S ARTIFICIAL ICE MACHINE (1859)
Ferdinand Carré's artificial ice machine used ammonia as the cooling agent and the input of heat as the operational force. This device essentially is the same as a modern absorption refrigeration unit.

plications that require lower temperatures and can justify the system's complexity and deal with the toxicity of ammonia.

While absorption refrigeration relies on a chemical interaction to force a liquid to evaporate, a physical change in pressure can achieve similar results. This mechanical means was the basis of the work of Perkins and Gorrie and is used in most refrigeration units today. Certain materials, which are used as refrigerants, tend to transition between a liquid and a vapor state near standard atmospheric temperatures and pressures. Increasing the pressure on a refrigerant forces it to liquefy. As it condenses, it must release latent heat of vaporization. Then, when the latent heat of vaporization is dissipated, releasing the pressure forces the liquefied refrigerant to flash into a vapor, which it will do if it acquires latent heat of vaporization. In this process it cools a surrounding material.

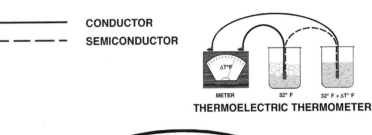

CONDUCTOR
SEMICONDUCTOR

THERMOELECTRIC THERMOMETER

METER   32° F   32° F + ∆T° F

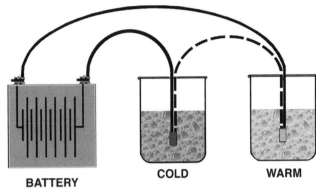

BATTERY   COLD   WARM

Figure 10.6 THERMOELECTRIC COOLING
A thermocouple consists of a conductor and a semiconductor; if the junctions are at different temperatures, an electric current is established. Since the voltage of the current is based on the temperature differential, if the temperature of one junction is known, the voltage can be used to determine the temperature of the other junction. If the system is reversed by applying an electric current to a thermocouple, a temperature differential is established between the two junctions.

While mechanical and absorption refrigeration are the primary cooling methods used in connection with ECS, there are other ways to force cooling through mechanical means. Thermoelectric cooling and the vortex tube are two of them.

Thermoelectric Cooling

Thermoelectric cooling is essentially the reverse of a thermoelectric thermometer. The thermoelectric thermometer is a thermocouple, which is an arrangement of a conductor and a semiconductor attached to a voltage meter. As indicated in the small insert in Figure 10.6, if the two junctions between the semiconductor and the conductor are at different temperatures, an electric current is formed. Metering the voltage of this current provides an indication of the temperature differential. If the meter is replaced by a source of direct current, such as a battery, an electric current is imposed on the device. As this current flows, there is a release of energy as the current moves from the conductor to the semiconductor and a comparable absorption of energy at the other junction.

Without any moving parts, a thermocouple can produce a lower temperature. Unfortunately, this process operates at only about 10% efficiency,[2] considerably less than an absorption refrigeration cycle, which generally has close to 70% efficiency, and definitely at a disadvantage relative to a typical mechanical refrigeration unit that operates at a COP of between 4 and 5 under normal cooling

conditions.[3] As a result, thermoelectric cooling has only limited practical applications. Although a variety of camping coolers use this cooling method since it will operate off of a standard automobile battery, the more logical applications of thermoelectric cooling take advantage of the fact that the method can provide spot or point-source cooling.

Vortex Tube

A vortex tube is also a device that can provide spot cooling. The tube, which is relatively small, with an overall length of 6 to 18 inches, operates on an input of compressed dry air at a pressure of around 100 psi. The air enters tangentially into the tube, spinning around at extremely high RPM. As the air spins around the circumference of the inlet, it is compressed until it can escape through the longer discharge tube, which has a larger diameter than the shorter inlet tube. As the air spins down the discharge tube, it induces suction on the input tube. Based on this performance, a vortex tube can effectively move abrasive granular materials that would destroy more conventional pumps or compressors.

---

[2]The efficiency of thermal devices is generally expressed as a coefficient of performance (COP), which is the ratio between the useful energy output and the energy applied.

[3]While a COP between 4 and 5 is normal during standard cooling loads, when the mechanical refrigeration cycle is used for heating rather than cooling, the temperature differentials are often significantly greater than for cooling, which lowers the COP. As a rule of thumb, we might assume an average COP of around 2 for a heat pump used during the heating season in much of the United States. While this is considerably less efficient than for cooling, which typically operates at a temperature differential of around 20° F to 25° F, it is twice as efficient as electric resistance heating, which has a COP of 1. However, this is based on the end use, and generally electricity provided by a regional power source is supplied at only around 30% efficiency.

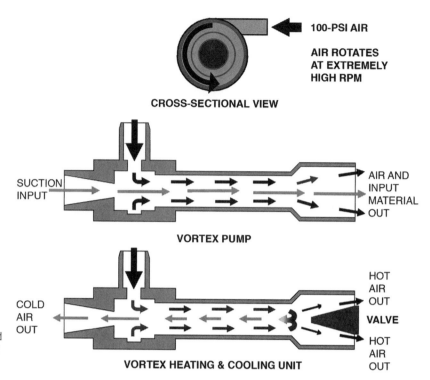

Figure 10.7 VORTEX TUBE
The vortex tube is based on a vortex pump, which is a simple device that uses high-pressure air to induce a material into the air stream. Typically, vortex pumps are used to move abrasive materials since the materials are entrained within the air stream, minimizing damage resulting from their abrasive nature. When a valve is added to the traditional output end of a vortex pump, an interesting things happens—hot air comes out of that end while cold air now comes out of what was the input end of the pump.

One difficulty with the vortex pump is controlling the rate of flow. The system only works with high-pressure air, and it is difficult to achieve a significant adjustment in the air volume in order to vary the rate of material flow. In 1928, George Ranque, a young French physics student, proposed adding a valve at the end of the discharge tube to control the flow rate. Since the air circulates around the edges of the tube, he proposed inserting a central plug into the end of the discharge tube rather than adding a more conventional valve that would confront the problem of abrasion from the granular material. He converted a vortex pump and when he initially operated the device, he observed an amazing phenomenon: air was now coming out of both ends of the device, and the air leaving the discharge end was warm, whereas the air leaving the former inlet end was cold. This phenomenon is diagrammed in Figure 10.7.

Again, as with thermoelectric cooling, the vortex tub, with no moving parts, can produce a lower temperature, but also, as with thermoelectric cooling, it does this at a COP of only around 0.10. As a result, vortex tubes are not used in ECS, but they are effective for applications that require spot cooling and have a source of high-pressure air available. One such application is cooling suits that miners wear; another is chilling drinking water in a diesel railroad engine.[4]

Standard ECS Refrigeration Process

The two primary refrigeration methods currently in use for environmental control are mechanical refrigeration and absorption refrigeration. The operation of both relies on the formation of a pressure differential for condensation and then evaporation of a refrigerant. The mechanical refrigeration cycle establishes this pressure differentially by means of a compressor, whereas the absorption refrigeration cycle utilizes a chemical reaction to enhance evaporation of the refrigerant.

As shown in Figure 10.8, both systems establish a division between high pressure and low pressure. A material, the refrigerant, is forced into the high-pressure side of the system, condensing into a liquid. The condensed liquid then is moved to the low-pressure side, where the liquid refrigerant flashes into a vapor because of the reduced pressure. When the refrigerant condenses in the high-pressure side, it must release latent heat of vaporization. When it flashes into a vapor (evaporates) in the low-pressure side, it must acquire latent heat of vaporization. That is, forcing the refrigerant to evaporate establishes the cooling that is the objective of the refrigeration cycle. The system gives

---

[4]Vortex tubes, which are currently manufactured by Exair Corporation, were initially available in the United States from Fulton Cryogenics.

Major early sales of vortex tubes were to railroads in order to allow them to meet a railroad engineers' union demand for chilled water in all diesel engines. With the rough conditions within an engine, conventional chilled drinking fountains were difficult to maintain; however, with the availability of high-pressure compressed air, the vortex tube provided an effective means of chilling drinking water without its low efficiency being a factor.

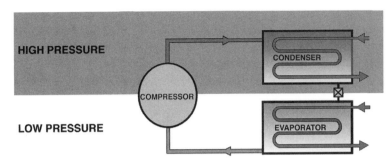

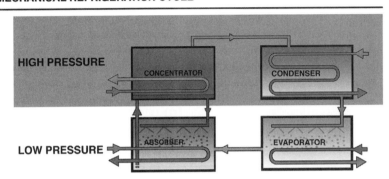

Figure 10.8 MECHANICAL REFRIGERATION AND ABSORPTION REFRIGERATION

A comparison of the mechanical and absorption refrigeration cycles indicates that both have a high-pressure side with a condenser and a low-pressure side with an evaporator.

off heat as a result of condensation and absorbs heat as a result of evaporation.

Older mechanical refrigeration systems used ammonia as the refrigerant but then switched to chlorofluorocarbons (CFCs)[5] and hydro-chlorofluorocarbons (HCFCs), with HCFC-22 used in most ECS refrigeration units. Unfortunately, while CFCs and HCFCs are effective refrigerants, both substances can deplete the critical ozone layer and, being carbon based, can contribute to global warming. As a result, in conformance with the Montreal Protocol, they are being phased out. CFCs are no longer manufactured and HCFCs are to be totally discontinued by 2030, although most manufacturers have committed to an earlier date. While both CFCs and HCFCs are now generally replaced by the more environmentally friendly hydrofluorocarbons (HFCs), other alternative refrigerants are being developed.

As previously mentioned, older absorption refrigeration systems used ammonia as the refrigerant, but most systems now used for ECS use water. Since at standard atmospheric pressures it takes a temperature of 212° F to force water into a vaporous form, an adjustment of atmospheric pressure to achieve effective environmental cooling by water evaporation is obviously not feasible. Vapor pressure is adjusted instead.

In a hot, arid environment, rather than rely on a refrigeration system, we can reduce temperatures by evaporative cooling. Spraying water into dry air increases the rate of evaporation of the water, and since the evaporative process requires the acquisition of latent heat of vaporization, sensible cooling is established. An absorption refrigeration system operates on basically the same principle, but since the reduced vapor pressure is not available naturally, it is established by spraying a desiccant into the evaporative chamber. Lithium bromide is the desiccant in most absorption units. By spraying both a concentrated solution of lithium bromide and water in the same chamber, the rate of water evaporation is increased; as a result, so is the exchange of sensible for latent heat, that is, cooling.

The high-pressure side of the refrigeration cycle forces the refrigerant to condense into a liquid. In a mechanical refrigeration system, a compressor establishes the high pressure, whereas in an absorption unit, heat is added to the solution of lithium bromide and water to force the boiling of the refrigerant—to increase the vapor pressure. As evaporation produces cooling by exchanging sensible heat for the required latent heat of vaporization, condensation releases heat as the latent heat of vaporization is converted into sensible heat.

Mechanical Refrigeration Cycle

The mechanical refrigeration cycle is diagrammed in Figure 10.9. A compressor produces the pressure

---

[5]In the early days of mechanical refrigeration, ammonia was one of the most commonly used refrigerants. However, since ammonia is a toxic material, with the development of CFCs in 1931, this apparently benign but now known to be ozone-depleting hydrocarbon became the refrigerant of choice.

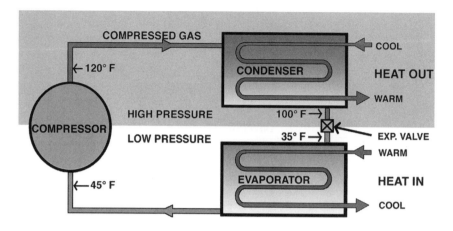

Figure 10.9 MECHANICAL REFRIGERATION CYCLE

The mechanical refrigeration cycle relies on a pressure differential that is established by a compressor and maintained by an expansion valve. The refrigerant is compressed, forcing it to condense into a liquid. Initially, since condensation entails the release of latent heat of vaporization, only a portion of the compressed refrigerant condenses, resulting in an increase in the temperature of the compressed gas. By passing the heated compressed refrigerant through a condenser, the excess heat in the compressed refrigerant can be released and the refrigerant will condense into a high-pressure liquid. This liquid then passes through the expansion valve into the low-pressure side of the unit, where the refrigerant flashes into a gas. Again, since this requires an exchange of latent heat of vaporization, although this time added to the refrigerant, the temperature of the refrigerant is reduced, which then allows for cooling of a medium that is passed over/through the evaporator.

difference in a mechanical refrigeration unit. In smaller units the compressor is typically a reciprocating compressor, but in larger units (100 tons or more) a centrifugal compressor is generally used. While electric motors are the standard power input, the compressor can be powered by a natural gas engine or by a steam turbine. However the compressor is powered, it produces a positive or high pressure on the discharge side and a negative or low pressure on the inlet side. Other devices, such a fan or a pump, also produce a pressure differential, but when the pressure differential is considerable, whether we are dealing with a gas such as air or a liquid such as water, we tend to refer to the device as a *compressor*. In order to maintain the developed pressure differential within the refrigeration system, an expansion valve is used to link the high- and low-pressure sides. The expansion valve tends to be a very small opening that can maintain the pressure differential. Sometimes the expansion valve is actually a valve that can be adjusted, but often it is merely a tube with a very small diameter through which the refrigerant must pass. In a way, the expansion valve is like a pinhole in a tire that slowly releases some of the air from the tire. Eventually the tire becomes flat, but in a mechanical refrigeration unit, as long as the compressor is operating, the difference between the high pressure and low pressure can be sustained.

Absorption Refrigeration Cycle

With absorption refrigeration, the pressure differential—which is in terms of vapor pressure, not air or atmospheric pressure—is developed by chemical means. In most

absorption units the chemical process is established by lithium bromide, a desiccant that readily absorbs water vapor. When the spray of concentrated solution of lithium bromide occurs in the same chamber, the water vapor is absorbed. This keeps the vapor pressure low so that the sprayed water readily vaporizes. Vaporization of the water requires the input of latent heat, and it gets this heat by cooling another material, typically the water used for space conditioning. By absorbing the water vapor, the lithium bromide solution is diluted. In order to keep the system running, this diluted solution of water and lithium bromide is heated, causing the water, which has a lower boiling temperature than the lithium bromide, to boil off. This reestablishes a concentrated solution of lithium bromide. Since the water vapor that is boiled out of the diluted solution is at a relatively high temperature, passing it over a cooler surface easily condenses it. This condensed water is again sprayed into a chamber into which the concentrated solution of lithium bromide is also being sprayed, continuing the cooling process.

While Figure 10.10 clearly shows the various components of an absorption refrigeration unit, generally the arrangement of the components is as shown in Figure 10.11. While this figure shows a pump used to return the diluted solution of lithium bromide and water to the concentrator, some absorption refrigeration units can operate without a pump, at least in the conventional sense. In 1926, Albert Einstein and Leó Szilárd developed an absorption refrigeration unit that used butane as the refrigerant, along with water and ammonia, and relied merely on the input of heat for its operation. There are also units that return the diluted

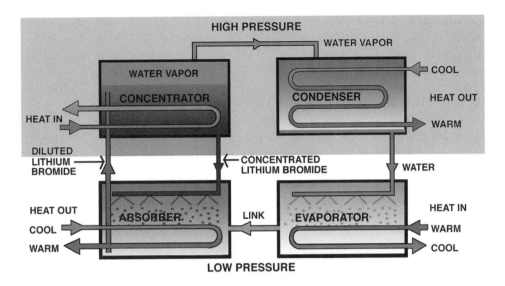

Figure 10.10 ABSORPTION REFRIGERATION CYCLE

This diagram, which is similar to the mechanical refrigeration cycle diagram, represents the various components of an absorption refrigeration unit. Heat is added to the concentrator, which is also sometimes referred to as the *generator*, in order to boil the water out of the dilute solution of water and lithium bromide. The water vapor is then condensed. The concentrated solution of lithium bromide and the water are then both discharged as a spray. Since lithium bromide is a desiccant, the lithium bromide spray absorbs water vapor, so that the sprayed water rapidly evaporates, providing the cooling action. At considerably different temperatures, heat is added to the absorption refrigeration cycle at both the concentrator and the evaporator, and heat is released from both the condenser and the absorber.

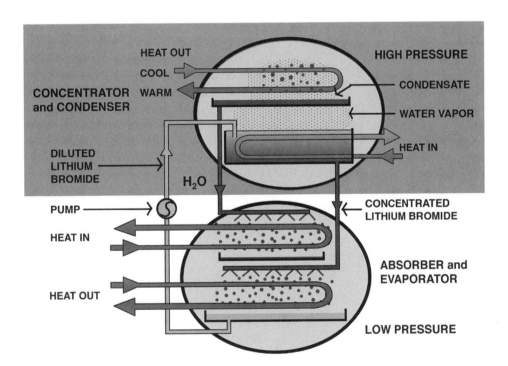

Figure 10.11 TYPICAL ARRANGEMENT OF AN ABSORPTION REFRIGERATION UNIT

The typical absorption refrigeration unit is comprised of two chambers. One chamber contains the concentrator and condenser, while the other includes the evaporator and absorber. As indicated in the diagram, by combining the generator and the condenser in the same chamber, the water vapor that is boiled off from the lithium bromide–water solution rises and condenses on the colder condensing coils, with the condensate readily collected in a pan. The water then flows into the second chamber, where it is discharged as a spray. Similarly, the concentrated lithium bromide solution flows into the second chamber, where it is discharged as a spray. Since the sprayed concentrated lithium bromide solution absorbs any water vapor in the chamber, the water spray readily evaporates, producing the desired cooling effect. Absorbing water vapor gives off heat and dilutes the lithium bromide–water solution. The diluted solution is then returned to the concentrator.

lithium bromide and water solution to the concentrator by means of a bubble pump that operates with the addition of heat in a manner similar to that of a coffee percolator.

Standard absorption refrigeration units operate with heat input at a high enough intensity to boil the water. The input can be by direct combustion or by hot water or steam. The unit generally has a COP of only around 0.67, so it does not make much sense to use electricity as the heat source since mechanical refrigeration, with a COP of between 4 and 5, is a much more efficient system. However, even with its relatively low COP, absorption refrigeration can be quite efficient if the heat input is from by-product steam or hot water. This makes a great deal of sense since the unit would be using energy that would otherwise be lost. It is also possible to hermetically seal the absorption unit and adjust the internal pressures so that the water will boil at less than 212° F. In this way, the absorption refrigeration cycle can operate with the intensity of heat that is readily available from a solar collector.

Refrigeration Components

Refrigeration units, whether mechanical or absorption, rely on heat being exchanged in a condenser and then in an evaporator so that the latent heat of vaporization can be "lost" and then reacquired so that the refrigerant can change from a high-pressure vapor to a liquid and then back again into a gas (see Figure 10.12).

Heat Exchanger

As its name implies, a shell-and-tube converter, which is a heat exchanger, includes a shell in which there are tubes.

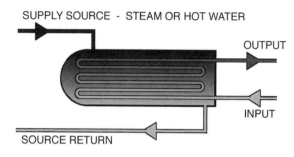

Figure 10.13 SHELL-AND-TUBE CONVERTER

As shown in Figure 10.13, one medium circulates through the tubes and the other passes through the shell. Since this brings the two media in close contact, heat will flow from the higher-temperature medium to the lower-temperature medium. This transfer tends to move both media toward a common temperature, resulting in one medium being heated and the other being cooled.

When used in heating and cooling distribution systems, which are discussed below in Water Systems, shell-and-tube converters are used to exchange heat between different loops or heating systems. For example, in a large complex such as a university, there could be hot water or steam that is centrally generated and then distributed to each building. In each building, the heat from the central supply would then be converted through a shell-and-tube converter into the water or steam distribution system for that building. The exchange can be from steam to water, water to water, or water to steam. Although today the output is typically water, the critical issue is not the final state of either medium but the relationship between the temperatures of each. That is, heat will always be transferred from the higher-temperature medium to the lower-temperature medium, which, based on variations

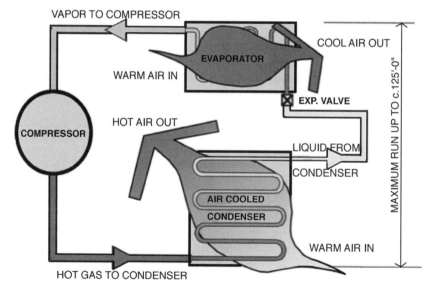

Figure 10.12 EXCHANGE OF TEMPERATURES IN A SMALL UNIT

A mechanical refrigeration unit must exchange heat in both the condenser and the evaporator. In smaller units, this exchange is generally to air. The evaporator is usually a direct-expansion coil that is inserted into the air-handling unit. The condenser, which is typically packaged along with the compressor, is typically located outside and is air-cooled. With an HFC refrigerant, the distance between the component units may be up to 125 feet, although in earlier systems using CFC and HCFC refrigerants, the maximum distance was only 60 feet.

in pressure, could mean that high-temperature hot water might transfer heat to steam. While water boils at 212° F at standard atmospheric pressure, in a contained system that can sustain higher pressures, temperatures well above 212° F can be achieved. As a result, it is quite feasible to generate steam from high-temperature hot water. When the exchange is for cooling, water is typically used for both media.

Condenser

Before the refrigerant can change from a high-pressure gas to a liquid, it must release its latent heat of vaporization. While in a mechanical refrigeration unit some of this occurs and causes an increase in the temperature of the refrigerant as it leaves the compressor, the major release of latent heat occurs in the condenser. In larger refrigeration units, which include most absorption units, the condenser is essentially a shell-and-tube converter, as diagrammed in Figure 10.13. The refrigerant transfers its latent heat to the water, which is then sent to a cooling tower where it can release heat to the surrounding atmosphere. Since the condensing refrigerant generally elevates the water to a temperature above the ambient outside-air temperature, this transfer of heat is relatively simple (see the description of the cooling tower below).

In smaller refrigeration units, the exchange of the latent heat of vaporization from the refrigerant occurs in an air-cooled condenser. In this system, rather than utilizing a water loop to exchange the heat to the outside air, the condenser is actually located outside so that it can be cooled by the outside air. This outside unit typically includes the compressor unit as well as a fan to force the air across the condenser (see Figure 10.14).

One potential problem with an air-cooled condenser is that as the outside temperatures increase, the load on the refrigeration unit probably also increases. As a result, the performance of the condenser diminishes as the demand increases. To solve this problem, especially in medium-sized units, sometimes the condenser is provided with a water spray. This type of unit, which has the confusing name *evaporative condenser*, relies on both a flow of outside air and the evaporation of water to condense the refrigerant. Since the intention is to rely on the water evaporating, eliminators are provided as a precaution against the loss of liquid water (see Figure 10.15).

While not formally evaporative condensers, most window-type air conditioning units now employ the condensate that comes from the cooling coils to enhance the operation of the condenser. Traditionally, this condensate was merely drained from the unit, often creating the potential for water to drip down on people passing below the air conditioner. Now the condensate is usually drained into the condenser side of the unit, where it is kicked up by the air-circulating fan. While this increases the unit's operational efficiency, it can be a source of bothersome noise if acoustical isolation is not effective.

The major components of a mechanical refrigeration unit (the compressor, the condenser, and the evaporator) must all be located within a reasonable distance of each other. Since the refrigerant is combined with oil, an excessively long run might result in the oil separating out from the refrigerant, causing potential blockages. To avoid this problem, the maximum distance separating the various components of refrigeration units using CFCs and HCFCs should not exceed around 60 feet. With new units, in terms of both the refrigerant used, typically HFCs, and the design, this distance has been increased to around

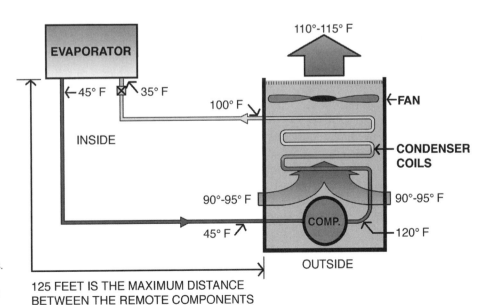

Figure 10.14 AIR-COOLED CONDENSER
Air-cooled condensers are standard with most smaller mechanical refrigeration units. The condenser is generally combined with the compressor, and the airflow is based on a fan.

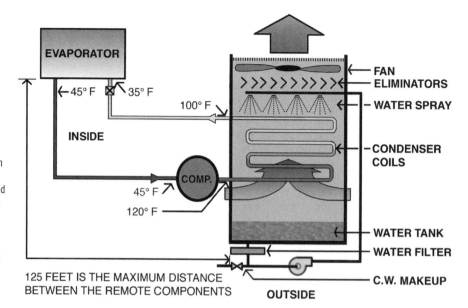

Figure 10.15 EVAPORATIVE CONDENSER
An evaporative condenser utilizes a water spray in addition to a flow of outside air to condense the refrigerant. With the evaporative process combined with the potential cooling from the outside air, as the outdoor temperatures increase, the outdoor relative humidity will typically be reduced. As a result, the combined effects tend to sustain the operation when the outdoor temperatures and the cooling loads both increase. Since environmental pollution can contaminate the water, a means of filtering the water should be included.

125 feet. While it could be difficult to comply with the 60-foot limit, for most refrigeration units using either an air-cooled condenser or an evaporative condenser and a newer refrigerant, the 125-foot limit is not an imposition. One reason is that these condensers are not generally used with larger systems.

With larger refrigeration units, for which the 125-foot limit would likely be a problem, the condenser is typically included as an integral part of the refrigeration unit rather than being located remotely. As a result, water is used as the agent to extract the latent heat of vaporization from the condenser, and this heat is then released in a cooling tower.

A cooling tower is not part of the refrigeration cycle since it is merely a device used to cool the water that is circulated through the condenser. However, while it is not a condenser, it operates somewhat like an evaporative condenser, relying on the exchange of energy as a result of the temperature differential between the water and the outside air and on the evaporation of some of the circulating water. Therefore, it must be located outside, typically on the roof of the structure. In a high-rise building, assuming 10–12 feet per floor, the distance between the condenser, which is often located in the basement or on a mechanical floor, and the cooling tower can easily exceed the 125-foot limit for circulating refrigerant; with water this is not a problem, although it does require energy input to circulate the water up to the cooling tower. The quantity of water circulated to a cooling tower is generally around 3 gallons per minute (GPM) for every ton of air conditioning (12,000 BTUH).

A cooling tower generally includes a water spray through which a current of air is passed (see Figure 10.16).

To increase the exchange of energy, the water spray is dispersed over an extended surface, typically wooden slats or perforated ceramic material. The air will cool the water both by temperature differential and by forced evaporation (as the air passes through the cooling tower, it is heated by the warm water, which lowers relative humidity of the air stream, thereby increasing the rate of evaporation). Since the intention is to rely on water evaporation, eliminators are again required. With the water being sprayed into rapidly moving air, droplets of liquid water are carried in the air stream; without the eliminators to capture these droplets, water would be lost without the benefit of any evaporative cooling. However, it is still possible that the air coming off a cooling tower will contain some droplets of liquid in addition to a high vapor content, which on being exposed to the lower temperatures outside of the cooling tower will partially condense.[6] As a result, when locating a cooling tower, it is important to consider the potential problems that this discharge might present. For example, if the cooling tower is located on a lower building, the discharge could create a continual monsoon-like condition for an adjacent higher building.

With today's increased air pollution, especially in built-up industrial areas, the spray of water often picks up various contaminants. One such contaminant is sulfur dioxide, which, if combined with the water, turns into sulfuric acid.

---

[6]I often ask my students how they might determine when the water in a kettle is boiling, assuming that there is no telltale whistle available. When they suggest that they know it is boiling when they see the steam rising up through the kettle spout, I congratulate them on their unique ability. Steam is a gas and, as such, it is not visible. What we see coming from the kettle when the water boils is not steam but droplets of liquid water that have condensed upon exchanging latent heat with the cooler room air. As these droplets disperse, they again vaporize and disappear.

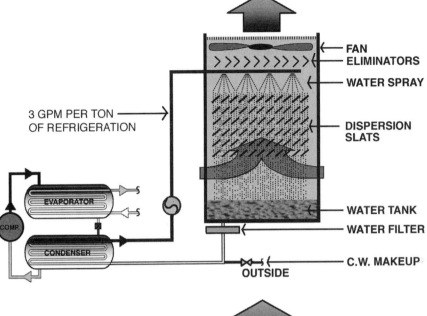

Figure 10.16 COOLING TOWER
A cooling tower is a device used to lower the temperature of water that is used to cool the water that extracts heat from a refrigeration unit—from the condenser in a mechanical refrigeration unit and from the condenser and absorber in an absorption refrigeration unit. The cooling is accomplished by heat exchange with the cooler air that is forced through the cooling tower and by evaporation of part of the circulated water. The movement of air can be draw-through, as indicated in the diagram, or blow-through. Since the system is open, the water can be contaminated by atmospheric pollution, which can be a serious problem in many areas.

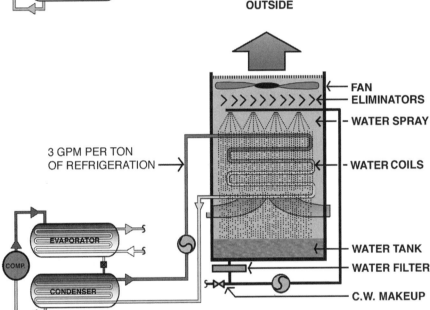

Figure 10.17 CLOSED COOLING TOWER
A closed cooling tower is similar to an open cooling tower except that the water circulated through the refrigeration unit is contained within a water loop, relying on a separate water circuit that is sprayed within the tower to accomplish the cooling. By providing this separation, water that is sprayed in the cooling tower and likely will become contaminated as a result of environmental pollution, particularly in industrial areas, will not circulate throughout the refrigeration system.

As a result, an open cooling tower, in which the water passing through the condensing unit is sprayed into the air, is replaced with a closed cooling tower, in which there is a separation between the water that is circulated through the structure and the condenser unit and the water that is sprayed into the cooling tower (Figure 10.17).

Evaporator

Somewhat like the condenser side, the evaporator side of a refrigeration unit can either be the direct means of cooling the air or it can cool water, which is then circulated to cooling coils. With direct cooling, the evaporator is called a *D-X cooling coil*, referring to the fact that the cooling is a result of direct expansion of the refrigerant. This is the system typically used in smaller installations, with one D-X coil for each refrigeration unit. With larger systems, when water is used as the cooling agent, the water can be circulated to cooling coils in a number of different air-handling units and, with adjustments in the amount of water circulated through a coil, can provide different amounts of cooling.

Heat Pump

A refrigeration unit is essentially a device to pump heat from a lower intensity level to a higher intensity level; however, the term *heat pump* is generally used to designated a mechanical refrigeration unit in which the heat exchange in the condenser as well as in the evaporator can be used for environmental control. That is, the term *heat pump* is used to denote a refrigeration unit that is used for heating and cooling.

While the process can be utilized in large units, the more effective application of the heat pump is for smaller systems. The advantage of the heat pump over electric resistance heating is the higher COP, although the overall efficiency is limited by the efficiency of the generation and distribution of electricity. With larger systems, more conventional heat generation or cogeneration of electricity can usually provide more efficiency. However, with smaller applications, the heat pump is an attractive system to use, and it definitely should be used when electricity is the primary source of energy input.

Since smaller refrigeration units used for cooling tend to pass the supply air directly over the evaporator, while the compressor and condenser are located remotely outside, the heating cycle of the heat pump requires reversing the direction of refrigerant flow. That is, the condenser for the cooling cycle becomes the evaporator for the heating cycle, which means that the refrigerant acquires heat from the cooler outside temperatures in order to raise the temperature inside. This works quite well when the outside temperatures are not below around 45° F, which is comparable to the colder side of the cooling cycle; however, the COP tends to drop as the temperature differential increases. As a result, when this occurs, most heat pumps revert to electric resistance heating, some partially and some completely. Some heat pumps are combined with more conventional heat sources, particularly a gas furnace. When there is no economical and/or energy advantage to using the heat pump cycle, the system converts to conventional heating.

An alternative is to replace the outdoor air as the source of heat during the heating season and as the heat sink during the cooling season with a more stable heat reservoir, such as a body of water or the earth. Such a system generally uses water as the basic exchange medium and is therefore referred to as a *water source heat pump* (WSHP).

Assuming a residence with a 50,000-BTUH heat loss based on a 70° F temperature differential located in an area with a 5000-DD winter heating season, how large a body of water would be required for the annual heating demand, which would be around 85 million BTU?

$$BTU = \frac{50,000 \text{ BTUH} \times 5000 \text{ DD}}{70° \text{ F}} = 85,714,285$$
$$\approx 85,000,000 \text{ BTU}$$

Since each BTU will raise the temperature of one pound of water by 1° F, we will need to set an acceptable change in water temperature to determine the amount of water that will be required to meet the heating demands. If the differential is too great, the water will freeze, which will complicate thermal exchange. Of course, in a location of 5000 DD and a maximum temperature differential of 70° F, an outside water body would likely freeze, but not completely since the ice will provide an insulation layer and the water will be in contact with the earth, which generally has a groundwater temperature of around 50° F. Assuming an allowable drop of 10° F, how much water would be required to supply the 100 million BTUs? Since a gallon of water weighs 8.33 pounds, a 10° F drop in a gallon of water relates to an exchange of 83.3 BTU. Based on this, roughly 1 million gallons of water are required; since there are around 7.5 gallons in 1 cubic foot, this relates to a volume of around 140,000 cubic feet, which is a sizable body of water. Of course, if we increase the allowable temperature drop from 10° F, we could reduce the amount of water required, although this would also reduce the system's operational efficiency.

Generally, for a water body to be an effective heat source, it should have a surface area of at least 20,000 square feet, which is about one-half an acre, and a depth of 8 to 10 feet. In exchanging heat with a body of water, we can either place a piping loop into the water body, which is considered a closed-loop system, or we can circulate the water from the pond or lake through the heat pump, which is considered an open-loop system. Since water quality, including mineral content and water acidity, can change and become problematic, open-loop systems are not recommended.

Sometimes groundwater is used in an open-loop system, with the water pumped from the aquifer, sent through the heat pump, and then returned to the ground. This method can be economical but it can also result in contamination or even depletion of the aquifer, so this method is not recommended. In fact, in some jurisdictions, it is appropriately prohibited.

An alternative to merely cooling a source of water would be to freeze water. With latent heat of fusion equal to 140 BTU per pound of water, a considerable amount of heat can be extracted by freezing water. For the above residence, without any credit for reducing the water temperature to 32° F, by freezing the water, each cubic foot of water could supply basically 8750 BTU, meaning that the necessary water volume would be less than 1000 cubic feet. In this approach, a closed volume of water would be used.

This essentially is what was studied in the Annual Cycle Energy System (ACES) project sponsored by the U.S. Department of Energy in the late 1970s.[7] The purpose of the project was to heat a home during the winter by

---

[7]V.D. Baxter, "Annual Cycle Energy System Performance and National Economic Comparisons with Competitive Residential HVAC Systems," presented at the ASHRAE meeting in Houston, Texas, January 1982.

generating ice that would then be used in the summer to cool the home. If the ice generated during the heating season did not meet the cooling demands during the summer—which it tended not to do in the test case at the University of Tennessee—since the system generated ice, it could do so in the summer during times of low electric demand, which further reduced the operational costs.

The ACES demonstration project used a heat pump to chill a brine solution. The chilled brine then passed through a heat exchanger located in the water-filled storage tank, freezing the water surrounding the coils. Unfortunately, in operation, the ice forming on the heat exchanger tended to reduce thermal transfer. While the ACES system never found wide application, the approach still suggests an intriguing method for providing environmental control.

While both a water-based heat source and the ACES method can improve the operational efficiency of a heat pump, the more common approach for WSHPs is earth integration, which unfortunately is often erroneously referred to as a *geothermal heat pump*. These systems pump water through the ground to exchange heat to or from the earth, depending on the phase of the cycle, heating or cooling. The system can use a horizontal loop or a vertical loop, depending on the amount of area that is available and the soil conditions. The horizontal loop tends to be more economical to install, but it requires 400 to 600 linear feet of piping for each ton of refrigeration. The piping is installed at least 5 to 6 feet below grade, either in trenches or in an excavated area that is then backfilled. When the climatic conditions are extreme, such as in the North or the Deep South, more earth cover is appropriate. When the area is excavated or wider trenches are dug, rather than straight pipe, slinky coil piping can be installed. The overlapping loops of pipe tend to reduce the ground area necessary for the installation, often requiring half or perhaps even less of the area required for conventional horizontal piping.

In extreme climates, when there is limited ground area or the terrain is rocky, vertical loops might be appropriate. Typically, the installation requires drilling 150- to 300-foot-deep holes in which to install hairpin-configured pipe loops. The holes are then grouted. Since the vertical loops are exposed to more stable and lower ground temperatures, the length of piping required is somewhat less than for a horizontal loop, although a vertical loop still needs around 300 to 500 linear feet of piping per ton of refrigeration.

PSYCHROMETRICS

The psychrometric chart plots the thermal characteristics of an air sample. The basic layout of the psychromet-ric chart, which was discussed in Chapter 6, is shown in Figure 10.18.

As a refresher, the sensible energy (i.e., the DBT) is plotted along the abscissa, with the origin, or point of zero sensible energy, lying off the chart to the left, with $32°$ F typically the lowest temperature indicated. The latent energy (i.e., the specific humidity) is plotted on the ordinate, with the point of zero specific humidity typically at the point where the ordinate crosses the abscissa (i.e., the lower right-hand corner of the chart). Movement from left to right indicates an increase in sensible energy, while movement upward indicates an increase in latent energy. Therefore, diagonal movement from left to right and upward or from right to left and downward indicates a change in sensible energy opposite to a change in latent energy (i.e., one increasing while the other is decreasing). At a certain angle, based on the geometry of the psychrometric chart, a movement in a diagonal direction will result in an exchange between sensible and latent energy while maintaining a constant amount of total energy. Such a change is called *adiabatic* and would parallel the adiabatic process line indicated in Figure 10.18. Since movement along the adiabatic process line retains the same total energy, this line can be extended to a scale that indicates the total energy content in the air sample in terms of BTU per pound of dry air. This total energy, both sensible and latent, is called *enthalpy* (*h*).

The psychrometric chart can be used to find the characteristics of any air sample. It can also be used to determine the characteristics of a mixture of two different air samples. If each air sample is plotted and a line is drawn between the two points, the mixed condition will lie on the line at the point that is based on the proportion that each of the initial conditions of the mixture comprises. Just remember that in determining the point along the line that defines the mixture, if there is an unequal amount of the components, the mix point will lie closer to that air sample that comprises the greater portion of the mixture. For example, Figure 10.19 indicates the mix point of one-third fresh air (FA) and two-thirds room air (RA).

While the proper definition of the *sensible heat ratio* (SHR) is the mathematical relationship of the sensible heat gain to the total heat gain, both sensible and latent, the SHR line used with the psychrometric chart has a slope that is based on the ratio of the sensible load to the latent load. As shown in Figure 10.20, the line indicates the slope of movement on the psychrometric chart that parallels the ratio of the sensible heat gain to the latent heat gain. Knowing this slope is important since it allows us to define the conditions of SA that can counteract the heat gain proportionally to the way it occurs. That is, the SA should balance the sensible heat gain with sensible cooling (i.e., lower temperature of the SA) and balance the latent heat

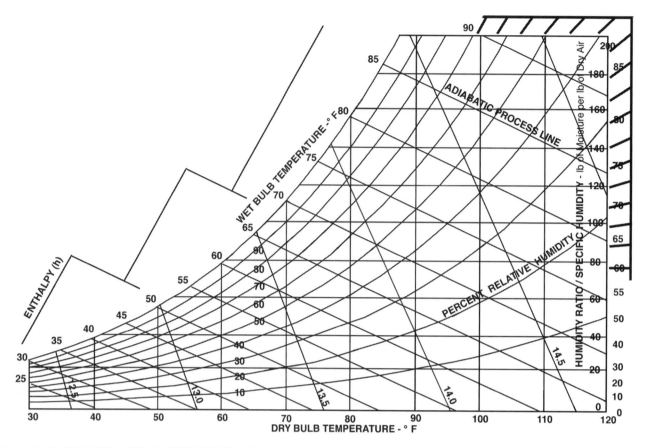

Figure 10.18 SCHEMATIC LAYOUT OF THE PSYCHROMETRIC CHART

The basic layout of the psychrometric chart, which graphically represents the thermal energy of an air sample, is shown. Horizontal movement relates to a change in sensible heat, while vertical movement indicates a change in latent heat. When there is an exchange between sensible and latent heat while a constant total amount of thermal energy is retained, it follows the slope of the adiabatic process line. Enthalpy (*h*) indicates the total amount of thermal energy within an air sample. Since the slope of the adiabatic process line represents conditions of temperature and humidity with constant energy, drawing a line that is parallel to the adiabatic process line and passes through the conditions of an air sample and extending the line to the enthalpy curve indicates the total energy content of the air sample.

gain with latent cooling (i.e., lower humidity of the SA). If the conditions of the SA do not fall on the SHR line that passes through the RA conditions, appropriate control will not occur.

As shown in Figure 10.20, we can graphically plot the heat gain, both sensible and latent, on a psychrometric chart, using a consistent percentage of the actual heat gain values, sensible and latent. These two plots establish a rectangle, and the slope of the diagonal of this rectangle is at the slope of the SHR line. By extending this line from the RA conditions and setting a temperature differential between the SA and RA, we can determine the appropriate SA conditions.

Although the heat gain will vary at different times, requiring that the ECS adjust to these variations, the intention in drawing the SHR line is to determine the appropriate temperature, humidity, and volume of SA that can balance the expected maximum load in order to maintain the room conditions. Of course, as the load changes, the ECS should be able to adjust to match these loads, which

means that in operation the slope of the SHR line changes, so the SA conditions should also change.

If the SA does not fall on the SHR line, the RA conditions cannot be maintained. Although the change in RA conditions shown in Figure 10.21 is not significant, there would be an increase in humidity. In terms of thermal comfort, with our ability to use various physiological means to adjust to varying thermal conditions, this slight adjustment of the RA conditions might not be serious, but for industrial processes, there might be less latitude, particularly for changes in relative humidity.

Instead of plotting the sensible and latent heat gains on the psychrometric chart as represented in Figures 10.20 and 10.21, we can utilize the SHR scale that is included in a number of psychrometric charts, along with a base point for this scale. The critical factor of the SHR line is its slope, and to establish this slope we merely need to draw a line passing through the base point and the appropriate calculated SHR located on the scale that is included on the right of the psychrometric chart (see Figure 10.22).

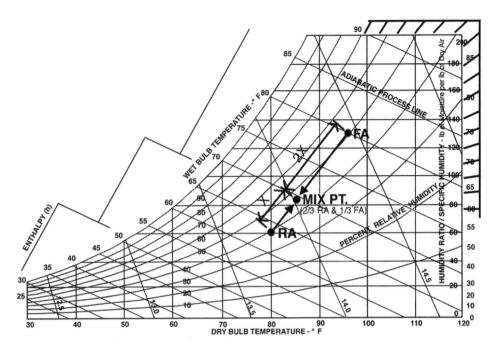

Figure 10.19 AIR MIXTURE POINT ON THE PSYCHROMETRIC CHART
The conditions of a mixture of two known air samples can be found by plotting both air samples on the psychrometric chart, drawing a line between the two points, and locating the mix point by proportioning the line as the ratio of the two mix air samples. (Note: This psychrometric chart is a schematic based on various published charts and is presented merely to demonstrate its various uses.)

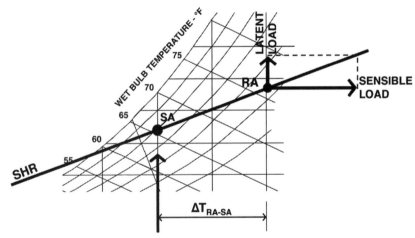

Figure 10.20 SHR DIAGRAM—1
The SHR line on the psychrometric chart is drawn at the slope that relates to the ratio of the sensible heat gain to the latent heat gain. By graphically plotting these loads on the psychrometric chart, the proper slope of the SHR line can be drawn. By extending the SHR line from the RA conditions and setting an acceptable temperature difference between RA and SA, the SA humidity that can maintain the RA conditions can be determined.

For convenience, the base point is generally set at what is assumed to be an appropriate summer interior condition, although this varies on different psychrometric charts. On the original Carrier psychrometric chart, this base point was set at 80° F and 50% relative humidity, while the Trane psychrometric chart used 78° F and 50% relative humidity, although the desired room conditions might be different. When the room condition is different from the base point of the psychrometric chart, the SHR line is drawn using the base point and then a line parallel to this line is drawn through the RA conditions for the design.

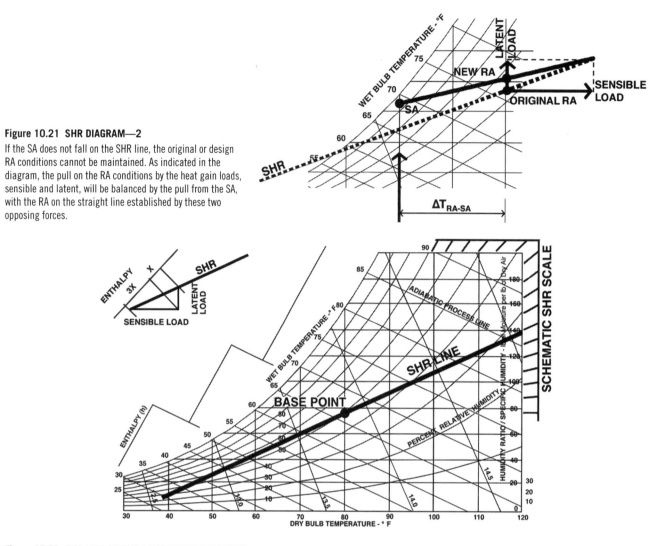

Figure 10.21 SHR DIAGRAM—2
If the SA does not fall on the SHR line, the original or design RA conditions cannot be maintained. As indicated in the diagram, the pull on the RA conditions by the heat gain loads, sensible and latent, will be balanced by the pull from the SA, with the RA on the straight line established by these two opposing forces.

Figure 10.22 SHR LINE ON THE PSYCHROMETRIC CHART
Some psychrometric charts include an SHR scale that is related to a base point. A line drawn from the base point to the calculated SHR will be at the slope that represents the relationship between the sensible load and the latent load. Rather than follow this approach, some other psychrometric charts include a SHR protractor that can set the slope of the SHR line based on the enthalpy scale. (Note: This psychrometric chart is a schematic based on various published charts and is presented merely to demonstrate its various uses.)

The critical value of the SHR line is its slope since this identifies the appropriate SA conditions that can effectively counteract the heat gain on a space, matching the system's sensible and latent responses with the sensible and latent loads. As a result, a line at the proper slope must be drawn through the intended design conditions for RA. If the base point of the psychrometric chart does not coincide with these conditions, the SHR line is drawn using the base point and then a line parallel to this line is drawn through the desired RA conditions (see Figure 10.23). This second line is then used to determine the SA conditions based on an assumed temperature differential between the SA and the RA.

The standard temperature differential between the SA and the RA is 20° F, although the range of acceptable temperature differentials is usually between 16° F and 24° F. Generally, 30° F is set as the maximum difference between the SA temperature and the RA temperature. If the SA temperature is far below the RA temperature, it is possible that this temperature will be less than the dew point temperature (DPT) of the RA conditions. If so, there could be problems with condensation that would develop on the SA grill.[8] Fortunately, the psychrometric chart can readily indicate the DPT for the intended RA conditions.

---

[8] If condensate develops on the metal supply-air grill, it will potentially run down the walls or, if the outlet is a ceiling diffuser, drip down. Often the SA temperatures drop below the DPT in the duct distribution spaces where humidity control might not exist. To avoid condensation on the exterior of these cold ducts, the recommendation is to insulate all cooling ducts with at least 2 inches of insulation. If this insulation is installed around the sheet metal duct, it must be wrapped with a vapor barrier.

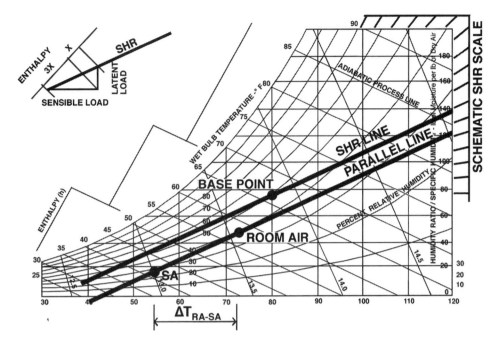

Figure 10.23 PARALLEL SHR LINE ON THE PSYCHROMETRIC CHART
If the SHR base point is not at the RA conditions, the SHR line is drawn using the base point and then a line parallel to this line is drawn through the RA conditions. Using this second line and a temperature differential between the SA and the RA, the SA conditions can be located. (Note: This psychrometric chart is a schematic based on various published charts and is presented merely to demonstrate its various uses.)

Now that we have a better understanding of the psychrometric chart's potential, let us use the chart to explore the cooling process. While we can assume that the system will return RA to the air-handling unit, which then becomes return air (both typically noted as RA since the conditions should be the same), with an air system some ventilation is also usually provided. Air-cooling systems are typically referred to as *air conditioning*, which should include more than just controlling temperature and humidity, hence the assumed fresh air ventilation. For our preliminary study, we can use the conventional standards for an air system: six air changes per hour, with one air change being fresh air and five air changes return air. Also, let us set 20° F as the temperature differential between the RA and SA. These parameters are presented in Figure 10.24.

Air conditioning generally involves lowering air temperatures, but typically it also requires reducing the humidity. While we should realize that we can cool an air sample by transferring heat from that sample to a lower medium, which basically means that we need to pass the SA over cooling coils, we might not understand how to lower the humidity. This is more complex since it entails causing condensation of water vapor out of the SA.

Condensation can be forced in several ways. Two of them were discussed in the explanation of the refrigeration process: changing pressure and chemical absorption. Theoretically, the atmospheric pressure could be increased

sufficiently to force condensation, but this is not really feasible, especially with an open system. So, a pressure change, at least in terms of the SA, will not work. In the chemical approach, the air supply could pass over a desiccant that would absorb moisture from the air stream. In this process, the absorbed moisture would condense into liquid, giving off heat. When the desiccant becomes saturated, it could be regenerated by adding heat in order to vaporize the absorbed liquid. This method does work, and it is sometimes used in conjunction with solar energy used as the regenerator, but it is rather labor intensive and somewhat cumbersome.

The psychrometric chart suggests an alternative approach for dehumidification. If an air sample is cooled, the conditions of that sample will move horizontally to the left. As the temperature drops, the relative humidity will increase, ultimately reaching 100% RH or saturation at the DPT. Since air cannot be supersaturated, any further cooling forces the conditions to move down the saturation curve, which means reducing the specific humidity of that air sample.

Theoretically, no reduction in the specific humidity will occur until the air sample reaches the saturation curve. As a result, when the lower specific humidity of the SA as defined on the SHR line is achieved, the temperature of the air sample might be less than the supply air temperature. If so, the air will have to be reheated. This process is shown in Figure 10.25.

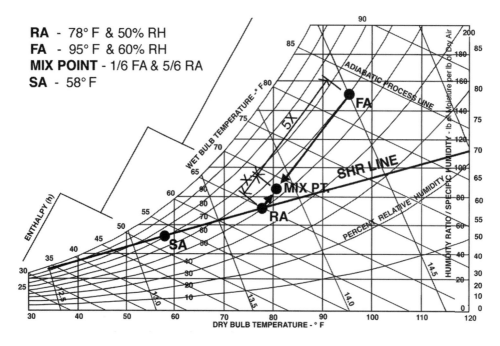

Figure 10.24 COOLING PROCESS EXAMPLE—STEP ONE

The cooling process can be graphically represented using the psychrometric chart. The first step is to plot the beginning conditions, which generally include RA, FA, the SHR line, the mix point conditions, and the SA based on an assumed temperature below the RA. (Note: This psychrometric chart is a schematic based on various published charts and is presented merely to demonstrate its various uses.)

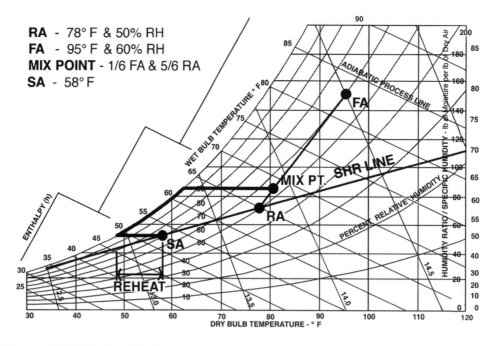

Figure 10.25 COOLING PROCESS EXAMPLE—STEP TWO

This diagram shows the theoretical cooling process with no reduction in specific humidity until the conditions of the combined RA–FA mixture reach the saturation curve. With continued cooling, the specific humidity is lowered until the specific humidity of the SA is achieved. However, this occurs at a temperature below the SA conditions, so the air must be reheated to reach the SA point located on the SHR line. (Note: This psychrometric chart is a schematic based on various published charts and is presented merely to demonstrate its various uses.)

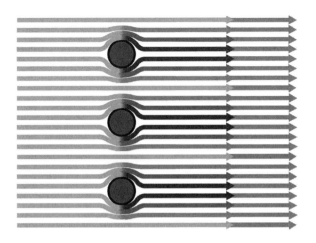

Figure 10.26 SCHEMATIC OF AIR PASSING OVER A COOLING COIL
As air passes across a cooling coil, there is some difference in the actual cooling, with the air that comes in direct contact with the coil experiencing a greater temperature reduction than the air that passes through the interstices. While the air will mix after passing over the coil, attaining an average temperature, since some of the air was cooled more than the average temperature indicates, some dehumidification might occur even though the average discharge temperature is higher than the DPT of the entering air.

The process is called theoretical since air passing over a cooling coil is not cooled evenly. As shown in Figure 10.26, some of the air comes in direct contact with the cold surfaces of the cooling coil, and some of the air passes through the interstices of the coil and experiences very little cooling. As the different air streams mix after passing through the coil, an average temperature of the air stream is established that might be higher than the DPT of the initial mixed-air conditions, and yet some dehumidification will have occurred in that portion of the air stream that came in direct contact with the cooling coils.

While the reduction in specific humidity that occurs when air passes across a dry cooling coil can be effective in reducing, or even eliminating, reheat in order to reach the appropriate SA conditions, in the early days of cooling it was difficult to determine what humidity reduction would actually occur. Although we tend to assume that air conditioning is used to provide thermal comfort, in the early days the focus was on providing the correct environmental conditions for industry and manufacturing, and for these purposes accurate control of the specific humidity was critical. Unfortunately, it was difficult to achieve the appropriate level of humidity control with dry cooling coils. This was the problem that Willis Haviland Carrier confronted, and why he proposed using a water spray cooling method that would move all the air up to the saturation curve and then provide controlled dehumidification as further temperature reduction was experienced.

Passing the air through a spray of chilled water rather than over a dry coil provides better control of the humid-

ity. With this approach, the mixture of RA and FA moves up the adiabatic process line until the saturation curve is reached. Even though a wet spray coil is used, after reaching the saturation curve further cooling results in dehumidification as well as sensible cooling. Again, once the proper humidity conditions are achieved, reheating is necessary to reach the proper SA conditions on the SHR line (see Figure 10.27).

While Carrier's water spray was quite effective and was the basis of the first system that could effectively control both temperature and humidity[9] (which is why Carrier is often called the father of air conditioning), it is now possible to get better performance data on dry cooling coils. The Trane Company,[10] a competitor of the Carrier Company, developed a psychrometric chart that included dry-coil cooling process lines. By following these lines, it was possible to see the adjustments in temperature and humidity produced by a cooling coil, thereby somewhat reducing the benefits of the spray cooling method (see Figure 10.28).

As shown in Figure 10.29, by using the cooling process lines for the previous example, we can see that not much will actually change; the amount of reheat is reduced by approximately 4° F. Interestingly, if the RA were at a lower temperature and humidity, which would mean that the overall air conditioning load would probably be increased, it might be feasible to eliminate the need for any reheat, especially if the temperature differential between RA and SA was increased slightly. As a result, adjusting the design expectations for the RA to a lower temperature and humidity should not require a proportional increase in the energy consumed by the control system.

As shown in Figure 10.30, the actual load on the cooling system is more than the space heat gain or cooling load. In addition to the reheat that might be necessary to ensure that the supply air falls on the SHR line, there is also the load imposed by providing outside air ventilation.

Whether a dry coil or a wet coil is used, if the chilled air does not move downward and cross the SHR line within the allowable range of RA–SA temperature difference, reheating the conditioned air might be required to achieve the SA conditions that can properly balance the heat gain—that is, matching the sensible-to-latent control to the sensible-to-latent load. While reheating may be considered a waste of energy, the "extra" cooling might be the only way to achieve the proper humidity level for the SA. However,

---

[9]In 1906, Willis Haviland Carrier obtained a U.S. patent for his "Apparatus for Treating Air." While Carrier is recognized as the father of air conditioning, the term *air conditioning* was actually proposed by Stuart H. Cramer.

[10]The three major U.S. companies manufacturing environmental control equipment are Carrier, Trane, and York, although many other reliable companies are also involved.

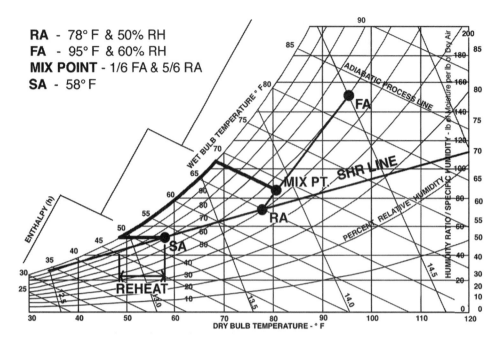

Figure 10.27 WATER SPRAY COOLING PROCESS

The water spray cooling process conditions the air by passing it through a water spray of chilled water. As the temperature continues to be lowered, there is a controlled drop in the humidity level. Cooling and dehumidification continue until the desired specific humidity is reached, and then the air is reheated to hit the appropriate SA conditions on the SHR line. (Note: This psychrometric chart is a schematic based on various published charts and is presented merely to demonstrate its various uses.)

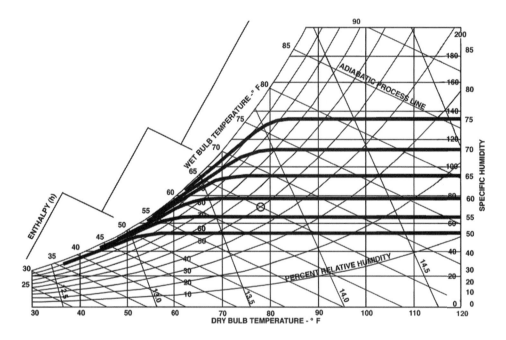

Figure 10.28 PSYCHROMETRIC CHART WITH DRY-COIL COOLING PROCESS LINES

The added cooling process lines represent the actual cooling and dehumidification that will occur with a dry cooling coil. The lines indicate that there is some effective dehumidification before the DPT is reached. As shown, as the temperature continues to drop after dehumidification begins, the distinction between the dry-coil performance and the theoretical performance becomes less and less. (Note: This psychrometric chart is a schematic based on various published charts and is presented merely to demonstrate its various uses.)

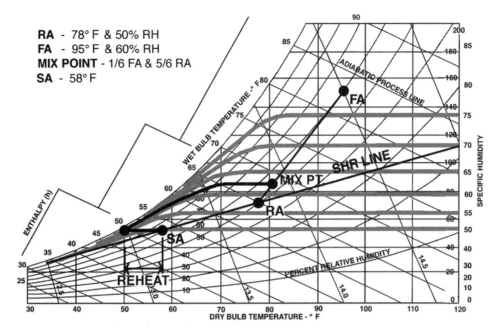

Figure 10.29 COOLING PROCESS EXAMPLE—DRY COOLING COIL

By using a dry cooling coil, some dehumidification occurs before the average temperature of the control air reaches the DPT of the mix point conditions. In this example, the benefit from the dry cooling coils over the spray cooling or the theoretical process is a reduction in the necessary reheat of only approximate 4° F. However, if the RA were cooler and drier and if the different between RA and SA were increased, it is possible that reheat might not be necessary. (Note: This psychrometric chart is a schematic based on various published charts and is presented merely to demonstrate its various uses.)

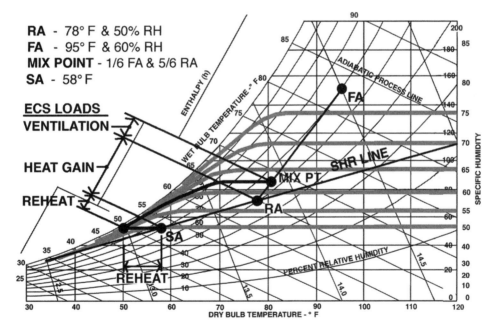

Figure 10.30 COOLING PROCESS EXAMPLE—REFRIGERATION LOAD

Whichever cooling approach is used, the BTU loads can be determined from the enthalpy values for each of the various points in the conditioning process. (Note: This psychrometric chart is a schematic based on various published charts and is presented merely to demonstrate its various uses.)

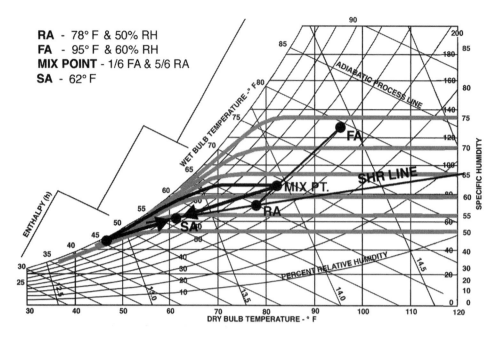

RA - 78° F & 50% RH
FA - 95° F & 60% RH
MIX POINT - 1/6 FA & 5/6 RA
SA - 62° F

Figure 10.31 COOLING PROCESS EXAMPLE – BYPASS
If the SHR line is reasonably flat, which means that there is no significant latent load, a bypass might avoid the need for reheating. A portion of the air remains at the conditions of the mix point by passing around the cooling coil rather than through it. The remainder of the air is cooled well below the SA temperature until it reaches a condition that, when combined with the air that was held at the original mix point conditions, establishes a new mixture that falls on the SHR line. This new mixture is the SA and is achieved without the need for any reheating. (Note: This psychrometric chart is a schematic based on various published charts and is presented merely to demonstrate its various uses.)

sometimes extra cooling might be used to avoid the need for reheating. It might be possible to leave a portion of the SA unconditioned and cool and dehumidify the remainder of the air well beyond the SA conditions, and then combine these two air samples to obtain a mixed condition that falls on the SHR line at a temperature that is acceptable for the SA. With this approach, which is called *bypass* and is shown in Figure 10.31, reheating can be avoided.

While a portion of the SA passes around the cooling coil and is not cooled at all, the other portion is cooled to below the desired SA conditions. As a result, even though some of the SA is not actually cooled, there are no savings in terms of cooling, but savings are achieved by eliminating the need for reheating, which should reduce the total refrigeration load as well as the reheat energy. Unfortunately, it is not always possible to achieve an effective bypass. In order to use the bypass, it must be possible to draw a line from the mix point of the RA and FA that passes across the SHR line and extends to a point near the saturation curve—to a point that the cooling process can reach. This is possible only if the latent cooling load does not comprise a significant portion of the total heat gain, which relates to a relatively flat SHR line.

Figure 10.32 shows the basic adjustments that occur in an air sample as a result of movement in various di-

rections on the psychrometric chart. In general, heat gain tends to pull the room conditions in the direction of the "B" arrow, so to correct for these loads the ECS should move in the opposite direction, denoted by the "F" arrow. Heat loss tends to pull the room conditions primarily to the left, in the direction of the "G" arrow. Since some dehumidification also results from the colder and drier outside air conditions, although the interior latent gain from people and equipment during the winter season might somewhat negate this, the "F" arrow represents the general pull on the room air conditions from winter loads, so during the heating season the ECS should move in the direction denoted by the "B" arrow.

HYDRONIC DISTRIBUTION SYSTEMS

Water is one of the primary means of distributing thermal energy from the point of heat generation to the point of use. While today *hydronic* tends to mean a water system, it actually includes both water and steam systems. In contrast to the present, most early hydronic heating was by means of steam.

A - HUMIDIFICATION
B - HUMIDIFICATION AND HEATING
C - HEATING
D - HEATING AND DEHUMIDIFICATION
E - DEHUMIDIFICATION
F - DEHUMIDIFICATION AND COOLING
G - COOLING
H - COOLING AND HUMIDIFICATION

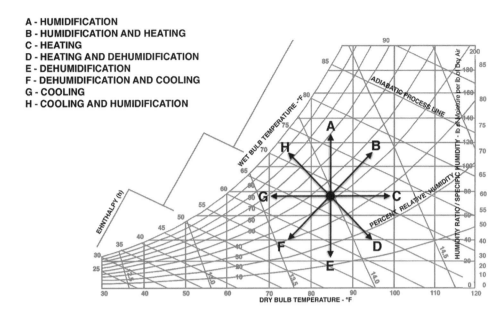

Figure 10.32 AIR CONDITIONING PROCESSES ON THE PSYCHROMETRIC CHART
Movement on the psychrometric chart relates to particular adjustments in the air conditions. In general, the summer season loads pull room conditions in the "B" direction, so the ECS requires an opposite pull in the "F" direction to counter the loads. In the winter the conditions reverse, with the loads pulling in the "F" direction, suggesting that the ECS needs to pull in the "B" direction. (Note: This psychrometric chart is a schematic based on various published charts and is presented merely to demonstrate its various uses.)

Steam Heating

Prior to electrification and the ready access to pumping devices, steam had the advantage. As a vapor that is lighter than air, steam tends to rise on its own and then releases its heat by condensing back into a liquid. In this process it releases approximately 1000 BTU for each pound of water, which is why the size of steam systems is often expressed in terms of pounds, with each pound related to 1000 BTUH heat output. When the steam has condensed into a liquid, the condensate can then flow by gravity back to the heating unit—the boiler.

A one-pipe steam system uses the same pipe to both distribute the steam and return the condensate (see Figure 10.33). The critical issue is to maintain the proper slope so that the condensate can flow back to the boiler. If this cannot be accomplished by gravity, the condensate is collected in a condensate set and then, when enough water has been collected, it is pumped back to the boiler. While the one-pipe system works effectively, sometimes a steam heating system is designed so that the major condensate is returned through a separate pipe, although the steam riser piping must still be sloped properly. As the steam rises up to the heat exchange device, which is typically a radiator, some of the steam will condense since the pipes will be surrounded by air temperatures well below 212° F, and this steam must also be able to drain back to the boiler. If it cannot drain back, then the water will form a trap in the

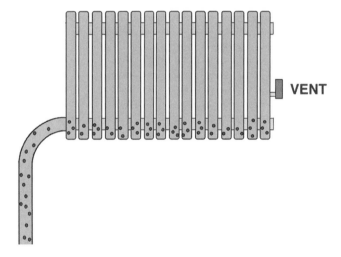

Figure 10.33 STEAM RADIATOR
A one-pipe steam system supplies the steam and returns the condensate in the same pipe, releasing around 1000 BTU for each pound of water condensed.

supply line, potentially preventing the steam from getting to the radiator (see Figure 10.34).

If it is not possible to provide a consistent slope back to the boiler or to a condensate set, such as what might happen in trying to pass by a door opening, a double loop can allow the condensate to drain while the steam can still pass. Since water seeks its own level, the bottom loop will fill with water and then will allow further condensate to drain back to the boiler.

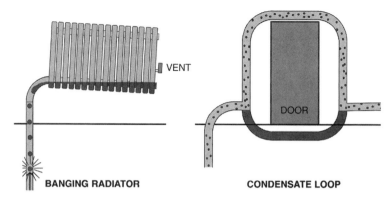

Figure 10.34 POTENTIAL PROBLEMS WITH STEAM PIPING
There are two potential problems with steam systems. If the slope is not properly maintained, condensate can build up and then drain back in a water slug that can explode when it confronts rising steam, resulting in a loud bang. Also, if there is an interruption in the natural drainage slope, as might exist by running down and up, condensate will collect and trap the steam flow. This trap can be eliminated by including an over loop, as shown in Figure 10.34.

BANGING RADIATOR   CONDENSATE LOOP

A banging radiator is an indication of improper drainage. Normally, the condensate should drain out of the radiator as it is produced, slowly and regularly. If, as shown in the left image in Figure 10.34, the radiator is sloped away from the steam pipe, the condensate will build up in the bottom of the radiator, and then, as it drains out in a slug of water, it will confront the rising steam. When the two meet, the water can explode in the pipe. Since the pipe is essentially vacated except for the steam, as the water hits the sides of the pipe, it makes a loud banging noise. Although we think of water as being soft, if we have ever taken a belly flop into water, we know that it is really rather hard. As the condensate slaps against the pipe, it sounds as though the pipe is being hit with a metal hammer. This gave rise to the legend that people in tenement housing use to bang on the radiators to let the superintendent know that they needed heat. Actually, the banging was probably the result of the water exploding against the pipes, which was more likely as the steam heating started up.

During normal operation, steam pressure fills the radiator and tends to force any condensate that has collected to flow back down the supply pipe. However, when the system shuts down, the steam pressure is eliminated and the condensate is not forced out of the radiator, especially if it is improperly sloped, as shown in Figure 10.34. So, as the system cools, all of the steam condenses and the bottom of the radiator tends to fill with water. Then as the system starts up again, the steam pressure confronts the accumulated water, forcing it out of the radiator, but now in large quantities—in a slug of water rather than in condensate drips. The result is the loud banging caused by the exploding water slug as it meets the rising steam. With a proper slope, even when the system shuts down and all of the steam condenses, the condensate will slowly drain back to the boiler.

Water can also circulate as a result of a change in density established when water is heated. When a change in density is used as the motive force, the arrangement is called a *gravity hot water system* and requires fairly large pipes. Large pipes are also required for steam heating, but this is because the volume of steam is about 1600 times the volume of liquid. The large pipes for gravity hot water are needed because the difference in hot water density does develop a significant pressure. Therefore, in order to minimize the resistance to water flow, both of the pipes in the gravity hot water system have to be rather large. Also, with a water system a separate return line is needed, so a gravity hot water system might need more distribution space than a steam system. The main supply and return pipes in a residential gravity hot water heating system are at least 4 to 6 inches in diameter.

Water Systems

With electrification and ready access to pumping devices, water became the preferred approach for hydronic heating. With forced circulation provided by a pump, the size of the pipes could be reduced significantly, typically to less than 2 inches in diameter for a residential system. Pumping also meant that the water system could be used for both heating and cooling. Water distribution systems also provide for easy adjustment of the thermal output by regulating the flow rate and/or the temperature of the water, and hot water can also be used as the energy source for absorption refrigeration.

The basic formula for thermal transfer, in terms of BTU is:

$$\text{BTU} = \text{Weight} \times \text{Specific Heat} \times \Delta T \,^{\circ}\text{F}$$

Since water weighs about 8.33 pounds per gallon and has a specific heat of 1.0, this general formula can be adjusted to provide a standardized formula for thermal transfer with water. In addition, the quantity of water is usually measured in terms of volume flow rate rather than weight.

The thermal transfer formula for water becomes:

$$\text{BTUH} = \text{GPM} \times 8.33\,\text{lb/Gal} \times 60\,\text{Min/Hr} \times \Delta T°\text{F}$$
$$= \text{GPM} \times 500\,\text{lb-min/gal-hr} \times \Delta T°\,\text{F}$$
$$\approx \text{GPM} \times 500 \times \Delta T°\,\text{F}$$

As the temperature of the water contained within the system changes, the volume of the water also changes. This requires the inclusion of an expansion tank that can accommodate an increased volume, avoiding any forced loss of water from the system. If water is lost as the temperature and volume increase, then make-up water will have to be added as the temperature drops and the volume decreases. With a system that is open to the atmosphere, the expansion tank must be located at the highest point of the system, but with a closed system, it can be located at any point.

Two-Pipe Water Distribution

With a two-pipe water distribution system, both heating and cooling are possible, but not simultaneously. In order to shift from heating to cooling or vice versa, there must be a switchover, circulating the water either through a heat exchanger connected with the boiler or through a heat exchanger connected with the chiller. A possible alternative arrangement would entail only one heat exchanger, with the water circulating through the shell coming either from the boiler or from the chiller (see Figure 10.35).

Although a two-pipe water distribution system does not allow for simultaneous heating and cooling within the same distribution zone, with proper zoning appropriate temperature control can be maintained. While simultaneous heating and cooling within a zone might not be possible, heating within one two-pipe distribution zone can occur while cooling is occurring within another two-pipe zone. For example, if five separate two-pipe water distribution zones are provided, one zone for each of the four orientation exposures and one for the interior, the various two-pipe water distribution systems should be able to provide effective thermal control. While the interior zone would normally require consistent cooling, the four exposure zones would likely require alternation between heating and cooling as the solar load changes during the day. As discussed previously, a southern exposure will often experience its maximum heat gain on a sunny winter day. During a sunny day in the winter heating season, when the other exposures are calling for hot water to control their heat loss, the two-pipe water distribution zones serving the interior and the southern zone would be pumping chilled

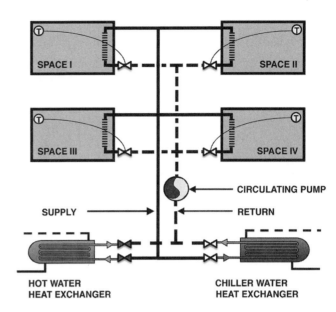

Figure 10.35 TWO-PIPE WATER DISTRIBUTION SCHEMATIC
The two-pipe water distribution system can both heat and cool, although not at the same time. With proper zoning, this is an effective means of providing an energy exchange medium for year-round environmental control.

water. Then in the evening, when there is no solar gain, all of the exterior zones would call for hot water, but the interior zone would continue to demand chilled water if the system continues to operate during hours of nonoccupancy. Even when not occupied, the exterior zones would continue to require heating during the winter season, although the interior temperature could be reduced.

Three-Pipe Water Distribution

With a three-pipe water distribution system, simultaneous heating and cooling are possible. One circulating pump, located in the return line, maintains a constant rate of flow. As the three-way valves respond to the room thermostats, either hot or chilled water will be circulated, depending on the particular demands of each space. Either 100% hot water, 100% chilled water, or a mixture of hot and chilled water can be provided as the thermostat adjusts the three-way mixing valve (see Figure 10.36).

While a three-pipe system offers considerable flexibility over the temperature of the water supplied to condition each individual space, since it has the ability to provide heating and cooling at the same time, it is not a very efficient system. If only heating were being provided, the hot water supply temperature might be at 220° F, with the return water at 200° F. A 20° F drop between the temperature of the supply and return water is standard for a hot water system. If only cooling were being provided, the temperature differential between the supply and return water

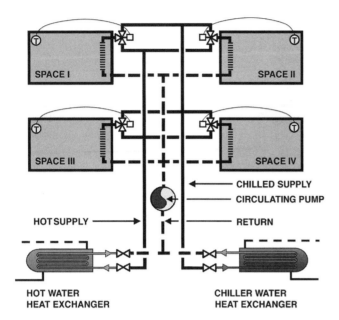

Figure 10.36 THREE-PIPE WATER DISTRIBUTION SCHEMATIC
The three-pipe water distribution system can both heat and cool, and do so at the same time. While this is a very effective way to provide temperature control, it does so rather inefficiently. Since there is a common return, hot and chilled water are combined in the return, forcing a significant increase in the heating and cooling return to achieve the supply temperatures.

is generally 10° F, with the supply at around 45° F and the return at around 55° F.

While the temperature differential (ΔT) between the supply and return water is usually less for cooling than for heating, for purposes of this explanation, let us assume that they are both 20° F. Therefore, if only heating were required and full demand existed, all the water circulated would have to be heated by 20° F. If only cooling were required, all the water circulated would have to be cooled by 20° F. Assuming a total water flow rate of 100 GPM, the heating and cooling loads can be found as follows:

$$BTUH_{heating} = 100 \text{ GPM} \times 500 \text{ BTUH/GPM-°F}$$
$$\times [220° \text{ F} - 200° \text{ F}]$$
$$= 1,000,000 \text{ BTUH}$$
$$BTUH_{cooling} = 100 \text{ GPM} \times 500 \text{ BTUH/GPM-°F}$$
$$\times [60° \text{ F} - 40° \text{ F}]$$
$$= 1,000,000 \text{ BTUH}$$

If both heating and cooling are provided at the same time and half of the water circulated through the system is for heating and half is for cooling, again both using a 20° F ΔT, then the common return water temperature would be the result of mixing equal quantities of 200° F and 60° F water. The temperature of the return water would be 130° F. As a result, the demands on the central heating and cooling equipment would be quite different from those

of the all-heating or all-cooling scenario.

$$BTUH_{heating} = 100 \text{ GPM} \times 500 \text{ BTUH/GPM-°F}$$
$$\times [220° \text{ F} - 130° \text{ F}]$$
$$= 4,500,000 \text{ BTUH}$$
$$BTUH_{cooling} = 100 \text{ GPM} \times 500 \text{ BTUH/GPM-°F}$$
$$\times [130° \text{ F} - 40° \text{ F}]$$
$$= 4,500,000 \text{ BTUH}$$

Assuming that half of the building required heating and the other half required cooling, the space heating demand would be 500,000 BTUH and the space cooling demand would be 500,000 BTUH. That is, the space heating and cooling demands would each equal half of the 1,000,000-BTUH load that would occur with either 100% heating or 100% cooling. However, using a three-pipe water distribution system to provide both hot and chilled water, the load on the central equipment with half heating and half cooling would be 4,500,000 BTUH for heating and 4,500,000 BTUH for cooling. This would be an 800% increase in the energy load in order to operate a three-pipe system to both heat and cool!

While a three-pipe water distribution system might provide for simultaneous heating and cooling, it obviously does so at a high price in terms of operational efficiency. In addition, since the same coil is used for both heating and cooling, it goes through a considerable temperature difference, from 40° F to 220° F, which can result in considerable thermal stress, reducing the life of the coil. Also, the coil design is not specific to either function: heating or cooling.

Four-Pipe Water Distribution

If simultaneous heating and cooling are required in the same zone, which perhaps should not be necessary if the ECS is properly zoned, then a four-pipe water distribution system might be appropriate. With a four-pipe system, the mixture of hot and chilled water is avoided and the demands on the central equipment are based on the space heating and cooling demands since the hot and chilled water are not combined. While a four-pipe system might be flexible, responsive to varying demands, and reasonably efficient, it is somewhat expensive since essentially two separate water distribution systems must be installed: one for heating and one for cooling. In addition, although not a major energy use, there are two circulating pumps (see Figure 10.37).

The most difficult periods of the year in terms of ECS control are spring and fall since the weather conditions often vary significantly, sometimes hot and sometimes cold. While a four-pipe water distribution system provides a

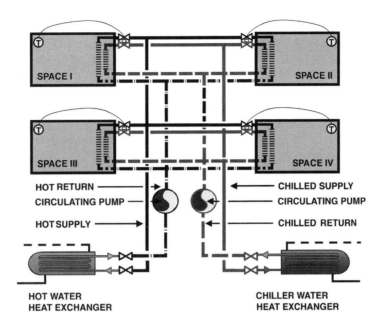

Figure 10.37 FOUR-PIPE WATER DISTRIBUTION SCHEMATIC
The four-pipe water distribution system is essentially the combination of two separate systems. It can both heat and cool, and do so at the same time. While this system is somewhat expensive to install, it provides the flexibility of a three-pipe system without the operational inefficiency of that approach.

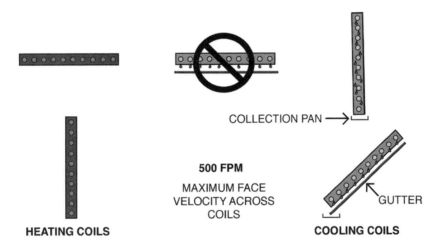

Figure 10.38 COIL ARRANGEMENTS
The orientation of cooling coils must allow for collection and dispersion of condensate, whereas coils used only for heating have no such limitation.

great deal of operational flexibility, it might make sense to limit its operation to these periods of changing weather, thereby somewhat reducing overall energy consumption. Of course this assumes that logical zoning has not been set aside on the assumption that the potential of the four-pipe system will suffice.

A four-pipe system generally uses separate heating and cooling coils, although it can be adapted to a common coil used for both heating and cooling. With separate coils, which do not experience the extreme range of temperature

differences that a combined coil has, each coil can be specifically designed for its intended function. With the two-coil arrangement, the thermostat controlling the space initially determines whether heating or cooling is required. Temperature control is then based on the rate of flow of the selected water, hot water for heating or cold water for cooling.

Figure 10.38 shows various arrangements of heat transfer coils. As suggesting in this figure, a particular requirement of a cooling coil is the collection and dispersion of condensate. As a result, a cooling coil generally cannot be installed horizontally, although a heating coil can be installed horizontally. A cooling coil also needs to have gutters that can carry the condensate off to the condensate drain. And when used for either heating or cooling, the face area of a coil should be based on a maximum velocity of 500 FPM.

HYDRONIC TRANSFER UNITS

In steam and gravity hot water systems, a cast iron radiator was the device typically used to deliver the heat to the occupied space. While the term *radiator* implies that thermal transfer was by means of radiation, most radiators were designed to promote convective thermal transfer. The device, which was usually a series of heavy cast iron sections joined together, had numerous vertical air passages between the sections so that air could flow readily by convection up through the radiator, moving across its hot surfaces. And with a somewhat shiny metallic finish, which was the standard finish for a cast iron radiator, the transfer of heat by radiation was actually reduced.

Heating Units

When pumped water distribution became more available, the large, bulbous cast iron radiators generally were replaced with nonferrous[11] linear thermal transfer devices that were smaller and tended to take up less interior space. These new devices basically include a pipe, generally copper, on which fins, typically aluminum, are placed. This assembly is generally referred to as *fin-tube* or *finned-tube radiation* (see Figure 10.39). Baseboard radiation is a smaller form of fin-tube radiation that is often used in residential applications.

As with all forms of fin-tube radiation, in baseboard radiation the hot water in the pipes heats the copper tubing, which, in turn, heats the aluminum fins. Since the pipe runs horizontally and the fins form a series of separated vertical surfaces, air can flow up between the fins. The piping and fins—the fin tube—are usually covered with a metal enclosure that can increase the convective airflow and also, being heated, will emit some radiation.

[11]Ferrous metals include iron and steel, and in terms of heat exchange devices they generally refer to cast iron radiators. Fin-tube radiation and most heating coils are constructed from aluminum and/or copper, both of which are nonferrous metals. Since cast iron has considerably more mass than nonferrous metals, it takes longer for ferrous components to heat up and cool down. For this reason, ferrous and nonferrous heat exchange devices should not be used in the same system.

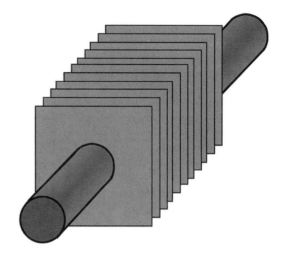

Figure 10.39 FIN TUBE
As its name implies, a fin tube unit is a metal tube, usually copper, on which extended fins, usually aluminum, have been applied. This greatly extends the effective surface area of the pipe, thereby increasing thermal exchange. In addition, with the fins oriented vertically, airflow between the fins also increases the thermal exchange. The fin tube is usually enclosed for protection of the fragile fins and to develop a stack effect.

With fin-tube heating, as the height of the enclosure increases, more air flows across the fin-tube unit, which increases the thermal exchange and heat output. The enclosure establishes a vertical air passage or stack that has a difference in pressure at the top and bottom, and increasing the height of this stack increases the pressure differential. With a greater pressure difference, more air is induced to flow across the fin tube, and this, in turn, increases the amount of heat exchange (see Figure 10.40).

As suggested in Figure 10.41, when the enclosure of the fin-tube unit is metal, the enclosure becomes a radiating source as well as establishing a stack effect. This can provide an effective way to compensate for the reduced radiant temperatures of windows. Fin-tube radiation is a linear heating device that is often extended along an exterior wall, with the actual fin tube located at the points of major heat loss, generally below the windows. That is, while the enclosure and the hot water or steam pipe usually run continuously along the exterior walls of a space, from wall to wall, the fin-tube section is sized to match the heat loss. Placing the fin tube below the windows will counteract the heat loss that is greatest through the windows and will provide a warmer surface that can balance the MRT of the space.

Baseboard and Fin-Tube Radiation

In nonresidential applications, which often have more heat loss per linear foot of exposure, rather than a baseboard unit, a larger fin-tube unit is used. This is essentially the

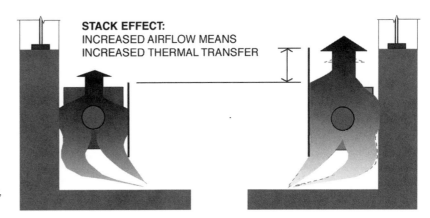

STACK EFFECT:
INCREASED AIRFLOW MEANS
INCREASED THERMAL TRANSFER

Figure 10.40 STACK EFFECT WITH FIN-TUBE RADIATION
The height of the enclosure of the fin-tube unit influences the amount of airflow that passes through the unit, which, in turn, increase the heat output.

RADIATION EMISSION
OFF OF THE HEATED
METAL ENCLOSURE

Figure 10.41 RADIATION FROM A FIN-TUBE ENCLOSURE
The height of the enclosure of the fin-tube unit influences the amount of airflow that passes through the unit, which in turn increase the heat output.

same type of device, except that the pipe and fins are larger. As indicated in Figures 10.42 and 10.43, because of the stack effect, as the height of the enclosure increases, the thermal output per linear foot also increases.

While Figure 10.43 shows a top outlet fin-tube unit, sometimes this configuration is not effective. The flat top provides a shelf, and if it is used to store things, as is often the case, the flow of air will be restricted. To avoid this and perhaps to eliminate a flat surface that might collect dust, slope-top units and front-opened units are also sometimes

used. Since removing the opening from the top of the unit reduces the overall effective height, the output per linear foot is also reduced (see Figure 10.44).

Baseboard and fin-tube units are linear devices. They are both rather effective in counteracting the heat loss along an exterior wall. In fact, the required length of fins, which provide the major thermal transfer components, often is less than the length of the wall along which the device is placed. In this situation, the enclosure and the distribution pipe can run the full width of the room, with the fin section sized to counter the heat loss. If this is done, the supply occurs at one end of the unit and the return at the other. Also, if the building exposure contains a row of several rooms, it is possible to have the hot water pipe continue from room to room, although this would mean that all of the linked spaces would be somewhat dependent on each other. The water in the pipe in each subsequent room would be at a lower temperature, requiring a longer section of fins in each subsequent room. Also, if one of the rooms located toward the beginning of the run had an open window, this room would require more heat, which might result in the subsequent rooms not having adequate heat.

Sometimes conventional fin-tube enclosures are not appropriate, particularly when the intention is to minimize the height of a windowsill and yet be able to supply heat along the base of the window. Since the clearance between the bottom of a fin-tube radiation unit and the

**OUTPUT (210° F)
@ 3 FPS**

SIZE	BTUH/LF
8" HIGH	700
12" HIGH	865

Figure 10.42 BASEBOARD RADIATION UNIT
The baseboard radiation unit, which is typically used in residential applications, is a linear output device. As its name implies, this unit was originally assumed as a replacement for conventional wood baseboards, thereby replacing the imposing cast-iron radiator with a device that would not be readily apparent within the space.

NOTE: OUTPUT VARIES WITH VELOCITY

4 FPS MAXIMUM

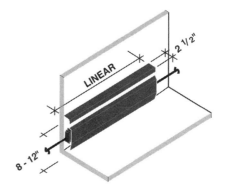

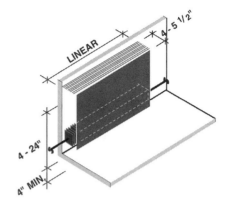

OUTPUT (210° F)
@ 3 FPS

SIZE	BTUH/LF
4" x 4"	1070
4" x 12"	1370
4" x 18"	1360
4" x 24"	1440
4" x 24" DBL	2220
5" x 5"	1590
5" x 12"	1820
5" x 18"	2040
5" x 24"	2120
5" x 24" DBL	2950

vs. 700 - 865 BTUH/LF
FOR BASEBOARD

Figure 10.43 FIN-TUBE RADIATION UNIT
The fin-tube radiation unit is a linear device that tends to have a higher output than a baseboard unit. This increased output results from the larger size of the unit, particularly its height.

TOP OUTLET　　**SLOPE TOP**　　**FRONT OUTLET**

Figure 10.44 VARIOUS ENCLOSURE ARRANGEMENTS FOR FIN-TUBE RADIATION
The effective height of a fin-tube enclosure can adjust the output per linear foot.

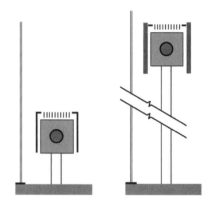
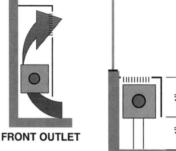

Figure 10.45 ALTERNATIVE ARRANGEMENTS FOR A FIN-TUBE RADIATION UNIT
Rather than use "standard" fin-tube enclosures, special designs are possible.

floor generally needs to be at least as large as the depth of the unit, a 4-inch fin-tube radiation unit requires a clearance of 4 inches below the unit. This results in a minimum overall height of 8 inches, but if an 8-inch sill is still too much, there are other alternatives.

Rather than install the fin-tube radiation along a wall, the unit can be freestanding. Such a unit was initially developed in order to adapt Le Corbusier's design for the Carpenter Center at Harvard University for the climate of Cambridge, Massachusetts. The design had wall-to-wall, floor-to-ceiling single glazing in the lobby area, with the intention of minimizing the interruption between inside and outside. To achieve this design intention and yet provide the appropriate heat, the unit shown in Figure 10.45 was proposed. However, while the unit was accepted and the interior–exterior connection was not significantly destroyed by it, the insurance and safety personnel were concerned that people would walk into the glazing, and they insisted on adding markers on the glass as a warning. This probably was fortunate since the freestanding fin-tube unit would provide a good way of tripping anyone who, not realizing that there was glass, tried to walk through the

"opening." Walking into the glass is dangerous enough. Falling into it could be catastrophic. In a subsequent project, this problem was addressed. Rather than set the unit at a minimum height, the fin tube was raised and set within a double wooden crash bar.

While these alternatives are effective, considering how a fin-tube unit works, rather than raise it as a freestanding unit, it should be apparent that it is also possible to lower the unit below the floor if the structural system permits (see Figure 10.46). In a sense, this is merely using the approach shown in the left image in Figure 10.45 but with the floor raised to the level of the top of the fin-tube enclosure. It is important to arrange this type of unit so that the cold air dropping down from the glass can enter the unit without having to cross the rising hot air leaving the unit; otherwise, the efficiency of the unit is considerably reduced. Also, since the unit is below the floor and is not exposed, the unit does not emit heat by radiation.

Sometimes the issue is not how to accommodate glazing that extends down to the floor but how to incorporate

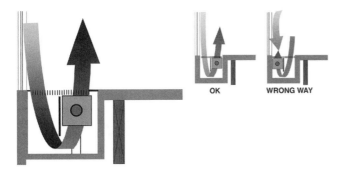

Figure 10.46 BELOW-FLOOR FIN-TUBE RADIATION
It is possible to install the fin-tube unit below the level of the floor assuming that the structure allows such. However, to maintain output from the unit it is important to place the intake so the natural convective airflow is not restricted.

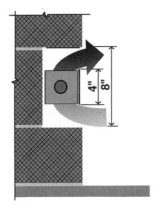

Figure 10.47 FIN-TUBE RADIATION UNIT RECESSED IN A CONCRETE BLOCK WALL
This recessed fin-tube unit was used in the Boston City Hall designed by Kallmann McKinnell & Knowles (1969).

a fin-tube unit without imposing physically. Following the idea suggested by the below-floor installation, a fin-tube unit can be recessed within the wall (see Figure 10.47). This is relatively easy with concrete block, although with the limit of only an 8-inch height, the BTUH output is reduced. In one installation, rather than for aesthetic rea-

sons, recessing the fin tube into the wall was necessary to meet code requirements concerning the allowable width of a stair landing.

The same consulting engineering firm that worked on Harvard University's Carpenter Center, Sidney J. Greenleaf & Associates of Cambridge, Massachusetts, initially proposed all of these alternative arrangements for fin-tube radiation. While they were developed in consultation with the architects for the projects, these innovations came from the engineer. Unfortunately, designers are not always able to work with a consultant who approaches the design of ECS with the same sensitivity as an architect, so we often need to take the lead.

The standard fin-tube radiation enclosures are not very attractive. When this is a problem, rather than change the basic approach, the solution might be to use a custom-fabricated enclosing unit. While this often entails an additional cost, it is often worthwhile to make the commitment.

Convector

If a large amount of heat is required at one point, as distinct from an extended surface, a convector can be used. This device, which is shown in Figure 10.48, is somewhat similar to the old cast iron radiators in terms of releasing a lot of heat in a limited area. A convector is not a linear device. Locations where a convector might be appropriate include a stairwell or alongside a large glazed opening that cannot be controlled from below.

Since the convector is not a linear device, the supply and return connections are generally located on the same side of the unit. As with the baseboard and fin-tube units, the output of the convector increases as the height of the enclosure increases. To increase the output even more, rather than merely rely on the stack effect, a fan can be added to the unit. Such a device, which is basically a convector with a fan, is called a *cabinet heater*.

OUTPUT (210° F) @ 3 FPS	
SIZE	BTUH/LF
4" x 14"	1500
4" x 20"	1700
4" x 32"	1800
10" x 14"	4000
10" x 20"	4250
10" x 32"	4750

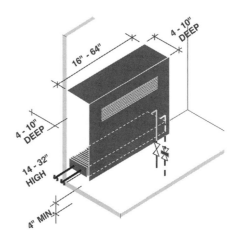

A CONVECTOR IS NOT A LINEAR UNIT

Figure 10.48 CONVECTOR UNIT
A convector unit is basically a modern radiator. Although it is not a linear device, the outputs are listed per linear foot, so a comparison with baseboard and fin-tube units is readily feasible.

OUTPUT (210° F)
@ 3 FPS

SIZE	COILS	MBH
36" x 9" x 24"	1	19.1
36" x 9" x 24"	2	32.8
40" x 12" x 27"	1	34.8
40" x 12" x 27"	2	59.0
44" x 14" x 28"	1	49.5
44" x 14" x 28"	2	78.1
60" x 14" x 30"	2	127.2

RANGE: 6330 TO 25,440 BTUH/LF

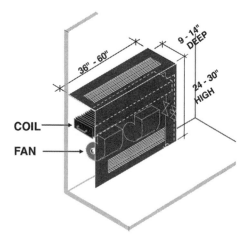

Figure 10.49 CABINET HEATER
Cabinet heaters are generally used in entrance vestibules. With the operation of the fan, there is a significant increase in the output, and the fan can be readily adjusted to match the load.

Cabinet Heater

A cabinet heater, shown in Figure 10.49, is often used in entry vestibules. Through natural convective transfer, the coil can release heat at a low rate for those times when the entry is not being used, but when the outside door is opened, the fan can quickly increase the airflow. As indicated for the output of typical cabinet heaters, with the high rate of air movement, a cabinet heater provides considerably more heat per linear foot than a fin-tube radiation unit or even a convector. With its ability to vary its intense output, the cabinet heater can quickly counteract the considerable heat loss that occurs when the outside doors to a vestibule are opened. As indicated by its name, the cabinet heater is only used for heating, although with the addition of the fan, it would be theoretically possible to use the device to cool air.

With the addition of a fan, the operation of the cabinet heater is not based on natural hot air convective flow, although as mentioned, this limited output can be effective in balancing the loads when major heat loss does not occur, as when the outside doors to a vestibule are opened. With this freedom, cabinet heaters can be installed in various ways, including remotely to the space that is conditioned (see Figure 10.50). Of course, with the inclusion of a fan, a cabinet heater needs an electrical connection as well as its own thermostat to control the fan operation.

While the cabinet heater and convector are not linear heating devices, it is interesting to compare the output of these units per linear foot (LF) to that of the linear units, fin-tube and baseboard radiation. A cabinet heater has an output range from about 6000 to about 25,000 BTUH/LF, while the output range for a convector is only about one-quarter as much, from 1500 to 4750 BTUH/LF. The output of fin-tube radiation ranges from about 1000 to about 3000 BTUH/LF, and the output for the two sizes listed for baseboard radiation is 700 and 865 BTUH/LF.

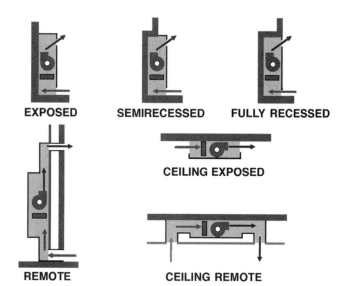

Figure 10.50 CABINET HEATER ARRANGEMENTS
Since a cabinet heater includes a fan, its location and orientation are not limited by natural convective airflow.

Assuming that the exterior wall of a space has a height of 10 feet, 50% of the wall is glazed, the temperature differential is 70° F, and there are standard "U" coefficients for the wall and window, the heat loss across each linear foot of exterior wall would be only 210 BTUH. With full glazing, the heat loss per linear foot would be 385 BTUH, which is still considerably below the output of even the smaller baseboard radiation unit, although this does not include any infiltration loss.

$$BTUH/LF = (5 \text{ sq ft} \times 0.55 \times 70° \text{ F})$$
$$+(5 \text{ sq ft} \times 0.05 \times 70° \text{ F})$$
$$= 210 \text{ BTUH/LF}$$

$$= 10 \text{ sq ft} \times 0.55 \times 70° \text{ F} = 385 \text{ BTUH/LF}$$

If the depth of the space extends about 20 feet from the exterior wall, each linear foot of exposure will be associated with an interior volume of 200 cubic feet. With infiltration at one air change per hour, the infiltration heat loss for each linear foot of exposure would be around 250 BTUH/LF.

$$BTUH = 200 \text{ cu ft} \times 0.018 \times 70° \text{ F} = 252 \text{ BTUH/LF}$$

Combining transmission loss and infiltration, the heat loss per linear foot of exposure would be about 450 to about 635 BTUH/LF, which can be easily controlled by baseboard or fin-tube radiation.

Radiant Panel Heating

For a space with limited heat loss, radiant panel heating is another means of heat exchange, although this method does not generally fulfill the basic principle of controlling heat loss at the point or place where it occurs since it is a distributed means of heating. While this might be a disadvantage, a major benefit of radiant panel heating is its minimal, if any, imposition on the design aesthetic. Also, although hot water is generally the heat source, electric resistance heating can be used. Since radiant panel heating does not require any visible expression, it is the preference of many designers.

The radiant panel can be installed within any room surface, although walls are not generally used since they normally have various openings that can impose on the installation. While including the radiant panel as part of an exterior wall might provide control at the point of loss, it would also establish a higher temperature within the exterior wall, significantly increasing the heat loss, so it is not recommended either. This leaves the floor and the ceiling. Since heating is the intention, the floor is a reasonable location, since the warm surface that is the premise of radiant panel heating will emit heat by convection as well as by radiation. However, the floor is also generally covered with various floor coverings and furniture, which can reduce the heat output. Even if this is considered in the initial design, future changes in finished flooring or furniture placement might have a major impact on the system's operation.

If the floor is used as the radiant panel, the maximum acceptable surface temperature is generally considered to be 95° F. At this temperature, the output would be 40 to 50 BTUH per square foot, but 95° F is actually hot to the touch, and a lower temperature is recommended. At a surface temperature of 85° F, the output is around 25 to 30 BTUH per square foot. Based on the previous suggested heat loss per linear foot of exterior wall with 50% window area, the radiant panel would have to extend into the

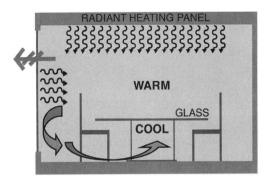

Figure 10.51 RADIANT PANEL HEATING IN THE CEILING
With radiant panel heating in the ceiling, air stratification can occur, with warm air collecting near the ceiling and cool air near the floor. With significant glazing, the cold air coming off of the glass can accentuate this stratification, and with a physical separation, perhaps by a dining table as shown, the temperature differential can be problematic.

room by at least 15 feet. While 50% window area might be high, the inclusion of furniture and floor covering will also reduce the radiant panel output, so the 15-foot extension into the room is reasonable.

If the ceiling is used, the surface temperature can be increased to around 110° F, which would produce an output of 60 to 70 BTUH per square foot. While it is unlikely that occupants would touch the ceiling, if the ceiling is relatively low and the surface temperature is 110° F, it could become quite noticeable in terms of its radiant emission. Of course, being at the top of the space, the hot surface is not an effective source of convective heating. For this reason, when radiant panel heating is installed in the ceiling, it is probably the purest or truest form of radiant heating. Unfortunately, this does not help to counteract the cold downdrafts that are established.

Figure 10.51 schematically shows how a ceiling radiant panel can result in some problems from downdrafts. In an actual residence that used ceiling-installed radiant panel heating, the architect was concerned with the stratification of the air that he anticipated would occur as a result of the dining room table. Therefore, he specified a glass dining table with the expectation that the radiant panel would be able to condition the cold air that would come off of the large, single-glazed windows and collect under the table. Unfortunately, he failed to remember that glass is not transparent to longwave radiation.

Figure 10.52 compares the output in BTUH for various hydronic heating devices, assuming a 4-foot unit for each. As might be surmised from the discussion above, the cabinet heater, with its fan resulting in significant airflow, has the highest output. With its reduced surface temperature, the radiant panel, which is assumed to be 4 feet wide and 10 feet deep, has the lowest output.

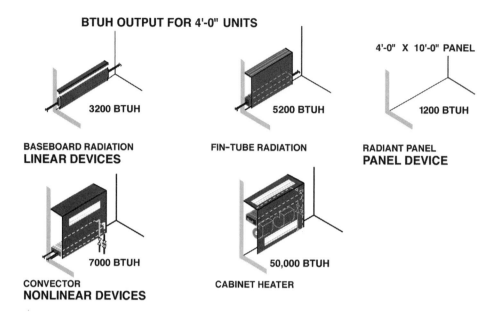

Figure 10.52 COMPARISON OF THERMAL OUTPUT FOR VARIOUS HEATING DEVICES
There is a considerable range in the output from different hydronic heating devices using the same hot water temperature. While the physical size of the heating elements is a factor, the difference in output is based mainly on the amount of air that flows across the heating elements.

Heating and Cooling Transfer Units

Cooling devices generally require some means of forcing the air across a heat exchange device—fin tube or cooling coil, the latter being more appropriate with cooling systems. When heating, the temperature differential is usually more than 100° F, with the actual difference based on room air of around 70° F and the hot water in the pipes, which is typically between 180° F and 220° F. The temperature differential, especially when put in an enclosure that establishes a stack effect, is adequate to develop a reasonable airflow. With cooling, assuming a room temperature of around 75° F and a water temperature of no less than 40° F, the temperature differential would be at best only around 35° F and sometimes less. Since this is not adequate to induce a significant airflow, a fan is generally required to move an adequate amount of air.

With a means of moving the air, a coil can be used for both heating and cooling, although there are some problems that can arise from the excessive temperature difference between the cooling temperature of around 40° F and the heating temperature of around 200° F and sometimes even higher. Since a pump is generally used to circulate the hot water, the system is normally closed.

As the temperature rises, the hot water expands, necessitating an expansion tank that can adjust for the varying water volume. The expansion tank typically contains air that is compressed as the heated water expands, but this generally also means that the internal pressures are above atmospheric conditions. As a result, the water does not boil at 212° F but tends to remain a liquid up to 220° F or higher. If the system can contain high pressures, then the water temperatures can be increased considerably. High-temperature hot water systems often circulate water at 500° F, although due to the pressures that are required, high-temperature hot water distribution is limited to central distribution and is not used in occupied zones. If a pipe containing water at 500° F sprang a leak, which the high pressures are apt to cause, the escaping water would immediately flash into steam.

In addition, cooling the air generally results in condensation. If the air entering the cooling coil is at medium to high humidity, the discharge air temperature could easily be below the dew point temperature. As a result, cooling coils, which should not be installed horizontally, must be designed to collect the condensate and discharge it someplace. For this reason, a standard heating coil should not be used for cooling.

If we tried to pump chilled water through a fin-tube unit, as suggested in Figure 10.53, the rate of airflow would be minimal, with the air that did come in contact with the fin tube being cooled close to the water temperature. This would likely result in condensation, but with no means of collecting it, the water would drip onto the floor. If this were not enough, since the cold air that does come off the fin tube would be at a low temperature, it would settle along the wet floor, and due to normal convective flow, it would not circulate. The room air would stratify, with cold air at the bottom of the room and warm air filling the upper region of the room, which is the occupied zone.

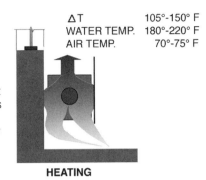

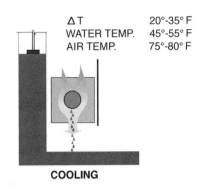

Figure 10.53 COMPARISON OF HEATING AND COOLING BY FIN TUBE
While the temperature differential between the heating hot water and the room air can produce effective airflow across a fin-tube unit, the temperature difference between the room air and the cooling water cannot. In addition, the low temperatures associated with cooling likely will result in condensation, which a fin-tube unit is not designed to control.

Fan-Coil Unit

If a device similar to a cabinet heater, which already has a fan, is provided with a coil that can be used properly for cooling, which means that there is either one multifunction coil or separate heating and cooling coils, the unit can both heat and cool. Such a unit, which is shown in Figure 10.54, is appropriately called a *fan-coil unit*.

In a way, the fan-coil unit is a small air-handling unit that is located within the conditioned space. Like a central air-handling unit, which typically circulates around six air changes per hour for heating and cooling, the fan-coil unit usually is sized to circulate this amount of air into the conditioned room. If the unit is also used to ventilate the space, the SA is usually comprised of five parts RA and one part outdoor FA.

A fan-coil unit often includes a direct outside-air inlet for the FA, but in areas of high pollution it might be appropriate to precondition the ventilation air. Since this is hard to do within a fan-coil unit, the outside "fresh" air can be filtered and cleaned by a central unit and then distributed to the fan-coil unit. Such centrally supplied ventilation air, which would still be sized at around one air change per hour, could be discharged into the room through the fan-coil unit or from a separate SA grill.

As shown in Figures 10.55 to 10.57, there are various ways by which ventilation air can be provided when a fan-coil unit is used. Since the fan-coil unit is the primary means of providing environmental control for each space, there is some logic in supplying the ventilation air through it rather than splitting the thermal control from the ventilation control. However, there are many reasons why a split system might be better. Typically, in order to supply air to the fan-coil unit, the air must come from the floor below. Since the floor slab likely provides the necessary 2-hour fire separation, a fire damper is required at each penetration of the slab. In addition, in order to service the air duct, it is necessary to work on the floor below, which might be occupied by another tenant.

These problems with supplying FA through the fan-coil unit can be reduced if there is a raised floor, which is sometimes advantageous in office buildings. It is also possible to supply the FA from air ducts installed as part of the exterior wall. This was first accomplished in the Blue Cross/Blue Shield Building in Boston designed by Paul Rudolph (see Figure 10.58). He developed a series of exterior vertical chases, which are similar to the appearance of the exterior structural columns. The supply-air ducts serving the various units are installed within these chases.

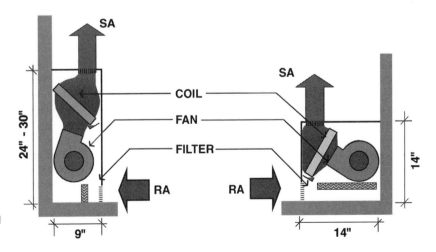

Figure 10.54 FAN-COIL UNIT
As its name implies, a fan-coil unit has both a fan and a coil. As such, if the coil is properly designed, the unit can be used for heating and cooling. The fan coil unit, which typically includes a means of filtering the circulated air and a way to provide ventilation, is essentially a localized air-handling unit.

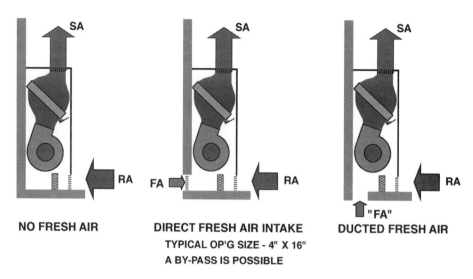

Figure 10.55 VARIOUS ARRANGEMENTS OF A FAN-COIL UNIT FOR VENTILATION
Fan-coil units often include a means of providing for ventilation.

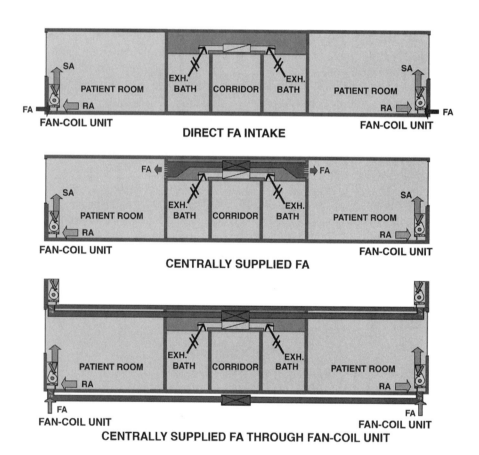

Figure 10.56 VARIOUS ARRANGEMENTS FOR FA SUPPLY WITH A FAN-COIL UNIT
This figure shows three typical arrangements for fan-coil units, perhaps as used in a nursing home. The units circulate six air changes each hour, with one air change ventilation and five air changes of recirculated room air. The FA can be outside air supplied directly to the fan-coil unit or preconditioned air from a central-air supply. Centrally supplied air can be provided from a separate ducted supply or through the fan-coil units. The exhaust from the bathrooms removes slightly less than the amount of ventilation air, thereby pressurizing the space to reduce infiltration.

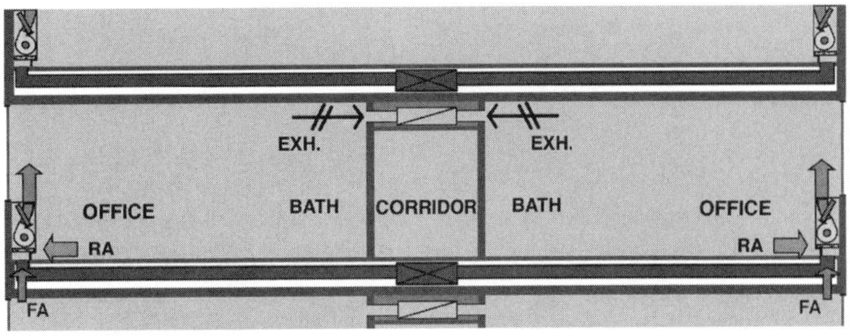

Figure 10.57 RAISED-FLOOR FA SUPPLY TO FAN-COIL UNITS
To avoid the problems caused by supplying FA from the floor below, it is possible to use a raised floor.

CENTRALLY SUPPLIED FA THROUGH FAN-COIL UNIT
FA FROM A CENTRAL SOURCE SUPPLIED TO
THE FAN-COIL UNITS THROUGH A RAISED FLOOR

Figure 10.58 BLUE CROSS/BLUE SHIELD BUILDING
The Blue Cross/Blue Shield Building in Boston was designed by Paul Rudolph in 1960. An extremely innovative design for the time, its Brutalist aesthetic was celebrated as an honest expression of structure, but the exterior elements actually encase the supply-air ducts.

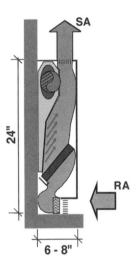

Figure 10.59 INDUCTION UNIT
The induction unit operates on the pressure of air that accounts for one-sixth to one-quarter of the total air circulated. As the pressurized air, which provides for ventilation, is released into the unit, it induces room air to flow through the unit, where it is heated or cooled.

If the fan-coil unit is adjusted to supply a significant amount of ventilation air, such as is required for a classroom, then the unit is typically referred to as a *unit ventilator*. Since more FA is supplied, the outside intake grill is somewhat larger than that for the typical fan-coil unit, although it is still smaller than the opening used with a unitized refrigeration system, whether it is a heat pump or just a cooling unit.

Induction Unit

If the ventilation air is supplied centrally, rather than a fan-coil unit, another device could be used—an induction unit (see Figure 10.59). Since a fan is merely a device that establishes a difference between inlet pressure and outlet pressure, if the centrally supplied ventilation air is emitted with "excess" pressure equal to the pressure that a fan would provide, the fan can be replaced with this air. High-pressure SA is ejected into the induction unit through a number of small openings somewhat resembling the openings in a gas burner. As the air leaves through these openings, room air equal to four to six times the

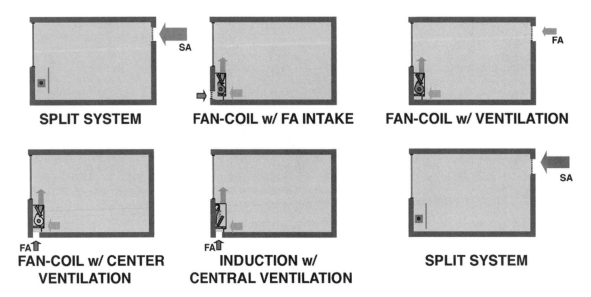

Figure 10.60 VARIOUS APPROACHES FOR PERIMETER CONTROL
This figure shows various ways in which heating, cooling, and ventilation can be provided. These variations are shown as a progression. Beginning with a split system, which historically meant that heating was by a perimeter hydronic system and that cooling and ventilation was by a central air system, the progression brings these together. However, with a better understanding of the intentions of the various components of an ECS, a split system might still provide a logical approach to environmental control.

volume of the ejected air is induced to flow across the heating and cooling coils.

The high-velocity discharge of air in an induction unit creates a noticeable sound. However, unlike a fan that produces a noise that tends to have harmonic vibrations that can be quite bothersome to some people, the sound produced by an induction unit can actually be beneficial. It is essentially a consistent white noise that can effectively mask other noises that could be problematic.

Another advantage of induction units is that, with no moving parts other than valves to control the flow of water, they do not require regular maintenance. This makes them an appropriate means of heating and cooling a perimeter space in which it might be rather inconvenient, if not totally unacceptable, to have a maintenance worker interfering with the activities of that space. An intensive care area in a hospital is such a space.

While induction units contain no moving parts, they operate as part of a complicated high-pressure air distribution system, and they rely on central hot and chilled water to accomplish heating and cooling. Because of the complexity of the system and the need for proper operation management, using induction units generally makes sense only when the system is large enough to include at least 150 such units.

Although it is an effective means for conditioning perimeter spaces, an induction-unit system is not very efficient to operate. This is because it relies on high-pressure air distribution, long distribution runs resulting from the necessary minimum number of units, and the probable continual operation of all units.

Split Systems

After the development of pumped water distribution and linear finned tubes, hydronic heating primarily involved baseboard and fin-tube radiation. With the advent of air conditioning application for thermal comfort, which essentially occurred around 1950, adding air conditioning to buildings that had hydronic heating meant developing what is called a *split system* since the cooling process typically involves an air system of some sort. As indicated in the first image in Figure 10.60, heating was by means of perimeter fin-tube radiation, and cooling (SA) was provided by a separate air system.

The split between heating and cooling was felt by many to be inappropriate. This conclusion seems to have been based on the belief that the environmental control system should be capable of controlling interior thermal conditions regardless of seasonal variations. Perhaps this attitude was based in part on the fact that the split system was an adaptation of an older system, which was somewhat of a "Rube Goldberg" contraption rather than a sophisticated design. Whatever the basis, this attitude tended to encourage the development of the fan-coil unit that could both heat and cool, and also seemed to prefer having various aspects of the system combined—fan-coil units that incorporated FA distribution or, ultimately, induction units.

While there might be some merit in a single system, on reflection it becomes apparent that perhaps the split system actually provides some critical advantages. Heat loss needs to be controlled at all times, at least in terms of maintaining interior spaces at temperatures of 50° F to 55° F. Below this level, standard interior finish materials can experience some deterioration, particularly from the resulting high humidity. Of course, there is also the critical need of keeping the temperatures above 32° F to avoid the chance that water in the pipes and various plumbing fixtures might freeze. So even if the building is not occupied, minimal heating is required, and this can be supplied by a perimeter system.

Interestingly, when the exterior temperatures are low—which is when the perimeter system would operate, regardless of whether the structure is or is not occupied—this is the time when a perimeter fin-tube radiation system is most effective. Also, it tends to take more energy to operate an air system than a water system to provide comparable heating. Although the air system might include ventilation that is not provided by the water system, the increased energy consumption is primarily connected with moving air. In addition, during times of nonoccupancy, an air system should not include FA if ventilation load if the system includes an economizing cycle. Another factor supporting a split system is that the building's owner has the greatest interest in maintaining at least acceptable minimum interior temperatures. Therefore, the cost of operating the perimeter fin-tube radiation system to maintain interior temperatures at 50° F to 55° F might be borne by the building's owner, with the air system being the responsibility of the tenant. As such, the air system, which might operate only when the space is occupied, can handle all the cooling and only the heating from the minimal temperature of around 50° F to the desired room temperature.

AIR DISTRIBUTION SYSTEMS

In order to maintain effective comfort conditions in the interior environment, there are five factors that need to be controlled: the four thermal factors that influence the processes of thermal transfer—dry bulb temperature (DBT), wet bulb temperature (WBT), mean radiant temperature (MRT), and air velocity—and air quality, a factor that affects our perception of the interior conditions in a manner analogous to our response to the thermal conditions. The purpose of the ECS is to control all five of these factors, which together establish the interior thermal conditions. While there is considerable interaction among the five factors, with the control of one often capable of counteracting the influence of another, the significance of each of these factors must be determined from actual conditions. For example, if there were a major glazed exposure, in the underheated period this would result in a considerable reduction in the MRT of the interior space. Although this problem might be somewhat balanced by an increase in the DBT, it is best resolved directly—by controlling the MRT. To accomplish this, there would need to be a way to control the radiant temperature of the space.

So, there really is no one best ECS. Each condition must ultimately determine the appropriate system to be used. In general, however, since we do wish to control as many of the five factors as possible, an air system is often the system of choice since it offers the greatest potential for achieving full environmental control. Although usually not very effective in controlling MRT except with special treatment, an air system can readily provide control of the other four factors: DBT, WBT, air velocity, and air quality.

Providing zone control with an air system can be accomplished either centrally, through the use of separate units or a multizone unit, and/or by various terminal control devices. There are basically four different terminal control methods for air distribution, which will be discussed after we consider how the air is distributed.

Duct Presssure

A pressure differential is necessary to move air. This pressure differential can be established by a difference in air temperature that results in a change of density and air movement. This is natural convection. In early warm air heating systems, this temperature-based pressure differential was used to move the air from a central furnace to the rooms to be heated. Since the effective pressure was not very strong, circulation of the air was limited, often necessitating that the warm air be supplied along an internal wall since this was closer to the furnace and supplying the air required less pressure. As air moves through a duct, it confronts resistance; the pressure must be powerful enough to overcome this resistance and impart some movement to the air—to add velocity pressure to the air.

Fans

While natural convection does work, today a fan is usually used to establish the necessary pressure differential. The discharge of the fan typically establishes a pressure above atmospheric conditions, which essentially pushes the air forward. The inlet of the fan, on the other hand, establishes a negative pressure, which pulls the air into the fan. As a result, in many systems, one fan can both supply the conditioning air and return RA to again be heated or cooled.

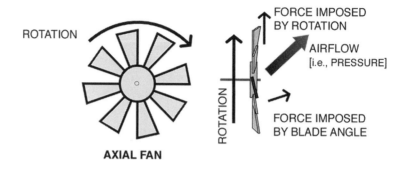

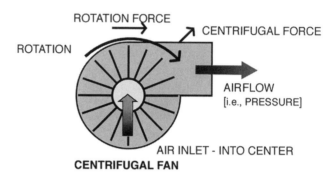

Figure 10.61 AXIAL AND CENTRIFUGAL FANS
There are basically two type of fans.

As shown in Figure 10.61, there are basically two types of fans—axial and centrifugal. The axial fan establishes movement of the air that is essentially parallel to the axis of rotation of the fan, whereas the centrifugal fan imposes movement that is perpendicular to the axis of fan rotation. Without an enclosure, an axial fan cannot develop a significant pressure differential, although it can move a large volume of air. This makes it an effective device for moving air when there is not much pressure to overcome, such as when generally circulating air within a space or when exhausting air from a space. These are the two major applications of the axial or propeller fan. If an axial fan is placed within a round enclosure, such as a round air duct, it can develop higher pressures, but as it does this, it also generates considerable noise, somewhat similar to that of a jet engine, which, of course, is a similar device. This type of axial fan is called a *tube-axial fan*. As the propeller blade spins, the air around it produces a great deal of turbulence, which limits the effective pressure. By adding air control devices that can redirect the spinning air in the direction of the air duct, more of the pressure that is produced by the rotating propeller can be captured rather than lost in the air turbulence. Such an axial fan is called a *vane-axial fan*.

With a centrifugal fan, as shown in Figure 10.62, the air is pulled into the center of the fan and then spun around within the paddle wheels of the device. As the air spins around, a force is imparted to the air as a result of the direction of movement, but there is also the addition of centrifugal force that is directed away from the center of

rotation. Together, the rotational and centrifugal forces are added to the air, but since the air is contained, it cannot move until it reaches the outlet opening. Air is released at this outlet with the pressure from both forces, which is higher than what is available from even the vane-axial fan. With the pressures that they can establish, centrifugal fans are generally those used in air-handling units. The size of the centrifugal fan basically determines the volume of air that it will move, while the rotational speed (RPM) establishes the pressure. As shown in Figure 10.63, the design of the paddle-wheel blades also has an impact on the pressure. If the blades are radial, a medium pressure is developed. If the blades are bent forward, a higher pressure results, and if they are bent backward, a lower pressure is produced.

As we will see, the proper fan for an air system is based on the volume of air and the pressure that is imparted to that air stream. The volume of air is based on the load established by the heat loss or heat gain, whereas the

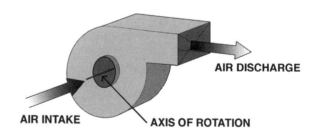

Figure 10.62 SCHEMATIC OF A CENTRIFUGAL FAN

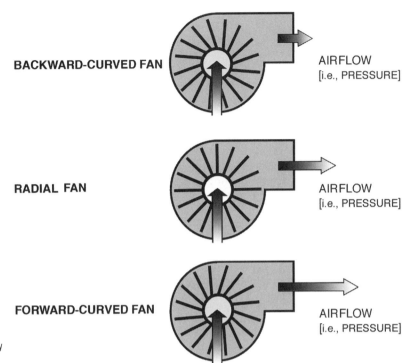

BACKWARD-CURVED FAN   AIRFLOW
[i.e., PRESSURE]

RADIAL FAN   AIRFLOW
[i.e., PRESSURE]

FORWARD-CURVED FAN   AIRFLOW
[i.e., PRESSURE]

Figure 10.63 VARIOUS CENTRIFUGAL FANS
The orientation of the blades in a centrifugal fan determines the pressure that is produced. Assuming that the same sized fans are rotating at the same speed, fans will move the same volume of air, but the pressure produced by a backward-curve fan will be less than a radial fan, and the pressure produced by the forward-curve fan will be higher.

pressure is set to match the resistance that will be confronted by moving the air from the air-handling unit to the farthest space to be conditioned, and perhaps to return it as well. Actually, the pressure must be enough to move the air through the supply ducts, leaving enough excess so that the air is discharged into the space with the proper velocity. The amount of air that is discharged from an SA grill is noted in terms of cubic feet per minute (CFM). The CFM, which is critical for the control of the space, is based on the open area of the SA grill times the velocity of air passing through it. Multiplying the square foot area times velocity in feet per minute produces CFM, the volume of SA.

Air Ducts

A fan establishes a pressure differential between the inlet and the outlet. How this pressure is used depends on a number of factors. An axial fan is often used merely to move air within a room. What is often referred to as a *window fan* is used for this purpose, as is the increasingly popular ceiling fan. Both of these fans establish a pressure differential, all of which essentially is used to develop velocity pressure to move the air. While we might assume that the basic purpose of using any fan is to move the air, to impart velocity pressure, in actuality most of the work provided by a fan in an air-handling unit is directed at producing pressure to overcome the resistance to airflow within the ducts. In a sense, this is like what we might experience by trying to blow up a balloon (see Figure 10.64). The intention is

to pump air into the balloon to cause it to expand, but we might confront the resistance of the balloon, and as hard as we blow, the balloon does not expand. If we are successful, and can inflate the balloon and then tie it off, an internal pressure will remain in the balloon to counteract the external atmospheric pressure, but this pressure will be static; it will not move. Of course, if after inflating the balloon we do not tie it but let it go, the balloon goes flying off, converting static pressure into dramatic velocity pressure.

A fan operates similarly, but how much air it will move is based on the total pressure imparted by the fan minus

Figure 10.64 BALLOONS
The experience of blowing up a balloon can provide insight in order to better understand the pressures that are involved with supplying air in an air system.

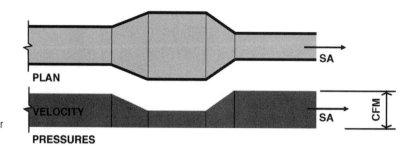

Figure 10.65 AIRFLOW DIAGRAM—1
As the cross section of an air duct changes, the velocity of the air also changes.

the resistance imposed by the ducting system. Figure 10.65 shows a partial plan of an air duct and the different velocities that will occur within the duct. The volume of air that comes out of the supply end of the duct establishes the velocity of air in the various sections of the duct. As the cross-sectional area of the duct changes, the air velocity, which is actually the velocity pressure, changes inversely.

Pressure Distribution

A fan provides pressure to the air stream. Some of this pressure is velocity pressure, which relates to the speed of the air in the duct; the balance is pressure to overcome the duct's resistance. The amount of resistance will vary according to the length of the duct run and the velocity of the airflow. Higher air velocity results in greater resistance.

The fan is located at the beginning of the duct run. Since it provides the pressure to overcome the resistance, which will not be confronted until the air moves down the duct, much of the pressure begins as static pressure. If this pressure were not static, it would be velocity pressure, which would mean that more air would be flowing in the duct; however, this is not desirable since the velocity of the air in the duct determines the volume of air being supplied.

In some ways, this is analogous to what we have probably experienced while riding a bicycle. If we pump the bike fast and hard, we can speed up and then allow the bike to coast. How far we can go will depend on how fast we get the bike going and the slope on which we continue. If we get going very fast, which means establishing high velocity pressure, and the bike's path continues to be relatively flat, we can go a good distance, but at the same speed while trying to coast up an incline, the bike will not go as far. When the bike coasts, the pressure we produced by pedaling is all that is available to move the bike. If we do not keep moving we can start pedaling again, but with an air system there is typically only the initial fan. There is no fan downstream. Also, while the extra pressure we produce on the bicycle is increased velocity, with the fan this would mean that too much air would flow through the duct, so the extra pressure must not move. It must be

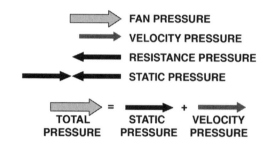

Figure 10.66 FAN PRESSURES
A fan produces a pressure differential between the inlet and the outlet. This is generally considered the total pressure, and it comprises static pressure and velocity pressure, with the static pressure essentially equal to the resistance confronted by the air distribution.

static. Rather than being directly analogous to the bicycle, perhaps this situation is more similar to that of the inflated balloon that will fly off if the internal air is quickly released.

All air distribution systems are basically self-balancing. If the fan does not provide enough initial pressure, then some of the velocity pressure must be used to overcome the friction loss. Since this would reduce the velocity of the SA and, as a result, its volume, the total resistance confronted by the airflow would also be reduced. This interchange would continue until a balance is achieved. In some instances, airflow can essentially be eliminated, which is somewhat like an unsuccessful attempt to blow up a balloon; we exert considerable pressure, but the balloon does not inflate.

Figures 10.65 through 10.72 graphically indicate various conditions related to air pressure in a duct system.

If the fan provides too much pressure, as shown in Figure 10.69, the static pressure will not be totally used to overcome the friction loss, and excess pressure will occur at the SA outlet. Since at the SA outlet the air is no longer contained, any excess pressure is converted into velocity pressure, thereby increasing the volume of SA. Again, with more air, there would be more total resistance and the system would self-balance, but with too much air supplied. However, if a balancing damper is added at the SA outlet, the damper can be closed to add resistance so that the velocity pressure discharges the intended volume of SA from the outlet.

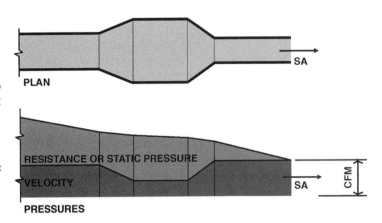

Figure 10.67 AIRFLOW DIAGRAM—2

If the size or cross section of the duct is not consistent, then the velocity of the air changes as the size of the duct changes. If the size of the duct increases, then the air in that portion of the duct slows down since the volume of air passing any point in the duct must be the same, at least in this diagram. The volume of air flowing down the duct is determined by the volume of air discharged at the end of the duct run. As the velocity is reduced, some of the velocity pressure is converted into static pressure, and as the size of the duct is reduced, the velocity must increase, requiring some of the static pressure to be converted into velocity pressure.

This is essentially how an air distribution system is designed. A fan is selected that can supply the appropriate volume at a total pressure that equals the velocity pressure of the fan discharge plus slightly more than the static pressure that is necessary to overcome the resistance to the farthest SA outlet. This ensures that there will be adequate pressure to get the air to the last outlet and, when reduced by the damper in this outlet that imposes a resistance equal to the slight extra pressure initially added, will supply the intended air volume.

While the previous airflow diagrams show only one SA outlet at the end of the duct, in actual installations an air duct typically supplies a number of outlets, each likely with a different resistance from the fan to the outlet (see Figure 10.70). With various outlets included in a duct run, it is likely that the resistance from the fan to each outlet will be different, although the fan produces only one total pressure, which must be sufficient for the outlet that has the greatest friction loss. As a result, the excess pressure at some of the SA outlets will be considerable, requiring the dampers to produce a greater pressure drop.

When a damper in an SA outlet produces a pressure drop, the pressure drop and the volume of air constitute the amount of energy that is not used productively—the energy that is lost. In order to reduce the amount of this lost energy, it is best to minimize the different pressures required to move the air from the fan to the SA outlets in a duct run. This can be accomplished by reducing the length of a duct run. This will lower the friction loss from the fan to the last outlet and reduce the difference in the pressure drop that the damper in the first outlet must provide compared with that in the last outlet.

Another factor in support of shorter duct runs is that the fans do not need to provide as much pressure, which correlates with energy consumption. The more fan pressure produced, the more energy is required to produce it,

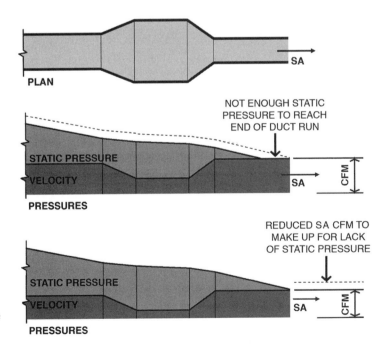

Figure 10.68 AIRFLOW DIAGRAM—3

Air distribution systems are essentially self-balancing. If the initial static pressure is not sufficient to overcome the friction loss for the intended airflow, the volume of air will be reduced, which, in turn, will reduce the friction loss. At the SA outlet, since any remaining pressure will no longer be contained, it will become velocity pressure.

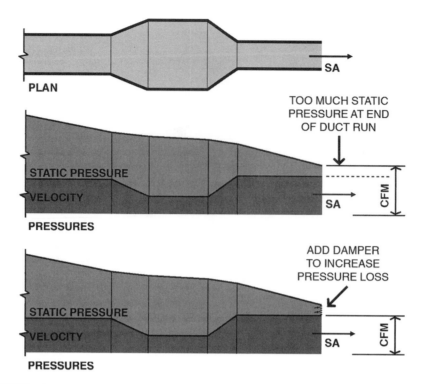

Figure 10.69 AIRFLOW DIAGRAM—4

If the initial static pressure supplied by the fan is too high, there will be excess pressure at the SA outlet. Since any pressure at the air outlet will no longer be contained, it will become velocity pressure, which will increase the volume of SA. In order to supply only the intended air volume, resistance can be added at the air outlet.

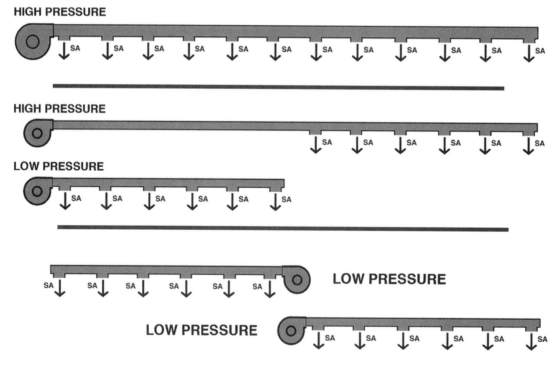

Figure 10.70 COMPARATIVE SA DUCT LAYOUTS

If the length of the run is considerable, the initial static pressure must be rather high in order to get the air to the farthest outlet. By splitting the system into a shorter run and a longer run, each handling half of the air, we can reduce the energy that would be lost while also cutting the resistance that the various dampers must contribute. Better yet, by relocating the air-handling units, it might be possible to avoid the need for a high-pressure run.

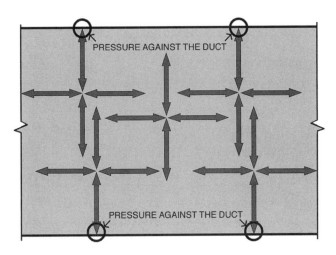

Figure 10.71 STATIC PRESSURE IN AN AIR DUCT
Static pressure in an air duct ultimately presses against the duct. The duct must be strong enough to resist this pressure.

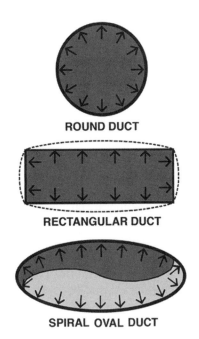

ROUND DUCT

RECTANGULAR DUCT

SPIRAL OVAL DUCT

Figure 10.72 STATIC PRESSURE AGAINST THE DUCT
The internal static pressure pushes against the sheet metal duct, forcing it to expand. While the thin sheet metal cannot resist bending moment, it does have high tensile strength, which favors the use of circular or oval ducts for high-pressure systems if the duct is configured as a continuous spiral of metal, similar to the core of a roll of toilet paper.

and when some of this energy is lost in order to balance the air distribution, it is an unjustified, or at least questionable, energy use.

The static pressure at the fan discharge is static because it is resisted. If it were not static, it would be dynamic, which means that it would be velocity pressure. Since it is static, its force is balanced by pressure in the air that is equal but opposite to it. However, at the edges of the air stream, where the air meets the enclosing metal duct, there is no additional air to oppose this pressure, so the metal duct must oppose it. This means that a metal duct provides a physical separation of the air stream from the surrounding that must be able to restrain the outward force of the static pressure. The longer the duct run, the greater the initial static pressure, so the stronger the duct must be (see Figure 10.71).

Air Duct Design

Air ducts are used to contain an air stream. Since the pressure necessary to move the air through an SA duct at the intended velocity is provided by a fan at the beginning of the duct run, the duct needs to resist the pressure that the fan produces (see Figure 10.71). With higher velocities and longer runs, the greater the initial pressure will be and the stronger the duct must be.

The Sheet Metal and Air Conditioning Contractors' National Association (SMACNA) sets ductwork standards. With low-pressure systems, which generally operate with a velocity of 1000 FPM, the sheet metal used for the ducts is usually between 22 and 26 gauge. These ducts are generally either in a rectangular or a round configuration. As rectangular ducts get larger, they often require a reinforcing frame. Low-pressure round ducts are generally made of flat sheet metal and are held in a circular form by an interlocking seam that has a limited ability to resist internal pressures. Flexible round ducts are also used, especially to make connections between rigid ductwork and air outlets. A flexible duct is generally merely a spiral metal coil that is wrapped with plastic, normally surrounded with a 2-inch fiberglass blanket, and then enclosed in a plastic wrap. As a result, most flexible ducts cannot contain high pressures and tend to produce a considerably higher pressure loss than sheet metal ducts.

High-pressure systems generally operate with a velocity of around 2000 FPM and sometimes up to 3000 FPM. With high velocities, there are also high internal pressures that require special consideration in the construction of the air ducts. Typically with high pressure, the ducts are constructed from a heavier-gauge metal (between 0 and 12 gauge), and rather than the simple mechanical connections that are used with low-pressure ducts, high-pressure ducts are usually welded. Also, in order to take advantage of the tensile strength of the sheet metal, instead of a rectangular shape, high-pressure ducts are usually of a round or oval configuration that is developed from a continuous spiral of sheet metal, similar to the core of a roll of toilet tissue (see Figure 10.72).

The movement of air in most systems relies on a pressure differential developed by a fan that is typically located at the beginning of the distribution run. The maximum

Table 10.1: SUPPLY-AIR DUCT EQUIVALENT SIZES

Circular	4	5	6	7	8	9	10	12	14	16	18	20	22
	Rectangular Dimensions in Inches												
6	8 x 4	6 x 5	5 x 6	5 x 7	4 x 8	4 x 9	3 x 10						
7	12 x 4	9 x 5	7 x 6	6 x 7	6 x 8	5 x 9	5 x 10	4 x 12	4 x 14				
8	16 x 4	12 x 5	9 x 6	8 x 7	7 x 8	6 x 9	6 x 10	5 x 12	5 x 14	4 x 16			
9		16 x 5	12 x 6	10 x 7	9 x 8	8 x 9	7 x 10	6 x 12	5 x 14	5 x 16	5 x 18		
10		20 x 5	16 x 6	12 x 7	12 x 8	10 x 9	9 x 10	7 x 12	7 x 14	6 x 16	5 x 18	5 x 20	
12			24 x 6	20 x 7	16 x 8	14 x 9	12 x 10	10 x 12	9 x 14	8 x 16	7 x 18	6 x 20	6 x 22
14				26 x 7	22 x 8	20 x 9	18 x 10	14 x 12	12 x 14	12 x 16	10 x 18	9 x 20	8 x 22
16					30 x 8	26 x 9	22 x 10	18 x 12	16 x 14	14 x 16	12 x 18	12 x 20	12 x 22
18						34 x 9	28 x 10	24 x 12	20 x 14	18 x 16	16 x 18	14 x 20	14 x 22
20								30 x 12	24 x 14	22 x 16	20 x 18	18 x 20	16 x 22
22								36 x 12	30 x 14	26 x 16	22 x 18	20 x 20	20 x 22

Notes: This table lists rectangular duct sizes that are equivalent to round ducts with the sizes are shown in inches. The rectangular equivalents are indicated only in even-numbered dimensions above 10 inches, although ducts may be available in increments of 1 inch. The listed sizes are based on the Trane Companys ductulator.

length of the run is based on the pressure that the fan can produce and that can be contained by the ductwork. As its name implies, low-pressure ductwork can only resist low pressures, and this limits the length of run in a low-pressure system to around 150 linear feet. With welded round or oval spiral ducts, high-pressure systems can resist higher pressures, which allows the distribution run to extend farther, up to around 400 linear feet.

Whether high-pressure or low-pressure, a fluid stream tends to have a circular cross section, which is something that perhaps we have observed. For example, even though many bathtubs have a square spout, the stream of water that comes out of it takes a circular form. Air also tends to take a circular form as it flows down a duct. Dividing the volume of air by the supply velocity indicates the required cross-sectional area of a supply duct, but this area is valid only for a circular duct. A rectangular duct must be slightly larger.

Preliminary Sizing of Air Ducts

Sizing a duct can be rather complicated; the process is made much easier using a ductulator or one of the many duct-sizing tables that are available (see Table 10.1). Although the actual sizing of air ducts might go beyond our level of involvement, we should be aware that rectangular ducts are typically based on an equivalent round duct. For example, a 12-inch by 24-inch duct has an internal area of 288 square inches, but the equivalent circular duct has a diameter of 18.3 inches, with an internal area of only 263 square inches.

Before we assume that we could use an 18.3-inch-diameter round duct, we should realize that round ducts

are available in 1-inch increments up to a 10-inch diameter and then only in even-numbered diameters. Rectangular ducts are generally available in full inches, with larger ducts often readily available only in even dimensions. Round ducts are available in 1-inch increments up to a 10-inch diameter, and then only in even-numbered diameters.

For estimating purposes, we can determine the necessary duct area by dividing the CFM by the air velocity. Legitimately, this area is appropriate only for round ducts, but we can use it for estimating purposes since we need to adjust this area to account for insulation that should be added to the duct and for space to accommodate installation. Table 10.2 lists the volume of air that can be supplied through a round duct at either 1000 or 2000 FPM.

The space used for SA distribution is generally rectangular in section. Horizontal runs typically are located in the corridors and installed in the space above a lowered ceiling. This space usually has a rectangular sectional configuration. As a result, even if the duct were round, it would require a space that is most easily allocated in terms of width times height, and this entails an area larger than the round duct by a factor of 1.27. This is the ratio of the area of a circle to the square of its diameter.

$$\text{Area of Circle} = \pi r^2 \quad \text{Area of Square} = (2r)^2 = 4r^2$$

$$\frac{\text{Area of Square}}{\text{Area of Circle}} = \frac{4r^2}{\pi r^2} = \frac{4}{\pi} = 1.27324$$

As indicated in Figure 10.73, in general at least 2 inches of insulation should be added to all SA ducts, and space must be allocated to allow for possible duct reinforcement and for basic installation. While the ratio of circle area to square area is a constant, the extra space required for

Table 10.2: ROUND DUCT AREAS AND AIR CAPACITIES

Diameter	Square Feet	@ 1000 FPM	@ 2000 FPM
4	0.09	85 CFM	175 CFM
5	0.14	135 CFM	270 CFM
6	0.20	195 CFM	390 CFM
7	0.27	265 CFM	535 CFM
8	0.35	350 CFM	700 CFM
9	0.44	440 CFM	880 CFM
10	0.55	545 CFM	1090 CFM
12	0.79	785 CFM	1570 CFM
14	1.07	1070 CFM	2140 CFM
16	1.40	1395 CFM	2790 CFM
18	1.77	1765 CFM	3535 CFM
20	2.18	2180 CFM	4360 CFM
22	2.64	2640 CFM	5280 CFM
24	3.14	3140 CFM	6280 CFM

insulation and installation varies proportionally with the size of the duct. Assuming a 12-inch by 12-inch duct and a 4-inch extended perimeter for the insulation and installation, the expanded duct area would be larger than the duct area based on the calculated SA area (CFM ÷ FPM) by a factor of 2.26.

12 in. × 12 in. = 144 sq in.   16 in. × 16 in. = 256 sq in.

Ratio of Duct Area to Installation Area = 144:256 = 1.78

Ratio of SA Area to Installation Area = 2.26

With larger ducts the factor by which the SA area should be calculated is less, but with small ducts, the factor actually increases. Recognizing these variations, in general we should assume that a reasonable allocation of building area for accommodating SA ducts is twice the calculated SA area. Since return-air ducts are also included with most systems, four times the SA area might be required.

The SA area is based on dividing the CFM of SA by the velocity of the system, which with low-pressure systems is 1000 FPM and with high-pressure systems is 2000 to 3000 FPM. The volume of air that is supplied, CFM, is actually determined by the heating or cooling load and the difference between the designed RA temperature and the SA temperature. With heating, this temperature differential (ΔT) might be up to 50° F, although it is generally less. The ΔT for cooling is set by the load conditions and the SHR, but it is often 20° F. Of course, while the ΔT is important, without knowing the BTUH load, we cannot determine the CFM. If we do know the BTUH load, we can calculate the CFM of supply air using the following formula:

$$CFM = \frac{BTUH_{sensible}}{(0.075 \text{ lb/cf} \times 0.24) \times 60 \text{ min/hr} \times \Delta T}$$

$$= \frac{BTUH_{sensible}}{1.08 \times \Delta T}$$

With air conditioning, the critical factor may not be temperature control but humidity control. When this is the situation, the volume of SA can be determined by the difference in specific humidity (W) between the SA and the RA.

$$CFM = \frac{BTUH_{latent}}{0.075 \text{ lb/cf} \times 1060 \text{ BTU/lb} \times 60 \text{ min/hr} \times \Delta W}$$

$$= \frac{BTUH_{latent}}{79.5}$$

It is also possible to determine the SA volume by using the psychrometric chart and the overall load, both sensible and latent. In this approach, the total load is divided by the enthalpy (h) difference between the SA and RA conditions, and then the appropriate weight of air is converted into the air volume selected for the SA conditions.

$$\text{Weight of SA per Hour} = \frac{BTUH_{totalload}}{h_{RA} - h_{SA}}$$

$$CFM = \frac{\text{Weight of SA per Hour}}{60 \text{ min/hr} \times \text{Specific Volume of SA}}$$

Unfortunately, in the preliminary design phase, we probably do not know what the BTUH loads are, so we are not able to determine the CFM of SA that will be needed. However, there is a rule of thumb that six to eight air changes per hour are reasonable for an air system. If the space has a floor-to-ceiling height of 10 feet, then six

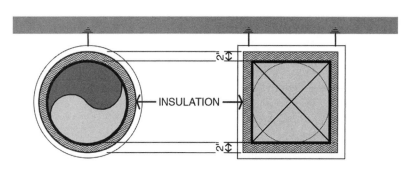

Figure 10.73 SA DUCT INSTALLATION
The amount of space that must be provided to accommodate an SA duct is considerably more than the duct size. With the allocation of building area to accommodate a circular duct or with conversion of this area to an equivalent rectangular size, the addition of at least 2 inches of insulation, and the provision of space for possible framing and for basic installation, almost twice the area found by dividing the CFM by the FPM should be assumed.

CONSTANT VELOCITY OR CONSTANT PRESSURE

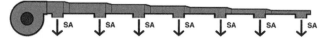

STATIC REGAIN

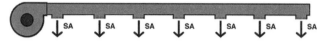

Figure 10.74 COMPARE CONSTANT-VELOCITY/PRESSURE WITH STATIC REGAIN
Although a constant velocity/constant pressure duct system is often considered easier to engineer but somewhat more expensive to install, static regain can result in reduced energy consumption and less cost overall.

air changes per hour relate to one CFM per square foot of space.

$$CFM = \frac{Room\ Volume \times 6\ ACH}{60\ min/hr}$$

$$= \frac{(Width \times Length \times Height) \times 6\ ACH}{60\ min/hr}$$

$$= \frac{Room\ Area \times 10\ ft \times 6\ ACH}{60\ min/hr} = Room\ Area$$

Based on the assumption that the volume of SA will be approximately the square foot area of space conditioned, the amount of space that should be allocated for the distribution of an air system can be readily determined by setting the velocity of the air, which for energy issues should be at 1000 FPM, and then increasing the SA area by a reasonable factor to accommodate the duct with insulation and installation:

$$Area = \frac{Area\ of\ Space\ to\ Be\ Conditioned}{FPM\ SA\ Velocity} \times Factor$$

There are several approaches to sizing the ducts within a distribution run (see Figure 10.74). As we have assumed already, one is constant velocity. Since there usually are several SA outlets on a run, the size of the ducts in a run with constant velocity will keep changing, getting smaller after each SA outlet. While the velocity remains consistent, the friction loss in the duct changes somewhat as the duct size changes. It is also possible to size the ducts based on constant pressure, which again will require changing the size of the duct after each SA outlet. Similar to what happens with the constant-velocity approach, with constant friction loss, the velocity tends to vary somewhat as the duct size changes. Generally, both the constant-velocity and constant-pressure design methods are relatively easy to engineer and tend to produce similar duct designs. Both approaches also result in a number of duct transi-

tions that are often expensive, especially in high-pressure systems.

Static regain is another approach to sizing the ducts, but this can get complicated and takes more engineering effort to take advantage of the potential energy benefits; however, it might end up being less expensive to install.[12] Essentially, static regain maintains the size of the duct, particularly in individual branches. With a constant duct area, the air velocity is reduced after each SA outlet, and as a result, the pressure associated with the reduction in air velocity is converted into static pressure, so it is now available to overcome friction loss in the duct (see Figure 10.75).

SA Dampers

Whether high pressure or low pressure, constant-velocity/pressure or static regain, the fan must provide enough pressure to overcome the friction loss to the farthest outlet, leaving just enough pressure to develop the intended exit velocity. Consequently, there will be excess pressure at each outlet before the last one. However, if the excess pressure at each of these intermediate outlets is not controlled, the volume of air supplied from each intermediate outlet will increase. That is, if the pressure is not restrained, it becomes velocity pressure, which means that more air will pass through the outlet. But if more air tries to flow through an outlet, there will be an increased pressure drop at that outlet. Since the system is self-balancing, the volume of air discharged through each outlet will increase until the total pressure drop from the fan to each outlet is equal.

If each SA outlet is the same size, based on the assumption that this would equalize the discharge volume, the results would be quite different (see Figure 10.76). Without some means of equalizing the pressure loss at each outlet, the amount of air supplied will increase the closer the outlet is to the fan, which is the beginning of the duct run. That is, the air pressures within the system would self-balance, which would unbalance the distribution of SA. However, if dampers are added to each outlet, the pressures within the system can be balanced and the volume of air supplied by each outlet will be equal (see Figure 10.77). This merely requires that each damper be adjusted to impose a pressure loss that matches the additional friction loss from that outlet to the last outlet. With the total pressure drop to all SA outlets equalized, the volume of air supplied

---

[12]This raises an interesting issue related to how compensation is provided for professional services, particularly if that compensation is based on a percentage of construction costs. There is little incentive to make the extra design and engineering effort that might be required to develop a less costly solution that might be more effective and perhaps more energy efficient as well.

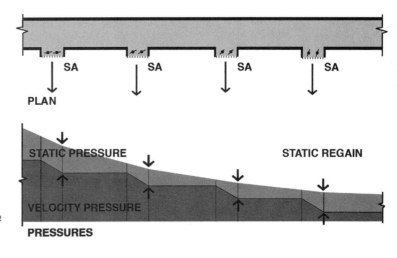

Figure 10.75 STATIC REGAIN
By maintaining the same duct size, the velocity within the duct keeps decreasing, which allows some of the velocity pressure to be converted into static pressure.

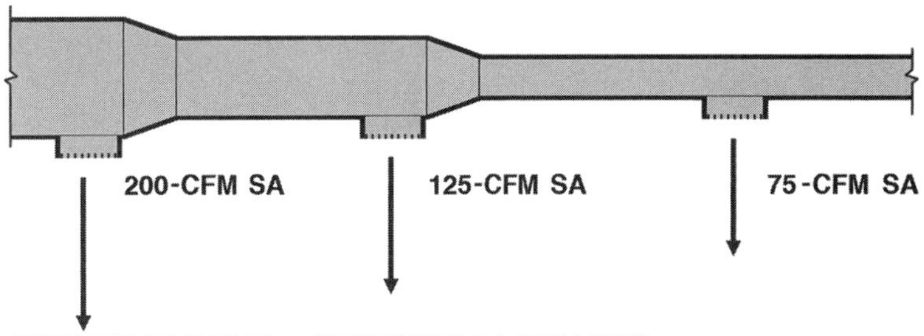

Figure 10.76 SA OUTLETS WITHOUT DAMPERS
The same sized outlets supply different volumes of air. The SA discharged through an outlets increases somewhat proportionally the closer the outlet is to the fan, which is the beginning of the duct run.

through each will also be equal, assuming they are the same size.

If there is a considerable difference in the distance from the fan to the various outlet on a duct run, the dampers closer to the fan need to be almost closed in order to add enough resistance to balance the distribution pressures. As a result, the air will rush through the narrow damper openings, creating the possibility of considerable damper blade vibration and/or whistling air, either one a serious potential noise problem. Even if the potential noise problem is controlled, there is still the problem of inefficiency. Duct systems with major differences in overall resistance tend to be inefficient since pressure, which entails the input of energy, must be added to a large volume of air even though

this pressure (energy) is not necessary for the actual distribution from the fan to the early outlets.

SA Outlets

After getting the air to the SA outlet, it is necessary to distribute it properly into the room so that it can control the heat loss or heat gain where it occurs. In doing this, the SA should not create noticeable drafts. Remember that air velocity is one of the five factors on which thermal comfort is based, and the recommended air velocity is 16 to 25 FPM. Air movement at more than 50 FPM is noticeable and considered drafty, and at 100 FPM, it can be quite troublesome since it will blow papers and other objects.

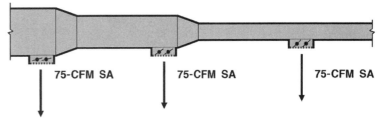

Figure 10.77 SA OUTLET WITH DAMPERS
The same sized outlets will supply the same volume of air if the pressure losses are equalized by properly adjusting the dampers.

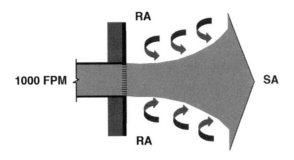

Figure 10.78 SA INDUCTION OF RA
When SA is discharged into a room, the edges of the air stream tend to induce RA. The amount of induced air, which is based on the spread of the discharge, will determine the length of throw. If the air is retained in a narrow stream, the throw will be extended, whereas if the stream is diffused, the throw will be reduced.

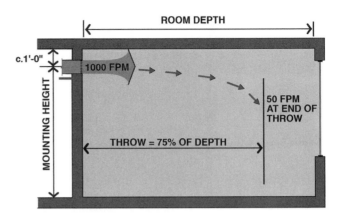

Figure 10.79 SIDEWALL SA DISTRIBUTION
A sidewall SA grill usually discharges air at 1000 FPM. Typically, the center of the outlet is located about 1 foot below the ceiling. This reduces the amount of RA induced into the SA stream, allowing for extension of the throw. The intention is to project the air about three-quarters of the way across the room so that it can condition the perimeter heat gain and/or loss yet decline in velocity to no more than 50 FPM before it drops into the occupied zone.

SA is usually discharged into a room at around 1000 FPM, so it is necessary to discharge it in a way that counteracts the heat loss or heat gain but does not cause drafty conditions in the occupied zones. Also, since the temperature and sometimes the volume of the SA change, it is necessary to consider how these variations will affect the distribution pattern.

An SA outlet can have various configurations. Ceiling diffusers formerly were usually round, although now they are more likely to be rectilinear, particularly square. Even with a round or square shape, the discharge pattern can be controlled. There are four-way, three-way, two-way, and one-way ceiling diffusers, often apparent by the arrangement of the exposed louvers, but there are also diffusers that conceal the control. Wall outlets range from a basic rectangle to a linear extended strip. When a linear grill is used—which can also be installed in a ceiling if the discharge is not directly downward— special adaptations are necessary to utilize the full length of the grill since an SA duct should not have an aspect ratio greater than 4:1. As a result, sometimes only a portion of a linear grill is actually used to supply air.

The most basic SA outlet is merely an opening in the duct, although most outlets are covered by a metal grill. While some are merely a perforated metal plate or simple grill, most SA outlets include vanes that can be adjusted to direct the pattern of discharge. With adjustable vanes oriented in both directions, it is possible to provide reasonable control of the discharge pattern. The length of the throw can be reduced by spreading or diffusing the air as it enters the room (see Figure 10.78). This is similar to experience with a water hose. The wider the spread of the water, the shorter the water jet; to project the water some distance, we need to narrow the water stream as much as possible. SA behaves in a similar way. As the air is discharged into the room, it tends to induce some RA to move along with it, and the more RA that is induced to move with the SA,

the shorter the throw. When the SA outlet intentionally spreads the air to reduce the throw, the outlet is called a *diffuser*. While ceiling outlets are normally diffusers to avoid blowing air down on people below, wall grills that supply a high volume of air are also usually diffusers, again to minimize drafts.

When a wall grill includes a damper, it is called a *register*. Interestingly, a wall grill with damper is called a register whether or not it is a diffuser, but a ceiling diffuser with a damper is still called a diffuser and not a register. A *punca drum* is an SA outlet that operates like the tight nozzle on a hose. It concentrates the air into a narrow stream to project it a long distance. A punca drum supply is commonly used on airplanes to supply air to each seat.

While the volume, temperature, and humidity of the SA are critical to control of the thermal conditions, the method of supply and distribution of the air within the space also has a strong impact on whether comfort conditions will be achieved (see Figure 10.79). Since the air is intended to counteract the loads on the space, it should be supplied in a manner that can accomplish this while maintaining comfort conditions in the occupied zone. It is not enough to merely balance the BTU gains or losses. While this might establish thermal stability, if it does so by exposing the occupants to drafts or major temperature gradients, comfort will not be achieved.

Return air[13] is also a factor to consider, primarily since the SA will not be able to enter the room unless a

---

[13]Return air is generally assumed to be room air (RA), at least in terms of thermal conditions. RA is expected to be at the design conditions, and yet this air is what is usually removed from the space and returned to the air-handling unit where it is heated or cooled so it will counteract the heat loss or heat gain when it is supplied back to the room. There

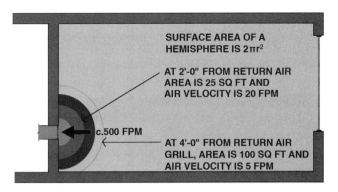

Figure 10.80 AIR VELOCITIES NEAR A RETURN AIR GRILL
The important issue concerning return air is that it does not affect SA distribution unless the return air inlet is located in the SA stream. The location of the return air inlet is not critical, although it can be effective in collecting cold downdrafts that might come off cold glazing. In general, the preferred location of the return air inlet is in the area of the room where the air might be stagnant. When cooling, this is generally closer to the floor; when heating, it is closer to the ceiling.

comparable amount of air is returned or exhausted. Otherwise, the room will be pressurized and this will oppose the proper release of the SA. Unfortunately this sometimes happens. For example, many houses still have only a central common return. While this works satisfactorily when the doors to the individual rooms are open, the air cannot circulate properly when the doors are closed, such as at night, when the bedroom doors might be closed for privacy. To solve this problem, sometimes the doors are undercut to release the air, although this also allows sound transmission. In nonresidential structures, door undercutting is also used, as are door louvers, which again result in sound transmission. Of course, the preferred arrangement is to provide a return air grill for every closed space.

A return air grill can release the air pressure in a room, but it cannot control the air distribution. This is done by the SA, which is discharged, usually at around 1000 FPM. Distribution control is a factor of pressure, which in the open conditions outside of the air ducts means velocity pressure. The velocity of return air at the intake is typically set at around 500 FPM, but unlike the SA that is ejected in one direction, the return air is pulled from all directions, and at a short distance from the return-air inlet, the area from which the return air is pulled is enlarged (see Figure 10.80). As a result, the placement of the return air grill does not have a major impact on SA distribution. An exception would be if the SA were to be directed toward the return air grill, which sometimes happens.

Let us assume a return air grill of 1 square foot with a return air velocity of 500 FPM. Since the air is pulled

from all directions, the area from which the air comes is hemispherical and has an area equal to $2\pi r^2$. At a distance of 1 foot, the area is equal to about 6.25 square feet, which means that the velocity is down to less than 100 FPM. At just 2 feet from the return air grill, the area is 25 square feet, which means that the 500-FPM pull of the return air is now causing an airflow at a velocity of only 20 FPM, which is approximately the air velocity that is desired to avoid a sense of stagnant air. At 4 feet from the return air grill, the velocity established by the pull of the return air would be theoretically only 5 FPM, which is less than the general airflow.

Another interesting factor regarding return air is that the conditions of the air are generally at the design conditions. Perhaps this seems illogical, but if we give it some thought, we realize that supposedly the SA has corrected the circumstances that are not at the design conditions. There are times when the return air grill might be located to intentionally capture air that is not at the design conditions. By placing the return air below a window, the cold downdraft coming off of the glass can be collected, keeping it from settling along the floor. Another example is pulling the return air through the light fixtures in order to extract the heat from the lamps, which can reduce the volume of air that needs to be circulated and increase the light output.

RA Distribution

For the heating cycle, the temperature difference between RA and SA should not exceed 50° F. For cooling, a 30° F temperature difference can be excessive. While the increased velocity of the SA is somewhat balanced by the increased air temperature when heating, these conditions tend to exacerbate each other when cooling. In addition to causing a cold draft, a large temperature differential can also cause condensation. Since the metal grill of the SA outlet will be at the SA temperature, it is likely that this will result in water condensing on the face of the outlet, especially if there is a large temperature differential.

During the cooling cycle, the temperature difference between RA and SA should be between 16° F and 24° F, with 20° F accepted as the standard. If a greater differential is required, perhaps to reduce the air volume or because of an excessive cooling load, up to a 30° F differential is possible, although not recommended, especially if the relative humidity in the room is higher than 30%.

Figures 10.81 through 10.87 show various ways that air might be supplied into a space that has exterior exposure.

The low-interior-wall air supply indicated in Figure 10.81 might have made some sense in the early days of

---

are instances when a return air grill is intentionally located so the air that it collects is not at the design conditions. For example, a return air grill might be located at the bottom of a window in order to draw in cold air that drops off the glass.

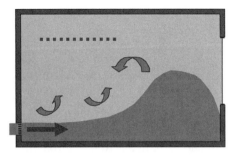

COOLING

HEATING

Figure 10.81 LOW WALL OUTLET
Locating the SA outlets low on an interior wall is not appropriate since it does not control the load at the point where it is produced. While it can spread hot air, it does so by blowing through the occupied zone. For cooling it is even less effective, with the cool air generally just collecting along the floor. This approach was quite common with early gravity warm air heating systems, and for these systems the distribution runs had to be limited. While these systems continue to be used, often converted to forced air and cooling, this approach is definitely not recommended for new work.

gravity heating, when airflow was dependent on the rising warm air and could not readily overcome the resistance of long horizontal duct runs, but today it doesn't make much sense. The SA is discharged directly into the occupied portion of the room, resulting in drafts. It also does not work well for cooling since the denser, cooler air will tend to remain on the floor and not circulate properly within the space.

Interestingly, even though this approach is inappropriate, many people appreciate the improvements in comfort that are provided by adding air conditioning, which probably suggests that our expectations for environmental control are not very high. In many buildings, especially residential ones, environmental control is quite basic. By contrast, most automobiles provide a level of control that far exceeds what is available in most buildings.

If an interior wall is to be used for the SA, it is better to raise the outlet higher on the wall, above the zone of occupation (see Figure 10.82). Typically, the outlet is located around 1 foot below the ceiling, which allows the ceiling plane to help the air flow to the exterior wall, where the load occurs. With the air supplied near the ceiling, there is less air above the discharge to be induced into the SA stream and slow it down, so the SA can travel farther into the space. Generally, an SA outlet located high on an interior wall can condition a space that has a depth equal to about two to two and a half times the floor-to-ceiling height, which, interestingly, is the same depth that a side window can usually illuminate.

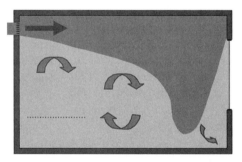

COOLING

Figure 10.82 HIGH WALL OUTLET
Locating the SA outlets high on an interior wall is quite effective for both heating and cooling. The critical issue is whether it can provide adequate control if there is a major heat loss as a result of considerable window area. The high distribution cannot counter the cold drafts coming off of the glass, suggesting the possible addition of perimeter fin-tube radiation.

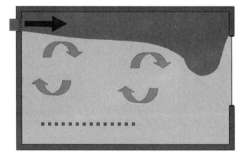

HEATING

HEAT LOSS AT THE WINDOW MIGHT NOT BE ADEQUATELY CONTROLLED

WITH BOTH LIMITED
GLASS AREA AND
DOUBLE GLAZING, THE
PROBLEM IS NOT
SIGNIFICANT

HEATING - SMALL DOUBLE-GLAZED WINDOW

IF THE PROBLEM IS
SIGNIFICANT, CONSIDER
USING A SPLIT SYSTEM

Figure 10.83 HIGH WALL OUTLET ALTERNATIVES
Using a high wall SA outlet in a space that has a major heat loss
can be problematic. A split system might be useful to counteract
the cold downdraft and provide radiant output to balance the MRT.

HEATING - LARGE SINGLE-GLAZED WINDOW

When sidewall outlets are located lower on the wall, the ceiling effect is not available and the length of throw is reduced considerably. If the outlets need to be lower, they still should be located above the occupied zone to avoid serious draft problems, especially since this arrangement also generally requires a longer throw. For this condition, a punca drum outlet is a reasonable selection to provide discharge control.

While sidewall outlets are an effective way to supply air into a space for both heating and cooling, there are some limitations if the heating load is considerable. If that is the situation, then a split system is recommended (see Figure 10.83).

A split system is a combination of an air system, used for cooling and ventilation and limited heating, and a hydronic perimeter system, used for heating. This system, which was formerly considered inappropriate due to its lack of "purity," is actually very effective. While cooling is not generally required if the space is unoccupied, heating is required when temperatures are low. Not only must the space remain above freezing if any water is present, but many materials start to deteriorate and condensation becomes a problem at temperatures below 45° F to 50° F. With a split system, the hydronic heating operates to maintain adequate minimum interior temperatures, whether or not the space is occupied, and the air system is operated only when the space is occupied and is used to ventilate and "refine" the temperature.

While supplying the air from a high point on an interior wall can reasonably control a perimeter space, especially if it is combined with fin-tube radiation to handle major heat loss, perhaps a better location for the air supply in a perimeter space is the floor at the base of the exterior wall, preferably below the windows (see Figure 10.84). With the air discharged upward to bathe the wall, the gain and loss can be controlled where they occur. During heat loss, this will also counteract any cold drafts that are dropping down. This is why perimeter fan-coil units and induction units are effective in controlling both heat gain and heat loss in a perimeter space.

As discussed for fan-coil units with central fresh air, supplying air from the floor typically requires penetrating the floor that provides a 2-hour fire separation. Also, since maintenance might be required on the ducts, if the lower floor is rented by another tenant, it might cause an imposition on this tenant. This problem can be avoided if the SA is run to the building's perimeter through a raised floor, or perhaps more easily by vertical supply distribution along the exterior wall (see Figure 10.85).

It is also possible to supply the air from the ceiling along the exterior wall (see Figure 10.85). While this will put control at the point of major gain and loss, it can create bothersome drafts, especially during the cooling cycle, and will not be very effective for heating. However, with a split system or at least a heated floor below, the settling of cold air off of the exterior wall can be ameliorated. Also, with the distinction between heating and cooling, it makes sense to alter the discharge pattern to reduce the downdraft that is developed with cold air.

Rather than direct high-velocity SA downward, a better solution in terms of ceiling supply is to diffuse the air across the ceiling (see Figures 10.86 and 10.87).

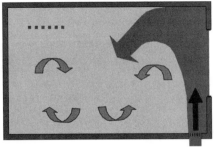

COOLING

HEATING

Figure 10.84 PERIMETER FLOOR OUTLET

Providing perimeter heating and cooling by an air system is most effective in terms of year-round control of the gain and loss and the room air distribution if the SA is discharged from the floor at the base of the exterior walls, particularly below window openings. However, this is often problematic since it probably requires penetrating the 2-hour rated floor construction and can impose on the occupants of the floor below if duct maintenance is necessary.

Spreading cool air across the ceiling and allowing it to settle down into the room works quite well for cooling interior spaces, and as a result, it is the method of supply that is usually used for interior spaces. It is also the preferred way to supply large volumes of air into a space since the distribution pattern can spread the air across 360°.

Ceiling diffusion is effective for cooling since the natural convective currents work in conjunction with the desired air circulation, but this method is not successful for heating. Since the density of warm air is less than the density of RA, the SA tends to remain at the top of the space. As a result, while ceiling diffusion might be effective for cooling and ventilating, it is not a good choice for heating perimeter spaces. If there are no interior walls that can accommodate a sidewall supply, ceiling diffusion might be an acceptable means of heating if it is augmented with perimeter radiation that operates when the exterior temperatures drop or the loads are nominal. This also assumes that the SA is distributed through a lowered ceiling, perhaps from a rooftop air-handling unit. This is a standard condition for many commercial spaces, which provide an added justification for ceiling diffusion—slab on grade.

When ceiling diffusion is used in an extended space that includes both an internal and perimeter zone, separate SA zones are required (see Figure 10.87). Even without a physical separation, once a space is around 20 feet from the building exterior, it essentially becomes an interior zone, requiring only cooling year round. However, the perimeter portion of the space needs to be conditioned in response to

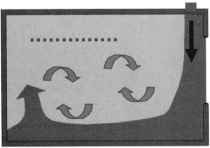

WITHOUT COOLING ADJUSTMENT
COOLING

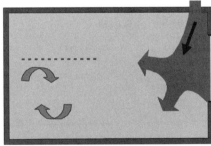

WITH COOLING ADJUSTMENT

Figure 10.85 PERIMETER CEILING OUTLET

When it is not feasible to supply air from below, it might be reasonable to provide perimeter heating and cooling from an air system by supplying the air from the ceiling along the exterior wall. This approach can result in unfortunate drafts since the air is discharged downward in a fairly tight pattern, although the problem is somewhat ameliorated by allowing reduced airflow when the space is above another conditioned space and there is no significant heat loss, particularly through glazing. Also, during cooling, the discharge should be adjusted to provide more diffusion and redirection across the ceiling.

HEATING

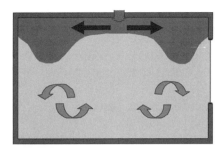

COOLING

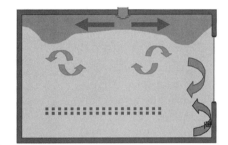

HEATING

WITH A CEILING DIFFUSER
AND LARGE GLAZED
EXPOSURES, PERIMETER
HEAT LOSS CANNOT BE
ADEQUATELY CONTROLLED

CONSIDER USING
A SPLIT SYSTEM

Figure 10.86 CEILING OUTLET IN A PERIMETER SPACE
The ceiling is the preferred location for SA discharge for interior spaces that have no heat loss. By spreading cool air across the ceiling, the air can slowly drop down and control the heat gain. However, good as ceiling diffusion is for cooling an interior space, it is not effective for heating a perimeter space.

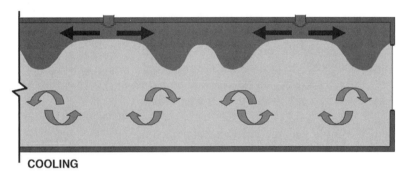

COOLING

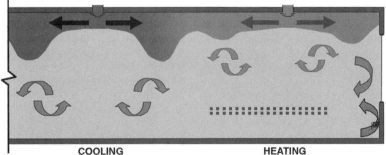

COOLING   HEATING
HEATING WITH INTERIOR ZONE COOLING

SPLIT
SYSTEM

Figure 10.87 CEILING OUTLET FOR A PERIMETER AND INTERIOR SPACE
When ceiling diffusers are used to supply a space that extends from the building's perimeter well into the interior, the diffusers handling the perimeter portion for a depth of up to around 20 feet should be in a separate zone.

the external loads on the space, which at times requires heating rather than cooling, which also will probably have to respond to heat gains that are different from those in the internal zone.

While a number of SA outlets might be required for proper air distribution within a space, often only one return air inlet is necessary, and as previously mentioned, the location of the return air grill does not have an impact on the distribution of the SA. If no return air is provided within a space, there could be a problem on the supply side. Unless air is removed, the pressure in the space could build up, impeding the release of the air supply.[14] Some means should be provided to allow for return or exhaust of the RA. While a return air grill is preferred, sometimes it is necessary to install a door louver or undercut the door to allow the RA to get to the return.

---

[14]The problem here is excessive pressurization. Some pressurization can be effective in reducing infiltration, but there is an assumption that the air left in the space exfiltrates through cracks and openings, avoiding excessive pressurization that could cut off the SA.

Displacement Ventilation

Conventional air systems are sometimes referred to as *mixed flow* since they mix the conditioned SA with the RA, relying predominantly on the difference in temperature between SA and RA. A relatively new method takes a slightly different approach called *displacement ventilation*. Figures 10.88 and 10.89 show the differences between conventional air supply and displacement ventilation.

Displacement ventilation is used predominantly for cooling in an interior zone. Cool ventilation air is supplied, generally from below through a raised floor, to control only the environment that immediately surrounds the occupants, allowing natural convection and perhaps radiant cooling to achieve comfort conditions. The air that is supplied is conditioned outside air to meet the ventilation requirements and to bathe the occupants in cooler air. This air is heated by the heat loss from the occupants and then rises to the ceiling, where it is collected and exhausted to the outside. As with fan-coil units with centrally supplied ventilation air or with induction units, there is no return air with a displacement ventilation system. It has also been suggested that indirect lighting be used with this approach. In this arrangement, the light is directed toward the ceiling, which is a radiant cooling panel; as a result, both the radiant and convective heat output from the lighting is controlled.

Displacement ventilation is an intriguing approach to environmental control. However, while it can certainly reduce the volume of air that has to be circulated, which can result in a major energy saving, it does have limitations.

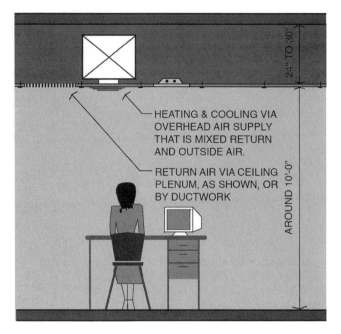

Figure 10.88 CONVENTIONAL MIXED-FLOW ENVIRONMENTAL CONTROL
Conventional mixed-flow environmental control supplies around 1 CFM per square foot, of which 20% is usually ventilation air and 80% is air that was returned from the space. With an economizing cycle, if the outside air is closer to the SA conditions, FA will be used rather than return air from the room. Also, when the building is not occupied, no FA is supplied, again unless it is closer to the SA conditions.

For one thing, with radiant panel cooling, the humidity level in the space must be fairly low. This should cause no discomfort if the relative humidity does not have to be less than around 25%, but to maintain such low humidity in many locations during the warmer periods of the year, the

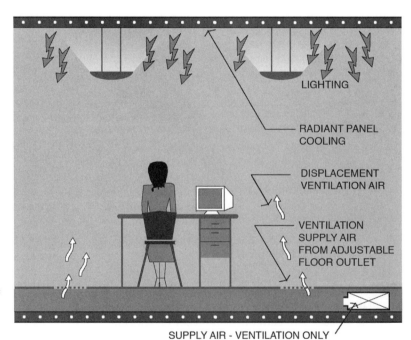

Figure 10.89 DISPLACEMENT VENTILATION ENVIRONMENTAL CONTROL
Displacement ventilation is an interesting approach to environmental control for an interior space that does not have a high latent load. When only ventilation air is circulated, the SA volume is only around 20% of the volume of air circulated in a conventional air system. Since this system also includes a radiant panel essentially for cooling, it is basically a version of a split system. Although some claim that it can also be used for heating, the basic application is for interior zones that typically have no heat loss and demand cooling at all times.

building must be sealed. This means that there cannot be any operable windows.

Sealed Buildings

Unfortunately, sealing the building is not merely a necessity for displacement ventilation. It is also a requirement for most high-rise structures that rely on central air distribution, although this requirement is based in part on how the systems are designed and engineered. As has been discussed, effective movement of air within an air distribution system is based on establishing the proper amount of pressure. Of course, this relates to the sizing of fans, but it is also connected to the height of a fin-tube radiation unit. If adding 4 inches to the height of a fin-tube enclosure can develop a stack effect that can increase the output by approximately 25%, a 10-story building can create a considerable stack effect.

A stack effect is based on a difference in the atmospheric pressure at the top and bottom of a vertical shaft. However, if the shaft is not exposed to variations in atmospheric pressure, the effect is controlled. The way to avoid variations in atmospheric pressure is to seal the building. When windows are open on different floors that are connected, a pressure differential will be developed. If we have ever waited in the lobby for an elevator in a high-rise building when the exterior doors were open, we probably have experienced the draft that can be produced.

Keeping a building sealed reduces the potential for problems resulting from the stack effect. This is one reason that revolving doors were developed—to allow people to enter and leave a building without opening a door and permitting air infiltratration. While vestibules are supposedly an alternative way to maintain a sealed building entry, unfortunately there generally is nothing that prohibits both doors being open at the same time. Hence the frequently seen sign: "Please use the revolving doors."

In a multistory structure with operable windows, various windows will be opened and closed, and the pressures within the building will vary each time this happens. These changes in pressure can wreak havoc on an air system that moves air between different floor levels. Unfortunately, a standard response is to seal the building, which means that the occupants must rely on mechanical control to maintain comfort. Even if the outside conditions are comfortable, many major buildings cannot enjoy the natural potential. In a sense, ECS create their own necessity.

It is possible to adjust the fan to respond to variations in pressure with advanced controls, but since the problem relates to distributing the air vertically across a number of floors, an alternative response might be to zone the air system horizontally. Limiting the number of floor served by the same air distribution systems can minimize, if not eliminate, the trouble presented by changes in the stack effect. With this approach, operable windows can again provide an opportunity to improve environmental conditions.

SA Duct Turns

There is a pressure loss in moving air through a duct, some of which comes from the resistance to moving the air in a contained duct. Some of this loss is the result of the friction between the duct and the laminar flow of the air, but much of it is from turbulence within the duct. In contrast to laminar flow, which is smooth and regular movement of a liquid or a gas, turbulence occurs when the air movement is agitated or irregular; this happens when there are duct transitions or changes in direction.

When an SA duct turns a corner, there tends to be considerable turbulence unless special devices to turn the air are provided. Without such devices, the air flows around the corner only because it strikes the sides of the duct and is deflected back. As the air bounces off the duct, it collides with oncoming air. Since the only path it can continue on is around the corner, the air does move on, but only after a great deal of crossover or turbulence, which produces considerable resistance or static loss (see Figure 10.90).

One way to attempt to minimize this turbulence is to use a long-sweep elbow, which generally has an inside turning radius equal to 1.5 times the width of the duct. However, while the curved sides of the duct tend to deflect the air in the direction of the turn, the various streams of air must still cross over each other. A long-sweep elbow with

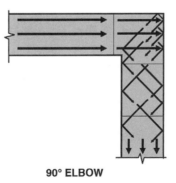

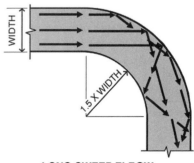

Figure 10.90 TWO OPTIONS FOR A 90° DUCT TURN
A 90° duct turn produces a great deal of turbulence. While the long-sweep elbow was developed to reduce turbulence, as can be seen in this diagram, the change of direction occurs for essentially the same reason that it does in the sharp 90° elbow—the air bounces off the sides of the duct. In both elbows, this forces the various air streams to cross over each other, which is a good example of turbulence.

90° ELBOW   **LONG-SWEEP ELBOW**

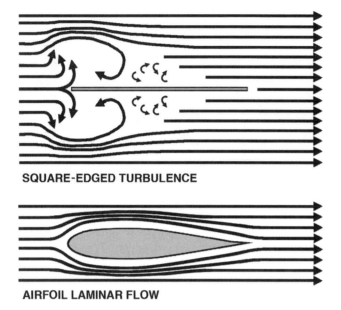

SQUARE-EDGED TURBULENCE

AIRFOIL LAMINAR FLOW

Figure 10.91 SQUARE-EDGED VERSUS AIRFOIL VANE
Even though it results in a wider vane, the airfoil design gradually deflects and redirects the air, reducing the turbulence as the air flows over an obstruction.

turning vanes further reduces turbulence by dividing the initial air stream into several narrow streams, although there is still some crossover within each pathway. With airfoil turning vanes, the turbulence can be further reduced since interference with laminar flow also results from the turning vanes themselves.

Portions of the initial air stream hit the square-edged end of the turning vanes and are deflected. While we might assume that the thin metal will not affect the airflow, the thin end of the metal deflects the air, creating turbulence. Beyond the end of the obstruction, as a result of the deflection of the air, the pressure is lowered, which causes some air to actually turn around. While it is considerably wider than a thin square-edged vane, the airfoil vane gradually deflects the air, and although the air is compressed, it retains laminar flow. These different conditions of airflow are diagrammed in Figure 10.91.

With the width of the airfoil vane and the imposed compression of the air stream, the air must travel faster, which means that some of the static air pressure is converted into velocity pressure. If the airfoil is irregular and the compression on the top is greater than on the bottom, more static pressure on the top of the airfoil is converted to velocity, resulting in uplift from the higher static pressure below the airfoil. This is the principle that the Wright brothers used to develop the first successful airplane.

Airfoil turning vanes create less turbulence than that resulting from the end of the flat turning vanes, but there is still the problem of air stream crossover. The turbulence from the crossover can be significantly lowered by reducing the size of the airfoil turning vanes and increasing their number. Also, since these smaller airfoil vanes are mass-produced and assembled in a set, rather than having to use long-sweep elbows, we can stay with a 90° elbow that includes a series of airfoil turning vanes. This will not only minimize the air turbulence, it will also likely cost less and require less space for duct installation (see Figure 10.92).

Air-Handling Units

In an air system, the air-handling unit is the device used to condition and distribute the SA. Figure 10.93 shows a schematic diagram of a draw-through air-handling unit. The air inlet to an air-handling unit usually is a mixing box in which return air and FA can be mixed. The air then passes through a filter, which is often placed in a zigzag pattern in order to increase the surface area and thereby reduce the velocity of the air stream. Another technique is to configure the filters in the shape of bags, a method that also reduces air velocity to increase the capture of particulate matter. Flat filters are also used, especially in residential systems. Filtration can also be provided by water sprays or by electronic filters that rely on an electrostatic charge to capture particulate matter. Devices intended to control odors, typically involving some sort of charcoal filter, might also be included.

Figure 10.92 TURNING VANES IN A 90° DUCT TURN
Adding turning vanes can reduce the crossover of the air streams and the turbulence that the crossover causes. By using airfoil turning vanes and increasing their number, turbulence can be further reduced. This also allows for a 90° duct turn, which reduces the required amount of space and typically costs less than fabricating the long-sweep turns.

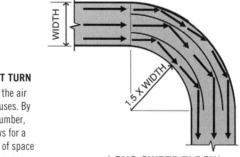

LONG-SWEEP ELBOW WITH TURNING VANES

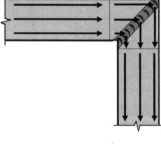

90° ELBOW WITH AIRFOIL TURNING VANES

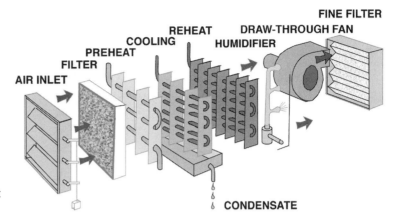

Figure 10.93 SCHEMATIC DRAW-THROUGH AIR-HANDLING UNIT

This is a schematic of the elements included in most air-handling units: air inlet or mixing box, filter, preheat coil, cooling coil, reheat coil, humidifier, and fan.

Heating and cooling coils are located downstream from the filter to avoid clogging the small openings in the coils. The coils are usually sized so that the air velocity across the face of the coil does not exceed 500 FPM. In cold regions, the first coil is typically a preheat coil that generally operates only when temperatures drop to a level where freezing might occur. This avoids exposing the cooling coils to temperatures that might freeze the water within. A bypass might also be provided so that, on the cooling cycle, only a portion of the SA is cooled, avoiding the need for reheat.

There are basically two types of air-handling units: *draw-through* and *blow-through*. These terms refer to whether the fan draws or blows the air through the unit. If the fan draws the air through, then all the air is mixed together in the fan. As a result, a draw-through unit can supply only one condition of air (see Figure 10.94). A blow-through unit can supply different conditions of air at the same time since the fan blows the air through the various control elements. When a blow-through unit supplies different conditions, it is a multizone air-handling unit (see Figure 10.95). There are different ways in which a multizone unit can be configured. Each zone might have its own coils, which would allow for heating or cooling in each zone, or the division of the zones might only relate to how the air is circulated.

The blow-through unit can also be configured with a double deck, which places the cooling coil above the heating coil.[15] In this way, the SA can be directed through the bypass, the cooling coil, or the heating coil, or in some proportion through each (see Figure 10.96). This increases the flexibility of a multizone, blow-through unit. The double-

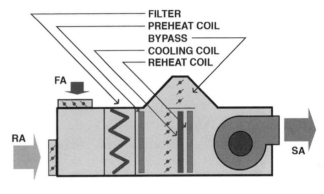

Figure 10.94 DRAW-THROUGH AIR-HANDLING UNIT

In a draw-through air-handling unit, the fan is placed at the end of the unit, drawing the air through the various control elements and discharging the air into the SA duct. Since the fan mixes all of the air, this unit can only supply one condition of air in terms of temperature and humidity.

deck unit can also supply a double-duct air system (see Figure 10.97).

A double-duct air system includes a warm air and a chilled air supply that are mixed at the point of use. This is similar to the way water temperatures are controlled at a sink faucet. With the possibility of different SA temperatures, a double-duct system can effectively meet a range of heating and cooling demands. For this reason, the same SA ducts often handle both interior and exterior zones. Since interior zones generally require only cooling, the SA ducts from a double-deck unit are often sized differently, with the chilled air duct at 100% capacity of the unit and the warm air duct at around 60%. This reduced percentage is somewhat related to the percentage of space that is in a perimeter zone and will require heating during a portion of the year, although some warm air might also be used to adjust for variations in the cooling loads in the interior zone.

While the velocity of air passing over heating and cooling coils should not exceed 500 FPM, the fan discharge velocity is typically around 2000 to 3000 FPM. As a

---

[15]When some of the air might pass through both coils, the cooling coil should be installed above the heating coil. This will ensure better mixing of the discharge air. With a major difference in temperature, the two streams of air will have different densities, which can maintain separation of the air streams. If the discharge splits shortly after leaving the air-handling unit, with some air going up and some down, it is possible that the upstream air will be warm while the downstream air will be chilled. Placing the cooling coil above the heating coil uses the density variations to help mix the air streams.

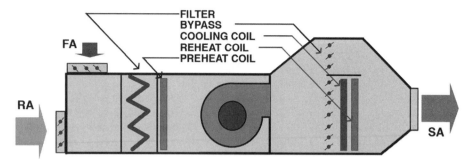

Figure 10.95 BLOW-THROUGH AIR-HANDLING UNIT
This is a blow-through air-handling unit, although the appropriate length for the convergence and divergence of the air stream is not shown. Since the fan is located before the coils and the bypass, it is possible to supply various conditions of air. The unit therefore has the potential to be a multizone air-handling unit that can supply up to 12 different air conditions.

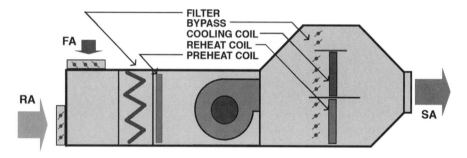

Figure 10.96 DOUBLE-DECK BLOW-THROUGH AIR-HANDLING UNIT
This is a blow-through air-handling unit similar to the unit shown in Figure 10.95 but with the discharge divided into two SA ducts. One duct carries chilled air and the other carries warm air.

result, space must be provided to accommodate a transition of the cross-sectional area of the air stream between the fan and the coils in a blow-through unit. Generally, to avoid excessive turbulence, the transition in the cross-sectional area of the air stream should be at an angle of 30° or less. Space must also be allocated after the coils to reduce the 500 FPM cross-sectional area of the air stream to the area of the air-handling unit discharge, which is 1000 FPM for a low-pressure system and 2000 to 3000 FPM in a high-pressure system. Space must also be provided to

allow the air to transition to the fan inlet. Since the air passing through a blow-through unit must transition into the fan, then from the fan to the coils, and then from the coils to the SA duct, blow-through units are longer than draw-through units, in which the air stream only has to transition from the coils to the fan inlet.

Although it is larger, there are advantages to a blow-through unit. If the fan blows the air through an air-handling unit, the unit can provide various conditions of SA. If more than one condition of SA is provided at the

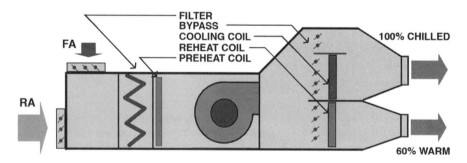

Figure 10.97 DOUBLE-DUCT, DOUBLE-DECK BLOW-THROUGH AIR-HANDLING UNIT
The double-deck air-handling unit can supply a double-duct air system. Since the volume of SA will be constant, relying on the various mixtures of warm and chilled air to provide the appropriate supply temperatures to match the different room loads, only one fan is required. As a result, the volume of air distributed in each of the ducts will vary. Based on these conditions and depending on the room loads, the chilled air duct might distribute 40% to 100% of the SA volume, while the warm air duct will usually carry 0% to 60% of the SA volume.

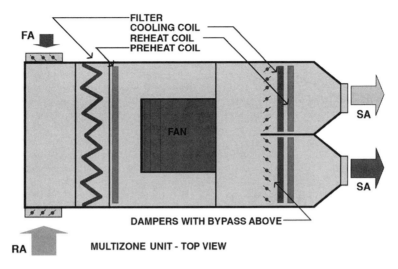

Figure 10.98 TOP VIEW OF A MULTIZONE AIR-HANDLING UNIT
While this diagram shows only two zones, a multizone unit can supply up to 12 different zones.

same time, the unit is called a *multizone air-handling unit*. Typically, one multizone unit can supply up to 12 different air conditions, but only with a blow-through unit. A draw-through unit ends with the fan, so all the air from the unit is mixed together and only one SA condition is possible.

The coils in a multizone air-handling unit can have different sections for the different zones. If the heating and cooling coils are arranged in a double-deck configuration, as shown in Figure 10.96, different conditions of SA can be achieved by arranging the ducting and dampers so that different paths of airflow can be provided for each zone. Without the double deck, separate coils are usually required for each zone.

Air-handling units are also available either as packaged units or as built-up units. In part, the decision on which to use is based on the ability to transport the air-handling unit to the construction site. With a built-up unit, the various components are assembled together at the construction site. However, while a number of components can be assembled at the site, the fan cannot. So, the largest fan tends to determine the maximum capacity of a built-up unit.

Regulations tend to restrict the maximum size of items transported on interstate highways to 12 feet wide and 12 feet high. Based on various manufacturers' data, a centrifugal fan that has a diameter of 12 feet and is 12 feet wide would have a maximum capacity of around 100,000 CFM. Since the rule of thumb suggests that six to eight air changes of SA, which converts to around 1 CFM per square foot of conditioned space, are required, a built-up air-handling unit with one fan could condition around 100,000 square feet of space. While a built-up unit could have two or more fans, there is not much reason to have such a large unit.

If a packaged unit is used, which has become the norm, the largest unit, which is again based on transportation limitations, can supply around 25,000 CFM, which can condition approximately 25,000 square feet of space. One advantage of packaged units is that they are usually encased in a weather enclosure that allows them to be installed on the roof, which precludes the need to construct building volume in which to locate the air-handling unit.

Multizone Air System

While separate air-handling units could be provided for each zone, as mentioned above, one multizone air-handling unit can provide different conditions of SA. But whether separate air-handling units or one multizone unit is used, each zone requires its own SA distribution duct. Figure 10.98 shows a possible arrangement of a multizone air-handling unit capable of supplying air for two different zones.

Generally, up to 12 different zones can be supplied by one multizone blow-through air-handling unit. The different temperatures for each zone can be determined in several ways: by passing the air either across the heating or cooling coil or through the bypass, or by providing separate heating and cooling coils for each zone. Regardless of how the different temperature zones are established, each zone is provided with its own SA duct off of the multizone air-handling unit, but since all the return air is mixed through the same fan, a common air return is typically used. This common return might be merely the fan in the multizone unit or it might be a separate fan, which is be required with an economizing cycle.

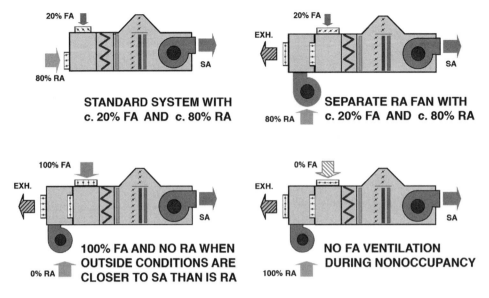

Figure 10.99 ECONOMIZING CYCLE DIAGRAMS

With a separate return air fan, the SA can vary from 100% FA and 0% RA to 0% FA and 100% RA. This flexibility, which is the essence of an economizing cycle, can provide significant energy savings.

Economizing Cycle

An economizing cycle adjusts the amount of outside air used in an air system (see Figure 10.99). Normally, when an air system is used for heating and cooling, most of the SA is conditioned RA that has been returned to the air-handling unit. The RA is recirculated since it is close to the SA conditions and usually requires less treatment than the outside air that is used for ventilation. However, if the outside air has a temperature and humidity that are closer to the SA conditions, it makes sense to use FA rather than the air returned from the room, but this means that a separate return-air fan must be provided. Even if the RA is not returned to the air-handling unit, it still needs to be removed from the room. Unless a volume of RA that is approximately equivalent to the volume of SA is removed from the space, the conditioned air cannot be supplied properly. Without removal of this air, the space would be pressurized, reducing the effective velocity pressure of the discharged air, which would lower the CFM of SA. With a separate return-air fan and adjustments to the mixing box in the air-handling unit, the SA can be comprised of 100% outside air.

In most nonresidential structures, SA is set at around six air changes per hour, with around one-sixth or 15% of the SA comprised of outside FA and around five-sixths or 85% comprised of return air, but the FA ventilation is required only when the buildings are occupied. When a building is not occupied, especially if the outside temperature and humidity are further removed from the SA conditions than the RA, it does not make sense to con-

tinue adding ventilation air to the SA. However, if no FA is included in the SA, the volume of SA would be reduced unless the volume of return air is increased, which usually requires a separate return air.

When the temperature and humidity of the outside air are closer than the temperature and humidity of the return air to the desired SA conditions, it makes sense to exhaust the return air and use 100% FA. This also requires a separate fan to extract air from the room and bring it to the air-handling unit where it can be exhausted or sent to the air-handling unit. That is, with a separate return-air fan and adjustable controls, it is possible to economize by using 100% FA, 100% return air, or a mixture of around 15% FA and 85% return air as the air supplied to the air-handling unit.

Warm Air Furnace

A furnace is a warm air heating device that is frequently used in residential structures. It typically includes a fan to move both the SA and return air, a basic filter to remove particulate matter from the air stream, and a direct combustion device, often a natural gas burner, although propane or oil can be used as the fuel (see Figure 10.100). When air conditioning is included, a DX coil is added in the bonnet or discharge duct of the furnace. A furnace is not a device to heat water, even in a residence. It is an air-handling unit with the capacity to generate its own heat source, and it might also be used as the motive force to move the air when cooling.

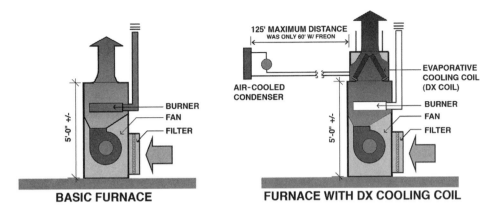

Figure 10.100 RESIDENTIAL FURNACE
The typical residential furnace is an air-handling unit that has a means of heat generation. If a DX coil is added, the unit can both heat and cool.

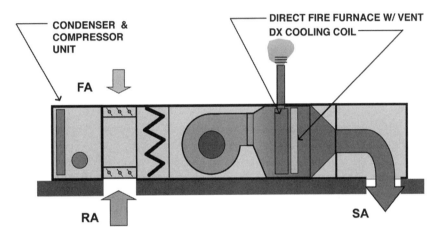

ROOFTOP AIR HANDLING UNIT - HEATING

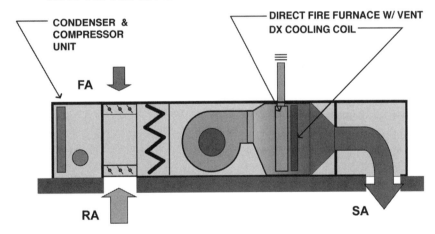

Figure 10.101 ROOFTOP AIR-HANDLING UNIT
The rooftop packaged air-handling unit has become a major means of providing environmental control in small nonresidential structures. Often the unit has a direct-fired heat generator, typically fueled by gas, and an attached refrigeration unit.

ROOFTOP AIR HANDLING UNIT - COOLING

Rooftop Packaged Air-Handling Unit

Figures 10.101 and 10.102 show various arrangements for packaged air-handling units that are designed for rooftop installation without the need for an architectural enclosure.

A packaged air-handling unit is an assembled unit that contains the essential components for conditioning the air. It can also come in a weather enclosure that allows the packaged unit to be located outside, typically on the roof. Such weather-enclosed, packaged air-handling units located on the roof have become a standard way of providing

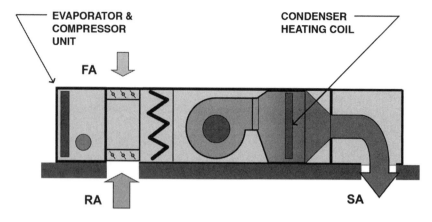

ROOFTOP AIR HANDLING HEAT PUMP UNIT - HEATING

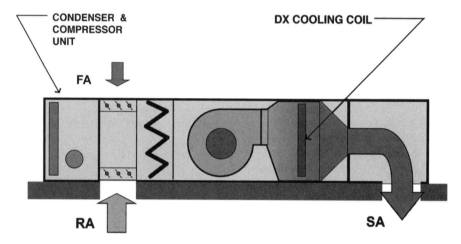

**Figure 10.102 ROOFTOP AIR-HANDLING
UNIT—HEAT PUMP**
Since rooftop air-handling units generally include
a refrigeration unit, it makes sense if this
refrigeration unit is configured as a heat pump.

ROOFTOP AIR HANDLING HEAT PUMP UNIT - COOLING

environmental control in small nonresidential structures. Generally, these units include a means of both heat generation and refrigeration. When refrigeration is included, it often makes sense to use a heat pump as the source for both heating and cooling.

AIR SYSTEM SUBZONE CONTROL

There are several ways of providing control for individual rooms or subzones with a central air system. While it is preferable to be able to control each individual space, at times several spaces are combined, establishing a subzone. When it is necessary to combine several rooms within a subzone, the combined spaces should have similar thermal characteristics; however, even when they do, it is difficult to ensure that proper control will be provided.

One approach is to provide a separate air-handling unit for each subzone. Fan-coil units and induction units, both

of which typically control only one room,[16] provide this control strategy, but at times, a small air-handling unit can be used to control a group of rooms. This method is often used in multifamily residential buildings that provide an individual air-handling unit, perhaps a direct-fired furnace, for each dwelling unit. This makes sense since most codes prohibit the exchange of air between dwelling units.

A multizone air-handling unit is another way to provide individual-room or subzone adjustments (see Figure 10.103). While each subzone is provided with SA that matches its loads, with this approach the air is supplied from a central source.

While zone control can be accomplished centrally through the use of separate units or a multizone unit, various terminal control devices are also available. There are basically three different methods to provide terminal control for an air distribution system: variable volume,

---

[16]Sometimes a single fan-coil unit can be extended to control more than one room. Generally, this merely requires adding an SA duct so that the discharge from the unit can be distributed to the second room.

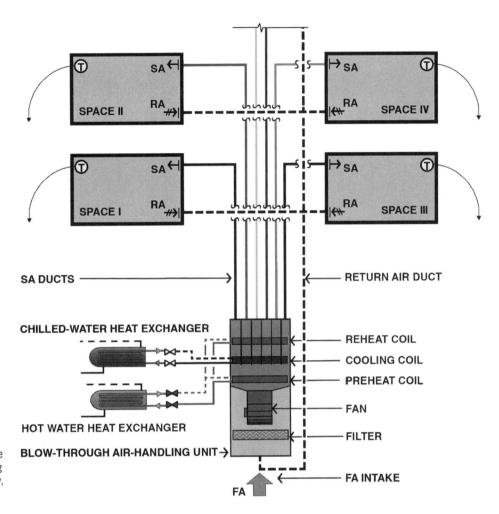

Figure 10.103 MULTIZONE SYSTEM DIAGRAM

This is a schematic diagram of a possible arrangement for a multizone air-handling unit. Each zone has a separate air supply, but all zones share a common return.

terminal reheat, and double duct. Variable volume and reheat systems are often combined and there are several different types of reheat, one of which uses the heat from the electric lights as the reheat source.

Terminal control refers to adjustment of the air conditions supplied from a central distribution run; the terminal control device is located just before the outlet or the branch duct for the space(s) to be conditioned. Often terminal control is used in larger structures for which a multizone unit cannot provide the number of zones that are required. Larger structures, especially those that do not have distributed air-handling capacity, generally require long runs for the air ducts, which probably need high-velocity air distribution. Since air is usually discharged into a space at around 1000 FPM, the terminal control unit is typically a means of reducing the velocity of the air, from around 2000 to 3000 FPM down to 1000 FPM. Since high-velocity air is noisy, the terminal control unit also provides sound attenuation.

Although we might assume that terminal control means that only one condition of distributed SA will work for all zones of a structure, terminal control is only in-

tended to adjust for minor variation in actual room loads. Terminal-control adjustments are limited, so the air supplied to the terminal unit should be appropriate for the particular building zone, relying on the terminal unit merely to temper this air for the specific conditions in the various subzones. As a result, with terminal control, separate air-handling units are assumed, one for each major zone. Of course, if the total area of the various zones has a combined floor area no larger than 25,000 square feet, a multizone air-handling unit might be used to supply the different zones, with terminal control providing adjustments for the particular requirements of each subzone.

Variable Air Volume System

Varying the SA volume is one of the basic ways to provide terminal control in an air distribution system (see Figure 10.104). Although this is a relatively simple and frequently used method of control, it cannot provide any adjustments to the SA conditions. Beyond having the air-handling unit establish a temperature and humidity based

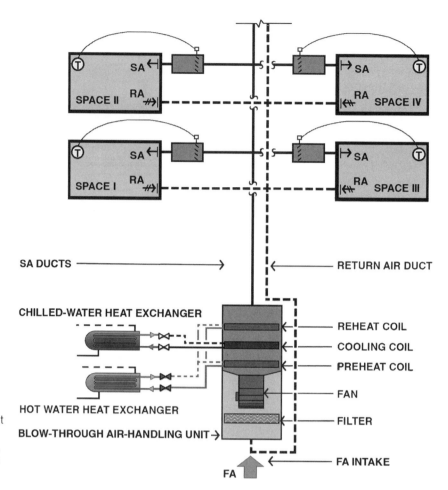

Figure 10.104 VARIABLE AIR VOLUME SYSTEM DIAGRAM
This is a schematic diagram of a possible arrangement for variable air volume terminal control. The terminal control units, which should include sound attenuation, can reduce the volume of SA when the space loads are less than the design maximum.

on the general demands of the zone it serves, the sole method of control with a variable air volume system is adjusting the amount of air being supplied into the various spaces. This system can only reduce or increase the amount of heating or cooling that will occur. At the terminal control point, it cannot adjust the SA temperature or humidity.

In the heating mode, the SA capacity is based on the assumed maximum heat loss, which presumes no heat gain from insolation, lights, or people. The expectation is that if any of these heat sources do exist in the space, the volume of the warm SA can be reduced. However, if there are no gains from people, which means that the space is unoccupied, we might wonder why the space needs to be heated, particularly to around 70° F, which is based on human comfort. During periods of nonoccupancy, temperatures of only around 50° F might be adequate, but there is an assumption that the space should be at the design conditions when it is first occupied.

If the system is capable of providing adequate heat, then when the space is occupied and the lights are turned on, the volume of air is reduced. Less air needs to be supplied since heat is now being contributed by the the people in the space. However, if the occupancy results in less warm air being supplied, then less ventilation air is also provided at a time when it becomes more necessary. Similarly, if the sun is allowed to penetrate into the space, less warm SA e is needed to achieve the design temperature. In addition, if the heat gain becomes excessive, a variable volume system includes no means of providing cooling.

For the cooling cycle, the basic volume of SA is based on the worst probable cooling load. In this case, it is assumed that there is solar gain, the lights are on, the equipment is running, and the space is fully occupied. If these cooling loads are not present, less air is supplied. On the cooling side, the reduction in SA volume does not tend to work against quality conditions, as it does with heating. As a result, variable volume terminal control is more effective for cooling than for heating.

While a variable air volume system can provide reasonable thermal control in a properly zoned structure, especially during the cooling cycle, in doing so it can alter the pattern of air distribution within the occupied space. The design of an air distribution system includes the selection of the air discharge device. This is usually through an air grill, which can be located in the ceiling; on the floor, usually along an exterior exposure; or on a wall, usually high on an interior wall. The size of the grill and its discharge pattern are based on the location of the grill and the volume of air to be supplied. If the amount of air changes, then the discharge pattern also will change. If there was an increase above the design volume, excessive noise and drafts would likely be established within the occupied zone. With a reduction in the volume of SA, the air might not reach the area it is intended to control and might drop into the occupied zone prematurely. In addition, with a changing volume, even if this does not cause thermal control problems or drafts, the fluctuation in noise and airflow can cause unacceptable distractions, to say nothing about the changing pressures in the major SA duct.

One method to avoid these potential problems is to use a variable volume system that has a pulsating supply. By providing the supply in rapid pulses of air rather than by a continuous air stream, the change in the volume of SA is accomplished by adjusting the pulse rate while maintaining a constant discharge velocity. By adjusting the pulses rather than the velocity, the air discharge pattern is essentially retained, and the distractions from the changing conditions are less noticeable. To operate properly, however, a pulsating system must include a means of returning to the air-handling unit any SA that is not discharged into the spaces. This requires special duct design.

While modern computer-based controls, connected to various sensing units, are able to adjust reasonably well to varying pressures in the SA in a variable air volume system, a simple mechanical method of adjusting to varying air pressure was developed a number of years ago by the Barber-Colman Company.[17] These adjustments are not only required with variable air volume terminal control, they are also necessary when balancing any air system. As one register is adjusted to provide a particular CFM supply, the pressures in the system change, altering the CFM from all other SA outlets. This is why balancing a system is critical and often quite difficult, and it is generally done by a specialist after the air system has been installed, shortly before occupancy (see Figure 10.105).

The device that Barber-Colman developed was a spring-controlled simple butterfly damper to be installed within an air duct. Theoretically, once the opening of the damper was set to provide the proper flow of air at normal pressure, any increase in the pressure would partially close the damper, which in turn would create more resistance equal to the increased pressure, thereby maintaining the prescribed CFM.

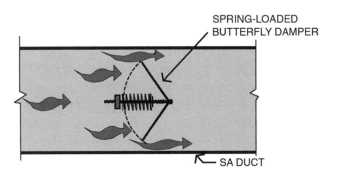

Figure 10.105 AUTOMATIC BALANCING DAMPER
This butterfly damper, developed by the Barber-Colman Company, provides a simple means of maintaining constant SA volumes with changing system pressure. When the amount of air discharged from an SA grill is adjusted, the pressure within the system is altered. If the total pressure increases, more air attempts to flow past the spring-loaded butterfly damper, but as it does so, the increased velocity pressure pushes against the blades of the damper, partially closing them. As the damper closes, it creates more resistance to airflow. If the system is properly designed, the increased resistance matches the unplanned increased velocity pressure, and the intended CFM flow is maintained.

Terminal Reheat System

When calculating the maximum heat loss, we normally assume that there are no solar or interior heat contributions; however, these normally do exist. On the other hand, when determining the maximum heat gain, solar and interior loads are included, although these might be less than what is assumed in the load calculations. In terms of solar gain, while the orientation, the season of the year, the time of day, and the weather conditions all help determine the maximum possible solar contribution, adjustable shading devices might affect the actual load. If the shading devices are adjustable, the expected maximum solar load might not actually exist. Similarly, while the calculations assumed an occupancy of a number of people, the space might actually be empty, which might also mean that the electric lights that were presumed to be on are not. So, it is possible that the interior loads, people, lights and equipment, and solar gain might not be as expected, thus requiring more or less heating during the winter season or more or less cooling during the summer season.

With a terminal reheat system, the central air-handling unit discharges air at a temperature that should be able to condition the spaces if all the probable heat-gain loads exist. If some or all of these gains are not present, the terminal reheat box adds the amount of heat (in BTU) that these loads would have imposed. This approach is very effective and efficient during the heating cycle. It can also provide nominal cooling concurrently with heating if the temperature of the centrally supplied air is less than the design RA temperature. If the common SA temperature is set at around 55° F to 65° F, cooling will occur if no

---

[17]The Barber-Colman Company is a major manufacturer of ceiling diffusers, registers, and grills used for air supply. Other manufacturers include Agitair, Krueger, Titus, and Tuttle & Bailey.

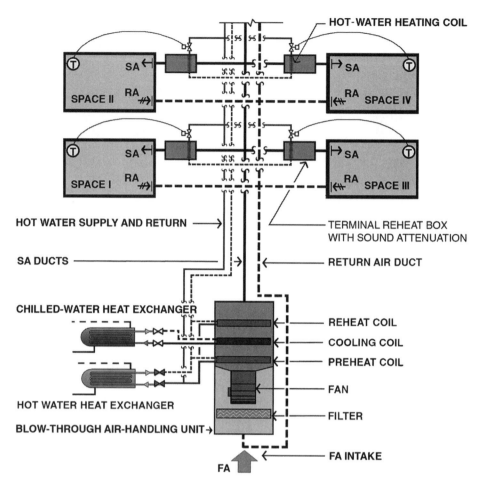

Figure 10.106 TERMINAL REHEAT SYSTEM DIAGRAM
This is a schematic diagram of a possible terminal reheat system. The terminal control units, which should include sound attenuation, can increase the temperature of the air supplied to the subzone.

additional heat is added in the terminal reheat box. That is, the basic approach with a terminal reheat system during the heating cycle is to discharge the air from the air-handling unit at a temperature that can do nominal cooling but is high enough so the terminal reheat boxes can achieve the warm air temperatures required to control the maximum calculated heat loss (see Figure 10.106).

During the cooling cycle in the overheated period of the year, terminal reheat can still offer effective thermal control, but it does so rather inefficiently since when a load does not exist, the reheat box adds the amount of heat that it was assumed would exist. Obviously, this is not efficient. For example, if the electric lights are on, it is expected that the SA can remove the heat that the lights release. If, on the other hand, the lights are off, the reheat box must add the heat that the lights would have emitted if they were on. So, instead of benefiting from turning off the lights, the cooling load remains constant. Similarly, even if there are venetian blinds, we cannot assume that the blinds will be adjusted to reduce the solar gain, so the solar gain

should be included in the heat gain calculations. If the occupants are energy conscious or perhaps just want to reduce the light level and close the blinds, the solar gain will be reduced. Unfortunately, the terminal reheat box now has to add heat to match the BTU of solar gain that the blinds block. Obviously, this suggests that the terminal reheat system is rather inefficient during the cooling cycle and justifies the fact that many states no longer permit terminal reheat to be used during the overheated period of the year. However, the system can effectively control the temperatures in the different spaces, and during the underheated period of the year it can do this quite efficiently.

Even with its inefficiency, with its ability to provide effective temperature control for individual spaces, terminal reheat sometimes remains the choice for year-round air conditioning when this control ability is required. This might include critical care areas in health facilities, such as operating rooms or labor and delivery rooms. It might also include spaces that have a very high ventilation load, especially laboratories that usually require 100% FA. Typically, during the overheated period of the year, it is necessary to lower the humidity of the FA; as discussed previously, this can be accomplished only by cooling the air well below the saturation curve. Sometimes this cold air is mixed with warmer air to arrive at the SA conditions, but when most or all of the air is to be dehumidified, there is no possibility of mixing the cold, dry air with any other air. That is, a reheat is required to achieve SA conditions. If so, it makes sense to provide this reheat in a terminal reheat box since this can also adjust for the demands of the individual spaces.

Interestingly, theaters and auditoriums might also legitimately use a terminal reheat system during all seasons of the year. These spaces have a high occupancy that establishes a high internal heat gain, both sensible and latent. During the underheated period of the year, while these spaces might require heating when not occupied, cooling is probably necessary when the spaces are occupied, even on the coldest days. The system might use outside air or chilled return air to provide the necessary cooling. If outside air is used during the underheated period, the air will probably need to be heated. So, in this instance, reheat would only mean adding more heat and not adding heat to compensate for energy expended to cool the air. That is, reheat would be additional heat rather than replacement heat.

If return air is used during times when the theater or auditorium is occupied, it will need to be dehumidified since half of the heat gained from the people is latent. Of course, there will also be a high ventilation requirement. If the two different air samples can be mixed to provide the desired SA conditions, then again, any reheat would be additional rather than replacement heat. If mixing the air samples is not effective and major cooling is required to develop the appropriate dehumidification, reheat will be required. Providing it at the terminal reheat box probably makes more sense then merely adding it through a reheat coil in the air-handling unit.

Once again, we should understand that some very logical and appropriate actions that make sense generally might not be reasonable for all situations. And the corollary also is true: things that are usually inappropriate and illogical might have legitimate applications.

The heat source used in the terminal reheat box can be steam, hot water, or electric resistance heating. If water is used, then it should be possible to distribute chilled water and develop a reheat/recool system that would not have the same inefficiency as the reheat system during the cooling cycle. Of course, special temperature controls would also be required (see Figure 10.107). With a terminal reheat/recool system, there is a potential for producing condensation during recooling, which would require special coils and a way to drain the condensate. However, if the central air-handling unit supplies air with a specific humidity that is less than the specific humidity that matches the DPT of the lowest temperature that the recool box can develop, condensation should not be a problem. If this is accomplished, there should be no condensation in the terminal box and the same coil can be used for heating and cooling.

Combined Terminal Reheat and Variable Air Volume System

The combination of terminal reheat and variable air volume in one system can provide reasonable control of the SA conditions that is both energy efficient and responsive to varying heating and cooling demands. With such a system, the reheat is used during the heating cycle, and the variable air volume is used during the cooling cycle. As with the conventional terminal reheat system, during the normal heating cycle, the main SA temperature is set at a minimum that would provide adequate control assuming a minimum demand for heating, such as might occur if the space were fully occupied with all lights on. If these heat gains are not present, the heating coil will open, providing additional heat so that the SA temperature and volume match the calculated maximum heat loss. During the cooling cycle, rather than operate the reheat, the variable air volume system takes over. In the cooling cycle, if the demand is less than the maximum calculated load, the volume of SA is merely reduced. Since lower occupancy means less internal heat gain, the volume of SA, which also means the amount of ventilation air, is reduced when there are fewer people present. While an adjustment in the volume of SA resulting from changes in occupancy might be a problem during the heating cycle, it does not have the same implications during the cooling cycle. During the cooling cycle, the reduction in SA volume occurs when there are fewer occupants, which means that the requirements for FA ventilation are in sync with the adjustments of the SA volume (see Figure 10.108).

With all air systems, but especially with the combined reheat and variable air volume system, proper zoning and controls are required for effective operation. Without these critical elements, the "opposing" sides of the system tend to compete against each other. While this probably would not result in the same inefficiencies as those of the standard reheat system when used for year-round control, it would tend to reduce the interior comfort level.

Terminal Induction Air System

The terminal induction air system is similar to the terminal reheat system, but rather than rely on a heating

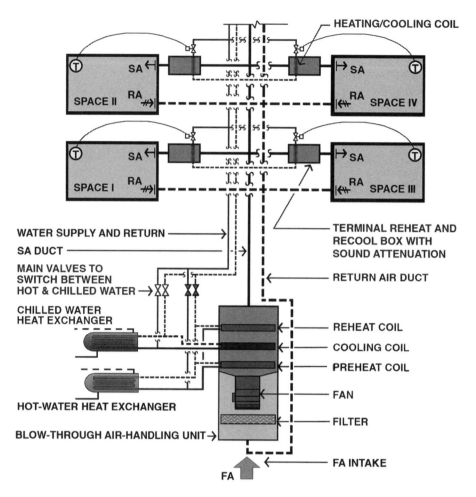

Figure 10.107 REHEAT/RECOOL SYSTEM DIAGRAM

This is a schematic diagram of a theoretical arrangement for terminal control that can both reheat and recool. In both situations, the main SA would be distributed at the temperature required to control the heat loss or heat gain load, assuming no internal loads—electric lighting, equipment, people, or direct solar gain that can be controlled with internal shading devices. During the heating cycle, the reheat box will make up for any gains that do not exist by adding additional heat. During the cooling cycle, if potentially variable internal loads do exist, the terminal box will add additional cooling to handle them.

system to provide the source for reheat, it utilizes an existing, available heat source—the interior electric lights. The RA is pulled through the fluorescent fixtures, where it is heated to around 95° F, providing a warm air source that can mix with the SA to increase its temperature (see Figure 10.109).

The lighting required for interior space accounts for considerable heat gain. With a lighting level of around 75 to 100 foot-candles, this could easily result in 2 to 4 watts of heat gain per square foot of space (see Table 10.3). This would convert into approximately 6 to 12 BTUH per square foot, or 1 ton of air conditioning (12,000 BTUH) for every 500 to 1000 square feet. In order to control just this lighting load within the space, it is necessary to circulate around 1 CFM of SA at a temperature 20° F below the RA temperature. (A 20° F ΔT is the standard temperature differential between the SA and the RA for cooling.)

BTUHsensible equals the product of the volume of air, the weight of air per cubic foot, the specific heat of air, and the temperature change in ° F. This converts into:

$$BTUH_{sensible} = CFH \times 0.018 \times \Delta T° \text{ F}$$

$$CFH = \frac{BTUH_{sensible}}{0.018 \times \Delta T° \text{ F}}$$

$$BTUH_{sensible} = CFM \times 1.08 \times \Delta T° \text{ F}$$

$$CFM = \frac{BTUH_{sensible}}{1.08 \times \Delta T° \text{ F}}, \text{ so}$$

$$\frac{6 BTUH_{sensible}}{1.08 \times 20° \text{ F}} \approx 0.3 \text{ CFM and } \frac{12 BTUH_{sensible}}{1.08 \times 20° \text{ F}} \approx 0.6 \text{ CFM}$$

If the return air is pulled out of the room through the light fixtures, most of the heat generated by these fixtures

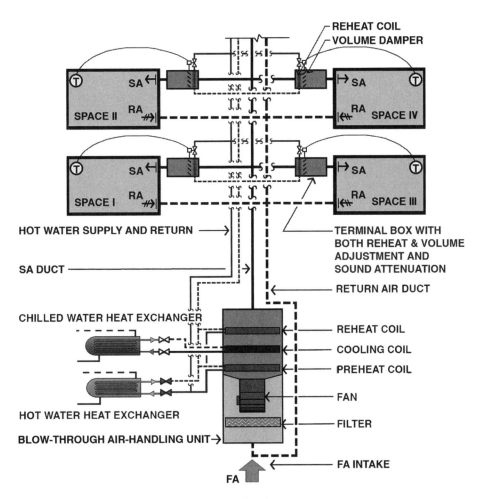

Figure 10.108 TERMINAL REHEAT AND VARIABLE AIR VOLUME SYSTEM DIAGRAM
This is a schematic diagram of an arrangement for terminal control that combines terminal reheat and variable air volume. The operation of this combined system relies on reheat during the heating cycle and variable air volume during the cooling cycle, thereby taking advantage of the attributes of each approach to SA control.

will be "absorbed." While the air removed from the room is at the RA conditions at about 75° F, whether it goes into the return air duct directly or initially passes through the lighting fixtures, if the air travels through the fixtures, it can easily reach 90° F to 95° F. This results in an effective temperature differential between the supply and return air that could be as much as 40° F. This would reduce the volume of air that has to be circulated to control the total cooling load. In addition, with the air passing through the fixture, the lighting efficacy is improved since fluorescent lights have the highest efficacy when the exterior bulb temperature is around 110° F.

Terminal induction requires light fixtures that are specially designed so that the RA can be pulled across the fluorescent lamps. These fixtures need to be installed at the bottom of a plenum, which is essentially an open area above the ceiling. Typically, a plenum or plenum chamber is a contained space through which air can flow. In a sense, it is a large air duct that usually has

a number of connections to different air passages, but other than these intended linkages, the plenum should be sealed.

Rather than supply air directly into a main duct and then take off the various distribution ducts from this main, a home furnace typically discharges the heated air into a plenum, which is also called the *bonnet*. The distribution ducts are attached to the plenum, and because the plenum is pressurized, the SA makes its way into the ducts. In this approach, distinct air streams are established without the need for complicated ductwork. In a sense, the pressurized air that pushes against the plenum's surfaces forms the pathways that direct the airflow.

Furnace plenums have a positive internal pressure, but the terminal induction air system relies on a ceiling plenum with negative pressure. As a result, if the ceiling is lay-in acoustical tile in an exposed-tee suspension system, special hold-down clips are usually required to keep the negative pressure from lifting the ceiling tiles. Also, the plenum

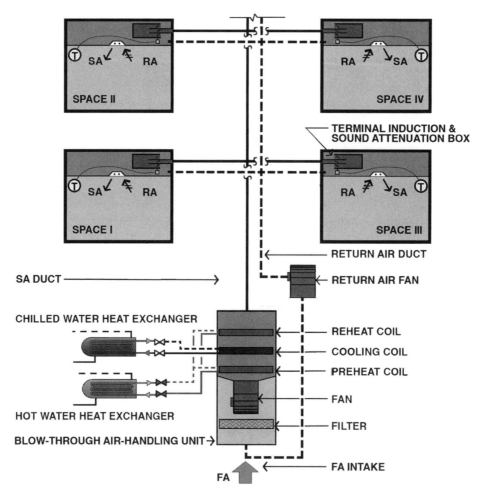

Figure 10.109 TERMINAL INDUCTION AIR SYSTEM DIAGRAM

This is a schematic diagram of a terminal induction air system. This is essentially a terminal reheat system, but rather than rely on a heating coil, terminal induction uses the heat from fluorescent light fixtures to provide heat. The room air, at around 75° F, is pulled through the light fixtures. By removing heat from the lamps, the efficiency of the lamps (efficacy) is increased and a source of "reheat" air is provided. If the SA requires additional heat, the heated room/return air is induced through the terminal induction box.

has to be common to a number of spaces; although not indicated in Figure 10.109, this is shown in Figure 10.110.

With terminal induction boxes installed in an air plenum that connects various spaces, the warm air emitted by the different lighting fixtures provides an air source that can be used for reheat if it is induced into those terminal induction boxes that call for an SA temperature higher than the temperature of the centrally distributed air. The temperature of the air emitted from an induction box will depend on the relative volumes of the centrally supplied air and the induced air and their temperatures.

The terminal induction air system provides considerable energy efficiency. As mentioned, the air that passes through the light fixtures lowers the temperature of the fluorescent lamps, which increases their light output. When the fluorescent lamps are cooled, the air is heated

to around 95° F, which means that the effective return air temperature is about 20° F warmer than the typical 75° F. Since the SA is around 55° F, the effective temperature differential is 40° F rather than the standard 20° F, which means that less air needs to be circulated to control the heat gain. In addition to allowing a reduction in the volume of air that needs to be circulated, the higher temperature of the return air can be used for reheat, thereby eliminating the need to generate a heat source. In fact, the heat could be used for heating perimeter spaces during the underheated period of the year, as well as for tempering the SA through a terminal induction box.

As discussed, the terminal induction air system is used primarily to adjust for variations in the heat gain in different spaces within an interior zone. While the assumption is that the lights are on, which until recently was typically true, the number of people and the use of equipment

Table 10.3: LIGHTING POWER DENSITIES

Building Occupancy/Use	Lighting Power Densities (watts/sq ft) 2004
Convention Center	1.2
Court House	1.2
Dining: Bar Lounge/Leisure	0.9 – 1.5
Dormitory	1.0
Exercise Center/Gymnasium	1.0
Healthcare Clinic	1.0
Hospital	1.2
Hotel/Motel	1.0
Library	1.3
Manufacturing Workshop	1.4
Museum	1.1
Office	1.0
Religious Building	1.3
Residential	0.7 – 1.0
Retail	1.5 – 1.7
School/University	1.2
Theaters	1.2 – 1.6
Warehouse	0.8

Note: These lighting power densities are based on recommendation from both NAIES and ASHRAE.

often vary. When these heat gains are less than assumed, the terminal induction process adds the amount of heat that would have been added. The induction system can also be used to heat the perimeter spaces by salvaging heat from the interior of the structure and supplying it to the spaces with an exterior exposure. This method of using the heat from the building's interior to condition the perimeter spaces is referred to as *bootstrap heating.*

Heat-of-Light

While not specifically a means of controlling the SA temperature, heat-of-light is a principle that we should consider, particularly since it relates to the terminal induction air system. As has been mentioned several times and is obvious to anyone who has touched an operating lamp, much of the electricity consumed by a light fixture, by the lamps and the ballasts, if they exist, results in heat. In fact, except for the minuscule amount of energy that is actually used to stimulate a visual sensation, all the consumed energy produces heat. Light is radiation, and when it is absorbed by a surface, it is converted from radiant energy into molecular activity, or sensible heat.

While a fluorescent lamp is around four times as efficient as an incandescent lamp in converting energy input into light output, essentially all of the energy that it consumes is converted into heat, some of which is emitted directly from the fixture into the space and some of which remains in the fixture. Initially, most of the heat remains in the fixture, but since the fixture is within the controlled environment, this heat ultimately becomes a gain in the occupied spaces. However, this heat can be extracted by pulling air through the fixture, with the heated air merely exhausted or, if possible, used productively, perhaps in a terminal induction system or in bootstrap heating (see Figure 10.111). To be effective, the air passing through each lighting fixture should be pulled into a plenum rather than through a return air duct.

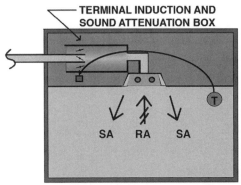

TERMINAL INDUCTION AND SOUND ATTENUATION BOX

SA   RA   SA

SCHEMATIC OF INDUCTION BOX

Figure 10.110 TERMINAL INDUCTION BOX SCHEMATIC

This is a schematic diagram of a terminal induction box and how the boxes might be arranged in a system. Usually the plenum is shared by a number of terminal induction boxes; thus, it is able to borrow heat from another space, which is generally necessary.

SA RA SA   SA RA SA   SA RA SA   SA RA SA   SA RA SA

COMMON PLENUM FOR A NUMBER OF SPACES

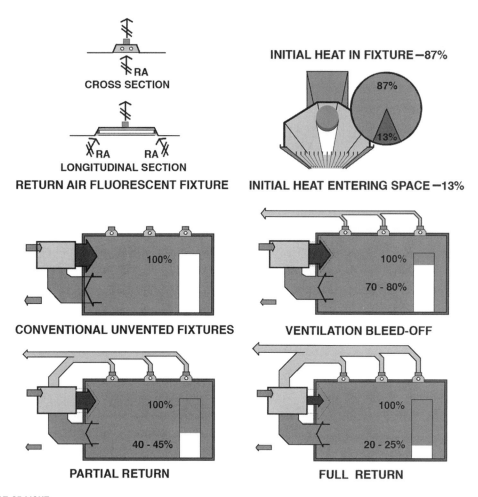

CROSS SECTION

LONGITUDINAL SECTION

RETURN AIR FLUORESCENT FIXTURE

INITIAL HEAT IN FIXTURE—87%

87%

13%

INITIAL HEAT ENTERING SPACE —13%

100%

CONVENTIONAL UNVENTED FIXTURES

100%

70 - 80%

VENTILATION BLEED-OFF

100%

40 - 45%

PARTIAL RETURN

100%

20 - 25%

FULL RETURN

Figure 10.111 HEAT-OF-LIGHT
Various benefits are possible by pulling the return air through the light fixtures. This effectively increases the temperature differential between the SA and the return air, permitting a reduction in the volume of air supplied to condition a. Exhausting the "superheated" return air rather than conditioning it to be supplied back to the space can reduce the load on the refrigeration equipment. Redirecting this "superheated" air to spaces requiring heating can also reduce the load on the heating equipment. And lowering the temperature of the fluorescent tubes increases the lighting efficacy.

Before electric lighting, when daylight was not available, illumination was usually by means of pyroluminescence—light produced by fire. This typically meant candle, kerosene, or gas flames that, in addition to providing light, produced heat and combustion by-products. When a fixture, such as a chandelier, included a number of burning flames, the heat and by-products could be considerable. To reduce the accompanying problems, the lights were often suspended below a perforated escutcheon or circular grill through which the heat and by-products could be vented to the outside (see Figure 10.112). When venting was not feasible, the fixture was frequently suspended below a simple decorative escutcheon that would concentrate the collected flame by-products so that the dirt was not spread across the ceiling, simplifying cleaning.

With conversion to electric light, the heat associated with the lamps was less, and there was no longer a

Figure 10.112 CHANDELIER EXHAUST AND SIMPLE ESCUTCHEON
Early chandeliers that burned candles, kerosene, or gas often relied on decorative escutcheons that could capture and/or vent the by-products from the flames.

Figure 10.113 SAARINEN'S LIGHT WITH AN SA DIFFUSER
This light hangs from a ceiling diffuser located in the First Christian Church in Columbus, Indiana, designed by Eliel Saarinen in 1942. While the combination of luminaire and diffuser is visually effective, it does not benefit from heat-of-light.

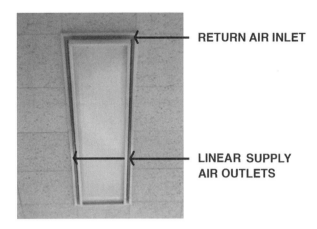

RETURN AIR INLET

LINEAR SUPPLY AIR OUTLETS

Figure 10.114 FLUORESCENT FIXTURE WITH SUPPLY AND RETURN
This fluorescent fixture includes both supply and return linear grills along its perimeter. Pulling RA through the fixture provides a potential of heat-of-light, whereas the inclusion of the SA outlets, which avoids the visual imposition of separate ceiling diffusers, does not provide any benefit from heat-of-light.

major accumulation of dirt resulting from the flames. This essentially eliminated the need for a vented escutcheon, although an electrical connection that was accessible and preferably concealed was now required. As a result, suspended electric fixtures continue to be hung from the center of escutcheon plates, although they do not have to be very large. However, decorative lighting fixtures are still often suspended from a major escutcheon that continues an aesthetic preference probably derived from the historic, more functional vented device.

This aesthetic, combined with a misunderstanding of the primary attributes of heat-of-light, has led to some intriguing designs that clearly do not rely on the more functional aspects of the original. While heat-of-light involves utilizing the heat produced by electric lights, which usually involves extracting the RA over or through the lighting fixtures, the connection between air movement and lighting fixtures has led to the use of the light fixture as a way to supply air to a room. While this can avoid the visual imposition of a number of ceiling diffusers, it does not benefit from the principles of heat-of-light.

In the First Christian Church in Columbus, Indiana, Eliel Saarinen combined ceiling diffusers with suspended light fixtures (see Figure 10.113). This was a very neat design. In a similar way, fluorescent fixtures are often used to supply air (see Figure 10.114). While a four-tube fluorescent fixture is usually 2 feet wide and a two-tube fixture is 1 foot wide, these dimensions are based mainly on the standard dimensions of ceiling tiles. Although the length of a fixture is set by the fluorescent lamp, usually 4 feet, its width can vary. By slightly narrowing the width of a fixture, a supply air bonnet, which is placed over the fixture, can include two linear SA grills, one on either side of the fixture.

Heat Reclamation

While heat-of-light is a way to reclaim heat from electric lights, the term *heat reclamation* generally refers to exchanging heat between incoming ventilation air and exhaust air. This exchange can be achieved by various means, including a heat pipe or a heat reclamation wheel, both of which provide a means of exchanging sensible heat between the two air streams. This can minimize the ventilation load imposed on the heating and cooling system. In the winter, this exchange preheats the ventilation air, while in the summer it precools it.

Nonresidential structures generally require mechanical ventilation, but residential buildings have typically relied on natural leakage through the normal cracks in windows, doors, and even structural enclosures to supply at least a minimal amount of FA. In response to the current commitment to higher energy efficiency, residential structures are typically constructed much more tightly than in the past, which has reduced the amount of infiltration, sometimes establishing a need for forced ventilation. Forced or mechanical ventilation, which generally requires an input of energy to operate, entails the exhaust of conditioned air as well as the supply of unconditioned, outside FA. However, heat reclamation, which provides a potential for energy savings, is possible if the passage of the exhaust air and the FA are thermally linked.

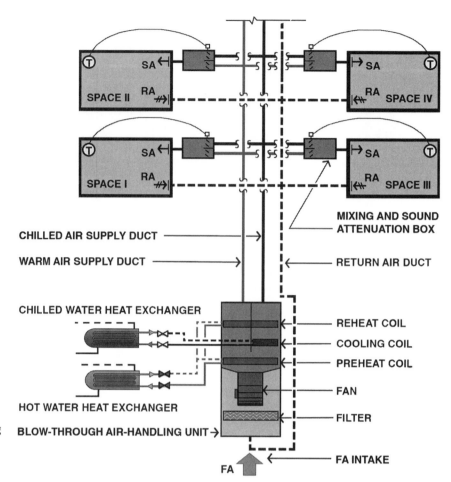

CHILLED AIR SUPPLY DUCT

WARM AIR SUPPLY DUCT

MIXING AND SOUND ATTENUATION BOX

RETURN AIR DUCT

CHILLED WATER HEAT EXCHANGER

REHEAT COIL

COOLING COIL

PREHEAT COIL

FAN

HOT WATER HEAT EXCHANGER

FILTER

BLOW-THROUGH AIR-HANDLING UNIT →

FA INTAKE

FA

Figure 10.115 DOUBLE-DUCT HIGH-VELOCITY AIR SYSTEM DIAGRAM

This is a schematic diagram of a double-duct high-velocity air system. Both warm and chilled air are supplied in separate ducts to the terminal mixing boxes, where they are mixed to match the load in the space(s) in which the SA from the mixing box is discharged.

Double-Duct High-Velocity Air System

The double-duct high-velocity air system can alternate simultaneously between providing SA that is at the maximum heating temperature, the minimum cooling temperature, or any temperature in between by mixing various proportions of the warm and cool air (see Figure 10.115). The system is designed to provide a full air supply from either the warm air or cool air ducts, although this does not necessarily mean that each main distribution duct has the same capacity. In a double-duct distribution system that serves only an exterior zone, equal volumes of warm and chilled air would probably be supplied, but for a system that is to condition both interior and perimeter zones or just an interior zone, 100% air volume would be provided for cooling but only a reduced amount, approximately 60%, would be needed for heating, since the interior zones typically do not generally require major heating.

The operation of a double-duct air system is quite simple—a consistent volume of SA at the appropriate temperature is provided by mixing warm and cool air. In addition to effectively controlling air temperature, air velocity,

and air quality, this system can control air humidity. Since cool air generally is less humid than warm air, by properly mixing the SA, reasonable control of the humidity can be achieved for each zone.

Unfortunately, while the thermal control offered by a double-duct system is quite effective, it tends to achieve it rather inefficiently, somewhat like a reheat system used during the cooling cycle. If, during the cooling season, the expected heat gains are not present in the subzone controlled by a terminal mixing box, the mixing box will add warm air to the SA. During the heating season, if there is a source of heat in the subzone that could reduce the demands on the system, the mixing box would counteract this benefit by adding cool air to the SA. Although neither of these adjustments specifically entails reversing a modification made to an air sample, such as heating and then cooling the air, the effect is not much different.

While this system is similar to the three-pipe water distribution system, it does not have the same inefficiencies based on using a common return. Although it is not totally reasonable, in terms of energy efficiency, to heat some air and cool other air and then mix the two together in order to achieve the desired temperature, at least with a double-duct air system no excessive extra load results from mixing all the return air in one duct. Since the RA temperature is set by the design intentions rather than by the control system, the common return air temperature with a double-duct system should be basically the same whether there is 100% heating, 100% cooling, or a mixture of both.

OVERALL SYSTEM SIZING AND SELECTION

Preliminary sizing can only provide a rough approximation that needs to be continually refined as the architectural design develops, load calculations are refined, and the various components of the ECS are engineered. However, there are some rules of thumb that can still be helpful in guiding our design efforts, as long as we clearly understand that these will need to be confirmed or, more likely, adjusted as things progress.

As previously mentioned, the volume of air that has to be circulated within a space to provide conditioning is roughly based on approximately six to eight air changes per hour. With a central air system, all of this air has to be distributed from the mechanical equipment areas to the spaces to be controlled and back again, but when only ventilation air is centrally distributed, such as with induction units or centrally served fan-coil units, the volume of air is approximately one air change per hour.

Most buildings today include some level of air conditioning, which typically involves some means of both adding and removing thermal energy so that the appropriate temperature and humidity of the air can be maintained. It also includes control of ventilation and the quality of the air. Air conditioning also generally implies refrigeration, although in hot arid locations, evaporative cooling is still an effective way of providing reduced temperature.

The amount of refrigeration is noted in terms of tons, with a ton of refrigeration equal to 12,000 BTUH. This relationship derives from the earliest form of refrigeration—making ice. A refrigeration unit can operate continuously, and in order to produce 1 ton of ice each day, the unit must extract from the water a total of 288,000 BTU. This is based on a ton equaling 2000 pounds and the latent heat of fusion of water being 144 BTU per pound. Since there are 24 hours in a day, the daily 288,000 BTU converts to 12,000 BTUH. That is, a refrigeration unit with a 12,000 BTUH capacity will be able to produce 1 ton of ice each day. Hence, 1 ton of refrigeration equals 12,000 BTUH.

$$12,000 \text{ BTUH} = \frac{1 \text{ lb} \times 144 \text{ BTUH per lb} \times 2000 \text{ lb per ton}}{24 \text{ hours per day}}$$

How many tons of refrigeration will actually be required for a design will depend on a number of complex factors. While we might wait until these are determined, initially it is reasonable to assume that 1 ton of refrigeration will be needed for approximately each 400 square feet of interior space. This is, of course, a rough figure, and the range can easily extend from 300 to 500 square feet per ton. For single-family residences, which generally have a lower percentage of the exterior walls in glazing than nonresidential structures and also have reduced interior heat gains, a ton of refrigeration is usually capable of conditioning around 500 square feet. Curtain-wall structures with high internal gains are often at the other end of the range, perhaps needing a ton of refrigeration for each 300 square feet, or even less, of interior floor space.

While we have discussed how to allocate building area for air supply distribution, there is also the issue of equipment rooms. Again, merely as a rough guide, a central air system typically requires an equipment room floor area that is equal to 2–5% of the gross floor area served. This area could be located at a central point or it can be distributed throughout the structure. While less area for the equipment is generally needed with a single central location, this arrangement does require more building space/volume for distribution and higher energy use than is usually needed for more localized distribution of the equipment.

Table 10.4 provides a guide to the selection of appropriate systems for various types of building occupancy. The systems checked for a particular application are those that are commonly used. This chart is not intended to limit system selection or to imply that a particular system included for an occupancy is appropriate for all situations. The specifics of each application and the nuance of each system must be considered in making an actual system selection. Economics, design objectives, local ordinances, and other factors will impact on the appropriate selection.

PASSIVE SOLAR SYSTEM

Figures 10.116, 10.117, and 10.119 to 10.121 present the basic criteria and methods to utilize insolation architecturally as the heat source. As with the other environmental issues discussed in this book, these diagrams are presented to introduce the critical concepts and principles related to solar design rather than to explain what should be done. While the discussion of this important opportunity for architectural design is limited here, it has been covered extensively in a number of excellent books. One of the best and most comprehensive of these was written by Edward Mazria in 1979: the expanded professional edition of *The Passive Solar Energy Book*.

Table 10.4: SUGGESTED SYSTEMS FOR VARIOUS BUILDING TYPES

Single-Purpose Occupancies	D-X Self-Contained ½ to 2 tons	D-X Self-Contained Over 2 tons	Fan-Coil Units With Fresh Air	Fan-Coil Units Without Fresh Air	Induction Units	Central Air Systems Multizone	Variable Volume	Terminal Reheat	Reheat & Variable Volume	Terminal Induction	Double Duct	Recirculation of Air Between Units
Residential — Medium	X	X										—
Residential — Large		X	X	X		X						—
Restaurants — Medium		X				X						N
Restaurants — Large		X				X	X	X	X			N
Stores		X	X	X		X	X					N
Churches		X				X						—
Theaters & Auditoriums						X						—
Multipurpose Occupancies												
Multifamily	X	X	X	X	X							N
Office Building			X	X	X	X	X	X	X	X	X	Y
Hospitals			X	X						X	X	N
Hotels & Dormitory Rooms	X		X	X								N
Motel Rooms	X		X	X								N
Residential Communal Spaces	X		X			X						Y
Schools & Universities			X		X	X		X	X	X	X	Y
Laboratories — Medium		X	X							X		N
Laboratories — Large		X								X		N
Museums		X				X	X	X	X	X	X	Y
Libraries		X				X	X	X	X	X	X	Y
Department Stores						X	X	X	X	X		Y
Shopping Centers		X	X	X		X	X	X	X	X		Y

Source: The information in this table is based on various resources, including "The ABC's of Air Conditioning," published by the Carrier Corporation, 1989.

The most basic approach to passive solar design is to orient the structure, particularly glazing, toward the south, at least in the Northern Hemisphere. Since the sun travels across the southern sky, achieving its maximum intensity during midday, in terms of solar time this orientation will maximize the solar access. While this fact is based on solar angles, Victor Olgyay's work suggested that an eastern shift would actually increase the daily solar gain during the winter season.[18] This shift is based on changing atmospheric conditions as the daily temperature increases and airborne moisture decreases. Olgyay's recommendation for the temperate zone was a 17.5° shift toward the east.

While there are differences in the ability of the sun to penetrate the atmosphere, solar intensity on a surface is also dependent on the angle of orientation to the solar rays, with the intensity varying with the cosine of the angle of incidence. Interestingly, within 15° to 20° from normal, there is no significant difference of intensity based on the changing cosine, which means that the critical factor is getting a basic southern exposure. Minor adjustments in orientation will have less of an impact than an ineffective architectural design and response.

Although definitely not limited to residential structures, passive solar design usually is most effective in

[18] V. Olgyay, *Design with Climate: Bioclimatic Approach to Architectural Regionalism* (Princeton University Press, Princeton, NJ, 1965), pp. 58–62.

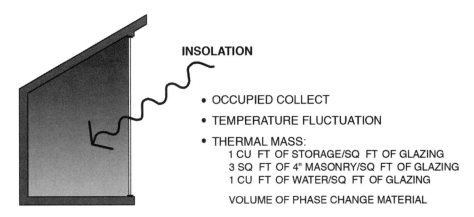

INSOLATION

• OCCUPIED COLLECT

• TEMPERATURE FLUCTUATION

• THERMAL MASS:
    1 CU FT OF STORAGE/SQ FT OF GLAZING
    3 SQ FT OF 4" MASONRY/SQ FT OF GLAZING
    1 CU FT OF WATER/SQ FT OF GLAZING

    VOLUME OF PHASE CHANGE MATERIAL

Figure 10.116 DIRECT GAIN—PASSIVE SOLAR SCHEMATIC

This schematic diagram includes the basic requirements for thermal storage with direct gain. Without adequate storage, solar gain will increase the interior temperatures and require cooling, which, during the underheated period of the year, would mean merely opening the windows. Unfortunately, while this would improve the thermal conditions while the sun is available, it would dissipate the heat, eliminating the potential to benefit from the solar gain when the sun is not available. Thermal storage can trap the heat and minimize the increase in room temperature during the period of direct solar access.

smaller structures that have a large surface-to-volume ratio—that is, that are skin dominated. While this category includes a variety of occupancy classifications, it clearly includes single-family residences.

Direct solar gain through southern-oriented glazing in the winter provides an effective means of counteracting heat loss, but the gain during the prime sunlit hours tends to exceed the concurrent heat loss. This is fortunate, since it means that the solar gain can be utilized beyond the time when it is directly available if some means is provided to capture the excess gain for use later, but it also means that if this heat is not captured and kept from increasing the air temperature, the interior temperature will become excessive. Hence the need for thermal mass, which can absorb the solar gain, limits the increase in room temperature, and is available to release heat when the sun is no longer available but room heat loss continues (see Figure 10.116).

The basic approach is to allow the solar gain to slightly increase the room air temperature, remaining within the comfort range. Since temperatures seek equilibrium, the increased air temperature will transmit its excess heat into the surrounding physical materials. The trick is to provide enough thermal mass in these materials to match the expected daily heat gain and to disperse this mass so that it can absorb the heat quickly to keep the room air temperature from increasing too much, even if only for a short time.

The rule of thumb is to provide 1 cubic foot of thermal mass, masonry or water, for every square foot of southern-oriented glazing. Since water can absorb the increased temperatures by relying on convective flow, if water is used as the thermal mass it can be reasonably concentrated. Solid masonry, on the other hand, needs to be spread out to

absorb the thermal energy, and the recommendation for this is to provide 3 square feet of 4-inch-thick material for each square foot of glazing. The location of the thermal mass is not critical, although if the direct sun does strike it, absorption will be improved. Generally, the thermal mass should be located "in sight" or in a direct line to the window opening. Also, the glazing should be insulated glass, perhaps with selective low emissivity (ε), to improve the "U" coefficient while not significantly reducing the solar gain.

The Trombe wall, named after the French engineer Félix Trombe (1906–1985), is an interesting approach to passive solar design, utilizing the same basic principles used in direct gain (see Figure 10.117). With direct gain, the occupied space is the solar collector and is surrounded by the means of thermal storage. With the Trombe wall, the solar collection and thermal storage are similar to those of direct gain, but they occur just outside of the occupied zone. This is basically the design developed by Edward Sylvester Morse, an American zoologist who had an interesting and diverse career. Morse's design for an air heater, which was patented in the 1880s, included a glazed box attached to a dark absorbing material.

Félix Trombe worked for a number of years on two French solar furnaces located in the Pyrénées. These furnaces included a large array of mirrors that reflected the sun onto a huge parabolic reflector that, in turn, focused the solar rays onto a small heating chamber, achieving extraordinarily high temperatures (around 5000° F) that are hard to generate on earth. However, Trombe realized that the sun should also be able to produce the far lower temperatures on which our thermal comfort is based. At the time, energy was inexpensive and residential construction generally included little, if any, insulation; in addition, in

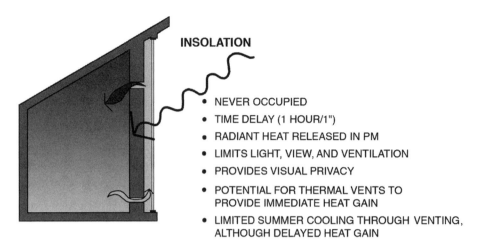

INSOLATION

- NEVER OCCUPIED
- TIME DELAY (1 HOUR/1")
- RADIANT HEAT RELEASED IN PM
- LIMITS LIGHT, VIEW, AND VENTILATION
- PROVIDES VISUAL PRIVACY
- POTENTIAL FOR THERMAL VENTS TO PROVIDE IMMEDIATE HEAT GAIN
- LIMITED SUMMER COOLING THROUGH VENTING, ALTHOUGH DELAYED HEAT GAIN

Figure 10.117 TROMBE WALL—PASSIVE SOLAR SCHEMATIC
This schematic diagram presents the basics of the Trombe wall, named after the French engineer who came up with the idea, Félix Trombe. Trombe worked on the solar furnace in the Pyrénées, at Mont-Louis and at Odeillo, where he developed his first modification of a structure to improve its solar performance.

the Pyrénées, the typical house was constructed from masonry. Trombe thought that if a glazed wall was installed in front of the south wall of such a typical house and was painted a dark color, the shortwave solar radiation would pass through the glazing and be absorbed by the dark wall, but the heat produced and the longwave radiation emitted by the wall would be trapped between the glazing and the masonry wall. This heat would then gradually migrate through the wall, arriving in the evening, when it could provide low-grade but effective radiant heat on the inside. If a low vent and a high vent were added, the warmer air temperature in the interstitial space of the collector would establish a natural convective airflow that could be harnessed if heat were needed before it started radiating through the wall by opening the vents. Usually, however, during the heating season, the vents would remain closed.

Trombe's design provided a significant improvement in performance over the conventional masonry design used in the typical Pyrénées residence. Trombe also suggested that, by adding operable sash to the enclosing glazed wall in front of the masonry wall, the heat gained during the warmer periods of the year could be released before it migrated through to the interior space and, in this process, draw room air into the collector and out through the vent. If a window on the north wall were open, then this would induce slow ventilation of the house by cool evening outside air. As intriguing as this method for cooling the house might have been, it turned out to be of limited benefit since the draft was not significant, although by venting the collector the heat gain from the sunlit hours could be dissipated, preparing for the next day's collection.

Since the Trombe wall relies on a major masonry wall oriented to the south, it allows for only limited exposure along this exterior wall. Combining this with the fact that

the release of heat is most effective in the evening hours, the Trombe wall might be an appropriate passive solar approach to be used for bedrooms. These spaces typically require privacy and security, and they are used mainly at times when the heat produced will be most appreciated. When the Trombe wall is employed for general living areas, such as a family room or living room, the sense of enclosure can be somewhat excessive. Also, while adding an exterior glazed wall over a masonry wall might make sense in the Pyrénées and elsewhere where masonry is the norm for residential construction, it might be less reasonable in places where the typical construction does not include solid masonry exterior walls.

Figure 10.118 shows a Trombe-wall used house in Princeton, NJ. This house, which was designed by Douglas Kelbaugh as his personal family residence in 1975, is a wonderful example of how innovative design can result from a thoughtful consideration of thermal performance.

By effectively turning the masonry wall horizontally, the Trombe wall collector can be converted into an attached solar space, which, for thermal purposes, is essentially still primarily a glass-enclosed thermal mass (see Figure 10.119). If the floor of this space is lowered below the main floor level, the vertical wall that fills this drop will add to the thermal mass, and the extension of this attached space beyond the interior space will reduce the inside–outside visual separation. With a lower floor level, it is possible to look over the extension. This also provides for natural convective transfer from the attached space to the higher structure, which is normally linked to the attached space by doors that can be open when this transfer is desired and closed when heat from the attached space is not needed or when the space might be too cold and would

Figure 10.118 DOUGLAS KELBAUGH HOUSE
This 1975 house in Princeton, New Jersey, was designed by Douglas Kelbaugh as his family residence. It includes a Trombe wall as the major architectural feature. This wall was somewhat modified in design in an attempt to increase the development of convective ventilation, but with only limited success. The design also includes a greenhouse that provides an increased sense of openness, counteracting the containment of the Trombe wall.

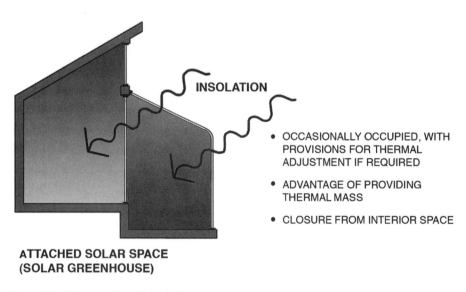

INSOLATION

- OCCASIONALLY OCCUPIED, WITH PROVISIONS FOR THERMAL ADJUSTMENT IF REQUIRED

- ADVANTAGE OF PROVIDING THERMAL MASS

- CLOSURE FROM INTERIOR SPACE

ATTACHED SOLAR SPACE (SOLAR GREENHOUSE)

Figure 10.119 ATTACHED GREENHOUSE—PASSIVE SOLAR SCHEMATIC
This schematic diagram presents the basics of an attached solar space. In a sense, this entails expanding the interstitial space of the Trombe wall system into a space that can be used selectively. While the attached solar space is usually in front of the interior space, the visually open nature of the attachment does not impose a major inside–outside separation, and if the space is lower than the interior space, as shown, there is more potential to provide thermal mass in the space and to allow for some direct gain and exposure for the interior space.

draw heat from the interior. Even if it cannot supply heat to the main spaces, when it is closed off, the attached space serves as a buffer, reducing heat loss. The attached solar space also provides a place that can be used at times when the thermal conditions are reasonable.

In the warmer seasons, both shading and venting should be provided to minimize solar gain, which should make the space reasonably comfortable except at times of high outside temperature and/or humidity. In the colder seasons, when the space is "working," it could get rather

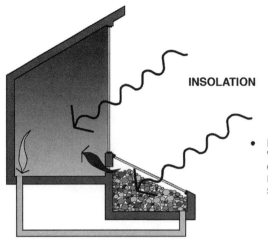

Figure 10.120 PASSIVE SOLAR COLLECTOR SCHEMATIC

This schematic diagram presents the basics of an attached greenhouse solar collector. In a sense, this entails expanding the interstitial space of the Trombe wall system into a space that can be used selectively. While the greenhouse is in front of the interior space, its visually open nature does not create a major inside–outside separation. If the greenhouse is lower than the interior space, as shown, there is more potential to provide thermal mass in the greenhouse and to allow for some direct gain and exposure for the interior space.

INSOLATION

PASSIVE SOLAR COLLECTOR

- PASSIVE SOLAR COLLECTOR WITH THERMAL STORAGE TO COLLECT AND STORE ENERGY FOR USE AT TIMES WHEN DIRECT SOLAR GAIN IS NOT AVAILABLE

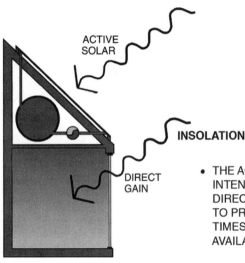

ACTIVE SOLAR

INSOLATION

DIRECT GAIN

ACTIVE SOLAR COLLECTOR WITH ROOM DIRECT GAIN

- THE ACTIVE SOLAR SYSTEM IS INTENDED TO SUPPLEMENT THE DIRECT GAIN, PASSIVE SYSTEM TO PROVIDE HEAT DURING THOSE TIMES WHEN THE SUN IS NOT AVAILABLE.

ACTIVE SOLAR

ACTIVE SOLAR COLLECTOR WITH NO DIRECT GAIN

- WITH NO DIRECT SOLAR GAIN , THE ACTIVE SYSTEM MUST PROVIDE HEAT DURING THE TIMES OF AVAILABLE SUN, MINIMIZING THE CONTRIBUTION THAT THE ACTIVE SYSTEM CAN PROVIDE WHEN THE SUN IS NOT AVAILABLE.

- WITH NO DIRECT GAIN, THE ACTIVE SYSTEM SUPPLANTS THE BASIC ARCHITECTURAL FUNCTION, WITH THE ARCHITECTURE BECOMING THE MEANS OF "CELEBRATING" THE MECHANICAL SYSTEM RATHER THAN HAVING THE MECHANICAL SYSTEM SERVE TO EXPAND THE CAPACITY OF THE ARCHITECTURE.

Figure 10.121 ACTIVE SOLAR COLLECTOR AND TECHNICAL CONFUSION
This schematic diagram shows how use of a technical potential or mechanical approach can confuse things and lead to an illogical design.

warm. At such times, using the space probably necessitates a trade-off with heating of the interior space. If the temperature in the space drops too much, it can be closed off from the main space. If it is necessary to use the space at those times for a special purpose, such as entertaining, then adding some heat during this limited time is probably acceptable, but this should definitely be limited to times of extraordinary need.

An attached solar space is often called a *greenhouse*, although there is no requirement to use it for plants, the original purpose for such a structure and the basis of its name. In fact, if it is used for horticultural purposes, special consideration must be given to the type of vegetation that can survive the temperature range and fluctuation that are likely to occur. While this space can be a wonderful green space, it is actually a solar collector with benefits. Unfortunately, the more it is used for other purposes, particularly if thermal comfort conditions must be maintained, the less effective the attached solar space usually is as a means of providing passive heating. That stated, this type of solar collector often becomes a wonderful living space.

Instead of a potentially occupiable space, it is possible to use an attached solar collector that can operate passively. As shown in Figure 10.120, the collector can be filled with a material the can capture and store the solar heat, releasing it as needed by natural convective airflow. While this approach has definite architectural potential, it is more of a passive mechanical device. Even a rooftop solar collector has an impact on the design's form and expression, although this approach to solar heating tends to be more technical than architectural. Unfortunately, sometimes this trend is carried so far that the direct architectural response to using solar energy is lost.

Figure 10.121 shows two approaches to active solar collection. In one approach, shown in the upper diagram, the active collector is effectively an extension of the approach used architecturally, capturing solar gain for use when direct gain is not available, which means at times when there is no solar gain. In the lower diagram, however, the architectural response is not effective. Since there is no potential for direct gain, reliance is solely on the active collector.

BIBLIOGRAPHY

Allen, E., and J. Iano. *The Architect's Studio Companion*. John Wiley & Sons, Inc., Hoboken, NJ, 1995.

Althouse, A.D., C.H. Turnquist, and A.F. Bracciano. *Modern Refrigeration and Air Conditioning*. Goodheart-Willcox, Tinley Park, IL, 2003.

Andrews, F.T. *The Architect's Guide to Mechanical Systems*. Reinhold Publishing Corporation, New York, 1966,

Bradshaw, V. *The Building Environment: Active and Passive Control Systems*. John Wiley & Sons, Inc., Hoboken, NJ, 2006.

Brown, G.Z., and M. DeKay. *Sun, Wind and Light: Architectural Design Strategies*. John Wiley & Sons, Inc., Hoboken, NJ, 1995.

Grondzik, W. T., A.G. Kwok, B. Stein, and J.S. Reynolds. *Mechanical and Electrical Equipment for Buildings*. John Wiley & Sons, Inc., Hoboken, NJ, 2010.

Heerwagen, D. *Passive and Active Environmental Controls*. McGraw-Hill Companies, New York, 2004.

Horuz, I. "A Comparison between Ammonia–Water and Water–Lithium Bromide Solutions in Vapor Absorption Refrigeration Systems." *International Communications on Heat Mass Transfer*, Vol. 25, No. 5, 1998, pp. 711–721.

Lechner, N. *Heating, Cooling, Lighting: Design Methods for Architects*. John Wiley & Sons, Inc., Hoboken, NJ, 2001.

Mazria, E. *The Passive Solar Energy Book* (Expanded Professional Edition). Rodale Press, Emmaus, PA, 1979.

Olgyay, V. *Design with Climate: Bioclimatic Approach to Architectural Regionalism*. Princeton University Press, Princeton, NJ, 1965.

"The ABC's of Air Conditioning." Carrier Corporation, Syracuse, NY, 1989.

Trane Air Conditioning Manual. The Trane Company, La Crosse, WI, 1995.

Whitman, W.C., W.M. Johnson, and J.A. Tomczyk. *Refrigeration and Air Conditioning Technology*. Thomson Delmar Learning, Clifton Park, NY, 2005.

11 PLUMBING

INTRODUCTION

The discussion of plumbing can be reasonably divided into two major areas: water supply and water removal. These areas can be divided further into several subcategories.

WATER SUPPLY	
Source of Water:	Rainwater Collection On-Site Wells Public Water Supply
Fixtures:	Sinks / Tubs / WC
Supply Distribution:	Supply Piping Domestic Hot Water
WATER REMOVAL	
Building Drainage:	Drainage Piping Venting
Waste Disposal:	Public Sewage On-Site Disposal

Early in his presidency, John F. Kennedy challenged America to send a man to the moon and back before the end of the 1960s. With the benefit of American ingenuity and with considerable financial support, the nation met this challenge. A critical objective of space exploration was to determine whether water was present on other planetary bodies since water is one of the necessities of life, at least as we define it. Whether or not water is present elsewhere, we must recognize that although water is critical for our existence, we have not been effective stewards of this important resource on our planet.

In the late 1960s and early 1970s, there was major concern about our water resources. But with the Arab oil embargo in 1973, the environmental focus shifted from water to energy. Rather than vacillate among specific issues that impact on our environment, we must realize that we need to address them all, especially since they are often interrelated. Sometimes, though, they are in conflict, and solving one problem can exacerbate another.

Although concern for our water resources has generated action that has reduced our water consumption, there is still a great deal that can and must be done. And while we legitimately might be concerned primarily with matters in the United States, we should not forget that water is a global resource and that elsewhere in the world, not only is this resource threatened, but there is already an extreme crisis in terms of availability of water to meet the personal and agricultural needs of the people. While as architects and designers we might not be able to resolve the global water problems, we must make some contribution to their resolution through our own activity, both personally and professionally. Specifically, we can reduce the amount of water used in the buildings we design, adjust the way we access water, and change the way that the water we do use impacts on the environment.

So, how much water do we need? Or perhaps, how much do we use?

Water Usage

Traditional water consumption in the United States is shown in Table 11.1. Since the passage of the Energy Policy Act of 1992, which established national standards for allowable water consumption in almost all plumbing fixtures, there has been a significant reduction in water consumption for domestic use. This policy prescribed the maximum volume of water for flushing toilets at 1.6 gallons and urinals at 1 gallon. In addition, the maximum flow permitted for both showerheads and sink faucets was set at 2.5 gallons per minute. While several years were allowed for full implementation, these requirements were not retroactive, so even though almost 20 years have passed, many plumbing fixtures still in use today unfortunately do not meet these standards. In addition, while the limitations in the number of gallons allowed for flushing toilets and urinals have resulted in significant reduction in water consumed for these purposes, the reduced flow for showers, the major means of personal hygiene, has not had as much impact since many homeowners had already switched to water-conserving showerheads in order to maintain adequate hot water.

Table 11.1: TRADITIONAL WATER USAGE IN THE UNITED STATES

Use		Gallons per Capita per Day (GCD)
Residential per Person per Day		70 GCD
Drinking and Cooking	c. 3 GCD	
Clothes Washing and Dishwashing	c. 14 GCD	
Bathing and Personal Hygiene	c. 25 GCD	
Toilets	c. 28 GCD	
Public Use: Parks, Fighting Fires		10 GCD
Commercial		85 GCD
Industrial		65 GCD
Mining		7 GCD
Irrigation and Agriculture		500 GCD
Thermoelectric Power Generation		477 GCD
Total per Capita U.S. Daily Use		**c. 1200 GCD**

Source: Adapted in part from information included in the U.S. Geological Survey's "Estimated Use of Water in the United States in 2000."

The 1.6 gallons per flush set by the Energy Policy Act is considerably less than what was traditionally necessary for proper toilet operation. Early toilets required up to around 7 gallons per flush, often at rather high pressure that was developed by raising the water tank well above the toilet bowl. Design adjustments to the drainage loop within the toilet bowl improved the siphon action, thereby reducing the water volumes and pressure necessary to flush the unit. By the mid-twentieth century, most new toilets required only around 5 gallons per flush, and by the 1980s they needed only 3.5 gallons. And while the current 1.6 gallons per flush has reduced our water consumption, unfortunately many older toilets are still being used that consume 3.5 to around 6 gallons per flush.

The 2.5 gallons per minute (GPM) for faucets and showerheads set by the Energy Policy Act has not had as great an impact in terms of lowering our water consumption. Showerheads used to deliver 5 to 8 GPM, so we might think that the reduction stipulated in the Energy Policy Act would have reduced water consumption for showers by about one-third to one-half. However, even before 1992, many showers were already using less water. A typical shower lasts for about 10 minutes, and at 5 to 8 GPM, each shower could require around 50 gallons of hot water, which would mean that even with a fairly good-sized hot water heater, one shower could use most of the available hot water. To avoid running out of hot water, many homeowners were already using flow restrictors in their showers that limited the water supply to around 2 to 2.5 GPM, which reduced water consumption before the passage of the Energy Policy Act. Although the Energy Policy Act sets 2.5 GPM as the maximum rate of flow, some new showerheads can provide a decent shower with water flows as low as 1.25 to 1.6 GPM.

There are lists that indicate the average water consumption for a variety of purposes. Most often these are presented in terms of per capita daily use in the typical U.S. home. In addition, each U.S. single-family residence consumes about 120 gallons per day for irrigation. This is an average; based on the climatic zone and the type of vegetation involved, the actual amount of water used for residential irrigation can vary considerably. In some locations, such as dry areas with nonnative vegetation, outdoor water use for a residence can exceed the assumed norm by a factor of 2 or 3—around 250 to 350 gallons per day. Of course, water is also consumed when people are away from home—for example, when at school, at work, or shopping. While this water is consumed directly, a considerable amount of water is also consumed indirectly through agricultural, industrial, and construction activities. As indicated in Table 11.1, these activities consume more than 15 times the amount of water used in our homes, with irrigation and agriculture accounting for

Table 11.2: HISTORIC WATER USE

Imperial Rome	38	GCD
London, 1912	40	GCD
American Cities before World War II	115	GCD
Los Angeles, Mid-1970s	182	GCD
Typical U.S. Home	70	GCD
U.S. Single-Family Home	50–75	GCD
U.S. Luxury Housing	100–150	GCD

Note: GDC refers to gallons per capita per day.
Source: Upper section adapted from data presented by Murray Milne.

around 500 GCD and thermoelectric power generation for almost the same amount.

Murray Milne, research professor in the Department of Architecture and Urban Design at the University of California, Los Angeles, suggests that water usage per person in the early 1900s was about the same as that in Imperial Rome. However, by the mid-twentieth century, water consumption had increased considerably.

The listings in the upper portion of Table 11.2 are suggested by Milne, whereas the bottom U.S. listings are from more traditional plumbing guides. It is interesting to note that while the 70 gallons per day per person that Milne lists is basically the same as the figure listed for U.S. single-family homes in a variety of tables, consumption in luxury housing is suggested to be twice as much. What might cause such a discrepancy? Do wealthy people take more baths rather than short showers? Do they wear more clothing and therefore have to do more laundry? It is not clear why this difference occurs.

We might also question why Milne suggests that daily water consumption per capita in pre–World War II American cities and in Los Angeles in the mid-1970s was 15 gallons and 182 gallons, respectively, whereas in the typical U.S. home, it was only 70 gallons. This distinction is the difference between what is used in the home compared to what is used on a per capita basis in all occupancies in a city. These include water used when people are away from home and water used in construction, commercial activities, and industry. Obviously, water used for irrigation and thermoelectric power generation, which combined account for almost 1000 GCD, is not included in these city figures.

While our involvement with water supply will probably be primarily in connection with the design of single-family residences, we should be aware that water is also used outside of the home. Interestingly, this water is often referred to as *domestic water* to distinguish it from water used for heating purposes or irrigation, although at times it is also called *tap water* or *service water*. Whatever it is called, we should be aware of how much is required. Table 11.3 lists the per capita demand for several different building

types, including residential occupancy, which is presented in several classifications.

Table 11.4 presents the typical U.S. water consumption prior to the Energy Policy Act and the more efficient usage after its passage. Major adjustments for reduced consumption assume water restrictors for the showerhead, shorter showers (5 minutes versus 8 minutes), 1.6-gallons-per-flush toilets rather than 3.5-gallons-per-flush units, and high-efficiency clothes washers. In addition to the reduction of water used for toilets, showers, and clothes washers, the assumption is that there will be no use of conventional potable water for irrigation and that there is a significant reduction in the amount of water lost due to leakage.

A 1.6-gallons-per-flush toilet uses 54% less water than a 3.5-gallons-per-flush toilet. Using a 2-GPM water restrictor and reducing the time from 8 to 5 minutes provides a 50% reduction in water used for showers. And since a front-loading clothes washer uses only around 15 gallons per cycle compared to a top-loading washer that requires 40 gallons, switching washers can produce a 67% reduction. Combined, these changes can produce an overall reduction of 44% in water consumption. Further reductions in water usage are also possible. Since, of the six toilet uses per day, four or even five are usually for light waste, dual-flush toilets that use only around 1 gallon for a light-waste flush could easily cut in half the water used for flushing toilets. And, as mentioned, showerhead flow can be reduced from 2.5 GPM to around 1.5 GPM, which can still provide an effective spray, and the time for a shower can be shortened to less than 5 minutes. Perhaps we might even consider whether a shower must remain on during soaping-up time. Sailors on a submarine typically get only 20 to 30 seconds to wet themselves, some no-water time for washing, and another 20 to 30 seconds for rinsing! Another effective means of reducing water consumption is possible by using both the clothes washer and the dishwasher only when they are full.

While the Energy Policy Act has reduced water consumption, it does not necessarily set the bar at the lowest level (or perhaps the highest level in terms of performance). There are a variety of ways in which water consumption can be further reduced, some of which are presented in Table 11.5, which assumes a family of four.

Table 11.4 indicates that per person daily water use is 73.2 gallons, which is slightly higher than the standard 70 GCD. By adding a factor for plumbing leaks but excluding irrigation, a family of four would use around 330 gallons per day at conventional rates of consumption. By adopting all of the water-saving recommendations in Table 11.4, water consumption can be reduced to 43 GCD. At this rate, a family of four would consume around 170 gallons per day, or only about half of the standard amount of water.

Table 11.3: PLANNING GUIDE FOR WATER SUPPLY

Building Usage	Per Capita Daily Usage	
	Gallons (GDC)	Liters
Airports (per Passenger)	3–5	11–19
Bath Houses (per Bather)	10	38
Camps		
Construction, Semipermanent (per Worker)	50	189
Day with No Meals Served (per Camper)	15	57
Luxury (per Camper)	100–150	378–568
Resorts, Day and Night, with Limited Plumbing (per Camper)	50	189
Tourist, with Central Bath and Toilet Facilities (per Person)	35	132
Cottages with Seasonal Occupancy (per Resident)	50	189
Courts, Tourist, with Individual Bath Units (per Person)	50	189
Clubs		
Country (per Resident Member)	100	378
Country (per Nonresident Member Present)	25	95
Dwellings		
Apartments, Multiple Family (per Resident)	40–60	151–227
Single Family (per Resident)	50–75	189–284
Luxury (per Person)	100–150	378–568
Rooming Houses (per Resident)	60	227
Boardinghouses (per Boarder)	50	189
Additional Kitchen Requirements for Nonresident Boarders	10	38
Hotels and Motels		
Hotels with Private Baths (Two Persons per Room)	60	227
Hotels without Private Baths (per Person)	50	189
Motels with Bath, Toilet, and Kitchen Facilities (per Bed)	50	189
Motel with Bed and Toilet (per Bed Space)	40	151
Institutions		
Other Than Hospitals (per Person)	75–125	284–473
Hospitals (per Bed)	250–400	946–1514
Schools		
Boarding (per Pupil)	75–100	284–378
Day, with Cafeteria, Gym, or Showers (per Pupil)	25	95
Day, with Cafeteria but No Gym or Showers (per Pupil)	20	76
Day, without Cafeteria, Gym, or Showers (per Pupil)	15	57
Parks		
Overnight, with Flush Toilets (per Camper)	25	95
Trailer, with Bath, No Sewer Connection (per Trailer)	25	95
Trailer, with Baths, Connected to Sewer (per Person)	50	189
Picnic		
With Baths, Showers, and Flush Toilets (per Picnicker)	20	76
With Toilet Facilities Only (per Picnicker)	10	38
Restaurants with Toilet Facilities (per Patron)	7–10	26–38
Without Toilet Facilities (per Patron)	$2\frac{1}{2}$–3	9–11
With Bar/Cocktail Lounge (Additional per Patron)	2	8
Stores (per Toilet Room)	400	1514
Swimming Pools (per Swimmer)	10	38
Theaters		
Drive-in (per Car Space)	5	19
Movie (per Auditorium Seat)	5	19
Laundries, Self-Service (per Washing)	50	189
Factories (per Person per Shift)	15–35	57–132
Highway Rest Area (per Person)	5	19

Table 11.3 (*Continued*)

Building Usage	Per Capita Daily Usage	
	Gallons (GDC)	Liters
Workers		
Construction (per Person per Shift)	50	189
Day (School or Office, per Person per Shift)	15	57
Service Stations (per Vehicle)	10	38
Livestock (per Animal)		
Cattle (Drinking)	12	45
Dairy (Drinking and Servicing)	35	132
Goat (Drinking)	2	8
Hog (Drinking)	4	15
Horse (Drinking)	12	45
Mule (Drinking)	12	45
Poultry		
Chickens (per 100)	5–10	19–38
Turkeys (per 100)	10–18	38–68
Sheep (Drinking)	2	8
Steer (Drinking)	12	45

Source: Adapted from B. Stein, J.S. Reynolds, W.T. Grondzik, and A.G. Kwok, *Mechanical and Electrical Equipment for Buildings* (John Wiley & Sons, Inc., Hoboken, NJ, 2006), Table 20.2.

By following the appropriate recommendations in Table 11.5, including the use of dual-action toilets, restricted showerheads, and leak control, an additional reduction in family water consumption can be realized, reducing the daily use by around 80 to 100 gallons per day. With all of these savings, a family of four might require only 100 gallons or less, which means only 25 GCD, or around one-third of standard use.

In addition to reducing water consumption, we should consider whether the same quality of water needs to be provided for all purposes. Most plumbing systems supply only potable water, although the water consumed by drinking or in association with food preparation accounts for just a small amount of the total water that we use. Tables 11.1 and 11.4 indicate that only 3 gallons, or slightly more than 4% of the 70 gallons typically

Table 11.4: WATER USAGE IN THE TYPICAL U.S. HOME

	Conventional Consumption		Water-Efficient Consumption	
	GCD	Percentage	GCD	Percentage
Drinking and Cooking	3.0	4.1	3.0	7.3
Dishwashers	3.5	4.8	3.0	7.3
Faucets	7.9	10.8	7.8	18.9
Toilets				
6 Flushes at 3.5 Gallons	21.0	28.7		
6 Flushes at 1.6 Gallons			9.6	23.3
Showers				
8 Minutes at 2.5 GPM	20.0	27.3		
5 Minutes at 2.0 GPM			10.0	24.3
Baths	1.2	1.6	1.2	2.9
Clothes Washers	15.0	20.5	5.0	12.1
Other Domestic Uses	1.6	2.2	1.6	3.9
Total Use per Capita	**73.2**	**100.0%**	**41.2**	**100.0%**
Consumption Use	73.2	60.6	41.2	95.4
Leaks	9.5	7.9	2.0	4.6
Irrigation	38.0	31.5	0.0	0.0
Total per Capita Use	**120.7**	**100.0%**	**43.2**	**100.0%**

Source: Adapted in part from American Water Works Association data.

Table 11.5: WAYS TO REDUCE RESIDENTIAL WATER CONSUMPTION

Action to Reduce Consumption	Savings per Family
• Replace Older Toilets with Toilets That Require No More Than 1.6 Gallons per Flush.	38 gal/day
• Even Better, Replace Older Toilets with Dual-Action, Ultra-Low-Flush Toilets That Require Only 1.2 or 1.4 Gallons per Flush for Heavy Waste and Only 1 Gallon per Flush for Light Waste.	48 gal/day
• Switch from 1.6-Gallons-per-Flush Toilets to Dual-Action, Ultra-Low-Flush Toilets (1/1.4 Gallons).	12 gal/day
• Use Restricted Showerheads That Use 1.5 GPM versus 2.5 GPM When Open and Reduce Shower Time from 8 to 5 Minutes.	50 gal/day
• Replace a Top-Loading, Agitator Washing Machine with a Front-Loading, Horizontal-Axis, High-Efficiency Clothes Washer. Assume Eight Loads per Family per Week.	30 gal/day
• Turn Water Off While Brushing Teeth and/or Shaving.	20 gal/day
• Replace the Old Dishwasher Requiring Over 10 Gallons per Cycle with a Newer Green Unit Requiring Only 4 Gallons or Less per Cycle, and Operate It Only When Full.	6 gal/day
• Peel and Clean Vegetables in a Bowl of Water Instead of Letting the Water Run.	20 gal/day
• Hand Wash Pots and Pans in a Basin and Then Rinse Them Off.	10 gal/day

• Practice Routine Commonsense Leak Detection Periodically:
   • Check Out Running-Water Noise.
   • "Zero Read" Water Meter for Leaks.
   • Replace Worn Valves, Washers, and O Rings.
	c. 20 gal/day

Note: Based on a family of four persons and six flushes (five plus one) per person per day.

used each day, are consumed by drinking and cooking. However, since the same water supply line typically supplies all of the plumbing fixtures, all of the water used is potable. Although clean water is appropriate for personal hygiene and clothes washing, this water does not have to be potable.

We need to rethink how water is supplied to the various plumbing fixtures. Perhaps dual or even triple water-supply systems need to be developed: a potable water system for consumption, a clean water system for personal hygiene, and a gray water system for toilets. Gray water is the drainage from the various plumbing fixtures other than toilets, whereas clean water might be fresh water that does not meet potable water standards. This could be gray water that has been partially treated.

The average size of the American family is 3.15 persons, although data also suggest that the typical U.S. residence has only around 2.5 persons, with a slightly higher number in single-family units compared to apartments or multifamily units. The difference between these numbers, 3.15 versus 2.5, might seem to be in conflict, but in actuality it probably indicates that not all members of a family necessarily reside in the same place. For example, when a dependent student attends school and does not live at home, that student remains a member of the family but is not necessarily included in the count of the number of individuals residing in the primary home. Family separations and divorce also affect the average number of individuals residing in a residence.

When we are involved in the design of a single-family residence, we probably will assume that the number of occupants will be a whole number, often set at four or five individuals or at the number of people who might reasonably be accommodated in the house. Assuming four persons and a 40-gallon-per-day consumption by each, the

Table 11.6: DAILY AND ANNUAL HOUSEHOLD WATER DEMAND

GCD	Family Size	Daily Demand	Annual Demand
30 GCD	3 Persons	90 gal/day	32,850 gal/yr
	4 Persons	120 gal/day	43,800 gal/yr
	5 Persons	150 gal/day	54,750 gal/yr
40 GCD	3 Persons	120 gal/day	43,800 gal/yr
	4 Persons	160 gal/day	58,400 gal/yr
	5 Persons	200 gal/day	73,000 gal/yr
50 GCD	3 Persons	150 gal/day	54,750 gal/yr
	4 Persons	200 gal/day	73,000 gal/yr
	5 Persons	250 gal/day	91,250 gal/yr
60 GCD	3 Persons	180 gal/day	65,700 gal/yr
	4 Persons	240 gal/day	87,500 gal/yr
	5 Persons	300 gal/day	109,500 gal/yr
70 GCD	3 Persons	210 gal/day	76,650 gal/yr
	4 Persons	280 gal/day	102,200 gal/yr
	5 Persons	350 gal/day	127,750 gal/yr

annual water demand for the residence would be around 60,000 gallons.

$$4 \text{ persons} \times 40 \text{ GCD} \times 365 \text{ days} = 58,400 \text{ gal}$$

Obviously, the overall demand for water will change if we adjust the number of people and the assumption about how much water is consumed daily by each person. Table 11.6 shows daily and annual water demand for various sizes of households and assumed daily water consumption per person.

As we address how much water we actually use,[1] we should consider how best to wash our dishes, by hand or in an automatic dishwasher. There are various opinions on this, but based on recent studies, including one done at the

---

[1] We should each keep a record of our personal daily water usage over a period of time, paying particular attention to ways that we might reduce this consumption, such as spending less time in the shower or turning off water when not in use, such as when brushing our teeth.

University of Bonn in Germany, it is now clear that automatic dishwashers generally use less water and less energy than washing dishes by hand. Most modern dishwashers use 7 to 10 gallons per wash cycle, and some newer units use only 4 gallons. Since modern kitchen faucets have a flow rate of around 2.5 GPM, this means only around 2 to 4 minutes of hand washing, which is hardly adequate to handle the approximately 12 place settings that a dishwasher can handle per wash cycle.

Of course, to realize the greatest water savings with a dishwasher, it should be run only when it is full, which relates to the dishes used each day by a family of four. This converts into water use of 2.5 GCD for dishwashing, but then there is also the water required to clean the cooking utensils and pots and pans, some of which can also be cleaned in the dishwasher. As an aside, even though an automatic dishwasher uses electricity, because it uses less hot water, overall an automatic dishwasher typically also consumes less energy than hand washing, and when the dry cycle is not used, the energy use is even less. Another advantage of the automatic dishwasher is a reduction in soap consumption, which can reduce the demands on the sewage system.

WATER SUPPLY

Once we have some basis to determine how much water is required, perhaps to meet the overall water demand for a residence or maybe only a particular use, we need to consider how this water can be provided. In the United States, most of the water consumed in buildings is supplied from a public water system, although some of these systems are actually private enterprises. Whether owned and operated by a local government agency or private enterprise, a public or community water system ensures that we have access to water that is clean and potable. It is also likely that this water is supplied with enough pressure to allow distribution throughout a typical single-family residence or low-rise building, although this is something that should be verified when determining the appropriate size for supply piping.

When there is no community water service, an independent water source needs to be developed; this must be done for around 15% of U.S. single-family residences. There are several possible alternatives, including using a source of surface water that might be on or near the site, drilling for water, or collecting rainwater. If there is a water body, such as a pond, lake, or stream, on or close to the building site, water can be pumped from this source. However, there is a high probability that this water will be contaminated, requiring a reasonable amount of treatment before use, particularly in a conventional plumbing approach that does not differentiate the use of the water supply. It is also possible, and if so probably preferable, to drill a well, but this depends on the geological conditions, which are not something that architects and designers typically determine. If this is feasible, then we would likely hire a specialist to determine the location where water is likely to be found, to drill the well, and to provide the necessary pumping and storage equipment. As with surface water, it is important to verify that the quality of the water is acceptable. Since groundwater generally consists of water that has percolated through the soil, it is usually reasonably clean, or at least cleaner than surface water, but we should not assume that it is of adequate purity but, rather, verify its quality. Again, this is not something that typically falls within the realm of the architect, although we are usually responsible for ensuring that things are done properly.

If the alternative of collecting rainwater is preferred, then probably we are involved since it is likely that the roof will be a major collecting surface and there are some architectural features that need to be provided. There is also the question of how the water that we collect will be used. Sometimes the reasonable approach is to use the collected rainwater, often referred to as *cistern water*, for flushing toilets and/or for washing and personal hygiene, relying on bottled water for the approximately 3 GCD consumed by drinking and cooking, although it is also possible that the water can be easily treated to meet potable quality standards.

Bottled water is an option for supplying clean potable water, but for regular use this should be supplied in 5-gallon or larger jugs. While bottled water clearly does not make up the majority of our daily water consumption, it is amazing how much bottled water is still consumed, especially water purchased in smaller liter-sized plastic containers. In an August 1, 2007, editorial in the *New York Times*, some interesting facts about bottled water were presented:

- The quality, purity, and even taste of most tap water are equal to, if not better than, those of most bottled waters.
- Annual water consumption at eight glasses per day:
     Tap water – 49 cents
     Bottled water – $1400
- 1.5 million barrels of oil are required each year to produce the plastic bottles consumed in the United States.
- Americans recycle only 23% of the plastic bottles they use.
- While some bottled water does come from a special water source, some is merely tap water, although generally tap water of decent quality.
- We tend to pay more for bottled water per liter than we do for gasoline.

Water Supply–Groundwater

When a public water supply is not available, we often rely on groundwater. It is possible that there is a spring on the property, but more likely it is necessary to drill down to the aquifer, an underground layer of water-bearing permeable rock or unconsolidated materials (gravel, sand, silt, or clay) (see Figure 11.1). If the aquifer is unconfined, it is generally located near the surface and is readily recharged by precipitation that percolates through the soil. The top of this aquifer, specifically the level of the saturated or water-filled part of the porous subsurface layer, is referred to as the *water table*. That is, the water table indicates the level at which water is located below grade. Above an unconfined aquifer is unsaturated soil. A confined aquifer lies below an impermeable layer, and it is not readily recharged by surface water.

Under certain conditions, similar to what is shown in Figure 11.2, a well can be drilled into a pressurized portion of a confined aquifer. If this happens, it is an *artesian well*, meaning that it would not be necessary to pump the water to the surface, although it is likely that the water supply would still have to pressurize in order to distribute the water to its ultimate place of use. Generally, this happens only in a valley since a portion of the underground water might actually be higher than the well. This produces what is sometimes referred to as a *head of water*, which is pressure developed by the increased height of the water. If this exists and there is a natural fissure in the impervious strata, a natural spring occurs. However, the conditions necessary to produce an artesian well or spring do not usually exist, so after drilling into the underground aquifer, the water has to be pumped out. Whether the pressure exists naturally or

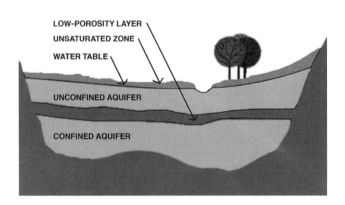

Figure 11.1 UNDERGROUND AQUIFERS—CONFINED AND UNCONFINED
An aquifer is an underground layer of water-bearing porous material from which the water can be extracted. The water table essentially is set at the top of the water-bearing material. Often there is, as shown, both an unconfined aquifer that is recharged by rainwater filtering through the unsaturated ground and a confined aquifer that is not readily recharged. When water, which can be extracted from either aquifer, is drawn from the unconfined aquifer, it tends to lower the level of the water table.

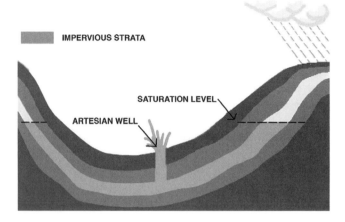

Figure 11.2 ARTESIAN WELL
If a confined aquifer is pressurized, generally because of a change in elevation, as shown, and a natural fissure exists through the confining layer of low-porosity material, the water can be released. This essentially forms a spring. When a well is drilled into a pressurized confined aquifer and the rise to grade is within the potential of the pressure, the water will flow out naturally. Such a pressurized well is referred to as an *artesian well*.

has to be supplied, raising a quantity of water to a higher elevation requires pressure.

The head of water that is produced is the pressure that water exerts as a result of its elevated height. A cubic foot of water weighs 62.428 pounds. Therefore, a volume of water that has a 1-square-inch footprint and a 12-inch height would weigh 0.43 pound.

$$62.428 \text{ lb} \div 144 \text{ sq in.} = 0.43 \text{ lb/sq in.}$$

A column of water exerts a pressure of 0.43 pound per square inch for each foot of height. For quick estimations, we can assume about $^1/_2$ pound per foot.

A pump is a device used to add pressure to water, and generally we must use a pump to increase the pressure to remove water from an aquifer and definitely to supply water to a higher level, such as a bathroom on the second floor of a house or, in a more extreme situation, to a water closet at the top of the Empire State Building. Traditional water pumps use atmospheric pressure to raise the water, and as a result, the maximum height that they can lift the water is about 34 feet. The atmosphere has weight, and this weight presses down on the earth. Standard atmospheric pressure, which is the weight per square inch of the atmosphere at sea level, is 14.7 pounds per square inch (psia). Since a 1-square-inch column of water 12 inches high weighs 0.43 pound, the atmospheric pressure can raise a column of water, but only to around 34 feet.

$$14.7 \text{ lb/sq in.} \div 0.43 \text{ lb/sq in./ft} = 34.186 \text{ ft}$$

The traditional hand-operated water pump creates a vacuum in the supply pipe, which eliminates the downward atmospheric pressure within the pipe. Without the downward pressure in the supply pipe, the atmospheric pressure pushes the water up. This is similar to what happens in a barometer. However, since a complete vacuum is not generally attained with hand pumps, they typically are effective for only about a 25-foot rise. If it is necessary to lift the water more than this, we cannot rely on suction and atmospheric pressure to raise the water. As a result, with deep wells and high-rise structures, we generally have to use a positive displacement pump that can "push" the water rather than "suck" it. With deep wells, this generally requires submerging the pump into the well so that the water is propelled by a pressure greater than 1 atmosphere (14.7 psia).

Wells are typically extended down to access water from the aquifer. While it is possible to drill down to reach an underground aquifer and insert a pump to extract the water, traditionally wells had to be dug by hand down far enough to reach the water table. As a result, these wells often had rather large diameters, which then made it possible for people to actually walk down to the water level (see Figure 11.3).

Rather than extend down to the water table, some wells were really only water storage vessels that collected surface water. In this arrangement, the well was located at a low point so that any precipitation that was not absorbed into the ground would flow into the well. While such wells provided a reasonable source of water, they were subject to contamination since there was no significant percolation through the soil. The well merely collected surface runoff.

Figure 11.3 POZZO DI S. PATRIZIO

St. Patrick's Well (Pozzo di S. Patrizio) in Orvieto, Italy, is an extremely impressive and fascinating architectural accomplishment. It was designed and built in the sixteenth century at the urging of the pope, who feared that the town would be besieged, requiring a water supply within the safety of the city. The well, a short distance from Orvieto's Duomo, is 175 feet deep and around 45 feet wide. A double-helix stair (two spiral stairs) provides access to the bottom of the shaft to collect water. This permitted convenient one-way movement—one stair down to the bottom and one up to grade—although going down and up 175 feet is probably not considered very convenient.

Water Supply—Rainwater Collection

In areas where a public water supply and access to groundwater are not readily available, rainwater is often the major source of water. While collected rainwater is sometimes the only source of water and is used for all water needs, many rainwater collection systems are used for everything but drinking and cooking. Rainwater itself is reasonably clean, although if the atmosphere is polluted, it can be contaminated. The drops of water might have formed on particles of nasty stuff or, as the rain falls to the ground, it can absorb various chemicals. A more common problem with collected rainwater results from the contaminants that are deposited on the collection or catchment surfaces and carried away with the rainwater. While these contaminants might have settled out of the air, they also probably include bird droppings and other such substances, as well as roofing materials that wear away. Using an initial collection bypass, filtering and treating the collected water, and proper control of the water storage can minimize the problems with collected rainwater. Of course, the intended use of the collected rainwater should determine the appropriate level of treatment.

Collecting rainwater is an attractive means of supplying water for certain purposes even when a public water supply is available. For one thing, this can reduce the use of potable water for functions like irrigation or flushing toilets. Also, by using collected rainwater for irrigation, the natural water cycle is essentially maintained since much of the water used for irrigation will recharge the ground water rather than overload the sewer system, which occurs in those urban areas that require rainwater coming off the roofs to be discharged into the sewer system. Of course, when a public water supply is not available and there is no access to groundwater, rainwater is the source of water for most, if not all, water use.

Sizing a rainwater collection system to meet a water demand is relatively simple. The process entails determining the amount of precipitation that is generally available and then matching the collection and storage capacity with the demand. When a match is not possible, the objective is to determine the percentage of demand that rainwater collection can supply. Figure 11.4 shows the annual precipitation for the United States. While this map provides an indication of how much precipitation might occur across the country, more detailed information is required to size a collection and storage system. The amount of precipitation at different U.S. locations is available from the National Oceanic and Atmospheric Administration (NOAA).[2]

---

[2]http://cdo.ncdc.noaa.gov/cgi-bin/climatenormals/climatenormals.
  pl?directive=prod_select&subrnum=.

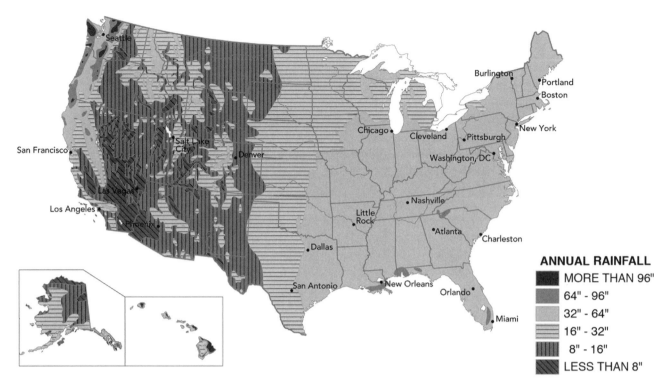

Figure 11.4 AVERAGE ANNUAL U.S. PRECIPITATION
This map presents a rough indication of the variations in annual rainfall across the United States. However, since the detail of the map is not refined and the range of rainfall for each plotted area is somewhat large, it is better to use data from the NOAA for actual calculations.

There are four critical issues for a rainwater collection system: the amount of precipitation, the collection or catchment area, the storage capacity, and the demand. While it is obvious that more water can be collected when there is more precipitation and/or there is a larger catchment area, sometimes the critical issue is when the rain might occur compared to when the demand might arise. Since these may not coincide, it is necessary to consider how much water must be stored and how this water can be secured and protected. There is also the question of how the precipitation occurs—during regular light rain or drizzle or during short, heavy rainfalls.

There are several steps in establishing a proper rainwater catchment area and storage facility:

■ Determine the gallons of water required over a year.
■ Determine the rainfall for the area on a monthly basis.
■ Determine the catchment area.
■ Determine the storage capacity.

Table 11.7 includes monthly and annual precipitation data for selected cities in the United States. A more extensive listing of locations is available from the NOAA Web page. Rainfall data, which should be the most up-to-date for these locations, can be searched by the particular city or zip code.

Once we know the amount of rainfall that is available and the catchment area, we can determine the yield either by using the graph presented in Figure 11.6 or by calculating the yield based on 1 inch of rain on a 1-square foot area equaling 0.6234 gallon of water. Generally, some of the precipitation is lost to evaporation or spillage, or it is of a nature that might not be collectable. Based on these losses, we usually assume that the catchment yield will be somewhere between 75% and 90% of the actual rainfall amount.

The percentage of rainwater that can be collected is based in part on the collection surface, which is usually the roof, and on the type of precipitation that might occur. If the roof is made of composite shingles, asphalt shingles, or cement tiles, which all have a rough surface, some rainwater will be trapped on the shingles or tiles. While a light drizzle of short duration is included in the data of precipitation received, it is questionable if much of this type of precipitation would actually be collected from these surfaces. It is likely that a drizzle would only wet the roof, resulting in little, if any, actual rainwater collection. If some of the precipitation is retained even temporarily on the roof surface and the surface is hot, there would be further loss due to evaporation. On the other hand, a slate or metal roof tends to trap very little precipitation, even if it is in the form of drizzle.

There is also a possibility that as rainwater runs over the roof, it will pick up contaminants, which might leach out from the roof surface and which we do not want to have

Table 11.7: MONTHLY AND ANNUAL PRECIPITATION FOR SELECTED U.S. CITIES

City, State	Jan	Feb	Mar	Apr	May	Jun	Jul	Aug	Sep	Oct	Nov	Dec	Annual
Phoenix, AZ	0.83	0.77	1.07	0.25	0.16	0.09	0.99	0.94	0.75	0.79	0.73	0.92	8.29
Los Angeles, CA	2.98	3.11	2.40	0.63	0.24	0.08	0.03	0.14	0.26	0.36	1.13	1.79	13.15
San Francisco, CA	4.45	4.01	3.26	1.17	0.38	0.11	0.03	0.07	0.20	1.04	2.49	2.89	20.11
Denver, CO	0.51	0.49	1.28	1.93	2.32	1.56	2.16	1.82	1.14	0.99	0.98	0.63	15.81
Hartford, CT	3.84	2.96	3.88	3.86	4.39	3.85	3.67	3.98	4.13	3.94	4.06	3.60	46.16
Washington, DC	3.21	2.63	3.60	2.77	3.82	3.13	3.66	3.44	3.79	3.22	3.03	3.05	39.35
Miami, FL	1.88	2.07	2.56	3.36	5.52	8.54	5.79	8.63	8.38	6.19	3.43	2.18	58.53
Tampa, FL	2.27	2.67	2.84	1.80	2.85	5.50	6.49	7.60	6.54	2.29	1.62	2.30	44.77
Tallahassee, FL	5.36	4.63	6.47	3.59	4.95	6.92	8.04	7.03	5.01	3.25	3.86	4.10	63.21
Atlanta, GA	5.02	4.68	5.38	3.62	3.95	3.63	5.12	3.67	4.09	3.11	4.10	3.82	50.20
Savannah, GA	3.95	2.92	3.64	3.32	3.61	5.49	6.04	7.20	5.08	3.12	2.40	2.81	49.58
Honolulu, HI	2.73	2.35	1.89	1.11	0.78	0.43	0.50	0.46	0.74	2.18	2.26	2.85	18.29
Boise, ID	1.39	1.14	1.41	1.27	1.27	0.74	0.39	0.30	0.76	0.76	1.38	1.38	12.19
Chicago, IL	1.75	1.63	2.65	3.68	3.38	3.63	3.51	4.62	3.27	2.71	3.01	2.43	36.27
Indianapolis, IN	2.48	2.41	3.44	3.61	4.35	4.13	4.42	3.82	2.88	2.76	3.61	3.03	40.95
Lexington, KY	3.34	3.27	4.41	3.67	4.78	4.58	4.80	3.77	3.11	2.70	3.44	4.03	45.91
New Orleans, LA	5.87	5.47	5.24	5.02	4.62	6.83	6.20	6.15	5.55	3.05	5.09	5.07	64.16
Portland, ME	4.09	3.14	4.14	4.26	3.82	3.28	3.32	3.05	3.37	4.40	4.72	4.24	45.83
Boston, MA	3.92	3.30	3.85	3.60	3.24	3.22	3.06	3.37	3.47	3.79	3.98	3.73	42.53
Detroit, MI	1.91	1.88	2.52	3.05	3.05	3.55	3.16	3.10	3.27	2.23	2.66	2.51	32.89
Grand Rapid, MI	2.03	1.53	2.59	3.48	3.35	3.67	3.56	3.78	4.28	2.80	3.35	2.70	37.13
Minneapolis–St. Paul, MN	1.04	0.79	1.86	2.31	3.24	4.34	4.04	4.05	2.69	2.11	1.94	1.00	29.41
Jackson, MS	5.67	4.50	5.74	5.98	4.86	3.82	4.69	3.66	3.23	3.42	5.04	5.34	55.95
Kansas City, MO	1.15	1.31	2.44	3.38	5.39	4.44	4.42	3.54	4.64	3.33	2.30	1.64	37.98
St. Louis, MO	2.14	2.28	3.60	3.69	4.11	3.76	3.90	2.98	2.96	2.76	3.71	2.86	38.75
Missoula, MT	1.06	0.77	0.96	1.09	1.95	1.73	1.09	1.15	1.08	0.83	0.96	1.15	13.82
Lincoln, NE	0.67	0.66	2.21	2.90	4.23	3.51	3.54	3.35	2.92	1.94	1.58	0.86	28.37
Las Vegas, NV	0.59	0.69	0.59	0.15	0.24	0.08	0.44	0.45	0.31	0.24	0.31	0.40	4.49
Albuquerque, NM	0.49	0.44	0.61	0.50	0.60	0.65	1.27	1.73	1.07	1.00	0.62	0.49	9.47
Buffalo, NY	3.16	2.42	2.99	3.04	3.35	3.82	3.14	3.87	3.84	3.19	3.92	3.80	40.54
New York, NY	3.56	2.75	3.93	3.68	4.16	3.57	4.41	4.09	3.77	3.26	3.67	3.51	44.36
Charlotte, NC	4.00	3.55	4.39	2.95	3.66	3.42	3.79	3.72	3.83	3.66	3.36	3.18	43.51
Cincinnati, OH	2.92	2.75	3.90	3.96	4.59	4.42	3.75	3.79	2.82	2.96	3.46	3.28	42.60
Cleveland, OH	2.48	2.29	2.94	3.37	3.50	3.89	3.52	3.69	3.77	2.73	3.38	3.14	38.71
Columbus, OH	2.53	2.20	2.89	3.25	3.88	4.07	4.61	3.72	2.92	2.31	3.19	2.93	38.52
Oklahoma City, OK	1.28	1.56	2.90	3.00	5.44	4.63	2.94	2.48	3.98	3.64	2.11	1.89	35.85
Portland, OR	5.07	4.18	3.71	2.64	2.38	1.59	0.72	0.93	1.65	2.88	5.61	5.71	37.07
Philadelphia, PA	3.52	2.74	3.81	3.49	3.88	3.29	4.39	3.82	3.88	2.75	3.16	3.31	42.05
Pittsburgh, PA	2.70	2.37	3.17	3.01	3.80	4.12	3.96	3.38	3.21	2.25	3.02	2.86	37.85
Charleston, SC	4.08	3.08	4.00	2.77	3.67	5.92	6.13	6.91	5.98	3.09	2.66	3.24	51.53
Memphis, TN	4.24	4.31	5.58	5.79	5.15	4.30	4.22	3.00	3.31	3.31	5.76	5.68	54.65
Dallas–Fort Worth, TX	1.90	2.37	3.06	3.20	5.15	3.23	2.12	2.03	2.42	4.11	2.57	2.57	34.73
Houston, TX	3.68	2.98	3.36	3.60	5.15	5.35	3.18	3.83	4.33	4.50	4.19	3.69	47.84
Salt Lake City, UT	1.37	1.33	1.91	2.02	2.09	0.77	0.72	0.76	1.33	1.57	1.40	1.23	16.50
Richmond, VA	3.55	2.98	4.09	3.18	3.95	3.54	4.67	4.18	3.98	3.60	3.06	3.12	43.91
Seattle, WA	5.13	4.18	3.75	2.59	1.77	1.49	0.79	1.02	1.63	3.19	5.90	5.62	37.07
Milwaukee, WI	1.85	1.65	2.59	3.78	3.06	3.56	3.58	4.03	3.30	2.49	2.70	2.22	34.81
Cheyenne, WY	0.45	0.44	1.05	1.55	2.48	2.12	2.26	1.82	1.43	0.75	0.64	0.46	15.45

Source: Adapted from data from NOAA.

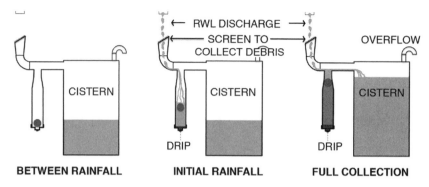

Figure 11.5 DIAGRAM OF A FIRST-FLUSH DIVERTER
This device keeps the initial rainwater from being collected in the cistern. The initial rain that comes off the collection surface fills the pipe column located before the entry into the cistern. This is the water that might be contaminated, so the contaminants are collected in the column. As the water fills the column, a float valve rises. When it gets to the top, this valve should keep the additional water flow, which should now be free of contaminants, from mixing with the contaminated water in the pipe column. The pipe column includes a slow-drip opening that will drain the column over time. As a result, if there is only a short time between rainfalls, the pipe column will still contain some water. This will reduce the amount of water that has to be diverted, which is logical since there should be fewer contaminants that need to be removed.

in the collected water. Zinc and copper are two of the most serious pollutants that might be contained in rainwater coming off a metal roof. While zinc and copper can be problems, the worst-quality water tends to be that collected from wood-shingle roofs. Wood roof shingles are usually treated chemically, and these chemicals leach out when the shingles deflect water, especially when they are relatively new. Composite shingles also present problems since they too can contain nasty chemicals. While we need to be cautious in selecting roofing materials when the roof will serve as the catchment for rainwater, we might consider the advantages of a slate or metal roof, although the finish of the metal is a critical issue that we would need to explore.

It is also important to consider whether the water initially available from a rain should be retained since this water is often coming off a surface that, in the interim between rainfalls, might have been contaminated by a variety of substances that should not be mixed with the stored water. If roofs and other impervious surfaces are able to collect rain, they will also collect dirt and debris, including deposits from birds and other animals—not necessarily things that are desired in a source of water.

To avoid contaminating the collected water, a bypass mechanism, often called a *first-flush diverter*, should be included so that the initial discharge from the catchment area is not collected in the cistern. With such a diverter, rainwater collection will not begin until there has been enough rain to clean off the collection surfaces. While there are obvious advantages to including a first-flush diverter, it will further reduce the amount of water that can be collected. If the rain is light and of short duration, all of the water from a rain may be diverted, with none collected. While some first-flush diverters need to be manually reset

before the next rain, most are designed with a slow-acting drain that adjusts the amount of water diverted.

Figure 11.5 shows a simplified first-flush diverter. The initial rain washes the roof, carrying away debris and pollutants that have collected on the roof since the last rain. As this initial runoff enters the collection system, it flows through a screen filter that removes leaves and other physical particles. The water then drops into a vertical diversion tube, which should be sized to collect around 10 gallons per 1000 square feet of catchment area. The diagrammed system indicates a float within the tube. When the diversion tube fills, the float closes off the opening, reducing the likelihood that the water that continues to come off the roof will mix with the contaminated water within the tube. Without the float valve, the water that flows into the cistern could pick up some of the contaminants that were initially washed off the roof and fed into the diversion tube.

There should be an opening at the bottom of the diversion tube to allow the collected water to slowly drip out. In this way, the diversion tube will empty after the rain, so that it will again be able to collect the initial runoff during the next rainfall. Given the rate at which the diversion tube empties, it is possible that if the next rainfall comes after only a short interval, the tube will still be partially full. In this case, less rainwater will be initially diverted, which makes sense since there should be less dirt and pollution to be removed. Since the diversion tube collects more than just contaminated water that ultimately drips out, it should be possible to open the bottom of the tube to clean it out on a regular basis.

To account for this initial bypass in addition to evaporation and other losses, the actual collection yield might be less than the 70% to 90% range suggested above. Rather than merely guess at the percentage, we should consider various issues: the usual nature of the precipitation that

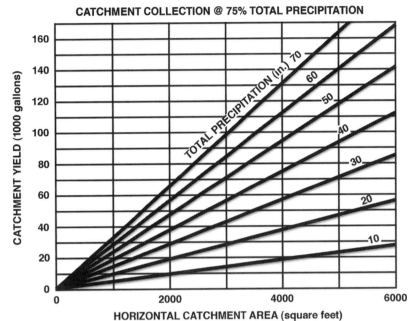

CATCHMENT COLLECTION @ 75% TOTAL PRECIPITATION

y-axis: CATCHMENT YIELD (1000 gallons)

x-axis: HORIZONTAL CATCHMENT AREA (square feet)

curve labels: TOTAL PRECIPITATION (in.) 70, 60, 50, 40, 30, 20, 10

Figure 11.6 CATCHMENT SIZING GRAPH
This graph indicates the amount of catchment area required to provide a particular yield or the yield that will result from a particular catchment area. Since annual precipitation of 40 inches is somewhat normal for much of the United States, this graph is effective only for general initial sizing of the rain catchment area or yield.

occurs in the location of the rainwater collection system; the actual collection surface(s) in terms of orientation, slope, and materials; the collection piping that includes gutters, rainwater leaders, and often horizontal drains to gather the water at one location; and the purpose for which the collected water will be used. All of these factors impact the percentage of water that can be collected.

Sizing the Rainwater Collection System

A catchment-sizing graph provides a simple way to match yield to collection area based on total expected precipitation. Such a graph typically assumes a percentage of the total precipitation that can be collected. The graph shown in Figure 11.6 is based on a collection for the system of 75% of the total precipitation.

The catchment-sizing graph can be used to determine either the catchment yield for a particular catchment area or the required catchment area to produce a desired yield. While we can begin with the total precipitation expected for the year or for a particular month, usually the graph is better used for a quick approximation on an annual basis. Since the monthly precipitation amounts are usually rather small, making it more difficult to interpolate accurate readings from the graph, the results cannot be definitive. Also, determining how much water can be collected is only the beginning. The water storage cistern must also be properly sized, especially since the time when the rain is available does not usually match the time when the water might be required. Also, even when an alternative water source is available for domestic water usage, it is reason-

able to incorporate a rainwater collection system to supply water for irrigation. Of course, for this purpose, when it is raining, cistern water is not needed—irrigation is needed when there is no rain.

Let us assume that we wish to develop a rainwater collection system for flushing toilets within a small multifamily condominium complex. This system will have a 75% collection yield and will be at a location with 40 inches of annual precipitation. If there are 20 units within the complex and the average occupancy of each unit is assumed to be 2.5 individuals, the total population would be 50 people, each of whom we might assume flushes the toilet six times a day. Before we go further, we should realize that the number of toilets per unit or the total number for the condominium complex is not important, at least for this exercise. While at times the number of toilets can have an impact on use, the question deals with the amount of water that will be used for 300 flushes a day.

With 50 people flushing six times a day, assuming standard water closets using 1.6 gallons per flush, the complex uses around 480 gallons each day, about 15,000 gallons each month, or a little over 175,000 gallons each year to flush toilets.

Gallons = 50 People × 6 Flushes × 1.6 Gallon/Flush
= 480 Gallons/Day

Figure 11.7 indicates a yield of up to only around 170,000 gallons. Although we could try to extend the graph, for this calculation it makes sense to assume only half of the desired yield, size a catchment area for that lower amount, and then double its size to determine what might actually be required. Assuming 40 inches of

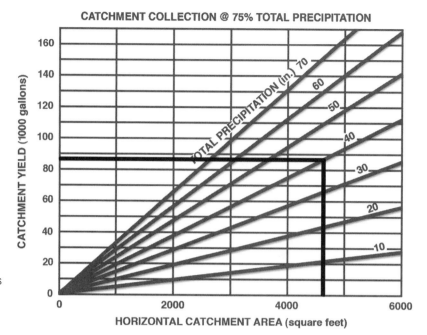

CATCHMENT COLLECTION @ 75% TOTAL PRECIPITATION

Figure 11.7 CATCHMENT SIZING GRAPH – EXAMPLE
This example is actually used to determine the catchment area required for a yield of 175,000 gallons with an annual precipitation of 40 inches; however, since this exceeds the yield range, only half of the required yield, 87,500 gallons, is assumed. This shows a catchment area of around 4600 square feet, which means that twice this area, or 9200 square feet, is required.

precipitation annually and a 75% collection yield, the catchment-sizing graph indicates that a total catchment area of around 4600 square feet is required to collect half of the demand, so the necessary catchment should have a total area of around 9200 square feet.

The reading of the graph requires interpolation, so it can provide only an approximation. If it is used for monthly precipitation, it is necessary to complete 12 readings using only several inches of precipitation for each. This attempt would soon demonstrate that using the graph, even though it is accurate, is not a precise way to determine either the yield or the catchment area. So, rather than use the catchment-sizing graph, which is merely a graphic plot of mathematically derived information, it is easier and more accurate to determine the yield or the required catchment area by using the simple calculation by which the graph was developed.

The calculation is based on the fact that 1 cubic foot of water contains 7.48 U.S. gallons. As a result, when 1 inch of rain falls over an area of 1 square foot, it amounts to one-twelfth of a gallon, or 0.6234 gallons. The basic formulas are:

$$\text{Yield (Gallons)} = \text{Catchment Area} \times 0.6234 \text{ Gallon/Inch} \\ \times \% \text{ Yield} \times \text{Inches of Precipitation}$$

$$\text{Required Catchment Area} = \\ \frac{\text{Required Gallons of Water}}{\text{Inches of Precipitation} \times \% \text{ Yield} \times 0.6234 \text{ gal/in.}}$$

An advantage of calculating the results over using the graph is that rather than assuming a prescribed percentage

of yield, which is usually set at 75%, a yield that is appropriate for the location and the conditions of the actual project can be readily applied.

Using the above catchment area formula, assuming 40 inches of annual precipitation and a 75% yield, the required catchment area for the 20-unit condominium toilet system is 9357 square feet rather than the 9200 square feet found by using the graph:

$$\frac{175,000 \text{ gal}}{40 \times 75\% \times 0.6234 \text{ gal/in.}} = 9357.3 \text{ sq ft}$$

Determining the yield from a catchment area, whether by calculating or by using the catchment-sizing graph, is only the beginning. Although we usually assume that water usage will be relatively stable day after day, such as with water used to flush the toilets in each small condominium, the rainfall not only will vary on a daily basis but also will vary considerably from month to month. As a result, we need to develop a water system that can collect the rain when it occurs and store it until it is needed, which requires a storage system capable of holding the excess water from the months when collection exceeds usage so that it will be available when the demand exceeds the rainfall. Since there is no assurance that the first month's collection will exceed, let alone match, the first month's demand, we should expect to charge the system for several months before it is actually put to use.

Table 11.8 presents rainwater collection and storage for the 20-unit condominium toilet system. The assumption is a catchment area of 9400 square feet, 75% yield, and the monthly precipitation as indicated. Basically, the table relates collection to usage, assuming that any net

Table 11.8: EXAMPLE OF RAINWATER COLLECTION AND STORAGE

Month	Rainfall (in.)	Catchment Yield (gal)	Usage (gal)	Net (gal)	Cumulative Capacity (gal)
May	4.59	20,173	14,880	5,293	5,293
June	4.42	19,426	14,400	5,026	10,319
July	3.75	16,481	14,880	1,601	11,920
August	3.79	16,657	14,880	1,777	13,697
September	2.82	12,394	14,400	(2,006)	11,691
October	2.96	13,009	14,880	(1,871)	9,820
November	3.46	15,207	14,400	807	10,626
December	3.28	14,416	14,880	(464)	10,162
January	2.92	12,833	14,880	(2,047)	8,115
February	2.75	12,086	13,440	(1,354)	6,761
March	3.90	17,140	14,880	2,260	9,022
April	3.96	17,404	14,400	3,004	12,026

gain is stored within a cistern so that this excess is available for the months when the amount collected is less than the amount used.

For several of the months, the table indicates that more water is consumed by flushing the toilets than is collected. However, there are a number of months when there is excess water, so if the cistern is large enough, the water demand should be met in those months when there is a deficiency by drawing down some of the excess water in the cistern. The first assumption might be merely to size the cistern to match the maximum monthly demand, which, for this example, is just below 15,000 gallons, but this would result in a cistern much larger than needed.

Instead, we might use the series of months for which the use exceeds the supply as the basis for sizing the cistern, which for this example would indicate a cistern of around 4000 gallons.

$$2006 + 1871 = 3,877 \text{ gal}$$

or

$$464 + 2047 + 1354 = 3865 \text{ gal}$$

Unfortunately, this would also be the wrong approach, resulting in a cistern that would be too small. Interestingly, for this example, the cistern should have a capacity of 7000 gallons. Table 11.9 is similar to Table 11.8, but it also includes a column that adjusts the cumulative capacity so that it does not exceed the capacity of the cistern. That is, the "Cumulative Capacity" column in both tables assumes an infinitely large cistern, whereas the maximum value in the last column in Table 11.9 is the capacity of the cistern.

Table 11.8 is set for a 6936-gallon cistern to show that for the month of February, only 1 gallon would be left in the cistern, indicating that this is the minimum-sized cistern that will work. In actuality, there should be a safety factor of around 10%. Based on this conclusion, a 7500-gallon cistern or perhaps even an 8000-gallon unit should be provided for this example.

Although both Tables 11.8 and 11.9 include information that seems to be relatively detailed, we should remember that all of it is based on some rather broad assumptions regarding the daily water consumption, the yield percentage, and the precipitation that will occur.

While the catchment-sizing graph is relatively easy to use, it is nearly impossible to use it to obtain precise information. Calculations based on the relationship

Table 11.9: EXAMPLE OF RAINWATER COLLECTION AND STORAGE

Month	Rainfall (in.)	Catchment Yield (gal)	Usage (gal)	Net (gal)	Cumulative Capacity (gal)	Cistern Capacity 6936 gal
May	4.59	20,173	14,880	5,293	5,293	6,936
June	4.42	19,426	14,400	5,026	10,319	6,936
July	3.75	16,481	14,880	1,601	11,920	6,936
August	3.79	16,657	14,880	1,777	13,697	6,936
September	2.82	12,394	14,400	(2,006)	11,691	4,930
October	2.96	13,009	14,880	(1,871)	9,820	3,059
November	3.46	15,207	14,400	807	10,626	3,866
December	3.28	14,416	14,880	(464)	10,162	3,401
January	2.92	12,833	14,880	(2,047)	8,115	1.354
February	2.75	12,086	13,440	(1,354)	6,761	1
March	3.90	17,140	14,880	2,260	9,022	2,261
April	3.96	17,404	14,400	3,004	12,026	5,265

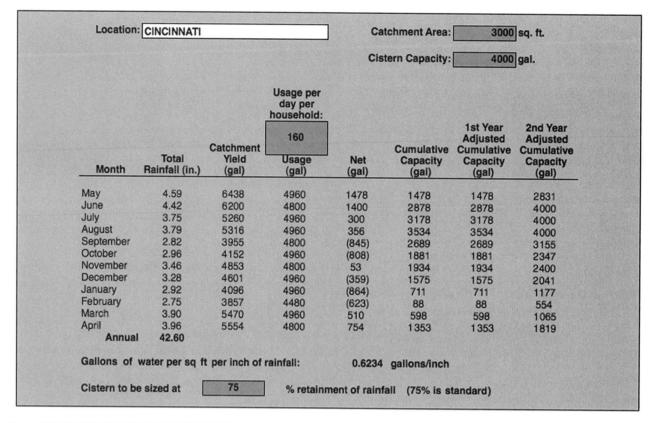

Month	Total Rainfall (in.)	Catchment Yield (gal)	Usage (gal)	Net (gal)	Cumulative Capacity (gal)	1st Year Adjusted Cumulative Capacity (gal)	2nd Year Adjusted Cumulative Capacity (gal)
May	4.59	6438	4960	1478	1478	1478	2831
June	4.42	6200	4800	1400	2878	2878	4000
July	3.75	5260	4960	300	3178	3178	4000
August	3.79	5316	4960	356	3534	3534	4000
September	2.82	3955	4800	(845)	2689	2689	3155
October	2.96	4152	4960	(808)	1881	1881	2347
November	3.46	4853	4800	53	1934	1934	2400
December	3.28	4601	4960	(359)	1575	1575	2041
January	2.92	4096	4960	(864)	711	711	1177
February	2.75	3857	4480	(623)	88	88	554
March	3.90	5470	4960	510	598	598	1065
April	3.96	5554	4800	754	1353	1353	1819
Annual	42.60						

Location: CINCINNATI   Catchment Area: 3000 sq. ft.   Cistern Capacity: 4000 gal.

Usage per day per household: 160

Gallons of water per sq ft per inch of rainfall: 0.6234 gallons/inch

Cistern to be sized at   75   % retainment of rainfall   (75% is standard)

Figure 11.8 EXAMPLE DATA PRODUCED BY A CATCHMENT-SIZING SPREADSHEET
This is an example of a catchment-sizing spreadsheet. A reasonable system size can be determined by manipulating the values for the rainfall, the percentage of collection, the catchment area and the cistern capacity.

between amount of precipitation, catchment area, yield percentage, and amount of water collected can provide accurate information, but the process can be somewhat tedious. Using a spreadsheet can provide effective results with minimal effort, although it does somewhat conceal how the responses are derived. Figure 11.8 shows an example of a catchment-sizing spreadsheet.

In the example above, we assumed that the rainwater would be used to flush the toilets. It makes sense to use rainwater for this or other purposes that do not require highly refined water, such as irrigation. But this means that separate water supply systems must be provided based on the type or quality of water and the intended use. As mentioned, when rainwater is the primary source of water, bottled water is often used for drinking and cooking, which means that there are two water supply systems, although not necessarily in an appropriate manner. We need to rethink how we access water and how we use it, and then propose an approach to water supply that is more appropriate than our current "one size fits all" approach.

While the tendency is to assume that water collection is based on rainwater, in many locations much of the precipitation comes in the form of snow, which can still charge the system. In determining how many inches of water can be obtained from snow, the conversion assumes that 10 inches of snow are basically equivalent to 1 inch of rain.

RAINWATER CONTROL

This discussion of rainwater collection as a means of providing water for irrigation and domestic usage includes the issue of storm water control and removal. This involves selecting gutters, rainwater leaders (RWL), and storm drains, all of which are sized based on expected maximum rainfall in terms of inches per hour. While the amount of precipitation over a period of time, typically a month or a year, is important for sizing a water collection system, the rate of rainfall is the critical issue in controlling runoff from roofs and paved areas.

Gutters, RWL, and storm drains are usually sized to handle the water flow from the most intense rainfall that might be expected for the building's location. Figure 11.9 is a map of the continental United States indicating the 100-year maximum rainfall contours, shown in terms of inches of precipitation per hour.

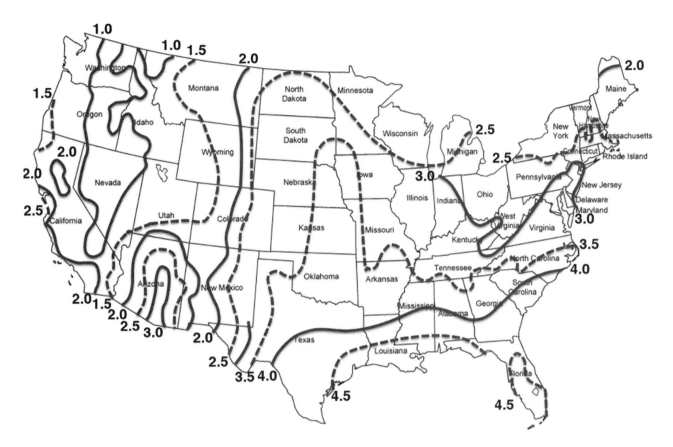

Figure 11.9 U.S. MAXIMUM 100-YEAR HOURLY RAINFALL IN INCHES PER HOUR

Adapted from B. Stein, J.S. Reynolds, W.T. Grondzik, and A.G. Kwok, *Mechanical and Electrical Equipment for Buildings* (John Wiley & Sons, Inc., Hoboken, NJ, 2006), Figure 20.22, and the *International Plumbing Code* (International Code Council, Inc., Falls Church, VA, 1997.

In addition to Figure 11.9, the 100-year maximum 1-hour rainfall can be found from climate data available from NOAA.[3] Table 11.10 lists the maximum rainfall rates for some of the major U.S. cities, organized by state.

When tabular data are presented on the NOAA Web site (see Figure 11.10), which is available for 18 states and southern California, the recommendation is to use the middle chart that presents the probable maximum rainfall in inches over different periods of time based on an average of various numbers of years. As more years are listed, the rainfall amounts tend to increase since there is a greater probability of a torrential downpour occurring. Also, as the precipitation period increases, the rate of rainfall tends to decrease. This suggests that it is likely that extremely heavy precipitation will not last for a long period of time.

For example, for Cincinnati, assuming a 100-year average recurrence interval (ARI), the projected rainfall in

5 minutes is 0.83 inch, whereas in 30 minutes, 1 hour, and 3 hours, the amounts are 2.23, 2.98, and 3.98 inches, respectively (see Figure 11.11). These rainfall amounts are also listed in tabular form in Table 11.11. Dividing each of these rainfall amounts by the number of minutes indicates that it is unlikely that a very heavy downpour will last long, which is something we should realize if we have ever confronted a downpour.

Although the sizing of the gutters, RWL, and storm drains is usually based on the maximum rainfall in 1 hour, often it makes sense to assume that the probable amount of rain will be between double the 30-minute and 60-minute values provided by NOAA, since this should accommodate the extremely large rainfall that might occur in less than an hour. Of course, it is likely that there will still be short periods of intense rain that will exceed the capacity based on this increased assumption of hourly rain, but these occasions should be relatively rare.

When the probable maximum rainfall that can be expected in 1 hour for the building site has been determined, we can proceed to size the various components of the rainwater collection system. Beginning with the gutters, we need to determine both the size of the gutter and the slope

---

[3] http://hdsc.nws.noaa.gov/hdsc/pfds/index.html. While this NOAA Web page links to data for most of the United States, currently only the links for 18 states and southern California (shown in purple in the U.S. map posted on the NOAA Web page) provide the information in tabular form. The other locations rely on contour maps similar to Figure 11.9.

Table 11.10: MAXIMUM RATES OF RAINFALL FOR SELECTED U.S. CITIES — INCHES IN 60 MINUTES

Location	Max. Rain (in.)	Location	Max. Rain (in.)	Location	Max. Rain (in.)	Location	Max. Rain (in.)
Alabama		**Idaho**		**Missouri**		**Pennsylvania**	
Birmingham	3.7	Boise	1.0	Independence	3.7	Erie	2.4
Huntsville	3.3	Idaho Falls	1.2	Jefferson City	3.4	Harrisburg	2.9
Mobile	4.5	Lewiston	1.0	St. Louis	3.2	Philadelphia	3.2
Montgomery	3.8	Twin Falls	1.1	Springfield	3.7	Pittsburgh	2.5
Alaska		**Illinois**		**Montana**		Scranton	2.8
Aleutian Islands	1.0	Chicago	2.7	Billings	1.8	**Rhode Island**	
Anchorage	0.6	Harrisburg	3.1	Glendive	2.5	Newport	3.0
Bethel	0.8	Peoria	2.9	Great Falls	1.8	Providence	2.9
Fairbanks	1.0	Springfield	**3.0**	Missoula	**1.3**	**South Carolina**	
Juneau	0.6	**Indiana**		**Nebraska**		Charleston	4.1
Arizona		Evansville	3.0	Omaha	3.6	Columbia	3.5
Flagstaff	2.3	Indianapolis	2.8	North Platte	3.5	Greenville	3.3
Phoenix	2.2	Richmond	2.7	Scotts Bluff	2.8	**South Dakota**	
Tucson	3.0	South Bend	2.7	**Nevada**		Lemmon	2.7
Arkansas		**Iowa**		Las Vegas	1.5	Rapid City	2.7
Eudora	3.8	Council Bluffs	3.7	Reno	1.2	Sioux Falls	3.4
Ft. Smith	3.9	Davenport	3.0	Winnemucca	1.0	**Tennessee**	
Jonesboro	3.5	Des Moines	3.4	**New Hampshire**		Knoxville	3.1
Little Rock	3.7	Sioux City	3.6	Berlin	2.2	Memphis	3.5
California		**Kansas**		Manchester	2.5	Nashville	3.0
Eureka	1.5	Goodland	3.5	**New Jersey**		**Texas**	
Lake Tahoe	1.3	Salina	3.8	Atlantic City	3.4	Corpus Christi	4.6
Los Angeles	2.0	Topeka	3.8	Peterson	3.0	Dallas	4.2
Lucerne Valley	2.5	Wichita	3.9	Trenton	3.2	El Paso	2.0
Needles	1.5	**Kentucky**		**New Mexico**		Houston	4.6
Palmdale	3.0	Bowling Green	2.9	Albuquerque	2.0	Lubbock	3.3
Redding	1.5	Lexington	2.9	Carlsbad	2.6	San Antonio	4.4
San Diego	1.5	Louisville	2.8	Gallup	2.1	**Utah**	
San Francisco	1.5	Paducah	3.0	**New York**		Bluff	2.0
San Luis Obispo	1.5	**Louisiana**		Binghamton	2.4	Cedar City	1.5
Colorado		Monroe	3.8	Buffalo	2.3	Salt Lake City	1.3
Craig	1.5	New Orleans	4.5	New York City	3.1	**Vermont**	
Denver	2.2	Shreveport	4.0	Schenectady	2.5	Bennington	2.5
Durango	1.8	**Maine**		Syracuse	2.4	Burlington	2.3
Stratton	3.0	Bangor	2.2	**North Carolina**		Rutland	2.4
Connecticut		Kittery	2.4	Asheville	3.2	**Virginia**	
Hartford	2.8	**Maryland**		Charlotte	3.4	Charlottesville	3.4
New Haven	3.0	Baltimore	3.6	Raleigh	4.0	Norfolk	4.0
Delaware		Frostburg	2.9	Wilmington	4.4	Richmond	4.0
Dover	3.5	Ocean City	3.7	**North Dakota**		Roanoke	3.3
Rehobeth Beach	3.6	**Massachusetts**		Bismarck	2.7	**Washington**	
District of Columbia		Adams	2.6	Fargo	2.9	Seattle	1.0
Washington	4.0	Boston	2.7	Minot	2.6	Spokane	1.0
Florida		Springfield	2.7	**Ohio**		Walla Walla	1.0
Daytona Beach	4.0	**Michigan**		Cincinnati	2.8	**West Virginia**	
Ft. Meyers	4.0	Detroit	2.5	Cleveland	2.4	Charleston	2.9
Jacksonville	4.3	Grand Rapids	2.6	Columbus	2.7	Martinsburg	3.0
Melbourne	4.0	Kalamazoo	2.7	Toledo	2.6	Morgantown	2.7
Miami	4.5	Sheboygan	2.1	Youngstown	2.4	**Wisconsin**	
Palm Beach	5.0	Traverse City	2.2	**Oklahoma**		Green Bay	2.5
Tampa	4.2	**Minnesota**		Boise City	3.4	Lacrosse	2.9
Tallahassee	4.1	Duluth	2.6	Muskogee	4.0	Milwaukee	2.7
Georgia		Grand Forks	2.5	Oklahoma City	4.1	Wausau	2.5
Atlanta	3.5	Minneapolis	3.0	**Oregon**		**Wyoming**	
Brunswick	4.0	Worthington	3.4	Medford	1.3	Casper	1.9
Macon	3.7	**Mississippi**		Ontario	1.0	Cheyenne	2.5
Savannah	4.0	Biloxi	4.5	Portland	1.3	Evanston	1.3
Thomasville	4.0	Columbus	3.5			Rock Springs	1.4
Hawaii	1.5 to 8	Jackson	3.8				

Source: Adapted from U.S. Weather Bureau data on 100-year 60-minute rainfall in inches.

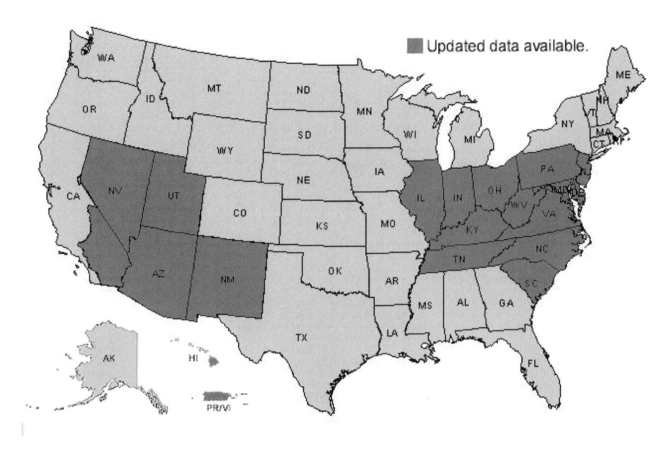

Figure 11.10 NOAA PRECIPITATION FREQUENCY DATA MAP

This is the link map on the NOAA Web page (http://hdsc.nws.noaa.gov/hdsc/pfds/index.html) that provides access to hourly rates of precipitation. Links to updated data are currently (2009) available only for 18 states and southern California, the darker areas shown above.

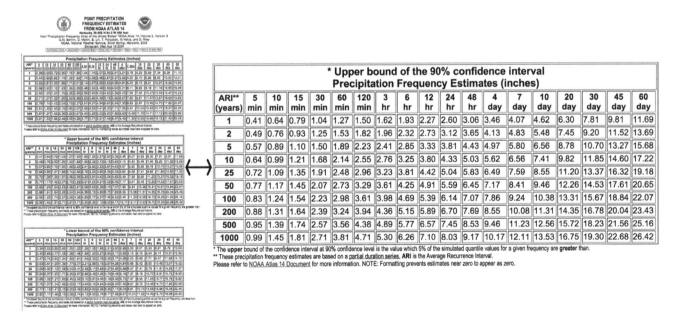

ARI** (years)	5 min	10 min	15 min	30 min	60 min	120 min	3 hr	6 hr	12 hr	24 hr	48 hr	4 day	7 day	10 day	20 day	30 day	45 day	60 day
1	0.41	0.64	0.79	1.04	1.27	1.50	1.62	1.93	2.27	2.60	3.06	3.46	4.07	4.62	6.30	7.81	9.81	11.69
2	0.49	0.76	0.93	1.25	1.53	1.82	1.96	2.32	2.73	3.12	3.65	4.13	4.83	5.48	7.45	9.20	11.52	13.69
5	0.57	0.89	1.10	1.50	1.89	2.23	2.41	2.85	3.33	3.81	4.43	4.97	5.80	6.56	8.78	10.70	13.27	15.68
10	0.64	0.99	1.21	1.68	2.14	2.55	2.76	3.25	3.80	4.33	5.03	5.62	6.56	7.41	9.82	11.85	14.60	17.22
25	0.72	1.09	1.35	1.91	2.48	2.96	3.23	3.81	4.42	5.04	5.83	6.49	7.59	8.55	11.20	13.37	16.32	19.18
50	0.77	1.17	1.45	2.07	2.73	3.29	3.61	4.25	4.91	5.59	6.45	7.17	8.41	9.46	12.26	14.53	17.61	20.65
100	0.83	1.24	1.54	2.23	2.98	3.61	3.98	4.69	5.39	6.14	7.07	7.86	9.24	10.38	13.31	15.67	18.84	22.07
200	0.88	1.31	1.64	2.39	3.24	3.94	4.36	5.15	5.89	6.70	7.69	8.55	10.08	11.31	14.35	16.78	20.04	23.43
500	0.95	1.39	1.74	2.57	3.56	4.38	4.89	5.77	6.57	7.45	8.53	9.46	11.23	12.56	15.72	18.23	21.56	25.16
1000	0.99	1.45	1.81	2.71	3.81	4.71	5.30	6.26	7.10	8.03	9.17	10.17	12.11	13.53	16.75	19.30	22.68	26.42

Figure 11.11 NOAA PRECIPITATION FREQUENCY DATA FOR CINCINNATI

This figure shows the precipitation frequency data for Cincinnati, Ohio. There are three tables for each site. The top one is the average, the middle one is the upper bound, and the bottom one is the lower bound. In sizing for maximum expected rainfall, the 100-year values from the middle table are typically recommended.

Table 11.11: EXAMPLE OF DECLINING RAINFALL INTENSITY WITH EXTENDED TIME

Period of Rainfall	Inches of Rain	Inches per Minute
5 minutes	0.83	0.166
30 minutes	2.23	0.075
60 minutes	2.98	0.050
180 minutes	3.98	0.022

Table 11.12: GUTTER SIZING—ROOF AREA FOR GUTTER SIZES AND SLOPES

Diameter of Gutters (Inches)	Horizontally Projected Roof Area (square feet) Rainfall Rate (inches per hour)					
	1	2	3	4	5	6
$1/16$ inch per foot slope (0.5%slope)						
3	680	340	226	170	136	113
4	1,440	720	480	360	288	240
5	2,500	1,250	834	625	500	416
6	3,840	1,920	1,280	960	768	640
7	5,520	2,760	1,840	1,380	1,100	918
8	7,960	3,980	2,655	1,990	1,590	1,325
10	14,400	7,200	4,800	3,600	2,880	2,400
$1/8$ inch per foot slope (1% slope)						
3	960	480	320	240	192	160
4	2,040	1,020	681	510	408	340
5	3,520	1,760	1,172	880	704	587
6	5,440	2,720	1,815	1,360	1,085	905
7	7,800	3,900	2,600	1,950	1,560	1,300
8	11,200	5,600	3,740	2,800	2,240	1,870
10	20,400	10,200	6,800	5,100	4,080	3,400
$1/4$ inch per foot slope (2% slope)						
3	1,360	680	454	340	272	226
4	2,880	1,440	960	720	576	480
5	5,000	2,500	1,668	1,250	1,000	834
6	7,680	3,840	2,560	1,920	1,536	1,280
7	11,040	5,520	3,860	2,760	2,205	1,840
8	15,920	7,960	5,310	3,980	3,180	2,655
10	28,800	14,400	9,600	7,200	5,750	4,800
$1/2$ inch per foot slope (4% slope)						
3	1,920	960	640	480	384	320
4	4,080	2,040	1,360	1,020	816	680
5	7,080	3,540	2,360	1,770	1,415	1,180
6	11,080	5,540	3,695	2,770	2,220	1,850
7	15,600	7,800	5,200	3,900	3,120	2,600
8	22,400	11,200	7,460	5,600	4,480	3,730
10	40,000	20,000	13,330	10,000	8,000	6,660

Source: Adapted from data for semicircular gutters from *Uniform Plumbing Code* (International Association of Plumbing and Mechanical Officials, Walnut, CA, 1997).

Table 11.13A: VERTICAL RAINWATER LEADER SIZING – CIRCULAR LEADER

Diameter of Leader (inches)[a]	Horizontally Projected Roof Area (square feet) Rainfall rate (inches per hour)											
	1	2	3	4	5	6	7	8	9	10	11	12
2	2,880	1,440	960	720	575	480	410	360	320	290	260	240
3	8,800	4,400	2,930	2,200	1,760	1,470	1,260	1,100	980	880	800	730
4	18,400	9,200	6,130	4,600	3,680	3,070	2,630	2,300	2,045	1,840	1,675	1,530
5	34,600	17,300	11,530	8,650	6,920	5,765	4,945	4,325	3,845	3,460	3,145	2,880
6	54,000	27,000	17,995	13,500	10,800	9,000	7,715	6,750	6,000	5,400	4,910	4,500
8	116,000	58,000	38,660	29,000	23,200	19,315	16,570	14,500	12,890	11,600	10,545	9,600

[a]Sizes indicated are the diameter of circular piping. This table is applicable to piping of other shapes, provided the cross-sectional shape fully encloses a circle of the diameter indicated in this table. For rectangular leaders, see Table 1106.2(2). Interpolation is permitted for pipe sizes that fall between those listed in this table.
Source: Adapted from the *2009 International Plumbing Code*, International Code Council, Inc., Falls Church, VA, 2009.

Table 11.13B: VERTICAL RAINWATER LEADER SIZING – RECTANGULAR LEADER

Dimensions of Common Leader Sizes width x length (inches)[a]	Horizontally Projected Roof Area (square feet) Rainfall rate (inches per hour)											
	1	2	3	4	5	6	7	8	9	10	11	12
$1^3/_4$ x $2^1/_2$	3,410	1,700	1,130	850	680	560	480	420	370	340	310	280
2 x 3	5,540	2,770	1,840	1,380	1,100	920	790	690	610	550	500	460
$2^3/_4$ x $4^1/_4$	12,830	6,410	4,270	3,200	2,560	2,130	1,830	1,600	1,420	1,280	1,160	1,060
3 x 4	13,210	6,600	4,400	3,300	2,640	2,200	1,880	1,650	1,460	1,320	1,200	1,100
$3^1/_2$ x 4	15,900	7,950	5,300	3,970	3,180	2,650	2,270	1,980	1,760	1,590	1,440	1,320
$3^1/_2$ x 5	21,310	10,650	7,100	5,320	4,260	3,550	3,040	2,660	2,360	2,130	1,930	1,770
$3^3/_4$ x $4^3/_4$	21,960	10,980	7,320	5,490	4,390	3,660	3,130	2,740	2,440	2,190	1,990	1,830
$3^3/_4$ x $5^1/_4$	25,520	12,760	8,500	6,380	5,100	4,250	3,640	3,190	2,830	2,550	2,320	2,120
$3^1/_2$ x 6	27,790	13,890	9,260	6,940	5,550	4,630	3,970	3,470	3,080	2,770	2,520	2,310
4 x 6	32,980	16,490	10,990	8,240	6,590	5,490	4,710	4,120	3,660	3,290	2,990	2,740
$5^1/_2$ x $5^1/_2$	44,300	22,150	14,760	11,070	8,860	7,380	6,320	5,530	4,920	4,430	4,020	3,690
$7^1/_2$ x $7^1/_2$	100,500	50,250	33,500	25,120	20,100	16,750	14,350	12,560	11,160	10,050	9,130	8,370

[a]Sizes indicated are nominal width °— length of the opening for rectangular piping.
[b]For shapes not included in this table, use the "equivalent" circular diameter, D, of the rectangular piping found from D = (width x length)$^1/_2$ and then use this equivalent diameter in Table 11.13A to find the projected roof area that can be accommodated.
Source: Adapted from the *2009 International Plumbing Code*, International Code Council, Inc., Falls Church, VA, 2009.

at which it will pitch toward the drain, which is usually an RWL. Both the size of the gutter and its slope are potential critical design issues. The larger the gutter, the more apparent it will be, but the more it slopes, the more it is likely to contrast with the eave line and thereby make it more prominent as well. One way to reduce the size of a gutter is to increase its slope, since the flow of the water in the gutter will be quicker with a steeper slope. The corollary is that if we reduce the slope of a gutter, we must increase its size.

Tables 11.12 through 11.14 can be used to size the rainwater collection system. Each of these tables is based on the horizontally projected roof area for various sized components of the rainwater collection system, based on the expected maximum rainfall in inches per hour.

While Table 11.12 can help determine the slope that might be used, generally gutters are installed with a pitch of only around $1/_2$ inch per 10-foot run, which is about $3/_6$ inch per foot. As a result, this least slope portion of the table is usually used to size the gutters. But while we take this approach, we should realize that buildings do settle, and this could mean that gutters that were installed with a reasonable slope to drain might not always maintain it. For this reason, we might consider installing an RWL at both ends of any gutter that is longer than 15 feet or so, and we probably should always use two RWL with gutters that

Table 11.14: HORIZONTAL STORM DRAIN SIZING

Size of Pipe (in.)	Flow at 1/8" Slope (GPM)	Maximum Allowable Horizontal Projected Roof Area (sq ft) Rainfall Rates (in./hr)					
		1	2	3	4	5	6
3	34	3,288	1,644	1,096	822	657	548
4	78	7,520	3,760	2,506	1,880	1,504	1,253
5	139	13,360	6,680	4,453	3,340	2,672	2,227
6	222	21,400	10,700	7,133	5,350	4,280	3,566
8	478	46,000	23,000	15,330	11,500	9,200	7,670
10	860	82,800	41,400	27,600	20,700	16,580	13,800
12	1,384	133,200	66,600	44,400	33,300	26,650	22,200
15	2,473	238,000	119,000	79,333	59,500	47,600	39,650

Size of Pipe (in.)	Flow at 1/4" Slope (GPM)	Maximum Allowable Horizontal Projected Roof Area (sq ft) Rainfall Rates (in./hr)					
		1	2	3	4	5	6
3	48	4,640	2,320	1,546	1,160	928	773
4	110	10,600	5,300	3,533	2,650	2,120	1,766
5	196	18,880	9,440	6,293	4,720	3,776	3,146
6	314	30,200	15,100	10,066	7,550	6,040	5,033
8	677	65,200	32,600	21,733	16,300	13,040	10,866
10	1,214	116,800	58,400	38,950	29,200	23,350	19,450
12	1,953	188,000	94,000	62,600	47,000	37,600	31,350
15	3,491	336,000	168,000	112,000	84,000	67,250	56,000

Size of Pipe (in.)	Flow at 1/2" Slope (GPM)	Maximum Allowable Horizontal Projected Roof Area (sq ft) Rainfall Rates (in./hr)					
		1	2	3	4	5	6
3	68	6,576	3,288	2,192	1,644	1,310	1,096
4	156	15,040	7,520	5,010	3,760	3,010	2,500
5	278	26,720	13,360	8,900	6,680	5,320	4,450
6	445	42,800	21,400	14,267	10,700	8,580	7,140
8	956	92,000	46,000	30,650	23,000	18,400	15,320
10	1,721	165,600	82,800	55,200	41,100	33,150	27,600
12	2,768	266,400	133,200	88,800	66,600	53	44,400
15	4,946	476,000	238,000	158,700	119,000	95,200	79,300

Source: Adapted from the *2009 International Plumbing Code*, International Code Council, Inc., Falls Church, VA, 2009.

are 30 feet or more in length. This will not only reduce the overall drop of the gutter, it will accommodate any adjustments in slope as the building settles. At a slope of 1/6 inch per foot, a 40-foot gutter would have an overall drop of 2 1/2 inches. With a 1/4-inch-per-foot slope, the drop would be 10 inches, but if the gutter has a double pitch to a drain at both ends, the overall drop would be only half since the run would be half.

The visual impact of the slope of the gutter is not critical when the gutter is built in. With this approach, the size and slope of the drainage unit are not usually exposed; however, built-in gutters tend to be significantly more expensive and over time can cause problems if they leak. If a gutter leaks, where does the water go? With an exposed gutter, it merely drips down. While this is unsightly, it is not a serious problem. With a built-in gutter, any leaking water would still be contained within the supporting structure, if not within the actual walls of the building. Unfortunately, the leak could exist for some time before it is apparent, and by then (or because of it) there might be considerable damage to the eaves. It is also possible for the leaking water to run into the building's interior, depending on the configuration of the wall section, whereas with exposed hung-on gutters that are installed beyond the structural enclosure, this is not likely (see Figure 11.12).

Table 11.12 is used to size the gutters. It shows the maximum roof area that can be handled by a gutter of a particular size and slope, assuming a maximum hourly rainfall, which is listed at 2, 3, 4, 5, and 6 inches. Table 11.13 is used to size the RWL. It shows the maximum roof area that can be handled by an RWL or vertical drainpipe of a particular size. Table 11.14 is used to size the horizontal storm drain. It shows the maximum roof area that can

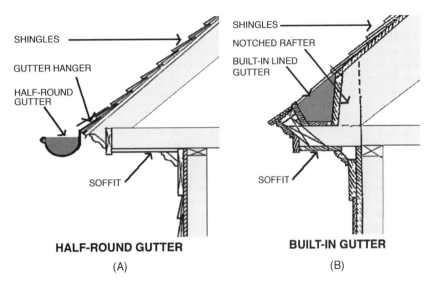

HALF-ROUND GUTTER

(A)

BUILT-IN GUTTER

(B)

Figure 11.12 GUTTERS – HALF-ROUND AND BUILT-IN
There are basically two types of gutters: built-in and attached or hung-on.

be handled by different-sized and -sloped horizontal storm drains carrying rainwater runoff from the roof. In each of these tables, the roof area is the horizontal projected area or footprint of the roof. While a sloped roof, which helps drainage, has a larger surface area than a flat roof, it does not increase the water collection area.

If the roof has shingles, the slope should be at least 2:12, which means that there should be a rise of at least 2 inches for every 12 inches of horizontal run. However, the preferable slope is 4:12 or more. If the slope is between 2:12 and 4:12, two layers of #15 felt underlayment below the shingles should be installed to help reduce the potential for water leakage, as well as to reduce the exposure of the shingles by increasing the overlap.

Flat roofs are not actually flat, or at least they should not be. If they were, the water would merely pool on the roof. Instead, a "flat" roof should be pitched so that the water is directed toward the drains. The minimal slope is $1/8$ inch per foot, although it is strongly recommended that the slope be at least $1/4$ inch per foot. This slope can be established by tilting the structural deck or by tapering the above-deck insulation.

One thing we should recognize, in determining both the slope of a "flat" roof and the slope of a gutter, is that buildings move, especially over time. Some movement is the result of structural deformation, but some of it is also due to settling of the structural foundation. Settlement can be limited by providing a solid foundation set on firm ground, well below any frost line that might occur, but even with a good foundation, some settling or movement will likely oc-

cur in most situations. Probably the only way to avoid this is to have the foundation sit on bedrock, which rarely occurs with smaller structures like single-family residences. Movement is especially likely when the foundation rests on clay. Clay can contain varying amounts of moisture. As the amount of moisture changes, the volume of the soil also changes. When there is a very dry period, the clay shrinks and the building foundation settles down. When the rains return and wet the clay, the clay expands and the structure moves, but not necessarily back to its original position.

In due course, most buildings settle and move, so gutters and roofs with minimal slopes might not remain pitched in the same direction. If this happens, it is likely that the rainwater will not flow to the drain.

In locations where there are low temperatures and significant quantities of snow, other problems are likely to occur. The snow that collects on the roof will likely melt as a result of heat loss from the interior spaces. Obviously, with more thermal resistance in the ceiling and roof assembly and/or venting (which is discussed below), this melting will be reduced but probably not totally eliminated. When the snow melts on a sloped roof, the water will run down toward the edge of the roof. Since the gutter is usually extended beyond the edge of the enclosing walls, as the water from the melting snow gets beyond this exterior wall, it is no longer in contact with the heat that is escaping from the building interior. As a result, the water might freeze. If this happens, the ice can build up, forming an ice dam that will trap any additional water running off the roof.

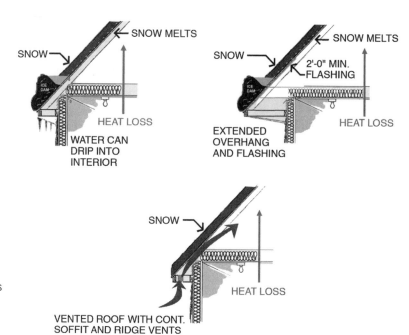

Figure 11.13 ICE DAM PROTECTION

To avoid possible problems from ice dams, the roof overhang should be extended and flashing should be extended at least 2 feet from the edge of the roof. While these actions can help protect against the problems from ice dams, venting the roof, as shown in the bottom diagram, can help eliminate the formation of ice dams by reducing the heat transfer that causes the snow to melt.

As more water runs down the roof, the ice dam increases, ultimately trapping any additional water and preventing it from draining off the roof. If this happens and the snow keeps melting, the water has no place to go but instead migrates upward under the shingles and potentially into the interior of the structure (see Figure 11.13).

Installing flashing along the bottom edge of the roof can reduce the possibility of water problems resulting from an ice dam. The flashing should be a minimum of 2 feet wide, extending up from the edge of the roof. Increasing the roof overhang can also help. With an extended overhang, any ice dam that might form should be well beyond the outside of the structure, so if any water gets under the shingles, most likely it will drip outside of the enclosing walls. Although this would still create some serious water damage problems to the structure, at least it is less likely to occur within the building. Combining an extended roof overhang with wide flashing can provide better protection, but the most effective action is to vent the roof. If the roof is vented, it is less likely that the warmer interior temperatures will melt the snow. Of course, it is vital to ensure that there is adequate thermal insulation below the vent-air passage.[4] To get the best results, we should consider combining roof venting, flashing, and an extended overhang.

Another problem that can occur with freezing temperatures relates to the RWL. If melting snow is not trapped by an ice dam, the water will be collected by the gutter and then drain into the RWL. At this point, two conditions could exist that could potentially create a problem: the RWL might be clogged and/or it might be located in shadow. If the RWL is clogged, perhaps by leaves and other debris that have washed off the roof, the flow of water could be slowed, if not stopped. This could cause the RWL to fill with water that could freeze because the water is no longer

---

[4]Venting the roof also allows any moisture from the building's interior that migrates through the insulation to dissipate, thereby reducing the probability that this moisture will condense and destroy the insulation, if not the structure.

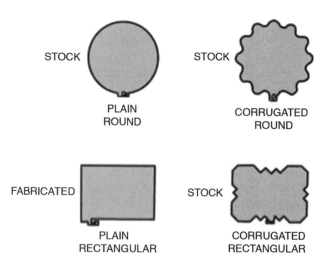

Figure 11.14 RWL, CORRUGATED TO ALLOW FOR EXPANSION

Since RWL can fill with water that would expand upon freezing, they are often corrugated to permit some expansion.

Figure 11.15 GARGOYLES ON NOTRE DAME CATHEDRAL, PARIS
While these gargoyles are clearly decorative, they are also functional waterspouts.

flowing or because the temperature drops. Also, if the RWL is located in shadow, then it is quite possible that the water, which could be at least partially the result of sun shining on the snow, could freeze when it drops in the RWL. Since the RWL is outside and in the shade, it could be well below freezing even though some of the snow is melting. If the water runoff refreezes when it enters the RWL and comes in contact with the cold RWL surfaces, layers of ice could build up, eventually clogging the leader, which would then fill with more water that will also freeze. Water expands as it freezes, so if the RWL fills with water that freezes, this would produce tremendous internal pressure that will likely cause the leader to burst. To counteract this tendency, RWLs are usually corrugated in some way so that they can deform rather than burst open (see Figure 11.14). We must also consider how to handle the discharge from RWL (see Figure 11.17).

RWL are sometimes called *downspouts*, although this term legitimately refers to an opening that discharges water onto the ground. While this typically occurs at the bottom of an RWL, downspouts might also be elevated, with the water dropping some distance. One of the more

familiar examples of this type is the gargoyle often used in Gothic cathedrals. In fact the word *gargoyle* is derived from the French *gargouille*, a legendary water-spouting dragon that lived in the Seine; this French word was apparently derived from the Latin root word *gar*, which was related to the gurgling sound of water. While the nonwaterspout sculptural grotesque figures that adorn various Gothic cathedrals are often called *gargoyles*, this term legitimately should only be used to denote waterspouts (see Figure 11.15).

There are also downspouts that are linked with a chain along which the water travels. These rain chains, which typically lead the rainwater to a storage vessel or drain, are supposedly intended to reduce the impact and the potential damage that the dropping water can cause, although they tend to be mainly decorative. They also provide a wonderful source of acoustical perfume (see Figure 11.16).

WATER DISTRIBUTION

An on-site water supply, however provided, typically requires pumps, storage tanks, surge tanks, and various means of water treatment. While these require some architectural accommodations, typically their actual design is not the responsibility of the architect but is handled by the drilling contractor and/or plumber. In more complex projects, consulting engineers would take the lead. Critical as this might be for certain projects, typically water is delivered to the project site from a public water supply system, which tends to be similar to what might be provided on-site but, of course, at a considerably larger scale.

Once a water supply is available at the site, the next consideration is the proper sizing of the water service piping and ensuring that there is adequate water pressure to distribute the water to the points of use and to operate the fixture once it gets there. The amount of pressure required for distribution is related to the volume of water supplied, the diameter of the pipes, the length of the pipes, and the height that the water must be raised. The appropriate pipe size for each portion of the distribution system is based on three interrelated factors: the amount of flow in GPM, the imposed resistance or pressure loss, and the water velocity. More water can be supplied through a given-sized pipe if the velocity is increased, but this comes at the price of greater resistance and increased noise. If there is adequate pressure, the increased resistance might not be critical, but noise is another matter. To keep the noise level within reasonable limits, the water velocity should not exceed 6 feet per second (FPS) if the pipes are within an occupied area and enclosed by at least $1/2$-inch gypsum board. If the pipes are exposed, the velocity should be less than 4

Figure 11.16 RAIN CHAINS AT MYOHONJI TEMPLE, KAMAKURA, JAPAN

Built in 1260, the Myohonji Temple is one of the oldest Nichiren sect temples in Kamakura, Japan. There are two rain chains that frame the entry to the temple.

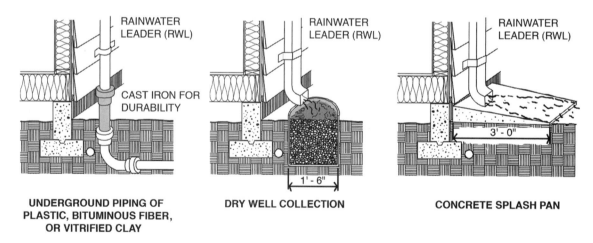

Figure 11.17 RWL BASE CONDITIONS

The water discharged from an RWL can cause problems. With a concentrated amount of water flowing at one point, there could be ground washout, which can be controlled by adding a dry well to collect the water or a splash pan to spread the water out. There are also rolled-up perforated vinyl tubes that can be attached to the downspout. As the water drops in the RWL, these tubes are extended, allowing the water to discharge over a larger ground area. There is also the option shown in the right image, which discharges the water into a storm drain that can then disperse the water on the site or connect to a public sewer, preferably a storm sewer rather than a combination sewer. When a storm drain is included, the footing drain usually connects to this system, but it should not be located at the base of an RWL to reduce the possibility that the water coming off of the roof will overcharge the footing drain. Adapted from diagrams in B. Stein, J. S. Reynolds, W.T. Grondzik, and A.G. Kwok, *Mechanical and Electrical Equipment for Buildings* (John Wiley & Sons, Inc., Hoboken, NJ, 2006), Figure 20.16.

FPS, the speed at which the water flow will be audible. If the supply pipe is located within an unoccupied area—for example, in a basement—any noise that results from a higher velocity might not be a problem. Under these conditions, the water velocity can be increased to 10 FPS, which should be considered the upper limit. In addition to the noise developed by the water flow, it is likely that the high velocity will also produce pipe vibrations, which will generate additional noise. To avoid having these vibrations transmitted into the structure, it is important to support the pipes resiliently.

While the velocity of the water flow is important, the critical issue in designing the water distribution system is the amount of water that must be supplied, and this depends on the number of plumbing fixtures supplied by the system. When many fixtures are supplied, it is unlikely that all of them will be used at the same time. As the number of fixtures within a system increases, the expected requirement for water supply in GPM should be adjusted to a lower percentage of the total possible demand that is set by all of the plumbing fixtures. The process of setting the demand begins with determining the total number of plumbing fixtures that the system must supply.

A variety of plumbing fixtures are generally included in a plumbing system, including the following:

Drinking fountains	Lavatories (sinks)
Tubs and showers	Water closets (toilets)
Kitchen sinks	Clothes washers
Dishwashers	Hose bibbs (hose faucets)

In addition, heating and cooling systems, especially boilers, humidifiers, cooling towers, and so on, have service water requirements.

Each plumbing fixture requires or consumes a certain amount of water, which has to be supplied at sufficient pressure for proper operation. The required amount of water, which is sometimes established in terms of flow rate and at other times in terms of quantity, is presented in terms of water supply fixture units that can then be converted into a GPM demand. Of course, the overall water demand is established by the number of fixtures present, which in turn is based on the type of building occupancy and the number of occupants. Table 11.15 presents the recommended minimum number of plumbing fixtures for various occupancies.

The number of occupants is determined by the applicable building code, usually on a stipulated allocation of square feet per person, and unless we have information to the contrary, we should assume that there is an equal number of men and women. However, for certain occupancies, particularly places of assembly, the water closet (WC) allocation is higher for female than male occupants.

Since more time is typically required for women to use the facilities than for men, the disproportionate allocation between men and women makes sense. Most jurisdictions allow 50% of the required WCs to be replaced by urinals. Interestingly, while not widely used, there are female urinals, which also may be substituted for 50% of the required WCs for women. However, female urinals do not provide the same advantage of reducing the time of use for women that standard urinals provide for men, so there is no significant advantage to female urinals and they are not generally used.

In addition to the number of fixtures, codes generally require that in nonresidential occupancies, toilet facilities should be located so that it is not necessary to travel more than one floor or 500 feet to get to a restroom. In addition, when there are more than 15 employees in a tenant space, we should provide separate toilet facilities for them. There are different interpretations as to whether separate facilities have to be provided for men and women. Generally, separate facilities should be provided for each sex, especially when the total number of occupants, including both employees and customers, exceeds 15. Most codes also require public drinking fountains for nonresidential occupancies, although in places where water is served, such as restaurants, or where bottled water coolers are available, they are generally not necessary. While drinking fountains were sometimes located within public restrooms, modern codes do not permit this, although since plumbing is not far away, they are typically located near a restroom entry.

As shown in Table 11.16, each fixture requires a particular water flow rate in GPM and a minimum pressure (psi). But while the GPM required by each fixture is important, a water distribution system is sized to meet the demand established by the water supply fixture units (WSFU) associated with each fixture. While related to the GPM value for the fixture, WSFU values are different, although with public fixtures they tend to be quite similar. Once the total WSFU served by each portion of the distribution system is known, the demand GPM for that segment of the supply system can be determined and used to size the piping that can deliver this volume of water. That is, the fixture requirements in terms of gallons per minute (gpm) required for each fixture are used to find the WSFU, which are then used to determine the expected GPM demand.

gpm ➡ WSFU ➡ GPM

Table 11.17 lists the WSFU for various plumbing fixtures. These values are presented for cold, hot, and total water used. The cold and hot WSFU are used to size the separate cold and hot water supply pipes, and the total or combined WSFU is used to size the common water supply line before the division into separate lines, that is, before the hot

Table 11.15: MINIMUM NUMBER OF PLUMBING FACILITIES

Occupancy	Walter Closets Urinals [b]		Lavatories	Bathtubs/ Showers	Drinking Fountains	Others
	Male	Female				
Assembly						
Theaters	1 per 125	1 per 65	1 per 200	—	1 per 1000	1 Service Sink
Nightclubs	1 per 40	1 per 40	1 per 75	—	1 per 500	1 Service Sink
Restaurants	1 per 75	1 per 75	1 per 200	—	1 per 500	1 Service Sink
Halls, Museums, etc.	1 per 125	1 per 65	1 per 200	—	1 per 1000	1 Service Sink
Coliseums, Arenas	1 per 75	1 per 40	1 per 150	—	1 per 1000	1 Service Sink
Churches, Synagogues, Mosques [d]	1 per 150	1 per 75	1 per 200	—	1 per 1000	1 Service Sink
Stadiums, Pools, etc.	1 per 100	1 per 50	1 per 150	—	1 per 1000	1 Service Sink
Business[e,f,g]	1 per 25		1 per 40	—	1 per 100	1 Service Sink
Educational	1 per 50		1 per 50	—	1 per 100	1 Service Sink
Factory and Industrial	1 per 100		1 per 100	—	1 per 400	1 Service Sink
High Hazard[e,f]	1 per 100		1 per 100	—	1 per 1000	1 service sink
Institutional						
Residential Care	1 per 10		1 per 10	1 per 8	1 per 100	1 Service Sink
Hospitals, Ambulatory Nursing Home Patients[i]	1 per 50		1 per Room [j]	1 per 15	1 per 100	1 Service Sink per Floor
Day Nurseries, Sanitariums, Nonambulatory Nursing Home Patients, Etc.[i]	1 per 15		1 per 15	1 per 15	1 per 100	1 Service Sink
Employees, Other Than Residential Care [i]	1 per 25		1 per 35	—	1 per 100	—
Visitors, Other Than Residential Care	1 per 75		1 per 100	—	1 per 500	—
Prisons [i]	1 per cell		1 per cell	1 per 15	1 per 100	1 Service Sink
Asylums, Reformatories, etc. [i]	1 per 15		1 per 15	1 per 15	1 per 100	1 Service Sink
Mercantile [e,f,g]	1 per 500		1 per 750	—	1 per 1000	1 Service Sink
Residential						
Hotels, Motels	1 per Guest Room		1 per Guest Room	1 per Guest Room	—	1 Service Sink
Lodges	1 per 10		1 per 10	1 per 8	1 per 100	1 Service Sink
Multiple Family	1 per Dwelling Unit		1 per Dwelling Unit	1 per Dwelling Unit	—	1 Kitchen Sink per Dwelling Unit, 1 Automatic Clothes Washer Connection per 20 Dwelling Units
Dormitories	1 per 10		1 per 10	1 per 8	—	1 Service Sink
One- and Two-Family Dwellings	1 per Dwelling Unit		1 per Dwelling Unit	1 per Dwelling Unit	—	1 Kitchen Sink per Dwelling Unit; 1 Automatic Clothes Washer Connection per Dwelling Unit [l]
Storage[e,f]	1 per 100		1 per 100	—	1 per 1000	1 Service Sink

[a] Based on one fixture being the minimum required for the number of persons indicated or any fraction of the number of person indicated. The number of occupants shall be determined by the building code. Unless otherwise shown, the required water closets, lavatories, and showers or bathtubs shall be distributed evenly between the sexes based on the percentage of each sex anticipated in the occupant load. The occupant load shall be composed of 50% of each sex, unless statistical data approved by the code official indicate a different distribution.

[b] In each bathroom or toilet room, urinals shall be substituted for more than 50% of the required water closets.

[c] Drinking fountains shall not be installed in public restrooms. Where water is served in restaurants or where bottled water coolers are provided in other occupancies, drinking fountains shall not be required.

[d] Fixtures located in adjacent buildings under the ownership or control of the church, synagogue, or mosque shall be made available during the period the "main structure" is occupied.

[e] Separate employee facilities shall not be required in occupancies in which 15 or fewer people are employed. Separate facilities for each sex shall not be required in structures or tenant spaces with a total occupant load, including both employees and customers, of 15 or fewer in which food or beverage is served for consumption within the structure or tenant space.

[f] Access to toilet facilities in occupancies other than assembly or mercantile shall be from within the employees' regular working area. The required toilet facilities shall be located not more than one story above or below the employees' regular work area, and the path of travel to such facilities shall not exceed a distance of 500 feet.

[g] In mercantile and assembly occupancies, employee toilet facilities shall be either separate facilities or public customer facilities. Separate employee facilities shall not be required in tenant spaces of 900 ft or less where the travel distance from the main entrance to a central toilet area does not exceed 500 ft and where such central facilities are located not more than one story above or below the tenant space.

[h] Emergency showers and eyewash stations shall be provided with a supply of cold water as required by the manufacturer. Waste connect shall not be required for emergency showers and eyewash stations.

[i] Toilet facilities for employees shall be separate from facilities for inmates or patients.

[j] A single-occupant room with one water closet and one lavatory serving not more than two adjacent patient rooms shall be permitted where such room is provided with direct access from each patient room and with provisions for privacy.

[k] For day nurseries, a maximum of one bathtub shall be required.

[l] For attached one- and two-family dwellings, one automatic clothes washer connection shall be required for 20 dwelling units.

Source: Adapted from data from the *International Plumbing Code* (International Code Council, Inc., Falls Church, VA, 1997).

Table 11.16: FLOW AND PRESSURE FOR TYPICAL PLUMBING FIXTURES

Fixture Served	Minimum Flow (GPM)	Pressure (psi)	Maximum Flow Rate or Quantity
Bathtub	4	8	
Bidet	2	4	
Combination Fixture	4	8	
Dishwasher, Residential	2.75	8	
Drinking Fountain	0.75	8	
Laundry Tray	4	8	
Lavatory, Private	2	8	2.5 GPM at 80 psi
Lavatory, Public	2	8	0.5 GPM at 80 psi
Lavatory, Public (Metering or Self-Closing)	2	8	0.25 gal per Metering Cycle
Showerhead	3	8	2.5 GPM at 80 psi
Showerhead with Temperature Control Valve	3	20	2.5 GPM at 80 psi
Sink, Residential	2.5	8	2.5 gal at 60 psi
Sink, Service	3	8	2.5 gal at 60 psi
Urinal, Valve	15	15	1.5 gal per Flush[a] or 1.0 gal per Flush
Water Closet, Flush Valve, Siphonic	25	15	4.0 gal per Flush[a] or 1.6 gal per Flush
Water Closet, Tank, Close Coupled	3	8	1.6 gal per Flush

[a]The higher maximum flow listed is for public use in places of assembly, and for patients, inmates, and residents in hospitals, nursing homes, sanitariums, prisons, asylums, and reformatories.

Note that the pressures listed are maximum, not minimum.

Source: Adapted from data from the *International Plumbing Code* (International Code Council, Inc., Falls Church, VA, 1997).

water heater. In a single-family residence, this total WSFU occurs primarily only for the water service line. However, if the hot water is generated by "instantaneous" heaters located close to the point of use—for example, within a second-floor bathroom—then the water line supplying the bathroom would be sized on the basis of total WSFU.

The total WSFU is not the sum of the cold and hot water that might be used. When using a fixture that is supplied with both cold and hot water, 100% of either might be used, but most often we use some of each. Therefore, adding the demand for cold and hot water assumes a higher result than is logical. At the same time, realizing that many fixtures, such as showers, tend to use a full flow whether it is all cold, all hot, or a mixture of the two, we might wonder why the total WSFU is consistently higher than either the cold or hot.

Since the total WSFU does not equal the sum of the cold and hot WSFU, it is clear that when the cold and hot water pipes are sized for the potential maximum flow in each, the actual flow rates generally will never meet these rates in both pipes at the same time. However,, it is likely that the total WSFU will be realized at times of full use, although the system is typically not at this level of demand either. That is, the actual use keeps changing. Unfortunately, if the supply piping is sized at a high velocity, which relates to a higher pressure drop, changes in demand will adjust the flow rate, which can cause drastic and abrupt changes in the discharge temperature unless special control valves are used.

After the total WSFU has been determined, we need to use Figure 11.18 to convert this to the demand in GPM. This figure includes two curves. Curve 1, the upper curve, is used if the WCs use flush valves, and curve 2 is used if the WCs are flush tanks. Since flush valves require the full flush volume in a very short time, they impose a higher GPM demand on the water supply system. Flush tanks, on the other hand, can acquire the required flush volume over a longer time period, although they will use the full flush volume in a rather short time. The volume of water required to flush a WC (1.6 gallons) or urinal (1 gallon)

Table 11.17: WATER SUPPLY FIXTURE UNITS (WSFU)

Fixture	Occupancy	Type of Supply Control	Load Values in WSFU		
			Cold	Hot	Total
Bathroom Group	Private	Flush Tank	2.7	1.5	3.6
Bathroom Group	Private	Flush Valve	6	3	8
Bathtub	Private	Faucet	1	1	1.4
Bathtub	Public	Faucet	3	3	4
Bidet	Private	Faucet	1.5	1.5	2
Combination Fixture	Private	Faucet	2.25	2.25	3
Dishwashing Machine	Private	Automatic	2.7	1.4	1.4
Drinking Fountain	Offices, etc.	$3/8''$ Valve	0.25	3	0.25
Kitchen Sink	Private	Faucet	1	1	1.4
Kitchen Sink	Hotel, Restaurant	Faucet	3	3	4
Laundry Trays (1–3)	Private	Faucet	1	1	1.4
Lavatory	Private	Faucet	0.5	0.5	0.7
Lavatory	Public	Faucet	1.5	1.5	2
Service Sink	Offices, etc.	Faucet	2.25	2.25	3
Showerhead	Private	Mixing Valve	1	1	1.4
Showerhead	Public	Mixing Valve	3	3	4
Urinal	Public	Flush Tank	3		3
Urinal	Public	$3/4''$ Flush Valve	5		5
Urinal	Public	$1''$ Flush Valve	10		10
Washing Machine (8 lb)	Private	Automatic	1	1	1.4
Washing Machine (8 lb)	Public	Automatic	2.25	2.25	3
Washing Machine (15 lb)	Public	Automatic	3	3	4
Water Closet	Private	Flush Tank	2		2
Water Closet	Private	Flush Valve	6		6
Water Closet	Public	Flush Tank	5		5
Water Closet	Public	Flush Valve	10		10
Water Closet	Public or Private	Flushometer Tank	2		2
Hose Bibb	Private	Faucet	2.5		2.5
Second Hose Bibb	Private	Faucet	1		1

Source: Adapted from data from the *International Plumbing Code* (International Code Council, Inc., Falls Church, VA, 1997).

Figure 11.18 ESTIMATE CURVES FOR GPM FLOW BASED ON TOTAL WSFU

Curve 1 is used for systems that include flush-valve fixtures, which are typical in nonresidential occupancies, and curve 2 is used for systems with flush-tank WCs. Using curve 2, at 20 WSFU or less, the demand GPM tends to equal the WSFU. Using curve 1, the demand GPM at lower WSFU, up to around 60 WSFU, might actually exceed the WSFU. Adapted from various sources, including the *Uniform Plumbing Code* (International Association of Plumbing and Mechanical Officials, Walnut, CA, 1997)

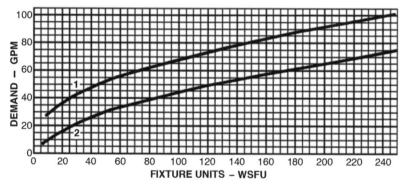

is based on the flushing action and not on the means of supply. That is, while the rate of supply in terms of GPM is different for flush-valve or flush-tank fixtures, the number of gallons used per flush is the same.

When the total WSFU for a particular portion of the water supply system has been established, we can use Figure 11.18 to determine the GPM demand. To do this, we locate the WSFU on the abscissa, rise from this point to the proper curve, and then read the demand GPM on the ordinate on the left.

Again, to determine the water supply demand in GPM, we must find the WSFU for each fixture, determine the total WSFU for each segment of the supply system and ultimately for the whole building, and then use the total WSFU value to determine the demand GPM. When the GPM demand has been determined, we can use Figure 11.19 to size the supply pipes.

Various materials are used for the water supply. Figure 11.19, which is based on copper pipe, can be used for all smooth-bore pipe ranging in size from $3/8$-inch

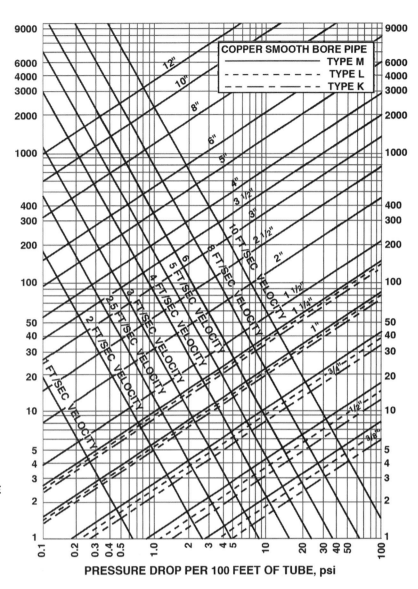

Figure 11.19 FRICTION LOSS CHART FOR SMOOTH PIPE
This chart provides the relationship between pipe size, GPM flow, fluid velocity, and pressure drop per 100 linear feet of tube. Velocities in excess of 6-8 FPS are not recommended due to excessive noise and pressure drop. Adapted from data from *2009 International Plumbing Code*, International Code Council, Inc., Falls Church, VA, 2009.

diameter up to 6 inches. The full range of copper pipe extends from $1/4$-inch diameter up to 24 inches, although in single-family residences, $1/2$-inch diameter is the standard small size used, with 1-inch diameter generally the largest. Copper pipe increases in size in $1/4$-inch increments from $1/2$ inch up to $1 1/2$ inches, then by $1/2$-inch increments up to $3 1/2$ inches, then by 1-inch increments up to 6 inches, and then by 2-inch increments up to 24 inches, although 12 inches is the maximum size readily available. A critical issue with the larger-sized copper pipes is how they are connected.

The standard means of connecting copper pipe is through male and female fittings that are connected by solder. Usually the pipe is the male component that is inserted into a female fitting, such as an elbow, tee, or plumbing valve. When the materials have been cleaned and assembled, the joint is heated until applied solder will

melt and fill the joint by capillary action. As cooling occurs the solder solidifies, expanding as it does, creating a watertight connection. Once we understand how this process works, it becomes clear that sweat connections are not really feasible with large-diameter piping since it is difficult to control the temperatures necessary to achieve effective results.

Figure 11.19, sometimes referred to as the *pipe-sizing chart*, plots a number of items. The ordinate denotes the flow of water in GPM, while the abscissa indicates the pressure loss in psia per 100 linear feet of pipe length. The lines that slope upward from right to left relate to the flow velocity in feet per second, and the lines that slope upward from left to right show different pipe sizes arranged by the standard diameters used in plumbing. The four smaller-sized pipes are shown with three different lines, one for each of three different types of copper.

Table 11.18: DIMENSIONS AND PHYSICAL CHARACTERISTICS OF COPPER PIPE

Nominal Size (in.)	Outside Diameter	Type K		Type L		Type M	
		Wall Thickness	Inside Diameter	Wall Thickness	Inside Diameter	Wall Thickness	Inside Diameter
$3/8$	0.500	0.049	0.402	0.035	0.430	0.025	0.450
$1/2$	0.625	0.049	0.527	0.040	0.545	0.028	0.569
$3/4$	0.875	0.065	0.745	0.045	0.785	0.032	0.811
1	1.125	0.065	0.995	0.050	1.025	0.035	1.055
$1^1/4$	1.375	0.065	1.245	0.055	1.265	0.042	1.291
$1^1/2$	1.625	0.072	1.481	0.060	1.505	0.049	1.527
2	2.125	0.083	1.959	0.070	1.985	0.058	2.009
$2^1/2$	2.625	0.095	2.435	0.080	2.465	0.065	2.495
3	3.125	0.109	2.907	0.090	2.945	0.072	2.981
$3^1/2$	3.625	0.120	3.385	0.100	3.425	0.083	3.459
4	4.125	0.134	3.857	0.110	3.905	0.095	3.935
5	5.125	0.160	4.805	0.125	4.875	0.109	4.907
6	6.125	0.192	5.741	0.140	5.845	0.122	5.881

Copper, which is the preferred material for water-supply piping, comes in three wall thicknesses:

■ Type K – heavy wall for underground
■ Type L – medium wall for medium pressure
■ Type M – light wall for low pressure

With small-diameter pipes, the change in wall thickness adjusts the free area inside the pipe and hence the three different lines (see Table 11.18).

For example, the free cross-sectional area within a $1/2$-inch pipe is 0.218 square inch if the pipe is type K copper, 0.233 square inch if it is type L copper, and 0.254 square inch if it is type M copper. Based on these slight variations in the thickness of the wall of the pipe, a nominal $1/2$-inch type L pipe has an internal free area that is 7% larger than the same-size type K pipe, whereas a nominal $1/2$-inch type M pipe has an internal free area that is 9% larger than the same-size type L pipe. With larger diameter pipes, the difference is negligible, so Figure 11.19 does not include any distinction between the types of copper.

With round pipes, as well as with circular ducts and exhaust flues, small changes in diameter can result in significant changes in the actual area and, as a result, in performance. For example, since the area is based on the square of the radius, the difference in the interior area of a 5-inch- and a 6-inch-diameter air duct is considerable. While 6 inches is only 20% larger than 5 inches, the area within a 6-inch duct is just under one and a half times that of a 5-inch duct. Double the diameter, and the area increases by a factor of 4 (see Table 11.19).

Table 11.19: COMPARATIVE AREAS WITH CHANGING DIAMETERS

Pipe Diameter (in.)	Area Formula	Interior Area
$3/8$	$\pi\,(3/16)^2$	0.11 sq. in.
$1/2$	$\pi\,(1/4)^2$	0.20 sq. in.
$3/4$	$\pi\,(3/8)^2$	0.45 sq. in.
1	$\pi(1/2)^2$	0.79 sq. in.
$1^1/2$	$\pi\,(3/4)^2$	1.77 sq. in.
2	$\pi\,(1)^2$	3.14 sq. in.
$2^1/2$	$\pi\,(1^1/4)^2$	4.91 sq. in.
3	$\pi\,(1^1/2)^2$	7.07 sq. in.
4	$\pi\,(2)^2$	12.57 sq. in.
5	$\pi\,(2^1/2)^2$	19.63 sq. in.
6	$\pi\,(3)^2$	28.27 sq. in.

Copper water lines are sometimes referred to as *pipe* and sometimes as *tubing*. Some believe that the difference is based on whether the line is rigid (a pipe) or flexible (tubing). However, the distinction is actually supposed to relate to whether the size is defined in terms of the outside dimensions (a tube) or the inside dimensions (a pipe). While this sounds reasonable and should provide some clarity in terms of understanding what dimensions refer to, unfortunately the terms are often used interchangeably. Since we are here concerned with the flow within the pipe, the interior dimensions are critical, which often is how tubing is sized. However, there are times when the exterior dimensions of a pipe might be an issue. The message is that we should verify the actual dimensions of the plumbing lines and not assume that the name by which they are referred to indicates a specific condition.

Calling copper pipe tubing is not the only possible problem with copper water lines. Unfortunately, copper is rather expensive and there is a good chance that it could be stolen during construction, so we might choose to consider alternative materials. Galvanized steel pipe, which was the major type of piping used for water supply prior to 1950, is still an alternative that we might consider, although hopefully not too seriously. It has a limited life and there are now some better choices, particularly plastic. But when considering plastic, we must take care to use the proper plastic. Some plastics are suitable for cold water but not for hot water, and some are not recommended for water that might be consumed. It is important to always check the applicable regulations for the jurisdiction in which we are working to verify the types of plastic that are acceptable for the intended use.

When we consider using plastic piping, polyvinyl chloride (PVC) is probably the type that will initially come to mind. PVC is a very popular plastic that effectively resists many chemicals, although it does not generally stand up well to hot water. As a result, if we use PVC for plumbing supply, we should use it only for cold water lines. PVC pipe is either white or gray. Chlorinated polyvinyl chloride (CPVC), which has a distinctive yellowish color, can resist hot water and is therefore effective for use for both hot and cold water supply. Both PVC and CPVC pipe are connected using solvent welding. Cross-linked polyethylene (PEX) is another plastic pipe that can handle both hot and cold water. PEX is actually a whitish color, although it is available in distinctive blue and red colors to denote cold and hot water. It is also flexible and can be connected in a variety of ways that rely on compression assembly. Kitec is a composite flexible pipe comprised of thin-walled aluminum pipe sandwiched between an inner and an outer layer of PEX plastic. While Kitec is an interesting alternative, unfortunately there have been problems with the special brass fittings that are used to connect the pipe. The fittings are prone to dezincification, which is a form of corrosion. Brass is a copper-zinc alloy. As the water that flows through the Kitec piping comes in contact with the brass fittings, zinc tends to leach out. This tends to constrict the flow, potentially increasing internal water pressure that can reduce water flow, weaken the fittings, and potentially result in leaks.

Whatever type of pipe is chosen, Figure 11.19 can be used for smooth-bore pipes with the interior dimensions indicated. The GPM demand for the WSFU that are served by the pipe determines a horizontal line in the chart. There are then three variables from which we can select one that will, in turn, determine the other two. Generally, the point is set on the GPM line by selecting either the velocity or the pipe size. Whichever is selected will then determine the other factor as well as the friction loss in terms of psi per 100 feet of pipe.

As discussed, water flowing in a pipe starts to generate apparent noise at a velocity of around 4 FPS, but if the pipe is enclosed by at least $1/2$-inch gypsum board, the noise should not become apparent until around 6 FPS. Based on this, we usually size piping so the velocity is less than 6 FPS, but the maximum might be increased to 10 FPS in building service areas, although this would result in significant pressure loss. While lower velocities will cost more initially, the reduced flow will be much quieter, changes in pressure will be reduced, and the chances for water hammer will be greatly diminished. If the supply must be pumped, the lower velocities will also require lower pump pressure, which means less energy consumption over the life of the system.

In selecting the size of a water supply pipe, it is better to oversize than undersize the pipe since this will reduce both the noise level and the pressure loss. A lower pressure loss will provide better performance at times of full demand since the adjustments in pressure with changes in GPM flow will not be as great. The changes shown in Figure 11.19 are basically logarithmic. As a result, a similar change in GPM will result in a smaller change in pressure loss when the basic pressure loss is at the lower portion of the scale than when it is at the higher portion of the scale.

For example, as shown in Figure 11.20, a $1/2$-inch pipe would have a friction loss of around 6 psi per 100 linear feet with a 2.5-GPM flow, such as the flow drawn by a shower. If a second shower served by the same $1/2$-inch line were turned on, the flow would increase to 5 GPM, with the friction loss increased to 20 psi. If a $3/4$-inch pipe were used instead for the same conditions, the friction loss would change from 1 psi per 100 linear feet to 3 psi. With the smaller $1/2$-inch pipe, the addition of 2.5 GPM relates to a 233% increase in pressure loss or an actual increase of 14 psi. For the same increase in GPM with the larger $3/4$-inch pipe, the percent increase is 200%, almost as much, but the actual pressure loss per 100 linear feet is only 2 psi higher. As a result, when the second shower is turned on, there would be a significant pressure drop with the smaller pipe that would cause a change in water flow for the person in the first shower. With the larger pipe, the pressure drop would be relatively insignificant, hardly affecting the water supply to the first shower. A related situation, one that might be experienced personally, happens when one person is taking a shower and someone else flushes a toilet. Once again there is a pressure drop, and if it is considerable, such as occurs with a $1/2$-inch supply pipe, the result could be a shocking increase in the shower

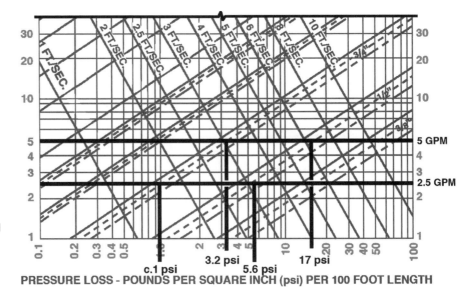

Figure 11.20 PRESSURE LOSS CHART FOR SMOOTH PIPE – EXAMPLE
The plotted conditions show that when the initial velocity is kept low and is then doubled, the change in pressure loss is less, in terms of both ratio and psi, than when the initial velocity is higher and the volume is doubled.

water temperature. Of course, the shock might come again but from a decrease in temperature when the toilet tank is filled.

The plumbing code now requires that showers be supplied from a balanced-pressure, a thermostatic, or a combined balanced-pressure/thermostatic mixing valve, any one of which should alleviate, although not necessarily eliminate, any problem of a temperature change resulting from a variation in line pressure. These mixing valves only provide on/off control and cannot adjust the flow rate, which usually is set at the U.S. prescribed 2.5 GPM. Once on, movement of the valve handle adjusts the discharge temperature, which is not to exceed 120°F. If the pressure or temperature of the water in the supply lines, hot or cold, should change, the valve should automatically adjust to keep the discharge at the selected temperature. Of course, with a large supply pipe, there is less proportional change in line pressure with a change in flow, which should reduce any change in the shower temperature.

The listed pressure loss per 100 linear feet shown in Figure 11.19 is based on a straight pipe. However, there are normally various bends within any run, as well as various plumbing fittings and valves, all of which resist water flow and increase the resistance well above what occurs merely as a result of the basic flow. If we know what bends and fittings exist, we can determine the pressure loss that each will provide, but in the preliminary design the general approach is to assume a 50% additional pressure loss from the probable plumbing fittings and bends. Once the actual plumbing layout is known, the pressure loss can be determined more accurately. Generally, the actual pressure loss is less than the estimate base on the 50% rule, and unless the pressure exceeds around 60 to 80 psi (see Table 11.16), this should not cause any serious problems; how-

ever, above this level, some problems could occur. In general, the internal pressures should be less than 100 psi since at this pressure valve packing might not be sufficient to avoid leaks. However, high pressures are likely to occur only in rather large projects, in which consulting engineers are generally responsible for the plumbing design. So, while we should be aware of the issues, it is unlikely that we will be directly involved with such complications, although with smaller projects, the plumbing design is often our responsibility.

Stop Valves

Figure 11.21 shows various stop valves that are used to control water flow. As their name implies, they are used to shut off the flow, but some are also used to adjust the rate of flow. There are four basic types of plumbing valves—globe valves, gate valves, butterfly valves, and ball valves— the last two developed more recently. Gate valves and globe valves have been around for some time and are still used regularly. There is also the check valve, which is intended to prohibit backflow.

Globe valves, which are probably the most common type of valve, are designed to adjust the rate of flow and are the valves generally used in plumbing faucets. The name of this valve derives from the spherical form of its body. As shown in Figure 11.21, the supply into a globe valve is located so that when the valve is closed, the water pressure in the supply line is not forced against the valve handle. When there is water flow through this portion of the valve, the line should be open, reducing the probability that the water pressure will leak through the valve stem. If a globe valve is installed backward, there is a chance that the valve will leak.

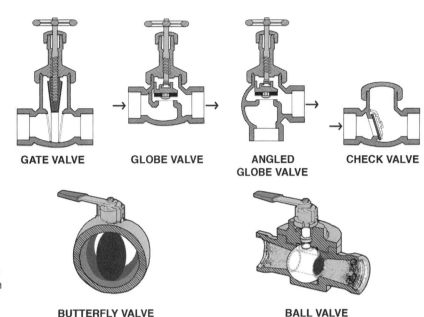

GATE VALVE   **GLOBE VALVE**   **ANGLED GLOBE VALVE**   **CHECK VALVE**

BUTTERFLY VALVE   **BALL VALVE**

Figure 11.21 PLUMBING VALVES
All of these valves can be used to stop the flow and are, therefore, legitimately stop valves. The globe valve can also throttle the flow and, because of this attribute, is the valve used in most plumbing fixtures. The check valve is a special valve that is intended to prohibit, stop, or reverse flow within a line.

Gate vales are intended for on/off control and are usually installed to isolate a portion of a plumbing line or to turn off the water to a fixture, for example in order to replace a washer in a faucet. In comparison to globe valves, gate valves impose relatively low resistance to water flow. When they are open, which is when the issue of resistance would be of concern, they impose little restriction to water flow. The gate valve usually includes a wedge-shaped solid piece of metal, somewhat like a sliding gate. This "gate" is raised or lowered (assuming that the valve handle is above the pipe and not to the side) in slotted grooves, one on either side of the gate. When the valve is closed, there should be a tight fit of the wedged gate in the slotted grooves, typically brass against brass, which stops any flow of water.

Based on their design, gate valves are not effective for adjusting the rate of water flow. In fact, trying to use a gate valve to adjust the rate of flow can damage the valve. Since the operation of the valve entails the insertion of the wedge-shaped gate into slotted grooves, at partial closure the flow of liquid will cause the gate to vibrate within the grooves, potentially damaging the finished surface of both the gate and the grooves on which closure is dependent. For this reason, gate valves should not be used to throttle the fluid flow. They will not effectively reduce the flow, and it is likely that they will be damaged in the attempt, potentially destroying their ability to completely stop the flow when required.

Butterfly valves include a round disk that is twisted within the fitting, essentially within the pipe. When the disk is oriented parallel to the pipe, fluid can flow, but when the disk is turned at 90°, it cannot. The butterfly valve can be used to throttle the flow by being turned partially between the two extreme positions. Since the operating handle on a butterfly valve is typically a simple lever handle that is oriented parallel to the valve disk, it is easy to operate and provides a clear indication of whether the valve is open, closed, or somewhere in between. Ball valves are similar in some ways to the butterfly valve, but rather than relying on a circular disk, they use a ball through which there is a clear opening. Ball valves, which also usually have a lever handle, are sometimes used to throttle the flow, although this is not the intended purpose for this type of valve.

The valve handle is connected to the operating mechanism within the valve by the valve stem. This means that the stem must extend from inside to outside the valve and still be free to move. To keep the water, which is under pressure, from leaking out through the stem opening, some pliable material, which will allow the stem to move and yet keep water from leaking, has to be packed between the stem and the enclosing components. There is a limit, however, to the internal pressures that this packing can resist. Also, in time the effectiveness of the packing can, and usually does, diminish. As a result, to reduce the likelihood that the valves will leak, the internal pressures in standard plumbing water supply systems should be less than 100 psi. Where water pressures have to be higher, perhaps when pumping water to the upper levels of a high-rise structure, special fittings must be used, and these should be located where potential leaks will not result in serious problems. This generally means that high-pressure fittings are not located within occupied areas.

Although the traditional handle for a plumbing control valve is round, lever handles are now used, particularly with butterfly valves and ball valves. There are two advantages to the lever handle. One is that the handle's position makes it readily apparent whether the valve is

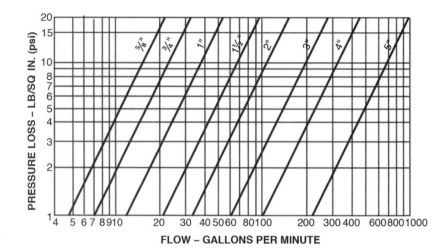

Figure 11.22 PRESSURE LOSS IN WATER METERS

open or closed. Generally, if the handle is parallel to the pipe, the valve is open. Another advantage of lever handles is that they are often quicker to operate, although the wheel handle control on gate and globe valves can provide assistance to overcome resistance, which might be helpful if the valve has not been adjusted for some time. Based on this, there are also butterfly valves and ball valves that use a wheel handle connected via planetary gears to convert hand force to move a fairly large valve against significant pressures.

The check valve allows water to flow in only one direction. The valve can swing open in only one direction, so if the flow is in reverse, the valve will close. Check valves are usually spring controlled so that they will close if there is no flow. Since pressure is needed to open the check valve, this basically means that the valve is open only when the water flow is in the intended direction. Such a valve is a safety feature intended in part to avoid water contamination. For example, if a water supply is connected to a hot water boiler, there is a chance that the internal pressure could build up in the boiler when the water is heated, which could produce some backflow into the supply pipe. If a check valve is installed, any backflow should be prevented, although there is no guarantee.

The water meter is another source of resistance within the water supply system, although this resistance is not typically assumed to be included in the 50% rule. Figure 11.22 shows the pressure loss of meters of various sizes, based on pipe diameter, for different flow rates.

The basic objective in designing the water supply system is to ensure that there is the necessary volume and adequate pressure at the end of the supply line for the operation of the plumbing fixtures. Generally, the concern is that there is sufficient pressure, although it is important not to exceed the maximum pressure, 100 psi, which might cause the valves to leak. While most plumbing fixtures require at least 8 to 10 psi, flush valves require at least 15 psi, and modern shower-mixing valves should have at least 20 psi to operate effectively. So, when designing a water supply system, we must ensure that the initial system pressure—for example, at the water main in the street if we are using public water—is sufficient to overcome the resistance in the piping and fittings and to raise the water from the entry point up to the highest point of use and still be adequate to operate the fixture. It is also important to make certain that excessive noise will not be produced and that the pressures do not exceed the limits at any point within the system.

WATER SUPPLY DESIGN EXAMPLE

What would be the appropriate size of a cold water supply pipe for the two-story residence diagrammed below that has the following plumbing fixtures?

- Two full baths on the upper level, one with two lavatories
- A half-bath or restroom on the lower level
- A kitchen with a sink and dishwasher
- A clothes washer on the upper level
- Two outside hose bibbs

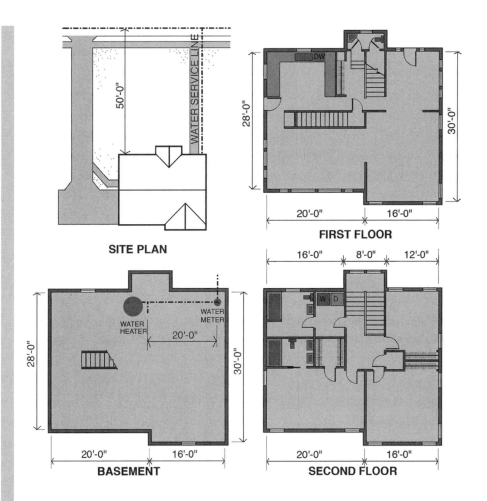

SITE PLAN

FIRST FLOOR

BASEMENT

SECOND FLOOR

Based on the simple description, there are four lavatories, three WCs, two shower/bath units, a kitchen sink, a dishwasher, a clothes washer, and two outside hose bibs. To size the water service for the house, we need to determine the total WSFU, but to design the plumbing distribution in the house, we should separate the distribution into hot and cold water.

Fixtures		WSFU
4 Lavatories	4 at 0.7	2.8
3 WCs	3 at 2.2	6.6
2 Shower/Bath Units	2 at 1.4	2.8
Kitchen Sink	1 at 1.4	1.4
Dishwasher	1 at 1.4	1.4
Clothes Washer	1 at 1.4	1.4
2 Hose Bibs		3.5
	1 at 2.5	
	1 at 1.0	
	Total WSFU	**19.9**

Assuming 20 WSFU, Figure 11.18 indicates that the GPM demand is about 15 GPM. From Figure 11.19, assuming a $^3/_4$-inch pipe, the water velocity for 15 GPM would be around 10 FPS, and there would be around a 22-psi pressure loss for each 100 linear feet of piping. While this velocity will produce considerable noise, since most of this portion of the water service would be underground and the portion that is not will probably be in a nonoccupied area such as a basement, perhaps this velocity is acceptable, assuming that there is adequate pressure. With a 1-inch pipe, the velocity would be 5.5 FPS and the pressure loss per 100 linear feet would be only 6.0 psi.

Once in the residence, the water is distributed to the various points of use, with some usually going to a hot water heater. Let us assume that a common water line distributes cold water to the two bathrooms on the upper level. While we could use the bathroom group approach, it is better to use the individual plumbing fixtures to determine the WSFU. The bathroom group method basically assumes that only one individual will likely use a bathroom at a time. Since one bathroom, probably the master bathroom, has two sinks, perhaps the modesty or privacy level of this family does not demand individual use. If so, it is likely that the shower might be running concurrently with a lavatory and the filling of the WC flush tank.

Fixtures		WSFU
3 Lavatories	3 at 0.5	1.5
2 WCs	2 at 2.2	4.4
2 Shower/Bath Units	2 at 1.0	2.0
	Total WSFU	**7.9**

If the bathroom group approach were used, the WSFU would be only 5.9.

Fixtures		WSFU
1 Lavatory	1 at 0.5	0.5
2 Bathroom Groups	2 at 2.7	5.4
	Total WSFU	**5.9**

Let us proceed using the WSFU based on the plumbing fixtures rather than the bathroom group. Since the laundry is located on the second floor, the WSFU for the cold water line serving the second floor is 8.9 WSFU, based on 7.9 WSFU for the two bathrooms and 1 WSFU for the clothes washer.

While Figure 11.18 converts WSFU to a GPM demand, since the WSFU is so low, the WSFU and GPM are essentially the same, so for 8.9 WSFU, rounding off, we can assume 9 GPM. Using Figure 11.19, assuming a $^1/_2$-inch pipe, the velocity for 9 GPM would be over 10 FPS and therefore rather noisy. (We should note that there are no velocity lines in Figure 11.19 above 10 FPS, so we must extrapolate as best we can.) The velocity would be around 12 FPS, and the pressure loss per 100 linear feet would also be 49 psi. With a $^3/_4$-inch pipe, the velocity would be around 6 FPS and the pressure losses would be significantly less at 9.1 psi per 100 linear feet.

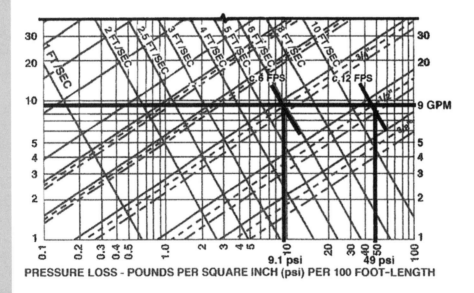

PRESSURE LOSS - POUNDS PER SQUARE INCH (psi) PER 100 FOOT-LENGTH

Example 1 Friction Loss Chart for Smooth Pipe

Since the hot water heater is located in the basement, the hot water line running to the second floor would have to handle both bathrooms and the clothes washer. The WSFU for this portion of the supply system will be the same as for the cold water, except that since the toilets do not use hot water, they are not included.

Fixture		WSFU
3 Lavatories	3 at 0.5	1.5
2 Shower/Bath Units	2 at 1.0	2.0
1 Clothes Washer	1 at 1.0	1.0
	Total WSFU	4.5

As with the cold water, since the WSFU is so low, the GPM equals the WSFU. For 4.5 GPM, the velocity and pressure for a $1/2$-inch pipe would be around 5.8 FPS with a pressure loss of 14 psi per 100 linear feet. If the pipe is increased to $3/4$ inch, which would reduce the noise level, the water velocity would be around 2.8 FPS, and the pressure loss would be about 2.7 psi per 100 linear feet of pipe.

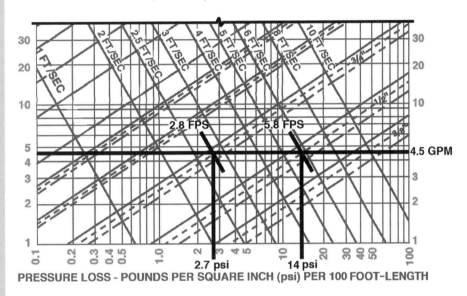

PRESSURE LOSS - POUNDS PER SQUARE INCH (psi) PER 100 FOOT-LENGTH

Example 2 Friction Loss Chart for Smooth Pipe

Rather than a central hot water heater, whether a storage heater or an instantaneous heater, which in terms of energy savings is suggested, let us assume that a terminal hot water heater is used for all of the plumbing applications on the second floor. If this heater is located close to the bathrooms and clothes washer, then the main cold water line running to the bathrooms would have to be sized for the combined or total WSFU shown in Table 11.17.

Fixture	Cold		Hot and Cold	
	Units	WSFU	Units	WSFU
3 Lavatories	3 at 0.5	1.5	3 at 0.7	2.1
2 WC	2 at 2.2	4.4	2 at 2.2	4.4
2 Shower/Bath Units	2 at 1.0	2.0	2 at 1.4	2.8
1 Clothes Washer	2 at 1.0	1.0	1 at 1.4	1.4
	Total WSFU	8.9	Total WSFU	10.7

Based on a total WSFU of 10.7, which again is at the low end, rather than that used in Figure 11.18, we can assume basically 11 GPM. From Figure 11.19, a $3/4$-inch supply pipe would have a velocity of 7.3 FPS and a pressure loss of 12 psi per 100 linear feet of run. Unfortunately, at 6 FPS, some noise will be generated when the water flow is at the full demand rate; however, if this pipe is installed in a manner that keeps it from a close connection with critical occupied areas, this noise should not be a problem. If this does not seem acceptable, the supply line should be increased to a 1-inch pipe, which might make sense since the water to the clothes washer will be going on and off during the wash cycle. For comparison, the velocity in a 1-inch pipe would be about 4 FPS and the pressure loss would be only 3.5 psi per 100 linear feet.

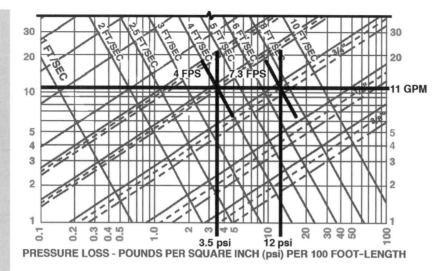

PRESSURE LOSS - POUNDS PER SQUARE INCH (psi) PER 100 FOOT-LENGTH

Example 3 Friction Loss Chart for Smooth Pipe

So far, the process has been primarily concerned with staying within the range of velocities to keep the noise within accepted levels, although consideration has also been given to the pressure loss per 100 linear feet. Having set the basic distribution piping sizes, we must then determine the total pressure required by the system—the pressure that has to be at the service entry in order to overcome the pressure loss in the piping and fittings, to raise the water to the highest point of use, and to have adequate pressure at that point, which is generally set at 20 psi if the use is for a shower, 15 psi for a flush valve urinal or WC, or 8 psi for most other fixtures. (Table 11.16B includes the required pressures and water flow rates for typical plumbing fixtures.)

Based on the above and on some other assumptions, we can determine the probable pressure loss in pounds per square inch. Even with a rough plan of the residence, we need to assume the length of the various segments of the water supply system. For this exercise, the underground run from the street to the house is 50 feet, and we can assume that there are about 30 feet of piping within the basement before the initial takeoff. These 30 feet include rising from the basement floor up to the ceiling. In addition to the pressure loss from these 80 feet of pipe, there is the 50% additional loss to account for the pressure loss from fittings and pipe bends, the basement floor-to-ceiling rise, and the water meter.

One-inch pipe with pressure loss of 6.7 lb per 100 ft (assume 50 ft from the street and 30 ft within the basement)

$$6.7 \text{ psi}/100 \text{ ft} \times .8 = 5.4 \text{ psi}$$
$$5.4 \text{ psi} \times 1.5 = 8.1 \text{ psi} \quad \textbf{8.1 psi}$$

Water meter friction loss is

$$1.7 \text{ psi} \quad \textbf{1.7 psi}$$

Cold water line from basement to second floor (assume 40 ft of $^3/_4$-inch pipe)

$$9.25 \text{ psi}/100 \text{ ft} \times .4 = 3.7 \text{ psi}$$
$$3 \text{psi} \times 1.5 = 5.6 \text{ psi} \quad \textbf{5.6 psi}$$

Vertical rise from service entry to showerhead (assume 25 ft)

$$25 \text{ ft} \times 0.43 \text{ lb/ft} = 10.8 \text{ psi} \quad \textbf{10 psi}$$
20 psi required at end of run   **20 psi**

45.4 psi required at the water main

Water Supply Pressure

For most single-family residences that have public water service, the pressure at the service entry into the house is more than adequate to distribute the water and provide sufficient pressure at the highest point of discharge. In fact, at times the pressure is too great, and it is necessary to install a pressure-reducing valve in order to avoid problems. One reason for this is that the public water service that supplies residential customers also typically supplies the fire hydrants, and these require pressures of around 100 psi. If the pressure is too high, a pressure-reducing valve should be installed to reduce potential problems, which include leakage (as already discussed) as well as poor operation of automatic valves that are used in clothes washers and dishwashers.

While the public water system can maintain enough pressure within the system by using pumps, generally water is pumped up to an elevated storage tank, which itself is usually located at a topographical high point, with system pressure established by the overall elevation of the tank (see Figure 11.23). In addition to establishing a pressure head, a storage tank makes it unnecessary to match the rate of water flow from the water treatment plant into the storage tank with the rate of actual usage. While the water can be pumped into the tank at a reduced rate, the drawdown can be at a much higher rate to meet the peak water demand.

However the pressure in the water main is established, generally this pressure, even at 100 psi, is not adequate for a high-rise building. With 0.43 pound required for each foot of elevation and assuming a 12-foot floor-to-floor dimension, 5.16 pounds are required to pump the water up one floor level. If elevating the water was all that the water main pressure had to do, 100 psi could raise the water about 19 floors, but, in addition to the pressure needed to elevate the water, there is also the need to overcome the resistance from the piping system and still leave around 15 to 20 psi at the end of the run for proper operation of the plumbing fixture. As a result, 100 psi pressure at the street main is probably only adequate for a structure up to 10 stories high.

In higher structures, additional pressure is required. While there are various ways that this can be provided (see the four diagrams in Figure 11.24 that present different supply arrangements for high-rise structures), in general, in order to avoid excessive pressures, the distribution system is divided into zones, each of which extends for approximately 16 floors. In this way, the discharge pressures at the plumbing fixtures within a zone will stay within an acceptable range—not too high and not too low.

If the water comes from a public water system, it generally has sufficient pressure to distribute the water throughout a building of up to around 4 or 5 floors and perhaps even more but generally not more than 10 floors. With higher structures, the water generally must be pumped up to the higher levels. While the pressure can be increased as the water enters the structure, even enough to supply it up to 100 stories or more, the internal pressure necessary to reach such a height would be excessive for normal plumbing control valves. Therefore, it is necessary to reduce the number of floors served within any plumbing zone to around 16 floors. This applies whether the water is pumped upward to the fixtures or is pumped upward to a

Figure 11.23 WATER STORAGE TANKS
Elevating a water storage tank establishes system pressure as well as a means of meeting variations in supply demand. The image on the left is the 172-foot-high water tower in Eden Park in Cincinnati, Ohio, that was built in 1894. The image on the right is the water tower designed by Eero Saarinen for the GM Tech Center in the later 1940s.

(a)   (b)

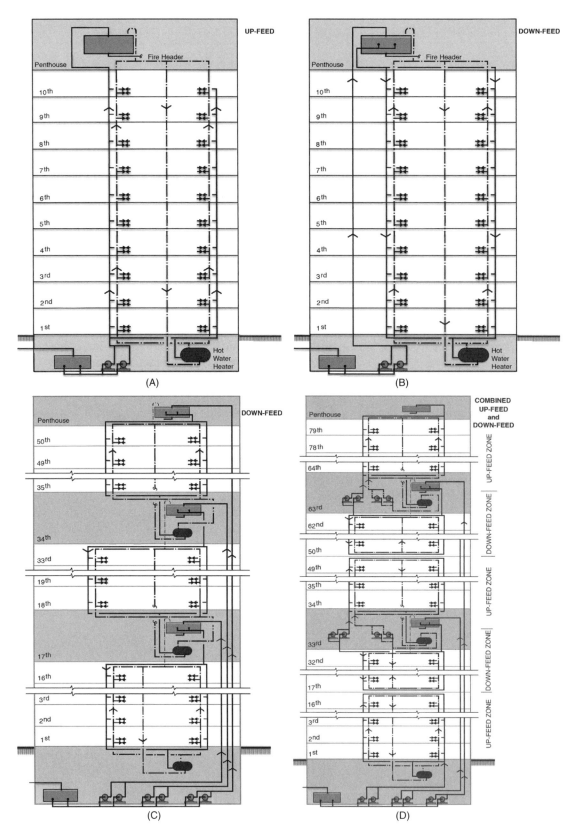

Figure 11.24 HIGH-RISE WATER SUPPLY

When the pressure in the public main is not adequate, it is necessary to pressurize the building's water distribution system in either an up-feed (A), or a down-feed (B). When pumps are added, a surge tank should be installed to reduce the possibility of establishing pressure variations within the public supply. With the up-feed system, the pumps must be capable of meeting the highest GPM demand, whereas with the down-feed system, the pumps need not be related to this demand. Both systems show a storage tank, although the tank for the up-feed system is typically smaller and is intended for fire suppression rather than water supply. When there are more than 16 floors in a building, it is typical to establish various plumbing supply zones (see C & D). Accepting the 16-floor limit, this might mean locating a mechanical floor, or at least a portion of that floor, at 16-story increments. However, if the structure uses both up-feed and down-feed, these mechanical floors can be at a 32-floor spacing, as shown in (D).

water storage tank from which the water is then supplied by gravity to the fixtures below. With either approach, the range of pressure within a plumbing zone should be at least around 15 psi, which is the minimum pressure required for a flush valve, and at most around 100 psi, above which valves might leak. Assuming a 12-foot floor-to-floor height, this establishes the 16-floor limit. If the water is pumped up to the fixtures, the pressure would be highest at the bottom of the zone and would decrease with the elevation floor by floor. If the water comes from an upper-level storage tank, as indicated in Figure 11.24B, the pressure increases as the water drops down, so again, the highest pressure will be at the bottom of the zone.

Theoretically, the pressure that the pump needs to provide is the same for both up-feed and down-feed. However, with the up-feed system, the pump must be able to supply the full demand GPM, whereas with the down-feed system, the pump can slowly add water to the storage tank that should be able to meet the peak GPM demand. There is also the option combining up-feed and down-feed systems, as shown in Figure 11.24D, which provides the advantage of locating the plumbing service floors at a 32-floor spacing rather than after only 16 floors.

Water Hammer Arrester

While excessive water velocities will generate noise, noise can also result from water hammer, which can occur if the flow is stopped quickly. Although we generally think of water, which is a fluid, as being flexible or relatively "soft," anyone who has experienced a belly flop knows that water is not really very forgiving. When water flows at a high rate and is then stopped suddenly, which might occur with an automatic shutoff valve in a clothes washer or a quick-acting faucet, the rushing water can create a water hammer. At the worst, this can sound like the pipe's being hit by a metal hammer (hence the name), but often the noise is more like that of a rubber mallet, creating a thud and a subsequent rattle of the pipes. In any event, water hammer can be rather annoying.

Water hammer can be eliminated by adding an air cushion in the plumbing supply line. This cushion, which can absorb the pressure that is exerted on the pipes when a valve is closed quickly, was traditionally formed by simply capping a 2-foot vertical extension of the water line past the takeoff to the fixture control valve (see Figure 11.25). Since the extension is capped, when the system is filled with water, air is trapped in the extension, establishing a shock absorber that reduces the impact of the abrupt stoppage of the water. Sometimes the capped segment of pipe is increased in size to provide a larger volume of air. While some water can enter the pipe as the system is filled, a sub-

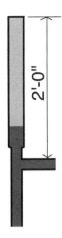

Figure 11.25 WATER HAMMER ARRESTER
Extending the supply pipe beyond the takeoff to a valve by 2 feet will establish an air cushion that can eliminate water hammer. In response to the concern that over time water that has migrated into the air chamber can become contaminated, many jurisdictions now require manufactured water hammer arresters that include a piston that supposedly will prevent this problem.

stantial column of compressed air will remain to arrest the water hammer problem. However, although this system is effective, recently some questions have been raised about whether, over time, the air in the pipe extension will be gradually absorbed into the water, allowing the water to rise up into the pipe, eventually reducing the effectiveness of the air column in stopping the water hammer. Another concern is that the water trapped within the pipe column can become contaminated with bacteria and other unpleasant materials. The thought is that impurities exist in any water system, although at very low levels, but that over time these can build up in the stagnant water that remains within the water hammer arrester. If this happens and there is a pressure drop within the system, this contaminated water could get into the water supply stream. While this is a possibility, perhaps more as a result of effective lobbying by manufacturers, many jurisdictions now prohibit simple pipe-column water hammer arresters and require devices that are specifically designed as a hammer arrester. The difference between the two systems is that the cushioning effect is provided by a shock-absorbing piston rather than merely a shock-absorbing column of air. With the piston, less water will ultimately be trapped within the arrester device, thereby apparently reducing the potential for water contamination.

Domestic Hot Water

The procedure for sizing the domestic hot water supply is similar to that for sizing the cold water supply: identify all of the fixtures that use hot water, determine the hot water WSFU, and then find the GPM demand. This information

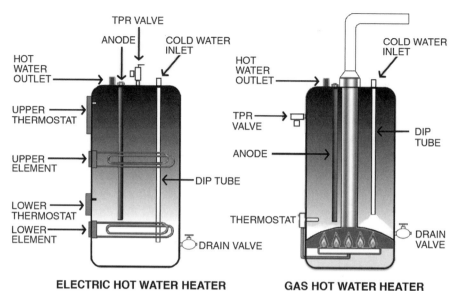

Figure 11.26 HOT WATER HEATERS
Hot water heating in most single-family residences is provided by a storage tank heater that typically uses either a gas flame or two electric resistance units as the heat source. The intention is to heat the water to the desired temperature, usually around 120° F to 140°F, and maintain it at that temperature. When hot water is drawn off from the top of the tank, cold water is dispersed at the bottom of the tank in a way that should maintain thermal stratification. In a well-insulated heater, maintaining the water temperature when there is new addition of cold water should require only several short periods of heating each day.

ELECTRIC HOT WATER HEATER

GAS HOT WATER HEATER

is then used to size the supply pipe, similarly to the simple calculation example above, and to size the hot water heater.

The water can be heated in several ways. The most common approach is to use a hot water heater that is combined with a water storage tank, with the heating provided by either a gas flame or an electric resistance heater. These units are designed to slowly heat a large volume of water, which is set by the expected hot water demand. The rate of heating, called the *recovery rate*, is typically about half of the actual demand in terms of gallons per hour. Since these units are intended to store a volume of heated water, maintaining the temperature at 120° F to 140° F, it is important that they be very well insulated. Older units often were not and were, therefore, a source of considerable energy loss, but newer units are better insulated and have greater energy efficiency.

In addition to ensuring that the hot water storage tank is properly insulated, we must also make sure that the hot water supply pipes are insulated. Since the hot water is between 120° F and 140° F, there is around a 60° F temperature differential between the hot water and the interior temperatures.

As shown in Figure 11.26, the cold water connection to a hot water heater is typically at the top of the heater, but the cold water flows through the dip tube and is discharged at the bottom of the tank. This way the cold water does not mix with the hot water and lower its temperature. One indication that there might be a problem with a hot water heater is that the temperature of the hot water drops very quickly shortly after initial use. This shows that perhaps the cold water dip tube has deteriorated or broken and that cold water is entering at the top of the tank and mixing with the hot water. If this happens, the hot water is quickly

diluted with cold water, lowering the temperature of the water drawn from the tank. If, as intended, the cold water enters at the bottom of the tank or the temperature of the stored water drops, the thermostat reads this change in temperature and activates the heater.

There are various recommendations for sizing residential hot water heaters. Obviously, larger families require hot water heaters with more storage capacity and a higher recovery rate. HUD-FHA recommends minimum residential water heater capacities. These capacities are shown in Table 11.20, listed according to the type of heat source. In addition, this table includes the recommended storage capacity and recovery rate for the different heat sources that are typically used in single-family residences.

If space heating is provided by hot water or steam, the space-heating boiler can provide the domestic hot water. This generally requires that a loop of domestic water supply piping be inserted into the boiler water or through a heat exchanger connected to the boiler. When domestic hot water is required, cold water flows through the boiler or heat exchanger and is heated. This heated water then either flows into a domestic hot water storage tank, from which the hot water for the fixtures is actually drawn, or is directly distributed through the hot water supply lines. In the latter arrangement, the space-heating boiler operates basically as a "tankless" heater. Usually temperature controls are added to the boiler in order to maintain the boiler water temperature at around 180° F, which is adequate to heat the domestic water to around 120° F to 140° F. During the heating season, the boiler temperatures are usually kept above this level so that when heating is required, there is no major delay until the boiler water is heated up. While a boiler is usually shut down during the summer, if it is used to heat the domestic hot water, the boiler must

Table 11.20: Minimum Residential Water Heater Capacities (HUD-FHA)

Number of Baths	1.0–1.5			2.0–2.5				3.0–3.5				
Number of Bedrooms	1	2	3	2	3	4	5	3	4	5	6	STD
Gas												
Storage, gal	20	30	30	30	40	40	50	40	50	50	50	**50**
Input, 1000 BTUH	27	36	36	36	36	38	47	37	38	47	50	
1-Hr Draw, gal	43	60	60	60	70	72	90	72	82	90	92	
Recovery, gph	23	30	30	30	30	32	40	32	32	40	42	**50**
Electric												
Storage, gal	20	30	40	40	50	50	66	50	66	66	80	**80**
Input, kW	2.5	3.5	4.5	4.5	5.5	5.5	5.5	5.5	5.5	5.5	5.5	
1-Hr Draw, gal	30	44	58	58	72	72	88	72	88	88	102	
Recovery, gph	10	14	18	18	22	22	22	22	22	22	22	**22**
Oil												
Storage, gal	30	30	30	30	30	30	30	30	30	30	30	**30**
Input, kW	70	70	70	70	70	70	70	70	70	70	70	
1-Hr Draw, gal	89	89	89	89	89	89	89	89	89	89	89	
Recovery, gph	59	59	59	59	59	59	59	59	59	59	59	**60**

Source: Adapted from HUD-FHA recommendations.

continue to operate. This might seem rather wasteful, but space-heating boilers are usually well insulated and have considerable capacity. As a result, the domestic hot water demands can generally be met during the summer with one or two short periods of boiler operation to heat the boiler water to 180° F. If space heating is provided by steam, heat will not be distributed through the system since the maintained water temperatures are below 212° F. Space heating will only occur when steam is produced. If space heating is provided by hot water, the system needs to include a temperature control valve that keeps the hot water from flowing by gravity through the piping system used for space heating. The flow control valve should remain closed and should open only when the space thermostat calls for heat and starts the supply pump. Such flow control should be provided even without domestic hot water heating so that heat is not distributed until the space thermostat calls for it, which, of course, would mean that heat is only used for domestic hot water during the summer.

Combining domestic hot water with space heating can increase the operational efficiency of the heating system. During the winter, space-heating demands are generally well below the capacity of the system since the outdoor temperature rarely drops to the low design temperature (e.g., 0°–5° F). For this reason, the boiler has extra capacity, which, if used to heat the domestic hot water, will increase the system's efficiency. At times when the capacity of the boiler is needed to meet a major heat loss, there could be a slight problem in meeting both demands, but generally at extremely low temperatures, which occur rarely, there is less expectation of full comfort.

Instantaneous or *demand* hot water heaters, also sometimes called *tankless* heaters, do not have storage tanks. These units have a high-capacity heater that can heat the water as it flows through. When the hot water line is opened at a fixture, water starts to flow through the demand hot water heater, signaling a flow switch that activates the heater. When the flow stops, the heater turns off. The heating is usually provided by either a gas flame or an electric resistance coil; the use of gas is more prevalent with larger units.

Water heating can occur centrally, with the hot water then distributed to the points of use, or at different locations near, if not directly at, the point of use. While the United States has traditionally used centralized hot water heating, especially in residential occupancies, there is increased support for the point-of-use approach, which tends to rely on demand heaters, since this tends to be more efficient, particularly in terms of water consumption. The main water efficiency comes from not having to waste water while waiting for the hot water to arrive from a centrally located hot water heater. There is also some efficiency in terms of energy use. With distributed domestic hot water heating, less hot water is left in the pipe after the hot water is turned off. Since the hot water that remains in the pipe cools down over time, the heat that was added to the water is therefore essentially lost. A hot water line serving two second-floor bathrooms in a single-family residence, which would likely be a $^3/_4$-inch pipe with an overall length of at least 50 feet, would contain over 1 gallon of water. Assuming that the hot water temperature is 130° F, as this hot water cools to around 70° F, it will lose 500 BTU. This is not a large amount, but the loss is repeated several times each day.

We can install a hot water loop in order to avoid any delay in getting hot water from a faucet and the associated water loss, which can be considerable in a large building

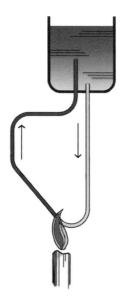

Figure 11.27 HOT WATER LOOP
Water can flow as a result of variations in density established by temperature differentials.

(see Figure 11.27). Relying merely on density variations or using pumps, a hot-water can maintain a supply of hot water at all of the hot-water-consuming fixtures, thereby ensuring that hot water is available without delay. While this means that there is less water loss, since the hot water is maintained throughout the system, even when not in use, more energy tends to be consumed in heating the water.

As with the residential example just mentioned, the hot water in the pipes cools down, which is why a recirculating system would be used—to avoid the delay and waste of water before there is hot water in the plumbing fixture. While the heat loss can be reduced by insulating the hot water lines, which should be done in any event, this will not eliminate the heat loss. If a recirculating pump is used to move the hot water through the loop, then there is also the added energy consumed by the pump. Of course, both the waste of water and the energy loss can be reduced with localized water heating using demand hot water heaters.

According to the U.S. Department of Energy, homes that use 40 gallons or less of hot water each day can save around one-third of the energy used to heat hot water in conventional storage-tank heaters. Even in homes that use more hot water, demand heaters are still usually more efficient. The major problem with demand heaters is that they typically produce no more than 5 GPM, which is often less than the demand even in a single-family residence. This is for gas demand heaters. Electric demand heaters cannot match this output and are typically limited to about 2 GPM. This limitation can actually be the basis for improved performance since it generally means that several demand heaters are needed, and these can be located close to the points of use. This can result in approximately 50% savings in energy compared to conventional heaters.

Unfortunately, neither storage-tank hot water heaters nor tankless demand heaters have a very long life. While the actual useful life can vary considerably, in part dependent on the quality of the water, the standard life of a storage tank heater is about 10 to 15 years, whereas the life of demand heaters is around 15 to 20 years.

Figure 11.28 WATER HAND PUMPS
When access to water was relatively easy, sometimes hand pumps could be located inside, providing an early means of indoor plumbing, although typically the pump was located outside over the well. Today we probably consider the hand pump merely as an interesting remnant of former times that might be used as a quaint artifact in an outdoor space, although it is still the source of water for many.

Figure 11.29 PUMP AT RANTHAMBORE, INDIA
Women in Ranthambore, India, gather at the local community pump to get water that they then have to carry back to their homes.

Figure 11.30 WATER CARRIERS
Women in India must carry the water that they in their homes from the local community well.

PLUMBING SUPPLY FIXTURES

While we expect water to be supplied to the various plumbing fixtures that are now located conveniently inside our buildings, in terms of the history of architecture this is a relatively new possibility, especially for typical buildings. When hand pumps were the means of supplying water, it was sometimes possible to locate the pump inside (see Figure 11.28). While this might be considered as indoor plumbing, modern indoor plumbing typically relies on the supply of water under pressure and basically dates from the mid-1800s, although it was not until the 1950s when most residences in the industrialized world included indoor plumbing.

Indoor plumbing is still not available for around one-third of the world population. Even in the United States, particularly in the Navajo Nation, there are homes without indoor plumbing. While the Navajos tend to rely on hauling water in large containers loaded in the back of their pick-up trucks, many people around the world still must personally carry their daily water needs from a community well or water source. Figures 11.29 and 11.30 show some of these conditions from Ranthambore, India.

Figure 11.31 PITCHER AND BOWL
Before modern plumbing supply, personal hygiene relied on filling a bowl with water from a pitcher and then depositing the used water into the chamber pot to be dumped outside later.

Figure 11.32 LAVATORY SINK WITH DOUBLE FAUCETS
Early sinks were supplied by separate hot and cold water faucets. The expectation was that the water would be added to the basin and then used.

When our personal hygiene relied on water that was carried to the point of use, the water was usually poured into a bowl and then used (see Figure 11.31). This established a method of use that continued with piped water supply, which generally meant that the cold and hot water would be supplied by separate faucets (see Figure 11.32). While these separate supplies now tend to be considered a problem, the early expectation was that, as with the pitcher, the water would be added to the basin and then used. The combined faucet, which supplied the cold and hot water from the same spout, was able to take advantage of the convenience of piped running water. With this arrangement, the water temperature could be adjusted and then used directly as it came out of the faucet. This became even more feasible with the development of the single-handled faucet, although it also tends to increase water consumption.

Double-handled faucets, referred to as center-set faucets, typically have the control valves set apart either at eight inches or four inches. As shown in Figure 11.34, the three component of an eight-inch center-set faucet, the two faucets and the spout, are typically mounted independently on the sink, whereas with the four-inch center-set faucet, the components are usually combined into one unit. Figure 11.33 shows a single unit, although this is single-handle faucet that requires only one opening through the basin. Figure 11.35 also.

Al Moen came up with the idea of a single-handle faucet in 1937 after he scalded his hand. At the time, Moen was a college student. He continued to refine his idea and about 10 years later was able to sell his revised design to a manufacturer, the Ravenna Metal Products of Seattle, Washington, which is today known as the Moen Company and is part of the Fortune Brands Home & Hardware LLC. Now available from a number of different manufacturers, the single-handle faucet has become rather standard for many applications, especially both lavatory and kitchen sinks.

With the temperature of the discharged water controlled, the basin now tends to be used merely as a receptacle for the water to the point where it is often no longer provided with a means of closing off the drain. However, these new counter-top sinks often take a form that resembles a bowl similar to what was used with a pitcher of water.

Fixture Placement

The minimum clearance between various plumbing fixtures is stipulated within the *International Plumbing Code* and is shown in Figure 11.36. In general, spacing of fixtures should be at a minimum of 30 inches centerline-to-centerline, and there should be at least 15 inches from a fixture centerline to an adjacent wall or partition. When a toilet tissue holder is mounted on a sidewall or a partition, the distance from the fixture centerline to the partition should not exceed 24 inches in order to avoid an extended reach. In terms of clearance in front of any fixture, at least 21 inches should be provided, although this should definitely be recognized as a recommended minimum. Even though the plumbing code does not formally apply to single-family residences, these clearance recommendations still should be followed.

Except for toilet rooms with single-occupancy or in day-care and child-care facilities, each water closet and urinal should be provided with a means to ensure privacy. Water closets should be enclosed by walls or partitions provided with a door, whereas urinals need to be separated by walls or partitions, which are to extend at least 18 inches

Figure 11.33 LAVATORY SINK WITH SINGLE-HANDLE FAUCET
While the lavatory sink continues to retain a means of stopping the drain, with the temperature-controlled water supplied from a common spout, the discharge from the faucet can be used directly.

Figure 11.34 EIGHT-INCH CENTER SET FAUCET ON RECEPTACLE
With the hot and cold water each controlled by a single handle and the water supplied from a common spout, the discharge from the faucet can be used directly, adjusting the basic way that a lavatory is used.

off the wall or 6 inches beyond the outermost front lip of the urinal, whichever is greater. For both water closets and urinals, the privacy partitions should extend from no higher than 12 inches above the floor to a height of at least 5 feet.

While these partitions should provide a reasonable level of privacy, care must also be given to limiting the possible view into the toilet room, although with single-occupancy facilities this is not critical. In general, this is most easily achieved by establishing an entry vestibule that cuts off any direct view into the toilet room. The simple issue of the swing of the door can also be a factor in terms of providing privacy.

In addition to these general spacing requirements, consideration must also be given in terms of ADA accessibility in terms of public restrooms. While a wheelchair can negotiate a 90° turn in a 36-inch-wide corridor, it takes 60 inches for a pivot (see Figure 11.37). As such, even though the minimum dimensions of a handicapped toilet stall tend to be around 60 inches square (see Figure 11.38), this really provides merely minimal accessibility. In fact, some jurisdictions allow the handicapped stalls to be only 48 inches wide, and some even permit stalls with only a 36-inch width. With these narrower stalls, obviously it is not feasible to turn a wheelchair around, and considerable maneuvering is necessary in order to transfer from a wheelchair onto the toilet. Since the wheelchair must remain in front of the toilet, these narrow stalls also require a greater depth, generally at least 66 inches, although 6 feet would be better.

In public or employee men's toilet rooms, at least one urinal must be installed to accommodate handicapped access. This requires that the rim of the urinal be no more than 17 inches above the finished floor, and while not specified by the ADA, generally the urinal lip should extend a minimum of 14 inches from the finished wall on which the urinal is mounted. In addition, there should be at least a

Figure 11.35 COUNTER-TOP LAVATORY SINK
Newer sinks seem to replicate the original bowl used before central plumbing was available, although these new basins are merely receptacles without the ability to hold the water.

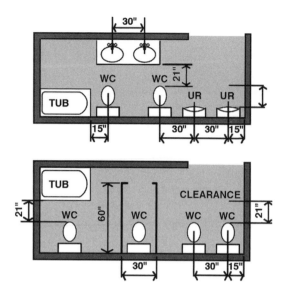

Figure 11.36 FIXTURE CLEARANCE
The minimal clearances between plumbing fixtures are shown. (Adapted from the *2009 International Plumbing Code,* International Code Council, Inc., Falls Church, VA, 2009).

30-inch-wide and 48-inch-deep clearance in front of the urinal. If automatic flush control is not provided, the control must be mounted no more than 44 inches above the floor.

WATER REMOVAL

Water removal has two basic components: building drainage and waste disposal. Building drainage is primarily a result of the ability to supply water to a structure and, because of this, is a relatively recent aspect of plumbing. Previously, without a water distribution system, while water was still used within buildings, the method of removal was no more complicated than the method of access: basically, merely carry it out as it was carried in. When a

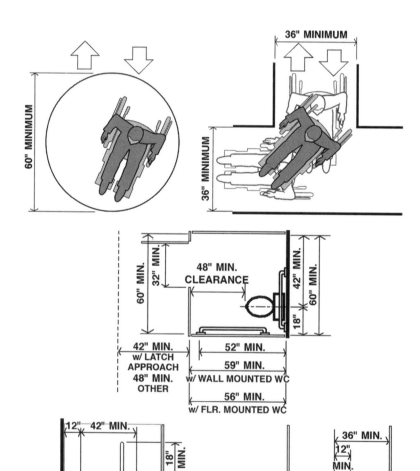

Figure 11.37 WHEELCHAIR TURNING CLEARANCE
While a wheelchair can turn 90° in a 36-inch corridor, it takes 60 inches for a pivot.

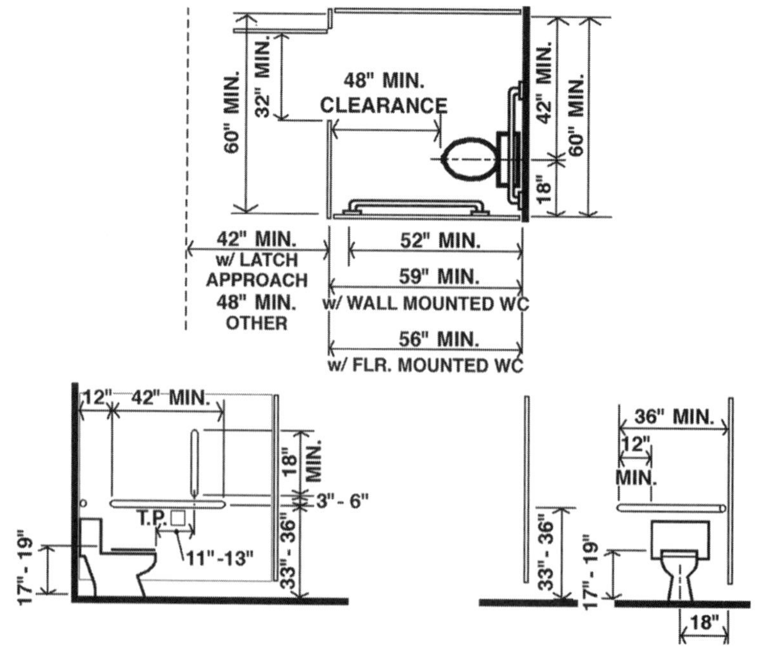

Figure 11.38 WATER CLOSET HANDICAPPED ACCESS
In addition to meeting these minimum dimensions, consideration should be given to the ease of movement into and within the toilet room for individuals with access limitations.

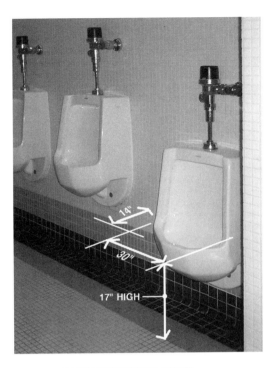

Figure 11.39 URINAL FOR HANDICAPPED ACCESS
At least one urinal should be mounted with the rim at no more than 17 inches above the finished floor and projecting at least 14 inches from the back wall. Clearance of 30-inch width and 48-inch depth should also be provided in front of the urinal. Note that this image does not include the privacy partitions that are required by the *2009 International Plumbing Code*.

Figure 11.40 AKROTIRI TOILET
This limestone toilet seat is from excavations at Akrotiri on the island of Santorini, Greece, and dates from the second millennium B.C.E.

Figure 11.41 TEL EL ARMANA TOILET
This limestone toilet seat is from excavations at Tel El Armana in Egypt and dates from around 1350 B.C.E.

pressurized water supply distributed through a system of pipes started to be used, a comparable method of removal was necessary to handle the increased volume of water flow. This advance also brought an increase in water consumption, largely as a result of improved personal hygiene. Just as a reminder, the Saturday night bath was considered quite a luxury and something that most people rarely engaged in. Bathing was often must less frequent, whereas today the daily shower is an expectation.

While the current demands of water removal are relatively new, the need for waste disposal, which relates primarily to urination and defecation, has not changed as much as the method by which this waste is handled. The standard method for managing personal waste removal today was available to a limited number of people in certain societies in ancient times, although most people merely went outside and performed the necessary functions. This is still the method for some people in certain areas.

The Evolution of the Toilet

While flush toilets were used in ancient times, as found in ancient ruins along the eastern Mediterranean Sea and throughout the Roman Empire, for a long period of hu-

man history, urination and defecation were handled in a less than hygienic manner. Akrotiri on the island of Santorini, Greece, was destroyed by a volcanic eruption in the second millennium B.C.E. Archeologists working at this site have found signs of a clear connection with the Minoan civilization, including some plumbing developments. Figure 11.40 shows a toilet found in these excavations.

Excavations at Tel El Armana in Egypt have also produced remnants of a toilet that was used around 1350 B.C.E. (see Figure 11.41). The form of this remnant is very similar to the keyhole-shaped, water-flushed latrines that were used throughout the Roman Empire.

The ruins at the Palace of Knossos show clear indications of a rather well-developed plumbing system,

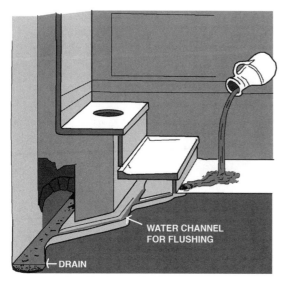

Figure 11.42 LATRINE AT KNOSSOS
The ruins at Knossos provide indications of a latrine from around 1700 B.C.E. that was cleaned by water. As indicated, this latrine was flushed by water poured from a water jug.

Figure 11.43 ROMAN LATRINE AT OSTIA
Wherever and whenever a large number of people gather, there is a need to provide accommodations for personal hygiene. Throughout the Roman Empire this meant that at the public baths and stadia, latrines were provided. These typically followed the basic design shown at Ostia, consisting of a number of keyhole openings over a trough through which water ran to remove the waste.

including flush toilets and baths. The latrine, which dates from around 1700 B.C.E., apparently included a bench seat with an opening over a drainage channel. Water was poured from a water vessel into this channel to carry away the waste (see Figure 11.42). Thus, this latrine is often considered to be the first flush toilet.

While the indication is that the latrine emptied into an open channel, the Palace at Knossos apparently also included terra-cotta drainpipes that were slightly tapered so that they could easily fit together, allowing the water to flow with a rush to prevent sediment from being accumulated. These pipes are similar to the terra-cotta drainpipes that were also used during Roman times.

The Romans built upon these past developments in plumbing, achieving significant success in terms of both water supply, in part through the renowned system of aqueducts, and waste collection and sewage control. Whenever a large number of people gather in one location, there is always a need to accommodate their hygiene needs. The Romans addressed these needs by providing public latrines that generally followed the same basic design of keyhole openings that deposited waste into an open trough through which water flowed to carry away the discharge. Interestingly, as shown in Figure 11.43, which is the latrine at the baths at the Roman port of Ostia, a front trough was also typically provided that allowed for regular and easy maintenance.

Historically, sewage management meant merely carrying off the waste rather than treating it. In Rome the major sewer was the Cloaca Maxima, the remnants of which still exist along the Tiber River. The Cloaca Max-

ima, which literally means "great sewer," is believed to have been constructed around 510 B.C.E. under the orders of Lucius Tarquinius Superbus (535–496 B.C.E.), the seventh and last king of Rome. Although it was apparently intended merely to control an existing stream that flowed through the Forum as well as to drain the marshy land, the Cloaca Maxima ended up serving as a sewer that carried waste away from this intensely built-up area of Rome. This sewer, which was maintained until well after the fall of the Roman Empire, provided drainage from the Roman Forum to the Tiber River (see Figure 11.44).

With the fall of the Roman Empire, which spread throughout much of Western civilization, most of the plumbing techniques that had been developed were lost. Interestingly, during medieval times, the latrines or garderobes, which were private rooms used as privies in many castles, were merely locations where people could deposit their waste, often directly into the moat, providing one more reason why a moat might be an effective means of protection at times of attack (see Figures 11.45 and 11.46).

In America and elsewhere, where castles with moats were not a tradition, the outhouse, similar to the one shown in Figure 11.47, was often the major way of handling elimination. While there are examples of outhouses that are connected to a building, typically a residence, as its name implies, the particular nature of an outhouse is that one goes outside to use it. In many areas, outhouses continued to be used until after World War II. Figure 11.48 shows a 1950s development in Brisbane, Australia, that relied on

Figure 11.44 ROMAN CLOACA MAXIMA
This was the sewer that drained the Roman Forum into the Tiber River.

Figure 11.45 DUNSTAFFNAGE CASTLE LATRINE
The ruins of this Scottish castle, located near Oban, show an old latrine projecting from the wall. When this facility was used, the waste dropped into the moat that surrounded the castle.

outhouses, which the Australians call *dunnies*. Even today, the outhouse is still used in some places.

The Closet

At times, rather than go outside to use an outhouse or go to the particular location of a latrine, the preference for depositing human waste was to use a closet, which could be brought to where one wanted to use it and then carried elsewhere to dispose of the waste (see Figure 11.49). While today a closet is a place for storing things, particu-

larly clothing, it was formerly a container that was used to hold human waste, hence a place to store, at least for a while, human urine and feces. The closet, which generally included a seat located above a receptacle, provided a convenient way for people to relieve themselves without having to go outside. Often the closet itself had carrying handles so that the whole closet could be removed and emptied, but there were also closets containing a receptacle that could be removed and emptied, somewhat like a modern portable training potty that young children use.

The closet was sometimes used in less than private circumstances. While current standards suggest that one attends to personal elimination privately, the arrangement of the Roman latrines suggests that perhaps their use was a somewhat social event. In a related way, while the closet was an individual device, it was not necessarily used in

Figure 11.46 DOUNE CASTLE LATRINE
Doune Castle in Scotland, which is still accessible, also includes a wall latrine. The grill has been added as a safety precaution.

Figure 11.47 AMERICAN OUTHOUSE
Prior to the development of modern plumbing, perhaps the major way of handling elimination in America was the outhouse.

that the term *throne* is still sometimes used to denote a toilet.[5]

One of the more interesting closets was developed in the 1860s by an English preacher, Henry Moule. Reverend Moule's proposal was for an earth closet. It included a container that held earth that could be readily deposited on the accumulated contents of the closet, which supposedly increased the times between required emptying (see Figure 11.50).

Interestingly, Moule developed his earth closet in reaction to the increasing use of water closets in England, which was causing water pollution and was a major cause of a cholera epidemic. His hope was that he could overcome the appeal of the water closet by providing an improved closet that was convenient to use. Of course, the logical response and the one that was ultimately given, although only after an order of Parliament, was the development of effective sewage treatment, and this, in turn, allowed for the expanded use of the water closet.

Chamber Pots

Before the development of the water closet and the necessary means of treating its discharge, chamber pots were

Figure 11.48 AUSTRALIAN DUNNIES
The small structures lined up behind these houses, which were built around 1950 in Brisbane, Australia, are called *dunnies*, the Australian term for toilet, although they are actually outhouses. From the John Oxley Library, State Library of Queensland.

private. In fact, the handles typically attached to the closet made it possible to move it readily to the place of use as well as to remove it in order to dispose of the contents.

Related to this is the apparent custom of Louis XIII of France, and perhaps also of his son, Louis XIV, of holding an audience while sitting on a closet. His throne actually included a commode so that he could relieve himself while continuing to fulfill his royal obligations. It is on this basis

also used to avoid the trek to the outhouse. But these were typically used only for urine and then primarily at night. Most chamber pots were ceramic and usually were attractively decorated, since they were part of the accoutrements

---

[5]This is based on various sources, including Dr. Bindeshwar Pathak, the founder of the Sulabh International Social Service Organization, a pioneering nonprofit voluntary organization (nongovernment organization, or NGO) in the field of sanitation in India and the organization that runs the Sulabh International Museum of Toilets.

of a bedchamber. They typically included a cover and were also usually part of a set of items used for personal hygiene, which usually included a bowl, a pitcher for clean water, a slop jar to collect waste, and a chamber pot (see Figure 11.51).

Chamber pots were generally used only when it was not convenient to go out to the outhouse. The used chamber pots were then emptied, hopefully into the outhouse, although there are clear indications that this was not always done. It is suggested that in many locations, the tradition was merely to throw the waste out the window, which, since they were primarily used during the night, made walking in the city early in the morning rather dangerous. Some suggest that the chamber pot might have been used for collecting feces as well as urine, although this was not usual.

Flush Toilets

The flush toilet reemerged in the eighteenth century, but its modern development apparently began in 1596, interestingly as part of a publication by Sir John Harington. Harington wrote *A New Discourse of a Stale Subject, Called the Metamorphosis of Ajax*, a critical and unrelenting assault on the hypocrisy of the English society. This book was loaded with double meanings and literary allusions, including a discourse on obscenity in the guise of a discussion on the design of a flushable toilet. Harington was the godson of Queen Elizabeth, who, as can be imagined, was

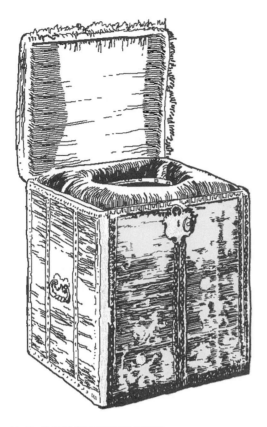

Figure 11.49 CLOSET AT HAMPTON COURT
This sketch of the close stool or closet at Hampton Court, which dates from the seventeenth century, is based on an image in Lawrence Wright, *Clean and Decent, the Fascinating History of the Bathroom and the Water-Closet*, Routledge, London, 1960.

Figure 11.50 REV. HENRY MOULE'S EARTH CLOSET
This shows the working of Moule's earth closet, which was also available in a much more refined configuration. Image by Musphot on Wikimedia Commons.

Figure 11.51 CHAMBER POT AND SLOP JAR
This figure shows a chamber pot and a covered slop jar. When a chamber pot had a cover, it was generally intended to be used by one person. When a chamber pot did not have a cover, it was part of a set that included a covered slop jar; after the chamber pot was used, its contents were deposited into the slop jar and held until the slop jar could be emptied. Since chamber pots were used by both men and women, it was convenient and more hygienic to lift the pot when using it.

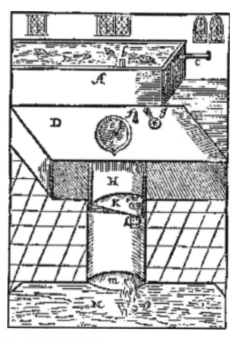

Figure 11.52 JOHN HARINGTON'S CLOSET
This diagram shows the flushing toilet that Harington built at Richmond. It clearly indicates how complicated his system might have been. The notations in the diagram are as follows: A — the cistern, B — the little washer, C — the waste pipe, D — the seat board, E — the pipe that comes from the cistern, F — the screw, G — the scallop shell to cover it when it is shut down, H — the stool pot, I — the stopple, J — the current, K — the sluice, N — the vault into which it falls.

incensed at his attack on society and indirectly on her. In an attempt to get back into her good graces, Harington constructed one of his water-flushing toilets for the queen at Richmond Palace. Figure 11.52 shows a schematic of this device, which is similar to one that Harrington made for himself.

The term *toilet*, while used today to imply the device or the space in which one can relieve oneself, derives from the French *toilette* and initially referred to the process of dealing with one's personal appearance—dressing and grooming—rather than hygiene. As Harington used various allusions and associations in his *Metamorphosis of Ajax*, today we often use various terms to designate the toilet, often without clarifying whether the reference is to the device, which legitimately is a WC, or the space in which it is located. Our general interpretation of the term *closet* tends to confuse things even more.

Many terms are used to designate this important facility. Some of the terms that tend to refer specifically to the device include *can, commode, crapper, necessary, potty,* and *throne*. Those used to indicate the space include *bathroom* (which, of course, suggests another act of *toilette*), *convenience, head, john, lavatory* (another term that relates to another act of *toilette*), *loo, privy, restroom, washroom,* and *WC*. Of course, there are others as well.

We might assume that the term *john* was adopted as a way of referring to the toilet in recognition of John Harington's contributions to the modern WC, but this would not be correct. However, there is a connection with the term *jack* or *jakes* that has been used since the Middle Ages as a way of referring to a privy, and it is supposedly *jakes* that gave rise to Harington's use of *Ajax* in the title of his book. Interestingly, the use of *john* as a reference to a toilet is almost exclusively American.

Loo is common in England and apparently derives not from someone named Louis/Lewis but from the French term *l'eau*—"the water." As mentioned above, chamber pots were convenient containers that people could use during the night, avoiding the need to go outside. Then in the morning, when it was time to "clean up," the tradition in France was to open the bedroom window, yell out "Gardez l'eau" ("Watch the water"), and dump the contents of the chamber pot onto the street below, sometimes soaking those who did not react quickly enough to the warning. Supposedly, when English travelers to France returned to England, some who remembered this morning ritual adopted the term, somewhat Anglicized, to refer to the device that we now call by various terms.

There is also the classic term *crapper* that has been attributed as a way to honor Thomas Crapper, a London plumber who was responsible for major improvements in the design of the toilet flushing system. The flippant claim is that American GIs passing through England after the First World War often saw the toilets that were clearly embossed with the Crapper name. However, *crop* is an old term that means "residue left over from rendering fat" or just "dirt." The British etymologist Michael Quinion suggests that the term might actually derive from the old term *croppin ken* that was used for a privy. Since *ken* was slang for "house," the original meaning should be clear. Over time, *croppin ken* apparently became *crappin ken*, from whence the word *crap* evolved to become accepted as a reference for the toilet or for what is put into it, although the term is generally considered rather vulgar slang.

The flushing toilet that Sir John Harington installed for Queen Elizabeth was a complicated device that wasn't easy to operate (see Figure 11.52). To provide guidance to the servants, he wrote:

Always remember the chamberlain at noon and at night

Empty it and leave it half a foot deep in fair water.

And this being well done, and orderly kept,

Your worst privy may be as sweet as your best chamber.

As Harington's little verse implies, the noxious gases that are released from human feces are a major problem with all closets. While water can flush the waste away, since the pipe that carries things away is by necessity connected to the closet, there is a strong probability that if they are not controlled, these gases will migrate back through the closet and contaminate the space in which the closet is located. So, one of the critical requirements for any effective closet is a means of keeping the sewer gases from passing back through the closet and contaminating the space in which the closet is located.

Harington's design for the toilet, intriguing as it might have been, was not a great success, perhaps in part because he built just two, with the one at Richmond Palace being the only one about which we have any clear information, and he did not refine his design. Almost 200 years passed before Alexander Cummings developed the first effective WC with a controlled water supply. While Harington's device was rather large and difficult to operate in terms of removing the waste and controlling the noxious fumes, Cummings' closet was rather small and relatively easy to use (see Figure 11.53). He received a patent for his design in 1775.

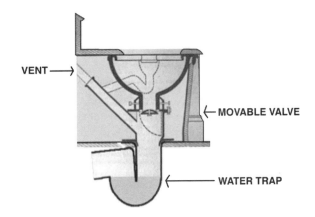

VENT →

← MOVABLE VALVE

← WATER TRAP

Figure 11.53 CUMMINGS' WC
This early WC incorporated various ways to control the noxious gases related to the disposal of human waste, particularly feces.

Cummings' closet incorporated basically three strategies to control gases: a water trap (standing water) in the sewer pipe, a movable valve, and standing water in the bowl. It also included a vent tube, located between the water trap and the vent, which would release any gases that might get by the water trap and avoid a buildup of pressure. As with modern toilets, collection was in a bowl that was partially filled with water, but unlike WCs today, a valve was used to retain the water in the bowl. After use, the valve was opened, allowing the waste to flow out. More water was added to the stream before the valve was closed, and then the bowl was partially filled again with clean water. While this closet should have worked reasonably well, unfortunately the valve became contaminated fairly quickly, and the hygienic qualities that Cummings tried to provide in terms of controlling sewer gases were canceled out by the mess that accumulated.

Other designs were proposed, many again relying on some physical device to hold water in the bowl. Interestingly, most of these were of English origin. Perhaps this was due to English sensibilities, but there are two interpretations here. One is that, as mentioned in terms of how English travelers apparently reacted to the French custom of dumping out the contents of chamber pots, the English are rather particular and pristine in their personal hygiene. The other is that many of the historic works on plumbing developments are English, which again might be related to English sensibilities, as can be seen if we read two of the more enjoyable accounts: Wallance Reyburn's *Flush with Pride: The Story of Thomas Crapper* and Lawrence Wright's *Clean and Decent, The Fascinating History of the Bathroom and the Water-Closet.*

Another explanation for the leadership coming from England is that a WC relies on an effective sewage system, which was unavailable in most place. However, after the cholera epidemic of 1832, which prompted Moule to develop his earth closet, the British government passed laws that required houses to have flushing toilets, which then forced the development of an effective sewage system. Although it was not until the 1860s that London had a workable system, it preceded most other major cities, not only in England but throughout the world. As a result, Britain led the world in the development of both decent sewage systems and workable WCs.

Interesting historic information is also available on the Internet, particularly at www.theplumber.com/h_index.html. This link is to the table of contents on the History of Plumbing, which is only a small part of a great deal of material on all aspects of plumbing posted by PlumbingSupply.com, a plumbing supplier from Chico, California.

George (J.G.) Jennings is credited with coming up with the basic design of the WC that is still used today. His closet, referred to as *Jennings' Syphonic Closet* or the *Closet of the Century*, was introduced in 1900 and received the Grand Prix at the Paris Exhibition that year. After many attempts to control the sewer gases, which included various water traps and valves, Jennings came up with the combination of using a water trap to seal the pipe, maintaining the water level in the closet bowl, and relying on a siphon to extract the water and waste from the bowl (see Figure 11.54).

Perhaps because of the bad connotations of using an indoor facility, Jennings included two water traps between the collection bowl of the closet and the sewer line. This double water trap made sense since, at that time, the use of vents to release the pressure within the drainage system

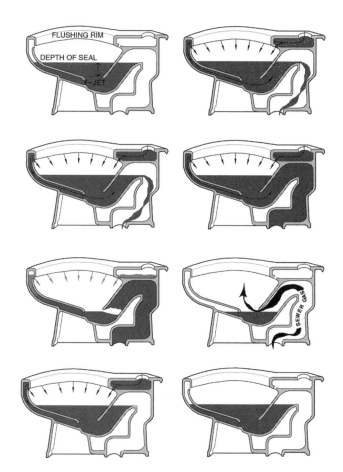

Figure 11.55 WATER CLOSET SIPHON FLUSH SEQUENCE
This series of diagrams shows the process of the siphon flush. Basically, as water enters the bowl, the drain fills with water, establishing a siphon that then drains the bowl of the water and its contents. When the siphon breaks as the water level drops, water continues to be added until the trap is reformed.

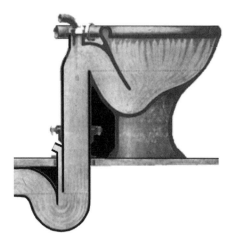

Figure 11.54 JENNINGS' SYPHONIC CLOSET
This early WC was one of the first to incorporate a water trap as a way to control the noxious gases related to the disposal of human waste, particularly feces. This is essentially the approach used today.

was not yet prevalent, and as a result, it was difficult to maintain the trap.

While Jennings is given the credit for the basic design of the modern closet, Thomas Crapper was the individual who developed the flushing mechanism that is essentially the one we use today. Although he is often credited for inventing the WC, Crapper was merely an ingenious and industrious London plumber who kept improving the flushing mechanism. His major contribution was his Water Waste Preventer, which controlled both the supply of water to the flush tank while filling the drained closet bowl and the release of the accumulated water in the tank into the closet to begin the siphoning action.

Figure 11.55 shows the basic stages of the siphoning action in a water closet. When a toilet is flushed, water that either comes from a flush tank or flows through a flush valve washes down the closet bowl, cleaning it and raising the water level in the bowl. As the water rises, some water begins to drain out of the bowl, but, ultimately, the drainage passageway fills and creates a siphon. Once a

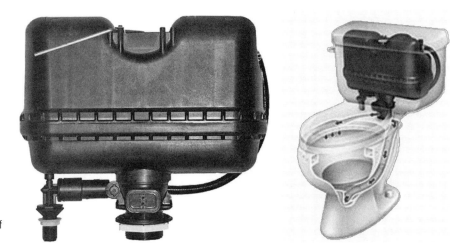

Figure 11.56 SLOAN FLUSHMATE TANK TOILET
This pressurized flushing system relies on the pressure in the water supply. As the water enters the tank, the pressures in the supply line and the tank are equalized, but unlike the standard flush tank, which is open, this enclosed tank is then able to use this line pressure to eject the water into the toilet bowl to forcefully remove the contents. (From Sloan *FLUSHMATE*® a division of Sloan Valve Company).

siphon is formed, the water is drained from the bowl, along with its contents. The siphoning action is reinforced by the ejection of some water into the drain. After the water and any contents are removed, the siphon is broken, but the flushing mechanism continues to add water into the bowl, raising the water level in order to reestablish the critical water.

While raising the water level in the closet creates a siphon that is the major means of draining the bowl of its contents, water is also inserted from the jet at the bottom of the bowl to establish a current that helps move the waste matter up and out. To increase this ejection force, some early WCs had raised tanks to raise the pressure of the flushing action. Generally, these units required a lot of water per flush, sometimes over 6 gallons. With improvements in the design of the discharge piping, the siphoning action was enhanced, allowing the volume of water to be reduced. Through additional improvements, water consumption per flush was reduced from over 6 gallons to 3.5 gallons, which was generally standard at the end of the twentieth century, and now to 1.6 gallons or less per flush, which meets or exceeds the current U.S. requirements established by the Energy Policy Act of 1992. Some of the early low-consumption toilets did not work very well, often requiring several flushes to clean the closet. While the current toilets look the same, the drainage is through a smooth passageway that has a consistent and somewhat reduced cross-sectional drain. These changes have reduced the water flow required to flush a toilet while improving the suction developed by the siphon.

Improvements to the discharge passageway allow WCs to use no more than 1.6 gallons per flush, with some using only 1.4 gallons or even 1.2 gallons per flush to remove heavier matter. Some toilets are dual flush and require only 1 gallon to flush merely liquid content. When the challenge to lower water requirements was initially proposed, some manufacturers attempted to increase the flushing pressure to lower water consumption. This involved placing the tank well above the bowl. Another approach was to pressurize the water supply. The Sloan Flushmate tank toilet was one of the more successful attempts at this, and with the improvements to the drainage system, these toilets apparently now require only 1 gallon per flush for all types of matter.

The Flushmate relies on the pressure in the water supply line to increase the discharge pressure as the water enters the closet bowl. While the water tank appears to be similar to other toilets, the water is stored in a sealed container located within the tank rather than merely in the tank itself. Since the container is closed and provided with an entry control valve, the water in the tank retains the pressure of the water line. When the toilet is flushed, this pressure is then used to deliver the water into the closet bowl (see Figure 11.56). While the increased pressure does allow for lower water quantities, it means that the flush is accompanied by a rather loud noise.

Another approach is to use a small pump to increase the pressure of the water as it is discharged into the bowl. Of course, this unit requires an electrical connection. The Kohler Power Lite Toilet is an example of such a toilet, and with the electrical connection, the benefit of a heated toilet seat is also included.

The toilet used in the United States and most of Western Europe is designed to have the user sit down during use, although males can urinate into these units while standing. While we tend to think that this is the preferred method, in much of the world toilets do not include a seat. Various terms are used to denote these toilets, such as *Turkish toilet, Asian toilet*, and *squat toilet* (which indicates how they are used for defecation and female urination) (see Figure 11.57).

In deference to varying customs, some toilets are designed to be used in either manner, either sitting or squatting (see Figure 11.58).

Figure 11.57 ASIAN TOILET
In many locations, often outside the Western world, rather than a raised bowl on which the user sits, the toilet is an opening in the floor over which the user squats. These toilets are called by various terms, including *Asian toilet*, *Turkish toilet*, and even *squat toilet*.

Another difference in toilet use relates to how one cleans up after defecation. While the Western world tends to use toilet paper, many places rely on a water wash rather than a paper wipe (see Figure 11.59). While there are some religious implications concerning the method of cleaning, sometimes the method used is merely based on the custom of the area.

When paper is used, it should be specifically designed for this purpose. While the size of toilet paper is clearly different from that of facial tissues and hand towels, we should also be aware that toilet paper is specifically designed to disintegrate when placed in water. As a result, the paper does not remain as a solid that must be carried through the sewage lines. Facial tissues and paper towels do not dissolve in water, and, as a result, they can pose serious problems if they are flushed down the toilet.

Some toilets and urinals do not use any water. Composting toilets not only do not use water, they convert the waste into compost that can then be used as soil rather than having to be processed through a sewage treatment system. Although some people might assume that these toilets are not very different from the traditional outhouse, most composting toilets are actually quite advanced and capable of controlling odors. In fact, they are often installed so that they can be used within a building. This is quite an accomplishment, since the nature of the waste placed in a composting toilet generally requires a direct deposit. On the other hand, since waterless urinals only handle liquid, these units can be located anywhere. However, this requires a drain line, and some separation must be maintained from this line. This separation is provided in most waterless urinals by a special drain that uses a sealing liquid. This liquid is less dense than urine, so the urine can pass through while the seal is retained (see Figure 11.60).

Figure 11.58 SIT OR SQUAT
Two examples of combination toilets from India.

Figure 11.59 WASH OR WIPE
In deference to various traditions, this facility includes the option of either washing or wiping.

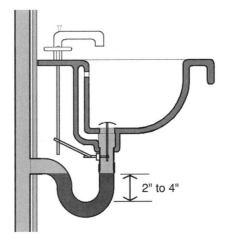

Figure 11.61 WASHBOWL TRAP
The lavatory and most plumbing fixtures should have a water trap that retains a column of water 2 to 4 inches high.

Figure 11.60 WATERLESS URINAL
Waterless urinals rely on a liquid seal to close the connection with the drain line. The density of the liquid in the seal is less than the density of the urine, which allows the urine to pass through the seal. After a number of uses (7000, as recommended by Sloan), the seal needs to be renewed. In addition, since water is not used to wash down the unit, regular cleaning is recommended; however, whereas a waterless urinal requires higher maintenance than a conventional urinal, each waterless urinal can save around 40,000 gallons or more of water each year. The actual water savings is based on the number of uses.

Water Traps

Urine and feces release various gases that are not appreciated in occupied spaces. These are sewer gases, and some means has to be provided to block their release. This is generally accomplished by placing a column of standing water between a plumbing fixture and the drain line to close off or seal the connection between the two. This standing-water seal is called a *trap*, and generally it should have a height of 2 to 4 inches (see Figure 11.61) As has been discussed, toilets have traps, but these become part of the siphon during the flushing process. Since this means that the column of water is siphoned out, after a toilet is flushed and water refills the tank, some water must also be added to the closet bowl to restore the trap. With toilets and urinals that use a flush valve, although a tank does not need to be filled, the flush valve has to release some water after the flush in order to restore the trap. With most other plumbing fixtures, there is no such means of adding water after use that might, as with the toilet, have drained the trap.

Since these other plumbing fixtures do not incorporate a means of restoring the water seal after use, the trap must be designed so that a siphon is not created, even with full flow through the drain line. Although the drains from most fixtures do not fill during normal use, particularly given how they tend to be used today, if a fixture (e.g., a sink) is filled and then emptied, the trap could be siphoned dry if some way to prevent this is not provided.

To avoid siphoning the trap, all plumbing fixtures, other than toilets and urinals, should be vented. (The drain from toilets and urinals should also be vented, but this is not intended to eliminate the potential of siphoning from these fixtures.) This means that an air release must exist at

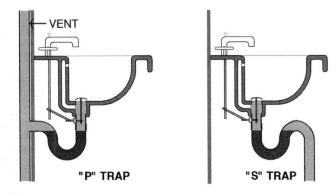

Figure 11.62 WASHBOWL TRAP CONFIGURATIONS
If an S-trap is filled, a siphon will be created and the trap will not be maintained. With a P-trap, there is an air release at the top of the inverted-U portion of the drain line, which prohibits the formation of a siphon and the elimination of the trap.

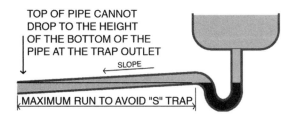

Figure 11.63 MAXIMUM DRAIN LENGTH TO VENT
If an S-trap is filled, a siphon will be created and the trap will not be maintained. With a P-trap, there is an air release at the top of the inverted-U portion of the drain line, which prohibits the formation of a siphon and the elimination of the trap.

Table 11.21: MAXIMUM ALLOWABLE LENGTH OF FIXTURE DRAIN TO VENT

Drain Slope (in./ft)	Drain Diameter			
	$1^1/_4$ in.	$1^1/_2$ in.	2 in.	$2^1/_2$ in.
$1/_8$ in./ft	10 ft	16 ft	20 ft	24 ft
$1/_4$ in./ft	6 ft	8 ft	10 ft	12 ft
$1/_2$ in./ft	3 ft	4 ft	5 ft	6 ft

Note: The actual length of the horizontal drain between the trap and the vent must be less than the listed distances to avoid forming a potential siphon.

the top of any potential siphon. As a result, the usual requirement is to use *P-traps* rather than *S-traps*, the names of which indicate the configuration of the trap—a P-trap looks like a "P" and an S-trap looks like an "S." With an S-trap, if the drain line fills with water, a siphon will be formed and the water in the trap will be extracted. While we could then slowly add more water to restore the water seal to a height of between 2 and 4 inches, this is not a reliable way to ensure that the trap is maintained. Although S-traps are not permitted by most codes, they still exist in many older structures. Since, as mentioned above, the normal use of these fixtures fortunately does not generally result in filling of the drain line, it is unlikely that these S-traps create a serious problem. Still, they should be avoided.

As indicated in Figure 11.62, the major difference between the P-trap and the S-trap is that at the point after the actual U-shaped trap where the drain line drops down, the P-trap also has a line or vent that rises. This line forms a vacuum break that prohibits a siphon from forming. However, since the drainage flows by gravity, there is a limit to how far after the actual trap the horizontal drain can run before this vacuum break. If the distance and the slope are such that the top of the horizontal run drops below the bottom of the pipe at the trap, essentially an S-trap would be established (see Figure 11.63).

The vent, which should have a diameter that is at least half the diameter of the drain line that it serves but no less than $1^1/_4$ inches, must be close enough to the P-trap to ensure that the sloping horizontal drain line does not drop too much and thereby establish an S-trap. The maximum drop must be less than the inside diameter of the horizontal drain. Table 11.21 lists the maximum horizontal run for various-sized drains, which will avoid establishing an effective S-trap at three different slopes.

While most drainage systems rely on venting to the outside in order to provide a way to both release sewage

gases and avoid major pressure variations within the drain, there are alternative ways to achieve these benefits. The Sovent system is one such alternative. By incorporating a series of aerator fittings and double offsets, this system reduces the velocity of the liquids and solids as they enter the vertical portion of the drainage system, thereby supposedly eliminating back-pressure problems. The release of the sewer gases is accomplished the same way as with the standard vent: the stack extends up through the roof to the outside. In some jurisdictions, it might be feasible to use a wet vent for some of the fixtures. A wet vent essentially is a vertical drain line that is somewhat oversized so that it can do double duty: carry drainage and vent the line. This is similar to what is referred to as a *circuit vent* (see Figure 11.66).

Water Contamination Protection

While a siphon that might drain the trap is a problem, a siphon that might establish a link between the supply and the drainage circuits could be extremely dangerous. As such, it is critical to ensure that a siphon is not established between the supply and the water in the fixture. Unfortunately, such a siphon apparently did occur in the early 1900s at the Boston City Hospital. The story is that someone was cleaning contaminated vials by running

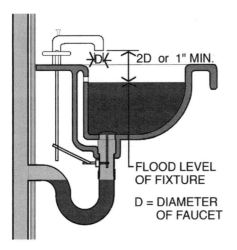

Figure 11.64 BACKFLOW PREVENTION
The outlet from the supply faucet must be separated by a minimum of 1 inch or two times the diameter of the faucet, whichever is greater.

water into a slop sink from a hose that was extended from the faucet. This sink was on an upper floor, and when there was a drop in the main supply line pressure, the water started to flow backward, dropping down from the upper floors. This negative pressure created a siphon, and contaminated water in the sink was drawn into the water supply line and ultimately discharged through a faucet on a lower level of the hospital. Unfortunately, this contaminated water was consumed by a number of people, supposedly resulting in several deaths.

Since drops in the line pressure can occur, particularly as more water is drawn from the pipe, conditions that could pull water from the fixture and/or create a backflow siphon must be avoided. The basic approach to ensure that water from the fixture cannot be pulled into the supply line is to always keep an air gap between the supply discharge and the flood level of any fixture. The normal requirement is to have an air gap that is at least 1 inch or twice the diameter of the faucet outlet (see Figure 11.64). When this guideline might not be possible, such as with a flush valve on a WC or urinal, or might be violated, such as with a hose extension off of an outside hose connection, the faucet must include an antisiphon control valve.

Today, all flush valves are designed to provide a vacuum break, which will avoid creating a siphon. But when we consider that garden hoses are often connected to devices that are discharging weed killer and other poisonous chemicals, it is a wonder that our water supply is not regularly contaminated. The advantage here is that the garden hose is typically at a low level within the residential water system and precedes other supply outlets within the house. As a result, backflow siphoning is less likely to occur, but

such an arrangement still creates the potential for serious problems. To reduce the possibility of such events, all hose bibbs should be antisiphon faucets. Similarly, laundry tubs and slop sinks often have threaded faucets, so these should also use only vacuum-break control valves.

Interestingly, many old bathtubs had a supply spigot that was located within the tub. While these tubs were supposed to have overflow limits that would keep the water level below the bottom of the faucet, these limits were often ineffective, and in many situations they were eliminated. As a result, these old bathtubs create a potential backflow problem. In comparison, the water supply to newer tubs is from a faucet that is usually installed on the wall above the top of the tub, and certainly above the flood level of the tub.

Even when there is a significant distance between the flood level and the faucet outlet and/or a proper antisiphon faucet has been specified, if a hose extension is attached to an outlet, this can potentially develop a backflow siphon. Perhaps this is a good reason to include, as part of the bath unit, a properly designed hand shower that includes an antisiphon device.

WATER DRAINAGE

Water drainage entails various components, some of which run horizontally and some vertically. A *stack* is a vertical pipe, but there are various classifications. A *soil stack* is a vertical pipe that carries black water, which is the discharge from a WC or urinal. A *waste stack* is a vertical pipe that carries gray water, which is the discharge from plumbing fixtures other than a WC or urinal, so this drainage water, while no longer pure, supposedly includes no feces or urine. There is also both a stack vent and a vent stack. The difference between them is that a *stack vent* is a vertical pipe that vents a stack, either a waste stack or a soil stack, whereas a *vent stack* is a vertical pipe that is not intended to carry any drainage and is generally not an extension of a stack that does—a subtle but distinct difference. We can remember which is which if we consider that there are soil stacks, waste stacks, and vent stacks, each of which is a vertical pipe intended for either soil conveyance, waste drainage, or venting. That is, the word before *stack* indicates the purpose of the stack. A stack vent, on the other hand, is a vent for a stack, probably a soil stack or a waste stack. A *storm leader* is another vertical drain pipe that is similar to an RWL, although it is located within the structure, whereas an RWL is typically outside the building enclosure.

As discussed, the connection of a vent line at each trap eliminates the possibility of forming a siphon. The vent

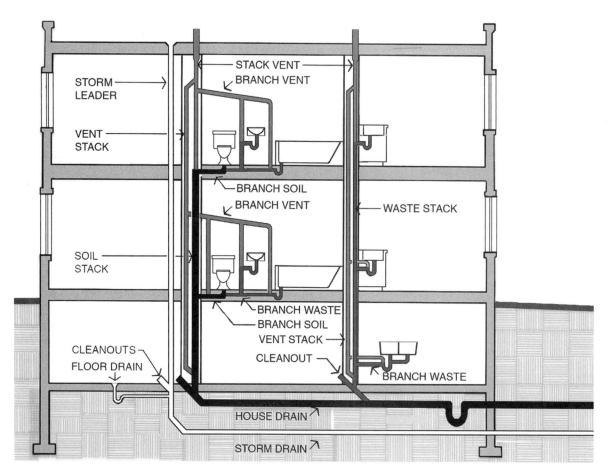

Figure 11.65 TYPICAL RESIDENTIAL SANITARY DRAINAGE

This schematic section, which is for a small apartment building, shows the various components of a residential sanitary drainage system. Adapted from B. Stein, J.S. Reynolds, W.T. Grondzik, and A.G. Kwok, *Mechanical and Electrical Equipment for Buildings* (John Wiley & Sons, Inc., Hoboken, NJ, 2006), Table 22.9.

also tends to maintain equal pressures within the drainage system. This helps reduce the chance of developing a negative pressure or a vacuum, which could extract the water from the trap, or a positive pressure that could blow the trap. The vent also has another benefit. As its name implies, it can vent or expel the sewer gases to the outside, thereby reducing the possibility that these noxious fumes will migrate through the trap seal into the interior space.

Figure 11.65 is a rough schematic of various drain lines. It includes a storm drain that extends beyond the building line. Unfortunately, storm and sanitary drainage are still often combined in a public sewage system. When they are, the lines should remain separate within the structure and not be combined until at least 5 feet beyond the building line. While the storm drain in this example is internal to the building, the storm drainage from most single-family residences is provided by external gutter and RWL.

If there are floor drains, it is important to determine their purpose. If they are merely to provide protection against possible basement leaks and/or to drain condensate from a cooling coil, then they can be connected to the storm drain, as indicated in Figure 11.65. If they will be used to carry away waste from a plumbing fixture, such as a clothes washer, then they should be connected to the sanitary sewer system. If they are intended to collect drainage that might be contaminated, such as from a garage in which auto repairs are done, the floor drain might need to be connected to a holding tank so that the chemicals are not put into the sewage system or deposited in such a way that they could contaminate the groundwater. All floor drains should have a trap, and when they connect to a sanitary sewer system, these traps must be vented. While the floor drain in Figure 11.65, which is connected to the storm drain, is not vented, if the storm system does connect with the sanitary sewer, it must be vented. In addition, regardless of the expected use of the floor drain, when it is in the basement or at a similar low point, perhaps a backflow preventer should be added to the floor drain line. Further, if the floor drain has a trap, there must be a simple way to add water to maintain the water seal.

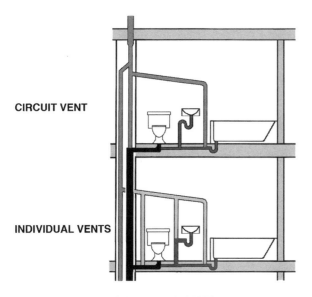

CIRCUIT VENT

INDIVIDUAL VENTS

Figure 11.66 CIRCUIT VERSUS INDIVIDUAL VENTS
A venting system provide an escape path for the gases that can build up within the drainage system, keeping them from penetrating through the traps into the occupied spaces. Adapted from B. Stein, J.S. Reynolds, W.T. Grondzik, and A.G. Kwok, *Mechanical and Electrical Equipment for Buildings,* (John Wiley & Sons, Inc., Hoboken, NJ, 2006), Table 22.10.

Venting

When water and solid material drop within a stack, they act somewhat like a plunger. This action tends to build up the pressure, pushing gases within the drains forward. If a vent stack is connected at the bottom of the soil or waste stack, any significant pressure buildup will be released. While this buildup of positive pressure can be problematic, the potential negative pressure that the dropping water and waste can develop is more critical since this could suck the water out of a trap. In fact, some think that this is the major benefit from the venting system, and they believe that rather than vent each individual fixture trap, a circuit vent can do the job. Figure 11.66 presents both individual venting and circuit venting for the same plumbing fixtures. Those who endorse circuit venting claim that if a circuit vent is provided for each drainage branch, it will afford pressure relief similar to that provided by individual fixture vents. However, this claim is not accepted by all jurisdictions, and most codes do not permit circuit vents.

As implied in the discussion and as shown in Figures 11.65 and 11.66, vent piping goes up while drainage goes down. However, when the fixture is not located adjacent to a wall, such as in an island counter, there is likely no concealed path in which the vertically rising vent piping can be installed. Fortunately, there are several ways to deal with this problem. However, as with circuit vents, some methods are not allowed in certain jurisdictions, so it is

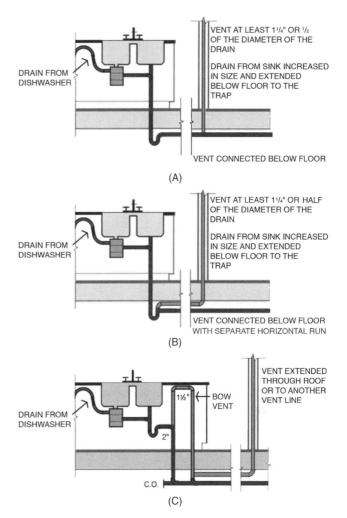

Figure 11.67 ISLAND SINK VENTING
A shows the trap and vent below the floor. B shows the trap and vent below the floor but with a split between the drain and vent. C shows a bow vent with the trap above the floor and a looped vent.

always important to check the local codes when somewhat nonstandard approaches are considered.

One approach to deal with venting an island sink is to increase the size of the drain by one step and locate the trap below the floor level, where it might be possible to vent the trap conventionally (see Figure 11.67A). If the fixture is a kitchen sink located in an island, this probably means that the trap will be in the basement, which should not be too difficult to accomplish. However, since there is no wall near the sink, it is likely that there will be no convenient way to extend the vent upward from the basement trap. Assuming that the drain is from a kitchen sink, the standard $1\frac{1}{2}$-inch drain would have to be increased to 2 inches if it is placed below the floor. With a 2-inch-diameter horizontal drain with a minimal slope of $\frac{1}{8}$ inch per linear foot, the vent would have to be within 16 feet of the trap. While this seems reasonable, it is also possible to split the vent

Table 11.22: DFU BY TRAP SIZE

Fixture Drain or Trap Size (in.)	DFU Value
$1^1/_4$	1
$1^1/_2$	2
2	3
$2^1/_2$	4
3	5
4	6

Table 11.23: DFU BY FIXTURE TYPE

Fixtures	DFU	Minimum Trap Size in.
Automatic Clothes Washers: Commercial Residential	3 2	2 2
Bathroom Group: WC, Lavatory, Bidet, and Bathtub or Shower	6	
Bathtub (with or without Overhead Shower or Whirlpool Attachments	2	$1^1/_2$
Bidet	2	$1^1/_4$
Combination Sink and Tray	2	$1^1/_2$
Dishwashing Machine, Domestic	2	$1^1/_2$
Drinking Fountain	$1/_2$	$1^1/_4$
Floor Drains	2	2
Kitchen Sink, Domestic	2	$1^1/_2$
Kitchen Sink, Domestic, with Food Waste Grinder and/or Dishwasher	2	$1^1/_2$
Laundry Tray (One or Two Compartments)	2	$1^1/_2$
Lavatory	1	$1^1/_4$
Shower Compartment, Domestic	2	2
Sink	2	$1^1/_2$
Urinal	4	–
Urinal, 1 gal (3.8 L) per Flush or Less	2	–
Wash Sink (Circular or Multiple), Each Set of Faucets	2	$1^1/_2$
WC, Flushometer Tank, Public or Private	4	–
WC, Private Installation	4	–
WC, Public Installation	6	–

and drain near the trap, which would allow the vent to slope upward while the drain slopes downward (see Figure 11.67B). This will probably require that the trap be lowered somewhat so that the "horizontal" portion of the vent can have some rise as it extends to the point where it can then run vertically upward and then extend through the roof.

It might also be possible to use a bow vent, although this is not allowed in all jurisdictions. The bow vent, as shown in Figure 11.67C, extends a vent loop that fits just below the countertop height. The expectation is that this loop rises up to basically the flood level of the sink and then drops down to below the floor, where it is extended to a vertical vent stack. As this figure shows, the bow-vent line should remain free of water, preventing siphon formation and releasing any buildup of pressure. Of course, if the drain line gets clogged and the sink totally fills, then the bow vent could fill with water. However, this would not remove the trap seal and allow sewer gases to escape through the sink into the kitchen.

Sizing of Drainage Piping

Sizing the drains is somewhat similar to the approach used in sizing the supply lines, but it is also necessary to size the vents. The drainage system includes the essentially horizontal runs, which are called *branches*, and the vertical runs, which are called *stacks*, plus the vents. The size of the branches and stacks is based on drainage fixture units (DFU), which in turn can be based on the size of the drainpipe and trap or on the particular fixture. DFU based on trap size are presented in Table 11.22, and those based on the fixture are presented in Table 11.23. The diameter of the vent is based on the size of the line being vented, although the vent diameter might need to be increased as the overall length of the vent run is extended. An increase in the length of the vent creates more resistance to the flow of air, which can be decreased by increasing the diameter of the vent. Remember that one of the purposes of the vent is to relieve pressure, and as the vent line gets longer, there

is more resistance to airflow, but this can be reduced by increasing the diameter of the vent.

Drainpipes, both horizontal branches and vertical stacks, are not to be reduced in the direction of flow. This implies that in the reverse direction the size of the lines can get smaller, which makes sense since this portion of the drainage system would carry less drainage. However, the diameter of a stack at its upper end must not be less than 50% of the diameter of that stack at its bottom. This limitation avoids the potential restriction of airflow into and out of the stack.

Once the DFU that are to be handled by various portions of the drainage system have been determined, Table 11.24 can be used to size the horizontal branches and the stacks. However, unlike WSFU, which are used to find the expected GPM demand, DFU are used directly to determine the appropriate size of the drainage pipes.

As Table 11.24 shows, the drainage pipes are separated into two categories: branches, or horizontal lines,

Table 11.24: HORIZONTAL FIXTURE BRANCHES AND STACKS

Diameter of Pipe(in.)	Any Horizontal Fixture or Branch	One Stack of Three Stories in Height for Two Intervals	More Than Three Stories in Height	
			Total Branch Stack	Total at One Story or Internal
$1^1/_4$	1	2	2	1
$1^1/_2$	3	4	8	2
2	6	10	24	6
$2^1/_2$	12	20	42	9
3	20	30	60	16
4	160	240	500	90
5	360	540	1100	200
6	620	960	1900	350
8	1400	2200	3600	600
10	2500	3800	5600	1000
12	3900	6000	8400	1500

Table 11.25: BUILDING DRAINS AND SEWERS

Diameter of Pipe (in.)	Maximum Number of Fixture Units That May Be Connected to Any Portion of the Building Drain or the Building Sewer			
	$^1/_{16}$ in.	$^1/_8$ in.	$^1/_4$ in.	$^1/_2$ in.
2			21	26
$2^1/_2$			24	31
3		20	27	36
4		180	216	250
5		390	480	575
6		700	840	1000
8	1400	1600	1920	2300
10	2500	2900	3500	4200
12	3900	4600	5600	6700

and stacks, or vertical lines. In addition, the stacks are divided into those that are three stories in height or have three intervals (connections) and those that are more than three stories in height. This last stipulation implies that this arrangement also includes more than three intervals.

The numbers listed in Table 11.24 indicate the maximum number of DFU that may be connected to the listed pipe sizes. As can be noted, a vertical stack can handle more DFU than a branch of the same diameter. In addition, when a stack serves more than three stories, it has a DFU capacity significantly more than what can be added from any branch and is more than the listed maximum DFU for the same-size stack that serves only three or fewer stories. These differences are based on the assumption that it is unlikely that all horizontal branches will discharge their allowable drainage at the same time.

The diameter of a stack is sized based on the total DFU that flows through its base. As it rises, the diameter of the stack can be reduced as long as the total DFU that flows through the smaller stack is less than the listed maximum DFU for that diameter in Table 11.24 and as long as the upper smaller diameter is no less than 50% of the diameter at the bottom of the stack. In addition, the size of a drain must not be reduced in the direction of the drainage flow.

At the bottom of a stack, a stack is connected to a horizontal pipe. When it is within the footprint of the structure, such a pipe is referred to as the *building drain* or *house drain*.

When it is outside the building envelope, generally beginning 5 feet away from the building foundations, it is called the *sewer line*.

The capacity of a building drain or building sewer, which is still listed in terms of DFU, is based on the diameter and slope of the pipe. While a slope as low as $^1/_{16}$ inch is included in Table 11.25, such slopes are not recommended since it is likely that with normal building settlement, these minimal slopes might not be sustained. If the slope is $^1/_8$ inch per foot, the drop would be $12^1/_2$ inches for a total run of 100 linear feet, and at $^1/_4$ inch per foot, the drop would be just over 2 feet.

The recommended slope of a horizontal building drain or sewer is $^1/_4$ to $^1/_2$ inch per linear foot. Horizontal runs with slopes greater than $^1/_2$ inch per linear foot are not recommended, particularly for those lines that carry black water. If the pitch of the drain or sewer is increased, the liquid will tend to flow rapidly, but at the increased rate it could leave behind solid matter. The result could be a potential buildup of solid matter in the pipe that could restrict subsequent drainage flows. While slopes greater than $^1/_2$ inch per foot are to be avoided, this restriction no longer applies at slopes of 45° or greater, which is above the angle of repose.

Sizing of Vent Piping

The vents must also be sized correctly. The basic requirement is that a vent be at least $1^1/_4$ inches, or one-half the size of the trap or drain that it serves, whichever is larger. In addition, as the distance to the outside point of release increases, the diameter of the vent might have to get larger. Since the vent is intended to avoid the buildup of pressure

Table 11.26: SIZE AND DEVELOPED LENGTH OF STACK VENTS AND VENT STACKS

Diameter of Soil or Waste Stack (in.)	Drainage Fixture Units Being Vented (dfu)	Maximum Developed Length of Vent (feet) — Diameter of Vent (in.)										
		1¼	1½	2	2½	3	4	5	6	8	10	12
1¼	2	30	150									
1½	8	50	100	—	—	—	—	—	—	—	—	—
½	10	30										
2	12	30	75	200	300							
2	20	26	50	150	—	—	—	—	—	—	—	—
2½	42		30	100								
3	10		42	150	360	1,040						
3	21		32	110	270	810	—	—	—	—	—	—
3	53		27	94	230	680						
3	102		25	86	210	620						
4	43			35	85	250	980					
4	140			27	65	200	750	—	—	—	—	—
4	320			23	55	170	640					
4	540			21	50	150	580					
5	190				28	82	320	990				
5	490			—	21	63	250	760	—	—	—	—
5	940				18	53	210	670				
5	1,400				16	49	190	590				
6	500					33	130	400	1,000			
6	1,100				—	26	100	310	780	—	—	—
6	2,000					22	84	260	660			
6	2,900					20	77	240	600			
8	1,800						31	95	240	940		
8	3,400					—	24	73	190	720	—	—
8	5,600						20	62	160	610		
8	7,600						18	56	140	560		
10	4,000							31	78	310	960	
10	7,200					—		24	60	240	740	—
10	11,000							20	51	200	630	
10	15,000							18	46	180	570	
12	7,300							31	120	380	940	
12	13,000						—	24	94	300	720	
12	20,000							20	79	250	610	
12	26,000							18	72	230	500	
15	15,000							—	40	130	310	
15	25,000						—		31	96	240	
15	38,000								26	81	200	
15	50,000								24	74	180	

Source: Adapted from the *International Plumbing Code*, International Code Council, Inc., Falls Church, VA, 2009.

within the drainage system, an extended vent line could mean that the resistance to airflow will become excessive.

While the intention is to extend each vent line to the outside, sometimes this can be accomplished by collecting various vent lines together, typically in the attic in many single-family residences, and have only one vent penetrate the roof. Of course, when the vents are not brought together, each stack vent or vent stack must extend through the roof. If the diameter of a vent is small, the recommendation is to expand it to 4 inches before it goes through the roof, especially in locations where freezing temperatures

are expected. If the vent line is narrow, moisture that might be released through this line could freeze, with a buildup of ice ultimately clogging the vent. Also, small vents are more likely to be blocked by small debris that might collect in the vent, including deposits by animals or birds if they attempt to take advantage of the warmth provided by the vent.

In addition to being increased to at least a 4-inch diameter, the vent needs to extend above the roof by at least 6 inches. Where snow is expected, the vent should extend higher; the recommendation is that it exceed the probable depth of accumulated snow on the roof. If the roof is occupied, then the vent should discharge at about 7 feet above the roof level so that the sewer gases are not discharged within the occupied zone.

The vent size is determined by the DFU, the diameter of the stack, and the developed length of the vent, which means the distance of the run to the outside. The DFU are based on information from Table 11.23 or Table 11.24, the stack diameter from Table 11.24, and the allowable developed length of the vent from Table 11.26. When using Table 11.26, the horizontal line of the listed stack diameter for which the listed DFU is not exceeded by the connected DFU for the calculation is selected. For example, if a 4-inch stack carries 53 DFU, which exceeds the 43-DFU maximum allowed for the first 4-inch stack line, the second line of the 4-inch stacks should be selected, which can handle up to 140 DFU. Since the stack is 4 inches, the vent must be at least 2 inches in diameter. For a 2-inch diameter, the maximum developed length of the vent from the beginning point of the vent to the extension through the roof cannot exceed 27 feet. If this distance is less than the run of the vent, then a 2-inch vent would be acceptable. If the vent is $2^1/_2$, 3, or 4 inches, the length of the vent could be increased to a total of 65, 200, or 750 feet, respectively. There is no allowable extension of the length of the vent for using a vent with a diameter that exceeds the diameter of the drain.

Materials Used for Drainage and Vent Piping

Drainage lines used to be mainly galvanized steel for lines smaller than 3 inches in diameter and cast iron for the larger lines. Connections with galvanized steel were generally made with male-female screw fittings, whereas hub-and-spigot connections were used with cast iron (see Figure 11.68). Hub-and-spigot connections involved a larger hub into which the end of the prior section of pipe was inserted. In the traditional way of making a hub-and-spigot connection, the space between the pipe and the enlarged hub was tightly packed with oakum and sealed with molten lead, which expanded upon solidifying. While not the prime material for larger-diameter drainage pipes, cast iron is still used today, although now the hub-and-spigot connections, called *compress joints*, use vinyl gaskets rather than lead and oakum. However, most cast iron drains no longer have a hub, and the no-hub cast iron sections are typically assembled by means of rubberized *slip sleeves* that are connected to each pipe by a compression stainless steel retaining clip or clamp. When a plastic or copper drain line is connected to cast iron, the connection between the cast iron and the other material is usually provided by a slip-sleeve joint.

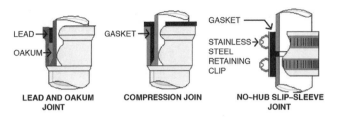

Figure 11.68 CAST IRON CONNECTIONS
There are various methods of connecting sections of cast iron drains. Traditionally, this entailed lead and oakum joints, which were somewhat labor intensive. Today, if hub-and-spigot joints are used, these usually rely on a gasketed compression joint. But more often a slip joint is used.

Copper is another material that we can use for drainage lines. While type K, L, or M copper can be used, generally DWV copper, which is specifically configured for use as drain, waste, or vent piping (hence DWV), is preferred. While rather expensive, copper is long-lasting. Joints between pipes are usually male-female soldered joints, similar to the joints used with supply piping. Plumbing solder used to be lead, but since ingestion of lead is to be avoided, non-lead solder is used today. This is particularly important for water supply piping since if any excessive solder is used, some of it could flow into the interior of the supply pipe and contaminate the supply water. Nonlead solder is now used even on drain lines.

Plastic is the material most often used today for drainage lines and venting. There are various types of plastic that can be used for drainage, including PVC DWV, acrylonitrile butadiene styrene (ABS), and polyolefin. As with copper, plastic fittings are typically male-female connections, although they are solvent welded. Once set, these joints cannot be undone, so if a problem occurs, they must be cut out and replaced. Slip-sleeve joints can also be used with plastic, and, as mentioned, are the way that plastic is connected to cast iron.

While cast iron lines last a long time, they do not last forever. There are many installations that have been in use for more than 75 or 100 years without showing any signs of deterioration, but cast iron can crack and leaks can form. Problems with cast iron and the smaller galvanized steel drains can occur especially if caustic materials are drained through them. When it was expected that a drain might have to handle such materials, Pyrex glass lines were sometimes used since glass does not react to the chemicals. Plastic drainage pipes were developed, in part, to provide an inexpensive alternative to handle caustic materials.

Whatever material is used for the drains, the interior of drain lines should be smooth so as not to catch any solid material. To meet this requirement, drainage fittings are designed somewhat differently than fittings that might be used for supply piping. When the pipes are assembled, there should not be any ridges or rough edges that might obstruct the smooth flow of the sewage (see Figure 11.69).

Figure 11.69 COMPARISON OF FITTINGS
Since drainage lines carry solid material, it is important that the fittings have no projections or edges that might trap solid material or restrain free flow.

SEWAGE TREATMENT

After the wastewater and soil are drained from a structure, what happens to them? While it is possible to handle the sewage on site, the simplest method, which has become standard, is to connect to a public sewage system. But with this approach, there are still several options, particularly in terms of how sanitary sewage and storm drainage are handled.

While sanitary sewage requires considerable treatment, storm water, even though it is not pure, does not demand anywhere near the same level of treatment. Sanitary sewage is discharged at a reasonably consistent flow rate, whereas storm water is not, and at times it can definitely overload the system. Even though this is apparent, many public sewage systems combine storm and sanitary sewage; as a result, there are times when the system is unable to treat the combined effluent properly. When the effluent flow exceeds the capacity of the treatment plant, there must be a way to hold the excess sewage temporarily until it can be treated; otherwise, some untreated sewage will be discharged into the natural water drainage system. When heavy precipitation overloads the sewer, there is also a strong possibility that it will cause the sewage system to back up. This situation is bad enough if it is only storm water, but it is overwhelming if it includes sanitary discharge (black water).

We can help reduce potential problems with combined sewers and undersized storm water systems by incorporating storm water holding tanks as part of our site development. This requires incorporating on-site holding tanks that can retain storm water either until the sewer system can handle it, at which time the water can be drained into the sewer, or as the water slowly percolates into the ground without creating any site runoff. The latter approach reduces the load on the sewage treatment plant and recharges the groundwater.

Another critical issue is the location and depth of the public sewer. While it is possible to pump sanitary waste coming from a building up to the sewer line, the obviously preferred approach is to have the sewage flow by gravity. The critical issue here is the invert or elevation of the sewer line as it drains out of a manhole. The *invert* is the vertical distance from the bottom of the interior of the discharge pipe to the top of the manhole, which is typically the level of the street. This information determines whether gravity drainage is possible and, if so, the appropriate slope of the building sewer.

If a public sewer is not available, we might choose to collect the sewage in a holding tank that can be periodically drained, with the collected material removed to a treatment facility. With this approach, the sewage is held in a below-grade tank that should be capable of retaining the sewage without contaminating the ground. Such a holding tank should be provided with a warning device that can signal when the tank is about three-quarters full, allowing enough time for arranging to have the tank pumped out.

Sometimes a sewage-holding tank is called a *cesspool*. This term is not accurate since, although both are essentially holes in the ground that contain sewage, a cesspool is not watertight, whereas a holding tank must be. If a cesspool were used to hold sewage, the liquid would slowly migrate into the ground, but without any treatment, this would result in significant ground contamination. As a result, cesspools are generally no longer permitted, although when gray-water and black-water sewage are kept separate, a cesspool might be used to hold gray water until it can percolate into the ground. For this application, however, such an underground perforated vessel is perhaps more legitimately called a *drywell*. There is also a *seepage pit*, which is also an underground tank in which sewage is deposited, but a seepage pit is used to receive the output from a septic tank when using a conventional drain field or leaching field is not possible. However, the use of seepage pits might also be prohibited.

Septic Tank

While holding sewage and then having it removed for treatment elsewhere is a possibility, when a site does not have access to a public sewage system, the general approach is to develop some method of on-site sewage treatment. The *septic tank* is the standard method of on-site sewage treatment, and apparently one-quarter to one-third of all U.S. homes still utilize such a system.

It is thought that the French were the first to use an underground sewage disposal system similar to our modern septic system in the latter part of the nineteenth century. This approach relies on the fact that human waste decomposes through the action of its own bacteria. Such a system includes a holding tank, but this tank is different from a holding tank used for sewage that is to be removed for treatment off-site. This holding tank is used to slow and divert

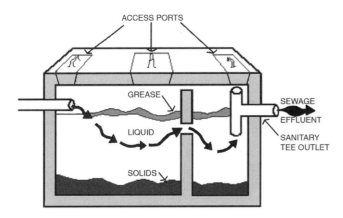

Figure 11.70 TWO-COMPARTMENT SEPTIC TANK
The septic tank is used to separate solid material from sewage and to initiate the digestive process.

the flow of the effluent in order to separate out any solid material and to retain the sewage in order for the anaerobic process to begin the breakdown of the effluent. Today most tanks are concrete, although fiberglass and plastic tanks are also used. All of these tanks should last for at least 50 years, although some retrofitting might be appropriate after around 20 to 25 years. In the past, some tanks were steel, but corrosion problems limited their effective life to only around 10 to 15 years.

Septic tanks, which are watertight containers set into the ground and covered with around 12 inches of earth, usually include two compartments (see Figure 11.70). The first compartment separates the effluent. The heavier materials, including any solids that might have been put into the system as well as feces, tend to sink to the bottom, forming a layer of sludge. The lighter materials, such as grease and fats, float to the top and form a scum layer. Initial digestion of the waste material also occurs in the tank. This digestion process is based on the bacterial microbes that are contained within the waste essentially "eating" themselves. The process is anaerobic (without oxygen), and it produces gases such as hydrogen sulfide and methane that promote further digestion of the solids. The liquid ultimately leaves the holding tank and flows to the drain field. As Figure 11.70 shows, discharge from the septic tank is by means of a sanitary tee that keeps the floating scum from flowing out of the tank.

The septic tank, which for a family of four should have a capacity of 1000 to 1500 gallons, accomplishes several functions: it separates liquid from solid material, initiates the anaerobic digestion of sewage, retains the solid material that has not digested (hopefully until it digests more), and releases effluent fluid. The general intention is that it will take at least 30 hours for the effluent to pass through the holding tank, allowing the solid waste to decompose more

completely. The release from the septic tank then flows to the drain field, where it is distributed through a number of 4-inch-diameter perforated pipes so that this liquid can slowly percolate through the soil. As mentioned above, in some systems the effluent might be sent to a seepage pit rather than to the drain field, although this is not permitted in a number of jurisdictions. Any solid material that breaks down and is retained in the holding tank must ultimately be removed from the tank.

While most of the sewage treatment occurs in the septic tank, the effluent that is discharged from the tank is still not fully clarified. The remainder of the treatment occurs in the drain fields, which might also be referred to as *drainage fields, disposal fields, leaching fields,* or *absorption fields.* Sometimes rather than *field* the term *bed* is used (e.g., *absorption bed*). The effluent that comes out of the septic tank, which still contains some untreated sewage, is distributed relatively evenly across the area of the drain field through perforated pipes. Generally, this distribution is accomplished by initially sending the discharge from the septic tank into a distribution box that can then distribute the flow evenly into the various lines within the drain field. As the liquid flows out of the perforated distribution pipes, this "rich" water encourages microscopic plant and bacterial growth that provide further clarification of the wastewater. As this clarified discharge water filters down through the ground, it is filtered by the sand and dirt in the ground, which provides further refinement. However, if the soil is too permeable, the rapid flow of the discharge through the soil can drastically reduce the final decomposition of the effluent. Table 11.30 lists the characteristics of five typical soils in terms of the design of drain fields.

The best soils for treating the effluent are thick and permeable, containing neither too much sand nor too much clay. Thick layers of soil that are relatively uniform, not wet, and have good aggregation (can be easily broken into small aggregates) work the best. Generally, it is helpful to have a site and soil study conducted by a soils engineer or a specialist in sanitation before proceeding with the design of the leaching field.

Unfortunately, while a septic system is a very efficient way to digest human waste, it does not work as well in breaking down other materials that might be added to the system, such as food items, particularly grease, and most household cleaners and soaps. These can greatly reduce the efficiency of the system. As a result, when using a septic system for sewage treatment, care is needed to avoid draining materials that cannot be effectively digested by the anaerobic process. Fortunately, there are cleaners and soaps that are septic system friendly.

With proper use and maintenance, a septic system should provide effective sewage treatment for many years.

Table 11.27: SUGGESTED SCHEDULE OF SEPTIC TANK INSPECTION AND PUMPING

Tank Size (gal)	Number of People Using the System									
	1	2	3	4	5	6	7	8	9	10
	Septic Tank Pumping Frequency in Years									
500	5.8	2.6	1.5	1.0	0.7	0.4	0.3	0.2	0.1	—
750	9.1	4.2	2.6	1.8	1.3	1.0	0.7	0.6	0.4	0.3
900	11.0	5.2	3.3	2.3	1.7	1.3	1.0	0.8	0.7	0.5
1000	12.4	5.9	3.7	2.6	2.0	1.5	1.2	1.0	0.8	0.7
1250	15.6	7.5	4.8	3.4	2.6	2.0	1.7	1.4	1.2	1.0
1500	18.9	9.1	5.9	4.2	3.3	2.6	2.1	1.8	1.5	1.3
1750	22.1	10.7	6.9	5.0	3.9	3.1	2.6	2.2	1.9	1.6
2000	25.4	12.4	8.0	5.9	4.5	3.7	3.1	2.6	2.2	2.0
2250	28.6	14.0	9.1	6.7	5.2	4.2	3.5	3.0	2.6	2.3
2500	30.9	15.6	10.2	7.5	5.9	4.8	4.0	3.5	3.0	2.6

Source: Adapted from a table developed by Karen Mancl and presented in *Septic Tank Maintenance*, Publication AEX-740-01, Ohio State University Extension Fact Sheet, http://ohioline.osu.edu/aex-fact/0740.html.

The following suggestions are recommended for proper maintenance:

- Reduce the amount of water per capita, definitely no more than 50 GCD and perhaps as low as 30 GCD.
- Keep materials such as chemicals, nonbiodegradable soaps, sanitary napkins, and other materials that do not degrade biologically out of the wastewater.
- Avoid using the garbage disposal unit, particularly for vegetable scraps. Instead, compost these food wastes.
- Do not pour grease or cooking oils down the sink drain.
- Know where the septic tank and the drain field are located, and avoid interfering with the land above them..
- Keep water runoff away from the septic tank and the drain field.
- Maintain adequate vegetative cover over the drain field.
- Keep automobiles and heavy equipment off the land above the septic tank and the drain field.
- Periodically remove the solids from the septic tank (see Table 11.27).

If the septic tank fills with solids, these solids can flow out of the tank and into the pipes in the drain field, causing severe damage. While some solids will get into the drain field, this should not be a problem. However, if the tank is not properly cleaned out and maintained, the solids flowing into the drain field could become excessive and block the drain holes in the field piping. If this occurs, the sewage will probably back up and/or the effluent will flood the drain field. If pipes in the drain field get clogged with solid material, it is generally necessary to replace the drain field with a new one in a different location. While this should not be necessary if the system is properly serviced, when initially considering how a septic system can be accommodated on a project site, it is reasonable to designate an area for a possible replacement field as well as for the initial drain field.

Since liquid, which comprises the major portion of the sewage, is supposed to flow through the tank, it should be clear that a septic tank should never fill with solids. If solids fill 25% to 33% of the tank, it is definitely time to pump out the tank; when this is done, the solids should be removed from both compartments. The piping, especially the sanitary tee fitting at the discharge, should also be checked and repaired if necessary. If this tee fitting is damaged, the effluent discharge will likely include grease and fat, and these will likely clog the pipes in the drain field.

Table 11.27 shows a recommended schedule for inspecting and pumping out a septic tank. While this table is a helpful guide, it is preferable to clean out the septic tank after a few years of use, and to do this sooner rather than later. We can use Table 11.27 to schedule the initial cleaning at around half of the time listed, which should ensure that the amount of collected material is well below the tank's capacity. Then, based on the amount of solid material that has accumulated over the particular period of use, a reasonable cleaning schedule can be established. We might choose to adjust the schedule if the septic system is not used regularly, perhaps at a vacation home. On the other hand, if a garbage disposal unit is used, we will have to inspect and pump out the septic tank more frequently. Whatever schedule is appropriate, since it will likely be every 3 to 5 years, it is important to establish a system to ensure that the owner will perform the proper maintenance. If not, there can be some unfortunate consequences. Since a septic system generally does not require much attention, establishing a known schedule of

Table 11.28: SEPTIC TANK CAPACITY

Single-Family Dwellings – No. of Bedrooms	Multiple Dwelling Units or Apartments – One Bedroom Each	Other Uses: Maximum DFU	Minimum Septic Tank Capacity gal)
1 or 2		15	750
3		20	1000
4	2 units	25	1200
5 or 6	3	33	1500
	4	45	2000
	5	55	2250
	6	60	2500
	7	70	2750
	8	80	3000
	9	90	3250
	10	100	3500

Extra bedrooms: 150 gallons each.

Extra dwelling units over 10: 250 gallons each.

Extra fixture units over 100: 25 gallons per fixture unit.

Septic tank sizes allow connection disposal of domestic food waste units without further volume increase.

For larger or nonresidential installations in which sewage flow rate is known, size the septic tank as follows:

    1. Flow up to 1500 GCD: flow x 1.5 = septic tank cap.

    2. Flow over 1500 GCD: (flow x 0.75) + 1125 = septic tank capacity in gallons.

    3. Secondary system should be sized for total flow per 24 hours.

Source: Adapted from the *Uniform Plumbing Code* (International Association of Plumbing and Mechanical Officials, Walnut, CA, 1997).

Table 11.29: SIZE OF THE SEPTIC TANK BASED ON DAILY WATER USAGE

Average Sewage Wastewater Flow (gal/day)	Minimum Septic Tank Required Effective Capacity (gal)
0–500	900
601–700	1200
801–900	1500
1001–1240	1900
2001–2500	3200
4501–5000	5800

Table 11.30: SEPTIC TANK & DISPOSAL AREA DESIGN CRITERIA FOR FIVE TYPICAL SOILS

Type of Soil	Required ft^2 of Disposal Area/100 Gal	Maximum Absorption Capacity, Gal/ ft^2 of Disposal Area for a 24-hr Period	Maximum Allowable Septic Tank Size Gallons
Coarse sand or gravel	20	5	7,500
Fine sand	25	4	7,500
Sandy loam or sandy clay	40	2.5	5,000
Clay with considerable sand or gravel	90	1.1	3,500
Clay with small amount of sand or gravel	120	0.83	3,000

Source: Adapted from *Uniform Plumbing Code* (International Association of Plumbing and Mechanical Officials, Walnut, CA, 1997)

maintenance is important. When problems with a septic system become apparent, it is often too late to solve them readily, to say nothing of the unpleasantness of having to deal with the issue; remember that a septic system is a sewage treatment system.

While a specialist usually is responsible for the design of a septic system, we can determine the basic requirements by using a few tables. Table 11.28 shows the minimum septic tank capacities based on the size of various residential units or DFU served. Table 11.29 indicates the minimum septic tank size based on the gallons of sewage, and as mentioned, Table 11.30 lists the maximum absorption capacities for different soil conditions. Table 11.31 provides dimensions to be used in laying out the trenches in the drain field. Figure 11.71 and Table 11.32 provide information on the layout and placement of the various elements of the septic tank treatment system.

Based on different sources, we can develop various estimates of the proper size for the septic tank and drain field. For example, while according to Table 11.28 a two-bedroom single-family house requires only a 750-gallon

septic tank, Table 11.29 stipulates that the recommended minimum size for a septic tank is 900 gallons. Another source of confusion is the number of people and the ultimate water usage if the size of the tank is based on the number of bedrooms. How many people occupy each bedroom? Should we assume that there are two occupants in each bedroom or only in the master bedroom? And then there is the correlation between the different ways that the septic system can be sized: based on gallons of water consumed daily by each person, which might be 70 GCD or the more reasonable 40 GCD with our modern water-conserving toilets and other fixtures; on the DFU; or on a stipulated gallons-per-day flow for a residence of a particular size.

We can develop a preliminary estimate of the size of the septic tank and drain field from the number of people that the system must serve. But, in general, it is best to develop the system design on the basis of projected water consumption. So the design of the water supply system has a direct impact on the sizing of the sewage treatment system.

In laying out the drain field, we should attempt to set 50 feet as the maximum length of run for each line and should definitely not exceed 100 linear feet per run. Table 11.31 also indicates that the lines in the drain field area should be set at least 1 foot below grade but not more than around 5 feet, with at least 12 inches of filtering material added below the pipe. Also, assuming that each trench is 24 inches wide, which is about midway between the 18-inch minimum and the 36-inch maximum trench width, the suggestion to provide 150 square feet per person converts to around 75 linear feet of pipe within the drain field per person. With the minimal 6-foot spacing between the drain field lines, the drain field area per individual would be around 450 square feet. On this basis, a drain field for a family of four should have an area of around 1800 square feet.

Table 11.31: DRAIN FIELD TRENCHES

Field Trenches	Minimum	Maximum
Length of Drain Line(s)	—	100 ft
Bottom Width of Trench	18 in.	36 in.
Spacing of Lines, o.c.	6 ft	—
Depth of Earth Cover Over Lines	12 in.	—
Grade of Lines	18 in. Preferred Level	3 in./100 ft
Filter Materials Over Drain Lines Under Drain Lines	2 in. 12 in.	— –
Disposal Area		
Trench Bottom:	Minimum 150 sq ft per System	
Trench Side Wall:	Minimum 2 sq ft/ft of Length Maximum 6 sq ft/ft of Length	

Source: Adapted from the *Uniform Plumbing Code* (International Association of Plumbing and Mechanical Officials, Walnut, CA, 1997).

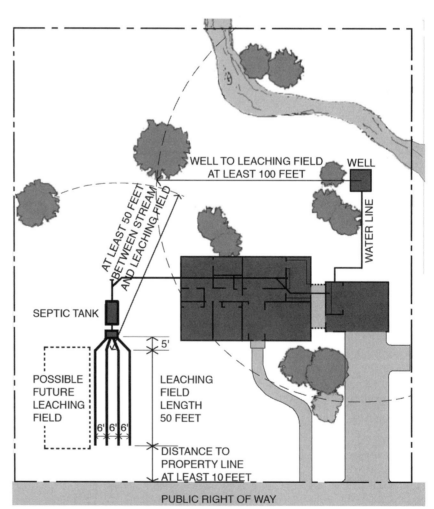

Figure 11.71 LOCATION OF ON-SITE SEWAGE DISPOSAL SYSTEMS

This layout shows various requirements for laying out a septic system. Adapted from B. Stein, J.S. Reynolds, W.T. Grondzik, and A.G. Kwok, *Mechanical and Electrical Equipment for Buildings* (John Wiley & Sons, Inc., Hoboken, NJ, 2006), Figure 27.37.

Table 11.32: RECOMMENDED CLEARANCES FROM DISPOSAL SYSTEMS

Minimum Clear Horizontal Distance Required from:	Building Sewer (ft)	Septic Tank (ft)	Drain Field (ft)	Seepage Pit (Cesspool) (ft)
Property Line Adjoining Private Property	Clear	5	10	10
Buildings or Structures	2	5	10	10
Streams/Creeks	50	50	50	100
Water Supply Wells	50	100	100	150
On-Site Domestic Water Service Line	1	5	10	10
Public Water main	10	10	10	10
Large Trees	—	10	—	10
Septic Tank	—	—	5	—
Distribution Box	—	—	5	5

Source: Adapted from the *Uniform Plumbing Code* (International Association of Plumbing and Mechanical Officials, Walnut, CA, 1997) and various local codes.

Aerobic Sewage Treatment

While a properly designed septic system is an effective means of treating residential sewage, sometimes the site conditions are not adequate for this approach. In this situation, we might choose to use an aerobic treatment unit (ATU), which is essentially a small sewage treatment plant. By adding oxygen to the sewage holding tank and mixing the mixture, aerobic bacteria are able to break down the waste material within a relatively short period of time, reducing the further refinement of the effluent required within an extended drain or leaching field. These aerobic systems can effectively treat the sewage so that the effluent can be sufficiently refined for it to be returned to the natural water flow—into a surface stream or percolated through the soil into the underground aquifer. It is also possible to combine an aerobic system with a reduced drain field, which is in essence an active septic system. These systems are referred to as *aerobic septic systems*. While effective, aerobic systems have a higher initial cost, require a continual source of electrical power, and must be regularly maintained. In addition, all aeration treatment units should be equipped with an alarm system that can detect both failure of the system and high water levels.

Sand filters can also be added to either a septic tank system or an aerobic treatment system to provide additional refinement of the effluent before it is discharged into the natural water flow. The sand filters reduce the amount of suspended solids, and microorganisms attached to the particles of sand aerobically digest the organic material. Constructed wetlands are another possible way to promote sewage treatment. These wetlands include trenches or cells lined with materials that impede permeation of the effluent and contain various forms of vegetation. The roots of the plants transpire oxygen and aerate the water, establishing aerobic conditions, which in turn helps the microorganisms attached to the medium lining the cells and the roots of the vegetation to refine the sewage.

BIBLIOGRAPHY

2009 International Plumbing Code. International Code Council, Inc., Falls Church, VA, 2009.

Grondzik, W.T., A.G. Kwok, B. Stein, and J.S. Reynolds. *Mechanical and Electrical Equipment for Buildings*. John Wiley & Sons, Inc., Hoboken, NJ 2010.

Krishna, H. J. *The Texas Manual on Rainwater Harvesting*, 3rd ed., Texas Water Development Board, Austin, TX, 2005.

Lambton, L. *Temples of Convenience and Chambers of Delight*. Pavilion Books Limited, London, 1998.

Milne, M. "Residential Water Re-Use." California Water Resources Center Report No. 46. University of California/Davis, 1979.

Reyburn, W. *Flush with Pride: The Story of Thomas Crapper*. Permanent Press, New York, 1999.

Uniform Plumbing Code. International Association of Plumbing and Mechanical Officials, Walnut, CA, 1997.

Wright, L. *Clean and Decent, the Fascinating History of the Bathroom and the Water-Closet*. Penguin Books, London, 1960.

12 ELECTRICITY

INTRODUCTION

BASIC PRINCIPLES

SOURCES OF ELECTRIC POWER

ELECTRICAL TRANSMISSION AND DISTRIBUTION

BUILDING DISTRIBUTION

GENERAL GUIDELINES FOR RESIDENTIAL APPLICATIONS

INTRODUCTION

"Plugging In"
Peg plugged in her 'lectric toothbrush,
Mitch plugged in his steel guitar'
Rick plugged in his CD player'
Liz plugged in her VCR,
Mom plugged in her 'lectric blanket,
Pop plugged in the TV fights,
I plugged in my blower-dryer—
Hey! Who turned out all the lights?[1]

Shel Silverstein

Electricity is a form of energy that occurs naturally only in rare forms that typically are unusable, such as lightning. However, electricity is an extremely powerful and important form of energy that has been largely responsible for many modern technological improvements. This is especially so in the area of architecture. With the harnessing of electricity, in various forms but particularly through electric lighting, architecture in both form and use has been significantly altered.

As a form of energy, electricity is unlike most other forms of energy in that it cannot be stored easily. While bat-

teries can store electric energy or even generate it through chemical means, this is not the type of electricity that is generally used in architectural applications. Batteries provide direct-current (d-c) electricity, whereas most architectural applications, the major exceptions being certain older elevator equipment and some communications systems, use alternating-current (a-c).

Fundamentally, electricity is energy that results from the movement or flow of electrons. This flow, which is referred to as *current* or *amperage*, occurs basically at the speed of light and typically in what are referred to as *conductors*. Materials can be classified into three types: conductors, semiconductors, and insulators. By reflecting on the nature of light, we can gain an understanding of how these different classifications are established and what opportunities they provide.

As we saw in our discussion of the nature of light, humans have pondered the nature of various physical phenomena since ancient times. In the area of light, this exploration vacillated between two theories: the corpuscular or photon theory, which assumed that light was itself a substance referred to as a *photon*, and the wave theory, which assumed that light was related to a variation in another substance. Pythagoreans considered light as a series of particles, which is the basis of the corpuscular theory, while the Aristotelians tended to support the wave theory.

---

[1]S. Silverstein, *Falling Up* (HarperCollins Publishers, New York, 1996), p. 8.

The resolution of the nature-of-light dilemma seemed to come in the early 1800s with Thomas Young's double-slit experiment, which clearly demonstrated that light is a waveform, but then there was the question about the substance in which these waves existed and traveled. The response was that light waves existed in a material called *ether.* About 100 years after Young's experiment, Max Planck developed a formula to explain radiation emitted from an incandescent solid. The formula indicated that the energy is emitted in discrete bundles, which Planck called *quanta.* His notion of radiation occurring in discrete bundles suggested that perhaps the corpuscular theory of light was correct. A few years later, Albert Einstein combined these two theories into what is currently assumed to be the valid explanation of light. Einstein applied Planck's quantum theory to the wave theory. Shortly afterward, Niels Bohr proposed that light is emitted when electrons make a transition from a higher to a lower orbit around the nucleus of an atom. His thesis was that electrons could travel only in certain successively larger orbits. As an electron drops from a higher to a lower orbit, it releases energy in the form of electromagnetic radiation. The frequency of this radiation is determined by the energy released by the electron when it shifts orbits. The number of electrons dropping into a lower orbit determines the brightness, or intensity, of the radiation.

Based on the work of these scientists, today we understand that light is electromagnetic radiation, which is a combination of an electric field and a magnetic field, and has the characteristics of a wave but is released in quantum units. However, while electromagnetic radiation extends across an extremely wide range of frequencies, light falls within only a narrow portion of this range, between 4.3×10^{18} and 7.5×10^{18} Hz.

BASIC PRINCIPLES

Now, what does this have to do with electricity?

Electromagnetic radiation, which under certain conditions is in the form of visible light, is released when electrons drop from a higher to a lower orbit. With some materials, the process can be reversed, with light causing electrons to move. This is the *photoelectric phenomenon,* which is used by a light meter to indicate the amount of incident electromagnetic radiation. The incident light results in a flow of electrons that deflects a meter by an amount proportional to the intensity of the radiation.

Electricity entails the movement or flow of electrons, which are negatively charged particles. When the photoelectric phenomenon produces a usable electric current, we tend to use the term *photovoltaic* rather than merely

photoelectric. Photoelectric refers to the excitation of electrons by light, whereas *photovoltaic* refers to light-activated systems intended to produce a usable electric current.

So, we come back to the distinction between materials with respect to electricity, with some materials being conductors, some insulators, and some falling in between these two categories as semiconductors. Conductors have a particular atomic structure. They have an outer shell of orbiting electrons, called the *valence shell,* which typically contains only one or two electrons. These materials, often metallic, can conduct electricity since the electrons in the valence shell are readily disengaged from their orbit and are free to flow to establish an electric current. Materials that have more than five electrons in the valence shell are considered insulators since it is difficult to disengage any of these outer electrons from their orbit around the nucleus of the atom. That is, there is a bond between these electrons that resists the flow of electrons through the material. Semiconductors have three, four, or five electrons in their valence shell or outer orbit.

Copper and aluminum are the materials most often used as electrical conductors. Interestingly, aluminum has three electrons in its outer orbit. However, due to its chemical nature, the bond between these electrons is apparently not strong, allowing the electrons to flow from atom to atom. While aluminum is an effective conductor, it is now generally used only for high-voltage distribution lines since its coefficient of thermal expansion and its tendency to oxidize can cause electrical connections to fail. Copper, although a rather expensive semiprecious metal, remains the preferred conductor for most low-voltage wiring, that is, below 12,000 volts.

For protection, conductors are usually insulated by surrounding them with materials with more than five electrons in the outer valence or by separating them from each other. Either of these methods prevents contact or arcing between the conductors. Of course, surrounding a conductor with a nonconducting material prevents the conductor from making direct contact with the wire, so exposed conductors are not used within buildings where different electric lines are typically in close proximity to each other.

For an electric current to flow, there must be a difference in the electric potential. We usually refer to this electric potential by the term *voltage,* although it is also noted as *EMF* or merely *E,* for electromotive force. Voltage is electrical pressure and is similar to pressure in a hydraulic system, while current or amperage is similar to the water flow in that system. The resistance to the flow is called just that in d-c circuits, and its electrical term is *ohm.* With a-c circuits, due to the nature of electricity, resistance is compounded by other factors such as inductance. As a result, the more proper reference for a-c current is *impedance* rather than *resistance*, although in standard discussion, *resistance* is often used for both a-c and d-c circuits.

In a *d-c* electric circuit the current flows in only one direction, so we can assume that a d-c circuit relies on electrons actually traveling down a conductor. In an a-c circuit the current continually reverses. At 60 cycles per second or Hertz, which is the standard U.S. electrical frequency, the current will flip-flop 60 times per second. Even though the electrons basically remain in the same location in an a-c circuit, an electric current does flow. So, obviously, an electric current is not based on the actual flow of the electrons down a conductor, at least with an a-c circuit, but on the movement of the electrons.

Another possible question relates to the speed of an electric current. Electricity seems to travel rather quickly, approximating the speed of light. If an electric current requires the movement of electrons, this is improbable, particularly in a d-c circuit. In a d-c circuit, the electrons flow in only one direction and travel at the rather slow speed of around 3 inches per hour. However, if we consider electricity as the flow of energy rather than as the physical movement of the electrons, which are tangible objects, it is reasonable that the flow of electricity attains a speed close to that of light.

Theoretically, if electricity were to flow across a vacuum, it would travel at the speed of light. If it flows through a gas, it moves almost at the same speed, perhaps at around 95% that of light, but in a physical conductor, an electric current moves at only around 75% of the speed of light. Still, we might wonder how this is possible.

While it is sometimes compared to hydraulics or a flow of water, which entails the movement of a physical object from point to point, an electric current is a flow of an energy field. In a way, this is similar to what happens with a Newton's pendulum (see Figure 12.1). If the ball at one end of the pendulum is raised and dropped, the ball at the other end swings upward and the movement is essentially repeated, with the two end pendulums swinging somewhat as if they were only one pendulum. Although the three intermediate balls do not move, they must obviously transmit the energy from one end of the pendulum to the other. This is what happens with an electric circuit. Whether it is d-c or a-c, the energy flows through the conductor.

Another way of thinking about an electric current is to compare it with a garden hose. We probably know from experience that water typically flows out of a hose as soon as we turn on the hose bibb, regardless of the length of the hose. However, if we use a new hose or one that was drained and stored for the winter, water will not flow out of the end of the hose when the water is turned on. Water will not come out of the hose until the hose fills with water. Once it is full, there is no delay, although it does take time for the fresh water coming out of the hose bibb to reach

Figure 12.1 NEWTON'S PENDULUM
The movement of the hanging balls in a Newton's pendulum indicates the principles of an electric current and the rate at which it flows.

the end of the hose. This is similar to the reason we often have to wait for hot water when turning on a shower in the morning. In a d-c circuit the electron flow is like the flow of water, but the flow of electricity is similar to the water flow that occurs when a hose is full or when the hot water has reached the shower.

Generation and Distribution of Electricity

The work of James Clerk Maxwell (1831–1879), a Scottish mathematician and theoretical physicist, showed that there was a connection between light, electricity, and magnetism. Realizing that these three forms of energy are different manifestations of the same phenomenon, Maxwell demonstrated that an electric current flowing through a conductor creates a magnetic field. Similarly, moving a magnetic field in relation to a conducting material, for example a copper wire, can establish an electric current, and it is this principle of physics that permits the generation of electricity—a series of wire coils rotating through a magnetic field.

If we think in terms of basic principles (perhaps relying on our own likely experience of playing with magnets), magnets have both a positive and a negative charge or force. Since the outer valence electrons can move and are negatively charged, when a conductor is placed in a magnetic field, these electrons tend to move toward the positive

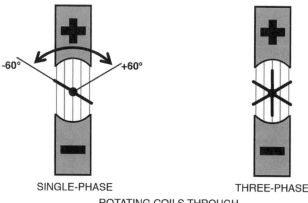

SINGLE-PHASE   THREE-PHASE
ROTATING COILS THROUGH
A MAGNETIC FIELD

Figure 12.2 ELECTRIC GENERATOR DIAGRAM
As the coil of wire moves through the magnetic field, an electric current is
established, but this only occurs from −60° to +60°, as shown. Since this
means that the effective movement is limited to 120°, which is one-third of the
total rotation of 360°, if three loops are combined and set at a 120° separation,
three phases of electricity can be developed.

portion of a magnetic field (opposite forces are attracted to
each other) and move away from the negative portion
of the magnetic field (similar forces are repelled by each
other). As a result, relative movement between a magnetic
field and an electrical conductor will cause the electrons to
move in the conductor, which is electricity—movement of
electrons. If this movement is in one direction, the electricity is d-c, and if it keeps changing directions, it is a-c.

When a coiled wire loop passes through a magnetic
field, an electric current is produced. As implied by the left
diagram in Figure 12.2, this would occur only for the short
period of the time when the coiled wire loop passes through
the magnetic field, that is, when the coil moves between the
two poles of the magnet. Assuming rotation is clockwise,
when a coiled wire loop rotates from approximately −60°
from vertical to +60° from vertical, it passes through the
magnetic field. From +60° to +120° the coil of wire does
not cut through the magnetic field and, as a result, electricity is not generated in that wire loop. By placing three
coiled wire loops on the armature at 60° angles from each
other, as one wire loop passes out of the magnetic field,
another enters. This arrangement, which is used in most
generating systems, generates three-phase electricity.

As each loop rotates, the different ends of the coiled
wire loop are alternately exposed to the positive and then
the negative pole of the magnet. As a result, the generated
electric current consistently changes direction in the loop,
so a-c is produced.

Reversing this process by running an electric current
through the coil produces a changing electromagnetic
field. Since this field has a positive and then a negative
charge, depending on the direction of the current, rota-

tional movement is induced. Opposite charges are attracted
to each other, while similar charges are repulsed. So, a
generator and a motor are basically the same—one producing an electric current from rotational movement and
the other producing rotational movement from an electric
current.

An electric motor has an armature that can rotate
through an electro-magnetic field. With a single-phase motor, only one electro-magnetic field is available to induce
rotation of the armature, and, as a result, a single-phase
motor is not very powerful. With a three-phase electric
motor, there are three electro-magnetic fields, one from
each phase of the three-phase electricity. With three in-
puts per rotation, a three-phase moter develops a more
consistent push. As a result, when more powerful motors
are required, three-phase electricity is recommended. In
other uses of electricity, such as for lighting or resistance
heating, three phases are not required. For these applications, only one of the phases is typically used. In order to
maximize efficiency, the electricity produced from all three
phases should be utilized in a balanced manner. This requires some consideration of the electric circuitry to ensure
that there is a reasonable balance in electrical consumption, but this is normally not an architectural concern.
Balanced use of all three phases of electricity is generally
addressed by the electric utility in terms of how it handles its distribution or, with large buildings or industrial
complexes, by the consulting engineers.

While generators naturally produce a-c, depending on
how the electrical connections are made with the rotating
coils, either a-c or d-c can be produced. As each of the
coiled wire loops rotates through the magnetic field, the
direction of the current within the loop will constantly
alternate as it is exposed to different poles of the magnetic
field. However, as shown in Figure 12.3, the current that is
actually supplied, a-c or d-c, depends on the arrangement
of the connections to a generator. Since the electrons flip-
flop in direction, if the two ends of the rotating wire loop
remain in contact with the same electric conductor, then
a-c is produced. However, if the ends of the wire loop are
in contact with a split ring take-off, d-c is generated.

Figure 12.4 shows the type of electricity, in terms of frequency and voltage, supplied worldwide. In North America, the generation of electricity has the coils of wire rotating at 60 cycles per second or Hertz (Hz). In most areas
other than North America, electricity is generated at 50
Hz. The change in cycles per second impacts on certain
equipment, especially motors, since cycles per second determines the number of motor rotations, but for most uses
the difference in cycles is not critical.

Another variation in electrical standards in different
global areas is the voltage of electricity used. In North
America, the standard voltage is 120 volts, although the

DOUBLE RING FOR A-C CURRENT

SPLIT RING FOR D-C CURRENT

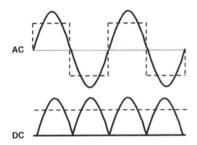
AC

DC

Figure 12.3 ELECTRIC GENERATION–DISTINCTION BETWEEN A-C AND D-C
The type of electric current produced, d-c or a-c, is based on how the output of the generator is extracted. A double-ring connection to the rotating wire coil produces a-c. A split-ring connection produces d-c. In either case, the output is not consistent or flat, which means that voltage is generally indicated as the mean rather than the specific voltage at any instant.

actual voltage used in an area is usually set by the local utility company. The voltages used in North America range from 110 to 127 volts. While 120 volts is becoming the standard, in certain areas the actual voltage might be 110 volts and in others 115 volts. In Europe and most of the world, the standard voltage used in electric circuits within buildings is 240 volts, again with a range from 220 to 240 volts. So, if we purchase a lamp abroad and then try to

use it in a 120-volt circuit, the resulting lighting would not be adequate. Conversely, if we try to use an American appliance abroad, there could be a serious problem due to excessive voltage.

While 120 volts is the American standard, 240-volt electricity is also used for major electrical appliances such as cooktops, ovens, and clothes dryers. When more electric power is required, there is a benefit in using a higher voltage. Since voltage is the electric potential or force, when the load is more demanding, a higher voltage means less current. The higher voltage is typically double the basic voltage. If the basic voltage in an area is 110 volts, then the higher voltage would be 220 volts, and if it is 115 volts, it would be 230 volts.

According to basic theory, particularly Ohm's Law, an electric current is the result of voltage divided by resistance or, stated in reverse, voltage is the product of current times resistance. This can be shown by the following formula:

$$I = \frac{V}{R} \text{ or } V = IR$$

where

> I is current,
> V is voltage
> R is resistance

In basic electric circuits, wattage is power and is the product of current times voltage. As a result:

$$W = I^2 R = I(IR)$$

where

> W is wattage

Figure 12.4 TYPICAL VOLTAGES AND HERTZ ACROSS THE WORLD

Electricity in North America is generally set at 120 volts at 60 Hz. This is also the standard for southern Japan, Saudi Arabia, and much of northern South America, excluding a portion of Brazil and Peru. Northern Japan and Madagascar are somewhat unique, using 120–127 volts but at 50 Hz. Throughout most of the world, the standard is 220 to 240 volts at 50 Hz, although again, as an anomaly, 220 to 240 volts at 60 Hz is used in some areas in South America and in Korea, both North and South.

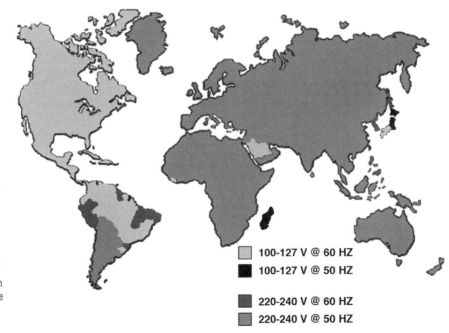

☐ 100-127 V @ 60 HZ
■ 100-127 V @ 50 HZ

☐ 220-240 V @ 60 HZ
☐ 220-240 V @ 50 HZ

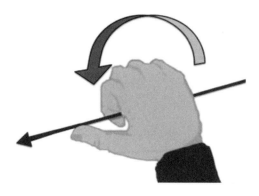

Figure 12.5 RIGHT-HAND RULE
If the thumb of the right hand is pointed in the direction of an electric current, the fingers of the right hand point in the direction of the magnetic field established by the electric current.

But since $V = IR$, watts equal volts times amps:

$$W = VI$$

With a-c circuits, rather than resistance, we should use impedance. Impedance is a combination of resistance, inductance, and reactance. Inductance and reactance basically result from the fact that relative movement between a magnetic field and a conductor establishes an electric current and an electric current develops a magnetic field. When the current is a-c, since the direction of the current keeps changing, the developed magnetic field also keeps changing directions, which establishes relative movement between this developed magnetic field and the conductor, producing an electric current. So, an alternating electric current generates a secondary electric current, and this phenomenon is most pronounced when the initial electric current is in a coiled wire. Let us clarify this situation.

The direction of the magnetic field induced by an electric current follows the right-hand rule (see Figure 12.5). By orienting the thumb of the right hand in the direction of the electric current, the direction of the fingers indicates the direction of the magnetic field. As we can see by flipping our right hand back and forth, with the direction of the electric current constantly changing, the direction of

the magnetic field will also keep changing. Since an electric current is generated when there is relative movement between a conductor and a magnetic field, by its nature an alternating electric current tends to generate an electric current, which is also a-c. But this is not some wonderful "perpetual motion" phenomenon since the electric current induced by an a-c current actually opposes the initial current. When a conductor is coiled, such as in a transformer or a motor, the magnetic field produced by the a-c current is concentrated, and as a result, a more significant counterflow electric current is generated by the initial current. This generated current, which is called *reactance*, tends to oppose the initial current, and as a result it acts like resistance, although it is legitimately called *inductance*.

Inductance is the tendency of an electric device to induce an opposing voltage in an electric circuit. This tendency is especially pronounced when the wire is coiled or wound. The induced current flows in the opposite direction from the primary current, reducing the main current flow. This is called *inductive reactance*, and it tends to put the voltage and the current out of phase with each other, causing the amperage to lag behind the voltage (see Figure 12.6). As a result of this phenomenon, with a-c circuits wattage is based on volts, amps, and also a power factor (pf).

$$W = VI \times \text{pf}$$

The power factor, which is the cosine of the angle by which the amperage lags behind the voltage, tends to reduce the energy available in an a-c circuit. To adjust for this power factor, it is usually necessary to install a capacitor in the electric circuit. A capacitor, sometimes referred to as a *condenser*, in its simplest form consists of two metal plates brought close to each other but insulated from each other. A capacitor, which may include more than two plates, is said to have a capacity to store a charge of electrons and, in this way, tends to maintain the voltage. One effect of capacitive reactance in a circuit is to make the current "lead" the voltage. That is, by adding a capacitor, we can get the current to lead, and thereby counteract the effect of the inductance that tends to cause the voltage to lead.

Figure 12.6 VOLTAGE AND AMPERAGE CURVES
An a-c circuit, by the nature of the changing magnetic field that it produces, induces an opposing current within the same wire. This opposing current causes the voltage and amperage to shift out of phase. Since power is basically determined by volts times amps, this shift in the two results in reduced power. Note that both voltage and amperage follow the sine wave and are not constant. Therefore, the listed voltage, amperage, and power are typically the mean of each.

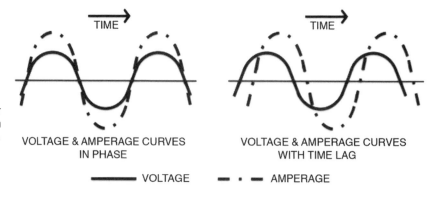

VOLTAGE & AMPERAGE CURVES
IN PHASE

VOLTAGE & AMPERAGE CURVES
WITH TIME LAG

——— VOLTAGE   — · — AMPERAGE

All of this is rather technical, and it is something that needs to be handled by a qualified consulting engineer, but it is important that we be aware of it since it can be critical in terms of operational efficiency.

Since the power factor is not included, merely multiplying volts times amps with an a-c circuit produces *volt-amperes* rather than watts. However, in purely resistive circuits, such as those for incandescent lighting or electric heating, impedance and resistance are essentially equal, so the power factor is essentially 1.0 and the basic formula of watts equaling volts times amps gives reasonable results. When there are motors or many fluorescent or HID lights, which rely on ballasts, a form of transformer, then the power factor applies more significantly.

Since electric power is essentially the product of volts and amps, to increase the power it is necessary to increase the voltage and/or the amperage. With an increase in the current, more electricity has to flow through the electrical conductor in order to deliver the same power. The more current that flows, the more resistance develops. This is similar to trying to push more water through a pipe of a given size or more air through a duct of a given size. Or, as we might understand from personal experience, it is like trying to accommodate more cars on the same-sized roadway. As the road gets overloaded, traffic becomes clogged, but the same-sized road can accommodate more people if more people ride in each vehicle, especially if the vehicles are buses rather than cars. Similarly, with electricity, to get more power we can increase the voltage rather than the current, which is the logical thing to do—more electric power with less resistance.

In trying to reduce overall resistance to the flow of electricity, we might question the logic of using a-c, which has to deal with inductance and reactance in addition to basic resistance. On initial consideration, it seems that d-c rather than a-c should be used for power distribution, especially over long distances. With high voltage, less electric current needs to be supplied through the transmission lines, and with d-c the problems of reactance and inductance do not have to be confronted. However, since there are serious potential dangers from high voltages, the high voltage would have to be lowered before the electricity is distributed into buildings where people will come into close contact with it. How can this change in voltage be accomplished?

The reactance and inductance associated with an a-c current provide an effective and reasonably efficient way to change voltages. If two separate electric circuits are linked together, an alternating current in one circuit can establish an a-c electric current in the linked circuit. The linkage is achieved by wrapping both circuit conductors around a common metal core. As a result, the incoming a-c circuit establishes a changing magnetic field that is transmitted through the metal core to the outgoing circuit. Since this is

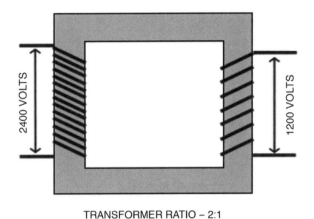

TRANSFORMER RATIO – 2:1

Figure 12.7 ELECTRIC TRANSFORMER DIAGRAM
The electric transformer is used to change the voltage of a-c electricity. Since an a-c circuits develops a changing magnetic field, by coiling wire from two different circuits around a common metal core, the current in one circuit will be transferred to the second circuit, with the voltage changed according to the ratio of the number of coils from each circuit that are wrapped around the common metal core.

a dynamic magnetic field, an electric current is established, and the ratio of the voltages in the two circuits is based on the ratio of the number of windings of each circuit around the common metal core (see Figure 12.7).

Such a device, which is called a *transformer*, changes the electric voltage, and it does this quite efficiently. Although the connection between a flow of electricity and a magnetic field exists with both a-c and d-c current, it is only with a-c that the direction of the current constantly changes, allowing for the voltage adjustment. While changing voltage is relatively easy with a-c, it is not readily achieved with d-c. (Changing d-c voltage is more feasible today with the development of modern solid-state electronics.)

Two entrepreneurs who were active in the early development of the modern electrical system, Thomas Alva Edison (1847–1931) and George Westinghouse (1846–1914), were at opposite sides of the a-c versus d-c generation dilemma, which has been referred to as the *war of the currents*. While we recognize Edison as the individual responsible for the development of the first practical incandescent lamp, we sometimes forget that perhaps his real genius consisted of realizing that unless there was a readily available source of electricity, there would be little demand for the incandescent lamp. As a result, Edison actively pursued the generation and distribution of electricity, and in this effort he was committed to using d-c.

Nikola Tesla (1856–1943) was an inventor and physicist (a mechanical and electrical engineer) who arrived in the United States just before he turned 28. He had already achieved certain recognition for his scientific contributions, and based on this and with a letter of recommendation, he obtained a position with the Edison Machine Works company. Tesla was hired to improve the efficiency of Edison's d-c generator and motor, which were rather inefficient. Edison apparently promised Tesla a significant amount of money (suggested to have been around $1 million at today's values) if he was successful. While Tesla completed this assignment, he also began exploring a-c and its potential for providing further efficiencies.

Edison was convinced that d-c was the way to go, and he apparently gave Tesla a hard time due to his interest in a-c. He also reneged on his offer to remunerate Tesla for his accomplishments on the generator and motor designs. Believing that Edison had taken advantage of him, Tesla quit working for Edison but, without any contacts, he was forced to work as a common laborer. However, Tesla continued to work independently on his electrical experiments and eventually was able to form his own company, Tesla Electric Light and Manufacturing.

Tesla then started working with George Westinghouse, and together they began to push a-c; as they sometimes say, the rest is history. With its clear advantage in terms of its ability to change voltage, a-c won the war. With a-c, electricity could be boosted to a rather high voltage at the generating plant, thereby allowing efficient long-distance electric power transmission. The voltage could then be adjusted to a lower voltage for electric distribution to consumers and once again converted to standard voltages (e.g., 120/240 or 120/208 volts) for building delivery and use.

In retrospect, it is interesting to consider what might have happened if d-c had won. Without the ease of voltage conversion, electrical generation would have to occur relatively close to the point of use. This is what Edison pursued in his electrical system installations, such as in New York City. With electrical generation located close to the place of use, the by-product, steam, is available for use as an energy source for both space heating and cooling, such as in many areas of New York City. As a result, significant improvements in the basic efficiency of electrical generation might have been realized.

Power plants typically use steam as the motive force for generating electricity. Regardless of how this steam is produced, by burning fossil fuels or by nuclear reactors, after leaving the generator the steam must be condensed into a liquid before it can be returned to the boiler to repeat the cycle. As a result, only a portion of the energy added to the water to create the high-pressure steam necessary to run a generator is actually used by the generator. A major portion of the energy (285 watts or 970 BTU per pound of water) is the latent heat of vaporization, and this energy must be lost before the water can return to the boiler.

For this reason, the typical total operational efficiency of electricity tends to be only around 30%. Since half of

our electricity is coal generated, at such low efficiency this amounts to significant contributions to environmental pollution. Recent data indicate that coal accounts for 50.8% of all U.S. electrical generation, with oil and natural gas accounting for 3.1% and 16.7%, respectively. Nuclear power accounts for 19.7% of our electricity, with hydroelectric power and renewable energy production accounting for only slightly more than 9% of the total electrical generation (see Figure 12.8).

SOURCES OF ELECTRIC POWER

Regardless of the fuel source, when electricity is generated by steam turbines, most of the input energy is not used for production of electricity but is lost as the steam is condensed after it leaves the turbines. In addition, there are losses in distribution, even with high voltage. As a result, the overall efficiency of electrical production and distribution, as noted above, tends to be only about 30%, which, of course, cannot be discounted even with high efficiencies in terms of end use.

Figure 12.8 indicates that almost 50% of the electricity in the United States is generated in coal-burning power plants. When this percentage is combined with the amount produced by burning natural gas and petroleum, over 70% of the electricity consumed in the United States is produced in fossil fuel–based power plants, with around 20%

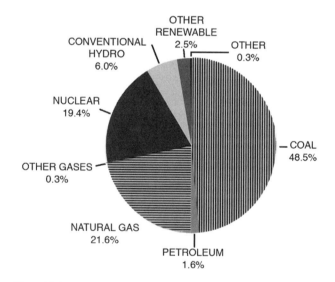

Figure 12.8 U.S. POWER GENERATION BY FUEL SOURCE AND EFFICIENCY
Based on 2007 U.S. government statistics, renewable energy sources account for around 8.8% of total power generation. Actually, a small amount of power is produced by pumped-storage hydroelectric power generation, although this process actually produces somewhat less power than is required to pump the water to the storage tanks. Generation by steam turbines, regardless of the fuel source, is inefficient, with most of the energy lost in the condensation of the steam after it leaves the turbines. There are also losses in distribution, even with high voltage. Overall efficiency tends to be only about 30%.

generated in nuclear plants. Furthermore, excluding hydroelectric power, Figure 12.8 indicates that only 2.5% of the electricity consumed in the United States is produced from renewable sources, which are typically assumed to include solar energy and wind power. With such a small percentage of U.S. power coming from renewable sources, there is clearly an opportunity for a significant increase in the proportion of electricity generation provided by renewable sources. With the potential that they both offer, solar and wind power provide attractive options. Unfortunately, since much of the sun and wind are not necessarily located near most of the areas of electricity demand, this might require major adjustments in the electricity distribution grid and development of alternative methods of energy conversion. One possibility is to convert the power obtained from the sun and wind to hydrogen. Hydrogen can be stored and distributed through pipelines, and it can be used in place of both natural gas and gasoline. Hydrogen can also produce electricity by means of electrochemical conversion in a fuel cell. However, hydrogen itself is generally obtained through the electrolysis of water, which is a critical resource in short supply in many locations, especially where there tends to be an "excess" of sun. If ocean water is available at these sites, it could be used as the source of hydrogen, and when the hydrogen is converted into electricity, whether by using it as a fuel source for combustion or in a fuel cell, pure water is the major by-product. So, hydrogen could provide a double benefit. Rather than causing serious environmental degradation, hydrogen could provide two needed resources: clean energy and water. While there are many obstacles to be overcome, generating hydrogen from solar energy or wind power could provide a source of power that could help meet the demands for electricity, even if these demands are not coincident in terms of time or location with the availability of these alternative forms of energy, sun and wind.

The continued excessive use of fossil fuels poses a number of problems that greater use of renewable sources could help solve. There are basically three problems associated with fossil fuels: they are limited resources; they possess a higher value that is not realized when serving merely as combustible fuels; and they produce serious environmental problems when they are burned, particularly by increasing atmospheric pollution and our carbon footprint.

Hydroelectric power generation is also basically solar dependent. While it is generally assumed to be a clean source of energy, hydropower can have a negative impact on our environment, particularly the way it is used today. Historically, hydropower entailed distributed, small-scale operations such as water wheels and mills. Small-scale hydroelectric plants were also popular in the early days of electrical use, but these were abandoned to achieve the benefits of scale. As a result, most hydropower today comes from large dams that, with their immense scale, can cause considerable environmental damage, although no increase in particulate matter or in the concentration of atmospheric carbon dioxide. However, there are small hydroelectric generators that can be used if there is a source of running water.

While it does not provide a significant amount of electricity today, at least in the United States, geothermal power is another possible source of energy. Although not a renewable source of energy, it produces basically no environmental pollution and consumes no nonrenewable resources. Geothermal energy comes from the heat developed and stored in the Earth from the decay of radioactive particles. This heated material, called *magma*, comprises the outer layer of the Earth's core. At certain locations the magma rises up through the surrounding mantle to the Earth's upper crust. When this magma breaks through the upper crust, this generally occurs in the form of volcanic action. But even when magma doesn't break through the Earth's upper crust, if it rises high enough, it heats groundwater, which can then be released, such as occurs with the geysers at Yellowstone National Park. Whether it emerges on its own or is pumped out, geothermal power provides a source of steam. This steam can then be used to generate electricity and for other environmental purposes.

There are three basic ways to use geothermal energy to generate electricity: dry steam, flash, and binary cycle. In the dry steam system, steam is released from the geothermal reservoir directly into the generator/turbine. With the flash system, water at high pressure and high temperature, well above boiling, is pumped out of the ground. This high-pressure, high-temperature water is then released into the generator, where it flashes into steam and turns the turbine. The binary cycle uses the heated groundwater to heat another water circuit. In this approach, the heated groundwater, which is not at a sufficient temperature or pressure to turn the turbine, is used to heat another fluid. If this secondary fluid is under reduced pressure, it will boil at a temperature less than 212° F, and the steam that is produced is used to turn the turbine.

While geothermal energy comprises only a small portion of the electricity consumed in the United States—less than 0.5% of annual use—the Geothermal Energy Association (GEA) claims that the United States is the world leader in terms of the amount of electric power generated from geothermal energy. At present, geothermal power plants produce electricity in seven states: Alaska, California, Idaho, Hawaii, New Mexico, Nevada, and Utah. GEA claims that California produces by far the most electricity from geothermal energy. Not only does it get almost 5% of its electricity from geothermal energy and produce around 85% of what is produced in the United States, the amount of geothermal energy produced in California apparently exceeds all of the geothermal energy produced worldwide.

While using less geothermal energy than California, Iceland, with its special geological conditions, has the highest percentage of its energy use, including heating as well as electricity, provided by geothermal power. There are five major geothermal power plants that produce around 25% of the electricity use in Iceland. In addition, about 90% of the space heating and hot water is produced by geothermal energy. With its significant production of electricity from hydropower, Iceland is the only country where essentially all of its energy, excluding that for transportation, comes from nonfossil fuel or nuclear sources—that is, from renewable sources.

Nuclear power currently provides about 20% of the electricity consumed in the United States. While nuclear power does not create the environmental problems associated with fossil fuels or large-scale hydropower, it has its own problems, primarily the disposal of the radioactive fuel. Given the environmental problems connected with our conventional approach to energy production, perhaps we should embrace the nuclear potential, but from a source located 93 million miles away. The amount of solar radiation available far exceeds our energy needs. The Earth's solar gain in 1 day equals around 1/100th of the annual energy used worldwide. Stated another way, the Earth receives more energy from the sun in 1 hour than all of humankind uses in a whole year.

(Obviously, this discussion of the various alternative methods of generating electricity has been rather cursory. The potential of any of these approaches for providing all or part of the electric demand for a particular project can and should be explored further. Helpful information is available from numerous sources, many of which are accessible on the Web. However, diligence is needed to ensure that any recommendations provided by these sources are legitimate and not merely self-generated endorsements.)

Electrical Usage

The amount of electricity generated or consumed is expressed in terms of energy, which is equal to power times time. Since wattage is the indication of electric power, electrical energy is denoted by the watt-hour or, more typically, by the kilowatt-hour (kWh). While there is a tendency to consider the amount of electricity required in terms of watts, to determine the energy consumption related to this wattage, it is necessary to convert this value into kilowatt-hours by multiplying the watts by the length of time that they are used. When doing this, it is important to recognize that the usage of or demand for this wattage is typically not continual. That is, the actual energy used is usually considerably less than what wattage implies, except for those electric loads that are continuous.

Utility companies charge for electricity in terms of kilowatt-hours. While this is what most consumers actually purchase, we should recognize that considerable capital investment is required in order to generate and distribute this electricity, and the utility companies, which are usually for-profit enterprises, must obtain adequate compensation for their investment. So, while most consumers—typically residential users and other small-scale operations—tend to purchase electrical energy, apparently paying merely for what they use, larger consumers must provide an adequate payment to the utility company to cover its capital investment, whether or not they actually consume any electrical energy. That is, large consumers typically have to pay a demand charge that is set at the level of electrical consumption that they might have over a period of time, say 30 minutes or even 15 minutes. This determines the capacity that the utility company must have in order to meet the demand, if it exists. That is, while there might be a reduction in the amount of fuel that the utility company must use when a large consumer has reduced its electrical consumption, the system capacity to meet the maximum electric demand must be available even when it is not used. As a result, large consumers of electricity generally must pay a major portion of their maximum electrical charge, even if considerably less electricity is used, which unfortunately means that there is little incentive to reduce consumption.

Since peak use might establish a continually high demand charge, one of the intentions of the design of an electrical system is to balance consumption so that excessive peaks do not occur. There are various ways to do this; they usually entail first attempting to lower electrical consumption by increasing efficiency and then spreading out usage so that consumption remains reasonably level over time. In some situations, if there is a period of time when the local utility company has excess generating capacity, there might be an opportunity for a reduction in charges if the electrical usage can be postponed until that time period, typically the evening, when industrial and commercial demands for electricity tend to be lower. One example of this, which does not necessarily relate to large consumers, involves the use of storage heaters, which consume electricity when there is little system demand but can release heat as it is needed, which is often long after the energy input has been discontinued.

While the control of electric demand is beyond the scope of services provided by most architects and designers, it can have a major impact on life-cycle costing and building operations. By being aware of this critical issue, we should be prepared to ensure that our consulting engineers have adequately addressed this aspect of electrical usage.

Table 12.1: PER CAPITA ELECTRICAL CONSUMPTION BY COUNTRY

	Country (Rank by Country)	Consumption per Country (kWh/year)	Consumption per capita (kWh/year)	Date of Information
1	Iceland (86)	9,312,000,000	31,147	2006
2	Norway (26)	111,500,000,000	24,011	2006
3	Finland (32)	88,270,000,000	16,850	2007
4	Canada (7)	530,000,000,000	16,279	2006
5	Qatar (76)	13,190,000,000	15,939	2006
6	Kuwait (51)	39,540,000,000	15,211	2006
7	Sweden (23)	133,600,000,000	14,769	2006
8	Luxembourg (100)	6,748,000,000	14,605	2006
9	United States (1)	3,892,000,000,000	12,924	2007
10	United Arab Emirates (41)	57,880,000,000	12,484	2006
11	Bahrain (88)	8,742,000,000	11,820	2006
12	Cayman Islands (161)	546,100,000	11,719	2007
	World	14,280,000,000,000	3,240	est. 2006
	European Union	2,711,000,000,000	5,828	est. 2006

Source: Adapted from *The World Factbook* (U.S. Central Intelligence Agency, Washington, DC. December 2003 to December 2008).

Another concern is the ability to provide power continuously. While we usually assume that the various electrical utilities are up to this task, there have been brownouts and blackouts, to say nothing of the power losses that can occur after major weather events. For example, the remnants of Hurricane Ike in 2008, which in its full power pretty much wiped out Galveston, Texas, did extensive damage in a large area of the midwestern United States. As a result, many locations experienced serious power outages that extended for some time.[2]

When normal electric service is not available, emergency power is critical for many building occupancies. To allow for proper egress, short-term power is required for fire alarms and emergency lighting. Power might also be required for fire protection systems and at times for emergency elevator operation. There is also the potential need for standby power, which provides continued operation of equipment that is critical for economic or business purposes. For example, standby power might be required for continued operation of computers and critical research equipment.

Emergency power can be provided by batteries or on-site generators. Obviously, with batteries, there is a limit to how long the backup power will last. With on-site generators, which should be able to operate for an extended period of time until normal power is again available, there might

be a delay between the time normal power is lost and the emergency power becomes operational. When situations are critical, an uninterruptible power system (UPS) might be appropriate. A UPS ensures continuous electricity service for special needs for which even a momentary power loss would have serious consequences. In such a system, power is always supplied by batteries that are kept charged by the standard electricity service and, if there is a power loss, by an on-site emergency generator. While not specifically intended for this purpose, the operation of a standard laptop computer is similar to that of a UPS.

Electrical Consumption

While it is generally assumed that the highest per capita consumption of electricity occurs in the United States, data suggest otherwise. In fact, according to the *World Factbook* from the U.S. Central Intelligence Agency, the United States ranks only ninth in per capita electrical consumption. Interestingly, the countries whose electrical consumption exceeds or generally matches that of the United States are located either in rather cold or hot climates, suggesting that their consumption is used largely for temperature control. While the United States does use considerable air conditioning, which usually relies on electricity, heating is more likely provided by burning fossil fuels. Perhaps a more important statistic is that U.S. per capita consumption is four times the world average.

Tables 12.1 and 12.2 list per capita annual electrical consumption. The listing in Table 12.1 is in order of the

---

[2]In Cincinnati, which felt the brunt of the aftermath from Hurricane Ike, 80% of the customers in the metropolitan area lost electricity, with the average outage lasting for 3 to 4 days.

Table 12.2: ELECTRICAL CONSUMPTION BY COUNTRY

	Country	Consumption per Country (kWh/year)	Consumption per capita (kWh/year)	Date of Information
1	United States	3,892,000,000,000	12,924	2007
2	China	2,859,000,000,000	2,180	2006
4	Russia	985,200,000,000	6,969	2007
5	Japan	982,500,000,000	7,702	2006
6	Germany	549,100,000,000	6,663	2006
7	Canada	530,000,000,000	16,279	2006
8	India	517,200,000,000	466	2006
9	France	447,300,000,000	7,328	2006
10	Brazil	402,200,000,000	2,117	2007
11	South Korea	368,600,000,000	7,516	2007
12	United Kingdom	348,500,000,000	5,774	2006
	World	14,280,000,000,000	3,240	est. 2006
	World Average by Country	78,330,606,630	3,240	est. 2006
	European Union	2,858,000,000,000	5,828	est. 2006

Source: Adapted from *The World Factbook* (U.S. Central Intelligence Agency, Washington, DC, December 2003 to December 2008.

countries in terms of per capita consumption, whereas the listing in Table 12.2 is in order of the total annual electrical consumption by country

In terms of total electrical consumption by country, the United States ranks first. Interestingly, China has the second highest consumption of any country, but this is due primarily to the number of people, since in terms of per capita consumption, China ranks 91st.

In the last 50 years, there has been approximately a tenfold increase in overall U.S. electrical consumption, of which about one-third is for residential use. The average monthly consumption per U.S. household is 877 kWh, although this varies according to the geographic location. The highest consumption is in the southeastern portion of the country, where there is a very high demand for air conditioning, and the lowest, interestingly, is in New England, with a ratio of almost 2:1. Of this usage, 35% is for air conditioning, heating, and hot water, which tends to support the previously mentioned notion that electrical use in countries with very high per capita consumption is in part for space conditioning. Table 12.3 lists the U.S. residential electrical consumption in terms of the percentage allocated for various uses.

Table 12.4 shows usage if gas rather than electricity is used for domestic hot water heating, clothes drying, and range-top cooking.

Electric rates in the United States, particularly for residential use, have been increasing significantly with rising energy costs. In the last 5 years, there has been approximately a 25% increase nationally, although some regions have had a much larger increase and others less. The difference in the charge for electricity service can change significantly among different governmental jurisdictions, even if these are essentially at the same location, and among different utility companies.

The rising costs for electricity should encourage less usage and, when it is used, greater efficiency. However, even when the end use of electricity is efficient, the overall efficiency of use is limited by the fact that power generation and distribution tend to be only around 30% efficient. Recognizing this, we should understand that there are many reasons to reduce our use of electricity and perhaps switch to methods of electrical generation that do not have as negative an effect on the environment as do most current methods.

Table 12.3: RESIDENTIAL CONSUMPTION OF ELECTRICITY (2001)

Use	Percent Usage
Air Conditioning	16.0
Space Heating	10.2
Water Heating	9.1
Refrigerators	13.7
Lighting	8.8
Clothes Dryers	5.8
Televisions	4.4
Cooking	5.3
Other	25.8

Source: Adapted from information from the *Residential Energy Consumption Surveys* of 1993 and 2001 by the Office of Energy Markets and End Use, U.S. Energy Information Administration, Washington, DC.

Table 12.4: RESIDENTIAL CONSUMPTION OF ELECTRICITY— ADJUSTED FOR USE OF GAS

Use	Percent Usage
Air Conditioning	19.8%
Space Heating	12.6%
Refrigerators	16.9%
Lighting	10.9%
Televisions	5.4%
Cooking	2.5%
Other	31.9%

Note: Residential consumption is adjusted for using gas rather than electricity for various applications.

Source: Adapted from information from the *Residential Energy Consumption Surveys* of 1993 and 2001 by the Office of Energy Markets and End Use, U.S. Energy Information Administration, Washington, DC.

Electric Regulations

The National Electric Code (NEC), which is the basic electric code for most jurisdictions, regulates most electrical applications. The NEC is published by the National Fire Protection Association (NFPA).

Generation of Electric Power

Today most electricity is generated at rather large-capacity central power plants. In the United States, the average power plant has a generating capacity of 750 to 1000 megawatts (MW). Since 1 megawatt is equal to 1 million or 10^6 watts, this means that the typical power plant has a capacity of 750 million to 1 billion watts. The largest coal-burning power plant has a capacity of 4 gigawatts (GW) or 4 billion watts, and the largest nuclear power plant has a capacity more than twice this size.

These capacities are a long way from those of the first central electrical generating plant, the Pearl Street Station built by Thomas Edison and his Edison Electric Illuminating Company of New York. This plant included six generators, each with a capacity of 100 kilowatts,[3] for a total capacity that was less than 1/1000th that of the typical generating plant today. The Pearl Street Station went on line on September 4, 1882, and initially supplied 4400 lamps. The plant continued to operate for 8 years.

Since the plant generated and distributed d-c, the distribution was limited to a one-sixth-square-mile area. Edison,

who had initially worked with the telegraph, intentionally chose not to add to the maze of aboveground wiring and committed to underground distribution. This, of course, posed problems in terms of how to protect the wires. The solution was to use heavy copper wire placed in wooden troughs that were buried underground. Initially, Edison tried to insulate the copper with tar, but when this system tended to break down, he developed a complex procedure of wrapping the copper with muslin that was then coated with a mixture of paraffin wax, tar, linseed oil, and asphalt. Along with the wires, by-product steam from the generators was also distributed, making this installation not only the first commercially viable, central electrical generation system, but also the first cogeneration system that utilized both the electric power and steam developed by the facility. Unfortunately, while central electrical generation and distribution continued to develop and expand, cogeneration did not, partially because the expansion of electrical distribution relied on a switch from d-c, which Edison used, to a-c, which was endorsed by Westinghouse and Tesla.

In the contest between Edison and Westinghouse over which electric current, d-c or a-c, should be used, sometimes referred to as the *war of current*, Edison claimed that a-c was unsafe, primarily because it relied on high voltage to reduce losses over long distribution lines. In his tactic of using fear in support of d-c, attempting to associate a-c with danger and death, he even seems to have become involved with the way electrocution would be handled. At the time, New York was considering switching from hanging to the electric chair for its executions.

The inventor of the electric chair, Harold Brown, had also expressed concern over the safety of a-c. Not to miss an opportunity, Edison and Brown linked up, and with this support, Brown undertook various experiments that demonstrated that in a comparison between a-c and d-c, a dog could survive exposure to 1000 volts of d-c but would be killed by only 800 volts of a-c. Based on these experiments, Edison, who apparently objected to capital punishment, then endorsed electrocution, particularly if a-c was used. After New York adopted and used electrocution, Edison used this unique application of electricity as a further charge in his arsenal of fear against a-c—claiming that a-c clearly killed.[4]

Actually, Edison was correct in that a-c is often distributed at very high voltages, which are clearly more dangerous than low voltages, recognizing that voltage is an indication of the electromotive force. However, this criticism is somewhat unfair since the potential ability of a-c to adjust the voltage, increasing it for distribution and then lowering it when used near people, is necessary to establish

---

[3]Based on information provided by the Consolidated Edison Company of New York (Con Edison), the ultimate successor to the Edison Electric Illuminating Company, on its Web page, http://www.coned.com/.

[4]R. Moran, "The Strange Origins of the Electric Chair," *Focus Magazine, The Boston Sunday Globe*, August 5, 1990.

a major electrical distribution system. Safety should always be a factor, but the higher the voltage, the lower the amperage, which improves efficiency.

The Niagara Falls Power Company Competition

The war of current was ultimately played out at Niagara Falls, New York, with the development of what is likely the earliest large-scale hydroelectric plant, which went online on August 26, 1895. The power of Niagara Falls had been used as a source of energy for some time; however, this was basically for mechanical power. The water from the upper Niagara River had been diverted through a number of channels and was used to turn several water wheels that, through complex belting systems, then operated machinery. With the development of electricity, it became apparent that the energy of the falls could be used to generate electric power and that this could then be distributed farther than was possible with the belting systems.

While initially a small d-c generator was installed, with the produced electricity used in the general vicinity of the falls, the magnitude of the power that was possible from the falls led to a major competition for hydroelectric generation that involved a number of individuals including Edison, Tesla, Westinghouse, and even Lord Kelvin, along with financiers such as J.P. Morgan, John Jacob Astor, Edward Dean Adams, and William K. Vanderbilt. The goal was to develop an electrical generating and distribution system that could power not only the local Niagara community but also the City of Buffalo, as far as 26 miles away. While ultimately a-c won out, primarily because it was the only way that electrical energy could be distributed over such a long distance, the supporters of d-c, primarily Edison, managed to extend the fight for quite some time. Of course, with the various prominent financiers also involved, some of this extended confrontation was motivated by attempts to establish control. As expressed by Quentin Skrabec in his book on Westinghouse, "The Niagara project [was] one of the greatest competitive battles in the annals of American business."[5]

Lord William Thomson Kelvin (1824–1907), the renowned Scottish mathematician and physicist, was instrumental in ultimately resolving the argument between a-c and d-c. He was a strong proponent of d-c, and his position was used to help undermine the adoption of a-c, but then in 1893, in the midst of the Niagara "debate," Lord Kelvin switched positions and advocated for a-c. With his support, the logic of using a-c carried the argument and Westinghouse a-c generators were selected to be used. While Westinghouse had committed to two-phase gen-

eration, the selection was for poly-phase or three-phase generation, which is now the standard.

In 1890, Edison had formed the Edison General Electric Company, which then merged with the Thomson-Houston Company to form the General Electric Company. While this new entity continued as the major manufacturer of Edison's generators and other electrical devices, following the merger Edison's management position was essentially eliminated. Without Edison's dominance, during the period of exploration between a-c and d-c, General Electric seems to have "hedged its bets" and began developing an a-c generator and other a-c-related equipment. As such, General Electric was a competitor of Westinghouse for the contract to build the a-c generators for the Niagara Falls Power Company. While it did not get this contract, it did get the contract for building the transformers to step up the voltage of the generated power, from 2000 volts to 10,000 volts to be fed into the distribution lines. So, while Edison had fought against a-c, using the somewhat legitimate argument that it was dangerous because of the high voltages associated with it, the company that he started fought for and won the contract for the transformers used at Niagara Falls, which produced the high voltages that Edison apparently feared and depended on the selection of a-c as the current to be used.

While the capacity of Edison's Pearl Street Station was around 600 kW, the initial capacity of the Niagara Falls Power Company's hydroelectric plant was around 37,000 kW. This was provided by 10 Westinghouse a-c generators, each with an output of 5000 horsepower. With power conversion of 1 horsepower equaling 746 watts, each of the generators developed 3730 watts of power. Obviously, the Niagara Falls hydroelectric plant was quite large,[6] but a number of smaller hydroelectric plants were also quite prevalent in the early days of electrification. Unfortunately, most of these smaller plants, which sometimes supplied only single users, were abandoned for the apparent convenience of central power generation, and typically, these environmentally responsive systems were replaced with pollution-emitting, coal-burning power plants.

Renewable Power

Hydroelectric Power

There are a number of large hydroelectric installations in the United States and across the world. In the United States, the largest and second largest dam and hydroelectric plants

---

[5]Q.R. Skrabec, *George Westinghouse: Gentle Genius* (Algora Publishing, New York, 2006), p. 177.

[6]The current capacity of the hydroelectric plants at Niagara Falls is 2,700,000 kW on the U.S. side and 2,338,000 kW on the Canadian side. Combined, this is about 135 times the capacity of the initial plant that went online in 1895.

Figure 12.9 DAM AT OLD STURBRIDGE VILLAGE
A vertical drop in water was established on the Wright family farm in 1795 with the construction of the millpond and a dam. This difference in elevation, which remains today at approximately 6 to 8 feet, depending on the water levels, was used to power a gristmill and a sawmill. They both continue to exist and operate on water power, but in the 1980s another use of the water power was added —two hydroelectric generators.

are the Grand Coulee Dam (6800 MW) and the Glen Canyon Dam (1300 MW).[7] When it was built in 1936, Hoover Dam, located 35 miles from Las Vegas, was both the largest concrete structure and the largest electric-power generating plant in the world. Its current generating capacity is around 2000 MW.

Old Sturbridge Village in Sturbridge, Massachusetts, is a living museum that re-creates life in rural New England from the late 1700s to the mid-1800s. This historic museum is located on a farm that was owned by the Wright family and includes the original sawmill and gristmill, as well as a millpond that was dug in 1795 and then repaired and improved in 1846. The Wright millpond dam, which is shown in Figure 12.9, had a water drop of about 6 to 8 feet. While significantly less than the drop at Niagara Falls (70–173 feet) or at other major hydroelectric plants, this drop is more than adequate for electrical generation. In fact, in addition to continuing to power the sawmill and gristmill, which are shown in the left-hand image in Figure 12.10, today this historic millpond generates electricity for 50 local households. This is accomplished by two small hydroelectric generators that can be observed in the right-hand image in Figure 12.10.

Actually, with a head of around 5 feet and a flow rate of at least 40 GPM, it is possible to generate enough power

24 hours per day, 7 days a week, to meet the electrical needs of a single-family residence, although a 10-foot drop and a 100-GPM flow are often recommended. Obviously, the amount of power that can be produced is based on the size and efficiency of the generator; the pressure available from the head of water, which is determined by the drop of the water; and the water flow, with the critical factors being essentially the combined effects of head and flow. As long as the conditions fall within the limits of the particular units, an increased flow can usually compensate for a low head, and vice versa.

A micro-hydroelectric system can deliver 120/240-volt a-c electric current to meet the power needs of a small building, such as an individual residence. If the water supply is not sufficient to meet the peak electric demands, it is possible to use a relatively small volume of water to generate d-c current at low voltage, often 12 volts, although both 24 and 48 volts are sometimes used. With this arrangement, the power would be generated continuously and used to charge batteries from which current can be drawn as needed. It is also possible to push the current, which would have to be generated at or converted to 60 cycles, 120 volts, into the electric grid as it is produced and then to draw electricity from the grid as needed. With this method, batteries are not necessary, but there has to be a connection to the electric grid. As the electricity produced on-site is added to the grid, the electric meter would flow backward; then, when current is drawn from the grid, the meter would flow forward.

The most common micro-hydrogenerator relies on the Pelton wheel or turbine, which is essentially a series of cups attached to a hub. With a jet of water flowing into the cups, the resulting forces cause the turbine to spin, and this rotational force is then used to turn the micro-generator.

Often when the natural water flow is reduced, which might occur during the drier periods of summer, there is likely to be a significant amount of available sun. As a result, a system that combines a hydroelectric generator and an array of photovoltaic solar cells should be able to meet the electricity demand, with the two methods balancing each other as the availability of the renewable sources changes.

Wind Power

Wind, which has been used since ancient times as a source of power, is another potential means for generating electricity. Somewhat similar to hydroelectric power, wind power can be produced by micro units or at major wind farms that use large wind generators. In the United States, wind power currently produces over 10,000 MW of electricity, and the Department of Energy has announced the

---

[7]While the Grand Coulee Dam is the largest hydroelectric plant in the United States, it is only the fourth largest producer in the world. The three top producers of hydroelectric power are the Three Gorges Dam in China (20 MW), the Guri Dam in Venezuela (10,000 MW), and the Itaipu Dam on the border between Paraguay and Brazil (12,500 MW) (information from the U.S. Department of the Interior, Bureau of Reclamation).

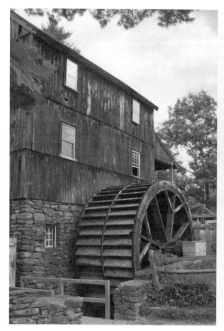 

Figure 12.10 HISTORIC GRISTMILL AND HYDROELECTRIC GENERATORS

At Old Sturbridge Village there is an interesting contrast in water power applications. The drop in water level is used to operate an historic gristmill and two modern hydroelectric generators that develop 70 kW of electricity that can supply electricity to 50 households in the local community. One of the hydroelectric generators is visible in the center of the circle.

goal of meeting 6% of the total U.S. electric demand by wind power by 2020.

While many people object to using modern wind turbines, particularly in wind farms, because of their visual impact on the environment, related historical structures that had basically the same purpose, providing power, and did so in a mechanically expressive form, are often revered for their beauty, even by those who disparage the modern wind turbine. Figure 12.11 shows several well-known historic "windmills," along with a modern wind turbine that is used to general electricity on Prince Edward Island. Additional historic windmills are shown in Figure 12.15.

As with hydropower, the electrical output of a wind turbine depends on the size of the turbine and the wind speed. Turbines are now available in a range of power ratings, from around 250 watts to over 5 MW (see Figure 12.12).

VENETIAN WINDMILL, CRETE

WIND PUMPS, ZAANDIJK, HOLLAND

WINDMILL, CRETE

WIND TURBINE, PRINCE EDWARD ISLAND

Figure 12.11 HISTORIC WIND POWER STRUCTURES AND A WIND TURBINE AT PEI

While some people object to wind turbines because of their impact on the natural beauty of the environment, historic structures built to harness the power of the wind have been appreciated for their extraordinary beauty and charm.

Figure 12.12 WIND POWER AT NORTH CAPE, PRINCE EDWARD ISLAND
On Prince Edward Island, Canada, around 10% of the electric power is currently generated by wind power. North Cape, which is an experimental facility, has a capacity of more than 10.5 MW of power, which is enough to power over 4000 homes. The wind farm was developed in two phases, the first in 2001 and the second in 2003, with each having a capacity of 5.28 MW.

According to the American Wind Energy Association (AWEA), a 10-kW turbine can generate about 10,000 kWh over a year, which should be quite adequate to meet the electric demands of a typical single-family residence. Of course, the turbine size should be based on the electric demand of the particular residence or occupancy, and with reasonable conservation, a wind turbine with a capacity of 2 to 6 kW might be sufficient. This is somewhat similar to what generally should be done when developing an on-site water collection system: in recognition of the limitations of on-site power generation, it makes sense to reduce the electric demand that is generally set on the assumption of an unlimited source of power from a central power utility.

Smaller wind turbines usually require an annual average wind speed of at least 9 MPH. With larger turbines, such as those used in wind farms, a higher average wind speed is required, typically 13 MPH or more.[8]

In addition to the need to meet the annual average wind speeds, the location and placement of the wind turbine are critical. With larger turbines, this is determined in large part by the physical size of the units themselves, but with the smaller turbines that might be used for a single small structure, location and placement are more critical. AWEA recommends that a minimum area of 1 acre be provided for each wind turbine, with the turbine installed at least 30 feet above any physical wind barrier within a 500-foot radius, which encompasses an area of almost 20 acres. These wind barriers can include topography and vegetation as well as physical structures. The elevation of the turbine is critical since wind speeds increase at higher elevations, and wind power is based on the cube of the wind speed. So, a small increase in wind speed can produce a significant increase in wind power (see Figure 12.13).

While wind power can effectively generate electricity,[9] wind turbines can also create noise and vibration. Both of these potential problems, which tend to increase with increased wind velocity and turbine speed, vary according to the type of turbine used. These problems are exacerbated if the turbine is installed directly on the roof of a structure.

The thought that a turbine might be installed on a roof seems contrary to the recommendation that the turbine be 30 feet above any surrounding wind barrier. However, if the building is essentially an isolated freestanding structure and the aerodynamics are proper, the building can be considered part of the elevating support structure for the turbine. In fact, depending on the form of the building, the effect might be to increase the wind velocity at the turbine. This is likely with a pitched roof that deflects the wind without creating significant turbulence.

While most wind turbines rotate on a horizontal axis, there are turbines that are configured with a vertical axis, predominantly the Savonius and Darrieus turbines (see Figure 12.14). The Savonius turbine is named after Sigurd Savonius, the Finnish engineer who developed it in the 1920s, although apparently there were previous attempts to develop a similar type of turbine. The Darrieus turbine is named after Georges Jean Marie Darrieus, a French

---

[8] Adapted from information from AWEA.

[9] Before rushing to embrace wind power as a way to meet our electricity demands, we should consider a few issues. The major issue is whether or not the location has sufficient wind to justify this approach. The U.S. Department of Energy's (DOE) Web page for Energy Efficiency and Renewable Energy (http://www.eere.energy.gov/) provides a link to information on the potential for wind power for different U.S. locations, as well as links to other interesting information on renewable energy. For many if not most locations, wind is perhaps even less dependable than sunlight as a source of energy. Many people find wind generators to be visually distracting. While some people think that wind generators are ugly, others consider them attractive, as well as an effective means of reducing some of the more serious forms of environmental pollution. Fortunately, as indicated in the DOE Web page, there are locations with relatively consistent wind that are not close to areas where the noise and/or the visual appearance of wind generators will be a distraction.

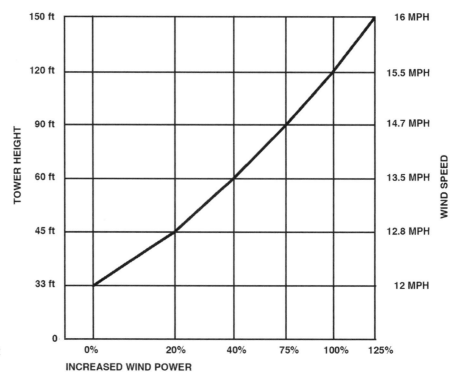

Figure 12.13 WIND POWER BASED ON TOWER HEIGHT
Wind power is related to the cube of the wind velocity, and as the elevation increases, the velocity tends to increase. While the increase in height, shown on the left, might result in only a modest increase in wind speed, shown on the right, because power is related to the cube of velocity, these limited wind-speed increases result in a significant increase in wind power.

Figure 12.14 VERTICAL WIND TURBINES
While traditionally wind power is developed from a unit that uses a horizontal axis of rotation, vertical wind turbines are also available. These do not need to be adjusted with changes in the direction of the wind. The Darrieus turbine, shown on the left, does not start easily, particularly at low velocities, whereas the Savonius turbine, shown on the right, begins spinning at low wind speeds. As a result, these turbines are often combined to generate wind power. The image of the Darrieus wind turbine is by the author. The image of the Savonius wind turbine is derived from an image by Eric Scheide and used with permission.

DARRIEUS WIND TURBINE

SAVONIUS WIND TURBINE

aeronautical engineer who proposed this design in the 1930s.

One advantage of the vertical-axis turbines is that wind direction is not an issue. With horizontal-axis turbines the blades must be directed into the wind. When the prevailing breezes come from a particular direction, such as on Crete (see Figure 12.11) and other Greek islands, the orientation need not change, but when the breeze direction changes, a means of reorienting the blades is necessary. Sometimes this was done manually, but ways were also found to use wind power itself to reorient the blades. Sometimes, as with most modern wind turbines, reorientation involved only the blades, but the more traditional approach was to turn the top of the structure, and sometimes the whole structure was rotated (see Figure 12.15).

Solar Power

In addition to water power and wind power, solar power is a way of producing electricity, and this approach is often appropriate at the scale of the individual building. In terms of electricity, solar power typically implies the use

EAST ANGLIA   **HASTINGS**   **NEAR HASTINGS**

Figure 12.15 TURNING THE BLADES INTO THE WIND

These three English windmills show various ways of turning the blades into the wind. As shown left to right, these include: manually rotate the top of the tower, allow wind that rotates the rear wheel to rotate the top, and allow the rear wheel to rotate the whole structure.

Figure 12.16 PHOTOVOLTAIC ARRAY

The individual PV cell, which is around 4 inches square, typically develops around 1 volt. To produce 12-volt electricity, 12 cells are joined together in a module, and to develop usable current, the 12-volt modules are assembled together in an array.

of photovoltaic cells, although it is also possible to use this extraordinary source of energy in other ways.

Albert Einstein initially explained the photoelectric effect in 1905, and this potential source of energy was explored by a number of people and organizations. In the 1950s, Bell Laboratories studied the photoelectric effect as a potential way to provide electric power for remote communication systems. Based on their work, silicon cells emerged as an effective material that could, when used in the crystalline form that was treated with impurities to adjust the electron counts, generate a substantial voltage, which then was at around 6%.[10] With this improved efficiency and the development of a means of harnessing the output of these cells, the photoelectric effect evolved into a means of producing a usable electric current, and when it serves this purpose, it is referred to as the *photovoltaic effect* or simply *photovoltaics* (PV).

These early silicon cells required considerable energy to grow the silicon crystals and then to transform them into thin wafers that were doped, typically with boron and phosphorus, to develop the p-type and n-type surface characteristics. The energy required to prepare the photovoltaic

cells, particularly with the low output efficiency, tended to exceed the amount of power that they could be expected to generate in their lifetime, which was assumed to be about 20 years.[11] More recently, the process of generating the silicon crystals has changed and the operational efficiency has increased, making PV cells a reasonable potential source of electric power (see Figure 12.16).

The PV cells available today are generally made from amorphous silicon and tend to have an efficiency that ranges from about 10% to 18%. Some special cells have been produced for research purposes that are in the high 20% range, although the usual average efficiency is 14%. This cell efficiency relates to an overall module efficiency of captured sunlight to d-c energy of 11% to 12%.

With PV cells producing 12-volt d-c, the output can be readily stored in a battery array, but for application, this electric power often needs to be converted into 120-volt a-c, which can be accomplished by a solid-state inverter. With the photovoltaic output converted to 120-volt, 60-cycle a-c, it is also possible to link the photovoltaic-generated power with the electric grid, which can avoid the need for

[10]Solar Energy International, *Photovoltaics, Design and Installation Manual* (New Society Publishers, Gabriola Island, BC, Canada, 2004), p. 2.

[11]The lifetime of a cell is based primarily on the effects of environmental pollution on the doping and electrical connections rather than on the silicon crystal.

on-site storage of electricity. When the PV power exceeds the electric demand, the excess current can be fed into the electric grid, reversing the direction of the meter. While there are various ways that this can be handled, essentially it establishes an electric savings account from which electricity can be withdrawn if the demand exceeds the PV generation. This arrangement is also possible with both hydropower units and wind turbines.

In some locations, this exchange to and from the electric grid is handled equally, relying solely on the net current flow to determine any charges or credits. In other locations, where a considerable capital investment is necessary for the electric utility to supply electricity to its customers, the rate of exchange varies as the current flows in different directions through the meter. In these locations, the rate per kilowatt-hour is higher for the electricity purchased from the utility than for that purchased by the utility.

ELECTRICAL TRANSMISSION AND DISTRIBUTION

Figure 12.17 shows a schematic diagram of an electrical distribution system, from power plant to ultimate users. Power plants typically produce three-phase electricity at around 25,000 volts (25 kV). This electricity is then boosted up to a higher voltage, usually 110 kV or higher, sometimes up to 400 kV. This extra-high voltage (EHV), three-phase electricity is then sent via transmission wires to substations located in the general area of utilization (see Figure 12.18). The portion of the electrical distribution network that provides bulk transfer of electric power from the power plant to the substation is referred to as *electric power transmission*. At the substation the voltage is lowered, and the electricity is then sent through a number of different lines.

Electric distribution is actually the name of the portion of the electric network between the substation and the ultimate consumers, although there are generally two distribution segments, primary and secondary. *Primary distribution* is the portion of the electric distribution that runs from the electrical substation to the final step-down transformer. *Secondary distribution* is the portion from this final step that is then distributed to the consumer. The voltage in the primary distribution portion of the network will be lower than the voltage used for power transmission but higher than what is safe for use. The range of primary electric distribution voltage is usually between 2.4 and 35 kV.

Electric service to industrial and commercial structures that have a large electric demand is generally provided with three-phase electric service at the elevated primary-distribution voltage. In these situations, it is typically up to the consumer to reduce this service to the voltage of use, which means that the step-down transformers are the responsibility of these industrial or commercial users. On the other hand, customers with normal electric demands are provided with 120/240-volt service, usually single phase. For these customers, the higher voltage in the primary distribution portion of the network is reduced to the standard 120/240 volts by the utility company, and then this lower-voltage electricity is supplied to the customer via secondary distribution. With the lower voltage, however, the length of this secondary distribution should be limited to avoid excessive power loss. As a result, typically there are numerous secondary distribution circuits coming off of a primary distribution circuit, with each secondary distribution circuit serving only a few small customers.

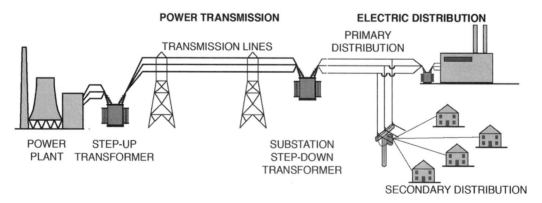

Figure 12.17 ELECTRICAL DISTRIBUTION DIAGRAM
An electrical distribution network is usually divided into various segments. The first segment is between the power plant and the step-down substation, and the electricity is at extra-high voltage. At the substation the voltage is reduced, and the electricity is then sent through the distribution segment, which might be further divided into primary distribution at the initial step-down voltage and secondary distribution at the standard service voltage.

Figure 12.18 POWER TRANSMISSION LINES
These power transmission lines are located on the Arizona side of Hoover Dam. As is typical, there are three lines, one for each phase of electricity generated. In addition to the three power lines, there might be an additional line or, as shown here, two. These are essentially grounded wires intended as lightning arresters. Power transmission lines are sometimes called *high-tension* lines, based on the historical use of "tension" as a term for electrical pressure or voltage.

The transformers used to step down the primary distribution voltage to the 120/240 volts delivered through the secondary distribution are generally pole mounted. When underground electric service is provided, the transformers are often located at grade, and these might belong to the customer rather than to the utility company. Even if the utility company provides these transformers, the installation of the underground service is typically the responsibility of the customer, whereas the utility company usually provides overhead service to the building without charge to the customer.

The electric distribution portion of the overall electric network handles all three phases of electricity, although each of these phases can be distributed separately. When the distribution includes three wires, all three phases are accessible, but when there is only one wire, only single phase is possible. With this approach, each phase of the generated electricity is distributed to a different but comparable service area, to balance the use of all three phases of electricity.

Electrical Distribution Transformers

Two types of transformers are typically used to adjust voltage between the primary and secondary distribution: a wye transformer and a delta transformer. When three-phase service is required, a wye transformer is used, and when single-phase service is adequate—which it is for most small-scale installations—a delta transformer is used to develop a service voltage of basically 120/240 volts.

In addition to changing the voltage, a transformer can "split" the voltage. That is, it can provide two voltages—one between two hot wires and one between a hot wire and ground (the neutral wire). With a delta transformer, the typical split is in a ratio of 1:2, such as 120/240 volts, but with a wye transformer, the split follows the basic geometry of the transformer, establishing a ratio of 1:1.732. If, as shown in Figure 12.19, the connection between a hot node and ground is 120 volts, the voltage between two hot nodes of a wye transformer will be 208 volts (120 V × 1.72 = 208 V).

As indicated in Figure 12.20, the transfer of the primary voltage with a three-phase wye transformer follows the geometry of the wye and results in a ratio based on twice the cosine of 30°. This transformer is primarily used when three-phase electricity is required, although it is not restricted to these conditions. A voltage of 120/208 volts can be used even when only single-phase service is required. However, care should be taken that appliances that require 240 volts are not connected to 208 volts and vice versa. While voltages of 220, 230, and 240 volts, like voltages of 110, 115, or 120 volts, can reasonably be exchanged for each other, this exchange is not appropriate between 208 and 240 volts. Note that 208-volt motors should not be used on 240-volt service, nor should 240-volt motors be used on 208-volt service. The appropriate voltage, 240 or 208 volts, should be used with appliances such as ovens. If not, the temperature settings will not be correct.

Sometimes the wye transformer is used to produce 277/480-volt service (see Figure 12.21). This voltage split

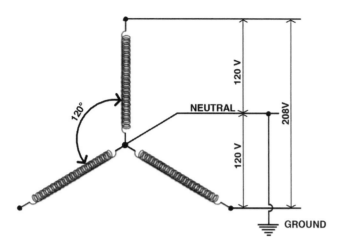

Figure 12.19 WYE TRANSFORMER FOR 120/208-VOLT SERVICE
This diagram shows the typical arrangement for a wye transformer used to provide the standard end-use 120/208 voltage used with three-phase electricity. The wye transformer is generally used for industrial applications and other occupancies that require major power. Elevators are an example of such a requirement, and as a result, 120/208 voltage is often the electric service provided to office buildings and large apartments buildings.

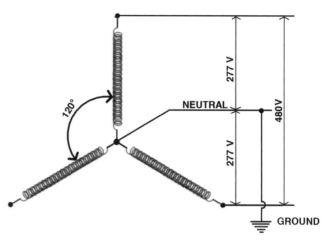

Figure 12.21 WYE TRANSFORMER FOR 277/480-VOLT SERVICE
The wye transformer, which is used with three-phase electricity, is generally used for industrial applications and other occupancies that require major power. When there is a major use of fluorescent lighting, 277/480 voltage is often produced since the 277 volts can be used for the lighting.

provides some advantage when there is a lot of fluorescent lighting. Higher voltage can reduce the power loss that is likely to exist in large buildings that have long runs for the lighting circuits. It can also reduce the energy loss associated with standard fluorescent ballasts. The "double voltage" from the wye transformer developing 277 volts is single-phase, 480 volts, which might be appro-

priate for certain applications. If there are motors, these can be three-phase (3 Ø), 480-volt motors. If 120-volt service is required, as is usual for most buildings, this can be readily obtained from the 480-volt single-phase circuit by step-down transformers located where appropriate, either centrally or distributed.

A delta transformer is generally used to adjust the voltage with single-phase electricity. With this transformer, the voltage between one phase and the neutral or ground is one-half of the voltage between two phases of the three-phase distribution.

As noted in Figure 12.22, each leg of the delta transformer is formed by connecting two of the three phases of current and can deliver 240 volts. 240 volts can then be divided into two 120-volt circuits by providing a neutral that is connected to the midpoint of the coil and is grounded. Figure 12.23 is a more fully developed diagram

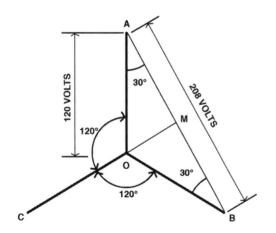

Figure 12.20 WYE TRANSFORMER STRUCTURE DIAGRAM
Since there are three phases in the circle, each phase has a 120° angle, so angle AOB is 120°. If a line is drawn from A to B, forming an isosceles triangle, the two new angles, AOM and OBM, are both 30° and angles OMA and OMB are both right angles, or 90°. The length of line AM is equal to cosine 30° times line AO. Similarly, the length of line BM is equal to cosine 30° times line BO. But since line AO and line BO are both equal and graphically represent 120 volts, line AMB, which represents the voltage to be obtained by connecting two phases, graphically shows that this voltage is twice 120 volts times cosine 30°. Since cosine 30° equals 0.867, twice this value is 1.732, which times 120 volts equals 208 volts.

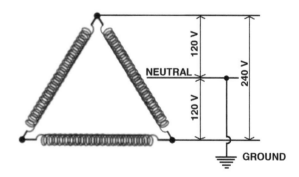

Figure 12.22 DELTA TRANSFORMER FOR 120/240-VOLT SERVICE
The delta transformer is the basic transformer used with single-phase electricity, although the source of current is typically a connection between two phases of the three-phase distribution.

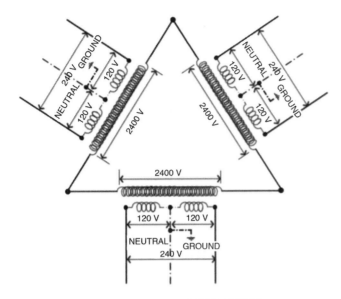

Figure 12.23 EXPANDED DELTA TRANSFORMER DIAGRAM
This expanded diagram of the delta transformer shows how each leg can be divided into split voltage. Of course, while each leg is shown at 120/240 volts, the voltage from the different legs could be different.

of a delta transformer, with all three phases of current being adjusted to 120/240 volts. We should remember that rather than 120/240 volts, the transformer could produce 110/220, 115/230, or even 127/254 volts.

When electricity is transmitted from the generating plant to a substation, there are three wires, one for each phase of the generated electricity. These three wires are quite obvious, as can be seen in Figure 12.18, but there is also usually a fourth wire, which is grounded and serves as a lighting arrester. At the substation, the power-transmission voltage is lowered by a transformer, although there are often several transformers involved with larger substations. As shown in the transformer diagrams, the transformers rely on the electric current flowing between two phases to establish a lower-voltage current. With three such connections, again there are three phases of electricity. After the substation, electric distribution also involves three wires, one for each phase, but these wires do not always run together. When they do, the next step-down

transformer uses the current between two phases, as in the substation. When only one distribution wire is accessible, this wire is actually a link between two phases, so a transformer can develop current at a different voltage. In a sense, a single wire is simply one leg of the three-phase transformer, most easily seen in terms of a delta transformer (see Figure 12.24)

Power transmission generally entails four wires, one for each of the three phases and the grounded lightning arrester. Interestingly, the single-phase electric distribution within a structure also uses four wires. In many ways, the purpose of the fourth wire is similar for both systems. In building distribution, this fourth wire is the ground that is not normally intended to carry any current. It provides a safety feature. If there is an electric "leak," it will be carried to ground, hopefully opening the circuit protection, the fuse or breaker.

The other three wires are the two hot wires and one neutral wire. These wires are intended to carry an electric current, although in a truly balanced system the neutral wire would not. The neutral wire is connected to ground, and the electric potential between it and either of the hot wires is typically 120 volts. The potential between the two hot wires is 240 volts, which, of course, is double the 120 volts. This higher voltage is used for appliances that demand more power since this can be provided with only half as much current at 240 volts as at 120 volts.

For certain 240-volt applications, the neutral wire is not necessary since it will not carry any current. The current flow is merely between the two hot wires. However, many 240-volt appliances also have some 120-volt applications. For example, while the heating elements in an electric stove rely on only 240 volts, the oven light and the clock need 120 volts. Similarly, a 240-volt electric clothes dryer needs 120 volts for its controls, light, and drum motor.

Electric Ground

As suggested by Figure 12.25, the current in an electric circuit flows either between two hot wires or between a hot

Figure 12.24 DELTA TRANSFORMER FOR 120/240-VOLT SERVICE FROM A SINGLE WIRE
Even when only one distribution wire is accessible, this wire is actually connected between two phases of the generated power. As such, various takeoffs from this line will deliver single-phase current at the desired voltage, which is typically 120/240 volts.

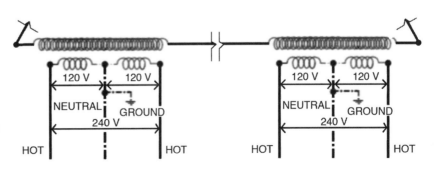

Figure 12.25 STANDARD A-C VOLTAGES
An electric circuit that runs between the two hot wires will have an electric potential of 240 volts. A circuit that runs between either of the hot wires and the neutral will have an electric potential of 120 volts.

wire and ground. In a single-phase circuit coming from a delta transformer, which is what is used in most residential and small-scale structures, the hot-to-hot connection provides double the voltage of the hot-to-ground connection, 240 volts versus 120 volts.

In an electric circuit, ground is actually ground, and one way to develop the electric potential is by connecting a hot wire to ground. Since the use of the electric potential occurs within some device, the device is connected to both a hot wire and a neutral wire that is actually connected to the ground. Although both this neutral wire and the ground wire run from the device to ground, they are quite different. In a 120-volt circuit, the neutral wire carries a current to ground when the connected electrical device is in operation; therefore, this wire must be insulated similarly to the hot wire. The ground wire, on the other hand, is not necessarily insulated. It is not intended to carry any current unless there is a problem, and then the intention is that the electric flow will be sufficient to cut off the power supply by opening the circuit breaker or "blowing" the fuse on the hot wire. When the ground wire is insulated, it is color coded green.

Both wires, the neutral and the ground, are connected in the electric panel to a conductor that is physically extended into the ground. The physical connection to ground is by means of what the NEC refers to as a *grounding electrode*, and in most installations, two grounding electrodes are now required. The traditional way of making the ground connection is to connect the ground conductor from the electric panel box to the water supply pipe on the supply side of the water meter, assuming that the meter is located in the structure. To serve as a grounding electrode, the water supply line must be an underground metal pipe, usually copper, that is in direct contact with the earth for at least 10 feet. Obviously, if a plastic pipe is used to supply the water, it cannot serve as an electric ground.

The ground conductor must be connected to the water supply line no more than 5 feet from the point of entrance into the structure. While this limits the exposed length of run that will carry current, we might be concerned that we could get an electrical shock if we were to touch that portion of the pipe. However, even though the pipe is

exposed and is carrying current, it should provide a better ground conductor than what we would offer even if we were grounded. However, if the underground water line were replaced by a plastic pipe connected to the pipe outside of the entrance into the structure, safety would definitely be an issue, and this might not be apparent if the portion of the water supply that enters the structure is not replaced.

In part for this reason, the NEC now requires that a second grounding electrode must supplement the ground connection to the water-supply pipe. While there are several ways that this can be accomplished, the usual method is to use a metal rod or pipe electrode that is at least 8 feet in length and is driven into the ground.

BUILDING DISTRIBUTION

Electrical Connections

Figure 12.26 shows a sculpture by Claes Oldenburg, a Swedish sculptor who is best known for his extremely large replicas of everyday objects. This sculpture is a replica of a three-way plug extension, which is both a celebration of electrical connections and an editorial comment on the need for proper consideration of this aspect of electrical design.

When it was first generally available, electricity was used primarily for lighting and industrial applications. Usually, the electrical connections for both of these applications were fixed. However, since the incandescent lamp (what we typically call a *light bulb*) had a limited life, it was necessary to develop a way to readily replace the lamp. Both screw and bayonet sockets served this purpose, with

Figure 12.26 GIANT THREE-WAY PLUG
This 1970 sculpture by Claes Oldenburg is located on the campus of Oberlin College in Ohio.

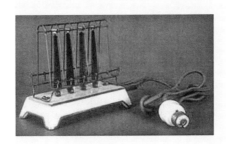

Figure 12.27 EARLY ELECTRICAL CONNECTORS

The rough image at the near right shows an early electric toaster that used a screw-type electrical connector to obtain power from a typical lighting socket. Even after the slotted receptacle became standard for 120 volts in the United States, often an electrical connection still relied on a lighting socket, as indicated by the screw adaptor shown at the far right.

the screw socket becoming the preferred method of connecting a lamp to a lighting fixture. However, the size of the screw base was not standardized until 1909, when it was licensed by the Edison General Electric Company to other manufacturers under the Mazda trademark.

As additional uses of electricity developed, there was a need to have a way to make nonfixed electrical connections, sometimes considered temporary although they might remain connected for a long period of time. Initially this entailed using a device that was essentially a modified base of a lamp that could be screwed into a screw-type lighting socket (see the left image in Figure 12.27). That is, the initial "plug" was often a device that was screwed into a lighting socket, although subsequently the double flat-prong plug and slotted receptacle became the standard means of making these electrical connections in a 120-volt circuit in the United States.[12] However, even after this standard was adopted, electrical connections were often still made with lighting sockets using a screw adaptor (see the right image in Figure 12.27).

The double flat-prong plug and slotted receptacle were initially developed in 1904 by Harvey Hubbell. A shown in Figure 12.28, this often entailed a slotted receptacle that was inserted into a screw base. Hubbell's double-slotted receptacle was an advance from the screw socket method of connecting an electrical device. Not only did it avoid the problem of twisting wires that was associated with using a screw connection to which the wires were connected, but it also was safer to use, at least after it was installed in a screw socket or was itself hard wired to an electric circuit. Since screw sockets were rather large and, when used as an electrical connector, were often hot wired and not controlled by a switch, the electrical contacts were exposed, establishing a considerable potential for an electric shock. In deference to this possibility, hot connection was through the base pin rather than through the sides of the socket.

The openings in the Hubbell slotted receptacle were small, and it was unlikely that one might insert a finger into the opening. And while the plug had protruding and exposed metal prongs, the plugs were always dead until they were plugged into a receptacle. With its advantages, Hubbell's device was quickly embraced as the preferred way to make electrical connections for 120-volt circuits, and it became the standard for North America.

Interestingly, as can be seen in Figure 12.28, Hubbell's receptacle also included slightly different-sized slots to ensure correct polarity for the connection—hot-to-hot and neutral-to-neutral. This required what is called a *polarized plug*—a plug with an enlarged neutral prong. With such, the plug can only be inserted one way into the receptacles. Unfortunately, receptacles from other manufacturers often were not polarized, which meant they could not accept a polarized plug. It wasn't until 1948 that codes required receptacles to be polarized.

Figure 12.28 SCREW-IN PLUG ADAPTOR

Early electrical connections used the screw socket that is still used for incandescent lamps. To accommodate the flat-prong plugs, often an adaptor, as shown here, was provided to convert the screw-socket receptor to a slotted receptacle. Of course, with no means of turning off the power to the screw-socket receptor, these adaptors were somewhat dangerous.

---

[12]While in North and Central America the standard receptacle slots and plug prongs are rectangular, except for the ground (see Figure 12.29), elsewhere they are usually round (see Figure 12.30).

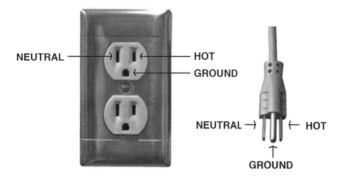

Figure 12.29 TYPICAL GROUNDED 120-VOLT PLUG AND RECEPTACLE
The standard grounded 120-volt plug and receptacle is arranged so that the connection will maintain hot-to-hot and neutral-to-neutral. When the plug includes a ground prong, this is assured, assuming that the circuit and the plug are properly wired. If the plug is not grounded but is polarized, then the neutral will have a wider prong that can only be inserted into the wider slot in the receptacle, again maintaining hot-to-hot and neutral-to-neutral.

The grounded receptacle was developed in the late 1920s by Philip Labre when he was a student at the Milwaukee School of Engineering. While grounding clearly provided a significant safety improvement, it was not required until 1947 and then only for laundry rooms. Subsequently it was required for outdoors and basements, and then in 1962, the NEC required grounding for all branch circuits.

Most electrical appliances use 120 volts provided by a hot wire and a neutral wire, often also with a ground wire. If an electrical appliance has an on-off switch, it is logical to connect it to the electrical circuit so the electrical power can be cut off as it flows into the appliance. In this way, when the switch is off, the wiring within the unit is not hot since it is only connected to the neutral wire. While a polarized plug can ensure that the connection is proper, a three-prong grounded plug can do the same. In addition, the grounded plug can provide a means for opening the electric circuit if there is any leaking current (see Figure 12.29).

When a plug does not include a ground prong and is also not polarized, there is no assurance of a proper electrical connection. When a proper electrical connection, hot-to-hot and neutral-to-neutral, is critical, a grounded plug or a polarized plug should be used. This will reduce the chances of a crossed connection, especially since electrical wiring and the contacts in receptacles are now color coded, decreasing the chance that the installation is faulty, although there is no guarantee that these simple controls will be followed, especially by the home handyman.

Unfortunately, if the ground prong on a plug is removed, which might be done when confronting an ungrounded receptacle, the two prongs are often the same size. So without the benefit of the ground or a distinction between the prongs of the plug, there is a clear possibility that the electrical connection will be reversed. Another problem is that there is no assurance that a receptacle that has a ground slot is actually grounded. Since grounded receptacles have been required since 1962, grounded receptacles are generally the only type of receptacle that can be purchased in most hardware stores. As a result, these receptacles are often installed without a ground connection when an ungrounded receptacle must be replaced. Because of this, it is important to verify that an apparently grounded outlet in an older structure is actually grounded. By the way, ungrounded receptacles are available from most electrical supply stores, but it is preferable to ground the replaced receptacle by adding a ground wire. In fact, with new work, as distinct from a repair, the NEC indicates that the existing code requirements must be met, and this includes providing grounding for all circuits.

Using an adapter to connect a grounded plug into an ungrounded receptacle can also override the intended safety controls. These adapters usually have a ground wire or metal tab that is to be connected to the screw holding the cover plate on the receptacle, suggesting that this will provide the missing ground connection. But it is unlikely that there is any ground at the receptacle—if there was, there would be a grounded receptacle. A rare exception would be if the outlet installation predates the general use of grounded receptacles but included a metal electrical box connected to a grounded metal conduit system. But more likely, the only thing that connecting the green wire or tab accomplishes, besides providing a false sense of security, is to reduce the chance that the converter will be lost.

Early on, electrical connections were standardized within North America, settling on the slotted receptacle, with one slot connected to the hot wire and the other to the neutral wire. Both of these wires ran to the electric panel box, where there was a fuse to limit the current that could flow within the circuit. After the fuses, the hot wires were collected together and connected to the electric service line. The neutral wires were also collected together in the electric panel box, but they connected to ground. With the addition of grounded circuits, the ground wires would also run to the electric panel box, where they would then be combined with the neutral wires. That is, the ground wires ultimately connected with the neutral wires; however, unlike the neutral wires, the ground wires were not intended to regularly carry current. Of course, this is essentially the same arrangement used today, although the circuit breakers usually replace the fuses and the hot wires connect to two legs of a 120/240 volt electric service.

While the basic 120-volt electrical connection was standardized for North America, most of the world uses 240-volt electricity, which demands a distinct connector. However, while this generally means circular rather than slotted receptors, the arrangement of these receptors varies by country or geographical area and sometimes even by region within a country. Figure 12.30 shows some of the connectors that are used for the standard electrical connections along with an indication of where each of these might be used.

While plugs and receptacles vary for different countries, which can be a problem when traveling, they also vary according to the voltage and amperage supplied. The intention is to match the demands of an appliance with the capacity of an outlet, which can be critical in terms of safety and proper operation. While connecting a 120-volt device to a 240-volt outlet would be quite dangerous, a mismatch of current can be problematic, although probably not unsafe. The problem with mismatching amperage is when the device draws more current than can be supplied by the circuit to which it is connected. That is, a 30-amp load should not be connected to a 20-amp circuit. However, there is no particular problem connecting a 15-amp load to a 20-amp circuit since the current that will be drawn is determined by the appliance rather than the circuit.

With the different transformers and various wiring arrangements, it is necessary to make certain that electrical devices are properly connected. When they are hard wired, the electrical contractor hopefully ensures this, but with the many electrical appliances that are not hard wired, the electric plug (male) and receptacle (female) are the means of control. The receptacle is a wiring device with the conducting elements recessed behind the mating surface. Often referred to as an *outlet* (sometimes as a *convenience outlet* or a *duplex outlet* when the device can accommodate two plugs), an electrical receptacle is normally connected directly to the source of power. As a result, it is live, although it is possible to include an on–off switch on the circuit prior to the connection with the receptacle. If such a switch is provided, it should disconnect the hot wire rather than the neutral wire.

It is important to ensure that appliances with high current demands are not connected to outlets that are incapable of supplying the required amperage. While this is important for all connections, it is especially true for 240-volt ones. The National Electrical Manufacturers Association (NEMA) has established standards for different wiring devices ranging from 15 amps to 60 amps and 120 volts to 600 volts. NEMA also distinguishes between straight blade and twist-locking connections. The straight blade connections are intended for lighter-duty, general-purpose electrical devices, whereas locking units are for connecting equipment where accidental disconnection would be a problem, which generally means heavy-duty commercial

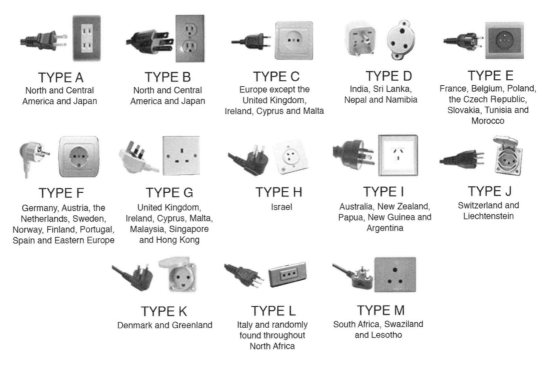

Figure 12.30 ELECTRIC PLUGS AND RECEPTACLES
Different plugs are used in different locations even when the voltage and frequency might be the same.

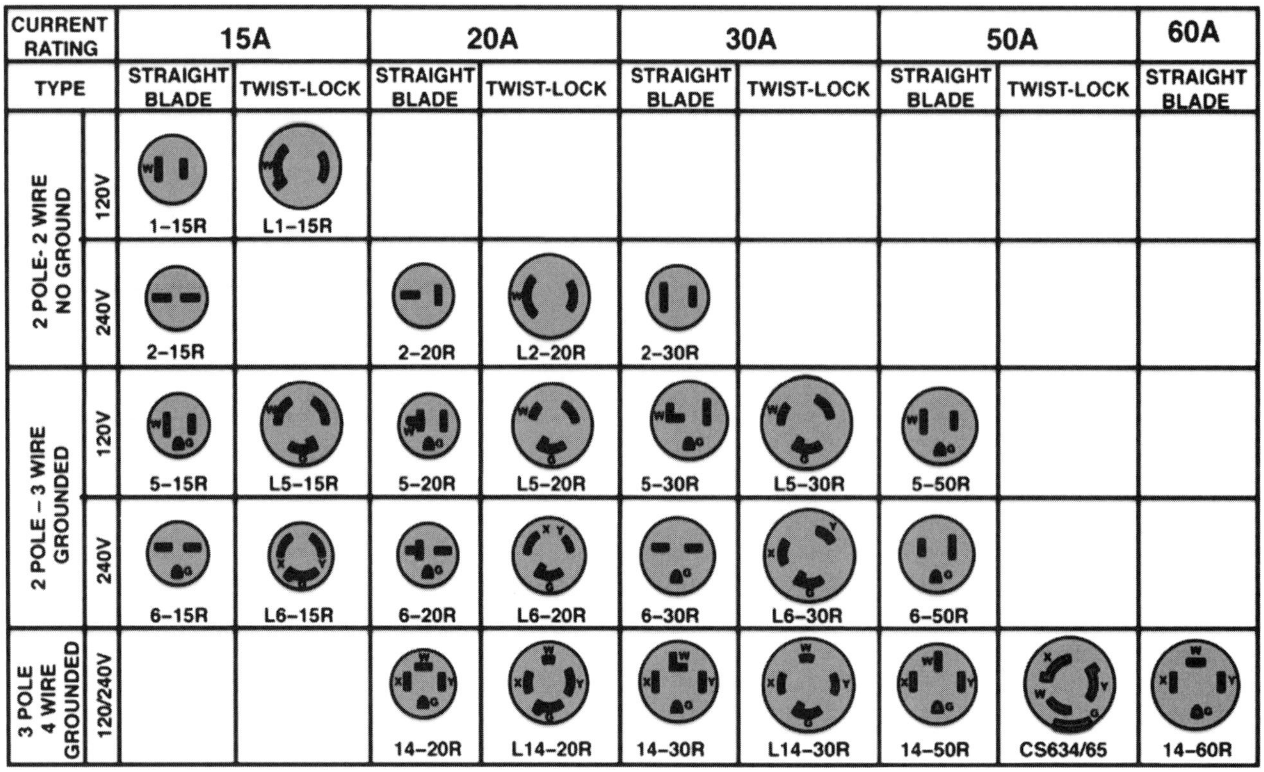

CURRENT RATING		15A		20A		30A		50A		60A
TYPE		STRAIGHT BLADE	TWIST-LOCK	STRAIGHT BLADE	TWIST-LOCK	STRAIGHT BLADE	TWIST-LOCK	STRAIGHT BLADE	TWIST-LOCK	STRAIGHT BLADE
2 POLE- 2 WIRE NO GROUND	120V	1–15R	L1–15R							
2 POLE- 2 WIRE NO GROUND	240V	2–15R		2–20R	L2–20R	2–30R				
2 POLE – 3 WIRE GROUNDED	120V	5–15R	L5–15R	5–20R	L5–20R	5–30R	L5–30R	5–50R		
2 POLE – 3 WIRE GROUNDED	240V	6–15R	L6–15R	6–20R	L6–20R	6–30R	L6–30R	6–50R		
3 POLE 4 WIRE GROUNDED	120/240V			14–20R	L14–20R	14–30R	L14–30R	14–50R	CS634/65	14–60R

Figure 12.31 VARIOUS NEMA RECEPTACLE CONFIGURATIONS

This figure shows some of the standard NEMA Receptacle Configurations. "W" denotes a neutral wire, which is typically white, "G" denotes a ground connection, and "X" and "Y" denote hot wires in a 120/240-volt connector.

and industrial equipment. Of course, heavy-duty equipment can be hard wired, but when they are, a disconnect switch should be included to be able to shut off power to the equipment.

The intention of the NEMA-designated outlet configurations for different electric demands is to prevent inappropriate and potentially dangerous electrical connections. Figure 12.31 presents a limited number of NEMA receptacle configurations. The notation for each of these ends in "R" indicating a receptacle. In similar but reversed diagrams, the notations end in "P," indicating that plug rather than receptacle configurations are shown. Notations beginning with "L" indicate twist-locking connectors.

Wiring

The NEC of the NFPA establishes the basic requirements for electric circuits. The size of the circuit conductor is chosen based on the acceptable current-carrying capacity. The rated capacity of a circuit is denoted by the term *ampacity*, whereas the term *amperage* refers to the current. At smaller sizes, the conductor is usually a copper wire, and it is sized in terms of the American Wire Gauge (AWG), with smaller-diameter wires having a larger gauge. The typical wire sizes used for electric circuits are 14 AWG for 15 amps, 12 AWG for 20 amps, and 10 AWG for 30 amps. At 6 AWG or larger, the conductor is typically referred to as a *cable* and is comprised of several smaller wires twisted together. This conversion to a multiple-wire cable is partly to improve the carrying capacity, since with larger cross sections of wire, less of the wire actually serves as a conductor, but the main advantage of a cable is that the conductor is more flexible. It is for this reason that appliance power cords, which are usually only 16 AWG, considerably smaller than 6 AWG, consist of cables—twisted wires but each with a smaller cross section.

The notation of the wire size by gauge continues as the wires get larger, from 0 AWG up to 0000 AWG, which is sometimes noted as 4/0 AWG. Conductors larger than 4/0 AWG have the designation MCM (thousand circular mil [Kmil]), with the number referring to the Kmil dimension, which increases as the conductor increases.[13]

---

[13]With smaller wires the gauge notation of the wire size gets smaller as the wire gets larger, but with larger wires the notation changes, increasing along with the wire size.

When multiple wires are combined together, even when the wires are smaller than 6 AWG, the combined assembly is also called a *cable*. In residential construction, the electrical wiring generally involves a hot wire or two, a neutral wire, and a ground wire that are combined in a nonmetallic (NM-B) sheathed cable. Most often this cable is referred to by the brand name ROMEX®.[14] NM-B usually contains two or three insulated conductors, most often with a copper ground wire that is typically uninsulated. These wires are then combined within an insulated plastic jacket. When only two insulated wires are provided, one is typically white, to be used as the neutral, and the other is black, to be used as the hot. When three insulated wires are provided, the third wire is usually red and is also intended to be hot. If the ground wire is insulated, it is green.

While NM-B cable is still used for residential construction and perhaps other small-scale installations in various jurisdictions, it is becoming increasingly necessary to install all electrical wiring in nonresidential occupancies within an electrical conduit. Even in a single-family residence, electrical conduit might be required where the electrical wiring within the occupied zone is exposed (i.e., not concealed with finish construction such as gypsum board). Based on this, exposed NM-B wiring can run across a ceiling in a basement. While these electric wires do not need to be enclosed in conduit, wires that drop down from the ceiling to a switch or outlet and are not installed behind a finished surface must be within a conduit.

Conduit and Raceways

The NEC requires that wiring in nonresidential occupancies be installed in conduit. Electrical conduit is generally a rigid metal tube, although some conduit is nonmetallic and some is flexible. Nonmetallic conduit is usually made from plastic or a cementitious composition and is used in low-hazard installations, often underground, where metal conduit would tend to deteriorate. Metal conduit, which can be made from various metals, is generally steel and is available in three categories: heavy-wall or rigid steel conduit, intermediate conduit (IMC), and electric metallic tubing (EMT). As a protection against deterioration, mainly from moisture, steel conduit is usually galvanized, but it might be enameled or enclosed in a thin plastic covering. Conduit is available in different sizes, ranging from 1/2 inch up to 4 inches in diameter, with the size determined by the number of wires, each of which is individually insulated. The conduit is not intended as insulation, as the external

jacket of NM-B is, but as a way to protect the wire against injury and to provide a raceway through which the wires can be fed after rough construction. A continuous metal conduit can also provide a system ground path.

Since the electric wires are typically fed through the conduits after they have been installed, the design and configuration of the conduit system must allow for this. All changes in direction in the conduit must be achieved by means of a gradual bend or through an accessible electrical connection box through which the wires can be pulled or fed. Even with gradual bends, the change in angle between pull boxes cannot exceed 360°.

Normally when an electrical conduit is used, especially with concrete construction, it is installed early during the construction process. All critical electrical outlets and connections are located and interconnected by the conduit, but the wiring is not installed until later, during the finishing phases of construction. In this manner, provisions are made to allow for proper electric distribution, but the wiring is not exposed to potential damage during the rough phases of construction. It also permits a way to run the electric circuits through monolithic construction. For example, with wood frame construction, voids are provided within the structure, which allows for installation of the electric wiring just prior to enclosure by the finish materials (e.g., gypsum board). However, with concrete construction, voids are not usually provided within the structural assembly. For example, if the floor construction is a concrete waffle slab and it is to be left exposed without a dropped ceiling, the only way that wiring can run through the structural floor is by installing conduit in the concrete. While the wiring could be installed in the conduit, there is no need to do so since it can be fished through later, thereby avoiding potential damage that might occur during completion of the formwork, installation of reinforcing, and pouring of the concrete. Perhaps we might question why NM-B sheathed cable is not simply buried directly in the concrete. Although this might work, the wiring would be exposed to some rough conditions including heavy traffic, potential dislodging during the concrete pour, moisture, and thermal movement, to say nothing of the total inability to adjust the wiring once the concrete is installed. Also, concrete does move, especially with changes in temperature[15] and over time, and any direct connection between

---

[14]ROMEX® was originally developed by the Rome Wire Company. It is now a registered trademark currently held by the Southwire Company, although Romex is often used generically, similar to PLEXIGLAS® or KLEENEX®.

[15]Reinforced concrete is possible in large part because the coefficients of thermal expansion of both the concrete and the steel, which is used as the reinforcement, are basically the same. If this were not so, the bond between concrete and steel would be broken as the temperature changed. Since the coefficient of thermal expansion for copper is not equal to that of concrete, changes in temperature could cause a break in the wires. This becomes even more critical because the temperature of the electric wires changes as a result of carrying a variable electric current.

the electric wires and the concrete slab would likely result in serious problems.

As mentioned, some conduit is flexible. This is especially important when making electrical connections to machinery. If nonflexible conduit were used, the vibration of the machinery would tend to telescope through the conduit and potential noise problems might develop. Making the final connection to an electrical device by a flexible conduit also eliminates the necessity of making complicated rigid connections between the electric box and the device. Another reason for using flexible conduit is that it might be necessary to move an electrical appliance after it is wired—for example, when a fluorescent lighting fixture is installed in a lay-in tile ceiling. While this might not seem necessary, particular labor union statutes might require it. That is, there are strict contract regulations that might prohibit a worker from one trade union from adjusting the work regulated by another trade union. With a flexible conduit connection, nonelectricians are generally permitted to move the lights without creating a labor union infraction.

There are two types of flexible metal conduit: Greenfield and "BX." Both of these entail a spirally wound strip of interlocking steel strips, which is somewhat similar to the support of a gooseneck lamp. The difference between the two types of conduit is that Greenfield is merely the flexible conduit through which the wires must be pulled after the conduit is installed, whereas "BX" includes the insulated wires. If the flexible conduit will be exposed to moisture, it can be provided with a liquid-tight plastic cover or jacket.

Other raceways for electrical wiring are also utilized. With the need for electric service and communication connections for various types of equipment, combined with a desire for flexibility, under-floor distribution systems have become reasonably standard in office space. This often requires special structural considerations and, while providing the potential for change, it usually imposes some restrictions on workstation layout since the points of connection are fixed. That is, while an under-floor system can provide a tremendous number of potential points of connection, they are all set and cannot be changed easily. For these reasons, the flexibility of the hung ceiling with lay-in tiles remains an attractive alternative way of providing for future adjustments in electric service. While the open ceiling can accommodate the running of additional wires, if regular change is expected, the installation of ceiling-mounted service trays might be appropriate. Although the ceiling distribution offers some advantages, it does have the problem of making the final connection. While the electrical drop can occur within a partition, in most situations, especially in the open office, partitions are few and even when they do occur, they don't necessarily extend up to the ceiling. Alternative methods of providing the electric drop are available, such as a pole raceway, a nonstructural column in which the wires are run, but these are not necessarily very attractive.

There are other options for providing flexibility, including some carpeting systems that include low-voltage wiring. And there is some suggestion that microwaves might soon be able to provide a potential means of energy distribution.

Wire Sizing

While 16 AWG wire was once used for wiring and is still used within individual luminaires and electrical appliances, the smallest wire allowed by the NEC for electric circuits is 14 AWG, which must be limited to circuits controlled by a 15-amp protection device (fuse or circuit breaker). This is based on the carrying capacity that will not result in an excessive temperature rise. As current flows through a wire, there is resistance, and this produces heat. The more resistance there is, the more heat is generated. Since resistance is based on the current flow per unit area of the conductor, as the amount of current increases, the wire size must increase to keep any potential temperature increase within an acceptable limit, which is often set at 140° F or 60° C. Based on this requirement, the wires for 15-, 20-, and 30-amp circuits must be at least 14, 12, and 10 AWG, respectively.

Since there is no assurance that the connected electric loads will be within these limits, each circuit has to be protected. This is accomplished by installing a breaker or fuse in each circuit to limit the current to the rated ampacity of the wiring for that circuit. While these protective devices should ensure that the current in a circuit will not exceed the rated ampacity of the wire, generating excessive heat, the NEC limits the actual connected load to 80% of the rating for a circuit. Based on this limitation, a maximum of 12 amps should be connected to a 15-amp circuit, a maximum of 16 amps to a 20-amp circuit, and a maximum of 24 amps to a 30-amp circuit.

Today, copper is the wire that is primarily used for electrical wiring within structures, with aluminum used mainly for transmission lines. Aluminum wiring was used for a while in buildings until it became clear that this wiring could create problems, especially in the 120-volt electric circuits used in most buildings, particularly single-family residences. There are two problems with aluminum: the tendency to oxidize when exposed to air, and expansion and contraction that exceed what occurs with copper as a result of temperature change.

Like most metals, aluminum oxidizes when exposed to air. While aluminum is an electrical conductor, aluminum oxide is not. It acts as an electrical insulator, impeding the flow of current. If the aluminum wire at an electrical connection oxidizes, this could create additional resistance, leading to a greater increase in temperature, which involves more thermal movement.

While oxidation is a problem with an electrical connection, it generally has no effect on the carrying capacity of most of the aluminum wire. As an electrical conductor, the aluminum wire is encased in a plastic insulator. Without access to air, there is no oxidation. Of course, this assumes that the extruded aluminum wire has not been exposed to air for an extended period of time prior to being encased in the insulation.

However, there is a possible problem in terms of sequencing the electric work. Since the insulation has to be removed from the wire in order to make a connection, this should be done only at the time when the wire is being connected to the electrical junction to minimize oxidation. Some would argue that since the oxidation is brittle, even if the wire were exposed for a period of time, any oxidation that developed would probably be removed in the process of making the electrical connection. However, there is an equal chance that this loosened oxidation would be trapped between the wire and the mechanical connector.

A proper clean and tight connection at an electrical junction, such as at an outlet or switch, generally should result in a seal for the portion of the aluminum wire that comes in direct contact with the electrical connection. This will keep any oxygen from reaching the concealed aluminum, thereby reducing the potential for oxidation and the problems that this could cause.

Even without oxidation, as the amount of current carried by the aluminum wire changes, there will be a variation in both resistance and temperature, which will exceed what would occur in a comparable copper wire. As a result, even without oxidation, there is more thermal expansion and contraction in aluminum wire than in copper wire. This has a definite impact on a mechanical connection that, over time, can cause it to loosen.

Although the coefficient of thermal expansion for aluminum is quite different from those of other metals, aluminum is not used as the mechanical connector in an electric device, such as a receptacle or a switch, even for aluminum wiring. Aluminum is not a hard metal, so it would not be an effective connector. But with the difference in thermal expansion between aluminum wiring and the metals that are used as electrical connectors, there is an increased possibility that an aluminum wire connection will progressively loosen, further compounding the problems. With a loosening connection, there is a greater chance of oxidation occurring, which would exacerbate the problems, possibly leading to breaking the connection or, even worse, arcing electricity.

To address these problems, aluminum wiring is sometimes coated with a thin layer of copper. In addition, only special electrical fittings designed for use with aluminum wiring are used, and special care must be taken when making the physical electrical connections. While the NEC still permits the use of aluminum wiring in residential construction if the wire is 12 AWG or larger and the proper precautions are followed, many insurance companies will not cover a structure with aluminum wiring. As a result, the obvious recommendation is to avoid aluminum wiring in buildings, particularly in structures that are not likely to have regular professional facility maintenance.

An electric current involves the movement of electrons in a conductor, and as they move, the electrons confront other electrons. This causes resistance, which in turn causes a rise in temperature. The higher the current is, the more electrons flow and the greater the resistance is, which means a larger increase in temperature. If the temperature increases too much, it can damage the insulation on the conductor. Therefore, the highest temperature that will not damage the insulation sets the limit on the current that can be carried by a conductor. A temperature of 60° C (140° F) is the standard maximum temperature, although some insulations can handle higher temperatures. Table 12.5, which shows the conductor sizes for both copper and aluminum wiring, presents ratings for three temperatures: 60° C, 75° C, and 90° C, although the NEC clearly sets the current limits for 14, 12, and 10 AWG, the three wire sizes most frequently used in building circuitry, to 15, 20, and 10 amps, respectively, regardless of the allowable temperature rise.

Generally, copper wiring is used for electric wiring in most structures. Table 12.6, which lists the standard ampacity limits, assumes a 60° C rise limit. In addition, there is the 80% rule, which sets the actual connected current to only 80% of the maximum ampacity of the wires. Since wiring in free air can more readily dissipate any temperature rise, the NEC allows approximately a 50% increase for these wires. These alternative current limits are also included in Table 12.6.

Electric Service

The NEC sets the minimum electric service for a single-family residence at 100-amp, 120/240-volt, single-phase, three-wire service. Not long ago, a 60-amp, 120-volt, single-phase, two-wire service was considered adequate for a residence, but based on the requirement to connect no more than 80% of the rated ampacity, this supports less than a 50-amp usage, which is far less than what has become the normal residential demand in the United States.

Table 12.5: CONDUCTOR SIZING FOR COPPER AND ALUMINUM WIRING BASED ON ALLOWABLE AMPACITIES OF INSULATED CONDUCTORS RATED 0 THROUGH 2000 VOLTS, 60° TO 90° C (140° to 194° F); NOT MORE THAN THREE CURRENT-CARRYING CONDUCTORS IN RACEWAY, CABLE, OR EARTH (DIRECTLY BURIED) AND BASED ON AMBIENT TEMPERATURE OF 30° C (86° F)

Temperature Rating of Conductor						
	60° C 140° F	75° C 167° F	90° C 194° F	60° C 140° F	75° C 167° F	90° C 194° F
Size	Copper			Aluminum- or Copper-Clad		
AWG or MCM	Type A	Type B	Type C	Type A	Type B	Type C
14 AWG	20	20	25	–	–	–
12 AWG	25	25	30	20	20	25
10 AWG	30	35	40	25	30	35
8 AWG	40	50	55	30	40	45
6 AWG	55	65	75	40	50	60
4 AWG	70	85	95	55	65	75
3 AWG	85	100	110	65	75	85
2 AWG	95	115	130	75	90	100
1 AWG	110	130	150	85	100	115
0 AWG	125	150	170	100	120	135
2/0 AWG	145	175	195	115	135	150
3/0 AWG	165	200	225	130	155	175
4/0 AWG	195	230	260	150	180	205
250 MCM	215	255	290	170	205	230
300 MCM	240	285	320	190	230	255
350 MCM	260	310	350	210	250	280
400 MCM	280	335	380	225	270	305
500 MCM	320	380	430	260	310	350
Ambient Temperature	For ambient temperatures other than 30° C (86° F), multiply the allowable ampacities shown above by the appropriate factor shown below					
°C	°F					
21–25	70–77	1.08	1.05	1.04	1.08	1.05	1.04
26–30	78–86	1.00	1.00	1.00	1.00	1.00	1.00
31–35	87–95	0.91	0.94	0.96	0.91	0.94	0.96
36–40	96–104	0.82	0.88	0.91	0.82	0.88	0.91
41–45	105–113	0.71	0.82	0.87	0.71	0.82	0.87

Wire Types

C-A	TW, UF
C-B	RHW, THHW, THW, THWN, XHHW, USE, ZW
C-C	TBS, SA SIS, FEP, FEPB, MI, RHH, RHW-2, THHN, THHW, THW-2, THWN-2, USE-2, XHH, XHHW, XHHW-2, ZW-2
A-A	TW, UF
A-B	RHW, THHW, THW, THWN, XHHW, USE
A-C	TBS, SA SIS, THHN, THHW, THW-2, THWN-2, RHH, RHW-2, USE-2, XHH, XHHW, XHHW-2, ZW-2

Source: Adapted from the 2005 National Electric Code, NFPA, Quincy, MA (2005), Table 310.16.

Table 12.6: CONDUCTOR SIZING FOR COPPER WIRES

Conductor Size (AWG)	Allowable Ampacity (60° C Rise)[a]	Maximum Connected Amperage (at 80%)[b]	Allowable Ampacity in Free Air[c] (60° C Rise)	Maximum Connected Ampacity in Free Air (at 80%)
14	15 A	12 A	15 A	12 A
12	20 A	16 A	20 A	16 A
10	30 A	24 A	30 A	24 A
8	40 A	32 A	60 A	48 A
6	55 A	44 A	80 A	64 A
4	70 A	56 A	105 A	84 A
3	85 A	68 A	120 A	96 A
2	95 A	76 A	140 A	112 A
1	110 A	88 A	165 A	132 A
0	125 A	100 A	195 A	156 A
2/0	145 A	116 A	225 A	180 A
3/0	165 A	132 A	260 A	208 A
4/0	195 A	156 A	300 A	240 A
250MCM	215 A	172 A	340 A	272 A
300 MCM	240 A	192 A	375 A	300 A
350 MCM	260 A	208 A	420 A	336 A
400 MCM	280 A	224 A	455 A	364 A
500 MCM	320 A	256 A	515 A	412 A
600 MCM	355 A	284 A	575 A	460 A
700 MCM	385 A	308 A	630 A	504 A
750 MCM	400 A	320 A	655 A	524 A
800 MCM	410 A	328 A	680 A	544 A
900 MCM	435 A	348 A	730 A	584 A
1000 MCM	455 A	364 A	780 A	624 A
1250 MCM	495 A	396 A	890 A	712 A
1500 MCM	520 A	416 A	980 A	784 A
1750 MCM	545 A	436 A	1070 A	856 A
2000 MCM	560 A	448 A	1155 A	924 A

[a]No more than three current-carrying conductors in a raceway, conduit, or directly buried in earth. The ampacities listed are based on conductor Types TW or UF. With Type RHW, THHW, THW, THWN, XHHW, or ZW, the rated values are approximately 20% higher
[b]Adjusted to 80% of rated amperage.
[c]Single-insulated conductor in free air.
Source: Adapted from the 2005 National Electric Code, NFPA, Quincy, MA (2005), Tables 310.16 and 310.17.

While there are tables that suggest the size of appropriate electric service for various occupancies, these are often far from accurate. Instead of using these tables, we can calculate the size of the electric service that should be provided, whether it is for a residence or for another type of occupancy. This is relatively simple to do, and by using the process, we should gain a better understanding of some critical issues that should facilitate our design efforts.

Since we are dealing with a-c electricity, we should do the calculation in terms of volt-amperes rather than watts. We need to determine the volt-amperes required for the lighting, for miscellaneous power, and for the various electrical appliances and equipment that will be used. The lighting and miscellaneous power are usually calculated in terms of square footage, which for a single-family residence is usually 3 volt-amperes per square foot for lighting and 0.5 volt-ampere per square foot for miscellaneous power.

Miscellaneous power relates to the volt-amperes provided by the various undedicated convenience outlets. When a receptacle is intended for a particular electrical device, this device should be added to the list of electrical appliances rather than included under the miscellaneous power allocation, which for a single-family residence is assumed to be 0.5 volt-amperes per square foot. Often each of these dedicated outlets should be connected to a separate circuit.

Determining the electric demand for the electrical appliances and equipment is an important design step requiring us to gather information about the devices, determine where they will be located, and develop the design to accommodate them in terms of dimensions and operation. While in an actual project we should get the specifications for the appliances and equipment that we expect will be used, there are some generic tables that provide an initial approximation of the electric service requirements.

Table 12.7 presents the volt-amperes per square foot for lighting and miscellaneous power for different occupancies. Since some of the listed volt-amperes are presented in ranges, we have to select what seems appropriate based on the expectations for the specific project. Being engaged in the design of the building, we should be able to determine whether the higher, mid-range, or lower values should be used.

Once the expected electric demand for lighting and miscellaneous power is determined, we need to select the appropriate volt-amperes for the various appliances and equipment and add these to the demand estimate. Volt-amperes, circuit, and protection information for various residential appliances and equipment are presented in Table 12.8. While some of the appliances included in this table do not demand a high level of volt-amperes, they are included since they are typically dedicated uses and often should be on a separate electric circuit.

The estimated demand, which is based on the expected maximum rate of electrical usage, is used to determine the appropriate size of electric service. Recognizing that the demand is expressed in volt-amperes, we can derive the amperage by dividing this by the voltage of the electric service, which is typically 240 volts. We must then multiply the resulting amperes by 1.25, the inverse of 0.80, to determine the proper service that will not exceed 80% of the ampacity that the NEC allows.

The minimum circuit breaker or fuse ampacity listed in Table 12.8 is 20 amps. Accepting 16 amps as the maximum connected load at 120 volts, the maximum volt-amperes for a 20-amp circuit is 1920 volt-amperes. For a 15-amp circuit, the maximum permissible volt-amperes is 1440 volt-amperes, which is more than the connected volt-amperes for many of the appliances that are listed with a 20-amp circuit. Today, the recommended minimum circuit ampacity to be used in new construction is 20 amps; however, in many existing structures, especially residential units, 15-amp circuits are still quite common.

Electric Service Calculations

What would be the proper electric service for a 2000-square-foot single-family residence with standard lighting and miscellaneous power requirements plus the following specific electrical appliances: electric range, dishwasher, waste disposal unit, refrigerator, clothes washer, electric clothes dryer, and 4 tons of air conditioning?

From Tables 12.7 and 12.8 we find the following:

Electric Service Calculation

Appliance	Connected Volt-Amperes	Volts	Min. Rec. Circuit Breaker Size
Electric Range	7500	120/240	40 A
Refrigerator	750	120	20 A
Dishwasher	1200	120	20 A
Waste Disposer	500	120	20 A
Clothes Washer	500	120	20 A
Electric Clothes Dryer	5000	120/240	30 A
4 Tons Air Cond.	4000	120/240	30 A

Lighting and Misc. Power	Connected Volt-Amperes	Volts	Rec. Circuits and Breaker Size
Lighting at 3 V-A/ft^2	6000	120	4 at 20 A
Misc. Power at 0.5 V-A/ft^2	1000	120	-
Electric Load	**26,450**	**120/240**	

While 120 volts can serve some of the load, the electric service is 240 volts. Therefore, to determine the amperage load, we need to divide the total electrical load of 26,450 volt-amperes by 240 volts. The amperage load is 110 amps.

$$\frac{26,450 \text{ V} - \text{A}}{240 \text{ V}} = 110 \text{ amps}$$

While it seems that perhaps we have just missed the ability to use a 100-amp service, with the NEC requirement to connect no more than 80% of the rated ampacity, the electric demand is actually just below 140 amps:

$$\frac{26,450 \text{ V} - \text{A}}{240 \text{ V} \times 1.25} = 137.6 \text{ amps}$$

Table 12.7: ELECTRICAL LOAD ESTIMATING CHART

	Volt-Amperes per Square Foot			
			Air Conditioning	
Type of Occupancy	Lighting	Miscellaneous Power	Electric	Nonelectric
Auditorium				
General	1.0–2.0	0.0	12–20	5.0–8.0
Stage	2.0–4.0	0.5	–	–
Art Gallery	2.0–4.0	0.5	5–7	2.0–3.2
Bank	1.5–2.5	0.5	5–7	2.0–3.2
Cafeteria	1.0–1.6	0.5	6–10	2.5–4.5
Church, Synagogue, Mosque	1.0–3.0	0.5	5–7	2.0–3.2
Computer Area	1.2–2.1	2.5	12–20	5.0–8.0
Department Store				
Basement	3.0–5.0	1.5	5–7	2.0–3.2
Main Floor	2.0–3.5	1.5	5–7	2.0–3.2
Upper Floor	2.0–3.5	1.5	5–7	2.0–3.2
Dwelling (Not Hotel)				
0–3000 ft^2	3.0	0.5	–	–
3001–120,000 ft^2	2.0	0.25	–	–
Above 120,000 ft^2	1.0	0.15	–	–
Garage (Commercial)	0.5	0.15	–	–
Hospital	2.0–3.0	1.0	5–7	2.0–3.2
Hotel				
Lobby	1.0–3.0	0.5	5–8	2.0–3.5
Rooms (No Cooking)	1.0–3.5	0.5	3–5	1.5–2.5
Industrial Loft Building	1.0–2.0	1.0	–	–
Laboratories	3.0–4.0	5.0–20.0	6–10	2.5–4.5
Library	1.5–3.5	0.5	5–7	2.2–3.2
Medical Center	2.0–4.0	1.5	4–7	1.5–3.2
Motel	1.0–2.5	0.5	–	–
Office Building	1.5–3.5	1.5	4–7	1.5–3.2
Restaurant	1.5–2.5	0.25	6–10	2.5–4.5
School	1.5–3.5	1.5	3.5–5	1.5–2.2
Shops				
Barber and Beauty	3.0–5.0	1.0	5–9	2.0–4.0
Dress	2.0–5.0	0.5	5–9	2.0–4.0
Drug	2.0–3.0	0.5	4–7	2.0–4.0
Five and Ten	2.0–3.0	0.5	4–7	1.5–3.2
Hat, Shoe, Specialty	2.0–3.0	0.5	4–7	1.5–3.2
Warehouse (Storage)	0.3	–	–	–
In the Above, Except Single Dwellings:				
Halls, Closets, Corridors	0.5	–	–	–
Storage Spaces	0.25	–	–	–

Nominal sizes for electric service are 100, 150, 200, 300, 400, and 600 amps. However, the service sizes that are available from a particular utility company might differ. This is particularly true for 300-amp service, which is not provided by some utilities. For our calculation example, a 150-amp, 120/240-volt, single-phase, three-wire electric service should be selected.

Interestingly, sometimes it is no more expensive to install a larger service. For example, a 200-amp service might cost no more than a 150-amp service based upon the availability and prevalent use of the different sizes of equipment. The labor involved should be basically the same.

Having determined the proper electricity demand and, from that, the proper electricity service, we should determine the appropriate circuitry. Before doing this, per-haps an explanation of the distinction between expected demand and correct circuitry is appropriate. This is best explained in terms of miscellaneous power.

According to Table 12.7, a single-family residence has an electric load for miscellaneous power based on 0.5 volt-ampere per square foot. For the 2000-square-foot residence, this totals only 1000 volt-amperes. Based on 120 volts and including the 80% requirement, this suggests that only 10 amps of miscellaneous power are required, which means that only one 15-amp miscellaneous-power circuit would be necessary. However, a 2000-square-foot residence would typically have at least eight 20-amp circuits for miscellaneous power: two in the kitchen, one for the exterior, and five based on the recommended one per 400 square feet.

What accounts for this difference?

Table 12.8: LOAD, CIRCUIT, AND PROTECTION CHART FOR RESIDENTIAL APPLIANCES

Appliance	Typical Connected Volt-Amperes[a]	Volts	Wires	Circuit Breaker or Fuse	Circuit on Outlets
Kitchen					
Electric Range	7500	120/240	3 #8	40 A	1
Electric Cooktop	4000	120/240	3 #10	30 A	1
Broiler	2500	120/240	3 #12	20 A	1
Wall Oven	4000	120/240	3 #10	30 A	1
Wall Ovens – Double	7500	120/240	3 #8	40 A	1
Microwave	1200	120	2 #12	20 A	1 or More[b]
Dishwasher	1200	120	2 #12	20 A	1
Waste Disposer	500	120	2 #12	20 A	1
Refrigerator	750	120	2 #12	20 A	1[c]
Freezer	500	120	2 #12	20 A	1[d]
Coffee Maker	1000	120	2 #12	20 A	1
Toaster	1100	120	2 #12	20 A	1
Toaster Oven	1250	120	2 #12	20 A	1
Miscellaneous Power	–	120	2 #12	20 A	2 Circuits Req.
Laundry					
Clothes Washer	350–500	120	2 #12	20 A	1
Electric Clothes Dryer	5000	120/240	3 #10	30 A	1
Gas Clothes Dryer	350	120	2 #12	20 A	1 or More
Hand Iron/Ironer	1650	120	2 #12	20 A	1 or More
Living Area					
Workshop	1500	120	2 #12	20 A	1 or More
Portable Heater	1500+	120	2 #12	20 A	1
Laptop Computer	50	120	2 #12	20 A	1 or More
Computer and Monitor	300	120	2 #12	20 A	1
Audio Center	200	120	2 #12	20 A	1 or More
DVD or VCR Player	25	120	2 #12	20 A	1 or More
Television	200	120	2 #12	20 A	1 or More
Fixed Utilities					
Fixed Lighting	1200 per 400 sq ft	120	2 #14	20 A	1 per 400 sq ft
	1800 per 600 sq ft	120	2 #12	20 A	1 per 600 sq ft
Central Air Conditioning	1000 per ton	120/240			
For 2000-sq ft Residence	5000[e]	120/240	3 #10	30 A	1
Unit Air Conditioners					
<1 ton or 1 hp	1200	120	2 #12	20 A	1
≥1 ton or 1 hp	1600	120/240	3 #12	20 A	1
Heating Plant (Furnace)	600	120	2 #12	20 A	1
Electric Hot Water Heater	4000	120/240	3 #10	30 A	1
Attic Fan	300	120	2 #12	20 A	1 or More

[a]Whenever possible, use the manufacturer's equipment ratings
[b]If built in, the microwave should be on its own circuit.
[c]A separate circuit is recommended to avoid potential overload, causing destruction of contents.
[d]While a separate circuit is still recommended, both a refrigerator and a freezer might be connected to the same circuit.
[e]Based on a 5-ton cooling load, determined at 400 square feet per ton. With an efficient design, this can be reduced.

Residential Spacing of Outlets and Required Wiring

The NEC suggests that each nondesignated receptacle (i.e., a duplex outlet or convenience outlet for which there is no assigned or specific connection) draws a current of 1.5 amps. Assuming 120 volts, this 1.5-amp current implies that each receptacle should be wired for 180 volt-amperes. In addition, the NEC states that within a residential occupancy, no point along a wall is to be more than 6 feet from an electrical receptacle. This means that receptacles need

to be placed at 12 feet on-center, except when a doorway or some other obstruction intervenes. If one does, a receptacle must be located within 6 feet of either side of the obstruction. Accepting the 12-foot spacing and assuming typical residential room dimensions of approximately 12 feet by 12 feet (some rooms will be larger and some will be smaller), each room requires at least four electrical receptacles, one on each wall. This suggests that four receptacles are required for each 144 square feet, which converts to one receptacle for every 36 square feet. At 180 volt-amperes per outlet, this relates to 5 volt-amperes per square foot, or

10 times what is suggested in Table 12.7 for miscellaneous power.

Rather than base the miscellaneous power load on this new figure, thereby increasing the estimated electric demand for which the electric service is sized, we must realize that there is a distinction between demand and circuitry. The demand, which is used to size the electric service, is the maximum electrical usage that is expected to occur at any given time, whereas the circuitry relates to the wiring that permits proper electrical distribution.

Assuming that each nondesignated receptacle is potentially used for 1.5 amps, adjusting for the 80% rule, only 8 outlets can be connected on a 15-amp circuit or 10 outlets on a 20-amp circuit. If there is to be at least one convenience outlet for each 36 square feet, rounding off, a 20-amp miscellaneous power circuit is required for each 400 square feet. With 15-amp circuits, one miscellaneous power circuit is needed for each 300 square feet.

In general, other than specifying the spacing of the receptacles in a residence, the NEC does not require any special arrangements regarding miscellaneous power outlets. However, there is a stipulation for a minimum of two 20-amp miscellaneous-power circuits to serve the kitchen, pantry, breakfast room, and dining room. While this was significant when 15-amp circuits were generally used, with the recommended general use of 20-amp circuits, it tends not to be a particular necessity. However, in addition to the two circuits for the food-service areas, the NEC now requires that two 20-amp circuits, which do not serve any other areas, be dedicated for the kitchen countertops. The NEC further stipulates that these countertop outlets are to be spaced so that no point along the wall line is more than 2 feet, measured horizontally, from a receptacle. The length of the counter occupied by a sink or range is not included in this 2-foot distance limitation. The receptacles are to be located above the countertops, but by no more than 20 inches, and they are to be protected with a ground fault interrupter (GFI). While the GFI requirement was previously applicable only to locations within 6 feet of a sink, it has recently been changed to apply to all countertop receptacles. The NEC also stipulates that any kitchen island or peninsular countertop that is larger than 24 inches by 12 inches shall have at least one electrical receptacle, with the assumption that if these surfaces are larger, the 2-foot countertop distance limit also applies.

Circuit Protection—GFCI, AFCI, and Other Devices

A GFI is a special protection device that is required in areas where any leaking electricity would cause an extreme hazard. This hazard can occur when it is possible to make contact with an electric ground, such as in a bathroom, kitchen, or laundry, all of which include plumbing, or where the standing surface is connected to the ground, as in a garage, basement, or outside where persons would actually be on the ground. While any leaking electricity can pose a problem, it becomes critical when, by making contact with an electrical device, we provide a ground connection. To avoid this grounding potential, electricians, who have to touch the wires, sometimes when they are hot, generally wear rubber-soled shoes and use non-conductive wood or fiberglass ladders rather than metal ladders.

Most protective devices, such as fuses and circuit breakers, open the circuit when there is a current overload. This overload results in a temperature increase that tends to melt the metal in the fuse or open the switch in a circuit breaker. Generally, circuit breakers rely on a bimetallic strip comprised of two metals that have different coefficients of thermal expansion. As a result, if an excessive current raises the temperature of the bimetallic strip, the difference in the expansion on the two sides of the metal strip causes the strip to bend, which releases the catch, forcing the spring-activated breaker to open. While these devices are effective in protecting against continual overloads, they do not interrupt the circuit until enough excessive current flows to increase the temperature sufficiently to open the circuit. Even though their purpose is to open a circuit if there is excessive current, most fuses and circuit breakers are intentionally designed with a time delay so that the circuit will not open if the overload is of short duration, such as occurs when lights are initially turned on and when motors are started.

As a result, if someone was effectively grounded, perhaps by touching a water faucet, and then came in contact with leaking electricity, a normal fuse or circuit breaker would not provide adequate safety protection. While a fuse or breaker relies on a temperature increase to interrupt the electric current, a GFI does not operate on heat. It works by comparing the current that flows out of the GFI with the current that flows back in. If there is any difference in the two flows, even in the low range of milliamps, the device opens and breaks the circuit.

Whatever the electrical device is, it does not collect energy but, instead, relies on the flow of current, harnessing it as it flows from hot to neutral. The device is somewhat like a water wheel that captures the energy in a moving water stream, transmitting the captured energy to a mechanical apparatus, such as a saw or grain mill. Similarly, an electric device receives and sends electric current, and if the current that leaves is not equal to the current that came in, a portion of the current must have gone elsewhere—that is, some of it must have leaked. By comparing the current going out with the current coming in, the GFI can determine if any electricity has leaked and, if so, will open the circuit.

A GFI can be located within the electrical device itself, the receptacle to which the device is connected, a receptacle from which the connected receptacle derives its current, or the circuit breaker. If it is in the circuit breaker or in a receptacle from which a subcircuit is extended, then all electrical connections on that circuit are protected. Such a device is actually a ground fault circuit interrupter (GFCI), whereas if it is located only in a single receptacle or in the device itself, legitimately it is a GFI, although this distinction is often not realized or used.

The arc fault circuit interrupter (AFCI) is a new NEC requirement for use in dwelling unit bedrooms. An AFCI is a device that is intended to provide protection from the effects of an arc fault by recognizing the unique characteristics of arcing and opening the circuit. The NEC states that "all 120-volt, single-phase 15- and 20-ampere branch circuits supplying outlets installed in dwelling unit bedrooms shall be protected by [an AFCI to] provide protection of the branch circuit."[16]

Unfortunately, the term *dwelling unit bedroom* has raised questions about the intent of this new requirement. If such a safety device is appropriate for a bedroom in a private residence, it seems logical that it should also be required in all sleeping spaces— dormitories, hotels, and so on. And if an arc fault is a potential problem that can be detected, why is it more problematic in a bedroom?

When an electrical device has a switch, the intention is to disconnect the electric power and to do this as current enters the appliance rather than leaves it, thereby limiting any potential danger. Similarly, in switching electric circuits or protecting them with fuses or circuit breakers, the intention is to open the hot wire, not the neutral. While we might assume that installing a fuse or circuit breaker on the neutral wire as well as on the hot wire of a circuit would provide double protection, this is definitely not true. In fact, we should never install a fuse or circuit breaker on the neutral wire. Since a protection device operates to open the circuit if excessive current is flowing, there is an equal chance that if excessive current were flowing through a doubly protected circuit, the device in the neutral wire would be the one to open. If this happens, while the appliance or light fixture would not operate, the wiring within the appliance or fixture would still be hot, creating a dangerous condition if one attempted to repair the fault that had caused the circuit to blow while assuming that the power was off. While we understand the problem with adding a protection device on the neutral wire as well as the hot wire, double fusing was traditionally done with knob-and-tube wiring.

[16]NEC National Electric Code, 2005: 210.12 (B).

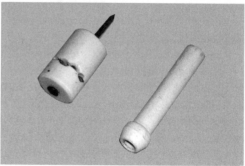

Figure 12.32 KNOB-AND-TUBE WIRING
Before the development of ROMEX®, knob-and-tube wiring was generally used for electrical installations. With this approach, the hot and neutral wires were kept separate. The knobs and tubes were both ceramic, with the knobs used to support each of the wires and the tubes used as added insulation when the wires passed through materials. While there are some questions as to the safety of these old systems, generally they are much better in this regard than early nonmetallic sheathed wiring.

Today electric circuits are developed using either nonmetallic sheathed cable or several insulated wires located in the same conduit, but in early electrical installations knob-and-tube wiring was used. With knob-and-tube wiring, rather than combine the hot and neutral conductors within the same jacket, the wires were physically separated. While they ultimately had to come close together when connected to an electrical device, each wire remained in its own insulated jacket (see Figure 12.32). This made sense since the insulation available then had limitations. It was not flexible, and over time, exposure to increased temperatures from the current flowing through the wires made the insulation rather brittle. With the wires physically separated, air was the prime insulator, at least for isolating the hot and neutral wires from each other. When the conductors had to go through joists or studs, ceramic tubes were inserted through the structural member and then the insulated wires were fished through the tubes. The knobs, which were used to fasten the wires, were comprised of two grooved ceramic pieces. When these pieces were assembled with the grooves aligned and facing each other, they provided a passage between which the wires could pass and yet be secured

Although it is an old method, knob-and-tube wiring installation does not pose any serious safety problems.

One exception when knob-and-tube wiring could potentially present a hazard is when the space through which the conductors run is filled with thermal insulation, especially if this added insulation causes moisture and/or is comprised of combustible materials. As with their response to aluminum wiring, some insurance companies will not cover a structure if the electric wiring is knob-and-tube. Interestingly, there doesn't seem to be a comparable reaction to the early combined cables, which predate the use of thermoplastic insulation and are probably not as safe as knob-and-tube wiring. Of course, the nonmetallic sheathed cables manufactured today are effective and safe.

Since the hot and neutral wires in a knob-and-tube installation were not directly linked, at times it was easier to jump between circuits than to maintain the linkage between the same hot and neutral conductors. While an electric circuit should legitimately include a linked set of a hot conductor and a neutral conductor, if a hot wire in a knob-and-tube circuit were to be controlled by a switch and then extended to a light fixture, rather than running a wire from the light back to the proper neutral conductor for that circuit, another neutral might provide a more direct connection back to the electric panel box. If the hot wire of one circuit were jumped to the neutral of another, the neutral in that second circuit could carry excessive current. For this eventuality, fusing both the neutral wire and the hot wire of a circuit would make sense in terms of protecting the wires, but it could also create a potentially dangerous situation.

Unfortunately, jumping circuits is still sometimes done. This is not good practice and should be avoided. When a circuit is protected with either a GFCI or AFCI, both of which compare the current in the two legs of a circuit, jumping circuits will cause the GFCI or AFCI breaker to open.

Ground wires are not intended to carry any current under normal conditions. Therefore, the problems associated with jumping circuits do not apply to ground wires, which can help when adding a ground to an existing circuit. If a different circuit that includes a ground wire is accessible from an ungrounded circuit, it would be acceptable to connect to this ground. If it is not feasible to add a ground, the NEC allows a GFI receptacle to be substituted for a grounded receptacle. Interestingly, all GFI receptacles include a grounded connection, which makes sense since this means that they can receive a grounded plug. However, grounding is not required for a GFI to work; in fact, if the GFI works properly, there should never be any need for the ground since the GFI should open as soon as any current leaving the device is not equal to the current that is returning. The advantage of including a ground with a GFI is that if there is a potential for an electric leak, the leak might flow through the ground and thereby open the GFI, if not the circuit breaker.

While it is often feasible to add a separate ground wire when replacing an existing receptacle in an ungrounded electric circuit, another option is merely to install a GFI receptacle, without a ground. In fact, this will exceed the safety that a simple grounded receptacle can provide. However, in taking this approach, it is important to not connect the ground terminal on the GFI unit to the neutral wire of the circuit, since this could override the safety benefit that the GFI provides.

Another potential use of a GFI beyond its original intention of providing protection in locations where there is a high potential of someone being grounded, such as contacting plumbing lines, is when a child might insert an item into a receptacle. Although there are plastic inserts that can protect against this, the GFI can provide protection while still allowing use of the outlet.

Color coding is an important and effective means of controlling an electrical system that, in addition to proper wire selection, circuit breakers, GFIs, and AFCIs, can help ensure that the system is safe. In standard building wiring, white wire is to be used only for the neutral conductor, which is the wire that connects an electrical device to ground. However, while white is the standard color, the neutral conductor might also be gray. The hot wires, which, paired with a neutral wire, complete the circuit, are to be either black or red. Black is the usual color, but with a 240-volt circuit, both a hot-red wire and a hot-black wire will be required, along with a white neutral. A voltage of 240 volts is achieved by connecting a device between the hot-black and hot-red wires. Black-to-neutral and red-to-neutral both develop 120 volts of power. Green is the color assigned for the ground wire. This wire, which might be a bare copper wire included in the nonmetallic cable, is not intended to carry any current, but is provided to do so if there is an electric leak. The ground wire runs back to the panel box, where it is then connected to the ground. If it does carry current, the intention is that this will overload the circuit, opening the breaker or blowing the fuse and thereby deenergize the circuit.

With standard-voltage three-phase circuitry, a blue wire is also hot. So, with three-phase service, black, red, and blue indicate the standard hot wires. With higher-voltage three-phase circuits, brown, orange, and yellow wires are hot. With both of these three-phase systems, the neutral wire is still either white or gray.

The connections within electrical devices are also coded—brass, silver, and green. Connectors with a brass screw are to be connected to the hot line, whereas those with a silver screw are to be connected to the neutral line. Green, of course, represents the ground.

While color coding is extremely helpful, unfortunately it does not guarantee that the electrical connections are proper. We need to be especially concerned when working on buildings, particularly older structures, which predate some regulations, and/or single-family residences that have been previously remodeled. Even though clear regulations regarding electrical installations have existed for some time, these are not always properly followed, especially by journeyman electricians. Unfortunately, even when a licensed electrician has done the installation, there is no guarantee that the standards have been properly followed. Often we will find that the white wire, which is clearly intended only as a neutral wire, is actually the hot wire. We can also find that while the white neutral wire is suppose to be joined to the silver-colored screw anchor on the outlet or fixture and the black (or red) hot wire is to be connected to the brass-colored screw anchor, this is not always done.

Electricity can be dangerous, so care should be taken to ensure that the wiring systems are properly installed. As a safety precaution, when we are involved with a renovation project, it is always reasonable to check that the existing conditions are proper. So, the message is: beware!

GENERAL GUIDELINES FOR RESIDENTIAL APPLICATIONS

While the following guidelines are primarily applicable for a single-family residence, they suggest proper action for many types of occupancies.

1. In general, the electric load from lighting will be 3 volt-amperes per square foot and the load from miscellaneous power will be 0.5 volt-ampere per square foot. With these loads, lighting circuits should be based on about 500 square feet for a 15-amp circuit and 650 square feet for a 20-amp circuit. Miscellaneous power circuits should be based on 250 to 300 square feet for a 15-amp circuit and 300 to 400 square feet for a 20-amp circuit. At least two 20-amp miscellaneous power circuits are to be installed in the kitchen, pantry, and dining areas, and at least one GFI circuit in the garage and outside. Furthermore, two dedicated 20-amp miscellaneous power circuits, GFI protected, are to serve the kitchen counters. In addition to these miscellaneous circuits, the appropriate number of individual circuits for special appliances is required.

    Assuming 20-amp circuits:

    a. Lighting at about 650 square feet for each circuit
    b. Miscellaneous power at about 300 to 400 square feet for each circuit
    c. At least two circuits for kitchen, pantry, and dining areas that may be included within the count of basic miscellaneous power
    d. At least two dedicated 20-amp GFI circuits for the kitchen counters
    e. At least one 20-amp circuit for the garage and outside areas
    f. Separate circuits for special appliances:
        (i) Air conditioners
        (ii) Electric hot water heaters
        (iii) Major electric appliances (ovens, clothes dryers, etc.)
        (iv) Refrigerator
        (v) Computers
        (vi) Other appliances

2. Protect all electrical receptacles in areas of potential grounding with a GFI or GFCI. This includes circuits that serve the outside, garage, bathroom, laundry room, and kitchen.

3. Protect all circuits supplying receptacle outlets in sleeping areas with an AFCI.

4. Locate electric receptacles so that no point along a wall is more than 6 feet from an outlet. While this generally means that electric outlets should be no more than 12 feet apart (12 feet on-center), when a door or other interruption exists, it is important to meet the 6-foot stipulation versus the 12-foot on-center distribution.

5. Separate the electric circuits that serve lighting and miscellaneous power. When this is done, problems with one will not result in problems with the other. So, if a lighting circuit goes down, a utility light could be connected to an electric outlet within the area without lights. If the miscellaneous power circuit blows, which is the more likely type of circuit to exceed the rated amps, there would still be light to allow people to find their way and, if necessary, to address the electrical problem.

6. Provide at least two different miscellaneous power circuits in each room.

7. Avoid placing all lighting in one area of a structure on the same electric circuit.

8. In rooms without an overhead light, provide a switched receptacle outlet that is intended to supply a lighting device. To gain some advantage, this receptacle should be remote from the switch.

9. In bedrooms, provide a duplex receptacle (convenience outlet) convenient to the location of each bed. With double, queen, or king-sized beds, provide a receptacle on either side of the bed. Also, consider including a switch for the light that can be controlled from the bed.

10. Install a light in each closet, controlled by a door switch or wall switch. The closet light must be located where it will not pose a safety problem, as might occur if the light were too close to the clothing. Even with separation, since incandescent lights usually become rather hot, some jurisdictions require any closet light to be fluorescent rather than incandescent. The NEC still allows incandescent lights in a closet if the light is surface-mounted or recessed and completely enclosed. This provision reduces the potential that clothing and other potentially combustible materials will come in direct contact with the hot incandescent lamp.

11. Provide a convenient means of disconnecting electric service to appliances rated over 300 volt-amperes or $^1/_8$ horsepower that are permanently connected or with plugs that are not easily accessible. Since the disconnecting mechanism is to be within sight of the appliance, it might be necessary to use a subpanel in the areas where these appliances are located, such as the kitchen.

CALCULATION EXERCISES: RESIDENTIAL ELECTRIC SERVICE REQUIREMENTS

1. The standard nominal sizes for 120/240 single-phase electric service are 100, 150, 200, 300, 400, and 600 amps. For a single-family residence of 2500 square feet plus a two-car garage, with the following specific electrical appliances in addition to the standard lighting and miscellaneous power requirements, what would be the electric demand in terms of volt-amperes? For this demand, what would be the proper size of electric service that should be provided? What would be the required wire size for this service?
   Electric Appliances: Electric Cooktop, Double Electric Ovens, Side-by-Side Refrigerator/Freezer, Dishwasher, Waste Disposal, Clothes Washer, Electric Clothes Dryer, and 4 Tons of Air Conditioning

2. For a single-family residence of 1250 square feet plus attached carport, with the standard lighting and miscellaneous power requirements plus the following specific appliances, what would be the electric demand in terms of volt-amperes? For this demand, what would be the proper size of electric service that should be provided? What would be the required wire size for this service?
   Electric Appliances: Gas Range, Refrigerator/Freezer, Dishwasher, Waste Disposal, Clothes Washer, Gas Clothes Dryer, and 2.5 Tons of Air Conditioning

3. For a single-family residence with 2000 square feet plus attached carport, with the standard lighting and miscellaneous power requirements plus the following specific appliances, what would be the electric demand in terms of volt-amperes? For this demand, what would be the proper size of electric service that should be provided? What would be the required wire size for this service?
   Electric Appliances: Electric Range, Refrigerator/Freezer, Dishwasher, Waste Disposal, Clothes Washer, Electric Clothes Dryer, and 12 1-KWh Baseboard Electric Heaters

4. For a multifamily apartment complex comprised of 40 1200-square-foot units, what would be the proper electric service that should be provided? Each unit has the standard lighting and miscellaneous power requirements plus the appliances indicated below. The complex includes four washer and dryer combinations, 100 tons of air conditioning, and 4000 square feet of common area. What would be the electric demand in terms of volt-amperes for each unit and for the complex? What would be the proper size of the main breaker for the panel box in each apartment, and what size wire should serve this panel box?
   Electric Appliances: Electric Range, Refrigerator/Freezer, Dishwasher, and Waste Disposal

Answers to Calculation Exercises

1. The standard nominal sizes for 120/240 single-phase electric service are 100, 150, 200, 300, 400, and 600 amps. For a single-family residence with 2500 square feet plus a two-car garage, with the following specific electrical appliances in addition to the standard lighting and miscellaneous power requirements, what would be the electric demand in terms of volt-amperes? For this demand, what would be the proper size of electric service that should be provided? What would be the required wire size for this service?

Electric Appliances

Electric Cooktop	4000 V-A
Double Electric Ovens	7500 V-A
Refrigerator/Freezer	750 V-A
Dishwasher	1200 V-A
Waste Disposal	500 V-A
Clothes Washer	500 V-A
Electric Clothes Dryer	5000 V-A
4 Tons Air Conditioning	4000 V-A
Lighting	2500 × 3 = 7800 V-A
Miscellaneous Power	2500 × 0.5 = 1250 V-A

Service

Volt-Ampere Demand: 32,500 V-A

(32,500 V-A × 1.25)/ 240 V = 170 amps
Electric Service: 200 amps

Wire Size: 3 Wire #000 AWG

2. For a single-family residence with 1250 square feet plus attached carport, with the standard lighting and miscellaneous power requirements plus the following specific appliances, what would be the electric demand in terms of volt-amperes? For this demand, what would be the proper size of electric service that should be provided? What would be the required wire size for this service?

Electric Appliances

Gas Range	300 V-A
Refrigerator/Freezer	750 V-A
Dishwasher	1200 V-A
Waste Disposal	500 V-A
Clothes Washer	500 V-A
Gas Clothes Dryer	350 V-A
2.5 Tons Air Conditioning	2500 V-A
Lighting	1250 × 3 = 3900 V-A
Miscellaneous Power	1250 × 0.5 = 625 V-A

Service

Volt-Ampere Demand: 10,625 V-A7

(10,625 V-A × 1.25)/ 240 V = 55 amps
Electric Service: 100 amps

Wire Size: 3 Wire #2 AWG

3. For a single-family residence with 2000 square feet plus attached carport, with the standard lighting and miscellaneous power requirements plus the following specific appliances, what would be the electric demand in terms of volt-amperes? For this demand, what would be the proper size of electric service that should be provided? What would be the required wire size for this service?

Electric Appliances

Electric Range	7500 V-A
Refrigerator/Freezer	750 V-A
Dishwasher	1200 V-A
Waste Disposal	500 V-A
Clothes Washer	500 V-A
Electric Clothes Dryer	5000 V-A
Baseboard Electric Heat (12 1-KWh Strip Heaters)	12,000 V-A
Lighting	2000 × 3 = 6000 V-A
Miscellaneous Power	2000 × 0.5 = 1000 V-A

Service

Volt-Ampere Demand: 34,450 V-A

(34,450 V-A × 1.25)/ 240 V = 180 amps
Electric Service: 200 amps

Wire Size: 3 Wire #000 AWG

4. For a multifamily apartment complex comprised of 40 1200-square-foot units, what would be the proper electric service that should be provided? Each unit has the standard lighting and miscellaneous power requirements plus the following specific appliances. The complex includes four washer and dryer combinations, 100 tons of air conditioning, and 4000 square feet of common area. What would be the electric demand in terms of volt-amperes for each unit and for the complex? What would be the proper size of the main breaker for the panel box in each apartment, and what size wire should serve this panel box?

Electric Appliances

Typical Unit

Electric Range	7500 V-A
Refrigerator/Freezer	750 V-A
Dishwasher	1200 V-A
Waste Disposal	500 V-A
Lighting	3(1200) = 2600 V-A
Miscellaneous Power	0.5(1200) = 600 V-A

Complex

4 Washers and Dryers	22,000 V-A
Lighting	3(4000) = 12,000 V-A
Miscellaneous Power	0.5(4000) = 2000 V-A
Air Conditioning	100 × 1000 = 100,000 V-A

Service

Volt-Ampere Demand: 13,150 V-A
(13,150 V-A × 1.25)/240 V = 68.5 amps
Apartment Circuit: 70 amps

Wire Size: 3 Wire #2 AWG
Volt-Ampere Demand for 40 Units: 526,000 V-A

Volt-Ampere Demand: 662,000 V-A
(662,000 V-A × 1.25)/240 V = 3500 A
Electric Service: 3500 amps

BIBLIOGRAPHY

Bradshaw, V. *The Building Environment: Active and Passive Control Systems.* John Wiley & Sons, Inc., Hoboken, NJ, 2006.

"Central Electric Light and Power Stations, 1907." Report of the Bureau of the Census, U.S. Department of Commerce and Labor. Government Printing Office, Washington, DC, 1910.

Grondzik W.T., A.G. Kwok, B. Stein, and J.S. Reynolds. *Mechanical and Electrical Equipment for Buildings.* John Wiley & Sons, Inc., New York, 2010.

Heerwagen, D. *Passive and Active Environmental Controls.* McGraw-Hill Companies, New York, 2004.

Hewitt, P.G. *Conceptual Physics: A New Introduction to Your Environment.* Little, Brown and Company, Boston, 1974.

Irwin, W. *The New Niagara: Tourism, Technology, and the Landscape of Niagara Falls.* Pennsylvania State University Press, University Park, PA, 1996.

NFPA 70: National Electrical Code. National Fire Protection Association, Inc., Quincy, MA, 2005.

Shuttleworth, R. *Mechanical and Electrical Systems for Construction.* McGraw-Hill Book Company, New York, 1983.

Skrabec, Q.R. *George Westinghouse: Gentle Genius.* Algora Publishing, New York, 2006.

Solar Energy International. *Photovoltaics, Design and Installation Manual.* New Society Publishers, Gabriola Island, BC, Canada, 2004.

Trout, C.M. *Electrical Installation and Inspection.* Delmar Publishers, Albany, NY, 2002.

13 FIRE PROTECTION AND EGRESS

FIRE SAFETY EGRESS

STAIRS

FIRE EGRESS

FIRE CONTROL—PREVENTION AND SUPPRESSION

FIRE SAFETY EGRESS

While we generally do not expect them to happen, terrible calamities can occur, and if they do, we should be reasonably prepared to minimize their impact. Toward this end, we need to consider how our designs can potentially limit the impacts of possible catastrophic events. For example, the structure must be designed to resist potential movements from earthquakes. The structure also must be protected against fire so that occupants are allowed adequate time to get out; this requires us to provide acceptable means of egress.

Although we hope that things will not go wrong, there are many cases in which they have. Sometimes because the designers and building managers did not properly consider what could happen, the results have been worse than perhaps they might have been. The fire in the Cook County Administration Building in Chicago on October 17, 2003, resulted in loss of life, in large part because of a failure to analyze potential dangers (see Figure 13.1).

There was a small fire in a storage room on the 12th floor of this building. This storage room was close to one of the main fire stairs in this 35-story building. While the fire was relatively small, like most fires it produced a lot of smoke. The combination of the proximity of the fire to the fire stair, the rapid action by the Chicago Fire Department, and the reasonable response of the occupants to evacuate the building resulted in the death of six people.

In order to combat the fire, the firefighters opened the 12th-floor door to the fire stair, which allowed smoke to rise up in the stair shaft. As people from the upper floors started coming down the fire stair, they confronted the smoke rising up the stair shaft, which was acting like a chimney. Afraid to continue down, they tried to get out of the fire stair but found that the doors were locked. They were trapped!

Fortunately, someone did open the door on the 27th floor, allowing many who were trying to avoid the smoke to get out of the fire stair. Thirteen people were overcome by smoke, and six of them could not be revived.

Even though the fire was relatively small, there was a call for the evacuation of the whole building. If the people on the upper floors had remained in their offices, they would have been safe. However, when the severity of a fire is not known, it is often reasonable to assume that when a fire alarm is sounded, the whole building should be evacuated. To further complicate matters, while some believe that total evacuation of large buildings should not be called for except by professional firefighters, in many places people are required to leave a building if a fire alarm is sounded. There is also the memory of the tragedy of September 11, 2001, when two very large structures were

Figure 13.1 COOK COUNTY ADMINISTRATION BUILDING
What was actually a relatively small fire in 2003 caused loss of life because the doors of the fire stairs were locked and a number of people were trapped in the smoke-filled stairwell. Source: "County Building Fire," Chicago Tribune photo by Charles Osgood, October 17, 2003. All rights reserved. Used with permission.

16-year-old bar boy lit a match while trying to replace a light bulb that a patron had removed. (Supposedly the patron wanted to kiss his girlfriend and wanted some privacy.) What happened next is unclear, but it is known that the artificial palm trees and drapery quickly caught fire. It took only 15 minutes for the fire to engulf the building, and many people were trapped, unable to get out (see Figure 13.3, which shows some of the mayhem as attempts were made to combat this blaze).

The impact of this tragic fire was extensive, and as a result, some very important building code requirements were developed: finishes and decorations to be nonflammable, limits on occupancy based on floor area and the number of fire exits, emergency lighting, exit signs, fire doors not to be locked, fire doors to open outward, and revolving doors to be flanked by swing doors. In addition, the Coconut Grove fire provided the impetus for the development of the

totally destroyed, resulting in 2752 fatalities[1] (see Figure 13.2). As a result, regardless of what they might be told, many people believe that when a fire alarm is sounded, the proper thing to do is to evacuate the building.

If the fire stair in the Cook County Administration Building had a smoke tower or had been provided with a fire suppression system, the stair tower would not have acted as a chimney even with the opened fire door on the 12th floor. If the building had a sprinkler system, perhaps the fire might never have developed enough to produce the smoke problem in the first place. Of course, the more critical issue was that the doors were locked, trapping people in the fire stair.

While 6 people died in the Cook County Administration Building fire, 492 people were killed in the November 28, 1942 Coconut Grove Night Club fire in Boston. This was almost half of all the people who were in the club when the fire started. It is believed that the fire began when a

Figure 13.2 WORLD TRADE CENTER, NEW YORK CITY – SEPTEMBER 11, 2001
The fire at the World Trade Center, which ultimately caused the collapse of both towers, was the result of terrorist attacks and was intensified by jet fuel. As a result, architectural errors were not the cause of this terrible calamity, but the event still raises a number of critical issues related to architectural design that must be considered, particularly how to accommodate both emergency egress and access for fire fighters. Photo by Aaron Petz and used with permission.

---

[1]The currently accepted number of people killed as a result of the attack at the World Trade Center on September 11, 2001, is 2752. This does not include the 10 hijackers that died, but it does include the 127 passengers and 20 crew members who were on the two planes that crashed into the towers.

Figure 13.3 COCONUT GROVE FIRE IN BOSTON
The 1942 fire at the Coconut Grove Night Club in Boston caused many deaths but led to numerous important regulations that have improved fire safety. Source: U.S. Fire Administration photo archives.

Life Safety Code of the National Fire Protection Association (NFPA).

Authorities estimated that possibly 300 of those killed in the Coconut Gove fire could have been saved if the exit doors had swung outward. Since this obvious design requirement and the others that were adopted following this calamity all seem to be quite reasonable, we might wonder why it took such a terrible loss of life before they were incorporated into our building codes. In addition to the above-listed requirements that were adopted following the Coconut Grove fire, fire sprinklers, which had been introduced in 1874 to protect warehouses, came into widespread use to provide life safety for building occupants.

As noted, since the Coconut Grove fire apparently started when flammable decorations and draperies were ignited by a match, building codes require fire rating of the finishes used in most structures, especially places of assembly. However, the February 20, 2003 fire at The Station nightclub in West Warwick, Rhode Island, which caused 100 fatalities and over 200 injuries, clearly resulted when pyrotechnic devices called *gerbs* were activated during the performance of the heavy metal band Great White and then ignited the flammable foam used for soundproofing around the stage area. The fire at The Station was one of the deadliest nightclub fires in U.S. history.[2]

The third deadliest nightclub fire[3] occurred at the Beverly Hills Supper Club in Southgate, Kentucky, across the

river from Cincinnati. It occurred on May 28, 1977 and resulted in 165 fatalities and over 200 injuries. Unfortunately, the club had neither a sprinkler system nor an audible fire alarm system, both of which were code requirements for places of assembly. The severity of the fire and the resulting deaths and injuries were compounded by a number of factors, most of which were additional code violations. The club had noncompliant electrical wiring, and because of several renovations and additions to the club, there were various concealed layers of construction. The fire began in these concealed layers, apparently because of an electrical fault, and developed rather extensively before becoming apparent to the occupants. In addition, the club had flammable carpeting, finishes that released toxic fumes when burned, and the fire stairs were not properly enclosed.

As presented in the article "Thirty Years Later: The Beverly Hills Supper Club Fire" in the on-line publication *Fire Engineering*:

"Poor building design was a major contributing factor to the significant number of deaths and injuries," said Chris Jelenewicz, Engineering Program Manager with the Bethesda, Maryland–based Society of Fire Protection Engineers. "Additionally, many lives were lost because the fire burned out of control for a considerable amount of time before the occupants were notified that an emergency existed in the building." . . .

Fire investigators believed the cause of the fire to be electrical failure. The fire started in a combustible concealed space in an unoccupied room, where it burned

---

[2]The fire at The Station was 12th deadliest in terms of fatalities in U.S. fires.

[3]The fire at the Coconut Grove was the nightclub fire that caused the highest number of deaths, with the second highest number of fatalities occurring in the 1940 fire at the Rhythm Club in Natchez, Mississippi.

unnoticed for a significant amount of time. Once the fire was discovered by staff, instead of notifying the occupants to exit the facility, the staff unsuccessfully attempted to extinguish the fire. Soon after the fire was first observed, the fire spread quickly throughout the building via the main corridors. . . .

In addition, the building was not equipped with a sprinkler system or a fire alarm/detection system.

"Because of the delay in notification, the lack of fire protection systems and an insufficient number of fire exits, the occupants just didn't have enough time to get out alive," said Jelenewicz.

Most of the deaths were due to the inhalation of smoke or toxic gases. Many of the dead were reported to be piled on top of each other. Others were left sitting dead at their tables.

Additional contributing factors to the number of deaths and injuries included combustible interior finishes, a delay in calling the fire department and the lack of an evacuation plan.

As a result of this fire, many building requirements were enhanced to make night clubs and other buildings with large populations safer from fire. Some of these requirements included provisions for improved exiting systems, safer interior finishes, emergency planning and the installation of fire alarm and automatic fire suppression systems.

Moreover, the fire provided new insight for the fire protection engineering community on how humans behave in fires. For example, in the Beverly Hills fire, it was observed that the wait staff assisted in the evacuation of the patrons. These types of observations showed how the roles and responsibilities of building occupants influence decisions made during a fire.

"The Beverly Hills Supper Club Fire reminds us of the threat that is posed by fire and the importance of designing buildings that keep people safe from fire," said Jelenewicz.[4]

Once again, "As a result of [the Beverly Hills Supper Club] fire, many building requirements were enhanced to make night clubs and other buildings with large populations safer from fire." But when are we going to learn?

Tables 13.1 and 13.2 list some of the worst U.S. fires. The first table lists them in chronological order, and the second lists them by the number of fatalities that occurred in each fire.

While both the 1871 Peshtigo forest fire in northeast Wisconsin and the 1906 San Francisco earthquake and subsequent fire claimed many lives, they are not usually included in listings of the worst U.S. fires since both of these calamities included a very large geographical area and numerous structures. However, the actual damage caused by these tragedies might actually exceed what is listed. For example, while the U.S. Army reported that the fatalities resulting from the San Francisco earthquake and fire were 498 deaths in San Francisco, 102 deaths in the San Jose area, and 64 deaths in Santa Rosa, recent research by Gladys Hansen and Emmet Condon suggests that the total death toll from the earthquake might have been more than 3000. While there might be questions about the total number of fatalities, records on property destruction from the San Francisco earthquake and fire suggest that this was one of the most expensive property losses and was roughly equal to the property loss from the 2001 World Trade Center disaster.[5]

There are many good reasons for us to be aware of the possibility that a fire may occur in the buildings we design and to address this potential in our work. While it might not be possible to prevent all fires, through a thoughtful and considered design effort we can decrease the likelihood that one will occur and reduce its impact if it does occur, including minimizing injuries and deaths and reducing property loss.

U.S. Fire Statistics

Each year in the United States, there are generally more than 1.5 million fires, with over 500,000 of them occurring in structures.[6] Typically, there are more fires in New York City than in the entire country of Japan! Although Americans believe that their building regulations and standard of living make the United States one of the safest places in terms of fires, the statistics suggest otherwise. The 1973 Federal Emergency Management Agency (FEMA) publication, *America Burning*, was one of the early attempts to bring awareness to this reality. It suggested that, despite stringent building code regulations, fire was a critical issue in the United States:

---

[4]"Thirty Years Later: The Beverly Hills Supper Club Fire," *Fire Engineering,* http://www.fireengineering.com/articles/article_display.html?id=293277.

[5]RMS Special Report, "World Trade Center Disaster," Risk Management Solutions, Inc., Newark, CA, 2001. This report indicates that over 28,000 buildings were destroyed, resulting in an estimated monetary loss that exceeded $400 million in 1906 dollars or around $10 billion in 2009 dollars.

[6]M.J. Karter, Jr., "NFPA Reports: U.S. Fire Loss for 2007," *NFPA Journal,* September/October 2008.

Table 13.1: LISTING, IN CHRONOLOGICAL ORDER, OF SOME OF THE WORST U.S. FIRES

Year	Fire	Fatalities
1871	Great Chicago Fire, Chicago, Illinois	250+
1871	Peshtigo Forest Fire, Northeast Wisconsin (+16 Towns Destroyed and 1.2 Million Acres Scorched)	1152
1876	Conway's Theater, Brooklyn, New York	285
1903	Chicago Iroquois Theater, Chicago, Illinois	602
1906	San Francisco Earthquake and Fire, San Francisco, California	700–800
1908	Lakeview Grammar School, Collinwood, Ohio	175
1908	Rhodes Opera House, Boyertown, Pennsylvania	170
1911	Triangle Shirtwaist Company , New York, New York	146
1929	Cleveland Clinic Hospital, Cleveland, Ohio	125
1929	Eddystone Ammunition Co. Plant Explosion, Eddystone, Pennsylvania	133
1930	Ohio State Penitentiary, Columbus, Ohio	320
1937	Consolidated School Explosion, New London, Texas	294
1940	Rhythm Night Club, Natchez, Mississippi	207
1942	Coconut Grove, Boston, Massachusetts	492
1944	Ringling Brothers and Barnum and Bailey Circus Fire, Hartford, Connecticut	168
1946	Winecoff Hotel, Atlanta, Georgia	119
1958	Our Lady of the Angels School, Chicago	95
1977	Beverly Hills Supper Club, Covington, Kentucky	165
1980	MGM Grand Hotel/Casino, Las Vegas, Nevada	85
1990	Happy Lands Social Club, Bronx, New York	87
1995	Alfred P. Murrah Federal Building Explosion, Oklahoma City, Oklahoma	168
2001	The World Trade Center, New York, New York	2752
2003	The Station Nightclub, West Warwick, Rhode Island	100

Source: Adapted from the *1984 NFPA Fire Almanac* (National Fire Protection Association, Quincy, MA, 1984) and James Cornell, *The Great International Disaster Book* (Pocket Books, New York, 1976).

"In an America that has only lately grown conscious of its ecological responsibilities, there is a need also to develop an awareness of fire's role as one of the greatest wasters of our natural resources. Appallingly, the richest and most technologically advanced nation in the world leads all the major industrialized countries in per capita deaths and property loss from fire. While differing reporting procedures make international comparisons unreliable, the fact that the United States reports a deaths-per-million-population rate nearly twice that of second-ranking Canada leaves little doubt that this nation leads the other industrialized nations in fire deaths per capita. Similarly, in the category of economic loss per capita, the United States exceeds Canada by one-third."[7]

"15 years later, America Burning Revisited, *the report from a national workshop organized by FEMA, suggested that, "The characteristics of the nation's fire problem have changed little since the publication of* America Burning. *. . . Eighty percent of our fire deaths continue to occur in residences."*[8]

In the more than 20 years since this second report was published with more rigorous code regulations, widespread use of fire suppression systems (sprinklers), and broad adoption of smoke detectors, conditions have improved somewhat, although not significantly. As indicated by the 2008 statistics available from the U.S. Fire Administration, a unit of FEMA, the conditions remain pretty much as they were when *America Burning* and *America Burning*

---

[7] *America Burning*, The Report of The National Commission on Fire Prevention and Control (Federal Emergency Management Agency, Washington, DC, 1973), pp. 1–2.

[8] *America Burning Revisited*, Report of a National Workshop–Tyson's Corner, Virginia, November 30–December 2, 1987 (Federal Emergency Management Agency, Washington, DC, 1987), p. 22.

Table 13.2: LISTING, IN ORDER OF FATALITIES, OF SOME OF THE WORST U.S. FIRES

Fatalities	Fire	Year
2752	The World Trade Center, New York, New York	2001
1152	Peshtigo Forest Fire, Northeast Wisconsin (+16 Towns Destroyed and 1.2 Million Acres Scorched)	1871
700–800	San Francisco Earthquake and Fire, San Francisco, California	1906
602	Chicago Iroquois Theater, Chicago, Illinois	1903
492	Coconut Grove, Boston, Massachusetts	1942
320	Ohio State Penitentiary, Columbus, Ohio	1930
294	Consolidated School Explosion, New London, Texas	1937
285	Conway's Theater, Brooklyn, New York	1876
250+	Great Chicago Fire, Chicago, Illinois	1871
207	Rhythm Night Club, Natchez, Mississippi	1940
175	Lakeview Grammar School, Collinwood, Ohio	1908
170	Rhodes Opera House, Boyertown, Pennsylvania	1908
168	Ringling Brothers and Barnum and Bailey Circus Fire, Hartford, Connecticut	1944
168	Alfred P. Murrah Federal Building Explosion, Oklahoma City, Oklahoma	1995
165	Beverly Hills Supper Club, Covington, Kentucky	1977
146	Triangle Shirtwaist Company, New York, New York	1911
133	Eddystone Ammunition Co. Plant Explosion, Eddystone, Pennsylvania	1929
125	Cleveland Clinic Hospital, Cleveland, Ohio	1929
119	Winecoff Hotel, Atlanta, Georgia	1946
100	The Station Nightclub, West Warwick, Rhode Island	2003
95	Our Lady of the Angels School, Chicago	1958
87	Happy Lands Social Club, Bronx, New York	1990
85	MGM Grand Hotel/Casino, Las Vegas, Nevada	1980

Source: Adapted from the *1984 NFPA Fire Almanac* (National Fire Protection Association, Quincy, MA, 1984) and James Cornell, *The Great International Disaster Book* (Pocket Books, New York, 1976).

Revisited were published (see Tables 13.3 and 13.4). The statistics for 2008 indicate that:

- There were an estimated 1.5 million fires.
- Fire killed more Americans than all natural disasters combined.
- There were 3438 fatalities as the result of fire.
- There were around 17,000 injuries as the result of fire.
- Eighty-four percent of all civilian fire deaths occurred in residences.
- Direct property loss due to fires was estimated at $15.5 billion.[9]

Table 13.3: ALL U.S. FIRE STATISTICS, 1999–2008

Year	Fires	Deaths	Injuries	Direct Dollar Loss in Millions
1999	1,823,000	3,570	21,875	$10,024
2000	1,708,000	4,045	22,350	$11,207
2001	1,734,500	6,196	21,100	$44,023
2002	1,687,500	3,380	18,425	$10,337
2003	1,584,500	3,925	18,125	$12,307
2004	1,550,000	3,900	17,875	$9,794
2005	1,602,000	3,675	17,925	$10,672
2006	1,642,500	3,245	16,400	$11,307
2007	1,557,500	3,430	17,675	$14,639
2008	1,451,500	3,320	16,705	$15,478
Average	**1,634,150**	**3,869**	**18,846**	**$14,979**

Source: Adapted from "National Fire Protection Association Fire Loss in the U.S. 2008," U.S. Fire Administration, Washington, DC, 2008.

[9]QuickStats presented at: http://www.usfa.dhs.gov/statistics/quickstats/index.shtm and adapted from data from "National Fire Protection Association Fire Loss in the U.S. 2008," U.S. Fire Administration, Washington, DC, 2008, and "Firefighter Fatalities in the United States in 2008," U.S. Fire Administration, Washington, DC, 2008.

Table 13.4: U.S. RESIDENTIAL FIRE STATISTICS, 1999–2008

Year	Fires	%	Deaths	%	Injuries	%	Direct Dollar Loss in Millions	%
1999	383,000	21%	2,920	82%	16,425	75%	$5,092	51%
2000	379,500	22%	3,445	85%	17,400	78%	$5,674	51%
2001	396,500	23%	3,140	51%	15,575	74%	$5,643	13%
2002	401,000	24%	2,695	80%	14,050	76%	$6,055	59%
2003	402,000	25%	3,165	81%	14,075	78%	$6,074	49%
2004	410,500	26%	3,225	83%	14,175	79%	$5,948	61%
2005	396,000	25%	3,055	83%	13,825	77%	$6,875	64%
2006	412,500	25%	2,620	81%	12,925	79%	$6,990	62%
2007	414,000	27%	2,895	84%	14,000	79%	$7,546	52%
2008	403,000	28%	2,780	84%	13,560	81%	$8,550	55%
Average	399,800	24%	2,994	77%	14,601	77%	$6,445	43%

Note: Percentages (%) indicate the total percentage for the United States for residential fires.
Source: Adapted from "National Fire Protection Association Fire Loss in the U.S. 2008," U.S. Fire Administration, Washington, DC, 2008.

STAIRS

As noted, one of the things that must be addressed is the exiting system, and stairs are often a major part of this system, particularly in multistory structures. So, let us begin by considering how to design an effective stair, not just as a means of egress during an emergency, but as a viable way of moving between floors. Perhaps with better-designed stairs, both in terms of the actual stair run and the quality of the space, we could reduce the use of elevators, particularly when moving between only two or three floors.

First of all, we should clarify what a stair is. Perhaps we can agree that all stairs are a series of horizontal "platforms" arranged in a manner that provides a consistent vertical and horizontal displacement. These platforms, which are called *treads,* typically have a depth of around 10 to 12 inches, although it may be greater. The horizontal displacement of the treads is usually equal to the tread depth. The vertical displacement, which is referred to as the *riser height,* is usually 6 to 8 inches. A riser and a tread are usually considered to be a step.

Generally, for an assembly of steps to be considered a stair, there must be at least three risers, although in some jurisdictions, a stair must have at least four risers. While these distinctions might seem petty, what actually constitutes a stair is important for several reasons. One reason is that the code requirements governing stair design do not apply if the arrangement of steps is not actually a stair. Another reason is that when there are only a few risers, rather than *stair* they perhaps should be called *danger.*

When there are just a few risers, sometimes it is hard to determine that there actually is a change in level. With only one, two, or even three risers, people have a tendency not to recognize the change in level or to see that there are stairs. This can be dangerous, especially when approaching the steps from the upper level. The steps are often not visible from that level, especially at a distance, and as a result, there might not be adequate awareness of the danger. If there were a handrail at the steps, it would suggest the presence of the change in level, but while handrails are required with a stair, they are not required with only a few steps. As a result, it makes sense to avoid conditions in which there are just a few risers in a run, especially in a public space. This is especially true for only one step (see Figure 13.4).

Interestingly, one step does not seem to pose a significant problem when it occurs at a doorway. When exiting a building, traditionally there was always a step down, and as a result, we tend to be prepared for a level change as part of the transition. Of course, this is different from a few steps within a space since at a door there is a clear sense of a transition, although not necessarily in terms of a level change. By the way, the entry step provides some benefits, particularly in terms of moisture control in cold climates. However, in conformance with the Americans with Disabilities Act access requirements, the entry step is disappearing in most public structures. Perhaps a step at a doorway will become more of a concern when it is no longer expected.

Riser and Tread Dimensions

A stair is a run of steps that includes four or more risers. *Architectural Graphic Standards* presents a simple diagram, developed by Paul Vaughan, AIA, of Charleston, West Virginia, that relates the dimensions of risers and treads for various stairs. This diagram also presents information on

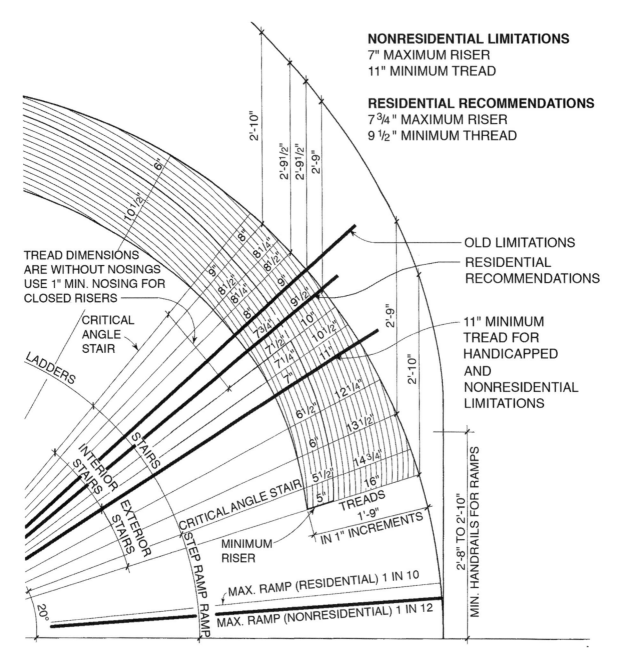

Figure 13.4 TREADS AND RISERS GRAPH
This graph is adapted from a graph that was developed by Paul Vaughan, AIA, and is used with permission of John Wiley and Sons.

handrail heights. A set of rule-of-thumb formulas is also included as part of the original figure presented in *Architectural Graphic Standards*.[10]

Interior Stairs

1. Riser + tread = 17 or $17^1/_2$ inches;
   thus, $7^1/_2$-inch rise + 10-inch tread = $17^1/_2$ inches

2. Riser × tread = 70 or 75;
   thus, 7.5-inch rise × 10-inch tread = 75 inches
3. 2 risers + tread ≥ 24 inches and ≤ 26 inches
4. Within any flight, $^3/_{16}$-inch maximum variation in riser height or tread depth

Exterior Stairs

Exterior stairs generally are not as steep as interior stairs, since space for wider treads and lower risers is usually available outdoors. Also, more dangerous conditions can

---

[10]Ramsey/Sleeper, *Architectural Graphic Standards* (John Wiley & Sons, Inc., Hoboken, NJ, 1989), p. 9.

exist (ice, snow, rain). Wider treads and lower risers make exterior steps safer. The following formula has been devised by Thomas Church in *Gardens Are for People*[11]:

$$2 \text{ risers} + \text{tread} = 26 \text{ inches}$$

thus an exterior stair with 6-inch risers requires 14-inch treads.

A more general recommendation for the ratio between riser and tread is that the sum of two risers plus one tread should equal 24 to 26 inches. This ratio achieves a very comfortable stair slope for both ascending and descending while allowing a little more design latitude.

$$2 \text{ risers} + \text{tread} = 24 \text{ to } 26 \text{ inches}$$

For public occupancies, current codes generally tend to require that riser heights not exceed 7 inches and that tread depth be at least 11 inches. Based on these dimensions, the 2 risers + tread formula results in 25 inches, which is midway between the recommendation for 24 to 26 inches. While the riser height can be greater than 7 inches within a private residence or dwelling unit, many codes limit residential risers to less than 8 inches and sometimes to no more than $7^3/_4$ inches. Similarly, within a residence, the tread depth can be reduced to a minimum of 9 inches. With two 8-inch risers and one 9-inch tread, the 2 risers + tread formula again results in 25 inches.

Another guide that some use is that the product of riser height times tread depth should equal 70 to 75:

$$\text{riser} \times \text{tread} = 70 \text{ to } 75$$

Assuming the standard public stair 7-inch riser and 11-inch tread, the results would be 77, which is just above the maximum. With an 8-inch riser and a 9-inch tread, the product of the two falls within the range.

Most codes also set 4 inches as the minimum riser height, which is less than the lowest riser presented in Figure 13.4 and the similar graph in *Architectural Graphic Standards*. Assuming a 4-inch riser, the 2 riser + tread formula indicates that the tread depth should increase to at least 16 inches.

Within any stair run, the riser and tread dimensions should be consistent, with a maximum variation of $^3/_8$ inch stipulated by most codes. This consistency is important since when we walk up or down a stair we typically set our gait by our initial movement, which is based in large part on what we observe as we approach the stair. Once we begin to climb or descend a stair, we normally do not continue to look where we are stepping. As a result, if a riser height exceeds what we have experienced on walking the stair,

we are likely to catch our toe if we are on the way up or land rather hard if we are walking down. In either situation, we could have a problem, although on the way up this could cause us to trip. If one riser is less than expected based on the rest of the risers within a run, we can still have some difficulty, but generally one shorter riser is more disturbing or disruptive than potentially dangerous.[12]

Interestingly, if a stair is obviously irregular, we tend to have less trouble than when a stair appears to be regular but is not. If a run of stairs has riser heights that are obviously variable, we can observe this as we approach the stair and will likely pay attention to where we step rather than rely on our initial determination of how to proceed that we tend to use with stairs that appear to be consistent.

Winder treads, such as those used with spiral stairs, are generally no longer permitted except perhaps in private residences and for special conditions. When winders are permitted, typically the minimum tread depth is 9 inches at a point 12 inches from the interior curve, with a 6-inch minimum depth at any point on the stair. Within any flight of winding stairs, the greatest winder tread depth at the 12-inch walk line should not exceed the smallest by more than $^3/_8$ inch.

Stair Dimensions

Several other factors also apply to stair design. In terms of width, 36 inches is recommended as the minimum dimension for a residential stair. In nonresidential occupancies, the minimum width is usually set at 44 inches, although 4 feet is generally suggested as the appropriate minimum width for a public stair since the additional 4 inches make it easier for two people going in opposite directions to pass without necessitating any body distortions to avoid colliding. Of course, 4 feet is also a standard building module. A 5-foot width is even better and is recommended for any stair that is intended to be used regularly by people going up and down.

Interestingly, in the Vontz Center for Molecular Studies designed by Frank Gehry for the University of Cincinnati Medical Center, the central stairs are only 40 inches wide (see Figure 13.5). When asked why they were so narrow,

---

[11] Thomas Church, *Gardens Are for People* (University of California Press, Berkeley, CA, 1995).

[12] A number of years ago, when attending a conference at Tulane, a group of us were outside enjoying the warm winter climate during a break in the sessions. We were sitting on the entry stairs to the architecture building, and being respectful, we were not preventing others from using the stair. However, we noticed that a number of people tripped on the top step as they were entering the building. While this could have been attributed to the distraction we were causing, I decided to compare the riser heights. Using a piece of paper, I was able to ascertain that the top riser was around $^1/_2$ inch higher than the other risers in the stair run, which apparently resulted when a coating was applied to the top landing.

Figure 13.5 VONTZ CENTER STAIR
The central stair in the Vontz Center for Molecular Studies at the University of Cincinnati Medical Center, designed by Frank Gehry, has a width of only 40 inches. This is rather narrow, considering that, in addition to making it difficult for two people to pass on the stair, this stair is the major architectural feature in the central open space of the research facility.

rather than admit what seems to be the real reason (that there was not enough space to make them any wider), Gehry apparently suggested that this was intentional so that the various medical researchers working in the building, who tend to work somewhat in isolation, would meet other researchers. This is not a good idea; researchers who are intensely focused on their own work, probably work of critical importance, will be delayed as they contort themselves to pass someone going in the other direction—not necessarily a good way to appreciate the meeting or to provide the basis for a continuing association. No wonder these central stairs are not often used even though they are the main architectural feature in the central open space of this research facility.

Another factor is the clearance height between the stair and any overhead element, such as the next higher stair (see Figure 13.6). This is usually set at a minimum of 6 feet 8 inches (80 inches) of vertical clearance above the nose of any stair tread. There is also a limitation on a maximum vertical rise of 12 feet before a landing is necessary. Previously, certain codes limited a stair run to a maximum of only 15 risers before a landing was required. However, using a riser of just under 7 inches, a stair run that extends a full 12 feet (144 inches) would have 21 risers (144 inches/21 = $6^7/_8$ inches). With a shorter riser height, the stair run could include even more

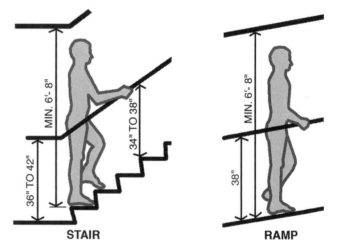

Figure 13.6 STAIR AND RAMP RAIL AND CLEARANCE LIMITATIONS
Since a guardrail is not to have an opening large enough to allow a 4-inch-diameter ball to pass through, the area below a continuous rail might exceed this allowance.

than 21 risers between landings and still conform to most current codes.

Exterior stairs, which fall into the public category, must adhere to the requirements for public stairs (see Table 13.5). That is, the maximum height of the riser is 7 inches and the minimum depth is 11 inches. Monumental stairs

Table 13.5: REQUIREMENTS FOR EXIT STAIRS

	New Stair	Exisitng Stairs	
		Class A	Class B
Minimum Width Clear of All Obstructions[a] Total Occupant Load[b] = 50 or More Total Occupant Load[b] = Less Than 50	44 in. 36 in.	44 in. 36 in.	44 in. 36 in.
Maximum Height of Risers	7 in.	$7^1/_2$ in.	8 in.
Minimum Height of Risers	4 in.		
Minimum Tread Depth	11 in.	10 in.	9 in.
Minimum Headroom	6 ft 8 in.	6 ft 8 in.	6 ft 8 in.
Maximum Height between Landings	12 ft	12 ft	12 ft
Minimum Dimensions of Landings in the Direction of Travel	Equal to Width of Stair. With a Straight Stair Run; This Need Not Exceed 4 ft.		
Doors Opening Immediately on Stairs, without a Landing at Least the Width of the Door	No	No	No

[a] A 3/2-inch projection at and below the handrail is allowed.
[b] Occupant load includes all floors served by the stair. There isno decrease in dimensions in the direction of travel.

do not necessarily have to conform to these dimensional requirements for riser and tread, although it is hard to see why they would not.[13]

Handrails and Guardrails

Handrails are required for all stairs. The height of the handrail is to be no less than 34 inches and no more than 38 inches directly above the front nose of the treads. If the stair is less than 44 inches in width or if it serves only one individual dwelling unit, just one handrail is necessary, but generally two handrails, one on either side of the stair, are required. An intermediate handrail is required for each portion of the stair that is 88 inches or more in width.

As implied by its name, a handrail is intended to be gripped by the hand. As such, the rail should be configured in a manner and size that will permit this. If the rail is circular, as with a pipe rail, the diameter must be no less than $1^1/_4$ inches or more than 2 inches. While a standard 2×4, or perhaps a 2×6, is only $1^1/_2$ inches wide, which falls within these allowable dimensions, it would not be an acceptable handrail since it is not a shape that can be effectively grasped. However, a 2×4 or a 2×6 could serve as a handrail if it were formed so that one could take hold of the top of it (see Figure 13.7).

In addition to having an acceptable shape and size, a handrail must have adequate clearance from any wall or

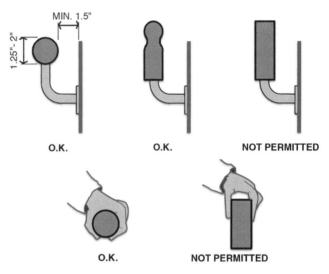

Figure 13.7 HANDRAIL LIMITATIONS

Handrails are intended to be held by the hand, which requires a configuration that makes this possible and a free distance from the wall of at least $1^1/_2$ inches. Pipe rails should be between $1^1/_4$ and 2 inches since when they are either too small or too large, it is difficult to get a good grasp on the rail.

partition. A minimal distance of $1^1/_2$ inches is suggested for such clearance. If the rail were 2 inches in diameter, it would project into the stair by $3^1/_2$ inches. Most codes do not count this projection into the stair as a reduction in the stair's width. In fact, most codes allow the handrails to extend into the required stair width up to $4^1/_2$ inches.

Stairs that are open on one or more sides must have guardrails on the open sides. A stair landing or any platform that is open and is 30 inches or more above the

---

[13] This is a link to the Safety Is Us Web page that addresses stairs, stairways, and handrail safety requirements issued by OSHA: http://safetyis .us/stairs.htm.

adjacent level must also be provided with guardrails. Guardrails typically must be at least 42 inches high; however, some jurisdictions allow a guardrail along the side of a stair to be reduced in height. This is permitted with the intent of the guardrail also serving as the handrail, but there are various allowable heights, such as 34 to 38 inches by some regulations and 36 to 37 inches by others. The height is measured as the vertical distance above the tread to the top of the rail in line with the nose of the tread or the face of the riser at the forward edge of the tread. A guardrail along the open side of a stair is sometimes referred to as a *stair rail.*

Another requirement for guardrails is that they must be configured so that a 4-inch sphere cannot pass through. This is a fairly recent requirement, reducing what used to be the 6-inch rule. The intention of this rule is to prevent the head of an infant from passing through the rail. Earlier stairs often were quite open and did not protect a child from falling through the stair rail. The current 4-inch limitation provides greater assurance that the intention of this regulation will be met.

A corollary of the switch to the 4-inch-sphere rule is that if spindles or balusters are used to form the stair rail, it is now necessary to have three balusters for each tread. Furthermore, with a 7-inch riser and a 10-inch or larger tread, a 4-inch sphere could pass under any barrier that was set on the stairs, resting or running from nose to nose of the treads (see Figure 13.8). The size of this opening increases with an increase in either the riser or tread dimensions, suggesting that the standard nonresidential 7/11 design really is not compliant with this code regulation unless some element is added below a continuous stair rail to reduce the opening. To avoid this and yet ensure that a 4-inch sphere cannot pass through the space below a stair rail, a 10-inch tread should be used with a riser that is no higher than $6\frac{1}{2}$ inches and an 11-inch tread with a riser of only $6\frac{1}{4}$ inches.

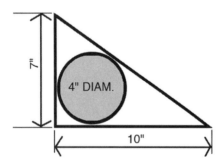

Figure 13.8 OPENING BELOW A STAIR RAIL
Since a stair rail must not have an opening large enough to allow a 4-inch-diameter ball to pass through, the area below a continuous rail might exceed this allowance.

FIRE EGRESS

September 11, 2001 should impress upon us all that fire egress is something that we must take seriously.

2752 people were killed in the destruction of the World Trade Center, including 411 emergency workers who responded to the scene and died as a result of their attempts to rescue people and fight the fires. There were also 147 fatalities in the two planes that struck the towers. While the full occupancy of the two towers was around 50,000, NIST estimates that, at the time of the attack, there were around 17,400 people in the towers. Most of the people who were below the impact floors were able to be evacuated safely, although, with the exception of 18 people who were in the impact zone in the south tower and yet managed to escape, those in the impact zone and above were not so fortunate.

As tragic as this event was and as important as it is that we not become complacent in any way, it is still somewhat reassuring that so many people survived. In less than 2 hours, even with the shock and extraordinary confusion that overwhelmed us all, almost 15,000, or around 85% of the people, were able to get out. While we can take some comfort in the fact that so many people were able to get out, fortunately, at the time that the first plane struck the north tower at the World Trade Center, the towers were only partially occupied. If not, the number of fatalities would have been much worse.

A lesson for us to learn from this tragedy is that, while we cannot protect against all eventualities, providing proper egress from a building is a serious responsibility. And to meet this responsibility, we need to know what the egress requirements are and, recognizing that they are merely the minimum, use them as a starting point and not as the goal.

The minimal requirements for fire egress are stipulated by building codes based on the type of occupancy, the number of occupants, and whether or not the structure is sprinkled. These requirements typically indicate the number of exits that must be provided; the width of the doors, corridors (passageways), and fire stairs; and the acceptable length of travel.

Exit Units

Various tables are available to determine the allowable or necessary dimensions of the various components of the emergency egress system. Since the requirements vary in different codes, we should always check the requirements for the jurisdiction in which a building is to be located. However, there is considerable general agreement among the current codes, although there are often slight differences in the specific stipulations.

Table 13.6: SUMMARY OF PROVISIONS FOR OCCUPANT LOAD AND EXIT CAPACITY

Occupancy	Occupant Load (sq ft)	Egress Width per Person	
		Doors, Corridors Horizontal Exits, Ramps	Stairs
Assembly			
Less Concentrated Use without Fixed Seating	15 Net (1.4)	0.2	0.3
Concentrated Use without Fixed Seating	7 Net (0.65)	0.2	0.3
Fixed Seating	Actual Number of Seats	0.2	0.3
Educational			
Classrooms	20 Net (1.9)	0.2	0.3
Shops and Vocational	50 Net (4.6)	0.2	0.3
Care Centers	35 Net (3.3)	0.2	0.3
Health Care		NAS AS	NAS AS
Sleeping Departments	120 Gross (11.1)	0.5 0.2	0.6 0.3
Treatment Departments	240 Gross (22.3)	0.5 0.2	0.6 0.3
Residential	200 Gross (18.6)	0.2	
Board and Care	200 Gross (18.6)	0.2	0.3
Mercantile			
Street Floor and Sales Basement	30 Gross (3.7)	0.2	0.3
Multiple Street Floors (Each)	40 Gross (3.7)	0.2	0.3
Other Floors	60 Gross (5.6)	0.2	0.3
Storage – Shipping	300 Gross (27.9)	0.2	0.3
Malls	See NFPA Code		
Business	100 Gross (9.3)	0.2	0.3
Industrial	100 Gross (9.3)	0.2	0.3
Detention and Correctional	120 Gross (11.1)	0.2	0.3

NAS, no area sprinkler; AS, area sprinkler.

Source: Adapted from NFPA 101® from the *Fire Protection Handbook,* 16th ed., © 1997, National Fire Protection Association, Quincy, MA, 02269.

Table 13.6 provides a basis for determining the number of occupants for different occupancies and then the appropriate widths per person for the different egress elements. While there are considerable differences in terms of the amount of square footage per occupant, the egress widths per person are fairly consistent at 0.3 inch per person for stairs and 0.2 inch per person for the other elements (doors, corridors, horizontal exits, and ramps).

Obviously, the limited width of 0.2 or 0.3 inch cannot by itself accommodate anyone. While the required overall egress width is set by the product of the number of occupants multiplied by one of these dimensions, the design of an egress system is usually based on the notion of a 22-inch-wide *unit of exit.*[14] When the calculations indicate a fractional number of units, the standard procedure is to either add 12 inches, when the fraction is $1/2$ or less, or increase to the next whole number of units when it is more.

That is, acceptable widths are usually set at 36, 44, 56, 66, 78, 88, 100, 110 inches, and so on.

If a corridor serves fewer than 50 occupants, most codes permit a reduction in the corridor width to 36 inches. A 36-inch corridor provides one and a half exit units and, based on a 0.2-inch egress width per person, should be able to service 180 people.

36 in./0.2 in. per person = 180 people

The standard minimum width of a corridor, especially if it serves 50 or more people in a public building, is 44 inches or two units of exit. At the 0.2-inch egress width per person, a 44-inch corridor should be able to handle up to 220 people.

44 in./0.2 in. per person = 220 people

What corridor width would be required for 250 people? At 0.2 inch per person, a 50-inch corridor would be required, so using the unit of exit approach, the corridor should be at least 56 inches wide (2 units at 22 inches and one fractional unit at 12 inches). But will such a corridor really accommodate more people than a 44-inch-wide

---

[14]While *unit of exit* is perhaps the legitimate term used in many building codes, *exit unit* or merely *unit* are often used to indicate a prescribed width, usually 22 inches, for both a corridor and a stair. This represents the width that is apparently required for a person. At 44 inches, two people should be able to walk abreast.

Table 13.7: CAPACITY OF A UNIT OF EXIT

	Stairs at 0.3 Inch per Person	Other at 0.2 Inch per Person
22-Inch Unit of Exit	73 Persons	110 Persons
12-Inch Fractional Unit	40 Persons	60 Persons

corridor? That is, does a partial exit unit really provide any increase in the capacity of a door, corridor, or stair?

While we ponder this, perhaps it is still helpful to know the capacity of each unit of exit (see Table 13.7). At the 0.3-inch egress width per person stipulated for stairs, a unit of exit can handle 73 persons. At the 0.2-inch egress width per person stipulated for most horizontal exit elements, a unit of exit can supposedly accommodate 110 persons. However, there are studies that suggest that only 40 to 45 persons per minute can be handled by a 22-inch unit of exit. And there are observations that only 24 persons per minute are actually able to move in a unit of exit, and this under peak flow conditions!

In general, while 44 inches is the minimum width of most corridors in terms of fire egress, 60 inches, or 5 feet, is the recommended minimum width, and 8 feet is quite common. Since 5 feet and 8 feet equal almost three and four exit units, respectively, at 24/40 persons per unit suggested by these studies and observations, the 5-foot corridor can accommodate only 72 at 24 persons per unit or 120 at 40 persons per unit. The capacity of the 8-foot corridor would be 96 or 160 persons.

Table 13.8 lists the Building Officials and Code Administrators (BOCA) National Building Code's widths of egress for various use groups. As indicated in this table, the egress widths are based on whether or not the structure is sprinkled. While less restrictive egress requirements for sprinkled buildings seem to make sense, a number of code officials are now questioning this, particularly based on findings from actual fires. Perhaps it is not that the distinction is wrong but rather that the egress requirements are not stringent enough.

Egress width through doors is based on the clear opening when the door is open to 90°. Sometimes, rather than

Table 13.8: BOCA NATIONAL BUILDING CODE–WIDTHS OF EGRESS COMPONENTS

		Width per Occupant			
		For Doors, Corridors, and Ramps		Stairs	
Use Group	Occupant Load: Square Feet per Occupant	S	U	S	U
A-1: Assembly, Theaters	Actual Number of Fixed Seats	0.15″	0.2″	0.2″	0.3″
A-2: Assembly, Night Clubs, and Similar Uses	15 Net	0.15″	0.2″	0.2″	0.3″
A-3: Assembly	7 Net for Lecture Halls	0.15″	0.2″	0.2″	0.3″
	15 Net for Exhibition Halls				
A-4: Assembly, Churches	18″ of Pew Space per Occupant	0.15″	0.2″	0.2″	0.3″
A-5: Assembly, Outdoor	18″ of Bleacher Space per Occupant	0.15″	0.2″	0.2″	0.3″
B: Business	100 Gross	0.15″	0.2″	0.2″	0.3″
E: Educational	20 Net for Classrooms	0.15″	0.2″	0.2″	0.3″
	50 Net for Workshops				
F-1: Factory and Industrial	100 Gross	0.15″	0.2″	0.2″	0.3″
F-2: Factory and Industrial Low Hazardous	100 Gross	0.15″	0.2″	0.2″	0.3″
H: Hazardous Occupancies	See BOCA National Building Code	0.2″	NP	0.3″	NP
I-1: Institutional Residential Care	Sleeping Areas: 120 Gross	0.2″	0.2″	0.2″	0.4″
	Treatment Areas: 240 Gross				
I-2: Institutional Incap.	Same	0.2″	0.7″	0.3″	1.0″
I-3: Institutional Restrain.	Same	0.2″	0.2″	0.3″	0.3″
M: Mercamtile	Basement and Ground Floor: 30 Gross	0.15″	0.2″	0.2″	0.3″
	Other Floors: 60 Gross. Storage,				
	Stock, and Shipping: 300 Gross				
M: Mercantile Enclosed Shopping Mall	See BOCA National Building Code	0.15″	NP	0.2″	NP
R-1: Residential Hotels	200 Gross	0.15″	0.2″	0.2″	0.3″
R-2: Residential Multifamily	Same	0.15″	0.2″	0.2″	0.3″
R-3: Residnetial One- and Two-Family	Same	0.15″	0.2″	0.2″	0.3″
S: Storage	300 Gross	0.15″	0.2″	0.2″	0.3″
Open Parking Garages	200 Gross	0.15″	0.2″	0.2″	0.3″

S, sprinkled; U, unsprinkled; NP, not permitted.

90°, the statement is that the clear opening is based on when the door is in the "full open position," which would add about 2 inches to the clear width if the door were able to swing 180°. That is, the door itself projects into the door opening when it is at 90°. The doorstop on the latch side also projects into the opening, whereas the stop on the hinge side is contained within the projection of the door when opened at 90° but not when opened at 180°. A door is generally around $1^3/_4$ inches thick in public structures, but sometimes it can be up to 2 inches thick. The hinges project the door into the opening by about 1 inch, although the throw of the hinge could be more. The stop on the door-frame typically projects $^1/_2$ inch. Together these add up to $3^1/_4$ inches, although 4 inches is often assumed.

While the door handle projects further into the opening, as with handrails this is generally not considered to reduce the width of the opening. However, if the door is provided with vertical pull/push hardware that extends the full height of the door, the handle projection should be added to the reduction of the door width to determine the effective width of the clear opening.

Generally, passage doors (hinged or swing doors, as distinct from sliding or revolving doors) have a width of 36 inches or less. Since the clear opening for a door at 90° is about 4 inches less than the door width, a 36-inch door has a clear opening of 32 inches. If a wider opening is required, double doors can be used, although this assumes no central mullion and might not be appropriate for fire doors. In some situations, typically only for Class C openings that require a door rated at $^3/_4$ of an hour, double doors will be permitted if these include a sealing astragal that will close the opening between the doors when they are shut. Fire doors with a higher rating generally must include a central mullion, which basically means that, when more than a 32-inch opening is required, essentially two doors must be installed next to each other. However, it is possible to specify a removable central post or mullion that can be removed if a wider opening is necessary to move furniture or equipment.

At times, the doors might need to provide adequate clearance for moving equipment or furniture, such as beds in a hospital. Rather than double doors with a removable mullion, a single wider hinged door can be used, although this width should not be greater than 48 inches. Doors that are wider than 36 inches tend to be somewhat difficult to operate, but the convenience of the extra width might justify this imposition.

When the fire doors are for a Class C opening located along a corridor, it might be reasonable to provide a double door frame with doors that can be retained in an open position by magnetic holders that will release the doors if the fire alarm is activated. With automatic closers, once the holders release the doors, they will close, providing fire sep-aration while remaining operable to allow passage. Since these doors are not normal passage doors, it is possible to use two 48-inch doors, which will provide closure across a nominal 8-foot-wide corridor.

To minimize smoke or fire transmission across a fire door, the seal is critical, particularly at the head and along the jambs. Since a door must be able to open and close during normal use, providing and maintaining an effective seal is not easy. As a result, codes are beginning to require the addition of an intumescent strip along the head and jambs of a fire door.

An *intumescent* material will expand at significantly elevated temperatures, usually around 300° F. This means that even in the event of a fire, the door should initially be usable as a means of egress, but if the fire becomes extreme, the intumescent strip will expand and seal any gap between the door and the frame, limiting the passage of smoke or flame. Fire doors with extended ratings might require double intumescent strips, one of which is continuous.

Number and Locations of Exits

In addition to having doors of proper width, there must also be enough doors. While only one door is generally required for a room that has a maximum occupancy of fewer than 50, a room with a potential occupancy 50 or more persons must have a minimum of two doors that are located remotely. The stipulation for remote location is usually based on the one-half diagonal rule. This rule, which applies to individual rooms, floors, and overall buildings, states that the two exits must be separated by a distance that is at least one-half the dimension of a diagonal line that would be drawn across the area under consideration. This is clarified in Figure 13.9.

The stipulation for at least two doors from a room with an occupancy of 50 or more should improve egress from the space in case of an emergency since the occupants will likely separate into two groups, each going to one of the doors. Based on this, when there are two doors in a room, each should be sized to accommodate at least half of the occupants. Of course, it is possible that one of the doors might not provide proper egress during an emergency, in which case all of the occupants would have to use only one door. If there are more than two doors, then it is still possible that one of them is not functional. With three doors, one of which not usable for some reason, the assumption is that the people would then disperse to the other two doors, which means that each of these doors would have to handle half of the occupants. In part to respond to this potential loss of one of multiple exits, codes generally require that each exit be sized to handle at least 50% of the occupants.

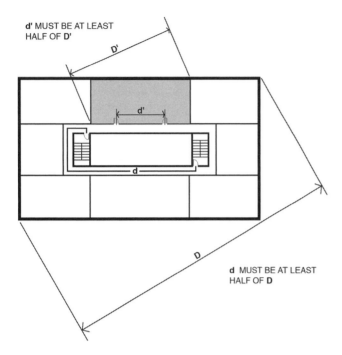

Figure 13.9 PLACEMENT OF EXIT DOORS AND EXIT STAIRS
This diagram presents the one-half diagonal rule that requires that the travel distance between fire exits must not be less than half of the diagonal distance across the floor area served by the two exits.

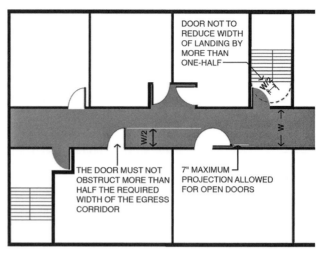

Figure 13.10 DOOR SWINGS
The projection of a door into a path of egress can be problematic. By providing a vestibule or recess off the corridor, doors will not create a dangerous condition in normal times or a reduction in egress capacity during an emergency. Similarly, an alcove or an enlarged stair landing can reduce the time imposition of the in-swinging door in a fire stair.

Obviously, if there are only two exits, each must be sized for at least 50% of the occupant load, but even if there are more than two exits, each is still to be sized for at least 50% of the total occupant load being served. While there are some exceptions to this requirement for places of assembly, this requirement applies to exit doors and fire stairs.

In some ways, this 50% requirement might tend to encourage limiting the number of exits (doors or fire stairs) that are provided since the size of each door would not be reduced by having more than two. This might be an unfortunate response since multiple exits can improve egress during an emergency and also provide effective choices of ways that people can move through a building during normal times. An increase in emergency egress makes sense since, as mentioned, observations of actual conditions indicate that the capacities of the emergency exits are not likely to be met during an emergency. In addition, an increase should improve the day-to-day experience within a building, which seems to be a legitimate and important objective of design.

Door swings must also be considered (see Figure 13.10). In general, doors should swing in the direction of egress; however, if the rated occupancy for a room is fewer than 50 people, this is not generally required. When a door swings outward, it can interfere with the exit passageway. While the best arrangement is a recessed entry that allows an out-swinging door to open without reducing the width of the passageway, most codes allow a door to project into a corridor as long as it does not reduce the required width of the passageway by more than half. This applies to doors swinging into corridors and into stairs. The assumption for this allowance is that the door is in the 90° open position for only a limited time since codes typically also stipulate that when a door is fully opened to 180°, it should not project into a corridor more than 7 inches. (When a door includes a closer, 90° is often the limit to which it can be open, but after people have passed through the door, the closer should close the door, reestablishing the full-width passageway.)

Another factor to be considered is that in public buildings, at times of emergency, most people tend to rush toward the way they entered even if this is not the closest exit or the largest exit. As a result of a study of the 2003 fire at The Station Nightclub in West Warwick, Rhode Island, which resulted in 100 fatalities, the National Institute of Standards and Technology (NIST) proposed a number of recommendations for improving safety. As stated in the report, although the nightclub patrons recognized the danger fairly quickly after the pyrotechnics started the fire, about two-thirds of the people attempted to get out through the main entrance, and many were unsuccessful since this entrance could not accommodate the crush. The NIST report recommended that in a public facility like a nightclub or theater, the main entrance should be capable of handling the evacuation of at least two-thirds of the maximum permitted number of occupants. Furthermore, the report recommended that occupant loads and the

Figure 13.11 EXIT SIGN FROM MoMA
For most people, the placement of the exit sign over the door probably suggests that this is the exit; however, the little arrow in the sign indicates that this is not so.

computation of the number and width of exits be based on the assumption that at least one exit will not be accessible during an emergency. The NIST report went on to suggest that the trade-offs between sprinkler installation that affect the evacuation time be eliminated and that additional research should be conducted to study human behavior during emergency situations.[15]

Exit Signage

Obviously, signage is an important factor in providing for effective egress during an emergency. As we can observe in Figure 13.11, which shows a view from the Museum of Modern Art (MoMA) in New York City, designed by Yoshio Taniguchi, sometimes the signage has not been adequately thought out. As might be noted after careful scrutiny of the image, the EXIT sign has an arrow indicating the direction toward the exit. The sign is not intended to suggest that the door below the sign is an exit—since it is not. However, especially if there were an emergency and people panicked, the clear implication is that this door is in fact the exit.

Contrary to what we might observe in real situations, the intention of emergency signage is to clearly mark all exit ways and exits so that people can evacuate a building in a quick and orderly fashion. The signage in the exit way or access corridor should clearly indicate the direction to a fire-rated enclosed stair or, when allowed, entry into a fire-separated structure. The fire-rated enclosed stair or separated structure, sometimes referred to as a *horizontal exit*, is considered to be the exit, and these must be clearly noted by signage. Generally, codes require that an exit sign must be provided to clearly denote each exit and to give directions to that exit. This requires that an exit sign be provided at every point where the direction to the nearest exit is not clearly apparent. To achieve this, it is also usually stipulated that no point in an exit access corridor should be more than 100 feet from the nearest visible exit sign. Also, any door, passage, or stair that is not an exit or a way to an exit and is likely to be mistaken for such must be clearly indicated as "Not an Exit" or by some similar notation.

Every exit sign is to have a design, size, and color that are visible. Each sign is to display the word "EXIT" in legible letters not less than 6 inches in height and with a line width of at least $^3/_4$ inch. Nothing should be placed within the exit way that might obscure or reduce the ability to clearly see the exit signs. Each exit sign must also be illuminated, internally or externally, at a recommended minimum brightness of 5 foot-lamberts for at least 90 minutes following a loss of power. In addition, the means of egress must have a minimum illumination of 1 foot-candle, which again must be available for at least 90 minutes during a power loss.[16] Obviously, in addition to these requirements that should provide reasonable visual awareness of the path of egress, it is also important that nothing be placed within the exit way that would reduce the egress width to less than that required for the occupancy load served, be a hazard of any kind, or impair expeditious egress.

Egress Requirements for Dwelling Units

The exit requirements for private dwelling units generally stipulate only one means of egress from an individual residence as long as there are no more than 10 occupants and the maximum length of travel within the dwelling unit does not exceed 75 feet. This applies even if the individual residence is a multistory unit. However, even though a residential unit needs only one exit, that exit has to be directly to the outside or, if within a multifamily structure, to a floor that has the prescribed number of exits required by the floor area and/or occupancy load exiting on that floor. These exits, typically a minimum of two, are to be

[15]National Institute of Standards and Technology (NIST) http://www.nist.gov/public_affairs/factsheet/mar_3_rifindings.htm.

[16]Code of Federal Regulations, Title 29, Volume 5 (U.S. Government Printing Office via GPO Access CITE: 29CFR1910.37, revised as of July 1, 2002).

Table 13.9: TRAVEL DISTANCE LIMITS IN FEET

Occupancy	Dead-End Limit		Travel Distance	
	Unsprinkled	Sprinkled	Unsprinkled	Sprinkled
Assembly	20	20	150	200
Educational	20	20	150	200
Health Care	30	30	NA	200

Residential
  Hotels and Dorms
  Apartments
  One- and Two-Family
	
	35
	35
	NR
		
		50
		50
		NR
			
			175
			175
			NR
				
				325
				325
				NR

Mercantile	20	50	100	200
Office	20	50	200	300

located according to the appropriate remoteness and travel distance.[17]

Additionally, all sleeping rooms must have at least one emergency means of escape, which can be provided by a door opening or a window, in addition to the normal access door. When a window provides this emergency exit, it must have a sill height that does not preclude its use as an emergency exit, although this height varies according to the applicable code. The range for the maximum sill height for an emergency exit seems to run from 41 to 44 inches above the floor. The opening must also have a net clear opening of at least 5.7 square feet, except if it is on the ground level, when the clear opening can generally be reduced to 5 square feet. In developing this opening, there must be a vertical clearance of at least 24 inches and a horizontal clearance of at least 20 inches. Recognizing that 5.7 square feet equals more than 821 square inches, when either the vertical or the horizontal dimension is at the minimum, the other dimension must exceed the minimum by a considerable amount. For example, if the height is only 24 inches, the width would have to be just over 34 inches to meet the 821-square-inch area requirement. If the width is 20 inches, the height would have to be around 41 inches. In addition, it must be possible to open these emergency escapes and rescue openings from inside the sleeping room without the need for special tools or keys.

In other than a residential unit, basements must have two means of egress, but a basement in a residential unit that has no habitable space[18] generally requires only one means of access and egress. However, if a residential basement contains a habitable space, this space must also have a secondary means of emergency egress and rescue. If this emergency egress is through an opening that is below grade, either a *window well* or an entry bulkhead must be provided. If it is a window well, it must have an area of at least 9 square feet, with each horizontal dimension no less than 3 feet. If it is deeper than 44 inches, a permanently affixed ladder, which is accessible when the window is fully opened, must be provided. This ladder should not project more than 6 inches into the well. If the emergency exit is through an entry bulkhead, when the bulkhead panels are in the open position, it has the same minimum requirements as an emergency egress window—a minimum net clear opening of 5 square feet, with minimum dimensions of 24 inches and 20 inches. In addition, if the height from the basement's finished floor to the exterior grade adjacent to the bulkhead entry is less than 8 feet, the stairs do not need to conform to all of the stair design requirements, particularly in terms of handrails and the dimensions for risers and treads.

Exit Placement and Access

The maximum travel distance to reach the closest fire exit is based on the type of occupancy and whether or not the structure is sprinkled (see Table 13.9). While a rated corridor (which typically has a 1-hour separation), is part of the overall egress system, it does not specifically qualify as a fire exit. A fire exit is generally considered a 2-hour-rated fire stair, a fire-protected horizontal passage across an acceptable fire barrier, or direct egress to an unconstrained exterior space.

While most tables on travel distances distinguish between sprinkled and unsprinkled structures, current discussions suggest that the reductions for a fire suppression sprinkler system have reduced the standards (raised the allowable distances) beyond reasonable levels. That is, a number of code officials believe that recent events

---

[17]Based on a presentation by R.W. Sullivan Engineering and available at http://www.rwsullivan.com/code/faq/egress.htm.

[18]A habitable space is generally defined as a place used for sleeping, living, and/or eating. Bathrooms, halls, closets and storage spaces, and utility rooms are not considered habitable spaces. Kitchens are sometimes considered habitable spaces and sometimes not.

indicate that we are not adequately protecting building occupants.

For example, the tragedy of September 11, 2001, has raised the question of how we can provide access for firefighters responding to an emergency without decreasing the means of egress for the building occupants. One of the observed problems at the World Trade Center was the conflict involving firefighters attempting to climb up the fire stairs while the occupants were trying to come down. Not only were the fire stairs typically sized based on the egress demands from only one floor, without considering the cumulative effect of simultaneous evacuations from all floors in a multistory structure, they were not required to concurrently accommodate the reverse flow of firefighters trying to get to the fire.

Although elevators are not to be used for emergency egress, they allow firefighters to readily gain access to the upper levels of a high-rise structure. There has been consideration about providing special lifts, perhaps modified elevators, for improved firefighter accessibility, efficiency in fighting fires, and overall safety. To ensure that the firefighters are not overcome with smoke, however, any elevator that is used for such access should be in a pressurized shaft.

In most situations, if a fire alarm is activated, all of the elevators are programmed to return to the ground level to allow the discharge of any passengers. If normal electrical power is lost, emergency backup power should be provided, although this can be at a reduced level sufficient to sequence through the elevators, lowering one car at a time until all the cars are at ground level. With the cars at ground level and with adequate power, firefighters could then gain secure access (key operated) to the protected elevators to ride to the upper levels of the structure.

There are also thoughts about permitting protected elevators to be used as a means of emergency egress. This could increase egress capacity in tall buildings and also assist evacuation of people with disabilities. While people with disabilities can now readily access buildings, these individuals, especially those with mobility limitations, are not provided with adequate means of egress during a time of emergency.

Since people with impairments that limit their mobility cannot be expected to use the stairs, and since currently they are not supposed to use the elevators during an emergency, they are relegated to areas of refuge, which are placed in or adjacent to fire stairs (see Figure 13.12). These individuals are supposed to remain in these supposedly secure areas until the emergency is over or they can be evacuated by professional firefighters.

While not as tenuous as an area of refuge, sometimes during an emergency, rather than leading to the outside, the exit is to an adjacent building or a portion of the same

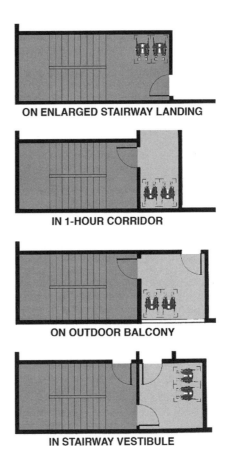

ON ENLARGED STAIRWAY LANDING

IN 1-HOUR CORRIDOR

ON OUTDOOR BALCONY

IN STAIRWAY VESTIBULE

Figure 13.12 AREAS OF REFUGE
Adapted from E. Allen and J. Iano, *The Architect's Studio Companion*, John Wiley & Sons, Hoboken, NJ, 1995, p. 229.

structure that is typically isolated by a 4-hour separation that is, through a horizontal exit (see Figure 13.13).

Fire Doors

When a horizontal exit relies on a fire separation within what is essentially the same structure, the connection between the building's segments might be provided by a doorway in which the doors are normally held opened. In this way, while a fire separation can be established if the fire alarms are activated, which will release the hold-open mechanism, during nonemergency conditions the separation might not be very apparent. While these closed doors continue to offer a means of movement between the different portions of the building, sometimes openings between fire-separated areas in the same building are closed during an emergency by fire-rated rolling shutters. Unlike the passage doors that close, when these shutters, which some call *overhead doors*, close, passage through the opening is not possible.

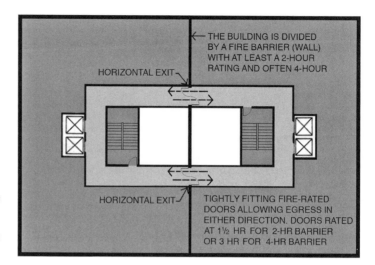

Figure 13.13 HORIZONTAL EXIT
At times, rather than exit from a building during an emergency, people move to an adjacent structure or into a fire-separated portion of the same structure. Often, as the diagram implies, a horizontal exit is used to gain access to a second means of egress rather than as a place of refuge. Adapted from E. Allen and J. Iano, *The Architect's Studio Companion*, John Wiley & Sons, Hoboken, NJ, 1995, p. 230.

As mentioned previously, after the Coconut Grove fire in Boston, code officials prescribed that all exit doors were to be swinging doors that opened in the direction of egress. This basically eliminated the use of sliding doors.[19] As a result, until recently, the only way to establish a clear opening through what needs to be a fire-rated separation was to use double doors that were held open and yet would close automatically during an emergency. To provide an opening larger than what is possible with double doors, it was necessary to use a fire-rated rolling shutter and, in order to maintain a means of egress after the shutter was closed, to include an adjacent swing passage door. While it is possible that a rolling shutter might include a passage door or be able to be opened manually to permit people to pass through the opening, generally when the shutter is lowered, passage across the fire separation is not possible, at least through that opening. So, this connection between the building areas that people would naturally be aware of as a means of egress would not be accessible during an emergency, although a clearly marked adjacent passage door might reduce the tendency to try to get out this way.

As a result of changes in fire and building codes since 2000, including a change in the NFPA regulations, sliding doors can now be used to provide fire separation for most occupancies other than those that typically involve the presence of flammable materials. Since there is no limitation on the width of the sliding doors, we are now able to include rather wide openings in what is actually a line of fire separation. This new option is especially attractive for public buildings like museums, schools, and airports, where various building zones that should be separated for fire safety are intentionally linked together for convenient public circulation and spatial dynamics.

The basic standards for a fire door indicate that no tool, key, or special knowledge can be required to open the door in the direction of egress. Furthermore, it should take no more than 15 pounds of pressure to release any latch or fully open the door, although up to 30 pounds of pressure may be required to initiate the opening. The intention of this requirement is to ensure that on closing, the fire door establishes an effective seal. These same standards apply to the fire-rated sliding-door systems that are now available.

The fire-rated sliding doors that are now being used are power operated and linked to a backup power system. While the power assist ensures that the doors close properly, when they are closed they can be opened manually with very little pressure, thereby providing for emergency egress. These doors also provide a major advantage: in an emergency, a person in a wheelchair making contact with an accordion-style horizontal sliding door will cause it to retract automatically. The sliding doors include a mechanism, similar to that provided on elevator doors, that automatically stops closure if an obstruction occurs, waits for a moment, and then resumes closing.

There are no limitations on the opening width for a fire-rated sliding door, although the height is limited to 28 feet. With such latitude in the size of the opening, these doors are usually custom designed. They are usually installed in a space that is intended to have an open character and are typically closed only to provide fire protection in an emergency. To keep them from being too conspicuous, when they are open they are typically stored in a recessed space enclosed by a panel that blends in with the finished wall surface. As a result, the closing mechanism must be capable of opening the covering panel when the system is activated.

Activation generally occurs with detection of smoke, fire alarm activation, operation of a manual pull station,

---

[19]Breakaway sliding doors are permitted in certain jurisdictions.

or perhaps the activation of a sprinkler flow valve. The speed of closure is to be not less than 6 inches per second or more than 24 inches per second.

Even after it is closed, a sliding door can be opened by releasing a latch placed toward the leading edge of the door. After they are closed, most systems require only a force of 5 pounds or less to open the door. The release of the latch initiates the automatic operator that retracts the door to a preset width, typically 36 inches, pauses for a moment, and then closes again. If the door starts to close while people are still passing through, as with the initial closing, the touch-sensitive mechanism will cause the door to retract. If power is not available, the door can be manually opened to allow passage.

General Fire Egress Requirements

Most codes require fire stairs to be enclosed with a 2-hour fire separation, which means that a fire should not be able to bridge the enclosure for 2 hours. While the physical enclosure of the stair should have a 2-hour fire rating, the doors into the stair need be rated at only $1^{1}/_{2}$ hours. Similarly, when a 1-hour fire separation is required, which is typically all that is necessary for a corridor that provides an exit way to a fire stair, the doors are to be rated at only $^{3}/_{4}$ of an hour. One important aspect of all rated doors is that they are to be provided with an automatic door closer and a latch that will retain the door in the closed position.

Since there is a time rating with a fire separation, the expectation is not that a fire cannot cross the barrier but that there will be enough delay to allow the occupants to exit the structure and the firefighters to get the fire under control and, hopefully, extinguished. Of course, this time is not guaranteed, as we saw on September 11, 2001. The first tower at the World Trade Center collapsed about $1^{3}/_{4}$ hours after the plane crashed into the building and started the fire, which was intensified by the released jet fuel. The second tower collapsed in just under an hour after it was hit.

As indicated in some of the tables, different portions of an exit system have different maximum allowable travel distances. The *exit enclosure* portion of the exit system is usually the fire stair, which should have a direct connection to the outside, although it is acceptable to connect to the outside through an exit passageway (see Figure 13.14) or a through a fire-controlled vestibule or lobby. Some codes permit what is essentially a passageway to serve as an entry vestibule or lobby. When passage from the ground level of an exit stair to the outside is through a lobby area, there is a question as to what fire separation, if any, is required (see Figure 13.15)

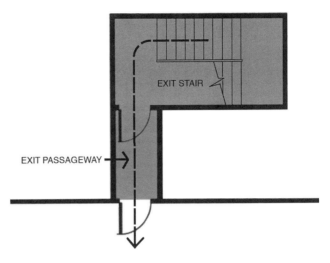

Figure 13.14 EXIT PASSAGEWAY
Generally, a passageway is a corridor that leads to an exit, which is typically a fire-rated stair enclosure. An exit passageway is a corridor or passageway that links an interior fire stair to the outside. While other passageways typically need only a 1-hour rating, an exit passageway is expected to have a 2-hour rating. Adapted from E. Allen and J. Iano, *The Architect's Studio Companion*, John Wiley & Sons, Hoboken, NJ, 1995, p. 232.

Table 13.10, which is based on information presented in *The Architect's Studio Companion* by Edward Allen and Joseph Iano, shows the maximum travel distance from the most remote point to the nearest exit enclosure. The implication is that these listed dimensions include the travel distance between the entry into the corridor or exit way

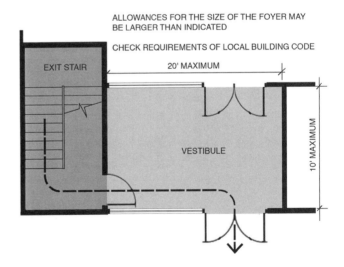

Figure 13.15 EXIT DISCHARGE THROUGH AN ENTRY VESTIBULE
Certain codes permit passage through an entry vestibule as the way to link a fire stair to the outside. Unfortunately, this often does not retain effective fire separation, even when the size of the vestibule is limited, as shown in the diagram. Obviously, if the arrangement were as shown, a door could/should have been provided to link the fire stair directly to the outside while still retaining the door into the vestibule. Adapted from E. Allen and J. Iano, *The Architect's Studio Companion*, John Wiley & Sons, Hoboken, NJ, 1995, p. 232.

Table 13.10: MAXIMUM ALLOWED TRAVEL DISTANCES, DEAD-END CORRIDOR LENGTHS, AND MINIMUM DOOR, CORRIDOR, AND STAIR WIDTHS

Use Group	Maximum Travel Distance from Most Remote Point to Nearest Exit Enclosure — S	U	Highest Room Occupancy That May Have Only One Door	Maximum Length of Dead-End Corridor	Minimum Clear Corridor Width	Minimum Clear Door Width	Minimum Stair Width	Additional Requirements
A-1: Assembly, Theaters	250'	200'	<50 Persons or <75' of Travel in the Room	20'	44" for Occupancy of 50+ Persons and 36" w/ 50 or Fewer	32"	44" for Occupancy of 50+ Persons and 36" w/ 50 or Fewer	See Detailed Requirements for Row Spacing, aisles, and Exits
A-2: Assembly, Nightclubs and Similar Uses	250'	200'	Same as Above	20'	Same as Above	32"	Same as Above	
A-3: Assembly	250'	200'	Same as Above	20'	Same as Above	32"	Same as Above	
A-4: Assembly, Churches	250'	200'	Same as Above	20'	Same as Above	32"	Same as Above	
A-5: Assembly, Ooutdoors	400'	400'	Same as Above	20'	Same as Above	32"	Same as Above	
B: Business	250'	200'	Same as Above	20'	Same as Above	32"	Same as Above	
E: Educational	250'	200'	Same as Above	20'	Same Except 72" for 100+ Occupants	32"	Same as Above	
F-1: Factory and Industrial	250'	200'	Same as Above	20'	44" for Occupancy of 50+ Persons and 36" w/ 50 or Fewer	32"	Same as Above	In a Sprinkled One-Story Building w/ Automatic Heat and Smoke Vents, the Max. Travel Distance Is 400'
F-2: Factory and Industrial, Low Hazard	400'	400'	Same as Above	20'	Same as Above	32"	Same as Above	
H: Hazardous Occupancies	Consult BOCA National Building Code							
I-1: Institutional, Residential Care	250'	200'	Same as Above	20'	96" Where Beds Must Be Moved	44" Where Beds Must Be Moved	Same as Above	Window Egress Is Required for Each Room in an Unsprinkled Building
I-2: Institutional, Incapacitated	250'	150'	1000 sq ft	20'	Same as Above	Same as Above	Same as Above	Each Floor Must Be Divided by at Least One Smokeproof Wall with Horizontal Exits.
I-3: Institutional, Restrained	200'	150'	<50 Persons or <75' of Travel in the Room	20'	44" for Occupancy of 50+ Persons and 36" w/ 50 or Fewer	Same as Above 28"	Same as Above	

Use Group								
M: Mercantile	250'	200'	Same as Above	30'	Same as Above	32"	Same as Above	
M: Mercantile, Enclosed Shopping Malls	200' In Mall Space Itself	NP	Same as Above	Twice the Width of Mall Space Itself, 20' for Corridors	20' for the Mall Space 66" for Corridors	32"	Same as Above	
R-1: Residential, Hotels	250'	200'	Same as Above	20'	44" for Occupancy 50+ Persons and 36" w/ 50 or Fewer	32"	Same as Above	Window Egress Is Required for Each Room in an Unsprinkled Building
R-2: Residential, Multifamily	250'	200'	Same as Above	20'	Same as Above	32"	Same as Above	Same as Above
R-3: Residential, One- and Two-Family	250'	200'	Same as Above	20'	Same as Above	28"	Same as Above	Same as Above
S-1: Storage, Moderate Hazard	250'	200'	Same as Above	20'	Same as Above	32"	Same as above	In an Unsprinkled One-Story Building with Automatic Heat and Smoke Vents the maximum Max. Travel Distance Is 400'
S-2: Storage, Low Hazard	400'	300'	Same as Above	20'	Same as Above	32"	Same as Above	Same as Above
Open Parking Garages	250'	200'	Not Applicable	20'	Same as Above	32"	Same as Above	Exit Stairway May Be Open

S–sprinkled; U–unsprinkled.

Source: Adapted primarily from information presented in E. Allen and J. Lano, *The Architect's Studio Companion* (John Wiley & Sons, Inc., Hoboken, NJ, 1995).

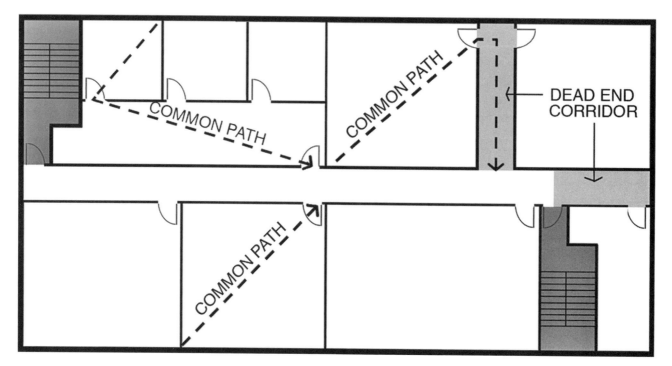

Figure 13.16 DEAD-END CORRIDOR AND COMMON PATH

Even though two means of egress are to be provided, a limited portion of an egress path may precede the point at which two egress options are available. Both a dead-end corridor and a common path provide only one choice of egress. As shown, a dead-end corridor is a corridor that is an extension of or a branch off of a corridor that does connect to two exits. A common path, which might include passage down a dead-end corridor, is the path from the remotest location within a room or a suite of rooms to the point from which there are two means of egress. Adapted from E. Allen and J. Iano, *The Architect's Studio Companion*, John Wiley & Sons, Hoboken, NJ, 1995, p. 231.

and the entry into the fire stair or exit enclosure plus the distance from the most remote location within the room or suite of rooms to the door to the corridor or exit way. Generally, codes have stipulated the maximum length of travel from the room door into the corridor or exit way to the fire door into the closest fire stair or exit enclosure, so the lengths listed in Table 13.10 are longer than traditional limits.

Distance is also limited for that portion of travel necessary before two means of egress are available, but this is considered in two ways: dead-end corridors and common paths. Figure 13.16 shows various conditions when there is only one possible path prior to meeting the general requirement for two means of egress. A dead-end corridor is generally a branch off of a main corridor that links at least two fire stairs. As such, although the dead-end corridor is part of an exit way that generally has a 1-hour fire separation, it provides only one means of egress until it meets the main corridor. The common path also provides only one means of egress until it links with the main corridor or exit way, but it begins with the most remote location within any occupied space. As such, the common path might merely be the length of travel within a room or a suite of rooms that has a single door opening into a corridor that extends to at least two fire stairs. If the door from an office or a suite

of rooms is into a dead-end corridor rather than the main portion of the corridor, the common path would include movement within the office or the suite of rooms plus the length of travel down a dead-end corridor.

The maximum travel distance indicated in the various tables is not the distance to the farthest fire stair. Rather, it is the maximum allowed distance to the closest fire stair. As a result, the distance to the second fire stair can exceed this distance. There is no stipulated limit as to how far away the second stair might be, although most situations tend to limit it to twice the maximum allowable distance to the closest fire stair. As shown in Figure 13.17, the closer a room exit is to the near stair (D_B), the greater the distance (D'_B) will likely be to the second means of egress. And, in general, the spacing between fire stairs should be around twice the allowed maximum travel distance to a fire stair.

Figure 13.18 shows the essential parts of an egress system and Table 13.10 presents the maximum travel distances that are allowed from the most remote point to the nearest fire stair, indicated as the *exit enclosure*. In addition, this table shows the maximum length of a dead-end corridor, the highest room occupancy that needs only one door, and the minimum widths of doors, corridors, and fire stairs. The travel distances are listed for both sprinkled and unsprinkled structures, and as might be surmised, the

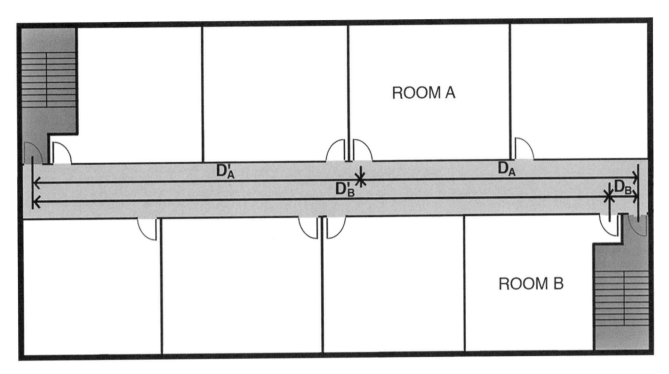

Figure 13.17 TRAVEL DISTANCE TO TWO FIRE STAIRS
The maximum distance allowed to a fire exit is generally the distance to the closest fire stair. Obviously, in this diagram, as the room exit is closer to one fire stair, the further is the distance to the second fire stair. The maximum distance to a fire stair for Room A would apply to D_A but not to D'_A, although the second exit is not much farther than the allowed distance. Assuming that D_A is equal to the maximum distance permitted, it is apparent that for Room B the distance to the second stair, D'_B, would be considerably longer than this limit.

sprinkled conditions generally permit longer travel, although, according to this table, not by very much.

Table 13.11 also presents the limits for dead-end corridors and travel distance to the closest fire enclosure, as well as for common paths. While these limits tend to be similar to those listed in Table 13.10, there are differences. Table 13.12 presents a simplified comparison between limits shown in Tables 13.10 and 13.11. What we can learn

from this is that there are differences between codes, so it is important to check with the particular jurisdiction in which a building will be located to verify the applicable restrictions and then base our design on these.

Changes in code requirements often occur following major tragedies when the reviews of these events conclude that the injuries and fatalities that occurred might have been reduced if the building's design and/or construction

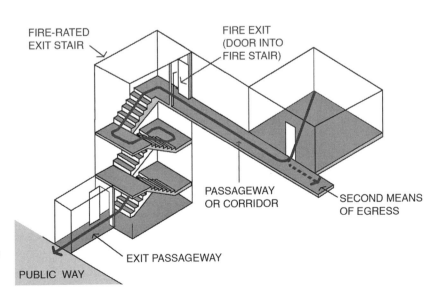

Figure 13.18 EGRESS DIAGRAM
This diagram shows various parts of the egress system. Adapted from E. Allen and J. Iano, *The Architect's Studio Companion*, John Wiley & Sons, Hoboken, NJ, 1995, p. 221.

Table 13.11: COMMON PATH, DEAD-END, AND TRAVEL DISTANCE LIMITS

Type of Occupancy	Common Path Limit		Dead-End Lim		Travel Distance Limit	
	Unsprinkled	Sprinkled	Unsprinkled	Sprinkled	Unsprinkled	Sprinkled
	(ft)	(ft)	(ft)	(ft)	(ft)	(ft)
Assembly:						
New	20/75	20/75	20	20	150	200
Existing	20/75	20/75	20	20	150	200
Educational:						
New	75	75	20	20	150	200
Existing	75	75	20	20	150	200
Day-Care Center: New	NR	NR	20	20	150	200
Day-Care Center: Existing	NR	NR	20	20	150	200
Health Care:						
New	NR	NR	30	30	NA	200
Existing	NR	NR	NR	NR	150	200
Ambulatory Care: New	NR	NR	30	30	150	200
Ambulatory Care: Existing	NR	NR	50	50	150	200
Detention and Correctional:						
New II, III, IV	50	100	50	50	150	200
New V	50	100	20	20	150	200
Existing II, III, IV	50	100	NR	NR	150	200
Residential:						
Hotels and Dormitories: New	35	50	35	50	175	325
Hotels and Dormitories: Existing	35	50	50	50	175	325
Apartments: New	35	50	35	50	175	325
Apartments: Existing	35	50	50	50	175	325
Board and Care						
Small, New and Existing	NR	NR	NR	NR	NR	NR
Large, New	NA	125	NA	50	NA	325
Large, Existing	110	160	50	50	175	325
Lodging and Rooming Houses	NR	NR	NR	NR	NR	NR
One- and Two-Family Dwellings	NR	NR	NR	NR	NR	NR
Mercantile:						
Class A, B, C: New	75	100	20	50	100	200
Class A, B, C: Existing	75	100	50	50	150	200
Mall: Open Air	NR	NR	0	0	NR	NR
Mall: Covered						
New	75	100	20	50	100	400
Existing	75	100	50	50	200	400
Business:						
New	75	100	20	50	200	300
Existing	75	100	50	50	200	300
Industrial:						
General	50	100	50	50	200	250
Special Purpose	50	100	50	50	300	400
High Hazard	0	0	0	0	75	75
Aircraft Servicing:	50	50	50	50		
Hangars: Ground Floor						
Hangars: Mezzanine Floor	50	50	50	50	75	75
Storage:						
General: Low Hazard	NR	NR	NR	NR	NR	NR
General: Ordinary Hazard	50	100	50	100	200	400
General: High Hazard	0	0	0	0	75	75
Parking Garages:						
Open	50	50	50	50	200	300
Enclosed	50	50	50	50	150	200
Aircraft Storage Hangars:						
Ground Floor	50	100	50	50		
Mezzanine Floor	50	75	50	50	75	75
Underground Spaces in Grain Elevators	50	50	NR	NR	200	400

NR—no requirement.

Table 13.12: COMPARISON OF MAXIMUM TRAVEL DISTANCES

Occupancy	Maximum Travel Distance from Most Remote Point Down Exit Way (Corridor) to Nearest Exit Enclosure			
	Sprinkled (ft)	Unsprinkled (ft)	Sprinkled (ft)	Unsprinkled (ft)
Assembly	250	200	200	150
Business	250	200	300	200
Educational	250	200	200	150
Factory and Industrial	250	200	250	200
Factory and Industrial, Low Hazard	400	400		
Hazardous Occupancies	Consult BOCA National Bldg Code		75	75
Institutional, Residential Care	250	200	200	150
Mercantile	250	200	200	100
Mercantile, Enclosed Shopping Malls	200	Not Permitted in the Mall	400	100
Residential, Hotels	250	200	325	175
Residential, Multifamily	250	200	325	175
Residential, One- and Two-Family	250	200	NR	NR
Storage, Moderate	250	200	400	200
Storage, Low	400	300	NR	NR
Open Parking Garages	250	200	300	200

NR – no requirement.

had been different. This clearly happened following the Coconut Grove Night Club fire, and there are numerous code adjustments that are being considered as a result of The Station Nightclub fire and, of course, the horrendous tragedy of the World Trade Center.

"Comparison of Codes, Standards, and Practices in Use at the Time of the Design and Construction of the World Trade Center 1, 2, and 7,"[20] a report prepared by Joseph C. Razza and Raymond A. Grill for NIST, includes a table that compares various codes that were in place on September 11, 2001: the New York City Building Code, the New York State Building Code, the Chicago Building Code, the BOCA Building Code, and the NFPA 101 Life Safety Code. A summary of the significant differences suggests that the New York City Building Code requirements were perhaps the most "forward thinking," providing the most restrictive requirements in terms of offering various means to minimize the impact of fire while maximizing the means of safe egress. And yet, after September 11, 2001, there were attempts to increase the requirements to provide a higher level of safety in the future. Although some design-

ers might object to the restrictions that codes can impose on design creativity, it is important to remember that their purpose is not antithetical to but, in fact, fundamental to true architectural quality, for there is no higher objective of architectural design than to achieve an environment that can support the fullest measure of human endeavor.

Fire Egress–Smoke Control

One critical issue concerning fire safety, particularly in providing effective egress, is smoke. Smoke is generally the significant life-threatening factor that confronts people as they attempt to evacuate a building in which there is a fire. Unfortunately, the stairs can increase the impact of the fire since they tend to operate as a flue or chimney through which the by-products of the fire, particularly smoke, rise. If the fire is located at a lower floor level, opening the door at this level into the fire stair allows smoke to infiltrate the stair enclosure, which can make the stair potentially impassible. This problem becomes much greater when the building is higher than 60 feet, and that is when most codes require some means of smoke control. Comparable control is also usually required if the stair extends more than 30 feet below grade.

There are two approaches to controlling smoke in fire stairs: mechanical pressurization and ventilation. Fire stair

---

[20]J.C. Razza and R.A. Grill, "Federal Building and Fire Safety Investigation of the World Trade Center Disaster: Comparison of Codes, Standards, and Practices in Use at the Time of the Design and Construction of World Trade Center 1, 2, and 7," National Institute of Standards and Technology, Washington DC, 2005 (http://wtc.nist.gov/NCSTAR1/PDF/NCSTAR%201-1E.pdf).

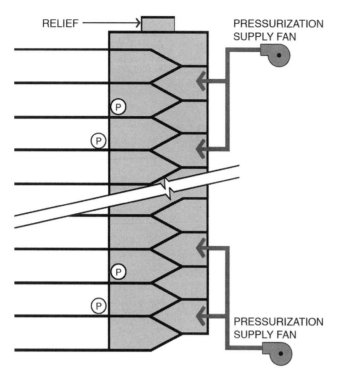

Figure 13.19 STAIR PRESSURIZATION
To keep smoke from filling the fire stair during a fire, with the activation of the fire alarm, fans blow outside air into the stair shaft. This increases the pressure, preventing smoke from entering the stair shaft, even when a door is open. Since the fire doors are to swing in the direction of movement, the pressure must not be excessive to keep them from opening.

pressurization essentially means that if there is a fire, which is noted by a detector or by manual operation of a fire alarm, mechanical fans will turn on and blow outside air into the stairwell. This action causes the stairwell to be pressurized. As a result, smoke, which could potentially make the stair impassible, should not be able to infiltrate into the stair (see Figure 13.19).

Ventilation, the other method of keeping smoke from filling the fire stair, basically relies on the fact that the density of smoke will cause it to rise; this is why it can cause a serious problem with a stair extending through many floors in a high-rise building. While this aspect of smoke can be a problem, it can be harnessed to reduce the possibility of smoke entering the fire stair. Since smoke will take the easiest path, the objective is to provide a clear opening before the entry into the fire stair. This opening can be provided in various ways, but essentially they all provide free passage to the outside. The simplest way to achieve this is to place the stair at the edge of the structure, with the entry into the stair through an open passage. If the stair is located within the building, the entry into the stair can be adjacent to a vertical shaft that is open to the outside at both the top and bottom. As a result of the different elevations of these openings, there will be a

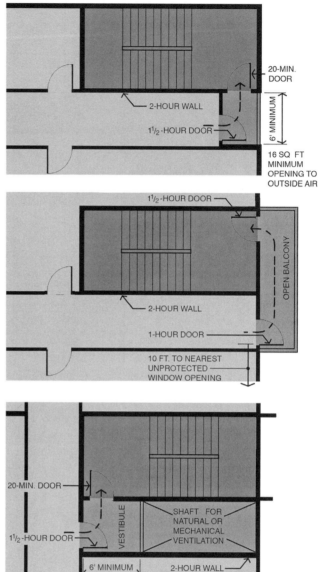

Figure 13.20 STAIR TOWER SMOKE CONTROL
By having the path into a fire stair pass by an opening to the outside, any smoke that might exist on the entry floor will tend to rise up the air shaft or directly outside rather than through the stair tower. Adapted from E. Allen and J. Iano, *The Architect's Studio Companion*, John Wiley & Sons, Hoboken, NJ, 1995, p. 227.

significant pressure differential, called the *stack effect*, that will establish an upward airflow that will draw in smoke before it can enter the stair. While the draft can be quite effective in high-rise structures, sometimes the addition of a mechanical exhaust is necessary to enhance smoke protection. Again, the fan would operate at times when there is an indication that a fire exists (see Figure 13.20).

Smoke is probably the major health hazard related to fire. In addition to limiting its access to fire stairs, we must limit its infiltration through a building, especially in those passageways that people need to use to evacuate the structure. Data suggest that 80% of all fatalities from fire are due to smoke. In addition, of the 20% of those deaths that are due to the fire itself, many might have been initiated by smoke-induced mental confusion.

Fortunately, smoke is lighter than air, so it tends to rise within a space and then spread across the ceiling. The higher the ceiling, the longer it will take before the layer of smoke will increase to the point where is fills the occupied zone. Also, by installing dropped elements called *curtain boards,* the spread of smoke across the ceiling will be somewhat limited. Water curtains can also inhibit the flow of smoke, but they can only delay the spread of smoke, not eliminate it if the fire continues. They are used to allow time for the occupants to get out and to slow the spread of the fire to give the firefighters a better chance of getting things under control.

It is also possible to vent smoke through special roof hatches that open when a fire has been detected. This is somewhat similar to venting the smoke at the entry to a fire stair, and it is also possible to use the other method used with the stair—pressurization. Rather than exhaust the buildup of smoke through a relief hatch, sometimes smoke control is provided by mechanically injecting a large volume of outside air into the space as a way of opposing the flow of smoke and/or diluting it. But while both of these methods can help control smoke so that people will be able to evacuate the premises, they also tend to fan the fire—less smoke but perhaps a more intense fire.

Reducing the smoke is important. Being lighter than air, the smoke collects at the top of a space. As the amount smoke increases, it tends to fill more and more of the upper portion of a space, leaving a smaller and smaller portion of the space clear. Therefore, and perhaps as seen in a movie, TV show, or unfortunately in real life, it might be necessary to crawl along the floor in order to maintain access to reasonably breathable air. Because this would likely force a person into basically a prone position in an attempt to avoid the smoke, many jurisdictions now require that exit signs be located near the floor as well as at standard height (see Figure 13.21). These lower exit signs are to be installed at least 6 inches but no more than 8 inches above the floor. Since exit signs are a way to guide occupants to the exit if they need to evacuate a building, we need to consider what might occur if there is a fire and design for such an eventuality, even though we sincerely hope that it will never happen.

As we design, we must give serious attention to providing the means for rapid and effective egress for all occupants. While we obviously do not expect a fire or other catastrophic event to occur that would necessitate evacuation, they do happen, and when they do, they can produce extreme damage for property and people. Fires can spread at extraordinarily rapid speeds, often doubling in size every

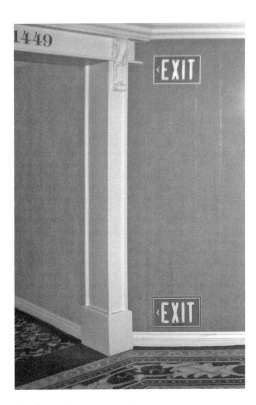

Figure 13.21 DOUBLE EXIT SIGNAGE
Since smoke tends to fill the upper regions of the exit passageway, it might be necessary to crawl along the floor into order to get to the exit enclosure, the location of which is shown by the exit signs. As a result, certain jurisdictions now require the installation of a lower exit sign with the bottom of the sign at least 6 inches but not more than 8 inches above the floor.

30 seconds, and there are probably both more fires and, unfortunately, more fatalities from fires than most of us assume. While it is impossible to prevent all fires, as designers we can take actions that will definitely reduce their potential occurrence and harm. Providing smoke control and effective egress is critical to meeting this responsibility.

Fire Egress and Protection—Escalators and Elevators

Escalators generally are not an acceptable way of meeting egress requirements. To fulfill part of the egress requirements, they would have to comply with the stipulations for exit stairs, such as riser-to-tread dimensions and fire enclosure, neither of which is typical with escalators. However, while escalators might not be counted in the required egress allotment, they can be used during an emergency. Since the direction in which an escalator moves can be reversed, even up units can provide a way out in an emergency. Of course, reversing the direction of an escalator requires authorization, so this might not be feasible, but anyone can easily stop an escalator. Also, if a fire alarm is activated, escalators generally stop automatically, and of course, if power is lost they will stop.

The escalator opening between floors provides a means of readily expanding any fire unless some form of protection is provided. There are various methods to accomplish this:

Fire Enclosure: Escalators can be installed within a fire-rated enclosure, somewhat similar to a fire stair, although this is not typically done.

Sprinkler-Vent: A combination automatic fire or smoke detection system that automatically establishes a water curtain around the escalator opening and the mechanical air exhaust.

Spray-Nozzle: A system of high-velocity water-spray nozzles, somewhat similar to the water curtain but at higher pressure.

Rolling Shutter: Automatic fire-rated rolling shutters that completely close the escalator opening at the top of each run. Obviously, with this type of fire protection, the escalator cannot be used during an emergency.

Partial Enclosure: Similar to an enclosed escalator that parallels a fire stair. With this protection, fire-rated doors that are normally open are automatically shut when an alarm is sounded.

In addition to these methods, fire protection demands that the escalator mechanisms (trusses return treads, motors, etc.) be enclosed within fire-rated construction.

The installation of elevators and escalators must meet the requirements of the American Society of Mechanical Engineers (ASME), specifically ASME A17.1 Safety Code for Elevators and Escalators, which also includes requirements for moving walks and other vertical movement devices.

Elevators also are not currently accepted as a means of egress during an emergency. While this situation is being reviewed, most codes demand that all public use of elevators stop if smoke or fire is detected. As mentioned above, generally, with notice of a fire, all elevators are to return automatically to the main access floor, where they are to remain for possible use by emergency personnel. In high-rise buildings, the elevators can be vital for providing firefighters access to the upper floors; however, when such access is expected, provisions must be made for control of smoke and emergency power.

Even though elevators are not intended as a means of egress during an emergency, elevator hoistways must be fire rated similarly to fire stairs. The enclosing walls must be rated at a minimum of 2 hours, and all elevator doors must be rated at a minimum of $1^{1}/_{2}$ hours.

Typically, an elevator should not operate unless all of its doors are closed. However, as a safety precaution, each elevator door is also to be provided with door closers that should close the door if, for some reason, the normal operation does not shut the elevator door as the cab leaves the landing. When closed, all elevator doors are to be held closed by a locking mechanism that can only be released if the elevator is at the landing or when an authorized individual overrides the lock, usually for repairs, for maintenance, or during an emergency. Interestingly, even though most elevator cars no longer have an escape hatch, to avoid being trapped within the elevator shaft, the enclosing doors should be operable from the hoistway side without the need for any special tool.

FIRE CONTROL—PREVENTION AND SUPPRESSION

Generally, there are three objectives for building fire safety: protection of life, protection of property, and continuity of operation. But sometimes the emphasis related to these objectives seems to be placed on fire suppression. Necessary and vitally important as suppression might be, unfortunately it is after the fact. Architects and designers should work aggressively to develop designs and select building and finish materials that help prevent fires from occurring. The commitment must be to prevention of fires and not merely protection from them. To reduce the potential for fires to even start, it is necessary to ensure that at least one of the three prerequisites for a fire is not present. These prerequisites include an available fuel source, a high temperature, and oxygen.

Fuel is readily supplied by many standard building materials, but with proper selection and care of these materials, including how they are supplied, located, and finished, the potential that a fire will occur can be reduced. While high temperatures can result from faulty equipment, particularly those that use electricity, or even from excessive solar impact, through thoughtful design, considered selection of equipment appropriate for the intended applications, and effective collaboration with consulting engineers and contractors, again the inherent danger of high temperatures can be minimized. Unfortunately, although there are some methods that can eliminate the presence of oxygen, removing this prerequisite is not generally something that architects and designers can accomplish. In fact, while some fire suppression systems rely on eliminating oxygen as a contributing factor in fire, such as through the application of chemicals like halon, this approach also tends to purge people. While it might be an effective way to protect property, it could work its magic at a very high cost!

The message is that we need to be careful and get reliable guidance before selecting fire suppression chemicals.[21]

Oxygen comprises around 21% of the normal mixture of air. While people can deal with changes in the level of oxygen without any serious effects, if the percentage drops below 17%, there can be severe problems. Even at this level, which will greatly reduce the ability to breathe and oxygenate the blood, there is sufficient oxygen to sustain a fire.

Water is the major means of suppressing a fire. Whether the water is spread by a sprinkler system or applied by a firefighter, either from the outside or the inside, the intention is to both cool and smother the fire. The blanket of water absorbs considerable heat since if its temperature rises to 212° F, the liquid must acquire latent heat of vaporization—a lot of heat for every gallon of water. Also, in its liquid state, water coats the burning material, cutting off the flow of oxygen to the fire.

While Philip Pratt is credited with having developed the first automatic fire sprinkler system in 1872, a few years later Henry Parmelee received a patent for an improved design that was used fairly extensively. Automatic sprinkler systems are now considered essential in all high-rise structures and are often mandated by code. They are effective, and the NFPA claims that there are no recorded incidents of a fire causing the death of more than two people in a fully sprinkled building in which the system operated properly, excluding explosions and flash fires and instances in which firefighters in the process of fighting the fire were the casualties.[22]

Sprinkler systems are usually designed by consulting engineers, who have experience and focus on working in this area, or by actual sprinkler contractors. Sprinkler systems fall into two categories: wet and dry. A wet system is filled with water that will be released if a fire is present and generates enough heat to cause the sprinkler head to open. The sprinkler head is kept closed by the pressure exerted by a glass vial that contains a liquid. If there is a fire, the temperature will increase, causing the liquid in the vial to expand. This breaks the vial, allowing the sprinkler head to open. If the system is filled with water, which should be under pressure, the water will immediately spray out, but only through that sprinkler head. Unlike what is typically seen in movies, all the sprinkler heads do not open when one does. Each head is opened the same way—by exposure to high temperature.

If the sprinkler system is dry, which probably means that the system is not always maintained at temperatures above freezing, once a sprinkler head is opened, there is a delay until the water can get to the fire location. Since this delay can be considerable, sometimes rather than a dry system where freezing temperatures are likely to occur, a protected wet system is used. This involves adding some antifreeze to the water that initially fills the system, but of course, a noncombustible antifreeze must be used.

The design of the sprinkler system involves locating sprinkler heads so that, if activated, the water spray will cover any and all areas. Since each sprinkler head has a particular spray pattern and spread, based on its design, mounting height, and discharge orientation, the layout of the system is relatively straightforward. While there is some latitude in terms of sprinkler head spacing and placement to fit effectively with a particular building design, there are limits that must be observed. The sprinkler system cannot be modified to accommodate an architectural design if this would result in reduced coverage.

The water that is initially discharged by the sprinkler can come from a source within the structure or from the public water supply. When a sprinkled building, typically a high-rise structure, has a water storage tank, the lower portion of the tank is usually not used for domestic water consumption but is allocated for fire protection; however, this water can only last for a limited time. If the sprinkler system is supplied directly from the public water main, the pressure level could drop below what is needed to maintain proper water distribution. For either situation, a Siamese fitting is provided at street level. This is a special connection that allows a fire pumper can to connect to the sprinkler system, thereby continuing to supply water under pressure (see Figure 13.22).

Siamese fittings are also connected to fire standpipes, a large-diameter piping system that can supply water through the building, eliminating the need to extend fire hoses. Standpipes, which are also directly connected to a water supply, used to have an access valve located on each floor near the access to a fire stair. These valves were typically placed within a cabinet that included a fire hose, usually 100 feet in length, which was already connected to the valve. While standpipes are still provided, today the location is often prescribed to be within the fire stair and a hose is not necessarily included.

There are several possible problems with including a hose. One problem is that the presence of the hose might

---

[21] Some time ago, before the obvious problem with halon applications became clear, my architectural firm was involved in the design of several community-oriented medical facilities, each of which included a fairly substantial medical records area. In response to the concern about protecting these records, which were hard copy rather than electronic, as is the norm today, we were told to avoid using a water suppression system for the file area. Unfortunately, the chemical systems that were available, worked effectively, and were relatively inexpensive had the side effect that if they were activated while someone was in the record room, the occupants might have ended up being deactivated.

[22] G. Craighead, *High-Rise Security and Fire Life Safety* (Elsevier Inc., Boston, 2009), p. 367.

Figure 13.22 SIAMESE HOSE CONNECTIONS
As noted in the sign, this Siamese fitting connects to both the sprinkler and the standpipe system in an office building at Rockefeller Center in New York City. This fitting provides a way for a fire pumper to supply pressurized water to both of these firefighting systems.

imply that a nonprofessional can use it to attempt to extinguish a fire. Such unknowledgeable attempts at heroic action are not generally effective and could delay the call for trained firefighters. Another problem is that the hose, after an extended period of nonuse, might not be sound. In this case, it could also delay things when a professional firefighter arrives since time would be required to recognize that there is a problem with the hose, disconnect it, and then connect another hose, assuming that the professional had the foresight to assume that the existing hose would not be useful.

The location of the standpipe in the corridor near the fire stair meant that the firefighter would have to enter the area of the fire in order to connect to the standpipe. With the standpipe located in the stair, which is protected by at least a 2-hour fire-rated enclosure and by some means of smoke control, the firefighter can connect to the standpipe and arrange the hoses prior to entering the area of conflagration. To avoid getting tangled up with the inward-opening fire door, rather than at the floor level, most standpipes are now located on a mid-landing of the fire stair.

Standpipes can be divided into various classifications. Class I systems include $2\frac{1}{2}$-inch hose connections for use by professional firefighters who are trained in handling heavy streams of pressurized water. Class II systems include a $1\frac{1}{2}$-inch hose connection and are intended to be used only by trained building staff. These systems are only appropriate for structures that include support staff with the proper training, which is somewhat rare. Therefore, these systems are not recommended and are becoming less prevalent.

BIBLIOGRAPHY

America Burning. Report of the National Commission on Fire Prevention and Control. Federal Emergency Management Agency, Washington, DC, 1973.

America Burning Revisited. Report of a National Workshop, Tyson's Corner, Virginia, November 30– December 2, 1987. Federal Emergency Management Agency, Washington, DC, 1987.

Bradshaw, V. *The Building Environment: Active and Passive Control Systems.* John Wiley & Sons, Inc., Hoboken, NJ, 2006.

Craighead, G. *High-Rise Security and Fire Life Safety.* Elsevier Inc., Boston, 2009.

Ramsey, C.G. and Sleeper, H.R. *Architectural Graphic Standards.* John Wiley & Sons, Inc., Hoboken, NJ, 1989.

Grondzik, W.T., A.G. Kwok, B. Stein, and J.S. Reynolds. *Mechanical and Electrical Equipment for Buildings.* John Wiley & Sons, Inc., Hoboken, NJ, 2010.

14 ELEVATORS AND ESCALATORS

ELEVATORS

ELEVATOR SYSTEM DESIGN

ELEVATORING

ESCALATORS

MOVING WALKWAYS

ELEVATORS

Elisha Graves Otis is regarded as the individual whose contributions helped make the elevator a safe and reliable means of passenger movement, which has allowed the development of high-rise structures. Otis was an inventive man who confronted challenges head on. As a young family man, he designed and built a gristmill in Vermont, but when this did not provide an adequate income, he converted it to a sawmill. As his family grew and his income did not, he gave up the sawmill and went to work as a bedstead maker. He continued to pursue alternative ventures, ending up in Yonkers, New York, with the intention of converting an abandoned sawmill into a bedstead factory. To do so, he needed to find a way to move materials up and down within the building. While hoisting systems had existed since ancient times, they all had problems, including the catastrophic potential of falling if the support cables failed. In considering how to move materials, Otis came up with a relatively simple safety brake that eliminated the danger of falling.

The hoist platform was guided by side rails but was supported by the cables. As long as the support cables remained intact and were connected to the hoist platform, the weight of the platform kept the cables taut. However,

if these support cables broke, not only would the platform start to fall, but also the tension in the cables would be released. Otis' device relied on the tension in the support cables to restrain a spring-activated braking mechanism. So, if there were failure, the brakes would automatically engage, which meant that the spring would drive a toothed wedge against the guide rails of the hoist system, preventing the unsupported platform from falling any further.

Otis set up the Otis Steam Elevator Works and began making elevators, but sales were rather limited. Then came the 1854 New York World's Fair, and Otis saw his opportunity to dramatically demonstrate the benefits and ease of major vertical movement afforded by elevators, secured by the safety that his brake provided.

The Latting Observatory was an eight-sided, 350-foot-tall wooden tower built to provide fair visitors with a spectacular view of the city. Otis agreed to supply a steam-powered elevator for the observatory that could be used to convey the people to the top of this tower as long as he could also use it to demonstrate his safety brake. His demonstration involved his standing on the hoist platform when it was suspended up in the air and then having the suspension cable cut with an axe (see Figure 14.1). As the platform began to plunge and the spectators gasped in horror, the brakes engaged and all was safe.

Figure 14.1 OTIS'S ELEVATOR BRAKE DEMONSTRATION – 1854
Otis demonstrated his elevator safety brake at the 1854 World's Fair in New York City. With the recognition that elevators were a safe means of providing vertical movement, they became increasingly accepted, creating the opportunity for high-rise designs.

While Otis' brake assumed that the actual support cables would be cut, modern elevator safety brakes rely on a separate brake cable that engages the brake if this cable is restrained. This cable is connected through a governor that locks up if it exceeds the allowable speed. With the brake cable restrained, any further movement engages the elevator brake, somewhat similar to the way we engage the brakes in a car.

Elevators are standard devices used in almost all new multistory buildings, providing a convenient, efficient, and dependable way of traveling between floors. In fact, it is claimed that elevators are the most widely used and safest form of public transportation in the world today. In the United States there are apparently more elevator trips each year than trips by all other modes of public transportation, including air, rail, and bus. This statistic relies on the fact that there are half a million or more elevators in the United States, accounting for 1 billion or more passenger-miles each year.

While elevator travel remains perhaps the safest form of public transportation, there are elevator accidents that result in injuries and fatalities. Various sources, including the Consumer Product Safety Commission, suggest that elevators account for around 15,000 personal injuries and just under 30 deaths each year in the United States. Some of these are related to elevator-worker events, some of which are the result of worker error, but there are also passenger casualties, most of which involve malfunctions of the safety systems or faulty installations.

Escalators are a related form of personal transportation, and these also account for personal injuries and deaths, but some of them, especially the deaths, might be the result of people tripping, falling, and being injured by the escalator rather than actually caused by the escalator. Of course, to the injured party, this distinction is not significant. A major cause of injury by escalators relates to items, including body parts, being caught in the toothed escalator treads and/or between the treads and the escalator sides. While escalators are supposed to be controlled by safety mechanisms that should stop movement if there is resistance to the advance of the stair treads (similar to what is provided with an automatic overhead garage door or the doors on an elevator), unfortunately sometimes these do not work as intended.

Adequate elevator service is based on the intended use of the building, economic considerations, and the architectural design, particularly the building's configuration. While elevators are typically designed by elevator specialists, as architects and designers we should be aware of the basic design issues so that our initial designs are not contrary to what will be needed, and also so that we can engage in a constructive collaboration with our specialist.

There are basically two different types of elevators: traction and hydraulic. Traction elevators are cable supported, whereas hydraulic elevators are piston supported.

Traction Elevators

A traction elevator is supported by four to eight cables that are hung over a grooved-sheave pulley, with the configuration of each cable interlocking with the sheave grooves to keep the cable from slipping. Most traction elevators now use only four cables, each of which is capable of supporting the loaded elevator car,[1] so there is redundancy. Cables, which are comprised of a number of wires bundled together, are used to support the elevators since they can provide some flexibility, although the number of individual wires needed to provide the required strength means that these cables are rather large. Even with advanced design, the flexibility of these large cables is somewhat limited. As a result, the curvature of the typical elevator cable cannot be too tight, which in turn means that the support pulley must have a sizable diameter.

---

[1] While *elevator car* is used in this textbook, often *elevator cab* denotes the same component of the elevator system.

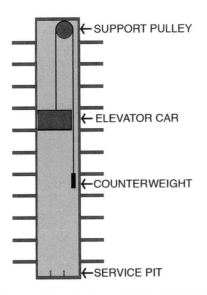

→ SUPPORT PULLEY

← ELEVATOR CAR

←COUNTERWEIGHT

←SERVICE PIT

Figure 14.2 BASIC COMPONENTS OF A TRACTION ELEVATOR
Traction elevators are supported from overhead by a number of cables, usually four. These cables are comprised of a bundle of wires and extend from the elevator car over the overhead pulley to a counterweight. The cables have a distinct surface configuration that matches the sheaves of the overhead pulley that locks them together, so as the elevator motor turns the pulley, the elevator car moves. Due to the thickness of the cables, the minimum cable bending radius establishes the necessary diameter of the pulley.

Figure 14.2 shows the basic arrangement of a traction elevator, which is available in two basic arrangements: geared and gearless. A geared traction machine, which uses gears to adjust the ratio between the actual motor revolutions (rpm) and the rotation of the elevator sheave pulley, is a lower-speed elevator and generally used for a building that is less than 150 feet or 15 stories tall. While the motor needs to have a variable speed, with the limited length of rise there is not sufficient run to reach high speeds. Geared traction machines have a medium efficiency.

An elevator needs to accelerate and decelerate relatively slowly to avoid jostling the passengers. As a result, it takes a number of floors for a comfortable transition between standing still and the highest speed or from this speed to a stop. If the elevator starts or stops too quickly, it can be rather harsh on the passengers.

With a gearless traction machine, the sheaved pulley that supports the cables is directly connected to the motor shaft. These machines are used with medium- to high-speed elevators. They are typically used in buildings that have a height of 250 feet or more since their potential speed would not be realized in installations with shorter runs. These machines have reasonably high efficiency; initially, however, they are usually more expensive than geared machines. For buildings between approximately 150 and

250 feet in height, the choice between geared and gearless machines must be based on the performance expectations and whether initial or life-cycle costs are more critical.

The changing rate of elevator car movement is based on adjusting the speed of the elevator motor, which of necessity is a rather large, high-power motor. Prior to recent developments in solid-state electronics, it was not possible to adjust the speed of an a-c motor, so, by default, elevators had to rely on d-c motors. Since electric service is a-c, elevators generally used a d-c motor-generator set (MG system). The a-c current ran an a-c motor that generated d-c current, which was then used in a variable-speed d-c elevator motor. Besides the obvious complications of this method, MG systems, often referred to as *Ward-Leonard systems*, suffer from high power consumption and costly maintenance. Generally, to avoid the necessity of having to stop and start the large motors if the elevator was to continue in service, the motor-generator set continued to run for a short time, around 2 minutes, after the elevator stopped. While this tended to reduce the stress and strain on the equipment, it resulted in extra energy consumption.

Today's advanced all-digital static d-c controls now allow d-c motors to essentially use a-c current directly by converting or rectifying the a-c curent to d-c current. This approach, which is referred to as the *thyristor Leonard elevator control system*, has greatly improved efficiency and reliability, although it tends to draw increased current during elevator car acceleration. With this system, there is no need to keep the motor running.

It is now also possible to use an asynchronous a-c motor that is serviced by a variable-voltage, variable-frequency (VVVF) a-c electricity to achieve adjustable elevator car speeds. VVVF, which is now the system of choice, is more efficient and reliable and provides more refined operational control. It also can regenerate electricity when the heavier part of the elevator-counterweight unit falls.

In older elevator systems, the potential energy that is released when there is "free fall" is not harnessed, but with contemporary electronics, it is possible to use this energy and the rotation of the elevator motor that it produces to generate electricity that can be fed into the building's electric distribution system, if not into the electric grid. Since a motor and an electric generator are essentially the same, when free fall turns the motor, it can generate electricity. It is estimated that VVVF traction machines can regenerate around 75% of the energy input.

A counterweight is used to reduce the load on the elevator motor. With the elevator car supported from one end of the traction cable and the counterweight from the other, the loads are somewhat balanced. If the counterweight actually equaled the weight of the elevator car plus the passengers, the elevator motor would basically only have to move the balanced system rather than lift a load. Of course, it is unlikely that the weights of the two will be equal since it is impossible to control the number of passengers. Sometimes the car is full, but sometimes it is empty.

Generally, the counterweight unit is set at the actual weight of the elevator car plus 40% of the maximum car capacity. As a result, at times the motor must be engaged to lower the elevator car, which might seem to be counterintuitive, but then at other times the elevator car can rise without any need for the motor, other than as a way to control the speed and hopefully to generate electricity. Whenever the greater weight in the counterweighted system drops, it turns the motor, rather than the reverse.

In addition to the change in weight resulting from a changing number of passengers, there is also the adjustment as a result of the unbalanced length of the traction cables on either side of the support pulley as the elevator car goes up and down. These are rather substantial cables, and there are at least four of them. As the amount of cable on one side of the support pulley increases, this weight often becomes the major load on the elevator motor. As the height of the elevator run increases, so does the amount of cable that might unbalance the system. When this unbalance becomes significant, an underslung cable might be appropriate (see Figure 14.3).

Since the intention is to balance the weight on either side of the support pulley, when the elevator run is long, it

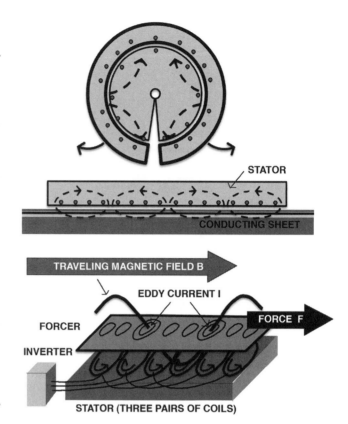

Figure 14.4 LINEAR INDUCTION MOTOR
The linear induction motor is essentially an unrolled standard circular motor.

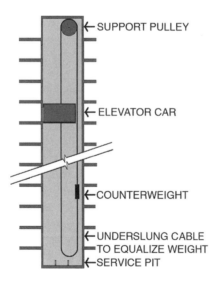

Figure 14.3 ELEVATOR WITH UNDERSLUNG CABLE
Since they must wrap over the support pulley, the cables must be somewhat longer than the height of the elevator run. As the building gets higher, the cables get longer, and as a result, they also get heavier. In order to balance the cable weight, which is often greater than the weight of the loaded elevator car, the cables are underslung.

makes sense to extend the support cables beyond the counterweight back to the elevator car. While this increases the load that has to be supported by the pulley, which in turn must be supported by the building structure, it reduces the load, and particularly a changing load during a particular run, that the elevator motor must lift.

The linear induction motor is another new development in elevator design. While the traditional motor results in rotational movement around an axis, the linear induction motor, as its name implies, causes linear movement. The basic principle of the standard motor still applies—that is, the electric current establishes a magnetic field that repulses and attracts a second magnetic field—but since, as shown in Figure 14.4, the stator is "unrolled" in the linear motor, it produces a linear rather than a rotational force, and this linear force extends along its length.

Figure 14.5 shows a design in which the counterweight is combined with a linear induction motor that can travel along the guide rails. With this arrangement, the motor no longer needs to be located above the hoistway. However, as implied in the diagram, the traction cables must be capable of a rather sharp bend, which is now feasible since flatter ribbon cables can be used in place of the traditional large round steel cables.

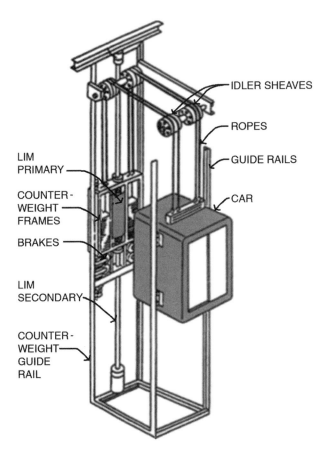

Figure 14.5 LINEAR INDUCTION ELEVATOR

The linear induction motor offers the potential of eliminating the elevator machine room and using the motor as part of the counterweight. As indicated, the bending radius of the support cables is much tighter than with conventional traction elevators and is possible as a result of the new flat cables.

Several companies, mainly in places other than the United States, are working to develop an elevator that uses a linear induction motor as its primary drive, but to date this new approach remains mainly in the proposal stage. The linear induction motor is currently being used in elevators, but to open and close the elevator doors rather than as the means of lifting and lowering the elevator car.

Another interesting development is the new machine roomless (MRL) traction elevators, which, as its name implies and as is promised by the linear induction elevator motor, can sit within the elevator hoistway or shaft (see Figure 14.6). There are several such units that eliminate the need for a penthouse elevator room already available on the market, including the Otis Gen 2 Elevator and the KONE MRL Elevator.

The MRL elevator motors, which rely on the use of flat cables that can adjust to a smaller-diameter sheave pulley, are still relatively new to the United States, although they have been used in Europe and Asia for some time. When they are used, it is generally in relatively low-rise structures where hydraulic elevators have usually been the elevator of choice. The MRL provides some benefits over the standard hydraulic elevator. One major advantage is that MRL elevators can potentially save a significant amount of energy, estimated at up to 75%, compared to hydraulic units. They also provide superior performance and faster speeds, and they do not carry the environmental liability of hydraulic elevators—the potential loss of hydraulic oil into the ground.

Tables 14.1 and 14.2 provide some comparative data for various elevator designs.

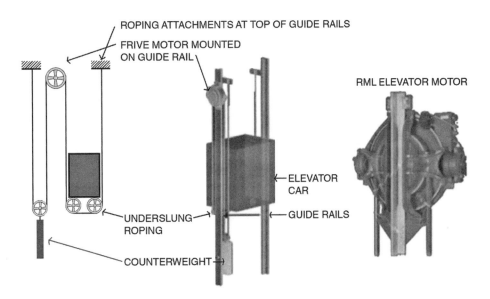

Figure 14.6 MRL ELEVATOR MOTOR

The MRL elevator motor eliminates the need for an elevator machine room that is typically located above the hoistway. This arrangement relies on using flat cables that can bend at a sharper radius than conventional support cables. Adapted from the KONE MRL elevator and images from B. Stein, J.S. Reynolds, W.T. Grondzik, and A.G. Kwok: *Mechanical and Electrical Equipment for Buildings*, John Wiley & Sons, Inc., Hoboken, NJ, 2006.

Table 14.1: COMPARATIVE CHARACTERISTICS OF ELEVATOR DRIVE SYSTEMS

Type	Rise (ft)	Speed (FPM)	Control	Initial Cost	Operating Cost	Performance
Geared a-c	250 300	150–350 150–450	Thyristor VVVF	Medium High	Medium Low	Fair Excellent
Geared d-c	175 250	50–450 50–450	UMV Thyristor	High Medium	High Low	Excellent Very good
Gearless d-c	Unlimited	400–1200	UMV Thyristor	High Medium	High Low	Excellent Very good
Gearless a-c	Unlimited	400–2000	VVVF	Medium	Low	Excellent
Hydraulic	65	≤200	Hydraulic Pump	Low	High	Fair

Source: Adapted from B. Stein, J.S. Reynolds, W.T. Grondzik, and A.G. Kwok, *Mechanical and Electrical Equipment for Buildings* (John Wiley & Sons, Inc., Hoboken, NJ, 2006), Table 31.3.

Table 14.2: COMPARATIVE ENERGY USE FOR VARIOUS ELEVATOR SYSTEMS

Elevator	Relative Energy Use
Hydraulic Elevators	10
UMV Motion Control	7–7.5
Geared d-c Traction Motor UMV Motion Control	6–6.5
Gearless d-c Traction Motor Thyristor Control	5–5.5
Geared d-c Traction Motor Thyristor Control	4–4.5
Gearless d-c Traction Motor VVVF a-c Traction Motor	2.5–3

Source: Adapted from B. Stein, J.S. Reynolds, W.T. Grondzik, and A.G. Kwok, *Mechanical and Electrical Equipment for Buildings* (John Wiley & Sons, Inc., New York, 2006), Table 3.12.

Hydraulic Elevators

While a traction elevator car is hung from above from cables that move the elevator car up and down as the support pulley or sheave rotates, a hydraulic elevator car is usually supported from below on a piston that rises or lowers as hydraulic oil is added to or removed from the piston cylinder. The standard hydraulic elevator has a cylinder that extends into the ground to the depth of the piston. When hydraulic oil is pumped into the cylinder, the piston rises, and when a valve is opened, the weight of the elevator car and passengers pushes the oil back to the oil holding tank and the car is lowered. Whether going up or down, a traction elevator requires energy input if the heavier side of the elevator car and counterweight assembly is rising, but a hydraulic elevator draws energy only when it rises. Going down requires only a release of pressure.

Hydraulic elevators are limited in terms of both maximum rise, based on the height of the piston, and speed.

Typically, the height limit is 60 to 65 feet and the fastest speed is around 150 FPM. The traditional hydraulic elevators require that a hole be drilled into the ground. This hole, which needs to be as deep as the intended rise of the elevator, is then encased in a pipe, usually PVC, and the hydraulic cylinder and piston are then inserted into the hole. It is also possible to use telescoping concentric tubes, which permit a shallower ground tube.

The equipment room for a traction elevator is usually located above the elevator hoistway, although generally the space that is required demands that the room extend beyond the actual dimensions of the shaft. On the other hand, the elevator equipment for a hydraulic elevator is usually located next to the base of the shaft, although it is possible to run the hydraulic lines from a remote equipment room. Similarly, with a traction elevator, although the top pulley must be able to support the weight of the car and counterweight, it is possible to locate the drive sheaves at the bottom of the hoistway rather than at the top. Of course, with MRL and linear induction motors, the elevator machine is actually located within the hoistway.

There are hydraulic elevators that do not require any drilling into the ground. These holeless hydraulic units can be arranged in a number of ways, including telescoping pistons or 2:1 roping supports. Since the piston cylinder sits within the range of the elevator movement, some extension of the lift height beyond the height of the hydraulic cylinder is required, as well as a way to suspend the elevator car rather than merely support it from below. Figure 14.7 shows a holeless unit with a 2:1 roping arrangement that raises the elevator car twice the distance that the piston rises. While this figure indicates rear support that must rely on the guide rails to keep the car level, other approaches to arranging the suspension are possible.

As indicated in Tables 14.1 and 14.2, hydraulic elevators are not very efficient. This is true for the standard operation, and when you consider that the new VVVF traction elevators can generate electricity when there is "free fall,"

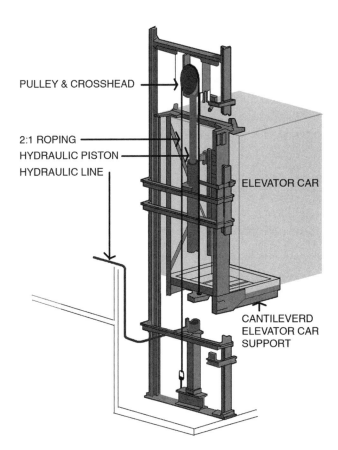

PULLEY & CROSSHEAD

2:1 ROPING
HYDRAULIC PISTON
HYDRAULIC LINE

ELEVATOR CAR

CANTILEVERD
ELEVATOR CAR
SUPPORT

Figure 14.7 A 2:1 ROPED HYDRAULIC HOLELESS ELEVATOR
This hydraulic elevator is sometimes used in low-rise structures with relatively light elevator usage, which generally means residential applications. Since the car is suspended by cables that are raised and lowered by the hydraulic piston, the installation is above grade. With the 2:1 roping, the rise of the elevator car will be twice the rise of the piston. Adapted from a design of the Corbett Elevator Co. and an image from B. Stein, J.S. Reynolds, W.T. Grondzik, A.G. and Kwok: *Mechanical and Electrical Equipment for Buildings* (John Wiley & Sons, Inc., Hoboken, NJ, 2006), Figure 32.7.

fectively encasing the hydraulic unit, including safety controls, to remove any leaking fluids and/or by replacing the hydraulic fluid with a substance that is less harmful to the environment. The use of biodegradable hydraulic fluids should reduce the environmental impact. Hydraulic fluids are used in many applications in addition to elevators, so there are a number of available fluid types: synthetic compounds, mineral oil, water-based mixtures, and water. Interestingly, early hydraulic lifts used water as the hydraulic fluid, although the compressibility of water does not allow it to perform as well as current hydraulic oils.

One advantage of hydraulic elevators is their ability to support heavy loads, and since the load is a critical factor with freight elevators and speed generally is not, freight elevators often continue to be hydraulic units. With freight elevators, the car size is also important, as is the convenient location near a loading dock and the service flow within the structure. While it is important to provide decent pedestrian movement within a building to access passenger elevators, people sometimes can move in ways that large, heavy equipment cannot. As indicated in Table 14.4, many structures should have separate freight elevators, based on occupancy and building size. When a separate freight or service elevator is not provided, one passenger elevator should be identified for this function. This will require accommodations in the architectural design to allow the elevator to function properly in this manner. This not only means being able to add protective blankets when it is used in that capacity, but also considering the connection between the elevator and the building's loading area, the dimensions of the elevator car (especially the height), and the ability to get large items into and out of the car.

something that hydraulic elevators cannot provide, the energy disadvantage of hydraulic elevators is clear. However, some companies are trying to develop a means of energy conservation that could improve hydraulic elevator performance. The basic idea is to somehow use the pressure that is released as the elevator car drops down to help elevate a rising elevator, thereby reducing the energy required by the hydraulic pumps. While this is an interesting concept, the apparently necessary linkage between the elevators obviously limits its potential, especially since a major use of hydraulic elevators currently tends to be in smaller buildings where frequently there is only one elevator and the demands on elevator performance are less. Of course, this can also be used to rationalize lower efficiencies.

In addition to the lower efficiency of hydraulic elevators, there is also the likelihood that some of the hydraulic oil will leak and contaminate the ground, including the underground aquifer. This problem can be reduced by ef-

ELEVATOR SYSTEM DESIGN

When we design a building, we obviously are concerned not only with how people can get into and out of the structure, but also with how they can move through it. With a multistory structure, this must include the design of the elevator system—where the elevators are located, what kind of elevators are to be used, how many there are, and the speed of service they will provide.

The basic approach to elevator design is to size the system in terms of how many building occupants it can handle in 5 minutes (300 seconds). This will be based on the number of elevator cars, the cab size, the elevator speed, and the number of floors served. In addition to determining how many people can be serviced in 5 minutes, we must consider the overall travel time for the typical elevator trip. This includes the average waiting time or interval after one arrives at the elevator lobby and the elevator begins to move, as well as the time it takes to get to one's floor level.

The terms used in these calculations include the following:

Average Lobby Time or **Average Lobby Waiting Time:** the average time spent by an individual between arriving in the lobby and leaving the lobby in an elevator

Handling Capacity (HC): the maximum number of passengers that can be handled in a given period of time—usually 5 minutes

Percent Handling Capacity (PHC): the HC expressed as a percentage of the building's occupancy, again in 5 minutes

Interval (I) or **Lobby Dispatch Time:** the average time between the departure of elevators from the lobby

Registration Time: the waiting time at an upper floor after registering a call for an elevator

Round-Trip Time (RT): the average time required for an elevator car to make a round trip, starting from the lower terminal and returning to it, and for peak traffic, including a statistically determined number of floor stops on the way up and an express return trip

Travel Time or **Average Trip Time (AVTRP):** the average time spent by passengers from the moment they arrive in the lobby to the time they leave the elevator at an upper floor

Zone: the grouping of floors in a building that is considered as a unit with respect to elevator service and has linkages between elevator stops

Since HC is the number of occupants that can be handled in a 5-minute period, the basic formula for determining HC is relatively simple:

$$HC = \frac{300 \times p \times N}{RT}$$

where:

p = passengers per elevator car

N = number of elevator cars

RT = round trip time in seconds

300 = 5 minutes x 60 sec/min

Since the interval (I) between elevator cars is found by

$$I = \frac{RT}{N}$$

the HC can be also determined by:

$$HC = \frac{300 \times p}{I}$$

Table 14.3: PRELIMINARY ELEVATOR SELECTION DATA

Building Type	Normal Passenger Load per Car	Car Travel (ft)	Recommended Car Speed (FPM)
Office	12–24	<100	100–150
		100	200
		125	300
		150	400
		175	500
		250	600
		350	700
		>350	1000+
Mercantile	16–24	<100	100–150
		100	200
		150	350
Apartment	6–13	<100	100–150
		100	200
		125	300
		150	350
		175	400
		250	500
		350	700
		>350	1000+
Hotel	10–22	125	350
		200	500
		250	600
		350	700
		>350	1000+
Hospital	6–24	<100	100–150
		100	200
		150	300

The options that can be used in selecting the appropriate elevator car size and the proper speeds definitely have an impact on the round-trip time in a building. Table 14.3 lists the normal passenger capacity for various building types and the recommended car speeds that should be used for different maximum car-travel distances. As we look at this table, we might question why the ultimate listed maximum travel is only 350 feet or why the maximum speed is no higher than 700 FPM. The 350-foot travel distance relates to the height of a building of only around 30 to 35 floors, and buildings are often taller than this (although some might question the logic of building higher). Also, there are elevators that have speeds considerably higher than 700 FPM.

Both limitations make sense since Table 14.3 presents recommendations for a single elevator zone. If a building is taller than 30 to 35 floors, the recommendation is to divide the structure into elevator zones, each of which serves a maximum of about 18 to 20 floors. Furthermore, when there are multiple elevator zones, the elevators that serve the upper zones will have a portion of their run that does not have any stops. As the elevator car moves through these express floors, speeds higher than 700 FPM become feasible.

While elevators can now travel at more than 1200 feet per minute, it takes some time before an elevator car can reach these high speeds and basically the same amount of time for the car to come to a stop. The rate of acceleration or deceleration should be low enough so as not to jostle the passengers. Generally, this means that the change in speed is between 140 and 220 FPM/second. Assuming a mid-position of around 180 FPM/second, it would take almost three floors before an elevator could reach 700 FPM or come to a stop comfortably from such a speed. Therefore, unless the elevator goes further than six floors between stops, it is unlikely that it could attain a speed of 700 FPM, let alone travel any distance at this speed. As a result, it makes sense to use high-speed elevators only when a building is high enough to include an express elevator.

Tables 14.4 and 14.5 provide some preliminary recommendations for sizing the elevator system for various building types and building size.

Elevator car capacity is listed in terms of maximum pounds that the car can carry. The occupancy conversion is based on an assumed 150 pounds per person. By dividing the various elevator car capacities by 150 pounds per person, the quotient found, rounded to the whole number, is the listed number of individuals in Table 14.6. On further thought, considering the platform dimensions of the various cars, we find that the listed car occupancies range from about 4 square feet per person in the smaller cars to less than 2.5 square feet per person in the larger cars. In some ways, this seems to run contrary to intuition, which suggests that it is less likely that someone would enter an elevator car already containing a number of people who are tightly packed together. Confronted with this situation, it seems less likely that the person would enter the elevator car and instead would choose to wait for the next car.

The theoretical elevator car capacity tends to exceed the actual number of passengers who tend to ride in an elevator. Generally, a "full" car will have only 75 to 80%

of the listed capacity, but even this seems to be higher than what riders might seem to prefer. Table 14.6 lists both the maximum number of passengers who can theoretically be carried by an elevator car and the more likely normal number, which is set at 80% of the listed maximum number of passengers. In *The Vertical Transportation Handbook*, George R. Strakosch suggests that, in order to feel comfortable, most people prefer to have at least 3 square feet

Table 14.5: ELEVATOR EQUIPMENT RECOMMENDATIONS

Building Type	Car Capacity (lb)	Minimum Car Speed (FPM)	Rise (ft)
Office Building	2500 3000 3500	350–400 500–600 700 800 1000+	0–125 126–225 226–275 276–375 Above 375
Mercantile	3500 4000 5000	200 250–300 350–400 500	0–100 101–150 151–200 Above 200
Apartment Building	2000 2500	100 200 250–300 700	0.75 76–125 126–200 Above 200
Hotel	2500 3000	350–400 500–600 700 800 1000+	0–125 126–225 226–275 276–375 Above 375
Hospital	3500 4000	150 200–250 250–300 350–400 500–600 700	0–60 61–100 101–125 126–175 176–250 Above 250

Source: Adapted from B. Stein, J.S. Reynolds, W.T. Grondzik, and A.G. Kwok, *Mechanical and Electrical Equipment for Buildings* (John Wiley & Sons, Inc., Hoboken, NJ, 2006), Table 31.9.

Table 14.4: APPROXIMATE NUMBER OF ELEVATOR SHAFTS

Use	Number of Shafts	Capacity of Elevator (lb)
Office Buildings	One per 35,000 sq ft of Area Served, Plus One Service Elevator for Each 265,000 sq ft of Area Served	2500 or 3500 (3500 is typical)
Apartment Buildings	One per 75 Units, Plus One Service Elevator for 300 Units or More in a High-Rise Building	2500
Hotels	One per 75 Rooms, Plus One Service Elevator for Up to 100 Rooms and One Service Elevator for Each Additional 200 Rooms	2500 or 3000

Source: Adapted from a table in E. Allen and J. Iano, *The Architect's Studio Companion* (John Wiley & Sons, Inc., Hoboken, NJ, 1995), p. 174.

Table 14.6: ELEVATOR CAR CAPACITIES AND SIZES

Elevator Type	Car Capacity (lb)	Passengers		Approx. Shaft	
		Normal	Listed	Width	Depth
Traction	1200 2000 2500 3000 3500 4000	6 10 12 16 19 21	8 13 16 20 23 26	6'-6" 7'-6" 8'-6" 8'-6" 8'-6" 10'-0"	5'-0" 6'-0" 6'-8" 7'-2" 8'-0" 8'-0"
Hydraulic	1500 2000 2500 3000 3500 4000	8 10 12 16 19 21	10 13 16 20 23 26	6'-6" 7'-6" 8'-6" 8'-6" 8'-6" 9'-0"	4'-6" 5'-0" 5'-6" 6'-0" 7'-0" 7'-0"

Table 14.7: ELEVATOR CAR CAPACITIES

Car Capacity (lb)	Car Area (sq ft)	Number of Passengers per Car				
		Normal	Listed	At 3 sq ft	At 2 sq ft	At 1.5 sq ft
1200	15	6	8	5	7	10
1500	19	8	10	6	9	12
2000	24	10	13	8	12	16
2500	29	12	16	9	14	19
3000	32	16	20	10	16	21
3500	38	18	23	12	19	25
4000	42	20	26	14	21	28

Table 14.8: RECOMMENDED ELEVATOR INTERVAL AND LOBBY WAITING TIMES

Facility Type	Interval (sec)	Waiting Time (sec)
Office Building		
Excellent Service	15–24	9–14
Good Service	25–29	15–17
Fair Service	30–39	18–23
Poor Service	40–49	24–29
Unacceptable Service	50+	30+
Residential Building		
Prestige	50–70	30–42
Middle-Income	60–80	36–48
Low-Income	80–120	48–72
Dormitories	60–80	36–48
Hotels — First Quality	30–50	18–30
Hotels — Second Quality	50–70	30–42

Source: Adapted from several tables from G.R. Strakosch (ed.), *The Vertical Transportation Handbook* (John Wiley & Sons, Inc., Hoboken, NJ, 1998).

of elevator car area, although, when necessary, they will crowd into an elevator car allotting only around 2 square feet per person. Strakosch also suggests that when there is a crush, the area per person might even be reduced to only $1^1/_2$ square feet. This could happen at peak-use times when an elevator car is willingly filled at about the 2-square-feet allotment, and then a few more people push their way into the car. Based on these allocations, we could rewrite the car capacities in Table 14.6 as shown in Table 14.7.

Based on the comparisons presented by Table 14.7, it seems reasonable to accept the densities presented as the normal elevator car capacities from this table. In this way, as we develop a preliminary design for an elevator system, we assume that the elevator cars will carry less than the maximum number of passengers who might actually crush into an elevator car. This approach will not only result in a better-performing system, it should also reduce the likelihood that, on further development of the elevator system, we will have to increase significantly the number of elevators that will be required. While we should expect that our preliminary elevator layout will be appropriate for the building we are working on, if we must adjust our elevator design assumption, it would be better to be able to reduce the number and/or size of the elevators than to be forced to find a way to increase them.

Another interesting (some might say peculiar) thing is that the average waiting time for an elevator is not half of the interval between times when two elevators leave the ground-floor lobby (see Table 14.8). It seems logical to assume that the arrival of people at the building during the period of maximum load, generally in the morning at the beginning of the work day, would be reasonably dispersed, with some arriving just after one elevator leaves and others just before the next elevator does. However, field measurements indicate otherwise, suggesting that the average waiting time is actually equal to 60% of the interval time between two elevators leaving the lobby. Perhaps this is

the result of some weird natural phenomenon that causes a large group of people to arrive just a second too late to catch the previous elevator, thereby skewing the waiting time. There is also the possibility that since at peak times the elevators are basically full, some people choose to wait for the next elevator car rather than rush to crowd into the elevator that is about to leave as they arrive in the lobby. In any event, when determining the overall average trip time, we should assume 60% of the interval time. Of course, when there are more elevator cars, the waiting time should be less, meaning that the 10% adjustment (60% rather than 50%) should not be critical since the interval time would be reduced.

As shown in Table 14.8, the acceptable waiting time changes for the type of building in terms of both occupancy and quality. One particular comparison that we might consider as we explore what might be appropriate for a building is that a 50-second interval, which at 60% means a 30-second average waiting time, is apparently not acceptable for an office building but is in fact considered the goal for a prestigious residential building. When an elevator system does not meet the standard for maximum acceptable waiting time, people tend to get upset. According to a study done by Mitsubishi Electric, while people are willing to wait some time for a bus or train, often more than 10 to 15 minutes beyond the expected time, they tend to become rather irritated when there is even a short delay in the arrival of an elevator. Mitsubishi Electric has suggested that with elevators, irritation as people wait increases proportionally to the square of the actual waiting time.[2]

---

[2] http://www.mitsubishi-elevator.com/innovations/control_system.html.

Perhaps our own elevator experiences can guide us in determining the appropriate expectations for an elevator system better than merely relying on design standards. We have probably had the experience of waiting (and waiting and waiting) for an elevator in a hotel, perhaps becoming further frustrated by the pressure to check out and make a tight travel connection. Or maybe the experience came from living in a multistory dormitory and confronting an interminable delay in trying to get back to our room so that we could get our books and then arrive in time for class or for an exam.

Fortunately, for both of these problems, modern computer-activated controls can improve the elevator response. Before these controls existed, an elevator starter was usually in charge of managing elevator operations for any major installation. This individual could readily observe when a problem occurred and manually override operations to get it resolved. While personal intervention is no longer likely to be an option, it is possible to program the computerized controls to override normal elevator operations if there is no response to an elevator call within a prescribed time. Of course, this cannot resolve problems that result from a faulty elevator system design.

Rather than merely accept the recommended times provided by various sources or elevator specialists, we should consider the level of performance that might be in sync with the underlying intentions of our architectural design. Even though elevators are considered to be part of the technical or mechanical operations, they are still a critical part of any high-rise building, and we should not relinquish all responsibility for their design. While we might never be proficient in the specific delineation of an elevator system, we should understand what is possible, not just what is standard, and take major responsibility for determining what is appropriate for a particular design.

ELEVATORING

Elevatoring is a term used by George R. Strakosch, editor of *The Vertical Transportation Handbook*, to indicate the process of applying elevator technology to determine the basic design of an elevator system. While Table 14.4 provides a guide that can be used to suggest a preliminary proposal for an elevator design, reinforced by the information presented in Table 14.5, we really need to test whether the suggestions in these tables are valid for a particular building by determining whether the handling capacity of the system will fall within an acceptable range. Strakosch suggests that this probably requires as much judgment as the application of hard technical data.

As presented above, HC is the number of passengers that an elevator system can handle in 5 minutes. This can be presented in several ways:

$$HC = \frac{300 \times p \times N}{RT}$$

$$HC = \frac{passengers/car \times 300}{I}$$

If the interval is 30 seconds, which is a reasonable assumption for an office building:

$$HC = 10 \times Passengers/Car$$

The first step is to determine the number of people that have to be accommodated within the 5-minute period of time—that is, the HC. This number is generally based on a percentage of the number of total building occupants, as suggested in Table 14.9, which is based on building type and building classification.

Since Table 14.9 gives a percentage of building occupancy, this occupancy must also be determined. This should not be too difficult since it is likely that the building's design is based in part on accommodating this population. If specific occupancy numbers are not available, Table 14.10 can be used as a guide. This table provides a way to determine building occupancy based on the net building area, which in turn is related to the gross building area adjusted for the floor level. As indicated in the table, the net area per person for various residential occupancies is often based on the number of beds. When this is not known, an average of about 200 square feet of net area per person may be used. Of course, any of these numbers can be adjusted to better match the overall objectives of the building design.

Table 14.11 can be used to establish a reasonable percentage of the gross building area from which to compute

Table 14.9: EXPECTED HC BY BUILDING TYPE

Facility	Percent of Building Occupancy to Be Carried in 5 Minutes
Office Building	
Center City	12–14
Investment	11–13
Single-Occupancy	14–16
Residential	
Prestige Apartment Building	5–7
Other Apartment Building	6–8
Dormitory	10–11
Hotel – Luxury	12–15
Hotel – Market	10–12

Source: Adapted from B. Stein, J.S. Reynolds, W.T. Grondzik, and A.G. Kwok. *Mechanical and Electrical Equipment for Buildings* (John Wiley & Sons, Inc., Hoboken, NJ, 2006), Table 31.6.

Table 14.10: ESTIMATED POPULATION OCCUPANCY OF TYPICAL BUILDINGS

Building Type	Density
Office Buildings Diversified (Multiple Tenancy)	Net Square Feet per Person
Normal	110–130
Prestige	150–250
Single Tenancy	
Normal	90–110
Prestige	130–200
Apartment Houses	Persons per Bedroom
High-Rent Housing	1.5
Moderate-Rent Housing	2
Low-Cost Housing	2.5–3.0
Hotels	Persons per Sleeping Room
Normal Use	1.3
Conventions	1.9
Hospitals	Visitors and Staff per Bed
General Private	3
General Public (Large Wards)	3–4
Schools	Net Square Feet per Person
Classrooms	15
Laboratory	100 .
Library	Based on Seating
Courthouse	Per Courtroom 30 people

Source: Adapted from several tables from various publications including B. Stein, J.S. Reynolds, W.T. Grondzik, and A.G. Kwok, *Mechanical and Electrical Equipment for Buildings* (John Wiley & Sons, Inc., Hoboken, NJ, 2006) and G.R. Strakosch (ed.), *The Vertical Transportation Handbook* (John Wiley & Sons, Inc., Hoboken, NJ, 1998).

the net area of an office building. This table essentially indicates that with multiple elevator zones, at the upper floors within a high-rise structure, the number of elevator shafts continuing up through the structure likely decreases. As a result, a higher percentage of the gross floor area becomes available as usable space. The percentages indicated in this table are applicable for office buildings with 15,000 to 20,000 gross square feet per floor.

Table 14.11: OFFICE BUILDING OCCUPANCY EFFICIENCY

Building Height			Net Usable Area as Percentage of Gross Area
0–10 Floors	Floors	1–10	Approximately 80%
0–20 Floors	Floors	1–10	Approximately 75%
		11–20	Approximately 80%
0–30 Floors	Floors	1–10	Approximately 70%
		11–20	Approximately 75%
		21–30	Approximately 80%
0–40 Floors	Floors	1–10	Approximately 70%
		11–20	Approximately 75%
		21–30	Approximately 80%
		31–40	Approximately 85%

Source: Adapted from G.R. Strakosch (ed.), *The Vertical Transportation Handboook* (John Wiley & Sons, Inc., Hoboken, NJ, 1998), Table 10.2.

As in many aspects of design, it is often necessary to make an initial proposal that, through various iterations, can develop into a reasonable idea. The design of an elevator system is similar to this, and Tables 14.12 to 14.14 provide some basic information that can be used for a preliminary elevator design proposal that can then be verified through some simple calculations.

The average trip time or time to destination is the sum of the lobby waiting time plus the travel time to a stop at the medium floor and is, as stated, merely an average of all the trips. The actual trip time will vary for each passenger based on the floor level to which that person travels, the number of stops that are made prior to reaching that floor, the number of people who have to exit the elevator at each stop, the floor-to-floor distances, the speed of the elevator, and the interval between the time when the passenger

Table 14.12: SUGGESTED PASSENGER ELEVATOR SPEEDS

Building Class:	Small (FPM)	Average) (FPM)	Large or Prestige (FPM)	Service (FPM)
Office Buildings				
Up to 5 Floors	200	300–400	400	150–200
5 to 10 Floors	400	400	500	300
10 to 15 Floors	400	500	500	400
15 to 25 Floors	500	700	700	500
25 to 35 Floors	–	1000	1000	500
35 to 45 Floors	–	1000–1200	1200	700
45 to 60 Floors	–	1200–1400	1400–1600	800
Over 60 Floors	–	1800	1800	800
Stores				
2 to 5 Floors	150	200	300	150–200
5 to 10 Floors	400	400	500	400
10 to 15 Floors	500	500	500–700	400
Garages				
2 to 5 Floors	200	200	200	–
5 to 10 Floors	200	300	400	–
10 to 15 Floors	300	400	500	–

Residential	Hotels and Motels	Apartments	Dormitories
2 to 6 Floors	150	150	150
6 to 12 Floors	300	200	200
12 to 20 Floors	400–500	400	400
20 to 25 Floors	500	500	500
25 to 30 Floors	700	500	700
30 to 40 Floors[a]	700–1000	700–1000	700–1000
40 to 50 Floors[a]	1000–1200	1000–1200	1000–1200

Institutional	Hospitals	Nursing Homes	Courthouse	Museum	Jail
2 to 6 Floors	200–400	200	400	400	200
6 to 12 Floors	400–500	400	500	500	400
12 to 20 Floors	700	500	700	700	500
20 to 25 Floors	800	500–700	800	–	–
25 to 30 Floors	1000	–	1000	–	–

[a]For buildings of this height, division into zones with an express run should be considered.

Source: Adapted from G.R. Strakosch (ed.), *The Vertical Transportation Handbook* (John Wiley & Sons, Inc., Hoboken, NJ, 1998), Tables 10.7, 11.1, and 12.1.

Table 14.13: SUGGESTED PASSENGER ELEVATOR CAPACITY

	Small (lb)	Average (lb)	Large or Prestige (lb)
Office Buildings			
Downtown	3000	3500	4000
Suburban	2500	3000	3500
Professional	2500	3500	4000
Stores	3500	3500	4000
Garages	2500	3000	3500
Industrial	4000	4000	4000
Residential			
Hotel		3500	
Motel		2500–3000	
Apartments		2500	
Dormitories		3000	
Institutional			
Hospitals		5000	
Long-term Care		3500	
Schools		6000	
Courthouse		4000	
Museum		6000	
Sports Arena		6000	
Jail		3500	

Source: Adapted from G.R. Strakosch, G.R. (ed.), *The Vertical Transportation Handbook* (John Wiley & Sons, Inc., Hoboken, NJ, 1998), Tables 10.6, 11.1, and 12.1.

arrives at the elevator lobby on the ground floor and the elevator begins its run.

In a commercial environment, a trip time of less than 1 minute is considered quite desirable. Trip times of 75, 90, and 120 seconds are considered to be acceptable, annoying, and at the limit of toleration, respectively. In the more

Table 14.14: SUGGESTED INTERVALS FOR PASSENGER ELEVATORS

	Up-Peak (sec)	Up-Peak with 10% Down Traffic (sec)	Two-Way (sec)
Commercial Buildings			
Multiple-Tenant Office	23–28	28–33	33–43
Single-Tenant Office	20–25	25–30	30–40
Professional Office	–	–	30–50
Stores	–	–	30–50
Parking Garages	40–50	–	40–60
Industrial Buildings	25–30	–	30–40
		Two-Way (sec)	
Residential Buildings			
Hotels and Motels		40–60	
Apartments		50–70	
Dormitories		50–70	
Institutions			
Hospitals		30–50	
Long-term Care		40–70	
Schools		40–50	

Source: Adapted from G.R. Strakosch (ed.), *The Vertical Transportation Handbook* (John Wiley & Sons, Inc., Hoboken, NJ, 1998), Tables 10.5, 11.1, and 12.1.

relaxed atmosphere of a residential building, the maximum trip times within each category can be increased.

The success of a preliminary elevator system design is generally based on the expected average trip time, round-trip time, and lobby waiting time, all of which can be determined from data available in various tables and graphs. The data presented here have been derived from various sources including Strakosch (1998) and Stein et al. (2006) (see Bibliography).

While the average trip time and lobby waiting time will influence the adequacy of an elevator design, the development of a design is primarily based on establishing the expected round-trip time. Since there are many variables that affect the performance of an elevator system, any calculation of round-trip time must be based on certain assumptions and averages. For example, although some elevators provide service between only two floor levels, most elevators serve a number of levels, and obviously, the more floors that are served by an elevator, the longer the probable trip time. Regardless of the number of floors served, the actual number of stops will vary considerably. As we have most likely experienced, sometimes the elevator we are riding has to stop at each floor to let someone get off; at other times, we are lucky and essentially have an express run to our stop. Therefore, in order to gain a reasonable understanding of the likely or average elevator performance, it is appropriate to proceed using various assumptions based on observed behavior, both of people and of equipment, and accepted probabilities.

Table 14.15 indicates the probable number of stops that an elevator will make based on the number of floors served and the number of passengers per trip, which is a factor of the size of the elevator car. In terms of the number of floors, the table uses the notation "Upper Floors Served," which indicates that the lobby level is not included in the count. A review of the table confirms that with more floors served and/or more passengers per car, there are likely to be more stops in each elevator run.

The time that should be allotted for the elevator stop at the ground-level lobby, which is presented in Table 14.16, is based on a minimum of 8 seconds plus 0.8 additional second for each passenger over eight individuals. This lobby time applies whether the passengers are merely entering, leaving, or some going in and some going out, although generally during the highest peak times, most passengers are arriving and therefore are entering the elevators at the lobby level.

When an elevator arrives at a stop, there must be adequate time to allow passengers to leave or enter the car. Three seconds, which is generally adequate for one or two passengers to transfer, is typically set as the time that the elevator doors will remain open. This is referred to as the *dwell time*. When more passengers must transfer at a stop,

Table 14.15: PROBABLE ELEVATOR STOPS

Upper Floors Served	Passengers per Trip														
	2	4	6	8	10	12	14	16	18	20	22	24	26	28	30
2	1.5	2.0	2.0	2.0	2.0	2.0	2.0	2.0	2.0	2.0	2.0	2.0	2.0	2.0	2.0
4	2.0	2.7	3.3	3.6	3.8	3.9	3.9	4.0	4.0	4.0	4.0	4.0	4.0	4.0	4.0
6	2.0	3.2	4.0	4.6	5.0	5.3	5.5	5.7	5.8	5.8	5.9	5.9	6.0	6.0	6.0
8	2.0	3.3	4.4	5.3	5.9	6.4	6.8	7.0	7.3	7.5	7.6	7.7	7.8	7.8	8.0
10	2.0	3.4	4.7	5.8	6.5	7.2	7.7	8.2	8.5	8.8	9.0	9.2	9.4	9.5	9.5
12	2.0	3.5	4.9	6.0	7.0	7.8	8.5	9.0	9.5	9.9	10.2	10.5	10.8	11.0	11.3
14	2.0	3.6	5.0	6.3	7.3	8.3	9.0	9.7	10.3	10.8	11.3	11.6	12.0	12.2	12.5
16	2.0	3.6	5.1	6.5	7.6	8.6	9.5	10.3	11.0	11.6	12.1	12.6	13.0	13.4	13.9
18	2.0	3.7	5.2	6.6	7.8	8.9	9.9	10.8	11.6	12.3	12.9	13.4	13.9	14.4	15.0
20	2.0	3.7	5.3	6.7	8.0	9.2	10.3	11.2	12.1	12.8	13.5	14.2	14.7	15.3	16.0
22	2.0	3.7	5.4	6.8	8.2	9.4	10.5	11.6	12.5	13.3	14.1	14.8	15.4	16.0	17.0
24	2.0	3.8	5.4	6.9	8.3	9.6	10.8	11.9	12.8	13.8	14.6	15.4	16.1	16.7	17.3
26	2.0	3.8	5.5	7.0	8.5	9.8	11.2	12.2	13.1	14.1	15.1	16.0	16.8	17.4	17.7

Source: Adapted from G.R. Strakosch (ed.), *The Vertical Transportation Handbook* (John Wiley & Sons, Inc., Hoboken, NJ, 1998), Chart 4.1.

an additional second for each passenger above two should be added to the dwell time. Such an extended time is usually created when the presence of an individual in the door opening is sensed either by a pressure-activated mechanical switch on the edge of the elevator door or by a photoelectric device connected with the elevator-door operating mechanism.

The dwell time for an elevator stop set by a call to pick up a passenger is also usually 3 seconds when there is only one elevator car. This dwell time is again assumed adequate for up to two passengers. If there are more than two new passengers, an additional second for each additional passenger should be added to the transfer time for that car-call stop. So, if there were a car call to a floor where five passengers were waiting for an elevator, the transfer time for that floor would be 6 seconds.

$$TT = 3\sec DT + (5-2)\sec EPT = 6\sec TT$$

where:
    TT is Transfer time
    DT is dwell time
    EPT is extra passenger time

Table 14.16: ELEVATOR LOBBY TIMES

	Number of Passengers Entering or Leaving										
	8	10	12	14	16	18	20	22	24	26	28
Lobby Time	8	10	11	13	14	16	18	20	21	23	24

Source: Adapted from G.R. Strakosch (ed.), *The Vertical Transportation Handbook* (John Wiley & Sons, Inc., Hoboken, NJ, 1998), Table 4.2.

When an elevator is called to a floor where there is a bank of elevators, which is sometimes referred to as a *landing call* as distinct from a *car call,* additional dwell time is required in order to let the passengers get to the elevator car that actually arrives. With up to four cars in a row and with both an audio signal to indicate that a car is arriving and a landing lantern to denote which car that might be, we should assume a dwell time of 4 seconds for a landing call. Strakosch suggests that without a landing lantern to indicate which car is arriving, the dwell time should be extended to 5 seconds for two side-by-side cars, with an added 4 seconds for each additional car in a row. For a landing call, the dwell time, whether or not it has been extended in response to the number and placement of the cars, is presumed adequate to allow only one passenger to enter the elevator, so we should also extend the transfer time by a second for each additional passenger. Assuming an audio signal and a landing lantern, if four passengers were waiting for an elevator at a bank of four cars, the transfer time for the landing call would be 7 seconds. If there were no audio signal and landing lantern, following Strakosch's recommendation, the transfer time would be 16 seconds.

$$TT = 4\sec DT + (4-1)\sec EPT = 7\sec$$
$$TT = (5+8)\sec DT + (4-1)\sec EPT = 16\sec$$

Since the dwell time for four elevator cars and no landing lanterns seems excessive, we might be tempted to reduce the 4 seconds of extended time for each additional car since this seems to be more time than is necessary to allow a person to move to the elevator that ultimately arrives for the landing call. However, the more logical approach, especially for our role in the design of the elevator system, would be to ensure that both an audio alarm and a landing lantern are provided, and that the lantern not only indicates which elevator might be arriving, but also denotes the direction in which the arriving elevator is going.

Since the transfer time does not include the time required to open and close the elevator doors, an allocation for this operation also needs to be added to the overall time for an elevator stop. Table 14.17 includes door opening and closing times as well the total time for the door operation. The total time includes an additional half-second for car startup. After the doors are closed, it takes a short time to ensure that they are locked before the elevator brake can be released and the elevator motor can restart. As a critical safety measure, it should not be possible to start the elevator motor unless the doors are closed and the elevator-door lock is activated. This verification adds additional time to the overall door operation.

As an aside, when an elevator stops at a landing, a complicated set of actions must occur before the doors can open. One expectation is that the elevator car will stop at essentially the same level as the landing. For a decent

installation, $1/4$ inch is the maximum allowable deviation. When we consider our own experience in trying to stop an automobile, we should appreciate that this leveling is accomplished automatically whether the stop occurs after the elevator car has traveled only one floor or after a long express run, or whether the car is full or has only one or two passengers. When the car does come to a stop, by stopping the elevator motor, the car is then locked into position by setting the brake. Only then should the elevator doors open.

The elevator doors are actually a double set of doors: the hoistway door or doors and the elevator gate or gates. In addition to providing an opening into the elevator shaft only when an elevator car is at that landing, the hoistway doors must provide fire separation when the doors are closed. Since the rating of the elevator-shaft enclosure is typically set at 2 hours, the hoistway elevator doors should be rated at $1^1/2$ hours. The elevator gates, which often were basically just what their name implies, are now generally comprised of solid panels. These gates should be configured to match the operation of the hoistway doors in both method of operation and speed.

As can be seen in Table 14.17 the size of the door and the type of door opening affect the time required for door operation. A two-speed door includes two door panels, both of which slide in the same direction but at different speeds so that they both open or close at the same time. In general, when minimizing elevator trip time is a concern, a center-opening door with a width of at least 48 inches should be specified. As noted in the table, since the travel distance for each door panel is only half that of a single door, a center-opening door opens and closes in less time. While a wider door increases the time required for the doors to open and close, the greater opening width generally reduces the time for both loading and exiting passengers. At 48 inches, two people can enter or leave at the same time, or one person can leave as another is entering (see Figure 14.11).

Table 14.18 provides running times for various floor-to-floor heights and elevator car speeds. These numbers include the time required to start and stop the run, as well as the time required to position the elevator car so that the floor levels are the same for both the landing and the car before the elevator doors open. In some installations, the elevator doors may begin to open before the car reaches a full stop. With this approach, which can cut almost 1 second of travel time, the interlock with the door safety switch must still be engaged and the width of the opening must remain less than what might permit someone to pass through, which generally is no more than 8 inches. While this limited opening width should definitely prevent any passenger from falling through the hoistway door, it does present a potential problem: a passenger's limb might be caught between the opening and the moving elevator car.

Table 14.17: ELEVATOR DOOR OPERATING TIME

Door Type	Width (in.)	Open (sec)	Close (sec)	Total (sec)
Single-Slide	36	2.5	3.6	6.6
Two-Speed	36	2.1	3.3	5.9
Center-Opening	36	1.5	2.1	4.1
Single-Slide	42	2.7	3.8	7
Two-Speed	42	2.4	3.7	6.6
Center-Opening	42	1.7	2.4	4.6
Two-Speed	48	2.7	4.5	7.7
Center-Opening	48	1.9	2.9	5.3
Two-speed	54	3.3	5	8.8
Center-Opening	54	2.3	3.2	6
Two-Speed	60	3.9	5.5	9.9
Center-Opening	60	2.5	3.5	6.5
Two-Speed Center-Opening	60	2.5	3	6

Note: Single-Slide refers to a single door panel sliding in one direction. Two-Speed refers to a door with two panel door with both panels sliding in the same direction. Center-Opening essentially refers to two panel doors with each sliding in a different direction. Two-Speed Center-Opening refers to two two-panel doors that slide in different directions.
Source: Adapted from a table in G.R. Strakosch (ed.), *The Vertical Transportation Handbook* (John Wiley & Sons, Inc., Hoboken, NJ, 1998), Table 4.3.

Table 14.18: ELEVATOR RUNNING TIME—CAR STOP TO CAR STOP

Elevator Speed	Run Heights									Each Additional 10 ft
	9	10	11	12	13	14	15	20	30	
100 FPM	7.6	8.2	8.8	9.4	10.0	10.6	11.2	14.2	20.2	6.0
150 FPM	6.7	7.1	7.5	7.9	8.3	8.7	9.1	11.1	15.1	4.0
200 FPM	5.8	6.1	6.4	6.7	7.0	7.3	7.6	9.1	12.1	3.0
300 FPM	5.2	5.4	5.6	5.8	6.0	6.2	6.4	7.4	9.4	2.0
400 FPM	4.8	5.0	5.1	5.2	5.4	5.6	5.7	6.5	7.0	1.5
500 FPM	–	–	4.3	4.4	4.5	4.6	4.7	5.2	6.4	1.2
700 FPM	–	–	4.3	4.4	4.5	4.6	4.7	5.2	6.1	0.86
1000 FPM	–	–	4.3	4.4	4.5	4.6	4.7	5.2	5.8	0.6

Note: The times listed for speeds of 100 FPM and 150 FPM include 0.75 second for leveling. Higher speeds include 0.5 second for leveling.
Source: Adapted from G.R. Strakosch (ed.), *The Vertical Transportation Handbook* (John Wiley & Sons, Inc., New York, 1998), Chart 4.2.

With information about our building design and the data provided in Tables 14.15 to 14.18, we can calculate the expected round-trip time to use in testing a preliminary design of the elevator system, verifying both the 5-minute handling capacity and the probable lobby waiting time. These calculations will indicate the appropriateness of the preliminary elevator design proposal.

One of the first things that should be done in developing a design for the elevator system is to select the number of floors that will be served by each elevator zone, the elevator speed for each zone, and the capacity of the elevator cars. We also need to determine the floor-to-floor height. Generally, the ground-level or lobby floor height is greater than the typical floor-to-floor height. Also, we should realize that an elevator that serves 16 floors actually travels through only 15 levels, which is one level less than the number of floors served.

The up run time is based on an assumed number of stops that are presented in Table 14.15. By dividing the number of stops into the overall height that the elevator travels, which is the distance between the lobby-floor level and the level of the top floor serviced by the elevator, we can determine the typical length of run, stop-to-stop, that the elevator will have to travel. By using this typical length of run, we can use Table 14.18 to provide the average time that it will take the elevator to travel stop-to-stop. The time required to operate the elevator doors and the dwell time for all the stops, including that for the ground-level lobby, must then be added to the run time. Since we are trying to determine the round-trip time, we have to add the time needed for the elevator to return to the lobby from its last stop. This return time is usually determined by one of the typical stop-to-stop travel times plus the remaining length of travel, assuming the elevator speed as the basis of travel time. The typical stop-to-stop time includes an allowance for both accelerating to running speed and

decelerating from this speed to a stop, so including one stop-to-stop run will account for this in the return run. We then have to reduce the overall length of the return run by the length of the typical stop-to-stop run and, using this length and the elevator speed, determine the time for the return run.

Calculation Procedures

Let us consider the probable round-trip time for an elevator system for a 17-floor office building that has a height from the lobby floor to the second floor of 20 feet and a typical office-level floor-to-floor height of 12 feet. Interpreting from the data in Tables 14.4, 14.5, 14.6, 14.12, and 14.13, we would probably conclude that a 3500-pound elevator car that travels at 500 FPM would be appropriate for this office. Let us also assume that the elevator door is a 48-inch-wide center-opening unit. Since the building has 17 floors including the ground-floor level, the elevator system will serve 16 floors. From Table 14.8, we can see that our 3500-pound car will normally carry 18 passengers, and based on Table 14.15, there will be 11 probable stops for each elevator run during peak times.

To determine the overall height that the elevator must rise, we need to add the distance between the level of the lobby floor and the lowest or first floor above the lobby that is served by the elevator to the product of the typical floor height multiplied by one less than the number of upper floors served by the elevator.

$$\text{Total Rise} = (\text{Lobby Floor Height}) + [(\text{Floor-to-Floor Height}) (\text{Upper Floors Served} - 1)]$$
$$= 20\,\text{ft} + (12\,\text{ft} \times 15) = 200\,\text{ft}$$

By dividing this total rise of 200 feet by the 11 probable number of stops, which was obtained from Table 14.15, the average length of run between elevator stops can be determined:

$$\frac{\text{Total Rise}}{\text{Probable Number of Stops}} = \frac{200\,\text{ft}}{11\,\text{Stops}} = 18.18\,\text{ft}$$

Interpolating between the appropriate values from Table 14.18, using an 18.18-foot run height and a 500-FPM elevator speed, we find that the typical run time between each elevator stop will be 5.02 seconds. With 11 stops and an average of 5.02 seconds for each partial run, it will take 55.22 seconds for the elevator to reach the last stop.

$$\begin{aligned}\text{Time to Run Up} &= \text{Number of Stops} \\ &\quad \times \text{Time Between Stops} \\ &= 11 \times 5.02\,\text{sec} = 55.22\,\text{sec}\end{aligned}$$

The time it will take the elevator car to return from the top stop to the ground-floor lobby is essentially the distance divided by the elevator speed. However, the return run must include time to start and stop the elevator car, so we should reduce the overall travel distance by the assumed distance of each stop and add the time for that run. That is, we can find the time for the return run by adding the time for the elevator to go between stops, 5.02 seconds in this example, to the results of reducing the total elevator-rise height by the height of the typical run from stop to stop, multiplying this value by 60 seconds, and dividing this by the speed of the elevator.

$$\frac{[\text{Total Rise} - (\text{Typical Stop-to-Stop Rise})] \times 60\ \text{sec}}{\text{Elevator Speed in FPM}}$$
$$+ \text{Stop-to-Stop Time (sec)}$$

$$\begin{aligned}\text{Time to Run Down} &= \frac{(200\,\text{ft} - 18.18\,\text{ft}) \times 60\,\text{sec}}{500\,\text{FPM}} \\ &\quad + 5.02\,\text{sec} = 26.8\,\text{sec}\end{aligned}$$

The standing times, which include the lobby time, the transfer times at each stop, and the door operation times, must also be added to the time. With 11 car stops and a total of 18 passengers, it is reasonable to assume that the standard dwell times at each elevator stop should be adequate to allow the one or two passengers to exit the elevator car.

Standing Time:

Lobby Time	18 passengers	16 sec
Transfer Time	11 stops at 3 sec	33 sec
Door Time	(11 stops + lobby) × 5.3 sec	63.6 sec

Running Time:

Run-Up Time	(11 × 5.02 sec)	55.22 sec
Run-Down Time		26.8 sec
Total Round-Trip Time		194.6 sec

To review: the overall round-trip time is basically determined by the overall height and number of floors served by the elevator and by the size of the elevator car. These factors, in turn, establish the probable number of stops that will likely occur during any elevator run, which sets the average distance between stops. Using the speed of the elevator, adjusted for the time it takes to accelerate and decelerate, the time for the elevator to run from stop to stop can be determined. This time, multiplied by the number of stops, establishes the time for the actual travel of the elevator during the up-run. There is also the time for the elevator to travel back to the lobby. The assumption is that during the down-run or return to the lobby, there are no stops since we are determining conditions during peak load times, which generally means that almost all of the traffic is going in the same direction. The time for the elevator to travel up and back is only a portion of the time for the overall round trip. The time that the elevator stays at the lobby and at each stop, which includes the time required to open and close the elevator doors and the time required for people to transfer out of the elevator, must be added to the travel time to determine the overall round-trip time.

The information needed to accomplish a simple calculation can be found from the following tables:

- Table 14.15: Probable Elevator Stops
- Table 14.16: Elevator Lobby Times
- Table 14.17: Elevator Door Operating Time
- Table 14.18: Elevator Running Time — Car Stop to Car Stop

In addition, the time that the elevator is assumed to remain at each upper-level stop, which is the dwell time and is generally assumed to be only 3 seconds, needs to be added to the run time.

While we can use the tables and calculate the expected round-trip times for elevator service within an elevator zone, we can also use a set of graphs to determine the overall time in seconds that an elevator round trip will require for the number of local floors served and the speed of the elevator. Figure 14.8, which assumes a floor-to-floor height of 10 feet, includes four graphs, each based on an elevator car size: a 2500-pound car, a 3000-pound car, a 3500-pound car, and a 4000-pound car. For each different-weight car, these graphs include a plot for 200 FPM, 300 FPM, 400 FPM, 500 FPM, and 700 FPM. Figure 14.9 is similar to Figure 14.8, except that it is based on a floor-to-floor height of 12 feet. The graphs in these figures were generated from calculations.

The difference between the curves for 500 FPM and 700 FPM tends to be less than that for lower speeds even though the 100-FPM spread between these lower speeds is only half that between 500 and 700 FPM. What we

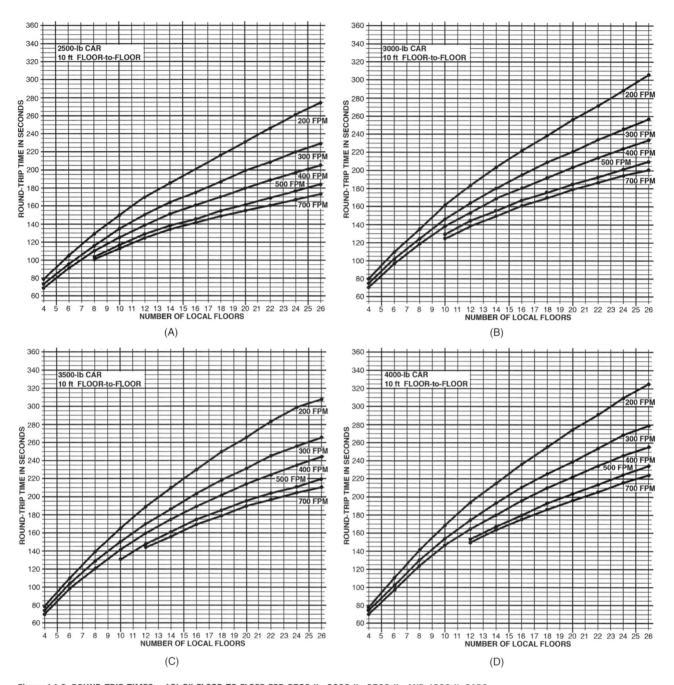

Figure 14.8 ROUND-TRIP TIMES – 10'-0" FLOOR-TO-FLOOR FOR 2500-lb, 3000-lb, 3500-lb, AND 4000-lb CARS

should realize from this is that when we are not dealing with an express run, there is little advantage in exceeding 500 FPM and very little reason to select an elevator that has a speed greater than 700 FPM except for an express run. In fact, by analyzing each of the plots, we would see that the advantage gained from increasing from 500 to 700 FPM derives mainly from the reduced time for the return run, with a reduction in the run-up time of less than 1 second. We would also find that within the service portion of an

elevator run—that is, excluding the return run and any express run—except with the slower elevators, at least half of the run-up time is the time spent with the elevator car stopped at a landing.

Generally, an elevator service zone should be limited to no more than 18 to 20 upper floors. When a building has 20 to 30 upper floors, it might still make sense to divide the structure into two elevator zones. The benefit from a division into zones is that the average trip time and

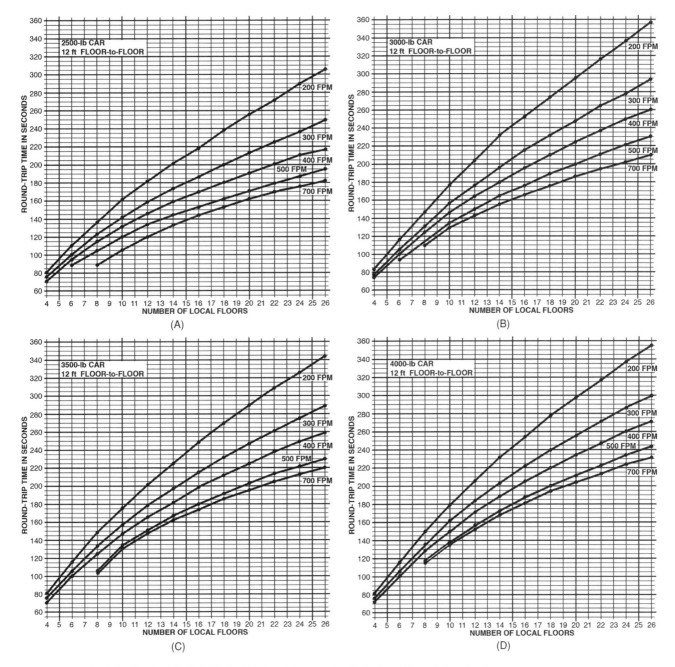

Figure 14.9 ROUND-TRIP TIMES – 12'-0" FLOOR-TO-FLOOR FOR 2500-1b, 3000-1b, 3500-1b, AND 4000-1b CARS

the round-trip time will be less since there will be fewer potential stops that need to be made for each run. Assuming that the ground level or first floor is not included in any service zone, which is the standard assumption, a 36-story structure would have two zones, the lower elevator zone serving the 2nd to 19th floors and the upper zone the 20th to 36th floors. Since the upper-zone elevators would have an express run through the lower zone, if the division of floors is not even, it makes sense to reduce the number of floors served by the upper zone since the time needed to

get to this zone must be added to the overall trip time. This also makes sense since the occupancy levels often tend to be higher for the upper zones, given the likelihood that there is more net rentable space with fewer elevator shafts extending up through the building.

Understanding the round-trip times for different elevator speeds, there is little justification in using elevators with a speed higher than 500 or 700 FPM in the lower zone. Higher speeds would not really be effective since it is unlikely that, with stops on various floors, the elevator cars could ever attain such speeds. However, the express run for elevator cars serving the upper zone would benefit from higher speeds, but with only a 20-floor express run, it is reasonable to evaluate the benefit against the additional cost, and if a higher speed were proposed, perhaps this should be no higher than 1000 FPM. If we are working on a high-rise structure with express runs that pass through more than one elevator service zone, selecting a higher speed might be justified. While 1600 FPM is probably the upper speed readily available, there are elevators that can run at 2000 FPM. The elevators installed at Taipei 101 in Taiwan supposedly can reach a speed of over 3300 FPM, which is equivalent to a little less than 40 miles per hour!

When an elevator runs to an upper zone, the time for the express run has to be added to the time for the round-trip run for the number of floors served by that elevator. The time for the express run is typically given for only one direction, but since the speed is the same whether the elevator car is rising up or dropping down, double this time has to be added to determine the round-trip time.

Calculating the time for an express run is rather basic. As for the down run time in the calculation above, we need to multiply the rise by 60 seconds and divide by the elevator speed in FPM.

$$\text{Express Run Time} = \frac{\text{Height of Express Run} \times 60 \text{ sec}}{\text{Elevator Speed in FPM}}$$

Figure 14.10 includes simple graphic correlations of elevator speeds and express-run heights with the time in seconds required for a one-way run. The height of the express run is shown in terms of the number of floors for both 10-foot and 12-foot floor-to-floor heights and for actual physical dimensions in feet. While the times for these express runs assume that the elevator essentially moves at its rated speed throughout the run, time is also added to account for acceleration or deceleration for express speeds higher than 700 FPM. The assumption is that any elevator with an express run has a rated speed of at least 700 FPM, and when adding the time for the express runs, up and down, to the time for local service, the time necessary to accelerate up to 700 FPM and to decelerate from this speed to a full stop has already been included. As a result, the express-run time for a 700-FPM speed is incorporated into the overall time by using the above formula. With express runs for elevators with speeds higher than 700 FPM, however, the time required to change speed between 700 FPM and the listed elevator speed, which should be achieved during the express run, must be accounted for. Figure 14.10 already includes these additional acceleration and deceleration times for speeds of 1000, 1200, 1500, and 2000 FPM.

Tables 14.19A–C include data similar to those presented in Figure 14.10, but they assume that the floor-to-floor heights are set at 10, 12, and 14 feet.

In determining how many elevator cars are needed to meet the service expectations, we will find that it is

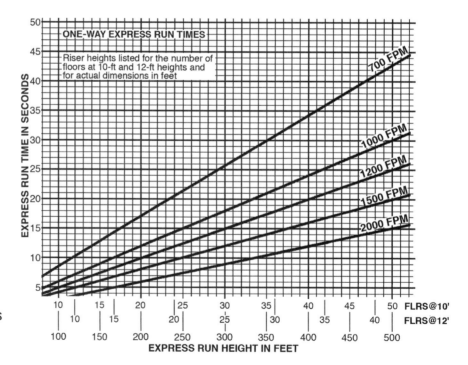

Figure 14.10 ONE-WAY EXPRESS RUN TIMES
Derived from calculations based on Strakosch (1998).

Table 14.19A: ONE-WAY EXPRESS RUN TIMES – 10'-0"
FLOOR-TO-FLOOR

Floors	Seconds for Express Run Car Speed					
	500	700	1000	1200	1600	2000
5	6.0	4.3	3.5	3.3	3.3	3.3
6	7.2	5.1	4.1	3.8	3.7	3.7
7	8.4	6.0	4.7	4.3	4.1	4.1
8	9.6	6.9	5.3	4.8	4.4	4.4
9	10.8	7.7	5.9	5.3	4.8	4.8
10	12.0	8.6	6.5	5.8	5.2	5.1
11	13.2	9.4	7.1	6.3	5.6	5.4
12	14.4	10.3	7.7	6.8	5.9	5.7
13	15.6	11.1	8.3	7.3	6.3	6.0
14	16.8	12.0	8.9	7.8	6.7	6.3
15	18.0	12.9	9.5	8.3	7.1	6.6
16	19.2	13.7	10.1	8.8	7.4	6.9
17	20.4	14.6	10.7	9.3	7.8	7.2
18	21.6	15.4	11.3	9.8	8.2	7.5
19	22.8	16.3	11.9	10.3	8.6	7.8
20	24.0	17.1	12.5	10.8	8.9	8.1
25	–	21.4	15.5	13.3	10.8	9.6
30	–	25.7	18.5	15.8	12.7	11.1
35	–	30.0	21.5	18.3	14.6	12.6
40	–	34.3	24.5	20.8	16.4	14.1
45	–	–	27.5	23.3	18.3	15.6
50	–	–	30.5	25.8	20.2	17.1
55	–	–	33.5	28.3	22.1	18.6
60	–	–	36.5	30.8	23.9	20.1

Table 14.19B: ONE-WAY EXPRESS RUN TIMES – 12'-0"
FLOOR-TO-FLOOR

Floors	Seconds for Express Run Car Speed					
	500	700	1000	1200	1600	2000
5	7.2	5.1	4.1	3.8	3.7	3.9
6	8.6	6.2	4.8	4.4	4.1	4.1
7	10.1	7.2	5.5	5.0	4.6	4.6
8	11.5	8.2	6.2	5.6	5.0	5.0
9	13.0	9.3	7.0	6.2	5.5	5.3
10	14.4	10.3	7.7	6.8	5.9	5.7
11	15.8	11.3	8.4	7.4	6.4	6.0
12	17.3	12.3	9.1	8.0	6.8	6.4
13	18.7	13.4	9.8	8.6	7.3	6.8
14	20.2	14.4	10.6	9.2	7.7	7.1
15	21.6	15.4	11.3	9.8	8.2	7.5
16	23.0	16.5	12.0	10.4	8.6	7.8
17	24.5	17.5	12.7	11.0	9.1	8.2
18	25.9	18.5	13.4	11.6	9.5	8.6
19	27.4	19.5	14.2	12.2	10.0	8.9
20	28.8	20.6	14.9	12.8	10.4	9.3
25	–	25.7	18.5	15.8	12.7	11.1
30	–	30.9	22.1	18.8	14.9	12.9
35	–	36.0	25.7	21.8	17.2	14.7
40	–	41.1	29.3	24.8	19.4	16.5
45	–	–	32.9	27.8	21.7	18.3
50	–	–	36.5	30.8	23.9	20.1
55	–	–	40.1	33.8	26.2	21.9
60	–	–	43.7	36.8	28.4	23.7

often better to use more smaller cars than fewer larger cars. The main advantage of this approach is that it will reduce the interval time, so each individual trip time, which includes that wait, will be shorter. Also, with smaller cars, it takes less time for the passengers to get on and off, and the elevator doors might even tend to open and close more quickly if they are smaller, although the width of the doors should probably not be reduced to less than 42 inches. As mentioned before, while it might take more time to open and close a larger door since it has further to travel, the wider opening should reduce the time needed for people to get on and off the elevator. While 3'-0" doors will satisfy Americans with Disabilities Act requirements, a minimum width of 3'-6" is recommended, and 4'-0" is preferred since this will permit two people to walk abreast or allow one person to leave the elevator while another one enters (although this is not really within the norms of etiquette, which suggest that it is appropriate to allow passengers to leave before entering an elevator car). When the elevator doors are larger, they are typically two-panel doors that move at the same time—one panel moving faster than the other so that they close at the same time (see Figure 14.11).

Grouping of Elevator Cars

When we have done a rough calculation and determined how many elevators are required and how they will be distributed in terms of elevator zones, we must consider how to arrange them. One basic premise is to locate the elevators that serve the same zone relatively close to each other to reduce the time delay for loading passengers. There is also the question of where people can wait for an elevator,

Table 14.19C: ONE-WAY EXPRESS RUN TIMES – 14'-0" FLOOR-TO-FLOOR

Floors	Seconds for Express Run Car Speed					
	500	700	1000	1200	1600	2000
5	8.4	6.0	4.7	4.3	4.1	4.1
6	10.1	7.2	5.5	5.0	4.6	4.6
7	11.8	8.4	6.4	5.7	5.1	5.0
8	13.4	9.6	7.2	6.4	5.6	5.4
9	15.1	10.8	8.0	7.1	6.2	5.9
10	16.8	12.0	8.9	7.8	6.7	6.3
11	18.5	13.2	9.7	8.5	7.2	6.7
12	20.2	14.4	10.6	9.2	7.7	7.1
13	21.8	15.6	11.4	9.9	8.3	7.5
14	23.5	16.8	12.2	10.6	8.8	8.0
15	25.2	18.0	13.1	11.3	9.3	8.4
16	26.9	19.2	13.9	12.0	9.8	8.8
17	28.6	20.4	14.8	12.7	10.4	9.2
18	30.2	21.6	15.6	13.4	10.9	9.6
19	31.9	22.8	16.4	14.1	11.4	10.1
20	33.6	24.0	17.3	14.8	11.9	10.5
25	–	30.0	21.5	18.3	14.6	12.6
30	–	36.0	25.7	21.8	17.2	14.7
35	–	42.0	29.9	25.3	19.8	16.8
40	–	48.0	34.1	28.8	22.4	18.9
45	–	–	38.3	32.3	25.1	21.0
50	–	–	42.5	35.8	27.7	23.1
55	–	–	46.7	39.3	30.3	25.2
60	–	–	50.9	42.8	32.9	27.3

not be in the way of other people, and avoid having other people interfere with passengers trying to enter an elevator car. Figure 14.12 shows standard arrangements for grouping various numbers of elevator cars. Generally,

eight cars are the most that we can effectively group together.

Elevator Hoistway Enclosures

The interior dimensions of the elevator shaft or hoistway are based upon the size of the elevator car and the method of support. Generally, the shaft for a traction elevator is slightly larger than that for a hydraulic elevator. While these dimensions are for each elevator car, when a shaft includes a bank of elevator cars, the clear opening within the shaft typically includes an allowance for some separation between these dimensions to accommodate the installation of the individual guide rails (see Table 14.20).

Elevator shafts must be protected with a fire enclosure, usually with a 2-hour fire rating, similar to a fire stair. As a result, the elevator doors into the shaft, as distinct from the elevator car doors, which are often called *gates*, are to be rated at $1\frac{1}{2}$ hours. The shaft also needs to extend both above and below the actual space in which the elevator car travels. Generally, a pit of around 8'-0" should be provided, which will allow a service person to work below the elevator cab when it is at its lowest level. To accommodate the elevator equipment and the necessary supports with an overhead traction elevator, the shaft and penthouse should extend above the level of the top floor served by the elevator by around 25'-0". When the elevator equipment is located at the bottom of the shaft, the extension above the top floor level may be reduced, although the minimum height above the top floor served must be around 12'-0" (see Figure 14.13).

Obviously, these dimensions are approximate. When we are involved with an actual project, we should verify the dimensions with our elevator design consultant, who, as mentioned above, is often connected with a particular elevator company. Unless we expect to use custom-designed elevators, we can also investigate the specification data

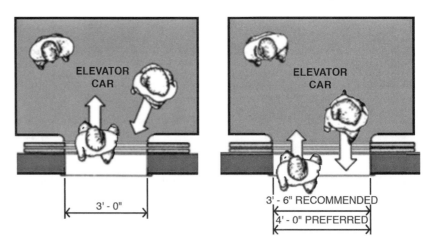

Figure 14.11 ELEVATOR CAR DOORS

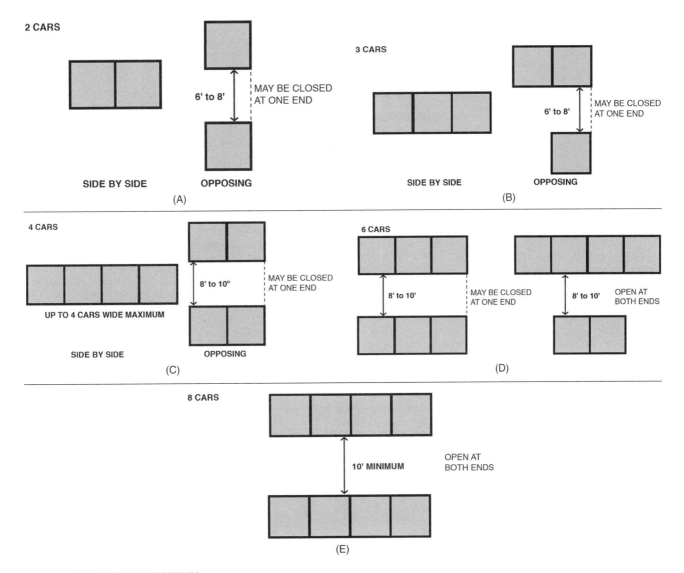

Figure 14.12 ELEVATOR CAR GROUPINGS

Table 14.20: ELEVATOR SHAFT SIZES

Elevator Type	Car Capacity (lb)	Approximate Shaft Size	
		Width	Depth
Traction	1200	6'-6"	5'-0"
	2000	7'-6"	6'-0"
	2500	8'-6"	6'-8"
	3000	8'-6"	7'-2"
	3500	8'-6"	8'-0"
	4000	10'-0"	8'-0"
Hydraulic	1500	6'-6"	4'-6"
	2000	7'-6"	5'-0"
	2500	8'-6"	5'-6"
	3000	8'-6"	6'-0"
	3500	8'-6"	7'-0"
	4000	9'-0"	7'-0"

from the major elevator manufacturers (Fujitec, Hitachi, KONE, Mitsubishi, Otis, Schindler Group, Richmond Elevator, ThyssenKrupp, and Toshiba). There are some custom elevator manufacturers, such as the Schumacher Elevator Company, and a number of companies that can provide custom elevator cars and/or elevator entrances. While the major manufacturers often produce similar-sized units, most will also develop elevators to meet custom designs.

Tables 14.21 and 14.22, which relate to Figures 14.15 and 14.16, respectively, present specification data from Fujitec for both its gearless and geared elevators.

As can be noted by perusing Figures 14.14 and 14.15, with a traction elevator, the elevator penthouse or equipment room is typically located above the top floor served by the elevator, although it may be located on a lower level. When it is above the top elevator stop, the equipment room

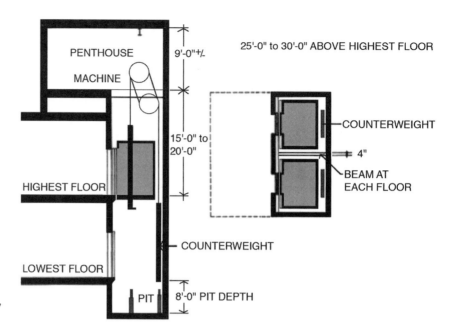

Figure 14.13 ELEVATOR SHAFT DIAGRAM
Adapted from a figure in E. Allen and J. Iano, *The Architect's Studio Companion* (John Wiley & Sons, Inc., Hoboken, NJ, 1995), p. 175.

Table 14.21: GEARLESS ELEVATOR SPECIFICATIONS DIMENSIONS

"Size" of Car (lb)	Speed (ft/min)	Inside Car Dimensions			Opening Size		Hoistway Size		Overhead	Pit	Machine Room Size		
		A ft-in.	B ft-in.	CH ft-in.	W ft-in.	H ft-in.	X ft-in.	Y ft-in.	OH ft-in.	P ft-in.	MX ft-in.	MY ft-in.	MH ft-in.
2200	400	5'-3"	4'-11"	7'-7"	2'-11"	6'-11"	22'-2"	7'-9"	17'-11"	7'-1"	25'-11"	28'-7"	8'-2"
	500						22'-2"	7'-9"	18'-6"	8'-2"	25'-11"	28'-7"	8'-2"
	600						22'-8"	7'-10"	19'-6"	9'-6"	26'-7"	28'-10"	8'-2"
	700						22'-8"	7'-10"	20'-10"	10'-10"	26'-7"	28'-10"	8'-2"
	800						22'-8"	8'-0"	22'-10"	13'-3"	26'-7"	28'-10"	8'-2"
	1000						23'-7"	8'-0"	25'-1"	13'-9"	28'-7"	29'-2"	9'-10"
	1200						24'-7"	8'-0"	25'-5"	14'-1"	28'-7"	29'-2"	10'-6"
	1400						24'-7"	8'-2"	26'-11"	17'-9"	28'-7"	29'-2"	10'-6"
2500	400	5'-11"	4'-11"	7'-7"	3'-3"	6'-11"	24'-1"	7'-9"	17'-11"	7'-1"	27'-11"	28'-7"	8'-2"
	500						24'-1"	7'-9"	18'-6"	8'-2"	27'-11"	28'-7"	8'-2"
	600						24'-7"	7'-10"	19'-6"	9'-6"	28'-7"	28'-10"	8'-2"
	700						24'-7"	7'-10"	20'-10"	10'-10"	28'-7"	28'-10"	8'-2"
	800						24'-7"	8'-0"	22'-10"	13'-3"	28'-7"	28'-10"	8'-2"
	1000						24'-7"	8'-0"	25'-1"	13'-9"	29'-2"	29'-2"	9'-10"
	1200						24'-7"	8'-0"	25'-5"	14'-1"	29'-2"	29'-2"	10'-6"
	1400						25'-7"	8'-2"	26'-11"	17'-9"	29'-2"	29'-6"	10'-6"
3000	400	6'-7"	4'-11"	7'-7"	3'-7"	6'-11"	26'-1"	7'-9"	17'-11"	7'-1"	29'-10"	28'-7"	8'-2"
	500						26'-1"	7'-9"	18'-6"	8'-2"	29'-10"	28'-7"	8'-2"
	600						26'-7"	7'-10"	19'-6"	9'-6"	29'-10"	28'-7"	8'-2"
	700						26'-7"	7'-10"	20'-10"	10'-10"	30'-2"	28'-10"	9'-2"
	800						26'-7"	8'-0"	22'-10"	13'-3"	30'-2"	28'-10"	9'-2"
	1000						26'-7"	8'-0"	25'-1"	13'-9"	30'-2"	29'-2"	9'-10"
	1200						26'-7"	8'-0"	25'-5"	14'-1"	30'-2"	29'-2"	10'-6"
	1400						27'-7"	8'-2"	26'-11"	17'-9"	31'-2"	29'-6"	10'-6"
3500	400	6'-7"	5'-9"	7'-7"	3'-7"	6'-11"	26'-1"	8'-6"	17'-11"	7'-1"	29'-10"	30'-2"	9'-2"
	500						26'-1"	8'-6"	18'-6"	8'-2"	29'-10"	30'-2"	9'-2"
	600						26'-7"	8'-8"	19'-6"	9'-6"	29'-10"	30'-2"	9'-2"
	700						26'-7"	8'-8"	20'-10"	10'-10"	30'-2"	30'-6"	9'-10"
	800						26'-7"	8'-10"	22'-10"	13'-3"	30'-2"	30'-6"	9'-10"
	1000						26'-7"	8'-10"	25'-1"	13'-9"	30'-2"	30'-10"	9'-10"
	1200						26'-7"	8'-10"	25'-5"	14'-1"	30'-2"	30'-10"	10'-6"
	1400						27'-7"	9'-0"	26'-11"	17'-9"	31'-2"	31'-2"	10'-6"

Source: The dimensions in this table, which are related to dimensions shown Figure 14.14, are based on data from Fujitec America, Inc. Actual dimensions should be verified by the selected elevator manufacturer.

Table 14.22: GEARED ELEVATOR SPECIFICATIONS DIMENSIONS

"Size" of Car (lb)	Speed (ft/min)	Inside Car Dimensions			Opening Size		Hoistway Size		Overhead	Pit	Machine Room Size		
		A ft-in.	B ft-in.	CH ft-in.	W ft-in.	H ft-in.	X ft-in.	Y ft-in.	OH ft-in.	P ft-in.	MX ft-in.	MY ft-in.	MH ft-in.
2000	400″ 500″ 600″ 700″ 800″	5'-3″	4'-11″	7'-7″	3'-7″	6'-11″	14'-7″ 14'-7″ 14'-9″ 14'-11″ 14'-11″	7'-9″ 7'-9″ 7'-10″ 7'-10″ 8'-0″	17'-11″ 18'-6″ 19'-6″ 20'-10″ 22'-10″	7'-1″ 8'-2″ 9'-6″ 10'-10″ 13'-3″	18'-4″ 18'-4″ 18'-8″ 18'-8″ 18'-8″	16'-1″ 16'-1″ 16'-9″ 16'-9″ 16'-9″	8'-2″ 8'-2″ 8'-2″ 8'-2″ 8'-2″
2500	400″ 500″ 600″ 700″ 800″	5'-11″	4'-11″	7'-7″	3'-7″	6'-11″	15'-11″ 15'-11″ 16'-3″ 16'-3″ 16'-3″	7'-9″ 7'-9″ 7'-10″ 7'-10″ 8'-0″	17'-11″ 18'-6″ 19'-6″ 20'-10″ 22'-10″	7'-1″ 8'-2″ 9'-6″ 10'-10″ 13'-3″	19'-8″ 19'-8″ 20'-0″ 20'-0″ 20'-0″	16'-1″ 16'-1″ 16'-9″ 16'-9″ 16'-9″	8'-2″ 8'-2″ 8'-2″ 8'-2″ 8'-2″
3000	400″ 500″ 600″ 700″ 800″	6'-7″	4'-11″	7'-7″	3'-7″	6'-11	17'-3″ 17'-3″ 17'-7″ 17'-7″ 17'-7″	7'-9″ 7'-9″ 7'-10″ 7'-10″ 8'-0″	17'-11″ 18'-6″ 19'-6″ 20'-10″ 22'-10″	7'-2″ 8'-1″ 9'-6″ 10'-10″ 13'-3″	20'-12″ 20'-12″ 21'-4″ 21'-4″ 21'-4″	16'-5″ 16'-5″ 16'-9″ 16'-9″ 16'-9″	8'-2″ 8'-2″ 8'-2″ 8'-2″ 8'-2″
3500	400″ 500″ 600″ 700″ 800″	6'-7″	5'-9″	7'-7″	3'-7″	6'-11	17'-3″ 17'-3″ 17'-7″ 17'-7″ 17'-7″	8'-6″ 8'-6″ 8'-8″ 8'-8″ 8'-10″	17'-11″ 18'-6″ 19'-6″ 20'-10″ 22'-10″	7'-1″ 8'-2″ 9'-6″ 10'-10″ 13'-3″	20'-12″ 20'-12″ 21'-4″ 21'-4″ 21'-4″	17'-1″ 17'-1″ 17'-5″ 17'-5″ 17'-5″	8'-2″ 8'-2″ 8'-2″ 8'-2″ 8'-2″

Source: The dimensions in this table, which are related to dimensions shown Figure 14.15, are based on data from Fujitec America, Inc. Actual dimensions should be verified by the selected elevator manufacturer.

is usually directly above the hoistway, but often extending beyond the hoistway limits. As shown in Figure 14.14, if there are elevators on either side of the elevator lobby, the elevator equipment room typically extends from hoistway to hoistway.

Example of Elevator Design

What would be an appropriate initial design for the elevators that serve a 50-story investment office building that has 20,000 square feet of rentable office space on each of the 49 floors above the ground level?

Before we jump in and look at the numbers, we should consider what type of elevator we should propose and what elevator size, speed, and number of elevator zones we should probably use. An initial factor to consider is the height of the building. While 50 stories suggests an overall height of around 500 to 600 feet, if the offices have hung ceilings with at least a 9-foot height above the finish floor (AFF), we should proceed assuming 12-foot floor-to-floor spacing and an overall height of at least 600 feet. Based on these dimensions and supported by information in Table 14.1, we should select a gearless a-c VVVF elevator.

Table 14.3 provides some preliminary selection data that recommend using an elevator with a speed of 1000 FPM, at least for the upper zones. Table 14.4 indicates that we should consider one elevator for every 35,000 square

feet plus a service elevator for each 265,000 square feet. This table also suggests using elevator cars with a capacity of 2500 to 3500 pounds, with the added notation that a 3500-pound car is the typical size.

$$1,000,000 \text{ sq ft} \div 35,000 \text{ sq ft per Elevator Car} = 28.57$$
$$1,000,000 \text{ sq ft} \div 265,000 \text{ sq ft per Service Car} = 3.77$$

Table 14.5 gives recommendations for elevator selections, and for our exercise, its recommendations are consistent with our initial idea. And from Table 14.6, we note that a 3500-pound elevator car has a capacity for 23 people, although at a likely number of passengers per car under peak conditions of only 80% of this maximum, we should proceed with each car at 19 passengers per trip. Based on the problem statement, the gross area of the occupied space, which excludes the ground level, is 980,000 square feet. To simplify our investigation, let's assume that the building has a gross area of 1 million square feet, which means we should assume 28 to 30 passenger elevators and 3 to 4 service elevators. And with 49 office floors, we should probably divide the building into three elevator zones: one including floors 2 to 19, the second 20 to 35, and the third 36 to 50.

Now we need to check out if this approach, with 28 to 30 passenger cars, will provide the 5-minute handling capacity appropriate for our building. Using Table 14.11, we can assume that the average net usable area for the overall building is around 75% of the gross area, which is

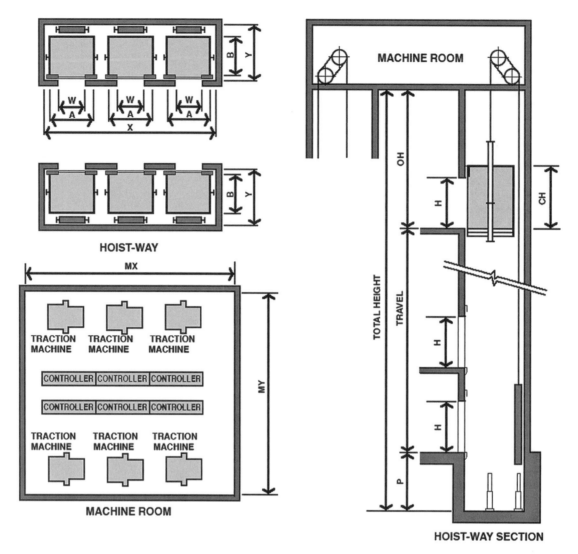

Figure 14.14 GEARLESS ELEVATOR SPECIFICATIONS
These drawings are adapted from material available from Fujitec America, Inc. The various dimensions, denoted by letters in the drawings, relate to data in Table 14.21.

approximately 750,000 net square feet. And at 120 net square feet per occupant, the midpoint in the suggested density presented in Table 14.10, we should expect a total of around 6250 individuals who have to be accommodated by our elevator system design.

This is general information about the overall building. Interpreting from Table 14.11, the net usable area of the bottom elevator zone will be around 75%, the middle zone 80%, and the top zone 85%. While this is still an assumption that we would have to confirm as we further develop the building design, we can use it for our initial elevator proposal. Once we know the net square feet of occupied space, we can determine the estimated number of occupants per elevator zone by dividing the net area of each zone by the 120 net square feet per occupant suggested by Table 14.10. Table 14.9 indicates that the elevator system should be capable of handling 11 to 13% of the occupants

in 5 minutes, so we will be fine if we use the more traditional 12% percent as the PHC. This indicates that the HC of the three elevator zones should be 255, 240, and 238, respectively.

BOTTOM ZONE (2–19)

17 floors × 75%(20,000 sq ft) = 255,000 sq ft
Total occupants = 255,000 ÷ 120 sq ft/person
= 2125 persons
With PHC of 12%: HC = **255 passengers**

MIDDLE ZONE (20–35)

15 floors × 80%(20,000 sq ft) = 240,000 sq ft
Total occupants = 240,000 ÷ 120 sq ft/person
= 2000 persons
With PHC of 12%: HC = **240 passengers**
Express run of 20 floors or 240 ft

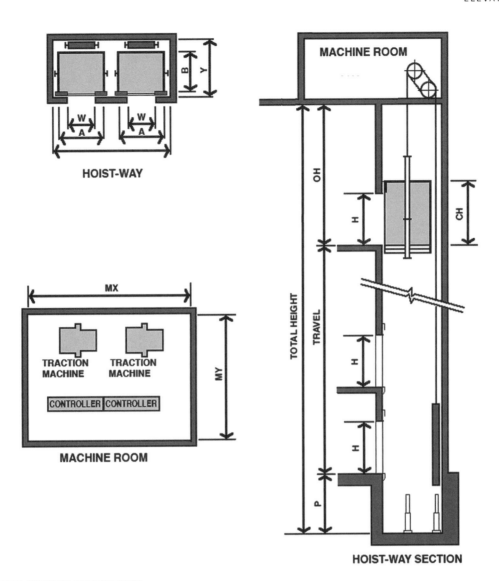

Figure 14.15 GEARED ELEVATOR SPECIFICATIONS
These drawings are adapted from material available from Fujitec America, Inc. The various dimensions, denoted by letters in the drawings, relate to data in Table 14.22.

TOP ZONE (36–50)

14 floors × 85%(20,000 sq ft) = 238,000 sq ft
Total occupants = 238,000 ÷ 120 sq ft/person
= 1983 persons
With PHC of 12%: HC = **238 passengers**
Express run of 36 floors or 432 ft

Assuming that our building should provide elevator service at the level of "good service," Table 14.8 recommends an interval time (I) between elevator cars leaving the lobby during peak service of no longer than 25 to 29 seconds, which means an average waiting time of 18 to 23 seconds.

While 1000 FPM used to be considered the maximum elevator speed, we are now able to exceed it. However,

with our building height, it seems reasonable to propose 1200 FPM for the express runs. At this speed, the express run to the 20th floor will take 15.3 seconds and the run to the 36th floor will take 25 seconds. For the round trip, these times have to be doubled to 30.6 and 50 seconds, respectively. For the local runs, recognizing that speeds above 700 FPM are unlikely to be achieved, we can use 700 FPM as the speed for the local round-trip times. Based on the use of 3500-pound cars, the lower local zone should have a round-trip time of 153 seconds. For the middle local zone, the round-trip time will be 137 seconds. For the top local zone, the round-trip time will be 134 seconds.

Combining the time for the local runs with the round-trip express runs, the overall round-trip times would be:

BOTTOM ZONE (2–19)

Local round-trip run: 153.0 seconds
Total round-trip time: 153.0 seconds
Interval time: 15.3 seconds

MIDDLE ZONE (20–35)

Local round-trip run: 137.0 seconds
Express round-trip run: 30.6 seconds
Total round-trip time: 167.6 seconds
Interval time: 16.8 seconds

TOP ZONE (36–50)

Local round-trip run: 134.0 seconds
Express round-trip run: 50.0 seconds
Total round-trip time: 184.0 seconds
Interval time: 18.4 seconds

Assuming 10 elevators allocated to each elevator zone, the interval time between each car will be 15.3 seconds for the bottom zone, 16.8 seconds for the middle zone, and 18.4 seconds for the top zone. All of these times fall well below the suggested maximum of 25 to 29 seconds.

The HC for each elevator zone is found by the following formula:

$$HC = (300 \times p \times N) \div RT$$

$$HC_{BOTTOM\ ZONE} = (300 \times 19\ Persons/Car \times 10\ Cars) \div 153.0\ sec = \textbf{372 Persons}$$

$$HC_{MIDDLE\ ZONE} = (300 \times 19\ Persons/Car \times 10\ Cars) \div 167.6\ sec = \textbf{340 Persons}$$

$$HC_{TOP\ ZONE} = (300 \times 19\ Persons/Car \times 10\ Cars) \div 184.0\ sec = \textbf{309 Persons}$$

Our initial proposal of three elevator zones, each with 10 3500-pound cars, clearly will not only meet the design expectations but will exceed them both in terms of HC and in terms of interval time (I). Taking an easy approach, we might assume that the elevators for each elevator zone will be arranged with an equal number of elevators on opposite sides of an elevator lobby area. With 10 elevators, this would mean two rows of five cars, which exceeds the recommended arrangement. So, since we have some latitude, perhaps rather than 10 elevator cars, we should consider whether 8 cars per elevator zone would work.

BOTTOM ZONE (2–19)

17 floors × 75%(20,000 sq ft) = 255,000 sq ft
Total occupants = 255,000 ÷ 120 sq ft/person
                = 2125 persons
With PHC of 12%: HC = **255 passengers**
Local round-trip run: 153.0 seconds
Total round-trip time: 153.0 seconds
Interval Time: 19.13 seconds

MIDDLE ZONE (20–35)

15 floors × 80% (20,000 sq ft) = 240,000 sq ft
Total Occupants = 240,000 ÷ 120 sq ft/person = 2000 persons
With PHC of 12%: HC = **240 passengers**
Express run of 20 floors or 240 ft
Local round-trip run: 137.0 seconds
Express round-trip run: 30.6 seconds
Total round-trip time: 167.6 seconds
Interval Time: 20.95 seconds

TOP ZONE (36–50)

14 floors × 85% (20,000 sq ft) = 238,000 sq ft
Total occupants = 238,000 ÷ 120 sq ft/person = 1983 persons
With PHC of 12%: HC = **238 passengers**
Express run of 36 floors or 432 feet
Local round-trip run: 134.0 seconds
Express round-trip run: 50.0 seconds
Total round-trip time: 184.0 seconds
Interval Time: 23 seconds

With only eight cars, the HC for each elevator zone is found by the following formula:

$$HC = (300 \times p \times N) \div RT$$

$$HC_{BOTTOM\ ZONE} = (300 \times 19\ Persons/Car \times 8\ Cars) \div 153.0\ sec = \textbf{298 Persons}$$

$$HC_{MIDDLE\ ZONE} = (300 \times 19\ Persons/Car \times 8\ Cars) \div 167.6\ sec = \textbf{272 Persons}$$

$$HC_{TOP\ ZONE} = (300 \times 19\ Persons/Car \times 8\ Cars) \div 184.0\ sec = \textbf{247 Persons}$$

While the number of people that can be carried within 5 minutes is reduced by 20%, we would still have acceptable conditions with only eight cars. This also means that the elevator lobby will require only four cars on either side, which is better than 10 cars. Furthermore, in doing our calculations, we assumed only 19 passengers per car, although the listed maximum for a 3500-pound car is 23 passengers, so our design is not pushing the envelope of acceptable elevator service.

Although Tables 14.4 and 14.5 were helpful in providing an initial approach for our elevator design, we should realize that our initial design was somewhat liberal. So, while we might begin with the recommendations in these tables, we really need to go through the design process before proposing a design for the elevators. Even then, we should realize that this design is still preliminary and should be confirmed with an elevator design consultant.

ESCALATORS

While it is often stated that the escalator, electric stairway, or moving stairs was first used at the Paris Exposition of 1900, a patent for an escalator-like device was issued in 1859 to Nathan Ames of Saugus, Massachusetts. It is suggested that his design was rather advanced for the time, and perhaps that is why it was never realized. Some 30 years later, the earliest working moving stair was presented by Jesse Reno as a novelty ride at Coney Island in New York City in 1896. Reno's design involved wedge-shaped supports that were attached to a conveyor belt. Others individuals also worked on developing a moving stair, but as the general belief suggests, the first step-type escalator intended for public use was presented at the Paris Exposition. Again, the person responsible for it was Elisha Graves Otis, and it was Otis who coined the term *escalator*, a term for which the Otis Elevator Company retained exclusive rights until 1950, when it was declared to be in the public domain. Actually, the design that Otis presented, which was based on patented designs that Otis purchased, included the adjustment of the steps into a flat platform at both the bottom and top of the escalator run. Without this adjustment, a moving stair presented challenges in getting both on and off, so this improvement was critical in having the escalator accepted for public use. Figure 14.16 shows the basic components of a modern escalator.

Escalators are used for moving people up to five floors, although they are generally considered to be effective for a level change of only one or two floors and to do so without creating any waiting time. In comparison with an elevator, an escalator can carry a large number of passengers up one or two floors more quickly and without any waiting time, except perhaps when the number of people trying to use the escalator exceeds its capacity. Before the development of modern automatic elevator controls, another major advantage was that the escalator did not require an operator. It was totally automatic.

Today the design of the escalator for U.S. applications has been standardized, although these standards are not always followed. The U.S. stipulation is that escalators are to be inclined at a 30° angle above the horizon, operate at a speed of 100 FPM, and be either 32 or 48 inches wide. These widths relate to step widths of 24 and 40 inches, respectively.

In terms of escalator speed, some publications suggest that the "standard" speed in the United States is 90 FPM and that it may be increased to 120 FPM. Some even imply that escalators may have speeds of up to 180 FPM. Historically, escalators were available with speeds of 90 FPM (0.45 mps) and 120 FPM (0.60 mps), but recently the speed has been set at 100 FPM (0.5 mps) for U.S. installations, although some manufacturers still list their escalators as operating at other speeds. While escalators operating above 100 FPM have been used, they tend to create some difficulty in getting on and off, although they are still permitted by the ASME-A17.1 Safety Code. Outside the United States, speeds above 100 FPM are somewhat common, and in some locations where there are

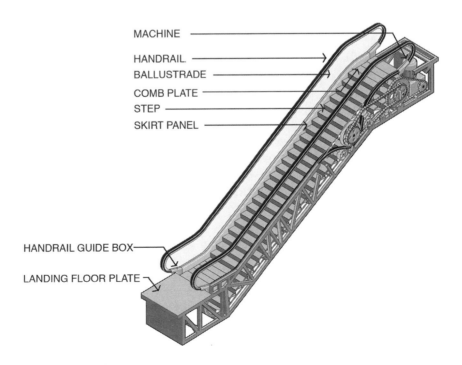

MACHINE

HANDRAIL

BALLUSTRADE

COMB PLATE

STEP

SKIRT PANEL

HANDRAIL GUIDE BOX

LANDING FLOOR PLATE

Figure 14.16 BASIC ESCALATOR
This shows the basic components of an escalator. (Adapted from a similar diagram by Otis Elevator Company.)

exceedingly long escalator runs, speeds as high as 200 FPM have been used.

While higher escalator speeds do pose some safety problems, they also increase the handling capacity. As a result, some have suggested that a two-speed escalator can operate at 120 FPM during times of peak load and then at 90 or 100 FPM at other times. There are several benefits to this approach. One, of course, is that it allows a higher handling capacity at peak times while allowing the casual rider, who generally uses the escalator outside of peak times, easier and safer access and egress. In addition, since the escalator will operate at the lower speed most of the time, there should be a reduction in energy use as well as less wear and tear on the equipment.

Escalators tend to run continuously, even when they are not carrying passengers. As a result, much of the time, they consume energy without providing any apparent benefit. Of course, in locations that are closed at certain times, the escalators are usually turned off when there are no potential passengers, but when buildings are not closed or in public spaces, the escalators generally keep running, even for the extended times when no one uses them. Since this is obviously wasteful, some have suggested that escalators should be set up to start automatically when someone approaches it and then stop after the person has completed the ride. Since the time it takes someone to go the full length of a run is set, it is feasible to install an infrared motion detector at the escalator entry that will activate automated controls to start the motor and then, after a prescribed time, turn it off. If by chance someone was still on the escalator when it stopped, he or she could readily walk the remaining distance.[3]

Unfortunately, turning escalator motors on and off is not necessarily a good idea. In fact, it might waste more energy than would be spent by keeping them running. However, with new VVVF motors, it is now feasible to adjust escalator speeds, and this seems to be a better approach to reducing energy consumption. While these variable-speed escalators are not yet code approved, they are being tested in the New York City subways. The intention is to install various infrared motion sensors that will detect whether any passengers are riding an escalator, and when no one is using it, the speed will be reduced to just 15 FPM. If the sensors detect the presence of a passenger approaching the escalator, the controls will gradually accelerate the escalator so that it achieves its full speed of 100 FPM in a few seconds. After a set time with no additional passengers detected, the controls will again reduce the speed to 15 FPM.

The length of an escalator is based on its 30° incline angle and the length of the prescribed horizontal platforms

that must be provided at the top and bottom of the incline. The actual rise takes a horizontal length equal to the floor-to-floor height times the cotangent of 30°, which is the tangent of 60°. The bottom landing is typically 6'-0" and the top landing is 7'-6". So, the basic formula for the required escalator overall length is:

$$\text{Length} = 13\text{'-}6\text{''} + (1.732 \times \text{Floor-to-Floor Height})$$

As the rise of the escalator increases, the overall length of the unit also increases, but since standardized components are used, there is a limit to the free span of an escalator run, and this is based on the capacity of the structural member. The sides of an escalator are structural trusses with a standard depth that is basically set by the design of the escalator. These same trusses, which are available in either a standard or heavy weight, are used for both the 32-inch and 48-inch escalator widths. The potential loading per linear foot of the narrower unit is about half that of the wider unit, although based on the theoretical maximum load, the structural design of the narrower escalator is based on its carrying 60% of the load that the wider unit carries. While we could explore the structural design, the basic fact is that the allowable span for a truss of the same weight is longer for the 32-inch escalator than for the 48-inch escalator.

In addition to changing the weight of the truss, it is possible to increase the allowable span or escalator rise by including an intermediate support. Of course, if the escalator is continuously supported, as is possible in a subway installation when the escalator basically sits on the ground, the side trusses of the escalator do not carry any load, and the length of the run is limited only by the capacity of the escalator motor.

The longest single-run escalators are installed in various subway stations. Perhaps the longest is at the Park Pobedy station of the Moscow Metro. This escalator is over 400 feet in length. The longest single-run escalator in the United States is part of the Washington, D.C., Metro. It is located in Silver Springs, Maryland, near the Wheaton Mall and has a length of 230 feet. The longest free-span escalator in the world is located at the CNN Center in Atlanta (see Figure 14.17). It has an overall length of 205 feet and rises through eight floor levels. To extend this far, the structural support is provided by two trusses within which the escalator is installed. So, even though it is freestanding, as with the long escalators serving subway systems, the escalator trusses are not the means of support.

As indicated in Table 14.23, the free span of the escalator can be extended if a heavier truss is used. Unfortunately, this extension is limited, providing an additional rise of only 2 feet. Since the incline of the escalator is 30° above the horizon, the ratio of the free span to the rise of an escalator

---

[3]You might enjoy viewing a YouTube presentation, "Stuck on an Elevator," http://www.youtube.com/watch?v=oRBchZLkQR0.

Figure 14.17 WORLD'S LONGEST FREESTANDING ESCALATOR
This escalator, at the CNN Center in Atlanta, is called the world's longest freestanding escalator. It has an overall length of 205 feet and rises through eight floors, although, as can be seen, the escalator is actually supported by a separate structural truss. Photo by Marco F. Duarte, Ph.D. and used with permission.

is the sine of 30°, or 2:1. So, a 2-foot increase in the rise of an escalator requires a 4-foot extension of the escalator span (see Figures 14.18 and 14.19).

Table 14.24 shows the theoretical maximum, the nominal, and the observed numbers of passengers that the two escalator widths can carry in 1 hour and in 5 minutes. Since the length of run has some effect on the number of people who can complete the ride within 5 minutes, the

5-minute capacities indicate the number of passengers who can either get on or get off the escalator, not those who can begin and complete their ride within this limited period of time. Table 14.25 indicates the time that it takes to complete some basic escalator runs.

Since it is generally assumed that there will be one person per step on a 32-inch escalator and two persons per step on a 48-inch escalator, it would seen that the

Table 14.23: APPROXIMATE MAXIMUM ESCALATOR RISE

Unit Size (in.)	Type	Supports	Maximum Rise (ft)
32	Standard	Ends	22
48			16
32	Standard	Ends plus Center	30
48			20
32	Heavy	Ends	24
48			18
32	Heavy	Ends plus Center	40
48			20

Source: Adapted from B. Stein, B., J.S. Reynolds, W.T. Grondzik, and A.G. Kwok, *Mechanical and Electrical Equipment for Buildings* (John Wiley & Sons, Inc., Hoboken, NJ, 2006), Table 33.2.

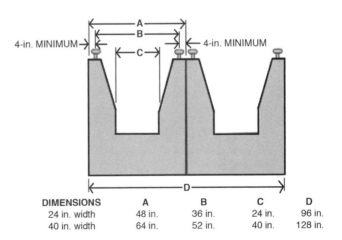

DIMENSIONS	A	B	C	D
24 in. width	48 in.	36 in.	24 in.	96 in.
40 in. width	64 in.	52 in.	40 in.	128 in.

Figure 14.18 ESCALATOR DIMENSIONS
Adapted from G.R. Strakosch (ed.), *The Vertical Transportation Handboook* (John Wiley & Sons, Inc., Hoboken, NJ, 1998), Figure 9.9.

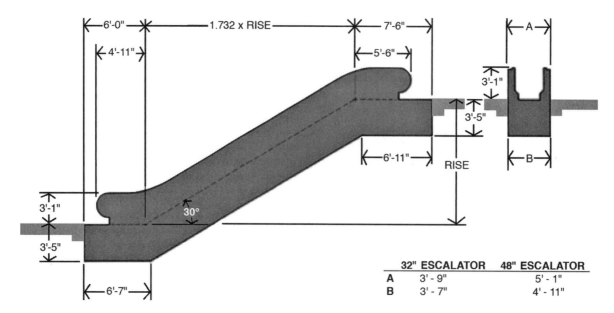

Figure 14.19 ESCALATOR SECTION
Adapted from G.R. Strakosch (ed.), *The Vertical Transportation Handboook* (John Wiley & Sons, Inc., Hoboken, NJ, 1998), Figure 9.10.

passenger capacity of a 48-inch escalator should be twice that of a 32-inch escalator. However, the ratio between the two listed maximum capacities is basically 1:1.6. This is because the assumption is that somehow $1^1/_4$ people ride on each step of a 32-inch escalator. While this obviously is assuming an average rather than some gruesome surgical procedure, from experience we should recognize that it is unlikely that such a density will occur. In fact, as is noted in the observed capacities, typically only every other step is occupied on a 32-inch escalator, and the rider arrangement on a 48-inch escalator is generally either two persons on every other step or one person on each step, somewhat

staggered left and right. That is, the observed loading for a 48-inch escalator is 50% of the maximum, while for a 32-inch escalator it is only 40%.

This suggests that the way people actually use an escalator is similar to the way they use an elevator. People tend not to stand as close together on an escalator as is theoretically possible. While listed capacities for escalators are based on passengers standing on each step, usually they only use every other step, and even though the wider escalator can readily accommodate two people on a step, only people who are close to each other (the pun has some relevance) will share an escalator step.

Table 14.24: ESCALATOR PASSENGER CAPACITY

Size (in.)	Tread Width (in.)	Speed (FPM)	Maximum[a] per Hour	Nominal[b] per Hour	Observed[c] per Hour
32	24	90	5040	3780	2016
32	24	100	5580	4185	2232
32	24	120	6750	5062	2700
48	40	90	8100	6075	4050
48	40	100	9000	6750	4500
48	40	120	10,800	8100	5400

Size (in.)	Tread Width (in.)	Speed (FPM)	Maximum[a] in 5 min	Nominal[b] in 5 min	Observed[c] in 5 min
32	24	90	420	315	168
32	24	100	465	348	186
32	24	120	562	420	225
48	40	90	675	506	337
48	40	100	750	562	375
48	40	120	900	675	450

[a] Theoretical maximum.
[b] Heavy loading, based on 75% of the theoretical maximum.
[c] Typical observed loading.

Table 14.25: ESCALATOR RIDE TIMES

Rise (ft)	Length of Run (ft)	Speed (FPM)	Ride Time (sec)
10	20	100	12
20	40	100	24
30	60	100	36
40	80	100	48

The nominal capacity listed for escalators relates to the peak loading. Using these figures and assuming a 100-FPM speed, the 5-minute carrying capacity for a 32-inch escalator is 348 people, and for a 48-inch escalator it is 562 people. Based on these nominal capacities, we can compare the service between escalators and elevators. Assuming three floors at a 12-foot floor-to-floor spacing, it would take seven 3500-pound elevators at 500-FPM speeds to match the carrying capacity of a 48-inch escalator that extends for three floors. The comparison between a 32-inch escalator and elevators suggests that more than four elevators would be required to provide a comparable carrying capacity. Of course, in both of these examples, assuming that the passengers can disembark on each floor, three escalators would be required, one for each floor-to-floor connection.

Safety is a critical factor with escalators. One problem that escalators pose is the sharp edge of the nosing of the escalator tread. Another potential problem seems to derive from what is actually a safety feature—the configuration of the nosing of each tread. Each escalator tread is comprised of what is essentially a metal grate. The tread is created by a series of vertical metal plates that are spaced apart. This arrangement allows the tread to pass through a comb device as the tread passes below the floor. The comb device is actually a safety switch, something like what is activated by the rubber bumper on an elevator door. If an object is jammed between the combs and the recesses of a tread, the escalator is supposed to stop. Unfortunately, things do get caught in these recesses, and the pressure activation is not always sensitive enough to avoid harm. Sometimes it is not that something is crushed in the thread-comb overlap, but that something is caught in it and as a result problems occur. For example, if a passenger is wearing shoes with loose or untied laces, these laces could get caught in the tread-comb overlap. As a result, the person, without any awareness, would be stopped abruptly as he or she tried to walk forward since the person is at the end of the escalator run, and this would probably cause the person to fall down. A third possible danger is getting caught between the moving treads and the sides of the escalator. This can result in slicing off the side of a shoe, but if the rider is wearing open sandals or, worse, is barefoot, the results could be considerably more traumatic. To minimize this problem, many escalators now have side brushes that act as a buffer that extends along the side rails.

Escalators, or more precisely the escalator opening, can also present a problem in terms of fire safety. Whenever there is an opening between floors and a fire occurs, the opening can establish an updraft that will permit rapid dispersal of smoke and increased airflow that can spread the fire. There are several ways that this possibility can be reduced. Perhaps the best and most effective response is to close off the opening with a fire shutter. If a fire alarm is activated, the fire shutter would roll across the escalator opening and form a fire-rated closure. While this should eliminate the problem, since it would close off the connection between the floors, it would also eliminate any possible use of the escalator as a means of egress. As mentioned, the escalator should stop when a fire alarm is activated, or it can be stopped manually, providing a means of emergency egress, although since a stationary escalator does not conform to code requirements for a fire stair, it cannot be used to meet the requirements for fire egress (see Figure 14.20).

Dropping the ceiling level around an escalator and forming a dense water spray or curtain around the opening can also reduce the rise of smoke. The ceiling drop can be accomplished in several ways. A curtain board could be installed around the opening or, as shown in Figure 14.20, rather than just a curtain board, a dropped soffit could be used. Both essentially establish a vertical drop before the escalator opening. Any smoke would have to build up a depth along the ceiling equal to the vertical drop before it could roll into the opening. The advantage of a dropped soffit is that it can include a duct system that could mechanically exhaust the smoke, keeping it from rising in the opening. With a mechanical exhaust combined with fresh air intake, the escalator opening should remain relatively smoke free and the dispersal of smoke throughout the building should be reduced.

MOVING WALKWAYS

Moving walkways were initially used at the 1893 World's Columbian Exposition held in Chicago. While other demonstrations of this movement system were included in subsequent expositions, the first commercial installation of a moving walkway in the United States did not occur until the 1950s. This was a system called Speedwalk, built by the Goodyear Company for Hudson & Manhattan Railroad's Erie Station in Jersey City, New Jersey. This walkway, which operated for only a few years, moved at a 10% grade and operated at a speed of 1.5 mph.[4]

---

[4] "Passenger Conveyor Belt to Be Installed in Erie Station," *New York Times*, October 6, 1953.

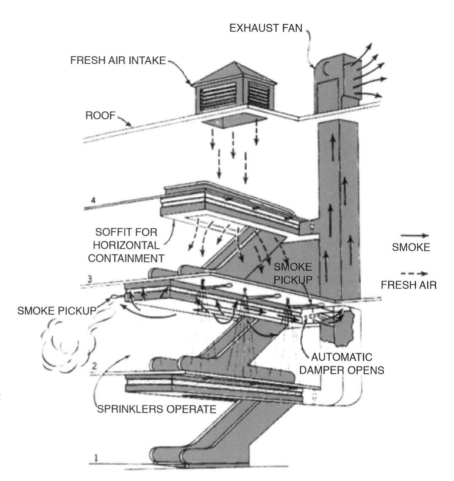

Figure 14.20 FIRE PROTECTION FOR ESCALATOR OPENING
Adapted from B. Stein, J.S. Reynolds, W.T. Grondzik, and A.G. Kwok, *Mechanical and Electrical Equipment for Buildings* (John Wiley & Sons, Inc., Hoboken, NJ, 2006), Figure 33.13.

Apparently the first moving walkway installed at an airport, which is now the major location of moving walkways in the United States, occurred in 1958 at Love Field in Dallas, Texas.[5] Moving walkways, which have been called *high-capacity continuous people movers*, are quite effective in airport terminals since these are rather large complexes through which passengers often have to travel considerable distances in a relatively short time (see Figure 14.21).

Moving walkways and ramps are similar to escalators, except that the wedge-step platforms are replaced with a continuous, flat moving belt. Walkways are basically level, although they can incline up to a 5° slope. If they are inclined more than 5°, they are essentially the same device, but they are then referred to as a *moving ramp*. Interestingly, while a walking ramp generally can have a slope no greater than 1 in 12, which means a slope angle of just under 5°, a moving ramp is permitted to have a slope as great as 15°. This is an incline of 1 in 3.73 (see Table 14.26).

While *escalator* is the accepted term used for a moving stair, many terms are used to denote a moving walkway, some indicating whether it is level or inclined. Some of

Figure 14.21 MOVING WALKWAY AT CVG AIRPORT

the names currently used, beginning with the more obvious and leading to the more imaginative, include *moving walkway, moving ramp, power ramp, movator,* and *travelator.*

The typical speeds of moving walkways and ramps are 100 to 150 FPM, although speeds of up to 180 FPM are

---

[5]http://en.wikipedia.org/wiki/Moving_sidewalk#cite_note-2.

Table 14.26: MOVING WALKS/RAMPS COMMERCIAL RATING

Angle of Incline	Pallet Width (in.)	Ramp Speed (FPM)		
0°–3° Walk	32	100	130	150
	40	100	130	150
10°, 11°, 12° Ramp	62	90	100	130
	32	100	130	150
	40	90	100	130

Source: Adapted from S. Stein, J.S. Reynolds, W.T. Grondzik, and A.G. Kwok, *Mechanical and Electrical Equipment for Buildings* (John Wiley & Sons, Inc., Hoboken, NJ, 2006), Table 33.5.

Table 14.27: MAXIMUM PERMISSIBLE OPERATING SPEEDS OF MOVING RAMPS

Angle of Incline	Maximum Speed (FPM)	
	Level Entrance	Sloping Entrance
0°–3°	180	180
3°–5°	180	160
5°–8°	180	140
8°–12°	140	130
12°–15°	140	125

Source: Adapted from B. Stein, J.S. Reynolds, W.T. Grondzik, and A.G. Kwok, *Mechanical and Electrical Equipment for Buildings* (John Wiley & Sons, Inc., Hoboken, NJ, 2006), Table 33.5.

allowed (see Table 14.27). Since walking speed is usually 120 to 240 FPM, walking on a moving walkway moving at 180 FPM would mean an overall speed of around 300 to 420 FPM. This relates to a speed of around 3.5 to almost 5 MPH. While most walkways are constant-speed devices, new proposals suggest that while it is necessary to provide lower speeds for access to and egress from the walkway, it might be feasible to provide higher speeds in the middle of the run. These walkways are referred to as *accelerating moving walkways* (AMWs).

There is also an *in-line accelerating moving walkway* that has been proposed by Loder Transport Systems. Apparently this walkway is a discontinuous system with a series of sections that operate at different speeds. This system involves simple thin slider belts that move over flat metal plates. The lower-speed entry section moves passengers to the higher-speed central sections, which ultimately deliver the passengers to a lower-speed exit section at the end of the run. While Loder has been providing such a system for baggage and heavy material movement, it apparently has not yet been put into passenger service.

As with fixed ramps, the entry to and exit from a moving inclined ramp must be level.

BIBLIOGRAPHY

Allen, E., and J. Iano. *The Architect's Studio Companion.* John Wiley & Sons, Inc., Hoboken, NJ, 1995.

Bangash, M.Y.H., and T. Bangash. *Lifts, Elevators, Escalators and Moving Walkways/Travelators.* Taylor & Francis, London, 2006.

Grondzik, W.T., A.G. Kwok, B. Stein, and J.S. Reynold. *Mechanical and Electrical Equipment for Buildings.* John Wiley & Sons, Inc., Hoboken, NJ, 2010.

Strakosch, G.R. (ed.). *The Vertical Transportation Handboook.* John Wiley & Sons, Inc., Hoboken, NJ, 1998.

INDEX